Victorian

Wiley Blackwell Anthologies

Editorial Advisers

Wiley Blackwell Anthologies is a series of extensive and comprehensive volumes designed to address the numerous issues raised by recent debates regarding the literary canon, value, text, context, gender, genre, and period. While providing the reader with key canonical writings in their entirety, the series is also ambitious in its coverage of hitherto marginalized texts, and flexible in the overall variety of its approaches to periods and movements. Each volume has been thoroughly researched to meet the current needs of teachers and students.

Victorian Literature

AN ANTHOLOGY

EDITED BY
VICTOR SHEA AND WILLIAM WHITLA

WILEY Blackwell

This edition first published 2015
© 2015 John Wiley & Sons, Ltd

Registered Office
John Wiley & Sons, Ltd, The Atrium, Southern Gate, Chichester, West Sussex, PO19 8SQ, UK

Editorial Offices
350 Main Street, Malden, MA 02148-5020, USA
9600 Garsington Road, Oxford, OX4 2DQ, UK
The Atrium, Southern Gate, Chichester, West Sussex, PO19 8SQ, UK

For details of our global editorial offices, for customer services, and for information about how to apply
for permission to reuse the copyright material in this book please see our website at
www.wiley.com/wiley-blackwell.

Library of Congress Cataloging-in-Publication Data

Victorian literature : an anthology / edited by Victor Shea and William Whitla.
    pages   cm. – (Blackwell anthologies)
  Includes bibliographical references and index.
  ISBN 978-1-4051-8865-4 (hardback) – ISBN 978-1-4051-8874-6 (paper)   1. English literature–19th century.
I. Shea, Victor, 1960– editor.   II. Whitla, William, 1934– editor.
  PR1145.V524 2015
  820.8′008–dc23

2014007436

A catalogue record for this book is available from the British Library.

Cover image: *A Private View at the Royal Academy, 1881* by William Powell Frith. One of the three focuses in the
painting is the group of aesthetes listening to Oscar Wilde (with notebook and sunflower in his lapel). To
Wilde's left are the actors Ellen Terry and Sir Henry Irving. Further over his opponents glower, led by the
journalist George Augustus Sala (white waistcoat). To Wilde's right is the actress Lillie Langtry, a society
wit and beauty, beside William Thomson, archbishop of York (in top hat). See:
http://en.wikipedia.org/wiki/A_Private_View_at_the_Royal_Academy,_1881.

Set in 10.5/12pt Dante by SPi Publisher Services, Pondicherry, India
Printed and bound in Malaysia by Vivar Printing Sdn Bhd

1   2015

About the Website

www.wiley.com/go/victorianliterature

Victorian Literature: An Anthology features a fully-integrated website which includes additional texts and contexts. Web materials are listed in the table of contents alongside items that appear in the book itself and are also cued throughout the text – just look for the grey boxes.

The website includes the following:

- Additional context sections
- Additional texts
- Timelines
- Photographs
- Appendices
- Further Reading
- Index of Authors and Titles

Contents

This anthology includes extensive additional material on an accompanying website at www.wiley.com/go/victorianliterature. The table of contents lists items that appear in the book as well as those which are available online. All online materials are marked with the web icon: ☙

Literature and the Arts 81

Religion and Science   113

Gerald Massey (1828–1907)   628

Elizabeth Siddal (1829–62)   631

Christina Rossetti (1830–94)   634

Plates and Illustrations

Colour Plates

(Between pages 500 and 501)

Black and White Illustrations

Web Plates and Illustrations

Web Plates

Illustrations

Preface

Increasingly scholars take a generous view of the multi-faceted term "Victorian," dating it not only from Victoria's reign, but sometimes from her birth in 1819 – or at least from the Great Reform Bill of 1832, when she was thirteen. Our approach to one common historical norm, the long nineteenth century (1789–1914), allows us to make contrasts and comparisons across a wide span of time and to include texts that were published before and after Victoria's reign by writers who came into prominence during that reign.

Overview

Our selection of ninety-five authors and five contexts is combined in both printed book and webpage. We intend that the book and its website be considered a single text, a representation of Victorian literature in its variety and complexity. The Table of Contents lists the contexts in the book, the additional web context sections, and the authors in both the print book and web book. For a complete list, see the Index of Authors and Titles on the Web. Also on the Web are links to chronologies of the Victorian period, weblinks, maps, tables, illustrations, photographs, links to recorded voices, and bibliographies.

Throughout, we usually use the first published versions, representing them in the texts first read by their contemporaries. All are provided with fresh and comprehensive annotation of concepts, names, places, foreign expressions, and ideas where necessary, as well as cross-references to other texts.

Highlights, Innovations, and New Materials

Many longer texts are included complete, including short stories by Doyle and Kipling; long poems by Barrett Browning, FitzGerald, Tennyson, Robert Browning, Arnold, Dante Rossetti, Christina Rossetti, Morris, Swinburne, and Hopkins. Substantial prose extracts are also included from Carlyle, Sarah Stickney Ellis, Newman, Martineau, Mill, Darwin, Ruskin, Nightingale, and Pater.

We have also gathered materials not usually anthologized: working-class literature, including diaries and poems; writings on women's status and campaigns, from Sarah Ellis to Martineau and Norton; writing on the Crimean War (diaries, poems, and a war correspondent's column); poems on the theme of Sappho as model and ideal poet; comic verse and hymns; dialect and rural poetry; radical and patriotic writing; same-sex love literature; and tribute poems, from one author to another.

Contexts and Multimedia

For more than half a century, Victorian literature has been allied in college and university courses with Victorian Studies, the interdisciplinary examination of the era. It is now accepted that Victorian literature should be read within and against the multilayered cultural conditions in which the writing was produced and read. Further, many texts that were formerly relegated to "background" categories, as properly in the domain of, for instance, politics or science, religion or art history, are now accorded status within literary study itself. We have responded to this academic reality by including five categories: The Condition of England; Gender, Women, and Sexuality; Literature and the Arts; Religion and Science; and Empire. These five context sections are only a few among many possible configurations. Some subdivisions within these contexts, like Progress, Industrialization, and Reform, or the Woman Question, or Geology and Evolution are frequently anthologized; some others, like Pollution, Protection, and Preservation (WEB), dealing with environmentalism and animal rights, or Working-Class Voices protesting social conditions and advocating reform, are rarely anthologized. The sections and selections are chosen and arranged to represent particular viewpoints or are especially illuminating in a disputed, often confrontational, area. Such readings are significant in the social and cultural conditions in which they are published. Hence, our context section on Literature and the Arts includes literary controversies about the novel but extends them by emphasizing the relations between the literary and other arts. For instance, Gothic medievalism is appealed to as an ideal in architecture and life by Pugin – but also by Ruskin and the Pre-Raphaelites in painting, poetry, and printing – and as an occasion for sneering dismissal in Dickens. Our reading of Martineau's painting of *Kit's Writing Lesson* (see Plate 8) allows us to move beyond a simplistic view of limited disputes over literary styles or genres to consider them within wider aesthetic debates among the arts, as well as within political debates involving the impact of literacy and the introduction of universal education.

A general introduction gives an overview of the age, not only of the course of literary changes and movements but also of some intellectual and cultural cross-currents of the time.

We also include three kinds of visual and aural materials. First, the published volume is enhanced with a series of coloured and black-and-white illustrations relevant to the cultural conditions or the authors' works. For instance, each of the introductions to the contexts begins with a discussion of a particular painting or architectural monument to highlight the materials presented in that section, like the representation of the moment when Victoria is told she has become queen, as engraved by the little-known Henry Tanworth Wells (see Figure 5) – with its significant bodily gestures serving to introduce the context of Gender, Women, and Sexuality. Second, a series of nineteenthcentury photographs from the original plates, along with Victorian writings on photography, present direct evidence of how the camera and the Victorian eye saw and interpreted the world around them. Third, thanks to improvements in camera and recording technology, we give access through the Web to early movies of the funeral procession of Queen Victoria and Victorian working and street scenes, and recordings of a number of leading Victorians, some reading their poetry, others giving portions of a speech, conducting or playing music, or recordings of characteristic sounds, like the chiming of Big Ben in 1890. Such materials greatly extend our apprehension of the age as very different from ours but also remarkably similar – and closer than we could have imagined.

The Canon and its Extensions

Literature is understood by us, as in recent scholarly discussion of the nineteenth century, in the broadest sense – literature as writing, reflected here in the range of some 100 authors, arranged chronologically by birth date, with each author's works presented in the order of their publication. The canon of major poets and prose writers whose works have traditionally represented Victorian literature is fully included in texts by Carlyle, Tennyson, the Brownings, Mill, Ruskin, Newman, Arnold, Dante Gabriel and Christina Rossetti, Hopkins, and Wilde, to name only a dozen of what Arnold called the enduring "touchstones" of persistently and rewardingly memorable writing. We also include natural scientists and social and religious thinkers who contributed to Victorian culture. Within the authors' section, almost half are women; many more female authors have a place in the context sections. More broadly still, we have recognized the opening up of the canon to writers not part of established culture, to those rarely included in general anthologies, and only occasionally gathered into specialized collections: dialect and regional writers, working-class men and women, writers that today would be called gays and lesbians, children's authors, hymn writers, and writers in the empire writing about home, and those writing about their experiences in their new home, either in London or the periphery of empire.

Women's Presence

A wide selection is included of what might be called the "new canon" of women writers – some already well-known, like Christina Rossetti, Barrett Browning, and George Eliot – others, only now coming to be recognized, like Webster and Field, and still others very little known or read, like such working-class women as Hamilton, Johnston, Luck, and Seacole. Some women writers established many of the Victorian gender codes, like Ellis and Beeton; others rebelled against the codes, like Grand and Levy; while still others, like Oliphant and Gaskell, wrote within the norms. Our authors' list includes almost forty women and the context sections have writings by thirty-three women.

Major and Minor Genres

We cover a breadth of genres. The varieties of Victorian poetry express the continuities and innovations within the literary tradition: dramatic monologues, pastoral elegies, lyrics, and short epigrams; sonnets and sonnet sequences; long poems like *In Memoriam* or *The Rubáiyát*; the classical poems of Swinburne and Field; the working-class poetry of Janet Hamilton and Elizabeth Duncan Campbell; the dialect verse of William Barnes and Ellen Johnston; and children's verse by Lear, Christina Rossetti, and Stevenson. We also include several varieties of prose: short fiction; autobiography and other forms of life-writing (such as diaries and personal letters); cookbooks and conduct guides; discursive prose from Carlyle, Norton, Eliot, Arnold, Newman, Pater, and others; plays by Boucicault and Wilde; and travel writing by Elizabeth Rigby, Isabella Bird, and Victoria herself. We situate controversies about these genres and their conflicting aesthetic programmes in such categories as comedy and melodrama, realism and romance, and sentiment and sensation. The dominant genre of the period, the novel, is discussed in several places: in our introductions and in the Debates about Literature section of Literature and the Arts; however, precluded by restrictions of space, we limit our selections of novels to extracts in the various context sections.

Editorial Procedures

Authors are arranged chronologically by date of birth, and selections from each author are arranged as far as possible in order of publication. Similarly, writings in the context sections are in chronological order of publication under each heading. Exceptions are explained in the notes. Poems are accorded line numbers as in the editions from which we take our copy-text. Prose extracts are not lineated.

Headnotes: Each author is provided with a short headnote giving the details of parentage, place of birth, education, course of their literary career, and other relevant biographical information. It concludes with a highly abbreviated list of references: the standard or scholarly edition, if available, the major collection of letters, a recent scholarly biography, and a reliable link to a current (where possible academic) scholarly webpage.

Annotation: We have provided useful factual information about people, references and allusions to specific works, places, events, translations of foreign words, and the sources of major ideas alluded to or not explained in the text. Occasionally, therefore, we have mentioned that such and such a text is the subject of critical or textual debate, or that this or that idea was a source of controversy to the Victorians – and often also to readers in the twenty-first century. While offering some guidance in such cases, we have generally restricted our interpretation to giving, for instance, some comment on structure, in the case of some longer poems (such as Tennyson's *In Memoriam* and Hopkins's "The Wreck of the Deutschland"), or explanations of some of the scientific or religious ideas alluded to, as, for instance, in the writings of Darwin, that might be unfamiliar to current readers. We have tried to avoid annotating words that occur in the *Concise Oxford Dictionary*, but occasionally have done so where a word is archaic or obsolete, or if it has a specific contextual or nineteenth-century meaning. Particular Victorian or earlier usage is identified with a reference to the *Oxford English Dictionary* (*OED*). Dialect and other special uses are often indicated by marginal glosses. The first note includes brief contextual or historical explanations, comments on compositional details, and finally, publication data, including copy-text information.

Such methods of annotation draw attention to three major sources of allusion among Victorian writers, the Authorized (King James) version of the Bible, the Greek and Latin authors, and Shakespeare. We have given titles only, without the authors' names, for well-known works by Homer, Virgil, Ovid, Dante, Shakespeare, Spenser, and Milton, and we use Arabic not Roman numerals for divisions of classical and other texts. Exceptions are those Victorian texts whose sections were originally numbered in Roman numerals.

Copy-text: We have been explicit about our choice of copy-text, indicating in each author's headnote or in the first note the source and date from which a text is derived. In almost every instance we have chosen the first published appearance in print, when it became accessible to the Victorian reading public. Problematic cases are explained in the first note. We have followed the copy-text with respect to orthography (so, occasionally, "Shakspere," in interests of historical accuracy and contemporary controversy), contractions (such as linger'd, watch'd, and heav'n), punctuation (with the exceptions noted below), indentation and spacing (with respect to poetry), capitalization, small caps (except for the opening words of a paragraph or poem), and italics.

Emendations: Exceptions to copy-text readings, such as the addition of later and well-known titles or editorial emendations, are added in brackets [thus]. Ellipses are indicated by three or four spaced periods. Authorial ellipses are indicated by two unspaced periods. We follow American usage for quotation marks, placing terminal punctuation within quotation marks, except that [;"] has been normalized to [";]. Translations are acknowledged when they are by specific translators; unacknowledged translations are by the editors. We have cited the King James version (with Apocrypha) of the Bible as that known by the Victorians, with the important exception of Hopkins, who used the Douay-Rheims, the standard Roman Catholic version.

We have generally ignored MS readings or textual variants throughout, except in a limited number of cases. For instance, the poems of the Brontës underwent several processes of revision, in some instances when moving from their place in the mythology of Angria or Gondal, their imaginary worlds, and in others when Charlotte edited her sisters' poems after their deaths. In another well-known case, D. G. Rossetti revised his poems frequently in manuscript as well as in trial editions, proofs, and published editions. We have given some of these readings for "The Blessed Damozel." We have included a range of such revisions by giving the MS or other readings, either flush-right or in footnotes. Words or letters that a writer has struck out in the MS are indicated thus: ~~strike out~~. Letters over-written are indicated within parentheses and are marked with an editorial comment: Thus (This) < overwritten>. Words or letters that a writer has added to the MS above the line are indicated thus: \word added/, and those added below the line are indicated thus: /word added\. Dialect words are glossed in the margins, cued with the degree character [°].

Acknowledgements and Permissions

We are grateful to the staff and collections of the Bodleian Library, Oxford, the libraries of York University (Clara Thomas Archives and Special Collections, Scott Library, Steacie Science Library) and the University of Toronto: Architecture and Design Library, Engineering and Computer Science Library, Massey College (Robertson Davies Library), Royal Ontario Museum Library, Sigmund Samuel and Gerstein Science Library, Trinity College (John W. Graham Library), Victoria College (E. J. Pratt Library), Emmanuel College Library, and especially the Thomas Fisher Rare Books Library. We also especially gratefully acknowledge the Robarts Library of the University of Toronto. A number of individuals have given wise advice and material help concerning particular aspects of the book, among whom we include Stacey Alison-Cassin, Florence Boos, Anne Dondertman, Hildo el Blanco, Danny Dean, Paul Fayter, Barbara Gates, the late Barbara Godard, Tony Hay, Linda K. Hughes, Gregory Kelly, the late Richard Landon, David Latham, Bernard Lightman, Marilou McKenna, Margaret Norman, Mike Sanders, Ann B. Shteir, Nancy Whitla, and Lisa Wood. Ivan Vestergaard has provided invaluable technical assistance. The staff at Wiley Blackwell has been full of patience and helpful advice at the various stages of book production, from proposals through preliminary to final submissions, and through the editorial process, including particularly Emma Bennett, Ben Thatcher, Bridget Jennings, and Felicity Marsh. We are also grateful to the anonymous appraisers of early proposals, and the careful and helpful readers of successive drafts of some of the authors and context sections. The editors and publisher thank the Faculty of Liberal Arts & Professional Studies, York University, for the financial support it provided to this work.

For copyright materials, we acknowledge a number of particular resources:

For materials from the Munby Collection held by Trinity College Library, Cambridge we acknowledge the kind permission of the Master and Fellows of Trinity College, Cambridge, and the Librarian, David McKitterick.

For Chartist materials, Mark Craik, Chartist Ancestors, and his webpage: http://www.chartists.net/Memorabilia-and-ephemera.htm.

For advice about nineteenth-century photography and for making their collection of early photographs available to us, we are grateful to Ann and Harry Malcolmson of Toronto.

For use of the manuscripts of Charles Stuart Calverley and related materials, we are grateful to Sybil Rampen of the Joshua Creek Heritage Art Centre, Oakville, his descendant.

For permission to use materials and illustrations in the Robarts Library and the Thomas Fisher Rare Books Library of the University of Toronto, we are grateful to the late Richard Landon, former Director, and to Anne Dondertman, Director of the Thomas Fisher Rare Books Library; and to Marie Korey, former Librarian of the Robertson Davies Library and the McLean Collection of Massey College.

Preface

For the various art galleries who have graciously allowed reproduction of works in their custody, as set out in the captions to them. For plates and illustrations we are grateful to Her Majesty Queen Elizabeth II for materials in the Royal Collection; the Boston Museum of Fine Arts; the Bridgeman Art Library; the Delaware Art Museum; the Fogg Art Museum and the President and Fellows of Harvard College, Harvard University, Cambridge; The India Office, London; the Master and Fellows of Keble College, Oxford; the Manchester Museum and Galleries; the Philadelphia Museum of Art and the John Howard McFadden Collection; Royal Holloway College; the Tate Gallery, London; and the Victoria and Albert Museum. As well we are grateful for the collections of York University Libraries, Toronto; the Robarts Library of the University of Toronto; the Gerstein Science Library, the Thomas Fisher Rare Books Library, and Massey College Library, Toronto. We have made every effort to acknowledge copyright materials; if any have been overlooked inadvertently, the publishers will be happy to make the necessary acknowledgements at the first opportunity.

Abbreviations

?	uncertain, approximation
=	meaning, as in word definitions
>	that is, suggesting, as in word definitions
<	from, derived from, from the root of, in derivations of words
abbrev.	abbreviation
adj.	adjective
adv.	adverb
alt.	alternative
Anon.	Anonymous
arch.	archaic
BA	Bachelor of Arts
BCE	Before the Common Era
BCP	Book of Common Prayer (1662)
bk.	book
c.	*circa* (about)
CE	Common Era
cent.	century
ch., chs	chapter, chapters
cm	centimetres
col., cols	column, columns
colloq.	colloquial
d.	died
d.	penny, pence
dial.	dialect
Douay	Douay-Rheims Roman Catholic translation of the Bible (1582–1609)
ed., eds	edited by; edition; editors
esp.	especially
et al.	(Lat. *et alii*) and others
f.	folio
ff.	and following
fig.	figure
fl.	flourished
Fr.	French
ft.	foot/feet
Gael.	Gaelic
gen.	general
Ger.	German

Gk.	Greek
Heb.	Hebrew
i.e.	(Lat. *id est*) that is
ILN	*Illustrated London News*
Ital.	Italian
KJV	King James Version of the Bible (1611)
km.	kilometre
Lat.	Latin
l.	*lire*/pound
l./ll.	line/s
lb.	pound/s
MA	Master of Arts
ME	Middle English
MP	Member of Parliament
MS, MSS	manuscript, manuscripts
n., nn.	note, notes
naut.	nautical usage
n.d.	no date
No.	number
obs.	obsolete
ODNB	*Oxford Dictionary of National Biography*
OE	Old English
OED	*Oxford English Dictionary*
OFr.	Old French
ON	Old Norse
Op.	*opus* (Lat. work)
oz	ounce/s
p.a.	*per annum*, a year
para.	paragraph
passim	(Lat. here and there), throughout
pl.	plural
PRB	Pre-Raphaelite Brotherhood
pt.	part
R.	rupee
RA	Royal Academy
s. or /	shilling, as in 5/6, five shillings and sixpence
sic	(Lat. *sicut*) it is so (identifies unusual spelling or grammar as original)
Sc.	Scene
Scots.	Scottish dialect
sect.	section, sections
Sp.	Spanish
Sr.	sister
stz.	stanza, stanzas
s.v.	(Lat. *sub verbo*) under the word, directing a reader to a proper word entry
trans.	translated by
UK	United Kingdom
US	United States (adj.)
USA	United States (n.)
v.	(Lat. *vide*) see, see entry
viz.	(Lat. *videlicet*) namely
vol., vols	volume, volumes
vs.	(Lat. *versus*) against

Introduction

Victorian Representations and Misrepresentations

The six decades of Victoria's reign (1837–1901) – and the longer nineteenth century (1789–1914) – witnessed tremendous changes for Britain: from rural village roads meandering around large estates to dynamic and sprawling cities; from a coach-and-four to complex, interlocking railway systems; from sail to steam; from penny post to world telegraph (see Plate 2, "Scientific Progress"). Such transformative changes brought challenging problems and multiple ambiguities. The latter prompted early twentieth-century thinkers like Lytton Strachey to use "Victorian" as a dismissive term implying over-stuffed rooms, over-zealous prudery, and over-large families – each associated with Queen Victoria and with her age.

Victorian and Victorianism have now become complex historical and cultural terms, signifying overlapping temporalities and locations. As a time-span, Victorian signifies both Victoria's historical reign as well as a cultural period extending from late Romanticism, about 1830 or earlier, to the Edwardian era in the early twentieth century. As a geographical locator, Victorian signifies England in the nineteenth century, but may also include Scotland, Ireland, and Wales, and, certainly later in the century, the term expands to include India and the wide reaches of the British Empire.

Victorianism signifies the conventions and social expressions characteristic of either Victoria's reign, or, more generally, of her epoch. Cultural historians try to use the terms as descriptive and value-neutral. Not tidy or neat categories, the sets of values and codes are general assumptions that allow readers to make specific connections between, for instance, literature and art, poetry and politics, novels and industry.

In a sense, Victorian also designates a set of styles, kinds of fashion and etiquette, architecture and design, and writing and speaking – the arts in general. Though not coined until about 1851, the year of the Great Exhibition, "Victorian" was applied with highest approval, celebrating enlightened national institutions, the wealth of commerce, the extension of water and steam power to industry throughout the land, and the success of international trade. Problems of definition, then, relate to the kind of "Victorian" referred to, as well as to the decade to which the term is applied.

Victorian Literature: An Anthology, First Edition. Edited by Victor Shea and William Whitla.
© 2015 John Wiley & Sons, Ltd. Published 2015 by John Wiley & Sons, Ltd.

"The Terrific Burning"

On the evening of 16 October 1834, less than three years before Victoria's accession, an art student at the Royal Acadeny (RA) recorded in his diary that "both Houses of Parliament had been destroyed by fire. Most of the students had witness[ed] the conflagration ... and they all describe it as being the most grand and imposing sight they ever saw. The appearance of the Abbey lighted up by the flames, they say, was most splendid and lately a scene of the most terrific grandeur. Some of the students who were on the river were in with same boat with Turner." As was his custom, J. M. W. Turner (1775–1851), the greatest painter of his age, viewed the awesome yet sublime catastrophe from many viewpoints, making notes and possibly sketches, many later worked over, resulting in two famous canvases exhibited the following year.

The *Burning of the Houses of Lords and Commons*, as Turner called his painting (see Plate 1), recorded what to many observers seemed apocalyptic: a divine judgement against the passage of the Reform Bill of 1832 to its detractors and a fortuitous destruction of added-on buildings of reprehensible design to others. Those Tories who feared extending the franchise had been shocked by the riots in Bristol in 1831 when over 100 houses were burned, including the Bishop's Palace, the Mansion House of the mayor and civic government, and three jails. Such an incendiary attack by an enraged populace when their representation at the Westminster Parliament was defeated by the Lords at an earlier stage of the Reform Bill now paled when the House of Lords itself burned to the ground. Architectural opponents of earlier tampering and patchwork with the ancient Gothic House of Lords objected to piecemeal stylistic additions when the Lords had recently been demolished and rebuilt (1824–27) both in neo-Classical style by Sir John Soane (1752–1837) and in neo-Gothic by James Wyatt (1746–1813); its burning, they claimed, was one more sign of God's displeasure with these aesthetic sins.

While rumours circulated wildly that the fire that destroyed the Palace of Westminster, as it is formally named, was purposely set, it was in fact the result of an archaic financial technology concerning the tallying up of tax accounts for the royal treasury. In a system going back to William the Conqueror (d. 1087), "tallies" were squared hazelwood sticks notched to show substantial amounts paid or deposited and then split, so that half went to the payer, usually the sheriff who collected the tax, and half to the Exchequer, marked with the names of lenders, payers, county, and when the debt or loan should be repaid. The system continued until 1826, but, despite periodical destruction of old tallies, two cartloads had accumulated in the tally-room of the old Palace of Westminster. The Board of Works eventually decided to burn them in the stoves of the House of Lords. The two workers assigned were overly enthusiastic, and, despite being warned by Mrs Wright, the housekeeper of the Lords, that two tourists she was showing about could not see the tapestries depicting the defeat of the Spanish Armada for the smoke, they continued their reckless stoking of the stoves. All left by five o'clock when Mrs Wright locked the chambers, but by six the over-heated flues ignited some wooden panelling. Within nine hours all of the medieval and later buildings were destroyed, except Westminster Hall (eleventh to fourteenth century). The burnt structures dated in part to the time of Edward the Confessor (c.1003–66), a warren of added-on buildings where Parliament and the royal courts had met since the thirteenth century.

To the artist Benjamin Robert Haydon (1786–1846) it was sublime visually and inspiring politically: "The terrific burning, ... from the bridge it was sublime. ... The feeling among the people was extraordinary – jokes and radicalism universal." Thirty years later Dickens would explain the circumstances of the fire in "A Speech on Administrative Reform":

Ages ago a savage mode of keeping accounts on notched sticks was introduced into the Court of Exchequer, and the accounts were kept, much as Robinson Crusoe kept his calendar on the desert island. In the course of considerable revolutions of time ... a multitude of accountants, book-keepers, and actuaries were born, and died. Still official routine inclined to these notched sticks, as if they were pillars of the constitution. ... However, they never had been useful, and official routine required that they never should be, and so the order went forth that they were to be privately and confidentially burnt. It came to pass that they were burnt in a stove in the House of Lords. The stove, overgorged with these preposterous sticks, set fire to the panelling; the panelling set fire to the House of Lords; the House of Lords set fire to the House of Commons; the two houses were reduced to ashes. Architects were called in to build others; we are now in the second million [pounds] of the cost thereof; the national pig is not nearly over the stile yet; and little old woman, Britannia, hasn't got home to-night (27 June 1855).

At the time of the speech Dickens was writing in *Little Dorrit* (1855–56) about another old and useless institution, the bumbling and deliberate obfuscation of the Circumlocution Office that made impossible the proper functioning of civil society. In questioning the cost of rebuilding the Palace of Westminster, he also recognized the epochal change the fire had caused.

Among those watching the conflagration on the evening of 16 October 1834 were two observers and architects with specialized interest. One was Charles Barry (1795–1860), returning from Brighton by coach, who saw the glow in the sky from afar and hurried to Westminster to see it close at hand, realizing, as his biographer says, that while "preservation or restoration was out of the question ... the erection of a new building was inevitable, on a scale and with an opportunity" that could scarce be imagined. Although chiefly specializing in Italianate buildings, Barry won the competition to design a Gothic Parliament. Another witness to the burning was Augustus Pugin (1812–52), a master of Gothic architecture and design. While he rejoiced, as did all of England, that Westminster Hall had been saved, he also thought that there was "much to rejoice in a vast quantity of Soane's mixtures and Wyatt's heresies [having] been effectually consigned to oblivion. Oh it was a glorious sight to see his composition mullions ... and battlements flying and cracking." The brilliant, eccentric, and short-lived Pugin feared the officials' "diabolical plans and detestable details." Nevertheless, he was to become Barry's collaborator, and to him were entrusted the thousands of Gothic interior details for ceiling decorations, floor tiles, carved doorways, fireplaces, tables and chairs and desks, brass ornaments, light fixtures, wallpapers, and the tower for Big Ben.

The Battle of the Styles

The Select Committee of Parliament stipulated that the new building was to be either Gothic or Elizabethan, the two styles most strongly associated with the chivalric and romanticized past demanded by national pride and cultural mystique. They replaced the neo-Classical style that smacked of either republicanism – recently adopted by the United States in the design of the Capitol in Washington – or the debaucheries of the reigns of the Hanoverian Georges. All ninety-seven entries complied. Barry's winning submission was clearly neo-Gothic in its detail, but it was also neo-Classical in its symmetry and balance, with the two houses of parliament and their anterooms flanking the central lobby. Pugin bemoaned the fundamentally neo-Classical arrangement of the building's parts: "All Grecian, Sir," he complained, "Tudor details on a classic body." Pugin's criticism was based on the implications of building styles: the virtues of medieval architecture, still visible in the ancient churches and cathedrals of England, for him made possible a culture united in the Catholic religion and feudal monarchy and able to care for itself by an interlocking system of rights, patronage, duties, obligations, and service. To Pugin, the defects of his contemporary society could be paralleled to the decline in architecture, to a debased and utilitarian neo-Classical functionalism. When he was deeply engaged in the first stages of the Westminster designs, Pugin set out his analysis of society and architecture in *Contrasts* (1836; second edition 1841), articulating the battle of the styles that would continue throughout the nineteenth century (see Figure 1 and Figure 2). The new Houses of Parliament incorporated novel engineering features while referring deferentially to England's medieval heritage. It was both nostalgic and prophetic: the beams and girders throughout are of cast iron, supported on brick, anticipating the second great monument of the Victorian era, the Crystal Palace of 1851 by Joseph Paxton (1803–65), which was made of iron and glass. All of the glass panels of the roofs and walls of the Crystal Palace, which housed the Great Exhibition, could be installed by the glaziers on wheeled carts that ran on the ribs of the structure: it was a triumph of pre-fabricated and modular construction that prefigures the architecture of the twenty-first century.

The decoration of Westminster fell to the Fine Arts Commission, appointed in 1841, under the chairmanship of Prince Albert. It announced competitions for narrative paintings, frescoes, sculptures, and bas-reliefs, with subjects drawn from British history or the works of Shakespeare, Spenser, or Milton, ensuring that both history and literature had a place in the deliberations of the nation. Hence, the Palace of Westminster narrated its own historical past, chronicling its pedigree on its walls, documenting its literary lineage in its pantheon of writers. It provided the links between old and literally burnt-out technology and the new order: the old wooden tally-sticks contrasting with the mechanics of new construction, whose heating and ventilation were absolutely up to date. It was the refurbished temple of the new political reform of 1832. Little here, however, reflected the "hungry Forties," the human costs of industry, or many cities' squalor. This present state of England was painted and plastered and bricked over by the Palace of Westminster. Carlyle in *Past and Present* (1843) presented the "Condition of England Question" in terms of an opposition, privileging the past as the better vision, an idealized bygone already slipping away. But such oppositions could be read from either end, as Dickens was to show.

"The Best of Times, the Worst of Times"

Dickens begins *A Tale of Two Cities* (1859) by opposing England and France, London and Paris – but less as polarities than as complementary aspects of a complex set of cultural phenomena: "It was the best of times, it was the worst of times, it was the age of wisdom, it was the age of foolishness, it was the epoch of belief, it was the epoch of incredulity, it was the season of Light, it was the season of Darkness, it was the spring of hope, it was the winter of despair, we had everything before us, we had nothing before us. . . ." Carlyle had drawn attention to these complementarities in *The French Revolution* (1837), significantly reappearing in a revised edition just two years before Dickens published his novel, and one of its important sources. Dickens's oppositions were summoned forth by other Victorians: Carlyle called it "Past and Present"; Disraeli, "Rich and Poor"; Ruskin, "beautiful and ugly"; Rossetti, Patmore, and others, "Body and Soul"; and Darwin, "Progress and Degeneration." Such social binaries arise from historical, social, aesthetic, and personal differences. But like all binaries, they each are true only in both extremes. We can add that they are each also weighted with value systems, and they each, on both sides, negotiate the Victorian social and cultural formation.

Demographics and Underlying Fears

Almost overwhelming data describing society poured in with the first modern census in 1851. The total population of England and Wales had increased to 27.5 million from 15.9 million ten years earlier in 1841. By Victoria's death in 1901, the 1841 figures had increased by a factor of more than two and a half, to 41.6 million. At the beginning of the nineteenth century, 34 per cent of the population was urban; by 1841, 45 per cent; by 1851, 50.2 per cent; and by the end of Victoria's reign, 77 per cent. Farm workers, especially from Ireland, migrated to England to work in the mill towns, and many millions more emigrated to North America, especially during the potato famine of the late 1840s. Throughout the nineteenth century single and widowed women far exceeded single and widowed men, accounting for "the spinster problem." In 1851, for instance, there were just over a million unmarried women 25 years of age and over, and three-quarters of a million widows, representing 8.9 per cent of the population, figures that grew throughout the century. Most younger women sought work in domestic service, family employment, or, for the lower end of the working class, as seamstresses doing piecework or as factory operatives; middle-class women sought work as teachers or governesses. Older women relied on income from property, or if they were without regular income depended upon poor relief under the New Poor Law of 1834 (see also Plate 3).

Underlying the Victorian quest for social stability in the face of such demographic inequalities was the fear of the breakdown of the class structure and political unrest. These fears combined with doubts about the value and utility of knowledge in relation to the certainty of faith: established knowledge was fragmenting. People feared that Britain would follow France in the steps of revolution, as happened there from 1789 to 1799 and the aftermath – with European monarchies overthrown to be replaced with Napoleonic dynasties, resulting in a European war that was massively destructive, both economically and sociologically. After Napoleon's naval defeat at Trafalgar (1805), his failed march into Russia (1812), and the collapse at Waterloo (1815), Europe faced a long and painful recovery.

Power, Industry, and the High Cost of Bread and Beer

Although England, unlike most countries of Europe, was spared the direct devastation of the continental wars, the country was being transformed by the Industrial Revolution, first in agriculture with mechanical threshing machines, invented about 1784. Soon widely available, they made possible the harvesting of much larger fields, leading to the enclosures of common land in the late eighteenth and early nineteenth centuries, eliminating many small tenant farmers. By 1830 the Swing Riots of agricultural workers suffering from low wages and increased unemployment resulted in hangings, transportation, and the flight from farming to the towns where the New Poor Law criminalized destitution and poverty, forcing thousands into workhouses.

A second major impact of industrialization was the union of coal and iron in the mining and manufacturing sectors, especially in the mechanization of the textile industry. The traditional producers of cloth by hand spinning and weaving were superseded by water- and then steam-driven machines, located in mills that quickly were surrounded by growing towns of ill-housed and poorly-fed workers. Steam engines required coal, putting new pressures on the mechanization of the mining industry. Further changes came from the transportation and distribution of goods by means of railways and steam locomotives, which transformed both landscape and work. They represented the new ideals of industrialism: efficiency, speed, production, and profit, and nothing could impede their progress.

Industrialism, and the concomitant progress in engineering, invention, and the related sciences, also had many benefits, enabling the Thames to be embanked to protect against the daily tides and flooding, and a multitude of other improvements that came to be regarded as necessities: plumbing for water provision and sewage disposal, the surfacing of roads, the building of steamships for shipping and travel, the telegraph, the penny post, and, not least, for literacy and literature, the manufacture of cheap paper and new technologies for printing.

The high price of wheat, and so of bread, was maintained by the Corn Laws of 1804 and 1814 that remained in place for thirty years, benefiting wealthy landowners but leaving the people hungry. In 1798 a handloom weaver could earn about 30s a week, and his bread cost him 1s 8d a pound. After the introduction of steam-weaving machines by 1831, hand-weavers' incomes had collapsed to 5s 6d a week. With the increase of bread prices to 2s 8d a pound because of Corn Law protectionism, the handloom weaver's wages would allow only one pound of bread a week for him and his whole family: a starvation diet. Under pressure from the Anti-Corn Law League and free-trade reformers, the Corn Laws were repealed in 1846 (to take effect in 1849), bringing hope for cheaper bread. However, repeal meant that Britain was flooded with cheaper grain from abroad and agricultural labourers were thrown out of work in increasing numbers. In 1865 a town labourer was even worse off than a hand-weaver of the 1830s, the labourer earning 3s 9d a week and having to pay 1s 8d for a pound of bread.

The prices of beer or porter, another commodity staple, also fluctuated throughout the nineteenth century. In 1840 beer could be had for 1d a pint, but by 1888 the cost of a pint had more than tripled to 3½d. And, as might be expected, beer was too often adulterated, with molasses, harmless enough, to give it colour, various herbs and drugs to increase flavour, water to extend it, and sulphuric acid to give it bite. Despite the rise in prices and the problems of adulteration, the production and importance of beer increased steadily throughout the period. In 1834 there were 134 commercial brewers, each producing over 10,000 barrels per year. By 1865 in the United Kingdom, 25 million barrels of beer were produced. The measurement of the barrels determined the structures of some of the most notable British architectural achievements. For instance, the basement piers, columns, and girders of St. Pancras Station and Hotel (1868) were built according to the measurement of the beer barrels from the largest British breweries at Burton-on-Trent to maximize storage efficiency.

The cost of food and the rate of wages played a direct role in political and social change throughout the century. Corn Law riots for lower taxes after 1815 culminated in massacre in 1819 at St. Peter's Field in Manchester (known ever after as Peterloo). Protests continued, and joined cause a little later with the agitation of the Chartists, demanding increased suffrage and parliamentary reform. Reform riots and rebellion could not forever be put down, nor their issues forever be denied, especially when they were combined with rational demands for political representation for large industrial towns like Birmingham and Manchester, demands that finally culminated in the passage of the Great Reform Bill of 1832, fought almost to the end by the House of Lords. The electorate would expand twice more in the century with the Reform Bills of 1867 and 1884, by which time there was almost universal male suffrage. Women would not begin to gain the vote until 1918.

At mid-century, three years of potato-crop failures in Ireland (1845–47) brought waves of famine and emigration – thousands of Irish to England (especially to the industrial north), and 1.5 million in famine (or "coffin") ships, riddled with dysentery, tuberculosis, and cholera, to North America. The Whigs under Lord John Russell (1792–1878) ended emergency aid for Ireland and thrust the starving Irish into the hopeless cruelty of the Irish Poor Laws. The embittered Irish would demand Home Rule under the leadership of John Stuart Parnell (1846–91), a demand that Parliament would deny them three times. The image of the penurious and drunken Irishman, fomenting violence, insurrection, and breeding beyond any reasonable means of support, became a living embodiment of Malthusian cries for control of the geometrically growing population in the face of an arithmetically growing food supply.

The Classes and the Masses

At the top of the social hierarchy that the artist George Cruikshank called "The British Bee Hive" (see Figure 3) was the Queen Bee herself, immured from the troubles in her realm, now suddenly the figure who was looked to for hope and stability in troubling times, arriving on the throne after a tight race between her age and her uncles (see GENDER: INTRODUCTION). "The British Bee Hive" worked as a metaphor for social harmony only if the drones and workers produced enough to keep the society functioning. Those below the queen and her court were the classes and the masses, living lives which varied from the comfort and pleasure of the rich to the desperation of the poor. Disraeli described the divisiveness of the bee-hive, the human costs of the industrial revolution, as splitting England into "two nations," "the rich and the poor." Social power is an amalgam composed of a number of attributes held by everyone in varying degrees: social status by birth, wealth (old wealth in property, or new money through business), living and working conditions (home/s, profession, servants, addresses), authority (by age or position, in family, profession, or society), life-style, education (school attended or apprenticeship), religion (Church of England followed by Non-conformists, Roman Catholics, Jews, and atheists), and cultural pursuits (from musical accomplishments, hunting and shooting, horseback-riding, gambling, opera and theatre, or travel to modest entertainments, like beer-drinking or gossiping with neighbours).

To enter society, one had to set a foot on the ladder, preferably by birth or inheritance, or, if necessary, by marriage. One began by arriving in London for "the season" (covering the sitting of Parliament from late January until mid-July or early August), when the social elite entertained each other at their London homes with extravagant dinners and balls, parties and socializing – the men with politics; the women with society gossip; and the children of marriageable age with the chance to "come out" by being presented at court, thereby declaring their nuptial eligibility. The lady of the house drove about "town," leaving calling cards with those she intended to notify of her arrival – and then she sat back and waited for an invitation to a dinner or a ball – especially if she were suddenly wealthy from the long-anticipated demise of a rich relation, or a particularly fortuitous marriage.

Meanwhile, in both fiction and in fact, the servants in the houses of the rich cooked, washed, scrubbed, lit coal fires, served dinner, dressed their masters and mistresses, taught the children, and bought food and drink (plenty of both) while their lesser brothers and sisters, those not in "domestic service," sewed shirts, ran weaving machines in the mills of Manchester, worked in a livery service tending horses or cabs, served in the army or navy, worked as farm labourers, or just begged in the street.

All seemed to be driven by a number of inexorable engines, more certain than steam and more unrelenting. The gospel of Work was first, so elaborately and symbolically portrayed in Ford Madox Brown's painting *Work* (1852–65; see Plate 5 and CONDITION (WEB p. 32). But it was not only Work that was a driving force in life; so too was Duty, a personal as well as a national virtue since Horatio Nelson required it of "every man" at the Battle of Trafalgar (1805), and Samuel Smiles described it in *Duty* (1880). Next in line after Duty was Faith, the social order of conduct and obedience in spiritual and moral matters.

This Victorian class structure and its social codes effectively kept most people in their place. "Knowing your place" meant behaving according to your social status; it also meant conforming, and from such conformity came the political virtue of social stability. But it was also a social put-down, especially to women or the lower classes when they demanded equal rights and opportunities. Class structure was usually subdivided into oversimplifications of "upper," "middle," and "lower," often with further refinements, like "upper middle" or "lower middle." As a positive attribute, class can be identified with those who have most of it, the upper classes, but it permeated all levels and was revealed to an onlooker by a thousand small details: bodily demeanour (pulling the forelock or removing the cap before authority or "your betters"), attire (kinds of shoes and hat), walk, gait, and stance (with the presence of a cane or not), means of travel (carriage – with how many horses – or by hired hansom cab, or by foot), with servants or as a servant, accent and dialect (a decisive giveaway, denoting place of birth and first associations – by county, by school, or by district in London), friendships and associates, jewellery or other marks of wealth, fingernails and palms of the hand (labouring or professional or leisured), ability to read or write, associations with what schools (village, grammar, public, university – or none), and so on. Each of these class markers was usually not absolute – though some, like accent, were pretty decisive.

Middle-class husbands ran the banks and industries that fuelled the self-confident achievements of entrepreneurship. Such men read *The Times* and *The Spectator* and smoked cigars after dinner apart from the ladies. Their employees in the office or on "the floor" in the factories were lucky to see the *Police News* once in a while for the pictures, and to read a little if literate, on the occasional visit to the local pub for a pint.

For the working poor, in the mills and on the streets, earning a living by standing over a noisy machine for fourteen hours a day or sweeping the streets of horse droppings and all the other garbage so m'lady could cross without soiling her clothes, thereby earning a few pennies, might keep a little shared roof over their heads and a very little food on the table – if there were a table at all. Responses to this "Condition of England," included Parliamentary measures for reform, like the various Factory Acts regulating working conditions; new political ideologies, like Utilitarianism, following the teachings of Jeremy Bentham; new political parties like the Liberal-Unionists, breaking from the Liberal Party in objecting to Irish Home Rule; and massive projects of urban and rural charity, sponsored by the churches and numerous philanthropic societies. Nevertheless, many, many thousands remained untouched by legislation, relief, or good will. Theirs was a story of the survival of the fittest, a Darwinian principle written graphically on the faces and bodies of the poor, as Dickens reminded his readers of *Oliver Twist* (1838) and as Luke Fildes depicted in his painting *Applicants for Admission to a Casual Ward* (1874; see Plate 3).

The Dynamics of Gender

The girl Sissy Jupe cannot define a horse as the boy Bitzer can in the opening of *Hard Times,* even though she was raised to train horses. Hence, the visible girl, unable to answer, is rendered invisible by her failure to understand the utilitarian and masculinist strategies of classroom definitions. Her plight, like those rendered invisible by distinctions of class, was the common lot of Victorian women. Women were often, like children, to be seen and admired, but not to be heard or counted as a presence. Their place was not important except to provide comfort, care, and offspring. Women were even more invisible to the law, education, the church, government and administration, and the military. Women were included by law with the husband as one person in marriage with no independent legal rights; they had no access to the vote (universal suffrage without a property qualification was not a reality in the United Kingdom until 1928), to the education that boys received, or to positions in the church, government, or army except as conveyors of mercy as a religious sister, as a teacher or governess, or as a nurse. Despite such restrictions, many women were well taught by loving and learned parents, excelling at intellectual pursuits, learning languages to become legends in their time, like George Eliot and Elizabeth Barrett Browning. Many women writers, like Harriet Martineau and Margaret Oliphant, took on numerous journalistic columns in the weeklies and monthlies to earn enough to sustain life.

Women's lot was very much circumscribed by the common law concept of coverture, was supported by the doctrine of separate spheres for men (business and profession) and women (hearth and family; see Figure 6), and was compromised by the sexual double standard (the purity of women and the possibility of a kept woman for a married man; see Plate 10 and Plate 15). Space and time too were gendered. Many buildings and areas of cities were entirely male preserves, and other areas were open to women only at certain times. For instance, some pleasure gardens and entertainment halls, discouraging middle-class women at any time, catered to male entertainment, engaging certain women, usually prostitutes, to provide it. Women could ride in Hyde Park if properly accompanied, but they could not even enter such male clubs as the Reform Club (1836, Liberal), the Carleton (1832, Tory), or the Athenæum (1830, the arts and the church). Church attendance, in families, was organized according to pew rent and social hierarchy. Travel in public, such as on a train, had to be chaperoned for single women, unless their means were much reduced, as is the case with Jane Eyre in her travels to seek employment in 1847.

Denied access to university education until late in the century, middle-class women sought fulfilment in marriage, or in their limited prospects for work, in spinsterhood, or in prostitution with its associated fears of violence and disease – all subjects for journal articles, novels, and political agitation. Marriage across class divides was a particular goal for the genteel poor to improve their circumstances, as well as for the aristocrat who had gambled away his inheritance. The prospect of a rich baron for the former or a wealthy widow for the latter seemed almost too good to be true, although its dream-quality motivated such rags-to-riches novels as Trollope's *Michael Armstrong: The Factory Boy* (1839–40) and true love across class barriers, as in Gilbert and Sullivan's *H. M. S. Pinafore, or The Lass that Loved a Sailor* (1878).

The plight of women, not just in seeking the vote but in the wider issues of rights, responsibilities, and access to means of education, work, and professions, came to be called "the woman question." Later in the century the image and ideology of the "New Woman" meant that women could claim their rights and act on their abilities, taking up jobs formerly only a male preserve, or simply standing up to conventional or systemic patriarchy.

Religion and the Churches

Patriarchy was particularly entrenched in the church, at once an agent of stability and of conservative reaction. The church was an instrument of power and authority, had a distinct role in government, and exercised control over every person at each stage of human life, from birth through marriage to death. Since the Reformation under Henry VIII (1491–1547) and the Settlement under Elizabeth I (1533–1603), the Church of England (Anglican) had been the national state church, known as the Established Church, with the monarch as its head. Church doctrine is summarized in various church formularies, the most important historically being the Thirty-Nine Articles of Religion (1563), settling matters of dispute from the time of the Reformation between the Anglican Church and both the Calvinist churches of Europe and the Roman Catholic Church. The order for church worship is set out in the Book of Common Prayer (BCP) (1662), a document frequently quoted by Victorian writers. The United Kingdom was divided into dioceses, each presided over by a bishop, with over 11,000 "livings" or parishes with an income (usually a tithe, ten percent, of each parishioner's income, paid in either cash or "kind"). However, as with the absence of representation in the pre-reform political system, most of the large towns and cities of the industrial Midlands and the north were without effective dioceses, and these came into existence gradually throughout the nineteenth century in Birmingham, Manchester, Preston, and elsewhere.

In theology and practice, the Anglican Church was divided into three parties. The Low Church or evangelicals stressed the literal meaning of the Bible, the sinfulness of human beings, and the avoidance of ritual or ceremony. The Broad Church took a liberal approach to theology, acknowledged recent German scholarship on the Bible that pointed to difficulties in both the texts and their meanings, and found an acceptable accommodation with new modes of thought in science (especially geology). The third party was the High Church, originally the old Tory group of conservative supporters of the Established Church in the Tory Party. As a new phenomenon, the High Church group that rallied around Newman, Keble, and Pusey at Oxford, was called either the Oxford Movement or the Tractarians (named after a series of the movement's publications, the *Tracts for the Times*). In the *Tracts* they set out their efforts to recover ancient and medieval theology and ceremony – later evolving into the Ritual Movement.

Two large impulses for spiritual renewal and revitalization were characteristic of the whole of Victoria's reign. First was the evangelical revival, drawing on the piety and deep religious fervour inherited from the Methodist revival or Wesleyanism in the late-eighteenth and early-nineteenth centuries. It had a profound effect on the religious observance and moral fervour of both the dissenting churches and the evangelical wing of the Anglican Church. It stressed Romantic individualism and the personal experience of religion, urging a direct encounter with the person of Christ in an act of conversion. This experience brought a certainty about the state of one's heart and soul that could be transferred to matters of empirical fact. Hence everything including scientific data and human relations could be read with the eyes of faith or the human heart. Congregations espousing evangelicalism espoused moral reform and imperatives – good works, social action on behalf of the oppressed or deprived or depraved – for children, animals, prisoners, and captives. Other aspects of the evangelical revival involved a strict Sunday observance, support for the temperance movement, and a huge increase in donations to charitable causes.

The other agent of spiritual renewal was the Oxford Movement, founded, as we have said, by Newman, Pusey, and Keble with the *Tracts for the Times* and inaugurated by Keble's *Sermon on National Apostasy* (1833). The movement grew, fuelled by the charismatic sermons of Newman, to stress the authority, doctrine, and practice of the early church; the role of tradition; the theology of the Fathers of the early church in the first five centuries; personal holiness; the revival of religious orders; and romantic religion. The Oxford Movement merged into Ritualism later in the century, in the use of colour in church decoration and vestments, of incense and candles, and of elaborate ceremonial.

Until the repeal of the Test and Corporations Acts in 1828 nonconformists (Presbyterians, Methodists, Baptists, and Congregationalists) were excluded from all public office and attendance at Oxford and Cambridge. Roman Catholics were similarly excluded until 1829 with the passing of the Catholic Emancipation Act. In 1850 the Vatican re-established the Catholic hierarchy in Britain with twelve dioceses, presided over by Nicholas Wiseman as the first Archbishop of Westminster, amidst riots demanding "No Popery!"

Despite these movements for revival, challenges to religious belief were seen on every side by the increasing secularization of society, the rise of scientific knowledge, and the growing perception of orthodox religion as irrelevant. The publication in 1860 of *Essays and Reviews* by seven writers associated with Oxford, most of them clergy, brought the claims of secularization to the forefront of religious debate. Tens of thousands of clergy protested, including most supporters of both the evangelicals and the Oxford Movement, while only a handful of liberals and Broad Church affiliates, along with a notable collection of scientists, supported them. Meanwhile, honest doubters like George Eliot, George Henry Lewes, and James Anthony Froude, along with Thomas Huxley and his circle, made both the name and the intellectual position of agnosticism acceptable. The sea of faith for which Arnold yearned in "Dover Beach" was in ebb-tide: Newman had abandoned the Oxford Movement, along with many followers, to join the Church of Rome. Over the century, the Anglican monopoly on public office and higher education was steadily eroded: Dissenters, Roman Catholics, Jews, and atheists (after the Charles Bradlaugh case was finally settled in 1886) were able to take the oaths, sit in Parliament, and take degrees at the universities.

Political Structures

With the exception of the Crown, Victorian political structures were, like the church, exclusively a male preserve, though a preserve that was undergoing large changes after the Reform Bill of 1832. Political power was held by the prime minister, chosen by the governing party (the one holding a majority of seats in the House of Commons) and the cabinet. Those elected very likely had both standing and wealth in their local county or borough, usually holding the land on which many of their electors lived; indeed, until 1838 MPs who sat as county members were required to have an annual income of £600 and borough members £300 (at a time when an agricultural worker would make about £20 annually). The vote was public, with persuasive influence, intimidation, and bribery. The Ballot Act of 1872 introduced the secret ballot, and the Corrupt and Illegal Practices Prevention Act (1883) more or less ended intimidation and bribery and limited the amount that could be spent on elections. The House of Lords was not elected, membership being largely hereditary – but otherwise dependent on appointment by the government (life peers), membership in the senior judiciary, or possession of a bishopric or archbishopric. The nobility consisted in order of precedence, of dukes, marquesses, earls, viscounts, and barons (all entitled to a place in the Lords), and the lesser nobility, not members of the peerage, the baronets (titled as "Sir").

Debates in both houses could be lengthy, as *Hansard*, the official record of parliamentary debates, makes clear. The House of Commons met four days a week during the "session" (from late January until mid-July or early August), sitting from 3:45 in the afternoon until late in the evening or early morning, with members leaving for dinner and returning in evening clothes to continue, not always worried over the question of quorum (as low as three in the Lords). Many of these procedures and practices found their way into the everyday life of London, providing copy for the newspapers that reported on parliamentary debates and having an important impact on all aspects of society.

The traditional political parties from the eighteenth century were the Whigs and the Tories – during the 1830s they gradually evolved into the Liberals and the Conservatives. The Whigs had pushed through the 1832 Reform Bill that enfranchised part of the middle classes, joining with the small number of parliamentary Radicals, who advocated universal male suffrage. Their alliance gradually came to be known as the "Liberal Party." Richard Cobden and John Bright as the leaders of the Anti-Corn Law League (established 1839) sought the support of the working classes, especially after the failure of the Chartist movement in 1848. After many years in power, the Whig-Liberals under Lord John Russell were defeated by the Tories (1866). The Tories then combined with John Bright and the Reform League, forming a minority government led by the Earl of Derby and Benjamin Disraeli that was able to introduce and pass the Second Reform Bill in 1867, legislation that doubled the electorate by giving the vote to most middle-class males. Thereafter the two parties fell under the dominating leadership of Disraeli for the Conservatives, and William Ewart Gladstone for the Liberals. The best of the parliamentary novels of the second half of the century treat the elaborate political bargaining, machinations, and skull-duggery required to gain and maintain political power: for instance, Anthony Trollope's six "Palliser" novels (1864–73) set out the dynasty of Plantagenet Palliser who aims to become the Chancellor of the Exchequer, recounting the procedures of parliament and their influence on the lives of those around him.

Empire

Parliament oversaw not only domestic affairs but also an ever-increasing empire during what became known as "Britain's imperial century." Whether one claims the British Empire began in 1169 with the Norman invasion of Ireland, or in 1600 with the granting of a charter to the East India Company, or in 1607 with the founding of Virginia, the nineteenth century is marked by an astonishing expansion of British territorial acquisitions. During Victoria's reign, Britain became the undisputed world power, doubling its size to one-sixth of the Earth's land mass, over 36 million square kilometres, and about one quarter of the world's population, over 400 million people. To the Victorians, the empire was divided into two parts: on the one hand, the settler or "white" colonies of Canada, Australia, New Zealand, and South Africa; and on the other, India and the "coloured" empire. The settler colonies were seen as extensions of the British family, the locale of wide-spread emigration for those from the home island wanting to get a fresh start. India, and later in the century in the Scramble for Africa, its African possessions, were conceived as conquered territories, as exotic fields of opportunity and adventure, being held for the good of the "coloured" inhabitants whose backwardness made them the necessary recipients of the three Cs: Christianity, Civilization, and Commerce.

Despite the British hegemony of the nineteenth century being known as the *Pax Britannica*, there was constant warfare throughout the world between Britain and a broad range of enemies: against Asians in Afghanistan (1838–42), European nations and Russia in the Crimea (1854–56), Africans in the Zulu Wars (1879), and the Dutch Boers in two wars (1880–81; and 1899–1902). Soldiers and administrators, and often their families, spread out across the world, and, for good or bad, spread British culture throughout the world. At the same time, imperial subjects influenced British ways in language, diet, and literature, influencing travel writing, adventure fiction, war reports, and a broad range of cookbooks, diaries, scientific studies, natural histories, and missionary journals – all feeding a voracious appetite among English readers for the new and foreign.

Genres and Literary Hierarchies

At home, there were significant shifts in the dominant, most popular, and most prestigious, forms of literature. While the Battle of the Styles raged in architecture between the neo-Gothic and the neo-Classical throughout the nineteenth century, it was also played out in the novel, the dominant literary form of the nineteenth century, replacing the long Romantic poem, as well as the lyric, as the most popular genre. The power of the Gothic novel of the late eighteenth century and Georgian period continued into various Victorian crime genres – from the popular penny dreadfuls to the mysteries of Wilkie Collins and Conan Doyle late in the century. Under Thackeray, Dickens, Trollope, Gaskell, Eliot, and many others, the Victorian novel flourished in periodical publications, reappearing in three-decker versions for multiple readers in the circulating libraries. At the same time, impulses concerning realism, naturalism, and impressionism affected the direction and style of English novels, as George Eliot explained in her famous chapter (17) in *Adam Bede* – and as many others demonstrated in both theory and practice.

Prose fiction overshadowed all other types of writing in the periodicals. It was most exhaustively reviewed, and it made fortunes, offered hope to struggling aspirants of either sex, and lined the publishers' pockets. The Gothic emerged in Victorian medievalism, in Carlyle's *Past and Present* (1843), Morris's *The Defence of Guenevere* (1858), Charles Reade's *The Cloister and the Hearth* (1861), and in the cluttered and realistic treatments of London by Dickens and Thackeray. The neo-Gothic, however, was not limited to re-creations of a medieval setting or ethos: it crept into the definitions of the scientist and his laboratory, the criminal, and the fugitive or exile, from direct representation in Mary Shelley's

Frankenstein (1818/1831) to Robert Browning's "Laboratory" (1844), Stevenson's *Strange Case of Dr. Jekyll and Mr. Hyde* (1886), and Wilde's *The Picture of Dorian Gray* (1890) to indirection in numerous settings of the macabre, psychologically deranged, and sensationally ghoulish, as in Sweeney Todd's meat pies in *The String of Pearls* (1846–47) and Jerry Cruncher's "resurrections" or grave robbings in *A Tale of Two Cities* (1859). Stage setting and novelistic decor called forth the Marshalsea Prison and Mrs Clennam's dreadful house and imprisoning chair in *Little Dorrit* (1855–57), all the terrors of Miss Havisham's rat-ridden cake in *Great Expectations* (1861), the Murgatroyds' dead ancestors in *Ruddigore* (1887), and Dracula's castle and bloodletting in Bram Stoker's novel (1897).

Fiction, though pre-eminently popular, remained inferior to poetry in the literary hierarchies established by genre and gender, and novelists were inferior to poets at the society dinner. The long poem directly competed with the novel from the publication of Barrett Browning's *Aurora Leigh* (1856). Three other long poems appeared over several years in the 1860s and 1870s: Tennyson's *Idylls of the King*, his romanticized neo-Gothic version of the epic of England that linked it to his own century of morally fraught action in an atmosphere of doubt, darkening to despair; Robert Browning's *The Ring and the Book*, a sensational Renaissance murder story, told many times over with neo-Classical order and symmetry and neo-Gothic details; and William Morris's *The Earthly Paradise*, a juxtaposition of both classical and northern tales, a combination of neo-Classical and neo-Gothic. The long poem continued to be both the goal and the triumph of generic aspirations, in many ways clinging to its place at the top of the hierarchy as an echo of the classical epic, but above all, as a work of great national significance.

Hence, in the decade after the deaths of Byron, Keats, and Shelley, poetry was the medium of choice for the writers of the next generation, as in Tennyson's *Poems Chiefly Lyrical* (1830) and Browning's *Dramatic Lyrics* (1842). Others worked in translation (Fitzgerald's *The Rubáiyát of Omar Khayyám*, 1859), and many more experimenting with compilations of earlier genres, new formats, and cross-generic structures, like Patmore's *The Angel in the House* (1854–62). Older forms were renewed, like the sonnet and sonnet sequence, the idyll, the ballad, iambic pentameter narrative verse, terza rima, and linked quatrains, while new interest in psychology, what Browning called "incidents in the development of a soul," yielded the dramatic monologue. The Romantic Ode, along with other generic forms, lost some of its conventional stability and became subject for patriotic fervour (in Tennyson's laureate poems), or encomia (as in Swinburne's praise of Hugo, Baudelaire, and Mazzini), or even mockery, in a notable example by Ellen Johnson, "Nelly's Lament for the Pirnhouse Cat" (1867). She is a representative of many new voices, often women, who write and publish in mill-town newspapers in the north of England, working-class, self-taught, pursuing lives of endless privation, all recorded in memoirs and verse that chronicles their loves, labours, and losses in moving detail.

The Fine Arts and Popular Entertainment

The fine arts blossomed under public patronage in the Palace of Westminster, but they were also supported to a massive degree by private money in every art form. New middle-class wealth, flowing from industrial and commercial entrepreneurship, needed to surround itself with paintings, sculpture, and music, housed in new and impressive country houses and city homes. Such arts were especially derived from the notion of revivalism, particularly from classical Greece and Rome, from French and English medieval Gothic, and later in the century from sixteenth-century Italian art and architecture. From these revivals in painting, literature, and architecture came also an interest in classical, medieval, and Renaissance subjects (for instance in Bulwer-Lytton's *Last Days of Pompeii*, 1834; the huge outpouring of Arthurian literature and painting, and Browning's monologues on Italian painters (1855)). In architecture, Harvey Elmes's St. George's Hall in Liverpool (1840) is the largest and most impressive neo-Classical revival building; the Houses of Parliament (1836–68) and the Courts of Justice (1874–82) are pre-eminent examples of neo-Gothic; and Charles Barry's Reform Club (1837) and especially the India and Foreign Offices (1861–68) in Whitehall are renowned samples of Italian Renaissance revival, all using the conventional architectural language of their periods.

Elsewhere in London, as well as in every town and city in England, four kinds of buildings were erected, each with distinctive architecture: neo-Gothic churches, a neo-Classical bank, whose solid Grecian columns declared the stability of world currency through the pound sterling; a building for civic government, either neo-Classical or neo-Gothic, as in Alfred Waterhouse's town hall at Manchester (1868); and finally, a railway station, with or without an attached hotel. The models for the stations were the highly innovative train sheds and attached hotels in London, such as King's Cross Station (Lewis Cubbitt, 1851–52), Paddington Station (Isambard Kingdom Brunel and Matthew Wyatt, 1852–54, depicted in William Powell Frith's painting, *The Railway Station*, 1862), and St. Pancras Station and Hotel (train shed by William Henry Barlow, 1865–67; hotel by George Gilbert Scott, 1868–77), a model for the Empire (see Plate 18).

In painting, too, the effects of traditional hierarchies and controversies were well established and continued throughout most of the nineteenth century. Sir Joshua Reynolds in his *Discourses* (1769–90), as the first president of the RA (founded 1768), had set out the hierarchy of painting: first, history and biblical paintings in the grand manner, then, portraiture, followed by domestic and genre scenes, landscape (surprisingly low in the scale), and finally, animals, still life, and flowers. Exhibiting at the Academy was a mark of entry into the ranks of elite and established artists, and election as an associate was a guarantee of success. The annual exhibitions of the RA were a social occasion and the subject of fierce competition; its Schools were the acknowledged route to artistic eminence. Increasingly, however, the authority of the Schools and the Academy's canons of beauty, composition, subject matter, and technique were resisted and rejected: in London the Free Exhibition in 1850 expressed such revolt on behalf of the Pre-Raphaelites led by D. G. Rossetti (see Plate 13), just as the *Salon des refusées* showing the rejected paintings from the official Salon Exhibition of 1863 did later in Paris with Manet's *Le déjeuner sur l'herbe* and Whistler's *Symphony in White No. 1: The White Girl* (see Plate 20 for Whistler's second version).

Patronage from new-found wealth meant that new walls and homes were ready to be decorated, first, in emulation of the old country houses of the nobility, with Old Masters, but increasingly with contemporary painters. Even the humble cottage and the industrial tenement could decorate a wall with an illustrated broadside, penny print, or cheap engraving of a religious or fine art subject – all increasingly available in vast numbers and at low prices.

Thematically, the acceptable subjects were biblical, historical, and literary, another cross-over in the arts, with some unexpected topics like fairy painting, as well as common phenomena like shipwrecks or fallen women. In a parallel with literature and architecture, classical and medieval subject matter in painting vied with "modern life." The popularity of a romanticized Middle Ages from Scott and Tennyson was continued by the Pre-Raphaelites, sometimes combined in volumes of poetry and engravings together, as in the publisher Edward Moxon's famous *Poems* of Tennyson (1857). Artists' modes of expression varied from the inheritors of the Romantic landscape painters like Turner to the photographic realism of the Pre-Raphaelites and their followers and to the social realism of later Victorian painters like Luke Fildes (1843–1927; see Plate 3) and the war paintings of Elizabeth Thompson, Lady Butler (1846–1933; such as *The Roll Call*, 1874, purchased by the queen). Elsewhere, the arts-and-crafts movement alluded to folk traditions and flat design (in the works of William Morris and his company; see Figure 7) or to impressionistic techniques by Whistler (see Plate 20), or to the art nouveau captivation to the whip-like line in such artists as Aubrey Beardsley (1872–98).

Music, like the other arts, was divided into hierarchies. In "classical music" – that is so-called art music or, as *Macmillan's Magazine* would have it, "the higher class of music" (March 1860) – England was notorious in Europe for not exporting world-class composers or performers. The chief agent for promoting concerts at home was the Philharmonic Society (1813), an orchestra founded by a group of professional musicians that was able to commission great works for its repertoire (such as Beethoven's *Choral Symphony*, no. 9 and Mendelssohn's *Italian Symphony*) and to bring noted composers such as Hector Berlioz (French, 1803–69) and Richard Wagner (German, 1813–83) to conduct their works. Concerts were usually a mix of vocal and orchestral selections, mostly from Romantic German and Italian composers. Mendelssohn had become a favourite of the royal family and played for them privately, writing in 1842 that Victoria and Albert, who both had voice training, sang some of his songs to his accompaniment.

The popularity of Italian opera (by Bellini, Donizetti, and Rossini) dominated the English musical stage, but with Prince Albert came a wider musical appreciation, with German operas by Gluck, von Weber, and Myerbeer. One of the few popular English-language operas was *The Bohemian Girl* by Michael William Balfe (Irish, 1808–70), which premiered in 1843; its famous aria "I Dreamt I Dwelt in Marble Halls" became one of the best-loved Victorian songs.

By far the most popular stage performances of music in the final quarter of the century were the thirteen operas by Gilbert and Sullivan. Such favourites as *H.M.S. Pinafore* (1878), *The Pirates of Penzance* (1879), and, most successful of all, *The Mikado* (1885), mocked parliament, the law, the armed forces, the Pre-Raphaelites and Aesthetes, the nobility, the class system, women's education, the monarchy and republicanism, and Gothic melodrama – all in infectious music and witty lyrics. The profits enabled the Savoy Theatre to be opened in 1881 specifically to perform their operas; it also was the first theatre in the world to be illuminated with electricity.

The social politics of gender dominated music as it did the other arts, including literature in Victorian England, especially in domestic settings. Playing the piano was considered an appropriate feminine virtue. Victorian hostesses would urge their guests to adjourn to the music room, to hear a specially invited pair of musicians perform the songs of Schubert, Mendelssohn, or Schumann. Two lovers could dally over a song and the keyboard. More informally, on Sundays, when most forms of entertainment were closed, the family could gather at the piano for hymns, or such favourites as Henry Bishop's "Home Sweet Home" (1827) or Arthur Sullivan's "The Lost Chord" (1877).

Church music, choral societies (from the woollen mills in Yorkshire – such as the Huddersfield Choral Society founded in 1836 and still in existence – to the thousand singers in the Albert Hall for Handel festivals), and the choirs and village organist in thousands of parish churches shared in the proliferation of Victorian hymns and the recovery of older composers such as the Tudor musicians William Byrd and Thomas Tallis and later composers like Purcell and Handel.

Music was also important in popular entertainment, but the essential ingredient was expendable leisure, leisure that could include a night at a ball or the opera for the wealthy or that allowed the middle-class family to enjoy the Christmas pantomime. Leisure also allowed for gender-separated recreation – clubs for the men or visiting for the women – or family activities for all (excursions, walking or riding trips, visits to places of entertainment, such as the seaside or a local park). For the working classes, leisure came only on Sundays, or, for the street dwellers, in any moment free for such activities as the Penny Gaffs (boy street actors) whom Henry Mayhew described as dancing and singing before 1,200 spectators who paid a penny admission:

> Rude pictures of the performers are arranged outside, to give the front a gaudy and attractive look... and on a Monday night as many as six performances will take place, each one having its two hundred visitors.... Singing and dancing

formed the whole of the hours' performance, and, of the two, the singing was preferred.... The "comic singer" ... was received with deafening shouts ... [He] sang a song, the whole point of which consisted in the mere utterance of some filthy word at the end of each stanza. Nothing, however, could have been more successful.... There were three or four of these songs sung in the course of the evening, each one being encored, and then changed. One written about "Pine-apple rock," was the grand treat of the night, and offered greater scope to the rhyming powers of the author than any of the others (*London Labour*, 1851, vol. 1, 'Of the 'Penny Gaff''').

Or, to keep the entertainment more decorous, it could be confined to the home itself. The enormous revival of the ballad tradition gave rise to both popular and parlour songs and to their street manifestations in the sung broadside. Music was a chief ingredient at balls in private homes for dancing the newly imported waltz and polka but also in the pleasure palaces for men, such as Kate Hamilton's near Leicester Square or Vauxhall and Cremorne Gardens – pleasure gardens for assignations, food and drink, concerts, and fireworks. Supper clubs and night houses (varying from the respectable to the unmentionable) offered food, often of a questionable sort, plentiful and strong libations, and assorted pleasures of the flesh. By 1870 there were 347 music halls in London, developed from the pubs of the 1850s into theatres licensed for popular music, but not for the performance of dramatic works.

For families there were trips and excursions; in the south Brighton attracted day-trip visitors to the sea from London after the rail connection opened in 1841; in the north-west, Blackpool provided seaside amusements for Preston and Liverpool, and in the south-east, Ramsgate in Kent was popular, as recorded in William Powell Frith's large painting, *Ramsgate Sands* (1852–54), bought by Victoria. Throughout London and at the seaside too was the travelling Punch-and-Judy show, with the puppets displaying the abusive violence and comic drolleries of that ill-matched family. Other excursions could be undertaken to major attractions – the "Views of London" at the Panorama in Leicester Square, or Madame Tussaud's Wax Museum in Baker Street (from 1836). Zoos were attractions in big cities (the Zoological Society of London, founded in 1820, opened to the public in 1847). Travelling menageries, like Wombwell's, appeared at county fairs with brass bands – and such popular "lion queens" as Nellie Chapman (d. 1899). Families travelled not just to see the exotic beasts but also to be seen (see Figure 9). Some lion tamers entered the cages for performances of derring-do, as did the most famous of all, Isaac van Amburgh (1811–65), whose portrait painted in oils by Landseer (1839) was also bought by Queen Victoria. Later in the century, travelling menageries were attached to circuses, most notably that of the American showman, P. T. Barnum (1810–91), whose prize exhibit for many years was the largest elephant in the world, Jumbo, along with acrobats, freak shows, and equestrian performers.

Some of the most violent sports, such as bear-baiting, cock-fighting, and dog-fights, were abolished with the Cruelty to Animals Act of 1835, but they continued illegally. The chief sport for the aristocracy was riding to hounds in the fox-hunt and hunting deer in Scotland and big game in Africa or India. Team sports, especially cricket and rugby at the public schools, and rowing at Oxford and Cambridge, were the sports or "games" that well-to-do English males learned at school; indeed, such sports came with a masculinist and later imperialist ethic and with the stamp of approval from evangelical religion in the belief that a healthy mind should dwell in a healthy body. Standardization and control of the various sports was effected by codifying their rules: the Cambridge rules for football or soccer (1848; revised 1863) and for cricket (from the Marylebone Cricket Club, MCC, the owner of Lord's cricket ground in London, founded in 1787) were formalized. Boxing under the Marquess of Queensberry rules (1867) tried to bring prize-fighting with bare knuckles under control. Horse-racing took place at the great racetracks like the Derby at Epsom Downs (as in Frith's painting *The Derby Day*, 1858), as well as at Ascot, Newmarket, and Cheltenham; at all races betting on the horses was part of the sport. Ball and mallet sports included the most popular sport for both men and women playing together, lawn croquet in the 1860s, which was eclipsed by tennis and golf in the 1870s and by polo in the 1880s (the first modern club was the Calcutta Club, formed in 1862). With the movement towards women's higher education in the 1870s, women were soon involved in a large number of sports for recreation: archery, badminton, lawn tennis, lacrosse, rounders, bicycle-riding, and numerous others.

Revolutions in Mass Media and the Expansion of Print Culture

The audience for writers also broadened the concept of literature from the undoubted classics to the most recent sensational railway novel, from *Hansard* recording parliamentary oratory to proliferating provincial newspapers of every political stripe. Innovations in the paper and printing industry, including the application of steam power to presses and the sophisticated distribution of newspapers and journals, books and magazines, facilitated this increased readership. The culture and economy of the changing print culture recorded its own life in print, in engravings, both wood and steel, in photographs and telegraphs, on paper with pens, and by the end of the century on typewriters. Even more remarkably, it became possible to record their voices on wax cylinders, and their images, including the funeral of Victoria, in moving pictures. Suddenly the world shrank in size: everywhere was almost next door; and time was equally diminished: the "news" really became what was new, enforcing dramatic transformations on how governments and the governed, parliament and the citizenry, reacted to what seemed to be most pressing, most sensational, most urgent.

No less for the Victorians than for us was literature being reshaped by the print and information revolutions. What was free speech for the Romantics seemed at first to shrink with the Victorians with the crackdown on the Chartists and their numerous radical publications – "incitings to riot," it was claimed, for which the perpetrators were locked up and deprived of pens. One such former Chartist, Thomas Cooper, visited Disraeli, who saw fit to turn the other political cheek, so to speak, enabling him to find a publisher and so have his radical diary of prison life published. That a prison diary, or the diaries of the war in the Crimea by a Creole woman, Mary Seacole, or the diary of a working Dumfries cotton factory worker like James Burn, could now be seen as literature is as amazing as the fact that the reading public could revel in sensational three-decker novels and purchase shady "literature" in Holywell Street for the private delectation of the fastidious gentleman.

Free speech, except for what was treasonous, seditious, libellous, or pornographic, had the effect of encompassing almost everything within the purview of literature. Science (in Darwin), philosophy (in J. S. Mill), history (in Macaulay), economics (in Engels), and theology (in Jowett) – all set their sights to writing better and for a wide reading public. The prevalence of learned articles every month on archaeology or German criticism, on Italian politics or on flowers and lichens by the seashore, from about sixty well-thumbed weighty periodicals published in Edinburgh and London, meant that the unending thirst for knowledge was slaked, if not quenched, as those indefatigable Victorians were striving both to understand their complex and transforming world and to write themselves into it.

Such multifarious writing is the stuff of this anthology. Not neglecting the "greats," those common denominators of Victorianism like Tennyson and Dickens and Elizabeth Barrett Browning, we also seek to *read* them in complex ways – through the shifting lenses of their contemporaries, writing from different parts of the country and the empire, from different classes and with vastly different experiences, and in different genres and media. To hold this kaleidoscope together is a daunting, challenging task for any reader, but also a rewarding and humbling experience. The Victorians did so much. A glimpse of how much can be seen by turning the following pages.

Part One
Contexts

The Condition of England

Introduction

Augustus Welby Northmore Pugin (1812–52), English architect, designer, and polemicist, a convert to Roman Catholicism, is remembered today as one of the most successful advocates for the revival of Gothic architecture. Known pre-eminently with Sir Charles Barry as one of the two architects of the new Houses of Parliament, he is the designer responsible from 1840 for all of its Gothic ornament, decoration, and furnishings. One year before Victoria's accession, Pugin self-published the book that would put him in the forefront of the "battle of the styles," a conflict between Gothic and Greek revival models of architecture. The long title of the book, *Contrasts; or a Parallel Between the Noble Edifices of the Fourteenth and Fifteenth Centuries and Similar Buildings of the Present Day; Shewing the Present Decay of Taste* (1836), sums up its content, methodology, and argument: a prefatory essay of thirty-five pages in five sections, an appendix, and nineteen drawings that juxtapose idealized or "noble" medieval buildings and their depraved modern counterparts. A second public edition in 1841, the one best known, doubled its length, and added five new plates.

In his preface, Pugin sticks to architecture, saying very little directly about what would soon be called the "Condition of England Question." That phrase is attributed to Thomas Carlyle in the title of the first chapter of *Chartism* (1840; see under SOCIAL FORMATION in this section) where he describes the condition of the English working-classes during the Industrial Revolution in the immediate aftermath of the New Poor Law Amendment Act (1834), legislation that in effect had criminalized poverty. Not one to neglect a good phrase, Carlyle used it again to begin *Past and Present* (1843): "The condition of England ... is justly regarded as one of the most ominous, and withal one of the strangest, ever seen in this world. England is full of wealth, of multifarious produce, supply for human want in every kind; yet England is dying of inanition." Like Pugin, Carlyle uses an idealized past, an imaginary feudal England, to attack his contemporaries; unlike Pugin, he explicitly and savagely denounces the entire present social formation, especially the aristocratic and middle-class leaders of the country, who were doing little to help the poor.

In one passage of the preface, while discussing architecture, Pugin, using the present tense, does name some key components of the "Condition of England Question" similar to that which Carlyle would soon target. Pugin writes:

> The erection of churches, like all that was produced by zeal or art in ancient days, has dwindled down into a mere trade.... They are erected by men who ponder between a mortgage, a railroad or a chapel, as the best investment of their money, and who, when they have resolved on relying on the persuasive eloquence of a cushion-thumping popular preacher, erect four walls, with apertures for windows, cram the room full of seats, which they readily let; and so greedy after pelf are these chapel-raisers, that they form dry and spurious vaults underneath, which are soon occupied, at a good rent, by some wine and brandy merchant (28).

Pugin here alludes to what Carlyle (and later Marx) would call the cash nexus, the system of capitalism overdetermining all human relationships, producing, according to them, shoddy workmanship, a landscape disfigured by railways, a nation of shopkeepers and merchants whose sole concern was their profit margin. The chief impact of Pugin's argument for ethical historicism, however, was not made through vitriolic prose, but through his illustrations.

An etching added in 1841 juxtaposes a "Catholic Town in 1440" (titled in Gothic letters) and "The Same Town in 1840" (see Figure 1). The medieval version is dominated by church spires, with no fewer than thirteen churches (of course, all Roman Catholic) listed in a key at the bottom of the drawing; it also contains a guildhall. People can freely enter and leave the town; its streets inside the walls lined

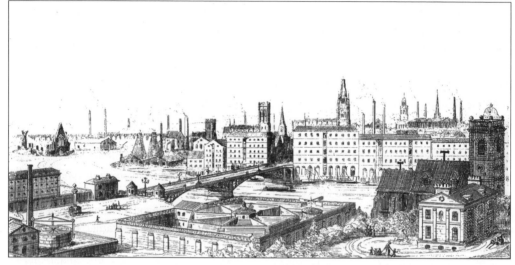

THE SAME TOWN IN 1840

1. St Michaels Tower, rebuilt in 1750. 2. New Parsonage House & Pleasure Grounds. 3. The New Jail. 4. Gas Works. 5. Lunatic Asylum. 6. Iron Works & Ruins of St Maries Abbey. 7. Mr Evans Chapel. 8. Baptist Chapel. 9. Unitarian Chapel. 10. New Church. 11. New Town Hall & Concert Room. 12. Wesleyan Centenary Chapel. 13. New Christian Society. 14. Quakers Meeting. 15. Socialist Hall of Science.

Catholic town in 1440.

1. St Michaels on the Hill. 2. Queens Cross. 3. St Thomas's Chapel. 4. St Maries Abbey. 5. All Saints. 6. St Johns. 7. St Peters. 8. St Alkmunds. 9. St Maries. 10. St Edmunds. 11. Grey Friars. 12. St Cuthberts. 13. Guild hall. 14. Trinity. 15. St Olaves. 16. St Botolphs.

Figure 1 Augustus Welby Northmore Pugin (1812–52), "Catholic Town in 1440; The Same Town in 1840." In *Contrasts* (1836, second edition 1841). Etching. 26 × 21 cm. Source: courtesy of the Thomas Fisher Rare Books Library, University of Toronto.

with trees. In the modern version, by contrast, the skyline is dominated by industrial chimneys spewing smoke, replacing the spires. Reading from right to left are the one Anglican church "rebuilt in 1750" in a neo-Georgian replacement of Gothic, with a Georgian parsonage and "pleasure grounds"; next is the "New Jail" in the centre, an octagonal structure built in the manner of Bentham's panopticon, where the warders could observe all inmates; then, a gasworks and behind that a lunatic asylum. Across the iron bridge with its toll gate are seven chapels of various dissenting denominations as well as a "Socialist Hall of Science."

A second added plate, "Contrasted Residences for the Poor" (Figure 2) captures the "condition of England" in even sharper relief. In fact, this plate could have served as a frontispiece to Carlyle's *Past and Present*. Its two levels, "Antient Poor Hovse" and a "Modern Poor House," each contain six panels, a large central one framed by five others. In the ancient house, in the first frame a poor man wears a cape with a staff in his hand; in the next, two monks, one the "Master," distribute alms before a door; the "Diet" consists of beef, mutton, bacon, ale and cider, milk porridge, wheat bread, and cheese; in "The Poor Brother's Convoy" a deceased pauper receives ceremonial burial; "Enforcing Discipline" is through religious instruction by exhortation (preaching) and the sacraments: communion and the anointing of the sick. At the centre, in the largest panel, is an ornately designed Gothic complex with a huge open courtyard, replete with trees and a separate garden for each of the inhabitants. In the modern version each panel provides a parallel to its medieval counterpart with the same caption: one of the poor men cowers on straw in a barred cell, placed there under the New Poor Law; "The Master" holds whips and handcuffs, with leg-irons hanging on the wall behind; the "Diet" for three meals is "2 oz." of bread, 1 pint of gruel; 2 oz. bread, 1 pint of gruel; and 1 oz. of bread, ½ pint of gruel and oatmeal and potatoes. A "poor man's" coffin labelled "For Dissection" is being loaded or unloaded on a wagon by three labourers wearing

hats and casually smoking pipes beneath a sign: "A Variety of Subjects Always Ready for Medical Students," instead of the fourteen vested figures interring the dead with full religious ritual. Discipline is enforced in the Poor House by the Master's ordering a keeper to imprison a mother with two children in a locked cell. At the centre, the Gothic poor house with its open courtyard and gardens has been replaced by a large, enclosed, prison-like octagonal structure, like the "New Jail" in Figure 1, with no windows, again in the manner of a Benthamite panopticon. The religious building has been removed to become a tiny structure in the background, while the foreground is barren and treeless.

Obviously Pugin is here distorting while glorifying the condition of the poor in medieval England, as does Carlyle; nevertheless, Pugin's two illustrations provide a map of many of the crucial social transformations that created the condition of England, controversies which would rage throughout Victoria's reign: the secularization of society, industrialization with concomitant pollution and social displacement, forced labour for the destitute, the substitution of incarceration for charity (see Plate 3: Fildes, *Applicants for Admission to a Casual Ward*), and the belief in science and rationalization on the model of utilitarianism – all are represented in Pugin's "contrasts": all are topics that run throughout the writings in this section. The transformations that Pugin calls repulsive are in many of these writings represented as a steady social improvement. Notably absent from Pugin's representation of his present is any awareness of a sense of progress, of the advantages of political reform based on democratic principles, or of education and mass literacy. For him, the nostalgic solution for the social dislocation was a return to the spiritual, moral, social, and political authority of the Roman Catholic Church, whose power and validity are represented in the architecture of the "Noble Edifices of the Fourteenth and Fifteenth Centuries." Macaulay follows a similar pattern, contrasting present to past; however, he draws completely opposite conclusions – the movement away from the authority of the church is social

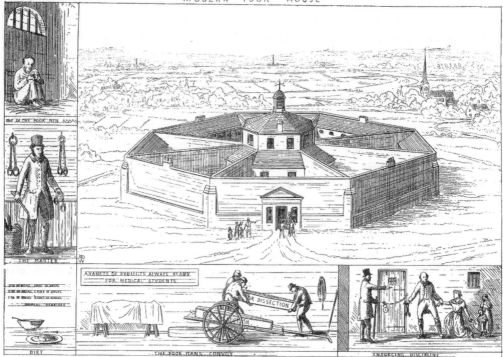

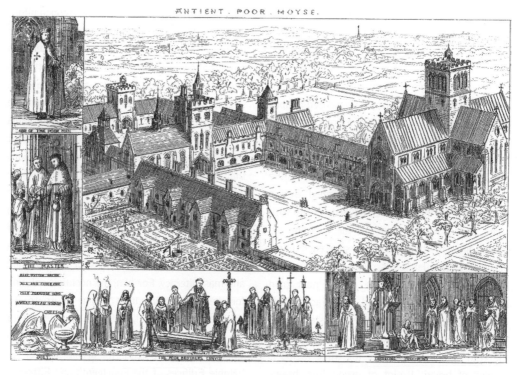

Figure 2 Augustus Welby Northmore Pugin (1812–52), "Contrasted Residences for the Poor" (1846). In *Contrasts* (1836, second edition 1841). Etching. 26 × 21 cm. Source: courtesy of the Thomas Fisher Rare Books Library, University of Toronto.

progress and human improvement through rationality, science, technology, and industrialization. Both Macaulay and Pugin read the signs of the times with one of the dominant modes of contrast used by Victorians, a temporal contrast that viewed the present through the lens of the past. Such contrasts between present and past were used throughout the nineteenth century to discuss the condition of England; for instance, at the end of Victoria's reign, advances in all areas of endeavour, such as progress in shipping, transportation, travel, and street lighting, were illustrated in a tribute to her Jubilee (see Plate 2: "Scientific Progress").

We arrange our selections about the condition of England under five headings: the VICTORIAN SOCIAL FORMATION; PROGRESS, INDUSTRIALIZATION AND REFORM (WEB); WORKING-CLASS VOICES (WEB); EDUCATION AND MASS LITERACY; and POLLUTION, PROTECTION, AND PRESERVATION (WEB). Our first category, the Victorian social formation, demonstrates how Victorians drew contrasts between the different classes and their lives, work, and appearances. Pugin mitigates the class structure within an idealistic and holistic social structure dominated by the church; Disraeli in *Sybil* (1845) claimed that "the Privileged and the People formed Two Nations," enunciating the contrast between the classes that relied on financial resources and economic stability – a stability that was shifting throughout the Victorian era, from landowners to business and industrial magnates, and from rural farm-workers displaced from impoverished fields to perhaps equally impoverished urban factory workers, living in squalor and obsessed with mere survival.

Such a divided country demanded reform, considered under our second category covering progress, industrialization, and reform. The gloominess of Carlyle and Pugin's assessment of their contemporaries can be contrasted to the optimism of Macaulay and Prince Albert's arguments for progress. Following the end of the Napoleonic Wars in 1815, and in the ensuing social chaos from industrial urbanization, political struggles for reform erupted in the industrial Midlands. The boom-and-bust in the various stages of the cotton industry's adaptation of new technology, such as the move from water power to steam in the 1840s, meant that in the county of Lancashire alone there were 2,650 cotton mills employing almost a half million workers, many poorly housed, overworked, and ill-fed. Resistance to reform on the part of those born into privilege had to be set against the abject suffering of the poor. Yet the Reform Bills of 1832, 1867, and 1884 increased male suffrage and began reforms in other areas, such as education and social welfare. Such massive shifts in social and political power depended upon all kinds of technological developments: a sewage system for metropolitan London; the move from gas to electric lighting; a vast railway system with armies of embankment builders, tunnel diggers, and steel rail layers; steam machinery in the mills; and steam presses for newspapers – all of these fundamentally changed the ways people interacted with each other and with their environment.

New working-class voices, our third category, began to be heard above or along with the clatter of looms and the roar of steam. The Chartists demanded just wages, fair working conditions, and the male franchise; they quickly engulfed the nation, expressing their unrest in both mass meetings and mass writing. The poor and disempowered continued to insist that they have a say in their own society, writing their own autobiographies and setting out their ideals in often inflammatory prose and verse. For instance, the Chartist poet Thomas Cooper (WEB p. 57), who in his autobiography describes seeking the help of Benjamin Disraeli in order to get his poems published following his release from prison. Others saw the necessity of providing universal education for the poor as it became increasingly clear that political reform could not be stopped.

Our fourth section, EDUCATION AND MASS LITERACY, sets out these educational goals in a variety of voices: from the great public schools by Thomas Arnold at Rugby and, fictionalized by a former student there, Thomas Hughes. It was in fiction that many of the demands for educational reform were often set forth, as in Dickens's parody of the degrading effects of Utilitarian education gone berserk in the first chapter of *Hard Times*. These were demands not only for education for boys, but also for men in the Working Men's College movement and numerous opportunities for the increasingly diverse education of women. Inns, pubs, and eating rooms throughout the realm continued to carry the newspapers and a number of leading journals for their patrons, but the explosion caused first by the steam printing press and then by the illustrated newspapers like the *Illustrated London News*, gave to the greatly increasing reading public, as announced in its first edition, "the very form and presence of events as they transpire, in all their substantial reality" (14 May 1842). Literacy became the coveted possession of many thousands with a related increase in sensational and thrilling reading material – and a concomitant fear on the part of the middle and governing classes that good taste was threatened by a flood of street literature, thrillers, and general vulgarity. A parallel burst of information on all topics came with the great journals like the *Edinburgh*, *Quarterly*, and *Cornhill*, as well as the numerous publications of the Society for the Diffusion of Useful Knowledge (founded 1826) whose *Penny Magazine* had a circulation of 200,000 a week in 1832.

With the demands of industry for more production and the related growth in urbanization came tremendous pollution, along with demands for better air and water and the protection of the environment: our fifth section, POLLUTION, PROTECTION, AND PRESERVATION (WEB). As these writings show, all kinds of worthy causes were in competition for the public eye and for public funds, all seeking to demonstrate that the Victorian era was not nearly so spiritually adrift as Pugin had considered it to be just before the reign of Victoria began.

In 1909, eight years after Victoria's death, Charles F. G. Masterman (1873–1927), a Liberal politician and journalist, published a survey of the social and political state of his society, entitled again, *The Condition of England*.

Like Pugin and Carlyle he was critical of the conditions of his time, but unlike them, when he contrasted the present with the past, he was optimistic for the future: "The nineteenth century—in the life of the wage-earning multitudes—was a century of disturbance. The twentieth promises to be a century of consolidation." He gives a caveat, claiming in the first chapter that if one were to draw only on the great Victorian literary figures, the picture of the era would be pessimistic:

> Select ten, say, of the greatest writers of the Victorian era, and attempt from the picture which they present to effect a reconstruction of the Victorian age. The product is a human society so remote from all benignant ways as to demand nothing less than the advent of a kindly comet which will sweep the whole affair into nothingness. Our fathers led their decent, austere lives in that Victorian age … inspired by their vigorous, if limited, creeds. They wrangled about politics and theology: they feasted at Christmas, and in the summer visited the seaside: they gave alms to the poor, and rejoiced that they lived in nineteenth-century England. But to the prophets of their age they were unclean from crown of head to sole of foot, a people who had visibly exhausted the patience of God.

Masterman then cites many of the writers included in our *Anthology*, Carlyle, Ruskin, Meredith, Arnold, Morris, Tennyson, Froude, Thomson, and others, as examples of harsh critics of the Victorian condition of England: "Literature has no tolerance for the existence of comfort and security which to so many people seems the last word of human welfare. And no reconstruction, from the works of genius, the great novelists, artists, critics, of the vanishing present, can provide any judgment much more satisfying to our pride than the judgment of summarized theft and fraud and violence which is the weekly enjoyment of many million readers. We know—at once—that this is a one-sided verdict."

In a like manner, the majority of the selections that follow represent the "Condition of England" in a largely negative light – castigating its industrialization and class relations, its political and social deprivations, and what we now call its environmental issues; nevertheless, such a depiction is too simplistic, as our selections also indicate. To many, the age was not a single, bleak expanse of gloom, but an era marked by opportunity – from the building of the Houses of Parliament and the Great Exhibition of 1851 to the Diamond Jubilee – and more than opportunity: it had become an age of progress and prosperity, of achievement and expansion. This later condition of England was the envy of the world – but it remained a complex, many-layered, contradictory, and still elusive condition.

1. The Victorian Social Formation

Edward Bulwer-Lytton (1803–73): *Pelham, or, Adventures of a Gentleman* (1828)

From Chapter 1[1]

I am an only child. My father was the younger son of one of our oldest earls; my mother the dowerless daughter of a Scotch peer. Mr. Pelham was a moderate whig, and gave sumptuous dinners;—Lady Frances was a woman of taste, and particularly fond of diamonds and old china.

Vulgar people know nothing of the necessaries required in good society, and the credit they give is as short as their pedigree. Six years after my birth, there was an execution in our house. My mother was just setting off on a visit to the Duchess of D—; she declared it was impossible to go without her diamonds. The chief of the bailiffs declared it was impossible to trust them out of his sight. The matter was compromised—the bailiff went with my mother to C—, and was introduced as *my tutor.* "A man of singular merit," whispered my mother, "but *so* shy!" Fortunately, the bailiff was abashed, and by losing his impudence he kept the secret. At the end of the week, the diamonds went to the jeweller's, and Lady Frances wore paste.[2] ...

My father went down to run his last horse at Newmarket,[3] and my mother received nine hundred people in a Turkish tent.[4] Both were equally fortunate, the *Greek*[5] and the *Turk*; my father's horse *lost*, in consequence of which he pocketed five thousand pounds; and my mother looked so charming as a Sultana, that Seymour Conway fell desperately in love with her.

Notes

The Victorian Social Formation

[1] *title* from the opening of the life of Henry Pelham, a dandy and man about town. Silver fork novels, of which this is a famous example, represent high society and fashionable life, and were very popular in the 1820s and 1830s. Associated with the Regency period, they simultaneously celebrate and satirize the upper classes. Our text: second edition 1828.

[2] *paste* imitation diamonds.

[3] *Newmarket* town in Suffolk with centuries-old race track, associated with aristocratic decadence.

[4] *Turkish tent* Turkish dress became fashionable in the eighteenth century, partly from the influence of Lady Mary Wortley Montagu (1689–1762), wife of the ambassador to Constantinople, who brought exotic costumes to the London social world from 1725 on. She popularized Turkish fashion in *Turkish Embassy Letters* (1763). By the 1780s the harem craze continued in art and music, as in the fashionable operas of Mozart like *The Abduction from the Seraglio* (1782). Although Pelham's mother is indulging in a showy display of high fashion, reform-minded Victorian women would later adopt Turkish dress to indicate a radical political or social agenda, especially Turkish pantaloons as a bicycling costume associated with freedom of movement for women in the 1880s and 1890s.

[5] *the Greek* archaic phrase meaning a cheat or swindler, here referring to Pelham's father's fixing of a horse race.

Mr. Conway had just caused two divorces;[6] and of course, all the women in London were dying for him—judge then of the pride which Lady Frances felt at his addresses. The end of the season was unusually dull, and my mother, after having looked over her list of engagements, and ascertained that she had none remaining worth staying for, agreed to elope with her new lover.

The carriage was at the end of the square. My mother, for the first time in her life, got up at six o'clock. Her foot was on the step, and her hand next to Mr. Conway's heart, when she remembered that her favourite china monster[7] and her French dog were left behind. She insisted on returning—re-entered the house, and was coming down stairs with one under each arm, when she was met by my father and two servants. My father's valet had discovered the flight (I forget how), and awakened his master.

When my father was convinced of his loss, he called for his dressing-gown—searched the garret and the kitchen—looked in the maid's drawers and the cellaret—and finally declared he was distracted. I have heard that the servants were quite melted by his grief, and I do not doubt it in the least, for he was always celebrated for his skill in private theatricals. He was just retiring to vent his grief in his dressing-room, when he met my mother. It must altogether have been an awkward *rencontre*, and, indeed, for my father, a remarkably unfortunate occurrence; for Seymour Conway was immensely rich, and the damages would, no doubt, have been proportionably high. Had they met each other alone, the affair might easily have been settled, and Lady Frances gone off in tranquillity;—those d—d[8] servants are always in the way!

I have, however, often thought that it was better for me that the affair ended thus,—as I know, from many instances, that it is frequently exceedingly inconvenient to have one's mother divorced.

I have observed that the distinguishing trait of people accustomed to good society, is a calm, imperturbable quiet, which pervades all their actions and habits, from the greatest to the least: they eat in quiet, move in quiet, live in quiet, and lose their wife, or even their money, in quiet; while low persons cannot take up either a spoon or an affront without making such an amazing noise about it. To render this observation good, and to return to the intended elopement, nothing farther was said upon that event. My father introduced Conway to Brookes's,[9] and invited him to dinner twice a week for a whole twelvemonth.

Not long after this occurrence, by the death of my grandfather, my uncle succeeded to the title and estates of the family. He was, as people justly observed, rather an odd man: built schools for peasants, forgave poachers, and diminished his farmers' rents; indeed, on account of these and similar eccentricities, he was thought a fool by some, and a madman by others. However, he was not quite destitute of natural feeling; for he paid my father's debts, and established us in the secure enjoyment of our former splendour. But this piece of generosity, or justice, was done in the most unhandsome manner; he obtained a promise from my father to retire from Brookes's, and relinquish the turf; and he prevailed upon my mother to take an aversion to diamonds, and an indifference to china monsters.

Notes

[6] *divorces* until the Divorce Act (1857), divorces could be obtained only through the church courts first, and then by an act of Parliament – both very expensive (see GENDER: WOMAN; NORTON, LETTER). The allegation that Conway committed adultery, thereby causing divorces, implies that the aggrieved husbands were rich.

[7] *monster* expensive collectibles, porcelain lions or dragons imported from China, a fad beginning in the early eighteenth century.

[8] *d—d* conventional spelling for "damned" from the mid-eighteenth century, here an upper-class curse directed at the servant class. This self-censorship in the typographic use of the dash for the missing letters enabled publishers to escape punishments that might be incurred under the Profane Oaths Act (1745), finally replaced by the Criminal Law Act (1967).

[9] *Brookes's*, usually spelled "Brooks's," an exclusive Whig gentleman's club in London, associated with heavy gambling. Bulwer-Lytton was a member.

WEB p. 3

William Cobbett (1763–1835): From *Rural Rides* (1830)
Victoria (1819–1901): From *Letters* (20 June 1837)
 ["I am *Queen*"]

Thomas Carlyle (1795–1881): *Chartism* (1840)

From Chapter 1: "Condition-of-England Question"[10]

A feeling very generally exists that the condition and disposition of the Working Classes is a rather ominous matter at present; that something ought to be said, something ought to be done, in regard to it. And surely, at an epoch of history when the "National Petition"[11] carts itself in waggons along the streets, and is presented "bound with iron hoops, four men bearing it," to a Reformed House of Commons;[12] and Chartism numbered by the million and half, taking nothing by its iron-hooped Petition, breaks out into brickbats, cheap pikes, and even into sputterings of conflagration, such very general feeling cannot be considered unnatural! To us individually this matter appears, and has for many years appeared, to be the most ominous of all practical matters whatever; a matter in regard to which if something be not done, something will *do* itself one day, and in a fashion that will please nobody. The time is verily come for acting in it; how much more for consultation about acting in it, for speech and articulate inquiry about it! . . .

The melancholy fact remains, that this thing known at present by the name Chartism does exist; has existed; and, either "put down," into secret treason, with rusty pistols, vitriol-bottle and match-box, or openly brandishing pike and torch (one knows not in which case *more* fatal-looking), is like to exist till quite other methods have been tried with it. What means this bitter discontent of the Working Classes? Whence comes it, whither goes it? Above all, at what price, on what terms, will it probably consent to depart from us and die into rest? These are questions. . . .

Delirious Chartism will not have raged entirely to no purpose, as indeed no earthly thing does so, if it have forced all thinking men of the community to think of this vital matter, too apt to be overlooked otherwise. Is the condition of the English working people wrong; so wrong that rational working men cannot, will not, and even should not rest quiet under it? A most grave case, complex beyond all others in the world; a case wherein Botany Bay,[13] constabulary rural police, and such like, will avail but little. Or is the discontent itself mad, like the shape it took? Not the condition of the working people that is wrong; but their disposition, their own thoughts, beliefs and feelings that are wrong? This too were a most grave case, little less alarming, little less complex than the former one. In this case too, where constabulary police and mere rigour of coercion seems more

Notes

[10] *title* named after the People's Charter of May 1838, the Chartists demanded six reforms: universal male suffrage; the secret ballot; removal of property qualifications for Members of Parliament; salaries for Members of Parliament; balanced electoral districts with equal numbers of electors; and annual parliamentary elections.

[11] *Petition* Chartists presented a large petition to Parliament in June 1839 that was rejected, leading to riots and loss of life. Later protests in Birmingham, London, and elsewhere would culminate in public riots in 1848.

[12] *Commons* the Reform Parliament of 1832 had made first steps in lowering the property and income qualifications for the franchise, but subsequent governments did not extend the vote to working-class men, as the Charter had demanded.

[13] *Botany Bay* near Sydney in south-east Australia, established by Britain in 1788 as a penal colony for deported criminals, sentenced to transportation, marking the beginning of colonization in Australia. After riots in November 1839 in Newport three Chartists would be transported to Australia.

at home, coercion will by no means do all, coercion by itself will not even do much. If there do exist general madness of discontent, then sanity and some measure of content must be brought about again,—not by constabulary police alone. When the thoughts of a people, in the great mass of it, have grown mad, the combined issue of that people's workings will be a madness, an incoherency and ruin! Sanity will have to be recovered for the general mass; coercion itself will otherwise cease to be able to coerce....

Surely Honourable Members ought to speak of the Condition-of-England question too. Radical Members,[14] above all; friends of the people; chosen with effort, by the people, to interpret and articulate the dumb deep want of the people! To a remote observer they seem oblivious of their duty. Are they not there, by trade, mission, and express appointment of themselves and others, to speak for the good of the British Nation? Whatsoever great British interest can the least speak for itself, for that beyond all they are called to speak. They are either speakers for that great dumb toiling class which cannot speak, or they are nothing that one can well specify....

What are the rights, what are the mights of the discontented Working Classes in England at this epoch? He were an Oedipus,[15] and deliverer from sad social pestilence, who could resolve us fully! For we may say beforehand, The struggle that divides the upper and lower in society over Europe, and more painfully and notably in England than elsewhere, this too is a struggle which will end and adjust itself as all other struggles do and have done, by making the right clear and the might clear; not otherwise than by that. Meantime, the questions, Why are the Working Classes discontented; what is their condition, economical, moral, in their houses and their hearts, as it is in reality and as they figure it to themselves to be; what do they complain of; what ought they, and ought they not to complain of?—these are measurable questions; on some of these any common mortal, did he but turn his eyes to them, might throw some light. Certain researches and considerations of ours on the matter, since no one else will undertake it, are now to be made public. The researches have yielded us little, almost nothing; but the considerations are of old date, and press to have utterance. We are not without hope that our general notion of the business, if we can get it uttered at all, will meet some assent from many candid men.

Thomas Carlyle (1795–1881): *Past and Present* (1843)

From Book I, Chapter 1: "Midas"[16]

The condition of England, on which many pamphlets are now in the course of publication, and many thoughts unpublished are going on in every reflective head, is justly regarded as one of the most ominous, and withal one of the strangest, ever seen in this world. England is full of wealth, of multifarious produce, supply for human want in every kind;

Notes ──────────────────────────────────────

[14] *Honourable Members ... Radical Members* members of the House of Commons in general, and especially radical members who advocated social and political reforms. The term was first applied in the eighteenth century to Charles James Fox (1749–1806), and later to the followers of Thomas Paine (1737–1809) against Edmund Burke (1729–97) at the time of the French Revolution. In Carlyle's time, Radicals referred to the supporters of the People's Charter, such as Richard Cobden (1804–65) and John Bright (1811–89). They led the parliamentary Radicals from 1839 with the establishment of the Anti-Corn Law League, opposing duties on imported grain that raised the price of wheat and bread, good for landowners, but not for agricultural and other workers.

[15] *Oedipus* in Sophocles play (429 BCE), Oedipus seeks to deliver the city of Thebes from the plague by finding out why the gods have sent it, little realizing that he is its cause for unknowingly killing his father and marrying his mother.

[16] *title* Carlyle conflates the two versions of the story of Midas, king of Phrygia, told in Ovid's *Metamorphoses*: how Bacchus (Dionysus) granted his wish that "whatever I touch may turn to gold," thoughtlessly including his food and daughter (II: 85–145) – in Carlyle a metaphor for the Victorians' pursuit of money. The second version tells how Midas awarded the prize for music to Pan instead of Apollo. In retaliation Apollo replaced Midas' "stupid ears" with the ears of "the slow-going jackass" (II: 146–190).

yet England is dying of inanition. With unabated bounty the land of England blooms and grows; waving with yellow harvests; thick-studded with workshops, industrial implements, with fifteen millions of workers understood to be the strongest, the cunningest and the willingest our Earth ever had; these men are here; the work they have done, the fruit they have realized is here, abundant, exuberant on every hand of us: and behold, some baleful fiat as of Enchantment[17] has gone forth, saying, "Touch it not, ye workers, ye master-workers, ye master-idlers; none of you can touch it, no man of you shall be the better for it; this is enchanted fruit!"[18] On the poor workers such fiat falls first, in its rudest shape; but on the rich master-workers too it falls; neither can the rich master-idlers, nor any richest or highest man escape, but all are like to be brought low with it, and made "poor" enough, in the money sense or a far fataller one.

Of these successful skilful workers some two millions, it is now counted, sit in Workhouses, Poor-Law Prisons; or have "out-door relief" flung over the wall to them,— the Workhouse Bastille[19] being filled to bursting, and the strong Poor-Law broken asunder by a stronger.[20] They sit there, these many months now; their hope of deliverance as yet small. In Workhouses, pleasantly so named, because work cannot be done in them. Twelve hundred thousand workers in England alone; their cunning right-hand lamed, lying idle in their sorrowful bosom; their hopes, outlooks, share of this fair world, shut in by narrow walls. They sit there, pent up, as in a kind of horrid enchantment; glad to be imprisoned and enchanted, that they may not perish starved. The picturesque Tourist,[21] in a sunny autumn day, through this bounteous realm of England, describes the Union Workhouse on his path. "Passing by the Workhouse of St. Ives[22] in Huntingdonshire, on a bright day last autumn," says the picturesque Tourist, "I saw sitting on wooden benches, in front of their Bastille and within their ring-wall and its railings, some half-hundred or more of these men. Tall robust figures, young mostly or of middle age; of honest countenance, many of them thoughtful and even intelligent looking men. They sat there, near by one another; but in a kind of torpor, especially in a silence, which was very striking. In silence: for, alas, what word was to be said? An Earth all lying round, crying 'Come and till me, come and reap me';—yet we here sit enchanted! In the eyes and brows of these men hung the gloomiest expression, not of anger, but of grief and shame and manifold inarticulate distress and weariness; they returned my glance with a glance that seemed to say, 'Do not look at us. We sit enchanted here, we know not why. The Sun shines and the Earth calls; and, by the governing Powers and Impotences of this England we are forbidden to obey. It is impossible, they tell us!' There was something that reminded me of Dante's Hell in the look of all this; and I rode swiftly away." ...

At Stockport Assizes,—and this too has no reference to the present state of trade, being of date prior to that,—a Mother and a Father are arraigned and found guilty of poisoning

Notes

[17] *Enchantment* the spell of death imposed by a wicked fairy in Charles Perrault's *Sleeping Beauty* (1697), ameliorated to a hundred-year sleep by a good fairy, who casts all of the inhabitants into suspended animation.

[18] *fruit* see Genesis 2: 17.

[19] *Workhouses ... Bastille* the number of workhouses greatly increased as a result of the Poor Law Act of 1834 that required even able-bodied paupers to seek relief by residing in a parish workhouse or union workhouse (for a union of parishes), called by Carlyle in *Chartism*, a "Poor-Law Bastille," using the term from the hated prison in Paris stormed as a symbol of tyranny in the French Revolution of 1789. The term "Bastile" was in currency in *The Book of the Bastile; or, the History of the Working of the New-Law* (1841) by George R. Wythen Baxter, a vast

collection of reports that attacked the New Poor Law; see MASSEY, n. 3.

[20] *stronger* "*The Return of Paupers for England and Wales, at Ladyday*, 1842, is, 'In-door 221,687, Out-door 1,207,402, Total 1,429,089.'—(*Official Report*)" [author's note]. Ladyday, the feast of the Annunciation in the calendar of the Church of England, dates the report to 25 March 1842.

[21] *Tourist* Carlyle's derogatory description of himself as seeking scenes of rural beauty dotted with medieval ruins, as in William Cobbett's *Rural Rides* (1830) and William Taylor's *Notes of a Tour in the Manufacturing Districts of Lancashire* (1842) (both of which Carlyle had read), is here juxtaposed ironically to rural blight.

[22] *St. Ives* in 1842 Carlyle had visited this workhouse, built in 1838 for 200 inmates.

three of their children, to defraud a "burial-society"of some 3*l*.8*s*. due on the death of each child: they are arraigned, found guilty; and the official authorities, it is whispered, hint that perhaps the case is not solitary, that perhaps you had better not probe farther into that department of things.[23] This is in the autumn of 1841; the crime itself is of the previous year or season. "Brutal savages, degraded Irish," mutters the idle reader of Newspapers; hardly lingering on this incident. Yet it is an incident worth lingering on; the depravity, savagery and degraded Irishism being never so well admitted. In the British land, a human Mother and Father, of white skin and professing the Christian religion, had done this thing; they, with their Irishism and necessity and savagery, had been driven to do it. Such instances are like the highest mountain apex emerged into view; under which lies a whole mountain region and land, not yet emerged. A human Mother and Father had said to themselves, What shall we do to escape starvation? We are deep sunk here, in our dark cellar; and help is far.—Yes, in the Ugolino Hunger-tower[24] stern things happen; best-loved little Gaddo fallen dead on his Father's knees!—The Stockport Mother and Father think and hint: Our poor little starveling Tom, who cries all day for victuals, who will see only evil and not good in this world: if he were out of misery at once; he well dead, and the rest of us perhaps kept alive? It is thought, and hinted; at last it is done. And now Tom being killed, and all spent and eaten, Is it poor little starveling Jack that must go, or poor little starveling Will?—What an *inquiry*[25] of ways and means! ....

To whom, then, is this wealth of England wealth? Who is it that it blesses; makes happier, wiser, beautifuller, in any way better? Who has got hold of it, to make it fetch and carry for him, like a true servant, not like a false mock-servant; to do him any real service whatsoever? As yet no one. We have more riches than any Nation ever had before; we have less good of them than any Nation ever had before. Our successful industry is hitherto unsuccessful; a strange success, if we stop here! In the midst of plethoric plenty, the people perish; with gold walls, and full barns, no man feels himself safe or satisfied. Workers, Master Workers, Unworkers, all men, come to a pause; stand fixed, and cannot farther. Fatal paralysis spreading inwards, from the extremities, in St. Ives Workhouses, in Stockport cellars, through all limbs, as if towards the heart itself. Have we actually got enchanted then; accursed by some god?—

Midas longed for gold, and insulted the Olympians. He got gold, so that whatsoever he touched became gold,—and he, with his long ears, was little the better for it. Midas had misjudged the celestial music-tones; Midas had insulted Apollo and the gods: the gods gave him his wish, and a pair of long ears, which also were a good appendage to it. What a truth in these old Fables!

Benjamin Disraeli (1804–81): *Sybil* (1845)

From Book 2, Chapter 5 [The Two Nations][26]

"It is a community of purpose that constitutes society," continued the younger stranger; "without that, men may be drawn into contiguity, but they still continue virtually isolated."

Notes

[23] *Stockport ... things* reported in the *Examiner* (1 Nov. 1840); a coroner's jury found the parents guilty of murder of their children to secure the payments of £3 8s. 6d. per child from the Philanthropic Burial Society. The *Examiner* (17 Aug. 1841) reported that in the criminal trial the father was convicted of murder.

[24] *Hunger-tower* in *Inferno* 33: 1–90 Dante tells of imprisoned Count Ugolino da Pisa whose children urge him to cannibalism to avoid watching him starve.

[25] *inquiry* changed to "a committee" in 1845 to stress the role of a parliamentary committee of "ways and means." Ways and Means committees dealt with government budgets in relation to specific pieces of legislation.

[26] *title* this social-problem novel, the second of Disraeli's Young England trilogy, is a harsh critique of Chartism from the position of aristocratic conservatism or benevolent paternalism. In this famous passage, the hero Charles Egremont meets Stephen Morley, a radical who eventually becomes

"And is that their condition in cities?"

"It is their condition everywhere; but in cities that condition is aggravated. A density of population implies a severer struggle for existence, and a consequent repulsion of elements brought into too close contact. In great cities men are brought together by the desire of gain. They are not in a state of co-operation, but of isolation, as to the making of fortunes; and for all the rest they are careless of neighbours. Christianity teaches us to love our neighbour as ourself;[27] modern society acknowledges no neighbour."

"Well, we live in strange times," said Egremont, struck by the observation of his companion, and relieving a perplexed spirit by an ordinary exclamation, which often denotes that the mind is more stirring than it cares to acknowledge, or at the moment is capable to express.

"When the infant begins to walk, it also thinks that it lives in strange times," said his companion.

"Your inference?" asked Egremont.

"That society, still in its infancy, is beginning to feel its way."

"This is a new reign," said Egremont, "perhaps it is a new era."

"I think so," said the younger stranger.

"I hope so," said the elder one.

"Well, society may be in its infancy," said Egremont slightly smiling; "but, say what you like, our Queen reigns over the greatest nation that ever existed."

"Which nation?" asked the younger stranger, "for she reigns over two."

The stranger paused; Egremont was silent, but looked inquiringly.

"Yes," resumed the younger stranger after a moment's interval. "Two nations; between whom there is no intercourse and no sympathy; who are as ignorant of each other's habits, thoughts, and feelings, as if they were dwellers in different zones, or inhabitants of different planets; who are formed by a different breeding, are fed by a different food, are ordered by different manners, and are not governed by the same laws."

"You speak of —" said Egremont, hesitatingly.

"THE RICH AND THE POOR."[28]

At this moment a sudden flush of rosy light, suffusing the grey ruins, indicated that the sun had just fallen; and through a vacant arch that overlooked them, alone in the resplendent sky, glittered the twilight star. The hour, the scene, the solemn stillness and the softening beauty, repressed controversy, induced even silence. The last words of the stranger lingered in the ear of Egremont; his musing spirit was teeming with many thoughts, many emotions; when from the Lady Chapel there rose the evening hymn[29] to the Virgin. A single voice; but tones of almost supernatural sweetness; tender and solemn, yet flexible and thrilling.[30]

Notes

the villain of the novel. The phrase "the two nations" had been coined by Dr William Channing of Boston, a Unitarian minister, in 1841: "In most large cities there may be said to be two nations, understanding as little of one another, having as little intercourse as if they lived in different lands. In such a city as London the distance of a few streets will carry you from one stage of civilization to another, from the excess of refinement to barbarism, from the abodes of cultivated intellect to brutal ignorance, from what is called fashion to the grossest manners; and these distinct communities know comparatively nothing of each other" (*A Discourse on the Life and Character of The Rev. Joseph Tuckerman*).

[27] *ourself* see Matthew 22: 36–40.

[28] *POOR* see Plato *Republic* 8.551d; Engels uses an almost identical phrase in his discussion of Irish immigrants in Manchester in *The Condition of the Working-Class in England in 1844* (1845).

[29] *hymn* very likely either the ninth- century evening hymn, *Ave Maris Stella* (Lat. Hail, O star of the ocean), or the early eleventh-century hymn used at the last or evening office of the Day (Compline), *Salve, Regina, Mater misericordiae* (Lat. Hail, O Queen, Mother of mercy).

[30] *thrilling* the singer is Sybil, the titular heroine and love-interest of the novel.

George Cruikshank (1792–1878): *The British Bee Hive.* Process engraving (1867)[31]

Figure 3 George Cruikshank (1792–1878), *The British Bee Hive* (1867). Process Engraving. 26 × 19.5 cm. Source: courtesy of the Thomas Fisher Library, University of Toronto.

Notes

[31] *title* Cruikshank was a renowned British cartoonist and book illustrator of such works as Dickens's *Oliver Twist* (1838) and Grimm's *Fairy Tales* (1853). The metaphor comparing society to the ordered culture of the bees with their queen derives from Bernard Mandeville's *Fable of the Bees* (1714). First designed in 1840, the etching was published separately in 1867 with a tract opposing the Second Reform Bill and its extension of the franchise. In his old age the former radical preferred the *status quo*, each worker in his place: "If Universal Suffrage were

Matthew Arnold (1822–88): *Culture and Anarchy* (1869)

From III [Chapter 3: "Barbarians, Philistines, Populace"][32]

For the middle class, for that great body which, as we know, "has done all the great things that have been done in all departments,"[33] and which is to be conceived as moving between its two cardinal points of our commercial member of Parliament and our fanatical Protestant Dissenter,[34]—for this class we have a designation which now has become pretty well known, and which we may as well still keep for them, the designation of Philistines. What this term means I have so often explained[35] that I need not repeat it here. For the aristocratic class, conceived mainly as a body moving between the two cardinal points of our chivalrous lord and our defiant baronet,[36] we have as yet got no special designation. Almost all my attention has naturally been concentrated on my own class, the middle class, with which I am in closest sympathy, and which has been, besides, the great power of our day, and has had its praises sung by all speakers and newspapers....

For *Philistine*[37] gives the notion of something particularly stiff-necked and perverse in the resistance to light and its children; and therein it specially suits our middle class, who not only do not pursue sweetness and light, but who even prefer to them that sort of machinery of business, chapels, tea-meetings, and addresses from Mr. Murphy,[38] which makes up the dismal and illiberal life on which I have so often touched....

I have in my own mind often indulged myself with the fancy of employing, in order to designate our aristocratic class, the name of *the Barbarians*.[39] The Barbarians, to whom we all owe so much, and who reinvigorated and renewed our worn-out Europe, had, as is well known, eminent merits; and in this country, where we are for the most part sprung from the Barbarians, we have never had the prejudice against them which prevails among the races of Latin origin. The Barbarians brought with them that staunch individualism,

Notes

granted, if everything were allowed, or even a great part of what is asked for, and *everyone* had a vote, it would cease to be a monarchy and would become a REPUBLIC." In his metaphor, movement between the layers of the beehive is almost impossible, a good thing to him now because the system works "wonderfully well" and is "almost as perfect as it can be made by man." Cruikshank's beehive is hierarchical, with the queen and royal family above the British Constitution and parliament, with religion and law below, followed by the hierarchies of professions, followed by the ranks of domestics and other workers, all held up at the foundational level by the economic power of business, the banks, and the military power of the army and navy, as well as merchant shipping. Cruikshank's earlier designs had taken a far more radical political approach, but are similar in illustrating society in a hierarchical pyramid.

[32] *title* Arnold's three terms refer to his division of the three classes of English society, "Barbarians" (the aristocracy), the "Philistines" (the middle classes), and the "Populace" (the working classes). For *Culture and Anarchy*, see ARNOLD, n. 30 (WEB p. 391).

[33] *departments* Arnold quotes from a lead article on middle-class education in *Daily News* (7 Dec. 1864).

[34] *commercial member ... Dissenter* the two poles of the Liberal Party: by the first, its interest in commerce, Arnold refers to Sir Thomas Bazley (1797–1883), MP for Manchester and a leading cotton manufacturer; and by

the second, protestant dissent, he refers to the Rev. William Cattle, Wesleyan minister from Walsall, a Midlands industrial town north-west of Birmingham, who was associated with William Murphy (1834–72) in promoting anti-Catholic riots in 1867. When this chapter was first published in the *Cornhill Magazine* (June 1868), these names were included, but were removed in the edition of 1869.

[35] *explained* chiefly in his essay "Heinrich Heine" (1863).

[36] *baronet* in the 1869 edition Arnold omitted the names of the people he refers to, Francis Charteris, Lord Elcho (1818–1914), a Conservative MP and his inherited title, and Sir Thomas Bateson (1819–90), Conservative MP for Devizes, who inherited his baronetcy, the lowest rank of the titled. Arnold heard both speak in the Commons on 4 June 1866 in the debate on the second Reform Bill.

[37] *Philistine* for Philistine, see ARNOLD, n. 38 (WEB p. 398).

[38] *Murphy* William Murphy (see n. 34), anti-Catholic lecturer who inflamed his hearers to riot in June 1867 in Birmingham; see ARNOLD, nn. 49 and 52 (WEB p. 397, 398).

[39] *Barbarians* Arnold's linking of the aristocrats to the Barbarians and personal freedom draws on a commonplace from Edward Gibbon's *Decline and Fall of the Roman Empire* (1776–88): "The most civilized nations of modern Europe issued from the woods of Germany; and in the rude institutions of those barbarians we may still distinguish the original principles of our present laws and manners" (pt. 1, ch. 9).

as the modern phrase is, and that passion for doing as one likes,[40] for the assertion of personal liberty.... The stronghold and natural seat of this passion was in the nobles of whom our aristocratic class are the inheritors; and this class, accordingly, have signally manifested it, and have done much by their example to recommend it to the body of the nation, who already, indeed, had it in their blood. The Barbarians, again, had the passion for field-sports;[41] and they have handed it on to our aristocratic class, who of this passion too, as of the passion for asserting one's personal liberty, are the great natural stronghold. The care of the Barbarians for the body, and for all manly exercises; the vigour, good looks, and fine complexion which they acquired and perpetuated in their families by these means,—all this may be observed still in our aristocratic class. The chivalry of the Barbarians, with its characteristics of high spirit, choice manners, and distinguished bearing,—what is this but the attractive commencement of the politeness of our aristocratic class? In some Barbarian noble, no doubt, one would have admired, if one could have been then alive to see it, the rudiments of our politest peer. Only, all this culture (to call it by that name) of the Barbarians was an exterior culture mainly. It consisted principally in outward gifts and graces, in looks, manners, accomplishments, prowess. The chief inward gifts which had part in it were the most exterior, so to speak, of inward gifts, those which come nearest to outward ones; they were courage, a high spirit, self-confidence. Far within, and unawakened, lay a whole range of powers of thought and feeling, to which these interesting productions of nature had, from the circumstances of their life, no access. Making allowances for the difference of the times, surely we can observe precisely the same thing now in our aristocratic class....

That part of the working class, therefore, which does really seem to lend itself to these great aims, may, with propriety, be numbered by us among the Philistines. That part of it, again, which so much occupies the attention of philanthropists at present,—the part which gives all its energies to organising itself, through trades' unions and other means, so as to constitute, first, a great working-class power independent of the middle and aristocratic classes, and then, by dint of numbers, give the law to them and itself reign absolutely,—this lively and promising part must also, according to our definition, go with the Philistines; because it is its class and its class instinct which it seeks to affirm—its ordinary self not its best self; and it is a machinery, an industrial machinery, and power and pre-eminence and other external goods, which fill its thoughts, and not an inward perfection. It is wholly occupied, according to Plato's subtle expression,[42] with the things of itself and not its real self, with the things of the State and not the real State. But that vast portion, lastly, of the working class which, raw and half developed, has long lain half-hidden amidst its poverty and squalor, and is now issuing from its hiding-place to assert an Englishman's heaven-born privilege of doing as he likes, and is beginning to perplex us by marching where it likes, meeting where it likes, bawling what it likes, breaking what it likes,[43]—to this vast residuum we may with great propriety give the name of Populace.[44]

Thus we have got three distinct terms, *Barbarians, Philistines, Populace*, to denote roughly the three great classes into which our society is divided; and though this

Notes

[40] *likes* in chapter 2 of *Culture and Anarchy*, called "Doing as One Likes," Arnold extends the ideal of British liberty to anarchic individualism; see also ARNOLD, n. 43 (WEB p. 395).

[41] *field-sports* included hunting, shooting, and fishing, associated with traditional aristocratic values. These came under attack in the nineteenth century by such social reformers as Arnold's father, who banned the boys at Rugby from engaging in them, substituting alternatives such as cricket and football to promote a new type of masculinity, that of the Christian gentleman (see this section, EDUCATION, n. 13).

[42] *expression* see *Charmides* 169c–172c, where Socrates separates a knowledge about knowledge or a science of science (Gk. *episteme*) from a knowledge (Gk. *gnosis*) about specific things. See TENNYSON, n. 29 (WEB p. 339).

[43] *likes* references to the Hyde Park riot of 23 July 1867; see also ARNOLD, n. 48 (WEB p. 397).

[44] *Populace* etymologically the common people (Lat. *popolo*, the people, as opposed to the nobility or the wealthy; in derogatory terms, the masses, the mob); in Arnold, the lowest part of the working-classes, without a vote and on

humble attempt at a scientific nomenclature falls, no doubt, very far short in precision of what might be required from a writer equipped with a complete and coherent philosophy,[45] yet, from a notoriously unsystematic and unpretending writer, it will, I trust, be accepted as sufficient.

WEB p. 12

Ada Nield Chew (1870–1945): "A Living Wage for Factory Girls at Crewe"(1894)
Eliza Davis Aria (1866–1931): "My Lady's Evening in London" in *Living London* (1901–3)

---

2. Education and Mass Literacy

WEB p. 16

Statistical Society of London: "Newspapers and Other Publications in Coffee, Public, and Eating Houses" (1839)

Illustrated London News (14 May 1842):
From "Our Address"[1]

In presenting the first number of the ILLUSTRATED LONDON NEWS to the British Public, we would fain make a graceful entrée into the wide and grand arena, which will henceforth contain so many actors for our benefit, and so many spectators of our career. In plain language, we do not produce this illustrated newspaper without some vanity, much ambition, and a fond belief that we shall be pardoned the presumption of the first quality by realizing the aspirations of the last. For the past ten years we have watched with admiration and enthusiasm the progress of illustrative art, and the vast revolution which it has wrought in the world of publication, through all the length and breadth of this mighty empire.[2] To the wonderful march of periodical literature it has given an impetus

---

Notes

the edge of or immersed in poverty, but now organizing itself to assert its demands for access to the middle class. See CONDITION: PROGRESS; ARNOLD, *CULTURE* (CONCLUSION) (WEB p. 40).

[45] *philosophy* refers to the newly developing field of sociology; see, for instance, Herbert Spencer, *Social Statics: or, the Conditions Essential to Human Happiness Specified, and the First of Them Developed* (1851).

EDUCATION AND MASS LITERACY

[1] *title* the *ILN* was founded in 1842 by Herbert Ingram (1811–60), with Mark Lemon (1809–70), the editor of *Punch*, as advisor. First published at sixpence for sixteen pages with thirty-two wood engravings, it continued weekly publication until 1971. The world's first pictorial newspaper, the *ILN* appealed to the middle classes and claimed that its printed text and realistic graphics covered politics, stressing the interests of the reformers—"your Poor-laws—your Corn-laws—

your Factory-bills—your Income-taxes!" The *ILN* covered the workings of the justice system in illustrations of the courts and crime, natural disasters, foreign news, leisure, and literature and the fine arts. Soon it was selling 65,000 copies a week, increasing to 300,000 copies during the Crimean War (1853–56). In the second issue (21 May 1842), the *ILN* explained its aims further in "Our Principles." See LITERATURE: NEW TECHNOLOGIES; KNIGHT, *OLD*; AND JACKSON, *PICTORIAL* (WEB p. 146–47).

[2] *empire* illustrations proliferated in letterpress printing of books on architecture, art, and literature (well-known artists illustrated the novels of Dickens and Thackeray and the poems of Tennyson), as well as botany, geology, history, and every other subject, from UK and colonial presses. Ingram lured many of Dickens's artists to also draw for him, including George Cruikshank (1798–1872) and "Phiz" (Hablot K. Browne (1815–82)).

and rapidity almost coequal with the gigantic power of steam.[3] It has converted blocks into wisdom, and given wings and spirit to ponderous and senseless wood.[4] It has in its turn adorned, gilded, reflected, and interpreted nearly every form of thought. It has given to fancy a new dwelling-place—to imagination a more permanent throne. It has set up fresh land-marks of poetry, given sterner pungency to satire, and mapped out the geography of mind with clearer boundaries and more distinct and familiar intelligence than it ever bore alone....

And there is now no staying the advance of this art into all the departments of our social system. It began in a few isolated volumes—stretched itself next over fields of natural history and science—penetrated the arcanæ of our own general literature—and made companionship with our household books.[5] At one plunge it was in the depth of the stream of poetry—working with its every current—partaking of the glow, and adding to the sparkles of the glorious waters—and so refreshing the very soul of genius, that even Shakspere came to us clothed with a new beauty,[6] while other kindred poets of our language seemed as it were to have put on festive garments to crown the marriage of their muses to the arts. Then it walked abroad among the people, went into the poorer cottages, and visited the humblest homes in cheap guises, and perhaps, in roughish forms; but still with the illustrative and the instructive principle strongly worked upon, and admirably developed for the general improvement of the human race. Lastly, it took the merry aspect of fun, frolic, satire, and *badinage*; and the school of *Charivari*[7] began to blend itself with the graver pabulum of Penny Cyclopædias and Saturday Magazines[8]....

The public will have henceforth under their glance, and within their grasp, the very form and presence of events as they transpire, in all their substantial reality, and with evidence visible as well as circumstantial....

Notes

[3] *steam* steam was first used by *The Times* in 1814 in a printing press made by the German firm of Koenig and Bauer, increasing the number of pages from about 250 on hand-presses to 2,000 per hour. In 1828 *The Times* used Applegarth and Cowper's machines to print both sides of 4,200 sheets per hour; in 1848 the same firm supplied *The Times* with a rotary machine to print 12,000 two-sided impressions an hour. By 1854 the *ILN* was printed on a steam-driven rotary machine.

[4] *wood* boxwood was used for wood engravings, cut into the end grain for relief printing. Many thousands of prints could be printed from a block, and a number of blocks could be screwed together for larger engravings, a number of engravers working simultaneously on parts of an engraving to meet deadlines. The process of electrotyping meant that by using electricity the woodblocks could be reproduced with a thin layer of copper in a mould, later rebacked with metal for longer print runs.

[5] *books* in *The Times* (14 May 1842), for example, there is an advertisement for a number of lavishly illustrated books: Col. Howard Vyse's *Pyramids of Gizeh* "with numerous plates," Parisian books of fashion, John Fisher Murray's *The Environs of London*, *Fletcher's Family Devotion* ("embellished with … elegant engravings"), the *Pictorial Waverley* by Walter Scott (2,100 illustrations) as well as the illustrated Abbotsford edition, in weekly numbers, and John Lindley's *Elements of Botany*.

[6] *beauty* a large number of editions of Shakespeare were published in the nineteenth century, including reprints of the most famous, John Boydell's *Dramatic Works of Shakspeare* [*sic*] (9 vols, 1803, with accompanying plates selling for 60 guineas), John Thurston, *Illustrations of Shakspeare* (1826), John Valpy, *Plays and Poems of Shakspeare* (15 vols, 1832–34), Frank Howard, *The Spirit of the Plays of Shakspeare* (5 vols, 1833), and Charles Heath, *The Heroines of Shakspeare* (1848), to name only a few up to the decade of the publication of the first number of the *ILN*.

[7] *Charivari* a boisterous and noisy mock serenade of newly-weds (often pronounced shivaree), a reference to the leading comic illustrated magazine, *Punch, or the London Charivari*, founded in 1841 by Mark Lemon.

[8] *Magazines* the *Penny Cyclopædia* was published by the Society for the Diffusion of Useful Knowledge from 1833 to 1843. It also issued the *Penny Magazine* from 1832 to 1845, both Whig publications for the working and middle classes. Their competing publication was the *Saturday Magazine*, an illustrated Anglican publication issued from 1833 to 1844 by the Committee of General Literature and Education of the Society of the Promotion of Christian Knowledge.

Illustrated London News (7 Jan. 1843): Dedicatory Sonnet[9]

> To the great public,—that gigantic soul
>   Which lends the nation's body life and light,
>   And makes the blood within its veins grow bright
> With gushing glory,—we this muster-roll[10]
> Of all the deeds that pass neath its controul   5
>   Do dedicate.—The page of simple news
> Is here adorned and filled with pictured life,
> Coloured[11] with thousand tints—the rainbow strife
>   Of all the world's emotions—all the hues
> Of war—peace—commerce;—agriculture rife   10
> With budding plenty that doth life infuse
>   And fair domestic joy—all—all are here
>   To gild the *new*, and from the bygone year
> Present a gift to take—to cherish and to use.

Arthur Penrhyn Stanley (1815–81): *Life and Correspondence of Thomas Arnold, D.D.* (1844)[12]

From "Letter of Inquiry for a Master" by Thomas Arnold (1795–1842)

What I want is a man who is a Christian and a gentleman,[13] an active man, and one who has common sense, and understands boys. I do not so much care about scholarship, as he will have immediatcly under him the lowest forms[14] in the school; but yet, on second thoughts, I do care about it very much, because his pupils may be in the highest forms; and besides, I think that even the elements are best taught by a man who has a thorough knowledge of the matter. However, if one must give way, I prefer activity of mind and an interest in his work, to high scholarship: for the one may be acquired far more easily than the other. I should wish it also to be understood that the new master may be called upon to take boarders in his house, it being my intention for the future to require this of all masters as I see occasion, that so in time the boarding-houses[15] may die a natural death. . . .

Notes

[9] *title* printed at the end of the preface to volume 1 of the collected *ILN*, dated "6 January 1843"; published 7 January 1843.

[10] *muster-roll* in the army, a list of officers and men called out for enumeration; here the collection of individual numbers of the *ILN* collected into volume format.

[11] *Coloured* a transferred epithet, applying colours, shades, or meanings to the black-and-while illustrations. In 1855, the Christmas Supplement of the *ILN* launched colour journalism with its title-page, Christmas scene, and two other full-page prints.

[12] *title* Arnold, British educator and historian, father of Matthew Arnold, became headmaster of Rugby School in 1828 and through his reforms (introducing sports and encouraging self-reliance) influenced the development of the new English public school ethos. Arnold was appointed Regius Professor of Modern History at Oxford University in 1841. The two letters are included in Stanley's biography to explain the values of a Christian gentleman that Dr Arnold was seeking in his assistant masters at Rugby.

[13] *gentleman* Arnold's main purpose was character building by fostering ethical rather than intellectual development, though both were important to him. Arnold shifted the emphasis from a feudal notion of gentleman (stressing military training and blood sports) to ideals of compassion for the disadvantaged, moral earnestness, self-discipline, and fair play.

[14] *forms* both the traditional public schools and the English grammar schools in the nineteenth century divided students into six forms or levels of study, each in two parts, a "lower" and an "upper" section. Beginning little boys of 9 or 10 started in the lower or upper second if they had been to a preparatory school; the upper sixth provided the prefects for the school and prepared students for Oxford and Cambridge entrance examinations.

[15] *boarding-houses* until Arnold's headmastership, most of the boys at Rugby were boarded out in the homes in the town and so could not be kept to a discipline of study, sports, and a regular life; instead, they were free to gamble, carouse, and hunt. Arnold built residential "houses" by extending the

With this to offer, I think I have a right to look rather high for the man whom I fix upon, and it is my great object to get here a society of intelligent, gentlemanly, and active men, who may permanently keep up the character of the school, and make it "vile damnum,"[16] if I were to break my neck to-morrow. . . .

From "Letter to a Master on his Appointment"

The qualifications which I deem essential to the due performance of a master's duties here, may in brief be expressed as the spirit of a Christian and a gentleman,—that a man should enter upon his business not ἔμ παρέργον[17] but as a substantive and most impor-tant duty; that he should devote himself to it as the especial branch of the ministerial calling[18] which he has chosen to follow that belonging to a great public institution, and standing in a public and conspicuous situation, he should study things "lovely and of good report;"[19] that is, that he should be public-spirited, liberal, and entering heartily into the interest, honour, and general respectability and distinction of the society which he has joined; and that he should have sufficient vigour of mind and thirst for knowledge to persist in adding to his own stores without neglecting the full improvement of those whom he is teaching. I think our masterships here offer a noble field of duty, and I would not bestow them on any one whom I thought would undertake them without entering into the spirit of our system heart and hand. . . .

William Wordsworth (1770–1850): "Illustrated Books and Newspapers" (1846)[20]

Discourse was deemed Man's noblest attribute,
And written words the glory of his hand;
Then followed Printing with enlarged command
For thought—dominion vast and absolute
For spreading truth, and making love expand.   5
Now prose and verse sunk into disrepute,
Must lacquey a dumb Art that best can suit
The taste of this once-intellectual Land.
A backward movement surely have we here,
From manhood,—back to childhood; for the age—   10
Back towards caverned life's first rude career.[21]

Notes ───

dormitories in one of the early buildings, School House, and by buying up town residences. Assistant masters were in control, though authority was decentralized under prefects, selected from the sixth-form boys. The house system was extended throughout the public schools during the 1850s.

[16] *vile damnum* (Lat. a cheap loss, or sacrifice); see Tacitus, *Annals*: 2.85.5, where 4,000 freedmen of Rome, adherents of Egyptian and Jewish religions, were transported to Sardinia to quell brigandage, and "a cheap loss" if they died of the pestilential climate.

[17] *ἔμ παρέργον* (Gk. *em parergon*, as a supplemental or secondary work or business); see Plato, *Symposium* 222c.

[18] *calling* Arnold's assistant headmasters were all Church of England clergymen, as was customary throughout the public schools in the nineteenth century. The first lay headmaster at Rugby would be appointed in 1903.

[19] *report* see Philippians 4: 8.

[20] *title* Wordsworth's sonnet was written in February 1846 upon viewing a copy of the *ILN*, and was first published in 1850. In 1896 an editor, William Angus Knight (1836–1916), added the following footnote to the poem: "Had Wordsworth known the degradation to which many newspapers would sink in this direction, his censure would have been more severe" (*Poetical Works* 8: 185). On 27 April 1850, four days after Wordsworth's death, the *ILN* published a large engraving of Wordsworth's home at Rydal Mount, with the caption: "We announce the death of William Wordsworth, one of the last and most illustri-ous of a race of poets now all but extinct. . . . We have no wish, now that the tomb is about to receive his mortal remains, to submit to the cold analysis of criticism the inspiration of his genius" (296).

[21] *career* the conventional analogy between human develop-ment of an individual from child to adult and collective

Avaunt this vile abuse of pictured page!
Must eyes be all in all, the tongue and ear
Nothing? Heaven keep us from a lower stage!

Anon. [Thomas Peckett Prest (?) (1810–59)]: "The String of Pearls: A Romance" in *The People's Periodical and Family Library* (1846–47).[22]

From Chapter 38 [Sweeney Todd]

Sweeney Todd walked into his back-parlour, conveying with him the only light that was in the shop, so that the dim glimpse that, up to this time, Johanna[23] from the outside had contrived to get of what was going on, was denied to her; and all that met her eyes was impenetrable darkness....

The moment his back was turned, the seeming farmer who had made such a good thing of his beasts, sprang from the shaving-chair,[24] as if he had been electrified; and yet he did not do it with any appearance of fright, nor did he make any noise. It was only astonishingly quick, and then he placed himself close to the window, and waited patiently with his eyes fixed upon the chair, to see what would happen next.

In the space of about a quarter of a minute, there came from the next room a sound like the rapid drawing of a heavy bolt, and then in an instant the shaving-chair disappeared beneath the floor; and the circumstances by which Sweeney Todd's customers disappeared was evident.

There was a piece of the flooring turning upon a centre, and the weight of the chair when a bolt was withdrawn, by means of a simple leverage from the inner room, weighed down upon one end of the top, which, by a little apparatus, was to swing completely round, there being another chair on the under surface, which thus became the upper, exactly resembling the one in which the unhappy customer was supposed to be "polished off."[25]

Hence was it that in one moment, as if by magic, Sweeney Todd's visitors disappeared, and there was the empty chair. No doubt, he trusted to a fall of about twenty feet below,

Notes

development of human kind from primitive to civilized is reversed. Wordsworth equates *ILN* illustrations with the cave-dwelling prehistoric humans, a point of controversy then with the discovery of human artifacts with mammoth and other bones in Kent's Cavern in Devon by the Rev. John MacEnery (1797–1841), Irish Roman Catholic priest and archaeologist, in 1841, as well as the publications in periodicals of the time of the Ajanta cave paintings in India, which date from the second century BCE.

[22] title the *People's Periodical* was published by Edward Lloyd (1815–90), with "The String of Pearls" running from 21 November 1846 to 20 March 1847. The authorship is disputed, the chief contenders being Prest or James Malcolm Rhymer (1814–84), the author of *Varney the Vampire, or, The Feast of Blood* (1845–47). Prest wrote a string of lampoons of Dickens's novels (*The Penny Pickwick*, 1837–38, *Oliver Twiss*, 1838, *David Copperful*, 1838 and *Nickelas Nicklebery*, 1838). *Varney the Vampire* and *The String of Pearls* are "penny dreadfuls," or "bloods," melodramatic fiction, often horror and crime stories, each serialized as an eight-page weekly number, with a woodcut illustration, on pulp paper, costing a penny, aimed at young working-class readers. The pejorative terms were adopted for this fiction in the 1870s by middle-class journalists, in opposition to the moralizing reward-book literature

presented as school and church prizes. See LITERATURE: DEBATES; JOHNS (WEB p. 126).

Before serial publication was completed, this novel was transformed into a stage success by George Dibdin Pitts (1799–1855) as *The String of Pearls; or The Fiend of Fleet Street* (1847); many other stage and novelistic adaptations and expansions followed with the same title or as *Sweeney Todd, the Demon Barber of Fleet Street*, as in Stephen Sondheim's "musical thriller" (1979) and a motion picture starring Johnny Depp and directed by Tim Burton (2007).

[23] *Johanna* Johanna Oakley is the heroine of the story (set in 1785), the lover of Mark Ingestrie who was lost at sea. His friend Lieutenant Thornhill comes to London to find her, bring news of Mark's death, and present her with a string of pearls, a gift from Mark. Thornhill's dog outside Todd's barbershop alerts his friends when he too disappears.

[24] *shaving-chair* according to Partridge's *Dictionary of Slang*, to "shave" someone was to rob them, as Todd did to his victims. A "barber's chair" was vulgar slang for a prostitute.

[25] *off* "I'll polish him off" is a phrase commonly associated with Sweeney Todd, as from chapter 1 when he says: "Now, sir, I suppose you want to be shaved, and it is well you have come here, for there ain't a shaving-shop, although I say it, in the city of London that ever thinks of polishing anybody off as I do."

on to a stone floor, to be the death of them, or, at all events, to stun them until he could go down to finish the murder, and — *to cut them up for Mrs Lovett's pies!* after robbing them of all money and valuables they might have about them. . . .

It was a full minute before Todd ventured to look from the parlour into the darkened shop, and then he shook so that he had to hold by the door to steady himself.

"That's done," he said. "That's the last, I hope. It is time I finished; I never felt so nervous since the first time. Then I did quake a little. How quiet he went; I have sometimes had a shriek ringing in my ears for a whole week."

It was a large high-backed piece of furniture, that shaving-chair, so that, when Todd crept into the shop with the light in his hand, he had not the remotest idea it was tenanted; but when he got round it, and saw his customer calmly waiting with the lather upon his face, the cry of horror that came gargling and gushing from his throat was horrible to hear.

"Why, what's the matter?" said Sir Richard.

"O God, the dead! the dead! O God!" cried Todd, "this is the beginning of my punishment. Have mercy, Heaven! oh, do not look upon me with those dead eyes!"

"Murderer!" shouted Sir Richard, in a voice that rang like the blast of a trumpet through the house.

In an instant he sprang upon Sweeney Todd, and grappled him by the throat. There was a short struggle, and they were down upon the floor together, but Todd's wrists were suddenly laid hold of, and a pair of handcuffs were scientifically put upon him by the officers, who, at the word "murderer," that being a preconcerted signal, came from the cupboard where they had been concealed.

"Secure him well, my men," said the magistrate, "and don't let him lay violent hands upon himself. Ah! Miss Oakley, you are in time. This man is a murderer. I found out all the secret about the chair last night, after twelve, by exploring the vaults under the old church.[26] Thank God, we have stopped his career."

From Chapter 39

What excitement there is now to get at the pies when they shall come! Mrs Lovett lets down the square, moveable platform that goes upon pulleys into the cellar; some machinery, which only requires a handle to be turned, brings up a hundred pies in a tray. These are eagerly seized by parties who have previously paid, and such a smacking of lips ensues as never was known. . . .

How the waggish young lawyers' clerks laughed as they smacked their lips, and sucked in the golophious gravy of the pies, which, by the by, appeared to be all delicious veal this time, and Mrs Lovett worked the handle of the machine all the more vigorously, that she was a little angry with the officious stranger. What an unusual trouble it seemed to be to wind up those forthcoming hundred pies! How she toiled, and how the people waited; but at length there came up the savoury steam, and then the tops of the pies were visible.

They came up upon a large tray, about six feet square, and the moment Mrs Lovett ceased turning the handle, and let a catch fall that prevented the platform receding again, to the astonishment and terror of everyone, away flew all the pies, tray and all, across the counter, and a man, who was lying crouched down in an exceedingly flat state under the tray, sprang to his feet.

Mrs Lovett shrieked, as well she might, and then she stood trembling, and looking as pale as death itself. It was the doomed cook[27] from the cellars, who had adopted this mode of escape.

Notes ———————————————————————————

[26] *church* St Dunstan's Church, Fleet Street, just at Temple Bar, in whose crypt were found the bones of slaughtered victims.

[27] *cook* the cook is the long-lost Mark Ingestrie, imprisoned in the cellars to cook the barber's victims into Mrs Margery Lovett's admired meat pies.

The throngs of persons in the shop looked petrified, and after Mrs Lovett's shriek, there was an awful stillness for about a minute, and then the young man who officiated as cook spoke.

"Ladies and Gentlemen—I fear that what I am going to say will spoil your appetites; but the truth is beautiful at all times, and I have to state that Mrs Lovett's pies are made of *human flesh!*"

The Society for Promoting Working Men's Associations: "Lectures for April, 1853"[28]

HALL OF ASSOCIATION,

34, CASTLE STREET EAST, OXFORD STREET.

LECTURES FOR APRIL, 1853.

MONDAY, APRIL 4th,
THOMAS HUGHES, Esq.,
MODERN BALLADS.

MONDAY, APRIL 11th,
Rev. CHARLES KINGSLEY Junr.
(Author of " Alton Locke,")
THE FINE ARTS IN RELATION TO THE EDUCATION OF THE PEOPLE.

MONDAY, APRIL 18th,
GEORGE GROVE, Esq.,
(Secretary to the Crystal Palace Company,)
MECHANICAL PRINCIPLES EXEMPLIFIED IN COMMON THINGS.

MONDAY APRIL 25th,
Rev. F. McDOUGALL,
(Head of the Borneo Mission,)
BORNEO AND ITS CAPABILITIES.

To commence at half-past Eight, p.m. Admittance :—Reserved Seats, 1s. ; Hall, 2d.

EVENING CLASSES.

Directed by
TUESDAYS & SATURDAYS .. **Singing** .. PROFESSOR HULLAH.
Conducted by
THURSDAYS .... **French** .. J. M. LUDLOW, ESQ.
FRIDAYS .... **Drawing** .. GEO. W. TERRY, ESQ.

The following Classes are also in course of formation :—

Grammar .... T. HUGHES, ESQ.
Latin .... J. F. MACLENNAN, ESQ.
Book-keeping .... WILLIAM TATE, ESQ.

*To commence at half-past Eight, p.m.—Terms for each Class, 2s. 6d. per Quarter ;
Ladies for either the Singing or Drawing Class, 2s. 2d.*

⁎⁎⁎ Persons desirous of joining either of these Classes, are requested to give in their names to the Secretary at the Hall.

CONFERENCES are held' on the First Wednesday in every Month, at half-past Eight, p.m., REV. F. D MAURICE in the Chair. Subject of the adjourned Conference on Wednesday, April 6th, "**The best means of promoting the Education of the People.**"—*Admission Free.*

LADIES ADMITTED TO ALL THE LECTURES, AND CONFERENCES, AND TO THE SINGING AND DRAWING CLASSES.

YEARLY Subscription, admitting to all Lectures, Conferences, and Classes, of the Society for Promoting Working Men's Associations, £1 1s.; Quarterly, 6s. 6d.

Parties desiring to engage the Hall when it is vacant, are requested to apply to the Secretary, Mr. SHORTER, on the Premises.

Working Printers' Association, (R. ISHAM, Manager,) 4a, Johnson's Court, Fleet Street.

Figure 4 Society for Promoting Working Men's Associations, *Lectures for April* 1853. Letterpress Handbill. Source: courtesy of the Robarts Library, University of Toronto.

Notes

[28] *title* following the defeat of the *People's Charter* in 1848, Christian socialists such as Charles Kingsley, F. D. Maurice, and Thomas Hughes turned their attention to education for the working classes. In 1852 and 1853 they organized a series of lectures, classes, and conferences on diverse subjects at the Hall of Association in Castle Street, advertising

Charles Dickens (1812–70): *Hard Times* (1854)

Chapter 1: "The One Thing Needful"²⁹

"Now, what I want is, Facts.³⁰ Teach these boys and girls nothing but Facts. Facts alone are wanted in life. Plant nothing else, and root out everything else. You can only form the minds of reasoning animals upon Facts: nothing else will ever be of any service to them. This is the principle on which I bring up my own children, and this is the principle on which I bring up these children. Stick to Facts, sir!"

The scene was a plain, bare, monotonous vault of a schoolroom, and the speaker's square forefinger emphasised his observations by underscoring every sentence with a line on the schoolmaster's sleeve. The emphasis was helped by the speaker's square wall of a forehead, which had his eyebrows for its base, while his eyes found commodious cellarage in two dark caves, overshadowed by the wall. The emphasis was helped by the speaker's mouth, which was wide, thin, and hard set. The emphasis was helped by the speaker's voice, which was inflexible, dry, and dictatorial. The emphasis was helped by the speaker's hair, which bristled on the skirts of his bald head, a plantation of firs to keep the wind from its shining surface, all covered with knobs, like the crust of a plum pie, as if the head had scarcely warehouse-room for the hard facts stored inside. The speaker's obstinate carriage, square coat, square legs, square shoulders,—nay, his very neckcloth, trained to take him by the throat with an unaccommodating grasp, like a stubborn fact, as it was,—all helped the emphasis.

"In this life, we want nothing but Facts, sir; nothing but Facts!"

The speaker, and the schoolmaster, and the third grown person³¹ present, all backed a little, and swept with their eyes the inclined plane of little vessels then and there arranged in order, ready to have imperial gallons of facts poured into them until they were full to the brim.

Notes

by means of handbills of lectures. The Hall of Association was a renovation of the upper floors of a house occupied by the Working Tailors' Association. The Society for Promoting Working Men's Associations began the first of these lecture series from 23 November to 30 December, 1852 with the following subjects: "The Historical Plays of Shakespeare" (F. D. Maurice), "The Life and Genius of [Robert] Burns" (Walter Cooper, manager of the Working Tailors' Association), "Vocal Music" (John Hullah, professor of vocal music at King's College, London), "Proverbs" (R. C. Trench, professor of divinity at King's College), "Rivers" (William Johnson, master at Eton College), "Architecture and its Influence, Especially with Reference to the Working Classes" (F. C. Penrose), "Photography" (Nevil S. Maskelyne), "Entomology" (Viscount Goderich, MP), and "Popular Astronomy for Children" (S. C. Hansard). Evening classes were offered in grammar, English history, book-keeping, French, and singing. These lectures resulted in the formation of the London Working Men's College on 31 October 1854. As this range of courses in 1852 and 1853 indicates, the working-men's lectures combined practical subjects with the arts and humanities, a contrast to the Mechanics' Institutes (founded 1824) which were more restricted to practical education in science and technology.

²⁹ *title* originally published in Dickens's journal *Household Words* (1 Apr. 1854). For the title of the chapter, see Luke 10: 42, where Mary is praised for having chosen the better

course, of listening to Jesus, rather than being like Martha, who busied herself in preparing a meal, a contrast between reflective wisdom and expedient action. Matthew Arnold uses the same phrase in the Vulgate Latin version (*porro unum est necessarium*: but one thing is needful) for the title of chapter 5 of *Culture and Anarchy*, referring to the primary need for the education of the working classes.

³⁰ *Facts* an attack on Political Economy or laissez-faire economics, called "the dismal science" by Carlyle. The chapter satirizes Utilitarianism, a philosophy that promoted the usefulness of a thing or idea established by "facts" in a quantifiable world, as opposed to what Dickens in this novel calls "fancy" or imagination. Utilitarian materialism is based on the principles outlined by Jeremy Bentham (1748–1832), British radical philosopher, in which morality is based on utility or usefulness; its goal is the greatest happiness of the greatest number of people, displacing duty and obligation; in economics the calculation of self-interest is the sum of profit (=pleasure) set against loss (=pain), letting the market regulate itself (laissez-faire).

³¹ *person* the three people present are the speaker, Thomas Gradgrind of Coketown (a generic mill-town in the English Midlands), proprietor of the utilitarian model school and member of parliament; the teacher of the class, Mr M'Choakumchild; and an unnamed government school inspector, also a utilitarian.

WEB p. 17

Thomas Hughes (1822–96): *Tom Brown's Schooldays* (1857)
From Part 1, Chapter 8: "A War of Independence"

Elizabeth Rigby, Lady Eastlake (1809–93): From "The Englishwoman at School" in *Quarterly Review* (July 1878)[32]

The practice of teaching in this free country, whether in schools or in private families, as carried on by governesses and mistresses, has been entirely of an *amateur* kind.[33] Not one Englishwoman in fifty has ever devoted herself to learn the art professionally, and certainly not five in fifty have had by nature so strong a vocation for it as to excel without training. While all foreign women—Russian, Swedish, Danish, German, French, and Italian— destined for the career of a governess or schoolmistress, have been required by law to go through a course of study, submit to examinations, and obtain certificates and matriculations as their indispensable credentials, Englishwomen have embarked in the calling most important to the rising generation with scarcely any other qualifications beyond want and good-will.[34] ... As a rule, the governess class have been painfully and curiously unfitted for their duties, have only undertaken them of necessity, and from this very cause they contribute largely to the numbers of the dependent women whose misery is perpetually brought before us.[35] Under these circumstances, it was time that the subject of female instruction in this country should receive systematic investigation.... To be at school at all for a few years, is in itself a relative advantage when compared with the slip-slop programmes and irregular habits of too many homes—for here we speak of that class which keep no regular governess. If also the standard of instruction has been found incredibly low, it has been placed and kept at that level by the ignorance and indifference of parents; and in many cases in direct opposition to the judgment of the ladies at the head of such institutions....

It would be difficult to trace precisely the first stirrings in public opinion on behalf both of a better and cheaper form of instruction for girls. The need for it was sure to make

Notes

[32] *title* author and art critic, Rigby was the first woman to write regularly for the *Quarterly Review*, chiefly on her travels, on art, and, as here, on education. Until the age of 12, she was educated at home, primarily by her father, Edward Rigby (1747–1821), gynecologist and classical scholar, becoming fluent in French, German, and the classics. Following his death, she travelled widely in Europe and continued her education as an autodidact.

[33] *kind* governesses were expected to live in the employer's house, on the fringes of the family but, as a waged worker, not part of it; they usually took their meals alone. They were expected to teach the girls in the family the 3 Rs, music (piano), drawing and watercolours, a little French, and other accomplishments expected of a middle-class or upper middle-class girl (sewing, embroidery or other needlework, and conversation). Over 140 governesses appeared in novels from the 1814 to 1865, including *Jane Eyre* (1847) by Charlotte Brontë, Becky Sharp in Thackeray's *Vanity Fair* (1847), and Lady Isabel Vane in Mrs Henry Wood's *East Lynne* (1861). Until about the age of 8 boys were usually taught by a governess; subsequently they had tutors or were sent out to school.

[34] *good-will* the Governesses' Benevolent Institution was inaugurated at meetings in 1841 but became established in 1843 to offer impoverished governesses financial aid and relief (they earned only £20–25 per annum, whilst their charges could pay that for a new outfit) and to improve governesses' status and qualifications by providing lectures at Queen's College, London, followed by an oral examination and a certificate of competence. Later in the century many had qualified, but their credentials and wages were undercut by thousands of almost untrained governesses who would work for only their food and lodging. For governesses, see ABDY, "GOVERNESS"; see also Plate 7: Redgrave, *The Governess*.

[35] *before us* the 1861 census states that there were 24,770 governesses in England and Wales. Many were employed by the wealthy growing merchant and business class but numerous others worked for the middle classes, including tenant farmers and townspeople. While it might cost a family £70–£80 a year in the 1860s to send a girl to boarding school in Bath, a governess could be hired for £25 per annum. Brontë's fictional Jane Eyre earned £20 in 1847.

itself felt in a community like London, mainly composed of hard-working professional men, where fathers of large families could ill afford to send their daughters to boarding-schools, and where the average houses can spare but little accommodation for resident governesses. The institution of King's College and University College Schools[36] for London boys, similarly placed, doubtless first suggested corresponding plans for their sisters. We find accordingly that Queen's College (in Harley Street) was founded in 1848 chiefly by gentlemen connected with King's College, among whom the names of Professor Maurice and of the present Archbishop of Dublin were foremost as successive principals.[37] Bedford College[38] followed in 1849; both being furnished with a staff of distin-guished names as professors and lecturers. As examples also of the powers for organiza-tion and tuition inherent in women, the Camden Town Schools, conducted by Miss Buss, and the Cheltenham College by Miss Beale, were among the first and most prominent—both of late enriched by considerable endowments.[39] But the earliest public step in favour of women was taken about nineteen years ago, when the University of Cambridge first opened what are called its "Local Examinations" for candidates under eighteen years of age, to girls; an example followed some years later by Oxford.[40] . . .

We now come to the crowning of the edifice, a bolder and more direct step than any yet taken. For in the institutions for Female Education already described, the principal aim has been to certify the fitness of women for the position of teachers and governesses. But . . . "the real way to remedy the great need was to begin by teaching not all the actual, but all the possible teachers; that is, women at large."[41] . . . In short, all they aspired at was to become undergraduates in the garb of women; not on the fantastic and poetical pat-tern of those in Tennyson's "Princess,"[42] but in the prosaic sense of full conformity to

Notes

[36] *Schools* King's College was founded in 1829 by George IV (1762–1830) and Arthur Wellesley, Duke of Wellington (1769–1852). As a secular institution for "the youth of our middling rich people between the ages of 15 or 16 and 20 or later," it provided a religious and economic alternative to wealthy Anglicans at Cambridge and Oxford. It first offered degrees when it joined with University College in the University of London in 1836. University College School was established by University College London in 1830 as a secular day school. It was unusual in abolishing corporal punishment and rigid forms, teaching modern languages and science as well as classics and mathematics.

[37] *principals* F. D. Maurice (1805–72) was chaplain of Lincoln's Inn (law society) and in 1840 became professor of history and English literature at King's College of the University of London. He was a proponent of the Governesses' Benevolent Institution and supported the teaching of governesses at Queen's College from 1848, along with the education of girls. The first building was next door to the Governesses' Institution. Among the male lecturers was Charles Kingsley (1819–75). Distinguished "Lady Visitors" including Lady Augusta Stanley (d. 1876), Lady Janet Kay-Shuttleworth (1817–72), and Lady Charlotte Canning (1817–1861) attended each lecture for propriety. The first group of students included Dorothea Beale (1831–1906), Frances Mary Buss (1827–94), and Sophia Jex-Blake (1840–1912). Richard Chenevix Trench (1807–86) was professor of theology at King's College, London and succeeded Maurice as prin-cipal of Queen's; in 1856 he became dean of Westminster, and in 1864 Archbishop of Dublin. A renowned philolo-

gist, his work was in part the inspiration for the *Oxford English Dictionary*.

[38] *College* "Now removed to 8 and 9 York Place, Portman Square" [author's note]. Bedford College was founded by the Unitarian social activist and advocate of women's edu-cation, Elizabeth Jesser Reid (1789–1866), who drew sup-port from the non-sectarian University College London, especially the classicist, Francis W. Newman (1805–97).

[39] *endowments* Frances Mary Buss (see, n. 37) was a student of Maurice, Kingsley, and Trench at Queen's College. She assisted at her family's school in London. In 1850 it was renamed the North London Collegiate School and Buss remained as its principal to the end of her life. She also founded the Camden School for Girls in 1871, was its first headmistress, and founded the Association of Head Mistresses in 1874. Dorothea Beale (see, n. 37) was princi-pal of the Cheltenham Ladies College (founded 1853) from 1858 to her death; she also founded St Hilda's College, Oxford in 1893.

[40] *Oxford* women were first admitted in 1863 to the Cambridge Local Examinations. These examinations were established in 1858 for persons not members of the University of Cambridge. They were primarily used to raise standards in education by providing criteria for school inspectors. In 1873 Oxford and Cambridge created the Oxford and Cambridge Schools Examination Board.

[41] *large* quotation from one of the books that Eastlake is reviewing: *Reports Issued by the Schools' Enquiry Commission on the Education of Girls* (1870).

[42] *Princess* a long poem published in 1857 on the topic of wom-en's education; see TENNYSON, n. 35 (WEB p. 341).

University work and rules. Who could resist such modest pretensions? "The College for Women"—for they took the bull by the horns even in the name—first temporarily started at Hitchin, and since located at Girton—was established in 1868, its existence in the first instance, its rules and administration for years, being chiefly the work of a clever woman, Miss Emily Davies, who for a short period was mistress of the institution. The position was so chosen as to obviate all objections or difficulties on the score of distance, for Girton is only two miles from Cambridge.... Girton College has now stood its trial for ten years with increasing popularity, the applicants for admission being more numerous than the present size of the building can accommodate, assuring to its inmates the same three years' course of systematic study which men obtain at the Universities, the same curriculum as that of Cambridge, the same teaching by Cambridge Professors, the same examinations at the same academical periods, on the same subjects and with the same papers, that have been the portion for generations and generations of successive undergraduates.[43]

Notes

[43] *undergraduates* Emily Davies (1830–1921) and others established a college for women outside Cambridge on 16 October 1869, later renamed Girton College. Women were granted increasing academic rights at Cambridge, but only in 1947 did they receive full status as undergraduates able to graduate with degrees.

Gender, Women, and Sexuality

Introduction

In the year of Victoria's Diamond Jubilee (1897) an almost unknown painter published an engraving of the announcement to Victoria of her accession in 1837. Henry Tanworth Wells (1828–1903) in *Victoria Regina* captures the moment when the Victorian era formally begins. The engraving shows the light streaming upon a young woman clothed in white with a shawl draped over her shoulders. She extends her hand to one of the two older men kneeling before her. Behind her, lurking in the shadows outside the door, is an older female figure. Inside the room, the morning dawn is reflected in the large mirror on the wall, in front of which is a clock. An unlit candle stands atop a closed piano and leaning on an adjacent chair is the walking stick of one of the kneeling men (see Figure 5).

The engraving, and the two related paintings on which it is based, one in the Tate (1880) and one in the Royal Collection showing the scene in a larger perspective (RA1887), became iconic at the end of Victoria's reign. According to the *ODNB*, "The most popular of Wells's works was … a painting of Queen Victoria receiving the news of her accession, exhibited in 1887 at the RA as *Victoria regina*" (*s.v.* "Wells, Henry Tanworth"). An engraving of the large painting was featured as the frontispiece of the first volume of *The Letters of Queen Victoria* (1907), sanctioned by the royal family. Within a short time of her accession a version of this occasion was mounted by Madame Tussaud's Wax Museum in London, showing the two kneeling officials before Victoria with her mother standing prominently behind her, a representation that was used as a coloured lithographic advertisement for Madame Tussaud's late in the century; it also appeared on an advertisement for Wills's cigarettes, moving from official publications to popular entertainment to commercial exploitation. In a mocking account of the Tussaud group in Hall of Kings read as the Chamber of Horrors, J. B. Priestley wrote:

> Even the most innocent subject was touched with the macabre. The announcement to Queen Victoria of her accession demands an almost idyllic treatment; the young girl standing in her dressing-gown, with the Archbishop and Lord Conyngham kneeling before her. But once again the wax has had its own sinister way; and you would swear that the two men you see there are a couple of potential murderers and that the girl herself is about to stamp her foot and release a trap-door that will swallow them both. (*Saturday Review* 19 Jan. 1929)

Indeed, the moment is still iconic, being reproduced in the recent film *The Young Victoria* (2009) in ways that directly copy Wells's engraving.

For our purposes, however, the engraving represents important contradictions in gender relations in the nineteenth century. First, the new sovereign is a young female, and hence the lavish ceremonials are contradicted by the legal status of women. Second, the moment can be projected as crucial in the narrative arc of the fairy tale, in which the princess leaves home to find her prince charming. And third, the new reign will represent a radical shift in sexual norms from Regency profligacy to bourgeois respectability.

Victorian Literature: An Anthology, First Edition. Edited by Victor Shea and William Whitla.
© 2015 John Wiley & Sons, Ltd. Published 2015 by John Wiley & Sons, Ltd.

Figure 5 Henry Tanworth Wells (1828–1903), *Victoria Regina* (1897). Photogravure by Selmar Hess for Goupil & Co. 18 × 23 cm. Source: author's collection.

The two men in the engraving, as Priestly indicates, are important functionaries of state and church, the Lord Chamberlain (Francis, Lord Conyngham, 1797–1876) and the bewigged Archbishop of Canterbury (William Howley, 1766–1848). Conyngham was Lord Chamberlain from 1835 to 1839, responsible for the administration of the Royal Household. He was the chief officer of the court and the liaison officer between the monarchy and the House of Lords. To illustrate how small was the world of the court, and how bound up were relations and conventions of gender, it is worth noting that his mother, Elizabeth Marchioness of Conyngham (née Denison, 1769–1861), was the last mistress of Victoria's uncle, George IV. Conyngham's daughter, Jane Spencer, Baroness Churchill (1826–1900), became one of Victoria's Ladies of the Bedchamber (1854 to her death) and closest friends. She died one month before Victoria while accompanying her at Osborne in the Isle of Wight.

The engraving underlines an important shift in gender relations as the two men kneel before a woman just transformed into a queen. Victoria records in her diary (see CONDITION: SOCIAL FORMATION (WEB p. 5)) that Conyngham "knelt down and kissed my hand," highlighting both convention and ambiguity that continued throughout her reign. The phrase "to kiss hands" is still used as an official term for accepting a government ministry, symbolizing fealty and loyalty to the Crown. Here the kiss by Conyngham is the first of many symbolic gestures of loyalty that would be bestowed upon the queen over her long reign. Kissing the hand of a lady is also a custom from feudal Europe governed by the gender norms of the chivalric code. Had Victoria been male, they still would have kissed their new monarch's hand, but the chivalric gender codes would not be invoked. Victoria also wrote in her diary entry about the potential conflict between "duty towards my country" and doing "what is fit and right." Duty towards her country involved her position as sovereign ruler of about 26 million people in Great Britain, the head of an evolving system of constitutional monarchy, in which as queen she would still have a great deal of power. "Fit and right" could involve questions of propriety, partly the elaborate court etiquette but especially new conventions governed by gender norms. The scene in which, at 6 a.m. on 20 June 1837, two of the most powerful men in the kingdom were kneeling before an 18-year-old girl was highly incongruous, and this incongruity becomes magnified over the ensuing years, eventually involving the competing demands of women and men for the franchise, education, better working conditions, and divergent roles in the home, families, institutions, and public life.

The fact that Princess Alexandrina Victoria of Kent, the daughter of Edward, Duke of Kent (1767–1820), the fourth son of George III, was the new monarch was possible only because George's other profligate sons had failed to produce a legitimate heir. She was able to inherit the crown because she was the eldest legitimate child of the sons of George III. Her uncle, Prince Ernest Augustus, Duke of Cumberland (1771–1851), was the fifth son of George III; according to Salic law, which functioned in Germany and barred women from succession, he was able to inherit the title of King of Hanover, reigning from 1837 to 1851. He remained the heir presumptive of Great Britain until Victoria's first-born child, Victoria, later the Princess Royal (1840–1901), was born; she was replaced in order of succession with the birth of her brother Albert Edward (later Edward VII), born a year later. Hence, the complicated rules concerning succession were heavily controlled by questions of legitimacy and sex throughout. The positioning of females in this chain of legitimacy, while granting them somewhat secondary status but conferring power when no male is available, was contradicted, as many of the writings in this section demonstrate, by the position of women in general society until 1870 (see this section, WOMAN; NORTON),

who could not own property or inherit money if they were married.

The newly deceased king, William IV, had ten illegitimate children by an actress with whom he had lived for twenty years. The three previous monarchs had been "an imbecile, a profligate, and a buffoon," in Sidney Lee's phrase in a biography of Victoria one year after her death. When the Lord Chamberlain and the archbishop kneel to her, illuminated by the early morning light as a symbol of blessing on the new order, they hail both a new monarch and the first female monarch of Britain since Queen Anne in 1714. They looked as well towards the prospects for the reformation of morals from the debaucheries of the Regency and its aftermath. The engraving, printed at the end of her reign and celebrating her diamond jubilee, came at a time when viewers could read in the kneeling acclamation of a haloed queen the inscription of new roles for women, an adjustment of gender priorities, and a questioning of specific issues concerning sexuality.

Following her death, Victoria's son Edward VII authorized the publication of *The Letters of Queen Victoria* (1907) with the engraving of Wells's painting (1887) of the accession announcement as the frontispiece, as we say above. The editors introduce this moment of transition by emphasizing the difference between her uncles and herself. Avoiding the use of terms that would cast moral aspersions on the former monarchs, they focus instead on gender characteristics: "A word may here be given to the Princess's own character and temperament. She was high-spirited and wilful, but devotedly affectionate, and almost typically feminine. She had a strong sense of duty and dignity, and strong personal prejudices. Confident, in a sense, as she was, she had the feminine instincts strongly developed of dependance upon some manly advisor." Such a dependence for a male ruler on a *womanly* advisor would not be an asset but a sign of weakness, an obvious liability; nevertheless, deep-seated fears of a female ruler's upsetting of the balance of political power – as well as social conventions – resurfaced throughout the century, as was articulated early in a broadside "Petticoats for Ever" (1837):

For great alterations there'll certainly be,
And Petticoat now will be master you'll see.
So maids, wives, and widows, all merrily sing,
Petticoats for ever! and God bless the Queen!

This anxiety decreased when Victoria married Albert in 1840 and he became her "manly advisor." Explicit reference, however, to her "typically feminine" traits would surface repeatedly. For instance, she was widely praised as a model wife and mother, and was portrayed in settings of domestic concord, as in Landseer's *Windsor Castle in Modern Times* (1843; see Plate 4). But even here the gender and political roles are in contradiction: Albert remains sitting for his wife, having just returned from hunting. Any other man in the kingdom would stand when the queen enters. Other instances of her feminine traits in relation to her role as monarch recurred when instructing Lord Derby to rewrite the Proclamation of 1858 transferring the government of India from East India Company to the British Government: Victoria wrote he had to bear "in mind that it is a female Sovereign who speaks.... Such a document should breathe feelings of generosity, benevolence, and religious toleration" (see EMPIRE: GOVERNING (p. 169, n. 9)). Later in her rule, well after the death of Albert, she came under the influence of Disraeli, who flattered her with the Spenserian title of "the Faerie Queene." In an incredibly flirtatious and inappropriate letter of 25 February 1875, he writes to her in the third person after receiving from her a bouquet of flowers: "In the middle of the night, it occurred to him, that it might all be an enchantment, and that, perhaps, it was a Faery gift and came from another monarch: Queen Titania, gathering flowers, with her Court, in a soft and sea-girt isle, and sending magic blossoms, which, they say, turn the heads of those who receive them. They certainly would turn Mr. Disraeli's, if his sense of duty to your Majesty did not exceed, he sincerely believes, his conceit." Whatever the complications of using

literary allusions from *A Midsummer Night's Dream* to flatter Victoria, or the appropriateness of his giving or her receiving such compliments, the important thing is here to acknowledge the clear split between the appeal to her girlish femininity and the limitations invoked by Disraeli's observance of his "duty" to his sovereign.

Another set of gendered literary relations are inscribed in the moment of her accession captured in the engraving. The female figure lurking in the dark behind the door, probably her mother, is in contrast with the light pouring through the window, signifying the new dawn of the new realm. Hence, the moment refers to the transition in Victoria's life from being under the control of her overly protective mother, the Duchess of Kent, and, as court gossip would have it, the duchess's lover as well as comptroller and private secretary, Sir John Conroy (1786–1854). Victoria had been sequestered by them from 1822 to 1837 under the Kensington System, named after the palace in London where she and her mother had apartments. The system isolated Victoria from other members of her family, denied her companions of her own age and courtly attendants, and required her never to be separated from one of four people: her mother, Conroy, her governess, and her tutor. Required to sleep in her mother's room, she was subjected to a regime of bullying and constant oversight intended to weaken her mind and break her will, and to have her accept her mother as regent should she come to the throne before her eighteenth birthday. In the event, however, she turned 18 less than three weeks before she became queen on 20 June 1837. One of Victoria's first acts as queen was to banish Conroy and to distance herself from her mother's influence, thereby rejecting the educational and social norms fit for a wholly dependent woman that they had raised her with in hopes of maintaining their control. This rejection is foregrounded in the recent film *The Young Victoria*, immediately after her being told of her uncle's death by Conyngham and Howley. These conventions of the darkness and light and the sinister mother figure also suggest gender norms of the fairy tale, where the young female's transition from innocent child to sexual being and womanhood must be regulated by a transfer of authority from the house of the father to that of the husband. Fairy tales contain a deed of magic at the key moment of transition – the princess kissing the frog, the prince kissing the sleeping beauty, and so on. The precise moment captured in the engraving does not involve the young prince, however, but the enabling figures of the wise counsellors, in particular, the bowing in ritualistic homage, the kissing of the royal hand, and the magical incantation in which she was first called "Your Majesty."

The moment captured in the engraving is the first step in this process, the means by which the evil stepmother or stepfather may be rejected, preparing the way, as recorded in her diaries and biographies, and in the recent film, for her being swept off her feet by Prince Charming. In her letters about her first meeting with Albert, she describes him in such terms emphasized by her underlinings: "Albert's *beauty* is *most striking*, and he is so amiable and unaffected—in short, very *fascinating*" (12 Oct. 1839). Three days later she writes of him: "My mind is quite made up—and I told Albert this morning of it; the warm affection he showed me on learning this gave *me great pleasure*. He seems *perfection*, and I think that I have the prospect of very great happiness before me. I *love* him *more* than I can say, and I shall do everything in my power to render the sacrifice he has made (for a *sacrifice* in my opinion it is) as small as I can" (15 Oct. 1839). Although Albert is the charming prince, her mind being "quite made up" means, contrary to the conventions of the fairy tale, that she holds the power. She takes on the role of the Prince Charming who brings Albert home to her castle after she proposes to him. In this fairy tale, however, the princess would not live happily ever after. The blurb for a recent biography by Helen Rappaport, *A Magnificent Obsession* (2011), calls it "a story that began as fairy tale and ended in tragedy." Albert's death in 1861 would shatter the happy ending and would

relegate Victoria until the mid-1870s to another gendered identity, the secluded Widow of Windsor, rewritten again as another romance in the celebrations of imperial prowess in the Golden Jubilee of 1887 and the near-hysteria and jingoism of the Diamond Jubilee of 1897.

The mostly happy marriage between 1841 and 1861, however, foregrounded Victoria's role and function as monarch and also the contradictions in her role as wife and mother. Within her marriage, Victoria became a model of conventional sexuality – the producer of children, the wife and mother, and later the dutiful widow and grandmother of European royalty. Harriet Martineau, later a staunch women's rights advocate, in *The History of the Thirty Years' Peace A.D. 1816–1846* (1849), wrote of this moment of transition:

> As for the domestic respectability ... it was really refreshing to the heart and soul of the nation. A new generation was now on the throne; and there was no scandal as yet, nor any reason to suppose there ever would be any. Here was no corruption bred of the Royal Marriage-law, nothing illicit, nothing questionable; but instead, a young girl, reared in health and simplicity, who might be expected to marry soon— making her choice for herself, so that there was every hope that she might love her husband, and be a good and happy wife. (bk. 5, ch. 9)

Martineau refers to court scandals before Victoria: her three uncles and her father had as many as twenty-two illegitimate children. Victoria and Albert, on the other hand, would become models of respectability, having nine children, forty grandchildren, and eighty-eight great grandchildren. Sarah Stickney Ellis dedicated a conduct book, *The Wives of England* (1843), to the new queen, shortly after her marriage, again foregrounding the complications of rank, gender, and power: "Let us never forget, that in the person of our beloved QUEEN we have the character of a wife and a mother so blended with that of a sovereign, that the present above all others ought to form an era in British history, wherein woman shall have proved herself not unworthy of the importance attached to her influence and her name." In *The Daughters of England* (1842), Ellis had reminded readers of the conventional position of the queen in relation to her husband: "As women, then, the first thing of importance is to be content to be inferior to men—inferior in mental power, in the same proportion that you are inferior in bodily strength" (see Figure 10).

These contradictions between queen and wife, part of the gender norms of Victorian England, were constructed within an ideology of "separate spheres" – the notion that "masculine" and "feminine" spheres were natural and normal, appropriate because women were passive, men active. Women's place, therefore, was in the domestic, conserving, and nurturing realm, while men's was in the public realm of conflict, compromise, and action. Recent gender theory has rejected the idea that gender is a natural or neutral condition of existence, instead seeing it as a social construction. In our selections the social construction of separate spheres is demonstrated in popular conduct books and instructional manuals, where women are in effect placed in a compromising position: on the one hand, on the basis of their lesser intelligence, reasoning power, and emotionalism, they are relegated to a subordinate status; while on the other hand, under the codes of chivalry, they are idealized as embodiments of beauty, innocence, purity, and sanctity, and under biblically sanctioned marriage, they represent high moral virtue as the helpmate to the husband (Genesis 2: 18). Their superior status, however, is continually subordinated to the man's superior status in the active realm outside the home, the world of action in commerce, politics, and warfare. Pure and innocent, women exerted a moral influence on men as their divinely instituted "mission." Most prominently enunciated by Ellis, Ruskin, and Beeton, this dominant ideal exalted the woman as wife, mother and daughter, and as queen, "angel of the house," and, somewhat

contradictorily in Beeton, as the general of her domestic army.

Correspondingly, a masculine ideal consisted of the nostalgic recovery of the medieval chivalric knight, dutifully protecting his lady and country with feats of bravery and loyalty under the watchful eye of God (even in business and industry), as in such writers as Digby and Kipling. These dominant ideals of masculinity, now Victorian stereotypes, were also highly contested. As early as 1843 Reid challenged the idea that women are naturally passive, restricted to the home and children, a view extended later in movements for the reform of education, of the divorce laws, of suffrage, and of property rights, all now termed, "the Woman Question."

The woman question was dominated by the legal issue of "coverture," under which a married woman was not deemed to be a legal person because she was an appendage of her husband and her few rights were absorbed (or "covered") by him. Norton's letter to Victoria in 1855 makes explicit this legal concept's "grotesque anomaly which ordains that married women shall be 'non-existent' in a country governed by a female Sovereign." Norton's identification of Victoria as the single exception, however, needs qualification. These gender-based laws applied to middle-class women. To a degree, working-class women lived on the margins of these laws and norms: to live, they had to work, and for them the woman question did not concern property or voting rights but rather laws to accommodate their changing conditions, concerning employment – safety, the ten-hour day, and other rights. Furthermore, as Norton explains, women were merely the property of their husbands, and they could be abused, beaten, and treated as slaves by their masters. Education was completely different for men and women: upper- and middle-class men were educated as gentlemen in the classics, and from the 1860s in sciences and other forms of useful knowledge; similar classes of women learned the arts of refinement, training to be to be wives and hostesses. Unmarried middle-class women could work only as governesses or as writers; working-class women and men were lucky to learn to read or write. The almost universal acceptance of such gendered social norms was increasingly questioned and opposed: by the end of the century, in writers such as Grand, a new category of feminism emerges, the "New Woman," directly confronting the gender assumptions and legal status imposed upon her. As Grundy and "Ouida" illustrate, this figure was also attacked with ridicule and satire. Among other things, the "New Woman" was seen as a threat because of her promotion of sexual freedom.

Consistent with assumptions about gender and the law, sexuality was to be controlled by marriage, heterosexual love, and the middle-class home. As with Victoria and the royal family, sex, at least according to the stereotype, was to be tolerated to produce heirs for the legal transfer of property and inheritance. But as was the case with Victoria's uncles, the norms of sexual behaviour were elastic and inconsistent. The double standard, allowing men to keep a mistress or visit prostitutes, remained the accepted but invisible underside of the dominant norm. Our section on sexuality (Web) shows how these assumptions were extended into law by parliament and in organized social and political resistance movements concerning the control of prostitution, contagious diseases, homosexuality (a word not coined until 1892), censorship, and birth control. These norms, however, were applied somewhat differently to the working classes: for instance, the writings of Cullwick and Munby (Web), chronicling their sadomasochistic relationship between cleaning woman and gentleman-master, not published until the late twentieth century, press power relations to a breaking point over class, employment, and gender proprieties. Forms of censorship were exercised for privacy or discretion (as with Victoria's journals) or under the obscenity laws, which also governed publication, or under the criminal laws that governed conduct. Publications like *The Pearl* brazenly exhibited promiscuous and often illegal sex, while the heterosexual norm was re-enforced in law (Henry Labouchère's amendment (Web)) and also

challenged (Oscar Wilde's trials (Web), and the joint writings by Michael Field, and others). The emergence of scientific and anthropological discourse about sexuality, both physiological and psychological, is explored by Havelock Ellis (Web) and Symonds (Web) in relation to law, evolution, medicine, and history.

It is somewhat ironic, however, that in light of this revolutionary theorizing of sexuality, the queen's name became conventionally associated with prudery, denial, and avoidance of anything sexual. As the documents in this section will demonstrate, Victoria's reign also saw seismic changes in gender relations and the legal position of women. However, despite her unique position as the most powerful woman in a patriarchal society, indeed, arguably the most powerful person, Victoria vigorously opposed thinkers who challenged the gender orthodoxy. In a letter to her friend and advisor Theodore Martin (29 May 1870), she criticized Katharine Russell, Lady Amberley (1842–74), radical and suffragist, supporter of birth control, religious freedom, and free love, and the mother of Bertrand Russell (1872–1970), who would become one of the most prominent British philosophers and mathematicians of the twentieth century. Russell had dared to speak out in favour of woman's suffrage. Victoria wrote to Martin,

> The Queen is most anxious to enlist everyone who can speak or write to join in checking this mad, wicked folly of "Woman's Rights," with all its attendant horrors, on which her poor feeble sex is bent, forgetting every sense of womanly feeling and propriety. Lady— ought to get a GOOD WHIPPING. It is a subject which makes the Queen so furious that she cannot contain herself. God created men and women different—then let them remain each in their own position. Tennyson has some beautiful lines on the difference of men and women in "The Princess." Woman would become the most hateful, heartless, and disgusting of human beings were she allowed to unsex herself; and

where would be the protection which man was intended to give the weaker sex? The Queen is sure that Mrs. Martin agrees with her.

Whatever Mrs Martin might have thought, the readings in Gender, Women, and Sexuality lay out positions for and against "'Woman's Rights,'

with all its attendant horrors" as well as the "difference of men and women" and gender and sexual equality. Ironically, the struggles for power, for gender equality, woman's rights, and sexual self-determination, are rejected by the most powerful woman in the nineteenth century as "mad, wicked folly," with the threat of corporal punishment against a naughty girl.

1. Constructing Genders

Kenelm Digby (1800–80): *The Broad Stone of Honour: or, the True Sense and Practice of Chivalry* ([1822] 1877)

From Part 1, Section 14: "Godefridus"[1]

"The age of chivalry is gone!" calmly observe the calculating sophists,[2] who lead the mind of the moderns, and persuade them that the world is hastening, under their influence, to a period of increased light and civilization,—a most convenient maxim to establish from the declamation of an orator! for that is as much as to hold, that there is no longer occasion for men to be generous and devoted, faithful and indifferent to their own selfish interest, full of high honour; not aiming to follow the erring multitude, but emulous of imitating the example and of joining the society of the celestial citizens: an assertion, however, which carries with it the less weight from its being characteristic of a class of men, whose first principles are all contained in similar propositions, with whom every age is gone but that of economists and calculators. . . .

The error which leads men to doubt of this first proposition consists in their supposing that tournaments and steel, panoply, and coat-arms, and aristocratic institutions, are essential to chivalry; whereas these are, in fact, only accidental attendants upon it, subject to the influence of time, which changes all such things, new-moulding them into a countless diversity of forms, to suit each race of new-born fancies. . . .

Chivalry is only a name for that general spirit or state of mind which disposes men to heroic and generous actions, and keeps them conversant with all that is beautiful and sublime in the intellectual and moral world. It will be found that, in the absence of conservative principles, this spirit more generally prevails in youth than in the later periods of

Notes

CONSTRUCTING GENDERS

[1] *title* drawing on numerous classical and medieval examples, Digby constructs an influential notion of the chivalric gentleman, attacking modern society, particularly utilitarianism, rationality, and middle-class concerns with making money. The entire work is in four sections, each named after chivalric heroes: Godefridus (Godfrey, hero of the first crusade (1095–99)), Tancredus (Tancred de Hauteville, another hero of the first crusade), Morus (Sir Thomas More (1478–1535)), and Orlandus (from Ariosto's *Orlando Furioso* (1591)). Upon capturing Jerusalem in 1099, Godefridus, or Godfrey of Bouillon, was elected king, but he refused the title, not wanting a crown in the city where Christ died, opting instead for

the title Baron and Defender of the Holy Sepulchre. He died on 18 July 1100. The work was published anonymously in 1822 and 1823 with the subtitle "Rules for the Gentlemen of England"; expanded to four volumes in 1828–29 and 1844–48 under Digby's name, subtitled "The True Sense and Practice of Chivalry"; enlarged to five volumes in 1877. Our text: 1877.

[2] *sophists* see Edmund Burke (1729–92), *Reflections on the Revolution in France* (1790): "The age of chivalry is gone.—That of sophisters, economists, and calculators, has succeeded; and the glory of Europe is extinguished forever." To Digby, sophists were specious philosophers, particularly utilitarians.

men's lives; and, as the heroic is always the earliest age in the history of nations, so youth, the first period of human life, may be considered as the heroic or chivalrous age of each separate man: and there are few so unhappy as to have grown up without having experienced its influence, and having derived the advantage of being able to enrich their imaginations and to soothe their hours of sorrow with its romantic recollections. The Anglo-Saxons distinguished the period between childhood and manhood by the term "cnihthad,";[3] boyhood a term which still continued to indicate the connexion between youth and chivalry, when knights were styled children, as in the historic song beginning,

Child Rowland to the dark tower came[4]:

an excellent expression, no doubt; for every boy and youth is, in his mind and sentiments, a knight, and essentially a son of chivalry. Nature is fine in him. Nothing but the circumstance of a most singular and unhappy constitution, and the most perverted and degrading system of education, can ever totally destroy the action of this general law; therefore as long as there has been, or shall be, a succession of sweet springs in man's intellectual world; as long as there have been, or shall be, young men to grow up to maturity, and until all youthful life shall be dead, and its source withered for ever, so long must there have been, and must there continue to be, the spirit of noble chivalry.

Sarah Stickney Ellis (1799–1872): *The Daughters of England* (1842)

From Chapter 1: "Important Inquiries"[5]

As women, then, the first thing of importance is to be content to be inferior to men—inferior in mental power, in the same proportion that you are inferior in bodily strength. Facility of movement, aptitude, and grace, the bodily frame of women may possess in a higher degree than that of man; just as in the softer touches of mental and spiritual beauty, her character may present a lovelier page than his. Yet, as the great attribute of power must still be wanting there, it becomes more immediately her business to inquire how this want may be supplied.

An able and eloquent writer on "Woman's Mission," has justly observed, that woman's strength is in her influence.[6] And, in order to render this influence more complete, you

Notes

[3] *cnihthad* (OE *cniht*, boy, youth; ME *knyght*, military servant of a king or lord; *had/hod* hood; ME *knyghthode*).

[4] came Mad Tom's song in *King Lear* (3.4.187); see also the title and last line of Robert Browning's poem, "Childe Roland to the Dark Tower Came" (1855; see BROWNING (WEB p. 346)).

[5] *title* Ellis wrote several popular conduct books for girls and women, including *The Women of England* (1838), *The Wives of England* (1843), and *The Mothers of England* (1845). Conduct literature replaces the courtesy literature of the Middle Ages concerning the appropriate behaviour of knights and ladies within the courtly love conventions. Most famous of the conduct books was Castiglione's *The Book of the Courtier* (translated by Thomas Hoby in 1561) that set the model for the gentleman at court. On the other hand, Mary Wollstonecraft's pre-radical and first published work, *Thoughts on the Education of Daughters* (1787), and Hannah More's *Coelebs in Search of a Wife* (1809), reshaped the tradition towards women and the middle classes, in which Ellis's books became a defining moment. Her didactic treatises instructed the newly emerging middle classes on the proper

place or domestic sphere for Victorian females. Females were to accept their inferiority to men and to dedicate their lives to the advancement and interests of their fathers, brothers, and husbands. In *The Wives of England* (1843) she wrote: "One important truth sufficiently impressed upon your mind will materially assist in this desirable consummation [of happy married life]—it is the superiority of your husband simply as a man. It is quite possible you may have more talent, with higher attainments, and you may also have been generally more admired; but this has nothing whatever to do with your position as a woman, which is, and must be, inferior to him as a man" (ch. 1). The differences laid out here between active males and passive females is long established; see, for instance, Plato, *Timaeus* 90e; and Aristotle, *Politics* 1254b.

[6] *influence* Sarah Lewis (fl. 1830–50) published a conduct book, *Woman's Mission*, anonymously in 1839 based on *L'éducation des mères de famille* (1834) by Louis Aimé Martin (1782–1847), a disciple of Rousseau. Lewis argued that "women may be the prime agents of God in the regeneration of mankind" through "the cultivation of the religious

will find, on examination, that you are by nature endowed with peculiar faculties—with a quickness of perception, facility of adaptation, and acuteness of feeling, which fit you especially for the part you have to act in life; and which, at the same time, render you, in a higher degree than men, susceptible both of pain and pleasure.

These are your qualifications as mere women. As Christians, how wide is the prospect which opens before you—how various the claims upon your attention—how vast your capabilities—how deep the responsibility which those capabilities involve! In the first place, you are not alone; you are one of a family—of a social circle—of a community—of a nation. You are a being whose existence will never terminate, who *must* live for ever, and whose happiness or misery through that endless future which lies before you, will be influenced by the choice you are now in the act of making....

I must now take it for granted, that the youthful reader of these pages has reflected seriously upon her position in society as a woman, has acknowledged her inferiority to man, has examined her own nature, and found there a capability of feeling, a quickness of perception, and a facility of adaptation, beyond what he possesses, and which, consequently, fit her for a distinct and separate sphere;[7] and I would also gladly persuade myself, that the same individual, as a Christian woman, has made her decision not to live for herself, so much as for others; but, above all, not to live for this world so much as for eternity. The question then arises—What means are to be adopted in the pursuit of this most desirable end? Some of my young readers will perhaps be disposed to exclaim, "Why, this is but the old story of giving up the world, and all its pleasures!" But let them not be too hasty in their conclusions. It is not a system of giving up which I am about to recommend to them, so much as one of attaining. My advice is rather to advance than to retreat, yet to be sure that you advance in the right way. Instead, therefore, of depreciating the value of their advantages and acquirements, it is my intention to point out, as far as I am able, how all these advantages may be made conducive to the great end I have already supposed them to have in view—that of living for others, rather than for themselves—of living for eternity, rather than for time....

From Chapter 9: "Friendship and Flirtation"

This part of my subject necessarily leads me to the consideration of what, for want of a more serious name, I am under the necessity of calling flirtation; by which I would be understood to mean, all that part of the behaviour of women, which in the art of pleasing, has reference only to men. It is easy to understand whether a woman is guilty of flirtation

Notes

and moral portion" – through "maternal influence," especially in the family: "We are not one iota behind these fiery champions of womanhood, in exalted notion of its dignity and mission. We are as anxious as they can be that women should be roused to a sense of their own importance; but we affirm, that it is not so much social institutions that are wanting to women, but women who are wanting to themselves. We claim for them no less an office than that of instruments (under God) for the regeneration of the world,—restorers of God's image in the human soul. Can any of the warmest advocates of the political rights of woman claim or assert for her a more exalted mission,—a nobler destiny! That she will best accomplish this mission by moving in the sphere which God and nature have appointed, and not by quitting that sphere for another, it is the object of these pages to prove." The book was a best-seller, with seventeen British and five American editions up

to 1854. The attacks on the idea of "Woman's Mission" continued throughout the century, as evidenced by the comment in the satirical periodical *Judy* (6 July 1881): "There has been a great deal (too much) talked about 'Woman's Mission' of late by the shrieking sisterhood; did they, by any chance, ever hear that woman's true mission is—sub-mission?" See also NIGHTINGALE, n. 18.

[7] *sphere* like Sarah Lewis, Ellis was a proponent of the ideology of the two separate spheres of social function, a commonplace of Victorian commentary on gender roles, whereby woman's proper sphere was domestic and the family, while man's was business and the world. This concept informs much of the discussion of women's rights and differing roles throughout the nineteenth century; see, for instance, this section, CONSTRUCTING: REID, TAYLOR, and GRAND; GENDER: CONSTRUCTING; RUSKIN (WEB p. 77); and also MARTINEAU, n. 6.

or not, by putting her conduct to this simple test—whether, in mixed society, she is the same to women as to men.

Although nothing could be more revolting to the feelings of a true-hearted woman, than needlessly to make a public exposure of the weaknesses and follies of her own sex, yet something of this is not only justifiable, but necessary in the present case, in order to contrast the conduct of those who are truly admirable, with that which is only adopted for the purpose of courting admiration. Nor would I speak uncharitably, when I confess, that, like others, I have often seen a drooping countenance suddenly grow animated, an oppressive headache suddenly removed, and many other symptoms of an improved state of health and spirits as suddenly exhibited, when the society of ladies has become varied by that of the nobler sex; and never does female friendship receive a deeper insult, than when its claims are thus superseded by those, perhaps, of a mere stranger.

Though the practice of flirtation, or the habit of making use of certain arts of pleasing in the society of men, which are not used in that of women, is a thing of such frequent occurrence, that few can be said to be wholly exempt from it; yet we rarely find a woman so lost to all sense of delicacy, as to make an open profession of flirtation. Indeed, I am convinced, that some do actually practise it unconsciously to themselves, and for this reason I am the more anxious to furnish them with a few hints, by which they may be better able to detect the follies of their own conduct.

WEB p. 70

Sarah Stickney Ellis (1799–1872): *The Mothers of England* (1843).
From Chapter 10: "On the Training of Boys"
From Chapter 11: "On the Training of Girls"

Marion Kirkland Reid (c.1839–89): From *A Plea for Woman* (1843)[8]

Woman's sphere is a phrase which has been generally used to denote the various house-hold duties usually performed by her; but this is employing the phrase in a very limited sense, and one that requires explanation. Strictly speaking, a person's sphere comprises the whole range of his duties; but, taken in this limited sense, woman's sphere does not do this: for she has very many duties in common with man, besides those household requirements peculiar to her as a woman. The meaning usually attached to the phrase "duties of woman's sphere," would be much better expressed, were we to say, duties *peculiar* to woman's sphere. However, the phrase being an established one, we shall use it in its usual limited sense, having thus explained. . . .

Notes

[8] *title* a Scottish activist, Reid attended the World's Anti-Slavery Convention in London in 1840, where all the American and English women delegates were excluded from membership and could only sit in silence. Reid's book went through five American editions to 1852 with the title *Woman, Her Education and Influence*. She was later involved in the Ladies National Association for the Repeal of the Contagious Diseases Acts (see this section, WOMAN QUESTION, n. 14). Reid attacked the views of Ellis and Lewis "that female influence is the *only* influence—and there is no such thing as male influence" as well as the doctrine of separate spheres: "power to man and influence to woman" (see this section, CONSTRUCTING, n. 6).

The ground on which equality is claimed for all men is of equal force for all women; for women share the common nature of humanity, and are possessed of all those noble faculties which constitute man a responsible being, and give him a claim to be his own ruler, so far as is consistent with order, and the possession of the like degree of sovereignty over himself by every other human being. It is the possession of the noble faculties of reason and conscience which elevates man above the brutes, and invests him with this right of exercising supreme authority over himself. It is more especially the possession of an inward rule of rectitude, a law written on the heart in indelible characters, which raises him to this high dignity, and renders him an accountable being, by impressing him with the conviction that there are certain duties which he owes to his fellow-creatures. Whoever possesses this consciousness, has also the belief that the same convictions of duty are implanted in the breast of each member of the human family. He feels that he has a *right* to have all those duties exercised by others towards him, which his conscience tells him he ought to exercise towards others; hence the natural and equal rights of men.[9] ...

Having thus attempted to show, that although in one sense woman was made for man, yet in another and higher she was also made for herself; and that the more faithful she is to the higher end of her being, the development of her whole nature moral and rational, the better will she fulfil the lower one, of ministering to the happiness of man. I shall now try to find out whether there is any need of so many artificial distinctions between the sexes, or whether we might not safely rely on their natural distinctions for retaining each in its proper place.

The most striking difference between the sexes is in their relative proportion of bodily strength, the frame of man being always much stronger than that of woman. And since the physical structure of man is stronger than that of woman, and the mental powers are manifested through physical organs, there is a strong presumption that man must always exceed woman in force of mind as well as in strength of limb. Accordingly the contrast between the minds of the different sexes is of the same nature as that between their physical constitutions. The one sex is soft, gentle, yielding; the other hard, stern, severe. The mental, like the physical organization of woman, seems more delicate than that of man; her mind like her body, is less capable of long-continued or severe labour. But in estimating the difference between the sexes in point of intellectual vigour, there is great danger of rating woman too low. To prevent this, it is necessary to bear in remembrance, that the mind of woman never has been cultivated in the same degree as that of man; so that it is hardly possible to institute a fair comparison between them. The long course of neglect or scorn which has been the general fate of the female mind, must have repressed and deteriorated its powers. Although, therefore, we see that woman is at present inferior in vigour of mind, and may presume that she always must continue to be so in some respect, yet, on the other hand, it must also be admitted, that the partiality which has given so much greater an amount of mental cultivation to man than to woman, and the greater calls which he has had for exertion, have made this difference much greater than it would naturally be, were the same amount of culture and the same opportunities of exertion bestowed on both sexes....

It will be readily allowed that, in the great essentials of their nature, man and woman are the same. They are alike moral, accountable, and immortal beings; and it is on this account that they are entitled to the same rights. But we hope it will also be seen, that there are so many minor differences in their characters as to render it almost absurd to imagine that any elevation of woman's character or position could possibly derange the social economy. In short, all those differences from man in the character

Notes

[9] *men* in 1789 the French National Assembly adopted *The Declaration of the Rights of Man and of the Citizen* in the first phase of the French Revolution. It proclaimed that "Men are born free and remain free and equal in rights and that social distinctions may be founded only on the general good."

of woman, which are usually produced as reasons for depriving her of civil rights, weigh, with us, quite on the other side of the question, and force us irresistibly to the conclusion, that as there are so many natural differences between man and woman, there is no occasion for those artificial distinctions which had their foundation in the superior strength of man when war and spoil were the order of the day. Surely those differences, so strongly marked, may be allowed to do away with the fear of any violent convulsion, in the event of woman receiving all the privileges of rational and responsible creatures. The peculiar characteristics of the sexes, show them so fitted to play into each other's hands, that I cannot conceive the idea of their interests ever interfering with each other. It is certainly the true interest of each to help the other forward as much as possible, and of both to assist in every way in advancing the cause of truth and liberty.

Richard Pilling (1799–1874): From "Defence at his Trial" (1843)[10]

Suppose, gentlemen of the jury, you were obliged to subsist on the paltry pittance given to us in the shape of wages, and had a wife and six helpless children,[11] five of them under thirteen years of age to support, how would you feel? Though you were to confine me to a dungeon I should not submit to it. I have a nervous wife—a good wife—a dear wife—a wife that I love and cherish, and I have done everything that I could in the way of resisting reductions in wages,[12] that I might keep her and my children from the workhouse, for I detest parish relief.[13] It is wages I want. I want to be independent of every man and that is the principle of every honest Englishman; and I hope it is the principle of every man in this court.... I was twenty years among the handloom weavers,[14] and ten years in a factory, and I unhesitatingly say, that during the whole course of that time I worked twelve hours a day with the exception of twelve months that the masters of Stockport would not employ me; and the longer and harder I have worked the poorer and poorer I have become every year, until, at last, I am nearly exhausted. If the masters had taken off another 25%, I would put an end to my existence sooner than kill myself working twelve hours a day in a cotton factory, and eating potatoes and salt. Gentlemen of the jury,[15] I now leave my case in your hands. Whatever it may have been with others it has been a wage question with me. And I do say that if Mr. O'Connor[16] has made it a chartist question,[17] he has done wonders to make it extend through England, Ireland, and Scotland.

Notes

[10] *title* Pilling was a handloom weaver, and later a cotton-mill worker and Chartist, brought to trial as a member of the Power-Loom Weavers' Trade Society and the Stockport Chartist Working Men's Association for organizing a series of strikes of the power-loom weavers at Stockport. They escalated to a general strike in the cotton districts of Lancashire and Yorkshire in 1842 known as the Plug Riots. He was brought to trial with Feargus O'Connor and fifty-seven other Chartists at the Lancashire Assizes of April 1843 where, faced with large numbers of offenders being transported to Australia, he made the defence from which this selection is drawn, earning him an acquittal. Our text: *State Trials* (New Series 1839–43), iv, cols. 1097–1108.

[11] *children* Pilling had seven children, three of whom were able to work, though the second eldest, James, had to leave work in 1842, dying soon afterwards from tuberculosis.

[12] *wages* he claimed that when he began to work, at about 10 years of age, he was earning 16 s. a week, but in the depression after the Napoleonic wars his earnings dropped to 6 s. 6 d.

[13] *relief* after the Poor Law Act of 1834 all who sought relief, even able-bodied paupers, had to seek relief by residing in a parish workhouse. See CONDITION: VICTORIAN SOCIAL, n. 19.

[14] *weavers* after the Napoleonic wars, there were between 200,000 and 250,000 handloom weavers working in their own houses in Britain; by 1861 there were only 7,000, decimated by the invention of the power loom (by Edmund Cartwright, 1785) and its deployment in factories. J. P. Kay estimated in 1832 that weavers worked fourteen hours a day and earned from 5 s. to 7 s. a week, down from £1 10 s. in 1790. With the collapse of the cotton industry in the 1840s, rates of pay dropped to mere starvation earnings.

[15] *jury* women were not allowed to serve on juries in the United Kingdom until the Sexual Disqualification Removal Act of 1919.

[16] *O'Connor* Feargus O'Connor (1794–1855), British MP for Cork in Ireland and later for Nottingham, editor of the Leeds radical newspaper *The Northern Star*, and Chartist.

[17] *question* for Chartism, see CONDITION: VICTORIAN SOCIAL, nn. 10 and 11.

But it was always a wage question, and ten hours bill[18] with me. I have advocated the keeping up of wages for a long time, and I shall do so till the end of my days. And, if confined within the walls of a dungeon, knowing that as an individual I have done my duty; knowing that I have been one of the great spokes in the wheel by which that last reduction of wages was prevented—knowing that by means of that turn-out thousands and ten of thousands have eaten the bread which they would not have eaten if the turn-out had not taken place, I am satisfied, whatever may be the result.... And, now, Gentlemen of the jury, you have the case before you; the masters conspired to kill me, and I combined[19] to keep myself alive.

WEB p. 72

Anne Brontë (1820–49): *The Tenant of Wildfell Hall* (1848)
  From Chapter 33: "Two Evenings"

Isabella Beeton (1836–65): *The Book of Household Management* (1859–61)

From Chapter 1: "The Mistress"[20]

1.   As with the commander of an army, or the leader of any enterprise, so is it with the mistress of a house . Her spirit will be seen through the whole establishment; and just in proportion as she performs her duties intelligently and thoroughly, so will her domestics follow in her path. Of all those acquirements, which more particularly belong to the feminine character, there are none which take a higher rank, in our estimation, than such as enter into a knowledge of household duties; for on these are perpetually dependent the happiness, comfort, and well-being of a family....

3.   Early rising is one of the most essential qualities which enter into good Household Management, as it is not only the parent of health, but of innumerable other advantages. Indeed, when a mistress is an early riser, it is almost certain that her house will be orderly and well-managed. On the contrary, if she remain in bed till a late hour, then the domestics, who, as we have before observed, invariably partake somewhat of their mistress's character, will surely become sluggards. To self-indulgence all are more or less disposed, and it is not to be expected that servants are freer from this fault than the heads of houses....

9.   In conversation, trifling occurrences, such as small disappointments, petty annoyances, and other every-day incidents, should never be mentioned to your friends.... If the mistress be a wife, never let an account of her husband's failings pass her lips....

Notes

[18] *bill* the Ten Hours Movement began in the 1830s, led by the labour reformer, Richard Oastler (1789–1861) outside parliament and Lord Shaftesbury (1801–85) inside parliament, to limit the hours of textile workers, especially women and children. The Factory Act of 1833 limited the hours worked by children of 9 to 13 to eight hours a day, and those 14 to 18 to not more than twelve hours a day, each with a one-hour lunch break. The Ten Hours Bill (Factories Act of 1847), introduced by Shaftesbury, limited the workday for children under 18 and women to ten hours a day, a reform that Parliament had opposed up to that point; see also, DODD, n. 7 (WEB p. 294).

[19] *combined* joined a trade union; a "combination" is an archaic term for a trade union. In 1824 the Combination Acts passed late in the eighteenth century that made unions illegal were repealed, allowing for legal unionization.

[20] *title* in 1856 Beeton had married the magazine publisher Samuel Beeton, who undertook the publication of her writings on managing a household. It was issued in twenty-four monthly parts in 1859–61, for 3*d*. a part, under the auspices of *The Englishwoman's Domestic Magazine*, and in book form in October, 1861 (our text), priced 7*s*. 6*d*., selling 60,000 copies in the first year. It was a kind of conduct book, an encyclopedia of household economy. It also had advice on kitchen and household equipment, nursing in the family, legal matters, and recipes, beginning with accounts of the place of animals, fish, fowl, and vegetables and fruit in the order of nature. For an adaptation of Beeton in the context of India, see EMPIRE: GOVERNING; STEEL AND GARDINER.

13.   The dress of the mistress should always be adapted to her circumstances, and be varied with different occasions. Thus, at breakfast she should be attired in a very neat and simple manner, wearing no ornaments. If this dress should decidedly pertain only to the breakfast-hour, and be specially suited for such domestic occupations as usually follow that meal, then it would be well to exchange it before the time for receiving visitors, if the mistress be in the habit of doing so. It is still to be remembered, however, that, in changing the dress, jewellery and ornaments are not to be worn until the full dress for dinner is assumed. . . .

19.   The treatment of servants is of the highest possible moment, as well to the mistress as to the domestics themselves. On the head of the house the latter will naturally fix their attention; and if they perceive that the mistress's conduct is regulated by high and correct principles, they will not fail to respect her. If, also, a benevolent desire is shown to promote their comfort, at the same time that a steady performance of their duty is exacted, then their respect will not be unmingled with affection, and they will be still more solicitous to continue to deserve her favour. . . .

21.   The following table of the average yearly wages paid to domestics,[21] with the various members of the household placed in the order in which they are usually ranked, will serve as a guide to regulate the expenditure of an establishment:—

	When not found in livery[22]	When found in livery
The House Steward	From £40 to £80	—
The Valet	" 25 to 50	From £20 to £30
The Butler	" 25 to 50	—
The Cook	" 20 to 40	—
The Gardener	" 20 to 40	—
The Footman	" 20 to 40	" 15 to 25
The Under Butler	" 15 to 30	" 15 to 25
The Coachman	—	" 20 to 35
The Groom	" 15 to 30	" 12 to 20
The Under Footman	—	" 12 to 20
The Page or Footboy	" 8 to 18	" 6 to 14
The Stableboy	" 6 to 12	—

Notes

[21] *domestics* Beeton's hierarchy of servants places three men above the cook in the first (wealthier) list and three women above the cook in the second. In most households able to afford a range of domestics, the butler ran the house and the housekeeper was responsible for the female staff. The housekeeper controlled the keys; both had status from personal proximity to the master and mistress of the house. Below stairs, that is, in the servants' area of the basement, the cook was in control of the entire preparation of meals, apart from consultation about menus; the lady's maid and valet had higher wages because of their duties with respect to clothing, conversation, and attendance to dressing and personal service to the family. Incomes for social status vary throughout the century and the country. About the time that Beeton was writing, based on John Henry Walsh's *A Manual of Domestic Economy Suited to Families* (1856, 1874) and Leone Levi's *Wages and Earnings of the Working Classes* (1867), a wealthy aristocratic family would have an income of between £10,000 and £30,000 or more; a well-to-do upper middle-class family (wealthy manufacturers, bankers, or landed gentry) would have a yearly income between £5,000 and £10,000; other upper-middle-class families (barristers, physicians, other professional men, and businessmen) between £1,000 and £5,000; a middle-class family (civil servants, solicitors, senior clerks) between £500 and £800 or £1,000; and a lower middle-class family (journalists and teachers) between £200 and £500. As Beeton indicates, all of these would have some kind of servant living in. For instance, Robert Browning's father, a senior clerk in the Bank of England, earned £275 a year around 1845, enough for the family of four to live comfortably in a London suburb, with two servants, keeping a horse and small carriage. In the working-classes around 1860, a skilled worker (cabinet-maker, typesetter, master carpenter) could earn between £75 and £100 a year; a labourer, £40–60, and a textile worker in a Manchester mill, about £30; farmworkers, soldiers, domestics, and needleworkers earned between £12 and £20.

[22] *livery* the uniform worn by the domestic members of a household, usually adorned with the heraldry of the family. In the first edition there were several typos for the wages, corrected in later editions in 1861. We have followed the corrected figures.

	When no extra allowance is made for Tea, Sugar, and Beer	When an extra allowance is made for Tea, Sugar, and Beer
The Housekeeper	From £20 to £45	From £18 to £40
The Lady's-maid	" 12 to 25	" 10 to 20
The Head Nurse	" 15 to 30	" 13 to 26
The Cook	" 11 to 30	" 12 to 26
The Upper Housemaid	" 12 to 20	" 10 to 17
The Upper Laundry-maid	" 12 to 18	" 10 to 15
The Maid-of-all-work	" 9 to 14	" 7–1/2 to 11
The Under Housemaid	" 8 to 12	" 6–1/2 to 10
The Still-room Maid	" 9 to 14	" 8 to 13
The Nursemaid	" 8 to 12	" 5 to 10
The Under Laundry-maid	" 9 to 11	" 8 to 12
The Kitchen-maid	" 9 to 14	" 8 to 12
The Scullery-maid	" 5 to 9	" 4 to 8

These quotations of wages are those usually given in or near the metropolis; but, of course, there are many circumstances connected with locality, and also having reference to the long service on the one hand, or the inexperience on the other, of domestics, which may render the wages still higher or lower than those named above. All the domestics mentioned in the above table would enter into the establishment of a wealthy nobleman. The number of servants, of course, would become smaller in proportion to the lesser size of the establishment; and we may here enumerate a scale of servants suited to various incomes, commencing with—

About £1,000 a year—A cook, upper housemaid, nursemaid, under housemaid, and a man servant.
About £750 a year—A cook, housemaid, nursemaid, and footboy.
About £500 a year—A cook, housemaid, and nursemaid.
About £300 a year—A maid-of-all-work and nursemaid.
About £200 or £150 a year—A maid-of-all-work[23] (and girl occasionally).

WEB p. 73

Harriet Martineau (1802–76): From "Middle-Class Education in England: Boys" (1864)
Harriet Martineau (1802–76): From "Middle-Class Education in England: Girls" (1864)
John Ruskin (1819–1900): *Sesame and Lilies* (1862)
    From "Of Queen's Gardens"

Notes ───────────────────────────────────

[23] *maid-of-all-work* for diary entries on the workday of a maid-of-all-work, see GENDER: SEX; CULLWICK, *DIARIES* (WEB p. 89).

Eliza Lynn Linton (1822–98): From "The Girl of the Period" in the *Saturday Review* (14 Mar. 1868)[24]

Time was when the phrase, "a fair young English girl," meant the ideal of womanhood; to us, at least, of home birth and breeding. It meant a creature generous, capable, and modest. . . . It meant a girl who could be trusted alone if need be, because of the innate purity and dignity of her nature, but who was neither bold in bearing nor masculine in mind; a girl who, when she married, would be her husband's friend and companion, but never his rival; one who would consider their interests identical, and not hold him as just so much fair game for spoil; who would make his house his true home and place of rest, not a mere passage-place for vanity and ostentation to go through; a tender mother, an industrious housekeeper, a judicious mistress. We prided ourselves as a nation on our women. We thought we had the pick of creation in this fair young English girl of ours, and envied no other men their own. We admired the languid grace and subtle fire of the South; the docility and childlike affectionateness of the East seemed to us sweet and simple and restful; the vivacious sparkle of the trim and sprightly Parisienne was a pleasant little excitement when we met with it in its own domain; but our allegiance never wandered from our brown-haired girls at home, and our hearts were less vagrant than our fancies. This was in the old time, and when English girls were content to be what God and nature had made them. Of late years we have changed the pattern, and have given to the world a race of women as utterly unlike the old insular ideal as if we had created another nation altogether. The girl of the period, and the fair young English girl of the past, have nothing in common save ancestry and their mother-tongue; and even of this last the modern version makes almost a new language, through the copious additions it has received from the current slang of the day.

The girl of the period is a creature who dyes her hair and paints her face, as the first articles of her personal religion; whose sole idea of life is plenty of fun and luxury; and whose dress is the object of such thought and intellect as she possesses. Her main endeavour is to outvie her neighbours in the extravagance of fashion.[25] No matter whether, as in the time of crinolines, she sacrificed decency; or, as now, in the time of trains, she sacrifices cleanliness; no matter either, whether she makes herself

Notes

[24] *title* the self-educated Linton supported herself entirely from writing, from the age of 23, for such publications as the *Morning Chronicle* and Dickens's *Household Words* and *All the Year Round*. Her early novel, *Realities* (1851), caused a sensation for its attack on respectable Victorian morality, and other writings promoted agnosticism and radical politics. In 1858 she married the engraver W. J. Linton, a widower with seven children, but they separated amicably in 1867. This essay, published in the strongly anti-feminist *Saturday Review*, caused a sensation for its rejection of women's suffrage using vitriolic stereotypes, but she did not claim authorship until 1884. Her title became a cliché in the years following publication (see this section, WOMAN QUESTION, n. 22). Becoming increasingly conservative, and attracting the ire of the feminists, Linton's other attacks were levelled against women's rights and "Modern Mothers" (*Saturday Review*, 29 Feb. 1868): "Not content with bewildering men's minds, and emptying their husbands' purses for the enhancement of their own charms, women do the same by their children, and the mother who leaves the health, and mind, and temper, and purity of her offspring in the keeping of a hired nurse takes especial care of the colour and cut of the frocks and petticoats."

[25] *fashion* after alluding to national stereotypes of feminine qualities, Linton turns to style and fashion as expressive of new modes of dress for advanced women. She mentions the chief characteristic of the society dresses of the period, the crinoline or frame of steel and cloth that held out women's skirts in a wide dome-shape that gradually declined to a cone shape through the 1860s. Evening wear involved a train. Over the next two decades the hoops and train combined into various forms of the bustle, eventually spurned by the aesthetes and new women of the 1890s, themselves the objects of attack for innovations in fashion and lifestyle, especially with the advent of dress for sports and hygiene. See also GENDER: WOMAN QUESTION, n. 19 (WEB p. 83).

a nuisance and an inconvenience to every one she meets.... It was all very well in old-fashioned times, when fathers and mothers had some authority and were treated with respect, to be tutored and made to obey, but she is far too fast and flourishing to be stopped in mid-career by these slow old morals; and as she dresses to please herself, she does not care if she displeases every one else. Nothing is too extraordinary and nothing too exaggerated for her vitiated taste; and things which in themselves would be useful reforms if let alone become monstrosities worse than those which they have displaced so soon as she begins to manipulate and improve. If a sensible fashion lifts the gown out of the mud, she raises hers midway to her knee. If the absurd structure of wire and buckram, once called a bonnet, is modified to something that shall protect the wearer's face without putting out the eyes of her companion, she cuts hers down to four straws and a rosebud, or a tag of lace and a bunch of glass beads....

This imitation of the *demi-monde*[26] in dress leads to something in manner and feeling, not quite so pronounced perhaps, but far too like to be honourable to herself or satisfactory to her friends. It leads to slang, bold talk, and fastness; to the love of pleasure and indifference to duty; to the desire of money before either love or happiness; to uselessness at home, dissatisfaction with the monotony of ordinary life, and horror of all useful work; in a word, to the worst forms of luxury and selfishness, to the most fatal effects arising from want of high principle and absence of tender feeling. The girl of the period envies the queens of the *demi-monde* far more than she abhors them....

No one can say of the modern English girl that she is tender, loving, retiring, or domestic.... The legal barter of herself for so much money, representing so much dash, so much luxury and pleasure—that is her idea of marriage; the only idea worth entertaining. For all seriousness of thought respecting the duties or the consequences of marriage, she has not a trace.... If we must have only one kind of thing, let us have it genuine; and the queens of St. John's Wood in their unblushing honesty, rather than their imitators and make-believes in Bayswater and Belgravia.[27] For, at whatever cost of shocked self-love or pained modesty it may be, it cannot be too plainly told to the modern English girl that the net result of her present manner of life is to assimilate her as nearly as possible to a class of women whom we must not call by their proper— or improper—name. And we are willing to believe that she has still some modesty of soul left hidden under all this effrontery of fashion, and that, if she could be made to see herself as she appears to the eyes of men, she would mend her ways before too late....

She thinks she is piquante and exciting when she thus makes herself the bad copy of a worse original; and she will not see that though men laugh with her they do not respect her, though they flirt with her they do not marry her; she will not believe that she is not the kind of thing they want, and that she is acting against nature and her own interests when she disregards their advice and offends their taste.

[26] *demi-monde* (Fr. half-world); a class of women imitating French courtesans on the outskirts of society, usually supported by wealthy lovers, who lived stylishly with lavish food, fashions, and parties.

[27] *St. John's Wood ... Belgravia* these areas of London have particular connotations: St. John's Wood was a disreputable area where many wealthy men kept their mistresses in fancy houses. Bayswater was respectable; Belgravia, aristocratic.

Rudyard Kipling (1865–1936). "If—" (1910)[28]

If you can keep your head when all about you
    Are losing theirs and blaming it on you;
If you can trust yourself when all men doubt you,
    But make allowance for their doubting too;
If you can wait and not be tired by waiting,   5
    Or being lied about, don't deal in lies,
Or being hated don't give way to hating,
    And yet don't look too good, nor talk too wise;

If you can dream—and not make dreams your master;
    If you can think—and not make thoughts your aim,   10
If you can meet with Triumph and Disaster
    And treat those two impostors just the same;
If you can bear to hear the truth you've spoken
    Twisted by knaves to make a trap for fools,
Or watch the things you gave your life to, broken,   15
    And stoop and build 'em up with worn-out tools;

If you can make one heap of all your winnings
    And risk it on one turn of pitch-and-toss,[29]
And lose, and start again at your beginnings
    And never breathe a word about your loss;   20
If you can force your heart and nerve and sinew
    To serve your turn long after they are gone,
And so hold on when there is nothing in you
    Except the Will which says to them: "Hold on!"

If you can talk with crowds and keep your virtue,   25
    Or walk with Kings—nor lose the common touch,
If neither foes nor loving friends can hurt you,
    If all men count with you, but none too much;
If you can fill the unforgiving minute
    With sixty seconds' worth of distance run,   30
Yours is the Earth and everything that's in it,
    And—which is more—you'll be a Man, my son![30]

Notes

[28] *title* written in 1895 in honour of Dr Leander Starr Jameson, who in 1895 led a raid against the Boers in South Africa. This action, later known as the Jameson Raid, was a major cause of the second Boer War (1899–1902). Taken out of its historical context, the poem is often interpreted to articulate ideal qualities of masculinity. First published *American Magazine* (Oct. 1910); collected in *Rewards and Fairies* (1910), our text.

[29] *pitch-and-toss* a coin-tossing game.

[30] *my son* Kipling's only son John (born two years after the poem was written) would die in World War One at the Battle of Loos in 1915 at age 18.

2. The Woman Question

Sarah Stickney Ellis (1799–1872): *The Women of England* (1838)

From Chapter 2: "The Influence of the Women of England"[1]

Figure 6 Thomas Allom (1804–72), *Female Influence*. In Sarah Stickney Ellis, *The Women of England*. (Illustrated edition 1845 [First ed. 1839]). Wood-block Engraving. 11 × 19 cm. Source: courtesy of the Thomas Fisher Library, University of Toronto. Thomas Allom usually worked with the publisher H. Fisher & Son (who published this engraving) and became a noted architect, architectural draughtsman, and watercolorist, much in demand.

It is therefore not only false in reasoning, but wrong in principle, for women to assert, as they not unfrequently do with a degree of puerile satisfaction, that they have no influence. An influence fraught either with good or evil, they must have; and though the one may be above their ambition, and the other beyond their fears, by neglecting to obtain an influence which shall be beneficial to society, they necessarily assume a bad one: just in the same proportion as their selfishness, indolence, or vacuity of mind, render them in youth an easy prey to every species of unamiable temper, in middle age the melancholy victims of mental disease, and, long before the curtain of death conceals their follies from the world, a burden and a bane to society at large.

Notes

A superficial observer might with this class many of those exemplary women, who pass to and fro upon the earth with noiseless step, whose names are never heard, and who, even in society, if they attempt to speak, have scarcely the ability to command an attentive audience. Yet amongst this unpretending class are found striking and noble instances of women, who, apparently feeble and insignificant, when called into action by pressing and peculiar circumstances, can accomplish great and glorious purposes, supported and carried forward by that most valuable of all faculties— *moral power.*[2] . . .

It is not to be presumed that women *possess* more power than men; but happily for them, such are their early impressions, associations, and general position in the world, that their moral feelings are less liable to be impaired by the pecuniary objects which too often constitute the chief end of man, and which, even under the limitations of better principle, necessarily engage a large portion of his thoughts. There are many humble-minded women, not remarkable for any particular intellectual endowments, who yet possess so clear a sense of the right and wrong of individual actions, as to be of essential service in aiding the judgments of their husbands, brothers, or sons, in those intricate affairs in which it is sometimes difficult to dissever worldly wisdom from religious duty.

To men belongs the potent (I had almost said the *omnipotent*) consideration of worldly aggrandisement; and it is constantly misleading their steps, closing their ears against the voice of conscience, and beguiling them with the promise of peace, where peace was never found. Long before the boy has learned to exult in the dignity of the man, his mind has become familiarized to the habit of investing with supreme importance, all considerations relating to the acquisition of wealth. He hears on the sabbath, and on stated occasions, when men meet for that especial purpose, of a God to be worshipped, a Saviour to be trusted in, and a holy law to be observed; but he sees before him, every day and every hour, a strife, which is nothing less than deadly to the highest impulses of the soul, after another god—the mammon of unrighteousness—the moloch[3] of this world; and believing rather what men do, than what they preach, he learns too soon to mingle with the living mass, and to unite his labours with theirs. To unite? Alas! there is no union in the great field of action in which he is engaged; but envy and hatred, and opposition, to the close of the day. . . .

How often has man returned to his home with a mind confused by the many voices, which in the mart, the exchange, or the public assembly, have addressed themselves to his inborn selfishness, or his worldly pride; and while his integrity was shaken, and his resolution gave way beneath the pressure of apparent necessity, or the insidious pretences of expediency, he has stood corrected before the clear eye of woman, as it looked directly to the naked truth, and detected the lurking evil of the specious act he was about to commit. Nay, so potent may have become this secret influence, that he may have borne it about with him like a kind of second conscience, for mental reference, and spiritual counsel in moments of trial; and when the snares of the world were around him, and temptations from within and without have bribed over the witness in his own bosom, he has thought of the humble monitress who sat alone, guarding the fireside comforts of his distant home; and the remembrance of her character, clothed in moral beauty, has scattered the clouds before his mental vision, and sent him back to that beloved home, a wiser and a better man.

Notes

[2] *power* see this section, CONSTRUCTING, nn. 5 and 6; see also Figure 6.

[3] *moloch* used in several places in the Bible; see, for instance, Leviticus 18: 21. Used poetically to signify a demanding or costly sacrifice.

Harriet Taylor (1807–58): From "The Enfranchisement of Women" in *Westminster Review* (July 1851)[4]

Most of our readers will probably learn from these pages for the first time, that there has arisen in the United States, and in the most civilized and enlightened portion of them, an organised agitation on a new question—new, not to thinkers, nor to any one by whom the principles of free and popular government are felt as well as acknowledged, but new, and even unheard of, as a subject for public meetings and practical political action.[5] This question is, the enfranchisement of women; their admission, in law and in fact, to equality in all rights, political, civil, and social, with the male citizens of the community....

When a prejudice, which has any hold on the feelings, finds itself reduced to the unpleasant necessity of assigning reasons, it thinks it has done enough when it has re-asserted the very point in dispute, in phrases which appeal to the pre-existing feeling. Thus, many persons think they have sufficiently justified the restrictions on women's field of action, when they have said that the pursuits from which women are excluded are *unfeminine*, and that the *proper sphere* of women is not politics or publicity, but private and domestic life.

We deny the right of any portion of the species to decide for another portion, or any individual for another individual, what is and what is not their "proper sphere." The proper sphere for all human beings is the largest and highest which they are able to attain to....

We shall follow the very proper example of the Convention, in not entering into the question of the alleged differences in physical or mental qualities between the sexes; not because we have nothing to say, but because we have too much.... But if those who assert that the "proper sphere" for women is the domestic, mean by this that they have not shown themselves qualified for any other, the assertion evinces great ignorance of life and of history. Women have shown fitness for the highest social functions, exactly in proportion as they have been admitted to them....

Concerning the fitness, then, of women for politics, there can be no question: but the dispute is more likely to turn upon the fitness of politics for women. When the reasons alleged for excluding women from active life in all its higher departments, are stripped of their garb of declamatory phrases, and reduced to the simple expression of a meaning, they seem to be mainly three: the incompatibility of active life with maternity, and with the cares of a household; secondly, its alleged hardening effect on the character; and thirdly, the inexpediency of making an addition to the already excessive pressure of competition in every kind of professional or lucrative employment....

But, in truth, none of these arguments and considerations touch the foundations of the subject. The real question is, whether it is right and expedient that one-half of the human race should pass through life in a state of forced subordination to the other half. If the best state of human society is that of being divided into two parts, one consisting of persons with a will and a substantive existence, the other of humble companions to these persons, attached, each of them to one, for the purpose of bringing up *his* children, and making *his* home pleasant to him; if this is the place assigned to women, it is but kindness to educate them for this; to make them believe that the greatest good fortune which can befal them, is to be chosen by some man for this purpose; and that every other career

Notes

[4] *title* this essay first appeared anonymously, soon after Taylor's marriage to John Stuart Mill in April, 1851. It was reprinted in Mill's *Dissertations and Discussions* (1859) and was often wrongly attributed to him. It was published as a pamphlet by the National Union of Women's Suffrage Societies (1868).

[5] *action* Taylor refers to "a Convention of Women, held in the State of Ohio, in the spring of 1850. Of this meeting

we have seen no report. On the 23rd and 24th of October last, a succession of public meetings was held at Worcester in Massachusetts, under the name of a 'Women's Rights Convention.'" She cites a newspaper account of the latter by Jacob Gilbert Forman, "Women's Rights Convention at Worcester, Mass." (*New York Daily Tribune*, 26 Oct. 1850).

which the world deems happy or honourable, is closed to them by the law, not of social institutions, but of nature and destiny.

When, however, we ask why the existence of one-half the species should be merely ancillary to that of the other—why each woman should be a mere appendage to a man, allowed to have no interests of her own, that there may be nothing to compete in her mind with his interests and his pleasure; the only reason which can be given is, that men like it. It is agreeable to them that men should live for their own sake, women for the sake of men: and the qualities and conduct in subjects which are agreeable to rulers, they succeed for a long time in making the subjects themselves consider as their appropriate virtues. . . .

There are indications that the example of America will be followed on this side of the Atlantic; and the first step has been taken in that part of England where every serious movement in the direction of political progress has its commencement—the manufacturing districts of the North. On the 13th of February 1851, a petition of women, agreed to by a public meeting at Sheffield, and claiming the elective franchise, was presented to the House of Lords by the Earl of Carlisle.[6]

Caroline Norton (1808–77): From *A Letter to the Queen on Lord Chancellor Cranworth's Marriage and Divorce Bill* (1855)[7]

Madam,—I will not do your Majesty the injustice of supposing, that the very different aspect the law wears in England for the female sovereign and the female subject, must render you indifferent to what those subjects may suffer; or what reform may be proposed, in the rules more immediately affecting them. I therefore submit a brief and familiar exposition of the laws relating to women,—as taught and practised in those Inns of Court, where your Majesty received homage, and Prince Albert was elected a Bencher.[8]

Notes

[6] *Carlisle* see *A Petition of the Female Inhabitants of the Borough of Sheffield in the County of York, in Public Meeting Assembled, Praying Their Lordships to Take into Their Serious Consideration the Propriety of Enacting an Electoral Law which Will Include Adult Females within Its Provisions* (13 Feb. 1851), *Journals of the House of Lords*, Vol. 83, 23.

[7] *title* to obtain a divorce in mid-Victorian Britain, one had first to obtain a decree of divorce *a mensa et thoro* (Lat. from table and bed) from the ecclesiastical courts (not a dissolving of the marriage, but a kind of separation). Then a husband had to win a case against the wife's lover(s) in a civil court for "criminal conversation" by proving the wife's adultery with them. Only then could a case be brought forward in the House of Lords, the only court that could grant a divorce – all at great cost. A Royal Commission of 1850 recommended the formation of a divorce court to hear matrimonial cases, but only in the case of a wife's adultery would the marriage be dissolved; divorce *a mensa et thoro* would then be available to wives and husbands, but only on the grounds of adultery, gross cruelty, or extended desertion.

Lord Cranworth proposed a bill with these provisions in June 1854 but it died after the second reading. When the bill was reintroduced in 1856, Norton's "Letter" had provoked a sensation, arousing opposition to the entrenched double standard and garnering support for a married women's property bill. As it stood, according to common law any legacy, income, or property of a married woman separated from her husband belonged to her husband; it could be seized, along with her children, and it could be conferred upon his mistress. The underlying concept in law was the idea of "coverture," that at marriage a woman's legal rights and obligations were merged with those of her husband: she was known as a *feme covert* (Norman Fr. covered woman); before that, an unmarried woman was known in law as a *feme sole* (Norman Fr. single woman). William Blackstone in his *Commentary on the Laws of England* (1765–69) writes, "By marriage, the husband and wife are one person in law: that is, the very being or legal existence of the woman is suspended during the marriage, or at least is incorporated and consolidated into that of the husband: under whose wing, protection, and cover, she performs every thing; and is therefore called in our law-French a feme-covert." In 1856 there were two amendments, one allowing women legally separated by the ecclesiastical courts to be treated as a *feme sole*, able to own their own property and undertake contracts; and that a woman deserted by her husband could go before a magistrate to be declared a *feme sole*; both amendments were incorporated into the Matrimonial Causes Act of 1857, which removed divorce from the ecclesiastical courts to the civil courts, but otherwise its stipulations continued. The Married Women's Property Act (1870) allowed a woman to own outright any wages or property she earned by her own work, and in 1882 the act was extended to cover all property, including inheritance, investment, or gift, whenever given.

A married woman in England has *no legal existence*: her being is absorbed in that of her husband. Years of separation or desertion cannot alter this position. Unless divorced by special enactment in the House of Lords, the legal fiction holds her to be *"one"* with her husband, even though she may never see or hear of him.

She has no possessions, unless by special settlement; her property is *his* property.... An English wife has no legal right even to her clothes or ornaments; her husband may take them and sell them if he pleases, even though they be the gifts of relatives or friends, or bought before marriage.

An English wife cannot make a will. She may have children or kindred whom she may earnestly desire to benefit;—she may be separated from her husband, who may be living with a mistress; no matter: the law gives what she has to him, and no will she could make would be valid.

An English wife cannot legally claim her own earnings. Whether wages for manual labour, or payment for intellectual exertion, whether she weed potatoes, or keep a school, her salary is *the husband's*; and he could compel a second payment, and treat the first as void, if paid to the wife without his sanction.

An English wife may not leave her husband's house. Not only can he sue her for "restitution of conjugal rights," but he has a right to enter the house of any friend or relation with whom she may take refuge, and who may "harbour her,"—as it is termed,—and carry her away by force, with or without the aid of the police.

If the wife sue for separation for cruelty, it must be "cruelty that endangers life or limb," and if she has once forgiven, or, in legal phrase, "condoned" his offences, she cannot plead them; though her past forgiveness only proves that she endured as long as endurance was possible.

If her husband take proceedings for a divorce, she is not, in the first instance, allowed to defend herself. She has no means of proving the falsehood of his allegations. She is not represented by attorney, nor permitted to be considered a party to the suit between him and her supposed lover, for "damages." ...

If an English wife be guilty of infidelity, her husband can divorce *her* so as to marry again; but she cannot divorce the husband *a vinculo*,[9] however profligate he may be. No law court can divorce in England. A special Act of Parliament annulling the marriage, is passed for each case. The House of Lords grants this almost as a matter of course to the husband, but not to the wife. In only four instances (two of which were cases of incest), has the wife obtained a divorce to marry again.[10] ...

Notes

After her husband abducted her three sons (when the criminal conversation accusations failed and divorce became impossible (see n. 12)), Norton set out to change the law and was successful in gaining support to have the Infant Custody Act passed in 1839. It gave custody for children under 7 to the mother, and the non-custodial parent access, the first notable act to gain for women some rights over entrenched patriarchal authority. However, Norton did not gain from it, since her husband removed her children to Scotland, where the act did not apply.

[8] *Bencher* Queen Victoria opened the new hall for Lincoln's Inn at the Inns of Court, the law societies of Great Britain,

on 30 October 1845, and Prince Albert became a member of the Inn; on 30 November he was elected to be called to the Bar, and on 12 January 1846 he had accepted and became a Bencher or "Master of the Bench," a senior member of one of the Inns of Court.

[9] *a vinculo* (Lat. abbreviation for *a vinculo matrimonii*, from the bond of marriage).

[10] *again* in 1801Mrs Addison won her case in the House of Lords because of her husband's incestuous adultery with her married sister; the other three cases were brought by Louisa Turton (1831), again because of incest with her sister, Anne Battersby (1840) and Georgina Hall (1850), both because of adultery aggravated by bigamy.

From the date of my mother's death,[11] he [Mr. Norton] has withheld entirely, and with perfect impunity, my income as his wife. I do not receive, and have not received for the last three years, a single farthing from him.[12] He retains, and always has retained, property that was left in my home—gifts made to me by my own family on my marriage, and to my mother by your Majesty's aunt, H.R.H. the Duchess of York;—articles bought from my literary earnings,—books which belonged to Lord Melbourne; and, in particular, a manuscript of which Lord Melbourne himself was the author, (when a very young man,) which Mr Norton resolutely refused to give up.

He receives from my trustees the interest of the portion bequeathed me by my father, who died in the public service, holding an official appointment at the Cape of Good Hope, leaving a family of very young orphans, slenderly provided for. . . . Yet such portion as he was able to leave me, goes from the "non-existent" wife, to the existent husband, in the general trust-fund of our marriage.

I have also (as Mr Norton impressed on me, by subpœnaing my publishers) the power of earning, by literature,—which fund (though it be the grant of Heaven, and not the legacy of earth) is no more legally mine than my family property.

Now again, I say, is or is not this a ridiculous law (if laws be made to conduct to justice)? I cannot divorce my husband, either for adultery, desertion, or cruelty; I *must* remain married to *his name*; *he* has, in right of that fact (of my link to his name), a right to everything I have in the world—and I have no more claim upon *him*, than any one of your Majesty's ladies in waiting, who are utter strangers to him! I never see him:—I hear of him only by attacks on my reputation:—and I do not receive a farthing of support from him. . . .

But let the recollection of what I write, remain with . . . the one woman in England who *cannot* suffer wrong; . . . [where] with a Queen on the throne, all other married women are legally NON–EXISTENT. I remain, With the sincerest loyalty and respect, Your Majesty's humble and devoted Subject and Servant,

CAROLINE ELIZABETH SARAH NORTON.

Notes

[11] *death* Norton's mother was Caroline Henrietta Sheridan (née Callander) (1779–1851), who had married Thomas Sheridan, a colonial treasurer in the Cape of Good Hope. After his death she received a small pension and, by courtesy of the Prince Regent, rooms in Hampton Court Palace. She published three novels.

[12] *him* Norton married the Hon. George Chapple Norton (1800–75), brother of Lord Grantley, on 30 June 1827. He was educated as a barrister but did not practice. Thanks to the intervention of his wife on his behalf with the Whig prime minister, Lord Melbourne (1779–1848), he was awarded a stipendiary police magistracy for Lambeth at £1,000 p.a. In the case of *Norton v. Melbourne* (1836), Norton, a Tory, hoped to make £10,000 in damages by accusing Melbourne of "criminal conversation" (sexual intimacy) with his wife, the first step in moving towards divorce. The case was thrown out because of lack of evidence, when George Norton's witnesses were discredited as having been hired. However, the case damaged his wife's reputation, and, because of Melbourne's involvement, almost caused the government to fall. Although Norton had contracted to give his wife an allowance of £500 a year, he did not pay, and so she tried to charge her expenses to his accounts. In August 1853 Caroline Norton followed legal advice and allowed her creditors to sue her husband. From 20 August on, *The Times* reported on the case of her coachbuilders, in *Thrupp v. Norton*, focusing on the details of her and her publishers' being subpoenaed, and the details of their financial dealings, her loss to him of her legacy from her father and mother as well as that from Lord Melbourne, her earnings through writing (she was a respected poet and novelist, and contributed many articles to Victorian periodicals), and his failure to follow the terms of a contract he had signed. George Norton also had brought up in court the old Melbourne slander that he had provoked in June 1835; however, doing so damaged him more than his wife. Nevertheless, the husband still retained the rights of all property and income of his wife. George Meredith modelled some aspects of his heroine in *Diana of the Crossways* on Norton.

Harriet Martineau (1802–76), Florence Nightingale (1820–1910), Josephine Butler (1828–1906), and others: "Manifesto" of "The Ladies' National Association for the Repeal of the Contagious Diseases Acts" in *Daily News* (31 Dec. 1869)[13]

There are two Acts of Parliament—one passed in 1866, the other in 1869—called the Contagious Diseases Acts.[14] These Acts are in force in some of our garrison towns, and in large districts around them. Unlike all other laws for the repression of contagious diseases, to which both men and women are liable, these two apply to women only, men being wholly exempt from their penalties.[15] The law is ostensibly framed for a certain class of women, but in order to reach these, all the women residing within the districts where it is in force are brought under the provisions of the Acts. Any woman can be dragged into court, and required to prove that she is not a common prostitute. The magistrate can condemn her, if a policeman swears only that he "has good cause to believe" her to be one. The accused has to rebut, not positive evidence, but the state of mind of her accuser.[16] When condemned, the sentence is as follows:—To have her person outraged by the periodical inspection of a surgeon, through a period of twelve months; or, resisting that, to be imprisoned, with or without hard labour—first for a month, next for three months—such imprisonment to be continuously renewed through her whole life unless she submit periodically to the brutal requirements of this law. Women arrested under false accusations have been so terrified at the idea of encountering the public trial

Notes

[13] *title* this letter to the press was in fact an appeal to others to join what Josephine Butler later called "The Great Crusade." It caused a sensation; it was the first time British women took an active role in political debate apart from men. The *Saturday Review* dismissed the women as "the shrieking sisterhood" (19 Mar. 1870; see this section, WOMAN QUESTION, n. 22); the rest of the press joined what Butler called a "conspiracy of silence," led by *The Times* (staunchly pro-Acts)—until 1874. Accordingly, the Ladies' National Association (LNA) established its own journal, the *Shield*. The members of the LNA began a vigorous publication program of their own, including circulars, leaflets, and pamphlets, while Josephine Butler became president of the LNA, speaking throughout England to huge gatherings of working men. Branches were founded in every major city.

[14] *Acts* a Royal Commission on the Health of the Army (1857), in the aftermath of the Crimean War, reported huge numbers of hospitalizations for venereal disease and recommended a special police force in garrison towns with powers to arrest, examine, and hospitalize women suspected of being common prostitutes. The government prepared a bill in secrecy in 1864; it was introduced in the Commons late on July 20, passed on July 21, took a week in the Lords and became law on July 29 without a word of debate in either house (*27-28 Vict., c. 85*). In 1866 a second Act was passed, removing the temporary status from the previous bill, making the procedures permanent, and adding Chatham and Windsor to the eleven previous towns. The third Act of 1869 extended coverage to eighteen towns, based largely on a report of a Select Committee of the House of Commons that refused to hear evidence in opposition to the Acts. The Acts allowed special morals police to obtain warrants from a justice of the peace to apprehend any woman suspected of being a "common prostitute" for an internal physical examination with instruments (if pregnant up to the seventh month). If infected, she was sent to a lock hospital for nine months, and if free of disease, she was issued a certificate, but had to be re-examined every two weeks. Supported by the *British Medical Journal* and *The Lancet*, there was talk of extending the legislation to the whole country.

[15] *penalties* the Acts enforced a double standard, while turning a blind eye to the men infected and their culpability in transmitting disease to women.

[16] *accuser* governesses, seamstresses, and other working women could fall under the law, as in this evidence to the 1868 Parliamentary Committee: "Mr. E. K. Parsons, visiting surgeon of the Portsmouth Lock Hospital, was examined by the Committee, and asked whether, if the police by error bring up a really modest woman to the surgeon, mistaking her for a harlot, the woman signs a voluntary paper before the surgeon examines her. He replies: 'Yes, they all sign a voluntary submission, unless sent by order of a magistrate.' The questioner continues, 'But a modest woman would decline to sign that paper, would she not?' Reply: 'No; for this reason. The police, believing in the correctness of their own impression say, very well, if you do not sign then you go to the bench. And then the woman says in order to avoid that—Well, I do not mind going into a private room and speaking to Mr. Parsons. And she will sign the voluntary submission.' Question—'Therefore they (really honest women) sign a voluntary submission, under the fear of being taken before the magistrate!' Reply—'Unquestionably.' Mr. Parsons also says that the police are very apt to jump to the conclusion that a woman is a prostitute if they see her out at night." See Plate 7.

necessary to prove their innocence, that they have, under the intimidation of the police, signed away their good name and their liberty by making what is called a "voluntary submission" to appear periodically for twelve months for surgical examination. . . .

We, the undersigned, enter our solemn protest against these Acts—

1.   Because, involving as they do, such a momentous change in the legal safeguards hitherto enjoyed by women in common with men, they have been passed, not only without the knowledge of the country, but unknown to Parliament itself; and we hold that neither the representatives of the people nor the press fulfil the duties which are expected of them, when they allow such legislation to take place without the fullest discussion.[17]

2.   Because, so far as women are concerned, they remove every guarantee of personal security which the law has established and held sacred, and put their reputation, their freedom, and their persons absolutely in the power of the police.

3.   Because the law is bound, in any country professing to give civil liberty to its subjects, to define clearly an offence which it punishes.[18]

4.   Because it is unjust to punish the sex who are the victims of a vice, and leave unpunished the sex who are the main cause, both of the vice and its dreaded consequence; and we consider that liability to arrest, forced surgical examination, and where this is resisted, imprisonment with hard labour, to which these Acts subject women, are punishments of the most degrading kind. . . .

6.   Because these measures are cruel to the women who come under their action— violating the feelings of those whose sense of shame is not wholly lost, and further brutalizing even the most abandoned.

7.   Because the disease which these Acts seek to remove has never been removed by any such legislation. The advocates of the system have utterly failed to show, by statistics or otherwise, that these regulations have in any case, after several years' trial, and when applied to one sex only, diminished disease, reclaimed the fallen, or improved the general morality of the country. We have, on the contrary, the strongest evidence to show that in Paris and other continental cities, where women have long been outraged by this forced inspection, the public health and morals are worse than at home.[19]

8.   Because the conditions of this disease, in the first instance, are moral not physical. The moral evil through which the disease makes its way separates the case entirely from that of the plague or other scourges, which have been placed under police control or sanitary care. We hold that we are bound, before rushing into the experiment of legalising a revolting vice, to try to deal with the causes of the evil, and we dare to believe that with wiser teaching and more capable legislation those causes would not be beyond control.

Notes

[17] *discussion* a reference to the lack of parliamentary debate and the exclusion of hostile witnesses from parliamentary committees. However, at the Social Science Congress meeting in Bristol in October 1869, Dr Charles Bell Taylor (1829–1909) brought forward hard evidence against the success of the Acts and Francis Newman (1805–97) eventually managed to have the Acts discussed, though only men were allowed into the meeting. Soon after the National Association for Repeal was formed with Newman, John Stuart Mill, and F. D. Maurice on the general committee, but by December the LNA took over the campaign, publishing evidence from the Rescue Societies, hospitals, doctors, and prostitutes, contesting elections, provoking a Royal Commission in 1870 that responded: "There is no comparison to be made between prostitutes and the men who consort with them. With the one sex the offence is committed as a matter of gain, with the other it is an irregular indulgence of a *natural* impulse."

[18] *punishes* being a "common prostitute" was defined in law as an offence.

[19] *home* the LNA eventually managed to present evidence to parliament, and made the public aware of the failure of the Acts in a campaign of education and agitation. Dr Garth Wilkinson (1812–99) recounted direct evidence in *The Forcible Introspection of Women* (1870), as did William Logan (1813–79) in his guide to the literature on prostitution, *The Great Social Evil* (1871); Josephine Butler published ten works between 1870 and 1872. After a crisis in Gladstone's cabinet in 1874, James Stansfield (1820–98) resigned as president of the Local Government Board to become vice-president of the National Association, and it was he who introduced a bill stopping compulsory examination of women in 1883; final repeal came in 1886, though the Acts continued in the British colonies until 1895.

[signed] Harriet Martineau, Florence Nightingale, Josephine E. Butler, Elizabeth Garrett, Lydia Becker, Elizabeth C. Wolstenholme [and 122 more names]

WEB p. 79

Margaret Oliphant (1828–97): From "[Review of] Mill's *Subjection of Women*" (1869) [Anon.] "The Woman of the Future: *A Lay of the Oxford Victory*" (1884)

Sarah Grand (1854–1943): From "The New Aspect of the Woman Question" in *North American Review* (Mar. 1894)[20]

It is amusing as well as interesting to note the pause which the new aspect of the woman question has given to the Bawling Brothers[21] who have hitherto tried to howl down every attempt on the part of our sex to make the world a pleasanter place to live in. That woman should ape man and desire to change places with him was conceivable to him as he stood on the hearth-rug in his lord-and-master-monarch-of-all-I-survey attitude, well inflated with his own conceit; but that she should be content to develop the good material which she finds in herself and be only dissatisfied with the poor quality of that which is being offered to her in man, her mate, must appear to him to be a thing as monstrous as it is unaccountable. . . .

It would be as rational for us now to declare that men generally are Bawling Brothers or to adopt the hasty conclusion which makes all men out to be fiends on the one hand and all women fools on the other. We have our Shrieking Sisterhood,[22] as the counterpart of the Bawling Brotherhood. . . . Both the cow-woman and the scum-woman,[23] are well within range of the comprehension of the Bawling Brotherhood, but the new woman[24] is a little above him, and he never even thought of looking up to where she has been sitting apart in silent contemplation all these years, thinking and thinking, until at last she

Notes

[20] *title* the *North American Review* was the first American mass-circulation literary magazine. The by-line identifying the author referred to her as "Sarah Grand, author of *The Heavenly Twins*," her novel published in 1893. Frances Bellenden McFall (née Clarke) took the name "Madam Sarah Grand" in 1890 when she left her doctor husband to pursue her writing career, in which she was a prominent advocate of the "New Woman" social and political movement. The term "New Woman" was applied to women of the 1890s through to World War One who advocated female independence as a lifestyle rather than the campaign for the vote; it was marked by dress reform (for work and leisure, such as bicycling and sports), sexual freedom (downplaying marriage), and disregard for social conventions. The new woman was often mocked and attacked by anti-feminists in cartoons, novels, and the popular press.

[21] *Brothers* Grand coined the phrase "Bawling Brotherhood" to counter Linton's mocking characterization of feminists (see n. 22).

[22] *Sisterhood* see Eliza Lynn Linton, "The Shrieking Sisterhood," *Saturday Review* (12 Mar. 1870): "The silent woman who quietly calculated her chances and measures her powers with her difficulties so as to avoid the possibility of a fiasco, and therefore achieves a success according to her endeavour, does more for the real emancipation of her sex than any amount of pamphleteering, lecturing, or petitioning by the shrieking sisterhood can do." See also this section, CONSTRUCTING, n. 24.

[23] *cow . . . woman* that is, they are treated either as breeding cattle or as prostitutes.

[24] *woman* although Grand is often credited with coining the term in this essay, she first used it earlier (see n. 20). It then appeared on 17 August 1893 in the *Women's Herald* in an article, "The Social Standing of the New Woman," and was repeated in the following March in this article.

solved the problem and proclaimed for herself what was wrong with Home-is-the-Woman's-Sphere, and prescribed the remedy.

What she perceived at the outset was the sudden and violent upheaval of the suffering sex in all parts of the world. Women were awaking from their long apathy, and, as they awoke, like healthy hungry children unable to articulate, they began to whimper for they knew not what. They might have been easily satisfied at that time had not society, like an ill-conditioned and ignorant nurse, instead of finding out what they lacked, shaken them and beaten them and stormed at them until what was once a little wail became convulsive shrieks and roused up the whole human household. Then man, disturbed by the uproar, came upstairs all anger and irritation, and, without waiting to learn what was the matter, added his own old theories to the din, but, finding they did not act rapidly, formed new ones, and made an intolerable nuisance of himself with his opinions and advice. . . .

The man of the future will be better, while the woman will be stronger and wiser. To bring this about is the whole aim and object of the present struggle, and with the discovery of the means lies the solution of the Woman Question. Man, having no conception of himself as imperfect from the woman's point of view, will find this difficult to understand, but we know his weakness, and will be patient with him, and help him with his lesson. It is the woman's place and pride and pleasure to teach the child, and man morally is in his infancy. There have been times when there was a doubt as to whether he was to be raised or woman was to be lowered, but we have turned that corner at last; and now woman holds out a strong hand to the child-man, and insists, but with infinite tenderness and pity, upon helping him up. . . .

We have been reproached by Ruskin[25] for shutting ourselves up behind park palings and garden walls, regardless of the waste world that moans in misery without, and that has been too much our attitude; but the day of our acquiescence is over. There is that in ourselves which forces us out of our apathy; we have no choice in the matter. When we hear the "Help! help! help!" of the desolate and the oppressed, and still more when we see the awful dumb despair of those who have lost even the hope of help, we must respond. This is often inconvenient to man, especially when he has seized upon a defenceless victim whom he would have destroyed had we not come to the rescue; and so, because it is inconvenient to be exposed and thwarted, he snarls about the end of all true womanliness, cants on the subject of the Sphere, and threatens that if we do not sit still at home with cotton-wool in our ears so that we cannot be stirred into having our sympathies aroused by his victims when they shriek, and with shades over our eyes that we may not see him in his degradation, we shall be afflicted with short hair, coarse skins, unsymmetrical figures, loud voices, tastelessness in dress, and an unattractive appearance and character generally, and then he will not love us any more or marry us. And this is one of the most amusing of his threats, because he has said and proved on so many occasions that he cannot live without us whatever we are. O man! man! you are a very funny fellow now we know you! But take care. The standard of your pleasure and convenience has already ceased to be our conscience. On one point, however, you may reassure yourself. True womanliness is not in danger, and the sacred duties of wife and mother will be all the more honorably performed when women have a reasonable hope of becoming wives and mothers of *men*. But there is the difficulty. The trouble is not because women are mannish, but because men grow ever more effeminate. Manliness is at a premium now because there is so little of it, and we are accused of aping men in order to conceal the side from which the contrast should evidently be drawn.

Notes

[25] *Ruskin* see GENDER: CONSTRUCTING; RUSKIN (WEB p. 77).

Sydney Grundy (1848–1914): *The New Woman* (1894)

From Act 1[26]

SYLVESTER: Yes, I am Mrs. Sylvester's husband. I belong to my wife, but my wife doesn't belong to me. She is the property of the public. Directly I saw her photograph in a shop-window I realized the situation. People tell me I've a wife to be proud of; but they're wrong. Mrs. Sylvester is not my wife; I am her husband.

COLONEL: [*taking up a book*] This is what comes of educating women. We have created a Frankenstein. "*Man, the Betrayer*[27]—*A Study of the Sexes*—by Enid Bethune."

SYLVESTER: Oh, I know her. She comes to our house.

COLONEL: And has a man betrayed her?

SYLVESTER: Never. Not likely to.

COLONEL: That's what's the matter, perhaps?

SYLVESTER: Her theory is, that boys ought to be girls, and young men should be maids. [Colonel *throws down the book*.] That's how she'd equalize the sexes.

COLONEL: Pshaw! [*Takes up another book*.] "*Ye Foolish Virgins!—A Remonstrance*—by Victoria Vivash."[28]

SYLVESTER: Another soul! She's also for equality. Her theory is, that girls should be boys, and maids should be young men. Goes in for latchkeys and that sort of thing.

COLONEL: [*throws down the book*] Bah! [*Takes up a third*.] "*Naked and Unashamed*[29]—*A Few Plain Facts and Figures*—by Mary Bevan, M.D.*" Who on earth's she?

SYLVESTER: One of the plain figures. *She* comes to our house, too.

COLONEL: [*reads*] "*The Physiology of the Sexes*"! Oh, this eternal babble of the sexes! [*Throws book down*.] Why can't a woman be content to be a woman? What does she want to make a beastly man of herself for?

SYLVESTER: But my wife isn't a woman.

COLONEL: None of them are, my boy. A woman, who *is* a woman, doesn't want to be anything else. These people are a sex of their own, Sylvester. They have invented a new gender....

[*Enter Enid and Victoria, in hot argument....*]

ENID: I can't agree with you! Say what you will, I can't agree with you!

VICTORIA: That doesn't alter the fact. A woman has just as much right to a latchkey[30] as a man.

Notes

[26] *title* produced at the Comedy Theatre in London, 1 September 1894, this drawing room drama, a four-act comedy with no scene divisions, centres on four progressive women who challenge conventional sexual roles, and who are ridiculed by Grundy as only needing a man to bring them into social conformity. In Alfred Morrow's poster for the play, the "New Woman" of the title sits smoking a cigarette with a number of books scattered at her feet, among which is one with the title *The New Woman* (see Plate 6). This play can be compared to Oscar Wilde's *Lady Windermere's Fan* (1892), and Arthur Wing Pinero's *The Second Mrs. Tanqueray* (1893) and *The Notorious Mrs. Ebbsmith* (1895) for contemporary representations of the New Woman.

[27] *Man the Betrayer* the phrase is used by Jeanette Leonard Bilder in *The Critic* (vol. 42 1894).

[28] *Vivash* the character is modelled on a popular author of New Woman stories, George Egerton (Mary Chaelita Dunne Bright, 1859-1945), who in *Keynotes* (1893) and

Discords (1894) caused a scandal by representing liberated woman as demanding sexual parity with men. The title of her book echoes Matthew 25: 1–13.

[29] *Unashamed* the phrase "naked and unashamed" (see Genesis 2: 25) occurred in an essay on "Reticence in Literature" by Arthur Waugh (1866–1943) in the first number of *The Yellow Book* (Apr. 1894), a publication in which George Egerton (see n. 28) wrote and for which Aubrey Beardsley (1872–98) was the first art editor. There were about 100 female doctors in London during the period.

[30] *latchkey* house key, a symbol of a woman's freedom to come and go at will. Perhaps there is also a reference to publisher John Lane's series of "Keynotes," and especially to the short stories by George Egerton (see n. 28) who published *Keynotes* (1893) in the series that artist Aubrey Beardsley illustrated with initial keys in black and white.

ENID: But a man has no right to a latchkey.

VICTORIA: That's ridiculous!

ENID: Rudeness is not argument!

VICTORIA: Why make distinctions?

ENID: I make no distinctions. I admit that a woman has just as much right to come home with the milk[31] as a man but I say, a man has no right to come home with the milk; and I say more—no woman who respects herself has any *desire* to come home with the milk!

VICTORIA: Bother the milk! It isn't a question of milk. It's a question of making artificial distinctions between the sexes.

ENID: I say that there ought to be *no* distinction! Why should a man be allowed to commit sins—

VICTORIA: And woman not be given an opportunity?

ENID: Then do you *want* to commit sins?

VICTORIA: I want to be allowed to do as *men* do.

ENID: Then you ought to be ashamed of yourself; there!

VICTORIA: I only say, I ought to be allowed.

ENID: And *I* say that a man, reeking with infamy, ought not to he allowed to marry a pure girl—

VICTORIA: Certainly not! *She* ought to reek with infamy as well.

ENID: Victoria! [*Knock without.*]

VICTORIA: What is the difference between man and woman?

ENID: There is *no* difference! . . .

LADY WARGRAVE: Excuse my ignorance, but I have been away from England for so many years. Can this be the New Woman I have read about?

COLONEL: Everything's New nowadays! We have a New Art[32]—

ENID: A New Journalism[33]—

VICTORIA: A New Political Economy—

DOCTOR: A New Morality—

COLONEL: A New Sex!

LADY WARGRAVE: [*smiling*] Ah!

DOCTOR: Do you object to modernity?

LADY WARGRAVE: I've only one objection to new things; they are so old.

VICTORIA: Not the New Woman!

LADY WARGRAVE: No; *she* is generally middle-aged. . . .

 WEB p. 82

Ouida [Marie Louise de la Ramée] (1839–1908): From "The New Woman" (1894)

Notes

31 *milk* stay out very late; milk was delivered in London very early in the morning to be in time to be prepared by the servants for breakfast. Enid's character is based on the New Woman novelist and essayist Sarah Grand (Frances Elizabeth McFall, 1854–1943), who advocated social purity and sexual chastity (see this section, WOMAN QUESTION, n. 20).

32 *new art* an article in the *Quarterly Review* (Oct. 1895) on the plays of Arthur Wing Pinero and others begins, "Novelty is the keynote of the dying century. With the 'New Woman' and the 'New Humour' we have also the 'New Drama.' It is the way of expiring centuries, when phase is arbitrarily mistaken for finality, and growth readily regarded as departure." "New Art" is a translation of the French phrase for the art of the 1890s, *art nouveau*, an international aesthetic movement in design involving architecture, furniture, graphic arts, book design, and clothes, made fashionable in interior design in London by the firm of Liberty. It developed out of the Arts and Crafts movement of the 1880s; also known as *Jugendstil* (Ger. young style) in Germany.

33 *new journalism* a term used by Matthew Arnold in "Up to Easter" (1887), an attack on W. T. Stead's *Pall Mall Gazette*.

Literature and the Arts

Introduction

When Robert Braithwaite Martineau (1826–69) exhibited his painting *Kit's Writing Lesson* at the RA in 1852 (see Plate 8), he doubtless assumed the public could identify its allusion to one of the most popular books of the day, Dickens's *The Old Curiosity Shop*, which had come out more than ten years earlier (1840–41). But rather than painting the famous scene that had aroused most public sympathy – the death of Little Nell – Martineau paints the scene when Nell Trent teaches writing to young Kit Nubbles, a poor workshop boy.

Dickens describes the scene:

> The child … soon occupied herself in preparations for giving Kit a writing lesson…. When he did sit down he tucked up his sleeves and squared his elbows and put his face close to the copy-book and squinted horribly at the lines—how from the very first moment of having the pen in his hand, he began to wallow in blots, and to daub himself with ink up to the very roots of his hair—how if he did by accident form a letter properly, he immediately smeared it out again with his arm in his preparations to make another… and how there was all the way through, notwithstanding, a gentle wish on her part to teach, and an anxious desire on his to learn (ch. 3).

The interior of the Old Curiosity Shop itself had already been drawn twice: the first time, in the frontispiece to the first edition (1841) by George Cattermole (1800–68), and again in the extra-illustrated edition of 1841 by Thomas Sibson (1817–44), who also chose the scene when Nell teaches Kit to write, though with few extra details.

Martineau retains the setting inside the shop with its curios: in the background are two suits of armour, one against the wall behind Kit and the second through the door in the adjoining room. Behind the armour are shelves crammed with objects: a large copper pot, vases, candlesticks, a carved wooden reading stand, a chess board with ivory pieces on a cabinet, and a framed picture. Suspended from the ceiling are swords and a battle-axe. In the window are quatrefoils of stained glass showing the symbols of the Evangelists, small stained glass roundels, various pots, candlesticks, vases, dishes, stuffed birds, and an angel figure under glass. Dickens's description of the Old Curiosity Shop picks out the details, stressing their Gothic antiquity and strangeness, and their anthropomorphizing efforts to hide themselves from sight:

> The place through which he made his way at leisure was one of those receptacles for old and curious things which seem to crouch in odd corners of this town and to hide their musty treasures from the public eye in jealousy and distrust. There were suits of mail standing like ghosts in armour here and there, fantastic carvings brought from monkish cloisters, rusty weapons of various kinds, distorted figures in china and wood and iron and ivory; tapestry and strange furniture that might have been designed in dreams. The haggard aspect of the little old man was wonderfully suited to the place; he might have groped among old churches and tombs and deserted houses and gathered all the

Victorian Literature: An Anthology, First Edition. Edited by Victor Shea and William Whitla.
© 2015 John Wiley & Sons, Ltd. Published 2015 by John Wiley & Sons, Ltd.

spoils with his own hands. There was nothing in the whole collection but was in
keeping with himself; nothing that looked
older or more worn than he (ch. 1).

On the surface, the painting seems to catch a
living moment from these decaying surroundings, to capture a domestic childhood pleasure –
often depicted in genre paintings when the
dutiful mother teaches her small children to
read and write or the governess carries out her
assigned duties (see Plate 7).

Kit's Writing Lesson, then, translates
Dickens's realistic prose onto the canvas; but is
the painting realistic? When he was painting it,
Martineau was studying with the Pre-Raphaelite
artist William Holman Hunt. Hunt himself was
painting two highly symbolic paintings, *The
Light of the World* (1851–53; see Plate 11) and
The Hireling Shepherd (1852) while he "encouraged" Martineau, as he records in his autobiography. It seems impossible that Martineau's
work would not absorb some of the moral fervour and symbolic meaning of Hunt. Indeed, his
is almost the reverse of the meaning of *The
Hireling Shepherd:* a scene of moral neglect and
the seduction of a girl becomes a scene of moral
instruction carried out by the girl to liberate the
young boy.

Read symbolically, Martineau's painting
calls attention to a number of factors in the
relations between Victorian literature and other
nineteenth-century art forms. The Gothic objects
of the Middle Ages contrast with the modern
action in the room, the movement into literacy
by a working-class boy. The Gothic past has
here been relegated to the background as the
"ghosts" of a faded and disappearing "dream,"
the world identified by Dickens with Nell's gambling grandfather. Literary realism, the mode of
Dickens and most other Victorian novelists writing of their contemporary world, largely depends
upon the tropes of metonymy and synecdoche, a
substitution of one word for another associated
with it (the pen for literary culture), or the details
or parts for a whole, the objects for the man,
as Dickens says. But in the painting the Gothic

objects are relics, fragmented curiosities of a
symbolic past, here without a direct association
with the grandfather. Kit, in this modest debate
of styles, represents the modern, the acquisition
by the working class of the new property of the
mind and hand, though surrounded by the relics
of the useless Gothic past. His learning to write
and read will make him into one of those working-class readers for whom the steam presses
would run. But just as Kit had difficulty in writing his letters to gain meaning, so too Victorian
viewers had difficulty in reading meaning in
Pre-Raphaelite paintings. They lacked the reading skills (visual literacy) to interpret symbolic
meaning in paintings just as Kit lacks the writing skills (verbal literacy) to interpret literal
meaning.

Whether read as a Pre-Raphaelite or natural-
istic painting, *Kit's Writing Lesson* for our purposes draws attention to relations between
literature and other arts in at least four important ways. First it represents an ekphrasis or
reverse ekphrasis, the translation of a scene
from one artistic medium to another. Second,
the acquisition of literacy can be read both as
the origin of literary creation and as a self-
reflective commentary on the process. Third, the
buyer of the painting, Charles Edward Mudie
(1818–90), the founder, in 1842, of Mudie's
Lending Library, calls attention to the literary
and artistic marketplace, which underwent a
shift from aristocratic patronage and an elite
audience to a mass market with a mass audience
under tight moral controls until the advent of
free libraries. Fourth, in the battle of styles current in architecture and the other arts, the
painting clearly identifies with the literary, symbolic, and pictorial ideals of the embattled Pre-
Raphaelites, not only in choosing literary subject
matter that crosses over between literature and
painting but also in making Kit into a Pre-
Raphaelite himself, copying from life.

The Pre-Raphaelites rejected the teachings of
Sir Joshua Reynolds (1723–92), first president
of the Royal Academy, mocking him as "Sir
Sloshua" for his shadowy effects and blurred
outlines. Reynolds had praised the superiority of

painting to poetry because its apprehension by a viewer was immediate: "A painter ... has but one sentence to utter, but one moment to exhibit. He cannot, like the poet or historian, expatiate" (*Discourse 4*, 1771); "What is done by painting, must be done at one blow" (*Discourse 8*, 1778). To Reynolds high art is a rhapsodic moment into which a viewer is absorbed. Literature, however, is limited by its linearity, to being slowly comprehended over time. As Ruskin pointed out, the typology and symbolism of the Pre-Raphaelite painters demanded that they be read like a written text, slowly, to unfold their meaning – an exercise strongly resisted by the critics still under the influence of Reynolds. Victorian novels, typically running over 500 pages, perhaps more than any other literary form present the antithesis to Reynolds's "one sentence." For instance, Dickens's novels were published serially, sometimes over an entire year, thereby necessitating slow reading over interrupted time, allowing for modifications of plot and character according to readers' responses, a much more complex production process and audience exchange than Reynolds's "one blow."

Martineau's painting, referring directly to literature, reverses the conventional trope of ekphrasis, wherein the writer pauses a narrative trajectory to linger over the description of a work of art. The most famous instances are Homer's description of Achilles' shield (*Iliad* 18: 398 ff.) and Virgil's description of the carvings of the Trojan war on the bronze doors to the temple in Dido's Carthage (*Aeneid* 1:450 ff.). In the nineteenth century major examples are Keats's "Ode on a Grecian Urn" (1820), Ruskin's description of Turner's *Slavers* (see RUSKIN *STONES* and RUSKIN: MODERN PAINTERS, "OF WATER"; and Plate 19), and Wilde's *Picture of Dorian Gray* (1890; for the preface see WILDE). Pater's description of the *Mona Lisa* is the pre-eminent example in the nineteenth century, famously turned into verse by W. B. Yeats. Martineau's painting is a kind of reverse ekphrasis because the rhetorical figure is not representing art in a literary form, but the reverse, translating literature into painting. As Wilde

writes in the preface to *Dorian Gray*: "The critic is he who can translate into another manner or a new material his impression of beautiful things." In the nineteenth century, many representations of classical stories from Greek and Roman history were painted by Frederick Leighton (1830–96) or Lawrence Alma-Tadema (1836–1912) or the versions of Malory or Chaucer painted by Edward Burne-Jones (1833–98).

Victorian writers used ekphrasis for different purposes: for instance, Browning uses it in writing on Italian Old Master painters to comment on the present, Tennyson writes "The Palace of Art," Eliot writes on seventeenth-century Dutch realist painters, Michael Field on European painting and sculpture, Ruskin on Gothic architecture, the Pre-Raphaelites on their own paintings and poetry, Pater on Renaissance painting and sculpture, and Wilde and Symons on the French impressionists – all interrelations among the arts signalling Victorian explorations of Pater's adage in "The School of Giorgione": "Poetry, music, and painting are but translations into different languages of but one and the same fixed quality of imaginative thought, supplemented by certain technical qualities of colour in painting, of sound in music, and rhythmical words in poetry."

Martineau's painting has two further significances regarding the acquisition of writing and literacy. First, while it depicts Kit's act of writing as a moment of literacy, it also captures his first moment of literary creation, copying a letter as a first step in literary imitation or mimesis. In the painting, the letter and the line are the primary components of literature. From early in the century, Victorian women writers had looked back to the point of origin for poetry, to the paradoxical Sappho, linking her pen and her broken and fragmented tongue (her work is fragmentary) to the fading letters of her poems and the occasion of her suicide, hurling herself and her harp into the sea, while her writing remains imperishable. Such writers as Hemans, Landon, Norton, and Barrett Browning claimed Sappho as muse, adopting the origin of poetry, the inscribing of the letter as their own initiation into writing. Little Nell appears in a famous unfinished painting depicting the scene of writing, *Dickens's Dream*, by Robert William Buss (1804–75). Nell is at the right shoulder of the sleeping author, his desk and writing materials prominently placed in front of him. The pen is the tool of the writer, whether in the hand of Sappho or of Kit or of Dickens himself, who was so often portrayed as holding one (as by Daniel Maclise, 1837 or by William Powell Frith, 1859). It is the new tool of Kit's step from ignorance into enlightenment, from innocence to experience, shown also in his half-eaten apple. He is falling into art.

Second, the task conventionally accorded to Nell is her sewing – the humble sewing on of a button to her grandfather's shirt. Instead, her act of creativity is the liberating of Kit by teaching him his letters, freeing him into language over which, as Dickens says, he stumbles. He is being liberated from the imprisonment of his illiteracy that confines him as surely as the symbolic cage above his head confines the songbird, also a conventional metaphor for the poet. Martineau possibly refers to another convention, the moral education of the child Jesus by his mother, or to her teaching him reading (as in Botticelli's *Madonna of the Magnificat*, 1481), or to the scene in Millais's *Christ in the House of his Parents* (Plate 12) two years earlier where Christ learns carpentry but suffers an injury that is a typological anticipation of the crucifixion – a painting, as we shall see, that had elicited Dickens's contemptuous indignation.

The advent of mass literacy, coinciding with the advent of steam power, meant that Dickens, in *The Old Curiosity Shop*, could capitalize on the cheap press that increased readership and profits, a vast market, soon to include children and their reading. This scene of writing demonstrates the acquisition of literacy, the great task of universal education in the nineteenth century, whose effects can only be glimpsed in the proliferation of print: newspapers and novels, poetry and pamphlets, advertising and handbills – print was everywhere. Writing appears frequently in

the paintings of the period – from the elaborate posters and billboards to the smaller signs of literacy in such paintings as *Work* by Ford Madox Brown (see Plate 5), and Fildes's *Applicants for Admission to a Casual Ward* (Plate 3). In Holman Hunt's *The Awakening Conscience* (Plate 10) the printed sheets of music have fallen to the floor, parallel to the fallen, but now awakening, woman. In Concanen's *Modern Advertising* (see Plate 9) the massive lettering looms over the people and trains and threatens to overwhelm the station itself in its consuming alphabet.

The purchaser of Martineau's *Kit's Writing Lesson*, the English publisher Charles Edward Mudie, was the arbiter of censorship masquerading as good taste. Mudie pioneered in lending to members (at a guinea a year) three-decker novels a volume at a time, in any order. By insisting on three-decker publication, Mudie profoundly influenced novel writing, its structure and plot, the development of character, and the style. For many years the price of novels was kept artificially high by him. His subscribers were so numerous, with library branches in York, Manchester, and Birmingham, that he could dictate terms and prices to publishers and authors, refusing immoral books, and promoting middle-class literature that, as Mr Podsnap in Dickens's *Our Mutual Friend* (1864) says, "would not bring a blush to the cheek of a young person." Mudie's "Catalogue of New and Standard Works" and his "Select Library" promoted specific titles and so tight a moral code that it led to a feud with George Moore over *A Modern Lover* (1883; see LITERATURE: DEBATES; MOORE (WEB p. 123)). Such manipulation of the literary marketplace sometimes took a sensational turn, as in Robert Buchanan's attack on Dante Rossetti and other Pre-Raphaelite poets and painters, associates of Martineau. Such controversies, like the other debates about literature, came out of the rivalry of different generic forms and disputes about accepted or controversial subject matter. It seems probable that the "Fleshly School" controversy (see LITERATURE: PRE-RAPHAELITISM (WEB p. 128)) did more to help sell more books than to warn off nervous readers. Dickens's issuing of the Cheap Edition, in an effort to make his novels available at cheap prices for a wide readership, can be seen as an effort to circumvent the subscription libraries like Mudies. Dickens's *The Old Curiosity Shop*, serialized in a form that pre-dates Mudie by only one year, sold 60,000 copies in the first edition.

The Old Curiosity Shop – with its chamber of curios extended to the death of Little Nell, her burial in the mouldering Gothic church, and her grandfather's half-mad vigil at her tomb – exemplifies one aspect of the Gothic tradition, part of the battle of the styles in architecture that was re-enacted in its sister arts, painting and literature. Pervasive in our selections in this section run the implicit concessions to and the fading continuations of the attenuated generic hierarchies that the Romantic movement had inherited from the classical eighteenth century. Hence, our first selections in the debates about literature are concerned with how those hierarchies of genres and styles are re-articulated for the nineteenth century in terminology such as romance and realism, gothic and classical, medieval and modern, or melodrama and sensationalism. While these debates about the place of poetry were in progress, prose fiction was enjoying its emergence and triumph over all other genres, eventually also a victory for both women writers and for realism. However, the pull of nostalgia for other periods (especially the Middle Ages and ancient Greece and Rome) continued its appeal. We relate this shift away from poetry to prose by considering the battle of the styles in both kinds. It took place chiefly in architecture between the Gothic revival (represented by Pugin) and neoclassical architecture, as we demonstrate in the introduction to the "Condition of England." Melodrama, here by Braddon and adapted by Hazlewood, uses stock figures and situations from the Gothic to formulate widely popular new forms of literature. An analogue to this contrast between historical periods is the later struggle between realistic fiction, a prose that accurately represents an external world, and the psychological novel of

James, calling for a complex representation of the inner world of thoughts and feelings. At the same time, as Eliot foregrounds, female voices were challenging the conventions by exploiting sentiment, sensation, and melodrama.

Our second section foregrounds another site of contestation. When the Pre-Raphaelites burst upon the London art world and the literary establishment in the 1850s, they were greeted with howls of mockery and attack. They attempted to do what the Romantics had done, to follow nature, and also to imitate the styles and subject matter of the painters before Raphael (1483–1520). They presented contemporary social issues in paintings and verse as Dickens and Carlyle were doing in prose; the Pre-Raphaelites also cultivated an interest in medieval subjects drawn from Dante, Malory, and the ballad tradition. Such a conflation of past and present in both their art and poetry was praised by Ruskin and attacked by Dickens. These attacks came to full flower in Robert Buchanan's attack on the "Fleshly School of Poetry" as he called it, his acrimony spilling over into the 1870s. By that time, Walter Pater was re-labelling "Fleshly" as "Æsthetic" poetry. On the Web we exemplify transitions from the Fleshly controversy through aestheticism to symbolism and the sinuous lines of *art nouveau* in some writers and artists of the 1890s.

It was a century of writing and reading, certainly, but such quantities of print, such an appetite for news and reading material, could not be met without transformations in the power industries (gas and electricity), communications (the penny post and the telegraph, both domestic and international, and late in the century, the telephone), and technology, especially in print and transportation (paper, presses, rail, and steamships). In the third section, we discuss the impact of the new technologies and media on literature, first presenting new methods of making paper, type, and printing presses; all of them meant cheaper books (like Dickens's Cheap Edition), but they also lead to the revival of fine printing with William Morris's Kelmscott Press (see Figure 7), and a telling contrast by John

Figure 7 William Morris (1834–96), *The Works of Geoffrey Chaucer* (Kelmscott Press, 1896), with illustrations by Edward Burne-Jones and borders and type design by William Morris. Letterpress. 42.5 × 29.2 cm per leaf. Source: author's collection. In 1891 Morris set up the Kelmscott Press in Hammersmith to print books on hand-presses using linen handmade paper and type that he had designed himself. Many of his publications were in black and red ink, some also with blue. His books helped revolutionize printing: the Chaucer, his masterpiece, is one of the finest volumes in the history of the book in England, finished in 1896 just four months before Morris died. He designed the typeface, all of the hundreds of capital letters, fourteen borders, and the eighteen frames, and his friend and collaborator over many years did the eighty-seven wood-cut illustrations. The printed book culminated his years of self-taught calligraphy in which he produced unrivalled ornamentation in colours and gold on pages of vellum, like his four hand-illuminated copies of FitzGerald's *Rubáiyát* (1870s). The *Chaucer* brought together Morris's (and the Victorians') love of medieval literature; his fascination with intricate two-dimensional design; and his socialism, in harking back to pre-industrial methods of production before the division of labour destroyed the social function of work as an enhancement of life. See LITERATURE: NEW TECHNOLOGIES (WEB p. 148).

Southward of the printing at the time of Victoria's accession and her diamond jubilee.

The new technologies changed not only what and how the Victorians read but also what they heard and saw, with inventions in aural and visual culture, the phonograph and the camera: we *read* the Victorians, we look at their paintings and architecture, but it is also possible, through their own innovations in technology, to listen to them speak to us, almost as their own contemporaries would have heard them, as the intervening century seems to fall away. We include both weblinks to the voices of eminent Victorians and

also comments on the recording techniques at the end of the era. Finally, there is an exhibition of another new technology in another new art form, photography and writings on it.

Dickens, the master of writing skills and manipulator of literary tropes and symbols to accommodate setting to character, proves woefully inadequate in assessing the symbolism of a famous Pre-Raphaelite painting accomplished two years before Martineau's. In his 1850 review of Millais's *Christ in the House of His Parents*, commonly called, "The Carpenter's Shop," he reads the symbolic and typological realistic detail in terms of strict literal and contemporary realism, like an exaggerated account of the Curiosity Shop. He finds it "mean, odious, repulsive, and revolting." He absolutely refuses to read the painting symbolically; for instance, he interprets the cuts on the young Christ's hands not as anticipation of the stigmata, but a portrayal of an ugly and grubby reality: "You behold … a hideous, wry-necked, blubbering, red-headed boy, in a bed-gown; who appears to have received a poke in the hand, from the stick of another boy with whom he has been playing in an adjacent gutter and … a kneeling woman, so horrible in her ugliness, that … she would stand out from the rest of the company as a Monster, in the vilest cabaret in France, or the lowest ginshop in England" (see Plate 12; see this section, PRE-RAPHAELITISM; DICKENS).

Whether Dickens would have read the "red-haired boy" or Nell's "dislocated throat" in the "foreground" of *Kit's Writing Lesson* in a similar fashion we do not know, but it is useful to juxtapose Dickens's reductionist dismissal of the Pre-Raphaelites with Ruskin on Holman Hunt's *The Awakening Conscience*: "There is not a single object in all that room, common, modern, vulgar (in the vulgar sense, as it may be), but it became tragical, if rightly read" (see this section, PRE-RAPHAELITISM). To read "rightly" according to Ruskin, however, here implies one-to-one identifications or extensions, and, by implication, a single, correct interpretation, a theory of reading that is too one-dimensional for our purposes. Our selections, drawing relations between literature and the other arts, to be read "rightly," suggest multiple interconnections and continuities as well as broken links, layered approaches and diverse viewpoints, within a literary and artistic culture that was undergoing profound transformation.

1. Debates about Literature

Augustus Welby Northmore Pugin (1812–52): *Contrasts; Or, a Parallel between the Noble Edifices of the Fourteenth and Fifteenth Centuries and Similar Buildings of the Present Day, Shewing the Present Decay of Taste: Accompanied by Appropriate Text* (1836)

From Chapter 1: "On the Feelings which Produced the Great Edifices of the Middle Ages"[1]

On comparing the Architectural Works of the present Century with those of the Middle Ages, the wonderful superiority of the latter must strike every attentive observer; and the mind is naturally led to reflect on the causes which have wrought this mighty change, and to endeavour to trace the fall of Architectural taste, from the period of its first decline[2] in this country to the present day; and this will form the subject of the following pages.

Notes

DEBATES ABOUT LITERATURE

[1] *title* the leading Gothic architect in Britain in the nineteenth century, Pugin took as his ideal the Early Middle Pointed style (c.1300), and exemplified it as the most moral and spiritual architecture for Britain, then in a crisis of social inequality and turmoil. *Contrasts* is polemical, demanding the revival of the medieval Gothic style, and also "a return to the faith and the social structures of the Middle Ages." The "contrasts" were chiefly between the Neo-Classical urban style of the nineteenth century and its fourteenth- or fifteenth-century equivalent, part of the battle of the styles. Pugin published an enlarged second edition in 1841, our text. See CONDITION: INTRODUCTION.

[2] *decline* Pugin dates the beginning of the decline with the beginning of the Reformation in England – the calling of the Reformation Parliament in 1529 to deal with the annulment of the marriage of Henry VIII (1491–1547) to Katharine of Aragon (1485–1536), after which, in the Act of Supremacy (1534), the monarch became the supreme head of the country's ecclesiastical ruler. In his analysis of the Gothic style, Ruskin notes a different moment for the decline of architecture – in Venice in 1418 – in *The Stones of Venice*: see RUSKIN; STONES, headnote; see also this section, PRE-RAPHAELITISM, n. 32.

It will be readily admitted that the great test of Architectural beauty is the fitness of the design to the purpose for which it is intended, and that the style of a building should so correspond with its use that the spectator may at once perceive the purpose for which it was erected.

Acting on this principle, different nations have given birth to so many various styles of Architecture, each suited to their climate, customs, and religion; and as it is among edifices of this latter class that we look for the most splendid and lasting monuments, there can be but little doubt that the religious ideas and ceremonies of these different people had by far the greatest influence in the formation of their various styles of Architecture.[3]

The more closely we compare the temples of the Pagan nations with their religious rites and mythologies, the more shall we be satisfied with the truth of this assertion.

But who can regard those stupendous Ecclesiastical Edifices of the Middle Ages (the more special objects of this work), without feeling this observation in its full force? Here every portion of the sacred fabric bespeaks its origin; the very plan of the edifice is the emblem of human redemption[4] —each portion is destined for the performance of some solemn rite of the Christian church. Here is the brazen font where the waters of baptism wash away the stain of original sin; there stands the gigantic pulpit, from which the sacred truths and ordinances are from time to time proclaimed to the congregated people; behold yonder, resplendent with precious gems, is the high altar, the seat of the most holy mysteries, and the tabernacle of the Highest![5] It is, indeed, a sacred place; and well does the fabric bespeak its destined purpose: the eye is carried up and lost in the height of the vaulting and the intricacy of the ailes; the rich and varied hues of the stained windows, the modulated light, the gleam of the tapers,[6] the richness of the altars, the venerable images of the departed just,—all alike conspire to fill the mind with veneration for the place, and to make it feel the sublimity of Christian worship. And when the deep intonations of the bells from the lofty campaniles, which summon the people to the house of prayer, have ceased, and the solemn chant of the choir swells through the vast edifice,—cold, indeed, must he the heart of that man who does not cry out with the Psalmist, 𝕯omine delixi decorem domus tuæ, et locum habitationis gloriæ tuæ.[7]

Such effects as these can only he produced on the mind by buildings, the composition of which has emanated from men who were thoroughly embued with devotion for, and faith in, the religion for whose worship they were erected.

Their whole energies were directed towards attaining excellence; they were actuated by far nobler motives than the hopes of pecuniary reward, or even the applause and admiration of mankind. They felt they were engaged in the most glorious occupation that can fall to the lot of man, that of raising a temple to the worship of the true and living God.

Notes

[3] *Architecture* a reference to the ancient temples of Greece (such as those on the Acropolis in Athens, especially the Parthenon, 447–438 BCE, dedicated to Pallas Athena) and the Forum in Rome at the time of Augustus (63 BCE–14 CE).

[4] *redemption* the cross-shaped or cruciform ground plan of a church, with the vertical composed of the nave and choir, and the crosspiece or transverse being the north and south transepts.

[5] *Highest* a reference to both the tabernacle or sacred tent used by the people of Israel to house the Ark of the Covenant during their wanderings in the wilderness after the flight from Egypt (see Exodus 25–31; and Psalm 46: 4); a tabernacle was also the box in a church to keep the reserved sacrament of the Eucharist for the sick in time of need.

[6] *ailes ... tapers aisles* is an archaic spelling of aisles (see *OED*), the side-passages adjoining the nave of a church; *tapers* candles.

[7] *Domine ... tuæ* (Lat. Lord I have loved the beauty of your house, and the place where your glory dwells), Psalm 26: 8. Pugin printed the quotation in gothic script, like the manuscript and early printed books of devotion of the fourteenth and fifteenth centuries.

It was this feeling that operated alike on the master mind[8] and that planned the edifice, and on the patient sculptor whose chisel wrought each varied and beatified detail. It was this feeling that induced the ancient masons, in spite of labour, danger, and difficulties, to persevere till they had raised their gigantic spires into the very regions of the clouds. It was this feeling that induced the ecclesiastics of old to devote their revenues to this pious purpose, and to labour with their own hands in the accomplishment of the work;[9] and it is a feeling that may be traced throughout the whole of the numerous edifices of the middle ages, and which, amidst the great variety of genius which their varied styles display, still bespeak the unity of purpose which influenced their builders and artists.

They borrowed then ideas from no heathen rites, nor sought for decorations from the idolatrous emblems of a strange people. The foundation and progress of the Christian faith, and the sacraments and ceremonies of the church, formed an ample and noble field for the exercise of their talents: and it is an incontrovertible fact, that every class of artists who flourished during those glorious periods selected their subjects from this inexhaustible source, and devoted their greatest efforts towards the embellishment of ecclesiastical edifices.

Yes, it was, indeed, the faith, the zeal, and, above all, the unity, of our ancestors, that enabled them to conceive and raise those wonderful fabrics that still remain to excite our wonder and admiration.

WEB p. 116

Charles Dickens (1819–1870): *Oliver Twist* (1838)
From Chapter XLV: "Fatal Consequences" [Bill Sikes murders Nancy]

George Eliot (1819–80): From "Silly Novels by Lady Novelists" in *Westminster Review* (Oct. 1856)[10]

Silly novels by Lady Novelists are a genus with many species, determined by the particular quality of silliness that predominates in them—the frothy, the prosy, the pious, or the pedantic. But it is a mixture of all these—a composite order of feminine fatuity, that produces the largest class of such novels, which we shall distinguish as the *mind-and-millinery* species. The heroine is usually an heiress, probably a peeress in her own right, with perhaps a vicious baronet, an amiable duke, and an irresistible younger son of a marquis as lovers in the foreground, a clergyman and a poet sighing for her in the middle distance, and a crowd of undefined adorers dimly indicated beyond. Her eyes and her wit are both dazzling; her nose and her morals are alike free from any tendency to irregularity; she has a superb *contralto*[11] and a superb intellect; she is perfectly well-dressed and perfectly

Notes

[8] *mind* the names of only a few such master masons and sculptors have survived from the Middle Ages; exceptions are Abbot Suger (1081–1151), architect of St Denis, north of Paris; William of Sens (fl. 1170s) at Canterbury for the rebuilding of the choir after the fire of 1174; and Henry Yevele (c.1320–1400), who undertook the naves of Westminster Abbey (1362) and Canterbury Cathedral (1377–1400). Among the medieval sculptors is Giselbertus (c.1120–35), sculptor of the Cathedral of St Lazare at Autun in France; see Ruskin on workers: RUSKIN, n. 24.

[9] *work* a commonplace of nineteenth-century Romanticism about the common people's hitching themselves together to haul stone for the cathedrals, the so-called cult of the carts.

[10] *title* published three years before Eliot's first novel *Adam Bede*, this essay attacks not only the sentimental popular fiction of the day by women writers but also the lack of educational and vocational opportunities for women. Eliot mentions a number of novels, all published in 1856, including *Compensation* by Lady Henrietta Georgiana Maria Chatterton (1806–76) and *The Old Grey Church* by Lady Caroline Scott (1784–1857), as well as several anonymous novels, including *Rank and Beauty* and *The Enigma*.

[11] *contralto* in classical singing, the deepest female voice.

religious; she dances like a sylph,[12] and reads the Bible in the original tongues.[13] Or it may be that the heroine is not an heiress—that rank and wealth are the only things in which she is deficient; but she infallibly gets into high society, she has the triumph of refusing many matches and securing the best, and she wears some family jewels or other as a sort of crown of righteousness[14] at the end. Rakish men either bite their lips in impotent confusion at her repartees, or are touched to penitence by her reproofs, which, on appropriate occasions, rise to a lofty strain of rhetoric; indeed, there is a general propensity in her to make speeches, and to rhapsodize at some length when she retires to her bedroom. In her recorded conversations she is amazingly eloquent, and in her unrecorded conversations, amazingly witty. She is understood to have a depth of insight that looks through and through the shallow theories of philosophers, and her superior instincts are a sort of dial by which men have only to set their clocks and watches, and all will go well. The men play a very subordinate part by her side. You are consoled now and then by a hint that they have affairs, which keeps you in mind that the working-day business of the world is somehow being carried on, but ostensibly the final cause of their existence is that they may accompany the heroine on her "starring" expedition through life. . . .

Writers of the mind-and-millinery school are remarkably unanimous in their choice of diction. In their novels, there is usually a lady or gentleman who is more or less of a upas tree[15]: the lover has a manly breast; minds are redolent of various things; hearts are hollow; events are utilized; friends are consigned to the tomb; infancy is an engaging period; the sun is a luminary that goes to his western couch, or gathers the rain-drops into his refulgent bosom; life is a melancholy boon; Albion and Scotia[16] are conversational epithets. . . . But the most remarkable efforts of the mind-and-millinery writers lie in their philosophic reflections. The authoress of "Laura Gay"[17] for example, having married her hero and heroine, improves the event by observing that "if those sceptics, whose eyes have so long gazed on matter that they can no longer see aught else in man, could once enter with heart and soul into such bliss as this, they would come to say that the soul of man and the polypus are not of common origin, or of the same texture." Lady novelists, it appears, can see something else besides matter; they are not limited to phenomena, but can relieve their eyesight by occasional glimpses of the *noumenon*,[18] and are, therefore, naturally better able than any one else to confound sceptics, even of that remarkable, but to us unknown school, which maintains that the soul of man is of the same texture as the polypus.

The most pitiable of all silly novels by lady novelists are what we may call the *oracular* species—novels intended to expound the writer's religious, philosophical, or moral theories. There seems to be a notion abroad among women, rather akin to the superstition that the speech and actions of idiots are inspired, and that the human being most entirely exhausted of common sense is the fittest vehicle of revelation. To judge from their writings, there are certain ladies who think that an amazing ignorance, both of science and of life, is the best possible qualification for forming an opinion on the knottiest moral and speculative questions. . . .

Notes

[12] *sylph* a mythological creature, an elemental of the air. Alexander Pope (1688–1744) in *The Rape of the Lock* (1712) uses sylphs to parody the vanity of the heroine, Belinda.

[13] *tongues* the OT was originally written in Hebrew; the NT, in *koine* (Gk. common) Greek. In both cases, knowledge of them signified educational accomplishments beyond the norm for girls. See CONDITION: EDUCATION; EASTLAKE and GENDER: CONSTRUCTING; MARTINEAU (WEB p. 75).

[14] *righteousness* see 2 Timothy 4: 8.

[15] *upas tree* a legendary poisonous tree of Java; used figuratively for something having a widespread evil influence.

[16] *Albion and Scotia* ancient names for the British Isles (Albion) and Scotland (Scotia).

[17] *Gay* an anonymous novel first published in the *Athenæum* in 1856.

[18] *noumenon* an object or event that is known without the use of the senses, which is opposed to the phenomenon, known through the senses. In Kantian philosophy, it is impossible to know the *noumenon*.

Happily, we are not dependent on argument to prove that Fiction is a department of literature in which women can, after their kind, fully equal men. A cluster of great names, both living and dead, rush to our memories in evidence that women can produce novels not only fine, but among the very finest;—novels, too, that have a precious speciality, lying quite apart from masculine aptitudes and experience. No educational restrictions can shut women out from the materials of fiction, and there is no species of art which is so free from rigid requirements. Like crystalline masses, it may take any form, and yet be beautiful; we have only to pour in the right elements—genuine observation, humour, and passion. But it is precisely this absence of rigid requirement which constitutes the fatal seduction of novel-writing to incompetent women. Ladies are not wont to be very grossly deceived as to their power of playing on the piano; here certain positive difficulties of execution have to be conquered, and incompetence inevitably breaks down. Every art which has its absolute *technique* is, to a certain extent, guarded from the intrusions of mere left-handed imbecility. But in novel-writing there are no barriers for incapacity to stumble against, no external criteria to prevent a writer from mistaking foolish facility for mastery. And so we have again and again the old story of La Fontaine's ass, who puts his nose to the flute, and, finding that he elicits some sound, exclaims, "Moi, aussi, je joue de la flûte";[19]—a fable which we commend, at parting, to the consideration of any feminine reader who is in danger of adding to the number of "silly novels by lady novelists."

WEB p. 119

Margaret Oliphant (1828–1897): From "Sensation Novels" (1862)

Mary Elizabeth Braddon (1835–1915): *Lady Audley's Secret* (1862)[20]

From Chapter 1: "Lucy"

At the end of this avenue there was an old arch and a clock-tower, with a stupid, bewildering clock, which had only one hand; and which jumped straight from one hour to the next, and was therefore always in extremes. Through this arch you walked straight into the gardens of Audley Court....

Notes

[19] *flute* (Fr. me too, I play the flute); Jean de La Fontaine (1621–95), French fabulist, mistakenly cited as the author of "The Ass and the Flute" (1782) by Tomás de Iriarte (1750–1791), Spanish poet.

[20] *title* the author of over ninety novels and nine plays, Braddon is known today primarily for this work based on abandonment, arson, bigamy, murder, and madness, the stock themes of melodrama. The sensation novel as a genre emerged in the 1860s with works by Braddon, Wilkie Collins (1824–89: *The Woman in White* (1859)), and Charles Reade (1814–84: *Hard Cash* (1863)). The sensation novel was closely associated with the melodrama – Braddon, Collins, and Reade's novels were turned into plays. Melodrama (Gk. *melos*, song, with drama) was a mixed media form on the eighteenth- and nineteenth-century stage that used music for background effect while arousing pathos or sympathy for the plight of the hero or heroine. No device was spared to milk every ounce of emotion from each sentimental moment, often ending with a dramatic rescue amidst spectacular scenic and musical effects of avalanches, floods, railway decapitation, or other disasters. Originally imported from France, melodramas were episodic, and the characterization exaggerated, with unexplained outbursts of madness, rage, passionate love, accompanied by fireworks, drownings, and explosions, as in Dion Boucicault's *The Corsican Brothers* (1852) and *The Octoroon* (1859; see BOUCICAULT (WEB p. 366). The form was parodied in Gilbert and Sullivan's *Ruddigore* (1887; see LITERATURE: DEBATES (WEB p. 119). The six stock characters were a robust hero of only average intelligence and a heroine in distress, lovers whose sentimental romance was blocked by the plotting villain and his henchman as well as, often, an aged parent, and a drooling and interfering

A noble place; inside as well as out, a noble place—a house in which you incontinently lost yourself if ever you were so rash as to go about it alone; a house in which no one room had any sympathy with another, every chamber running off at a tangent into an inner chamber, and through that down some narrow staircase leading to a door which, in its turn, led back into that very part of the house from which you thought yourself the furthest; a house that could never have been planned by any mortal architect, but must have been the handiwork of that good old builder—Time, who, adding a room one year, and knocking down a room another year, toppling down a chimney coeval with the Plantagenets, and setting up one in the style of the Tudors; shaking down a bit of Saxon wall there, and allowing a Norman arch to stand here; throwing in a row of high narrow windows in the reign of Queen Anne, and joining on a dining-room after the fashion of the time of Hanoverian George I. to a refectory that had been standing since the Conquest,[21] had contrived, in some eleven centuries, to run up such a mansion as was not elsewhere to be met with throughout the county of Essex.[22] Of course, in such a house there were secret chambers: the little daughter of the present owner, Sir Michael Audley, had fallen by accident upon the discovery of one. A board had rattled under her feet in the great nursery where she played, and on attention being drawn to it, it was found to be loose, and so removed, revealing a ladder leading to a hiding-place between the floor of the nursery and the ceiling of the room below—a hiding-place so small that he who had hid there must have crouched on his hands and knees or lain at full length, and yet large enough to contain a quaint old carved oak chest half filled with priests' vestments which had been hidden away, no doubt, in those cruel days when the life of a man was in danger if he was discovered to have harboured a Roman Catholic priest, or to have mass said in his house.[23] . . .

Notes

servant. Their gestures were extravagant and became conventional, such as the villain's swirling of his cape, and the twirling of his mustachios. The sensation novels of the 1860s incorporated recognizable elements of the melodrama in terms of plot (quick complications and reversals), sensational actions, and extravagant characterization.

The complicated plot of *Lady Audley* is based in part on elements of the notorious contemporaneous murder trial of Constance Emily Kent (1844–1944). The novel begins with the marriage of a young, beautiful governess, Lucy Graham, about whom little is known, to Sir Michael Audley, a much older, rich widower. Soon after, his barrister nephew, Robert Audley, arrives at Audley Court with his friend, George Talboys, who has recently returned from Australia to find his wife, Helen Talboys, whom he had abandoned three years earlier. Lady Audley avoids George, and soon he disappears. After much detective work and numerous complicated melodramatic plot twists, Robert discovers that Lady Audley and Helen Talboys are one and the same. When confronted, she initially tries to kill Robert by setting fire to his hotel; however, he survives and confronts her again. This time she admits to adultery but claims that she is insane. She is taken to an asylum near Brussels, where she confesses to murdering George by pushing him down a well. The novel ends happily; as it turns out George survived the fall into the well, and Robert is happily married to George's sister Clara.

The novel was first serialized in *Robin Goodfellow* (July–Sept. 1861), but remained unfinished as the magazine

went bankrupt after eighteen chapters. It was restarted and completed in *Sixpenny Magazine* (Jan.–Mar. 1862), and then republished in *London Journal* (Mar.–Aug. 1863). It was published as a three-decker novel in October, 1862 (our text), and went through eight editions by the end of the year. The novel was immensely popular and was adapted several times for the stage (see this section, DEBATES; HAZLEWOOD).

[21] *Plantagenets . . . Conquest* a sequence which aligns Audley Court with a long stretch of English history. The appeal to ancient history is a convention of Romantic and post-Romantic Gothic literature: the Plantagenet dynasty ruled England from 1154 to 1485; the Tudors were the ruling dynasty of England from 1485 to 1603; the Saxons were medieval Germanic tribes who migrated to Britain in the fifth century after the collapse of Roman Britain in 410; the Normans were the French of Normandy who invaded Britain in 1066 and became the ruling class; Anne was the last Stuart monarch, queen of Great Britain and Ireland from 1702 to 1714; and George I was the first British monarch from the House of Hanover, ruling from 1714 to 1727. The Norman conquest of 1066 was led by William Conqueror (1028–87).

[22] *Essex* a county located northeast of London, originally the eastern kingdom of the Saxons.

[23] *house* a secret chamber or "priest hole," a hiding place built in the houses of Catholic gentry to avoid persecution against priests during the reign of Elizabeth I, from 1558 to 1603. Here, again, used to evoke the Gothic convention of a mysterious and dangerous history associated with the house of an aristocratic family in ruin; see, nn. 25, 27.

At the end of this dark arcade there was the shrubbery, where, half buried among the tangled branches and the neglected weeds, stood the rusty wheel of that old well of which I have spoken. It had been of good service in its time, no doubt; and busy nuns have perhaps drawn the cool water with their own fair hands; but it had fallen with disuse now, and scarcely any one at Audley Court knew whether the spring had dried up or not. But sheltered as was the solitude of this lime-tree walk, I doubt very much if it was ever put to any romantic uses.

From Chapter 37: "Buried Alive"[24]

"You have brought me to my grave, Mr. Audley," she cried; "you have used your power basely and cruelly, and have brought me to a living grave."

"I have done that which I thought just to others and merciful to you," Robert answered, quietly; "I should have been a traitor to society had I suffered you to remain at liberty after—after the disappearance of George Talboys and the fire at the Castle Inn. I have brought you to a place in which you will be kindly treated by people who have no knowledge of your story—no power to taunt or to reproach you. You will lead a quiet and peaceful life, my lady, such a life as many a good and holy woman in this catholic country[25] freely takes upon herself, and happily endures unto the end. . . .

Robert started as she mentioned the name of his lost friend; his face turned pale in the dusky light, and his breathing grew quicker and louder.

"He was standing opposite me as you are standing now," continued my lady. "You said that you would raze the old house to the ground; that you would root up every tree in the gardens to find your dead friend. You would have had no need to do so much; the body of George Talboys lies at the bottom of the old well, in the shrubbery beyond the lime-walk."

Robert Audley flung up his hands and clasped them above his head, with one loud cry of horror.

"Oh, my God!" he said, after a dreadful pause, "have all the ghastly things that I have thought prepared me so little for the ghastly truth, that it should come upon me like this at last?"

"He came to me in the lime-walk," resumed my lady, in the same hard, dogged tone as that in which she had confessed the wicked story of her life. "I knew that he would come, and I had prepared myself, as well as I could, to meet him. I was determined to bribe him, to cajole him, to defy him; to do anything sooner than abandon the wealth and the position I had won, and go back to my old life. He came, and he reproached me for the conspiracy at Ventnor.[26] He declared that so long as he lived he would never forgive me for the lie that had broken his heart. He told me that I had plucked his heart out of his breast and trampled upon it; and that he had now no heart in which to feel one sentiment of mercy for me." . . .

Robert Audley uttered no word of horror when the story was finished. He moved a little nearer towards the door against which Helen Talboys stood. Had there been any other means of exit from the room, he would gladly have availed himself of it. He shrank from even a momentary contact with this creature.

"Let me pass you, if you please," he said, in an icy voice.

Notes

[24] *title* Lady Audley is here entering the asylum under the name of Madame Taylor.

[25] *country* Belgium; for "catholic," see nn. 23, 27.

[26] *Ventnor* a seaside resort in the Isle of Wight where Lady Audley fakes her death. George visits the supposed site of her grave and commissions a gravestone with the following inscription: "Sacred to the Memory of HELEN, / THE BELOVED WIFE OF GEORGE TALBOYS, / Who departed this life / August 24th, 18–, aged 22, / Deeply regretted by her sorrowing Husband."

"You see that I do not fear to make my confession to you," said Helen Talboys, "for two reasons. The first is that you dare not use it against me, because you know it would kill your uncle to see me in a criminal dock; the second is, that the law could pronounce no worse sentence than this, a life-long imprisonment in a mad-house. You see I do not thank you for your mercy, Mr. Robert Audley, for I know exactly what it is worth."

She moved away from the door, and Robert passed her without a word, without a look.

Half an hour afterward he was in one of the principal hotels at Villebrumeuse,[27] sitting at a neatly-ordered supper-table, with no power to eat; with no power to distract his mind, even for a moment, from the image of that lost friend who had been treacherously murdered in the thicket at Audley Court.

Colin Henry Hazlewood (1820–75): *Lady Audley's Secret* (1863)

From Act V[28]

SCENE FIFTH—*The Lime Tree Avenue and Well, as in* ACT I. *Moonlight, which falls on the old Well. Phœbe is heard without calling for help, and is dragged on by Lady Audley, R. 2 E.*

LADY AUDLEY:Come, come. To the Hall! to the Hall!
PHŒBE:No, I will not; you mean mischief towards me, I am sure you do.
LADY AUDLEY:No, girl, no; I am your friend.

Enter Robert Audley, who, coming between them from L., takes Phœbe from Lady Audley's grasp.

ROBERT:[*to Phœbe*] Away to your husband, girl, and see if there is any help for him.
PHŒBE.: Thank you, bless you, sir. [*Exit hastily, L.*]
ROBERT: [*to Lady Audley*] Now, madam, we will come to a reckoning.
LADY AUDLEY [*recoils from him*]. Alive!
ROBERT:Aye, to punish and expose you. You thought to trap me, to silence me, by dooming me to a dreadful death. But Heaven be praised I was not sleeping when your wicked hands set fire to the house. No, I live to be your fate, and the avenger of my friend.
LADY AUDLEY: What will you do?—proceed without evidence? And who are *you* that dare accuse me? Who are you that oppose yourself to me so constantly? I have wealth, boundless wealth, and I will use it to crush you—to crush you, Robert Audley.
ROBERT: How?
LADY AUDLEY. Thus! [*Rushes towards him with poignard,[29] he wrenches it from her hand.*]
ROBERT: And thus I rob the serpent of its sting![30]
LADY AUDLEY: Let me pass.
ROBERT: Never! the law shall have its own.
LADY AUDLEY: And who is to be my accuser?

Enter Luke, supported by Peasants and Phœbe, L.

LUKE: I, thank Heaven! I am spared to do an act of justice before I end my guilty life. I accuse that woman of——

Notes

27 *Villebrumeuse* (Fr. town or city of fog); an imaginary Belgian location for the insane asylum (*maison de santé*) where Helen will spend the rest of her life.
28 *title* an actor and playwright, Hazlewood adapted another of Braddon's melodramatic novels, *Aurora Floyd*, in 1863. This play was first performed on 25 May 1863 at the Royal Victoria Theatre in London. It was a huge success, and prompted two more adaptations before the year's end. In the stage directions, "without" means off-stage; "R.2 E." means stage right, second entrance; "L." means left.
29 *poignard* a type of dagger.
30 *sting* see Proverbs 23: 32.

ROBERT: No! hold, hold. It will be better not to cast a stain upon my uncle's name. Say nothing I beg, I entreat of you.

LUKE: Then I will be silent, silent for ever—ever—ever.

[*Falls back in the arms of the Peasants.*]

LADY AUDLEY: [*aside*] He is dead, and I shall triumph over them all. [*The great bell of the Castle is now heard tolling.*]

Enter Alicia from back, followed by Servants.

ALICIA: Robert! Robert! my father is dead. Oh, pity me! pity and protect me! [*Goes to Robert.*]

ROBERT: Sir Michael dead! Now vengeance, take thy own! Friends, hear me:—I accuse that woman of the murder of my friend, George Talboys.

LADY AUDLEY: How and where?

LUKE: [*revives*] I—I will tell that. She pushed him down that well, [*points to well, all start*] but it will be useless to search there now, for George Talboys is——

Enter George Talboys, R. 2 E.

GEORGE: Here!

[*Luke falls back dead.*]

OMNES: Alive!

LADY AUDLEY: [*petrified*] Alive! alive! you alive!

GEORGE: Back, woman! and thank that man [*points to Luke*] that you have not my death upon your soul. You will be scorned, loathed, and despised by all. The blow you struck me rendered me an invalid for months. I have been silent until to-day, because I gave my word to that poor, dying wretch. [*Points to Luke.*] But now I am free—free to tell all. Speak to her, speak to her, Robert, and say I forgive her. [*Points to Lady Audley.*]

ROBERT: [*to Lady Audley*] You hear, woman!

LADY AUDLEY: [*vacantly*] But I do not heed. I have a rich husband. They told me he was dead—but no, they lied—see—see, he stands there! Your arm—your arm, Sir Michael. We will leave this place—we will travel. Never heed what the world says—I have no husband but you—none—none! It is time to depart, the carriage is waiting. Come—come—come!

GEORGE: What does she mean, Robert?

ROBERT: Mean! Do you not see she is mad?

OMNES: [*retreating from her*] Mad!

LADY AUDLEY: Aye—aye! [*Laughs wildly.*] Mad, mad, that is the word. I feel it here—here! [*Places her hands on her temples.*] Do not touch me—do not come near me—let me claim your silence—your pity—and let the grave, the cold grave, close over Lady Audley and her Secret.

Falls—dies—Music—tableau of sympathy—George Talboys kneels over her.

CURTAIN

WEB p. 121

George Meredith (1828–1909): From "On the Idea of Comedy and the Uses of the Comic Spirit" (1877)

Henry James (1843–1916): From "The Art of Fiction" in *Longman's Magazine* (Sept. 1884)[31]

I should not have affixed so comprehensive a title to these few remarks, necessarily wanting in any completeness, upon a subject the full consideration of which would carry us far, did I not seem to discover a pretext for my temerity in the interesting pamphlet lately published under this name by Mr. Walter Besant.... There is something very encouraging in his having put into form certain of his ideas on the mystery of story-telling.

It is a proof of life and curiosity—curiosity on the part of the brotherhood of novelists, as well as on the part of their readers. Only a short time ago it might have been supposed that the English novel was not what the French call *discutable*.[32] It had no air of having a theory, a conviction, a consciousness of itself behind it—of being the expression of an artistic faith, the result of choice and comparison. I do not say it was necessarily the worse for that; it would take much more courage than I possess to intimate that the form of the novel, as Dickens and Thackeray[33] (for instance) saw it, had any taint of incompleteness. It was, however, *naïf*[34] (if I may help myself out with another French word); and, evidently, if it is destined to suffer in any way for having lost its *naïveté*, it has now an idea of making sure of the corresponding advantages. During the period I have alluded to there was a comfortable, good-humoured feeling abroad that a novel is a novel, as a pudding is a pudding, and that this was the end of it. But within a year or two,[35] for some reason or other, there have been signs of returning animation—the era of discussion would appear to have been to a certain extent opened.[36]. . .

It goes without saying that you will not write a good novel unless you possess the sense of reality; but it will be difficult to give you a recipe for calling that sense into being.

Notes

[31] *title* James's famous essay, often cited as a fundamental statement in the transition from the Victorian to the modernist novel, is a response to "The Art of Fiction," a lecture by Walter Besant (1836–1901), an historian and author of numerous popular novels, the best known of which represent social problems in East London, *All Sorts and Conditions of Men* (1882) and *Children of Gibeon* (1886). Besant's lecture, given at the Royal Institution (25 April 1884) and published as a pamphlet (1884), argues that the novelist both delights and elevates, and in doing so fulfils an essential social role as teacher and entertainer. Despite this importance, however, novelists in general do not receive official recognition, social status, or class acceptability, and are "by the general mass undervalued." Unlike other professions, novelists do not "receive their share of the ordinary national distinctions" such as being mentioned in the honours lists or being knighted. He argues that "the practical man" or "the Philistine" feels "contempt" for the novelist as a "dreamer": "the telling of stories is inconsistent with a well-balanced mind; to be a teller of stories disqualifies one from a hearing on important subjects." Against this dismissal, Besant argues that fiction has laws, that it has a social purpose in society, and that the mastery of these laws and purposes is intuitive in the fiction writer. His lecture inaugurated the "Art of Fiction" debates: it was answered not only by James but also by Robert Louis Stevenson, H. Rider Haggard (1856–1925), and Andrew Lang (1844–1912). James's essay was republished in *Partial Portraits* (1888).

[32] *discutable* (Fr. discussable). James uses French to align himself with discussions by critics of the novel in France,

whom he considered more sophisticated than those (like Besant) in England.

[33] *Thackeray* William Dean Howells (1837–1920), American novelist and critic, had written "Henry James, Jr." in *Century Magazine* (Nov. 1882): "The art of fiction has, in fact, become a finer art in our day than it was with Dickens and Thackeray.... The new school derives from Hawthorne and George Eliot rather than any others; but it studies human nature much more in its wonted aspects, and finds its ethical and dramatic examples in the operation of lighter but not really less vital motives. The moving accident is certainly not its trade; and it prefers to avoid all manner of dire catastrophes.... This school, which is so largely of the future as well as the present, finds its chief exemplar in Mr. James; it is he who is shaping and directing American fiction, at least.... Since he has finally made his public in his own way of story-telling—or call it character-painting if you prefer,—it must be conceded that he has chosen the best for himself and his readers in choosing the form of fiction for what he has to say."

[34] *naïf* (Fr. innocent, naive).

[35] *two* for contemporaneous essays about the nature of fiction see Stevenson's "A Gossip on Romance," *Longman's Magazine* (Sept. 1882), and Howells's "Henry James, Jr." *Century Magazine* (Nov. 1882; see n. 33).

[36] *era ... opened* see ARNOLD, "FUNCTION OF CRITICISM": "But epochs of concentration cannot well endure for ever; epochs of expansion, in the due course of things, follow them. Such an epoch of expansion seems to be opening in this country."

Humanity is immense and reality has a myriad forms; the most one can affirm is that some of the flowers of fiction have the odour of it, and others have not; as for telling you in advance how your nosegay should be composed, that is another affair. It is equally excellent and inconclusive to say that one must write from experience; to our supposititious aspirant such a declaration might savour of mockery. What kind of experience is intended, and where does it begin and end? Experience is never limited and it is never complete; it is an immense sensibility, a kind of huge spider-web, of the finest silken threads, suspended in the chamber of consciousness and catching every air-borne particle in its tissue. It is the very atmosphere of the mind; and when the mind is imaginative—much more when it happens to be that of a man of genius—it takes to itself the faintest hints of life, it converts the very pulses of the air into revelations. . . .

A novel is a living thing, all one and continuous, like every other organism, and in proportion as it lives will it be found, I think, that in each of the parts there is something of each of the other parts. The critic who over the close texture of a finished work will pretend to trace a geography of items will mark some frontiers as artificial, I fear, as any that have been known to history. There is an old-fashioned distinction between the novel of character and the novel of incident, which must have cost many a smile to the intending romancer who was keen about his work. It appears to me as little to the point as the equally celebrated distinction between the novel and the romance[37]—to answer as little to any reality. There are bad novels and good novels, as there are bad pictures and good pictures; but that is the only distinction in which I see any meaning, and I can as little imagine speaking of a novel of character as I can imagine speaking of a picture of character. When one says picture, one says of character, when one says novel, one says of incident, and the terms may he transposed. What is character but the determination of incident? What is incident but the illustration of character? What is a picture or a novel that is *not* of character? What else do we seek in it and find in it? It is an incident for a woman to stand up with her hand resting on a table and look out at you in a certain way; or if it be not an incident, I think it will be hard to say what it is. At the same time it is an expression of character. If you say you don't see it (character in *that—allons donc!*)[38] this is exactly what the artist who has reasons of his own for thinking he *does* see it undertakes to show you. . . .

. . . I can think of no obligation to which the "romancer" would not be held equally with the novelist; the standard of execution is equally high for each. Of course it is of execution that we are talking—that being the only point of a novel that is open to contention. This is perhaps too often lost sight of, only to produce interminable confusions and cross-purposes. We must grant the artist his subject, his idea, what the French call his *donnée;*[39] our criticism is applied only to what he makes of it. Naturally I do not mean that we are bound to like it or find it interesting: in case we do not our course is perfectly simple—to let it alone. We may believe that of a certain idea even the most sincere novelist can make nothing at all, and the event may perfectly justify our belief; but the failure will have been a failure to execute, and it is in the execution that the fatal weakness is recorded. . . .

Notes

[37] *romance* the term romance has shifted in meaning from Hellenistic first-century Greek fiction to medieval heroic and chivalric romances dealing with the fanciful deeds. During the eighteenth century, the term novel began to be associated with realistic fiction such as Defoe's *Robinson Crusoe* (1721), as opposed to the fantastic tales associated with romance. To Stevenson, Haggard, and Lang, however, the term would applied to adventure novels, and especially with Haggard to what has been called imperial romance, with an emphasis on heroic action, often in the face of daunting odds, rather than character analysis. During the twentieth century the term "romance" had shifted away from adventure associated with masculine bravery to novels of love and marriage produced by Mills and Boon in Great Britain and Harlequin Enterprises in North America.

[38] *allons donc* (Fr. come now).

[39] *donnée* (Fr. given).

Mr. Besant has some remarks on the question of "the story," which I shall not attempt to criticise, though they seem to me to contain a singular ambiguity, because I do not think I understand them. I cannot see what is meant by talking as if there were a part of a novel which is the story and part of it which for mystical reasons is not—unless indeed the distinction be made in a sense in which it is difficult to suppose that anyone should attempt to convey anything. "The story," if it represents anything, represents the subject, the idea, the data of the novel; and there is surely no "school"—Mr. Besant speaks of a school—which urges that a novel should be all treatment and no subject.[40] There must assuredly be something to treat; every school is intimately conscious of that. This sense of the story being the idea, the starting-point, of the novel is the only one that I see in which it can be spoken of as something different from its organic whole; and since, in proportion as the work is successful, the idea permeates and penetrates it, informs and animates it, so that every word and every punctuation-point contribute directly to the expression, in that proportion do we lose our sense of the story being a blade which may be drawn more or less out of its sheath. The story and the novel, the idea and the form, are the needle and thread, and I never heard of a guild of tailors who recommended the use of the thread without the needle or the needle without the thread.

WEB p. 123

George Moore (1852–1933): From *Literature at Nurse, or, Circulating Morals* (1885)
Bennett George Johns (1820/21–1900): From "The Literature of the Streets" (1887)

2. Pre-Raphaelitism, Aestheticism, and Decadence

William Michael Rossetti (1829–1919): *The Germ: Or Thoughts Toward Nature in Poetry, Literature, and Art* (1850)

From "Introduction"[1]

In 1848 the British School of Painting was in anything but a vital or a lively condition. One very great and incomparable genius, Turner,[2] belonged to it. He was old and past his executive prime. There were some other highly able men ... On the whole the school had sunk very far below what it had been in the days of Hogarth, Reynolds, Gainsborough,

Notes ———————————————————————————————

[40] *subject* James attacks Besant for assuming it is possible to detach the "story" from the other elements of prose fiction. Over the next four years the debate between the advocates of plot and action (the supporters of romance or adventure fiction) and the advocates of complex character development (the supporters of realist fiction) continued in essays and reviews.

PRE-RAPHAELITISM, AESTHETICISM, AND DECADENCE
[1] *title* William Michael, a brother of Dante Gabriel and Christina Rossetti, married Lucy Madox Brown (1843–94), daughter of Ford Madox Brown, in 1874. A civil servant in the Department of Inland Revenue, Rossetti was also a

critic, editor, and biographer. He edited the journal of the Pre-Raphaelite Brotherhood (hereafter PRB; he spelled it "Præraphaelite"), *The Germ* (four issues, 1850). Rossetti's contemporaries offered different views concerning the meaning of "Pre-Raphaelite." A close associate Ford Madox Brown (1821–93), claimed the German painters in Rome known as the Nazarenes (including Peter Cornelius, 1784–1867, and Johann Friedrich Overbeck, 1789–1869) inspired the PRB with their Early Christian subject matter and style and semi-monastic brotherhood. Another member of the PRB, Holman Hunt (1827–1910), claimed the name arose from a rejection of Raphael's *Transfiguration* (see n. 7) in an argument in the Academy Schools in 1847.

and Blake,[3] and its ordinary average had come to be something for which commonplace is a laudatory term, and imbecility a not excessive one.

There were in the late summer of 1848, in the Schools of the Royal Academy[4] or barely emergent from them, four young men to whom this condition of the art seemed offensive, contemptible, and even scandalous. Their names were William Holman-Hunt, John Everett Millais, and Dante Gabriel Rossetti, painters, and Thomas Woolner, sculptor.[5] . . . They hated those forms of execution which are merely smooth and prettyish, and those which, pretending to mastery, are nothing better than slovenly and slapdash, or what the P.R.B.'s called "sloshy."[6] Still more did they hate the notion that each artist should not obey his own individual impulse, act upon his own perception and study of Nature, and scrutinize and work at his objective material with assiduity before he could attempt to display and interpret it. . . . They were to have no master except their own powers of mind and hand, and their own first-hand study of Nature. Their minds were to furnish them with subjects for works of art, and with the general scheme of treatment; Nature was to be their one or their paramount storehouse of materials for objects to be represented; the study of her was to be deep, and the representation (at any rate in the earlier stages of self-discipline and work) in the highest degree exact; executive methods were to be learned partly from precept and example, but most essentially from practice and experiment. As their minds were very different in range and direction, their products also, from the first, differed greatly; and these soon ceased to have any link of resemblance.

The Præraphaelite Brothers entertained a deep respect and a sincere affection for the works of some of the artists who had preceded Raphael;[7] and they thought that they should more or less be following the lead of those artists if they themselves were to

Notes

In 1851 William Michael published "Pre-Raphaelitism" in the *Spectator* (4 Oct.): "Their aim is the same [as the precursors of Raphael]—truth; and their process the same— exactitude of study from nature" (see Plate 13: Dante Gabriel Rossetti, *The Girlhood of Mary Virgin* (1849)). In 1901 William Michael published a facsimile of the original issues of *The Germ* and added an introduction, our source.

[2] *Turner* Joseph Mallord William Turner (1775–1851), English landscape artist, was the subject of Ruskin's *Modern Painters* (1843–56), defended against critics who mocked Turner's colour, perspective, and composition, as in the attack by Sir George Beaumont (1753–1827), who claimed in 1813 that Turner "had done more harm in misleading the taste than any other artist... but he had fallen into a manner that was neither true nor consistent." To Ruskin, Turner excelled in colour, expression, and imaginative power, especially in his truth to nature, points on which Ruskin also praised the Pre-Raphaelites, as in his letters to *The Times* (see this section, PRE-RAPHAELITISM: RUSKIN; "THE PRE-RAPHAELITES"). See also RUSKIN, n. 6.

[3] *Hogarth . . . Blake* William Hogarth (1697–1764), painter and satirist, is perhaps best known for his series of paintings and consequent engravings *The Harlot's Progress* (1731), *The Rake's Progress* (1735), and *Marriage à la Mode* (1743–45); Sir Joshua Reynolds (1724–92) a major eighteenth-century portraitist, specialized in the "Grand Style" that echoed the Italian masters, as in *Mrs. Siddons as the Tragic Muse* (1784); he was a founder and first president of the RA; Thomas Gainsborough (1727–88), landscape and portrait painter; William Blake (1757–1827), poet, painter, and etcher, author of the *Songs of Innocence and of Experience* (1789–94), *Milton* (c.1804–11), and *Jerusalem* (1804–20).

[4] *Academy* the Schools of the RA (founded 1769) were established by Joshua Reynolds, emphasizing drawing from casts of ancient monuments and sculptures, copying old masters, and using life models; in the first half of the nineteenth century a studentship lasted ten years. Turner and Blake had been students at the RA Schools.

[5] *Holman-Hunt . . . sculptor* William Holman Hunt (1827–1910); John Everett Millais (1829–96) won a place at the RA Schools at the age of 11 (1840) and had a long and successful career; Dante Rossetti (1828–82) was at the Academy Schools from 1845 to 1848; and Thomas Woolner (1825–92), sculptor, attended in 1842.

[6] *sloshy* the term was applied to the fuzzy or blurred outlines and the brownish-golden palette based on the unstable tar product, bitumen or asphaltum, used as a ground in many contemporary and earlier paintings; hence, their nickname given to "Sir Sloshua Reynolds."

[7] *Raphael* Raphael Sanzio (1483–1520), a High Renaissance painter much admired by the Victorian art establishment; the PRB objected to Raphael's *Sistine Madonna* (1513–14) and *Transfiguration* (1520) for their attitudinizing, theatricality, and lack of fidelity to nature. His satellites included Giulio Romano (1499–1546). The PRB studied artists earlier than Raphael in a folio copy of engravings (1828) by Carlo Lasinio (1759–1838) of the frescoes of the Campo Santo in Pisa, created by Giotto (1266–1337), Orcagna (1308–68), and Benozzo Gozzoli (1421–97). They also praised such early Florentine artists as Fra Angelico (1395–1455) and Botticelli (1445–1510). The National Gallery then contained no Italian artist before Raphael. For Robert Browning's treatment of some of these artists, see BROWNING, "FRA LIPPO LIPPI" and "ANDREA DEL SARTO."

develop their own individuality, disregarding school-rules. This was really the sum and substance of their "Præraphaelitism." ...

The Præraphaelite Brotherhood having been founded in September 1848, the members exhibited in 1849 works conceived in the new spirit.[8] These were received by critics and by the public with more than moderate though certainly not unmixed favour: it had not as yet transpired that there was a league of unquiet and ambitious young spirits, bent upon making a fresh start of their own, and a clean sweep of some effete respectabilities. It was not until after the exhibitions were near closing in 1849 that any idea of bringing out a magazine came to be discussed. The author of the project was Dante Gabriel Rossetti. He alone among the P.R.B.'s had already cultivated the art of writing in verse and in prose to some noticeable extent ("The Blessed Damozel"[9] had been produced before May 1847), and he was better acquainted than any other member with British and foreign literature.[10] ... By July 13 and 14, 1849, some steps were taken towards discussing the project of a magazine. The price, as at first proposed, was to be sixpence; the title, "Monthly Thoughts in Literature, Poetry, and Art"; each number was to have an etching. Soon afterwards a price of one shilling was decided upon, and two etchings per number: but this latter intention was not carried out.

Charles Dickens (1812–70): From "Old Lamps for New Ones" [Review of Millais's *Christ in the House of his Parents*; see Plate 12] in *Household Words* (15 June 1850)[11]

In the fifteenth century, a certain feeble lamp of art arose in the Italian town of Urbino.[12] This poor light, Raphael Sanzio by name, better known to a few miserably mistaken wretches in these later days, as Raphael (another burned at the same time, called Titian[13]), was fed with a preposterous idea of Beauty—with a ridiculous power of etherealising, and exalting to the very Heaven of Heavens, what was most sublime and lovely in the expression of the human face divine[14] on Earth—with the truly contemptible conceit of

Notes

[8] *spirit* Millais exhibited *Lorenzo and Isabella* and Holman Hunt exhibited *Rienzi* at the RA in 1849; Rossetti exhibited his first major oil, *The Girlhood of Mary Virgin*, at the Free Exhibition (see Plate 13). All signed their names, followed by the initials P.R.B.

[9] *Damozel* poem (1850) and painting (1875–78) by Dante Rossetti; see ROSSETTI, "BLESSED DAMOZEL" and Plate 14.

[10] *literature* Rossetti was bilingual in English and Italian and by October 1848 he had translated Dante's autobiography, *La Vita Nuova* (Ital. the new life), published in *The Early Italian Poets* (1861).

[11] *title* Dickens's title alludes to the story of Aladdin from the *Arabian Nights* where a sorcerer tries to gain possession of Aladdin's magic lamp by offering to his wife "new lamps for old," his cry as he goes through the streets. Dickens adapts the story as purveying new art for old art, tried and true. His attack on Millais's painting *Christ in the House of His Parents* (1850, sometimes known as *The Carpenter Shop*; see Plate 12) joined the chorus against it, completely rejecting the painting's religious allegory in favour of savagely dismissive references to working-class values and the squalor of the London poor. Because the painting presented the holy family in an everyday setting and occupation, instead of the conventional idealized family home at Nazareth, as in John Rogers Herbert's *Our Saviour Subject to His Parents in*

Nazareth (1847) it was regarded as "pictorial blasphemy" (*Athenæum*, 1 June 1850). Instead, Millais's painting combines the realistic with the symbolic, depicting a moment when Christ has injured himself in the hand, prefiguring the marks of the nails at the crucifixion, towards which many other symbols refer: the instruments of the passion (ladder, nails, hammer, and pliers), the dove of the Holy Spirit, the Virgin anticipating the pietà pose, as well as the symbolic sheep (the flock of the Good Shepherd) and John the Baptist with the symbolic water of baptism. Further, the separate gender spheres of work and life are here blended and the sexual and religious propriety of representing Christ as manly by his tears, also an anticipation of the agony in Gethsemane. See also Plate 13: Dante Gabriel Rossetti, "*The Blessed Damozel*" (1871–78).

[12] *Urbino* Raphael (see n. 7) was born in the city of Urbino in eastern Italy.

[13] *Titian* Italian Venetian painter, Titian (1488/90–1576) was the most important High Renaissance painter of Venice, excelling in portraits, landscapes, and religious and mythological subjects.

[14] *divine* see *Paradise Lost* 3. 41–43; and William Blake's "human form divine" in "The Divine Image" in *Songs of Innocence* (1789). Ruskin writes extensively on "Of Ideas of Beauty"; see RUSKIN, MODERN PAINTERS, headnote.

finding in poor humanity the fallen likeness of the angels of GOD, and raising it up again to their pure spiritual condition. This very fantastic whim effected a low revolution in Art, in this wise, that Beauty came to be regarded as one of its indispensable elements. In this very poor delusion, Artists have continued until the present nineteenth century, when it was reserved for some bold aspirants to "put it down."

The Pre-Raphael Brotherhood, Ladies and Gentlemen, is the dread Tribunal which is to set this matter right. Walk up, walk up;[15] and here, conspicuous on the wall of the Royal Academy of Art in England, in the eighty-second year of their annual exhibition, you shall see what this new Holy Brotherhood, this terrible Police that is to disperse all Post-Raphael offenders, has "been and done!"[16]

You come—in this Royal Academy Exhibition, which is familiar with the works of WILKIE, COLLINS, ETTY, EASTLAKE, LESLIE, MACLISE, TURNER, STANFIELD, LANDSEER, ROBERTS, DANBY, CRESWICK, LEE, WEBSTER, HERBERT, DYCE, COPE,[17] and others who would have been renowned as great masters in any age or country—you come, in this place, to the contemplation of a Holy Family. You will have the goodness to discharge from your minds all Post-Raphael ideas, all religious aspirations, all elevating thoughts; all tender, awful, sorrowful, ennobling, sacred, graceful, or beautiful associations; and to prepare yourselves, as befits such a subject—Pre-Raphaelly considered—for the lowest depths of what is mean, odious, repulsive, and revolting.

You behold the interior of a carpenter's shop. In the foreground of that carpenter's shop is a hideous, wry-necked, blubbering, red-headed boy, in a bed-gown; who appears to have received a poke in the hand, from the stick of another boy with whom he has been playing in an adjacent gutter, and to be holding it up for the con-templation of a kneeling woman, so horrible in her ugliness, that (supposing it were possible for any human creature to exist for a moment with that dislocated throat) she would stand out from the rest of the company as a Monster, in the vilest cabaret in France, or the lowest ginshop in England. Two almost naked carpenters, master and journeyman, worthy companions of this agreeable female, are working at their trade; a boy, with some small flavour of humanity in him, is entering with a vessel of water; and nobody is paying any attention to a snuffy old woman who seems to have mistaken that shop for the tobacconist's next door, and to be hopelessly waiting at the counter to be served with half an ounce of her favourite mixture. Wherever it is possible to express ugliness of feature, limb, or attitude, you have it expressed. Such men as the carpenters might be undressed in any hospital where dirty drunkards, in a high state of varicose veins, are received. Their very toes have walked out of Saint Giles's.[18] . . .

Notes

[15] *up* the circus showman's pitch for the freak show.

[16] *been and done* "vulgar or facetious expletive amplification of the past participle" (*OED*, s.v. be), citing an example from Dickens's *Pickwick Papers* (ch. 26).

[17] *Wilkie . . . Cope* the most acclaimed painters of the day, all members of the RA (except Danby who was an Associate Member), who regularly showed in the Academy exhibi-tion, though some had already died when Dickens was writing: Sir David Wilkie (1785–1841); William Collins (1788–1847); William Etty (1787–1849); Sir Charles Eastlake (1793–1865); Charles Robert Leslie (1794–1859); Daniel Maclise (1806–70); Joseph Mallord William Turner (1775–1851); Charles Frederick Stanfield (1793–1867); Sir Edwin Landseer (1802–73); David Roberts (1796–1864); Francis Danby (1793–1861); Thomas Creswick (1811–69); Frederick Richard Lee (1798–1879); Thomas Webster (1800–86); John Rogers Herbert (1810–90); William Dyce (1806–64); and Charles West Cope (1811–90).

[18] *Giles's* London slum dating from the eighteenth and nine-teenth centuries, with terrible overcrowding, no sanitation, and a high incidence of crime, partly because of the pre-valence of gin shops and prostitutes. Dickens alleges that the models and their representations are from this area and are tainted with prostitution, allegations later applied to Rossetti's poetry by Buchanan (see LITERATURE: PRE-RAPH-AELITISM; BUCHANAN, "FLESHLY" (WEB p. 128)).

In the first place, the Pre-Perspective[19] Brotherhood will be presently incorporated, for the subversion of all known rules and principles of perspective. It is intended to swear every P. P. B. to a solemn renunciation of the art of perspective on a soup-plate of the willow pattern;[20] and we may expect, on the occasion of the eighty-third annual Exhibition of the Royal Academy of Art in England, to see some pictures by this pious Brotherhood, realising HOGARTH'S[21] idea of a man on a mountain several miles off, lighting his pipe at the upper window of a house in the foreground.

Christina Rossetti (1830–94): Two Poems on the Pre-Raphaelite Brotherhood [1853]

The P.R.B. [I][22]

The two Rossettis (brothers they)
And Holman Hunt and John Millais,
With Stevens chivalrous and bland,
And Woolner in a distant land—[23]
In these six men I awestruck see   5
Embodied the great P.R.B.
D. G. Rossetti offered two
Good pictures[24] to the public view;
Unnumbered ones great John Millais,
And Holman more than I can say.   10

William Rossetti, calm and solemn,
Cuts up his brethren by the column.[25]

19 September 1853

Notes

[19] *Pre-Perspective* a parody of "Pre-Raphaelite," but also part of the widespread attack on faulty perspective in some Pre-Raphaelite paintings. Linear perspective refers to the methods used by artists to represent distance on a flat two-dimensional plane, suggested by the lines of objects which may be extended towards a vanishing point or points. For instance, Rossetti had had trouble with perspective in both *The Girlhood of Mary Virgin* (1849; see Plate 13) and *Ecce Ancilla Domini* (1850) with several vanishing points as may be demonstrated by extending the lines from the tiled floor and the edges of the books or the embroidery frame; on 4 May 1850 the *ILN* accused the PRB in the Academy exhibition of "disclaiming perspective." See also RUSKIN, n. 6.

[20] *pattern* designed by pottery manufacturer Thomas Minton (1765–1836) from about 1780 to 1790 and widely sold in the eighteenth and nineteenth century (and promoted by a fabricated story about the plate's portrayal of a forbidden love story in ancient China). The chief character in Meredith's *The Egoist* (1879), Sir Willoughby Patterne, is named for the design. Rossetti and others in his circle, as

well as Whistler and Wilde, took an interest in old Chinese and Japanese porcelain and began collecting it.

[21] *Hogarth's* see n. 3.

[22] *title* Rossetti did not publish these two poems on the PRB. For identification of the members, see n. 5. From *The Poetical Works of Christina Georgina Rossetti*, ed. William Michael Rossetti (1904). The date refers to its composition.

[23] *land* Thomas Woolner, distressed at having lost the competition for a statue of Wordsworth, decided to emigrate with two friends to the Australian gold fields in July 1852. His departure prompted Ford Madox Brown to explore the subject of emigration in his painting *The Last of England* (1855), emblematic of the huge wave of emigration that year, over 350,000.

[24] *pictures* Rossetti exhibited *The Girlhood of Mary Virgin* (see Plate 13) in the Free Exhibition in 1849 and his painting of the Annunciation, *Ecce Ancilla Domini* in the Free Exhibition of 1850.

[25] *column* from 1850 to 1852 William Michael Rossetti was the art editor for the *Spectator*, publishing numerous reviews.

The P.R.B. [II][26]

The P.R.B is in its decadence:
　　For Woolner in Australia cooks his chops,[27]
　　And Hunt is yearning for the land of Cheops;[28]
　　　　D. G. Rossetti shuns the vulgar optic;[29]
　　While William M. Rossetti merely lops　　　　　　　5
　　　　His B's in English disesteemed as Coptic;[30]
Calm Stephens in the twilight smokes his pipe,
　　But long the dawning of his public day;
　　　　And he at last the champion great Millais,
Attaining Academic opulence,　　　　　　　　　　　　10
　　Winds up his signature with A.R.A.[31]
So rivers merge in the perpetual sea;
　　So luscious fruit must fall when over-ripe;
And so the consummated P.R.B.

10 November 1853

John Ruskin (1819–1900): "The Præ-Raphaelites" [On Holman Hunt's *The Awakening Conscience*"; see Plate 10] Letter to *The Times* (25 May 1854)[32]

Sir,—Your kind insertion of my notes on Mr. Hunt's principal picture encourages me to hope that you may yet allow me room in your columns for a few words respecting his second work in the Royal Academy, the "Awakening Conscience."[33] Not that this picture

Notes

[26] *title* from *Dante Gabriel Rossetti: His Family-Letters With a Memoir* (ed. William Michael Rossetti, 2 vols, 1895); reprinted in *The Poetical Works of Christina Georgina Rossetti*, ed. William Michael Rossetti (1904). The date refers to its composition.

[27] *chops* see n. 23.

[28] *Cheops* Khufu or Cheops (twenty-fifth century BCE), a pharaoh of Egypt's Old Kingdom, is thought to have been the builder of the Great Pyramid of Giza. Hunt was also planning his trip to Palestine (he left in January 1854) where he would paint *The Scapegoat* (1854) on the shore of the Dead Sea.

[29] *optic* public scrutiny; by 1853 Rossetti was refusing to exhibit at all.

[30] *B's ... Coptic* William Michael Rossetti cuts off the heads in criticism of his "B's," an abbreviation for "Brothers," that is, other Pre-Raphaelite Brothers. William Michael later wrote "I, in my press-criticisms, made light of my P.R.B. colleagues (which is joke, not fact), and that my utterances met with no public regard (which is partial but not entire fact; for in these criticisms, appearing in a paper of such high repute as the *Spectator*, and being, in 1850 to 1852, nearly the only press reviews which upheld the Præraphaelite cause, did excite some attention, and I suppose some anger)." The "Coptic" is a joke at the frequent obscurity of his prose, as in this cited sentence.

[31] *A.R.A.* on 7 November 1853 Millais was elected an Associate of the RA, and therefore was joining the ranks of those whom the Brotherhood had vowed to oppose. He had narrowly missed being elected the year before, but he was one year short of the required age of 24.

[32] *title* in 1854 William Holman Hunt exhibited two paintings as a pair, *The Light of the World* (Plate 11) and *The Awakening Conscience* (Plate 10), at the RA. Both caused a sensation and were widely discussed. The latter, however, was a puzzle to viewers and critics alike, praised for the realistic detail but bewildering for its symbolism. The *ILN* spoke for many: "The attempt to discover its actual meaning has ... proved abortive." No one until Ruskin had traced the moral and allegorical meanings in the painting's realistic details. For another allegory of the fallen woman, see Plate 15: ROSSETTI, *FOUND*.

[33] *Conscience* Hunt designed the symbolic frame for the painting decorated with bells (warning) and marigolds (sorrow), according to Victorian flower symbolism, with a star above the girl's head; it included a verse from Proverbs: "As he that taketh away a garment in cold weather, so is he that singeth songs to an heavy heart" (25: 20). The model for the woman was Hunt's mistress, Annie Miller (1835–1925). According to Hunt, his other painting in the Academy exhibition, *The Light of the World* (see Plate 11) with its "spiritual subject called for a material counterpart ... representing in actual life the manner in which the appeal of the spirit of heavenly love calls to a soul to abandon a lower life." He sought to portray "the unintended stirring up of the depths of pure affection by the idle song of an empty mind ... [showing]"

is obscure, or its story feebly told. I am at a loss to know how its meaning could be rendered more distinctly, but assuredly it is not understood. People gaze at it in a blank wonder, and leave it hopelessly; so that, although it is almost an insult to the painter to explain his thoughts in this instance, I cannot persuade myself to leave it thus misunderstood. The poor girl has been sitting singing with her seducer; some chance words of the song "Oft in the stilly night"[34] have struck upon the numbed places of her heart; she has started up in agony; he, not seeing her face, goes on singing, striking the keys carelessly with his gloved hand.

I suppose that no one possessing the slightest knowledge of expression could remain untouched by the countenance of the lost girl, rent from its beauty into sudden horror; the lips half open, indistinct in their purple quivering, the teeth set hard, the eyes filled with the fearful light of futurity, and with tears of ancient days. But I can easily understand that to many persons the careful rendering of the inferior details in this picture cannot but be at first offensive, as calling their attention away from the principal subject. It is true that detail of this kind has long been so carelessly rendered that the perfect finishing of it becomes matter of curiosity, and therefore an interruption to serious thought. But, without entering into the question of the general propriety of such treatment, I would only observe that, at least in this instance, it is based on a truer principle of the pathetic[35] than any of the common artistical expedients of the schools. Nothing is more notable than the way in which even the most trivial objects force themselves upon the attention of a mind which has been fevered by violent and distressful excitement. They thrust themselves forward with a ghastly and unendurable distinctness, as if they would compel the sufferer to count, or measure, or learn them by heart. Even to the mere spectator a strange interest exalts the accessories of a scene in which he bears witness to human sorrow. There is not a single object in all that room, common, modern, vulgar (in the vulgar sense, as it may be), but it became tragical, if rightly read. That furniture, so carefully painted, even to the last vein of the rosewood—is there nothing to be learnt from that terrible lustre of it, from its fatal newness; nothing there that has the old thoughts of home upon it, or that is ever to become a part of home? Those embossed books,[36] vain and useless—they also new—marked with no happy wearing of beloved leaves; the torn and dying bird upon the floor; the gilded tapestry, with the fowls of the air feeding on the ripened corn;[37] the picture above the fireplace with its single drooping figure—the woman taken in adultery;[38] nay, the very hem of the poor girl's dress, which the painter has laboured so closely, thread by thread, has story in it, if we think how soon the pure whiteness may be soiled with dust and rain, her outcast feet failing in the street; and the fair garden flower, seen in the reflected sunshine of the mirror——these also have their language—

Notes

how the companion of the girl's fall might himself be the unconscious utterer of a divine message ... revealing the memory of her childish home, and breaking away from her gilded cage with a startled awakening while her shallow companion still sings on, ignorantly intensifying her repentant purpose."

[34] *Night* a song by Thomas Moore from his *National Airs* (1815) with music by Sir John Stevenson (1761–1833), written in 1818, becoming enormously popular. On the floor is another piece of music, *Tears, Idle Tears*, with words by Tennyson as one of the songs in *The Princess* (see TENNYSON (WEB p. 342)), and set to music by a number of composers, in this case by Tennyson's friend, the poet and painter Edward Lear (1812–88).

[35] *pathetic* pathetic fallacy is defined by Ruskin as the correspondence of nature or the external world (in this case the books, furniture, and ripened corn) to human feelings; see RUSKIN, MODERN, "PATHETIC FALLACY."

[36] *books* the black embossed book on the table has been identified as Henry Noel Humphrey's *The Origin and Progress of the Art of Writing* (1854), an expensive and edifying account of writing from its beginnings traced through different civilizations, illustrated with coloured lithographs.

[37] *corn* that is, wheat. The wallpaper shows grape-vines and wheat, symbols of the elements of the Eucharist, here incongruously combined with a sleeping cupid or shepherd. For "fowls of the air," see Mark 4: 4.

[38] *adultery* see John 8: 3–11.

Hope not to find delight in us, they say,
For we are spotless, Jessy—we are pure.[39]

I surely need not go on. Examine the whole range of the walls of the Academy; nay, examine those of all our public and private galleries, and, while pictures will be met with by the thousands which literally tempt to evil, by the thousand which are devoted to the meanest trivialities of incident or emotion, by the thousand so the delicate fancies of inactive religion, there will not be found one powerful as this to meet full in the front the moral evil of the age in which it is painted, to waken into mercy the cruel thoughtlessness of youth and subdue the severities of judgment into the sanctity of compassion.

I have the honour to be, Sir, your obedient servant,

THE AUTHOR OF "MODERN PAINTERS."
Denmark Hill.[40]

Walter Pater (1839–94): From "The Poems of William Morris" ["Æsthetic Poetry"] in Westminster Review (Oct. 1868)[41]

The "æsthetic"[42] poetry is neither a mere reproduction of Greek or medieval poetry, nor only an idealisation of modern life and sentiment. The atmosphere on which its effect depends belongs to no simple form of poetry, no actual form of life. Greek poetry, medieval or modern poetry, projects, above the realities of its time, a world in which the forms of things are transfigured. Of that transfigured world this new poetry takes possession, and sublimates beyond it another still fainter and more spectral, which is literally an artificial or "earthly paradise." It is a finer ideal, extracted from what in relation to any actual world is already an ideal.[43] Like some strange second flowering after date, it renews on a

Notes

[39] *pure* from "Elegy XXVI. Describing the Sorrow of An Ingenuous Mind, on the Melancholy Event of a Licentious Amour" by William Shenstone (1714–63). Ruskin quotes the same passage in his discussion of pathetic fallacy in *Modern Painters* (vol. 3. pt. 4, 1856).

[40] *Hill* following convention, Ruskin often did not sign his name to his books or letters to the editor but used the authorship of *Modern Painters*. Ruskin lived in this area of London with his parents from 1843 to 1872, during which he wrote most of his major works.

[41] *title* originally "The Poems of William Morris," an anonymous review in the *Westminster Review* (Oct. 1868) of three volumes: *The Defence of Guinevere* (1858), *The Life and Death of Jason* (1867), and the first volume of *The Earthly Paradise* (1868). The first part of the review was revised and published separately as "Æsthetic Poetry" in the first edition of *Appreciations* (1889). It was suppressed in the second (1890) and subsequent editions. The rest of the essay (also revised) became the conclusion to *Studies in the History of the Renaissance* (1873); see PATER, n. 18. Our text: 1889.

[42] *æsthetic* that is, Pre-Raphaelite poetry. In the *Westminster* version, this first sentence begins "This poetry" in reference to Morris's poetry. The change to "æsthetic" poetry" names a movement of the 1870s and 1880s, later called "art for art's sake," with which Pater is closely identified. In "The School of Giorgione" in *The Renaissance*, Pater writes: "As art addresses not pure sense, still less the pure intellect, but the 'imaginative reason' through the senses, [so] there

are differences of kind in aesthetic beauty." The phrase "imaginative reason" is from Matthew Arnold's "Pagan and Christian Religious Sentiment" (*Cornhill Magazine*, Apr. 1864), appropriated by Pater to mean aesthetic perception, developed from Coleridge and Ruskin (without their religious and moral aspects of beauty), anchored in the conditions and context of their creation: "All true criticism of philosophical doctrine, as of every other product of human mind, must begin with an historic estimate of the conditions, antecedent and contemporary, which helped to make it precisely what it was" (Pater, *Plato and Platonism*, 1893). For a previous derogatory use of æsthetic see LITERATURE: PRE-RAPHAELITISM, n. 18 (WEB p. 130).

[43] *ideal* a version of Plato's theory of forms or ideas, in which the artist creates an image or representation of an ideal that he sees, through the special insight of the artist or craftsman, in the world of pure forms; see *Republic*, the "Allegory of the Cave" (bk. 7). This statement is in tension with Pater's general view that the attributes of the external world, including beautiful objects and forms, can be perceived by the senses and can give pleasure, in what in the conclusion to *The Renaissance* has been called his Epicurean naturalism. Against the abiding morality of Ruskin, and the permanence of the Platonic forms, he also held that morality and beauty are relative, since the world is continually subject to change in all of its aspects, following both Heraclitus (*c*.535–475 BCE), Greek philosopher, and Charles Darwin.

more delicate type the poetry of a past age, but must not be confounded with it. The secret of the enjoyment of it is that inversion of home-sickness known to some, that incurable thirst for the sense of escape, which no actual form of life satisfies, no poetry even, if it be merely simple and spontaneous.[44]

The writings of the "romantic school," of which the æsthetic poetry is an after-thought, mark a transition not so much from the pagan[45] to the medieval ideal, as from a lower to a higher degree of passion in literature. The end of the eighteenth century, swept by vast disturbing currents,[46] experienced an excitement of spirit of which one note was a reaction against an outworn classicism severed not more from nature than from the genuine motives of ancient art; and a return to true Hellenism was as much a part of this reaction as the sudden preoccupation with things medieval.[47] The medieval tendency is in Goethe's *Goetz von Berlichingen*, the Hellenic in his *Iphigenie*.[48] At first this medievalism was superficial, or at least external. Adventure, romance in the frankest sense, grotesque individualism—that is one element in medieval poetry, and with it alone Scott and Goethe[49] dealt. Beyond them were the two other elements of the medieval spirit: its mystic religion at its apex in Dante and Saint Louis,[50] and its mystic passion, passing here and there into the great romantic loves of rebellious flesh, of Lancelot and Abelard.[51] That stricter, imaginative medievalism which re-creates the mind of the Middle Age, so that the form, the presentment grows outward from within, came later with Victor Hugo in France, with Heine[52] in Germany.

In the *Defence of Guenevere: and Other Poems*, published by Mr. William Morris now many years ago,[53] the first typical specimen of æsthetic poetry, we have a refinement upon this later, profounder medievalism. The poem which gives its name to the volume is a thing tormented and awry with passion, like the body of Guenevere defending herself from the charge of adultery, and the accent falls in strange, unwonted places with the effect of a great cry. In truth these Arthurian legends, in their origin prior to Christianity, yield all their sweetness only in a Christian atmosphere. What is characteristic in them

Notes

[44] *spontaneous* the "past age" is the poetry of the Romantic movement to which Pater refers in the next paragraph. The poetry of simplicity and spontaneity is that of Wordsworth, from which Pater distances his view of aesthetic poetry somewhat, in favour of one of the Aesthetic movement's favourites, Keats, with his theme of escape in, for instance, the "Ode to Melancholy" (1819).

[45] *pagan* classical.

[46] *currents* such disturbances would include the American Revolution (1776), the French Revolution (1789–92), the Industrial Revolution (c.1750–1850), and the Romantic movement (second half of the eighteenth century to c.1840).

[47] *Hellenism ... medieval* Hellenism here refers to the revival of Greek (or classical) ideals in literature, art, and architecture in the second half of the eighteenth century; the theorist of Hellenism was the German philosopher and theorist, Johann Joachim Winckelmann (1717–68), of whom Pater wrote an important essay in the *Westminster Review* (Jan. 1867), republished in *The Renaissance* (1873). Incongruously, the medieval revival, associated with Pugin and Morris, was in part a reaction to Hellenism, but it also coincided with it in the same art forms.

[48] *Goethe ... Iphigenie* the play by Goethe (see n. 49), *Goetz von Berlichingen* (1773), is based on the life of the German poet Götz von Berlichingen (c.1480–1562). *Iphigenie in*

Taurus (1779 in prose, 1786 in verse) is a reworking of Euripides' play of the same name (414–412 BCE).

[49] *Scott ... Goethe* Walter Scott (1771–1832), famous for his series of Scottish historical novels from *Waverley* (1814) to *Anne of Geierstein* (1829). Johann Wolfgang von Goethe (1749–1832), German writer and philosopher, wrote a number of tragedies, including the two parts of *Faust* (1808; 1831), and such novels as *The Sorrows of Young Werther* (1774) and two parts of *Wilhelm Meister* (1795–1821).

[50] *Dante ... Louis* Dante Alighieri (1265–1321), Italian poet and author of the *Divine Comedy* (1308–21); Louis IX of France (1214–70) participated in the seventh (1248) and eighth (1270) crusades and built the Sainte-Chapelle in Paris (1248).

[51] *Lancelot ... Abelard* Lancelot du Lac is one of the legendary knights of King Arthur in a number of medieval romances telling the well-known story of Lancelot's adultery with Arthur's Queen Guenevere. For Abelard, see DANTE ROSSETTI, n. 82.

[52] *Hugo ... Heine* Victor Hugo (1802–85), French author, wrote *Notre-Dame de Paris* (1831), the story of the hunch-back Quasimodo. Heinrich Heine (1797–1856), German poet and political activist, published *Buch der Lieder* (Ger. book of songs, 1727), winning great popularity in settings by major composers.

[53] *ago* 1858; for extracts from the collection, including the title poem of which Pater writes, see MORRIS.

is the strange suggestion of a deliberate choice between Christ and a rival lover. That religion, monastic religion at any rate, has its sensuous side, a dangerously sensuous side, has been often seen: it is the experience of Rousseau as well as of the Christian mystics.[54] The Christianity of the Middle Age made way among a people whose loss was in the life of the senses partly by its æsthetic beauty, a thing so profoundly felt by the Latin hymn-writers,[55] who for one moral or spiritual sentiment have a hundred sensuous images. And so in those imaginative loves, in their highest expression, the Provençal poetry, it is a rival religion with a new rival *cultus* that we see.[56] Coloured through and through with Christian sentiment, they are rebels against it. The rejection of one worship for another is never lost sight of. The jealousy of that other lover, for whom these words and images and refined ways of sentiment were first devised, is the secret here of a borrowed, perhaps factitious colour and heat. It is the mood of the cloister taking a new direction, and winning so a later space of life it never anticipated. . . .

The *Defence of Guenevere* was published in 1858; the *Life and Death of Jason* in 1867; to be followed by *The Earthly Paradise;*[57] and the change of manner wrought in the interval, entire, almost a revolt, is characteristic of the æsthetic poetry. Here there is no delirium or illusion, no experiences of mere soul while the body and the bodily senses sleep, or wake with convulsed intensity at the prompting of imaginative love; but rather the great primary passions under broad daylight as of the pagan Veronese.[58] This simplification interests us, not merely for the sake of an individual poet—full of charm as he is—but chiefly because it explains through him a transition which, under many forms, is one law of the life of the human spirit, and of which what we call the Renaissance is only a supreme instance. Just so the monk in his cloister, through the "open vision," open only to the spirit, divined, aspired to, and at last apprehended, a better daylight, but earthly, open only to the senses. Complex and subtle interests, which the mind spins for itself may occupy art and poetry or our own spirits for a time; but sooner or later they come back with a sharp rebound to the simple elementary passions—anger, desire, regret, pity, and fear: and what corresponds to them in the sensuous world—bare, abstract fire, water, air, tears, sleep, silence, and what De Quincey has called the "glory of motion."[59]

This reaction from dreamlight to daylight gives, as always happens, a strange power in dealing with morning and the things of the morning. Not less is this Hellenist of the Middle Age master of dreams, of sleep and the desire of sleep—sleep in which no one walks, restorer of childhood to men—dreams, not like Galahad's or Guenevere's, but full of happy, childish wonder as in the earlier world. It is a world in which the centaur and the ram with

Notes

[54] *Rousseau . . . mystics* Jean-Jacques Rousseau (1712–78), Swiss philosopher, was deeply religious, first as a Calvinist in Geneva, then as a Roman Catholic convert, and then again as a Calvinist. He had a number of intense love affairs, as he records in his *Confessions* (1782). Among the Christian mystics, St Anthony (third century) was besieged by the temptations of the flesh; both St Catherine of Alexandria (fourth century) and St Catherine of Siena (1347–80) had visions of a mystical marriage with Christ, and both had important cult followings in the later Middle Ages.

[55] *hymn-writers* for example, Bernard of Clairvaux (1090–1153), the leader of the Cistercian reform, stressing a powerful asceticism and a suppression of the senses, also wrote a number of hymns, including *Jesus dulcis memoria* (Lat. Jesus the very thought of thee, / With sweetness fills the breast), essentially a love song.

[56] *see* Provençal or Occitan poetry is the vernacular poetry of Provence in southern France from the eleventh and twelfth

centuries. The poets, often called troubadours, gathered around the noble courts, especially that of William IX of Aquitaine (1071–1126). One of the dominant themes was idealized love or *fin amors* or *amours courtois* (OFr. noble love; courtly love). This *cultus* (Lat. cult, specialized system of belief and practice) venerated an unattainable woman with passionate love and offers of service, a process in literature that Pater describes in the following (omitted) paragraphs. The tradition developed at the same time as the veneration of the Virgin Mary.

[57] *Paradise* published 1868–70.

[58] *Veronese* Paolo Cagliari, called Paulo (Paul) Veronese (1528–88), Venetian Renaissance painter. His *Rape of Europa* (c.1570) came into the National Gallery in London in 1831.

[59] *motion* Thomas De Quincey (1785–1859) published "The English Mail-Coach; or, the Glory of Motion" in *Blackwood's Edinburgh Magazine* (Oct. and Dec. 1849).

the fleece of gold are conceivable.[60] The song sung always claims to be sung for the first time. There are hints at a language common to birds and beasts and men. Everywhere there is an impression of surprise, as of people first waking from the golden age, at fire, snow, wine, the touch of water as one swims, the salt taste of the sea. And this simplicity at first hand is a strange contrast to the sought-out simplicity of Wordsworth.[61] Desire here is towards the body of nature for its own sake, not because a soul is divined through it. . . . .

The modern poet or artist who treats in this way a classical story comes very near, if not to the Hellenism of Homer, yet to the Hellenism of Chaucer, the Hellenism of the Middle Age, or rather of that exquisite first period of the Renaissance within it. Afterwards the Renaissance takes its side, becomes, perhaps, exaggerated or facile. But the choice life of the human spirit is always under mixed lights, and in mixed situations, when it is not too sure of itself, is still expectant, girt up to leap forward to the promise. Such a situation there was in that earliest return from the overwrought spiritualities of the Middle Age to the earlier, more ancient life of the senses; and for us the most attractive form of classical story is the monk's conception of it, when he escapes from the sombre atmosphere of his cloister to natural light. The fruits of this mood, which, divining more than it under-stands, infuses into the scenery and figures of Christian history some subtle reminiscence of older gods, or into the story of Cupid and Psyche[62] that passionate stress of spirit which the world owes to Christianity, constitute a peculiar vein of interest in the art of the fifteenth century. . . .

One characteristic of the pagan spirit the æsthetic poetry has, which is on its surface—the continual suggestion, pensive or passionate, of the shortness of life. This is contrasted with the bloom of the world, and gives new seduction to it—the sense of death and the desire of beauty: the desire of beauty quickened by the sense of death. But that complexion of sentiment is at its height in another "æsthetic" poet of whom I have to speak next, Dante Gabriel Rossetti.[63]

WEB p. 128

Robert Williams Buchanan (1841–1901): From "The Fleshly School of Poetry: Mr. D. G. Rossetti" (1871)
Dante Gabriel Rossetti (1828–82): From "The Stealthy School of Criticism" (1871)
Algernon Charles Swinburne (1837–1909): From *Under the Microscope* (1872)

Notes

[60] *conceivable* the Greek myth of the golden fleece of the winged ram, is part of the story that William Morris tells in *The Life and Death of Jason* (1867).

[61] *Wordsworth* the simplicity of life in the golden age is con-trasted with that of Wordsworth's simplicity found in the solitary lives of the rustic peasants of the Lake District, as in "The Solitary Reaper" (1798), as well as in the simplicity of diction that he claimed to be "the language of men" in "Preface to *Lyrical Ballads*" (1800).

[62] *Psyche* ancient legend of the love of Cupid (or Amor or Eros) for Psyche recorded in *The Golden Ass* by Apuleius (c.125–c.180). William Morris retells the story in the May tales of *The Earthly Paradise* (1868).

[63] *Rossetti* in the *Westminster Review* article (see n. 41), this unrepublished paragraph continues "sense of death. '*Arriéré!*' [Fr. Hold on!] you say, 'here in a tangible form we have the defect of all poetry like this. The modern world

is in possession of truths; what but a passing smile can it have for a kind of poetry which, assuming artistic beauty of form to be an end in itself, passes by those truths and the living interests which are connected with them, to spend a thousand cares in telling once more these pagan fables as if it had but to choose between a more and a less beautiful shadow?' It is a strange transition from the earthly paradise to the sad-coloured world of abstract phi-losophy. But let us accept the challenge; let us see what modern philosophy, when it is sincere, really does say about human life and the truth we can attain in it, and the relation of this to the desire of beauty." There then follow directly the paragraphs that make up the conclusion to *The Renaissance* (1873); see Pater. The next essay in *Appreciations* (1889) is Pater's essay on "Dante Gabriel Rossetti," first published in T. H. Ward's *The English Poets* (vol. 4, 1883).

James Abbott McNeill Whistler (1834–1903): From "Mr. Whistler's 'Ten O'Clock'" (20 Feb. 1885)[64]

Ladies and Gentlemen:

It is with great hesitation and much misgiving that I appear before you, in the character of The Preacher.[65] . . .

Art is upon the Town![66]—to be chucked under the chin by the passing gallant—to be enticed within the gates of the householder—to be coaxed into company, as a proof of culture and refinement.

If familiarity can breed contempt, certainly Art—or what is currently taken for it—has been brought to its lowest stage of intimacy.

The people have been harassed with Art in every guise, and vexed with many methods as to its endurance. They have been told how they shall love Art, and live with it. Their homes have been invaded, their walls covered with paper, their very dress taken to task—until, roused at last, bewildered and filled with the doubts and discomforts of senseless suggestion, they resent such intrusion, and cast forth the false prophets, who have brought the very name of the beautiful into disrepute, and derision upon themselves.[67]

Alas! ladies and gentlemen, Art has been maligned. She has naught in common with such practices. She is a goddess of dainty thought—reticent of habit, abjuring all obtrusiveness, purposing in no way to better others.

She is, withal, selfishly occupied with her own perfection only—having no desire to teach—seeking and finding the beautiful in all conditions and in all times, as did her high

Notes

[64] *title* Whistler was an American artist who studied in Paris before settling in London in 1860. In Paris he had made friends with such leading artists as Henri Fantin-Latour (1836–1904), Gustave Courbet (1819–77), Edouard Manet (1832–83), Claude Monet (1840–1926), and Édgar Degas (1834–1917), as well as such writers as Charles Baudelaire (1821–67) and Stéphane Mallarmé (1842–98). In London his painting *Nocturne in Black and Gold: The Falling Rocket* (1875) had elicited the comment from John Ruskin that it was "wilful imposture. I have seen, and heard, much of Cockney impudence before now, but never expected to hear a coxcomb ask two hundred guineas for flinging a pot of paint in the public's face." Whistler sued Ruskin for libel and won the case, but was awarded only a farthing (¼ penny). It was, however, a decisive victory in that it began to dislodge Ruskin's dominating theory that art is a primarily a moral force in society – in favour of art as the expression of an artist's subjective vision in interpreting what he saw (see SWINBURNE, n. 30 and Plate 20: Whistler, *Symphony in White No. 2*). This invitation-only lecture was organized by Helen D'Oyly Carte (1852–1913) and was delivered on 20 February 1885 in the Prince's Hall in Piccadilly, London. Oscar Wilde reviewed the lecture in the *Pall Mall Gazette* (21 Feb. 1885) as filled "with really marvellous eloquence on the absolute uselessness of all lectures of the kind." The lecture was translated into French by Mallarmé. Our text: *The Gentle Art of Making Enemies*, 1890.

[65] *Preacher* to indicate the mock seriousness of the occasion and his topic, Whistler adopts a sermonizing posture. As one of the best-known London dandies, here dressed in black before a black backdrop, he also ironically echoes Ecclesiastes 1: 2.

[66] *Town* a conventional name among the landed wealthy to distinguish London from the country.

[67] *themselves* in 1882 Oscar Wilde had lectured throughout the United States and Canada on "The House Beautiful," a lecture repeated in England in 1884. The title had been made popular by the American writer, Clarence Cook (1828–1900) in *The House Beautiful* (1878), and the topic by a variety of writers, including Charles Locke Eastlake, *Hints on Household Taste* (1868); Mary Eliza Haweis, *The Art of Decoration* (1881) and *Beautiful Houses* (1882); and Frederick George Stevens, *Artists at Home* (1884). A number of journals also recommended aesthetic interiors, including *The House Furnisher and Decorator* (founded 1871), *The Magazine of Art* (1878), and *The Journal of Decorative Art* (1881). Whistler also alludes to the attacks on aesthetic people and houses launched by, amongst other magazines, *Punch* through the 1880s, especially in cartoons by George du Maurier such as "The Six-Mark Teapot" (*Punch* 30 Nov. 1880), with the following dialogue: *Æsthetic Bridegroom*: "It is quite consummate, is it not?" *Intense Bride*: "It is, indeed! Oh, Algernon, let us live up to it!"

priest Rembrandt, when he saw picturesque grandeur and noble dignity in the Jews' quarter of Amsterdam, and lamented not that its inhabitants were not Greeks.[68] ...

Humanity takes the place of Art, and God's creations are excused by their usefulness. Beauty is confounded with virtue, and, before a work of Art, it is asked: "What good shall it do?"

Hence it is that nobility of action, in this life, is hopelessly linked with the merit of the work that portrays it; and thus the people have acquired the habit of looking, as who should say, not *at* a picture, but *through* it, at some human fact, that shall, or shall not, from a social point of view, better their mental or moral state. So we have come to hear of the painting that elevates, and of the duty of the painter—of the picture that is full of thought, and of the panel that merely decorates....

A favourite faith, dear to those who teach, is that certain periods were especially artistic, and that nations, readily named, were notably lovers of Art.

So we are told that the Greeks were, as a people, worshippers of the beautiful, and that in the fifteenth century Art was engrained in the multitude.

That the great masters lived in common understanding with their patrons—that the early Italians were artists—all—and that the demand for the lovely thing produced it....

Listen! There never was an artistic period.

There never was an Art-loving nation....

Nature contains the elements, in colour and form, of all pictures, as the keyboard contains the notes of all music.

But the artist is born to pick, and choose, and group with science, these elements, that the result may be beautiful—as the musician gathers his notes, and forms his chords, until he bring forth from chaos glorious harmony.

To say to the painter, that Nature is to be taken as she is, is to say to the player, that he may sit on the piano.

That Nature is always right, is an assertion, artistically, as untrue, as it is one whose truth is universally taken for granted. Nature is very rarely right, to such an extent even, that it might almost be said that Nature is usually wrong: that is to say, the condition of things that shall bring about the perfection of harmony worthy a picture is rare, and not common at all.

This would seem, to even the most intelligent, a doctrine almost blasphemous. So incorporated with our education has the supposed aphorism become, that its belief is held to be part of our moral being, and the words themselves have, in our ear, the ring of religion. Still, seldom does Nature succeed in producing a picture....

Set apart by them [the Gods] to complete their works, he [the artist] produces that wondrous thing called the masterpiece, which surpasses in perfection all that they have contrived in what is called Nature; and the Gods stand by and marvel, and perceive how far away more beautiful is the Venus of Melos[69] than was their own Eve.

Notes

68 *Greeks* Rembrandt (1606–69), Dutch artist, was an influence on Whistler in his atmospheric portrait paintings, like his portrait of his mother (*Arrangement in Grey and Black No.1*, 1871) and of Thomas Carlyle (*Arrangement in Grey and Black, No. 2*, 1872–73). Rembrandt painted his sitters in the costume of the day, and included people from the Jewish quarter of Amsterdam as models in his biblical paintings, such as *The Woman Taken in Adultery* (1644) in the National Gallery, London. Neither he nor Whistler clothed his characters in historical costume as was the vogue in some Victorian painters like Frederick Leighton (1830–96) and Albert Moore (1841–93).

69 *Melos* the marble statue of Venus de Milo, the Aphrodite of Melos (*c.*130 BCE), discovered in 1820 and now in the Louvre in Paris.

WEB p. 134

Arthur Symons (1865–1945): From "The Decadent Movement in Literature" (1893)
Richard Le Gallienne (1866–1947) "A Ballad of London" (1895)
W. B. Yeats (1865–1939): From "The Symbolism of Poetry" (1900)
  I
  III
Olive Custance, Lady Douglas (1874–1944)
  A Mood (1896)
  The White Statue (1896)
  Peacocks: A Mood (1902)

WEB p. 144

3. Literature and New Technologies

3.1 Book Publishing
  Charles Dickens (1812–70): From "Address" (1847) [Prospectus for the Cheap Edition]
  Charles Knight (1791–1873): *The Old Printer and the Modern Press* (1854)
    From Chapter 6
  Mason Jackson (1819–1903): *The Pictorial Press: Its Origin and Progress* (1885)
    From Chapter 1
  William Morris (1834–96): From *A Note by William Morris on His Aims in Founding the Kelmscott Press* (1898)
  John Southward (1840–1902): *Progress in Printing and the Graphic Arts During the Victorian Era* (1897)
    From Chapter 1
    From Chapter 2
    From Chapter 3
    From Chapter 12

3.2 Aural Culture
  [Anon.] "The Edison Phonograph" in *Illustrated London News* (1888)
  Recordings of Victorian Voices and Sounds
    George Frideric Handel (1685–1759): *Israel in Egypt* (1739; recorded 1888)
    Arthur Sullivan (1842–1900): "The Lost Chord" (piano and cornet) (1888)
    Arthur Sullivan (1842–1900): After-Dinner Toast (1888)
    Thomas Alva Edison (1847–1931): "Around the World on the Phonograph" (1888)
    William Ewart Gladstone (1809–1898): "The Phonograph's Salutation" (1888)
    Robert Browning (1812–1889): "How They Brought the Good News from Ghent to Aix" (1889)
    Alfred Tennyson (1809–1892): "The Charge of the Light Brigade" (1890)
    "Big Ben": Sounding the Hours at the Palace of Westminster (1890)

Religion and Science

Introduction

In 1853 Anne Wright published *The Globe Prepared for Man; A Guide to Geology*, a popular guide to a controversial science "prepared for the use of young people" (vi). The frontispiece is a coloured engraving, "A Volcano in a State of Eruption." After the preface and table of contents there is a geological chart, "Order of Rocks Covering the Globe, 8 or 10 Miles in Depth," setting out, matter of factly, the relationship between the strata of the earth's crust, the geological periods in which they developed, and the correspondent biological forms which appeared in these periods (see Figure 8). The chart is to be read in two ways, vertically and horizontally. Vertically it charts four major layers of the earth plus the "Alluvial Soil" of the present, laid out "8 or 10 Miles in Depth" in three separate columns. On the left, a name is given to an epoch attached to a kind of rock, from Hypogene or Primary Rocks, through Transition, Secondary, and Tertiary Rocks, to the "Present State of the Earth's Surface." These divisions structure the book: after two introductory chapters, there follow five sections or "Divisions," each titled with the name of a geological formation. In the centre of the chart, the type of rock or soil is again placed in vertical relations, moving base phase of granite (composed of hornblende, basalt, and porphyry [sic]), through, among others, sandstone, clay, sand, and "Alluvial Soil." On the right, a number of forms are represented, again in a vertical line, at the very bottom, non-organic "Metals," a "Depth of Granite, unknown," moving up through "Corals," "Trilobites," "Fishes," "Extinct Trees," all the way to "Extinct Animals," "Huge Animals," and, finally, "Human Family, and present animals & vegetables."

This chart lays out the parameters of the science of geology in the terms widely followed by the major practitioners of the day. For instance, the order of beings in the right-hand column had been categorized in 1817 by the French zoologist George Cuvier (1769–1832) in a work translated as *The Animal Kingdom* (16 vols, 1825–35); the term "Silurian" had just been put into currency in 1839 by the Scottish geologist Roderick Impey Murchison (1792–1871); and the term "Old Red Sandstone" had been coined in 1821 by another Scot, Robert Jameson (1754–1854), and had been the title of a best-selling volume of natural history in 1847 by yet another Scot, Hugh Miller (1802–56). In other words, despite minor differences in terminology, and the fact that it is written for youth, Wright's book describes the condition of the science in up-to-date and accurate terminology. Significantly, however, the chart by itself is completely silent on controversial factors that would make many of Wright's contemporaries say that it was unfit for the hands of youth, indeed, of any God-fearing Christian. These factors, concerning agency, causality, and temporality, were much in dispute among the major geologists of the day. How do you explain the transition between the white space at the bottom of the chart and its base of "Hornblende. Basalt. Porphry [sic]. Depth of Granite, unknown," in other words, the First Cause? How do you account for the transition on the right-hand column between the non-organic "Veins of Metals" at the core of the earth, in which there are "no fossils," and the first life forms, "Sea Weeds, a few Corals," in other words, the beginning of life? How do the spatial relations laid out in the chart relate to temporality at a time when most people followed the chronology devised in 1654 by James Ussher, Archbishop of Armagh, which said the world was created on 23 October 4004 BCE,

Victorian Literature: An Anthology, First Edition. Edited by Victor Shea and William Whitla.
© 2015 John Wiley & Sons, Ltd. Published 2015 by John Wiley & Sons, Ltd.

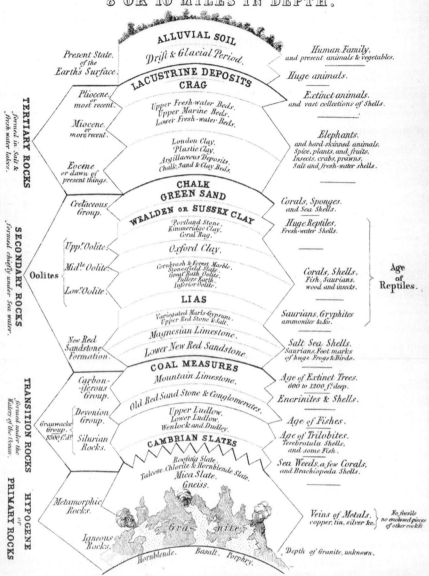

Figure 8 *Order of Rocks* in Mrs Wright, *The Globe Prepared for Man: A Guide to Geology* (1853). Engraving. 18 × 14 cm. Courtesy of the Gerstein Science Library, University of Toronto.

making the earth (at the time of Wright's publication) under 5,857 years old? The chart, using the latest scientific terms, elides such questions – these factors are dealt with intermittently but forcefully in the chapters that follow.

Anne Wright is identified as the author "Mrs. John Wright" on the title page (which also includes three biblical quotations); she was "The Author of 'The Observing Eye; or, Letters on Natural History,' 'The Passover Feasts,' Etc."

In the opening words of her preface, she lays out her purpose and the foundation for filling in the absences on her chart:

The discoveries made in Natural History by the study of GEOLOGY, excited a few years ago much alarm in the public mind, lest they should lead to statements at variance with the revealed account of the Creation.

But as the theories of imaginative minds have been made to yield to solid information, collected by the observation of excellent and learned men, this alarm has subsided. And the more the science has been pursued, upon the principle of a close investigation of facts, the more completely has it been found to harmonize with the Bible statements of the character and works of God; whilst at the same time, Geologists are free to own that it explains the cause of features in the outward works of Creation, unnoticed by the Word of Revelation, which dwells chiefly upon the moral and spiritual condition of man as he stands in connection with his Maker. (v)

The "alarm" she refers to in "the public mind" would, of course, ring much louder six years later, not just in relation to geology but to other sciences as well, with the publication of Darwin's *On the Origin of Species* (1859). Certainly by 1853 the "discoveries" of writers like Charles Lyell in *Principles of Geology* (3 vols, 1830–33) and particularly Robert Chambers in *Vestiges of Creation*, published anonymously in 1844, had indeed "excited" debate concerning the vast epochs of time needed to accommodate the antiquity of the world revealed in the fossil record, while providing "statements at variance with the revealed account of the Creation." Just eight years earlier, upon reading *Vestiges* when it came out, Adam Sedgwick, Woodwardian Professor of Geology at Cambridge from 1818 to 1873, sounded the "alarm" in a letter to Lyell: "If the book be true, the labours of sober induction are in vain; religion is a lie; human law is a mass of folly, and a base injustice; morality is moonshine; our labours for the black people of Africa were works of madmen; and man and woman are only better beasts!"(9 April 1845). Tennyson had finally finished his masterpiece *In Memoriam* (1850) only three years before Wright's book, in which he recorded this "variance" by asking "Are God and Nature then at strife, / That Nature lends such evil dreams?"

(LV). Tennyson juxtaposed the fossil evidence "From scarped cliff and quarried stone" to the understanding of humans, "Who trusted God was love indeed / And love Creation's final law" (LVI). One year after the publication of Tennyson's famous poem, John Ruskin in a letter to his friend Henry Acland would lament, "If only the Geologists would let me alone, I could do very well, but those dreadful Hammers! I hear the clink of them at the end of every cadence of the Bible verses" (24 May 1851). Such anxieties indeed call into question Wright's hopeful remark that by 1853 the "alarm" had "subsided."

The chart, then, lays out only half the story, the scientific; the preface, written by a woman whose publications included both natural history and religious topics, as well as several children's books, provides a litany of terms – "Natural History," "GEOLOGY," "variance," "revealed," "Creation," "theories of imaginative minds," "solid information," "observation," "science," "principle of close investigation of facts," "harmonize," "character and works of God," "outward works of Creation," "Word of Revelation," "moral and spiritual condition of man," and "Maker" – that were current in the attempts to negotiate, and indeed, in her case, to reconcile, the contradictions emerging between scientific evidence and the story of creation told in Genesis. The negotiation, however, was a difficult one. For instance, Wright ended every chapter like a catechism for her youthful readers, with a series of questions on the materials covered in that chapter – in none of the questions is there any mention whatsoever of the religious topics interspersed throughout every chapter of the volume. A glossary at the end of the volume has no religious expressions but is devoted exclusively to geological terms.

In answer to the questions implied by the absences in the chart Wright is explicit, as she claims repeatedly in remarks such as "After many experiments, they [geologists] have come to the conclusion, that the great Creator has been pleased to form the earth and all things that are upon it, out of a very few simple bodies, called elements" (14). The illustration of the erupting volcano in the frontispiece gives away Wright's primary means of reconciling the seeming "variance" between the developmental stages of different life forms (such as from "Sea Weeds" to "The Age of Trilobites"). Catastrophism, following George Cuvier and advocated in Britain by William Buckland (1784–1856) and Robert Jameson, posited that the earth had been subject to several sudden violent events or natural catastrophes, such as volcanic eruptions or universal floods (as in the story of Noah in Genesis 6–9), killing off existing life forms and inaugurating new ones. In this way the various levels of extinct life forms in the fossil record could be accounted for: "By many strong proofs we are therefore led to believe, that under the directing hand of God, explosions have repeatedly taken place amongst the gasses and fiery metals in the centre of the globe, which have frequently broken and tilted up the crust of the Earth" (40). Another way in which Wright accommodates the geological evidence to dominant religious beliefs of the day concerning the age of the earth is the "gap theory." It posited creation in six literal days, but with a huge time lapse at the beginning of the creation story in Genesis: "ages upon ages lie unrecorded between the end of the first verse, and the beginning of the second verse of Genesis" (10). We could go on – the point is that Wright never denies or contests the "facts" of the geological and fossil record, but she explains them using religious frameworks that were acceptable to the leading scientists of the day to negotiate, reconcile, or accommodate religion and science. As our selections in this section demonstrate, such negotiation took varied and complex forms.

The religion and science context has two sections: first, GEOLOGY AND EVOLUTION and second, RELIGIOUS FAITH AND UNCERTAINTY (WEB). They lay out the conventional intersection of the two fields in the nineteenth century. As the selections will show, the dominant move throughout this intersection between science and faith is not to reject one or the other but to reconcile the two. After the major theoretical texts on evolution by

Wallace and Darwin, a poem (KENDALL, "LAY OF THE TRILOBITE" (WEB p. 193)) written late in the century is evidence of how quickly the major aspects Darwin's position became commonplace. In fact, as early as one year after the publication of *The Descent of Man* (1871) debates on the relation of humans to the greater apes provoked satires of Darwin as a monkey and brought zoo-goers face to face with their supposed ancestors (see Figure 9).

The second section deals with ecclesiastical politics and the three parties of the Established Church; with higher criticism and attacks on the new scholarship from literalists resisting the historicity of the Bible; with devotional piety; and with a very popular form of poetry now often overlooked, hymns.

The conventions within Victorian Studies position relations between science and religion by foregrounding first geology, Genesis, and evolutionary science, with some attention paid to the reading of the biblical text following scientific principles in the higher criticism imported from Germany. Second, major developments in the nineteenth century in the fields of geology, palaeontology, and biology challenged orthodox religious beliefs about the creation of the world, the antiquity of the earth, the emergence and evolution of life forms, and the literal truths of the Bible. Hence, because religion and science chiefly engage each other over these issues, we have concentrated on them in this section. Technology as science is in every one of the other context sections: in the transportation, telecommunications, weaponry, and social Darwinism of EMPIRE; in theories of sexuality of GENDER, WOMEN, AND SEXUALITY; in print technology and developments in recording and photography of the LITERATURE AND THE ARTS; and in the industrial machinery and know-how of the CONDITION OF ENGLAND. To the Victorians, however, technology and science were closely linked, in evidence everywhere they looked. Such overlapping between science and technology is read as an important sign of the times by Lancelot Smith in Charles Kingsley's novel *Yeast* of 1851, the same year as

Figure 9 Gustave Doré (1832–83), *The Monkey House*. In Blanchard Jerrold and Gustave Doré, *London: A Pilgrimage* (1872), p. 110. Woodblock Engraving. 16 × 13 cm. Source: courtesy of The Robarts Library, University of Toronto. The viewpoint is from inside the monkey cage looking out towards the human spectators. While the monkeys are sitting relaxed in family groups, cradling their young, the humans are crowded against the enclosure, bewigged, their eyes peering through the wire enclosure, so that it looks as if they are wearing spectacles and giving them a more simian appearance than those inside the cage. The text reads: "'I always end with the monkeys,' said an illustrious *savant* to me, when we discussed the ways in which various people did the [Zoological] Gardens. . . . We were on the side of the monkeys; and we were with the majority." The phrase echoes the well-known comment attributed to Disraeli at the Oxford Diocesan Conference on 25 November 1864: "What is the question now placed before society? . . . That question is this: Is man an ape or an angel? I, my lord, I am on the side of the angels." The question had become more searching with the publication of Darwin's *The Descent of Man* in 1871. See RELIGION: GEOLOGY AND EVOLUTION; ROBINSON.

the Great Exhibition with its celebration of the manufacture of all nations. Smith is writing to his cousin, Luke, a Tractarian clergyman, rejecting his pious religion in favour of nature, secular and material progress, and the awakening of spiritual insight:

> Our ships do sail; our mills do work; our doctors do cure; our soldiers do fight.... So give me the political economist, the sanitary reformer, the engineer; and take your saints and virgins, relics and miracles. The spinning-jenny and the railroad, Cunard's liners and the electric telegraph, are to me ... signs that we are, on some points at least, in harmony with the universe; that there is a mighty spirit working among us, who ... may be the Ordering and Creating God. (p. 96)

This catalogue of technological advances is not only contemporaneous with Wright's book, but is also cited, as are the discoveries of geology by Wright, as evidence of a benevolent creator.

The readings of this section demonstrate that relations between Victorian religion and science involve much more than the conventional view of a conflict between two forms of evidence, faith and knowledge, believers and unbelievers, superstition and reason, the Book of Revelation and the Book of Nature, creation by a benevolent creator and evolution by uncaring natural laws, or the Bible and the scientific record. When considering these relations in their historical complexity, two major factors must be kept in the forefront: first, on a political level, the church controlled the institutions of knowledge but gradually lost that control over the course of the nineteenth century. Second, on an epistemological level, the major differences and controversies were not between religion and science. Rather, they lay between religious science, grounded in some form of the design argument of natural theology, and irreligious science, which, more often than not, compartmentalized the two fields. The latter claimed that there was no conflict in need of reconciliation but rather that the two fields were totally separate forms of knowledge.

Science became the authoritative discourse by the end of the nineteenth century, moving from a discipline dominated by amateurs and largely clerical gentlemen practising natural history to professional scientists employed in industry and the universities. Throughout the century there were two complementary movements: on the one side, the slow erosion of the monopoly control of the Anglican establishment over public offices, as well as political and educational institutions; and, on the other side, the slow shifts in educational policy, from a curriculum based entirely on the classics to, by the end of the century, one which was moving to be dominated by the sciences. Interest exploded early in the century, as evidenced by the number of endeavours for the promotion of science that

were founded: the British Association for the Advancement of Science (BAAS) in 1831, the Entomological Society (1833), the Geological Survey of Great Britain (1835), the Botanical Society (1836), the Microscopical Society (1839), the Pharmaceutical Society (1841), the Chemical Society (1841), the Ethnological Society (1843), and the Institution of Mechanical Engineers (1847). Many of these institutions had specialist journals, publishing their annual transactions for the general public. There were also significant institutional shifts in higher education: various university chairs were founded, such as in geology at Cambridge (1818) and Oxford (1819); the Royal College of Chemistry (1845), with the support of Prince Albert; the Honours School in Natural Sciences at Oxford (1850), and the Natural Sciences Tripos at Cambridge (1851); and Owens' College (1851), later Manchester University, specifically devoted to scientific education. The journal *Nature* (still one of the pre-eminent and most prestigious scientific journals) began publication in 1869 under the editorship of Norman Lockyer (1836–1920), an astronomer. The scientific method of these hard sciences became an imperial ideology, spilling over into the methodologies and ambitions of several social sciences, such as anthropology, ethnology, sociology, and psychology, each with its own society and journal: the Anthropological Society of London (1863), breaking away from by the Ethnological Society of London; the National Association for the Promotion of Social Science (1851); and the Psychological Association (1901). Along with this outburst of professionalization came a tremendous growth in popularizing science: The *Penny Cyclopædia of the Society for the Diffusion of Useful Knowledge* was published by Charles Knight from 1833 to 1843; Dickens's journal *Household Words* carried articles on popular science throughout its run from 1850 to 1859. The leading monthly and quarterly journals published learned articles on science – as well as on religion – and searching reviews of recent works, all by leading authorities. Mechanics Institutes promoting education for working-class men were established throughout Britain from the 1820s, promoting practical knowledge with an emphasis on scientific matters.

While this promotion and growth in science was taking place throughout Victoria's reign, the Established Church was steadily losing control of its power over the secular sphere. In 1828 the Corporation Act (1661) and the Test Act (1673) were repealed, thereby removing inhibitions against the dissenters; one year later, a similar bill gave relief to the Roman Catholics. Under the Act of Uniformity (1662), with its requirement of the swearing to the Thirty-Nine Articles, it was not possible for Catholics or Dissenters to take degrees at Oxford or Cambridge until reform in the 1850s. The separation of ecclesiastical control of knowledge was all but over by 1864, when Rowland Williams and H. B. Wilson, two clerics who had been dismissed from their university teaching positions for publishing heresy in *Essays and Reviews* (1860), won their appeal to the Privy Council when Lord Westbury's ruling, "dismissing Hell with costs," finalized the separation of the church and state in law. Nevertheless, throughout the century, certain factions of the clergy rallied against new formations of knowledge, particularly evolution and the higher criticism of the Bible.

Despite this seeming correspondence in the conflicting narratives, the rise of science and the decline of religious authority, it would be a grave mistake to conceive of the two fields as being locked in opposition. The majority of the promoters and practitioners of science, especially early in the century, were ordained clergy. The debate, except in extreme forms, was not, as stated earlier, between religion and science, but was about how to explain, reconcile, or rationalize the new discoveries in relation to faith. The fundamentals of geology and evolution were long accepted by most clergy. For instance, in 1860 at the famous meeting of the British Association, another writer in *Essays and Reviews*, Frederick Temple, gave a sermon promoting evolution; at the time he was headmaster of Rugby (1857–69), one of the prominent

public schools, where he built laboratories and promoted changes in the curriculum to encourage the study of natural science. He was promoted to bishop of Exeter in 1869, and in his eight *Bampton Lectures on the Relations between Religion and Science* (1884) he asserted that the "doctrine of Evolution is in no sense whatever antagonistic to the teachings of Religion" (p. 107). In 1896 he was appointed archbishop of Canterbury – clearly, his career path demonstrates that the mainstream and authoritative branch of the Established Church was not antagonistic to the discoveries of science.

The epistemology upon which the sciences could be accommodated to faith was grounded in many ways on the natural theology established in William Paley's *Natural Theology* (1802). Using an analogy, Paley forged a design argument: just as the complexity of a watch necessarily demanded that there be an intelligent designer, so too must the complexity found in nature be explained by an intelligent maker. The Bridgewater Treatises (1833–36) extended the design argument to a number of fields of enquiry: astronomy, physiology, physics, chemistry, biology, meteorology, and geology, all in accordance with natural theology. The will of the Right Honourable and Reverend Francis Henry Edgerton, Earl of Bridgewater (1759–1829), directed that £8,000 establish a series "On the Power, Wisdom, and Goodness of God, as manifested in the Creation," and that such works be illustrated "by all reasonable arguments, as, for instance, the variety and formation of God's creatures in the animal, vegetable, and mineral kingdoms; the effect of digestion, and thereby of conversion; the construction of the hand of man, and an infinite variety of other arguments: as also by discoveries, ancient and modern, in arts, sciences, and the whole extent of literature." In other words, natural theology allowed the discoveries of science to be an affirmation of an intelligent creator, not a challenge or denial: these are the grounds, for the most part, where the debates take place throughout Victoria's reign. Charles Lyell in *Principles of Geology*

(1830–33) concludes with the problem of measuring creation against human comprehension of time and space:

> We aspire in vain to assign limits to the works of creation in space, whether we examine the starry heavens, or that world of minute animalcules which is revealed to us by the microscope. We are prepared, therefore, to find that in time also the confines of the universe lie beyond the reach of mortal ken. But in whatever direction we pursue our researches, whether in time or space, we discover everywhere the clear proofs of a Creative Intelligence, and of His foresight, wisdom, and power.... To assume that the evidence of the beginning or end of so vast a scheme lies within the reach of our philosophical inquiries, or even of our speculations, appears to be inconsistent with a just estimate of the relations which subsist between the finite powers of man and the attributes of an Infinite and Eternal Being. (3: 384–85)

Darwin concludes the *Origin* with his famous "tangled bank" metaphor, where he asserts that the complexity in nature demonstrates "grandeur in this view of life, with its several powers, having been originally breathed into a few forms or into one" (p. 490). Even Huxley in explaining his coining of the word "agnostic" does not reject religion, but recognizes limits to what is knowable: "In matters of the intellect, follow your reason as far as it will take you, without regard to any other consideration. And negatively: In matters of the intellect, do not pretend that conclusions are certain which are not demonstrated or demonstrable" (pp. 186–87). What of religion is left after the recognition of such limits, or whether or not Huxley was being somewhat disingenuous, is debatable; nevertheless, the vast majority of scientists in the Victorian era struggled to explain their research in terms consistent with belief, just as the majority of religious thinkers strived to adapt their theology

in terms consistent with the new forms of scientific knowledge.

Until quite recently, it had been conventional to view the relationship between Victorian science and religion in terms of conflict and warfare. In her preface quoted above, Anne Wright writes rather tentatively about the geological "discoveries" that had "excited ... much alarm"; in the final paragraph of the book she sets out a reconciliation very much in line with the dominant mode of solving the problem using natural theology, in effect claiming there is really no problem:

> Thus we are able to perceive by the word of Revelation, that the Divine architect of this globe had two objects to set forth in its creation. First, the manifestation of His creative wisdom; and secondly the formation of a home for man, by whose redemption from sin and death, and preparation for a future throne of glory, is afforded unto principalities and powers in heavenly places, the grandest manifestation of His attributes of power, justice, mercy, and love. (339)

Just seven years later, reviewing Darwin's *Origin* in the *Westminster Review* (Apr. 1860), Huxley, who proudly declared himself to be Darwin's bulldog, would raise the level of excitement to a fever pitch, moving from metaphors of reconciliation to those of the battlefield:

> Extinguished theologians lie about the cradle of every science as the strangled snakes beside that of Hercules; and history records that whenever science and orthodoxy have been fairly opposed, the latter has been forced to retire from the lists, bleeding and crushed if not annihilated; scotched, if not slain. But orthodoxy is the Bourbon of the world of thought. It learns not, neither can it forget; and though, at present, bewildered and afraid to move, it is as willing as ever to insist that the first chapter of Genesis contains the beginning

and the end of sound science; and to visit, with such petty thunderbolts as its half-paralysed hands can hurl, those who refuse to degrade Nature to the level of primitive Judaism.

Such use of war metaphors, extending Wright's "alarm" to Huxley's triumphal death scene, would become the norm for characterizing relations between the two fields. John William Draper (1811–88), the American scientist who spoke directly before Wilberforce at the famous debate (see RELIGION: GEOLOGY; OXFORD DEBATE (WEB p. 182)), in *History of the Conflict between Religion and Science* (1875) sets out a history of strife between belief and knowledge from the Greeks and Romans to the present, but especially focussing on ascendancy of the Catholic Church and its treatment of Galileo. In his preface he writes of the "military fervor" of the church, of the impending "crisis" brought about by the "antagonism ... between Religion and Science" (p. vi). In this highly influential work, Draper combines the metaphors of warfare with an equally polarizing contrast between the "intellectual night" of the church and the "daybreak of better things" now dawning with the confrontation and defeat of superstition: "The history of Science is not a mere record of isolated discoveries; it is a narrative of the conflict of two contending powers, the expansive force of the human intellect on one side, and the compression arising from traditionary faith and human interests on the other." The conflict model was solidified further by another American, Andrew Dickson White (1832–1918), the first president of Cornell University, in a work whose title, *The History of the Warfare of Science with Theology in Christendom* (1895), established the dominant terms of reference. Thus, for most of the twentieth century, a narrative of good guys and bad guys, ignorance and reason, and so on, has governed the historical discussion. Twentieth-century political issues in the United States over control of education and the First Amendment to the Constitution over the separation of church and state, exemplified

in a number of court cases, for instance, in the Scopes Monkey Trial in Tennessee in 1925 on the illegality of teaching evolution, or more recently, the case in Dover, Pennsylvania in 2004 over the teaching of intelligent design, have kept the metaphors of warfare in the public eye, and have had a determinative effect on how the Victorian documents in the following section continue to be read. More recently, writers like Richard Dawkins in *The God Delusion* (2006) and Christopher Hitchens in *God Is Not Great: How Religion Poisons Everything* (2007) have extended the conflict model in the public realm promoting atheism through their popular books and their promotions on the talk-show circuit.

Since the 1990s, however, following the direction of such historians of science as John Hedley Brooke, Ronald Numbers, and Geoffrey Cantor, the field of religion and science has moved steadily away from the conflict model. In his ground-breaking study *Science and Religion: Some Historical Perspectives* (1991), Brooke rejects as too simplistic three views of historical analysis traditionally used to discuss religion and science: conflict, complementarity, and commonality. Instead, he offers an interpretive model of complexity based on historically specific circumstances and ideas and beliefs within which the texts and controversies are produced and read. For instance, in considering Huxley's outrageous extension of the war metaphor quoted above, we need to consider that he was an up-and-coming scientist outside the establishment. Most practising scientists were also clergymen, but Huxley was not a clergyman, no more was another popularizer of science, William Tyndall, and nor were they Oxford or Cambridge graduates. In order to be heard, therefore, one of their strategies was to dispense with the gentlemanly rhetoric to engage in bare-knuckle conflict. Such considerations of specific conditions – class positions, academic and church affiliations, family networks, and other allegiances – suggest Brooke's model of complexity. It is in accord with this model that we set out the following texts and annotation.

1. Geology and Evolution

WEB p. 180

Charles Lyell (1797–1875): *Principles of Geology* (1830–33)
    From Book 1, Chapter 1 (1830)
    From Book 3, Chapter 26 (1833)

Robert Chambers (1802–71): *Vestiges of the Natural History of Creation* (1844)

From Chapter 12: "General Considerations Respecting the Origin of the Animated Tribes"[1]

A candid consideration of all these circumstances can scarcely fail to introduce into our minds a somewhat different idea of organic creation from what has hitherto been generally entertained. That God created animated beings, as well as the terraqueous[2] theatre of their being, is a fact so powerfully evidenced, and so universally received, that I at once take it for granted. But in the particulars of this so highly supported idea, we surely here see cause for some re-consideration. It may now be inquired,—In what way was the creation of animated beings effected? The ordinary notion may, I think, be not unjustly described as this,—that the Almighty author produced the progenitors of all existing species by some sort of personal or immediate exertion.[3] But how does this notion comport with what we have seen of the gradual advance of species, from the humblest to the highest? How can we suppose an

Notes

Geology and Evolution

[1] *title* published anonymously as the self-proclaimed "first attempt to connect the natural sciences into a history of creation," and immediately causing a tremendous sensation, this bestseller's authorship was not revealed until the posthumous twelfth edition in 1884. In ten years the book went through ten editions, selling 24,000 copies. Chambers was a self-educated publisher, writer, and amateur naturalist who, in February 1832, began publishing *Chambers's Edinburgh Journal*, which included his articles summarizing the latest scientific developments for his middle-class readership. Although now usually read as a flawed precursor to Darwin's *Origin of Species* (1859), this book brought before a middle-class reading audience scientific concepts that challenged long-held religious notions regarding the creation of the earth and temporality. Popular among the public and the scientific community, *Vestiges* argued that "transmutation" (that is, evolution) was characteristic of the entire cosmos, including the solar system, Earth, the rocks, and all forms of life. Positing a divine author, the work concludes that some species known through the fossil record are extinct because of flaws, while the entire process as a kind of theological principle did not need special creation for each species. Tennyson eagerly read the first edition, and drew upon it heavily in *In Memoriam* to foreground an uncaring nature "red in tooth and claw" in the face of human suffering (see particularly, sects. XXXV and LV–LVI, and notes). *Vestiges* ranges from the formation of the solar system to speculations on the future of the human race, arguing a developmental hypothesis against the theological views of a special creation. The book begins by examining cosmic evolution based on the nebular hypothesis of Pierre Simon de Laplace (1749–1827), French mathematician and astronomer, who in 1796 had posited that the solar system, once a mass of gas, had cooled, resulting in the breaking off of hardened pieces which eventually became planets. Chambers then deals at length with the progressive development of plants and animals (including humans) from simple to complex forms. For progress in evolution, see n. 60. For the opposite argument, degradation from the original creation of perfect specimens, see n. 9. Chambers's time frame challenged traditional biblical interpreters from the seventeenth and eighteenth centuries, who relied on the dating of creation, including the geological record, in the year 4004 BCE, according to the chronology of James Ussher (1581–1656), Archbishop of Armagh, published in *Annales Vesti Testamenti* (Lat. The annals of the Old Testament; 1647), with his marginal dates printed in many bibles throughout the nineteenth century. *Vestiges* also had disturbing political overtones for many contemporaries: the connection of science with materialism implied a radical stance associated with the Jacobinism of the French Revolution.

[2] *terraqueous* (<Lat. both land and water).

[3] *the Almighty ... exertion* the position of the advocates of special or particular creation, or creationists (first used 1833, OED), based on a literalist reading of the creation narrative in Genesis, in which on the fifth day God creates the first animated beings, the sea creatures and birds (Genesis 1: 20–23).

immediate exertion of this creative power at one time to produce zoophytes, another time to add a few marine mollusks, another to bring in one or two conchifers, again to produce crustaceous fishes,[4] again perfect fishes, and so on to the end? This would surely be to take a very mean view of the Creative Power—to, in short, anthropomorphize[5] it, or reduce it to some such character as that borne by the ordinary proceedings of mankind. And yet this would be unavoidable; for that the organic creation was thus progressive through a long space of time, rests on evidence which nothing can overturn or gainsay. Some other idea must then be come to with regard to *the mode* in which the Divine Author proceeded in the organic creation. Let us seek in the history of the earth's formation for a new suggestion on this point. We have seen powerful evidence, that the construction of this globe and its associates, and inferentially that of all the other globes of space, was the result, not of any immediate or personal exertion on the part of the Deity, but of natural laws[6] which are expressions of his will. What is to hinder our supposing that the organic creation is also a result of natural laws, which are in like manner an expression of his will? More than this, the fact of the cosmical arrangements being an effect of natural law, is a powerful argument for the organic arrangements being so likewise, for how can we suppose that the august Being who brought all these countless worlds into form by the simple establishment of a natural principle flowing from his mind, was to interfere personally and specially on every occasion when a new shell-fish or reptile was to be ushered into existence on *one* of these worlds? Surely this idea is too ridiculous to be for a moment entertained....

To a reasonable mind the Divine attributes[7] must appear, not diminished or reduced in any way, by supposing a creation by law, but infinitely exalted. It is the narrowest of all views of the Deity, and characteristic of a humble class of intellects, to suppose him acting constantly in particular ways for particular occasions. It, for one thing, greatly detracts from his foresight, the most undeniable of all the attributes of Omnipotence. It lowers him towards the level of our own humble intellects. Much more worthy of him it surely is, to suppose that all things have been commissioned by him from the first, though neither is he absent from a particle of the current of natural affairs in one sense, seeing that the whole system is continually supported by his providence. Even in human affairs, if I may be allowed to adopt a familiar illustration, there is a constant progress from specific action for particular occasions, to arrangements which, once established, shall continue to answer for a great multitude of occasions. Such plans the enlightened readily form for themselves, and conceive as being adopted by all who have to attend to a multitude of affairs, while the ignorant suppose every act of the greatest public functionary to be the result of some special consideration and care on his part alone. Are we to suppose the Deity adopting plans which harmonize only with the modes of procedure of the less enlightened of our

Notes

[4] *zoophytes . . . mollusks . . . conchifers . . . fishes* a zoophyte is an obsolete term for a plant that produced animals as fruit in medieval bestiaries, or, in eighteenth- and nineteenth-century science, for animals that resembled plants, like sea anemones, sponges, and coral; George Johnston (1797–1855) published *A History of British Zoophytes* (1838), and in 1868 Thomas Hincks (1818–99) published *A History of British Hydroid Zoophytes* (2 vols). Molluscs are a very large class of marine invertebrate animals of very different appearances, from the largest, the giant squid, to the nautilus and sea snail. Conchifers are a very numerous set of bivalve sea animals, like the oyster, mussel, and scallop. Crustaceous fish are lobsters, crabs, shrimp, prawns, and many others. Hence Chambers alludes to the problem of particular creation for many thousands of very specialized sea creatures, only a fraction of which had been identified when he was writing.

[5] *anthropomorphize* to accommodate God's divine power in the creation of species to human standards and abilities in creative acts: hence, a faulty analogy; see n. 8.

[6] *laws* this phrase was most offensive to some religious critics of the book, who claimed that natural law denied the possibility of miracles and other forms of divine intervention. Chambers is arguing for gradual changes in the evolution of the earth according to natural laws, over long periods of time, a theory that was known as uniformitarianism. See n. 59; and TENNYSON, n. 98.

[7] *attributes* the eight Bridgewater Treatises, *On the Power, Wisdom, and Goodness of God as Manifested in the Adaptation of External Nature to the Moral and Intellectual Constitution of Man* (1833–40), one of the major sources for the analogy between nature and religion in the nineteenth century, are based on the attributes of God, namely omnipotence, omniscience, and omnibenevolence, as well as omnipresence, and general providence (sustaining the universe in existence and order).

race? Those who would object to the hypothesis of a creation by the intervention of law, do not perhaps consider how powerful an argument in favour of the existence of God is lost by rejecting this doctrine. When all is seen to be the result of law, the idea of an Almighty Author becomes irresistible, for the creation of a law for an endless series of phenomena—an act of intelligence above all else that we can conceive—could have no other imaginable source, and tells, moreover, as powerfully for a sustaining as for an originating power.[8]

Hugh Miller (1802–56): *The Foot-Prints of the Creator: or, the Asterolepis of Stromness* (1849)

From "Stromness and its Asterolepis. The Lake of Stennis"[9]

Very many ages must have passed ere, amid waves and currents, the water-worn debris which now forms the Great Conglomerate[10] could have accumulated over tracts of sea-bottom from ten to fifteen thousand square miles in area, to its present depth of from one to four hundred feet.... Myriads of fish, of forms the most ancient and obsolete,

Notes

[8] *power* the consistency and impermeability of the laws of nature, as divine laws, should, according to Chambers, demonstrate not only the power and goodness of God in creating the world (the argument of the deists of the mid-seventeenth to mid-eighteenth centuries who held that God was the author or creator of the world but remained aloof from creation thereafter) but also the continuing presence of God (omnipresence) in sustaining and extending creation. To Chambers, particular or special providence in the form of divine interference to abrogate or interfere with laws shows that the anthropomorphic analogy between human power (exercised in such efforts of particular creation and efforts to abrogate laws) and divine power is not applicable in light of the divine attributes; see n. 5.

[9] *title* a stonemason and geologist, Miller was well known for his books on geology, especially *The Old Red Sandstone; or New Walks in an Old Field* (1841), his autobiography, *My Schools and Schoolmasters* (1852), and *The Testimony of the Rocks*, published posthumously in 1857. He was a devout evangelical Christian and a member of the Free Church of Scotland (established in 1843), a break-away group from the Presbyterians under the leadership of Thomas Chalmers (1780–1847), whom Miller greatly admired. Chalmers, in *Evidences of Christianity* (1813), advocated the Great Gap theory at the opening of Genesis, positing that there was an earlier world created between the first and second verses of Genesis. Miller changed his views later in life, abandoning his earlier held Great Gap theory from Chalmers: in *The Testimony of the Rocks* (1857) Miller again made popular the idea that the biblical "days" are really tremendously long epochs or eras, a theory advanced by French naturalist Georges Buffon (1707–88). In the last phase of Miller's thinking, humankind is part of the last era (the sixth day in Genesis); he is the last stage of evolution and cannot expect to see those further developments proposed by Chambers at the end of *Vestiges*. Throughout his career, Miller's impact, then, was to foreground and popularize the notion of scriptural geology. Suffering from lung disease (silicosis) from stonemason's dust, and from depression, he committed suicide.

From 1840 Miller edited the paper of Chalmers's group, *The Witness*, in which *The Old Red Sandstone* (a study of the rock and fossil formations of the late Salurian and Devonian periods, more than 450 million years ago) was first serialized. *Foot-Prints of the Creator* (1849) was a reply to Chambers's *Vestiges* (see this section), presenting an anti-evolutionary argument for successive periods of divine creation, evidence for which Miller found in the fossil record. Using the example of part of a giant fossilized fish, a bone which he had discovered at Stromness in the Orkney Islands north of Scotland, Miller argued that it was found in the oldest Paleozoic era of geological formations, dating from the late Silurian to the Devonian period, in which the fish predominated, from about 440 to 400 million years ago. The Asterolepis (Gk. star-scale, from the star-like markings on its plates) represented a highly organized, extinct vertebrate, a fish with heavy body armour and a moveable jaw with teeth, that, according to *Vestiges*, should not have occurred in so old a formation. To Miller, this giant fish, extending to 6 metres in length, with a head larger than an elephant's skull, must have been created rather than developed in so old a geological formation. The fact that a giant form exists in a more ancient formation contradicts expected evolutionary sequence that smaller forms (in later formations) should precede larger forms. Miller follows the theories of the Swiss palaeontologist Louis Agassiz (1807–73) in *Recherches sur les poissons fossiles* (trans. *Research on Fossil Fish*, 5 vols, 1833–43), and in *Monographie des poissons fossiles du Vieux Gres Rouge, ou Systeme Devonien* (Fr. Monograph on the fossil fish of the Old Red Sandstone or Devonian System, 1844–45). On the basis of Miller's works and discoveries, Agassiz agreed to write the preface to *Foot-Prints*. Agassiz claimed that species had originally been created as perfect specimens, and rather than evolving to higher forms they had subsequently degenerated to become extinct. In agreement, Miller writes: "*Monstrosity through displacement of parts* constitutes yet another form of degradation; and this form, united, in some instances, to the other two [through defect of parts and through redundancy] we find curiously congregated on its banks or sheltered in its hollows; generation succeeded generation, millions and tens of millions perished mysteriously by sudden death: shoals after shoals were annihilated; but the productive powers of nature were strong, and the waste was kept up. But who among men shall reckon the years or centuries during which these races existed, and this muddy ocean of the remote past spread out to unknown and name-less shores around them? As in those great cities of the desert[11] that lie uninhabited and waste, we can but conjecture the terms of their existence from the vast extent of their cemeteries. We only know that the dark, finely-grained schists in which they so abun-dantly occur must have been of comparatively slow formation, and that yet the thickness of the deposit more than equals the height of our loftiest Scottish mountains. It would seem as if a period equal to that in which all human history is comprised might be cut out of a corner of a period represented by the Old Red Sandstone, and be scarce missed when away; for every year during which man has lived upon earth, it is not improbable that the Pterichthys[12] and its contemporaries may have lived a century. . . .

I traced the formation upward this evening along the edges of the upturned strata . . . and, imbedded in a grayish-coloured layer of hard flag, somewhat less than a hundred yards over the granite . . . I found what I sought,—a well-marked bone,—in all probability the oldest vertebrate remain yet discovered in Orkney. . . .

This nail-like bone formed a characteristic portion of the *Asterolepis*,—so far as is yet known, the most gigantic ganoid[13] of the Old Red Sandstone, and, judging from the *place* of this fragment, apparently one of the first.

Philip Henry Gosse (1810–88): *Omphalos: An Attempt to Untie the Geological Knot* (1857)

From Chapter 12: "The Conclusion"[14]

It is not necessary,—at least it does not seem so to me,—that all the members of this mighty commonwealth should have an actual, a diachronic existence; any more than that, in the creation of a man, his fœtal, infantile, and adolescent stages should have an actual,

Notes

exemplified in the geological history of the fish. . . . And it is, I am convinced, from a survey of the progress of degra-dation in the great ichthyic [fish, ancient and fossil fish] division,—a progress recorded, as 'with a pen of iron, in the rock for ever,' [Job 19: 24]—and not from superficial views founded on the cartilaginous or non-cartilaginous texture of the ichthyc skeleton, that the standing of the kingly fishes of the earlier period is to be adequately determined" (*Foot-Prints* (pp. 158–59)). Hence the gradual progressive evolution argued in *Vestiges*, that evolutionary transformation as found in fossils can occur without divine intervention, is called into question by Miller. For progress in evolution, see nn. 1, 8, and 60. The title of the first (unnumbered) chapter refers to Lake Stennis, a loch five kilometres north-east of Stromness near Hoy, one of the Orkney Islands, north of Scotland.

10 *Conglomerate* Old Red Sandstone outcrops covering a large area in the north-east of Scotland.

11 *desert* probably Palmyra, a vast archaeological site dating from the second millennium BCE and extensively rebuilt in the Hellenic and Roman periods, in the Syrian desert north of Damascus; a large number of funerary monuments are outside the ancient walls in the Valley of the Tombs.

12 *Sandstone . . . Pterichthys* for Miller's book, *Old Red Sandstone*, see n. 9. The Pterichthys is a genus of fossil fish with a heavily armoured body of the class of antiarch pla-coderms, a group that included the Asterolepis. They pos-sessed a backbone, jaws with grinding plates instead of teeth, a heavily-armoured, plated head and body, and two appendages perhaps used as claws for crawling or swim-ming located where fins are found in other kinds of fish. It was found in Old Red Sandstone in Scotland and dates from the Devonian period (see n. 9).

13 *ganoid* a fossil fish with plate-like scales.

14 *title* a member of the Plymouth Brethren, an evangelical sect, Gosse combined a belief in the inerrancy of scripture with the interests of a naturalist. He was one of the pre-eminent descriptive naturalists of the nineteenth century, perhaps the leading marine zoologist, and the author of at least forty-two books on natural science, both popular (like *The Aquarium—An Unveiling of the Wonders of the Deep Sea*, 1854 and *Evenings at the Microscope*, 1859) and technical (like *Actinologia Britannica—A History of the British Sea-Anemones and Corals*, 1860). This, his most famous (or infa-mous) book, was published in October 1857. The title *Omphalos* (Gk. navel) refers to the underlying question

diachronic existence, though these are essential to his normal life-history. Nor would their diachronism be more certainly inferrible from the physical traces of them, in the one case than in the other. In the newly-created Man, the proofs of successive processes requiring time, in the skin, hairs, nails, bones, &c. could in no respect be distinguished from the like proofs in a Man of to-day; yet the developments to which they respectively testify are widely different from each other, so far as regards the element of time. Who will say that the suggestion, *that the strata of the surface of the earth, with their fossil floras and faunas, may possibly belong to a prochronic development of the mighty plan of the life-history of this world,—* who will dare to say that such a suggestion is a self-evident absurdity? If we had no example of such a procedure, we might be justified in dealing cavalierly with the hypothesis; but it has been shown that, without a solitary exception, the whole of the vast vegetable and animal kingdoms were created,—mark! I do not say *may* have been, but MUST have been created—on this principle of a prochronic development, with distinctly traceable records. It was *the law of organic creation.*

It may be objected, that, to assume the world to have been created with fossil skeletons in its crust,—skeletons of animals that never really existed,—is to charge the Creator with forming objects whose sole purpose was to deceive us. The reply is obvious. Were the concentric timber-rings of a created tree formed merely to deceive? Were the growth lines of a created shell intended to deceive? Was the navel of the created Man intended to deceive him into the persuasion that he had had a parent?[15]

These peculiarities of structure were inseparable from the adult stage of these creatures respectively, without which they would not have been what they were. . . . The Man would not have been a Man without a navel. . . .

Admit for a moment, as a hypothesis, that the Creator had before his mind a projection of the whole life-history of the globe, commencing with any point which the geologist may imagine to have been a fit commencing point, and ending with some unimaginable acme in the indefinitely distant future. He determines to call this idea into actual existence, not at the supposed commencing point, but at some stage or other of its course. It is clear, then, that at the selected stage it appears, exactly as it would have appeared at that

Notes

of the book, "Did the biblical Adam have a navel?" Sir Thomas Browne (1605–82), English physician and author, had argued against Adam's having a navel in *Pseudodoxia Epidemica, or Enquiries into Common and Vulgar Errors* (1646–72). In the chapter "Of the Picture of *Adam* and *Eve* with Navels," Browne argues that navels are wrongly depicted in paintings by Raphael, Michelangelo, and others, but if indeed Adam and Eve had navels at creation, "the Creator affected superfluities, or ordained parts without use or office. . . . Now the Navell being a part, not precedent, but subsequent unto generation, nativity or parturition, it cannot be well imagined at the creation or extraordinary formation of *Adam*, who immediately issued from the Artifice of God; nor also that of *Eve*, who was not solemnly begotten, but suddenly framed, and anomalously proceeded from *Adam*" (bk 3, ch. 5). Gosse turns this argument on its head, arguing that Adam indeed had a navel when he was created whole, complete, and mature; similarly the earth comes into existence with its fossil record already implanted by a process Gosse calls prochronism, time already prepared for future development as though built upon a past that never existed (except in the mind of God), effects, as Gosse says, without a cause: "Perhaps it may help to clear my argument if I divide the past developments of organic

life, which are necessarily, or at least legitimately, inferrible from present phenomena, into two categories, separated by the violent act of creation. Those unreal developments whose apparent results are seen in the organism at the moment of its creation, I will call prochronic, because time was not an element in them; while those which have subsisted since creation, and which have had actual existence, I will distinguish as diachronic, as occurring during time."

To "untie the geological knot" in the book's subtitle is to solve an ancient unsolvable problem by a radical and ingenious move. Anticipating a large sale for a book that countered the geological reconcilers, Gosse ordered a print-run of 4,000 copies (the first edition of Darwin's *Origin* was 1,250). After polite first notices, the book sold poorly to negative reviews, and the remainder was pulped. After this series of attacks, Gosse defended his book with a supplement, *Geology and God: Which?* (1866), chiefly against the criticism that his book was based on a divine lie (Lat. *Deus quidam deceptor.* God who is sometimes a deceiver), a charge brought against him by his friend Charles Kingsley who refused to review the book because it would promote doubt.

[15] *parent* in a long footnote Gosse quotes from and refutes John Harris's *Pre-Adamite Earth* (1848), a treatise in support of the great gap theory (see n. 1).

moment of its history, if all the preceding eras of its history had been real. Just as the new-created Man was, at the first moment of his existence, a man of twenty, or five-and-twenty, or thirty years old; physically, palpably, visibly, so old, though not really, not diachronically. He appeared precisely what he would have appeared had he lived so many years.

Let us suppose that this present year 1857 had been the particular epoch in the projected life-history of the world, which the Creator selected as the era of its actual beginning. At his fiat it appears; but in what condition? Its actual condition at this moment:—whatever is now existent would appear, precisely as it does appear. There would be cities filled with swarms of men; there would be houses half-built; castles fallen into ruins; pictures on art-ists' easels just sketched in; wardrobes filled with half-worn garments; ships sailing over the sea; marks of birds' footsteps on the mud; skeletons whitening the desert sands; human bodies in every stage of decay in the burial-grounds. These and millions of other traces of the past would be found, *because they are found in the world now*; they belong to the present age of the world; and if it had pleased God to call into existence this globe at *this* epoch of its life-history, the whole of which lay like a map before his infinite mind, it would certainly have presented all these phenomena; not to puzzle the philosopher, but because they are inseparable from the condition of the world at the selected moment of irruption into its history; because they constitute its condition; they make it what it is.

Alfred Russel Wallace (1823–1913): From "On the Tendency of Varieties to Depart Indefinitely from the Original Type" in *Journal of the Proceedings of the Linnean Society. Zoology* (20 Aug. 1858)[16]

One of the strongest arguments which have been adduced to prove the original and permanent distinctness of species is, that *varieties* produced in a state of domesticity are more or less unstable, and often have a tendency, if left to themselves, to return to the normal

Notes

[16] *title* in September, 1855 Wallace had published "On the Law which has Regulated the Introduction of New Species" in the *Annals and Magazine of Natural History*, arguing that closely related species are found in geographical proximity and in the same geological period because one is descended from the other: "Every species has come into existence coincident both in space and time with a pre-existing closely allied species" (p. 186). His argument was based on his mapping of the geography and environment of the monkeys of the Amazon; Lyell read this paper and, forced to consider abandoning his belief in the immutability of species, alerted Darwin. However, Darwin did not follow up on Lyell's suggestion, although he began to correspond with Wallace and pressed on with his work on the *Origin*. Early in 1858 Wallace wrote this paper, "On the Tendency of Varieties," and sent it to Darwin, who received it on 18 June. Darwin immediately wrote to Lyell that he had now been "forestalled," claiming that if Wallace had seen his pencil sketch of 1842 (see DARWIN, n. 18), "he could not have made a better short abstract!"; furthermore, Darwin claimed that if he did not hurry *Origin* to publication, his own "originality ... will be smashed." Darwin sought Hooker's advice, had a medical relapse, and suffered through the final sickness and the death on 28 June from scarlet fever of his tenth and last child, Charles Waring Darwin. Hooker and Lyell persuaded the Linnean Society to hear, on 1 July 1858, a joint paper by Darwin and Wallace, both absent – Darwin burying his 18-month-old baby and Wallace in Borneo. The first part of the presentation was Hooker and Lyell's letter explaining how each naturalist "conceived the same very ingenious theory to account for the appearance and perpetuation of varieties and of specific forms"; second, extracts from Darwin's "Essay" of 1844; third, an abstract of Darwin's letter to Asa Gray of 5 September 1857; and finally, Wallace's paper. The documents were all printed in the *Proceedings of the Linnean Society* (20 Aug. 1858). Wallace's essay was published with the following subheadings (removed from our text): "Instability of Varieties supposed to prove the permanent distinctness of Species"; "The Struggle for Existence"; "The Law of Population of Species"; "The Abundance or Rarity of a Species dependent upon its more or less perfect Adaptation to the Conditions of Existence"; "Useful Variations will tend to Increase; useless or hurtful Variations to Diminish"; "Superior Varieties will ultimately Extirpate the original Species"; "The Partial Reversion of Domesticated Varieties explained"; "Lamarck's Hypothesis very different from that now advanced"; and "Conclusion."

form of the parent species; and this instability is considered to be a distinctive peculiarity of all varieties, even of those occurring among wild animals in a state of nature, and to constitute a provision for preserving unchanged the originally created distinct species.

In the absence of scarcity of facts and observations as to *varieties* occurring among wild animals, this argument has had great weight with naturalists, and has led to a very general and somewhat prejudiced belief in the stability of species. Equally general, however, is the belief in what are called "permanent or true varieties,"[17]—races of animals which continually propagate their like, but which differ so slightly (although constantly) from some other race, that the one is considered to be a *variety* of the other. Which is the *variety* and which the original *species*, there is generally no means of determining, except in those rare cases in which the one race has been known to produce an offspring unlike itself and resembling the other. This, however, would seem quite incompatible with the "permanent invariability of species,"[18] but the difficulty is overcome by assuming that such varieties have strict limits, and can never again vary further from the original type, although they may return to it, which, from the analogy of the domesticated animals, is considered to be highly probable, if not certainly proved.

It will be observed that this argument rests entirely on the assumption, that *varieties* occurring in a state of nature are in all respects analogous to or even identical with those of domestic animals,[19] and are governed by the same laws as regards their permanence or further variation. But it is the object of the present paper to show that this assumption is altogether false, that there is a general principle in nature which will cause many *varieties* to survive the parent species, and to give rise to successive variations departing further and further from the original type, and which also produces, in domesticated animals, the tendency of varieties to return to the parent form.[20]

The life of wild animals is a struggle for existence. The full exertion of all their faculties and all their energies is required to preserve their own existence and provide for that of their infant offspring. The possibility of procuring food during the least favourable seasons, and of escaping the attacks of their most dangerous enemies, are the primary conditions which determine the existence both of individuals and of entire species. These conditions will also determine the population of a species; and by a careful consideration of all the circumstances we may be enabled to comprehend, and in some degree to explain, what at first sight appears so inexplicable—the excessive abundance of some species, while others closely allied to them are very rare....

Why, as a general rule, are aquatic, and especially sea birds, very numerous in individuals? Not because they are more prolific than others, generally the contrary; but because their food never fails, the sea-shores and river-banks daily swarming with a fresh supply of small mollusca and crustacea. Exactly the same laws will apply to mammals. Wild cats are prolific and have few enemies; why then are they never as abundant as rabbits? The only

Notes

[17] *varieties* see Carl Linnaeus, *Somnus Plantarum* (Lat. sleep of plants, 1755), which argues that hybrid plants are common among plant breeders, and "if not admitted as new species, are at least permanent varieties."

[18] *species* see Carl Linnaeus, *Systema Naturae* (Lat. the system of nature, 1725): "The invariability of species is the condition for order [in nature]."

[19] *animals* on the analogy between domestic and wild animals, see n. 55.

[20] *form* Wallace's argument on the analogy between domesticated and wild animals, and the tendency of hybrid varieties to return to the type of the ancestor, is related to one of the fundamental differences between Wallace and Darwin.

While Wallace stressed the struggle for existence as the pressure on varieties and species to adapt to their changing environment, Darwin stressed the competition between individuals of the same species to survive in the struggle for food and to reproduce in the struggle for breeding partners. To Wallace, the variations in domesticated animals and birds follow the same laws that apply to animals in the wild, except that domestic animals are not subject to a true or valid struggle for existence but are protected from vicissitudes in food supply, predation, and environmental liabilities; when those conditions are removed, they revert to type rather than diverge from it. See also n. 53.

intelligible answer is, that their supply of food is more precarious. It appears evident, therefore, that so long as a country remains physically unchanged, the numbers of its animal population cannot materially increase. If one species does so, some others requiring the same kind of food must diminish in proportion. The numbers that die annually must be immense; and as the individual existence of each animal depends upon itself, those that die must be the weakest—the very young, the aged, and the diseased,—while those that prolong their existence can only be the most perfect in health and vigour—those who are best able to obtain food regularly, and avoid their numerous enemies. It is, as we commenced by remarking, "a struggle for existence," in which the weakest and least perfectly organized must always succumb.[21] ...

Most or perhaps all the variations from the typical form of a species must have some definite effect, however slight, on the habits or capacities of the individuals. Even a change of colour might, by rendering them more or less distinguishable, affect their safety; a greater or less development of hair might modify their habits. More important changes, such as an increase in the power or dimensions of the limbs or any of the external organs, would more or less affect their mode of procuring food or the range of country which they inhabit. It is also evident that most changes would affect, either favourably or adversely, the powers of prolonging existence. An antelope with shorter or weaker legs must necessarily suffer more from the attacks of the feline carnivora; the passenger pigeon with less powerful wings would sooner or later be affected in its powers of procuring a regular supply of food; and in both cases the result must necessarily be a diminution of the population of the modified species. If, on the other hand, any species should produce a variety having slightly increased powers of preserving existence, that variety must inevitably in time acquire a superiority in numbers. These results must follow as surely as old age, intemperance, or scarcity of food produce an increased mortality. In both cases there may be many individual exceptions; but on the average the rule will invariably be found to hold good. All varieties will therefore fall into two classes—those which under the same conditions would never reach the population of the parent species, and those which would in time obtain and keep a numerical superiority. Now, let some alteration of physical conditions occur in the district—a long period of drought, a destruction of vegetation by locusts, the irruption of some new carnivorous animal seeking "pastures new"[22]—any change in fact tending to render existence more difficult to the species in question, and tasking its utmost powers to avoid complete extermination; it is evident that, of all the individuals composing the species, those forming the least numerous and most feebly organized variety would suffer first, and, were the pressure severe, must soon become extinct. The same causes continuing in action, the parent species would next suffer, would gradually diminish in numbers, and with a recurrence of similar unfavourable conditions might also become extinct. The superior variety would then alone remain, and on a return to favourable circumstances would rapidly increase in numbers and occupy the place of the extinct species and variety. ...

Notes

[21] *succumb* according to his autobiography, *My Life* (1905), Wallace was suffering from malarial fever in February 1858 when he suddenly recalled having read Malthus's *Essay on Population* (1798) twelve years earlier (1846) and applied Malthus to his own views of the struggle for existence. The checks to increase in human population that Malthus identified – war, disease, accidents, and famine – also apply to the animal realm: "Why do some die and some live? And the answer was clearly, that on the whole the best fitted live. From the effects of disease the most healthy escaped, the strongest, the swiftest or the most cunning.... Then it suddenly flashed upon me that this self-acting process would necessarily *improve the race*, because in every generation the inferior would inevitably be killed off and the superior would remain – that is, *the fittest would survive*" (1: 361). Wallace's discussion in *My Life* goes on at some length through the various parts of the animal kingdom illustrating the effects of deprivations in the food supply, the predations of enemies, and the severities of the natural environment. For Darwin's similar revelation on reading Malthus twenty years earlier, see DARWIN, n. 17; and see also n. 35.

[22] *new* see the final words of Milton's "Lycidas" (1637).

We believe we have now shown that there is a tendency in nature to the continued progression of certain classes of *varieties* further and further from the original type—a progression to which there appears no reason to assign any definite limits—and that the same principle which produces this result in a state of nature will also explain why domestic varieties have a tendency to revert to the original type. This progression, by minute steps, in various directions, but always checked and balanced by the necessary conditions, subject to which alone existence can be preserved, may, it is believed, be followed out so as to agree with all the phenomena presented by organized beings, their extinction and succession in past ages, and all the extraordinary modifications of form, instinct, and habits which they exhibit.[23]

Charles Darwin (1809–82): *On the Origin of Species by Means of Natural Selection, or The Preservation of Favoured Races in the Struggle for Life* (1859)[24]

From "Introduction"

When on board H.M.S. "Beagle,"[25] as naturalist, I was much struck with certain facts[26] in the distribution of the inhabitants of South America, and in the geological relations of the present to the past inhabitants of that continent. These facts seemed to me to throw some light on the origin of species—that mystery of mysteries, as it has been called by one of our greatest philosophers.[27] ...

My work is now nearly finished; but as it will take me two or three more years to complete it, and as my health is far from strong, I have been urged to publish this Abstract. I have more especially been induced to do this, as Mr. Wallace,[28] who is now studying the natural history of the Malay archipelago, has arrived at almost exactly the same general conclusions that I have on the origin of species. Last year he sent to me a memoir on this

Notes

[23] *exhibit* Wallace's stress on different variants underlies another difference from Darwin. In Darwin, natural selection involves the struggle for existence between individual variants within the same population. In Wallace, however, new varieties adapt to changing environmental conditions over long periods of time, gradually differing from their ancestors, and such variations occur not only among individuals in a species, but in allied species as well as in a single species.

[24] *title* the first edition of 1,250 copies was published on 26 November 1859 and sold out on the day of publication. A month later, on 26 December, a second edition of 3,000 copies was printed, with the date 1860. When the sixth edition was published (dropping the "*On*" from the title) on 19 February 1872, some 12,750 copies were in circulation. For the third edition Darwin added "An Historical Sketch ... of Opinion on the Origin of Species," moving some material from the introduction there. Opposite the title page, Darwin printed a quotation from William Whewell's *Bridgewater Treatise*: (1833): "But with regard to the material world, we can at least go so far as this—we can perceive that events are brought about not by insulated interpositions of Divine power, exerted in each particular case [that is, special creation], but by the establishment of general

laws." A second quotation mentioned the theory of the two books from Bacon's *Advancement of Learning* (1605): "To conclude, therefore, let no man out of a weak conceit of sobriety, or an ill-applied moderation, think or maintain, that a man can search too far or be too well studied in the book of God's word, or the book of God's works; divinity or philosophy; but rather let men endeavour an endless progress or proficience in both." For the two-book theory, see TENNYSON, n. 307; and BEVINGTON, nn. 1 and 2.

[25] *Beagle* on its second voyage to South America (1831–36) under the command of Robert FitzRoy (1805–65). See DARWIN, nn. 2 and 8–11.

[26] *facts* this word recurs throughout the first paragraph of the introduction, stressing Darwin's empiricism, based here on his study of the relations between the fossils he had found in South America.

[27] *philosophers* Sir John Herschel (1792–1871), English astronomer, had so referred to the problem of the origin of species in a letter to Charles Lyell (see n. 29) in 1836. Darwin was struck with his discovery of fossils of large extinct mammals and two different species of rhea, large flightless birds, that coexisted in overlapping areas of Patagonia, raising questions about special creation.

[28] *Wallace* see, n. 16.

subject, with a request that I would forward it to Sir Charles Lyell,[29] who sent it to the Linnean Society,[30] and it is published in the third volume of the Journal of that Society. Sir C. Lyell and Dr. Hooker,[31] who both knew of my work—the latter having read my sketch of 1844—honoured me by thinking it advisable to publish, with Mr. Wallace's excellent memoir, some brief extracts from my manuscripts.

This Abstract,[32] which I now publish, must necessarily be imperfect. I cannot here give references and authorities for my several statements; and I must trust to the reader reposing some confidence in my accuracy. No doubt errors will have crept in, though I hope I have always been cautious in trusting to good authorities alone. I can here give only the general conclusions at which I have arrived, with a few facts in illustration, but which, I hope, in most cases will suffice....

The author[33] of the "Vestiges of Creation" would, I presume, say that, after a certain unknown number of generations, some bird had given birth to a woodpecker, and some plant to the misseltoe, and that these had been produced perfect as we now see them; but this assumption seems to me to be no explanation, for it leaves the case of the coadaptations of organic beings to each other and to their physical conditions of life, untouched and unexplained.

It is, therefore, of the highest importance to gain a clear insight into the means of modification and coadaptation. At the commencement of my observations it seemed to me probable that a careful study of domesticated animals and of cultivated plants would offer the best chance of making out this obscure problem. Nor have I been disappointed; in this and in all other perplexing cases I have invariably found that our knowledge, imperfect though it be, of variation under domestication, afforded the best and safest clue. I may venture to express my conviction of the high value of such studies, although they have been very commonly neglected by naturalists.

From these considerations, I shall devote the first chapter[34] of this Abstract to Variation under Domestication. We shall thus see that a large amount of hereditary modification is at least possible; and, what is equally or more important, we shall see how great is the power of man in accumulating by his Selection successive slight variations. I will then pass on to the variability of species in a state of nature; but I shall, unfortunately, be

Notes

[29] *Lyell* Charles Lyell (1797–1875), Scottish geologist, had become joint secretary of the Geological Society in 1823. He published *Principles of Geology* (3 vols, 1830–33; see RELIGION: GEOLOGY (WEB p. 180)) and was a friend of Darwin.

[30] *society* the Linnean Society founded in London in 1788, named after the Swedish naturalist, Carl Linnaeus (1707–78), who established the classification and naming of organisms. Darwin, Lyell, and Hooker were all members of the society's council.

[31] *Hooker* Joseph Dalton Hooker (1817–1911), British botanist, explored Antarctica (1839–43) and during the voyage read the proofs of Darwin's *Voyage of the Beagle*, given to him by Lyell. After Hooker's return, Darwin and he met and remained friends and colleagues for life. From 1844 Hooker was introduced to Darwin's views on evolution, and especially natural selection, and in 1847 he read and commented on Darwin's "Essay" outlining his theories (see n. 16; and DARWIN, n. 18).

[32] *Abstract* that is, *The Origin of Species*. After the papers by him and Wallace were read at the Linnean Society on 1 July 1858, Darwin had to revise or "abstract" what he had already written, omitting references and further supporting

information. He completed the remaining three and a half chapters in some haste for publication in 1859, and hence he referred to his completed work as an "abstract." For how Wallace's paper forced Darwin to compose and publish *Origin*, see n. 16; and DARWIN, n. 18.

[33] *author* for *Vestiges* and Darwin's initial reaction to it, see n. 1; In January 1845, Darwin, who had carefully read the work, commented that "his geology strikes me as bad, and his zoology far worse." By 1859 Darwin already suspected that the author of *Vestiges* was Chambers. Chambers would publish (still anonymously) an eleventh edition in December 1860, claiming that he and Darwin were arguing for the same thing. In this paragraph Darwin objects to Chambers's theory of transmutation by saltationism (Lat. *saltus*, leap, jump) – sudden, unexplained transformation from one species to another, or from an ancestral species to a quite different species, instead of Darwin's version – gradualism, the accumulation of small changes and adaptations. Darwin omitted this paragraph from "Introduction" in the third (March 1861) and subsequent editions.

[34] *chapter* Darwin gives a chapter-by-chapter outline of the entire volume in this and the following paragraphs.

compelled to treat this subject far too briefly, as it can be treated properly only by giving long catalogues of facts. We shall, however, be enabled to discuss what circumstances are most favourable to variation. In the next chapter the Struggle for Existence amongst all organic beings throughout the world, which inevitably follows from their high geometrical powers of increase, will be treated of. This is the doctrine of Malthus,[35] applied to the whole animal and vegetable kingdoms. As many more individuals of each species are born than can possibly survive; and as, consequently, there is a frequently recurring struggle for existence, it follows that any being, if it vary however slightly in any manner profitable to itself, under the complex and sometimes varying conditions of life, will have a better chance of surviving, and thus be *naturally selected*. From the strong principle of inheritance, any selected variety will tend to propagate its new and modified form. . . .

No one ought to feel surprise at much remaining as yet unexplained in regard to the origin of species and varieties, if he makes due allowance for our profound ignorance in regard to the mutual relations of all the beings which live around us. Who can explain why one species ranges widely and is very numerous, and why another allied species has a narrow range and is rare? Yet these relations are of the highest importance, for they determine the present welfare, and, as I believe, the future success and modification of every inhabitant of this world. Still less do we know of the mutual relations of the innumerable inhabitants of the world during the many past geological epochs in its history. Although much remains obscure, and will long remain obscure, I can entertain no doubt, after the most deliberate study and dispassionate judgement of which I am capable, that the view which most naturalists entertain, and which I formerly entertained—namely, that each species has been independently created—is erroneous. I am fully convinced that species are not immutable;[36] but that those belonging to what are called the same genera are lineal descendants of some other and generally extinct species, in the same manner as the acknowledged varieties of any one species are the descendants of that species. Furthermore, I am convinced that Natural Selection has been the main but not exclusive means of modification.

Notes

[35] *Malthus* the *Essay on the Principle of Population* (1798) by Thomas Robert Malthus (1766–1834), English divine and political economist, argued that the increase of population would involve a struggle for the necessities of life because the production of food would not keep pace with the demands, so that cycles of famine and disease would check population growth – all a refutation of the concept of increasing prosperity or meliorism. For Darwin's own account of discovering Malthus, see DARWIN, n. 17; for a similar revelatory reading of Malthus, see n. 21.

[36] *immutable* in these two sentences Darwin denies the fixity and constancy of species by arguing that species are changing or evolving; above all, he is seen to be denying the special creation of species by a divine power, thereby also denying the literal truth of the opening two chapters of Genesis. This view challenged the conventional biblical literalism that dominated the religious institutions and denominations in Britain. For instance, in 1864 nearly 11,000 clergymen would sign a "Declaration on the

Inspiration of the Word of God, and the Eternity of Future Punishment, by Clergymen of the United Church of England and Ireland," or the Oxford Declaration of the Clergy (1864), in protest against the acquittal of two of the writers of *Essays and Reviews:* "We, the undersigned Presbyters and Deacons in Holy Orders of the Church of England and Ireland, hold it to be our bounden duty to the Church and to the souls of men, to declare our firm belief that the Church of England and Ireland, in common with the whole Catholic Church, maintains without reserve or qualification the Inspiration and Divine Authority of the whole Canonical Scriptures as not only containing but being the Word of God; and further teaches, in the words of our Blessed Lord, that the 'punishment' of the 'cursed,' equally with the 'life' of the 'righteous,' is "everlasting." For biblical literalism, see this section, GEOLOGY: MILLER and GEOLOGY: GOSSE; see also RELIGION: RELIGIOUS; BURGON (WEB p. 210) and RELIGION: GEOLOGY; KINNS (WEB p. 191).

From Chapter 3: "Struggle for Existence"[37]

Hence, also, we can see that when a plant or animal is placed in a new country amongst new competitors, though the climate may be exactly the same as in its former home, yet the conditions of its life will generally be changed in an essential manner. If we wished to increase its average numbers in its new home, we should have to modify it in a different way to what we should have done in its native country; for we should have to give it some advantage over a different set of competitors or enemies.

It is good thus to try in our imagination to give any form some advantage over another. Probably in no single instance should we know what to do, so as to succeed. It will convince us of our ignorance on the mutual relations of all organic beings; a conviction as necessary, as it seems to be difficult to acquire. All that we can do, is to keep steadily in mind that each organic being is striving to increase at a geometrical ratio;[38] that each at some period of its life, during some season of the year, during each generation or at intervals, has to struggle for life, and to suffer great destruction. When we reflect on this struggle, we may console ourselves with the full belief, that the war of nature is not incessant, that no fear is felt, that death is generally prompt, and that the vigorous, the healthy, and the happy survive and multiply.[39]

From Chapter 4: "Natural Selection"[40]

Let it be borne in mind in what an endless number of strange peculiarities our domestic productions,[41] and, in a lesser degree, those under nature, vary; and how strong the hereditary tendency is. Under domestication, it may be truly said that the whole organisation becomes in some degree plastic. Let it be borne in mind how infinitely complex and close-fitting are the mutual relations of all organic beings to each other and to their physical conditions of life. Can it, then, be thought improbable, seeing that variations useful to man have undoubtedly occurred, that other variations useful in some way to each being in the great and complex battle of life, should sometimes occur in the course of thousands of generations? If such do occur, can we doubt (remembering that many more individuals are born than can possibly survive) that individuals having any advantage, however slight, over others, would have the best chance of surviving and of procreating their kind? On the other hand, we may feel sure that any variation in the least degree injurious would be rigidly destroyed. This preservation of favourable variations and the rejection of injurious variations, I call Natural Selection. Variations neither useful nor injurious would not be affected by natural selection, and would be left a fluctuating element, as perhaps we see in the species called polymorphic.[42]

Notes

[37] *title* in this chapter Darwin presents a view of nature opposed to that prevalent among natural scientists, religious leaders, and the general public, who by and large accepted the presuppositions of natural theology concerning the natural order, in which the harmonious and balanced processes of the reproduction and death are part of the benevolent plan of a divine creator. Instead Darwin argues that competition for life is a "struggle for existence" (in Malthus's phrase) in which warfare is the condition and either success or death and extinction are the results. In this conclusion to chapter 3, however, Darwin holds out a faint hope of consolation.

[38] *ratio* the core of Malthus's argument in *Essay on Population* is "population, when unchecked, increases in a geometrical ratio. Subsistence increases only in an arithmetical ratio. A slight acquaintance with numbers will shew the

immensity of the first power to the second." For Malthus, see n. 35; see also DARWIN, n. 17.

[39] *multiply* to consolidate his rhetorical appeal, Darwin echoes Genesis 1: 22.

[40] *title* two aspects of Darwin's theory of natural selection are discussed in this chapter: the struggle for existence (chapter 3), and the prevalence of variations that can be inherited.

[41] *productions* Darwin's first chapter "Variation under Domestication" dealt with relationships among domesticated plants (such as kinds of roses, orchids, or dahlias) and animals (such as kinds of dogs, sheep, or cattle) that are genealogical, as opposed to descent from different wild ancestors.

[42] *polymorphic* variant forms within the same species, as in the varieties of finches that Darwin found in the Galapagos Islands. Darwin discusses polymorphic variation under different conditions in nature in chapter 3.

We shall best understand the probable course of natural selection by taking the case of a country undergoing some physical change, for instance, of climate. The proportional numbers of its inhabitants would almost immediately undergo a change, and some species might become extinct. We may conclude, from what we have seen of the intimate and complex manner in which the inhabitants of each country are bound together, that any change in the numerical proportions of some of the inhabitants, independently of the change of climate itself, would most seriously affect many of the others. If the country were open on its borders, new forms would certainly immigrate, and this also would seriously disturb the relations of some of the former inhabitants. Let it be remembered how powerful the influence of a single introduced tree or mammal has been shown to be. But in the case of an island, or of a country partly surrounded by barriers, into which new and better adapted forms could not freely enter, we should then have places in the economy of nature which would assuredly be better filled up, if some of the original inhabitants were in some manner modified; for, had the area been open to immigration, these same places would have been seized on by intruders. In such case, every slight modification, which in the course of ages chanced to arise, and which in any way favoured the individuals of any of the species, by better adapting them to their altered conditions, would tend to be preserved; and natural selection would thus have free scope for the work of improvement.

We have reason to believe, as stated in the first chapter, that a change in the conditions of life, by specially acting on the reproductive system, causes or increases variability; and in the foregoing case the conditions of life are supposed to have undergone a change, and this would manifestly be favourable to natural selection, by giving a better chance of profitable variations occurring; and unless profitable variations do occur, natural selection can do nothing. Not that, as I believe, any extreme amount of variability is necessary; as man can certainly produce great results by adding up in any given direction mere individual differences, so could Nature, but far more easily, from having incomparably longer time at her disposal. Nor do I believe that any great physical change, as of climate, or any unusual degree of isolation to check immigration, is actually necessary to produce new and unoccupied places for natural selection to fill up by modifying and improving some of the varying inhabitants. For as all the inhabitants of each country are struggling together with nicely balanced forces, extremely slight modifications in the structure or habits of one inhabitant would often give it an advantage over others; and still further modifications of the same kind would often still further increase the advantage. No country can be named in which all the native inhabitants are now so perfectly adapted to each other and to the physical conditions under which they live, that none of them could anyhow be improved; for in all countries, the natives have been so far conquered by naturalised productions, that they have allowed foreigners to take firm possession of the land. And as foreigners have thus everywhere beaten some of the natives, we may safely conclude that the natives might have been modified with advantage, so as to have better resisted such intruders.[43]

As man can produce and certainly has produced a great result by his methodical and unconscious means of selection, what may not nature effect? Man can act only on external and visible characters: nature cares nothing for appearances, except in so far as they may be useful to any being. She can act on every internal organ, on every shade of constitutional difference, on the whole machinery of life. Man selects only for his own good; Nature only for that of the being which she tends. Every selected character is fully exercised by her; and

Notes

[43] *intruders* this passage on imperialistic conquest in relation to natural selection may be compared with his later comments on the evolution of race in *The Descent of Man* (1871); see also RELIGION: GEOLOGY; WALLACE, "ORIGIN" (WEB p. 188).

the being is placed under well-suited conditions of life. Man keeps the natives of many climates in the same country; he seldom exercises each selected character in some peculiar and fitting manner; he feeds a long and a short beaked pigeon on the same food; he does not exercise a long-backed or long-legged quadruped in any peculiar manner; he exposes sheep with long and short wool to the same climate. He does not allow the most vigorous males to struggle for the females. He does not rigidly destroy all inferior animals, but protects during each varying season, as far as lies in his power, all his productions. He often begins his selection by some half-monstrous form; or at least by some modification prominent enough to catch his eye, or to be plainly useful to him. Under nature, the slightest difference of structure or constitution may well turn the nicely-balanced scale in the struggle for life, and so be preserved. How fleeting are the wishes and efforts of man! how short his time! and consequently how poor will his products be, compared with those accumulated by nature during whole geological periods.[44] Can we wonder, then, that nature's productions should be far "truer" in character than man's productions; that they should be infinitely better adapted to the most complex conditions of life, and should plainly bear the stamp of far higher workmanship?[45]

It may be said that natural selection is daily and hourly scrutinising, throughout the world, every variation, even the slightest; rejecting that which is bad, preserving and adding up all that is good; silently and insensibly working, whenever and wherever opportunity offers, at the improvement of each organic being in relation to its organic and inorganic conditions of life. We see nothing of these slow changes in progress, until the hand of time has marked the long lapses of ages, and then so imperfect is our view into long past geological ages, that we only see that the forms of life are now different from what they formerly were. . . .

The affinities of all the beings of the same class have sometimes been represented by a great tree.[46] I believe this simile largely speaks the truth. The green and budding twigs may represent existing species; and those produced during each former year may represent the long succession of extinct species. At each period of growth all the growing twigs have tried to branch out on all sides, and to overtop and kill the surrounding twigs and branches, in the same manner as species and groups of species have tried to overmaster other species in the great battle for life. The limbs divided into great branches, and these into lesser and lesser branches, were themselves once, when the tree was small, budding twigs; and this connexion of the former and present buds by ramifying branches may well represent the classification of all extinct and living species in groups subordinate to groups. Of the many twigs which flourished when the tree was a mere bush, only two or three, now grown into great branches, yet survive and bear all the other branches; so with the species which lived during long-past geological periods, very few now have living and modified descendants. From the first growth of the tree, many a limb and branch has decayed and dropped off; and these lost branches of various sizes may represent those whole orders, families, and genera which have now no living representatives, and which are known to us only from having been found in a fossil state. As we here and there see a

Notes

[44] *periods* see Ecclesiastes 1: 3–4; and 2: 22–23.

[45] *workmanship* see the comparison between domestic and natural species, see n. 28.

[46] *tree* in this famous last paragraph of chapter 4 Darwin summarizes with the metaphor of a tree of life his long discussion of the one illustration in the *Origin*, a diagram that brings together in a branching pattern over thousands of generations divergence of character, natural selection, and the extinction of some strains. The branching pattern challenges the ancient hierarchical scheme of the great chain of being, moving from the lowest to the highest, from mineral to vegetal, to animal, and thence to human, angelical, and divine levels. While the tree image had long been used in genealogy (family tree), its use in biology was rare. Darwin, who kept with him on *The Beagle* a volume of Milton's works (see DARWIN, n. 15), is perhaps referring to the tree of life in the Garden of Eden in *Paradise Lost* (4: 218), a passage that derives from Genesis 2: 9.

thin straggling branch springing from a fork low down in a tree, and which by some chance has been favoured and is still alive on its summit, so we occasionally see an animal like the Ornithorhynchus or Lepidosiren,[47] which in some small degree connects by its affinities two large branches of life, and which has apparently been saved from fatal competition by having inhabited a protected station. As buds give rise by growth to fresh buds, and these, if vigorous, branch out and overtop on all sides many a feebler branch, so by generation I believe it has been with the great Tree of Life, which fills with its dead and broken branches the crust of the earth, and covers the surface with its ever branching and beautiful ramifications.

From Chapter 15: "Recapitulation and Conclusion"[48]

As this whole volume is one long argument, it may be convenient to the reader to have the leading facts and inferences briefly recapitulated.

That many and grave objections may be advanced against the theory of descent with modification through natural selection, I do not deny. I have endeavoured to give to them their full force. Nothing at first can appear more difficult to believe than that the more complex organs and instincts should have been perfected, not by means superior to, though analogous with, human reason, but by the accumulation of innumerable slight variations, each good for the individual possessor. Nevertheless, this difficulty, though appearing to our imagination insuperably great, cannot be considered real if we admit the following propositions, namely,—that gradations in the perfection of any organ or instinct, which we may consider, either do now exist or could have existed, each good of its kind,[49]—that all organs and instincts are, in ever so slight a degree, variable,—and, lastly, that there is a struggle for existence leading to the preservation of each profitable deviation of structure or instinct. The truth of these propositions cannot, I think, be disputed.

It is, no doubt, extremely difficult even to conjecture by what gradations many structures have been perfected, more especially amongst broken and failing groups of organic beings; but we see so many strange gradations in nature, as is proclaimed by the canon, "Natura non facit saltum,"[50] that we ought to be extremely cautious in saying that any organ or instinct, or any whole being, could not have arrived at its present state by many graduated steps.[51] There are, it must be admitted, cases of special difficulty on the theory of natural selection; and one of the most curious of these is the existence of two or three defined castes of workers or sterile females in the same community of ants but I have attempted to show how this difficulty can be mastered....

Notes

[47] *Ornithorhynchus ... Lepidosiren* the Ornithorhynchus is the platypus of Eastern Australia, one of only four egg-laying mammals; the Lepidosiren is the Amazonian lungfish that has rudimentary gills but breathes with lungs and has some characteristic bone structures that link it to land-based vertebrates.

[48] *title* Darwin divides his concluding chapter into three sections, marked off by spaces between them. First, he deals with difficulties and "grave objections" to evolution; second, he summarizes the main arguments in the order in which they are presented; and third, he looks to the present and the future and the role of evolution in all branches of science.

[49] *kind* see Genesis 1: 12.

[50] *Natura ... saltum* (Lat. nature does not make a jump); Darwin got the phrase from Linnaeus' *Philosophia Botanica*

(1751), but it is much older, having been used by the English botanist John Ray in *Methodus Plantarum* (1621), and earlier by Albertus Magnus (c.1200–80) in a line back to Aristotle.

[51] *steps* the notion is that nature is exhaustively full of minute gradations, and that gradations of structure occur gradually, a principle that in Darwin's view applies to the simplest hair on the skin as well as to the complexities of the human eye, thereby challenging the much loved argument from design used by such supporters of natural theology as William Paley. This complexity view is currently being advocated by a form of creationism, intelligent design, especially in applying it to such complex pathways of biochemical functions as the bacterial flagellum, the tail on certain cell bodies that by some is argued to be irreducibly complex.

That the geological record is imperfect all will admit; but that it is imperfect to the degree which I require, few will be inclined to admit. If we look to long enough intervals of time, geology plainly declares that all species have changed; and they have changed in the manner which my theory requires, for they have changed slowly and in a graduated manner. We clearly see this in the fossil remains from consecutive formations invariably being much more closely related to each other, than are the fossils from formations distant from each other in time.[52] ...

I have now recapitulated the chief facts and considerations which have thoroughly convinced me that species have changed, and are still slowly changing by the preservation and accumulation of successive slight favourable variations. Why, it may be asked, have all the most eminent living naturalists and geologists rejected this view of the mutability of species? It cannot be asserted that organic beings in a state of nature are subject to no variation; it cannot be proved that the amount of variation in the course of long ages is a limited quantity; no clear distinction has been, or can be, drawn between species and well-marked varieties. It cannot be maintained that species when intercrossed are invariably sterile, and varieties invariably fertile; or that sterility is a special endowment and sign of creation. The belief that species were immutable productions was almost unavoidable as long as the history of the world was thought to be of short duration; and now that we have acquired some idea of the lapse of time, we are too apt to assume, without proof, that the geological record is so perfect that it would have afforded us plain evidence of the mutation of species, if they had undergone mutation. ...

Several eminent naturalists have of late published their belief that a multitude of reputed species in each genus are not real species; but that other species are real, that is, have been independently created. ... These authors seem no more startled at a miraculous act of creation than at an ordinary birth.[53] But do they really believe that at innumerable periods in the earth's history certain elemental atoms have been commanded suddenly to flash into living tissues? Do they believe that at each supposed act of creation one individual or many were produced? Were all the infinitely numerous kinds of animals and plants created as eggs or seed, or as full grown? and in the case of mammals, were they created bearing the false marks of nourishment from the mother's womb?[54] Although naturalists very properly demand a full explanation of every difficulty from those who believe in the mutability of species, on their own side they ignore the whole subject of the first appearance of species in what they consider reverent silence.

Notes

[52] *time* in this and the previous paragraphs Darwin has explained the reasons for gaps in the fossil record, but he has also discussed the age of the earth as "utterly inappreciable by the human intellect." Such a view contradicted the widely held view among the religiously orthodox that the world was created in 4004 BCE; see n. 1. This dating had been challenged from the end of the eighteenth century, and especially by Lyell in *Principles of Geology* (1830–33), but Darwin's presentation of vast epochs of geological time, to allow for the small evolutionary changes to take place, was a much greater assault, questioning in the same argument the age of the earth, the act of creation out of nothing, and the creation of static and unchanging species. See also HOWITT, n. 3; and HUXLEY, n. 8.

[53] *birth* Darwin draws attention to the lack among some of his contemporaries of a clear distinction between species and variations. This lack of clarity means that they cannot assert that one species is a specially created form without calling into question why its variation is not specially created, but is the result of the operation of natural law; in the former case they invoke a miraculous intervention; in the latter, they deny the transmutation of species. He is very likely thinking of Philip Henry Gosse in *Omphalos* (1857), especially his theory of prochronism built in (see n. 14). Jean Louis Rodolphe Agassiz (1807–73), Swiss glaciologist renowned for his work on fossil fish, held that species and variations were the result of ideas in the mind of God, with variations of the same species of fish or bird in different and unconnected locations the creatures of special creative acts in "Geographical Distribution of Animals" in *Christian Examiner and Religious Miscellany* (March 1850).

[54] *womb* after challenging those who claim that species were specially created but that variations occur by the laws of evolution – itself a contradiction, since Darwin has shown that the variations accumulate to render species differentiation – he asks whether it is plausible to reject transmutation as impossible while accepting the possibility of special creation. In questioning whether, for instance, Adam and Eve had navels, he alludes to the famous book by Philip Gosse; see above, n. 14.

It may be asked how far I extend the doctrine of the modification of species.... Throughout whole classes various structures are formed on the same pattern, and at an embryonic age the species closely resemble each other. Therefore I cannot doubt that the theory of descent with modification embraces all the members of the same class. I believe that animals have descended from at most only four or five progenitors, and plants from an equal or lesser number.

Analogy would lead me one step further, namely, to the belief that all animals and plants have descended from some one prototype.[55] But analogy may be a deceitful guide. Nevertheless all living things have much in common, in their chemical composition, their germinal vesicles, their cellular structure, and their laws of growth and reproduction. We see this even in so trifling a circumstance as that the same poison often similarly affects plants and animals; or that the poison secreted by the gall-fly produces monstrous growths on the wild rose or oak-tree. Therefore I should infer from analogy that probably all the organic beings which have ever lived on this earth have descended from some one primordial form, into which life was first breathed.[56]

When the views entertained in this volume on the origin of species, or when analogous views are generally admitted, we can dimly foresee that there will be a considerable revolution in natural history.[57] Systematists will be able to pursue their labours as at present; but they will not be incessantly haunted by the shadowy doubt whether this or that form be in essence a species. This I feel sure, and I speak after experience, will be no slight relief. The endless disputes whether or not some fifty species of British brambles are true species will cease. Systematists will have only to decide (not that this will be easy) whether any form be sufficiently constant and distinct from other forms, to be capable of definition; and if definable, whether the differences be sufficiently important to deserve a specific name. This latter point will become a far more essential consideration than it is at present; for differences, however slight, between any two forms, if not blended by intermediate gradations, are looked at by most naturalists as sufficient to raise both forms to the rank of species. Hereafter we shall be compelled to acknowledge that the only distinction between species and well-marked varieties is, that the latter are known, or believed, to be connected at the present day by intermediate gradations, whereas species were formerly thus connected. Hence, without quite rejecting the consideration of the present existence of intermediate gradations between any two forms, we shall be led to weigh more carefully and to value higher the actual amount of difference between them....

A grand and almost untrodden field of inquiry will be opened, on the causes and laws of variation, on correlation of growth, on the effects of use and disuse, on the direct action of external conditions, and so forth. The study of domestic productions will rise immensely in value. A new variety raised by man will be a far more important and interesting subject for study than one more species added to the infinitude of already recorded

Notes

[55] *analogy ... prototype* in the theory of evolution, the wings of insects are analogous to the wings of vertebrates like birds and bats in that all enable their possessors to fly; however, the wings of each have evolved separately and differently. One of Darwin's fundamental analogies, however, is between artificial (domestic) selection and natural selection, an analogy that has attracted some attention as being derived in methodology from John F. W. Herschel's *Preliminary Discourse on the Study of Natural Philosophy* (1830). Exploiting this point, Samuel Wilberforce, in his review of *Origin* in the *Quarterly Review* (July 1860) argued that his analogy worked to disprove evolution, because all of breeders' experiments with pigeons confirmed that one species cannot be transmuted into another, over however many generations.

[56] *breathed* a month after the first edition, Darwin added a phrase to the last sentence in this paragraph in the second edition (see n. 24), so that it read "into which life was first breathed by the Creator." Darwin here proposes the possibility of universal common descent from "some one prototype" or "one primordial form," now known as the "last universal common ancestor."

[57] *history* from this point Darwin looks to the future of natural history.

species. Our classifications will come to be, as far as they can be so made, genealogies; and will then truly give what may be called the plan of creation. The rules for classifying will no doubt become simpler when we have a definite object in view.... We possess no pedigrees or armorial bearings; and we have to discover and trace the many diverging lines of descent in our natural genealogies, by characters of any kind which have long been inherited. Rudimentary organs will speak infallibly with respect to the nature of long-lost structures. Species and groups of species, which are called aberrant, and which may fancifully be called living fossils, will aid us in forming a picture of the ancient forms of life. Embryology will reveal to us the structure, in some degree obscured, of the prototypes of each great class....

In the distant future I see open fields for far more important researches. Psychology will be based on a new foundation, that of the necessary acquirement of each mental power and capacity by gradation. Light will be thrown on the origin of man and his history.[58]

Authors of the highest eminence seem to be fully satisfied with the view that each species has been independently created. To my mind it accords better with what we know of the laws impressed on matter by the Creator, that the production and extinction of the past and present inhabitants of the world should have been due to secondary causes, like those determining the birth and death of the individual. When I view all beings not as special creations, but as the lineal descendants of some few beings which lived long before the first bed of the Silurian system was deposited, they seem to me to become ennobled. Judging from the past, we may safely infer that not one living species will transmit its unaltered likeness to a distant futurity. And of the species now living very few will transmit progeny of any kind to a far distant futurity; for the manner in which all organic beings are grouped, shows that the greater number of species of each genus, and all the species of many genera, have left no descendants, but have become utterly extinct. We can so far take a prophetic glance into futurity as to foretel that it will be the common and widely-spread species, belonging to the larger and dominant groups, which will ultimately prevail and procreate new and dominant species. As all the living forms of life are the lineal descendants of those which lived long before the Silurian epoch, we may feel certain that the ordinary succession by generation has never once been broken, and that no cataclysm has desolated the whole world.[59] Hence we may look with some confidence to a secure future of equally inappreciable length. And as natural selection works solely by and for the good of each being, all corporeal and mental endowments will tend to progress towards perfection.[60]

It is interesting to contemplate an entangled bank,[61] clothed with many plants of many kinds, with birds singing on the bushes, with various insects flitting about, and with worms crawling through the damp earth, and to reflect that these elaborately constructed forms, so different from each other, and dependent on each other in so complex a manner, have all been produced by laws acting around us. These laws, taken in the largest sense, being Growth with Reproduction; Inheritance which is almost implied by reproduction;

Notes

[58] *history* Darwin adumbrates some of his own future work here, notably *The Descent of Man* (1871) and *The Expression of Emotions in Man and Animals* (1872).

[59] *world* Darwin here is rejecting the theories of catastrophism as advanced by Georges Cuvier amongst others, siding unequivocally with the uniformitarians like Charles Lyell, arguing that the geological record and all of the forms of life have undergone infinite changes over vast amounts of time in a gradual process. See n. 1.

[60] *perfection* here Darwin sees evolution as "progress towards perfection," as a movement towards patterns of natural selection that more adequately equip organisms to survive and reproduce. For progress in evolution, see nn. 1 and 8.

The poet May Kendall published "Ballad of the Ichthyosaurus" (*Punch*, 14 Feb. 1885) satirizing evolutionary progress in which the fossil reptile "aspires to better things." For the opposite argument, degradation from the original creation of perfect specimens, see n. 9. Darwin is not positing a teleological goal, an ideal of "perfection" towards which evolution pushes as a directional movement; instead, he sees that perfection manifest increasingly in the ability of organisms to survive.

[61] *bank* in the sixth edition, Darwin changed the phrase from "an entangled bank" to "a tangled bank." Samuel Johnson's *Dictionary* gives the meanings of "evolve" as "to unfold, to disentangle."

Variability from the indirect and direct action of the external conditions of life, and from use and disuse; a Ratio of Increase so high as to lead to a Struggle for Life, and as a consequence to Natural Selection, entailing Divergence of Character and the Extinction of less-improved forms. Thus, from the war of nature, from famine and death, the most exalted object which we are capable of conceiving, namely, the production of the higher animals, directly follows. There is grandeur in this view of life, with its several powers, having been originally breathed[62] into a few forms or into one; and that, whilst this planet has gone cycling on according to the fixed law of gravity, from so simple a beginning endless forms most beautiful and most wonderful have been, and are being, evolved.[63]

WEB p. 182

The Oxford Debate (30 June 1860): From Leonard Huxley, *The Life and Letters of Thomas Henry Huxley* (1900)
Alfred Russel Wallace (1823–1913): From "The Origin of Human Races and the Antiquity of Man Deduced from the Theory of 'Natural Selection'" (1864)
Samuel Kinns (1826–1903): From *Moses and Geology: Or, the Harmony of the Bible with Science* (1882)
From Chapter 1: "The Word is Truth"
May Kendall (1861–1943): "The Lay of the Trilobite" (1885)

Agnes Mary Frances Robinson (1857–1944)

Darwinism[64]

When first the unflowering Fern-forest[65]
   Shadowed the dim lagoons of old,
A vague, unconscious, long unrest
   Swayed the great fronds of green and gold.

Until the flexible stem grew rude,   5
   The fronds began to branch and bower,
And lo! upon the unblossoming wood
   There breaks a dawn of apple-flower.

Notes

[62] *breathed* in the second edition Darwin extended this phrase: "originally breathed by the Creator."

[63] *evolved* Darwin's only use of "evolve" or its cognates (such as "evolution") in the *Origin*. His usual word was "transmutation."

[64] *title* also known as Mary Duclaux (from her second marriage), Robinson was a prolific writer of literary criticism and poetry. Here, as in many poems at the end of the century, evolution is related to female emancipation. Robinson accepts the theory of evolution in general, but has moved away from Darwin. She bypasses both natural selection and the struggle for existence, each of them controversial even late in the nineteenth century, opting instead for a Lamarckian progressivism – that organisms strive towards their own improvement through their

willed or unconscious purposive action over millennia to modify and improve themselves. Robinson's poem describes a progressive urge that drove prehistoric ferns to evolve into trees, and apes into humans, and that still pushes humanity towards an invisible goal. First published in *Songs, Ballads, and a Garden Play* (1888), our text; republished in *The Collected Poems, Lyrical and Narrative* (1902).

[65] *Forest-ferns* plants with leaves that reproduce with spores rather than by seeds. They began to flourish on dry land in the Devonian Period (about 420–355 million years ago) and throughout the Carboniferous period (about 355–290 million years ago) and were distributed widely as vascular plants, varying from small ferns to very large ones, some climbing, some free-standing.

Then on the fruitful Forest-boughs
    For ages long the unquiet ape   10
Swung happy in his airy house
    And plucked the apple, and sucked the grape.[66]

Until in him at length there stirred
    The old, unchanged, remote distress,
That pierced his world of wind and bird   15
    With some divine unhappiness.

Not Love, nor the wild fruits he sought;
    Nor the fierce battles of his clan
Could still the unborn and aching thought,
    Until the brute became the man.[67]   20

Long since. .. And now the same unrest
    Goads to the same invisible goal,[68]
Till some new gift, undreamed, unguessed,
    End the new travail of the soul.

WEB p. 196

2. Religious Faith and Uncertainty

Henry Francis Lyte (1793–1847): "Abide with me!"(1847)

W. J. Conybeare (1815–1857): From "Church Parties" (1853)

John Ruskin (1819–1900): Letter to *The Times* (1854) [on Hunt's *Light of the World*]

Thomas Hughes (1822–1896): *Tom Brown's Schooldays* (1857)
    From Part 2, Chapter 9: "Finis"

Benjamin Jowett (1817–1893): From "On the Interpretation of Scripture" in *Essays and Reviews* (1860)

John William Burgon (1813–1888): *Inspiration and Interpretation* (1861)
    From Sermon 3. [On the literal inspiration of the Bible]

Sabine Baring-Gould (1834–1924): "Onward Christian Soldiers" (1864)

John Henry Newman (1801–90): *Apologia Pro Vita Sua*
    From "Part V. History of My Religious Opinions [from 1839 to 1841]"

Mrs Humphrey Ward [Mary Augusta Arnold Ward] (1851–1920): *Robert Elsmere* (1888)
    From Book 4, Chapter 26: "Crisis"

Notes

[66] *grape* the feminized ape (carrying within him the "unborn and aching thought" in line 19), contented with his lot in his "house" in the trees, suggests the separate spheres doctrine concerning women happy in their domestic life. This sphere is set against the "fierce battles" of the males in the next stanza. Overall, the apes becoming women are aspiring towards some kind of emancipation and new goals, perhaps of the franchise and education when they evolve into humans. Evolution was sometimes criticized as implying increased women's rights, as in Sarah Grand's *The Heavenly Twins* (1893), when Evadne's father is declared to be "ready to resent even the upward tendency of evolution when it presented itself to him in the form of any change ... more especially so if such change threatened to bring about an improvement in the position of women" (ch. 1).

[67] *man* a reference to the popularized view of Darwin as advocating the ape as an unquestioned human ancestor; see Figure 9.

[68] *goal* the teleological notion of a progress towards a (divinely ordained?) culmination is controversial in Darwin's presentation in *Origin*.

Empire

Introduction

The Victoria Terminus Station (VT) in Bombay, under construction since May 1878, was opened on Jubilee Day, 20 June 1887, as the main terminal and administrative offices of the Great Indian Peninsula Railway (GIPR). The English-trained architect, Frederick William Stevens (1848–1900), became famous as Bombay's premier neo-Gothic architect as he redesigned the centre of the city with at least nine splendid and elaborate edifices to display Britain's power and civilizing mission. He fused a Saracenic (Mughal) style with a British/Italian Neo-Gothic style, associating the British with the Mughal emperors, who had ruled most of the subcontinent from about 1526 to 1761, when their paramountcy was overtaken by the East India Company. The opening of the Suez Canal in 1869 had enhanced Bombay's status as the gateway to the subcontinent as travellers arriving on the west-coast port would board trains to take them inland. An 1895 coffee-table book, *Glimpses of India*, claimed, "It is Europe and England that made Bombay what it now is, the connecting link between Europe and Asia, the point where two civilizations meet and mingle.... Altogether Bombay looks like what Mr. Ruskin calls Venice, 'a gem set in the sea'" —a reference to the Venetian Gothic of the Doge's Palace that greatly influenced the architecture of the VT. A travel guide of 1889 by James Mackenzie Maclean describes the VT in detail as a "strikingly handsome structure" with an "architectural effect" surpassing "any of the fine public buildings for which Bombay is remarkable." Almost a century later, Jan Morris, well-known for nostalgic invocations of imperial glories, writes expansively in *Stones of Empire: The Buildings of the Raj* (1983) that the Victoria Terminus "could make a persuasive claim to be truly the central building of the entire British Empire — the building which expresses most properly the meaning of the imperial climax."

A watercolour (see Plate 18) by the architectural draughtsman Axel Herman Haig (1835–1921) had been commissioned by the architect, Stevens, in 1878 and was exhibited seven years before the building would be completed at the RA in 1880. This depiction joined a number of other iconic representations of railway stations, paintings that form an emerging convention in the nineteenth century (see Concanen, Plate 9; as well as John O'Connor's *St. Pancras Hotel and Station from Pentonville*, 1884). Haig's watercolour was both the visionary effect of Stevens's basic design and its prophetic prediction: a combination of Italian-derived neo-Gothic design combined with Hindu and Saracenic details and echoes, linking the monument both to the symmetrical architecture of the palaces of the Raj and to the contemporary examples of buildings serving similar functions in the imperial capital. The station is modelled to a large degree on St Pancras Station and the adjoining Midland Grand Hotel by Sir George Gilbert Scott (1811–78), built between 1866 and 1873. Its major colouristic feature, the use of polychrome brick and stone, especially in the alternating red and white stones of the Gothic arches, is exactly imitated in Bombay. Both monuments are based on Ruskin's ideal Gothic building, what he calls "the central building in the world," the Ducal or Doge's Palace in Venice. Haig projects the future terminal in ways close to its realization, an eclectic neo-Gothic building of towering spires, domes, elaborate arched windows, verandas, balustrades, and arched porticos; at the centre is an immense dome, atop of which is a fourteen-foot female statue,

Victorian Literature: An Anthology, First Edition. Edited by Victor Shea and William Whitla.
© 2015 John Wiley & Sons, Ltd. Published 2015 by John Wiley & Sons, Ltd.

"Progress," a flaming torch aloft in her right hand, a spoked wheel by her left side. In a niche below the clock under the central dome beneath "Progress" is a statue of Victoria, who in 1876 had been proclaimed Empress of India. She holds the orb and sceptre of imperial power. Groups representing "Engineering" and "Commerce" top the two gables of the projecting wings on the west side, and a representation of "Agriculture" is on the central gable of the south wing. These allegorical figures are dressed in classical togas, a further extension of western imperial conquest of the culture of India. In the tympana on the ground floor are representations of "Science," embodying astronomy, electricity, physical geography, medicine, chemistry, and mechanics; as well as "Trade," with the central figure of Peace promoting harmony between east and west to enable the exchange of goods. Figures of a lion, representing Great Britain, and a tiger, representing India, sit on columns at the entrance gates, in joint welcome. The carvings and wealth of sculptural details, which the painting does not show, include many flowers, animals, railway and GIPR symbols, and numerous gargoyles, drawing on a variety of indigenous cultures to portray Indian animals, flowers, and activities. In the finished building, much of this detailed ornamentation would be completed by Indian students of the Bombay School of Art under the direct supervision of Lockwood Kipling (1837–1911). Lockwood was the father of Rudyard Kipling, who would, of course, by the end of Victorian's reign, become, for better or for worse, the literary figure most closely connected, then and now, with the British Empire.

The Indo-Saracenic architectural revival in the late nineteenth century demonstrates how imperial relations were not simply the imposition of Western norms onto colonized peoples but also the attempt to synthesize and integrate Indian cultural norms with the British. Nevertheless, as an architectural form, it attempted to portray an invincible and insurmountable imperial power on a grand scale, echoing the style of the previous conquerors, while also referring unmistakably to the permanence and legitimacy of the Raj. The VT incorporates in its floor plans and sculptural details features of Mughal architecture, references to the Islamic empire that ruled India from 1526, reaching its artistic climax under the descendants of the third emperor, Akbar the Great (1542–1605), namely Jahangir (1569–1627) and Shah Jehan (1592–1666). Their work in red sandstone (like the Jehangir Palace in Agra) and the complex of towers, windows, and domes (like the Jehangir Mahal in Orchha), made important contributions to the VT. This fusion of styles symbolizes the technological triumph of the marriage of coal, iron, and stone in industrial capitalism and the civilizational progress of the railway, an icon to British modernity and the transformative power of empire to thrust India forward from its Moghul past.

The Victoria Terminus has not only survived as a monument, but still functions as the main railway station for the city, receiving and dispersing well over 2 million commuters a day. It is also still lauded as an architectural marvel, and in 2004 was named a World Heritage Site by UNESCO, praised on its website as "an outstanding example of Victorian Gothic Revival architecture in India, blended with themes deriving from Indian traditional architecture. The building was … a new style unique to Bombay."[1]

The meaning of the building has lately moved well beyond being a site of British imperial power – a symbol of either progress and civilization or the imposition of a colonial agenda. The terminus and the city have undergone massive cultural re-inscriptions, effacing colonial associations and realigning historical, political, and imperial value systems. The Great Indian Peninsula Railway, founded as a private charter

Notes ———————————————————————————————

INTRODUCTION
[1] See http://whc.unesco.org/en/list/945.

company in London in 1849, became the Central Railway, a state enterprise, after Indian independence in 1947. Its symbols are still, anachronistically, all over the building. Both the terminus and the city have been renamed. Bombay became Mumbai in 1996, in honour of Mumbadevi, a Hindu mother goddess. In the same year the VT was renamed the Chhatrapati Shivaji Terminus (CST; apparently the local people, and especially the cabbies, still call it the VT) in honour of the Maratha king Chhatrapati Shivaji (1630–80), who defeated the Muslim Mughals and re-established a Hindu empire in south-west India, which was eventually overthrown by the British in 1818. The city's international airport was also renamed after the Maratha king.

These changes came about under pressure from the right-wing Hindu nationalist party, Shiv Sena, which emerged from Mumbai in the late 1960s with first a pro-Marathi agenda and later broadened its base across India to pursue a Hindu nationalist agenda. Other buildings were also renamed in a nominal reconquest in celebration of a seventeenth-century Hindu imperial dynasty. The statue of Victoria in the main tower of the VT disappeared sometime in the early 2000s, and its location is unknown. More recently, the terminus appeared in the Oscar-winning *Slumdog Millionaire* (2008) directed by Danny Boyle. A climactic song-and-dance scene brings the lovers together while the end credits roll, showing a panorama of the VT/CST and the train shed, with the terminus's dedication plaque naming the architect, "Frederick W. Stevens," clearly visible. The song "Jai Ho" (which won an Oscar for best song) features vocals in three Indian languages, Urdu, Hindi, and Punjabi, fusing traditional Bollywood music with Western hip-hop and urban music and dance: the terminus has become an iconic setting for international filmic and musical acclaim. From 26 to 28 November 2008 the building took on yet another meaning for the world, as it and the Taj Mahal Hotel, another ornate Indo-Saracenic Victorian edifice, were the sites of a terrorist attack that killed 46 people and wounded 104 others.

If the contexts and meanings of what Jan Morris called the "central building of the entire British Empire – the building which expresses most properly the meaning of the imperial climax" – have since 1887 multiplied and shifted, so too have the contexts and meanings of Victorian imperialism. From a position in the twenty-first century, we cannot help but look at the Victorian Empire through a complex set of politically charged terms: imperialism and neo-imperialism; colonialism and post-colonialism; cultural imperialism and globalization; and so on. These concepts present political positionings to provide multiple views of the same phenomenon: for instance, in Mumbai/Bombay the Hindu nationalists could be said to represent a neo-imperialistic force eradicating the traces of the former imperialistic powers, the Mughal, Portuguese, and British empires – a bad thing perhaps for contemporary Muslims. At the same time, renaming the VT could be seen as a post-colonial insistence and empowerment against the colonial mindset imposed by the British before 1947 – a good thing for some contemporary Hindus. This same renaming could represent a resistance to cultural imperialism, the imposition of a dominant set of foreign cultural products, styles, and ideas. From the nationalist Hindu perspective represented by the Shiv Sena, such imperialism extends from the Saracenic architecture that came into the subcontinent with the Mughul invasions from the sixteenth century, to Valentine's Day, McDonald's, and the morality of American pop culture of today under globalization. On the other hand, the final scene of an Oscar-winning film could represent the successful fusion of India and Bollywood with globalized film, music, and dance styles, set in a building celebrated as an earlier example of is now called globalization: as UNESCO claims on its website, it "exhibits an important interchange of influences from Victorian Italianate Gothic Revival architecture, and from Indian traditional buildings ... characterized by Victorian Gothic Revival and traditional Indian features."

Writing at the time of the terminus's name change, Tim McGirk in *The Independent*

(23 Jan. 1996) offers us a different meaning to building, lamenting,

> Stone by stone, nameplate by nameplate, India is obliterating its memories of the British empire. The latest casualty is the grand Victoria Terminus railway station in Bombay – or Mumbai as the city's right-wing Hindu masters now call it.... After independence from Britain in 1947, all the blatant symbols of the British Raj were removed. In New Delhi, the statue of King George V was uprooted from India Gate, and boulevards with such as Kingsway and Queensway became Rajpath and Janpath.

The internal political affairs of naming public spaces so offending a British reporter fifty years after the end of the Raj is an instance of imperialist nostalgia, an idealist recasting of a projected stability of the past (Victorian) from a chaotic and disorderly present embracing a violent and dangerous past (Chhatrapati Shivaji). Opposite to such nostalgic projections has been criticism or dismissal of the Victorians as hypocrites who claimed to be bringing modernity and progress, as well the three Cs – Christianity, civilization, and commerce – to backwards people while, in reality, ruthlessly exploiting them, economically, politically, and ideologically. Broadly speaking, the latter attitude, dominant throughout most of the twentieth century, is still probably the most widespread.

The complexity inscribed in our selection of documents would dictate that such views of nostalgic yearning or judgemental dismissal are not adequate to informed readings of the Victorian empire. Victoria's reign saw huge transformations at home – but also vast changes in the ever-expanding empire and its relations with other imperial powers: almost constant imperial warfare; the development of military technology with such inventions as the Gatling gun, communications technology such as the telegraph, and travel technology such as the railway; the abolition of slavery; the introduction of free trade; several famines, most notably in Ireland from 1845 to 1850, and in India from 1876 to 1878; domestic political opposition to empire by such thinkers as William Morris and Wilfrid Scawen Blunt; instances of imperial subjects revolting against British dominance, such as in the Indian Rebellion of 1857–58 and the second Boer War of 1899–1902; the development of nationalist consciousness in colonial subjects, particularly in India and Ireland; the granting of responsible self-government to the white settler colonies such as Canada; the commercialization of global travel; the freedom for women to travel all over the world and to write about it; complex interactions with non-European empires, the Ottoman, Chinese, and Persian; an intensifying of competition with other European empires in the "scramble for Africa" after 1885; the development of scientific theories of race; and many other world-changing ideas and events.

We divide our extracts on empire into three sections: Celebration and Criticism, Governing the Colonies, and Imperial Travellers. The first section foregrounds diverse proposals and reactions to changes in imperial thought throughout the century, such as that of Carlyle and Mill on the abolition of sugar tariffs and their effects on former slaves and the plantation owners in the West Indies; Seeley on the notion of the white colonies' transformation and extension into one English "family," able to compete with the growing might of Russia and the United States; idealizations of the empire in Ruskin and Tennyson; and harsh critiques of its racism, economics, and violence by Labouchère, Hobson, and Blunt. The Web section focuses on two texts, the Imperial Federation Map of the World (1886) and a children's ABC.

The second section focuses on government. In the print book the focus is on governing India, stressing multiple ways in which the Raj exercised, or tried to exercise, control. Macaulay's "Minute on Education" outlines utilitarian reforms that would subsequently shape life in India, as they continue to do to this day. The preface to a boy's adventure novel by G. A. Henty combines imperial propaganda with the shaping of masculinity. Our excerpt from a woman's guide to the Anglo-Indian household indicates that control did not stop in officialdom but transcended the division of home and work, the running of the household here held up in direct parallel with the running of the Indian Empire. This section on the Web extends "governing the colonies" to the White Colonies, Ireland, and Africa.

The section on travel contains excerpts from women travellers Lady Eastlake, Isabella Bird, and Mary Kingsley, as well as the famous report on the charge of the Light Brigade by *The Times* war correspondent William Howard Russell (Web). The usual trajectory of imperial travel writing is reversed in the book contents of this section by excerpting descriptions of Britain by Indian and African colonial subjects. Malabari, an Indian social reformer, and Mukasa, an Ugandan government functionary, describe what they see in Britain in terms of critical curiosity as well as reverential awe. This trajectory also appears in Gandhi's account of London in 1878 (Web).

In the same year as the opening of the VT, Tennyson's "*Carmen Sæculare*, the Ode in Honour of Victoria's Golden Jubilee" (*Macmillan's Magazine* April 1887; see this section) hails the "Queen, and Empress of India, / Crown'd so long with a diadem" for reigning over "Fifty years of ever-broadening Commerce! / Fifty years of ever-brightening Science! / Fifty years of ever-widening Empire!" The ode addresses a diverse audience, pointing to, among others, the multitudes, the affluent, "the Mighty," "the Fortunate," "the Lord-territorial," "the Lord-manufacturer," "the hardy, laborious, / Patient children of Albion," "Canadian, Indian, Australasian," and "African." In this wide range of quick references, imperial and domestic matters receive equal treatment. Stanza eight contains the one addressee, "the Patriot Architect," who is given a sustained treatment, urging that he "shape for eternity ... a stately memorial," an "Imperial Institute, Rich in symbol," that "regally gorgeous" would speak to "All the centuries after us, Of this

great Ceremonial." The monument in question, the Imperial Institute, would be completed in 1893.

At the time of the poem's publication, the "Patriot Architect" had not been chosen. Two months later, in June 1887, Thomas Collcutt (1840–1924) won the competition, beating out forty competitors. A committee struck in 1886 to set out the terms of that competition had reported in December that the building should honour the jubilee by illustrating "the great commercial and industrial resources of the colonies and India." The rhetorical flourishes in their conclusion read very much like Tennyson's celebration of imperial progress: "An Imperial Institution ... would be an emblem of the Unity of the Empire, embracing as it does all parts of the Queen's dominions.... It would exhibit the vast area, the varied resources, and the marvellous growth, during Her Majesty's reign, of the British Empire. It would unite in a single representative act the whole of her people." The Victoria Terminus in Bombay, as we have seen, has been spoken of using the same lofty tropes.

Such language speaks to the centrality of empire near the end of the nineteenth century: "During her Majesty's reign" the empire had doubled in size to one sixth of the earth's land mass, over 14 million square miles, and about one quarter of the world's population, over 400 million people. From this vantage point, it would seem indeed that not only the "stately monument," but the "ever-widening Empire" itself, would "speak to the centuries" of imperial accomplishment after 1887. On 10 May 1893, Victoria finally opened the Imperial Institute: "I now declare it open, with an earnest Prayer that it may it never cease to continue and flourish as a lasting Emblem of the Unity and Loyalty of my Empire" (see Figure 10). Such optimism proved unfounded. The Imperial Institute was poorly received and never became "an emblem of the Unity of the Empire": by 1956, the same year as the Suez Crisis, which marks for many historians the symbolic end of British

Figure 10 Godefroy Durand (1832–c.1910), *The Imperial Institute: Opening Ceremony by Her Majesty the Queen.* In *The Graphic* (13 May 1893: Supplement). Steel Engraving. 29.9 × 22.5 cm. Source: courtesy of the Robarts Library, University of Toronto. Durand, originally from Belgium, became one of the staff illustrators for *The Graphic* in the 1870s, specializing in military, horse, and foreign views. Victoria opened the Imperial Institute on 10 May 1893 in South Kensington. The competition for the building to encourage emigration, trade, and commerce within the empire had been won in June 1887 by the architect Thomas Edward Collcutt (1840–1924) in a French early-Renaissance style. The motto over the entrance was "Strength and honour are her clothing" (Proverbs 31: 25). In Durand's fanciful drawing, Victoria stands beneath a trumpeting angel carrying the British flag. She is surrounded by the royal family, including the Prince of Wales (later Edward VII) on her left, and to her right the son of the Prince of Wales, George, Duke of York (later George V), whose betrothal to Princess Mary of Teck (on the queen's right) had just been announced. In front of her are the exotically attired members of the empire bearing their characteristic tribute, accompanied by national animals, the kangaroo, elephant, and the skins of bears and tigers, all bowing in tribute. See also EMPIRE: CELEBRATION; TENNYSON, "OPENING."

imperial power, the demolition of the building was proposed to allow for the expansion of Imperial College. In 1965, despite a vigorous public outcry to save the building, all that remained of the original building was the Queen's tower; by 1965, most of the territories attained during Victoria's reign had been decolonized. With exceptions such as Hong Kong (transferred to China in 1997 under the terms of an 1841 agreement), the Falkland Islands (subject to an irredentist claim by Argentina which calls it *Islas Malvinas*), and Gibraltar (subject to an irredentist claim by Spain), the formal political structure of the empire was all but gone, replaced by a loose association, the British Commonwealth.

The building in Mumbai designed by Stevens, on the other hand, is still both admired and functional, still described in laudatory terms, most commonly in travel guides promoting tourism – a genre and an industry that emerged during Victoria's reign. A current website, "Insight Guides: Inspiring your Next Adventure," briefly describes it under "Places to Visit in Mumbai (Bombay)": the

> Victoria Terminus ... was conceived as a symbol of the pride and power of the British Empire. It amalgamated all the stylistic eccentricities of the day – ornate domes, minarets, fancy arched windows and a staggering wealth of sculptural detail – and still forms an imposing spectacle. Re-named Chhatrapati Shivaji Terminus, the station remains one of the country's best-loved landmarks, in spite of its imperial past and more recent associations with the bloody terror attacks of 2008.

The writings in this section are meant to represent, in a similar fashion, a complex, multilayered, and contradictory set of relationships, to be read not *in spite of* but *because of* their multiple connections to the "pride and power of the British Empire."

1. Celebration and Criticism

Thomas Carlyle (1795–1881): From "Occasional Discourse on the Negro Question" in *Fraser's Magazine* (Dec. 1849)[1]

My Philanthropic Friends,—It is my painful duty to address some words to you, this evening, on the Rights of Negroes. Taking, as we hope we do, an extensive survey of social affairs, which we find all in a state of the frightfullest embroilment, and as it were, of inextricable final bankruptcy, just at present, and being desirous to adjust ourselves in

---

Notes ───

CELEBRATION AND CRITICISM

[1] *title* after a long campaign led by the abolitionist William Wilberforce (1759–1833), the Slave Trade Act (1807) abolished the trading of slaves in the British colonies; slavery itself was abolished in 1834 with the Slavery Abolition Act. The government paid compensation of £20 million to slave owners in 40,000 separate claims. The freed slaves were to be indentured to their former owners in an apprenticeship system that was to continue, in some cases, until 1840. In 1846, the same year as the repeal of the Corn Laws on imported wheat, the Sugar Duties Act eliminated protective tariffs on sugar imported into Britain, enraging the plantation owners of the West Indian colonies, who had believed that after abolition these tariffs would remain in place. Carlyle railed against these developments, almost calling for a reinstatement of slavery. His views were poorly received; John Stuart Mill published a vigorous response (see this section, MILL; NEGRO QUES-TION). He and Mill would clash again on racial matters in the 1860s in the Governor Eyre controversy. From the eighteenth to the mid-twentieth century, the term "Negro" was acceptable usage when referring to people of African origin. In 1853 Carlyle added twenty-three paragraphs to the *Fraser's* essay and published it as a pamphlet, changing the title to "Occasional Discourse on the Nigger Question." The term "nigger" is derived from Latin *negrum*, black; from Spanish and Portuguese *negro*, black. Although the *OED* cites several examples of the word "used by whites or other non-blacks as a relatively neutral (or occas. positive) term, with no specifically hostile intent" (s.v. "Nigger" 1.a), there can be no doubt, given the change in title in his 1849 essay, that Carlyle uses it as a term of abuse and contempt. For an extension of Carlyle's ideas on the West Indies, see EMPIRE: GOVERNING; WHITE COLONIES, FROUDE, *ENGLISH* (WEB p. 232).

that huge upbreak, and unutterable welter of tumbling ruins, and to see well that our grand proposed Association of Associations, the UNIVERSAL ABOLITION-OF-PAIN ASSOCIATION,[2] which is meant to be the consummate golden flower and summary of modern Philanthropisms all in one, do *not* issue as a universal "Sluggard-and-Scoundrel Protection Society,"—we have judged that, before constituting ourselves, it would be very proper to commune earnestly with one another, and discourse together on the leading elements of our great Problem, which surely is one of the greatest. With this view the Council has decided, both that the Negro Question, as lying at the bottom, was to be the first handled, and if possible the first settled; and then also, what was of much more questionable wisdom, that—that, in short, I was to be Speaker on the occasion. An honourable duty; yet, as I said, a painful one!—Well, you shall hear what I have to say on the matter; and you will not in the least like it. . . .

And now observe, my friends, it was not Black Quashee[3] or those he represents that made those West India Islands what they are, or can by any hypothesis be considered to have the right of growing pumpkins there. For countless ages, since they first mounted oozy, on the back of earthquakes, from their dark bed in the Ocean deeps, and reeking saluted the tropical Sun, and ever onwards till the European white man first saw them some three short centuries ago, those Islands had produced mere jungle, savagery, poison-reptiles and swamp-malaria: till the white European first saw them, they were as if not yet created,—their noble elements of cinnamon, sugar, coffee, pepper black and gray, lying all asleep, waiting the white Enchanter who should say to them, Awake! Till the end of human history and the sounding of the Trump of Doom,[4] they might have lain so, had Quashee and the like of him been the only artists in the game. Swamps, fever-jungles, maneating Caribs,[5] rattle-snakes, and reeking waste and putrefaction, this had been the produce of them under the incompetent Caribal (what we call Cannibal) possessors till that time; and Quashee knows, himself, whether ever he could have introduced an improvement. Him, had he by a miraculous chance been wafted thither, the Caribals would have eaten, rolling him as a fat morsel under their tongue; for him, till the sounding of the Trump of Doom, the rattlesnakes and savageries would have held on their way. It was not he, then; it was another than he! Never by art of his could one pumpkin have grown there to solace any human throat; nothing but savagery and reeking putrefaction could have grown there. These plentiful pumpkins, I say, therefore, are not his: no, they are another's; they are only his under conditions; conditions which Exeter Hall, for the present, has forgotten; but which Nature and the Eternal Powers have by no manner of means forgotten, but do at all moments keep in mind; and, at the right moment, will, with the due impressiveness, perhaps in rather a terrible manner, bring again to our mind also!

If Quashee will not honestly aid in bringing out those sugars, cinnamons, and nobler products of the West Indian Islands, for the benefit of all mankind, then I say neither will

Notes

[2] *Association* a reference to various philanthropic societies founded by Nonconformist sects, such as the Quakers and the Baptists. Such associations as the Central Emancipation Committee (1837) and the British and Foreign Anti-Slavery Society (1839) were formed at Exeter Hall, a building on The Strand, London, which opened in 1831. Its name became synonymous with the anti-slave movement, as well as with other philanthropic societies. Dickens also mocked these societies in *Bleak House* (1853) with Mrs Jellyby's "African project" in Borrioboola-Gha in the fourth chapter, entitled "Telescopic Philanthropy."

[3] *Quashee* a derogatory name for a West Indian black who supposedly is gullible or stupid (*OED*).

[4] *Doom* the final judgement; see Revelation 11: 15.

[5] *Caribs* (from Sp. *Caribe*), also carabal, a race native to the southern West Indies or Lower Antilles at the time of first contact with the Europeans; often used synonymously with cannibal to signify anthropophagy, the eating of human flesh by other humans, which was reported by the Europeans to be practised by certain Caribbean peoples, primarily as a ritual of war. The accuracy of these and subsequent reports is a matter of considerable historical controversy, as the term designates savagery and was used by imperial powers as a legal justification to enslave the indigenous people.

the Powers permit Quashee to continue growing pumpkins there for his own lazy benefit; but will sheer him out, by and by, like a lazy gourd overshadowing rich ground; him and all that partake with him,—perhaps in a very terrible manner....

John Stuart Mill (1806–73): From "The Negro Question" in *Fraser's Magazine* (Jan. 1850)[6]

SIR, Your last month's Number contains a speech against the "rights of Negroes," the doctrines and spirit of which ought not to pass without remonstrance.... If by the quality of the message we may judge of those who sent it, *not* from any powers to whom just or good men acknowledge allegiance. This so-called "eternal Act of Parliament"[7] is no new law, but the old law of the strongest,—a law against which the great teachers of mankind have in all ages protested:—it is the law of force and cunning; the law that whoever is more powerful than another, is "born lord" of that other, the other being born his "servant," who must be "compelled to work" for him by "beneficent whip," if "other methods avail not." I see nothing divine in this injunction. If "the gods" will this, it is the first duty of human beings to resist such gods.... The history of human improvement is the record of a struggle by which inch after inch of ground has been wrung from these maleficent powers, and more and more of human life rescued from the iniquitous dominion of the law of might. Much, very much of this work still remains to do; but the progress made in it is the best and greatest achievement yet performed by mankind, and it was hardly to be expected at this period of the world that we should be enjoined, by way of a great reform in human affairs, to begin *undoing* it....

According to him, the whole West Indies belong to the whites: the negroes have no claim there, to either land or food, but by their sufferance. "It was not Black Quashee, or those he represents, that made those West India islands what they are." I submit, that those who furnished the thews and sinews really had something to do with the matter. "Under the soil of Jamaica the bones of many thousand British men"—"brave Colonel Fortescue, brave Colonel Sedgwick, brave Colonel Brayne,"[8] and divers others, "had to be laid." How many hundred thousand[9] African men laid their bones there, after having had

Notes

[6] *title* published anonymously as a letter to the editor, signed "D," in answer to Carlyle's article above. Between the title and the article is the following note: "[If all the meetings at Exeter Hall be not presided over by strictly impartial chairmen, they ought to be. We shall set an example to our pious brethren in this respect, by giving publicity to the following letter. Our readers now have both sides of the question before them, and can form their own opinions upon it.—EDITOR]." The editor of *Fraser's* was John William Parker, Jr. (1820–60). The article was also reprinted in the *Daily News* (2 Jan. 1850).

Although Mill and Carlyle had been close friends in the 1830s, they became increasingly estranged as Carlyle moved to more extremist views on politics and race; however, Mill could also express views on racial inferiority in other writings. For instance, in *Representative Government* (1861) he would make comments about people who are too "rude" to be governed as a civilized nation: "Nothing but foreign force would induce a tribe of North American Indians to submit to the restraints of a regular and civilised government. The same might have been said, though somewhat less absolutely, of the barbarians who overran the Roman Empire." India, too, was not capable of representative

government on its own resources, but must rely on Britain: "Some [dependencies] are composed of people of similar civilisation to the ruling country, capable of, and ripe for, representative government: such as the British possessions in America and Australia. Others, like India, are still at a great distance from that state."

[7] *Parliament* quoting Carlyle in *Fraser's* article above; all subsequent quotations in Mill are from that article unless otherwise noted.

[8] *Fortescue ... Brayne* Carlyle mentioned three military leaders as heroic, Colonel Richard Fortesque (d. 1655), a commander in Cromwell's Model Army, sent to Jamaica in 1654 where he died of fever; Colonel Robert Sedgwick (1613–56), military leader in Massachusetts and England in the first Anglo-Dutch War; and Lieut.-General William Brayne (d. 1657), in 1656 appointed commander-in-chief in Jamaica where he died of fever.

[9] *thousand* when the British acquired Jamaica (1655), the slave population was about 400. It rose steadily as the sugar economy grew: to about 9,500 in 1673; about 86,500 in 1734; about 193,000 in 1775; and about 300,000 in 1800. It peaked at about 360,000 in 1810; and at abolition (1834) was a little below 300,000.

their lives pressed out by slow or fierce torture? They could have better done without Colonel Fortescue, than Colonel Fortescue could have done without them. But he was the stronger, and could "compel"; what they did and suffered therefore goes for nothing. Not only they did not, but it seems they *could* not, have cultivated those islands. "Never by art of his" (the negro) "could one pumpkin have grown there to solace any human throat." They grow pumpkins, however, and more than pumpkins, in a very similar country, their native Africa. . . .

No argument against the capacity of negroes for improvement, could be drawn from their not being one of these rare exceptions. It is curious withal, that the earliest known civilization was, we have the strongest reason to believe, a negro civilization. The original Egyptians are inferred, from the evidence of their sculptures, to have been a negro race: it was from negroes, therefore, that the Greeks learnt their first lessons in civilization; and to the records and traditions of these negroes did the Greek philosophers to the very end of their career resort (I do not say with much fruit) as a treasury of mysterious wisdom.[10] But I again renounce all advantage from facts: were the whites born ever so superior in intelligence to the blacks, and competent by nature to instruct and advise them, it would not be the less monstrous to assert that they had therefore a right either to subdue them by force, or circumvent them by superior skill; to throw upon them the toils and hardships of life, reserving for themselves, under the misapplied name of work, its agreeable excitements.

Were I to point out, even in the highest terms, every vulnerable point in your contributor's Discourse, I should produce a longer dissertation than his. One instance more must suffice. . . . The labour market admits of three possible conditions, and not, as this would imply, of only two. Either, first, the labourers can live almost without working, which is said to be the case in Demerara;[11] or, secondly, which is the common case, they can live by working, but must work in order to live; or, thirdly, they cannot by working get a sufficient living, which is the case in Ireland. Your contributor sees only the extreme cases, but no possibility of the medium. If Africans are imported, he thinks there must either be so few of them, that they will not need to work, or so many, that although they work, they will not be able to live.

John Ruskin (1819–1900): From *Inaugural Lecture* (1870)[12]

There is a destiny now possible to us—the highest ever set before a nation to be accepted or refused. We are still undegenerate in race; a race mingled of the best

Notes

[10] *wisdom* Mill gives a version of what was to develop in twentieth-century America as Afro-centrism, the view that African contributions to history and culture have been suppressed under colonialism and slavery.

[11] *Demerara* former Dutch colony on the northern coast of South America, captured by the British, first in 1796 and finally in 1803. Now called Guyana, it was the site of a famous and bloody slave rebellion in 1823, a revolt that the abolition movement in Britain used to rally its cause.

[12] *title* this lecture was given on 8 February 1870 as the newly endowed Slade Professor of Fine Art at Oxford on Ruskin's fifty-first birthday to a large crowd. In the Hilary term 1870 he would give six more lectures: "The Relation of Art to Religion"; "The Relation of Art to Morals"; "The Relation of Art to Use"; "Colour"; "Line"; and "Light." In

this first introductory lecture he lays out his beliefs: "The art of any country is the exponent of its social and political virtues." He addresses his privileged audience of Oxford undergraduates on the role of art in their education: "a youth is sent to our Universities, not (hitherto at least) to be apprenticed to a trade, nor even always to be advanced in a profession; but, always, to be made a gentleman and a scholar. . . . I conceive it to be the function of this Professorship, with respect to them, to establish both a practical and critical school of fine art for English gentlemen: practical, so that if they draw at all, they may draw rightly; and critical, so that being first directed to such works of existing art as will best reward their study, they may afterwards make their patronage of living artists delightful to themselves in their consciousness of its

northern blood.[13] We are not yet dissolute in temper, but still have the firmness to govern, and the grace to obey. We have been taught a religion of pure mercy, which we must either now betray, or learn to defend by fulfilling. And we are rich in an inheritance of honour, bequeathed to us through a thousand years of noble history, which it should be our daily thirst to increase with splendid avarice, so that Englishmen, if it be a sin to covet honour, should be the most offending souls alive.[14] Within the last few years we have had the laws of natural science opened to us with a rapidity which has been blinding by its brightness; and means of transit and communication given to us, which have made but one kingdom of the habitable globe. One kingdom;—but who is to be its king? Is there to be no king in it, think you, and every man to do that which is right in his own eyes? Or only kings of terror, and the obscene empires of Mammon and Belial?[15] Or will you, youths of England, make your country again a royal throne of kings; a sceptred isle,[16] for all the world a source of light, a centre of peace; mistress of Learning and of the Arts;—faithful guardian of great memories in the midst of irreverent and ephemeral visions;—faithful servant of time-tried principles, under temptation from fond experiments and licentious desires; and, amidst the cruel and clamorous jealousies of the nations, worshipped in her strange valour, of goodwill towards men?[17] . . .

And this is what she must either do, or perish: she must found colonies as fast and as far as she is able, formed of her most energetic and worthiest men;—seizing every piece of fruitful waste ground she can set her foot on, and there teaching these her colonists that their chief virtue is to be fidelity to their country, and that their first aim is to be to advance the power of England by land and sea: and that, though they live on a distant plot of ground, they are no more to consider themselves therefore disfranchised from their native land than the sailors of her fleets do, because they float on distant waves. So that literally, these colonies must be fastened fleets, and every man of them must be under authority of captains and officers, whose better command is to be over fields and streets instead of ships of the line; and England, in these her motionless navies (or, in the true and mightiest sense, motionless churches, ruled by pilots on the Galilean lake[18] of all the world) is to "expect every man to do his duty";[19] recognising that duty is indeed possible no less in peace than war; and that if we can get men, for little pay, to cast themselves against cannon-mouths for love of England, we may find men also who will plough and sow for her, who will behave kindly and righteously for her, who will bring up their

Notes

justice, and, to the utmost, beneficial to their country, by being given to the men who deserve it; in the early period of their lives, when they both need it most, and can be influenced by it to the best advantage." Said to have been a huge influence on Cecil Rhodes, the lecture closes with an exhortation (our selection) on the imperial obligations of the soon-to-be-educated gentlemen. In *The Pleasures of England* (1873) Ruskin would claim that the first three paragraphs of our extract are "of all the pieces of teaching I have ever given from this chair, the most pregnant and essential to whatever studies, whether of Art or Science, you may pursue, in this place or elsewhere, during you lives" (lecture 1, para. 3). He would resign the professorship in 1880 after suffering attacks of mental illness; in October 1883 after recovering, he was re-elected to the professorship; and in March 1885 he resigned again after quarrelling with university authorities. First published in *Lectures on Art, Delivered before the University of Oxford in Hilary Term, 1870* (1870).

[13] *blood* belief in Anglo-Saxon racial superiority.
[14] *if it... alive* see *Henry V* 4. 3. 29.
[15] *eyes ... Belial* for "right ... eyes" see Proverbs 12: 15; Mammon is Aramaic for riches, used in the Bible to signify greed (see, for instance, the parable of the Unjust Steward, Luke 16: 1–13). Belial (Heb. worthless) is used throughout the Bible to signify a demon or devil, as in 2 Corinthians 6: 15; the names Mammon and Belial are used by Milton for devils throughout Books 1 and 2 of *Paradise Lost*.
[16] *royal ... isle* see *Richard II* 2. 1. 41.
[17] *toward... men* see Luke 2. 14.
[18] *navies ... lake* for navies Ruskin refers to the common usage in calling the main section of a church as the "nave" (Lat. *navis*, ship); for pilots, see Milton, *Lycidas* (109).
[19] *expect ... duty* in a message to the navy at the Battle of Trafalgar (21 Oct. 1805), Horatio Nelson (1758–1805) said: "England expects that every man will do his duty" – a phrase that passed into popular patriotism; for imperial duty as a poetic trope, see HEMANS, n. 1.

children to love her, and who will gladden themselves in the brightness of her glory, more than in all the light of tropic skies.

But that they may be able to do this, she must make her own majesty stainless; she must give them thoughts of their home of which they can be proud. The England who is to be mistress of half the earth cannot remain herself a heap of cinders, trampled by contending and miserable crowds; she must yet again become the England she was once, and in all beautiful ways more; so happy, so secluded, and so pure.... She must guide the human arts, and gather the divine knowledge, of distant nations, transformed from savageness[20] to manhood, and redeemed from despairing into peace.

You think that an impossible ideal. Be it so; refuse to accept it if you will; but see that you form your own in its stead. All that I ask of you is to have a fixed purpose of some kind for your country and yourselves; no matter how restricted, so that it be fixed and unselfish. I know what stout hearts are in you, to answer acknowledged need; but it is the fatallest form of error in English youths to hide their hardihood till it fades for lack of sunshine, and to act in disdain of purpose, till all purpose is vain. It is not by deliberate, but by careless selfishness; not by compromise with evil, but by dull following of good, that the weight of national evil increases upon us daily. Break through at least this pretence of existence; determine what you will be, and what you would win. You will not decide wrongly if you resolve to decide at all. Were even the choice between lawless pleasure and loyal suffering, you would not, I believe, choose basely.

George William Hunt (c.1839–1904): "MacDermott's War Song" ["By Jingo"] (1877)[21]

"The Dogs of War"[22] are loose and the rugged Russian Bear,[23]
Full bent on blood and robbery,[24] has crawl'd out of his lair;
It seems a thrashing now and then, will never help to tame
That brute, and so he's out upon the "same old game."[25]

Notes

[20] *savageness* earlier in the lecture Ruskin argues that some semi-savages were unlike his contemporaries, who "cannot design, because we have too much to think of, and we think of it too anxiously. It has long been observed how little real anxiety exists in the minds of the partly savage races which excel in decorative art."

[21] *title* the song became enormously popular in British pubs and music halls partly through the singing of Gilbert Hastings MacDermott (1845–1901), who had bought the rights to the song from Hunt. It became one of the popular British nationalistic songs and was revived during World War I. The Russo-Turkish War (1877–78) war pitted the Turkish Empire against a coalition of Eastern Orthodox nations in the Balkans, led by the Russian Empire. The crisis concerned the regaining of Balkan territory lost to Russia by the Treaty of Paris (1856), which ended the Crimean War, and the declaration of independence of Poland from Russia and of Serbia and Montenegro from Turkey. The Bulgarian uprising of 1876 was repressed with brutal force and widespread slaughter by Russia and hired Bashi-Bazouk mercenaries and quickly engaged Europe against the "atrocities." Disraeli, then in power, supported Turkey as public opinion in England turned against his pro-Ottoman policy. Russia, supporting Bulgaria, and looking towards

a pan-Slavic and pan-Orthodox union, declared war on Turkey on 24 April 1877, and within two months had crossed the Danube. After the Russians successfully besieged Plevna in modern Bulgaria (the occasion for Hunt's song), the road was clear for Russia to proceed to Constantinople, whereupon Britain sent warships to prevent their entry into the city to preserve the remnants of the Turkish Empire, later consolidated by the Congress of Berlin (1878). Our text: G. W. Hunt, *MacDermott's War Song* (1877), Victorian sheet music.

[22] *war* see *Julius Caesar* 3. 1. 273. On 17 June 1876 on the eve of the Balkan crisis, *Punch* published a John Tenniel's cartoon of Russia reigning in four "dogs of war" (named Herzegovina, Serbia, Montenegro, and Bosnia) about to attack the Turkish Sultan, while a British policeman looks over the fence, warning Russia against releasing them.

[23] *Bear* a widely used symbol of Russia in British anti-Slavic rhetoric and cartoons from the seventeenth through the nineteenth century.

[24] *robbery* regaining possessions in the Balkans and the use of a fleet in the Black Sea lost after the Crimean War.

[25] *game* or the "Great Game" was a term applied to the strategic, diplomatic, and military rivalry between the British and Russian empires over the control of central Asia, especially Afghanistan, throughout the nineteenth century.

The Lion[26] did his best to find him some excuse 5
To crawl back to his den again, all efforts were no use;
He hunger'd for his victim, he's pleased when blood is shed,
But let us hope his crimes may all recoil on his own head.

[*Chorus*]
We don't want to fight but by jingo[27] if we do,
We've got the ships, we've got the men, and got the money too! 10
We've fought the Bear before[28] and while we're Britons true
The Russians shall not have Constantinople.

The misdeeds of the Turks[29] have been "spouted" thro' all lands,
But how about the Russians, can they show spotless hands?
They slaughtered well at Khiva,[30] in Siberia icy cold, 15
How many subjects done to death will never perhaps be told,

They butchered the Circassians,[31] man, woman, yes and child,
With cruelties their Generals their murderous hours beguiled,
And poor unhappy Poland[32] their cruel yoke must bear,
Whilst prayers for "Freedom and Revenge"[33] go up into the air. 20

[*Chorus*]
May he who 'gan the quarrel soon have to bite the dust,
The Turk should be thrice armed for "he hath his quarrel just,"
'Tis sad that countless thousands should die thro' cruel war,
But let us hope most fervently ere long it will be o'er;

Let them be warned, Old England is brave Old England still, 25
We've proved our might, we've claimed our right, and ever, ever will,
Should we have to draw the sword our way to victory we'll forge,
With the battle cry of Britons, "Old England and Saint George!"[34]
[*Chorus*]

J. R. Seeley (1834–95): *The Expansion of England* (1883)

From Course II, Lecture I: "History and Politics"[35]

I take it that every other country, France, Germany, the United States, every country
except perhaps Russia, has a simple problem to solve compared with that which is set

Notes

[26] *Lion* symbol of Great Britain, and used in the British coat of arms.

[27] *by jingo* a "minced oath" or euphemism for "by Jesus" dating from the seventeenth century, but revived in 1877 in this song. Jingoism is an extreme and bellicose form of patriotism, threatening sanctions and military force to protect national interests. In 1901, J. A. Hobson, in the context of the Second Boer War (1899–1902), would publish a harsh denunciation of this populism in *The Psychology of Jingoism*.

[28] *before* in the Crimean War.

[29] *Turks* the carnage in Serbia and Montenegro after their uprisings in 1876.

[30] *Khiva* in modern Uzbekistan, Khiva, a Turkish city, was taken in a battle by Russia in May, 1873. It is far from Siberia.

[31] *Circassians* a people on the north-east coast of the Black Sea (formerly Circassia), expelled from their homeland by Russia, especially in the Caucasian War (1817–64). They found refuge in the Ottoman Empire in Turkey, Syria, Jordan, and elsewhere.

[32] *Poland* eastern Poland had been occupied by Russia since the Congress of Vienna (1815) but was incorporated into the Russian Empire in 1864.

[33] *Freedom and Revenge* see Robert Southey, *Vision of Don Roderick* (1811).

[34] *George* this patriotic cry echoes Shakespeare's Henry V before Agincourt:

Follow your spirit; and, upon this charge
Cry "God for Harry! England and Saint George!" (3.1.31).

[35] *title* this work was originally two sets of eight lectures given in 1881. The first set deals with the beginnings of

before England. Most of those states are compact and solid, scarcely less compact, though so much larger, than the city-states of antiquity. They can only be attacked at home, and therefore their armies are a kind of citizen soldiery. Now distant dependencies destroy this compactness, and make the national interest hard to discern and hard to protect.... But this external difficulty is less serious than the internal difficulties which arise in a scattered empire. How to give a moral unity to vast countries separated from each other by half the globe, even when they are inhabited in the main by one nation! But even this is not the greatest of the anxieties of England. For besides the Colonies, we have India. Here at least there is no community of race or religion. Here that solid basis which is formed by immigration and colonisation is almost entirely wanting. Here you have another problem not less vast, not less difficult, and much less hopeful than that of the colonies. Either problem by itself is as much as any nation ever took in hand before. It seems really too much that both should fall on the same nation at the same time.

Consider how distracting must be the effect upon the public mind of these two opposite questions. The colonies and India are in opposite extremes. Whatever political maxims are most applicable to the one, are most inapplicable able to the other. In the colonies everything is brand-new. There you have the most progressive race put in the circumstances most favourable to progress. They have no past and an unbounded future. Government and institutions are all ultra-English. All is liberty, industry, invention, innovation, and as yet tranquillity. Now if this alone were Greater Britain, it would be homogeneous, all of a piece; and, vast and boundless as the territory is, we might come to understand its affairs. But there is at the same time another Greater Britain, surpassing this in population though not in territory, and it is everything which this is not. India is all past and, I may almost say, no future. What it will come to the wisest man is afraid to conjecture, but in the past it opens vistas into a fabulous antiquity. All the oldest religions, all the oldest customs, petrified as it were. No form of popular government as yet possible. Everything which Europe, and still more the New World, has outlived still flourishing in full vigour; superstition, fatalism, polygamy, the most primitive priestcraft, the most primitive despotism;[36] and threatening the northern frontier the vast Asiatic steppe with its Osbegs and Turcomans.[37] Thus the same nation which reaches one hand towards the future of the globe and assumes the position of mediator between Europe and the New World, stretches the other hand towards the remotest past, becomes an Asiatic conqueror, and usurps the succession of the Great Mogul.[38]

Notes

European imperialism up to the eighteenth century, from Columbus to the American Revolution, which he calls the "schism" of Greater Britain. In the second set of lectures Seeley focuses entirely on India, describing the differences between the English conquest of India and the "natural" tendency of expansion into other parts of the world where English emigrants formed, if not the majority of the population, certainly the power block. Famously, Seeley described "the extension of the English name into other countries of the globe, the foundation of Greater Britain," as almost an accident: "We seem, as it were, to have conquered and peopled half the world in a fit of absence of mind" (course 1, ch. 1). For Seeley, the study of history is entirely pragmatic: it is to educate the statesmen of his day so that they prevent the loss of the "white" colonies. Despite little hope that the differences between India and England could be reconciled, "Greater Britain" must retain India as part of what Kipling would later call "the white man's burden." By 1885, Seeley's book had sold over 80,000 copies, and had become the bible of the Imperial

Federation League, an influential group formed in July 1884 to promote the colonies as an organic extension of the British "family."

[36] *despotism* for a famous statement about an atrophied India, see this section, GOVERNING, n. 5. Oriental despotism is a commonplace among Western commentators, whose presumption is that Asians by necessity must be ruled by despotic governments, cutting them off from Western notions of progress. The idea goes back to Herodotus (c.484–425 BCE), Greek historian. Gibbon in *Decline and Fall* (1776) refers to "the effeminate luxury of oriental despotism" (bk. 1, ch. 6); Karl Marx on India often writes of an "Asiatic mode of production" cut off from the progressive forces of Western history.

[37] *Osbegs ... Turcomans* the Osbegs were a historical Turkic tribal confederation in Central Asia during the early medieval Turkic expansion from 600 to 1100 between Persia and the Oxus River (or present-day Iran and the Amu Darya River).

[38] *Mogul* the Mogul or Moghal Empire designates the conquest of the Indian subcontinent by the Timurid

WEB p. 223

Walter Crane (1845–1915): "Imperial Federation Map of the World Showing the Extent of the British Empire in 1886" (1886)

Alfred Tennyson (1809–92): "Opening of the Indian and Colonial Exhibition" (1886)[39]

I

Welcome, welcome with one voice!
In your welfare we rejoice,
Sons and brothers that have sent,
From isle and cape and continent,
Produce of your field and flood,   5
Mount and mine, and primal wood,
Works of subtle brain and hand,
And splendours of the Morning Land,
Gifts from every British zone!
        Britons, hold your own!   10

2

May we find, as ages run,
The mother featured in the son,
And may yours for ever be
That old strength and constancy
Which has made your Fathers great,   15
In our ancient island-state!
And—where'er her flag may fly
Glorying between sea and sky—
Makes the might of Britain known!
        Britons, hold your own!   20

3

Britain fought her sons of yore,
Britain fail'd: and never more,
Careless of our growing kin,
Shall we sin our fathers' sin,

Notes

dynasty from Persia from about 1526 to the mid-1700s, although the last emperor, Bahadur Shah II (1775–1862) of Delhi, hung on until the Indian Rebellion in 1857.

[39] *title* written in Tennyson's official capacity as Poet Laureate at the request of the Prince of Wales. The Colonial and Indian Exhibition opened on 4 May 1886 in

Men that in a narrower day—   25
Unprophetic rulers they—
Drove from out the Mother's nest
That young eagle of the West,
To forage for herself alone![40]
        Britons, hold your own!   30

4

Sharers of our glorious past,
Brothers, must we part at last?
Shall we not thro' good and ill
Cleave to one another still?
Britain's myriad voices call   35
"Sons, be welded, each and all,
Into one Imperial whole.
One with Britain, heart and soul!
One life, one flag, one fleet, one Throne!"
        Britons, hold your own!   40
        And God guard all![41]

Alfred Tennyson (1809–92): "*Carmen Sæculare*: An Ode in Honour of the Jubilee of Queen Victoria" (1887)[42]

I

Fifty times the rose has flower'd and faded,
Fifty times the golden harvest fallen,
Since our Queen assumed the globe, the sceptre.

Notes

South Kensington in London to great acclaim (see EMPIRE: CELEBRATION; CRANE (WEB p. 223)). The Prince of Wales said the exhibition was "to stimulate commerce and strengthen the bonds of union now existing in every portion of her Majesty's Empire." The Ode was first made public when it was printed in the "Official Programme" for the opening of the exhibition in the presence of Queen Victoria in the Royal Albert Hall. On that occasion the second verse of the National Anthem was sung in Sanskrit, translated into that language by Max Müller. Tennyson's Ode followed, set to music and conducted by Arthur Sullivan (1842–1900) and sung by soprano Emma Albani (1847–1930) and the large Royal Albert Hall Choral Society. Thereafter the poem was reprinted in newspaper accounts of the ceremony – in England, for instance, in *The Standard* (5 May 1886, 3; our text), and around the world. The Prince

of Wales sent a telegram to various colonies: "I should be glad if you would publish them [the proceedings, including Tennyson's Ode] in the *New Zealand Gazette*," as was done there and elsewhere. It was later republished in *Locksley Hall Sixty Year After and Other Poems* (1886).

[40] *alone* the entire stanza is about the American Revolution (1775–83), the watershed division between the first and second British Empire (see n. 35).

[41] *all* Tennyson added this line in MS to the proof sheets of the text for the official programme where it was included (each word was capitalized), as well as in newspaper reports following the event. The last line would be omitted from the version in *Locksley Hall* (1886).

[42] *title* the metre of the poem in the even-numbered sections is based, according to Tennyson, on Catullus' *Collis o Heliconii* (Hallam, Lord Tennyson, *Life ... Memoir*, 2. 400),

II

She beloved for a kindliness
Rare in Fable or History,   5
Queen, and Empress of India,
Crown'd so long with a diadem
Never worn by a worthier,
Now with prosperous auguries
Comes at last to the bounteous   10
Crowning year of her Jubilee.

III

Nothing of the lawless, of the Despot,
Nothing of the vulgar, or vainglorious,
All is gracious, gentle, great and Queenly.

IV

You then loyally,[43] all of you,[44]   15
Deck your houses, illuminate
All your towns for a festival,
And in each let a multitude
Loyal, each, to the heart of it,
One full voice of allegiance,   20
Hail the great[45] Ceremonial
Of this year of her Jubilee.

V

Queen, as true to womanhood as Queenhood,
Glorying in the glories of her people,
Sorrowing with the sorrows of the lowest!   25

VI

You, that wanton in affluence,
Spare not now to be bountiful,

Notes

Carmen 61, written in Aeolic stanzas of four glyconics and a pherecratean (a truncated glyconic). That is, the general verse form is modelled on the archaic Aeolic lyric form of Sappho and Alcaeus who wrote in the Aeolic dialect. The glyconic is a line of Greek or Latin verse in which the opening foot can be either long or short, followed by two more feet of roughly this pattern: ¯ ¯ or ˇ ˇ followed by two further feet, the rest of the line: ¯ ˇ ˇ ˇ ¯ ˇ, though additional syllables could be added, and the caesura varies in its location. It is a celebratory poem in honour of Victoria's golden jubilee, the fiftieth anniversary of her coronation. It also came to be identified with the building and completion of the Imperial Institute (see this section, INTRODUCTION). Other poems commemorated that event: Swinburne's The Union—A Song" (Nineteenth Century, 1893), Kipling's "Ode for the Opening of the Imperial Institute" (English Illustrated Magazine 1893), and John Douglas Sutherland Campbell, the Marquess of Lorne's "The Empire's Toasts" (The Graphic 20 May, 1893). First published in Macmillan's Magazine April 1887; republished as "An Ode on the Jubilee of Queen Victoria" in Demeter and Other Poems (1889) and signed "Tennyson."

[43] loyally joyfully (1889).

[44] you two additional lines were added after this line: "Set the mountain aflame tonight, / Shoot your stars to the firmament," (1889).

[45] great fair (1889).

Call your poor to regale with you,[46]
Make their neighbourhood healthfuller,
Give your gold to the Hospital,   30
Let the weary be comforted,
Let the needy be banqueted,
Let the maim'd in his heart rejoice[47]
At[48] this year of her Jubilee.

VII

Henry's fifty years are all in shadow,   35
Gray with distance Edward's fifty summers,
Ev'n her Grandsire's fifty half forgotten.[49]

VIII

You, the Patriot Architect,[50]
Shape[51] a stately memorial,
Make it regally gorgeous,   40
Some Imperial Institute,
Rich in symbol, in ornament,
Which may speak to the centuries,
All the centuries after us,[52]
Of[53] this year of her Jubilee.   45

IX

Fifty years of ever-broadening Commerce!
Fifty years of ever-brightening Science!
Fifty years of ever-widening Empire!

X

You, the Mighty, the Fortunate,
You, the Lord-territorial,   50
You, the Lord-manufacturer,
You, the hardy, laborious,

Notes

[46] *you* after this line, the following line was added "All the lowly, the destitute," (1889).

[47] *rejoice* after this line, the following line was added: "At this glad Ceremonial," (1889).

[48] *At* And (1889).

[49] *Henry… forgotten* all had long reigns: Henry III (1207–72) reigned for fifty-six years, from 1216 until his death; Edward III (1312–77) reigned for fifty years, from 1227 until his death; and George III (1738–1820), reigned for sixty years, from 1760. However, because of his mental illness, George, Prince of Wales, became Prince Regent in 1810 and ruled in this capacity until his father's death, after which he became George IV.

[50] *Architect* two months after this poem was first published, in June 1887, Thomas Collcutt (1840–1924) was chosen architect of the new Imperial Institute. After this line, Tennyson added another: "You that shape for Eternity," (1889). See this section, INTRODUCTION.

[51] *Shape* Raise (1889).

[52] *us* after this line the following line was added: "Of this great Ceremonial," (1889).

[53] *Of* And (1889).

[54] *Albion* ancient name for England.

Patient children of Albion,[54]
You, Canadian, Indian,
Australasian, African,   55
All your hearts be in harmony,
All your voices in unison,
Singing "Hail to the glorious
Golden year of her Jubilee!"

XI

Are there thunders moaning in the distance?[55]   60
Are there spectres moving in the darkness?
Trust the Lord of Light to guide her people,[56]
Till the thunders pass, the spectres vanish,
And the Light is Victor, and the darkness
Dawns into the Jubilee of the Ages.   65

WEB p. 226

Mrs Ernest Ames [Mary Frances Ames] (1853–1929): *An ABC for Baby Patriots* (1899)

Henry Labouchère [?] (1831–1912): "The Brown Man's Burden" (1899)[57]

Pile on the brown man's burden
To gratify your greed;
Go, clear away the "niggers"[58]
Who progress would impede;

Be very stern, for truly   5
'Tis useless to be mild
With new-caught, sullen peoples,
Half devil and half child.[59]

Notes

[55] *distance* Tennyson asked Charles Villiers Stanford to write the music for the Ode; he records in his *Pages from an Unwritten Diary* that Victoria suggested that Tennyson add the concluding section.

[56] *Lord ... to guide* Hand ... will lead (1889).

[57] *title* a parody of "The White Man's Burden" (see KIPLING), published anonymously in *Truth* in the same month as Kipling's poem (Feb. 1899), this poem was probably written by Labouchère, English Radical Liberal politician, writer, and theatre owner. He was the owner and editor of *Truth*, a journal he started in 1877. Labouchère was an agnostic, a rebel, and a radical thinker; he was also a virulent opponent of women's suffrage and a vocal anti-Semite. Labouchère is best known for his amendment

making homosexual acts a criminal offence (1885); see GENDER: SEX; LABOUCHÈRE, "AMENDMENT" (WEB p. 102). There are a number of other parodies and commentaries on Kipling's poem: see, for instance, Wilfrid Scawen Blunt (see n. 74), Ernest Crosby (1856–1907), American clergyman and writer, "The Real White Man's Burden" in *Swords and Ploughshares* (1902); and Hubert Harrison (1883–1927), West Indian–American writer and political activist, "The Black Man's Burden" in *When Africa Awakes* (1920).

[58] *nigger* the term was used not just in reference to Africans, but also Indians, Maoris (from New Zealand), and aborigines from Australia. See n. 1.

[59] *half child* see KIPLING, "THE WHITE MAN'S BURDEN" (7–8).

Pile on the brown man's burden;
And, if ye rouse his hate,   10
Meet his old-fashioned reasons
With Maxims[60] up to date.

With shells and dumdum bullets[61]
A hundred times made plain
The brown man's loss must ever   15
Imply the white man's gain.[62]

Pile on the brown man's burden,
Compel him to be free;
Let all your manifestoes
Reek with philanthropy.   20

And if with heathen folly
He dares your will dispute,
Then, in the name of freedom,
Don't hesitate to shoot.

Pile on the brown man's burden,   25
And if his cry be sore,
That surely need not irk you—
Ye've driven slaves before.

Seize on his ports and pastures,
The fields his people tread;   30
Go make from them your living,
And mark them with his dead.

Pile on the brown man's burden,
And through the world proclaim
That ye are Freedom's[63] agent—   35
There's no more paying game!

And, should your own past history
Straight in your teeth be thrown,
Retort that independence
Is good for whites alone.   40

Pile on the brown man's burden,
With equity have done;
Weak, antiquated scruples
Their squeamish course have run,

Notes

[60] *Maxims* both a fundamental principle and a type of machine gun invented in 1884 and widely associated with the British Empire. One year earlier in "The Modern Traveller" (1898), Hilaire Belloc (1870–1953) had written: "Whatever happens, we have got / The Maxim gun, and they have not."

[61] *bullets* Dum-Dum, a town 6.5 kilometres northeast of Calcutta, was the site of a British rifle and ammunition factory where the Mark IV or Dum Dum bullets were developed and manufactured. These bullets expanded dramatically upon impact, creating a large wound. They were used extensively in the Empire until the Boer War, when in 1899 the International Conference of The Hague prohibited their use.

[62] *gain* see KIPLING, "THE WHITE MAN'S BURDEN" (15–6).

[63] *Freedom's* see KIPLING, "THE WHITE MAN'S BURDEN" (43).

And, though 'tis freedom's banner   45
You're waving in the van,
Reserve for home consumption
The sacred "rights of man"![64]

And if by chance ye falter,
Or lag along the course,   50
If, as the blood flows freely,
Ye feel some slight remorse,

Hie ye to Rudyard Kipling,
Imperialism's prop,
And bid him, for your comfort,   55
Turn on his jingo[65] stop.

J. A. Hobson (1858–1940): *Imperialism: A Study* (1902)

From Part 2, Chapter 4: "Imperialism and the Lower Races"[66]

The statement, often made, that the work of imperial expansion is virtually complete is not correct. It is true that most of the "backward" races have been placed in some sort of dependence upon one or other of the "civilised" Powers as colony, protectorate, hinterland, or sphere of influence. But this in most instances marks rather the beginning of a process of imperialisation than a definite attainment of empire. The intensive growth of empire by which interference is increased and governmental control tightened over spheres of influence and protectorates is as important and as perilous an aspect of Imperialism as the extensive growth which takes shape in assertion of rule over new areas of territory and new populations....

During the last twenty years Great Britain, Germany, France, and Russia have bitten off huge mouthfuls of Africa and Asia which are not yet chewed, digested, or assimilated.[67] Moreover, great areas still remain whose independence, though threatened, is yet unimpaired....

There is nothing unworthy, quite the contrary, in the notion that nations which, through a more stimulative environment, have advanced further in certain arts of

Notes

[64] *man* the title of a famous pamphlet by Thomas Paine (1737–1809), published in 1791 in support of the French Revolution; also "The Declaration of the Rights of Man and of the Citizen" adopted during the revolution in 1789.

[65] *jingo* see above, Hunt, n. 27.

[66] *title* in the preface Hobson claims to proceed "rather by diagnosis than historical description." The book consists of two parts: first, "the economic origins are traced"; and second, "the theory and practice of Imperialism regarded as a 'mission of civilization'" are analysed. He claims to be treating a "social pathology," a "disease": "Our economic analysis has disclosed the fact that it is only the interests of competing cliques of business men—investors, contractors, export manufacturers, and certain professional classes—that are antagonistic; that these cliques, usurping the authority and voice of the people, use the public resources to push their private interests, and spend the blood and money of the people in this vast and disastrous

military game, feigning national antagonism which have no basis in reality." In the first chapter, Hobson provided a list of territories acquired by Britain since 1870: "For so small a nation to add to its domains in the course of a single generation an area of 4,754,000 square miles, with an estimated population of 88,000,000, is a historical fact of great significance." The book was extremely influential: Lenin's *Imperialism: the Highest Stage of Capitalism* (1916) draws its core argument entirely from Hobson. Immediately prior to this work, Hobson was a journalist for the *Manchester Guardian*, covering the Boer War (1899–1902), publishing *War in South Africa* (1900) and *Psychology of Jingoism* (1901).

[67] *assimilated* in the first chapter, Hobson claims: "the definite advance of Germany upon its Imperialist career began in 1884, with a policy of African protectorates and annexations of Oceanic islands. During the next fifteen years she brought under her colonial sway about 1,000,000

industry, politics, or morals, should communicate these to nations which from their circumstances were more backward, so as to aid them in developing alike the material resources of their land and the human resources of their people. . . . Force is itself no remedy, coercion is not education, but it may be a prior condition to the operation of educative forces. Those, at any rate, who assign any place to force in the education or the political government of individuals in a nation can hardly deny that the same instrument may find a place in the civilisation of backward by progressive nations.

Assuming that the arts of "progress," or some of them, are communicable, a fact which is hardly disputable, there can be no inherent natural right in a nation to refuse that measure of compulsory education which shall raise it from childhood to manhood in the order of nationalities. The analogy furnished by the education of a child is *primâ facie*[68] a sound one, and is not invalidated by the dangerous abuses to which it is exposed in practice.

The real issue is one of safeguards, of motives, and of methods. What are the conditions under which a nation may help to develop the resources of another, and even apply some element of compulsion in doing so? The question, abstract as it may sound, is quite the most important of all practical questions for this generation. For, that such development will take place, and such compulsion, legitimate or illegitimate, be exercised, more and more throughout this new century in many quarters of this globe, is beyond the shadow of a doubt. It is the great practical business of the century to explore and develop, by every method which science can devise, the hidden natural and human resources of the globe.

That the white Western nations will abandon a quest on which they have already gone so far is a view which does not deserve consideration. That this process of development may be so conducted as to yield a gain to world-civilisation, instead of some terrible *débâcle*[69] in which revolted slave races may trample down their parasitic and degenerate white masters, should be the supreme aim of far-sighted scientific statecraft.

Arthur Christopher Benson (1862–1925): "Land of Hope and Glory" (1902)[70]

Land of hope and glory, Mother of the free,[71]
How may we extol thee, who are born of thee?

Notes

square miles, with an estimated population of 14,000,000. Almost the whole of this territory is tropical, and the white population forms a total of a few thousands": France's "acquisitions since 1880 (exclusive of the extension of New Caledonia and its dependencies) amount to an area of over three and a half million square miles, with a native population of some 37,000,000, almost the whole tropical or sub-tropical, inhabited by lower races and incapable of genuine French colonisation"; and "Russia, the only active expansionist country of the North, stands alone in the character of her imperial growth, which differs from other Imperialism in that it has been principally Asiatic in its achievements." For Britain, see n. 66.

[68] *primâ facie* (Lat. at first sight, on the face of it).

[69] *débâcle* (Fr. disaster).

[70] *title* the son of Edward White Benson (later, archbishop of Canterbury from 1882 to 1896) and Mary Sidgwick (1841–1918), Benson was a poet, essayist, and master of Magdalene College, Cambridge. The lyrics were written for a famous melody by Edward Elgar (1857–1934). Elgar's melody was first

used in the *trio* section of the first of six marches for orchestra entitled *Pomp and Circumstance*. Written in 1901, the march was inscribed on the first page with a loose paraphrase and partial rewriting of the opening of a poem by John Warren, Lord de Tabley (1835–1895), "The March of Glory":

> Like a proud music that draws men on to die
> Madly upon the spears in martial ecstasy,
> A measure that sets heaven in all their veins
>   And iron in their hands.
> I hear the Nation march
> Beneath her ensign as an eagle's wing;
> O'er shield and sheeted targe
> The banners of my faith most gaily swing;
> Moving to victory with solemn noise,
>   With worship and with conquest, and the voice
>   of myriads.

Lord de Tabley exploits two military tropes, *dulce et decorum est pro patria mori* (Lat. how sweet and proper it is to die for one's native land) and *nos morituri te salutamus*

Truth and Right and Freedom, each a holy gem,
Stars of solemn brightness, weave thy diadem.

Tho' thy way be darkened, still in splendour drest,   5
As the star that trembles o'er the liquid West.

Throned amid the billows,[72] throned inviolate,
Though hast reigned victorious, thou has smiled at fate.

[Chorus]
Land of hope and glory, Fortress of the free,
How may we extol thee, praise thee, honour thee?   10

Hark, a mighty nation maketh glad reply;
Lo, our lips are thankful, lo, our hearts are high!

Hearts in hope uplifted, loyal lips that sing;
Strong in faith and freedom, we have crowned our King!

Dear Land of Hope, thy hope is crowned[73]   15
    God make thee mightier yet!

On Sov'ran brows, belov'd, renown'd,
    Once more thy crown is set.

Thine equal laws, by freedom gained,
    Have ruled thee well and long;   20

Notes

(Lat. we who are about to die salute you), the latter a greeting of gladiators hailing Caesar in the Roman amphitheatre, but applied here by de Tabley to the hailing of a personified glory as queen.

   Three versions of the lyrics exist. First, Elgar was commissioned to write a composition for a gala concert before the Edward VII's coronation. Elgar set to work on his *Coronation Ode* (1902) with some words from Benson, then asking him for more. Benson wrote words for the seven sections of the *Ode*, those for the concluding finale being known as "Land of Hope and Glory" set to Elgar's tune from *Pomp and Circumstance*. This version consists of the first stanza (four lines sung by a contralto, four by a soprano) followed by the chorus. It was published in April 1902 (our text) and was first performed in Sheffield on 26 October 1902 and a few days later in London in the presence of Edward VII and Queen Alexandra at a festival honouring the Empire and the Union Jack – with one flag issued to every audience member. Another British composer, Charles Villiers Stanford (1852–1924), wrote to Elgar that his *Ode* had "translated Master Rudyard Kipling into Music." For the second and third versions, see n. 73. The song is traditionally sung as an alternative English national anthem at rugby and football games, at national and royal celebrations (like the Golden Jubilee concert for Elizabeth II) and at the last night of the BBC Proms concerts with flags (for an audio and visual recording, see http://www.youtube.com/watch?v=gLKSDT_2zPA).

[71] *free* the stanza is to be sung by contralto (first four lines) and soprano (second four lines), followed by the chorus in the version of 1902.

[72] *billows* the imagery suggests the figure of Britannia as the queen of the oceans. For another patriotic use of such imagery, see Gilbert, *Iolanthe*, "When Britain Really Ruled the Waves."

[73] *crowned* this stanza, the second version, is now the standard wording used in popular celebrations. Elgar asked Benson for alternative words for an orchestral arrangement for solo voice, and it was first sung in June 1902 by Elgar's friend, the contralto Dame Clara Butt (1872–1936). She recorded it in 1911, as may be heard here: http://www.firstworldwar.com/audio/landofhopeandglory.htm

   In 1914 an additional stanza, the third version, was added to the 1902 / 1911 version to reflect the sentiments of Britain's involvement in the First World War:

Thy fame is ancient as the days,
    As Ocean large and wide;
A pride that dares, and heeds not praise,
    A stern and silent pride.
Not that false joy that dreams content
    With what our sires have won;
The blood a hero sire hath spent
    Still nerves a hero son.

By Freedom gained, by Truth maintain'd,
  Thine Empire shall be strong.

  [*Chorus*]
    Land of Hope and Glory, Mother of the Free,
    How shall we extol thee, who are born of thee?

    Wider still and wider shall thy bounds be set,   25
    God, who made thee mighty, make thee mightier yet.

    God, who made thee mighty, make thee mightier yet.

Wilfrid Scawen Blunt (1840–1922): From *My Diaries: Being a Personal Narrative of Events, 1888–1914* (1919)[74]

22nd Dec. [1900]—The old century is nearly out, and leaves the world in a pretty pass, and the British Empire is playing the devil in it as never an empire before on so large a scale. We may live to see its fall. All the nations of Europe are making the same hell upon earth in China, massacring and pillaging and raping in the captured cities as outrageously as in the Middle Ages.[75] The Emperor of Germany gives the word for slaughter and the Pope looks on and approves.[76] In South Africa our troops are burning farms under Kitchener's command, and the Queen and the two Houses of Parliament, and the bench of bishops thank God publicly and vote money for the work.[77] The Americans are spending fifty millions a year on slaughtering the Filipinos;[78] the King of the Belgians has invested his

Notes

[74] *title* a poet and writer, Blunt served in the diplomatic service from 1858 to 1869, and, paradoxically, as a Tory he became well known for his anti-imperial politics. He supported Irish and Egyptian nationalists, at one point being banned from Egypt for four years from 1882, and put into an Irish prison for three months in 1888. Among his many anti-imperial writings he published in 1899 a long poem, "Satan Absolved: A Victorian Mystery," where Satan praises "These Lords who boast Thine aid at their high civic feasts. / The ignoble shouting crowds, the prophets of their Press, / Pouring their daily flood of bald self-righteousness. / Their poets who write big of the 'White Burden' Trash! / The White Man's Burden, Lord, is the burden of his cash" (see n. 57); and a pamphlet at his own expense, "The Shame of the Nineteenth Century" (1900), a scathing indictment of the British Empire.

[75] *Europe … Ages* the Eight-Nation Alliance of Austria-Hungary, France, Germany, Italy, Japan, Russia, the United Kingdom, and the United States had an army of 20,000 in China to suppress the Boxer Rebellion (1900–1), a nationalist rebellion against foreign influence and Christianity. During the fighting, the allied troops were reported to have committed a number of atrocities. A witness, the Irish journalist George Lynch (b. 1868), would write in *The War of the Civilisations: Being the Record of a "Foreign Devil's" Experiences with the Allies in China* (1901): "there are things that I must not write, and that may not be printed in England, which would seem to show that this Western civilization of ours is merely a veneer over savagery" (ch. 10).

[76] *Emperor … approves* Wilhelm II or William II (1859–1941), last German Emperor (Kaiser), grandson of the British Queen Victoria, gave a speech to German troops departing for the Boxer Rebellion in July, 1900: "When you come upon the enemy, smite him. Pardon will not be given. Prisoners will not be taken. Whoever falls into your hands is forfeit.… May you in this way make the name German remembered in China for a thousand years so that no Chinaman will ever again dare to even squint at a German!" Leo XIII (1810–1903) was pope from 1878 to 1903.

[77] *South … work* Horatio Herbert Kitchener (1850–1916) was appointed commander-in-chief of the British army in the Boer War in August 1900 and soon after adopted a scorched earth policy, destroying Boer farms and livestock, and moving women and children to concentration camps. These camps had a death rate of 35%, mostly from rampant disease caused by poor conditions. Although British authorities and public opinion still fully supported their troops at the beginning of the twentieth century, many would soon turn against them when these tactics began to be reported in the press. See this section, IMPERIAL TRAVELLERS, n. 17.

[78] *Filipinos* following the Spanish–American War (1898), American troops and Philippine revolutionary forces engaged in a war that lasted from February 1899 to July 1902; the United States would occupy the Philippines until 1946. It was in this context that Kipling wrote "The White Man's Burden" (see n. 57).

whole fortune on the Congo, where he is brutalizing the negroes to fill his pockets.[79] The French and Italians for the moment are playing a less prominent part in the slaughter, but their inactivity grieves them.[80] The whole white race is revelling openly in violence, as though it had never pretended to be Christian. God's equal curse be on them all! So ends the famous nineteenth century into which we were so proud to have been born. . . .

31st Dec.[1900]—I bid good-bye to the old century, may it rest in peace as it has lived in war. Of the new century I prophesy nothing except that it will see the decline of the British Empire. Other worse Empires will rise perhaps in its place, but I shall not live to see the day. It all seems a very little matter here in Egypt, with the Pyramids watching us as they watched Joseph,[81] when, as a young man four thousand years ago, perhaps in this very garden, he walked and gazed at the sunset behind him, wondering about the future just as I did this evening. And so, poor wicked nineteenth century, farewell!

2. Governing the Colonies

2.1 India

Thomas Babington Macaulay (1800–59): From *Minute on Indian Education* (2 Feb. 1835)[1]

We now come to the gist of the matter. We have a fund to be employed as Government shall direct for the intellectual improvement of the people of this country. The simple question is, what is the most useful way of employing it?

Notes

[79] *pockets* Leopold II (1835–1909), king of the Belgians, cousin of Queen Victoria, was recognized at the Berlin Conference of 1884–85 to be the sole owner of the Congo; he exploited it ruthlessly for ivory and rubber, causing millions of deaths, until international outrage would force him in 1908 to give it to Belgium as a colony. In 1898 Conrad had written the most famous literary treatment of the subject in *Heart of Darkness*; see also Mark Twain's bitter satire, *King Leopold's Soliloquy* (1905).

[80] *them* at this time the French Empire consisted primarily of colonies in French Indochina (now Vietnam) and northern and central Africa (Algeria, Tunis, Mauritania, Senegal, Guinea, Mali, Ivory Coast, Benin, Niger, Chad, and Central African Republic); the Italians held Italian Somaliland in the Horn of Africa; in 1896, at the hands of Ethiopian forces at the Battle of Adwa, they had become the first European power to be defeated by Africans.

[81] *Joseph* a figure in the Old Testament who rose from a slave to the captain of Pharaoh's guard to be vizier or executive officer in Pharaoh's court with control of "all the land of Egypt." He rose to this position by interpreting Pharaoh's dreams as prophetic of abundant harvests and subsequent famine, and by offering plans for such a future (see Genesis 37–50). By present calculations, Blunt's dating is far off: Joseph's narrative dates from the fifth to the seventh centuries BCE when the pyramids were already two thousand years old: the Great Pyramid of Khafre at Giza dates from about 2480 BCE.

GOVERNING THE COLONIES

[1] *title* the British Parliament in 1813 had stipulated that the East India Company would spend at least one lakh (100,000) of rupees annually on the education of Indians, and thus continued a policy debate that had been ongoing since the governorship of Warren Hastings (1732–1818). He had advocated for education in indigenous languages, a part of a policy of non-intervention or non-disturbance of Indian ways of life. Macaulay served the East India Company in India from 1834 to 1838 as first Law Member of the Supreme Council, as well as president of the General Committee of Public Instruction, during which time he wrote this memorandum on the side of the anglicists, advocating for the Indian subjects to be educated in English. He was opposed to the orientalists, who wanted the languages of instruction to be Arabic, Sanscrit, and Persian, as well as English. Both sides, anglicists and orientalists, agreed on modernization: their difference concerned the language of instruction. Macaulay closes the "Minute" by advocating that the English close Arabic and Sanscrit schools, and cease to print books in those languages, after which he threatened to resign from the council if his position were not adopted. Governor General William Bentinck (1774–1839) gave his "entire concurrence to the sentiments expressed in this Minute," and, with small revisions, on 7 March Macaulay's "Minute" formed the basis of the English Education Act of 1835. Macaulay's biographer G. O. Trevelyan would write in 1876: "A new India was born in 1835. The very foundations of her ancient civilization began

All parties seem to be agreed on one point, that the dialects commonly spoken among the natives of this part of India,[2] contain neither literary nor scientific information, and are, moreover so poor and rude that, until they are enriched from some other quarter, it will not be easy to translate any valuable work into them. It seems to be admitted on all sides that the intellectual improvement of those classes of the people who have the means of pursuing higher studies can at present be effected only by means of some language not vernacular amongst them.

What, then, shall that language be? One half of the Committee maintain that it should be the English. The other half strongly recommend the Arabic and Sanscrit.[3] The whole question seems to me to be, which language is the best worth knowing?

I have no knowledge of either Sanscrit or Arabic.—But I have done what I could to form a correct estimate of their value. I have read translations of the most celebrated Arabic and Sanscrit works. I have conversed both here and at home with men distinguished by their proficiency in the Eastern tongues. I am quite ready to take the Oriental learning at the valuation of the orientalists themselves. I have never found one among them who could deny that a single shelf of a good European library was worth the whole native literature of India and Arabia. The intrinsic superiority of the Western literature is, indeed, fully admitted by those members of the Committee who support the Oriental plan of education....

The claims of our own language it is hardly necessary to recapitulate. It stands preeminent even among the languages of the West. It abounds with works of imagination not inferior to the noblest which Greece has bequeathed to us; with models of every species of eloquence; with historical compositions, which, considered merely as narratives, have seldom been surpassed, and which, considered as vehicles of ethical and political instruction, have never been equalled; with just and lively representations of human life and human nature;[4] with the most profound speculations on metaphysics, morals, government, jurisprudence, and trade; with full and correct information respecting every experimental science which tends to preserve the health, to increase the comfort, or to expand the intellect of man. Whoever knows that language, has ready access to all the vast intellectual wealth, which all the wisest nations of the earth have created and hoarded in the course of ninety generations. It may safely be said that the literature now extant in that language is of far greater value than all the literature which three hundred years ago was extant in all the languages of the world together. Nor is this all. In India, English is the language spoken by the ruling class. It is spoken by the higher class of natives at the seats of Government. It is likely to become the language of commerce throughout the seas of the East. It is the language of two great European communities which are rising, the one in the south of Africa, the other in Australasia; communities which are every year becoming more important, and more closely connected with our Indian empire. Whether we look at the intrinsic value of our literature, or at the

Notes

to rock and sway. Pillar after pillar in the edifice came crashing down." Our text: *Bureau of Education. Selections from Educational Records, Part I* (ed. H. Sharp 1920).

[2] *India* between 1894 and 1928, the British Raj would undertake the Linguistic Survey of India, in which 364 languages were recognized.

[3] *Sanscrit* the orientalists on the Board of Instruction included Henry Hayman Wilson (1786–1860) and Henry Prinsep (1792–1878), who wrote a critical response to Macaulay's "Minute." The orientalists, the dominant party since Hastings (see n. 1) and founders of the Asiatic Society in 1784, were not opposed to modernizing their Indian subjects,

but rather argued that science would be better absorbed if "engrafted" to the native languages. Their position is clearly laid out in a paper by Wilson, "Education of the Natives of India," *Asiatic Journal* (Jan. 1836).

[4] *nature* echo of John Dryden's *Essay of Dramatick Poesie* (1688): "A Play ought to be, *A just and lively Image of Human Nature, representing its Passion and Humours, and the Changes of Fortune to which it is subject; for the Delight and Instruction of Mankind.*" Samuel Johnson varies this statement in his *Preface to Shakespeare* (1765): "Nothing can please many, and please long, but just representations of general nature."

particular situation of this country, we shall see the strongest reason to think that, of all foreign tongues, the English tongue is that which would be the most useful to our native subjects.

The question now before us is simply whether, when it is in our power to teach this language, we shall teach languages in which, by universal confession, there are no books on any subject which deserve to be compared to our own; whether, when we can teach European science, we shall teach systems which, by universal confession, whenever they differ from those of Europe, differ for the worse; and whether, when we can patronise sound Philosophy and true History, we shall countenance, at the public expense, medical doctrines which would disgrace an English farrier—Astronomy, which would move laughter in girls at an English boarding school—History, abounding with kings thirty feet high, and reigns thirty thousand years long—and Geography, made up of seas of treacle and seas of butter.[5] ...

It is said that the Sanscrit and Arabic are the languages in which the sacred books of a hundred millions of people are written, and that they are, on that account, entitled to peculiar encouragement. Assuredly it is the duty of the British Government in India to be not only tolerant, but neutral on all religious questions. But to encourage the study of a literature admitted to be of small intrinsic value, only because that literature inculcates the most serious errors on the most important subjects, is a course hardly reconcilable with reason, with morality, or even with that very neutrality which ought, as we all agree, to be sacredly preserved. It is confessed that a language is barren of useful knowledge.[6] We are to teach it because it is fruitful of monstrous superstitions. We are to teach false History, false Astronomy, false Medicine, because we find them in company with a false religion. We abstain, and I trust shall always abstain, from giving any public encouragement to those who are engaged in the work of converting natives to Christianity.[7] ...

In one point I fully agree with the gentlemen to whose general views I am opposed. I feel, with them, that it is impossible for us, with our limited means, to attempt to educate

Notes

[5] *butter* these claims are commonplace among such commentators on India as James Mill (see this section, CELEBRATION, n. 36) and Charles Edward Trevelyan (1807–86), Macaulay's brother-in-law, who in 1838 in *On the Education of the People of India* would write, "The Hindu system of learning contains so much truth as to have raised the nation to its present point of civilization, and to have kept it there for ages without retrograding, and so much error as to have prevented it from making any sensible advance during the same long period. Under this system, history is made up of fables, in which the learned in vain endeavour to trace the thread of authentic narrative; its medicine is quackery; its geography and astronomy are monstrous absurdity; its law is composed of loose contradictory maxims, and barbarous and ridiculous penal provisions; its religion is idolatry; its morality is such as might be expected from the example of the gods and the precepts of the religion." (ch. 3).

[6] *knowledge* the utilitarians consistently called for "useful knowledge" to be the basis of any educational system in India. For instance, in a memorandum to the governor-general-in-council of Bengal (18 Feb. 1824) on the Muslim College in Calcutta and the Hindu College in Benares, James Mill had written, "The great end should not have been to teach Hindoo learning, or Mahomedan learning, but useful learning.... In professing ... to establish Seminaries for the purpose of teaching mere

Hindoo, or mere Mahomedan literature, you bound yourself to teach a great deal of what was frivolous, not a little of what was purely mischievous, and a small remainder indeed in which utility was in any way concerned." Unlike Macaulay, however, Mill had never set foot in India.

[7] *Christianity* in 1813, a new charter for the East India Company (see n. 1) allowed missionaries into India; up to that point the policy was to discourage missionary activity for fear of offending Hindu and Muslim sensibilities. One of the most prominent promoters of evangelical Christianity had been Charles Grant, (1746–1823), East India Company chairman, and like Macaulay's father Zachary, a member of the Clapham Sect of evangelical Christianity. In *Observations on the State of Society among the Asiatic Subjects of Great Britain* (1792), Grant had argued in favour of English education to the Indians for the purposes of conversion: "Are we forever to preserve the enormities of the Hindu system? ... The true cure of darkness is the introduction of light." He urged that the company establish "places of gratuitous instruction in reading and writing English." This book was presented to parliament in 1813 in the debates on the new charter, during which William Wilberforce (1759–1853) claimed of the Indians, "Their divinities are absolute monsters of lust, injustice, wickedness, and cruelty. In short, their religious system is one grand abomination."

the body of the people. We must at present do our best to form a class[8] who may be interpreters between us and the millions whom we govern; a class of persons, Indian in blood and colour, but English in taste, in opinions, in morals, and in intellect. To that class we may leave it to refine the vernacular dialects of the country, to enrich those dialects with terms of science borrowed from the Western nomenclature, and to render them by degrees fit vehicles for conveying knowledge to the great mass of the population.

Proclamation by the Queen in Council, to the Princes, Chiefs, and People of India[9]

One November 1858

Whereas, for divers weighty reasons, we have resolved, by and with the advice and consent of the Lords Spiritual and Temporal, and Commons, in Parliament assembled, to take upon ourselves the government of the territories in India, heretofore administered in trust for us by the Honourable East India Company: ...

And we, reposing especial trust and confidence in the loyalty, ability, and judgement of our right trusty and well-beloved cousin and councillor, Charles John Viscount Canning, do hereby constitute and appoint him, the said Viscount Canning, to be our first Viceroy and Governor-general[10] in and over our said territories, and to administer the government

Notes

[8] *class* the Indians educated on this model would come to be referred to as Macaulay's children; it is this class that later are referred to derisively as "babus," once a term of respect but converted into a term of ridicule for a half-educated, semi-literate, self-important, and sycophantic Indian clerk, such as the babu in Kipling's *Kim* (1901), Hurree Chunder Mookerjee.

[9] *title* on 2 August 1858 the Government of India Act was passed in parliament, transferring power to the Crown from the British East India Company, which had been granted its charter by Queen Elizabeth in 1600. The company had ruled virtually all of the Indian subcontinent since the Battle of Plassey in 1757 (see n. 15). The Company would be completely dissolved by East India Stock Dividend Redemption Act (1874). The Indian Rebellion (called by the British the Indian Mutiny, and by Marx the First War of Indian Independence) broke out on 10 May 1857 in Meerut when sepoys (Indian soldiers) refused to bite off the paper cartridges for their rifles which they believed were greased with beef and pork fat. The root causes of the rebellion, however, had long-standing causes, involving changes in army regulations governing the sepoys, grievances on the part of the native princes and nobility, seizures of land under the Doctrine of Lapse, (which declared vacant a native title if a ruler died without a male heir), and resentment regarding social reform directed by utilitarian and evangelical British leaders (see nn.1, 3). Fighting broke out in different areas of India, with the rebels fighting under various leaders. The armed phase of the conflict had ended on 20 June 1858 at Gwalior. On 15 August 1858 Queen Victoria wrote to the prime minister "to explain in detail to Lord Derby her objections to the draft of Proclamation for India. The Queen would be glad if Lord Derby would write it himself in his excellent language, bearing in mind that it is a female

Sovereign who speaks to more than 100,000,000 of Eastern people on assuming the direct Government over them after a bloody civil war, giving them pledges which her future reign is to redeem, and explaining the principles of her Government. Such a document should breathe feelings of generosity, benevolence, and religious feeling, pointing out the privileges which the Indians will receive in being placed on an equality with the subjects of the British Crown, and the prosperity following in the train of civilisation." The proclamation would be publically read on 1 November in Allahabad by the Viceroy Lord Canning. Our text: *House of Commons Papers*, Volume 18.

[10] *Governor-general* Charles John Canning, first Earl Canning (1812–62) was governor-general of India from 1856 to 1858, and the first Viceroy of India from 1858 to 1862; his wife, Charlotte Canning, Countess Canning (1817–1861), had been a Lady of the Bedchamber to Queen Victoria from 1842 to 1855; she is well known as an artist of Indian landscapes. Canning had earned the nickname "Clemency" Canning when he adopted a policy of pardoning the rebels who had not been involved in murder if they surrendered before 1 January 1859. In a letter (4 Sept. 1858) Canning wrote to Stanley (see n. 11) of a false report of the amnesty, adding that nevertheless he was anxious to issue an amnesty "the moment I feel that it will be respected." Upon hearing of Canning's offer of clemency, on 4 October 1857 while the siege of Lucknow was taking place, in a letter to his friend Angela Burdett-Coutts (1814–1906), Charles Dickens wrote: "I wish I were Commander in Chief in India. The first thing I would do to strike that Oriental race with amazement (not in the least regarding them as if they lived in the Strand, London, or at Camden town), should be to proclaim to them, in their language, that I considered my holding that appointment by the

thereof in our name, and generally to act in our name and on our behalf, subject to such orders and regulations as he shall, from time to time, receive from us through one of our Principal Secretaries of State.[11]

And we do hereby confirm in their several offices, civil and military, all persons now employed in the service of the Honourable East India Company, subject to our future pleasure, and to such laws and regulations as may hereafter be enacted.

We hereby announce to the native Princes of India that all treaties and engagements made with them by or under the authority of the Honourable East India Company are by us accepted, and will be scrupulously maintained, and we look for the like observance on their part.

We desire no extension of our present territorial possessions; and, while we will permit no aggression upon our dominions or our rights to be attempted with impunity, we shall sanction no encroachment on those of others.

We shall respect the rights, dignity, and honour of native Princes[12] as our own; and we desire that they, as well as our own subjects, should enjoy that prosperity and that social advancement which can only be secured by internal peace and good government.

We hold ourselves bound to the natives of our Indian territories by the same obligations of duty which bind us to all our other subjects, and those obligations, by the blessing of Almighty God, we shall faithfully and conscientiously fulfil.

Firmly relying ourselves on the truth of Christianity, and acknowledging with gratitude the solace of religion, we disclaim alike the right and desire to impose our convictions on any of our subjects. We declare it to be our royal will and pleasure that none be in anywise favoured, none molested or disquieted, by reason of their religious faith or observances, but that all shall alike enjoy the equal and impartial protection of the law; and we do strictly charge and enjoin all those who may be in authority under us that they abstain from all interference with the religious belief or worship of any of our subjects on pain of our highest displeasure.[13]

And it is our further will that, so far as may be, our subjects, of whatever race or creed, be freely and impartially admitted to offices in our service, the duties of which they may be qualified, by their education, ability, and integrity, duly to discharge.

We know, and respect, the feelings of attachment with which the natives of India regard the lands inherited by them from their ancestors, and we desire to protect them in all rights connected therewith, subject to the equitable demands of the State; and we will that generally, in framing and administering the law, due regard be paid to the ancient rights, usages, and customs of India. . . .

We deeply lament the evils and misery which have been brought upon India by the acts of ambitious men, who have deceived their countrymen by false reports, and led them into open rebellion. Our power has been shown by the suppression of that rebellion in the field; we desire to show our mercy by pardoning the offences of those who have been thus misled, but who desire to return to the path of duty. . . .

Notes

leave of God, to mean that I should do my utmost to exterminate the Race upon whom the stain of the late cruelties rested; and that I begged them to do me the favour to observe that I was there for that purpose and no other, and was now proceeding , with all convenient dispatch and merciful swiftness of execution, to blot it out of mankind and raze it off the face of the Earth."

[11] *State* the bill created the India Office and a new position of Secretary of State for India. The man to occupy the office was Edward Henry Stanley, fifteenth

Earl of Derby (1826–93), the son of the prime minister (see n. 9).

[12] *princes* under the British Raj a number of princely or native states remained nominally sovereign under Indian hereditary rulers; they were governed according to a form of indirect rule by the crown. At independence in 1947 there would be 565 princely states.

[13] *displeasure* in effect the proclamation reverses the evangelical impulse for conversion implemented after 1813 (see nn. 1, 7).

Our clemency will be extended to all offenders, save and except those who have been, or shall be, convicted of having directly taken part in the murder of British subjects. With regard to such the demands of justice forbid the exercise of mercy.[14] . . .

When, by the blessing of Providence, internal tranquility shall be restored, it is our earnest desire to stimulate the peaceful industry of India, to promote works of public utility and improvement, and to administer its government for the benefit of all our subjects resident therein. In their prosperity will be our strength; in their contentment our security, and in their gratitude our best reward. And may the God of all power grant to us, and to those in authority under us, strength to carry out these our wishes for the good of our people.

G. A. Henty (1832–1902): *With Clive in India: Or, The Beginnings of an Empire* (1884)

From "Preface"[15]

MY DEAR LADS,—In the following pages I have endeavoured to give you a vivid picture of the wonderful events of the ten years, which at their commencement saw Madras in the hands of the French, Calcutta at the mercy of the Nabob of Bengal, and English influence apparently at the point of extinction in India, and which ended in the final triumph of the English both in Bengal and Madras.[16] There were yet great battles to be fought, great efforts to be made before the vast Empire of India fell altogether into British hands; but these were but the sequence of the events I have described.

Notes

[14] *mercy* see n. 10.

[15] *title* the author of over 100 novels, Henty was among the most popular writers of boys' adventure fiction. This novel follows Henty's well-trodden formula for imperialist propaganda, aligning a fictional young lad with a heroic historical figure. In this case, a third-person narrative traces the exploits of Charlie Marryat, who at the age of sixteen, after the death of his father, acquires, through the influence of his uncle, a post as a clerk in the East India Company. The setting is the mid-eighteenth century, focusing on the exploits of Robert Clive (1725–74) and the Battle of Plassey (1757). This battle marked the beginning of the expansion of the company from three trading posts in Madras, Bombay, and Calcutta to virtual control of the whole subcontinent.

Typical is the address here to the readers before almost every novel, dividing the novel between the personal adventures of the boy hero and the serious matter, the history and geography of the empire. Upon his arrival in India, young Charlie quickly leaves the bureaucracy of the East India Company and joins the army. Through a series of battles, represented, as in all of Henty's novels, by large amounts of historical data, technical information, and battle plans drawn (close to plagiarized) from historical works, Charlie rises in rank in the company's army until, at the end of the novel, he returns home having acquired a fortune as a result of his having fought for the company and empire. The novel closes with a comment on the historical significance of the events represented in the novel: "It was now just ten years since they had sailed, and in that time they had seen Madras and Calcutta rise, from the rank of two trading stations, in constant danger of destruction by their powerful neighbours, to that of virtual capitals of great provinces. Not as yet, indeed, had they openly assumed the sovereignty of these territories; but Madras was, in fact, the absolute master of the broad tract of land extending from the foot of the mountains to the sea, from Cape Comorin to Bengal; while Calcutta was master of Bengal and Oressa, and her power already threatened to extend itself as far as Delhi. The conquest of these vast tracts of country had been achieved by mere handfuls of men, and by a display of heroic valour and constancy scarce to be rivalled in the history of the world."

[16] *ten years . . . Madras* Robert Clive, first Baron Clive (1725–74), British major-general and imperial administrator, established British supremacy in India at the Battle of Plassey (1757), conquering Bengal by defeating the nawab of Bengal and his French allies, ending a rivalry between the English and French East India Companies. Clive's rise to fame had begun in September 1746 when the French, under Joseph-François, Marquis Dupleix (1697–1763), French general and imperial leader, attacked Madras and had Clive, then a clerk, imprisoned with a number of others. Clive led a dangerous escape, after which he became a soldier. He eventually conquered Bengal; however, in 1772, a few years after his return to England, he was charged with corruption and abuse of authority as governor by a parliamentary committee. Although acquitted in 1774, depressed and addicted to opium, he committed suicide. Vilified during his lifetime as a corrupt official in India, his reputation was restored as a hero for the public school by Macaulay and others. In 1880 Browning published a

The historical details are, throughout the story, strictly accurate, and for them I am indebted to the history of these events written by Mr. Orme, who lived at that time, to the *Life of Lord Clive*, recently published by Lieutenant-colonel Malleson, and to other standard authorities.[17] In this book I have devoted a somewhat smaller space to the personal adventures of my hero, Charlie Marryat, with as much interest as you have manifested in the adventures of the many characters to whom I have hitherto introduced you.

Yours very sincerely,
G. A. Henty.

Flora Annie Steel (1847–1929) and Grace Gardiner (d. 1919): The Complete Indian Housekeeper and Cook: Giving the Duties of Mistress and Servants, the General Management of the House and Practical Recipes for Cooking in All its Branches (1888)

From "Preface to the First Edition"[18]

This book, it is hoped, will meet the very generally felt want for a practical guide to young housekeepers in India. A large proportion of English ladies in this country come to it newly married, to begin a new life, and take up new responsibilities under absolutely new conditions.

Few, indeed, have had any practical experience of housekeeping of any sort or kind; whilst those who have find themselves almost as much at sea as their more ignorant sisters. How can it be otherwise, when the familiar landmarks are no longer visible, and,

Notes

complex monologue, "Clive," narrated by a dissolute former soldier, in which Clive is a flawed hero, reliving former glories through his present addictions and despondency. In Grace Stebbing's *Winning an Empire: The Story of Clive* (1885) he is (as in Henty) presented as an imperial adventure hero; however, she also uses him as a moral example against gambling and drug addiction.

[17] *authorities* Robert Orme (1728–1801), British historian, joined the East India Company in 1743 and was appointed company historiographer in 1769; he wrote *History of the Military Transactions of the British Nation in Indostan from 1745* (1763–78) and *Historical Fragments of the Mogul Empire, the Morattoes and English Concerns in Indostan from 1659* (1782). George Bruce Malleson (1825–98), historian and soldier, joined the army of the East India Company in 1847. The *Life of Lord Clive* that Henty refers to is in Malleson's *The Founders of the Indian Empire* (1882), later reworked in *Lord Clive* (1893) in a series called "Rulers of India." It was a book written for children, extravagant in its hero-worship: "Caesar conquered Gaul for his country; Hannibal caused unrest to Rome for merely a quarter of a century; Wellington drove the French from Portugal and Spain. The achievement of Clive was more splendid than any one of those! … He founded for this little island in the Atlantic a magnificent empire."

[18] *title* in 1867 Steel married an Indian civil servant, Henry William Steel (1840–1923); she would live in India, mostly in the Punjab, until 1889, during which time she learned native languages and undertook several reforms,

particularly regarding the education of Indian women. She wrote some thirty books in her career, including novels, short stories, histories, a guide to household management for English women or memsahibs in India, and an autobiography in 1929; she was called the female Rudyard Kipling. Grace Anne Marie Louise Napier Gardiner was the junior partner in the joint authorship. Not much can be ascertained about her. She was the daughter of Sir Joseph Napier (1804–82), Conservative MP and Lord Chancellor of Ireland, and Charity Grace. She married John William Gardiner, a member of the Indian Civil Service, in November 1868, and went with him to India. They had a large family. She died on 3 August 1919. The *Complete Indian Housekeeper*, like Mrs Beeton's *Book of Household Management* (1859–61; see GENDER: CONSTRUCTING GENDERS), is as much a conduct book as a cookbook. Covering virtually every aspect of domestic life in India, the book, dedicated to "The English Girls to whom fate may assign the Task of Being House-Mothers in our Eastern Empire," deals with managing servants, their wages, prices for household items, and so on. The book does not address cooking until after 220 pages; only two recipes for curry and seven Indian dishes are included. Chapter 6, one of the longest (42 pages), is "Duties of the Servants." The book is the best-known among what became a crowded field in the last half of the nineteenth century. There were ten editions of *Complete Indian Housekeeper* published by 1921; our text: second edition, 1890.

amid the crowd of idle, unintelligible servants, there seems not one to carry on the usual routine of household work which in England follows as a matter of course?

The kitchen is a black hole,[19] the pantry a sink. The only servant who will condescend to tidy up is a skulking savage with a reed broom; whilst pervading all things broods the stifling, enervating atmosphere of custom, against which energy beats itself unavailingly, as against a feather bed....

From Chapter 1: "The Duties of the Mistress"

Housekeeping in India, when once the first strangeness has worn off, is a far easier task in many ways than it is in England, though it none the less requires time, and, in the present transitional period, an almost phenomenal patience; for, while one mistress enforces cleanliness according to European methods, the next may belong to the opposite faction, who, so long as the dinner is nicely served, thinks nothing of it being cooked in a kitchen which is also used as a latrine; the result being that the servants who serve one, and then the other stamp of mistress, look on the desire for decency as a mere personal and distinctly disagreeable attribute of their employer, which, like a bad temper or stinginess, may be resented or evaded.

And, first, it must be distinctly understood, that it is not necessary, or in the least degree desirable, that an educated woman should waste the best years of her life in scolding and petty supervision. Life holds higher duties,[20] and it is indubitable that friction and over-zeal is a sure sign of a bad housekeeper. But there is an appreciable difference between a care-worn Martha vexed with many things, and the absolute indifference displayed by many Indian mistresses, who put up with a degree of slovenliness and dirt which would disgrace a den in St. Giles,[21] on the principle that it is no use attempting to teach the natives....

The first duty of a mistress is, of course, to be able to give intelligible orders to her servants, therefore it is necessary she should learn to speak Hindustani. No sane Englishwoman would dream of living, say, for twenty years, in Germany, Italy, or France, without making the *attempt*, at any rate, to learn the language. She would, in fact, feel that by neglecting to do so she would *"write herself down an ass."*[22] It would be well, therefore, if ladies in India were to ask themselves if a difference in longitude increases the latitude allowed in judging of a women's intellect.

The next duty is obviously to insist on her orders being carried out. And here we come to the burning question, "How is this to be done?" Certainly, there is at present very little to which we can appeal in the average Indian servant, but then, until it is implanted by training, there is very little sense of duty in a child; yet in some well-regulated nurseries obedience is a foregone conclusion. The secret lies in making rules, and *keeping to them*. The Indian servant is a child in everything save age, and should be treated as a child; that is to say, kindly, but with the greatest firmness. The laws of the household should be those

Notes

[19] *black hole* slang for a military prison, here a reference to the legendary "Black Hole" of Calcutta, where, based on the account of a survivor, John Zephaniah Holwell (1711–98), supposedly 123 of 146 British prisoners perished on the night of 19 June 1756. The account has been largely discredited, but, nevertheless, it became an important component in imperialist hagiography, and served for many years as an example of Indian treachery and baseness. The best-known account to the Victorians was in Macaulay's essay "Lord Clive," *Edinburgh Review* (Jan. 1840): "Then the prisoners went mad with despair. They trampled each other down, fought for the places at the windows, fought for the pittance of water with which the cruel mercy of the murderers mocked their agonies, raved, prayed, blasphemed, implored the guards to fire among them. The gaolers in the meantime held lights to the bars, and shouted with laughter at the frantic struggles of their victims."

[20] *duties* compare the use of "duties" in the opening paragraph of Mrs Beeton's *Book of Household Management* (see GENDER: CONSTRUCTING GENDERS).

[21] *St. Giles* then a notoriously poor slum district in London, now in the borough of Camden.

[22] *ass* see *Much Ado About Nothing* 4. 2. 75.

of the Medes and Persians,[23] and first faults should never go unpunished. By overlooking a first offence, we lose the only opportunity we have of preventing it becoming a habit.

But it will be asked, How are we to punish our servants when we have no hold either on their minds or bodies?—when cutting their pay is illegal, and few, if any, have any sense of shame.

The answer is obvious. Make a hold.

In their own experience the authors have found a system of rewards and punishments perfectly easy of attainment. One of them has for years adopted the plan of engaging her servants at so much a month—the lowest rate at which such servant is obtainable—and so much extra as *bakshish*,[24] conditional on good service. For instance, a khitmatghar is engaged permanently on Rs. 9 a month,[25] but the additional rupee which invites the wage up to that usually demanded by good servants is a fluctuating assessment! From it small fines are levied, beginning with one pice[26] for forgetfulness, and running up, through degrees of culpability, to one rupee for lying. The money than returned to imperial coffers may very well be spent on giving small rewards; so that each servant knows that by good service he can get back his own fines. That plan has never been objected to, and such a thing as a servant giving up his place has never been known in the author's experience. On the contrary, the household quite enters into the spirit of the idea, infinitely preferring it to volcanic eruptions of faultfinding....

A good mistress in India will try to set a good example to her servants in routine, method, and tidiness. Half an hour after breakfast should be sufficient for the whole arrangements for the day; but that half hour should be given as punctually as possible. An untidy mistress invariably has *untidy*, a weak one, *idle* servants. It should never be forgotten that—although it is most true in India—if you want a thing done, you should do it yourself; still, having to do it is a distinct confession of failure in your original intention. Anxious housewives are too apt to accept defeat in this way; the result being that the lives of educated women are wasted in doing the work of lazy servants....

Finally, when all is said and done, the whole duty of an Indian mistress towards her servants is neither more or less than it is in England. Here, as there, a little reasonable human sympathy is the best oil for the household machine. Here, as there, the end and object is not merely personal comfort, but the formation of a home—that unit of civilisation where father and children, master and servant, employer and employed, can learn their several duties. When all is said and done also, herein lies the natural outlet for most of the talent peculiar to women. It is the fashion nowadays to undervalue the art of making a home; to deem it simplicity and easiness itself. But this is a mistake, for the proper administration of even a small household needs both brain and heart. A really clever woman always sees this, and, like George Eliot, the greatest of modern women, prides herself on being an excellent housekeeper; and—as was written of that charming author—"*nothing offends her more than the idea that her exceptional intellectual powers should be held to absolve her from ordinary household duties.*"[27] In regard to expenditure, the mistress of a house has it in her power to make debts, as to prevent them; for she, and she only, has the power of preventing that extravagance in small things, which is but the prelude to a like recklessness in greater matters....

Notes

[23] *Medes and Persians* unalterable laws; see Daniel 6: 8.

[24] *bakshish* (Persian a tip or gratuity).

[25] *khitmatghâr ... month* (*khitmatghâr*: Persian a waiter or servant); in 1890, a rupee was worth about 18*d*.; therefore, the servant's monthly wage was 162*d*., or a little under 14*s*., which makes about £7 8*s*. per annum. According to Mrs Beeton's scale for British servants thirty years earlier in 1860, this calculation would place the Indian headwaiter at the absolute bottom of the scale, the equivalent of the stable boy or the scullery maid.

[26] *pice* a coin worth one sixty-fourth of a rupee.

[27] *nothing ... duties* see *George Eliot's Life as Related in Her Letters and Journals; Arranged and Edited by her Husband J. W. Cross* (1885; 3: 308).

The great object is to secure three things—smooth working, quick ordering, and subsequent peace and leisure to the mistress. It is as well, therefore, with a view to the preservation of temper, to eat your breakfast in peace before venturing into the pantry and cookroom; it is besides a mistake to be constantly on the worry.

Inspection parade should begin, then, immediately after breakfast, or as near ten o'clock as circumstances will allow. The cook should be waiting—in clean raiment—with a pile of plates, and his viands for the day spread out on a table. With everything *en evidence*, it will not take five minutes to decide on what is best, while a very constant occurrence at Indian tables—the serving up of stale, sour, and unwholesome food—will be avoided. It is perhaps *not* pleasant to go into such details, but a good mistress will remember the breadwinner who requires blood-forming nourishment, and the children whose constitutions are being built up day by day, sickly or healthy, according to the food given them; and bear in mind the fact that, in India especially, half the comfort of life depends on clean, wholesome, digestible food.

Luncheon and dinner ordered, the mistress should proceed to the storeroom, when both the bearer and the *khitmutgâr* should be in attendance. Another five minutes will suffice to give out everything required for the day's consumption, the accounts, writing of orders &c., will follow, and then the mistress (with a sinking heart) may begin the daily inspection of pantry, scullery, and kitchen. But before she sets foot in the back purlieus, let her remember that if a mistress will not give proper appliances, she cannot expect cleanliness. If, however, this excuse is not valid, the author's advice is—*notice the least dirt quietly, with the order that before going for his mid-day recess the servant in fault shall come personally and report its removal.* Let the mistress then send another servant to see if this be true; but let her guard against giving herself the least trouble in the matter. For here, again, Indian servants are like children, gaining a certain satisfaction in the idea that at any rate they have been *troublesome*.

We do not wish to advocate an unholy haughtiness; but an Indian household can no more be governed peacefully, without dignity and prestige, than an Indian Empire. For instance, if the mistress wishes to teach the cook a new dish, let her give the order for everything, down to charcoal, to be ready at a given time, and the cook in attendance; and let her do nothing herself that the servants can do, if only for this reason, that the only way of teaching is to *see* things done, not to let others see *you* do them.

WEB p. 229

WEB p. 254

Behramji Malabari (1853–1912): *The Indian Eye on English Life, or Rambles of a Pilgrim Reformer* (1893)

From Chapter 2: "In and About London"[1]

What strikes an Asiatic most, on getting out at Victoria Station,[2] is the noise and bustle around him. Every man and woman—one might say every animal, and even some of the inanimate objects—seem to be full of life. The streets and thoroughfares of London present a sight in this respect, which it is impossible for the stranger to realize save with his own eyes. I happen to have read a good deal about this, but what

Notes

IMPERIAL TRAVELLERS

[1] *title* a social reformer who lobbied in Britain as well as India, Malabari was concerned with women's rights, particularly child brides and the forbidding of widows of remarriage. Friends with Max Müller (1823–1900) and Florence Nightingale, Malabari made three trips to Britain, the first in 1890. By that time he had published a volume of poems in Gujarati, and an English volume, *The Indian Muse in English Garb* (1877). His description of the urban poor is contemporaneous with William Booth (EMPIRE: GOVERNING (WEB p. 252)). This record of his travels went through four editions. Our text: first edition 1893.

[2] *Station* located in central London, one of the main railway stations in the city.

I actually see here exceeds my anticipation. To Crocodile[3] it is all a new world. He stands apart, gaping at the scene in bewildered admiration. The crowds of women in the streets, walking rapidly past, pushing and elbowing everyone who stands in the way, all intent on business or pleasure, are a sight not likely to be soon forgotten. For me it is a sight more striking than attractive. After all, a woman's place is at home rather than in the street. Of course, the climate and the conditions of life generally impose this outing upon not a few Englishwomen who are apparently unwilling to rough it in a crowd. But it is none the less painful on that account to see a delicate girl struggling to return home in the midst of a traffic heavier than we see in India during our annual fairs. This traffic is maintained every day by railway trains, running under ground[4] and above ground, by omnibuses, trams, cabs, private carriages, waggons, trucks, hand-barrows, tricycles, etcetera, to say nothing of the immense pedestrian crowds. In the large and more fashionable business quarters, such as Bond Street, Piccadilly, Oxford and Regent Streets,[5] into which the various agencies mentioned above pour vast multitudes every five minutes, and some of which are broad enough, besides the pavements, to hold a row of five carriages abreast, I stand breathless of an evening, watching what goes on before my eyes. Carriages, and pedestrians alike seem to have a hair-breadth escape of it now and again. But amid this surging ocean of humanity, the police-constables keep such order, the drivers are so skilful, and the pedestrians so alert, that accidents are very rare indeed. And yet the eye, if it can observe well, may detect a good deal of suffering among the gay or busy crowd. Here is some fashionable cad, nearly driving over a fragile old woman. She rushes, trembling, to the constable's side. There goes a knot of boy-sweepers,[6] running about between carriages, and even under them, in order to keep the ground clean. You could hardly expect greater agility from mice or squirrels. There is more safety, of course, on the pavements. But you are not quite safe here either, from dangers other than trampling. Few respectable women, I find, will venture out into some of these streets towards evening without a guide; so great is the rush therein of the unworthy ones of their sex, of their victims and tyrants. The back parts of not a few streets seem to have been given up to a Godless population, foreign and English. A large percentage of this, I should think, represents virtue first betrayed, and then crowded out, by vice. . . .

Water is about the last thing the average Britisher thinks of for a beverage. Ale and beer and stout are the A B C of his alphabet of bibacity. He may wash a dinner down with tea, coffee, or other non-intoxicants. But have these as an aid to digestion and a fillip to the spirits? No. Never. He must have a something strong, you know. As a race, the British are hard drinkers, partly because they are heavy eaters; and they can stand much. The majority of respectable householders ought to know where to draw the line; but I doubt if all of them can do this. Mr. and Mrs. John Bull[7] take a drop because it is so cold; then because they are so tired, or grieved, or disappointed. The habit grows on many till the victims are reduced to a state verging on lunacy.

Notes

[3] *Crocodile* the son of a poor friend from India who accompanied Malabari on his journey.

[4] *ground* the London Underground, the world's first subway system, was opened on 10 January 1863; by 1890, it ran the world's first electric trains.

[5] *Bond . . . Streets* all major streets in the shopping district of London's West End.

[6] *boy-sweepers* they cleared a path on the dirty urban streets for a gratuity. Henry Mayhew (see CONDITION: SOCIAL FORMATION (WEB p. 9)) wrote extensively on them in *London Labour and the London Poor* (1851).

[7] *Bull* a stout, cartoonish figure, in a top hat usually wearing a Union Jack as a vest, or waistcoat, the figure is a national personification of the English that was invented by John Arbuthnot (1667–1735) in 1712 in *The History of John Bull*, in which Mrs Bull also appears.

WEB p. 262

Mary Kingsley (1862–1900): *Travels in West Africa* (1897)
From Chapter VIII "From Ncovi to Esoon"

Ham Mukasa (1870–1956): *Uganda's Katikiro in England Being the Official Account of his Visit to the Coronation of His Majesty King Edward VII* (1904)[8]

From Chapter 5

The following day, June 14th, we went to the house of images of all kinds (the British Museum),[9] which contained many wonderful things of long ago, statues of the old kings of all countries and of Egypt. We saw also the body of a man said to be eight thousand years old. We could not understand whether this was true or not, because we see in the Bible that those who calculate the time from the Creation make it out to be nearly six thousand years;[10] and after this one is told that this body is eight thousand years old! Is not this a thing to be wondered at? We saw also other remains, 5,000, 4,500, 3,700, 2,000, 2,500 years old. On every statue they write its name, its age, and the country from which it comes, so that people can understand. . . .

This house of images, the British Museum, is very large indeed, about twenty times as large as the Namirembe Cathedral;[11] you can understand the size of it if I tell you that when you walk about in it it is just as if you were not in a house at all, and you think you are outside. The posts that support it are very large, as large as one of the largest of our trees, but of dressed stone; the outside posts are twice as high as the eaves of our cathedral. . . .

Notes

[8] *title* a translation from Luganda, this text traces the journey of Ham Mukasa (1868–1956), chief secretary to Apolo Kagwa (1864–1927), prime minister (Katikkiro) of the Kingdom of Buganda (now part of Uganda). Mukasa had converted to Christianity at a young age. The two Ugandans travelled from Africa to Britain to attend the coronation of Edward VII (1841–1910). Victoria died on 22 January 1901; Edward VII was to be crowned on 26 June but came down with appendicitis, delaying the ceremony until 9 August. The text was translated by Ernest Millar (1868–1917) of the Church Mission Society in Uganda; Millar, an Anglican missionary, had gone to Uganda in 1892 and for the most part remained there all his life.

[9] *Museum* established in 1753 and opened to the public in 1759, it has one of the largest and most comprehensive collections in the world of human artefacts from all ages from all over the world. Many items in its collection, most famously the Elgin Marbles of the Greek Parthenon, or the Rosetta Stone of Egypt, are now being considered by many as objects of imperial theft and plunder, with demands that they be returned to their country of origin. It does not occur to Makasa that many of these "wonderful things" have been taken wrongfully from his continent. The parenthetical identification was added by the translator.

[10] *old ... years* in 1896 E. A. Wallis Budge (1857–1934), Egyptologist and keeper of the Egyptian antiquities at the British Museum, excavated or purchased six of what are known as the Gebelein pre-dynastic mummies (c.3400 BCE), discovered in the same grave in the Egyptian desert. The bodies had been given to the British Museum in 1900; in 1901 the first body was put on display, nicknamed "Ginger" because of the colour of her hair. Mukasa contrasts their antiquity with the conventional date of creation of 4004 BCE that he had been taught by missionaries to Africa (see RELIGION: GEOLOGY, n. 1).

[11] *Cathedral* Uganda's Anglican cathedral was built first in Kampala in 1890 with a capacity for 800 people, but shortly after its construction it was abandoned because it had been built on swampy ground; a new and bigger cathedral, seating more than 3,000, was completed in July 1892, but a year later the building was ruined in a powerful storm; a third building seating 4,000 was completed by 1895 but abandoned in 1900 because of termites. While Mukasa was in England, a fourth cathedral was being built (it would be completed in 1904 and destroyed by fire in 1910).

We then went out to see the wonders of England. We went with Mr. Millar and his brother, Charles Millar,[12] and first went in our carriages to see the wonderful railways that go through the town underground.[13] The English truly are marvellous people! The railway was called "Central London,"[14] and is a hundred feet below the ground; we saw many roads, and trains passing, and the people who were there were like locusts in numbers. If your friend were to leave you for some time, you would get lost owing to the numbers of people. The roads there are very fine and wonderful; they have electric lamps,[15] which shine and act as suns. If any one were to take you there, and did not tell you that you were going underground, when you arrived you would not know that you were under the earth because the roads are so fine and the electric light is so bright, and the people are like locusts in numbers: and all these things make you silly, so that you would not understand that you were underground. . . .

From Chapter 6

The next day, June 23rd, we went back into London at half-past ten, and after a short rest went to see the glass house (Crystal Palace),[16] where they keep only the most beautiful things. There are figures of all the kings, and many great men and brave generals, like Sir Lord Roberts, who conquered the Transvaal at the Cape.[17] There are also copies of all the things made in their land; they pick out one thing, and put it there to show people how things are made in different places to which they cannot go themselves. We saw there live fish, and birds of all kinds. They chisel out stones and make them just like people, and put them there to remind people in after years what they were like. There were a number of statues of the kings from early times right down to the Queen (Victoria) and Edward VII., and of generals who had won great wars right down to Sir Lord General Roberts, who conquered the Boers while the Queen was still reigning. There is a statue in stone representing him on a horse; one wants to salute it and say, "Good morning, Roberts," though really it can neither see nor hear.

We saw how they bore gun-barrels, and saw also a slide for canoes in the game they play with them (water-chute). They make a large pond on a hill, and they make a slide of boards, which the canoes run down to get into the water below. They rush down very fast; a giddy person could not endure it. We saw also a great many people who had come to enjoy themselves, and there were many amusements, players on flutes, organs, and banjos, and many other instruments. We saw a very tall tower from which one can get a distant view over the city; perhaps you could see twenty or twenty-five miles—that is, as far or farther than Entebbe.[18] The tower is four or five times as high as Namirembe Cathedral, because when you are at the top men below look like little children. We saw

Notes

[12] *Millar* see n. 8.

[13] *underground* see n. 4.

[14] *London* a brand new underground line, also known as the Twopenny Line, had just opened on 30 July 1900.

[15] *lamps* electric street lights in Britain were introduced in November 1878; by the time Mukasa is writing the City of London Electric Lighting Act (1900) had made them the dominant mode over gas lights.

[16] *Palace* built in 1851 for the Great Exhibition; moved to Sydenham Hill in 1854 to become a place of public exhibits

and entertainment (see CONDITION: PROGRESS; ALBERT, "SPEECH" (WEB p. 26)). Parenthetical identification added by translator.

[17] *Roberts. . . Cape* Frederick Sleigh Roberts (1832–1914), Anglo-Irish soldier and army commander from the Indian Rebellion (1857) to the Second Boer War. The war began in 1899 and had concluded three weeks before this entry.

[18] *Entebbe* a city on Lake Victoria in present day Uganda, then the capital of the Uganda Protectorate, about 37 kilometres southwest of Kampala.

also large and small fish, and fish of all kinds in glass boxes, into which they pour water, and in which the fish live; when you look at them you would not think there was any glass there, as you can see them playing. When we saw all this we were amazed at the care of the English, who can feed unfeedable things like fish and keep them alive many years in their little lakes. The English are a wonderful people.

WEB p. 263

Mohandas Karamchand Gandhi (1869–1948): *An Autobiography, or, The Story of My Experiments with Truth* (1927)
   From Chapter 15: "Playing the English Gentleman"

Part Two
Authors

Walter Savage Landor (1775–1864)

British poet and classicist, Landor was born in Warwick into great wealth; after quarrelling with his father, he broke from the family. He was educated at Rugby and Oxford, from both of which he was expelled for his temper and outrageous pranks. He wrote in several genres in the classical languages as well as English; he is best known for his long poem, *Gebir* (1798) and for *Imaginary Conversations of Literary Men and Statesmen* (1824–53), a prose work of about 150 fictional dialogues between distinguished ancient and modern personages. Landor was a close friend of a number of leading literary figures of both the Romantic and Victorian periods, including Robert Southey, Samuel Taylor Coleridge, Charles Lamb, Charles Dickens, and Robert Browning. Dickens satirized his fierce temper and impetuous nature in *Bleak House* in the character of Laurence Boythorne. Landor lived in Italy from 1821 to 1835, returned to England, and then fled court action back to Italy in 1857, where he remained until his death; he is interred in Florence. Standard edition: *Complete Works*, eds T. E. Welby and Stephen Wheeler (16 vols, 1927–36); Jean Field, *Landor: A Biography of Walter Savage Landor* (2000); "Walter Savage Landor's Warwick"@: http://www.florin.ms/warwick.html.

To Robert Browning[1]

> There is delight in singing, though none hear
> Beside the singer: and there is delight
> In praising, though the praiser sit alone
> And see the prais'd far off him, far above.
> Shakspeare is not *our* poet, but the world's,   5
> Therefore on him no speech; and short for thee,
> Browning! Since Chaucer was alive and hale,
> No man hath walk'd along our roads with step
> So active, so inquiring eye, or tongue
> So varied in discourse. But warmer climes   10
> Give brighter plumage, stronger wing: the breeze
> Of Alpine heights thou playest with, borne on
> Beyond Sorrento and Amalfi,[2] where
> The Siren waits thee, singing song for song.

Notes

WALTER SAVAGE LANDOR

[1] *title* Landor wrote this tribute after receiving a copy of Browning's *Dramatic Romances and Lyrics* in early November 1845. Concerning lines 10–14, see Browning: "An Englishman in Italy." First published in *The Morning Chronicle* (22 Nov. 1845) where it is dated "Nov. 19, 1845." Reprinted in *The Works of Walter Savage Landor* (1846), and also prefixed to Ticknor-Fields' Boston edition of Browning's *Poems* (2 vols, 1850).

[2] *Amalfi* a spectacular road links these coastal towns overlooking the Bay of Naples and Mount Vesuvius in southern Italy. The unique Temple of the Sirens, dating from the ancient Greek occupation, is located at Sorrento.

Victorian Literature: An Anthology, First Edition. Edited by Victor Shea and William Whitla.
© 2015 John Wiley & Sons, Ltd. Published 2015 by John Wiley & Sons, Ltd.

"You smiled, you spoke, and I believed"[3]

You smiled, you spoke, and I believed,
By every word and smile deceived.
Another man would hope no more;
Nor hope I what I hoped before:
But let not this last wish be vain;　　　　　　　　5
Deceive, deceive me once again!

Dying Speech of an Old Philosopher[4]

I strove with none, for none was worth my strife:
　　Nature I loved, and, next to Nature, Art:
I warm'd both hands before the fire of Life;
　　It sinks, and I am ready to depart.

"I entreat you, Alfred Tennyson"[5]

I entreat you, Alfred Tennyson,
Come and share my haunch of venison.
I have too a bin of claret,[6]
Good, but better when you share it.[7]
Tho' 'tis only a small bin,　　　　　　　　5
There's a stock of it within.
And as sure as I'm a rhymer,
Half a butt of Rudesheimer.[8]
Come; among the sons of men is one
Welcomer than Alfred Tennyson?　　　　　　　　10

Notes

[3] title our text Works (1846).

[4] title English biographer John Forster (1812–76) says that Dickens and he had visited Landor in Bath to celebrate his birthday, and this quatrain was written after they left to return to London; he mailed it to Forster, who received it the next day: "It was his own version of the moral of his life in its aims and enjoyments; and, to all who could accept it, a very terse and conclusive summing-up of Epicurean philosophy." First published in The Examiner (3 Feb. 1849), signed "W. S. L.," commemorating Landor's seventy-fourth birthday on 30 January. Republished in The Last Fruit of an Old Tree (1853) without a title as the epigraph to the volume, the entire poem in small capitals. There is a handwritten facsimile in the biography of Landor by John Forster (bk. 7 sect. 9).

[5] title in 1838 Tennyson became a member of the Anonymous Club when he was living at Lincoln's Inn, London. Meeting at the Olde Cock Tavern in Fleet Street once a month for literary conversation, the members included Thomas Carlyle, J. S. Mill, and W. M. Thackeray. They occasionally composed verses in each other's honour, such as this example. Published in The Last Fruit of an Old Tree (1853).

[6] bin of claret an English term for the red wine of Bordeaux region in France. A bin is a partitioned section in a wine-cellar.

[7] share it an allusion to Horace's invitation to Virgil to join him for wine: "the season comes with thirst, Virgil, so if, O client of noble youths, you want to taste the Celenian wine, bring a little fragrant spikenard" (Odes 4. 12).

[8] Rudesheimer famous Rhenish white wine.

Charlotte Elliott (1789–1871)

Born in Clapham, then in the countryside south of London, the daughter of a silk merchant, Charles Elliott, and his wife, Eling Venn (from the Clapham Sect of Church of England social reformers), Elliott became a writer of humorous verse and a portrait painter. From about 1819 her health declined and she became bedridden for the rest of her life, subject to periods of extreme lethargy, pain, and severe depression. In 1822 the Swiss evangelist and hymn writer Henri Abraham César Malan (1787–1864) visited her and told her that she could find relief and comfort if she turned to Christianity: "Come just as you are, a sinner, to the Lamb of God." She marked her positive response as her spiritual birthday. She wrote over 150 hymns. No standard edition. *Selections from the Poems of Charlotte Elliott with a Memoir by her Sister* (1873?); *Leaves from the Unpublished Journals, Letters and Poems of Charlotte Elliott* (1874); the latter is available digitally from Baylor University's 19th Century Women Poets Collection: http://contentdm.baylor.edu/cdm/compoundobject/collection/ab-wpc/id/27582/rec/1.

"Him That Cometh to Me I Will in No Wise Cast Out." [Just As I Am][1]

John vi, 37.
Just as I am—without one plea
But that thy blood was shed for me,
And that thou bid'st me come to thee—
        O Lamb of God,[2] I come!

Just as I am—and waiting not
To rid my soul of one dark blot,
To thee, whose blood can cleanse each spot—
        O Lamb of God, I come!

Just as I am—though toss'd about,
With many a conflict, many a doubt,
Fightings and fears within, without—
        O Lamb of God, I come!

Just as I am—poor, wretched, blind;
Sight, riches, healing of the mind,
Yea, all I need, in thee to find—
        O Lamb of God, I come!

Notes

CHARLOTTE ELLIOTT

[1] *title* written in 1836 to raise money for a school for the children of poor clergy in Brighton, all seven verses were printed in Elliott's *Hours of Sorrow Cheered and Comforted* (1836) with the title, from John 6: 37, as given; it was also published in *The Invalid's Hymn Book* (first edition 1836), which contained 115 of her hymns (without the last verse); the title was later changed to "Just As I Am." Several hymn tunes have been used for this hymn, of which the most popular is "Woodworth" by William B. Bradbury (1816–68) used in *Hymns Ancient and Modern* (1861). See Plate 11: Hunt, *The Light of the World*.

[2] *God* one of the titles of Jesus Christ, from the words of John the Baptist (John 1: 29).

Just as I am—Thou wilt receive,
Wilt welcome, pardon, cleanse, relieve,
Because thy promise I believe—
    O Lamb of God, I come!

Just as I am—thy love unknown
Has broken every barrier down;
Now to be thine, yea, thine alone—
    O Lamb of God, I come!

Just as I am—of that free love
"The breadth, length, depth, and height"[3] to prove,
Here for a season, then above—
    O Lamb of God, I come!

John Keble (1792–1866)

Born near Fairford in Gloustershire, the son of a clergyman, John Keble (1745–1835), and Sarah Maule (1758–1823), the daughter of a clergyman, Keble was educated at Corpus Christi College, Oxford. He became a fellow of Oriel College (1812), later the centre of the emerging Oxford Movement led by John Henry Newman, who became one of his closest friends. He was ordained priest in the Church of England in 1816. After the great success of *The Christian Year* (1827), published anonymously, combining a Wordsworthian appreciation of nature with the analogy of the visible world to the spiritual world, Keble was appointed Professor of Poetry at Oxford (1831–41), delivering the required lectures in Latin (published 1844). In 1833 he gave the "Assize Sermon" in St Mary's Church, Oxford, for the opening of the law courts on the topic of "National Apostasy." To Newman and some others, the sermon marked the beginning of the Oxford Movement; to still others, like Isaac Williams (1802–65), it was "indiscreet and fruitless." In 1835, Keble was appointed vicar of a small village in Hampshire, Hursley, near Winchester, where he remained for the rest of his life. He married Charlotte Clarke (1806–66) and continued to be an important figure in the Oxford Movement, writing nine of the *Tracts for the Times*, editing the writings of the Elizabethan and Caroline divines like Richard Hooker (3 vols, 1836), and publishing other collections of poetry, *Lyra Innocentium* (1846), and thirteen volumes of parish sermons. Keble College, Oxford, was built as his memorial. No scholarly edition. Georgina Battiscombe, *John Keble: A Study in Limitations* (1963). Works online at Project Canterbury: anglicanhistory.org/keble.

Notes ———————————————————————————————————————

[3] *height* see Romans 8: 38–39.

From *National Apostasy Considered in a Sermon Preached in St. Mary's, Oxford, Before His Majesty's Judges of Assize on Sunday, July 14, 1833*[1]

1 Samuel 12: 23: *As for me, GOD forbid that I should sin against the LORD in ceasing to pray for you: but I will teach you the good and the right way.*

On public occasions, such as the present,[2] the minds of Christians naturally revert to that portion of Holy Scripture, which exhibits to us the will of the Sovereign of the world in more immediate relation to the *civil* and *national* conduct of mankind. We naturally turn to the Old Testament, when *public* duties, *public* errors, and *public* dangers, are in question. And what in such cases is natural and obvious, is sure to be more or less right and reasonable. Unquestionably it is a mistaken theology, which would debar Christian nations and statesmen from the instruction afforded by the Jewish scriptures, under a notion, that the circumstances of that people were *altogether*

Notes

JOHN KEBLE

[1] *title* Keble was chosen to deliver the sermon for the opening of the term of the civil and criminal courts in which the court officers and the judges were admonished to bear witness faithfully and administer justice impartially. It was a ceremonial occasion. Keble used it to accuse the nation of "apostasy," or the renunciation of religious faith. He outlined the reasons why the privileged position of the Church of England was in peril: widespread anti-clericalism; the repeal of discriminatory legislation against Nonconformists that excluded them from public office (the Test and Corporation Acts, 1828); Catholic emancipation that allowed local and national office, including sitting in parliament (the Catholic Emancipation Act, 1829); and the threat of a wider electorate because of the Reform Bill of 1832. An immediate cause of the charge of apostasy was the government's suppression of two archbishoprics and eight bishoprics in Ireland in the disestablishment of the Irish Church and the confiscation of their incomes (the Irish Church Temporalities Act, 1833). Keble and his associates, later becoming the High Church party, feared that the disestablishment of the Anglican Church in England was next. Others responded to the crisis differently. Coleridge wrote *On the Constitution of Church and State* (1830), where he introduced the notion of a "clerisy," the government-sponsored keepers of the national culture (see CONDITION: PROGRESS, n. 106 (WEB p. 40)). In *Principles of Church Reform* (1833) Thomas Arnold argued for an amalgamation of church and state as a community established "for the moral improvement of mankind," based not on doctrinal exclusions or articles of faith, but rather a shared Bible and a commitment to moral action. The positions of Coleridge and Arnold provided the basis for the Broad Church movement of liberal Anglicanism that was generally identified with the Whigs (Liberals) in politics and that avoided both the literalism of the evangelicals and the Anglo-Catholicism of the High Church parties; see RELIGION: RELIGIOUS FAITH; CONYBEARE (WEB p. 197).

Keble's homily is based upon an analogy between the Jews in the Hebrew scriptures and the contemporaneous Anglican Church. Under Samuel the Jews had demanded an earthly king (Saul) instead of relying on the heavenly king (God). When they had acknowledged their apostasy before God's prophet Samuel, they renewed their covenant with God, committing the nation to follow the ways of God and the words of the prophet (1 Samuel 12). Keble published the sermon with an "Advertisement" or preface: "The Legislature of England and Ireland, (*the members of which are not even bound to profess belief in the Atonement*), this body has virtually usurped the commission of those whom our Saviour entrusted with *at least one voice* [that is, the Established Anglican Church] in making ecclesiastical laws, on matters wholly or partly spiritual. The same Legislature has also ratified, to its full extent, this principle;—that the Apostolical Church in this realm is henceforth only to stand, in the eye of the State, *as one sect among many.* . . . How may they continue their communion with the Church *established*, (hitherto the pride and comfort of their lives), without any taint of those Erastian Principles [the state's supremacy over the church] on which she now is avowedly to be governed? What answer can we make henceforth to the partisans of the Bishop of Rome [the pope], when they taunt us with being a mere Parliamentarian Church?" Keble wished to preserve the traditional "middle way" (Lat. *via media*) of Anglicanism, eschewing both the continental reformers in Germany, France, and Switzerland who were, he concluded, Erastian, and the Roman Catholics who erred in the other direction. The sermon inaugurates the Oxford Movement: in the *Apologia* Newman wrote, "The following Sunday, July 14th, Mr. Keble preached the assize sermon in the University pulpit. It was published under the title of National Apostasy. I have ever considered and kept the day as the start of the religious movement of 1833." To Newman it was a highly symbolic confrontation between church and state; the assembled judges and the press reported no such response.

[2] *present* the opening of the law courts' sessions.

peculiar and unique, and therefore irrelevant to every other case. True, there *is* hazard of misapplication, as there is whenever men teach by example. There is *peculiar* hazard, from the sacredness and delicacy of the subject; since dealing with things supernatural and miraculous as if they were ordinary human precedents, would be not only unwise, but profane. But these hazards are more than counterbalanced by the absolute certainty, peculiar to this history, that what is there commended was right, and what is there blamed, wrong. And they would be effectually obviated if men would be careful to keep in view this caution:—suggested every where, if I mistake not, by the manner in which the Old Testament is quoted in the New:—that, as regards reward and punishment, GOD dealt formerly with the Jewish people in a manner analogous to that in which He deals now, not so much with Christian *nations*, as with the *souls of individual Christians*. . . .

That portion,[3] in particular, of the history of the chosen people, which drew from Samuel, the truest of patriots, the wise and noble sentiment in the text, must ever be an unpleasing and perplexing page of Scripture, to those, who would fain persuade themselves, that a nation, even a Christian nation, may do well enough, as such, without GOD, and without His Church. For what if the Jews *were* bound to the Almighty by ties common to no other people? What if He *had* condescended to know *them* in a way in which He was as yet unrevealed to all families of the earth besides? What if, as their relation to Him was nearer, and their ingratitude more surpassing, so they might expect more exemplary punishment? Still, after all has been said, to exaggerate their guilt, *in degree*, beyond what is supposed possible in any nation whatever now, what can it come to, in *kind* and in *substance*, but only this;— that they rejected GOD? that they wished themselves rid of the moral restraint implied in His peculiar presence and covenant? They said, what the prophet Ezekiel, long after, represents their worthy posterity as saying, "*We will be as the heathen, the families of the countries.*"[4] "Once for all, we will get rid of these disagreeable, unfashionable scruples, which throw us behind, as we think, in the race of worldly honour and profit." Is this indeed a tone of thought, which Christian nations cannot fall into? Or, if they should, has it ceased to be displeasing to GOD? In other words, has He forgotten to be angry with impiety and practical atheism? Either this must be affirmed, or men must own, (what is clear at once to plain unsophisticated readers), that this first overt act, which began the downfall of the Jewish nation, stands on record, with its fatal consequences, for a perpetual warning to all nations, as well as to all individual Christians, who having accepted GOD for their King, allow themselves to be weary of subjection to Him, and think they should be happier if they were freer, and more like the rest of the world. . . .

What are the symptoms, by which one may judge most fairly, whether or no a nation, as such, is becoming alienated from GOD and CHRIST?

And what are the particular duties of sincere Christians, whose lot is cast by divine Providence in a time of such dire calamity?

The conduct of the Jews, in asking for a king, may furnish an ample illustration of the *first* point: the behaviour of Samuel, then and afterwards, supplies as perfect a pattern of the *second*, as can well be expected from human nature.

The case is at least possible, of a nation, having for centuries acknowledged, as an essential part of its theory of government, that, *as* a Christian nation, she is also a part

Notes ———————————————————————————————————

[3] *portion* Keble bases his sermon on a text from 1 Samuel 11–12 where the Israelites had chosen Saul as their king, against the will of God and the instructions of the prophet Samuel.

[4] *countries* "Ezekiel 20: 32" [author's note].

of Christ's Church, and bound, in all her legislation and policy, by the fundamental rules of that Church, the case is, I say, conceivable, of a government and people, so constituted, deliberately throwing off the restraint, which in many respects such a principle would impose on them, nay, disavowing the principle itself; and that, on the plea, that other states, as flourishing or more so in regard of wealth and dominion, do well enough without it. Is not this desiring, like the Jews, to have an earthly king over them, when the LORD their GOD is their King? Is it not saying in other words, "We will be as the heathen, the families of the countries,"[5] the aliens to the Church of our Redeemer?

To such a change, whenever it takes place, the immediate impulse will probably be given by some pretence of danger from without,—such as, at the time now spoken of, was furnished to the Israelites by an incursion of the children of Ammon;[6] or by some wrong or grievance in the executive government, such as the malversation[7] of Samuel's sons, to whom he had deputed his judicial functions. Pretences will never be hard to find; but, in reality, the movement will always be traceable to the same decay or want of faith, the same deficiency in Christian resignation and thankfulness, which leads so many, as individuals, to disdain and forfeit the blessings of the gospel. Men not impressed with religious principle attribute their ill success in life,—the hard times they have to struggle with,—to any thing rather than their own ill-desert: and the institutions of the country, ecclesiastical and civil, are always at hand to bear the blame of whatever seems to be going amiss. . . .

These, which have been hitherto mentioned as omens and tokens of an Apostate Mind[8] in a nation, have been suggested by the portion itself of sacred history, to which I have ventured to direct your attention. There are one or two more, which the nature of the subject, and the palpable tendency of things around us, will not allow to be passed over.

One of the most alarming, as a symptom, is the growing indifference, in which men indulge themselves, to other men's religious sentiments. Under the guise of charity and toleration we are come almost to this pass; *that no difference, in matters of faith, is to disqualify for our approbation and confidence, whether in public or domestic life.* Can we conceal it from ourselves, that every year the practice is becoming more common, of trusting men unreservedly in the most delicate and important matters, without one serious inquiry, whether they do not hold principles which make it impossible for them to be loyal to their CREATOR, REDEEMER, and SANCTIFIER?[9] Are not offices conferred, partnerships formed, intimacies courted,—nay, (what is almost too painful to think of,) do not parents commit their children to be educated, do they not encourage them to intermarry, in houses, on which Apostolical Authority[10] would rather teach them to set a mark, as unfit to be entered by a faithful servant of CHRIST?

I do not now speak of public measures only or chiefly; many things of that kind may be thought, whether wisely or no, to become from time to time necessary, which

Notes

[5] *countries* Ezekiel 20: 32.

[6] *Ammon* see 2 Samuel 10.

[7] *malversation* corruption in public office.

[8] *Apostate Mind* mind of one who has repudiated religion; a religious traitor.

[9] *Sanctifier* reference to alternate names for the Trinity: Father, Son, and Holy Spirit.

[10] *Creator . . . Authority* sometimes called "apostolic succession": the claim of the Church of England to be in direct descent through its bishops from Jesus' conferring of authority to the apostle Peter (see Matthew 16: 18).

are in reality as little desired by those who lend them a seeming concurrence, as they are, in themselves, undesirable. But I speak of the spirit which leads men to *exult* in every step of that kind; to *congratulate* one another on the supposed decay of what they call an exclusive system.

Very different are the feelings with which it seems natural for a true Churchman to regard such a state of things, from those which would arise in his mind on witnessing the mere triumph of *any given set of adverse opinions*, exaggerated or even heretical as he might deem them. He *might* feel as melancholy,—he *could* hardly feel so indignant.

But this is not a becoming place, nor are these safe topics, for the indulgence of mere *feeling*. The point really to be considered is, whether, according to the coolest estimate, the fashionable liberality of this generation be not ascribable, in a great measure, to the same temper which led the Jews voluntarily to set about degrading themselves to a level with the idolatrous Gentiles? And, if it be true any where, that such enactments are forced on the Legislature by public opinion, is APOSTASY too hard a word to describe the temper of that nation?

The same tendency is still more apparent, because the fair gloss of candour and forbearance is wanting, in the surly or scornful impatience often exhibited, by persons who would regret passing for unbelievers, when Christian motives are suggested, and checks from Christian principles attempted to be enforced on their public conduct. I say, "their public conduct," more especially; because in that, I know not how, persons are apt to be more shameless, and readier to avow the irreligion that is in them;—amongst other reasons, probably, from each feeling that he is one of a multitude, and fancying, therefore, that his responsibility is divided....

Felicia Hemans (1793–1835)

Born in Liverpool, the daughter of a merchant, George Browne, Felicia Dorothea Hemans moved to Wales with her family after her father's business failed. She was educated at home, in her family's well-stocked library, under the direction of her mother Felicity Dorothea Browne (née Wagner, 1766–1827). A precocious child, she published a volume, *Poems*, at age 14 (as Felicia Dorothea Browne). In 1812 she married Alfred Hemans, an army captain, shortly after publishing her second volume, *The Domestic Affections and Other Poems*. There followed other collections, including *On the Restoration of the Works of Art to Italy* (1816), *Hymns on the Works of Nature, for the Use of Children* (1827), and *Records of Woman: With Other Poems* (1828). In all, she would publish nineteen volumes of poetry, drama, and other writings. In 1818 she and her husband separated, leaving her with five sons under the age of 6; her poetry sold well, enabling her to support her family. She was extremely popular in both Britain and the United States, celebrated as a "Poetess." Her reputation suffered later in the nineteenth century: she was dismissed as sentimental and moralistic; however, she has lately received new critical attention and interest as the leading female poet of her day. She died of a heart condition in Dublin and is buried at St Anne's Church. No standard edition: *The Poetical Works of Felicia Dorothea Hemans* (1914); *Felicia Hemans: Selected Poems, Letters, Reception Materials*, ed. Susan J. Wolfson (2000); *Felicia Hemans: Selected Poems, Prose and Letters*, ed. Gary Kelly (2001); *Felicia Hemans: Reimagining Poetry in the Nineteenth Century*, eds Nanora Sweet & Julie Melnyk (2001); "Felicia Hemans": http://digital.library.upenn.edu/women/hemans/biography.html.

Casabianca[1]

The boy stood on the burning deck
    Whence all but he had fled;
The flame that lit the battle's wreck,
    Shone round him o'er the dead.

Yet beautiful and bright he stood,   5
    As born to rule the storm;
A creature of heroic blood,
    A proud, though child-like form.

The flames rolled on—he would not go,
    Without his Father's word;   10
That Father, faint in death below,
    His voice no longer heard.

He called aloud:—"say, Father, say
    If yet my task is done?"
He knew not that the chieftain lay   15
    Unconscious of his son.

"Speak, Father!" once again he cried,
    "If I may yet be gone!
And"—but the booming shots replied,
    And fast the flames rolled on.   20

Upon his brow he felt their breath,
    And in his waving hair,
And looked from that lone post of death,
    In still, yet brave despair.

And shouted but once more aloud,   25
    "My Father! must I stay?"
While o'er him fast, through sail and shroud,
    The wreathing fires made way.

Notes

FELICIA HEMANS

[1] title "Young Casabianca, a boy about thirteen years old, son to the Admiral of the Orient, remained at his post (in the Battle of the Nile), after the ship had taken fire, and all the guns had been abandoned, and perished in the explosion of the vessel, when the flames had reached the powder" [author's note]. On 1 August 1798, about 9 p.m., one of Napoleon's ships, L'Orient, was attacked by the British under Admiral Horatio Nelson (1758–1805). After the ship caught fire and burned for an hour, the powder magazine exploded. Throughout, Giacomo Jocante Casabianca, son of the ship's commander, Louis de Casabianca (1762–98), stayed at his post. The death of the boy was also a theme of contemporary French poets Écouchard Lebrun (1729–1807) and André Chénier (1762–94). The event is recounted in Robert Southey's Life of Horatio, Lord Nelson (1813). He reports that Nelson was presented with a coffin made from the main mast of L'Orient as a trophy to be buried in, and it did carry his remains to England after he was killed at Trafalgar (1805). Going against British patriotic fervour and poetical frenzy after the Battle of the Nile, Hemans's poem, which turns to praise the French boy-hero, with its ballad form, became an oft-repeated piece of memory work in the elementary readers of the United States, and a popular example of imperial duty in Great Britain. There are numerous parodies. For other treatments of Victorian duty, see CLOUGH, n. 3; and HOPKINS, "FELIX RANDAL." The poem was first published in the Monthly Magazine (Aug. 1826).

They wrapt the ship in splendour wild,
  They caught the flag on high, 30
And streamed above the gallant child,
  Like banners in the sky.

There came a burst of thunder sound—
  The boy—oh! where was he?
Ask of the winds that far around 35
  With fragments strewed the sea!

With mast, and helm, and pennon fair,
  That well had borne their part—
But the noblest thing which perished there,
  Was that young faithful heart! 40

The Indian Woman's Death-Song[2]

An Indian woman, driven to despair by her husband's desertion of her for another wife, entered a canoe with her children, and rowed it down the Mississippi towards a cataract. Her voice was heard from the shore singing a mournful death-song, until overpowered by the sound of the waters in which she perished. The tale is related in Long's Expedition to the Source of St Peter's River.[3]

Non, je ne puis vivre avec un coeur brisé. Il faut que je retrouve la joie, et que je m'unisse aux esprits libres de l'air. (Bride of Messina, Translated by MADAME DE STAEL*)[4]*

Let not my child be a girl, for very sad is the life of a woman. (The Prairie)[5]

Down a broad river of the western wilds,
Piercing thick forest glooms, a light canoe
Swept with the current; fearful was the speed
Of the frail bark, as by a tempest's wing
Borne leaf-like on to where the mist of spray 5
Rose with the cataract's thunder.—Yet within,
Proudly, and dauntlessly, and all alone,
Save that a babe lay sleeping at her breast,
A woman stood: upon her Indian brow 10
Sat a strange gladness, and her dark hair wav'd

Notes

[2] *title* first published in *Records of Woman: With Other Poems* (1828).

[3] *River* William Hypolitus Keating (1799–1840), in *Narrative of an Expedition to the Source of St Peter's River … under the command of S. H. Long*, (2 vols, 1824), includes an account of a woman who "launched her light canoe, entered into it with her children, and paddled down the stream singing her death song.... Her voice was drowned in the sound of the cataract."

[4] *Staël* Madame de Staël (1766–1817) translated *Die Braut von Messina, Die, oder, Die Feindlichen Bruder* (Ger. The Bride of Messina, or the Hostile Brother, 1803), a tragedy by Friedrich Schiller (1759–1805). Her citation: (Fr. No, I am not able to live with a broken heart. I must find joy again, and what unites me with the free spirits of the air).

[5] *Prairie* slightly misquoted from James Fenimore Cooper's *The Prairie* (1827, ch. 26).

As if triumphantly. She press'd her child,
In its bright slumber, to her beating heart,
And lifted her sweet voice, that rose awhile
Above the sound of waters, high and clear,   15
Wafting a wild proud strain, her song of death.

———

Roll swiftly to the Spirit's land, thou mighty stream and free!
Father of ancient waters,⁶ roll! and bear our lives with thee!
The weary bird that storms have toss'd, would seek the sunshine's calm,
And the deer that hath the arrow's hurt, flies to the woods of balm.   20

Roll on!—my warrior's eye hath look'd upon another's face,
And mine hath faded from his soul, as fades a moonbeam's trace;
My shadow comes not o'er his path, my whisper to his dream,
He flings away the broken reed—roll swifter yet, thou stream!

The voice that spoke of other days is hush'd within *his* breast,   25
But *mine* its lonely music haunts, and will not let me rest;
It sings a low and mournful song of gladness that is gone,
I cannot live without that light—Father of waves! roll on!

Will he not miss the bounding step that met him from the chase?
The heart of love that made his home an ever sunny place?   30
The hand that spread the hunter's board, and deck'd his couch of yore?—
He will not!—roll, dark foaming stream, on to the better shore!

Some blessed fount amidst the woods of that bright land must flow,
Whose waters from my soul may lave the memory of this wo;
Some gentle wind must whisper there, whose breath may waft away   35
The burden of the heavy night, the sadness of the day.

And thou, my babe! tho' born, like me, for woman's weary lot,
Smile!—to that wasting of the heart, my own! I leave thee not;
Too bright a thing art *thou* to pine in aching love away,
Thy mother bears thee far, young Fawn! from sorrow and decay.   40

She bears thee to the glorious bowers where none are heard to weep,
And where th' unkind one hath no power again to trouble sleep;
And where the soul shall find its youth, as wakening from a dream,—
One moment, and that realm is ours—On, on, dark rolling stream!

Notes

⁶ *waters* "'Father of waters,' the Indian name for the
Mississippi" [author's note].

The Indian With His Dead Child[7]

Then the hunter turn'd away from that scene,
Where the home of his fathers once had been,
And burning thoughts flash'd o'er his mind,
Of the white man's faith and love unkind.

BRYANT[8]

In the silence of the midnight,
    I journey with the dead:
In the darkness of the forest boughs,
    A lonely path I tread.

But my heart is high and fearless,   5
    As by mighty wings upborne;
The mountain-eagle hath not plumes
    So strong as love and scorn.

I have raised thee from the grave-sod,
    By the white man's path defiled;   10
On to th' ancestral wilderness
    I bear thy dust, my child!

I have ask'd the ancient deserts
    To give my dead a place,
Where the stately footsteps of the free   15
    Alone should leave a trace:

And the rocking pines made answer—
    Go, bring us back thine own!
And the streams from all the hunter's hills,
    Rush'd with an echoing tone.   20

Thou shalt rest by sounding waters,
    That yet untamed may roll;
The voices of those chainless ones[9]
    With joy shall fill thy soul.

Notes

[7] *title* "A striking display of Indian character occurred some years since in a town in Maine. An Indian of the Kennebeck tribe, remarkable for his good conduct, received a grant of land from the state, and fixed himself in a new township, where a number of families were settled. Though not ill treated, yet the common prejudice against Indians prevented any sympathy with him. This was shewn on the death of his only child, when none of the people came near him. Shortly after, he gave up his farm, dug up the body of his child, and carried it with him two hundred miles through the forest, to join the Canada Indians."—TUDOR's *Letters on the Eastern States of America*" [author's note]. Letter 12 of William Tudor's *Letters on the Eastern States* (1820) is "On the Past, Present, and Future State of the Indians," although this event is not recounted in it.

The entire anecdote, almost verbatim, occurs in Rufus Merrill's *Stories About Indians* (1854) in the third series of *Merrill's Toy and Juvenile Books*. First published in *Blackwood's Edinburgh Magazine* (Apr. 1829) as the second of three poems, under the general title of "Songs of the Affections," signed "F. H."; collected in *Songs of the Affections, with Other Poems* (1830).

[8] *Bryant* the epigraph poem is not by William Cullen Bryant (1794–1878) but by Henry Wadsworth Longfellow (1807–82), from "The Indian Hunter" (1825). Between lines two and three of the citation are two more lines: "And heard by the distant and measured stroke, / That the woodman hew'd down the giant oak"; the epigraph was removed from later editions.

[9] *ones* in later editions: "that chainless host."

In the silence of the midnight 25
    I journey with the dead,
Where the arrows of my father's bow
    Their falcon-flight have sped.

I have left the spoilers' dwellings,
    For evermore behind; 30
Unmingled with their household sounds,
    For me shall sweep the wind.

Alone, amidst their hearth-fires,
    I watch'd my child's decay;
Uncheer'd I saw the spirit-light 35
    From his young eyes fade away.

When his head sank on my bosom,
    When the death-sleep o'er him fell,
Was there one to say—"A friend is near?"
    There was none!—Pale race, farewell! 40

To the forests, to the cedars,
    To the warrior and his bow,
Back, back! I bore thee laughing thence,
    —I bear thee slumbering now!

I bear him unto burial 45
    With the mighty hunters gone;—
I shall hear thee in the forest-breeze,—
    Thou wilt speak of joy, my son!

In the silence of the midnight
    I journey with the dead; 50
But my heart is strong, my step is fleet,
    My father's path I tread.

The Rock of Cader-Idris[10]

A Legend of Wales[11]

It is an ancient tradition of Wales, that whoever should pass a night alone on the summit of the Mountain Cader-Idris, would be found in the morning either dead, in a state of frenzy, or endowed with the highest poetical inspiration.[12]

I lay on that rock where the storms have their dwelling,
The birthplace of phantoms, the home of the cloud;
Around it for ever deep music is swelling,

Notes

[10] *title* Cader-Idris (Welsh: chair of Idris) is a mountain in north-west Wales. Idris is named after a learned giant in Welsh mythology who is supposed to have rested there. The first edition in *A Selection Of Welsh Melodies With Symphonies And Accompaniments By John Parry And Characteristic Words By Mrs Hemans* (1822 vol. 2) was printed

with the name of the melody after the title: "Air—'The Ash Grove.'" The poem was reprinted in *New Monthly Magazine* (Mar. 1834), our text.
[11] *Wales* this sub-title was added in 1834.
[12] *inspiration* this epigraph in the first edition read as follows: "There is a popular Welsh tradition, that on the summit of

The voice of the Mountain-wind, solemn and loud.
'Twas a midnight of shadows, all fitfully streaming,   5
Of wild gusts and torrents that mingled their moan,
Of dim-shrouded stars, as thro' gulphs faintly gleaming,
And my strife with stern nature was darksome and lone.

I lay there in silence:—a spirit came o'er me;
Man's tongue hath no language to speak what I saw!   10
Things glorious, unearthly, pass'd floating before me,
And my heart almost fainted with rapture and awe!
I viewed the dread Beings around us that hover,
Tho' veiled by the mists of Mortality's breath;
And I called upon Darkness the vision to cover,   15
For within me was battling of madness and death!

I saw them—the Powers of the Wind and the Ocean,
The rush of whose pinion bears onward the storm;
Like the sweep of the white-rolling wave was their motion,
I felt their dread presence, but knew not their form.   20
I saw them—the mighty of ages departed—
The dead were around me that night on the hill;
From their eyes, as they pass'd, a cold radiance they darted;
There was light on my soul, but my heart's blood was chill.

I saw what man looks on, and dies!—but my spirit   25
Was strong, and triumphantly lived thro' that hour,
And as from the grave I awoke, to inherit
A flame all immortal, a voice and a pow'r!
Day burst on that Rock with the purple cloud crested,
And high Cader-Idris rejoiced in the sun;   30
But oh! what new glory all nature invested,
When the sense which gives *soul* to her beauty was won![13]

The Last Song of Sappho[14]

What is Poesy, but to create
    From overfeeling, good or ill, and aim
At an exernal life beyond our fate?
    Bestowing fire from Heaven, and then, too late,

Notes

Cader-Idris, one of the highest mountains in North Wales, is an excavation in the rock resembling a couch, and that whoever should pass a night in that seat, would be found in the morning either dead, raving mad, or endowed with supernatural genius.—*See* Davis's *Celtic Remains.*" Edward Davies (1756–1831) published *Celtic Researches, on the Origin, Traditions and Language of the Ancient Britons; With Some Introductory Sketches on Primitive Society* (1804).

[13] *won* "One of the Welsh poetical Triads thus describes the attributes of Genius:—'The three primary requisites of genius: an eye that can see nature, a heart that can feel nature, and boldness that dares follow nature'" [author's note]; the note was omitted after the first edition.

[14] *title* after the first edition, the following headnote was included: "Suggested by a beautiful sketch, the design of the younger Westmacott. It represents Sappho sitting on a rock above the sea, with her lyre cast at her feet. There is a desolate grace about the whole figure, which seems penetrated with the feeling of utter abandonment." Richard Westmacott (the younger, 1799–1872) was a Fellow of the RA and eventually succeeded his father as professor of sculpture there; the sketch has not been identified or

Finding the pleasure given repaid with pain!
　　And vultures to the heart of the bestower,
Who, having lavish'd his high gift in vain,
　　Lies chain'd to his lone rock by the seashore.
　　　　　　BYRON's *Prophecy of Dante*.[15]

Sound on, thou dark unslumbering sea!
　　My dirge is in thy moan;
My spirit finds response in thee,
To its own ceaseless cry—"Alone, alone!"[16]

Yet send me back one other word,　　　　　　　　　5
　　Ye tones that never cease!
Oh! let your hidden leaves be stirr'd,
And say, deep waters! can you give me peace?

Away!—my weary soul hath sought
　　In vain one echoing sigh,　　　　　　　　　　10
One answer to consuming thought
In human breasts—and will the *wave* reply?

Sound on, thou dark, unslumbering sea!
　　Sound in thy scorn and pride!
I ask not, alien world! from *thee*,　　　　　　　　15
What my own kindred earth hath still denied!

And yet I loved that earth so well,
　　With all its lovely things!
Was it for *this* the death-wind fell
On my rich lyre, and quench'd its living strings?　　　20

Let them lie silent at my feet!
　　Since, broken even as they,
The heart, whose music made them sweet,
Hath pour'd on desert sands its wealth away.

Yet glory's light hath touch'd my name,　　　　　　25
　　The laurel wreath[17] is mine—
With a worn heart, a weary frame,
O! restless Deep! I come to make them thine!

Notes

located; Hemans also admired a sculpture, *Sappho* (1834), by John Gibson (1790–1866); Hemans draws on Ovid's *Heroides* for her account of Sappho (see LANDON, n. 1); she was also familiar with the tragedies about Sappho by Franz Grillparzer (1818) and by Mme de Staël (1821). First published in *Blackwoods Edinburgh Magazine* (Jan. 1831); republished *National Lyrics, and Songs for Music* (1834). It was reprinted in her posthumous collection, *Poetical Works* (1839).

[15] *Dante* Hemans quotes Byron's *Prophecy of Dante* (1819), from Canto 4. 11–19, but omits line 14: "And be the new Prometheus of new men," presumably because of its inappropriate application to Sappho; the Titan Prometheus stole fire from the gods to benefit humans (or taught humans the arts and sciences) and was punished by Zeus by being chained to a rock where his liver was consumed daily by an eagle, regenerating overnight. To Goethe and the English Romantics, especially Byron and Percy and Mary Shelley, Prometheus was a modern hero of pride and genius opposed by fate and force.

[16] *alone* possibly an echo of Sappho's Fragment 52: "The silver moon is set; / The Pleiades are gone; / Half the long night is spent, and yet / I lie alone" (tr. J. H. Merivale, 1813); see also CHRISTINA ROSSETTI, "SAPPHO" (14).

[17] *wreath* the nymph Daphne was pursued by Apollo and to escape him prayed to her father for assistance. She was transformed into the evergreen bay or laurel, which was

Give to that crown, that burning crown,
   Place in thy darkest hold!   30
Bury my anguish, my renown,
With hidden wrecks, lost gems, and wasted gold!
Thou sea-bird on the billow's crest,
   Thou hast thy love, thy home!
They wait thee in the quiet nest—   35
And I—unsought, unwatch'd for—I too come!

I, with this winged nature fraught,
   These visions, brightly free,
This boundless love, this fiery thought—
Alone, I come! O! give me peace, dark sea!   40

Janet Hamilton (1795–1873)

The daughter of a poor Lanarkshire shoemaker and farm labourer, Hamilton was born Janet Thomson in Shotts, Lanarkshire where her mother taught her to read and use the tambour frame to embroider silk. She was well acquainted with the Bible, Shakespeare, and Milton, and read widely in the Scottish poets, especially Robert Burns. The family moved about a good deal as farm labourers. She married John Hamilton in 1809, settling in Langloan, raising ten children and teaching them all to read. She resumed writing poetry in both English and Scots, publishing in Cassell's *Working Man's Friend*. Her published volumes included *Poems and Essays* (1863), *Poems of Purpose and Sketches in Prose* (1865), and *Poems and Ballads* (1868). She wrote about the hardships suffered by working women, in support of the temperance movement, and on national liberation in Italy and Greece. In 1868 she received a grant of £50 from the Royal Bounty after petitions were forwarded to Benjamin Disraeli. Standard edition: *Poems, Sketches, and Essays with a Life of Janet Hamilton by the Rev. George Gilfillan* (1880); John Young, *Pictures in Prose and Verse; or, Personal Recollections of the Late Janet Hamilton; Together with Several Hitherto Unpublished Poetic Pieces* (1877); *Working-Class Women Poets in Victorian Britain: An Anthology*, ed. Florence S. Boos (2008).

A Lay of the Tambour Frame[1]

Bending with straining eyes
   Over the tambour frame,
Never a change in her weary routine—

Notes

thenceforth sacred to Apollo (*Metamorphoses* 1. 452 ff.) and was used to make a wreath to crown the victor in literary and athletic contests in ancient Greece, revived when Petrarch (1304–74) was crowned with laurel in Rome (1341) and subsequently taken as the mark of poetic inspiration and literary acclamation. Sappho in some paintings and ancient sculptures is depicted as wearing a laurel wreath, as befitted her status as defined by an epigram attributed to Plato: "Some say the Muses are nine: how careless! Look, there's Sappho too, from Lesbos, the tenth," *Anthologia Palatina* (9.506). For other uses of laurel, see ELIZABETH BROWNING, n. 2; and ELIZABETH BROWNING, n. 27 (WEB p. 308); NORTON, "THE PICTURE OF SAPPHO" (57); and TENNYSON, *IN MEMORIAM*, SECT. XXXVII.

JANET HAMILTON
[1] *title* from Hamilton's *Poems and Ballads* (1868). Hamilton endorsed the pleasures of poetry for the working classes

Slave in all but the name.
Tambour, ever tambour,   5
   Tambour the wreathing lines
Of 'broidered silk, till beauty's robe
   In rainbow lustre shines.

There, with colourless cheek;
   There, with her tangling hair;   10
Still bending low o'er the rickety frame,
   Seek, ye will find her there.
Tambour, ever tambour,
   "With fingers cramped and chill;—
The panes are shattered, and cold the wind   15
   Blows over the eastern hill.

Why quail, my sisters, why,
   As ye were abjects vile,
When begging some haughty brother of earth
   "To give you leave to toil?"   20
It is tambour you must,
   Naught else you have to do;
Though paupers' dole be of higher amount
   Than pay oft earned by you.

No union strikes for you;—   25
   Unshielded and alone,
In the battle of life—a battle it is,
   Where virtue is oft o'erthrown.
O working men! O why
   Pass ye thus careless by,   30
Nor give to the working woman's complaint
   One word of kind reply?

Selfish, unfeeling men!
   Have ye not had your will?
High pay, short hours; yet your cry, like the leech,   35
   Is, Give us, give us still.
She who tambours—tambours
   For fifteen hours a day—
Would have shoes on her feet, and dress for church,
   Had she a third of your pay.   40

Sisters, cousins, and aunts[2]
   Are they; yet, if not so,
Say, are they not sisters by human ties,

Notes

in "The Uses and Pleasures of Poetry to the Working Classes" in *The Working Man's Friend and Family Instructor* (Dec. 1850: Supplement): "The working man who is a good English reader, and possessed of an intellectual cast of mind, seasoned with a dash of fancy and feeling … thanks to the facilities afforded by cheap literature, may yet indulge a taste for the sublime and beautiful, and be quite as capable of appreciating the treasures contained in the rich and varied stores of the higher walks of literature and the sublime effusions of the best poets, as if he had ascended through all the gradations of learning, from the parish school to the *finale* of a classical education in the patrician halls of Oxford or Cambridge."

[2] *aunts* a line later made famous by Gilbert and Sullivan in Sir Joseph Porter's song in *H.M.S. Pinafore* (1878): "I am the monarch of the sea, / The ruler of the Queen's Navee, /

And sympathy's kindly flow?
To them how dear the boon   45
    From brother's hand that came!
It would warm the heart and brighten the eyes,
    While bending o'er the frame.

Raise ye a fund to aid
    In times of deep distress;   50
While man helps man, to their sisters in need
    Brothers can do no less.
Still the tambourer bends
    Wearily o'er the frame.
Patterns oft vary, for fashions will change—   55
    She is ever the same.

Thomas Carlyle (1795–1881)

In rural Ecclefechan in Scotland, just north of the English border, Carlyle was born into Calvinistic piety and hard work. He attended Edinburgh University to study for the ministry, but, overwhelmed by religious doubts, he turned to mathematics and science, and then to literature and philosophy, being greatly influenced by the German transcendentalists; his first work was translating German literature.

In 1821 he met Jane Welsh (1801–66), an equally brilliant thinker and wit, and in 1826 they married, moving to Craigenputtock in 1828, where Carlyle wrote *Signs of the Times* (1829), *On History* (1830–33), and *Characteristics* (1831), as well as *Sartor Resartus* (1833–34), a puzzling and symbolic autobiography recounting his spiritual doubts and recovery. In London, from 1834, the Carlyles cultivated a wide circle of friends and intellectuals, including Harriet Martineau and J. S. Mill. Success came with his *French Revolution* (2 vols, 1837). A notable series of lectures, *On Heroes, Hero-Worship, and the Heroic in History* (1841), signalled a shift in his thinking towards the importance of powerful leaders in

delivering society from trivial compromises, anarchy, and futile bloodshed. Afterwards, he addressed "the condition of England" in a series of writings, offering a biting critique of the materialism, utilitarianism, and *laissez-faire* capitalism of his own age in *Past and Present* (1843). Bitterly opposing liberal views on democracy, prison reform, and human rights, and adopting a narrow view of internationalism and extending his view of powerful leaders to a kind of authoritarianism, he published his most notorious works, "Occasional Discourse on the Negro Question"(1849), *Latter-Day Pamphlets* (1850), and *Shooting Niagara, and After?* (1867).

Carlyle's style is satiric, paradoxical, and often ironic. He is repetitive, given to abuse, and filled with ambiguity, allusions to other literatures, filling his early writing with Germanisms and coinings – all detrimental to his receiving early recognition by the public. But his style is more accessible in the histories, replete with careful attention to documents and facts, stressing important and symbolic events, persons, and things that to him reveal universal truths.

Notes

Whose praise Great Britain loudly chants. / [Cousin Hebe:] And we are his sisters, and his cousins and his aunts! / [Relatives:] And we are his sisters, and his cousins, and his aunts!"

Carlyle's reputation was damaged by his later attitudes to race and attacks on democracy, subsequently identified by some with the rise of fascism in Germany, where he had always been popular, in part for being a leading promoter of German literature and philosophy in Victorian England. Although offered a burial place in Westminster Abbey, he is interred beside his parents at Ecclefechan. Standard edition: *The Strouse Edition of the Writings of Thomas Carlyle,* ed. Chris R. Vanden Bossche (4 of 8 vols now published, 1993–); *The Collected Letters of Thomas and Jane Welsh Carlyle,* eds C. R. Sanders, K. J. Fielding, *et al.* (35+ vols, 1970–): available online carlyleletters.dukejournals. org]; John Morrow, *Thomas Carlyle* (2006). "Thomas and Jane Carlyle": www.nd. edu/~carlyle.

WEB p. 269

Sartor Resartus
  From "Symbols" [bk. 3. ch. 3]
  From "Natural Supernaturalism" [bk. 3. ch. 8]

Past and Present

The "present" of *Past and Present* (Apr. 1843) is set in the previous year, 1842, when Carlyle wrote his chapters modelled on political pamphlets occasioned by the strikes, unrest, and Anti-Corn Law riots of July and August. He sets up four symbolic and antagonistic classes to represent England at war with itself: the poor and the almost-impoverished workers, whose symbols are the workhouses and cotton mills; the displaced rural agricultural workers, who grow wheat but cannot afford bread; the do-nothing, land-owning, pheasant-shooting aristocracy; and the entrepreneurial middle-class capitalists, who are "Worshippers of Mammon," seeking only success and money. Carlyle contrasts this present social and spiritual crisis with an idealized "past," a community of monks around the medieval Abbot Samson, whose records he found in a recently published chronicle.

Carlyle's method is dialectical, setting one political force against another, and above all contrasting the past with the present using the rhetorical figure of pleonasm, the repetition of phrases and images with variation, so that the meaning is piled up with excessive exaggeration and bombastic invective, an evangelical preaching of reform.

Two societies are set in dramatic contrast: British society in 1842–43 under the Tory government of Sir Robert Peel (caricatured as Sir Jabesh Windbag in bk. 1: "Proem," setting out the "Condition of England" and its need for remedies) and the harmonious order of the medieval abbey under Abbot Samson (bk. 2: "The Ancient Monk"). In Books 3 ("The Modern Worker") and 4 ("Horoscope") the two societies overlap and intersect. The parliamentary "Blue Books," or reports on contemporaneous social conditions in the factories, housing, health, and sanitation, are contrasted with his source for the medieval abbey, the *Chronicle* by Jocelin of Brakelond (d. 1211). Book 4 suggests how the reordering of society in the future could bring about a renewal of national life. Such economic and spiritual renewal would be based, according to Carlyle, on the heroic leadership of the hard-working "Captains of Industry," a "Working Aristocracy of talent" governing a "Chivalry of Labour." This fundamentally medieval notion of a social hierarchy is considered by Carlyle to be both noble and sacred. Such views, though strongly anti-democratic, influenced many Victorian social reformers, including Benjamin Disraeli, Charles Dickens, Elizabeth Gaskell, and William Morris.

"Hero-Worship" [bk. 1. ch. 6][1]

To the present Editor,[2] not less than to Bobus,[3] a Government of the Wisest, what Bobus calls an Aristocracy of Talent, seems the one healing remedy: but he is not so sanguine as Bobus with respect to the means of realising it. He thinks that we have at once missed realising it, and come to need it so pressingly, by departing far from the inner eternal Laws and taking up with the temporary outer semblances of Laws. He thinks that "enlightened Egoism,"[4] never so luminous, is not the rule by which man's life can be led. That "Laissez-faire," "Supply-and-demand," "Cash-payment for the sole nexus,"[5] and so forth, were not, are not, and will never be, a practicable Law of Union for a Society of Men. That Poor and Rich, that Governed and Governing, cannot long live together on any such Law of Union. Alas, he thinks that man has a soul in him, *different* from the stomach in any sense of this word; that if said soul be asphyxied, and lie quietly forgotten, the man and his affairs are in a bad way. He thinks that said soul will have to be resuscitated from its asphyxia; that if it prove irresuscitable, the man is not long for this world. In brief, that Midas-eared Mammonism,[6] double-barrelled Dilettantism,[7] and their thousand adjuncts and corollaries, are *not* the Law by which God Almighty has appointed this his Universe to go. That, once for all, these are not the Law: and then farther that we shall have to return to what *is* the Law,—not by smooth flowery paths, it is like, and with "tremendous cheers" in our throat; but over steep untrodden places, through stormclad chasms, waste oceans, and the bosom of tornadoes; thank Heaven, if not through very Chaos and the Abyss! The resuscitating of a soul that has gone to asphyxia is no momentary or pleasant process, but a long and terrible one.

To the present Editor, "Hero-worship," as he has elsewhere named it,[8] means much more than an elected Parliament, or stated Aristocracy, of the Wisest; for, in his dialect, it is the summary, ultimate essence, and supreme practical perfection of all manner of "worship," and true worships and noblenesses whatsoever. Such blessed Parliament and,

Notes

Thomas Carlyle

[1] *title* Carlyle's fullest treatment of heroes is *On Heroes, Hero-Worship, and the Heroic in History* (1841). The book originated as six lectures given in London in 1840, organized as the hero as (1) divinity; (2) prophet; (3) poet; (4) priest; (5) man of letters; and (6) king. They included discussions of such figures as Odin, Mohammed, Shakespeare, Luther, Burns, and Napoleon. Carlyle's view of the hero derives from Hegel, Fichte, and Novalis: the hero is the embodiment of the spirit of the people (the *Volksgeist*) and so also of the spirit of the time or age (the *Zeitgeist*). Heroes are the great men destined to lead nations, ideas, and the arts, embodying the triumph of individual will and work as opposed to anonymous forces and mechanisms.

[2] *Editor* as in *Sartor*, Carlyle adopts the persona of a fictitious editor.

[3] *Bobus* a fictional character, earlier referred to as "Bobus Higgins, Sausage-maker on the great scale," satirically representing the middle class and their views on democratic reform.

[4] *Egoism* the belief that individual self-interest is the basis for a rational society, as in Adam Smith's *Wealth of Nations* (1776): "It is not from the benevolence of the butcher, the brewer, or the baker that we expect our dinner, but from their regard to their own interest. We address ourselves, not to their humanity but to their self-love." More specifically,

he addresses Jeremy Bentham (1748–1832) and Utilitarianism. In *An Introduction to the Principles of Morals and Legislation* (1789) Bentham argued that the happiness of the community is the sum of individual human interests.

[5] *Laissez ... nexus* terms referring to political economy, the theory that markets regulate themselves according to supply and demand, without government interference, and that cash is the only bond between people. Carlyle first used the term "cash-payment nexus" in *Chartism* (1839).

[6] *Midas-eared Mammonism* in Greek mythology Midas was a king of Phrygia whose touch turned everything to gold; he was reputed to have long ears like a donkey; see *Metamorphosis* 11. The first chapter of *Past and Present* is entitled "Midas"; book 3, chapter 2 is entitled "The Gospel of Mammonism." Mammon (Heb. money) is money or greed personified as a god or demon; for the worship of money, see Luke 16: 13 and Matthew 6: 24.

[7] *double-barrelled Dilettantism* practice of an art or science without serious intent; here the unworking landed aristocracy, devoted to shooting on their estates rather than governing the nation; see book 3, chapter 3 of *Past and Present*, entitled "The Gospel of Dilettantism"; see also Carlyle, n. 50 (WEB p. 277).

[8] *named it* in *Sartor Resartus* (1833–34) and *On Heroes and Hero-Worship* (1841).

were it once in perfection, blessed Aristocracy of the Wisest, god-honoured and man-honoured, he does look for, more and more perfected,—as the topmost blessed practical apex of a whole world reformed from sham-worship, informed anew with worship, with truth and blessedness! He thinks that Hero-worship, done differently in every different epoch of the world, is the soul of all social business among men; that the doing of it well, or the doing of it ill, measures accurately what degree of well-being or of ill-being there is in the world's affairs. He thinks that we, on the whole, do our Hero-worship worse than any Nation in this world ever did it before: that the Burns an Exciseman, the Byron a Literary Lion, are intrinsically, all things considered, a baser and falser phenomenon than the Odin a God, the Mahomet a Prophet of God.[9] It is this Editor's clear opinion, accordingly, that we must learn to do our Hero-worship better; that to do it better and better, means the awakening of the Nation's soul from its asphyxia, and the return of blessed life to us,—Heaven's blessed life, not Mammon's galvanic[10] accursed one. To resuscitate the Asphyxied, apparently now moribund, and in the last agony if not resuscitated: such and no other seems the consummation.

"Hero-worship," if you will,—yes, friends; but, first of all, by being ourselves of heroic mind. A whole world of Heroes; a world not of Flunkeys, where no Hero-King *can* reign: that is what we aim at! We, for our share, will put away all Flunkeyism, Baseness, Unveracity from us; we shall then hope to have Noblenesses and Veracities set over us; never till then. Let Bobus and Company sneer, "That is your Reform!" Yes, Bobus, that is our Reform; and except in that, and what will follow out of that, we have no hope at all. Reform, like Charity, O Bobus, must begin at home. Once well at home, how will it radiate outwards, irrepressible, into all that we touch and handle, speak and work; kindling ever new light, by incalculable contagion, spreading in geometric ratio, far and wide,—doing good only, wheresoever it spreads, and not evil.

By Reform Bills, Anti-Corn-Law Bills,[11] and thousand other bills and methods, we will demand of our Governors, with emphasis, and for the first time not without effect, that they cease to be quacks, or else depart; that they set no quackeries and blockheadisms anywhere to rule over us, that they utter or act no cant to us,—that it will be better if they do not. For we shall now know quacks when we see them; cant, when we hear it, shall be horrible to us! We will say, with the poor Frenchman at the Bar of the Convention, though in wiser style than he, and "for the space" not "of an hour" but of a lifetime: *"Je demande l'arrestation des coquins et des lâches."* "Arrestment of the knaves and dastards":[12] ah, we know what a work that is; how long it will be before *they* are all or mostly got "arrested":—but here is one; arrest him, in God's name; it is one fewer! We will, in all practicable ways, by word and silence, by act and refusal to act, energetically demand that arrestment,—*"je demande cette arrestation-là!"*—and by degrees infallibly attain it. Infallibly: for light spreads; all human souls, never so bedarkened, love light; light once kindled spreads, till all is luminous;—till the cry, "*Arrest*

Notes

[9] *Burns ... God* Robert Burns (1759–96), Scottish poet, was granted a government post to collect taxes or duties; George Gordon, Lord Byron (1788–1824), English Romantic poet, was criticized by Carlyle as a "sham," although celebrated by contemporary society; Odin, is the Norse god of war, wisdom, and poetry; Mahomet, a variant spelling of Mohammad (570–632), was the founder of Islam. All except Byron are included in *On Heroes* (1841).

[10] *galvanic* electric shock that prompts a movement in muscles, associated with the Italian scientist, Luigi Galvani (1737–98), who in the 1790s applied electricity to stimulate motion in dead limbs, and, by extension, to restore life; associated by Carlyle with quackery.

[11] *Reform ... Bills* the Reform Bill of 1832 abolished rotten boroughs, and expanded the electorate to males with property of £10. It excluded women and the working class. Corn Laws put high duties on imported wheat, protecting the landed interest, the aristocracy who controlled parliament, at the expense of the industrialists and their workers because of higher food prices. The Anti-Corn Law League, formed in 1838, agitated for their repeal. The Corn Laws were abolished in 1846 when Britain entered an era of free trade. See CONDITION; PROGRESS, n. 11 (WEB p. 20).

[12] *dastards* Carlyle cites an incident on 20 May 1795 in the French Convention that he recounts in *The French Revolution* (1837), "Lion Sprawling its Last" (3.7.5).

your knaves and dastards" rises imperative from millions of hearts, and rings and reigns from sea to sea. Nay, how many of them may we not "arrest" with our own hands, even now; we! Do not countenance them, thou there: turn away from their lackered sumptuosities, their belauded sophistries, their serpent graciosities, their spoken and acted cant, with a sacred horror, with an *Apage Satanas*.[13] —Bobus and Company, and all men will gradually join us. We demand arrestment of the knaves and dastards, and begin by arresting our own poor selves out of that fraternity. There is no other reform conceivable. Thou and I, my friend, can, in the most flunkey world, make, each of us, *one* non-flunkey, one hero, if we like: that will be two heroes to begin with:—Courage! even that is a whole world of heroes to end with, or what we poor Two can do in furtherance thereof!

Yes, friends: Hero-kings and a whole world not unheroic,—there lies the port[14] and happy haven, towards which, through all These stormtost seas, French Revolutions, Chartisms, Manchester Insurrections,[15] that make the heart sick in these bad days, the Supreme Powers are driving us. On the whole, blessed be the Supreme Powers, stern as they are! Towards that haven will we, O friends; let all true men, with what of faculty is in them, bend valiantly, incessantly, with thousandfold endeavour, thither, thither! There, or else in the Ocean-abysses, it is very clear to me, we shall arrive.

Well; here truly is no answer to the Sphinx-question;[16] not the answer a disconsolate Public, inquiring at the College of Health,[17] was in hopes of! A total change of regimen, change of constitution and existence from the very centre of it; a new body to be got, with resuscitated soul,—not without convulsive travail-throes; as all birth and new-birth presupposes travail! This is sad news to a disconsolate discerning Public, hoping to have got off by some Morrison's Pill, some Saint-John's corrosive mixture[18] and perhaps a little blistery friction on the back!—We were prepared to part with our Corn-Law, with various Laws and Unlaws: but this, what is this?

Nor has the Editor forgotten how it fares with your ill-boding Cassandras in Sieges of Troy.[19] Imminent perdition is not usually driven away by words of warning. Didactic Destiny has other methods in store; or these would fail always. Such words should, nevertheless, be uttered, when they dwell truly in the soul of any man. Words are hard, are importunate; but how much harder the importunate events they foreshadow! Here and there a human soul may listen to the words,—who knows how many human souls? whereby the importunate events, if not diverted and prevented, will be rendered *less* hard. The present Editor's purpose is to himself full of hope.

For though fierce travails, though wide seas and roaring gulfs lie before us, is it not something if a Loadstar,[20] in the eternal sky, do once more disclose itself; an everlasting

Notes

[13] *Satanas* (Lat. get thee hence, Satan); see Matthew 4: 10.

[14] *there ... port* see TENNYSON, "ULYSSES" (44–45).

[15] *French ... Insurrections* these historical events position Carlyle's rejection of liberal or radical politics: France had had two revolutions at this point, the first from 1789 to 1799, and the second, the July Revolution of 1830; Chartism is the movement for political reform founded in 1838 on the basis of six points: universal manhood suffrage, secret ballot, payment for MPs, annual elections, abolition of property qualifications for voters, and equal electoral districts; in July and August, 1842, there were insurrections and riots in Manchester and other industrialist regions over the Corn Laws; see n. 11.

[16] *Sphinx-question* the mythical sphinx, half-woman, half-lion, asked a riddle of travellers: if they answered correctly, they could pass; if incorrectly, they were killed.

[17] *Health* James Morison (1770–1840), quack doctor, inventor and promoter of the sham cure-all, Morison's Pills,

founded the fraudulent British College of Health. Carlyle misspells his name.

[18] *Morrison's ... mixture* for Morrison, see n. 17. John St John Long (1798–1834), quack doctor, claimed he could cure consumption (tuberculosis) by means of his corrosive liniment applied with friction. He was tried in 1830 for manslaughter involving fraudulent claims about his cures when two of his patients died. Carlyle's brother John (1801–79), Scottish physician, wrote two articles on Long: "On Medical Quackery and Mr. St. John Long" (*Fraser's Magazine* May and Oct. 1830).

[19] *Troy* Cassandra, daughter of Priam, king of Troy, prophesied the fall of the city. Apollo granted her the gift of prophecy but later cursed her with the fate of never being believed. She also appears in Aeschylus' *Agamemnon* as a crazed doomsday prophet.

[20] *Loadstar* the North Star, used for navigation; a guide.

light, shining through all cloud-tempests and roaring billows, ever as we emerge from the trough of the sea: the blessed beacon, far off on the edge of far horizons, towards which we are to steer incessantly for life? Is it not something; O Heavens, is it not all? There lies the Heroic Promised Land; under that Heaven's-light, my brethren, bloom the Happy Isles,[21] —there, O there! Thither will we;

"There dwells the great Achilles whom we knew."[22]

There dwell all Heroes, and will dwell: thither, all ye heroic- minded!—The Heaven's Loadstar once clearly in our eye, how will each true man stand truly to *his* work in the ship; how, with undying hope, will all things be fronted, all be conquered. Nay, with the ship's prow once turned in that direction, is not all, as it were, already well? Sick wasting misery has become noble manful effort with a goal in our eye. "The choking Nightmare chokes us no longer; for we *stir* under it; the Nightmare has already fled."[23] —

Certainly, could the present Editor instruct men how to know Wisdom, Heroism, when they see it, that they might do reverence to *it* only, and loyally make it ruler over them,— yes, he were the living epitome of all Editors, Teachers, Prophets, that now teach and prophesy; he were an *Apollo*-Morrison, a Trismegistus[24] and *effective* Cassandra! Let no Able Editor hope such things. It is to be expected the present laws of copyright,[25] rate of reward per sheet, and other considerations, will save him from that peril. Let no Editor hope such things: no;—and yet let all Editors aim towards such things, and even towards such alone! One knows not what the meaning of editing and writing is, if even this be not it.

Enough, to the present Editor it has seemed possible some glimmering of light, for here and there a human soul, might lie in these confused Paper-Masses now intrusted to him;[26] wherefore he determines to edit the same. Out of old Books, new Writings, and much Meditation not of yesterday, he will endeavour to select a thing or two; and from the Past, in a circuitous way, illustrate the Present and the Future. The Past is a dim indubitable fact: the Future too is one, only dimmer; nay properly it is the *same* fact in new dress and development. For the Present holds in it both the whole Past and the whole Future;—as the LIFE-TREE IGDRASIL, wide-waving, many-toned, has its roots down deep in the Death-kingdoms, among the oldest dead dust of men, and with its boughs reaches always beyond the stars;[27] and in all times and places is one and the same Life-tree!

"Captains of Industry" [bk. 4. ch. 4][28]

If I believed that Mammonism with its adjuncts was to continue henceforth the one serious principle of our existence, I should reckon it idle to solicit remedial measures from any Government, the disease being insusceptible of remedy. Government can do much, but it can in no wise do all. Government, as the most conspicuous object in Society, is

Notes

[21] *For though ... Isles* the entire paragraph echoes Tennyson, "Ulysses" (60–63).

[22] *knew* see TENNYSON, "ULYSSES": "And see the great Achilles, whom we knew" (64).

[23] *fled* Jean Paul Friedrich Richter (1765–1825), German Romantic writer known as Jean Paul, from *Wahrhreit aus Jean Paul's Leben* [Ger. the truth of Jean Paul's life] (1826–28). Carlyle published two essays on Jean Paul (*Edinburgh Review* June 1827; and *Foreign Review* Jan. 1830) and translated two of his stories in *German Romance* (vol. 3, 1827).

[24] *Apollo ... Trismegistus ... Cassandra* for Morrison, see n. 17; Trismegistus (Gk. thrice-great) is the Greek name for Egyptian god Thoth, inventor of magic and writing and also associated with Hermes; a body of Hermetic writings (*Hermetica*), purportedly by Trismegistus, was a popular

source for medieval alchemists; here used to connote useless and fraudulent knowledge; for Cassandra, see n. 19.

[25] *copyright* in 1842 efforts were being made by writers, including Carlyle, to extend the terms of copyright; a bill was passed in July 1842 to lengthen the term from twenty-eight to forty-two years, or seven years after the author's death.

[26] *him* as with *Sartor Resartus*, Carlyle is pretending to be editing a bundle of old papers, in this case on the life of Abbot Samson.

[27] IGDRASIL ... *stars* holy ash tree of Old Norse mythology depicted in the *Poetic Edda* (thirteenth century), which spreads throughout the cosmos and universe and at whose roots are the laws and destiny of humans and gods.

[28] *title* while the phrase usually refers in the United States to nineteenth-century "robber barons," industrial capitalists

called upon to give signal of what shall be done; and, in many ways, to preside over, further, and command the doing of it. But the Government cannot do, by all its signalling and commanding, what the Society is radically indisposed to do! In the long-run every Government is the exact symbol of its People, with their wisdom and unwisdom; we have to say, Like People like Government.—The main substance of this immense Problem of Organising Labour, and first of all of Managing the Working Classes, will, it is very clear, have to be solved by those who stand practically in the middle of it; by those who themselves work and preside over work. Of all that can be enacted by any Parliament in regard to it the germs[29] must already lie potentially extant in those two Classes, who are to obey such enactment. A Human Chaos *in* which there is no light, you vainly attempt to irradiate by light shed *on* it: order never can arise there.

But it is my firm conviction that the "Hell of England" will *cease* to be that of "not making money"; that we shall get a nobler Hell and a nobler Heaven! I anticipate light *in* the Human Chaos, glimmering, shining more and more; under manifold true signals from without That light shall shine. Our deity no longer being Mammon,—O Heavens, each man will then say to himself: "Why such deadly haste to make money? I shall not go to Hell, even if I do not make money! There is another Hell, I am told!" Competition, at railway-speed,[30] in all branches of commerce and work will then abate:—good felt hats for the head, in every sense, instead of seven-feet lath-and-plaster hats on wheels,[31] will then be discoverable! Bubble-periods,[32] with their panics and commercial crises, will again become infrequent; steady modest industry will take the place of gambling speculation. To be a noble Master, among noble Workers, will again be the first ambition with some few; to be a rich Master only the second. How the Inventive Genius of England, with the whirr of its bobbins and billy-rollers[33] shoved somewhat into the backgrounds of the brain, will contrive and devise, not cheaper produce exclusively, but fairer distribution of the produce at its present cheapness! By degrees we shall again have a Society with something of Heroism in it, something of Heaven's Blessing on it; we shall again have, as my German friend[34] asserts, "instead of Mammon-Feudalism with unsold cotton-shirts and Preservation of the Game, noble just Industrialism and Government by the Wisest!"

It is with the hope of awakening here and there a British man to know himself for a man and divine soul, that a few words of parting admonition, to all persons to whom the Heavenly Powers have lent power of any kind in this land, may now be addressed. And first to those same Master- Workers, Leaders of Industry; who stand nearest, and in fact powerfulest, though not most prominent, being as yet in too many senses a Virtuality[35] rather than an Actuality.

Notes

and bankers who amassed immense fortunes, to Carlyle the wealthy industrialists would be the new working aristocracy of Britain. He imagined a kind of fealty between workers who were loyal to their taskmasters, as soldiers were loyal to their captains. The ideal of individual self-development in business and industry is exemplified by Samuel Smiles in *Self-Help* (1859) and *Lives of the Engineers* (1862).

[29] *germs* seeds.

[30] *railway-speed* George Stephenson (1781–1848), English engineer, built a steam engine for the Stockton and Darlington Railway in north-east England in 1825, the first public steam railway in the world. In 1830 the first regular intercity service was inaugurated, between Liverpool and Manchester, at 27 kilometres per hour.

[31] *wheels* see CARLYLE, n. 63 (WEB p. 279).

[32] *Bubble-periods* time of financial speculation, as occurred when the markets collapsed in 1837 and again in 1842. The name comes from the South Sea Bubble of 1720, with the collapse of the South Sea Company.

[33] *billy-rollers* iron rods two to three yards long with a pivot on each end that run on top of the feeding cloth in cotton mills. As Carlyle wrote to his brother Alexander (26 Mar. 1833), they were often used against "little children labouring for sixteen hours a day, inhaling at every breath a quantity of cotton fuz, falling asleep over their wheels, and roused again by the lash of thongs over their backs, or the slap of 'billy-rollers' over their little crowns."

[34] *friend* Teufelsdröckh in *Sartor Resartus*, but an invented citation.

[35] *Virtuality* Carlyle had originally titled this chapter "The Virtual Aristocracy" in the printer's copy.

The Leaders of Industry, if Industry is ever to be led, are virtually the Captains of the World; if there be no nobleness in them, there will never be an Aristocracy more. But let the Captains of Industry consider: once again, are they born of other clay than the old Captains of Slaughter; doomed forever to be no Chivalry, but a mere gold-plated *Doggery*,—what the French well name *Canaille*,[36] "Doggery" with more or less gold carrion at its disposal? Captains of Industry are the true Fighters, henceforth recognisable as the only true ones: Fighters against Chaos, Necessity and the Devils and Jötuns;[37] and lead on Mankind in that great, and alone true, and universal warfare; the stars in their courses fighting for them,[38] and all Heaven and all Earth saying audibly, Well-done! Let the Captains of Industry retire into their own hearts, and ask solemnly, If there is nothing but vulturous hunger for fine wines, valet reputation and gilt carriages, discoverable there? Of hearts made by the Almighty God I will not believe such a thing. Deep-hidden under wretchedest godforgetting Cants, Epicurisms, Dead-Sea Apisms; forgotten as under foulest fat Lethe[39] mud and weeds, there is yet, in all hearts born into this God's-World a spark of the Godlike slumbering. Awake, O nightmare sleepers; awake, arise, or be forever fallen![40] This is not playhouse poetry; it is sober fact. Our England, our world cannot live as it is. It will connect itself with a God again, or go down with nameless throes and fire-consummation to the Devils. Thou who feelest aught of such a Godlike stirring in thee, any faintest intimation of it as through heavy-laden dreams, follow *it*, I conjure thee. Arise, save thyself, be one of those that save thy country.

Bucaniers, Chactaw Indians,[41] whose supreme aim in fighting is that they may get the scalps, the money, that they may amass scalps and money: out of such came no chivalry, and never will! Out of such came only gore and wreck, infernal rage and misery; desperation quenched in annihilation. Behold it, I bid thee, behold there, and consider! What is it that thou have a hundred thousand-pound bills laid up in thy strong-room, a hundred scalps hung up in thy wigwam? I value not them or thee. Thy scalps and thy thousand-pound bills are as yet nothing, if no nobleness from within irradiate them; if no chivalry, in action, or in embryo ever struggling towards birth and action, be there.

Love of men cannot be bought by cash-payment; and without love, men cannot endure to be together. You cannot lead a Fighting World without having it regimented, chivalried: the thing, in a day, becomes impossible; all men in it, the highest at first, the very lowest at last, discern consciously, or by a noble instinct, this necessity. And can you any more continue to lead a Working World unregimented, anarchic? I answer, and the Heavens and Earth are now answering, No! The thing becomes not "in a day" impossible; but in some two generations it does. Yes, when fathers and mothers, in Stockport hunger-

---

Notes

[36] *Canaille* (Fr. pack of dogs) rabble, the masses of the people.

[37] *Jötuns* (Old Norse *jötunn* giant) in Norse mythology, the giants opposed to the gods under Odin; spirits of the elements of nature: fire, frost, and sea tempests.

[38] *them* see Judges 5: 20.

[39] *Epicurisms ... Lethe* Epicurus (341–270 BCE), Greek philosopher, taught that the human goal is to achieve a happy and peaceful life in a circle of friends, with all needs met. Pleasure, to him, is the absence of pain. His name came to be associated with the ideal of material pleasures and bodily comforts; Dead-Sea Apisms refers to a note to chapter 2 of George Sale's translation of the *Koran* (1734) that Carlyle had discussed earlier in *Past and Present* (bk. 3, ch. 3), in which David (not Moses, as Carlyle claims) comes to warn a group of erring people at the Red Sea

(not the Dead Sea as in Carlyle) of their danger; having ignored the patriarch, they are turned into apes; Lethe (Gk. forgetfulness) in Greek mythology is one of the rivers of Hades from which the shades drank on entering the realm of the dead in order to forget their past lives.

[40] *fallen* see *Paradise Lost* 1. 330.

[41] *Bucaniers, Chactaw Indians* buccaneers or pirates against the French and Spanish in the Caribbean in the seventeenth century; here, any kind of pirate, industrial or mercantile. Carlyle's spelling is French. The Choctaw Indians (Carlyle misspells them) inhabited the Mississippi and its tributaries' valleys in the south-eastern United States. In the eighteenth century they had integrated with the Europeans and supported the Thirteen Colonies against Britain. Not warlike but agricultural, the Choctaws, to Carlyle, are stereotypical scalping savages.

cellars, begin to eat their children,[42] and Irish Widows have to prove their relationship by dying of typhus-fever; and amid Governing "Corporations of the Best and Bravest,"[43] busy to preserve their gain by "bushing,"[44] dark millions of God's human creatures start up in mad Chartisms, impracticable Sacred-Months, and Manchester Insurrections;[45]— and there is a virtual Industrial Aristocracy only half-alive, spell-bound amid money-bags and ledgers; and an actual Idle Aristocracy seemingly near dead in somnolent delusions, in trespasses and double-barrels; "sliding," as on inclined-planes, which every new year they *soap* with new Hansard's-jargon[46] under God's sky, and so are "sliding" ever faster, towards a "scale" and balance-scale whereon is written *Thou art found Wanting:*[47]—in such days, after a generation or two, I say, it does become, even to the low and simple, very palpably impossible! No Working World, any more than a Fighting World, can be led on without a noble chivalry of Work, and laws and fixed rules which follow out of that,—far nobler than any chivalry of Fighting was. As an anarchic multitude on mere supply-and-demand, it is becoming inevitable that we dwindle in horrid suicidal convulsion, and self-abrasion, frightful to the imagination, into *Chactaw* Workers. With wigwam and scalps,—with palaces and thousand-pound bills; with savagery, depopulation, chaotic desolation! Good Heavens, will not one French Revolution and Reign of Terror[48] suffice us, but must there be two? There will be two if needed; there will be twenty if needed; there will be precisely as many as are needed. The Laws of Nature will have themselves fulfilled. That is a thing certain to me.

Your gallant battle-hosts and work-hosts, as the others did, will need to be made loyally yours; they must and will be regulated, methodically secured in their just share of conquest under you;—joined with you in veritable brotherhood, sonhood, by quite other and deeper ties than those of temporary day's wages! How would mere redcoated regiments, to say nothing of chivalries, fight for you, if you could discharge them on the evening of the battle, on payment of the stipulated shillings,—and they discharge you on the morning of it! Chelsea Hospitals,[49] pensions, promotions, rigorous lasting covenant on the one side and on the other, are indispensable even for a hired fighter. The Feudal Baron, much more,—how could he subsist with mere temporary mercenaries round him, at sixpence a day; ready to go over to the other side, if seven-pence were offered? He could not have subsisted;—and his noble instinct saved him from the necessity of even trying! The Feudal Baron had a Man's Soul in him; to which anarchy, mutiny, and

Notes

[42] *children* as reported in the *Examiner* (1 Nov. 1840), a coroner's jury found two parents guilty of the murder of their children to secure the payments of £3 8s. 6d. per child from the Philanthropic Burial Society. The *Examiner* (17 Aug. 1841) reported that in the criminal trial the father was convicted of murder. Carlyle uses the Stockport murders and the suggestions of cannibalism earlier in *Past and Present* (bk. I, ch. I, "Midas").

[43] *Irish Widows . . . Bravest* for Irish Widows, see CARLYLE, n. 64 (WEB p. 279); Carlyle had defined an aristocracy as "a corporation of the Best, of the Bravest" in his essay, "Chartism" (1839).

[44] *bushing* planting bushes at intervals to protect game of landholders from net poachers.

[45] *Chartisms . . . Sacred-Months . . . Insurrections* for Chartism and insurrections, see n. 15; the Chartist convention of 1839–40 to draw up plans for presenting the charter to Parliament considered a "Sacred Month," or a general strike but rejected it.

[46] *sliding. . . Hansard's-jargon* sliding scale (in which speculators gambled) on the duty applied to cheap imported

grain under the Corn Laws; see n. 11. Inclined planes were used to raise canal boats without locks, as on the Shropshire canal (1792) and elsewhere; soap denotes flattery; Thomas Chandler Haliburton discusses soft sawder as soap for flattery in *Sam Slick* (1837); *Hansard* is the official daily transcript of the British parliamentary debates, first published in 1812 by Thomas Curson Hansard, who took over the Parliamentary Debates that William Cobbett had issued in his *Political Register* from 1802.

[47] *Wanting* see Daniel 5: 27.

[48] *French . . . Terror* the French Revolution (1789–99) began with the storming of the Bastille prison in Paris on 11 July 1789. The Reign of Terror (1793–94) was inaugurated by the Committee of Public Safety under the control of Maximilien Robespierre (1758–94), with the purpose of ridding France of the enemies of the revolution, chiefly by the use of the guillotine in public executions.

[49] *Hospitals* built by Sir Christopher Wren (1632–1723), English architect, the Royal Hospital Chelsea was established by Charles II in 1681 for retired, elderly, and injured soldiers.

the other fruits of temporary mercenaries, were intolerable; he had never been a Baron otherwise, but had continued a Chactaw and Bucanier. He felt it precious, and at last it became habitual, and his fruitful enlarged existence included it as a necessity, to have men round him who in heart loved him; whose life he watched over with rigour yet with love; who were prepared to give their life for him, if need came. It was beautiful; it was human! Man lives not otherwise, nor can live contented, anywhere or anywhen. Isolation is the sum-total of wretchedness to man. To be cut off, to be left solitary; to have a world alien, not your world; all a hostile camp for you; not a home at all, of hearts and faces who are yours, whose you are! It is the frightfulest enchantment; too truly a work of the Evil One. To have neither superior, nor inferior, nor equal, united manlike to you. Without father, without child, without brother. Man knows no sadder destiny. "How is each of us," exclaims Jean Paul, "so lonely in the wide bosom of the All!"[50] Encased each as in his transparent "ice-palace"; our brother visible in his, making signals and gesticulations to us; —visible, but forever unattainable: on his bosom we shall never rest, nor he on ours.[51] It was not a God that did this; no!

Awake, ye noble Workers, warriors in the one true war: all this must be remedied. It is you who are already half-alive, whom I will welcome into life; whom I will conjure in God's name to shake off your enchanted sleep, and live wholly! Cease to count scalps, gold-purses; not in these lies your or our salvation. Even these, if you count only these, will not long be left. Let bucaniering be put far from you; alter, speedily abrogate all laws of the bucaniers, if you would gain any victory that shall endure. Let God's justice, let pity, nobleness and manly valour, with more gold-purses or with fewer, testify themselves in this your brief Life-transit to all the Eternities, the Gods and Silences. It is to you I call; for ye are not dead, ye are already half-alive: there is in you a sleepless dauntless energy, the prime-matter of all nobleness in man. Honour to you in your kind. It is to you I call; ye know at least this, That the mandate of God to His creature man is: Work! The future Epic of the World rests not with those that are near dead, but with those that are alive, and those that are coming into life.

Look around you. Your world-hosts are all in Mutiny, in confusion, destitution; on the eve of fiery wreck and madness! They will not march farther for you on the sixpence a day and supply-and-demand principle: they will not; nor ought they, nor can they. Ye shall reduce them to order, begin reducing them. To order, to just subordination; noble loyalty in return for noble guidance. Their souls are driven nigh mad; let yours be sane and ever saner. Not as a bewildered bewildering mob; but as a firm regimented mass, with real Captains over them, will these men march any more. All human interests, combined human endeavours, and social growths in this world, have, at a certain stage of their development, required organising: and Work, the grandest of human interests, does now require it.

God knows, the task will be hard: but no noble task was ever easy. This task will wear away your lives, and the lives of your sons and grandsons: but for what purpose, if not for tasks like this, were lives given to men? Ye shall cease to count your thousand-pound scalps, the noble of you shall cease! Nay the very scalps, as I say, will not long be left if you count only these. Ye shall cease wholly to be barbarous vulturous Chactaws, and become noble European Nineteenth-Century Men. Ye shall know that Mammon, in never such gigs and flunkey "respectabilities,"[52] is not the alone God; that of himself he is but a Devil, and even a Brute-god.

Notes

[50] *All* quotation of Jesus Christ in *Siebenkäs* (1796–97), a story by Jean Paul Richter (1763–1825), German Romantic writer. Carlyle had translated two stories of Richter's in *German Romance* (1827); he also wrote three essays on him (1827–30).

[51] *ours* see John 13: 23–25.

[52] *respectabilities* to have enough income to drive a horse and gig (two-wheeled cart) and keep a servant.

Difficult? Yes, it will be difficult. The short-fibre cotton; that too was difficult. The waste cotton-shrub,[53] long useless, disobedient, as the thistle by the wayside,—have ye not conquered it; made it into beautiful bandana webs; white woven shirts for men: bright-tinted air-garments wherein flit goddesses. Ye have shivered mountains asunder, made the hard iron pliant to you as soft putty: the Forest-giants, Marsh-jötuns bear sheaves of golden grain[54]; Ægir[55] the Sea-demon himself stretches his back for a sleek highway to you, and on Firehorses and Wind-horses ye career.[56] Ye are most strong. Thor red-bearded,[57] with his blue sun-eyes, with his cheery heart and strong thunder-hammer, he and you have prevailed. Ye are most strong, ye Sons of the icy North, of the far East,—far marching from your rugged Eastern Wilderness, hitherward from the grey Dawn of Time! Ye are Sons of the *Jötun*-land; the land of Difficulties Conquered. Difficult? You must try this thing. Once try it with the understanding that it will and shall have to be done. Try it as ye try the paltrier thing, making of money! I will bet on you once more, against all Jötuns, Tailor-gods, Double-barrelled Law-wards, and Denizens of Chaos whatsoever!

WEB p. 277

Past and Present
From "The Gospel of Mammonism" [bk. 3. ch. 2]

Maria Smith Abdy (1797–1867)

Little is known about the early life of Maria Abdy, the daughter of a London solicitor, except that she had some literary connections through her mother, Maria Smith. Her uncles James (1775–1839) and Horace Smith (1779–1849) were the authors of a well-known collection of satires and parodies, *Rejected Addresses* (1812). In 1821 Abdy married a clergyman, John Channing Abdy (d. 1845), and settled in the Southwark area of London. She published in the *New Monthly Magazine* and the *Metropolitan* and in such annuals or gift books as *Forget-Me-Not* (from 1828 to 1847) and *Keepsake* (from 1835 to 1857); such contributions were widely printed in annuals in the USA, making her, with Felicia Hemans, one of the most popular English poets there. She wrote in various veins, concerning

Notes

[53] *short-fibre cotton . . . cotton-shrub* American cotton had short fibres, a problem for spinning in separating the fibres until the cotton gin (1793); cotton is a shrub whose species has a number of cultivated, commercial subspecies; cotton-shrub, non-commercial waste, growing wild.

[54] *Forest-giants . . . grain* Carlyle uses a series of kennings (<ON *kenna*, to know, perceive) here and in the next few clauses, drawing on the Old Norse and Old English convention of using an allusive compound word as a figure of speech to stand in for a simpler idea, as the "whale's path" is a poetic allusion to the sea. So here *Forest-giants* alludes to steam machinery used in building the canals in Great Britain from the Bridgewater Canal of 1761 through the first half of the nineteenth century. For Jötuns see n. 37; Marsh-jötuns were steam machines used by the engineer

John Rennie (1761–1821) in draining the marshy Fens in the east of England, to whom Carlyle's term was later applied by Samuel Smiles in his *Lives of the Engineers* (1861).

[55] *Ægir* in Norse mythology the giant who rules the ocean and hosts celebrations of the gods.

[56] *Firehorses . . . career* kennings (see n. 54) for steamships and sailing ships to traverse Ægir's *back* (the ocean as a "sleek highway"); for horses and the chariot of fire, see 2 Kings 2: 11.

[57] *Thor red-bearded* in Norse mythology, Thor, the child of Odin, was the god of thunder and lightning and a protector of humanity. Thor's hammer, named Mjöllnir, never failed to hit its target and always returned to Thor's hand when thrown; it could split mountains and could also become small to be carried inside his clothes.

herself with social issues such as the plight of dressmakers and governesses and continuing the tradition of witty, clever satires as practised by her uncles. She collected her verse in a series of eight privately printed volumes, each entitled *Poetry* (1834–62). No standard edition. A. H. Beavan, *James and Horace Smith: A Family Narrative* (1899); the Orlando Project: http://orlando.cambridge.org/public/svPeople?person_id=abdyma.

A Governess Wanted[1]

"Our governess left us, dear brother,
    Last night, in a strange fit of pique,
Will you kindly seek out for another?
    We want her at latest next week:
But I'll give you a few plain credentials,   5
    The bargain with speed to complete;
Take a pen—just set down the essentials,
    And begin at the top of the sheet!

With easy and modest decision,
    She ever must move, act, and speak,   10
She must understand French with precision,
    Italian, and Latin, and Greek:
She must play the piano divinely,
    Excel on the harp and the lute,
Do all sorts of needlework finely,   15
    And make feather-flowers, and wax-fruit.

She must answer all queries directly,
    And all sciences well understand,
Paint in oils, sketch from nature correctly,
    And write German text, and short-hand: 20
She must sing with power, science, and sweetness,
    Yet for concerts must not sigh at all,
She must dance with etherial fleetness,
    Yet never must go to a ball.
She must not have needy relations,   25
    Her dress must be tasteful, yet plain,
Her discourse must abound in quotations,
    Her memory all dates must retain:
She must point out each author's chief beauties,
    She must manage dull natures with skill,   30
Her pleasures must lie in her duties,
    She must never be nervous or ill!

If she write essays, odes, themes, and sonnets,
    Yet be not pedantic or pert,
If she wear none but deep cottage bonnets,   35
    If she deem it high treason to flirt,

Notes

Maria Smith Abdy
[1] *title* first published in *The Metropolitan Magazine* (May 1836); reprinted in Abdy, *Poetry* (1838), second series. See Plate 7: Redgrave, *The Governess*; see also Bernstein, wanted a husband.

If to mildness she add sense and spirit,
    Engage her at once without fear,
I love to reward modest merit,
    And I give—forty guineas a-year!"   40

"I accept, my good sister, your mission,
    To-morrow, my search I'll begin,
In all circles, in every condition,
    I'll strive such a treasure to win;
And if, after years of probation,   45
    My eyes on the wonder should rest,
I'll engage her without hesitation,
    But not on the terms you suggest.

Of a bride I have ne'er made selection,
    For my bachelor thoughts would still dwell   50
On an object so near to perfection,
    That I blushed half my fancies to tell;
Now this list that you kindly have granted,
    I'll quote and refer to through life,
But just blot out—'A Governess Wanted,'   55
    And head it with—'Wanted a Wife!'"

Mary Howitt (1799–1888)

Born in Gloucestershire of Quaker parents, Samuel Botham (1758–1823) and Anne Wood (1764–1848), and receiving a strict Quaker education at various schools, Howitt met and married another Quaker, William Howitt (1792–1879), settling in Nottingham and, from 1843, in London. Together they embarked on a long collaboration in writing (over 180 books) and social activism. They published numerous volumes of poetry, including *The Forest Minstrel* (1823) and *The Desolation of Eyam and Other Poems* (1827). Mary Howitt published widely in annuals and keepsakes, as well as in *Tait's Edinburgh Magazine*. Her separate publications of poetry included *Sketches of Natural History* (1834), *The Seven Temptations* (1834), *Hymns and Fireside Verses* (1839), and *Ballads and Other Poems* (1847). For two years she and her husband published *Howitt's Journal* (1847–48), and she also published children's books, novels, popular history, short stories, and translated from Danish the tales of Hans Christian Andersen (1805–75) and the novels of the Swedish writer Fredrika Bremer (1801–65). They developed a wide circle of friends, including Charles Dickens, Elizabeth Barrett Browning, Elizabeth Gaskell, Anna Jameson, and Alfred Tennyson. The family moved away from the Quakers to join the Unitarians, and eventually the Spiritualists – and late in life Mary Howitt converted to Roman Catholicism. Throughout their lives she and William were advocates of social reform: the Anti-Corn Law League, anti-enclosure movements, the Married Women's Property Committee, women's emancipation, and the extension of the franchise. No standard edition. Mary Howitt, *My Own Story* (1845); *Mary Howitt: An Autobiography*, ed. Margaret Howitt (2 vols, 1889); Carl Woodring, *Victorian Samplers: William and Mary Howitt* (1952).

The Spider and the Fly[1]

An Apologue

A New Version of an Old Story

"Will you walk into my parlour?" said the Spider to the Fly,—
'Tis the prettiest little parlour that ever you did spy;
The way into my parlour is up a winding stair,
And I have many curious things to show when you are there."
"Oh no, no," said the little Fly; "to ask me is in vain,   5
For who goes up your winding stair can ne'er come down again."

"I'm sure you must be weary, dear, with soaring up so high;
Will you rest upon my little bed?" said the Spider to the Fly.
"There are pretty curtains drawn around, the sheets are fine and thin,
And if you like to rest awhile, I'll snugly tuck you in!"   10
"Oh no, no," said the little Fly; "for I've often heard it said,
They never, never wake again, who sleep upon your bed!"

Said the cunning Spider to the Fly, "Dear friend what can I do,
To prove the warm affection I've always felt for you?
I have within my pantry good store of all that's nice;   15
I'm sure you're very welcome—will you please to take a slice?"
"Oh no, no," said the little Fly, "kind Sir, that cannot be,
I've heard what's in your pantry, and I do not wish to see!"

"Sweet creature!" said the Spider, "you're witty and you're wise,
How handsome are your gauzy wings, how brilliant are your eyes!   20
I have a little looking-glass upon my parlour-shelf,
If you'll step in one moment, dear, you shall behold yourself."
"I thank you, gentle sir," she said, "for what you're pleased to say,
And bidding you good-morning now, I'll call another day."

The Spider turned him round about, and went into his den,   25
For well he knew the silly Fly would soon come back again:
So he wove a subtle web, in a little corner sly,
And set his table ready, to dine upon the Fly.
Then he came out to his door again, and merrily did sing,—
"Come hither, hither, pretty Fly with the pearl and silver wing;   30
Your robes are green and purple, there's a crest upon your head;
Your eyes are like the diamond bright, but mine are dull as lead!"

Alas! alas! how very soon this silly little Fly,
Hearing his wily, flattering words, came slowly flitting by;

Notes

MARY HOWITT
[1] *title* perhaps based loosely upon Aesop's *Fables*, Number 7,
"The Silkworm and the Spider" and Number 200, "The
Gnat and the Lion." Howitt's very popular poem's metre
and rhyme scheme were parodied by Lewis Carroll in
"The Lobster Quadrille" in *Alice in Wonderland* (1865). First
published in *The New Year's Gift* (1829); republished in
Sketches of Natural History; Or, Songs of Animal Life (1834),
our text.

With buzzing wings she hung aloft, then near and nearer drew,   35
Thinking only of her brilliant eyes, and green and purple hue—
Thinking only of her crested head—poor foolish thing! At last,
Up jumped the cunning Spider, and fiercely held her fast.
He dragged her up his winding stair, into his dismal den,
Within his little parlour—but she ne'er came out again!   40

And now, dear little children, who may this story read,
To idle, silly flattering words, I pray you, ne'er give heed:
Unto an evil counsellor close heart and ear and eye,
And take a lesson from this tale of the Spider and the Fly.

The Fossil Elephant[2]

The earth is old! Six thousand years[3]
    Are gone since I had birth;
In the forests of the olden time,
    And the solitudes of earth.

We were a race of mighty things;   5
    The world was all our own.
I dwelt with the Mammoth large and strong,
    And the giant Mastodon.[4]

No ship went over the waters then,
    No ship with oar or sail;   10
But the wastes of the sea were habited
    By the Dragon and the Whale.[5]

And the Hydra[6] down in the ocean caves
    Abode, a creature grim;
And the scaled Serpents huge and strong   15
    Coiled up in the waters dim.

Notes

[2] *title* first published in *Sketches of Natural History* (1834).

[3] *years* when Howitt was writing, the earth was thought by conventional religious authorities to have been created by God in 4004 BCE, according to the dating by James Ussher (1581–1656), Anglican archbishop of Armagh in Ireland, in his *Annales Veteris Testamenti* (Lat. Annals of the Old Testament, 1650). From 1701 many editions of the King James translation of the Bible contained the Ussher dates. Exactly contemporaneous with this poem are the Bridgewater Treatises "On the Power, Wisdom, and Goodness of God as Manifested in the Creation," and Charles Lyell's *Principles of Geology* (1833).

[4] *Mammoth . . . Mastodon* in 1796 Georges Cuvier (1768–1832), French naturalist, published a paper on fossil and living elephants, blaming the extinction of some species on a catastrophe that had wiped them out, later refining his theory to a series of catastrophes. He later named some fossil-elephant-like remains the mastodon, in fact a much earlier off-shoot from the same evolutionary tree. The mastodon, an extinct relative of the modern elephant, was widely distributed and existed between 33 million and 11 thousand years ago, predating the mammoth. In 1828 the English paleontologist Joshua Brookes (1761–1833) identified various fossil remains as those of a distinct species, the woolly mammoth (*Mammuthus primigenius*), existing about 300 thousand years ago.

[5] *Dragon . . Whale* for the sea beast, Leviathan, see Job 41: 1–41. In 1823 Mary Anning (1799–1847), British palaeontologist, made the sensational discovery at Lyme Regis in Dorset on the south coast of England of a complete long-necked *Plesiosaurus*, known as the "sea-dragon." Based on this discovery, Thomas Hawkins (1810–89) published *Book of the Great Sea Dragons* (1840). In 1828 Anning found a fossil skeleton of the *Pterodactylus*, the so-called flying-dragon.

[6] *Hydra* one of the labours of Hercules was the slaying of the many-headed serpent, called the Hydra.

The wastes of the world were all our own;
    A proud, imperial lot!
Man had not then dominion[7] given,
    Or else we knew it not.   20

There was no city on the plain;
    No fortress on the hill;
No mighty men of strength,[8] who came
    With armies up, to kill.

There was no iron then—no brass—   25
    No silver and no gold[9]
The wealth of the world was in its woods,
    And its granite mountains old.

And we were the kings of all the world;
    We knew its breadth and length;   30
We dwelt in the glory of solitude,
    And the majesty of strength.

But suddenly came an awful change![10]
    Wherefore, ask not of me;
That it was, my desolate being shows,   35
    Let that suffice for thee.

The Mammoth huge and the Mastodon
    Were buried beneath the earth;
And the Hydra and the Serpents strong,
    In the caves where they had birth!   40

There is now no place of silence deep,
    Whether on land or sea;
And the Dragons lie in the mountain-rock,
    As if for eternity!

And far in the realms of thawless ice,   45
    Beyond each island shore,
My brethren lie in the darkness stern,
    To awake to life no more!

And not till the last conflicting crash
    When the world consumes in fire,[11]   50
Will their frozen sepulchres be loosed,
    And their dreadful doom expire!

Notes

[7] *dominion* see Genesis 1: 26.

[8] *city ... strength* for city, see 2 Esdras 7: 6; for fortress, see 2 Chronicles 27: 4; and for mighty men, see Daniel 3: 20.

[9] *gold* a reference to the four classical ages of the world, the golden, silver, bronze, and iron; see *Metamorphoses* 1: 89–150.

[10] *change* the catastrophism of which Cuvier wrote (see n. 4).

[11] *fire* the Last Judgement, the Apocalypse, or the end of time; see Revelation 8:9; see also TENNYSON, "THE KRAKEN."

Thomas Hood (1799–1845)

A journalist and poet, Hood was born in London, the son of a bookseller. After leaving school at the age of 14, he worked first a clerk, then apprenticed as an engraver; he eventually became an editor and journalist for *London Magazine* in 1821, where he met such important Romantic poets and essayists as Wordsworth, Coleridge, de Quincey, and Hazlitt. Throughout his life he would edit a number of periodicals: *The Gem* (1829), *Comic Annual* (1830–42), and the *New Monthly Magazine* (1841–43); he also initiated his own publication, *Hood's Magazine and Comic Miscellany* (1844–45). Known primarily as a humourist to his contemporaries, he published his first book, *Odes and Addresses to a Great People* (1825),

co-authored with his brother-in-law, John Hamilton Reynolds (1794–1852), a work of satire with the epigraph: "Catching All the Oddities, the Whimsies, the Absurdities, and the littlest of Conscious Greatness by the Way"; however, as the two poems below demonstrate, he was also capable of serious topics. Throughout his life he was plagued by ill health and debt: he died of consumption on 3 May 1845. Standard edition: *The Works of Thomas Hood : Comic and Serious, in prose and verse* (9 vols, 1862); *The Complete Poetical Works of Thomas Hood*, ed. Walter Jerrold (1906); *The Letters of Thomas Hood*, ed. Peter F. Morgan (1973); Lloyd N. Jeffery, *Thomas Hood* (1972); "Thomas Hood": http://gerald-massey.org.uk/hood/index.htm.

The Song of the Shirt[1]

With fingers weary and worn,
With eyelids heavy and red,
A Woman sat, in unwomanly rags,
Plying her needle and thread—

Notes

THOMAS HOOD

[1] *title* in 1843 *The Times* campaigned against sweated labour, the New Poor Law, and the resulting reorganization of the work-houses. On 26 October it reported that a Mrs Biddell, a Lambeth widow, was arrested and came before a magistrate for having unlawfully pawned clothing that she had been employed to make up for a slopseller (a seller of cheap ready-made garments) who had required a deposit of two pounds for the clothes which he now demanded. The woman's husband had died a year earlier, leaving her with a small child and a baby. Her needlework could not sustain them. Faced with prison, the magistrate offered her the workhouse, which she accepted. The next day the paper repeated the story with further details in a long lead article, condemning the fact that seamstresses worked from fourteen to nineteen hours a day, seven days a week, for between four and seven shillings a week, not enough for food and lodging. Another article on the same day condemned such uncontrolled sweated labour as "white slavery." On 4 November *Punch* reprinted the opening of *The Times* leader in an article called "Famine and Fashion" and then attacked a system that paid needlewomen one penny an hour to make shirts. *The Times* continued its campaign, as did *Punch*, publishing a review of an imaginary book, *The Pride of London*, on 9 December, a savagely ironic mockery of "the disgrace of the metropolis."

Affected by this agitation, Hood wrote "The Song of the Shirt" and sent it in a private letter to Mark Lemon (1809–70), the editor of *Punch*, who accepted it over the objections of his staff, and printed it anonymously in the Christmas number (16 Dec. 1843), to enormous public acclamation. *Punch's* circulation tripled, turning around a floundering magazine to a success that lasted for 150 years. *The Times* reprinted the poem; it was translated into many languages, and incongruously, was printed on cotton handkerchiefs. The poem was set to music by March 1844 by J. H. Tully (1814–68) and was painted by Richard Redgrave (1804–88) as *The Sempstress* (1844). Redgrave used part of Hood's poem as a motto and details from the poem in the painting when it was exhibited to great success at the RA in May, the first of a number of paintings of the subject. The poem was turned into a popular play by Mark Lemon, *The Seamstress* (May 1844); John Leech (1817–64) published an illustration, *Bubble of the Year. Cheap Clothing*, of skeletons making shirts in a sweatshop under the oversight of a corpulent anti-Semitic proprietor, which appeared in *Punch's* almanac for 1845. For a discussion of contemporaneous conditions in the clothing industry, see CONDITION: PROGRESS; KINGSLEY, "CLOTHES" (WEB p. 31). See also ✍ WEBSTER, "CASTAWAY," n. 23.

Stitch! stitch! stitch!   5
In poverty, hunger, and dirt,
      And still with a voice of dolorous pitch
She sang the "Song of the Shirt!"

      "Work! work! work!
While the cock is crowing aloof!   10
      And work—work—work,
Till the stars shine through the roof!
It's O! to be a slave
      Along with the barbarous Turk,[2]
Where woman has never a soul to save,   15
      If this is Christian work!

      Work—work—work
Till the brain begins to swim!
      Work—work—work
Till the eyes are heavy and dim;   20
Seam, and gusset, and band,[3]
      Band, and gusset, and seam,
        Till over the buttons I fall asleep,
And sew them on in a dream!

      O! Men, with Sisters dear!   25
      O! Men! with Mothers and Wives!
It is not linen you're wearing out,
      But human creatures' lives!
        Stitch—stitch—stitch,
In poverty, hunger, and dirt,   30
Sewing at once, with a double thread,
      A Shroud as well as a Shirt.

      But why do I talk of Death?
      That Phantom of grisly bone,
I hardly fear his terrible shape,   35
      It seems so like my own—
      It seems so like my own,
      Because of the fasts I keep,
Oh! God! that bread should be so dear,[4]
      And flesh and blood so cheap!   40

Notes

[2] *Turk* the phrase "barbarous Turk" and the figure of the European woman held hostage in a harem became commonplaces of anti-Muslim rhetoric from the Renaissance on, as in Thomas Heywood's play *The Fair Maid of the West* (1631: 4. 7–8). The term regained European popularity at the time of the Greek War of Independence from the Ottoman Empire (1821–32).

[3] *band* special needlework procedures to prevent ravelling (seam), to strengthen the arms (gusset), and to shape the collar (band, neck band).

[4] *dear* bread remained expensive because of the controversial Corn Laws, protectionist tariffs that excluded the importation of foreign and cheaper corn (wheat and most grains) until British wheat prices reached a competitive price. The Corn Laws were enforced from 1815 to 1846 to give landowners profit on domestic grains. Parliament continuously refused to repeal the Corn Laws, despite support from such figures as Richard Cobden (1804–65). Hood's poem came just at the time when it appeared that Parliament would soon have enough votes to repeal (as happened under Sir Robert Peel in 1846), and so reduce the price of bread.

Work—work—work!
   My labour never flags;
And what are its wages? A bed of straw,
   A crust of bread—and rags.
That shatter'd roof—and this naked floor—   45
   A table—a broken chair—
And a wall so blank, my shadow I thank
   For sometimes falling there![5]

Work—work—work!
From weary chime to chime,   50
   Work—work—work—
As prisoners work for crime!
   Band, and gusset, and seam,
   Seam, and gusset, and band,
Till the heart is sick, and the brain benumb'd,   55
   As well as the weary hand.

Work—work—work,
In the dull December light,
   And work—work—work,
When the weather is warm and bright—   60
While underneath the eaves
   The brooding swallows cling
As if to show me their sunny backs
   And twit me with the spring.

   Oh! but to breathe the breath   65
Of the cowslip and primrose sweet—
   With the sky above my head,
And the grass beneath my feet,
For only one short hour
   To feel as I used to feel,   70
Before I knew the woes of want
   And the walk that costs a meal!

Oh but for one short hour!
   A respite however brief!
No blessed leisure for Love or Hope,   75
   But only time for Grief!
A little weeping would ease my heart,
   But in their briny bed
My tears must stop, for every drop
   Hinders needle and thread!"   80

With fingers weary and worn,
   With eyelids heavy and red,
A Woman sat, in unwomanly rags,

Notes

[5] *there* these details became conventional in numerous paintings and engravings of distressed seamstresses, following Richard Redgrave's painting of 1844 and Anna Blunden's *The Song of the Shirt, or, For Only One Short Hour* (1854).

Plying her needle and thread—
Stitch! stitch! stitch!
In poverty, hunger, and dirt,
And still with a voice of dolorous pitch,
Would that its tone could reach the Rich!
She sang this "Song of the Shirt!"

85

The Bridge of Sighs[6]

"Drown'd! drown'd!"

HAMLET[7]

One more Unfortunate,
Weary of breath,
Rashly importunate,
Gone to her death!

Take her up tenderly,
Lift her with care;
Fashion'd so slenderly,
Young, and so fair!

5

Notes

[6] *title* named after a famous bridge over a canal in Venice (Ital. *Ponte dei Sospiri*), linking the old prison with the Doge's palace, giving condemned prisoners their last view of the world before incarceration. On 26 March 1844, *The Times* reported that "a middle-aged woman, named Mary Furley" was charged with "murder, in having caused the death of George Furley, her infant son, aged 18 months, and also with having attempted to commit the additional crime of suicide." In her later trial it became clear that she had left the Bethnal Green workhouse some days earlier with a parish grant to enable her to become a seamstress to support her two children, though she could only make three shirts for 1¾ d. a day, insufficient to support her family. At her trial before Mr Justice Maule she was condemned to be executed with a stern lecture. The case was taken up in leaders by *The Times* as part of the continuing attacks on the New Poor Law and sweated labour (see n. 1): "The New Poor Law brought this poor creature to the verge of madness," inciting a public outcry that caused John Bright (1811–89), British Radical MP, to take up the case in Parliament, so that the Home Secretary commuted the sentence on 15 May to seven years' transportation.

Hood, meanwhile, though gravely sick and within a year of his death, began a new magazine, and a number of friends contributed to it, including Charles Dickens with "Threatening Letter to Thomas Hood from an Ancient Gentleman, by Favour of Charles Dickens," printed in *Hood's Magazine and Comic Miscellany* (May, 1844), immediately before "The Bridge of Sighs." In it Dickens, with savage irony, claims that the British constitution is in peril because of a lapse in public backbone in civic administration, first mentioning the law where only one judge remains rigorous: "He tried that revolutionary female the

other day, who, though she was in full work (making shirts at three-halfpence a piece), had no pride in her country, but treasonably took it in her head ... to attempt to drown herself and her young child; and the glorious man went out of his way, sir—out of his way—to call her up for instant sentence of Death; and to tell her she had no hope of mercy in this world—as you may see for yourself if you look in the papers of Wednesday the 17th of April." He claimed she had become famous in "every manufacturing town of this kingdom, and read aloud to crowds in every political parlour, beer-shop, news-room, and secret or open place of assembly, frequented by the discontented working-man." Already, by 10 April 1844, Hood wrote to his friend Frederick Oldfield Ward: "I have all but done a poem on 'the Bridge of Sighs'—i.e. Waterloo, and its Suicides." In his final version, Hood makes the mother much younger and relocates the scene to the Thames and Waterloo Bridge, a favoured scene for many suicides. The poem was frequently reprinted, often with engraved illustrations by such artists as John Everett Millais (1858), J. Moyr Smith (1870), and Gustave Doré (1878). It also became the subject for paintings, such as the eighth plate from George Cruikshank's *The Drunkard's Children* (1848), which shows a woman plunging from a bridge into the Thames; G. F. Watts's *Found Drowned* (1848–50); the many representations of the drowning Ophelia, such as that by John Everett Millais (1853); the third part of Augustus Egg's triptych *Past and Present* (1858); and Abraham Solomon's *Drowned! Drowned!* (1860); see also THOMSON, "CITY OF DREADFUL NIGHT," SECT. XIX.

[7] *Hamlet* words of the Queen to Laertes informing him that his sister, Ophelia, is drowned (4. 7. 184). This epigraph was later omitted in reprints of the poem, but the subject continued to be an archetype for Victorian suicides.

Look at her garments
Clinging like cerements; 10
Whilst the wave constantly
Drips from her clothing;
Take her up instantly,
Loving, not loathing.—

Touch her not scornfully; 15
Think of her mournfully,
Gently and humanly;
Not of the stains of her,
All that remains of her
Now is pure womanly. 20

Make no deep scrutiny
Into her mutiny
Rash and undutiful:
Past all dishonour,
Death has left on her 25
Only the beautiful.

Still, for all slips of hers,
One of Eve's family—
Wipe those poor lips of hers
Oozing so clammily. 30

Loop up her tresses
Escaped from the comb,
Her fair auburn tresses;
Whilst wonderment guesses
Where was her home? 35

Who was her father?
Who was her mother?
Had she a sister?
Had she a brother?
Or was there a dearer one 40
Still, and a nearer one
Yet, than all other?

Alas! for the rarity
Of Christian charity
Under the sun! 45
Oh! it was pitiful!
Near a whole city full,
Home she had none.

Sisterly, brotherly,
Fatherly, motherly 50
Feelings had changed:
Love, by harsh evidence,
Thrown from its eminence;
Even God's providence
Seeming estranged. 55

Where the lamps quiver
So far in the river,

With many a light
From window and casement,
From garret to basement,   60
She stood, with amazement,
Houseless by night.

The bleak wind of March
Made her tremble and shiver;
But not the dark arch,   65
Or the black flowing river:
Mad from life's history,
Glad to death's mystery,
Swift to be hurl'd—
Any where, any where   70
Out of the world!

In she plunged boldly,
No matter how coldly
The rough river ran,—
Over the brink of it,   75
Picture it—think of it,
Dissolute Man!
Lave in it, drink of it,
Then, if you can!

Take her up tenderly,   80
Lift her with care;
Fashion'd so slenderly,
Young, and so fair!
Ere her limbs frigidly
Stiffen too rigidly,   85
Decently,—kindly,—
Smoothe, and compose them:
And her eyes, close them,
Staring so blindly!

Dreadfully staring   90
Thro' muddy impurity,
As when with the daring
Last look of despairing
Fix'd on futurity.

Perishing gloomily,   95
Spurr'd by contumely,
Cold inhumanity,
Burning insanity,
Into her rest.—
Cross her hands humbly,   100
As if praying dumbly,
Over her breast!

Owning her weakness,
Her evil behaviour,
And leaving, with meekness,   105
Her sins to her Saviour!

Sarah Stickney Ellis (1799–1872)

Born at Ridgmount in Yorkshire, the fifth child of the Quaker farmer William Stickney (d. 1848) and Esther Richardson (d. 1803), Ellis attended a Quaker school at Ackworth and was also educated at home, encouraged to read by her father, as well as to ride and train her own horses and to paint in water-colour and oil. During the agricultural depression of the 1820s she helped support her family by painting and then by publishing an anti-slavery novel, *The Negro Slave* (1830), three series of *Pictures of Private Life* (1833–37), a collection of essays, *The Poetry of Life* (2 vols, 1835), and a triple-decker novel, *Home, or, The Iron Rule* (1836). In 1837 she married a Congregational missionary widower, William Ellis (1794–1872), and with him and his four children moved to Hoddesdon in Essex. There, in 1844, she opened the non-denominational Rawdon House School, teaching girls the usual curriculum as well as cookery and household management. It is for her four conduct books that Mrs Ellis (as she was known) became most renowned: *The Women of England, their Social Duties and Domestic Habits* (1839); *The Daughters of England, their Position in Society, Character and Responsibilities* (1842); *The Wives of England, their Relative Duties, Domestic Influence, and Social Obligations* (1843); and *The Mothers of England, their Influence and Responsibility* (1843). All displayed a tension between women's social and legal subordination to men in practical life and her endorsement of "separate spheres" in which women controlled the domestic aspects of a household: the tension was partially resolved by women's moral influence over the actions of men and the life of the home (for other writings by Ellis, see GENDER and GENDER (WEB p. 70)). A strong supporter of the temperance movement, she published short stories concerning the ravages of alcoholism in *Family Secrets, or, Hints to Those Who Would Make Home Happy* (3 vols, 1842), showing how compassionate middle-class wives or daughters could rescue the family. No standard editions. *The Home Life and Letters of Mrs. Ellis, compiled by Her Nieces* (1893). Orlando project through library access: http://orlando.cambridge.org/public/svPeople?person_id=ellisa.

From *Pictures of Private Life*[1]

"An Apology for Fiction"

To write a book which is intended, and calculated, solely for the readers of fiction, and prefix to it an apology addressed to the non-readers of fiction, appears somewhat paradoxical; yet as a member of a religious society,[2] whose sentiments are openly and

Notes

SARAH STICKNEY ELLIS

[1] *title* the title page to the 1827 collection of four short domestic novels bears the following epigraph: "Would you judge of the lawfulness or unlawfulness of pleasure, take this rule: whatever weakens your reason, impairs the tenderness of your conscience, obscures your sense of God, or takes off the relish of spiritual things;—in short, whatever increases the strength and authority of your body over your mind, that thing is sin to you, however innocent it may be in itself" (from a letter to John Wesley, 8 June 1725, by Susanna Wesley (1669–1742), the mother of Charles and John Wesley, the founders of Methodism). The preface is an apology for or defence of didactic fiction, written to exemplify the advice given by Wesley's mother to her son. This prescriptive fiction was often directed at children paralleling the advice in the conduct books for which Ellis became famous. Our text: the preface to *Pictures of Private Life* (second ed. 1833), written before her marriage under her maiden name.

[2] *society* Ellis was then a member of the Society of Friends, the Quakers.

professedly at variance with works of this description, I would not willingly oppose the peculiarities of many whom I regard with gratitude, esteem, and admiration, without offering in my own vindication some remarks upon the nature of fiction in general.

Fiction may, or may not be, subservient to the purposes of moral instruction. The following are some of the abuses to which it is most liable:—the delineation of unnatural characters, by the combination of such qualities as never did, and never could exist in one human being; and the placing such creatures of imagination in scenes and circumstances, where the common sympathies of our nature find no place; and where the mind of the reader, in order to follow them with interest, must be elevated to the highest pitch of absurdity, and the feelings strained beyond their proper and healthy tone; and when I add to this, the shameless prostitution of talent, with which some writers have confounded the nature of good and evil, making vice interesting, and virtue insipid, by investing the one with the fantastic drapery of romance, and stripping the other of all that can please the eye or charm the senses, by describing the most astonishing instances of integrity, generosity, and self-denial, as arising solely from an amiable heart, without the assistance of religion, or the control of good principle, I am willing to allow that fiction has often been, and is well calculated to be, a most powerful engine of demoralization.[3]

On the other hand, when a writer keeps steadily in view the developement of moral truth, when his characters are all of our "mixed essence," drawn from the scenes of every-day life,[4] animated with our feelings, weak with our frailties, led into our difficulties, surrounded by our temptations, and altogether involved in a succession of the same causes and effects which influence our lives, his productions may be called fictitious, but they cannot be false. To me they appear at least as lawful as those of the painter, and for this reason I have ventured to call my stories, Pictures of Private Life.

Suppose, for instance, an artist wished to exhibit to the public a personification of old age. Perhaps he would paint an old woman in her cottage. But this would not be all. In order to present the idea more complete, he must place before our eyes the interior of her habitation, her ancient furniture, the old fashioned chair on which she is resting, her crutch at her side, her knitting, or her spinning wheel, her kettle and her cat. Now, though such an old woman, with her furniture, such a chair, spinning wheel, crutch, kettle, and cat, never did exist, yet the picture may be true; because the idea of old age could not well be conveyed without the representation of the scene being thus filled up; and in proportion as the subject is more complex, the collateral circumstances will be more studied, and frequently more numerous. In the same way the fictitious writer labours, and for the same end; with this advantage, that the supposed lapse of time, affords him an opportunity of tracing causes to their effects. If, for instance, his subject be virtue, that virtue must be tried; and therefore he brings in a variety of circumstances all subservient to one purpose. Virtue must be contrasted with vice; and therefore other characters are introduced, and made to speak, and act, in a manner the most opposed to the words and actions of virtue. Virtue when allied to clay, must not be complete, and without flaw, because that would be unnatural, and convey an idea of a superhuman being; virtue must therefore sometimes fall away from its high purpose, in order that it may learn humility, and look more earnestly for the guiding hand of Providence; and, lastly, virtue must have its reward. In this manner the writer is involved in a great variety of imagery, and may sometimes have

Notes

[3] demoralization Ellis finds fiction a potential source of damage to society for its corrupting influence, a theme that goes back to Plato's attack on Homer for telling lies about the gods (Republic, bk. 10). In the next paragraph, however, she claims with Sir Philip Sidney (Apologie for Poetry, 1595) and others that literature (here fiction) may be an instrument for social good, as presenting truthful ideals and examples. See also LITERATURE, DEBATES, n. 31.

[4] life in chapter 17 ("In which the Story Pauses a Little") of Adam Bede (1859), George Eliot defends novels of everyday life grounded not in morality but on nature and fact.

the management of characters, which, if separately and independently considered, would not be worth his while to delineate.

Various means may be employed to produce the same end. As individuals we must all labour according to our calling. Some preach virtue, some only practise it, some make a picture of it, and some a poem, and some, (perhaps the lowest in the scale of moral teachers) adorn it with the garb of fiction, that it may ensure a welcome, where it would not otherwise obtain an entrance.

To meet with an attentive and willing listener, is no less difficult than to find an able teacher. Fiction may be compared to a key, which opens many minds that would be closed against a sermon. Nor is it without authority in the writings of sincere and zealous christians. The wide range of allegory affords innumerable subjects for instruction and delight, and many a weary wanderer through the valley of the shadow of death,[5] has been cheered by the remembrance of Bunyan's pilgrim.[6] But the scriptures themselves afford the highest evidence that this style of writing may be made serviceable, as a means of reproof and conviction. Let us confine our attention to one example. Where can we find anything comparable to the affecting story of the ewe lamb?[7] Had the prophet Nathan addressed the king of Israel at once as a violator of the laws of virtue, honour, and generosity, he would probably have found him so effectually defended by the pride of human nature, as well as by the dignity of his office, that he would have failed to reach his heart; but by the simple story of the ewe lamb, he touched at once upon that chord of feeling, which seemed ever ready to vibrate with sweetest melody, in the soul of the Royal Psalmist; and then followed that emphatic application "thou art the man!"[8]

It is in this manner, by the contemplation of ideal characters that we are sometimes led on towards conviction; our feelings become softened in sympathy with theirs, we unconsciously pronounce our own condemnation, and conscience makes the application.

Although willing to allow that fictitious writing is the most humble means of moral instruction, I am still earnest in endeavouring to maintain its utility, especially on the ground that it finds its way to the dense multitude who close their eyes upon the introduction of purer light.

Happy, happy is it for those whose hearts are open to receive "Christ as their Schoolmaster,"[9] who have learned to desire the "sincere milk of the word."[10] In their select and privileged communities, the bible spreads before them a wide field of never ending wonder and delight, and religion is a hallowed word, uniting all their sympathies into one bond of peace and love.

Let us look into the next stage of advancement towards moral excellence, and here we see religion obscured by the mists of party prejudice, still worshipped, but frequently disguised, and misunderstood. A little lower, and religion holds a disputed sway, contending with the spirit of the world, for a small portion of the heart. Lower still, and her power and her excellence are called in question; but before we arrive at that class by which her image is dethroned, and her institutions violated, let us regard that immense mass of beings whose perceptions are so imperfect, whose minds so unenlightened, and whose feelings so absorbed by the trifling affairs of a busy world, that they can hardly be said to have learned to think. It is from amongst these that I have ventured to lift up my voice; it is for these that

Notes

[5] *death* see Psalm 23: 4.

[6] *pilgrim* the hero, Christian, in *Pilgrim's Progress* (1678) by John Bunyan (1628–88).

[7] *lamb* for the story of the confrontation between Nathan the Prophet and King David, see 2 Samuel 12.

[8] *Royal Psalmist . . . man* King David, to whom was credited the authorship of the book of Psalms; for "thou art the

man" see 2 Samuel 12: 7, where David is reprimanded by Nathan the prophet for having Uriah the Hittite murdered in battle so David could marry his widow, Bathsheba.

[9] *Schoolmaster* see Galatians 3: 24.

[10] *word* see 1 Peter 2: 2.

I have thought, and felt, and written. In vain might instruction be laid before them in a weightier form. Their pursuit is pleasure, their food excitement. And since books of fiction are a kind which thousands will continue to write, and tens of thousands to read, I have endeavoured to do my little part towards blending with amusement some of those serious reflections, which in the often shifting scenes of a restless life, have occupied my own mind; not without earnest longings, that I myself were amongst those who are already prepared to receive truth without fiction, light without clouds, good without alloy.

Thomas Babington Macaulay (1800–59)

Born into a prominent evangelical family of the Clapham sect and educated at Trinity College, Cambridge, Macaulay was elected MP in 1830, the Whig member for the pocket borough of Calne. He was appointed to the Supreme Council of India where he codified criminal law and reformed the educational system (see EMPIRE, "GOVERNING"). In 1838 he returned to Britain and was re-elected MP, serving in cabinet from 1838 to 1847. During this time he published *Lays of Ancient Rome* (1842), an immensely popular set of four ballads on heroic moments in the Roman Republic (see MACAULAY, "LAYS" (WEB p. 280)). He collected a number of sharply polemical essays written for *Edinburgh Magazine* in *Essays Critical and Historical* (1843). Upon losing his seat in 1847, he set out to write his major work, *The History of England from the Accession of James the Second* (4 vols, 1848–55; vol. 5, 1861). Macaulay was made a peer in 1857. He died on 28 December 1859 and is interred in Westminster Abbey. Standard edition: *The Works of Lord Macaulay* (12 vols, 1898); *The Letters of Thomas Babington Macaulay*, ed. Thomas Pinney, (6 vols, 1974–81); George Otto Trevelyan, *The Life and Letters of Lord Macaulay* (1876); Robert E. Sullivan, *Macaulay: The Tragedy of Power* (2009); Thomas Babington Macaulay:http://www.columbia.edu/itc/mealac/pritchett/00general links/macaulay/index.html.

WEB p. 280

Lays of Ancient Rome
From "Horatius: A Lay Made About the Year of The City CCCLX"

The History of England from the Accession of James the Second (1848–61)

Macaulay's Whig interpretation of history aligns and judges events of an imperfect past to the degree that they lead to a present that is steadily improving, showing progress in the political, material, and cultural conditions of England (see also CONDITION, PROGRESS, MACAULAY, COLLOQUIES (WEB p. 18)). His writing combines a great deal of research in primary documents and commentaries with a popular style, with picturesque descriptions and a steady narrative pace. Macaulay claimed he wished to "produce something which shall for a few days supersede the last fashionable novel on the tables of young ladies." He intended to cover the period from 1685 to the first Reform Bill of 1832; however, at the time of his death he had written only up to the death of William III (1702). In publishing terms the result was an unqualified success: the first volumes (1848) sold 13,000 copies in the first four months; volumes three and four (1855), over 25,000 copies in two months. The final volume (1861), edited by his sister, Hannah (Lady Trevelyan), was released posthumously. Our text: 1848.

From Chapter 1: "Before the Restoration"[1]

[Introduction]

I purpose to write the history of England from the accession of King James the Second down to a time which is within the memory of men still living.[2] I shall recount the errors which, in a few months, alienated a loyal gentry and priesthood from the House of Stuart.[3] I shall trace the course of that revolution which terminated the long struggle between our sovereigns and their parliaments, and bound up together the rights of the people and the title of the reigning dynasty. I shall relate how the new settlement was, during many troubled years, successfully defended against foreign and domestic enemies;[4] how, under that settlement, the authority of law and the security of property were found to be compatible with a liberty of discussion and of individual action never before known; how, from the auspicious union of order and freedom, sprang a prosperity of which the annals of human affairs had furnished no example; how our country, from a state of ignominious vassalage, rapidly rose to the place of umpire among European powers; how her opulence and her martial glory grew together; how, by wise and resolute good faith, was gradually established a public credit[5] fruitful of marvels which to the statesmen of any former age would have seemed incredible; how a gigantic commerce gave birth to a maritime power, compared with which every other maritime power, ancient or modern, sinks into insignificance; how Scotland, after ages of enmity, was at length united to England, not merely by legal bonds, but by indissoluble ties of interest and affection;[6] how, in America, the British colonies rapidly became far mightier and wealthier than the realms which Cortes and Pizarro had added to the dominions of

Notes

THOMAS BABINGTON MACAULAY

[1] *title* in the opening chapter, after stating his intentions and giving the scope of his study, Macaulay quickly surveys English history from its beginnings to the Restoration of Charles II (1660).

[2] *living* James II (1633–1701), king of England and Ireland, and as James VI, king of Scotland, from 6 February 1685 to 11 December 1688, when he abdicated by fleeing to France.

[3] *Stuart* also the House of Stewart, the dynasty ruled Scotland from 1371 to 1603. With the death of Elizabeth I (1533–1603), rule of England and Ireland passed from the Tudor dynasty to the Stuarts: hence, they ruled England, Ireland, and Scotland from 1603 to 1694, and from 1702 to 1707, when, with the death of Queen Anne, the rights of succession passed to the House of Hanover. Macaulay is concerned primarily with the rule of James II, a believer in absolutism and the divine right of kings, who had converted to Catholicism while in exile in 1668; upon his ascension, he alienated his subjects by advocating policies which would overturn the exclusion of Catholics from public offices.

[4] *enemies* when Queen Mary, James's wife, gave birth to a Catholic heir in 1688, a group of Protestant nobles, fearing a Catholic dynasty, solicited William I of Orange (1650–1702), James's nephew and son-in-law, to invade England. James escaped to France without much resistance. The Glorious Revolution was settled when James's daughter Mary II (1662–94) was declared co-monarch with her husband, who became William III of England, Ireland, and Scotland. Subsequently, there were a number of Jacobite uprisings in Scotland and Ireland in 1689–90. James landed in Ireland in March 1689 with 6,000 French troops, and was finally defeated on 1 July 1690 at the Battle of the Boyne. In Scotland there were further outbreaks of Jacobinism in 1715 and 1745.

[5] *credit* in chapters 19 and 20, Macaulay discusses the origins of the national debt in 1692 and the establishment of the Bank of England in 1694; these undermined the power of the aristocracy, for whom wealth was measured in land, and also enabled the establishment of global capitalism ("gigantic commerce").

[6] *affection* the kingdom of Scotland can be traced back to the thirteenth century; the Act of Union (1 May 1707), passed by both the English and Scottish parliaments, created the United Kingdom of Great Britain, ending Scotland's existence as a separate state.

Charles the Fifth;[7] how, in Asia, British adventurers founded an empire not less splendid and more durable than that of Alexander.[8]

Nor will it be less my duty faithfully to record disasters mingled with triumphs, and great national crimes and follies far more humiliating than any disaster. It will be seen that even what we justly account our chief blessings were not without alloy. It will be seen that the system which effectually secured our liberties against the encroachments of kingly power gave birth to a new class of abuses from which absolute monarchies are exempt.[9] It will be seen that, in consequence partly of unwise interference, and partly of unwise neglect, the increase of wealth and the extension of trade produced, together with immense good, some evils from which poor and rude societies are free. It will be seen how, in two important dependencies of the crown, wrong was followed by just retribution;[10] how imprudence and obstinacy broke the ties which bound the North American colonies to the parent state;[11] how Ireland, cursed by the domination of race over race, and of religion over religion, remained indeed a member of the empire, but a withered and distorted member, adding no strength to the body politic, and reproachfully pointed at by all who feared or envied the greatness of England.[12]

Yet, unless I greatly deceive myself, the general effect of this chequered narrative will be to excite thankfulness in all religious minds, and hope in the breasts of all patriots. For the history of our country during the last hundred and sixty years is eminently the history of physical, of moral, and of intellectual improvement. Those who compare the age on which their lot has fallen with a golden age which exists only in their imagination may talk of degeneracy and decay: but no man who is correctly informed as to the past will be disposed to take a morose or desponding view of the present.

I should very imperfectly execute the task which I have undertaken if I were merely to treat of battles and sieges, of the rise and fall of administrations, of intrigues in the palace, and of debates in the parliament. It will be my endeavour to relate the history of the people as well as the history of the government, to trace the progress of useful and ornamental arts, to describe the rise of religious sects and the changes of literary taste, to portray the manners of successive generations, and not to pass by with neglect even the revolutions which have taken place in dress, furniture, repasts, and public amusements. I shall cheerfully bear the reproach of having descended below the dignity of

Notes

[7] *Fifth* on behalf of Charles V, Holy Roman emperor, Charles I of Spain (1500–58), Hernan Cortez (1485–1547) conquered the Aztec Empire in Mexico in 1521; Francisco Pizarro (c.1471–1541) conquered the Inca Empire of Peru in 1632. The first permanent English settlement in the Americas was in Jamestown, Virginia in 1607; by 1761, with the Treaty of Paris settling wars between the French and English, Britain was the most powerful European empire in the Americas.

[8] *Alexander* the East India Company received a royal charter from Elizabeth I on 30 December 1600 for exclusive trading rights in India and China; by 1757, after defeating the French at the Battle of Plassey, they became the government of British India, a role they continued until the Indian Rebellion of 1857–58. Alexander the Great of Macedonia (356–323 BCE) conquered Persia, Syria, Egypt, and Mesopotamia; when he tried to invade the Indian subcontinent in 327–326 BCE, his army revolted, forcing him to turn back.

[9] *exempt* following the Glorious Revolution, the new system of governing through the House of Commons often depended upon buying votes of members; without party discipline, there was no way of assuring a majority. The

figure most commonly and controversially associated with this practice was Robert Walpole (1676–1745), often called Britain's first prime minister (although no such title then existed), who dominated the House from 1721 to 1745. Macaulay writes of the "abuse" in chapter 15 of *History* in a section called "The Rise and Progress of Parliamentary Corruption in England."

[10] *retribution* reference to the Jacobite Rebellions in Scotland and Ireland (see n. 4). Macaulay discusses these at length in chapter 12, "The Revolution in Ireland," and chapter 13, "The Revolution in Scotland."

[11] *state* the Thirteen Colonies declared independence on 4 July 1776, forming the United States of America.

[12] *England* throughout the seventeenth and eighteenth centuries, Catholics in Ireland were discriminated against by a series of penal acts which deprived them of basic rights; the Act of Union (1801), following an uprising in 1798, united the Kingdom of Ireland with England. The Irish potato famines were ongoing at precisely the time Macaulay is writing. Macaulay had addressed these problems in a speech to the House of Commons, "The State of Ireland," 19 February 1844.

history, if I can succeed in placing before the English of the nineteenth century a true picture of the life of their ancestors.

The events which I propose to relate form only a single act of a great and eventful drama extending through ages, and must be very imperfectly understood unless the plot of the preceding acts be well known. I shall therefore introduce my narrative by a slight sketch of the history of our country from the earliest times. I shall pass very rapidly over many centuries: but I shall dwell at some length on the vicissitudes of that contest which the administration of King James the Second brought to a decisive crisis.[13]

From Chapter 3: "The State of England in 1685"

[The Clergy][14]

The rural clergy were even more vehement in Toryism than the rural gentry, and were a class scarcely less important. It is to be observed, however, that the individual clergyman, as compared with the individual gentleman, then ranked much lower than in these days. The main support of the Church was derived from the tithe; and the tithe bore to the rent a much smaller ratio than at present.[15] King estimated the whole income of the parochial and collegiate clergy at only four hundred and eighty thousand pounds a year;[16] Davenant at only five hundred and forty-four thousand a year.[17] It is certainly now more than seven times as great as the larger of these two sums. It follows that rectors and vicars must have been, as compared with the neighbouring knights and squires, much poorer in the seventeenth than in the nineteenth century. . . .

Thus the Anglican priesthood was divided into two sections, which, in acquirements, in manners, and in social position, differed widely from each other. One section, trained for cities and courts, comprised men familiar with all ancient and modern learning; men able to encounter Hobbes or Bossuet[18] at all the weapons of controversy; men who could, in their sermons, set forth the majesty and beauty of Christianity with such justness of thought, and such energy of language, that the indolent Charles[19] roused himself to listen and the fastidious Buckingham[20] forgot to sneer; men whose address, politeness, and

Notes

[13] *crisis* "In this, and in the next chapter, I have very seldom thought necessary to cite authorities: for, in these chapters, I have not detailed events minutely, or used recondite materials; and the facts which I mention are for the most part such that a person tolerably well read in English history, if not already apprised of them, will at least know where to look for evidence of them. In the subsequent chapters I shall carefully indicate the sources of my information" [author's note].

[14] *title* as with his description of the Tory squires, Macaulay here denigrates the seventeenth-century country clergy as a regressive force.

[15] *present* tithes were one-tenth of income or produce of the land given to the clergy as alms; the system changed in 1836 with the Tithe Commutation Act, which changed the ancient system to provide payment in money.

[16] *year* Gregory King (1648–1712), civil servant and economic statistician, wrote *Natural and Political Observations and Conclusions upon the State and Condition of England* (1696).

[17] *year* Charles Davenant (1656–1714), English economist, wrote *Two Discourses on the Public Revenues and Trade of England* (1698).

[18] *Hobbes … Bossuet* Thomas Hobbes (1588–1679), English philosopher, was author of *Leviathan* (1651); Jacques-Bénigne Bossuet (1627–1704), French theologian and famous orator, was a believer in divine right of kings.

[19] *Charles* Bossuet gave a famous oration at the funeral of the widow of Charles I, Henrietta Maria of France (1609–69), published as *Oraison funèbre d'Henriette de France* (Fr. funeral oration of Henriette of France; 1669), as well as at the funeral of her daughter, Henrietta Anne of England, Duchess of Orléans (1644–70), Charles II's sister. The latter was published as *Oraison funèbre d'Henriette d'Angleterre* (Fr.funeral oration of Henriette of England; 1670). In both orations, he argued strongly for a restoration of Catholicism in England.

[20] *Buckingham* George Villiers, second Duke of Buckingham (1628–87), English statesman and poet, was a Royalist who fought for Charles I during the Civil War; famous as a profligate and wit, he was pilloried by John Dryden in *Absalom and Achitophel* (1681).

knowledge of the world qualified them to manage the consciences of the wealthy and noble; men with whom Halifax[21] loved to discuss the interests of empires, and from whom Dryden was not ashamed to own that he had learned to write.[22] The other section was destined to ruder and humbler service. It was dispersed over the country, and consisted chiefly of persons not at all wealthier, and not much more refined, than small farmers or upper servants. Yet it was in these rustic priests, who derived but a scanty subsistence from their tithe sheaves and tithe pigs, and who had not the smallest chance of ever attaining high professional honours, that the professional spirit was strongest. Among those divines who were the boast of the universities and the delight of the capital, and who had attained, or might reasonably expect to attain, opulence and lordly rank, a party, respectable in numbers, and more respectable in character, leaned towards constitutional principles of government, lived on friendly terms with Presbyterians, Independents, and Baptists, would gladly have seen a full toleration granted to all Protestant sects, and would even have consented to make alterations in the liturgy, for the purpose of conciliating honest and candid nonconformists.[23] But such latitudinarianism was held in horror by the country parson. He was, indeed, prouder of his ragged gown than his superiors of their lawn and their scarlet hoods.[24] The very consciousness that there was little in his worldly circumstances to distinguish him from the villagers to whom he preached led him to hold immoderately high the dignity of that sacerdotal office which was his single title to reverence. Having lived in seclusion, and having had little opportunity of correcting his opinions by reading or conversation, he held and taught the doctrines of indefeasible hereditary right[25], of passive obedience,[26] and of nonresistance[27] in all their crude absurdity. Having been long engaged in a petty war against the neighbouring dissenters, he too often hated them for the wrongs which he had done them, and found no fault with the Five Mile Act[28] and the Conventicle Act,[29] except that those odious laws had not a sharper edge. Whatever influence his office gave him was exerted with passionate zeal on the Tory side; and that influence was immense. It would be a great error to imagine, because the country rector was in general not regarded as a gentleman, because he could not dare to aspire to the hand of one of the young ladies at the manor house, because he was not asked into the parlours of the great, but was left to drink and smoke with grooms and butlers, that the power of the clerical body was smaller than at present. The influence of a class is by no means proportioned to the consideration which the members of that class enjoy in their individual capacity. A Cardinal is a much more exalted personage than a

Notes

[21] *Halifax* George Savile, first Marquess of Halifax (1633–95), English statesman, was a vehement opponent of James II.

[22] *write* "'I have frequently heard him (Dryden) own with pleasure that, if he had any talent for English prose, it was owing to his having often read the writings of the great Archbishop Tillotson.' 'Congreve's Dedication of Dryden's Plays'" [author's note]. John Dryden (1631–1700), English poet and playwright, author of *Marriage à la Mode* (1672) and *All for Love* (1678), was the leading writer of the Restoration period and Poet Laureate to Charles II and James II; John Tillotson (1630–94), English divine, archbishop of Canterbury (1691–4), was known as a great orator; William Congreve (1670–1729), English playwright and poet, edited *The Dramatick Works of John Dryden* (6 vols, 1717).

[23] *Presbyterians ... nonconformists* these groups are Protestant but not part of the Church of England; the Corporation Act (1661) and Test Act (1673) excluded them from public and military office. The Test Act (1828) repealed these

exclusions. The liturgy is the standardized order of public worship; the Nonconformists wanted the Anglican liturgy purified of alleged "papacy."

[24] *hoods* academic head covering worn by Doctors of Divinity or Canon Law.

[25] *right* the divine right of kings, establishing succession through bloodlines legitimated by God.

[26] *obedience* a belief in the absolute right of the Crown, and that any disobedience is illegal and sinful, most famously articulated by George Berkeley (1685–1753), Irish bishop and philosopher, in *Discourse on Passive Obedience* (1711).

[27] *nonresistance* often used in parallel with "passive obedience."

[28] *Act* an act passed in 1665 forbidding dissenting clergy from living within 8 kilometres of a parish from which they had been banned, unless they swore an oath swearing obedience to the king and state.

[29] *Act* an act of 1664 forbidding religious meetings outside the auspices of the Anglican Church of over five people.

begging friar: but it would be a grievous mistake to suppose that the College of Cardinals has exercised greater dominion over the public mind of Europe than the Order of Saint Francis.[30] In Ireland, at present, a peer holds a far higher station in society than a Roman Catholic priest: yet there are in Munster and Connaught few counties where a combination of priests would not carry an election against a combination of peers.[31] In the seventeenth century the pulpit was to a large portion of the population what the periodical press now is. Scarce any of the clowns who came to the parish church ever saw a Gazette[32] or a political pamphlet. Ill informed as their spiritual pastor might be, he was yet better informed than themselves: he had every week an opportunity of haranguing them; and his harangues were never answered. At every important conjuncture, invectives against the Whigs and exhortations to obey the Lord's anointed resounded at once from many thousands of pulpits; and the effect was formidable indeed. Of all the causes which, after the dissolution of the Oxford Parliament,[33] produced the violent reaction against the Exclusionists,[34] the most potent seems to have been the oratory of the country clergy.

WEB p. 284

James Dawson Burn (1801?–c.1889)
From *Autobiography of a Beggar Boy*

John Henry Newman (1801–90)

The first of six children, Newman was born in London to a banker father, John Newman (d. 1824), and Jemima Fourdrinier (d. 1836). He was sent to Ealing School where he received a solid classical education. After his father's bank failed in 1816 in the aftermath of the Napoleonic Wars, Newman's health failed and he experienced a religious conversion towards Calvinistic Evangelicalism. In 1817 he entered Trinity College, Oxford, on a scholarship, and would remain at Oxford for twenty-eight years.

Although he did poorly in his examinations, he was elected (1822) to a fellowship at Oriel College, then one of the leading colleges for its intellectual endeavours. There he met some of his most important teachers, Richard Whately (1787–1863) and Edward Hawkins (1789–1882), and friends John Keble, Richard Hurrell Froude (1803–36), Edward Pusey (1800–82), and Robert Isaac Wilberforce (1802–57), but he had to give up his tutoring when he came into conflict with college authorities about

Notes

[30] *Cardinal … Francis* the College of Cardinals is advisory body to the pope whose main function is to pick a papal successor upon death or abdication; the Order of Saint Francis is a Catholic religious order of friars based on the rules and teachings of St Francis of Assisi (1181–1286). The order emphasized poverty and an identification with common people.

[31] *Ireland … peers* Munster and Connaught are provinces in western Ireland; the former has six counties, the latter, seven. Peers were appointed in Ireland by the English monarchs in their capacity as king or queen of Ireland, as well as England and Wales.

[32] *Gazette* the *London Gazette* is the official publication of the English government, first published in 1665.

[33] *Parliament* in the events leading up to the Civil War, Charles I, being advised he could not dissolve parliament at Westminster without violating the law, summoned a parliament at Oxford, which met twice in 1644–45. Only about a third of the lords and MPs attended.

[34] *Exclusionists* political faction opposed to religious toleration (see n. 23).

reforming the system. He published his first major work, *The Arians of the Fourth Century* (1833), and during the same year travelled round the Mediterranean with Hurrell Froude. He and his colleagues began to publish a series of tracts addressed to the clergy and interested laymen concerning the state of the Church of England and its heritage in the Caroline divines and the ancient church – a series of ninety, called *Tracts for the Times* (1833–41) – supplying a name for the movement of which he was the leader: "Tractarianism." In 1834 he published the first of six volumes of *Parochial Sermons*, given in Oxford when he was vicar of the University Church, St Mary the Virgin. At the same time he was studying the relationship between the Anglican Church as a *via media* (middle way) between the Roman Catholic and Calvinistic churches – especially in the light of the heretical controversies of the fourth to sixth centuries. The *Tracts* culminated with *Tract 90*, Newman's weighty analysis of the Thirty-Nine Articles of Religion as conformable to various aspects of medieval Catholic doctrine, arousing deep antagonism. He resigned his position at St Mary's (1843) and went into retreat at a small village, Littlemore, outside Oxford, and it was there that he was received into the Roman Catholic Church in 1845. Subsequently he brought his most recent research to fruition with *Essay on the Development of Christian Doctrine* (1845). In September 1846 Newman went to Rome to study for the Roman Catholic priesthood. He was ordained on 30 May 1847 and within a year had become the superior of the Birmingham Oratory for a group of priests living in commu-

nity under a rule but not religious vows. He published his first novel, *Loss and Gain* (1848), and later another novel, *Callista* (1855), and delivered various series of lectures: *Certain Difficulties Faced by Anglicans* (1850), *The Present Position of Catholics in England* (1851), and, most significantly, at the request of religious leaders in Ireland, *Discourses on the Scope and Nature of University Education* (1852). Eventually Newman was made rector of the new Catholic University of Ireland. After an attack on his veracity by Charles Kingsley, Newman responded with a series of pamphlets that became the famous justification of his own life: *Apologia Pro Vita Sua* (1864): see RELIGION: RELIGIOUS FAITH; NEWMAN (WEB p. 216). In the next year came *The Dream of Gerontius* (1865), a kind of oratorio-libretto, which is what it was eventually turned into by Edward Elgar (1900). In 1870 he published *A Grammar of Assent*. He returned to Oxford to become Trinity College's first honorary fellow when he received the invitation in December 1877. He died of pneumonia at the Birmingham Oratory. At his request, he was buried in the same grave as his long-time friend, the priest Ambrose St John (1815–75). Standard editions: *Collected Works* (36 vols, 1868–1881); *The Idea of a University*, ed. Frank M. Turner (1996); *Apologia Pro Vita Sua*, ed. Frank M. Turner (2008); *The Letters and Diaries of John Henry Newman*, ed. Charles Stephen Dessain (32 vols, 1961–); Frank M. Turner, *Newman* (2002); Ian Ker, *John Henry Newman: A Biography* (2009). Society for the Study of Cardinal Newman: http://www.cardinalnewmansociety.net/index.html.

The Idea of a University Defined and Illustrated

According to the Act of Uniformity (1662), all students at Oxford and Cambridge had to subscribe to the Thirty-Nine Articles of Religion of the Anglican Church before they were matriculated or admitted to their college: part of the Test Acts. In effect, this requirement meant that all those who were not members of the

Church of England were denied a place. In Ireland, the one university-level college was the Anglican establishment, Trinity College, Dublin, with a similar requirement: Roman Catholics had been excluded until 1794; after that they were admitted, but were denied all scholarships until 1834. These restrictions, religious tests on matriculation, and on taking an ordinary bachelor's degree, were abolished by the Oxford University Act (1854) and the Cambridge Act (1856). The Universities Tests Act (1871) in effect abolished tests in the Universities of Oxford and Cambridge. Hence, for most of the century, Roman Catholics were denied access to university education, even though three "Queen's Colleges" were established in 1845 at Belfast, Cork, and Limerick, but with all religious subjects disallowed. In response, Paul Cullen (1803–78), Roman Catholic Archbishop of Armagh and Primate of Ireland, asked Newman for advice in April, 1851, and proposed a series of lectures against "mixed education" (the teaching of Catholics and Protestants together). Newman gave advice, agreed to lecture, and also agreed to become the first president or rector of the new university in 1854, the Catholic University of Ireland, now the National University. Newman delivered the first five of his ten discourses in May and June, 1852, and broke them off in mid-stream to return to England for his libel trial with Giacinto Achilli (1803–50). In the *Present Position* he had attacked this former Dominican monk, who had been touring England denouncing Catholicism after he had been defrocked for sexual misconduct. Newman accused him of immorality, against which Achilli launched criminal proceedings against Newman. In the trial in 1852, midway through *The Idea of a University* lectures, the jury found Newman guilty (he could not prove all of his allegations) – though even *The Times* acknowledged the miscarriage of justice – and imposed a fine of £100 and the very substantial legal costs. Newman's first five discourses were published separately soon after delivery, and the final five were issued as a pamphlet in the autumn of 1852.

Answering Newman's request for advice about the topic of his discourses, Cullen said, "What we want in Ireland is to persuade the people that education should be religious.... The subjects ... might be the advantages of educating people and the sort of education they ought to receive—Mixed Education—Examination of the education given to Catholics in Trinity College and its effects—education in the Queen's Colleges, or education without any religion.... The services rendered by the Catholic Church and its Pontiffs to literature—But you will best know what points to select, and how to treat them." Accordingly, in his preface to the third edition (1873, with nine discourses) Newman began with the principle that a university is "a place of *teaching* universal *knowledge*" – a point to which he would return over and over in emphasizing his goal of "more intelligent members of society" through "cultivation of mind." Newman opposes training for professionalism by teaching the sciences, or any kind of usefulness (associated with radicals, Benthamites, and Utilitarians), with the Oxford model to educate for national leadership. Attacks on the narrowness of Oxford's classical education and its neglect of teaching and scholarship had been current from early in the nineteenth century in the *Edinburgh Review* in essays by John Playfair (Jan. 1808), Richard Payne Knight (July 1809), Sydney Smith (Oct. 1809), and by all three writers (Apr. 1810) in a review of *Reply to the Calumnies of the "Edinburgh Review" Against Oxford* (1810), a defence of the classics by Newman's old colleague from Oriel College, Edward Coplestone (1776–1849).

His claim to speak on this topic, as he says in Discourse I, is his own experience at Oxford of "the great principle of liberal education." That education was forged in the context of two controversies—the first, dating from 1808 to 1811, its "*inutility*," when Oxford's disconnectedness from the "duties of life" resulted in attacks on its curriculum, teaching methods, and examinations. Second was the controversy about Oxford's "*religious exclusiveness*," for reasons outlined above. Further, precisely when Newman was preparing his lectures, the Oxford Parliamentary Commission of 1850 on the studies and revenues of Oxford was preparing to report (1854), followed by the reforming Oxford Act (1855), giving space for teaching the sciences and languages other than the classics. In Discourse II Newman argues that theology is a legitimate branch of knowledge and must be included in university study. Discourse III relates the study of theology to other studies on the basis that all knowledge is one and unified. Discourse IV reverses the pattern by showing how other branches of knowledge relate to theology. In Discourse V Newman turns from an account of studies to students, showing that "knowledge [is] its own end." Though a student cannot study all fields of knowledge, he is exposed to an "intellectual tradition" that encompasses the whole circle of knowledge, and from it gains a "habit of mind" characteristic of a liberal education that has "freedom, equitableness, calmness, moderation, and wisdom; or what in a former Discourse I have ventured to call a philosophical habit." The transition from passive to active learning is covered in Discourse VI, the engagement with and illumination of new ideas, and the carrying of them forward to find "their true place in the universal system." Discourse VII deals with the use of a liberal education – first how knowledge is related to "Professional Skill" (as an end in itself, not designed for material benefit), and second, how it is useful in promoting the good, as "the *instrument* of good," and hence has a moral purpose. In Discourse VIII, on "Knowledge viewed in relation to Religion," Newman distinguishes between an intellectual culture with its "Religion of Philosophy" and Christianity – and to the latter, especially under the Roman Catholic Church,

Newman turns in Discourse IX – on the "Duties of the Church towards Knowledge" – where Catholic theology is given its place in the circle of knowledge, and where "liberal education" is cautioned to make a place for it. In Discourse VIII Newman defines a gentleman: "it is almost a definition of a gentleman to say he is one who never inflicts pain.... He is mainly occupied in merely removing the obstacles which hinder the free and unembarrassed action of those about him.... The true gentleman in like manner carefully avoids whatever may cause a jar or a jolt in the minds of those with whom he is cast; — all clashing of opinion, or collision of feeling, all restraint, or suspicion, or gloom, or resentment; his great concern being to make every one at their ease and at home."

The discourses were gathered together as the first edition in 1853: *Discourses on the Scope and Nature of University Education, Addressed to the Catholics of Dublin.* The second edition (1859) contained eight discourses, compressing the first two into one, and omitting the fifth. The third edition changed the title to *The Idea of a University Defined and Illustrated* in 1873 (our text) and again separated the first two, but continued to omit the original fifth discourse, and added ten other lectures and essays, giving the whole the title by which it is still known. We give extracts from the first and sixth of ten subsections, first numbered in the third edition.

From Discourse V: "Knowledge Its Own End"

A university may be considered with reference either to its Students or to its Studies; and the principle, that all Knowledge is a whole and the separate Sciences parts of one, which I have hitherto been using in behalf of its studies, is equally important when we direct our attention to its students. Now then I turn to the students, and shall consider the education which, by virtue of this principle, a University will give them; and thus I shall be introduced, Gentlemen, to the second question, which I proposed to discuss, viz, whether and in what sense its teaching, viewed relatively to the taught, carries the attribute of Utility along with it.[1]

Notes

John Henry Newman

[1] it the question of the utility of a university education had been raised by the debates of 1808 to 1811, and were further complicated by the push for useful and secular education by the founding of the University College London (1826) by the Utilitarians under Jeremy Bentham (1748–1832).

John Henry Newman

I have said that all branches of knowledge are connected together, because the subject-matter of knowledge is intimately united in itself, as being the acts and the work of the Creator. Hence it is that the Sciences, into which our knowledge may be said to be cast, have multiplied bearings one on another, and an internal sympathy, and admit, or rather demand, comparison and adjustment. They complete, correct, balance each other. This consideration, if well-founded, must be taken into account, not only as regards the attainment of truth, which is their common end, but as regards the influence which they exercise upon those whose education consists in the study of them. I have said already, that to give undue prominence to one is to be unjust to another; to neglect or supersede these is to divert those from their proper object. It is to unsettle the boundary lines between science and science, to disturb their action, to destroy the harmony which binds them together. Such a proceeding will have a corresponding effect when introduced into a place of education. There is no science but tells a different tale, when viewed as a portion of a whole, from what it is likely to suggest when taken by itself, without the safeguard, as I may call it, of others.

Let me make use of an illustration. In the combination of colours, very different effects are produced by a difference in their selection and juxtaposition; red, green, and white, change their shades, according to the contrast to which they are submitted. And, in like manner, the drift and meaning of a branch of knowledge varies with the company in which it is introduced to the student. If his reading is confined simply to one subject, however such division of labour may favour the advancement of a particular pursuit, a point into which I do not here enter, certainly it has a tendency to contract his mind. If it is incorporated with others, it depends on those others as to the kind of influence which it exerts upon him. Thus the Classics, which in England are the means of refining the taste, have in France subserved the spread of revolutionary and deistical doctrines.[2] In Metaphysics, again, Butler's Analogy of Religion, which has had so much to do with the conversion to the Catholic faith of members of the University of Oxford, appeared to Pitt and others, who had received a different training, to operate only in the direction of infidelity.[3] And so again, Watson, Bishop of Llandaff, as I think he tells us in the narrative of his life, felt the science of Mathematics to indispose the mind to religious belief,[4] while others see in its investigations the best parallel, and thereby defence, of the Christian Mysteries.[5] In like manner, I suppose, Arcesilas would not

Notes

[2] *doctrines* in England the study of the Greek and Latin languages, literatures, philosophy, and history, that is, "the classics," was part of the curriculum of the grammar schools and the public schools in preparation for continued study at Oxford and Cambridge. It was the elitist foundation for all professions. In France, according to Newman, such study, especially of Plutarch's *Lives of the Noble Greeks and Romans*, as in the life of Brutus, prepared for revolution and free thinking that rejected the gods. Deism held that human reason and the observation of the natural world were sufficient means of showing that the universe and humans are the creatures of an intelligent being without the aid of revelation or divine intervention. This view was widespread in the seventeenth and eighteenth centuries, inaugurated by the *De Veritate* (Lat. on truth, 1624) of Lord Herbert of Cherbury (1583–1648), and expanded in Matthew Tindal's *Christianity as Old as the Creation* (1730), more or less concluding with Conyers Middleton's *Free Inquiry* (1749), though with a long fall-out of scepticism.

[3] *infidelity* Joseph Butler (1692–1752) published the *Analogy of Religion* (1736) to defend Christianity against the Deists and others. In the *Apologia* Newman argued that to him it taught of "a visible Church, the oracle of truth and a pattern of sanctity, of the duties of external religion, and of the historical character of Revelation … [and that] Probability is the guide of life." In the *Eclectic Review* (Jan. 1864), Edwin Hood (1820–85) reports that William Pitt the Younger (1759–1806) declared to William Wilberforce that "Butler's work raised more doubts in his mind than it answered"; the article also lists a number of others who felt the same way.

[4] *belief* Richard Watson (1737–1816), professor of chemistry and divinity at Cambridge, wrote *Anecdotes of the Life of Richard Watson … Written by Himself* (1817).

[5] *Mysteries* biblical events and Christian beliefs that are not easily susceptible to rational argument, such as the doctrine of the Trinity; also the Christian sacraments.

have handled logic as Aristotle, nor Aristotle have criticized poets as Plato;[6] yet reasoning and poetry are subject to scientific rules.

It is a great point then to enlarge the range of studies which a University professes, even for the sake of the students; and, though they cannot pursue every subject which is open to them, they will be the gainers by living among those and under those who represent the whole circle. This I conceive to be the advantage of a seat of universal learning, considered as a place of education. An assemblage of learned men, zealous for their own sciences, and rivals of each other, are brought, by familiar intercourse and for the sake of intellectual peace, to adjust together the claims and relations of their respective subjects of investigation. They learn to respect, to consult, to aid each other. Thus is created a pure and clear atmosphere of thought, which the student also breathes, though in his own case he only pursues a few sciences out of the multitude. He profits by an intellectual tradition, which is independent of particular teachers, which guides him in his choice of subjects, and duly interprets for him those which he chooses. He apprehends the great outlines of knowledge, the principles on which it rests, the scale of its parts, its lights and its shades, its great points and its little, as he otherwise cannot apprehend them. Hence it is that his education is called "Liberal." A habit of mind is formed which lasts through life, of which the attributes are, freedom, equitableness, calmness, moderation, and wisdom; or what in a former discourse I have ventured to call a philosophical habit.[7] This then I would assign as the special fruit of the education furnished at a University, as contrasted with other places of teaching or modes of teaching. This is the main purpose of a University in its treatment of its students....

6

Now bear with me, Gentlemen, if what I am about to say, has at first sight a fanciful appearance. Philosophy, then, or Science, is related to Knowledge in this way:— Knowledge is called by the name of Science or Philosophy, when it is acted upon, informed, or if I may use a strong figure, impregnated by Reason. Reason is the principle of that intrinsic fecundity of Knowledge, which, to those who possess it, is its especial value, and which dispenses with the necessity of their looking abroad for any end to rest upon external to itself. Knowledge, indeed, when thus exalted into a scientific form, is also power;[8] not only is it excellent in itself, but whatever such excellence may be, it is something more, it has a result beyond itself. Doubtless; but that is a further consideration, with which I am not concerned. I only say that, prior to its being a power, it is a good; that it is, not only an instrument, but an end. I know well it may resolve itself into

Notes

[6] *Arcesilas ... Plato* Arcesilas(316–242 BCE), a noted sceptic and so opposed to Aristotle's teaching of the certainty of knowledge, was the head of the academy in Athens; Aristotle dealt favourably with poets in *On Poetry*, praising them for aesthetic qualities, while Plato assessed poets on moral grounds: poets should be praised and then exiled from the ideal state because they do not tell the truth (*Republic* 10).

[7] *Liberal ... habit* (<Lat. *liberalis* of or relating to a free man; < *liber* free; see *OED* A. 1: "originally, the distinctive epithet of those 'arts,' or 'sciences' that were considered 'worthy of a free man'; opposed to *servile* or *mechanical*. In later use, of condition, pursuits, occupations: Pertaining to or suitable to persons of superior social station; 'becoming a gentleman.'" The discussion of a philosophical habit is in Discourse III, sect. 4. In Part V of the *Apologia* Newman had given a completely different treatment of "Liberal," referring to those holding views opposed to the evangelicals and generally supporting the Broad Church around the time of the first Reform Bill, and believing that the Bible, though divinely inspired, was not literally true, that it should be read using all the resources of secular knowledge, including the use of myth, metaphor and other literary studies, archaeology, and science: see RELIGION: RELIGIOUS FAITH; CONYBEARE (WEB p. 197).

[8] *knowledge ... power* the phrase "knowledge is power" is often ascribed to Francis Bacon in its Latin version, *scientia potentia est*, though it has not been located in his writings. Instead it is found with a different meaning in Thomas Hobbes's *De Homine* (1658, on man): *scientia potentia est, sed parva* (Lat. knowledge is power, but a small power).

John Henry Newman

an art, and terminate in a mechanical process, and in tangible fruit; but it also may fall back upon that Reason which informs it, and resolve itself into Philosophy. In one case it is called Useful Knowledge,[9] in the other Liberal. The same person may cultivate it in both ways at once; but this again is a matter foreign to my subject; here I do but say that there are two ways of using Knowledge, and in matter of fact those who use it in one way are not likely to use it in the other, or at least in a very limited measure. You see, then, here are two methods of Education; the end of the one is to be philosophical, of the other to be mechanical; the one rises towards general ideas, the other is exhausted upon what is particular and external. Let me not be thought to deny the necessity, or to decry the benefit, of such attention to what is particular and practical, as belongs to the useful or mechanical arts; life could not go on without them; we owe our daily welfare to them; their exercise is the duty of the many, and we owe to the many a debt of gratitude for fulfilling that duty. I only say that Knowledge, in proportion as it tends more and more to be particular, ceases to be Knowledge. It is a question whether Knowledge can in any proper sense be predicated of the brute creation; without pretending to metaphysical exactness of phraseology, which would be unsuitable to an occasion like this, I say, it seems to me improper to call that passive sensation, or perception of things, which brutes seem to possess, by the name of Knowledge. When I speak of Knowledge, I mean something intellectual, something which grasps what it perceives through the senses; something which takes a view of things; which sees more than the senses convey; which reasons upon what it sees, and while it sees; which invests it with an idea. It expresses itself, not in a mere enunciation, but by an enthymeme:[10] it is of the nature of science from the first, and in this consists its dignity. The principle of real dignity in Knowledge, its worth, its desirableness, considered irrespectively of its results, is this germ within it of a scientific or a philosophical process. This is how it comes to be an end in itself; this is why it admits of being called Liberal. Not to know the relative disposition of things is the state of slaves or children; to have mapped out the Universe is the boast, or at least the ambition, of Philosophy.

Moreover, such knowledge is not a mere extrinsic or accidental advantage, which is ours to-day and another's to-morrow, which may be got up from a book, and easily forgotten again, which we can command or communicate at our pleasure, which we can borrow for the occasion, carry about in our hand, and take into the market; it is an acquired illumination, it is a habit, a personal possession, and an inward endowment. And this is the reason, why it is more correct, as well as more usual, to speak of a University as a place of education, than of instruction, though, when knowledge is concerned, instruction would at first sight have seemed the more appropriate word. We are instructed, for instance, in manual exercises, in the fine and useful arts, in trades, and in ways of business; for these are methods, which have little or no effect upon the mind itself, are contained in rules committed to memory, to tradition, or to use, and bear upon an end external to themselves. But education is a higher word; it implies an action upon our mental nature, and the formation of a character; it is something individual and permanent, and is commonly spoken of in connexion with religion and virtue. When, then, we speak of the communication of Knowledge as

Notes

9 *useful knowledge* the Society for the Diffusion of Useful Knowledge, founded in 1828 by Lord Brougham (1778–1868), and terminated in 1848, was associated with University College London and with the Mechanics Institutes. It published inexpensive books and booklets of instruction, chiefly about science, for working- and lower middle-class readers. It also circulated various weeklies, such as the *Penny Magazine* and *Penny Cyclopaedia*.

10 *enthymeme* an abbreviated form of argument in which one premise is followed by a conclusion: for instance, "Because he was an Irish Catholic, he was excluded from Trinity College, Dublin," an enthymeme omitting the major premise: "All Irish Catholics were excluded from Trinity College, Dublin."

being Education, we thereby really imply that that Knowledge is a state or condition of mind; and since cultivation of mind is surely worth seeking for its own sake, we are thus brought once more to the conclusion, which the word "Liberal" and the word "Philosophy" have already suggested, that there is a Knowledge, which is desirable, though nothing come of it, as being of itself a treasure, and a sufficient remuneration of years of labour.

From Discourse VII: "Knowledge Viewed in Relation to Professional Skill"[11]

1

I have been insisting, in my two preceding Discourses, first, on the cultivation of the intellect, as an end which may reasonably be pursued for its own sake; and next, on the nature of that cultivation, or what that cultivation consists in. Truth of whatever kind is the proper object of the intellect; its cultivation then lies in fitting it to apprehend and contemplate truth. Now the intellect in its present state, with exceptions which need not here be specified, does not discern truth intuitively, or as a whole. We know, not by a direct and simple vision, not at a glance, but, as it were, by piecemeal and accumulation, by a mental process, by going round an object, by the comparison, the combination, the mutual correction, the continual adaptation, of many partial notions, by the employment, concentration, and joint action of many faculties and exercises of mind. Such a union and concert of the intellectual powers, such an enlargement and development, such a comprehensiveness, is necessarily a matter of training. And again, such a training is a matter of rule; it is not mere application, however exemplary, which introduces the mind to truth, nor the reading many books, nor the getting up many subjects, nor the witnessing many experiments, nor the attending many lectures. All this is short of enough; a man may have done it all, yet be lingering in the vestibule of knowledge:—he may not realize what his mouth utters; he may not see with his mental eye what confronts him; he may have no grasp of things as they are; or at least he may have no power at all of advancing one step forward of himself, in consequence of what he has already acquired, no power of discriminating between truth and falsehood, of sifting out the grains of truth from the mass, of arranging things according to their real value, and, if I may use the phrase, of building up ideas. Such a power is the result of a scientific formation of mind; it is an acquired faculty of judgment, of clear-sightedness, of sagacity, of wisdom, of philosophical reach of mind, and of intellectual self-possession and repose,—qualities which do not come of mere acquirement. The bodily eye, the organ for apprehending material objects, is provided by nature; the eye of the mind, of which the object is truth, is the work of discipline and habit.

This process of training, by which the intellect, instead of being formed or sacrificed to some particular or accidental purpose, some specific trade or profession, or study or science, is disciplined for its own sake, for the perception of its own proper object, and for its own highest culture, is called Liberal Education; and though there is no one in whom it is carried as far as is conceivable, or whose intellect would be a pattern of what intellects should be made, yet there is scarcely any one but may gain an idea of what real training is, and at least look towards it, and make its true scope and result, not something else, his standard of excellence; and numbers there are who may

Notes

[11] *title* originally Discourse VIII; see headnote.

submit themselves to it, and secure it to themselves in good measure. And to set forth the right standard, and to train according to it, and to help forward all students towards it according to their various capacities, this I conceive to be the business of a University. . . .

6

You will see what I mean by the parallel of bodily health. Health is a good in itself, though nothing came of it, and is especially worth seeking and cherishing; yet, after all, the blessings which attend its presence are so great, while they are so close to it and so redound back upon it and encircle it, that we never think of it except as useful as well as good, and praise and prize it for what it does, as well as for what it is, though at the same time we cannot point out any definite and distinct work or production which it can be said to effect. And so as regards intellectual culture, I am far from denying utility in this large sense as the end of Education, when I lay it down, that the culture of the intellect is a good in itself and its own end; I do not exclude from the idea of intellectual culture what it cannot but be, from the very nature of things; I only deny that we must be able to point out, before we have any right to call it useful, some art, or business, or profession, or trade, or work, as resulting from it, and as its real and complete end. The parallel is exact:—As the body may be sacrificed to some manual or other toil, whether moderate or oppressive, so may the intellect be devoted to some specific profession; and I do not call *this* the culture of the intellect. Again, as some member or organ of the body may be inordinately used and developed, so may memory, or imagination, or the reasoning faculty; and *this* again is not intellectual culture. On the other hand, as the body may be tended, cherished, and exercised with a simple view to its general health, so may the intellect also be generally exercised in order to its perfect state; and this *is* its cultivation.

Again, as health ought to precede labour of the body, and as a man in health can do what an unhealthy man cannot do, and as of this health the properties are strength, energy, agility, graceful carriage and action, manual dexterity, and endurance of fatigue, so in like manner general culture of mind is the best aid to professional and scientific study, and educated men can do what illiterate cannot; and the man who has learned to think and to reason and to compare and to discriminate and to analyze, who has refined his taste, and formed his judgment, and sharpened his mental vision, will not indeed at once be a lawyer, or a pleader, or an orator, or a statesman, or a physician, or a good landlord, or a man of business, or a soldier, or an engineer, or a chemist, or a geologist, or an antiquarian, but he will be placed in that state of intellect in which he can take up any one of the sciences or callings I have referred to, or any other for which he has a taste or special talent, with an ease, a grace, a versatility, and a success, to which another is a stranger. In this sense then, and as yet I have said but a very few words on a large subject, mental culture is emphatically *useful*.

If then I am arguing, and shall argue, against Professional or Scientific knowledge as the sufficient end of a University Education, let me not be supposed, Gentlemen, to be disrespectful towards particular studies, or arts, or vocations, and those who are engaged in them. In saying that Law or Medicine is not the end of a University course, I do not mean to imply that the University does not teach Law or Medicine. What indeed can it teach at all, if it does not teach something particular? It teaches *all* knowledge by teaching all *branches* of knowledge, and in no other way. I do but say that there will be this distinction as regards a Professor of Law, or of Medicine, or of Geology, or of Political Economy, in a University and out of it, that out of a University he is in danger of being absorbed and narrowed by his pursuit, and of giving Lectures which are the Lectures of nothing more than a lawyer, physician, geologist, or political economist; whereas in a University he will just know where he and his science stand, he has come to it, as it were, from a height, he has taken a survey of all knowledge, he is kept from extravagance by the very rivalry of other studies, he has gained from them a special illumination and largeness of mind and freedom and self-possession, and he treats his own in consequence with a philosophy and a resource, which belongs not to the study itself, but to his liberal education.

This then is how I should solve the fallacy, for so I must call it, by which Locke[12] and his disciples would frighten us from cultivating the intellect, under the notion that no education is useful which does not teach us some temporal calling, or some mechanical art, or some physical secret. I say that a cultivated intellect, because it is a good in itself, brings with it a power and a grace to every work and occupation which it undertakes, and enables us to be more useful, and to a greater number. There is a duty we owe to human society as such, to the state to which we belong, to the sphere in which we move,[13] to the individuals towards whom we are variously related, and whom we successively encounter in life; and that philosophical or liberal education, as I have called it, which is the proper function of a University, if it refuses the foremost place to professional interests, does but postpone them to the formation of the citizen, and, while it subserves the larger interests of philanthropy, prepares also for the successful prosecution of those merely personal objects, which at first sight it seems to disparage.

William Barnes (1801–86)

Barnes lived almost his whole life in Dorsetshire in the rural west of England. A teacher, philologist, and Anglican clergyman, he took his divinity degree at St John's College, Cambridge, was fluent in Latin, Greek, and a number of European and Asiatic languages, and incorporated this knowledge in *A Philological Grammar* (1854), a *Glossary of Dorset Dialect* (1863), and other philological works. In 1861 he was awarded a civil list pension of £70 and the next year his financial position became secure on becoming the rector of Winterborne Came, a village 3 kilometres south of Dorchester. He was a friend of Alfred Tennyson, Thomas Hardy (who edited *Select Poems of William Barnes*, 1908), and Gerard Manley Hopkins, who wrote, "he is a perfect artist and of a most spontaneous inspiration; it is as if Dorset life and Dorset landscape had taken flesh and tongue in the man." Barnes experimented with a number of ways of printing his poems to show the way the Dorset dialect deployed diphthongs, sometimes with a dieresis (¨) over a letter, sometimes by printing a double vowel without a dieresis. For instance, the word "orchard" in the title to first poem is spelled "Orchet" (1859) and "Orcha'd" (1862). Conventional orthographic ways of writing the Dorset dialect for Barnes include the suffix *èn* for *ing*; the diphthong *eä* for *a*; *v* for *f*; *au* for *o*; and *z* for the initial *s*. Barnes published three collections of *Poems of Rural Life in the Dorset Dialect* (1844, 1859, 1862), recording a disappearing culture and way of speaking. Standard edition: *The Poems of William Barnes*, ed. Bernard Jones (2 vols,1962); James W. Parins, *William Barnes* (1984). The William Barnes Society: www.william-barnes-society.org.uk.

Notes

[12] *Locke* Locke argued against education for its own sake and in favour of producing individuals to conform to their social and economic environment. For instance, in *Some Thoughts Concerning Education* (1693), he argued, "The busy inclination of children being always to be directed to something that may be useful to them, the advantages proposed from what they are set about may be considered of two kinds: 1. Where the skill itself that is got by exercise is worth the having. Thus skill not only in languages and learned sciences, but in painting, turning, gardening, tempering and working in iron, and all other useful arts is worth the having. 2. Where the exercise itself, without any consideration, is necessary or useful for health" (sect. 202).

[13] *move* see Acts 17: 28.

My Orchet in Linden Lea[1]

'Ithin° the woodlands, flow'ry gleäded,°   °within; °gladed
 By the woak° tree's mossy moot,°   °oak °base of tree-trunk
The sheenèn° grass-bleädes, timber-sheäded,   °shining
 Now do quiver under voot°;   °foot
An' birds do whissle auver head,   5
An' water's bubblèn in its bed,
An' there vor me the apple tree
Do leän down low in Linden Lea.

When leaves that leätely wer a-springèn
 Now do feäde 'ithin the copse,   10
An' païnted birds do hush ther zingèn
 Up upon the timber's tops;
An' brown-leav'd fruit's a-turnèn red,
In cloudless zunsheen, auver head,
Wi' fruit vor me, the apple tree   15
Do leän down low in Linden Lea.

Let other vo'k meäke money vaster
 In the aïr o' dark-room'd towns,
I don't dread a peevish meäster;
 Though noo man do heed my frowns,   20
I be free to goo abrode,
Or teäke ageän my hwomeward road
To where, vor me, the apple tree
Do leän down low in Linden Lea.

Childhood[2]

Aye, at that time our days wer but vew,
An' our lim's wer but small, and a-growèn ;
An' then the feäir worold wer new,
An' life wer all hopevul an' gaÿ;
An' the times o' the sproutèn o' leaves,   5
An' the cheäk-burnèn seasons o' mowèn,
An' bindèn o' red-headed sheaves,
Wer all welcome seasons o' jaÿ.

Then the housen seem'd high that be low,
An' the brook did seem wide that is narrow,   10

Notes

WILLIAM BARNES

[1] *title* the poem was set to music as a song for voice and orchestra by Ralph Vaughan Williams (1872–1958), English composer, as "Linden Lea" (1901), his first publication. The poem was first published in the *Dorset County Chronicle* (20 Nov. 1856); our text: *Hwomely Rhymes: A Second Collection of Poems in the Dorset Dialect* (1859).

[2] *title* Hardy's selection prints only the first two stanzas. It was first published in the *Dorset County Chronicle* (1 Apr. 1858); our text: *Hwomely Rhymes: A Second Collection of Poems in the Dorset Dialect* (1859).

An' time that do vlee did goo slow,
An' veelèns° now feeble wer strong,   °feelings, emotions
An' our worold did end wi' the neämes
Ov the Sha'sbury Hill or Bulbarrow;³
An' life did seem only the geämes   15
That we plaÿ'd as the days roll'd along.

Then the rivers an' high-timber'd lands,
An' the zilvery hills, 'ithout buyèn,
Seem'd all comèn into our hands
Vrom others that own'd em avore;   20
An' all zickness, an' sorra, an' need,
Seem'd to die wi' the wold vo'k a-dyèn,
An' leave us vor ever a-freed
Vrom evils our forefaethers bore.

But happy be childern the while   25
They have elders a-livèn to love em,
An' teäke all the wearisome twile
That zome hands or other mus' do;
Lik' the low-headed shrubs that be warm,
In the lewth o' the trees up above 'em,   30
A-screen'd vrom the cwold blowèn storm
That the timber avore 'em mus' rue.

The Wife a-Lost⁴

Since I noo mwore do zee your feäce;
    Up steäirs or down below,
I'll zit me in the lwonesome pleäce,
    Where flat-bough'd beech do grow:
Below the beeches' bough, my love,   5
    Were you did never come
An' I don't look to meet ye now
    As I do look at hwome.

Since you noo mwore be at my zide,
    In walks in zummer het,   10
I'll goo alwone where mist do ride,
    Droo° trees a-drippèn wet: °through

Notes

³ *Sha'sbury ... Bulbarrow* Shaftesbury is a Dorset town 32 kilometres west of Salisbury, inhabited from Anglo-Saxon times. The town is now famous for the steep and cobbled Gold Hill (or Shaftesbury Hill), overlooking Blackmore Vale where Barnes was born. Bulbarrow Hill, 16 kilometres north of Dorchester, also overlooks Blackmore Vale, and is the site of an iron-age hill fort and a number of prehistoric burial barrows or mounds.

⁴ *title* written after the death of his wife, Julia Miles (1805–52), whom he had first seen in 1818 and married in 1827; to the end of his life, Barnes completed his diary entry each day with her name in Italian, "Giulia." First published in the *Dorset County Chronicle* (12 Aug. 1858); our text: *Hwomely Rhymes: A Second Collection of Poems in the Dorset Dialect* (1859).

Below the raïn-wet bough, my love,
    Where you did never come,
An' I don't grieve to miss ye now,   15
    As I do grieve at hwome.

Since now bezide my dinner-bwoard
    Your vaïce do never sound,
I'll eat the bit I can avword,°   °afford
    A-vield° upon the ground;   °in the field   20
Below the darksome bough, my love,
    Where you did never dine,
An' I don't grieve to miss ye now,
    As I at hwome do pine.

Since I do miss your vaïce an' feäce   25
    In praÿer at eventide,
I'll praÿ wi' oone sad vaïce vor greäce°   °one sad voice for grace
    To goo where you do bide;
Above the tree an' bough, my love,
    Where you be gone avore,
An' be a-waïtèn vor me now,   30
    To come vor evermwore.

Zummer An' Winter[5]

When I led by zummer streams
    The pride o' Lea, as naïghbours thought her,
While the zun, wi' evenèn beams,
    Did cast our sheädes athirt the water;
        Winds a-blowèn,   5
        Streams a-flowèn,
        Skies a-glowèn,
Tokens ov my jaÿ zoo fleetèn,°   °joy so fleeting
Heighten'd it, that happy meetèn.

Then, when maïd an' man took pleäces,   10
    Gaÿ in winter's Chris'mas dances,
Showèn in their merry feäces
    Kindly smiles an' glisnèn glances;
        Stars a-winkèn,
        Day a-shrinkèn,
        Sheädes a-zinkèn,   15
Brought anew the happy meetèn,
That did meäke the night too fleetèn.

Notes

[5] title our text: *Poems of Rural Life in the Dorset Dialect* (third collection, 1862).

From "Old Bardic Poetry" [Two Translations from the Welsh] in *Macmillan's Magazine* (Aug. 1867).

I   Cynddyl'an's Hall[6]

Cynddyl'an's hall is all in gloom—to-night;
No fire, no lighted room:
Amid the stillness of a tomb.

Cynddyl'an's hall is left alone—to-night
A hall with none to own.   5
O Death, take me where he is flown.

Cynddyl'an's hall is now unblest—to-night;
On Hydwyrth's rocky crest
No lord is there, no meal, no guest.

Cynddyl'an's hall! It makes me wan   10
To see cold hearths, and roofing gone.
My lord is dead, and I live on!

Cynddyl'an's hall is sad within—to-night;
For sons of Cyndrwyn,
Cynon, Gwion, and Gwyn.[7]   15

Notes

[6] *title* in a twelve-page article Barnes explains various Old Welsh poetic forms, interlacing his prose explanations with his translations. Barnes did not include these translated fragments in any of his collections. This translation is from an elegy attributed to the medieval prince, warrior, and poet Llywarch Hên (Old Welsh: Llywarch the Old), who lived in the sixth century in Wales and in the kingdom of Rheged in northern England. Various poems, some as late as the ninth century, are attributed to him, as well as a lost saga about his life. Barnes translates five of the sixteen stanzas (numbers 20, 23, 24, 27, and 32) of the *Canu Heledd* (Old Welsh: song of Heledd; one of the daughters of Cynddyl'an), concerning the death of Cynddyl'an and the destruction of his hall. Cynddyl'an ap Cyndrwyn (Cynddylan, son of Cyndrwyn) was a late sixth and early seventh century chieftain or prince of Pengwern in modern north Shropshire, who fought in the battle of Maserfield against the Saxons under Oswald of Northumbria (*c.*604–42), who died in the fray. Cynddyl'an was slain in defending Tren, his father's stronghold near Chester, by Oswald's brother, Oswi, who also destroyed the hall at Pengwern, commemorated in the poem.

Barnes calls this verse form, one of the earliest forms of British verse, "the warrior's triplet" (Old Welsh, *triban*

milwr), a "verse of three lines, each of seven or eight syllables, and all ending with syllables of one rhyme," in this case with a "mid-point word," "to-night" (Old Welsh *heno*) at the end of the first line of each stanza.

Barnes explains the form of the verses: "The poem on Cynddyl'an is of many strains [groups of stanzas], each of which is of more or fewer triplets on the same head [topic]; as on the hero, on his fallen palace, or on Pengwern, the field of battle: and almost every triplet begins with a *cymmeriad* (resumption) of the same word or thought, as a verse-head. The triplets on Cynddyl'an begin with his name, and those on his hall begin with 'The Hall of Cynddyl'an,' 'Ystavell Cynddyl'an.' The strain on the hall of Cynddyl'an is of triplets of a very sad cast:—

[quotes the 5 stanzas, as above].…

It may be seen that the above-quoted triplets have a special form. In that which begins with a *cymmeriad* in the words 'Cynddyl'an's Hall,' ('Ystavell Cynddyl'an'), and others, each takes after the first measure of the first line the word 'to-night' (*heno*); and thus the triplet shows the beginning of the form of verse called the Englyn, which is the form of the Welsh epigram."

[7] *Cynon … Gwyn* three brothers of Cynddyl'an.

II   An Englyn on a Yellow Greyhound[8]

Hound yellow, light of tread—the cunning foe
Of deer bedappled red;
He of the wind[9] gets not ahead,
Nor yet is by the wind outsped.

Harriet Martineau (1802–76)

Born in Norwich as the sixth of eight children, Martineau had a difficult childhood in the household of the cloth manufacturer Thomas Martineau (1764–1826) and his clever but formidable wife, Elizabeth Rankin (1770–1848). The family was of Huguenot descent and Unitarian. Harriet was sickly and isolated but had a good education. After her father's business failed (1825–29), she was thrown upon writing as a profession and became one of the most prodigious writers of her time, producing thirty-five books and hundreds of essays on philosophy, theology, sociology, travel literature, reviews of contemporary writing, education, abolition, and feminist causes. She moved to London in 1832 and enjoyed a wide literary circle that included Elizabeth Barrett, Charlotte Brontë, Edward Bulwer-Lytton, Thomas Carlyle, George Eliot, Thomas Malthus, John Stuart Mill, Harriet Taylor, Monckton Milnes, Florence Nightingale, and Sydney Smith. In the same year she began to publish *Illustrations of Political Economy*, a series of twenty-three tales appearing monthly to great success, followed by other publications welcomed by both Radicals and Whigs in the legislation following the Reform Bill of 1832, *Poor Laws and Paupers Illustrated* (1833) and *Illustrations of Taxation* (1834). Enabled by her royalties to travel, she spent two years in the United States (1834–36) and from the experience wrote two books, *Society in America* (1837) and the more popular *Retrospect of Western Travel* (1838), the two earning her £1,500. She moved on to other fields, publishing a novel, *Deerbrook* (1839), and a number of books on mesmerism. She became sick with an ovarian tumor (1839) and retired to a sick-bed for five years, claiming an eventual cure by mesmerism in letters to the *Athenæum* (Nov. and Dec. 1844). She toured Egypt and the Near East (1846–47) and published *Eastern Life: Present and Past* (1848). Increasingly interested in Positivism, she translated Auguste Comte's *Cours de philosophie positive* as *The Positivist Philosophy of Auguste Comte* (1853). Settling in the Lake District at Ambleside she wrote a guide to the Lakes and more than 1,600 lead editorials

Notes

[8] *title* this poem is translated from the *Englyn i Vilgi Melyn* (Old Welsh) in Edward Jones's *Musical and Poetical Relicks of the Welsh Bards* (1794). Barnes explains this poetic form: "The Englyn is a verse of four lines, with four fellow-rhymes.... It is of several forms; sometimes of four lines of even measure, though a more skilful, and not less common, form has the first line of ten syllables, the next of six, and the other two of seven. The first two lines, called the shaft (*paladr*), as of an arrow, has in it a rhyme-point for the other lines, and, beyond the rhyme-point, two or four syllables ending with the so-called 'cyrch' or mid-point word, as in the word 'heno' (to-night) in the triplets of Llywarch [for Llywarch, see n. 6]. The following has the form of an Englyn and gives nearly the substance of an Englyn of late time, on a 'Yellow Greyhound.' [he gives poem as above]. . .

The two lines down to 'red' are the shaft, and the other two are the head or wings, 'esgyll' (feathers), as of the arrow. Here 'tread' is the main-word to which the other lines rhyme."

Barnes follows this scheme carefully in his English translation of the Old Welsh:

Nôdyn, Ci melyn cymalau,° gwiw-lwybr	° joints, legs, tread
Gelyn bŷdd brŷcb-winau;°	° brown, red
Nid cynt yw na gwynt yn gwau,°	° ahead
Nid yw'r gwynt gynt nag yntau.°	° faster, sped)

The Welsh shows the rhyme-point as "cymalau," picked up in the final rhyme words of the three ensuing lines.

[9] *wind* "i.e. the wind with the scent" [author's note].

for the *Daily News* besides continuing to work on her *Autobiography* (1877), a candid account of spiritual and philosophical development, of living with myriad physical disabilities, and of the trials of a professional writer. Standard Editions: *Autobiography*, ed. Linda H. Peterson (2007); *The Collected Letters of Harriet Martineau*, ed. Deborah A. Logan (5 vols, 2007); *Harriet Martineau: Further Letters*, ed. Deborah A. Logan (2012); R. K. Webb, *Harriet Martineau: A Radical Victorian* (1960). Martineau Society: www.martineausociety.co.uk.

Society in America (1837)

From Chapter 3: "Morals of Politics"

Section VI: "Citizenship of People of Colour"[1]

Before I entered New England, while I was ascending the Mississippi, I was told by a Boston gentleman that the people of colour in the New England States were perfectly well-treated; that the children were educated in schools provided for them; and that their fathers freely exercised the franchise.[2] This gentleman certainly believed he was telling me the truth. That he, a busy citizen of Boston, should know no better, is now as striking an exemplification of the state of the case to me as a correct representation of the facts would have been. There are two causes for his mistake. He was not aware that the schools for the coloured children in New England are, unless they escape by their insignificance, shut up, or pulled down, or the school-house wheeled away upon rollers over the frontier of a pious State, which will not endure that its coloured citizens should be educated. He was not aware of a gentleman of colour, and his family, being locked out of their own hired pew in a church, because their white brethren will not worship by their side. But I will not proceed with an enumeration of injuries, too familiar to Americans to excite any feeling but that of weariness; and too disgusting to all others to be endured. The other cause of this gentleman's mistake was, that he did not, from long custom, feel some things to be injuries, which he would call anything but good treatment, if he had to bear them himself. Would he think it good treatment to be forbidden to eat with fellow-citizens; to be assigned to a particular gallery in his church; to be excluded from college, from municipal office, from professions, from scientific and literary associations? If he felt himself excluded from every department of society, but its humiliations and its drudgery, would he declare himself to be "perfectly well-treated in Boston?" Not a word more of statement is needed.

A Connecticut judge lately declared on the bench that he believed people of colour were not considered citizens in the laws. He was proved to be wrong. He was actually ignorant of the wording of the acts by which people of colour are termed citizens. Of course, no judge could have forgotten this who had seen them treated as citizens: nor could one of the most eminent statesmen and lawyers in the country have told me that it is still a doubt, in the minds of some high authorities, whether people of colour are citizens. He is as mistaken

Notes

HARRIET MARTINEAU

[1] *title* the enormous success of the monthly copies of *Illustrations of Political Economy*, (1832–34) as many as 10,000 a month in its last year, made it possible for Martineau to travel to the United States in 1834 where she remained for two years. On the way there, she outlined her forthcoming procedures in one of the earliest studies of sociology, *How to Observe Morals and Manners* (1838). She travelled extensively, from New York through the central American states, through the south to Mississippi and Virginia, with longer stays in Philadelphia, Baltimore, Washington, and Boston, ending with New England, Detroit, and Chicago.

[2] *franchise* Martineau was a strong advocate of abolition, supporting the radical position led by William Lloyd Garrison (1805–79), editor of the abolitionist newspaper, *The Liberator*. She also reports on the prejudice and bigotry that she found in the northern states.

as the judge. There has been no such doubt since the Connecticut judge was corrected and enlightened. The error of the statesman arose from the same cause; he had never seen the coloured people treated as citizens. "In fact," said he, "these people hold an anomalous situation. They are protected as citizens when the public service requires their security; but not otherwise treated as such." Any comment would weaken this intrepid statement.

The common argument, about the inferiority of the coloured race, bears no relation whatever to this question. They are citizens. They stand, as such, in the law, and in the acknowledgment of every one who knows the law. They are citizens, yet their houses and schools are pulled down, and they can obtain no remedy at law. . . .

While the mass of common men and women are despising, and disliking, and fearing, and keeping down the coloured race, blinking the fact that they are citizens, the few of Nature's aristocracy are putting forth a strong hand to lift up this degraded race out of oppression, and their country from the reproach of it. If they were but one or two, trembling and toiling in solitary energy, the world afar, would be confident of their success. But they number hundreds and thousands; and if ever they feel a passing doubt of their progress, it is only because they are pressed upon by the meaner multitude. Over the sea, no one doubts of their victory. It is as certain as that the risen sun will reach the meridian. Already are there overflowing colleges, where no distinction of colour is allowed;—overflowing, *because* no distinction of colour is allowed. Already have people of colour crossed the thresholds of many whites, as guests, not as drudges or beggars. Already are they admitted to worship, and to exercise charity, among the whites.

The world has heard and seen enough of the reproach incurred by America, on account of her coloured population. It is now time to look for the fairer side. The crescent streak is brightening towards the full, to wane no more. Already is the world beyond the sea beginning to think of America, less as the country of the double-faced pretender to the name of Liberty, than as the home of the single-hearted, clear-eyed Presence which, under the name of Abolitionism, is majestically passing through the land which is soon to be her throne.

Section VII: "Political Non-Existence of Women"

One of the fundamental principles announced in the Declaration of Independence is, that governments derive their just powers from the consent of the governed.[3] How can the political condition of women be reconciled with this?

Governments in the United States have power to tax women who hold property; to divorce them from their husbands; to fine, imprison, and execute them for certain offences. Whence do these governments derive their powers? They are not "just," as they are not derived from the consent of the women thus governed.

Governments in the United States have power to enslave certain women; and also to punish other women for inhuman treatment of such slaves. Neither of these powers are "just"; not being derived from the consent of the governed.

Governments decree to women in some States half their husbands' property; in others one-third. In some, a woman, on her marriage, is made to yield all her property to her husband; in others, to retain a portion, or the whole, in her own hands. Whence do governments derive the unjust power of thus disposing of property without the consent of the governed?

The democratic principle condemns all this as wrong; and requires the equal political representation of all rational beings. Children, idiots, and criminals,[4] during the season of sequestration, are the only fair exceptions.

Notes

[3] *governed* passed on 4 July 1776, the Declaration stated that the thirteen states were independent of Great Britain: "Governments are instituted among Men, deriving their just powers from the consent of the governed."

[4] *criminals* categories of persons legally incompetent under English law; a famous phrase referring to those excluded from the franchise, referred to an 1868 article, "Criminals, Idiots, Women, and Minors," by Frances Power Cobbe

The case is so plain that I might close it here; but it is interesting to inquire how so obvious a decision has been so evaded as to leave to women no political rights whatever. The question has been asked, from time to time, in more countries than one, how obedience to the laws can be required of women, when no woman has, either actually or virtually, given any assent to any law. No plausible answer has, as far as I can discover, been offered; for the good reason, that no plausible answer can be devised. The most principled democratic writers on government have on this subject sunk into fallacies, as disgraceful as any advocate of despotism has adduced. In fact, they have thus sunk from being, for the moment, advocates of despotism. Jefferson in America, and James Mill at home, subside, for the occasion, to the level of the author of the Emperor of Russia's Catechism for the young Poles[5]. . . .

The truth is, that while there is much said about "the sphere of woman,"[6] two widely different notions are entertained of what is meant by the phrase. The narrow, and, to the ruling party, the more convenient notion is that sphere appointed by men, and bounded by their ideas of propriety;—a notion from which any and every woman may fairly dissent The broad and true conception is of the sphere appointed by God, and bounded by the powers which he has bestowed. This commands the assent of man and woman; and only the question of powers remains to be proved. That woman has power to represent her own interests, no one can deny till she has been tried. The modes need not be discussed here: they must vary with circumstances. The fearful and absurd images which are perpetually called up to perplex the question,—images of women on wool-sacks in England, and under canopies in America,[7] have nothing to do with the matter. The principle being once established, the methods will follow, easily, naturally, and under a remarkable transmutation of the ludicrous into the sublime. The kings of Europe would have laughed mightily, two centuries ago, at the idea of a commoner, without robes, crown, or sceptre, stepping into the throne of a strong nation. Yet who dared to laugh when Washington's[8] super-royal voice greeted the New World from the presidential chair, and the old world stood still to catch the echo?

The principle of the equal rights of both halves of the human race is all we have to do with here. It is the true democratic principle which can never be seriously controverted, and only for a short time evaded. Governments can derive their just powers only from the consent of the governed.

Notes

(*Fraser's Magazine*, Dec. 1868), one year after women were excluded from the Reform Bill of 1867 (see MILL, n. 18).

[5] *Jefferson . . . Poles* Thomas Jefferson (1743–1826) was one of the founders of the United States of America, the drafter of the Declaration of Independence, and the third president of the United States. Martineau cites Jefferson's letter of 5 September 1816 to Samuel Kercheval: "Were our State a pure democracy . . . there would yet be excluded from their deliberations . . . women, who, to prevent depravation of morals, and ambiguity of issue, could not mix promiscuously in the public meetings of men." James Mill (1773–1836), British Utilitarian philosopher, was the author of an essay on "Government" for the *Encyclopædia Britannica* (1820) and also *Essays on Government, Jurisprudence, Liberty of the Press, Education, and Prisons and Prison Discipline* (1823), in which he moved from the British Radicals' support of absolute freedom and equality according to the early ideals of the French Revolution to principles closer to the Whigs under which the extension of the franchise (as in the Reform Act of 1832) would guarantee social stability and good government. After the Congress of Vienna (1815), Poland increasingly fell under the domination of Russia,

eventually disregarding the constitution under a viceroy, Grand Duke Constantine Pavlovich (1779–1831). The "Cadet Revolution" (or the November Uprising) of 1830–31 began when the cadets at the Military Academy in Warsaw revolted, soon joined by large sections of the population as far as Lithuania and the Ukraine – only to be crushed by the Russian army of Tsar Nicholas I (1796–1855).

[6] *woman* for the theory of gender-controlled separate spheres, see GENDER: INTRODUCTION; and GENDER: CONSTRUCTING GENDERS, n. 7; and REID.

[7] *America* in the House of Lords the Lord Speaker and the Lord Chancellor sit on a seat known as the woolsack, so named from the fourteenth century because of reliance upon the wool trade for the prosperity of the country. Judges sit on another woolsack. In America in the 1830s under Chief Justice John Marshall (1755–1835), when judges of the Supreme Court met with the House of Representatives they sat on a raised dais with a small architectural canopy over them.

[8] *Washington* George Washington (1732–99) became the first president of the United States (1789–97).

L. E. L. [Letitia Elizabeth Landon]
(1802–38)

Born in Chelsea, L. E. L. (as she was known) was a precocious reader and writer, publishing her first book, *The Fate of Adelaide: A Swiss Romantic Tale; and Other Poems*, in 1821, followed by *The Improvisatrice, and Other Poems* in 1824. On the death of her father in 1824, she had responsibility for the support of her mother, a sister, and a brother at Oxford. She became the chief reviewer for William Jerdan's *Literary Gazette*, in which she also published poems. She rapidly published volumes of poetry: *The Troubadour* (1825), *The Golden Violet* (1827), *The Venetian Bracelet* (1829), and *The Vow of the Peacock* (1835); as well, she published novels: *Romance and Reality* (1831), *Francesca Carrara* (1834), *Ethel Churchill* (1837), and *Duty and Inclination* (1838). After breaking off her brief engagement to John Forster (1812–76), English literary critic and biographer, following unfounded rumours concerning her promiscuity, she married George Maclean (1801–47), governor of the Gold Coast, accompanying him there in 1838. Two months after their arrival she was found dead with a bottle of prussic acid in her hands; it was unknown whether she had taken an overdose or committed suicide. Her *Poetical Works* in four volumes was published in 1839. Standard edition: *Poetical Works of Letitia Elizabeth Landon, L.E.L.* ed. F. J. Sypher (1990); *Critical Writings by Letitia Elizabeth Landon* ed. F. J. Sypher (1996); *Selected Writings* eds Jerome McGann and Daniel Riess (1997); Laman Blanchard, *Life and Literary Remains of L.E.L.* (2 vols, 1876); Glennis Stephenson, *Letitia Landon: The Woman Behind L.E.L.* (1995); "L.E.L.": http://www.rc.umd.edu/editions/lel/index.html.

Sappho's Song[1]

> Farewell, my lute!—and would that I
> > Had never waked thy burning chords!
> Poison has been upon thy sigh,
> > And fever has breathed in thy words.

Notes

L. E. L. [Letitia Elizabeth Landon]

[1] *title* no early records of the life of Sappho (fl. *c.*600 BCE) survive, except three complete poems and numerous fragments. One of the earliest Greek lyric poets and the only woman from ancient Greece whose poetry has survived in any form, she was from the island of Lesbos, a Greek island in the eastern Aegean Sea near the coast of Turkey. From the fragments it is clear that her circle included young women for whom poems of love and infatuation were written. Romantic and Victorian writers supposed that Sappho presided over a small academy preparing girls for marriage, while her circle seems to have been a religious and poetic band of women, international and variable in membership; her own story was known through the *Heroides* (Lat.: the heroines) of Ovid (43 BCE–17/18 CE), a collection of fifteen epistolary poems written in elegiac couplets from famous or legendary figures, followed by six further "double" poems in which three pairs write and respond to each other. The last of the single poems (poem 15), wholly unhistorical, purports to be a suicide letter by Sappho addressed to her (male) lover, Phaon, who had abandoned her, moving to Sicily; she is about to throw herself into the sea from the Leucadian cliffs as she laments the loss of her love, her lyre, and her poetic voice. Leucadia (Leukas) is one of the Ionian Islands off the west coast of Greece, north-west of the Peloponnese, with steep white cliffs.

In the nineteenth century Sappho became the archetype of the "poetess," a persona for women writers' elegiac

Yet wherefore, wherefore should I blame 5
    Thy power, thy spell, my gentlest lute?
I should have been the wretch I am,
    Had every chord of thine been mute.

It was my evil star above,
    Not my sweet lute, that wrought me wrong; 10
It was not song that taught me love,
    But it was love that taught me song.

If song be past, and hope undone,
    And pulse and head, and heart, are flame;
It is thy work, thou faithless one![2] 15
    But, no!—I will not name thy name!

Sun-god! lute, wreath are vowed to thee![3]
    Long be their light upon my grave—
My glorious grave—you deep blue sea:
    I shall sleep calm beneath its wave! 20

Revenge[4]

Ay, gaze upon her rose-wreathed hair,
    And gaze upon her smile;
Seem as you drank the very air
    Her breath perfumed the while:

And wake for her the gifted line, 5
    That wild and witching lay,
And swear your heart is as a shrine,
    That only owns her sway.

'Tis well: I am revenged at last,—
    Mark you that scornful cheek,— 10
The eye averted as you pass'd,
    Spoke more than words could speak.

Notes

themes of sentimental loss of a male lover, abandonment, loss of voice while composing, suicide for love and letters, and assurance of poetic fame after death. While some of Sappho's fragments had been translated from the seventeenth century and earlier (e.g. Ambrose Philips, Alexander Pope), Mary Robinson (1758–1800) set the vogue for the nineteenth century with her *Sappho and Phaon: A Series of Legitimate Sonnets* (1796), based on Ovid. Later Sappho poems include Landon's own "Sappho" (*Literary Gazette*, 4 May 1822); Felicia Hemans's "The Last Song of Sappho" (1831; see HEMANS); a response to it: Caroline Norton's "The Picture of Sappho" (1840: see NORTON); a section of "A Vision of Poets" by Elizabeth Barrett Browning (1844); Christina Rossetti's "Sappho" (*Verses: Dedicated to Her Mother*, 1847) and "What Sappho Would Have Said Had Her Leap Cured Instead of Killing Her" (unpublished in her lifetime); and "Ode to Sappho" (1848) by Elizabeth Oakes Smith (1806–93). Swinburne shifted the context of Sappho

from heterosexual love to the love of females in "Anactoria" and "Sapphics" (from *Poems and Ballads*, 1866); he is also credited by the *OED* with first using the term "lesbianism" in 1870. John Addington Symonds discussed Sappho in detail in *Studies of the Greek Poets* (1873), and "Michael Field" published *Long Ago* (1889), an entire volume of Sapphic lyrics. First published as part of Landon's long poem *The Improvisatrice* (1824: 141–60). An improvisatrice was a female poet who improvised poems on a line or subject proposed by a member of an audience, often in a salon setting.

[2] *one* Phaon.

[3] *thee* Phoebus Apollo is the sun god, the god of prophecy, music, and poetry, and the leader of the muses in Greek mythology. He is often depicted with a lyre. This line is suggested by Sappho's dedication of her lyre to Apollo before her death in Ovid's *Heroides*: "The grateful poetess Sappho hangs up this lyre to you Phoebus" (14. 183).

[4] *title* first published in *The Venetian Bracelet* (1829).

Ay, now by all the bitter tears
    That I have shed for thee,—
The racking doubts, the burning fears,—   15
    Avenged they well may be—

By the nights pass'd in sleepless care,
    The days of endless woe;
All that you taught my heart to bear,
    All that yourself will know.   20

I would not wish to see you laid
    Within an early tomb;
I should forget how you betray'd,
    And only weep your doom:

But this is fitting punishment,   25
    To live and love in vain,—
O my wrung heart, be thou content,
    And feed upon his pain.

Go thou and watch her lightest sigh,—
    Thine own it will not be;   30
And bask beneath her sunny eye,—
    It will not turn on thee.

'Tis well: the rack, the chain, the wheel,
    Far better hadst thou proved;
Ev'n I could almost pity feel,   35
    For thou art nor beloved.

Stanzas on the Death of Mrs. Hemans[5]

"The rose—the glorious rose is gone."
                Lays of Many Lands[6]

Bring flowers to crown the cup and lute,—
    Bring flowers,—the bride is near;
Bring flowers to soothe the captive's cell,
    Bring flowers to strew the bier!
Bring flowers! thus said the lovely song;[7]   5

Notes

[5] *title* Felicia Hemans had died on 16 May 1835. Landon had praised her in "On the Character of Mrs. Hemans's Writings" (*New Monthly Magazine*, 1835). For an answer to this poem, see ELIZABETH BARRETT BROWNING, "STANZAS." First published in *New Monthly Magazine* (July, 1835).

[6] *Lands* from Hemans's poem "The Nightingale's Death-Song," from *Lays of Many Lands* (1825): "The rose, the glorious rose is gone, / And I, too, will depart" (47–48).
[7] *song* reference to the model for this elegy, Hemans's "Bring Flowers" in *Lays of Many Lands* (1825).

And shall they not be brought
To her who linked the offering
   With feeling and with thought?

Bring flowers,—the perfumed and the pure,—
   Those with the morning dew,   10
A sigh in every fragrant leaf,
   A tear on every hue.
So pure, so sweet thy life has been,
   So filling earth and air   15
With odours and with loveliness,
   Till common scenes grew fair.

Thy song around our daily path
   Flung beauty born of dreams,
That shadows on the actual world   20
   The spirit's sunny gleams.
Mysterious influence, that to earth
   Brings down the heaven above,
And fills the universal heart
   With universal love.   25

Such gifts were thine,—as from the block,
   The unformed and the cold,
The sculptor calls to breathing life
   Some shape of perfect mould,
So thou from common thoughts and things   30
   Didst call a charmed song,
Which on a sweet and swelling tide
   Bore the full soul along.

And thou from far and foreign lands
   Didst bring back many a tone,   35
And giving such new music still,
   A music of thine own.
A lofty strain of generous thoughts,
   And yet subdued and sweet,—
An angel's song, who sings of earth,   40
   Whose cares are at his feet.

And yet thy song is sorrowful,
   Its beauty is not bloom;
The hopes of which it breathes, are hopes
   That look beyond the tomb.   45
Thy song is sorrowful as winds
   That wander o'er the plain,
And ask for summer's vanished flowers,
   And ask for them in vain.

Ah! dearly purchased is the gift,   50
   The gift of song like thine;
A fated doom is hers who stands
   The priestess of the shrine.

The crowd—they only see the crown,
    They only hear the hymn;—   55
They mark not that the cheek is pale,
    And that the eye is dim.

Wound to a pitch too exquisite,
    The soul's fine chords are wrung;
With misery and melody   60
    They are too highly strung.
The heart is made too sensitive
    Life's daily pain to bear;
It beats in music, but it beats
    Beneath a deep despair.   65

It never meets the love it paints,
    The love for which it pines;
Too much of Heaven is in the faith
    That such a heart enshrines.
The meteor wreath the poet wears   70
    Must make a lonely lot;
It dazzles, only to divide
    From those who wear it not.

Didst thou not tremble at thy fame,
    And loathe its bitter prize,   75
While what to others triumph seemed,
    To thee was sacrifice?
Oh, Flower brought from Paradise
    To this cold world of ours,
Shadows of beauty such as thine   80
    Recall thy native bowers.

Let others thank thee—'twas for them
    Thy soft leaves thou didst wreathe;
The red rose wastes itself in sighs
    Whose sweetness others breathe!   85
And they have thanked thee—many a lip
    Has asked of thine for words,
When thoughts, life's finer thoughts, have touched
    The spirit's inmost chords.

How many loved and honoured thee   90
    Who only knew thy name;
Which o'er the weary working world
    Like starry music came!
With what still hours of calm delight
    Thy songs and image blend;   95
I cannot choose but think thou wert
    An old familiar friend.

The charm that dwelt in songs of thine
    My inmost spirit moved;
And yet I feel as thou hadst been   100
    Not half enough beloved.

They say that thou wert faint, and worn
    With suffering and with care;
What music must have filled the soul
    That had so much to spare!   105

Oh, weary One! since thou art laid
    Within thy mother's breast—
The green, the quiet mother-earth—
    Thrice blessed be thy rest!
Thy heart is left within our hearts,   110
    Although life's pang is o'er;
But the quick tears are in my eyes,
    And I can write no more.

The Factory[8]

'Tis an accursed thing!—

There rests a shade above yon town,
    A dark funereal shroud:
'Tis not the tempest hurrying down,
    'Tis not a summer cloud.

The smoke that rises on the air   5
    Is as a type and sign;
A shadow flung by the despair
    Within those streets of thine.

That smoke shuts out the cheerful day,
    The sunset's purple hues,   10
The moonlight's pure and tranquil ray,
    The morning's pearly dews.

Such is the moral atmosphere
    Around thy daily life;
Heavy with care, and pale with fear,   15
    With future tumult rife.

There rises on the morning wind
    A low appealing cry,
A thousand children are resigned
    To sicken and to die!   20

We read of Moloch's[9] sacrifice,
    We sicken at the name,
And seem to hear the infant cries—
    And yet we do the same;—

Notes

[8] *title* for other works concerning factories, see NORTON, "A VOICE"; and CONDITION: PROGRESS (WEB p. 18). First published in *The Vow of the Peacock and Other Poems* (1835).

[9] *Moloch's* ancient god associated in the Bible with the Canaanites who required the sacrifice of sons and daughters; see, for instance, 2 Kings 23: 10; and Jeremiah 32: 35. In *Paradise Lost* Moloch is a leader of the fallen angels in Hell: 1: 392–405; and 2: 43–105.

And worse—'twas but a moment's pain   25
    The heathen altar gave,
But we give years,—our idol, Gain,
    Demands a living grave!

How precious is the little one,
    Before his mother's sight,   30
With bright hair dancing in the sun,
    And eyes of azure light!

He sleeps as rosy as the south,
    For summer days are long;
A prayer upon the little mouth,   35
    Lull'd by his nurse's song.

Love is around him, and his hours
    Are innocent and free;
His mind essays its early powers
    Beside his mother's knee.   40

When after-years of trouble come,
    Such as await man's prime,
How will he think of that dear home,
    And childhood's lovely time!

And such should childhood ever be,   45
    The fairy well; to bring
To life's worn, weary memory
    The freshness of its spring.

But here the order is reversed,
    And infancy, like age,   50
Knows of existence but its worst,
    One dull and darkened page;—

Written with tears, and stamp'd with toil,
    Crushed from the earliest hour,
Weeds darkening on the bitter soil   55
    That never knew a flower.

Look on yon child, it droops the head,
    Its knees are bow'd with pain;
It mutters from its wretched bed,
    "Oh, let me sleep again!"   60

Alas! 'tis time, the mother's eyes
    Turn mournfully away;
Alas! 'tis time, the child must rise,
    And yet it is not day.

The lantern's lit—she hurries forth,   65
    The spare cloak's scanty fold
Scarce screens her from the snowy north,
    The child is pale and cold.

And wearily the little hands
  Their task accustom'd ply;
While daily, some mid those pale bands,
  Droop, sicken, pine, and die.   70

Good God! to think upon a child
  That has no childish days,
No careless play, no frolics wild,   75
  No words of prayer and praise!

Man from the cradle—'tis too soon
  To earn their daily bread,
And heap the heat and toil of noon
  Upon an infant's head.   80

To labour ere their strength be come,
  Or starve,—is such the doom
That makes of many an English home
  One long and living tomb?

Is there no pity from above,—   85
  No mercy in those skies;
Hath then the heart of man no love,
  To spare such sacrifice?

Oh, England! though thy tribute waves
  Proclaim thee great and free,   90
While those small children pine like slaves,
  There is a curse on thee!

The Princess Victoria [I]¹⁰

And art thou a Princess?—in sooth, we may well
Go back to the days of the sign and the spell,
When a young queen¹¹ sat on an ivory throne
In a shining hall, whose windows shone
With colours its crystals caught from the sky,   5
Or the roof which a thousand rubies dye;
Where the summer garden was spread around,
With the date and the palm and the cedar crowned;
Where fountains played with the rainbow showers,
Touched with the hues of their comrade flowers;   10

Notes

¹⁰ *title* first published in *Fisher's Drawing Room Scrap Book for 1832*, of which Landon had been the editor from 1831 to 1839, writing most of the text for 100 guineas a year. The large folio volume usually had about thirty-five high-quality engravings with some accompanying text and was lavishly bound.
¹¹ *queen* either Scheherazade in *The Arabian Nights*, or the Queen of Sheba; see 1 Kings 10: 1–13.

Where the tulip and rose grew side by side,
One like a queen, and one like a bride;
One with its own imperial flush,
The other reddening with love's sweet blush;
When silver stuffs for her step were unrolled, 15
And the citron was served on a plate of gold;
When perfumes arose from pearl caskets filled
With odours from all sweet things distilled;
When a fairy guarded the throne from ill,
And she knew no rule but her own glad will: 20
Those were the days for a youthful queen,
And such, fair Princess, thou should'st have been.

But now thou wilt fill a weary throne,
What with rights of the people,[12] and rights of thy own:
An ear-trumpet now thy sceptre should be, 25
Eternal debate is the future for thee.
Lord Brougham[13] will make a six-hours' oration,
On the progress of knowledge, the mind of the nation;
Lord Grey[14] one yet longer, to state that his place
Is perhaps less dear to himself than his race; 30
O'Connell[15] will tell Ireland's griefs and her wrongs,
In speech, the mac-adamized prose of Moore's songs:[16]
Good patience! how weary the young queen will be
Of "the flower of the earth, and the gem of the sea!"
Mr. Hume,[17] with his watchwords "Retrenchment and Waste," 35
Will insist that your wardrobe in his care be placed;
The silk he will save! the blonde[18] he will spare—

Notes

[12] *people* often known as the "rights of man," a rallying cry of the Chartists in the 1830s, especially with "The People's Charter" of 1838. A typical slogan for the Chartists in Leicester, for instance, was "The rights of the people and nothing less." For the rights of man see GENDER: CONSTRUCTING, n. 9.

[13] *Brougham* Henry Brougham, first Baron Brougham and Vaux (1778–1868), Whig politician and Lord Chancellor in the government of Lord Grey (see n. 14) from 1830 to 1834. His greatest accomplishment was helping pass the first Reform Bill. In a previous debate on 7 February 1828 Brougham spoke for six hours on law reform. He was also one of the founders of the Society for the Diffusion of Useful Knowledge (1825) and an advocate of educational reform.

[14] *Grey* Charles Grey, second Earl Grey (1764–1845), was Whig prime minister of Great Britain (1830–34), during the time the Great Reform Bill was debated and passed, and slavery was abolished in the British Empire (1833). He was a noted parliamentary orator.

[15] *O'Connell* Daniel O'Connell (1775–1847), Irish political reformer, was first elected to the British Parliament in 1828, but as a Roman Catholic he could not take the Oath of Supremacy. He was denied his seat until the Emancipation Act (1829) allowed Roman Catholics,

Presbyterians, and others who were not members of the Church of England to become MPs. Known as the "Liberator" in working for Catholic emancipation, he also campaigned for the repeal of the Act of Union (1801) that made one the parliaments of Ireland and Great Britain.

[16] *mac-adamized ... songs* John Loudon McAdam (1756–1836), Scottish engineer, used small compacted stones as a road-bed on the Bristol Turnpike in 1816, later adapted by others by the overlay of stone dust and water, and, later still, with tar to make a solid, dust-free road. Such roadways were termed "macadamized." Thomas Moore (1779–1852), Irish poet, actor, and songwriter, published ten volumes of *Irish Melodies* between 1808 and 1834, including many of great popularity such as "The Harp That Once Through Tara's Halls," "Believe Me, if All Those Endearing Young Charms," "The Minstrel Boy," and "The Last Rose of Summer."

[17] *Hume* Joseph Hume (1777–1855), Scottish radical MP, was influenced by James Mill and the Benthamites on behalf of the working classes and educational reform. In Parliament he required a vote on all items of public spending to eliminate waste, and had the word "retrenchment" added to the Radical platform.

[18] *blonde* "silk lace ... the colour of raw silk, but now white or black" (*OED*).

I wish he may leave Your Grace any to wear.
That feminine fancy, a will of your own,
Is a luxury wholly denied to a throne;   40
And this is your future—how soon time will trace
A change and a sign on that fair and young face!
Methinks the best wish to be offered thee now
Is—God keep the crown long from that innocent brow.

The Princess Victoria [II]¹⁹

A fair young face o'er which is only cast
The delicate hues of spring,
Though round her is the presence of the past,
And the stern future gathers darkly fast;
As yet no heavy shadow loads their wing.   5

A little while hast thou to be a child,
Thy lot is all too high;
Thy face is very fair, thine eyes are mild,
But duties on thine arduous path are piled—
A nation's hopes and fears blend with thy destiny.   10

Change is upon the world, it may be thine
To soothe its troubled way,
To make thy throne a beacon and a shrine
Whence knowledge, power, and liberty may shine,
As yet they have not shone on mortal day.   15

There is much misery on this worn earth,
But much that may be spared:
Of great and generous thought there is no dearth,
And highest hopes of late have had their birth,
Hopes for the many, what the few have shared.   20

The wind that bears our flag from soil to soil,
Teaches us as it flies;
It carries in its breath a summer spoil,
And seeds spring up to stimulate man's toil.
So should our mind spread round its rich supplies.   25

Thou, Royal child, the future is thine own,
May it be bless'd in thee!
May peace that smiles on all be round thy throne
And universal truth, whose light alone
Gives golden records unto history.   30

Notes

¹⁹ *title* born on 24 May 1819, Victoria was 17 in November, 1836 when this poem was published in *Fisher's Drawing Room Scrap Book for 1837* (Nov. 1836). When she turned 18 the following May, she came of age to inherit the crown. William IV died on 20 June, 1837.

Elizabeth Duncan Campbell (1804–78)

Born in the parish of Tannadice, near Brechin in eastern Scotland, Elizabeth Duncan was the fifth of six daughters of a ploughman, James Duncan. Her mother died when she was 3 years old; to help the family she tended cows and gathered gorse branches and at the age of 7 started a long period of domestic work. First in a series of rural farmhouses she served in various positions, eventually becoming a cook at Barry's Hotel in Edinburgh. With one of her families she spent two years in France. Eventually she married a flax-dresser from Brechin, William Campbell, raising a family of four sons (all of whom died before her) and four daughters. She had learned the art of handweaving, moving to Arbroath and finally to Lochee. She published *Burns' Centenary: An Ode and Other Poems* (1862), a series of small privately issued pamphlets, each entitled *Poems* (in 1862, 1863, 1865, 1867), and *Songs of My Pilgrimage* (1875) with an introduction by George Gilfillan (1813–78), Scottish poet and clergyman. It also included her short autobiography. No standard edition, but some of her poems are gathered in *Working-class Women Poets in Victorian Britain: An Anthology,* ed. Florence Saunders Boos (2008). Writing Lives: Working-class Poetry: http://www.writinglives.org/links-resources/online-sources-for-working-class-poetry.

The Windmill of Sebastopol[1]

There's an ancient windmill, seen from Inkermann Hill—
Oft was it hailed with hearty good will,—
With soft steps and voice still
By our brave allies, when they strayed from home,
In the gloamin' to have a lark, (not now in Regent Park[2]); 5
But a password was in the dark, and they look't 'tween
Earth and sky to hark called—"Who goes?" "A friend!"
Or is it a Russian to stab us behind.

As in the wet mud they did tramp,
A mixture from ship and camp, 10
No Fleet Street[3] car and lamp

Notes

Elizabeth Duncan Campbell

[1] *title* an irregular ode with a complicated versification, composed mostly of alternating eight- and six-line stanzas, each made up of dimeters, tetrameters, and pentameters, with varying feet, iambic and anapestic predominating. Three repeated opening rhymes, with additional internal rhymes culminate in the use of "home" (sometimes as a second rhyme word) in the middle of seven of the fourteen stanzas, including six of the first seven stanzas. The word contrasts appropriately with "storm," "mourn," and similar rhymes in stanzas ten, eleven, and twelve. Campbell very likely refers to the windmill on what came to be known as Windmill Ridge and Windmill Ravine at Inkerman, 5 kilometres east of Sebastopol, the Russian stronghold on the Black Sea during the Crimean War (1853–56). The windmill, often referred to in dispatches, was at a major crossroads, and served to organize the placement of the allied troops for the Battle of Inkerman on 5 November 1854. Reports of the battle appeared on the same pages as the continuing siege of Sebastopol, as for instance, in the *Aberdeen Journal* (29 Nov. 1854), when the windmill is mentioned as one of the burial sites for the fallen, and on December 5 when the windmill was endangered: it was "our main magazine in this part of the camp" and contained "some hundred and eighty tons of powder." On that occasion it had narrowly escaped destruction and the 7th Fusiliers succeeded in covering the exposed roof with wet tarpaulins to prevent sparks from igniting the powder boxes. Campbell wrote at least nine other poems on the Crimean War. The poem was privately printed in *Poems* (1862). For discussion of the Crimean War, see TENNYSON, n. 311; see also EMPIRE: IMPERIAL TRAVELLERS; RUSSELL (WEB p. 258); LITERATURE: AURAL; RECORDINGS and PHOTOGRAPHY; FENTON (WEB pp. 158 and 172).

[2] *Park* park in central London.

[3] *Street* major thoroughfare in the City of London.

There fetched them home,
As did in Britain, when they chose to roam—
There they were dreary and sorrow their song.

Some love-sick and crying, while others were dying,   15
With pitiful moans on the ground lying,
Their life away flying;
Far from their kindred, loved ones and home,
There no sister did wait for a loved brother's sake,
No tinsel'd lacky op't the gate to let young master in,   20
And no lover's balmy kiss sweetened his dreams,
But round his head balls hissed in the tent-home he claimed.

There was no seam and book thrown in the nearest nook,
No child with witching look blessed the warrior's home;
But oft flew his thoughts home   25
To the dear ones that to him belonged,
And ruled on his heart's throne,
Though beyond the salt main.

His tent bed was cold and lone
In that land of pain,   30
Where no loving wife did wait
To hark his horse approach the gate,
When it chimed ten o'clock—
That is my husband's knock,
Bless him, he's come.   35

Quick the key turned the lock,
Hot did the supper smoke,
And happy love blessed their lot
In their dear English home;
But the door-bell now made her start,   40
And she pressed her child to her aching heart
In fear should the postman say—
Its father is slain.

O little gratitude is shown
To the warriors that guard our home: 45
Much blood has paid the sum
For our peaceful dreams,
And away their weary spirits flown,
'Mid war's dreadful screams.

When woe walk'd the Crimean hills, an angel watch'd the windmill,   50
And made it of use to our harassed men;
'Twas a landmark, a leading star,
All in that dreadful war,
When bombshells flew afar o'er bloody plains.

Elizabeth Duncan Campbell

And war has made the old mill dumb,   55
Stilled its⁴ clattering tongue,
Rusty's its wheel and drum, this heavy time,
There no miller's maid are found;
But the sentinel in his round—all ear to every sound,
While quick flying thoughts bound   60
His sad heart within.
Wending his weary way down by Careening Bay,⁵
He alone in the dark greets the old mill his friend,
With its battered walls, and its flails torn,
Stood the old mill forlorn, beating the winter storm,   65
Where sweet peace once hailed the morn
That land within.

Peace fled with scorn, and war made many mourn;
To the blast of the war horn
The war horse quickly turned to bound through the stream,—   70
Hard-toiled and care-worn its rider bent his weary form;
With hunger his heart torn, while snow drifted on the storm,
And dismal the night-winds wail on the wing.

Deep did the Russians mourn for their broad fields of yellow corn,
Home by the reapers borne, when peace was the theme;   75
Now deserted is cot and town,
Away are the inmates flown,
And a hundred thousand cut down
Of that unhappy band.

Where, O where are they gone?   80
For fire and sword flash along,
Famine and the death gong walk hand in hand,
Blowing their bugle and rifling the land;
Sorry must be the home—sick, hungry, cold and lone,
Where the camp with the hostile gun   85
Claims the command.

O think of the mother of the new born child,
Great One keep all hearts from ambition so wild,
As the spirit departed, that to death them condemned:
O Nicholas,⁶ proud Nicholas, pray what have you gained?   90
Ye earned it hard, and received your reward;
Merciless tyrant, war was your rhyme,
To kill and possess was a fancy of thine,
But death knocked at your door before it was time,
And bade you prepare at his banquet to dine;   95
He bore you away on pain-laden wings,—
Ye died by slow poison—a warning to kings!

Notes

⁴ *its* the text reads "it's."
⁵ *Bay* fourth bay on the coast south of Sebastopol, and the name given to a ravine that led down from the heights into it, held by the English and French armies.

⁶ *Nicholas* Nicholas I, tsar of Russia (1795–1855). From the following four lines, it is clear that the poem was written after his death on 2 March 1855, before the end of the war in February 1856.

The Crimean War[7]

I think it's a pity that kings go to war,
And carry their murd'rous inventions so far;
Since Adam did blunder[8] such blunders have been,
And I weep for those that's the victims of kings.
I weep for the coward, I weep for the brave,   5
I weep for the monarch, I weep for the slave,
I weep for all those that in battle are slain;
I've a tear and a prayer for the souls of all men.

There were many a cut and bloody scar
When those four nations went to war,   10
And many cries and helpless sighs
Reached the skies when starry,
From hill, and glen, and Russian plain,
Away the winds did carry;
When many men in war were slain   15
At capturing of the quarry.

There Death came in his muffled car,
And to and fro he drove afar,
And where the young man made a blunder,
He in Death's valley slew six hunder'.[9]   20

The King of kings,[10] with power and will,
Said blood of men shall dye the rills,
And stain the plain and Crimea hills,
'Neath glowing skies so starry.
The God of War, in Heaven's car,   25
Cried, haste, I shall not tarry;
Go, kill, kill, kill! for slain shall fill
The trenches and the quarry.

North Britain,[11] long God's favoured isle,—
May Peace and Plenty on thee smile,   30
In castle and in cot;
O ever shower your spirit there,
And hear the hoary-headed's prayer,
In this my native spot!
May true religion ever stand   35
In thee, my own dear native land!

And honest men rule Britain's Throne;
Its Freedom flourish when I'm gone;
For, think ye, I've forgot it?

Notes

7 *title* for the Crimean War, see above, "WINDMILL"; and especially TENNYSON, "CHARGE." From privately printed *Poems* (1867).

8 *blunder* Adam's original sin; see Genesis 2–3.

9 *hunder'* a reference to the Battle of Balaclava (25 October 1854) and an echo of the "six hundred" in Tennyson's "Charge."

10 *kings* see Revelation 17: 14; and 19: 16.

11 *Britain* Scotland.

When Bonnie[12] begged five hundred men,   40
To face up in the great Redan,[13]
For targets to be shot at;
Till he stepped in to claim the fame;
Fain would he Britain bloated.

Sebastopol of guns was full,   45
To shed the blood of sage and fool,
To wash that far-famed city;
And many more will feel Death's chill,
Ere Vengeance' cup be towering full,
Or hardened men feel pity.   50
There many mother lost her son
Before Sebastopol was won.

What pen can mark the dreadful hour
When fate of war did o'er them lower;
And brothers fought with will and power,   55
At the Malakoff and Mamelon tower,[14]
Their life and limbs not heeding;
When o'er the walls of the Redan
The iron-nervëd British ran,
To fall by hundreds bleeding.   60

By some mischance they left their guns,
And in confusion all did run,
Like butter-flies into the sun,
When rains a summer shower;
Before the fight was well begun,   65
And long before the setting sun,
A mile of Russian loaded guns
Quick down their lines did pour.

And who could paint the awful strife,
With nothing to defend their life,   70
At the attack upon the great Redan,
When to and fro commanders ran,
With nothing to confide in
But a stick, a stone, an empty gun;
Yet British hearts disdained to run,   75
Though deep in red blood wading.

Notes

[12] *Bonnie* Bonnie Prince Charlie (Charles Edward Stuart, 1720–88), the Young Pretender, led the Jacobite Rebellion in Scotland (1745), finally defeated at the Battle of Culloden (16 Apr. 1746). The reference here is very likely to the Highland Brigade of the British Army, composed of the 42nd Royal Highland Regiment, the 79th Cameron Highlanders, and the 93rd Sutherland Highlanders, all deployed at Sebastopol, taking part in the Battle of Inkerman and siege of Sebastopol, and all suffering tremendous losses.

[13] *Redan* a "v" shaped fortification; the "great Redan" was the major Russian fortification protecting Sebastopol.

[14] *tower* the Malakoff fortress, a tower of stone with redans, was the largest and strongest defence position for Sebastopol; it was attacked by the French on 7–8 September 1855, resulting in horrific hand-to-hand fighting with bayonets and great loss of life on both sides, followed by the evacuation of Sebastopol by the Russian army, and the effective end of the war. The Mamelon hillock, heavily fortified as part of the defences of Sebastopol, was taken by the French in June, 1855. See LITERATURE: NEW TECHNOLOGIES; PHOTOGRAPHS, FENTON (WEB p. 172).

But, ah! their noble hearts did wince,
When their eyes fell on the fearful trench
That circled round the great Redan,
Their limbs did shake, their face did wane,   80
Though men of noble breeding.
The Russian battery raised a cloud,
Like peals of thunder roaring loud,
With smoke and fire then hiding.

'Twas well for those that found a grave   85
Aside those walls when fighting brave,
It many a mother's tears did save
From seeing her son a British slave,
Tied up and get a flogging;
'Neath Britain's boasted Freedom's flag,   90
Deserters out their life must drag,
White fear their footsteps dogging.

Great One that has the will and power,
On erring mortals mercy shower,
And save us in our dying hour;   95
O spread your wings to keep's from harm;
Stretch over us your saving arm,
From Satan's wiles us screen;
For dear is saints and souls to Thee
And to Christ our Lord and King.   100

The Schoolmaster[15]

It may be that you're a poet,
    Yet I scarcely think 'tis so;
And I'm sure you're no patriot,
    Your mind runs rather low.
For all the high-class Latin   5
    That from your tongue may flow,
Your range of mind is narrow,
    You silly empty crow.

Although ye wore a chain of gold,
    Upon your vest right fine;   10
Ye kept me in the rain and cold,
    When no bright sun did shine.
My old feet wet with winter sleet,
    That you seemed not to regard;
Nor the east wind fan my withered cheek,   15
    While ye scanned my palace card.[16]

Notes

[15] *title* from privately printed *Poems* (1867).   [16] *card* her document to be admitted to school.

Then your jealous e'e cared not to see
     One so meanly bred as me,
Earn fame of high degree,
     That stamps the poet's roll.   20

'Tis not learning that makes the poet,
     Nor grammar from Latin riven,
The mind of the brave patriot,
     And that of the humble poet,
Glides down on a cloud from Heaven,   25
     Divine imagination's a gift from infinite God,
To cheer poor pilgrims on their way
     O'er Life's sharp thorny road.

We're like John Graham of Claverhouse,[17]
     Vile Cardinal Beaton's[18] tool,   30
He sported the face of an angel,
     But a demon possessed his soul.
You're proud, like a silly peacock,
     Spreading his tail to be seen;
You're as black as a rook on a tree top,   35
     Ho-hacke[19] with the broken wing.

The Death of Willie, My Second Son[20]

The balm of human kindness from his master's lips did flow,
And his mistress like a mother did alleviate my woe;
The blooming servant-maiden in pity shed her tears,
To smooth down my dread sorrow—they whispered in mine ears.

The bless'd sun veiled his brightness, the clouds their radiant hue,   5
The moon trailed bloody shadows across the azure blue;
The planets paled their lustre, and hid in darkness deep,
When sudden death in silence hushed my dear son asleep!

Notes

[17] *Claverhouse* John Graham of Claverhouse, first Viscount Dundee (1648–89), was a Scottish military leader who, after persecuting the Presbyterian Covenanters in the rebellions of the 1660s and 1670s, joined their ranks and led the clans, dying in the Battle of Killiecrankie against the British (July 1689).

[18] *Beaton* David Beaton (1494–1546), cardinal archbishop of St Andrews, was a strong opponent of Henry VIII and his anti-Rome reforms in the Anglican Church. Accordingly he forged links between Scotland and France, and was one of the supporters of James V of Scotland and of the infant Mary Queen of Scots in 1542. He became Lord Chancellor of Scotland (1543–46), when he waged several wars of religion with England and the English supporters in Scotland. He was brutally assassinated on 29 May 1546.

[19] *Ho-hacke* hawk.

[20] *title* Campbell prefaced the poem with the following note: "On the 20th April 1866, my son, William Campbell, was killed at Aberdeen, in the 35th year of his age. It was caused by a hair-teasing machine insufficiently covered, at which he was employed. They telegraphed for me to come to identity his corpse, which had been removed to the dead-house. There was a fearful wound in his brow over the left eye, and all his body was terribly mangled. Filled with deep and bitter grief for the sad fate of my poor son, I wrote this piece.— E.C." For his death, see CAMPBELL, n. 29 (WEB p. 290). From *Songs of My Pilgrimage* (1875).

O! were God's angels waiting to bear him on their wings
Beyond the reach of sorrow to the land of glorious things?   10
This is my heart's deep sadness, because I cannot know
That God in mercy saved him from everlasting woe.

No sound came from his sealed lips when death dealt him the blow,
I wept and kissed his gory brow—nigh bloodless as the snow—
I tucked him in his white shroud and hid him in the ground,   15
I saw how deep in earth he'll sleep with many a gory wound!

Oh! never a stone will mark the spot where wild flowers o'er him wave,
To tell the name or mournful lot of my son in his lowly grave;
Cold, cold and still in earth he'll lie till Time's last sands are run,
The winds will sigh and wild birds fly o'er the dust of my dear son.   20

The glorious sun in brightness for him no more shall shine,
And never more heart-lightness on earth will e'er be mine;
Hard pressed on fields of battle, thrice shipwrecked on the sea,
Oh, lo! from many a distant isle he wandered home to me.

His ever welcome footsteps and voice I'll no more hear,   25
No more tales in my ear he'll pour my heart to chill or cheer;
O! Nellfield lonely graveyard,[21] I'll often think of thee,
Where Willie sleeps 'mong strangers, by the silvery flowing Dee.[22]

WEB p. 287

From "The Life of My Childhood"

WEB p. 291

William Dodd (1804–c.1850)
   From *A Narrative of the Experiences and Sufferings of William Dodd, A Factory Cripple, Written by Himself*

WEB p. 295

Mary Jane Seacole (1805–81)
   The Wonderful Adventures of Mrs. Seacole in Many Lands
      From Chapter 8: I Long to Join the British Army Before Sebastopol
      From Chapter 13: My Work in the Crimea

Notes

[21] *graveyard* cemetery in Aberdeen.   [22] *Dee* river in Aberdeenshire, Scotland.

Elizabeth Barrett Browning (1806–61)

Born as Elizabeth Barrett Moulton-Barrett, she was the eldest of twelve children of Edward Moulton-Barrett (1785–1857), a repressive father who forbade his children to marry, and Mary Graham Clarke (d. 1828), whose family, like her husband's, owned extensive sugar plantations in Jamaica worked by slaves until imperial emancipation (1836). Happy amidst her large family in Hertfordshire, at age 6 Elizabeth learned French and read novels, at 8 immersed herself in translations of Homer, and at 11, already proficient in Latin, studied Greek with her brother, and wrote short novels, plays, and poetry. She also learned enough Italian to read Dante's *Inferno* and enough Hebrew to read the Old Testament. At 14 her first book, *The Battle of Marathon*, was privately published by her father. The abolition of slavery in 1833, which she supported, greatly decreased her father's income from his Jamaican sugar plantations and led to the sale of the family home. After her mother's death, the family moved in 1838 to 50 Wimpole Street in London, the same year that she published *The Seraphim and Other Poems*. She had become an invalid, probably with spinal tuberculosis, and lived a secluded life, ameliorated with laudanum, until she met Robert Browning, who wanted to meet the author of *Poems* (1844). They carried on a two-year correspondence during which they met, in May 1845, and she began in secret her *Sonnets from the Portuguese* (1850). They were clandestinely married on 26 September 1846 and in a few days left for Florence, where they lived on her independent income, Barrett Browning's father having disinherited her upon her marriage. Her health improved, she travelled, and had a son. Increasingly she took up contemporary social issues (anti-slavery, Italian unification, women's rights) in such poems as her long iambic pentameter poetic epic *Aurora Leigh* (1856), as well as *Casa Guidi Windows* (1851), and *Poems before Congress* (1860). She fell sick in 1860, died in Robert's arms in 1861, and was buried in Florence. Standard edition: *The Works of Elizabeth Barrett Browning*, ed. Sandra Donaldson (5 vols, 2009–10); *The Brownings' Correspondence*, eds Philip Kelley, Ronald Hudson, and Scott Lewis (14 vols, 1984–); Gardner B. Taplin, *The Life of Elizabeth Barrett Browning* (1958); Rebecca Stott and Simon Avery, *Elizabeth Barrett Browning* (2003). "The Elizabeth Barrett Browning Portal": http://www.florin.ms/ebbwebsite.html.

Stanzas Addressed to Miss Landon,

Suggested by Her "Stanzas on the Death of Mrs. Hemans"[1]

Thou bay-crown'd[2] living one—who o'er
The bay-crown'd dead art bowing,
And o'er the shadeless, moveless brow

Notes

ELIZABETH BARRETT BROWNING

[1] *title* the title was later changed (1850) to "Felicia Hemans. / To L. E. L., Referring to her Monody on the Poetess" (1850), joining the lines to make four-line stanzas. Felicia Hemans had died on 16 May 1835 and L. E. L. published "Stanzas on the Death of Mrs. Hemans" (see L. E. L., "Stanzas"). Elizabeth Barrett commemorates the death of Hemans by paying tribute to Landon's own memorial poem; her retitling links the poem to the tradition of the pastoral

monody from Milton's *Lycidas* (1638) to Shelley's *Adonais* (1821). Published in *New Monthly Magazine* (Sept. 1835), signed "B."; republished in *The Seraphim, and Other Poems* (1838) and *Poems* (1850).

[2] *bay-crown'd* for the bay or laurel wreath, see HEMANS, n. 17. The "dead" in the following line refers to Felicia Hemans. For laurels, see also ELIZABETH BROWNING, n. 27 (WEB p. 308).

Thy human shadow throwing;
   And o'er the sighless, songless lips   5
      The wail and music wedding—
Dropping o'er the tranquil eyes
      Tears[3] not of *their* shedding:

Go! take thy music from the dead,
      Whose silentness is sweeter;   10
Reserve thy tears for living brows,
      For whom such tears are meeter;
And leave the violets[4] in the grass
      To brighten where thou treadest
No flowers for *her*! Oh! bring no flowers—   15
      Albeit "Bring flowers," thou saidest.[5]

But bring not near her solemn corse
      A type of human seeming;
Lay only dust's stern verity
      Upon her dust undreaming.   20
And while the calm perpetual stars
      Shall look upon it solely;
Her spherèd soul shall look on *them*,
      With eyes more bright and holy.

Nor mourn, oh living one, because   25
      Her part in life was mourning:
Would she have lost the poet's flame
      For anguish of the burning?
The minstrel harp, for the strain'd string?
      The tripod,[6] for th' afflated   30
Woe? or the vision, for those tears
      Through which it shone dilated?

Perhaps she shudder'd while the world's
      Cold hand her brow was wreathing:
But wrong'd she ne'er that mystic breath   35
      Which breath'd in all her breathing.—
Which drew from rocky earth and man
      Abstractions high and moving,—
Beauty, if not the beautiful,—
      And love, if not the loving.   40

Notes

[3] *tears* see LANDON, "STANZAS ON THE DEATH OF MRS. HEMANS," last two lines. Tears were the mark of mourning and respect, as well as sentimental affection between women. See also TENNYSON, n. 41 and TENNYSON, SONGS FROM THE PRINCESS, "TEARS, IDLE TEARS" (1847) (WEB p. 342).

[4] *violets* in the *Language of Flowers* (1885) by Kate Greenaway (1846–1901) and earlier handbooks dating back to the sixteenth century, particular emotions and attributes were associated with flowers. Other editions of *The Language of Flowers* were published throughout the Victorian era.

Violets signify faithfulness and modesty; for example, Ophelia to her brother Laertes: "I would give you some violets, but they withered all when my father died" (*Hamlet* 4. 5. 182).

[5] *saidest* "Bring Flowers" is a poem by Felicia Hemans (1824) that is echoed in Landon's "Stanzas on the Death of Mrs. Hemans," (see LANDON, "STANZAS") and in Barrett's poem.

[6] *tripod* the stool on which the oracle at Delphi sat when delivering an inspired prophesy; hence, with the harp, symbols of poetic inspiration.

Such visionings have paled in sight
　　The *Saviour* she descrieth,
And little recks who wreath'd the brow
　　That on His bosom lieth.
The whiteness of His innocence　　　　　　　　45
　　O'er all her garments flowing,
There learneth she that sweet "new song"[7]
　　She will not mourn in knowing.

Be blessed, crown'd and living one:
　　And when thy dust decayeth,　　　　　　　　50
May thine own England say for thee
　　What now for her it sayeth,—
"Albeit softly in our ears
　　Her silver song was ringing,
The footsteps of her parting soul　　　　　　　55
　　Were softer than her singing."

L. E. L.'s Last Question[8]

"Do you think of me as I think of you,
My friends, my friends?"—She said it from the sea,
The English minstrel in her minstrelsy,[9]
While, under brighter skies than erst she knew,
Her heart grew dark, and gropëd, as the blind　　5
To touch across the waves friends left behind—
"Do you think of me as I think of you?"

It seemed not much to ask—as I of you?
We all do ask the same. No eyelids cover
Within the meekest eyes, that question over.　　10
And little in this world the Loving do
But sit (among the rocks?[10]) and listen for
The echo of their own love evermore—
"Do you think of me as I think of you?"

Love-learnèd she had sung of only love,—　　　15
And as child asleep (with weary head

Dropped on the fairy-book he lately read),
Whatever household noises round him move,
Hears in his dream some elfin turbulence,—
Even so, suggestive to her inward sense,   20
All sounds of life assumed one tune of love.

And when the glory of her dream withdrew,
When knightly gestes[11] and courtly pageantries
Were broken in her visionary eyes
By tears the solemn seas attested true,—   25
Forgetting that sweet lute[12] beside her hand
She asked not,—Do you praise me, O my land,—
But,—"Think ye of me, friends, as I of you?"

True heart to love, that pourëd many a year
Love's oracles for England,—smooth and well.   30
Would God, thou hadst an inward oracle
In that lone moment to confirm thee dear!
For when thy questioned friends in agony
Made passionate response, "We think of thee,"
Thy place was in the dust, too deep to hear.   35

Could she not wait to catch the answering breath?
Was she content, content, with ocean's sound,
Dashing his mocking infinite around
The craver of a little love?[13]—beneath
Those stars content, where last her song had gone?   40
They mute and cold in radiant life,[14]—as soon
Their singer was to be, in darksome death?[15]

Bring your vain answers—cry, "We think of thee!"
How think ye of her? in the long ago
Delights!—or crowned by new bays?—not so—   45
None smile and none are crowned where lieth she,
With all her visions unfulfilled save one,
Her childhood's—if the palm-trees in the sun.
And lo! their shadow on her sepulchre!

Do you think of me as I think of you?—   50
O friends, O kindred, O dear brotherhood
Of the whole world! what are we, that we should

Notes

[11] *gestes* (Fr. noble deeds < Lat. *gesta*: things done) a reference to the romances of chivalry (the *chansons de geste*, like the *Song of Roland, c.*1100) or collections of moralized tales of antiquity, like the *Gesta Romanorum* (Lat. deeds of the Romans; late thirteenth century).

[12] *lute* or lyre, the instrument sacred to Apollo, the leader of the Muses, and hence the instrument of poetic inspiration and accompaniment. For Landon's farewell to her lute, see LANDON, n. 2.

[13] *The craver ... love* in *Poems* (1850) this line reads: "One thirsty for a little love?—beneath." Christina Rossetti echoes this line in the epigraph and in repeated lines in her tribute poem to Letitia Landon; see CHRISTINA ROSSETTI, n. 68.

[14] *Stars ... radiant life* the second poem that Letitia Landon wrote on board ship while travelling to Africa was "The Polar Star," published in the *New Monthly Magazine* (Jan. 1839). It begins: "A star has left the kindling sky."

[15] *death* "Her lyric on the polar star, came home with her latest papers" [author's note, added in 1856].

For covenants of long affection sue?
Why press so near each other when the touch
Is barred by graves? Not much, and yet too much,   55
This, "Think upon me as I think of you."

But while on mortal lips I shape anew
A sigh to mortal issues,—verily
Above the unshaken stars that see us die,
A vocal pathos rolls; and HE who drew   60
All life from dust, and for all, tasted death,
By death and life and love, appealing, saith
DO YOU THINK OF ME AS I THINK OF YOU?

WEB p. 301

A Musical Instrument[16]

I

What was he doing, the great god Pan,
    Down in the reeds by the river?
Spreading ruin and scattering ban,[17]
Splashing and paddling with hoofs of a goat,
And breaking the golden lilies afloat   5
    With the dragon-fly on the river?[18]

Notes

[16] *title* Pan was the god of the rustic pastures, shepherds, and flocks, and was represented as an aggressively sexual half-man and half-goat, playing the reed or pan-pipe. In Greek mythology, Pan fell in love with the chaste nymph Syrinx, who escaped his amorous advances when she was transformed into a water reed, whereupon Pan collected the reeds together and played her mournful tune on them – a metaphor for the invention of the first musical instrument (*Metamorphoses* 1. 689 ff.). Pan taught the shepherd Daphnis to play the pipes, and when he composed poetry to the music he became the legendary inventor of pastoral poetry. Hence Pan is also associated with the

II

He tore out a reed, the great god Pan,
　　From the deep cool bed of the river.
The limpid water turbidly ran,
And the broken lilies a-dying lay,
And the dragon-fly had fled away,　　　　　　　　　　　10
　　Ere he brought it out of the river.

III

High on the shore sate the great god Pan,
　　While turbidly flowed the river,
And hacked and hewed as a great god can,　　　　　　15
With his hard bleak steel at the patient reed,
Till there was not a sign of a leaf indeed
　　To prove it fresh from the river.

IV

He cut it short, did the great god Pan,
　　(How tall it stood in the river!)　　　　　　　　　20
Then drew the pith, like the heart of a man,
Steadily from the outside ring,
And notched the poor dry empty thing
　　In holes, as he sate by the river.

V

"This is the way," laughed the great god Pan,　　　　25
　　(Laughed while he sate by the river!)
"The only way since gods began
To make sweet music they could succeed."
Then, dropping his mouth to a hole in the reed,
　　He blew in power by the river.　　　　　　　　　30

Notes

invention of poetry. In the Greek pastoral poets, Theocritus (third century BCE), Moschus (fl. 150 BCE), and Bion (fl. 100 BCE), Pan and his Arcadian countryside are often referred to, along with such shepherds as Daphnis. Pan was the only Greek god besides Asclepius (god of medicine) who died, so that his death represents the end of the ancient gods dethroned by Christianity, a theme examined in Elizabeth Barrett's "The Dead Pan" (1844). In this context, the etymology of Pan is related to Gk. *pan* (all) rather than Gk. *paein* (to pasture). Barrett Browning's last poem, it was first published in *Cornhill Magazine* (July 1860), with a full-page wood-block illustration (see http://www.nines.org/exhibits/How_A_Musical_Instrument_Embod) by Frederick Leighton (1830–96), a friend of the Brownings, who in 1862 would design the monument for Barrett Browning's grave in the English Cemetery in Florence. See: http://www.nines.org/exhibits/How_A_

Musical_Instrument_Embod. The poem was also published in *The Musical Quarterly* (21 July 1860), without numbers for the stanzas. It was reprinted in *Last Poems* (1862), a posthumous volume carried through the press by Robert Browning after Elizabeth's death on 29 June 1861. The end of the first line was used as a title for a novella, *The Great God Pan* (short version in *The Whirlwind*, 1890; expanded in 1894) by Arthur Machen (1863–1947), a horror story published in John Lane's series of decadent fiction, "Keynotes," illustrated by Aubrey Beardsley; for Pan, see also TENNYSON, IN MEMORIAM, SECT. XXI.

[17] *ban* curses.

[18] *river?* the question mark in the first edition at the end of the first stanza was removed in *Last Poems* (1862), making the second half of the stanza an answer to the question in the first two lines, but also closing off alternative readings.

VI

Sweet, sweet, sweet, O Pan,
   Piercing sweet by the river!
Blinding sweet, O great god Pan!
The sun on the hill forgot to die,
And the lilies revived, and the dragon-fly   35
   Came back to dream on the river.

VII

Yet half a beast is the great god Pan
   To laugh, as he sits by the river,
Making a poet out of a man.
The true gods sigh for the cost and pain,—   40
For the reed which grows nevermore again
   As a reed with the reeds in the river.

John Stuart Mill (1806–73)

The eldest of nine children, Mill was born in London, the son of the Scottish Utilitarian philosopher, James Mill (1773–1836), a brilliant but ill-tempered and demanding father, and Harriet Burrow (1782–1854), whose name is never mentioned in her son's *Autobiography*, but who is described in a cancelled passage as one "who without misgivings of any sort worked from morning till night for her [nine] children." Mill was a test-case for the principles of Utilitarian education, and he was taught by his father, with the help of Jeremy Bentham (1748–1832), philosopher and reformer, and Francis Place (1771–1854), English social reformer. Mill was sequestered from other children, and pushed to an extreme, learning Greek at the age of 3; Latin, geometry, and algebra at 8; and reading most of the literature, philosophy, and history of ancient Greece and Rome by the time he was 10, as well as calculus, logic, and political economy. He spent 1820–21 in France, studying chemistry, zoology, and logic at Montpelier University. Upon returning to London he joined his father in the London office of the East India Company. When he was 20 he suffered a nervous breakdown, caused, he claimed, by his rigorous education and suppres-

sion of feelings. Through reading the *Memoirs d'un père* (4 vols, 1804) of Jean-François Marmontel (1723–99), French historian, and Wordsworth's *Excursion* (1814), he began to recover, partly rejecting Utilitarianism, and developing new friendships. In 1830 he met Harriet Taylor (1807–58), already married to a London merchant, John Taylor (1796–1849); they had a close relationship for twenty-one years, and after Taylor's death they married in 1851. Mill acknowledged in his *Autobiography* and elsewhere how profoundly he was indebted to her in his political, philosophical, and economic writings, "in all that concerned the application of philosophy to the exigencies of human society and progress," from *Political Economy* to *On Liberty* which "was more directly and literally our joint production than anything else." Mill was elected MP for Westminster (1865–68), calling for equal votes for women in the Second Reform Bill (1867). As one of the leading philosophers of the nineteenth century, Mill wrote voluminously: *System of Logic* (2 vols, 1843); *Principles of Political Economy* (1848); *On Liberty* (1859); *Utilitarianism* (1863); *The Subjection of Women* (1869); and *Autobiography* (1873).

Standard Edition: *Collected Works*, ed. John Robson (33 vols, 1963–91); Richard Reeves, *John Stuart Mill: Victorian Firebrand* (2008). J. S. Mill at Utilitarian Net: www.utilitarian.net/ jsmill. See also Collected Works at Online Library of Liberty: http://oll.libertyfund.org/? option=com_staticxt&staticfile=show.php%3F collection=46&Itemid=27.

On Liberty

In his *Autobiography* Mill notes the profound impact made on him by his reading of Alexis de Tocqueville's *Democracy in America* (2 vols, 1835; 1840). Mill published two favourable reviews of it in the *Westminster Review* (Oct. 1835) and the *Edinburgh Review* (Oct. 1840), particularly stressing de Tocqueville's emphasis on equality in America. Mill claimed that his views had greatly advanced between the two reviews. The good result of democracy according to de Tocqueville, says Mill, is that "alone among all governments its systematic and perpetual end is the good of the immense majority." However, this advantage is balanced with a serious disadvantage: "that the interest of the majority is not always identical with the interest of all; and hence the sovereignty of the majority creates a tendency on their part to abuse their power over all minorities." Hence, a major task of democracies is to educate people to make a proper choice of those who govern them, a choice based on the education of individual talents both in the electorate and in the governing, for the betterment of civil life. Mill's worry concerned not only education, however, but chiefly the relationship between individual rights and the state's authority, between dissent and the power of public opinion, and between private political or social dissent and the tyranny of the majority opinion. "It is," says Mill "a tyranny exercised over opinions, more than over persons, which he is apprehensive of" (quotations from the 1835 review). He continues to wrestle with such problems as the legitimate roles of private and public opinion in his essay "Civilization" (*Westminster Review*, Apr. 1836). Here Mill examines what civilization, as a form of democracy, means in England: "The triumph of democracy, or, in other words, of the govern-ment of public opinion, does not depend upon the opinion of any individual or set of individuals that it ought to triumph, but upon the natural laws of the progress of wealth, upon the diffusion of reading, and the increase of the facilities of human intercourse." In such a civilization (or democracy), there is a danger largely ignored: "The individual becomes so lost in the crowd, that though he depends more and more upon opinion, he is apt to depend less and less upon well-grounded opinion; upon the opinion of those who know him."

In the tradition of John Milton's *Areopagitica* (1644) and John Locke's *Letters on Toleration* (1689–92), Mill's essay sets out the pre-eminence of the individual and the personal and public liberty that would allow a person's abili-ties to flourish, and the legitimate limits that might be placed on that liberty. Consideration of such a theme was urgent in light of a number of historical conditions: the emergence of greater democratic representation in Britain (after 1832) and elsewhere in Europe (after the revolutions of 1848); increasing expansion of ideas through co-operatives and associations (especially Radical groups); widening literacy and expanded media for expressing diverse opinions; the tyranny of public opinion and institutions as in the Cornwall and London trials of the summer of 1857 for blasphemy against Christianity; and the role of the Church of England in protecting the literalism of its beliefs, as would happen in the *Essays and Reviews* controversy of the next year (1860).

Freedom of thought, that takes up the first part of *On Liberty*, individual opinion – and rights and responsibilities – may be overdeter-mined, or even coerced by public opinion, especially, as Mill argues in the second part of his essay, by public opinion that is institutionalized in state government. Mill, then, had worked over these ideas for almost twenty-five years before he put them in order with the help of Harriet Taylor, writing and discussing and rewriting every sentence and paragraph together as he says in his *Autobiography*. He published it in February 1859, four months after the death of Taylor, and dedicated to her: "It belongs as much to her as to me."

Mill's treatise has five chapters. In his first chapter, "Introductory," he surveys the history and meanings of liberty. He also introduces his fundamental principle of liberty, that only for self-protection can liberty be interfered with, or, put another way, power can only rightfully be used "to prevent harm to others." Chapter 2, "Of the Liberty of Thought and Discussion," deals with freedom of thought and of speech, arguing that they should not be coerced or limited, suppressed or silenced — because the suppressed thought or speech might be true; or the censors might be wrong or ill-informed; or the government might be acting wrongly to protect certain beliefs for the supposed well-being of society; or the legal persecution of opinion, say for blasphemy or atheism, can be an instance of the tyranny of public opinion or social intolerance — all positions that need the correction of free discussion or debate with the dissenting opinion for four reasons: to correct false public opinion; to ensure that the premises and arguments of true public opinion be understood; to guarantee that true opinion not be lost; and to assure a place for partial truths between extremes of truth and falsity. In chapter 3, "Of Individuality, as One of the Elements of Well-Being," liberty of action is tested by individuals who hold unpopular or even illegal beliefs – and who act on them, incurring legal punishment or social stigma. In chapter 4, "Of the Limits to the Authority of Society over the Individual," those who live under the benefits of society must not infringe the interests of others. At the same time, the state has no interest in those opinions or actions of an individual that affect only that person. The final chapter, "Applications," examines particular examples to clarify the argument. He reiterates his argument. Society can use "advice, instruction, persuasion, and avoidance by other people" for an individual's own good, provided no harm is done to others, but cannot use coercion. At the same time, an individual is responsible for actions that do harm others, and is then rightly subject to society's strictures. A number of examples are given: crime, profit from crime, self-damage, the implications of bad contracts, and so on.

From "Introductory"[1]

The subject of this Essay is not the so-called Liberty of the Will, so unfortunately opposed to the misnamed doctrine of Philosophical Necessity; but Civil, or Social Liberty:[2] the nature and limits of the power which can be legitimately exercised by society over the

Notes

JOHN STUART MILL

[1] *title* first published 1859.

[2] *Will... Liberty* Mill contrasts free will, the ability of people to choose courses of action independent of constraints, and "Philosophical Necessity," the view that all human actions are determined by constraints such that no other action could occur. In his *Autobiography* Mill writes of being held captive by a belief in necessity while in his mental crisis: "I perceived, that the word Necessity, as a name for the doctrine of Cause and Effect applied to human action, carried with it a misleading association; and that this association was the operative force in the depressing and paralysing influence which I had experienced. I saw that though our character if formed by circumstances, our own desires can do much to shape those circumstances; and that what is really inspiriting and ennobling in the doctrine of freewill, is the conviction that we have real power over the formation of our own character" (ch. 5). Social Liberty is the condition and operation of liberty in society with respect to the individual and the corporate nature of civic actions and responsibilities. Civil Liberty here does not mean for Mill the rights and

individual. A question seldom stated, and hardly ever discussed, in general terms, but which profoundly influences the practical controversies of the age by its latent presence, and is likely soon to make itself recognised as the vital question of the future. It is so far from being new, that in a certain sense, it has divided mankind, almost from the remotest ages; but in the stage of progress into which the more civilized portions of the species have now entered, it presents itself under new conditions, and requires a different and more fundamental treatment.

The struggle between Liberty and Authority is the most conspicuous feature in the portions of history with which we are earliest familiar, particularly in that of Greece, Rome, and England. But in old times this contest was between subjects, or some classes of subjects, and the government. By liberty, was meant protection against the tyranny of the political rulers. The rulers were conceived (except in some of the popular governments of Greece) as in a necessarily antagonistic position to the people whom they ruled. They consisted of a governing One, or a governing tribe or caste, who derived their authority from inheritance or conquest, who, at all events, did not hold it at the pleasure of the governed, and whose supremacy men did not venture, perhaps did not desire, to contest, whatever precautions might be taken against its oppressive exercise. Their power was regarded as necessary, but also as highly dangerous; as a weapon which they would attempt to use against their subjects, no less than against external enemies. To prevent the weaker members of the community from being preyed upon by innumerable vultures, it was needful that there should be an animal of prey stronger than the rest, commissioned to keep them down. But as the king of the vultures would be no less bent upon preying on the flock, than any of the minor harpies, it was indispensable to be in a perpetual attitude of defence against his beak and claws. The aim, therefore, of patriots, was to set limits to the power which the ruler should be suffered to exercise over the community; and this limitation was what they meant by liberty. It was attempted in two ways. First, by obtaining a recognition of certain immunities, called political liberties or rights, which it was to be regarded as a breach of duty in the ruler to infringe, and which if he did infringe, specific resistance, or general rebellion, was held to be justifiable. A second, and generally a later expedient, was the establishment of constitutional checks; by which the consent of the community, or of a body of some sort, supposed to represent its interests, was made a necessary condition to some of the more important acts of the governing power. To the first of these modes of limitation, the ruling power, in most European countries, was compelled, more or less, to submit. It was not so with the second; and to attain this, or when already in some degree possessed, to attain it more completely, became everywhere the principal object of the lovers of liberty. And so long as mankind were content to combat one enemy by another, and to be ruled by a master, on condition of being guaranteed more or less efficaciously against his tyranny, they did not carry their aspirations beyond this point. . . .

What was now wanted was, that the rulers should be identified with the people; that their interest and will should be the interest and will of the nation. The nation did not need to be protected against its own will. There was no fear of its tyrannizing over itself. Let the rulers be effectually responsible to it, promptly removable by it, and it could afford to trust them with power of which it could itself dictate the use to be made. Their power was but the nation's own power, concentrated, and in a form convenient for exercise. This mode of thought, or rather perhaps of feeling, was common among the last generation

Notes

freedoms that are customary in society, such as those guaranteed under a charter of rights and freedoms (freedom of the press, religion, free association, and

so on), though some of these also fall under his consideration, such as freedom of expression. For "Necessity Supreme," see THOMSON, *CITY OF DREADFUL NIGHT*, XIV.

of European liberalism, in the Continental section of which it still apparently predominates.[3] Those who admit any limit to what a government may do, except in the case of such governments as they think ought not to exist, stand out as brilliant exceptions among the political thinkers of the Continent. A similar tone of sentiment might by this time have been prevalent in our own country, if the circumstances which for a time encouraged it, had continued unaltered. ...

It was now perceived that such phrases as "self-government," and "the power of the people over themselves," do not express the true state of the case. The "people" who exercise the power are not always the same people with those over whom it is exercised; and the "self-government" spoken of is not the government of each by himself, but of each by all the rest. The will of the people, moreover, practically means the will of the most numerous or the most active part of the people; the majority, or those who succeed in making themselves accepted as the majority; the people, consequently, may desire to oppress a part of their number; and precautions are as much needed against this as against any other abuse of power. The limitation, therefore, of the power of government over individuals loses none of its importance when the holders of power are regularly accountable to the community, that is, to the strongest party therein. This view of things, recommending itself equally to the intelligence of thinkers and to the inclination of those important classes in European society to whose real or supposed interests democracy is adverse, has had no difficulty in establishing itself; and in political speculations "the tyranny of the majority"[4] is now generally included among the evils against which society requires to be on its guard. ...

In England, from the peculiar circumstances of our political history, though the yoke of opinion is perhaps heavier, that of law is lighter, than in most other countries of Europe; and there is considerable jealousy of direct interference, by the legislative or the executive power, with private conduct; not so much from any just regard for the independence of the individual, as from the still subsisting habit of looking on the government as representing an opposite interest to the public. The majority have not yet learnt to feel the power of the government their power, or its opinions their opinions. When they do so, individual liberty will probably be as much exposed to invasion from the government, as it already is from public opinion. But, as yet, there is a considerable amount of feeling ready to be called forth against any attempt of the law to control individuals in things in which they have not hitherto been accustomed to be controlled by it; and this with very little discrimination as to whether the matter is, or is not, within the legitimate sphere of legal control; insomuch that the feeling, highly salutary on the whole, is perhaps quite as often misplaced as well grounded in the particular instances of its application. There is, in fact, no recognised principle by which the propriety or impropriety of government interference is customarily tested. People decide according to their personal preferences. Some, whenever they see any good to be done, or evil to be remedied, would willingly instigate the government to undertake the business; while others prefer to bear almost any amount of social evil, rather than add one to the departments of human interests amenable to governmental control. And men range themselves on one or the other side in any particular case, according to this general direction of their sentiments; or according to the degree of interest which they feel in the particular thing which it is proposed that the government should do, or according to the

Notes

[3] *predominates* Mill is thinking of the intellectual heirs of the French Enlightenment, including Wilhelm von Humboldt (1767–1835), German linguist, educationist, and philosopher, whom he cited in the epigraph to the volume, and Auguste Comte (1798–1857), French social reformer, whom Mill was writing against concerning the rights of individuals. But these ideas were even more characteristic of the British Utilitarians, like his father James Mill and Jeremy Bentham.

[4] *majority* the phrase was used by de Tocqueville in *Democracy in America* and was quoted by Mill and used by him in both of his reviews, especially in the second (see above, headnote).

belief they entertain that the government would, or would not, do it in the manner they prefer; but very rarely on account of any opinion to which they consistently adhere, as to what things are fit to be done by a government. And it seems to me that in consequence of this absence of rule or principle, one side is at present as often wrong as the other; the interference of government is, with about equal frequency, improperly invoked and improperly condemned.

The object of this Essay is to assert one very simple principle, as entitled to govern absolutely the dealings of society with the individual in the way of compulsion and control, whether the means used be physical force in the form of legal penalties, or the moral coercion of public opinion. That principle is, that the sole end for which mankind are warranted, individually or collectively, in interfering with the liberty of action of any of their number, is self-protection. That the only purpose for which power can be rightfully exercised over any member of a civilized community, against his will, is to prevent harm to others.[5] His own good, either physical or moral, is not a sufficient warrant. He cannot rightfully be compelled to do or forbear because it will be better for him to do so, because it will make him happier, because, in the opinions of others, to do so would be wise, or even right. These are good reasons for remonstrating with him, or reasoning with him, or persuading him, or entreating him, but not for compelling him, or visiting him with any evil in case he do otherwise. To justify that, the conduct from which it is desired to deter him, must be calculated to produce evil to some one else. The only part of the conduct of any one, for which he is amenable to society, is that which concerns others. In the part which merely concerns himself, his independence is, of right, absolute. Over himself, over his own body and mind, the individual is sovereign.

It is, perhaps, hardly necessary to say that this doctrine is meant to apply only to human beings in the maturity of their faculties. We are not speaking of children, or of young persons below the age which the law may fix as that of manhood or womanhood.[6] Those who are still in a state to require being taken care of by others, must be protected against their own actions as well as against external injury. For the same reason, we may leave out of consideration those backward states of society in which the race itself may be considered as in its nonage. The early difficulties in the way of spontaneous progress are so great, that there is seldom any choice of means for overcoming them; and a ruler full of the spirit of improvement is warranted in the use of any expedients that will attain an end, perhaps otherwise unattainable. Despotism is a legitimate mode of government in dealing with barbarians, provided the end be their improvement, and the means justified by actually effecting that end. Liberty, as a principle, has no application to any state of things anterior to the time when mankind have become capable of being improved by free and equal discussion. Until then, there is nothing for them but implicit obedience to an Akbar or a Charlemagne,[7] if they are so fortunate as to find one. But as soon as mankind have attained the capacity of being guided to their own improvement by conviction or persuasion (a period long since reached in all nations with whom we need here

Notes

[5] *others* Mill refers to this notion as the "harm principle," recurrent throughout chapter 1, a restriction on "doing as we like" (see n. 10). On this topic he was influenced by von Humboldt's *On the Limits of State Action* (1850) in such ideas as the limits of civil law and actions that are harmful to others: "Where rights are infringed on by such actions, it is clearly the duty of the state to restrict them, and compel the agents to repair the injury they have inflicted" (ch. 11).

[6] *womanhood* Mill's distinction in using gendered language alludes to a problem in law: under the legal status of "coverture" a married women at this time was not deemed to be a legal person; see GENDER: WOMAN QUESTION; TAYLOR, "ENFRANCHISEMENT" and also GENDER: WOMAN QUESTION; NORTON, LETTER.

[7] *Akbar ... Charlemagne* Akbar the Great (1542–1605) was the Moghul emperor of India from 1556 to his death. Charlemagne (c.742–814) ruled as the king of the Franks from 768 to 814. Pope Leo III (750–816) crowned him Emperor of the Romans in 800. Both extended their empires, but also fostered learning and culture.

concern ourselves), compulsion, either in the direct form or in that of pains and penalties for non-compliance, is no longer admissible as a means to their own good, and justifiable only for the security of others.

It is proper to state that I forego any advantage which could be derived to my argument from the idea of abstract right, as a thing independent of utility. I regard utility as the ultimate appeal on all ethical questions; but it must be utility in the largest sense, grounded on the permanent interests of man as a progressive being. Those interests, I contend, authorize the subjection of individual spontaneity to external control, only in respect to those actions of each, which concern the interest of other people. If any one does an act hurtful to others, there is a *primâ facie* case[8] for punishing him, by law, or, where legal penalties are not safely applicable, by general disapprobation. There are also many positive acts for the benefit of others, which he may rightfully be compelled to perform; such as, to give evidence in a court of justice; to bear his fair share in the common defence, or in any other joint work necessary to the interest of the society of which he enjoys the protection; and to perform certain acts of individual beneficence, such as saving a fellow-creature's life, or interposing to protect the defenceless against ill-usage, things which whenever it is obviously a man's duty to do, he may rightfully be made responsible to society for not doing. A person may cause evil to others not only by his actions but by his inaction, and in either case he is justly accountable to them for the injury. The latter case, it is true, requires a much more cautious exercise of compulsion than the former. To make any one answerable for doing evil to others, is the rule; to make him answerable for not preventing evil, is, comparatively speaking, the exception. Yet there are many cases clear enough and grave enough to justify that exception. In all things which regard the external relations of the individual, he is *de jure*[9] amenable to those whose interests are concerned, and if need be, to society as their protector. There are often good reasons for not holding him to the responsibility; but these reasons must arise from the special expediencies of the case: either because it is a kind of case in which he is on the whole likely to act better, when left to his own discretion, than when controlled in any way in which society have it in their power to control him; or because the attempt to exercise control would produce other evils, greater than those which it would prevent. When such reasons as these preclude the enforcement of responsibility, the conscience of the agent himself should step into the vacant judgment seat, and protect those interests of others which have no external protection; judging himself all the more rigidly, because the case does not admit of his being made accountable to the judgment of his fellow-creatures.

But there is a sphere of action in which society, as distinguished from the individual, has, if any, only an indirect interest; comprehending all that portion of a person's life and conduct which affects only himself, or if it also affects others, only with their free, voluntary, and undeceived consent and participation. When I say only himself, I mean directly, and in the first instance: for whatever affects himself, may affect others *through* himself; and the objection which may be grounded on this contingency, will receive consideration in the sequel. This, then, is the appropriate region of human liberty. It comprises, first, the inward domain of consciousness; demanding liberty of conscience, in the most comprehensive sense; liberty of thought and feeling; absolute freedom of opinion and sentiment on all subjects, practical or speculative, scientific, moral, or theological. The liberty of expressing and publishing opinions may seem to fall under a different principle, since it belongs to that part of the conduct of an individual which concerns other people; but, being almost of as much importance as the liberty of thought itself, and resting in great part on the same reasons, is practically inseparable from it. Secondly, the principle requires liberty of tastes and pursuits; of framing the plan

Notes

[8] *case* (Lat. at first appearance) case on first examination.   [9] *jure* (Lat. according to the law).

of our life to suit our own character; of doing as we like,[10] subject to such consequences as may follow: without impediment from our fellow-creatures, so long as what we do does not harm them, even though they should think our conduct foolish, perverse, or wrong. Thirdly, from this liberty of each individual, follows the liberty, within the same limits, of combination among individuals; freedom to unite, for any purpose not involving harm to others: the persons combining being supposed to be of full age, and not forced or deceived.

No society in which these liberties are not, on the whole, respected, is free, whatever may be its form of government; and none is completely free in which they do not exist absolute and unqualified. The only freedom which deserves the name, is that of pursuing our own good in our own way, so long as we do not attempt to deprive others of theirs, or impede their efforts to obtain it. Each is the proper guardian of his own health, whether bodily, or mental and spiritual. Mankind are greater gainers by suffering each other to live as seems good to themselves, than by compelling each to live as seems good to the rest.

Though this doctrine is anything but new, and, to some persons, may have the air of a truism, there is no doctrine which stands more directly opposed to the general tendency of existing opinion and practice. Society has expended fully as much effort in the attempt (according to its lights) to compel people to conform to its notions of personal, as of social excellence. The ancient commonwealths thought themselves entitled to practise, and the ancient philosophers countenanced, the regulation of every part of private conduct by public authority, on the ground that the State had a deep interest in the whole bodily and mental discipline of every one of its citizens; a mode of thinking which may have been admissible in small republics surrounded by powerful enemies, in constant peril of being subverted by foreign attack or internal commotion, and to which even a short interval of relaxed energy and self-command might so easily be fatal, that they could not afford to wait for the salutary permanent effects of freedom. In the modern world, the greater size of political communities, and above all, the separation between spiritual and temporal authority (which placed the direction of men's consciences in other hands than those which controlled their worldly affairs), prevented so great an interference by law in the details of private life; but the engines of moral repression have been wielded more strenuously against divergence from the reigning opinion in self-regarding, than even in social matters; religion, the most powerful of the elements which have entered into the formation of moral feeling, having almost always been governed either by the ambition of a hierarchy, seeking control over every department of human conduct, or by the spirit of Puritanism.[11] And some of those modern reformers who have placed themselves in strongest opposition to the religions of the past, have been noway behind either churches or sects in their assertion of the right of spiritual domination: M. Comte, in particular, whose social system, as unfolded in his *Traité de Politique Positive*,[12] aims at establishing (though by moral more than by legal appliances) a despotism of society over the individual, surpassing anything contemplated in the political ideal of the most rigid disciplinarian among the ancient philosophers.

Notes

[10] *like* Matthew Arnold would use a similar phrase ten years later, "doing as one likes" to suggest anarchy (see, ARNOLD, n. 43 (WEB p. 395)).

[11] *hierarchy . . . Puritanism* a conventional distinction between authoritarian Catholicism and individualistic Calvinism with a belief in original sin and particular salvation; de Tocqueville had coined the term "individualism" in *Democracy in America* (vol. 2) to describe the Puritanism that he found in America.

[12] *Positive* Auguste Comte (1798–1857), French philosopher and economist, the founder of Positivism, published *Système de politique positive* in 1851–54. In the second edition of *On Liberty* Mill corrected the title to *Système*. Mill would publish *Auguste Comte and Positivism* in 1865. Mill admired Comte's struggle to establish the grounds for sociology and a "science of society" but distrusted both his rigid organization of society that suppressed individual rights and also his view of women as inferior to men.

Apart from the peculiar tenets of individual thinkers, there is also in the world at large an increasing inclination to stretch unduly the powers of society over the individual, both by the force of opinion and even by that of legislation: and as the tendency of all the changes taking place in the world is to strengthen society, and diminish the power of the individual, this encroachment is not one of the evils which tend spontaneously to disappear, but, on the contrary, to grow more and more formidable....

It will be convenient for the argument, if, instead of at once entering upon the general thesis, we confine ourselves in the first instance to a single branch of it, on which the principle here stated is, if not fully, yet to a certain point, recognised by the current opinions. This one branch is the Liberty of Thought: from which it is impossible to separate the cognate liberty of speaking and of writing. Although these liberties, to some considerable amount, form part of the political morality of all countries which profess religious toleration and free institutions, the grounds, both philosophical and practical, on which they rest, are perhaps not so familiar to the general mind, nor so thoroughly appreciated by many even of the leaders of opinion, as might have been expected. Those grounds, when rightly understood, are of much wider application than to only one division of the subject, and a thorough consideration of this part of the question will be found the best introduction to the remainder. Those to whom nothing which I am about to say will be new, may therefore, I hope, excuse me, if on a subject which for now three centuries has been so often discussed, I venture on one discussion more.

The Subjection of Women[13]

From Chapter 1

The object of this Essay is to explain as clearly as I am able, the grounds of an opinion which I have held from the very earliest period when I had formed any opinions at all on social or political matters,[14] and which, instead of being weakened or modified, has been constantly growing stronger by the progress reflection and the experience of life: That the principle which regulates the existing social relations between the two sexes—the legal subordination of one sex to the other—is wrong in itself, and now one of the chief hindrances to human improvement; and that it ought to be replaced by a principle of perfect equality, admitting no power or privilege on the one side, nor disability on the other.

Notes

[13] *title* with Mary Wollstonecraft's *A Vindication of the Rights of Women* (1792) and Caroline Norton's "Letter to the Queen" (1855), Mill's short book is one of the crucial statements of the Romantic and Victorian eras. The four chapters of the book deal with four major topics concerning sexual equality: first, nature versus nurture – women are projected to be and are taught to be feminine and subordinate, but their natural inferiority has no evidential validity; second, the legal forms of the marriage and divorce laws and sufferance that enslaved married women must be removed to be replaced with a new concept of marriage as between equals, based on love and respect; third, how the subjection of women affects men and children as well as it does women; and fourth, how marriage is like a master–slave relationship. In the course of the essay Mill discusses property rights extensively, but he avoids the question of divorce. He also advocates the admission of women to suffrage; see women and the law in GENDER: WOMAN QUESTION, n. 7. Harriet Taylor had published "Enfranchisement of Women," in the *Westminster Review* (July 1851), which Mill reprinted in his *Dissertations and Discussions* (1859; vol. 2) with a fulsome eulogy of Taylor. Critics have raised questions about Mill's use of the bourgeois family as the norm as well as his acceptance of the two spheres theory as "a desirable custom" (see GENDER: CONSTRUCTING, n. 7). Although *The Subjection of Women* was written in 1861, it was not published until 1869, when Mill had a more supportive audience resulting from the agitation over the Contagious Diseases Acts and the campaign for the women's franchise. For Margaret Oliphant's critical review of *The Subjection of Women*, see GENDER: WOMAN QUESTION; OLIPHANT (WEB p. 79).

[14] *matters* while Mill accepted his father's arguments throughout his *Essay on Government* (in *Encyclopædia Britannica*, 1820) on almost all matters, he regarded his father's acquiescence to women's exclusion from suffrage as "as great an error as any of those against which the Essay was directed" (*Autobiography*, ch. 4).

The very words necessary to express the task I have undertaken, show how arduous it is. But it would be a mistake to suppose that the difficulty of the case must lie in the insufficiency or obscurity of the grounds of reason on which my conviction rests. The difficulty is that which exists in all cases in which there is a mass of feeling to be contended against. So long as an opinion is strongly rooted in the feelings, it gains rather than loses instability by having a preponderating weight of argument against it. For if it were accepted as a result of argument, the refutation of the argument might shake the solidity of the conviction; but when it rests solely on feeling, the worse it fares in argumentative contest, the more persuaded its adherents are that their feeling must have some deeper ground, which the arguments do not reach; and while the feeling remains, it is always throwing up fresh entrenchments of argument to repair any breach made in the old.[15] . . .

If the authority of men over women, when first established, had been the result of a conscientious comparison between different modes of constituting the government of society; if, after trying various other modes of social organization—the government of women over men, equality between the two, and such mixed and divided modes of government as might be invented—it had been decided, on the testimony of experience, that the mode in which women are wholly under the rule of men, having no share at all in public concerns, and each in private being under the legal obligation of obedience to the man with whom she has associated her destiny, was the arrangement most conducive to the happiness and well being of both; its general adoption might then be fairly thought to be some evidence that, at the time when it was adopted, it was the best: though even then the considerations which recommended it may, like so many other primeval social facts of the greatest importance, have subsequently, in the course of ages, ceased to exist. But the state of the case is in every respect the reverse of this. In the first place, the opinion in favour of the present system, which entirely subordinates the weaker sex to the stronger, rests upon theory only; for there never has been trial made of any other: so that experience, in the sense in which it is vulgarly opposed to theory, cannot be pretended to have pronounced any verdict. And in the second place, the adoption of this system of inequality never was the result of deliberation, or forethought, or any social ideas, or any notion whatever of what conduced to the benefit of humanity or the good order of society. It arose simply from the fact that from the very earliest twilight of human society, every woman (owing to the value attached to her by men, combined with her inferiority in muscular strength) was found in a state of bondage to some man. Laws and systems of polity always begin by recognising the relations they find already existing between individuals. They convert what was a mere physical fact into a legal right, give it the sanction of society, and principally aim at the substitution of public and organized means of asserting and protecting these rights, instead of the irregular and lawless conflict of physical strength. Those who had already been compelled to obedience became in this manner legally bound to it. Slavery, from being a mere affair of force between the master and the slave, became regularized and a matter of compact among the masters, who, binding themselves to one another for common protection, guaranteed by their collective strength the private possessions of each, including his slaves.[16] In early times, the great majority of the male sex were slaves, as well as the whole of the female. And many ages elapsed,

Notes

[15] *old* Mill's polemical rhetoric in this paragraph alludes self-consciously to the difficulty of his task ("task," "arduous," "difficulty," "argument" [six uses]), as well as to its contradictions ("insufficiency," "conviction" [two uses], "contended against," "instability," "solidity," "contest") and metaphors of legal and military battle ("case," "entrenchments," "breach").

[16] *slaves* here Mill introduces one of his key analogies, slave/housewife and the necessity for the emancipation of each. Another common analogy, especially among Chartist and other working-class writing in the 1830s–1840s, was that between the slave and the factory worker. "Gradual Oppression of the Labourer" by T. B. Smith (fl. 1830s–1840s) in *Northern Star* (28 Apr. 1838) explicitly compares the

some of them ages of high cultivation, before any thinker was bold enough to question the rightfulness, and the absolute social necessity, either of the one slavery or of the other. By degrees such thinkers did arise: and (the general progress of society assisting) the slavery of the male sex has, in all the countries of Christian Europe at least (though, in one of them, only within the last few years[17]) been at length abolished, and that of the female sex has been gradually changed into a milder form of dependence. But this dependence, as it exists at present, is not an original institution, taking a fresh start from considerations of justice and social expediency—it is the primitive state of slavery lasting on, through successive mitigations and modifications occasioned by the same causes which have softened the general manners, and brought all human relations more under the control of justice and the influence of humanity. It has not lost the taint of its brutal origin. No presumption in its favour, therefore, can be drawn from the fact of its existence. The only such presumption which it could be supposed to have, must be grounded on its having lasted till now, when so many other things which came down from the same odious source have been done away with. And this, indeed, is what makes it strange to ordinary ears, to hear it asserted that the inequality of rights between men and women has no other source than the law of the strongest. . . .

But, it will be said, the rule of men over women differs from all these others in not being a rule of force: it is accepted voluntarily; women make no complaint, and are consenting parties to it. In the first place, a great number of women do not accept it. Ever since there have been women able to make their sentiments known by their writings (the only mode of publicity which society permits to them), an increasing number of them have recorded protests against their present social condition: and recently many thousands of them, headed by the most eminent women known to the public, have petitioned Parliament for their admission to the Parliamentary Suffrage.[18] The claim of women to be educated as solidly, and in the same branches of knowledge, as men, is urged with grow- ing intensity, and with a great prospect of success; while the demand for their admission into professions and occupations hitherto closed against them, becomes every year more urgent. Though there are not in this country, as there are in the United States, periodical Conventions and an organized party to agitate for the Rights of Women,[19] there is a numerous and active Society organized and managed by women, for the more limited object of obtaining the political franchise. . . .

Notes

plight of the Negro slave and the factory worker. In "Lines on the Conviction of the Glasgow Cotton Spinners" (*Northern Star* 3 Feb. 1838), Smith extends his worker– abolitionist alliance internationally, urging his readers to take their wives and children with them to swear at "the altars of the Almighty" to "combine to blot this outrage" and "show the world each chain of slavery broke." See also NORTON, n. 9. Slavery had been abolished in the British Empire in 1834, and in the United States from Abraham Lincoln's Emancipation Proclamation (1863) to the Thirteenth Amendment to the Constitution (1865), and the Fourteenth Amendment (1868), guaranteeing equal protection under the law. During the period when Mill was writing his treatise (1861, see n. 13), the British cam- paign for American Emancipation was ongoing. Mill joined the London Emancipation Society (founded 1862) and in the same year discussed emancipation in "The Contest in America," in *Fraser's Magazine* (Feb. 1862).

[17] *years* Russia had abolished serfdom in 1861.

[18] *Suffrage* Mill presented a huge petition for women's suf- frage in parliament in June, 1866. In March 1866 the Conservative government introduced the second Reform Bill to extend the vote to prosperous members of the working class. In favour of extending the vote to women Mill also proposed an amendment to remove any reference to the sex of householders able to vote, changing the word "man" to "person" throughout the bill. Although he gained a sizeable measure of support in this first vote for female suffrage in the Commons the bill failed by 196 votes to 73.

[19] *Women* the Seneca Falls Convention in New York in July 1848 marked the collective beginning of the campaign for women's suffrage in the United States, led by Lucretia Mott (1793–1880), Elizabeth Cady Stanton (1815–1902), and Frederick Douglass (1818–95). The National Women's Rights Convention was held annually from 1850. In 1848 Gerrit Smith (1797–1874) made women's suffrage part of the platform of the US Liberty Party of the 1850s and 1860s. See GENDER: WOMAN QUESTION; TAYLOR, "ENFRANCHISEMENT."

All causes, social and natural, combine to make it unlikely that women should be collectively rebellious to the power of men. They are so far in a position different from all other subject classes, that their masters require something more from them than actual service. Men do not want solely the obedience of women, they want their sentiments. All men, except the most brutish, desire to have, in the woman most nearly connected with them, not a forced slave but a willing one, not a slave merely, but a favourite. They have therefore put everything in practice to enslave their minds. The masters of all other slaves rely, for maintaining obedience, on fear; either fear of themselves, or religious fears. The masters of women wanted more than simple obedience, and they turned the whole force of education to effect their purpose. All women are brought up from the very earliest years in the belief that their ideal of character is the very opposite to that of men; not self-will, and government by self-control, but submission, and yielding to the control of others. All the moralities tell them that it is the duty of women, and all the current sentimentalities that it is their nature, to live for others; to make complete abnegation of themselves, and to have no life but in their affections. And by their affections are meant the only ones they are allowed to have—those to the men with whom they are connected, or to the children who constitute an additional and indefeasible tie between them and a man. When we put together three things—first, the natural attraction between opposite sexes; secondly, the wife's entire dependence on the husband, every privilege or pleasure she has being either his gift, or depending entirely on his will; and lastly, that the principal object of human pursuit, consideration, and all objects of social ambition, can in general be sought or obtained by her only through him, it would be a miracle if the object of being attractive to men had not become the polar star of feminine education and formation of character. . . .

What is now called the nature of women is an eminently artificial thing—the result of forced repression in some directions, unnatural stimulation in others. It may be asserted without scruple, that no other class of dependents have had their character so entirely distorted from its natural proportions by their relation with their masters; for, if conquered and slave races have been, in some respects, more forcibly repressed, whatever in them has not been crushed down by an iron heel has generally been let alone, and if left with any liberty of development, it has developed itself according to its own laws; but in the case of women, a hot-house and stove cultivation has always been carried on of some of the capabilities of their nature, for the benefit and pleasure of their masters. . . . Of all difficulties which impede the progress of thought, and the formation of well-grounded opinions on life and social arrangements, the greatest is now the unspeakable ignorance and inattention of mankind in respect to the influences which form human character. Whatever any portion of the human species now are, or seem to be, such, it is supposed, they have a natural tendency to be: even when the most elementary knowledge of the circumstances in which they have been placed, clearly points out the causes that made them what they are . . . .

The general opinion of men is supposed to be, that the natural vocation of a woman is that of a wife and mother. I say, is supposed to be, because, judging from acts—from the whole of the present constitution of society—one might infer that their opinion was the direct contrary. They might be supposed to think that the alleged natural vocation of women was of all things the most repugnant to their nature; insomuch that if they are free to do anything else—if any other means of living, or occupation of their time and faculties, is open, which has any chance of appearing desirable to them—there will not be enough of them who will be willing to accept the condition said to be natural to them. If this is the real opinion of men in general, it would be well that it should be spoken out. I should like to hear somebody openly enunciating the doctrine (it is already implied in much that is written on the subject)—"It is necessary to society that women should marry and produce children. They will not do so unless they are compelled. Therefore it is necessary to compel them." The merits of the case would then be clearly defined. It would be exactly that of the slaveholders of South Carolina and Louisiana. "It is necessary that cotton and sugar should be grown. White men cannot produce them. Negroes will not, for any wages which we choose to give. *Ergo* they must be compelled."[20] An illustration still closer to the point is that of impressment.[21] Sailors must absolutely be had to defend the country. It often happens that they will not voluntarily enlist. Therefore there must be the power of forcing them. How often has this logic been used! and, but for one flaw in it, without doubt it would have been successful up to this day. But it is open to the retort—First pay the sailors the honest value of their labour. When you have made it as well worth their while to serve you, as to work for other employers, you will have no more difficulty than others have in obtaining their services. To this there is no logical answer except "I will not": and as people are now not only ashamed, but are not desirous, to rob the labourer of his hire, impressment is no longer advocated. Those who attempt to force women into marriage by closing all other doors against them, lay themselves open to a similar retort. If they mean what they say, their opinion must evidently be, that men do not render the married condition so desirable to women, as to induce them to accept it for its own recommendations. It is not a sign of one's thinking the boon one offers very attractive, when one allows only Hobson's choice,[22] "that or none." And here, I believe, is the clue to the feelings of those men, who have a real antipathy to the equal freedom of women. I believe they are afraid, not lest women should be unwilling to marry, for I do not think that any one in reality has that apprehension; but lest they should insist that marriage should be on equal conditions; lest all women of spirit and capacity should prefer doing almost anything else, not in their own eyes degrading, rather than marry, when marrying is giving themselves a master, and a master too of all their earthly possessions. And truly, if this consequence were necessarily incident to marriage, I think that the apprehension would be very well founded. I agree in thinking it probable that few women, capable of anything else, would, unless under an irresistible *entrainement*,[23] rendering them for the time insensible to anything but itself, choose such a lot, when any other means were open to them of filling a conventionally honourable place in life: and if men are determined that the law of marriage shall be a law of despotism, they are quite right, in point of mere policy, in leaving to women only Hobson's choice. But, in that case, all that has been done in the modern world to relax the chain on the minds of women, has been a mistake. They never should have been allowed to receive a literary education. Women who read, much more women who write, are, in the existing constitution of things, a contradiction and a disturbing element: and it was wrong to bring women up with any acquirements but those of an odalisque,[24] or of a domestic servant.

 WEB p. 320

Autobiography
    From Chapter 1: "Childhood and Early Education"
    From Chapter 5: "A Crisis in My Mental History. One Stage Onward"

Notes

[20] *compelled* see n. 16.

[21] *Ergo … impressment* (ergo Lat. therefore). Impressment was forced conscription into naval service that had been stopped after the Napoleonic wars but that was reaffirmed in 1835 and not outlawed completely until conscription in the First World War.

[22] *choice* in logic or everyday life, a false choice between nothing at all or whatever is offered. It is named after Thomas Hobson (1544–1630), a Cambridge-to-London hosteler who refused to hire out his horses except in turn.

[23] *entrainement* infatuation.

[24] *odalisque* female concubine in a harem; see PFEIFFER, n. 1.

Caroline Norton (1808–77)

The Hon. Caroline Elizabeth Sarah Norton, feminist, social reformer, and author, was one of three sisters, granddaughters of the Irish playwright Richard Brinsley Sheridan (1751–1816). Her father, Thomas Sheridan, died in 1817 in Cape of Good Hope (South Africa) while serving as colonial secretary. His death left the family penniless. Her two sisters married into the peerage; but Caroline entered into unhappy marriage with George Chapple Norton (1800–75), a barrister and MP, who abused her physically and mentally. She was the centre of a circle of writers and politicians, including Edward Bulwer-Lytton, Mary Shelley, and Benjamin Disraeli. She first published *The Dandies Rout* (1825), a novel, followed by poetry, *The Sorrows of Rosalie* (1829); after leaving her husband (1836), she supported herself by her writings. Her husband won her earnings as his own in court, abducted their three sons, and accused his wife of having an affair with Lord Melbourne (1779–1848), then Whig prime minister. In 1835 George Norton sued Melbourne for adultery. He lost the case, but in the course of it, Caroline Norton's reputation was seriously damaged. She became a champion for women's rights, vigorously campaigning for the Custody of Infants Act (1839), giving custody to the mother, and the Matrimonial Causes Act (1857), allowing women to inherit property. She also published *English Laws for Women in the Nineteenth Century* (1854) and the important *Letter to the Queen* (1855): see GENDER: WOMAN QUESTION; NORTON. After an affair with the Conservative politician Sidney Herbert (1810–61) and a close friendship with George Meredith (by which he was influenced in writing *Diana of the Crossways*, 1886), in 1877 she married Sir William Stirling Maxwell (1818–78), dying three months later. No standard edition; Jane Gray Perkins, *The Life of the Honourable Mrs. Norton* (1909); Alan Chedzoy, *A Scandalous Woman: The Story of Caroline Norton* (1992); Diane Atkinson, *The Criminal Conversation of Mrs Norton* (2012). "Victorian Women Writers Project": http://webapp1.dlib.indiana.edu/vwwp/welcome.do

From *A Voice from the Factories*[1]

I

When fallen man from Paradise was driven,[2]   <1–9>
Forth to a world of labour, death, and care;
Still, of his native Eden, bounteous Heaven
Resolved one brief memorial to spare,

Notes

CAROLINE NORTON

[1] title in a preface the poem is dedicated to the politician and factory reformer Anthony Ashley Cooper, seventh Earl of Shaftesbury (1801–85). In a prefatory letter Norton declares that the poem "strictly adhered to the printed Reports," the *Reports of Factory Commissioners* (1833, 1834). Seven other publications, as well as her own anonymous poem, first published as a pamphlet in 1836, were reviewed by Ashley in the *Quarterly Review* (Dec. 1836): *Report from the Committee on the Bill to Regulate the Labour of Children in the Mills* (1832); *Reports of Factory Commissioners* (1833, 1834); *Reports and Evidence of the Parliamentary Committee on the Factory Question* (1832); John Fielden, *The Curse of the Factory System*

(1836); M. T. Sadler, *Factory Statistics … on the Ten-Hours Factory Bill* (1836); *An Enquiry into the State of the Manufacturing Population, and the Causes and Cures of the Evils therein Existing* (1831); James Phillips Kay, *The Morals and Physical Condition of the Working Classes Employed in the Cotton Manufacture in Manchester* (1832); and Charles Wing, *The Evils of the Factory System* (1836). Ashley commented that the poem presents "by no means over-coloured pictures of our accursed system of white slavery," and demanded that Parliament limit the hours of children in the mills and other factories. The Factory Act of 1833 had required that children 9 to 13 could not work more than eight hours a day, and

And gave his offspring an imperfect share
Of that lost happiness, amid decay;
Making their first *approach* to life seem fair,
And giving, for the Eden past away,
Childhood, the weary life's long happy holyday.[3]

VII

Because we feel, for Childhood's years and strength,   <54–62>
Unnatural and hard the task hath been;—
Because our sickened souls revolt at length,
And ask what infant-innocence may mean,
Thus toiling through the artificial scene;—
Because at that word, Childhood, start to birth
All dreams of hope and happiness serene—
All thoughts of innocent joy that visit earth—
Prayer—slumber—fondness—smiles—and hours of rosy mirth.

VIII

And therefore when we hear the shrill faint cries   <64–90>
Which mark the wanderings of the little sweep;[4]
Or when, with glittering teeth and sunny eyes,
The boy-Italian's voice, so soft and deep,
Asks alms for his poor marmoset asleep;
They fill our hearts with pitying regret,
Those little vagrants doomed so soon to weep—
As though a term of joy for all was set,
And that *their* share of Life's long suffering was not yet.

IX

Ever a toiling *child* doth make us sad:
'Tis an unnatural and mournful sight,
Because we feel their smiles should be so glad,
Because we know their eyes should be so bright.
What is it, then, when, tasked beyond their might,
They labour all day long for others' gain,—
Nay, trespass on the still and pleasant night,
While uncompleted hours of toil remain?
Poor little Factory Slaves[5]—for You these lines complain!

Notes

limited children 14 to 18 to twelve hours a day. The poem is in Spenserian stanzas (invented by Edmund Spenser in *The Faerie Queene* (1590, 1596). The poem was reprinted by William Dodd in 1847 in *The Labouring Classes of England by an "Englishman"* published in Boston.

[2] *driven* see Genesis 3: 23–24.

[3] *holyday* a Romantic trope of lost innocence recollected in childhood, as in Wordsworth's "Ode: Intimations of Immortality" (1807: 64–66): "But trailing clouds of glory do we come / From God, who is our home: / Heaven lies about us in our infancy!"

[4] *sweep* chimney-sweep: little boys were apprenticed as sweeps from the age of 8 (by law from 1788, though largely unenforced, so boys could start at 5 or 6). Their small bodies enabled them to sweep their way through the chimneys; because of their work they were particularly subject to testicular cancer. See CAMPBELL, n. 3 (WEB p. 288).

[5] *slaves* a conventional analogy between slaves and their owners, workers and the factory owners, or workers and the machines; Mill extends the analogy to slave / housewife; see MILL, n. 16).

X

Beyond all sorrow which the wanderer[6] knows,
Is that these little pent-up wretches feel;
Where the air thick and close and stagnant grows,
And the low whirring of the incessant wheel[7]
Dizzies the head, and makes the senses reel:
There, shut for ever from the gladdening sky,
Vice premature and Care's corroding seal
Stamp on each sallow cheek their hateful die,
Line the smooth open brow, and sink the saddened eye.

XIV

Mark the result. Unnaturally debarred   <118–162>
All nature's fresh and innocent delights,
While yet each germing energy strives hard,
And pristine good with pristine evil fights;
When every passing dream the heart excites,
And makes even *guarded* virtue insecure;
Untaught, unchecked, they yield as vice invites:
With all around them cramped, confined, impure,
Fast spreads the moral plague which nothing new shall cure.

XV

Yes, this reproach is added; (infamous
In realms which own a Christian monarch's sway!)
Not suffering *only* is their portion, thus
Compelled to toil their youthful lives away:
Excessive labour works the Soul's decay—
Quenches the intellectual light within—
Crushes with iron weight the mind's free play—
Steals from us leisure purer thoughts to win—
And leaves us sunk and lost in dull and native sin.

XVI

Yet in the British Senate[8] men rise up,
(The freeborn and the fathers of our land!)
And while these drink the dregs of Sorrow's cup,
Deny the sufferings of the pining band.
With nice-drawn calculations at command,
They prove—rebut—explain—and reason long;
Proud of each shallow argument they stand,

Notes

[6] *wanderer* the sorrows of the mythical wanderer, always denied rest and death, were a staple of European literature. Folklore figures included the Wandering Jew, an anti-Semitic legend that portrays the wanderer as a person who mocked Christ's crucifixion; and the Flying Dutchman, condemned to wander on a ghost ship until he found love, as in Walter Scott's *Rokeby* (1812), Charles Maturin's *Melmolth the Wanderer* (1820), "Vanderdecken's Message Home; Or, The Tenacity of Natural Affection," *Blackwood's Magazine* (May 1821), and Richard Wagner's opera, *The Flying Dutchman* (1843).

[7] *wheel* see BARRETT BROWNING, "THE CRY OF THE CHILDREN," STZ. 7 (WEB p. 303, ll. 77–88).

[8] *Senate* House of Lords.

And prostitute their utmost powers of tongue
Feebly to justify this great and glaring wrong.

XVII

So rose, with such a plausible defence
Of the unalienable RIGHT OF GAIN,
Those who against Truth's brightest eloquence
Upheld the cause of torture and of pain:
And fear of Property's Decrease made vain,
For years, the hope of Christian Charity
To lift the curse from SLAVERY's dark domain,
And send across the wide Atlantic sea[9]
The watchword of brave men—the thrilling shout, "BE FREE!"

XVIII

What is to be a slave? Is't not to spend
A life bowed down beneath a grinding ill?—
To labour on to serve another's end,—
To give up leisure, health, and strength, and skill—
And give up each of these *against your will*?
Hark to the angry answer:—"Theirs is not
A life of slavery; if they labour,—still
We *pay* their toil. Free service is their lot;
And what their labour yields, by us is fairly got."

XXXIX

Wake, dreamer!—Choose;—to labour Life away,   <343– 351>
Which of these little precious ones shall go
(Debarred of summer-light and cheerful play)
To that receptacle for dreary woe,
The Factory Mill?—Shall He, in whom the glow
Of Life shines bright, whose free limbs' vigorous tread
Warns us how much of beauty that we know
Would fade, when *he* became dispirited,
And pined with sickened heart, and bowed his fainting head?

XLV

Enter with him. The stranger who surveys   <397–405>
The little natives of that dreary place
(Where squalid suffering meets his shrinking gaze),
Used to the glory of a young child's face,
Its changeful light, its coloured sparkling grace,
(Gleams of Heaven's sunshine on our shadowed earth!)

Notes

[9] *sea* British support for the abolition of slavery in the Caribbean and America after the passing of the Slavery Abolition Act (1833). The act prepared for the abolition of slavery within the British Empire, including emancipation on 1 August 1834, though in fact slaves remained indentured in an apprenticeship system to their former owners. William Wilberforce (1759–1833) and others founded the first British Anti-Slavery Society in 1823. See also MILL, n. 16.

Starts at each visage wan, and bold, and base,
   Whose smiles have neither innocence nor mirth,—
And comprehends the Sin original from birth.

XLVIII

   These then are his Companions: he, too young
   To share their base and saddening merriment,
   Sits by: his little head in silence hung;
   His limbs cramped up; his body weakly bent;
   Toiling obedient, till long hours so spent
   Produce Exhaustion's slumber, dull and deep.
   The Watcher's stroke,[10]—bold—sudden—violent,—
   Urges him from that lethargy of sleep,
And bids him wake to Life,—to labour and to weep!

<424–450>

XLIX

   But the day hath its End. Forth then he hies
   With jaded, faltering step, and brow of pain;
   Creeps to that shed,—his HOME,—where happy lies
   The sleeping babe that cannot toil for Gain;
   Where his remorseful Mother tempts in vain
   With the best portion of their frugal fare:
   Too sick to eat—too weary to complain—
   He turns him idly from the untasted share,
Slumbering sinks down unfed, and mocks her useless care.

L

   Weeping she lifts, and lays his heavy head
   (With a woman's grieving tenderness)
   On the hard surface of his narrow bed;
   Bends down to give a sad unfelt caress,
   And turns away;—willing her God to bless,
   That, weary as he is, he need not fight
   Against that long-enduring bitterness,
   The VOLUNTARY LABOUR of the Night,
But sweetly slumber on till day's returning light.

LVIII

   Nor should we, Christians in a Christian land,
   Forget who smiled on helpless infancy,
   And blest them with divinely gentle hand.—
   "Suffer that little children come to me:"[11]
   Such were His words to whom we bow the knee!
   These to our care the Saviour did commend;

<514–531>

Notes

[10] *stroke* not a caress but the stroke of a whip to rouse the sleeping boy.

[11] *me* see Mark 10: 14.

And shall we His bequest treat carelessly,
Who yet our full protection would extend
To the lone Orphan child left by an Earthly Friend?

LIX

No! rather what the Inspired Law imparts
To guide our ways, and make our path more sure;
Blending with Pity (native to our hearts),
Let us to these, who patiently endure
Neglect, and penury, and toil, secure
The innocent hopes that to their age belong:
So, honouring Him, the Merciful and Pure,
Who watches when the Oppressor's arm grows strong,—
And helpeth them to right—the Weak—who suffer wrong!

The Picture of Sappho[12]

I

Thou! whose impassion'd face
The Painter loves to trace,[13]
Theme of the Sculptor's art and Poet's story[14]—
How many a wand'ring thought
Thy loveliness hath brought,   5
Warming the heart with its imagined glory!

II

Yet, was it History's truth,[15]
That tale of wasted youth,
Of endless grief, and Love forsaken pining?
What wert thou, thou whose woe   10
The old traditions show
With Fame's cold light around thee vainly shining?

Notes

[12] *title* for Sappho and other Victorian poems on Sappho, see LANDON, n. 1. Norton is responding to Felicia Hemans's "The Last Song of Sappho" (1831); see HEMANS. Published in *The Dream and Other Poems* (1840).

[13] *trace* Norton's poem may also be based on the Westmacott sketch to which Hemans refers; however, a number of other representations of Sappho, Phaon, the cliffs, her lyre, and her death were available, such as the figure of Sappho amongst other famous poets in Raphael's fresco *Parnassus* (1510) in the Stanza della Segnatura in the Vatican, Louis David's painting *Sappho and Phaon* (1809), and Theodore Chasseriau's *Sappho Leaping into the Sea from the Leucadian Promontory* (1840). Throughout the nineteenth century Sappho continued to be a popular theme for artists: an etching by Queen Victoria (1841),

William Bell Scott's engraving (1873), Edmund Friedrich Kanoldt's *Sappho at the Leucadian Cliffs* (1879), and many later paintings and drawings, such as those by Gustave Moreau (*Sappho Leaping from the Leucadian Cliff*, 1864; and *Death of Sappho*, 1871), Lawrence Alma Tadema (*Sappho and Alcaeus*, 1881), Gustav Klimt (*Sappho*, 1888–90), and Charles-Auguste Mengin (*Sappho*, 1877).

[14] *sculptors . . . story* sculptures of Sappho include a number of ancient marbles, especially the Capitoline Museum bust of a Roman copy of a Greek original of the fifth century BCE; John Gibson's *Sappho* (1834: RA); Henri de Triqueti's *Sappho and Cupid* (1851: Royal Collection), and James Pradier's *Sappho* (1852: Musée d'Orsay); the story refers to Ovid's *Heroides*: "Sappho and Phaon" (see also LANDON, n. 1).

[15] *truth* as in Ovid's *Heroides*.

III

Didst thou indeed sit there
In languid lone despair—
Thy harp neglected by thee idly lying—   15
Thy soft and earnest gaze
Watching the lingering rays
In the far west, where summer-day was dying—

IV

While with low rustling wings,
Among the quivering strings   20
The murmuring breeze faint melody was making,
As though it wooed thy hand
To strike with new command,
Or mourn'd with thee because thy heart was breaking?

V

Didst thou, as day by day   25
Roll'd heavily away,
And left thee anxious, nerveless, and dejected,
Wandering thro' bowers beloved—
Roving where *he* had roved—
Yearn for his presence, as for one expected?   30

VI

Didst thou, with fond wild eyes
Fix'd on the starry skies,
Wait feverishly for each new day to waken—
Trusting some glorious morn
Might witness his return,   35
Unwilling to believe thyself forsaken?

VII

And when conviction came,
Chilling that heart of flame,
Didst thou, O saddest of earth's grieving daughters!
From the Leucadian steep[16]   40
Dash, with a desperate leap,
And hide thyself within the whelming waters?

Notes —————————————————————————————————————

[16] *steep* see LANDON, n. 1.

VIII

Yea, in their hollow breast
Thy heart at length found rest!
The ever-moving waves above thee closing—   45
The winds, whose ruffling sigh
Swept the blue waters by,
Disturb'd thee not!—thou wert in peace reposing!

IX

Such is the tale they tell!
Vain was thy beauty's spell—   50
Vain all the praise thy song could still inspire—
Though many a happy band
Rung with less skilful hand
The borrowed love-notes of thy echoing lyre.

X

FAME, to thy breaking heart   55
No comfort could impart,
In vain thy brow the laurel wreath[17] was wearing;
One grief and one alone
Could bow thy bright head down—
Thou wert a *woman*,[18] and wert left despairing!   60

Notes

[17] *wreath* for laurel, see HEMANS, n. 17.

[18] *woman* before and after she wrote this poem, Norton campaigned for the rights of women. Thanks partly to her case and her advocacy, the Infant Custody Act was passed in 1839 (see GENDER: WOMAN QUESTION, nn. 7 and 11). She had published *The Separation of Mother and Child by the Law of Custody of Infants Considered* (1837), prompting personal attacks against her concerning her supposed inadequacies as a mother and alluding again to the old 1835 slander concerning her alleged affair with Lord Melbourne. She responded to these reviewers with *A Plain Letter to the Lord Chancellor* (1839) using the pseudonym Pearce Stevenson, in which she presents her arguments to the chancellor, Lord Brougham (1778–1868) and also takes on an anonymous reviewer in the *British and Foreign Review*, arguing that in such disputes a woman loses her proper name (both her surname and her propriety) while a reviewer can hide behind anonymity. A woman is subsumed in a man, and so is reduced to a grammatical variant: over and over she stresses women's vulnerability and oppression and erasure of the term woman, often printing it in italics to highlight it: "To him [her reviewer] the word *woman* signifies a *bad woman*; he cannot conceive any other case; he cannot form to himself any other idea. . . . Did this author never see that very usual and customary sight, a modest and affectionate wife? Did he never see a woman watching the cradle of her sick child? Did he never see a mother teaching her little one to pray? Did he never see the welcome of a long absent son to his home, the embrace of the aged mother, the tears of the young sisters? Did he never see, hear, or read any of the instances of devoted fondness and unswerving faith shewn by women to their husbands, in danger, in temptation, in distress?" She asks, regarding the care of a woman for her children, and, more generally concerning woman's nature: "What is it [such argument] but to deny the position of the woman as a rational and accountable creature?" Hence the assertion at the end of the poem seeks to reclaim that title for Sappho, on the basis that Sappho is the archetypal "poetess" and woman, roles that Norton claimed for herself, as did other women poets writing on this theme like L. E. L., Hemans, and Elizabeth Barrett Browning.

Charles Darwin (1809–82)

Charles Darwin came from an illustrious family with at least ten fellows of the Royal Society: his father, a successful doctor, Robert Waring Darwin (1766–1848) was the son of Erasmus Darwin (1731–1802), botanist, poet, and philosopher. His mother was Susannah Wedgwood (1765–1817), his father's first cousin and the daughter of the pottery manufacturer Josiah Wedgwood (1730–95), renowned as both an industrialist and abolitionist. Darwin was also somewhat distantly related to Elizabeth Gaskell who included a fictionalized portrait of him as Roger Hamley in *Wives and Daughters* (1866). Darwin's schooling was unremarkable, and he withdrew first from medical studies at Edinburgh after two years, and then from divinity at Cambridge. In preparing for his BA examinations, he made a thorough study of the writings of William Paley: "I am convinced that I could have written out the whole of the "Evidences [of Christianity, 1794]" with perfect correctness.... The logic of this book and, as I may add, of his "Natural Theology [1802]," gave me as much delight as did Euclid.... I did not at that time trouble myself about Paley's premises; and taking these on trust I was charmed and convinced by the long line of argumentation" (*Autobiography*). Darwin had immersed himself in various aspects of natural history, working on insect collecting, marine biology of invertebrates, and plant taxonomy. When his botany professor John Henslow (1796–1861) recommended him for the position of naturalist on the exploratory voyage of *H.M.S. Beagle*, his career as a world-class naturalist was begun. He published the account in *The Voyage of the Beagle* (1839) and collected his observations on bird variations, fossils, and plant and insect species and variations, especially the tortoises and finches on the remote Galapagos Islands. After returning, Darwin was busy giving lectures at various scientific associations, and worked on his own theories of the relations among species and their ancestors.

The geology and fossil evidence gleaned on the *Beagle* confirmed what he had read in the work of geologist Charles Lyell, that the earth was millions of years old and that species had slowly changed over that time. He had, however, no mechanism to explain the process. A reading of Thomas Malthus's *An Essay on the Principle of Population* (1798) showed him that the pressures on the environment would cause those more strong to adapt, and, he thought, pass on favourable traits to successive generations, thereby enabling species to adapt, and gradually to form new species, a process to be measured only over millions of years. Refining his findings over the next twenty years, he was spurred towards publication when another naturalist, Alfred Russel Wallace (1823–1913), sent him a paper that also proposed a theory of natural selection. They agreed to present a joint paper to the Linnean Society in London in 1858 (for Wallace, see RELIGION: GEOLOGY; WALLACE; see also RELIGION: GEOLOGY, n. 30). In 1859 Darwin published *On the Origin of Species*. The book outraged many of his contemporaries for dismissing special creation; it amazed the scientific community, and completely redirected the course of natural science. Darwin's literary and religious readers were also caught up in the fascination with evolution, and the surprise that the earth was older than 6,000 years. Over the following years Darwin continued to publish, controversially applying his methods and observations to human beings in *The Descent of Man* (1871), followed by *The Expression of the Emotions in Man and Animals* (1872), *Insectivorous Plants* (1875), and studies of crustaceans and earthworms, and many other topics. His recurrent long bouts of ill health forced him to moderate his propensity to overwork; he died acclaimed by the scientific world and was honoured with burial in Westminster Abbey beside Sir Isaac Newton (1642–1727). Standard edition: *The Works of Charles Darwin*, eds Paul H. Barrett and R. B. Freeman (29 vols,

1986); *The Autobiography of Charles Darwin, 1809–1882*, ed. Nora Barlow (1958); *The Correspondence of Charles Darwin*, eds Frederick Burkhardt and Sydney Smith (17+ vols, 1985–); Adrian Desmond and James Moore, *Darwin* (1991); Janet Browne, *Charles Darwin* (2 vols, 1995–2002). "Darwin Online": darwin-online.org.uk.

From *Autobiography*[1]

On returning home from my short geological tour in North Wales, I found a letter from Henslow, informing me that Captain Fitz-Roy was willing to give up part of his own cabin to any young man who would volunteer to go with him without pay as naturalist to the Voyage of the *Beagle*.[2] I have given, as I believe, in my MS. Journal[3] an account of all the circumstances which then occurred; I will here only say that I was instantly eager to accept the offer, but my father strongly objected, adding the words, fortunate for me, "If you can find any man of common sense who advises you to go I will give my consent." So I wrote that evening and refused the offer. On the next morning I went to Maer to be ready for September 1st, and, whilst out shooting, my uncle[4] sent for me, offering to drive me over to Shrewsbury and talk with my father, as my uncle thought it would be wise in me to accept the offer. My father always maintained that he was one of the most sensible men in the world, and he at once consented in the kindest manner. I had been rather extravagant at Cambridge,[5] and to console my father, said, "that I should be deuced clever

Notes

CHARLES DARWIN

[1] *title* the autobiography was dated by Darwin 31 May 1876 on the first page of the MS. Darwin wrote an addendum in 1881. His son Frances (1848–1925) included the autobiography in *The Life and Letters of Charles Darwin* (vol. 1 1887: our text), adding the following "Preface": "My father's autobiographical recollections, given in the present chapter, were written for his children,—and written without any thought that they would ever be published. To many this may seem an impossibility; but those who knew my father will understand how it was not only possible, but natural. The autobiography bears the heading, 'Recollections of the Development of my Mind and Character,' and end with the following note:—'Aug. 3, 1876. This sketch of my life was begun about May 28th ... and since then I have written for nearly an hour on most afternoons.' It will easily be understood that, in a narrative of a personal and intimate kind written for his wife and children, passages should occur which must here be omitted; and I have not thought it necessary to indicate where such omissions are made. It has been found necessary to make a few corrections of obvious verbal slips, but the number of such alterations has been kept down to the minimum." Darwin's wife and son cut many passages and phrases from the first edition of 1887, most having to do with his religious opinions, all restored by Darwin's granddaughter in *The Autobiography of Charles Darwin, 1809–1882. With Original Omissions Restored* (ed. Nora Barlow 1958); for a sample, see http://www.update.uu.se/~fbendz/library/cd_relig.htm.

[2] *Beagle* our excerpt omits Darwin's childhood and university career. In August 1831 Darwin accompanied Adam Sedgwick (1785–1873), professor of geology at Cambridge, on a geological survey of north Wales. Sedgwick taught him how to draw geological maps, and

how to classify and describe rock specimens. Meanwhile, Darwin had been wanting a botanical expedition with Henslow (see headnote) and others to Tenerife in the Canary Islands, when Henslow was offered the position of naturalist on *H.M.S. Beagle*. He declined and recommended Darwin. Robert FitzRoy (1805–65) was captain of the *Beagle* for its second voyage from 1831 to 1836. He had risen in the navy from midshipman to lieutenant from 1820 to 1824, and while on the first voyage of the *Beagle* became its temporary captain after Pringle Stokes shot himself in 1828.

[3] *Journal* Darwin's *Journal of Researches* (better known as *The Voyage of the Beagle*, 1839) was published as the third volume of FitzRoy's *Narrative of the Surveying Voyages of H.M.S. Adventure and Beagle* (1839).

[4] *Maer ... uncle* the home of Darwin's uncle, Josiah Wedgwood II (1769–1843), the son of the founder of the Etruria Works, the manufacturer of Wedgwood china. Wedgwood was the father of Emma, who would become Darwin's wife in 1839; Darwin went to Maer Hall to shoot partridge.

[5] *Cambridge* earlier in the *Autobiography* Darwin had written: "My time was sadly wasted there, and worse than wasted. From my passion for shooting and for hunting, and, when this failed, for riding across country, I got into a sporting set, including some dissipated low-minded young men. We used often to dine together in the evening, though these dinners often included men of a higher stamp, and we sometimes drank too much, with jolly singing and playing at cards afterwards. I know that I ought to feel ashamed of days and evenings thus spent, but as some of my friends were very pleasant, and we were all in the highest spirits, I cannot help looking back to these times with much pleasure."

to spend more than my allowance whilst on board the *Beagle*"; but he answered with a smile, "But they tell me you are very clever."

Next day I started for Cambridge to see Henslow, and thence to London to see Fitz-Roy, and all was soon arranged. Afterwards, on becoming very intimate with Fitz-Roy, I heard that I had run a very narrow risk of being rejected, on account of the shape of my nose! He was an ardent disciple of Lavater,[6] and was convinced that he could judge of a man's character by the outline of his features; and he doubted whether any one with my nose could possess sufficient energy and determination for the voyage. But I think he was afterwards well satisfied that my nose had spoken falsely.

Fitz-Roy's character was a singular one, with very many noble features: he was devoted to his duty, generous to a fault, bold, determined, and indomitably energetic, and an ardent friend to all under his sway. He would undertake any sort of trouble to assist those whom he thought deserved assistance. He was a handsome man, strikingly like a gentleman, with highly courteous manners, which resembled those of his maternal uncle, the famous Lord Castlereagh, as I was told by the Minister at Rio.[7] ...

Fitz-Roy's temper was a most unfortunate one. It was usually worst in the early morning, and with his eagle eye he could generally detect something amiss about the ship, and was then unsparing in his blame. He was very kind to me, but was a man very difficult to live with on the intimate terms which necessarily followed from our messing by ourselves in the same cabin.[8] We had several quarrels; for instance, early in the voyage at Bahia, in Brazil, he defended and praised slavery, which I abominated, and told me that he had just visited a great slave-owner, who had called up many of his slaves and asked them whether they were happy, and whether they wished to be free, and all answered "No." I then asked him, perhaps with a sneer, whether he thought that the answer of slaves in the presence of their master was worth anything?[9] This made him excessively angry, and he said that as I doubted his word we could not live any longer together. I thought that I should have been compelled to leave the ship; but as soon as the news spread, which it did quickly, as the captain sent for the first lieutenant to assuage his anger by abusing me, I was deeply gratified by receiving an invitation from all the gun-room officers to mess with them. But after a few hours Fitz-Roy showed his usual magnanimity by sending an officer to me with an apology and a request that I would continue to live with him.

His character was in several respects one of the most noble which I have ever known.

The voyage of the *Beagle* has been by far the most important event in my life, and has determined my whole career; yet it depended on so small a circumstance as my uncle offering to drive me thirty miles to Shrewsbury, which few uncles would have done, and on such a trifle as the shape of my nose. I have always felt that I owe to the voyage the first real training or education of my mind; I was led to attend closely to several branches of

Notes

[6] *Lavater* Johann Kaspar Lavater (1741–1801), Swiss poet and physiognomist, published *Physiognomische Fragmente* (1775–78, trans. as *Essays on Physiognomy*, 1789). Lavater held that the physical appearance, especially the shape and measurement of the head, could indicate traits of character.

[7] *Castlereagh ... Rio* Robert Stewart, Lord Castlereagh (1769–1822), Tory MP and Foreign Secretary from 1812 to 1822, was the head of the Britain delegation during the Congress of Vienna (1815) but became unpopular because of the Peterloo Massacre (1819); see CONDITION, WORKING-CLASS VOICES, n. 29 (WEB p. 52). The British minister plenipotentiary at Rio de Janeiro was Henry Stephen Fox (1791–1846) from 1833 to 1836, at the time of Darwin's visit.

[8] *cabin* Darwin was chosen by FitzRoy as a travelling companion who would share in his scientific interests in

charting the coast of South America. They were to share cramped quarters (3 by 3.3 metres) for five years.

[9] *Bahia ... anything* the *Beagle* visited Bahia in north-eastern Brazil in February 1832. As a major centre of the sugar plantations it was also the most important slave centre for Brazil. Darwin is writing of his experiences in 1832, about one year before the abolition of slavery in the British Empire. The abolitionists in Britain, especially the Clapham Sect of evangelical Anglican reformers, exerted a great deal of pressure on the government to influence the newly independent Brazil to abolish slavery, which they would not do until 1888. Darwin's relatives, the Wedgwoods, were strong abolitionists; see also BARRETT BROWNING, n. 37 (WEB p. 311).

natural history, and thus my powers of observation were improved, though they were always fairly developed.

The investigation of the geology of all the places visited was far more important, as reasoning here comes into play. On first examining a new district nothing can appear more hopeless than the chaos of rocks; but by recording the stratification and nature of the rocks and fossils at many points, always reasoning and predicting what will be found elsewhere, light soon begins to dawn on the district, and the structure of the whole becomes more or less intelligible. I had brought with me the first volume of Lyell's "Principles of Geology,"[10] which I studied attentively; and the book was of the highest service to me in many ways. The very first place which I examined, namely St. Jago in the Cape de Verde islands,[11] showed me clearly the wonderful superiority of Lyell's manner of treating geology, compared with that of any other author, whose works I had with me or ever afterwards read. . . .

During these two years I also went a little into society, and acted as one of the honorary secretaries of the Geological Society.[12] I saw a great deal of Lyell. One of his chief characteristics was his sympathy with the work of others, and I was as much astonished as delighted at the interest which he showed when, on my return to England, I explained to him my views on coral reefs.[13] This encouraged me greatly, and his advice and example had much influence on me. During this time I saw also a good deal of Robert Brown[14]; I used often to call and sit with him during his breakfast on Sunday mornings, and he poured forth a rich treasure of curious observations and acute remarks, but they almost always related to minute points, and he never with me discussed large or general questions in science. . . .

As I was not able to work all day at science, I read a good deal during these two years on various subjects, including some metaphysical books; but I was not well fitted for such studies. About this time I took much delight in Wordsworth's and Coleridge's poetry; and can boast that I read the "Excursion" twice through. Formerly Milton's "Paradise Lost" had been my chief favourite, and in my excursions during the voyage of the *Beagle*, when I could take only a single volume, I always chose Milton.[15] . . .

After my return to England it appeared to me that by following the example of Lyell in Geology, and by collecting all facts which bore in any way on the variation of animals and plants under domestication and nature, some light might perhaps be thrown on the whole subject. My first note-book was opened in July 1837. I worked on true Baconian principles,[16] and without any theory collected facts on a wholesale scale, more especially with respect to domesticated productions, by printed enquiries, by conversation with

Notes

[10] *Geology* just before the *Beagle* set sail, FitzRoy had given Darwin the first volume of *Principles of Geology* (1830) by Charles Lyell (1797–1875; see RELIGION: GEOLOGY (WEB p. 180)), geologist and later a lifelong friend of Darwin's. Lyell believed that the earth's geological surface was formed gradually and uniformly over vast periods of time still in operation: uniformitarianism; see RELIGION, GEOLOGY, n. 1. In late 1832 Darwin received the second volume published the same year, and the third volume in the Falkland Islands in 1834.

[11] *St. Jago . . . islands* St. Jago is the largest island in the Cape Verde archipelago off the west coast of equatorial Africa that Darwin explored for three weeks in January and February 1832. It came to be regarded as a turning point in his view of geology as he resolved to publish on the topic, gradually accepting Lyell's uniformitarianism over the previously taught theory of successive cataclysms.

[12] *Society* founded in 1807, the Geological Society of London received a royal charter in 1825 from George IV. Presidents would include William Buckland, Adam Sedgwick, Charles Lyell, and T. H. Huxley.

[13] *reefs* Darwin's first monograph was *The Structure and Distribution of Coral Reefs* (1842).

[14] *Brown* (1773–1858), Scottish botanist and classifier of the flora of Australia.

[15] *Milton* Darwin read and reread Milton during these five years on the *Beagle*, and, as many recent scientists have pointed out, found many grounds of connection between Milton's views of creation and the fall of man and biological evolution.

[16] *note-book . . . principles* in his *Journal* for 1837 Darwin elaborates: "In July opened first notebook on 'Transmutation of Species,'" a reference to note-book "B" (first edited and

skilful breeders and gardeners, and by extensive reading. When I see the list of books of all kinds which I read and abstracted, including whole series of Journals and Transactions, I am surprised at my industry. I soon perceived that selection was the keystone of man's success in making useful races of animals and plants. But how selection could be applied to organisms living in a state of nature remained for some time a mystery to me.

In October 1838, that is, fifteen months after I had begun my systematic enquiry, I happened to read for amusement "Malthus on Population,"[17] and being well prepared to appreciate the struggle for existence which everywhere goes on from long-continued observation of the habits of animals and plants, it at once struck me that under these circumstances favourable variations would tend to be preserved, and unfavourable ones to be destroyed. The result of this would be the formation of new species. Here then I had at last got a theory by which to work; but I was so anxious to avoid prejudice, that I determined not for some time to write even the briefest sketch of it. In June 1842 I first allowed myself the satisfaction of writing a very brief abstract of my theory in pencil in 35 pages; and this was enlarged during the summer of 1844 into one of 230 pages, which I had fairly copied out and still possess.[18]

But at that time I overlooked one problem of great importance; and it is astonishing to me, except on the principle of Columbus and his egg,[19] how I could have overlooked it and its solution. This problem is the tendency in organic beings descended from the same stock to diverge in character as they become modified. That they have diverged greatly is obvious from the manner in which species of all kinds can be classed under genera, genera under families, families under sub-orders and so forth; and I can remember the very spot in the road, whilst in my carriage, when to my joy the solution occurred to me; and this was long after I had come to Down.[20] The solution, as I believe, is that the modified offspring of all dominant and increasing forms tend to become adapted to many and highly diversified places in the economy of nature.[21]

Notes

published by Gavin de Beer in 1960), in which he begins to set out his view that the fixity or stability of species is "undermined" in favour of transmutation or changes across species. Darwin's scientific method was that developed by Francis Bacon (1561–1626), English philosopher, scientist, and statesman, in his *Novum Organum* (Lat. new instrument, 1620), in which he argues for the inductive method of investigation, proceeding gradually to a generalization by an examination of evidence from all of the data.

[17] *Populations* Thomas Robert Malthus (1766–1834), English divine and political economist, published *Essay on the Principle of Population* (1798), showing that the increase of population would involve a struggle for the necessities of life because of shortages of food. See also RELIGION: GEOLOGY, n. 35; for Wallace's revelatory reading of Malthus, see RELIGION: GEOLOGY, n. 21. Darwin's positive use of Malthus contrasts with contemporaneous attacks on him by Chartist writers: see, for instance, CONDITION: WORKING-CLASS VOICES, nn. 1 and 2 (WEB pp. 45–46).

[18] *possess* Darwin had first set out his theory of evolution in a letter to Lyell in January 1842, following it up with the "Pencil Sketch" of thirty-five pages, expanded by July 1844 into his "Essay" (230 pages). In October Chambers published *Vestiges* anonymously and Darwin read it in November. In January 1847 Darwin persuaded Hooker to read his "Essay" and Hooker responded with both positive

comment and also a negative response to Darwin's rejection of continuous creation. Bouts of ill health and the publication of his two volumes on barnacles (*Cirripedia*, 1851–54) consumed physical and mental energy before he could return to his discussion of evolution in *Origin*. The thirty-five page MS. was printed by Francis Darwin as *The Foundations of the Origin of Species, a Sketch Written in 1842* (1909). It was reprinted in the same year by Francis Darwin together with the 1844 MS. in *The Foundations of the Origin of Species: Two Essays Written in 1842 and 1844*.

[19] *egg* allusion to the story that after discovering America, Columbus was told that it was easy. He challenged the scoffers to stand an egg on its end unaided. When they failed, he tapped it gently to slightly break the shell and succeeded, saying it is easy once one has led the way. The source is Girolamo Benzoni's *History of the New World* (1565).

[20] *Down* Down House, near the village of Downe, 22 kilometres southeast of London, was where Darwin and his family lived from 1842 to 1906, and where he wrote most of his major works.

[21] *nature* Darwin discusses the relation of adaptation to natural selection, the modification of species, and altered conditions in a number of places in the *Origin*, as, for example, at the beginning of the chapter on "Natural Selection" (see RELIGION: GEOLOGY, DARWIN, *ORIGIN*, CH. 4).

Early in 1856 Lyell advised me to write out my views pretty fully, and I began at once to do so on a scale three or four times as extensive as that which was afterwards followed in my "Origin of Species"; yet it was only an abstract of the materials which I had collected, and I got through about half the work on this scale. But my plans were overthrown, for early in the summer of 1858 Mr. Wallace, who was then in the Malay archipelago, sent me an essay "On the Tendency of Varieties to depart indefinitely from the Original Type"; and this essay contained exactly the same theory as mine. Mr. Wallace expressed the wish that if I thought well of his essay, I should sent it to Lyell for perusal.[22]

The circumstances under which I consented at the request of Lyell and Hooker to allow of an abstract from my MS., together with a letter to Asa Gray, dated September 5, 1857, to be published at the same time with Wallace's Essay, are given in the "Journal of the Proceedings of the Linnean Society," 1858, p. 45.[23] I was at first very unwilling to consent, as I thought Mr. Wallace might consider my doing so unjustifiable, for I did not then know how generous and noble was his disposition. The extract from my MS. and the letter to Asa Gray had neither been intended for publication, and were badly written. Mr. Wallace's essay, on the other hand, was admirably expressed and quite clear. Nevertheless, our joint productions excited very little attention, and the only published notice of them which I can remember was by Professor Haughton[24] of Dublin, whose verdict was that all that was new in them was false, and what was true was old. This shows how necessary it is that any new view should be explained at considerable length in order to arouse public attention.

In September 1858 I set to work by the strong advice of Lyell and Hooker to prepare a volume on the transmutation of species, but was often interrupted by ill-health, and short visits to Dr. Lane's delightful hydropathic establishment at Moor Park.[25] I abstracted the MS. begun on a much larger scale in 1856, and completed the volume on the same reduced scale. It cost me thirteen months and ten days' hard labour. It was published under the title of the "Origin of Species," in November 1859. Though considerably added to and corrected in the later editions, it has remained substantially the same book.[26]

It is no doubt the chief work of my life. It was from the first highly successful. The first small edition of 1250 copies was sold on the day of publication, and a second edition of 3000 copies soon afterwards. Sixteen thousand copies have now (1876) been sold in England; and considering how stiff a book it is, this is a large sale. It has been translated into almost every European tongue, even into such languages as Spanish, Bohemian, Polish, and Russian. It has also, according to Miss Bird, been translated into Japanese,[27] and is there much studied. Even an essay in Hebrew has appeared on it, showing that the theory is contained in the Old Testament![28] The reviews were very

Notes

[22] *perusal* see RELIGION: GEOLOGY, n. 16.

[23] *p. 45* for the joint presentation, see RELIGION: GEOLOGY, n. 16.

[24] *Haughton* Samuel Haughton (1821–97), Irish scientist and professor of geology at Trinity College, Dublin, was the first to respond to the Darwin–Wallace paper: "If it means what it says, it is a truism; if it means anything more, it is contrary to fact."

[25] *Park* near Farnham in Surrey where Edward Wickstead Lane (1822–91), English hydrotherapist, held a clinic from which Darwin greatly benefited.

[26] *book* see RELIGION: GEOLOGY, n. 24.

[27] *Japanese* "Miss Bird is mistaken, as I learn from Prof. Mitsukuri" [note by Francis Darwin]. The first Japanese edition of the *Origin* was published in 1896, but the ideas of Darwin were first introduced to Japan by Edward S. Morse (1838–1925), American zoologist and

first professor of zoology at the Imperial University of Tokyo. Francis Darwin's first reference is to Isabella Bird (1831–1904), who published *Unbeaten Tracks in Japan* (1880). In Letter 21 she reports of a Japanese bookseller: "He has translations of some of the works of Huxley, Darwin, and Herbert Spencer, which, he says, are bought by the young men attending the higher school. The *Origin of Species* has the largest sale." Francis' second reference is to Kakichi Mitsukuri (1857–1909), professor of zoology at the Imperial University and the successor to Morse.

[28] *Testament* possibly the attempts to find an accord between Genesis and geology through traditional commentaries (*Mishna*) on the Bible. Earlier attempts include the commentary on the *Mishna* by Rabbi Israel Lipschitz (1782–1860) of Danzig (especially a lecture of 1842 on the Torah and

numerous; for some time I collected all that appeared on the "Origin" and on my related books, and these amount (excluding newspaper reviews) to 265; but after a time I gave up the attempt in despair. Many separate essays and books on the subject have appeared; and in Germany a catalogue or bibliography on "Darwinismus"[29] has appeared every year or two.

The success of the "Origin" may, I think, be attributed in large part to my having long before written two condensed sketches, and to my having finally abstracted a much larger manuscript, which was itself an abstract.[30] By this means I was enabled to select the more striking facts and conclusions. I had, also, during many years followed a golden rule, namely, that whenever a published fact, a new observation or thought came across me, which was opposed to my general results, to make a memorandum of it without fail and at once; for I had found by experience that such facts and thoughts were far more apt to escape from the memory than favourable ones. Owing to this habit, very few objections were raised against my views which I had not at least noticed and attempted to answer.

It has sometimes been said that the success of the "Origin" proved "that the subject was in the air," or "that men's minds were prepared for it." I do not think that this is strictly true, for I occasionally sounded not a few naturalists, and never happened to come across a single one who seemed to doubt about the permanence of species. Even Lyell and Hooker,[31] though they would listen with interest to me, never seemed to agree. I tried once or twice to explain to able men what I meant by Natural Selection, but signally failed. What I believe was strictly true is that innumerable well-observed facts were stored in the minds of naturalists ready to take their proper places as soon as any theory which would receive them was sufficiently explained. Another element in the success of the book was its moderate size; and this I owe to the appearance of Mr. Wallace's essay; had I published on the scale in which I began to write in 1856, the book would have been four or five times as large as the "Origin," and very few would have had the patience to read it.

I gained much by my delay in publishing from about 1839, when the theory was clearly conceived, to 1859; and I lost nothing by it, for I cared very little whether men attributed most originality to me or Wallace; and his essay no doubt aided in the reception of the theory. I was forestalled in only one important point, which my vanity has always made me regret, namely, the explanation by means of the Glacial period of the presence of the same species of plants and of some few animals on distant mountain summits and in the arctic regions. This view pleased me so much that I wrote it out in extenso, and I believe that it was read by Hooker some years before E. Forbes published his celebrated memoir ("Geolog. Survey Mem.," 1846.) on the subject. In the very few points in which we differed,

Notes

palaeontology), and by Netzif (Naftali Zvi Yehuda Berlin, 1816–93), both of whom taught that the cycles of ages referred to in the Bible and the commentaries could encompass the geological record and the history of the fossils. The *Origin* would not be translated into Hebrew until 1930.

[29] *Darwinismus* German booksellers' term for "Darwinism" or what English bibliographers and booksellers would call "Darwiniana" or materials on Darwin and his theories. But the term was also used for an amalgamation of Darwin's views with those of others by Ernst Haeckel; see n. 34.

[30] *abstract* see n. 18.

[31] *Lyell … Hooker* for Lyell, see n. 10. Lyell had great trouble in accepting the idea of evolution, especially natural selection, because of his biblical literalism. Hence, he rejected evolution in nine editions of the *Principles of Geology*, finally giving a lukewarm acceptance in the tenth edition (1866–68). Joseph Dalton Hooker (1817–1911), botanist and explorer, was Darwin's closest friend. In January 1844 Darwin explained his views on transmutation of species and natural selection to Hooker, and subsequently Darwin showed Hooker his work as it progressed. Hooker facilitated with Lyell the joint presentation by Darwin and Wallace before the Linnean Society in 1858 and was the first scientist to support Darwin in print, in his *Flora Tasmaniae* (December 1859). Finally, Hooker with Huxley defended Darwin against Wilberforce and others at the famous Oxford debate of 1860; see RELIGION: GEOLOGY; OXFORD DEBATE (WEB p. 182).

I still think that I was in the right.[32] I have never, of course, alluded in print to my having independently worked out this view.

Hardly any point gave me so much satisfaction when I was at work on the "Origin," as the explanation of the wide difference in many classes between the embryo and the adult animal, and of the close resemblance of the embryos within the same class. No notice of this point was taken, as far as I remember, in the early reviews of the "Origin," and I recollect expressing my surprise on this head in a letter to Asa Gray.[33] Within late years several reviewers have given the whole credit to Fritz Müller and Häckel,[34] who undoubtedly have worked it out much more fully, and in some respects more correctly than I did. I had materials for a whole chapter on the subject, and I ought to have made the discussion longer; for it is clear that I failed to impress my readers; and he who succeeds in doing so deserves, in my opinion, all the credit.

This leads me to remark that I have almost always been treated honestly by my reviewers, passing over those without scientific knowledge as not worthy of notice. My views have often been grossly misrepresented, bitterly opposed and ridiculed, but this has been generally done, as I believe, in good faith. On the whole I do not doubt that my works have been over and over again greatly overpraised. I rejoice that I have avoided controversies, and this I owe to Lyell, who many years ago, in reference to my geological works, strongly advised me never to get entangled in a controversy, as it rarely did any good and caused a miserable loss of time and temper.

Whenever I have found out that I have blundered, or that my work has been imperfect, and when I have been contemptuously criticised, and even when I have been overpraised, so that I have felt mortified, it has been my greatest comfort to say hundreds of times to myself that "I have worked as hard and as well as I could, and no man can do more than this." I remember when in Good Success Bay, in Tierra del Fuego,[35] thinking (and, I believe, that I wrote home to the effect) that I could not employ my life better than in adding a little to Natural Science. This I have done to the best of my abilities, and critics may say what they like, but they cannot destroy this conviction.

Written May 1st 1881

I have said that in one respect my mind has changed during the last twenty or thirty years. Up to the age of thirty, or beyond it, poetry of many kinds, such as the works of Milton, Gray, Byron, Wordsworth, Coleridge, and Shelley, gave me great pleasure, and

Notes

[32] *in extenso ... right* (Lat. completely, fully); Darwin included a discussion of the dispersal of organic beings during the Glacial period in chapter 9 of *Origin* (1859), expanding it and moving the fuller discussion to chapter 12 in the sixth edition (1872). Edward Forbes (1815–54), British botanist and biogeographer, worked for the Geological Survey and proposed in an article to which Darwin refers, "On the Connexion between the Distribution of the Existing Flora and Fauna of the British Isles and the Geological Changes which have Affected the Area" (1846), that there was a sunken land bridge or continent from Ireland to Portugal, including the Azores, to explain the migration of similar species across sea barriers. Forbes opposed the transmigration of species on religious grounds, and Darwin rejected his theory of the supposed continent's subsidence.

[33] *Gray* in his letter to his lifelong friend, Gray (1810–88), American botanist, Darwin wrote, "Embryology is to me by far the strongest single class of facts in favour of change

of form, & not one, I think, of my reviewers has alluded to this" (10 Sept. 1860).

[34] *Müller ... Häckel* Johann Friedrich Theodor Müller (1821–97), German biologist, published *Für Darwin* (1864, trans. as *Facts and Arguments for Darwin*, 1868); Ernst Heinrich Philipp August Haeckel (1834–1919), German biologist and supporter of Darwin, whose vast *Generelle Morphologie* (1866) advanced a synthesis of Darwin's concepts with the German Romantic naturalism of Fichte, Schelling, Hegel, and Goethe, combined with Lamarck's progressive evolutionism, in a mix he called "Darwinismus." In disagreement with Darwin, he held that ontogeny (embryonic development) recapitulated phylogeny (the developmental history of the species). Buchanan uses asexual reproduction in attacking the sensuousness of the Pre-Raphaelites: see LITERATURE: PRE-RAPHAELITISM, n. 16 (WEB p. 130).

[35] *Fuego* on the southern tip of South America, visited by Darwin and the *Beagle* in late December 1832.

even as a schoolboy I took intense delight in Shakespeare, especially in the historical plays. I have also said that formerly pictures gave me considerable, and music very great delight. But now for many years I cannot endure to read a line of poetry: I have tried lately to read Shakespeare, and found it so intolerably dull that it nauseated me. I have also almost lost my taste for pictures or music. Music generally sets me thinking too energetically on what I have been at work on, instead of giving me pleasure. I retain some taste for fine scenery, but it does not cause me the exquisite delight which it formerly did. On the other hand, novels which are works of the imagination, though not of a very high order, have been for years a wonderful relief and pleasure to me, and I often bless all novelists. A surprising number have been read aloud to me, and I like all if moderately good, and if they do not end unhappily—against which a law ought to be passed. A novel, according to my taste, does not come into the first class unless it contains some person whom one can thoroughly love, and if a pretty woman all the better.

This curious and lamentable loss of the higher æsthetic tastes is all the odder, as books on history, biographies, and travels (independently of any scientific facts which they may contain), and essays on all sorts of subjects interest me as much as ever they did. My mind seems to have become a kind of machine for grinding general laws out of large collections of facts.[36] ...

My habits are methodical, and this has been of not a little use for my particular line of work. Lastly, I have had ample leisure from not having to earn my own bread. Even ill-health, though it has annihilated several years of my life, has saved me from the distractions of society and amusement.[37]

Therefore my success as a man of science, whatever this may have amounted to, has been determined, as far as I can judge, by complex and diversified mental qualities and conditions. Of these, the most important have been—the love of science—unbounded patience in long reflecting over any subject—industry in observing and collecting facts— and a fair share of invention as well as of common sense. With such moderate abilities as I possess, it is truly surprising that I should have influenced to a considerable extent the belief of scientific men on some important points.

Edward FitzGerald (1809–83)

Born as Edward Purcell in Bredfield House in Suffolk, his family name was changed to FitzGerald in 1818 when his mother Mary Frances FitzGerald (1779–1855) inherited a second fortune, becoming extremely wealthy. The family were rich Irish landholders. FitzGerald was sent to grammar school at Bury St Edmunds, and in 1826 to Trinity College, Cambridge where he knew Thackeray and Tennyson. In 1831 he published anonymously a poem, "The Meadows in Spring," in the *Athenæum,* one of his few original compositions. He moved from one rented location to another, staying with family and friends or on his own in London or the country. Required to escort his ostentatious mother in society he rebelled by becoming scruffy and unkempt for the rest of his life. In 1849 he edited the

Notes

[36] *facts* Darwin's condition towards the end of his life may be compared to John Stuart Mill's nervous breakdown and recuperation through reading poetry; see MILL, *AUTOBIOGRAPHY,* n. 27 (WEB p. 324).

[37] *amusement* Darwin suffered from bouts of ill health throughout his life, perhaps from Chagas disease contracted from parasites after an attack of the Benchuca bug, widespread in South America, or perhaps another disease. His sickness has never been definitively identified. He suffered from dizziness, sweating, skin diseases, and severe stomach complaints.

works of his friend the Quaker poet Bernard Barton (1784–1849), and in 1851 he published a philosophic prose dialogue on education, *Euphranor*, and a collection of aphorisms, *Polonius* (1852). In 1844 he had met Edward Byles Cowell (1826–1903), seventeen years his younger, and already a self-taught linguist. About 1850 Cowell convinced FitzGerald to study Spanish under his guidance, leading to his free translation of *Six Dramas of Calderon* (1853), the chief works of Pedro Calderon (1600–81), Spanish poet and dramatist. At Cowell's urging he took up Persian in 1852, resulting in a translation of Jámi's *Salámán and Absál* (1856), and in the same year Cowell introduced him to the quatrains of Omar Khayyám called *rubá'i*. Cowell also left for Calcutta in 1856 to teach at the Presidency College while maintaining a long correspondence with FitzGerald (Cowell later returned to England to become the first professor of Sanskrit at Cambridge in 1867). Later in 1856 FitzGerald married Lucy Barton (1808–98), the daughter of his old Quaker friend – and probably at his death-bed injunction – but at the end of a disastrous year they separated. FitzGerald eventually published anonymously (1859) seventy-five of the quatrains of Omar Khayyám, and eventually three further editions, each with different arrangements and with numerous variants. Two more translated plays of Calderon were privately printed in 1865. Late in his life he published a free translation of Aeschylus' *Agamemnon* (1869) and of Sophocles' two plays about Oedipus, *The Downfall and Death of King Oedipus* (1880–81) in two parts. Other diffuse publications included a glossary of Suffolk sailing terms, a calendar of the life of Charles Lamb, and a child's version of the story of Dickens's Little Nell from *The Old Curiosity Shop* (1840–41). Standard Edition: *The Variorum and Definitive Edition of the Poetical and Prose Writings of Edward FitzGerald*, ed. George Bentham (7 vols, 1902–3); *The Letters of Edward FitzGerald*, eds Alfred McKinley and Annabelle Burdick Terhune (4 vols, 1980); Robert Bernard Martin, *With Friends Possessed: A Life of Edward FitzGerald* (1985); *Rubáiyát of Omar Khayyám: A Critical Edition*, ed. Christopher Decker (1997); *Rubáiyát of Omar Khayyám*, ed. Daniel Karlin (2009); Exploring Khayâm: http://www.exploringkhayyam.com/journal/?currentPage=2; Dutch Omar Khayyám Society: http://www.omarkhayyamnederland.com/index.html.

The Rubáiyát of Omar Khayyám, The Astronomer-Poet of Persia[1]

FitzGerald provided a thirteen-page "Preface" to his first edition (not included here) in which he sets out a few of the details of Omar's life and historical and cultural context, and gives some words of explanation about his translation. Omar ibn Ibrahim al Khayyám (1048–1131)

Notes ———————————————————

EDWARD FITZGERALD

[1] *title* there are numerous variants, revisions, and rearrangements from edition to edition; the first (our text) and fourth/fifth editions are most often reprinted. FitzGerald printed the first edition (250 copies) at his own expense and distributed a few copies to his friends, although not a single copy was sold. Two years later, however, a friend of the Pre-Raphaelites found copies remaindered for a penny each, and it was bought by Dante Rossetti and Algernon Swinburne, and was soon read by William Morris, Edward Burne-Jones, and George Meredith, and its fame grew and was assured. Swinburne used the stanza form in his *Laus Veneris* (1866), and William Morris hand-illuminated four copies of the poem. At the head of the poem, the title is given as *Rubáiyát of Omar Khayyám of Naishápúr*. FitzGerald added twenty-two explanatory notes to the text (reprinted here), mostly explanations of Persian colloquialisms.

was born in Naishapur in north-east Persia, now Iran. He was a tent-maker, but also an eminent scholar and poet, renowned as a mathematician (for a treatise on algebra), a philosopher (the successor to the polymath Avicenna, c.980–1037, who had assimilated Aristotelian rationalism about being and existence with Neoplatonic metaphysics and Islamic theology), and an astronomer and poet. His somewhat unorthodox approach to Islam and to scholarship was protected by the patronage of the ruler, Malik-Shah (d. 1092). Of the many hundreds of quatrains attributed to him, it is unknown how many are actually his. The *rubá'i* (Persian: four) is a traditional stanza form in Persian poetry, consisting of four lines of verse, a quatrain, in which the first, second, and fourth rhyme. There are metaphors, similes, and other figures of speech in the first three lines, and the fourth line serves to sum them up in an epigrammatic conclusion, a convention not usually followed by FitzGerald. Each *rubá'i* is self-contained as an independent composition. If grouped together, the Persian tradition required them to be linked in a sequence based on the last letter of the rhyming word. FitzGerald retained the quatrain (in iambic pentameter) and the rhyme scheme (*aaxa*), but he abandoned use of the alphabetizing order. He retranslated and reshuffled the order of the poems in each of his four editions, each of different lengths or combinations: 1859 (75 quatrains), 1868 (110), 1872 (101), and 1879 (101). A fifth (posthumous) edition (1889) incorporated some of the MS corrections FitzGerald made to the fourth edition. The second and third editions are most closely related as well as the fourth and fifth. FitzGerald also did a translation of thirty-one of the quatrains in rhyming Latin verse (1857), later using it occasionally as one of his sources by translating the Latin back into English quatrains. Numerous editions were published later in the nineteenth and the first half of the twentieth centuries, many with lavish illustrations. William Morris undertook four hand-illuminated manuscripts of the *Rubáiyát*: Google: William Morris Rubaiyat Images.

FitzGerald used copies of two major MSS of the *Rubáiyát*: the Persian MS at the Bodleian Library in Oxford (Ousley 525, dated 1460, 158 quatrains). It was unknown until Cowell discovered it in 1856 and transcribed it, sending it to FitzGerald before he left for Calcutta; and the Calcutta MS 1548 that Cowell discovered in the collection of the Bengal Asiatic Society, Calcutta, which has 674 quatrains. Again Cowell had a transcription of this manuscript made, and sent it to FitzGerald. To nineteenth-century readers, *The Rubáiyát* was a masterpiece, encapsulating for the age their sensibility, doubts, and stress on the fleeting moment. Some recent critics have aroused controversy over the adequacy of FitzGerald's translation, his fictionalizing, paraphrasing, and exoticizing. His knowledge of Persian was limited to the work before Cowell left for India in 1856 and his correspondence with him, and his study of Sir William Jones's *Grammar of the Persian Language* (fourth edition, 1797) and Francis Johnson's *Dictionary of Persian, Arabic & English* (1852), and several travel books about Persia for local atmosphere. To the Victorians such issues of accuracy mattered little in the light of the poem's view of Persia as strange and enticing. About half of FitzGerald's quatrains paraphrase specific stanzas in these two MSS, and another 45 per cent are combinations of two or more quatrains in the MSS. In almost every stanza there is some phrase or idea that is not in the originals, and that is FitzGerald's addition. At least three quatrains are wholly invented by him. Omar's original contains much material that FitzGerald ignores or sets aside, concerning satire and parody, wide reflections on time and life, paradoxes, and piety and religious devotion, as well as spiritual questioning. Some of Omar's quatrains reflect the influence of Sufism, the devotional mysticism that is one aspect of Islam, in which an individual renounces luxury in favour of a life of simplicity, seeking union with God. At the same time, Omar paradoxically mocks Sufi pietism. For instance, wine is almost omnipresent in the *Rubáiyát*, even though it is forbidden in Islam. So it is a poem in praise of wine, and also of the many meanings of wine, including wine as a means of ecstatic vision, and sexuality as a union of souls, and even of the soul with the divine. FitzGerald accommodated Omar's ideas to his own religious scepticism, finding the poem both refreshingly materialistic and to a degree pantheistic. FitzGerald's poem sets out the reflections of an aging Omar throughout a single day (FitzGerald's own idea), beginning at dawn and ending at nightfall. Within that loose frame, some poems are grouped thematically, such as the "Book of Pots." The reflections are an Epicurean meditation on fate and death, a common theme in the nineteenth century. Intensely materialist, the *Rubáiyát* stresses the impermanence of things and the transience of human life. In the face of such flux and change, and even of the continuous presence of mortality, it emphasizes the need to make the most of the present, the *carpe diem* (Lat. seize the day) motif from Horace. It praises the virtues of courage and levity, virtues that again coincided well with Victorian injunctions concerning optimistic patriotism and the nobility of courageous duty. However, unlike the Victorians in their obsession with the past, and the elaborate preparations for the future (with property, insurance, and succession), the poem asserts that only the present has value.

I

Awake! for Morning in the Bowl of Night
Has flung the Stone that puts the Stars to Flight[2]:
    And Lo! the Hunter of the East has caught
The Sultán's Turret in a Noose of Light.

II

Dreaming when Dawn's Left Hand was in the Sky[3]   5
I heard a Voice within the Tavern cry,
    "Awake, my Little ones, and fill the Cup
Before Life's Liquor in its Cup be dry."

III

And, as the Cock crew, those who stood before
The Tavern shouted —"Open then the Door!   10
    You know how little while we have to stay,
And, once departed, may return no more."

Notes

[2] *Flight* "Flinging a Stone into the Cup was the Signal for 'To Horse!' in the Desert" [author's note]. FitzGerald wanted the first three stanzas printed on the first page of the poem, as a "Lever de Rideau" (Fr. curtain raiser). The opening call in the poem is like the muezzin's first call to prayer at dawn (see n. 23), but ironically the religious metaphors in the next stanza are a call to the temple of the tavern. See also Joel 1: 5; and a number of hymns that begin this way, such as Thomas Ken's "Awake my soul and with the sun" (1674).

[3] *Sky* "The '*False Dawn*'; *Subhi Kházib*, a transient Light on the Horizon about an hour before the *Subhi sádhik*, or True Dawn; a well known Phenomenon in the East. The Persians call the Morning Gray, or Dusk, '*Wolf-and-Sheep-While*.' 'Almost at odds with, which is which'" [author's note]. FitzGerald here cites *Macbeth* 3. 4. 125–26: "Macbeth: What is the night? Lady Macbeth: Almost at odds with the morning, which is which."

IV

Now the New Year[4] reviving old Desires,
The thoughtful Soul to Solitude retires,
　　Where the WHITE HAND OF MOSES on the Bough　　　15
Puts out,[5] and Jesus from the Ground suspires.

V

Irám indeed is gone with all its Rose.
And Jamshýd's Sev'n-ring'd Cup[6] where no one knows;
　　But still the Vine her ancient Ruby yields,
And still a Garden by the Water blows.　　　　　　　20

VI

And David's Lips are lock't[7]; but in divine
High piping Péhleví,[8] with "Wine! Wine! Wine!
　　Red Wine!"—the Nightingale cries to the Rose
That yellow Cheek[9] of her's to'incarnadine.[10]

Notes

[4] *Year* "New Year. Beginning with the Vernal Equinox, it must be remembered, and (howsoever the old Solar Year is practically superseded by the clumsy *Lunar* Year that dates from the Mohammedan Hijra) still commemorated by a Festival that is said to have been appointed by the very Jamshyd whom Omar so often talks of, and whose yearly Calendar he helped to rectify.

'The sudden approach and rapid advance of the Spring,' (says a late Traveller in Persia) 'are very striking. Before the Snow is well off the Ground, the Trees burst into Blossom, and the Flowers start from the Soil. At *Now Rooz* (their New Year's Day) the Snow was lying in patches on the Hills and in the shaded Vallies, while the Fruit-trees in the Garden were budding beautifully, and green Plants and Flowers springing upon the Plains on every side—

> And on old Hyem's Chin and icy Crown
> An odorous Chaplet of sweet Summer buds
> Is, as in mockery, set—

Among the Plants newly appear'd I recognized some old Acquaintances I had not seen for many a Year: among these, two varieties of the Thistle; a coarse species of the Daisy, like the Horse-gowan; red and white Clover; the Dock; the blue Corn-flower; and that vulgar Herb the Dandelion rearing its yellow crest on the Banks of the Watercourses.' The Nightingale was not yet heard, for the Rose was not yet blown: but an almost identical Blackbird and Woodpecker helped to make up something of a North-country Spring" [author's note].

Omar had helped reform the solar calendar, enabling the lunar calendar to replace it. In the second paragraph of this note, FitzGerald quotes from one of his sources of information on Persia, Robert Binning's *Journal of Two Years' Travel in Persia* (2 vols, 1857), itself citing *A Midsummer Night's Dream* (2. 1. 109–11). Binning also says that the

festival of *Now Rooz* was initiated by Jamshyd, a hero-king of Persian legend.

[5] *out* "Exodus iv. 6; where Moses draws forth his Hand—not, according to the Persians, '*leprous as Snow*,'—but *white* as our May-Blossom in Spring perhaps! According to them also the Healing Power of Jesus resided in his Breath" [author's note]. In this note FitzGerald refers to the Koran (Sura 3) where Jesus breathes life into a clay bird.

[6] *Cup* "Irám, planted by King Schedad, and now sunk somewhere in the Sands of Arabia. Jamshyd's Seven-ring'd Cup was typical of the Seven Heavens. 7 Planets, 7 Seas, &c. and was a *Divining Cup*" [author's note]. The Garden of Heaven (*Iram*: Persian: heaven) is now located in Shiraz, Iran, where it was rebuilt on an earlier site in the eighteenth century by the Seljuk dynasty, and restored and extended in the nineteenth century. Schedad was a legendary king of the Adites, the son of Ad, and grandson of Ham, great-grandson of Shem, the son of Noah. The legendary cup of Jamshyd, with its magical powers of seeing the future, also contained the wine of immortality. Seven is a symbolic number in Islam, as also in Judaeo-Christian religions, where it is the perfect number: for the days of the week and for Mohammed who ascended into the seven heavens in Jerusalem, commemorated in the seven panels of the Dome of the Rock in the Holy Sanctuary.

[7] *lock't* as the shepherd king, David was known as the author of the Psalms, but that book is closed and his life over, though he is celebrated in Islamic tradition.

[8] *Péhleví* "Péhlevi, the old Heroic *Sanskrit* of Persia. Háfiz also speaks of the Nightingale's *Péhlevi*, which did not change with the People's" [author's note]. Péhleví was a pre-Islamic Persian language. Háfiz of Shiraz (1325/6–1389/90) was a revered Persian lyric poet.

[9] *Cheek* "I am not sure if this refers to the Red Rose looking sickly, or the Yellow Rose that ought to be Red; Red, White, and Yellow Roses all common in Persia" [author's note].

VII

Come, fill the Cup, and in the Fire of Spring   25
The Winter Garment of Repentance fling:
    The Bird of Time has but a little way
To fly—and Lo! the Bird is on the Wing.

VIII

And look—a thousand Blossoms with the Day
Woke—and a thousand scatter'd into Clay: 30
    And this first Summer Month that brings the Rose
Shall take Jamshýd and Kaikobád[11] away.

IX

But come with old Khayyám, and leave the Lot
Of Kaikobád and Kaikhosrú forgot:
    Let Rustum lay about him as he will,[12]   35
Or Hátim Tai cry Supper—heed them not.

X

With me along some Strip of Herbage strown
That just divides the desert from the sown,
    Where name of Slave and Sultán scarce is known,
And pity Sultán Máhmúd[13] on his Throne.   40

XI[14]

Here with a Loaf of Bread beneath the Bough,
A Flask of Wine, a Book of Verse—and Thou
    Beside me singing in the Wilderness—
And Wilderness is Paradise enow.[15]

Notes

[10] *incarnadine* see *Macbeth* 2. 2. 59.

[11] *Kaikobád* the mythological founder of the second Persian dynasty, as recorded in Persia's national epic *Shah Namah* (Persian, book of kings, *c.*1000) of Firdusi (940–1020).

[12] *will* "Rustum, the 'Hercules' of Persia, whose exploits are among the most celebrated in the *Shah-náma*. Hátim Tai, a well-known Type of Oriental Generosity" [author's note]. Kaikhosrú is the successor to Kaikobád (see n. 11). Rustum is also one of the title characters in Matthew Arnold's narrative poem *Sohrab and Rustum* (1853), based on Firdusi's poem. Hátim Tai, a fifth-century Arabian poet, was a famous adventurer, renowned for his generosity, with which his name became synonymous.

[13] *Máhmúd* Mahmud of Ghazni (Afghanistan) ruled from 997 to 1030 in what is today eastern Iran, though his realm eventually included most of Iran, Afghanistan, Pakistan, and western India.

[14] *XI* this quatrain is perhaps the best known in the poem. In the 1879 version it reads as follows: "A Book of Verses underneath the Bough, / A Jug of Wine, a Loaf of Bread—and Thou / Beside me singing in the Wilderness— / Oh, Wilderness were Paradise enow!" This quatrain was one that FitzGerald had earlier translated into Latin: *Si cerebri cerealis esset apud me sinceri / Panis, esset et cruoris Amphora repleta Meri* . . . (Lat. If I had bread from grain, the source unspoiled, and a great jar of blood-red wine . . .).

[15] *enow* (arch. enough).

XII

"How sweet is mortal Sovranty!"—think some: 45
Others—"How blest the Paradise to come!"
  Ah, take the Cash in hand and wave the Rest;
Oh, the brave Music of a *distant* Drum!¹⁶

XIII

Look to the Rose that blows about us—"Lo,
Laughing," she says, "into the World I blow: 50
  At once the silken Tassel of my Purse
Tear, and its Treasure¹⁷ on the Garden throw."

XIV

The Worldly Hope men set their Hearts upon
Turns Ashes—or it prospers; and anon,
  Like Snow upon the Desert's dusty Face   55
Lightning a little Hour or two—is gone.

XV

And those who husbanded the Golden Grain,
And those who flung it to the Winds like Rain,
  Alike to no such aureate Earth are turn'd
As, buried once, Men want dug up again.   60

XVI

Think, in this batter'd Caravanserai¹⁸
Whose Doorways are alternate Night and Day,
  How Sultán after Sultán with his Pomp
Abode his Hour or two, and went his way.

XVII

They say the Lion and the Lizard keep   65
The Courts where Jamshýd gloried and drank deep¹⁹:
  And Bahrám, that great Hunter—the Wild Ass
Stamps o'er his Head, and he lies fast asleep.

Notes

16 *Drum* "A Drum—beaten outside a Palace" [author's note].
Wave: waive.

17 *Treasure* "That is, the Rose's Golden Centre" [author's note].

18 *Caravanserai* resting stop for caravans in the desert; a metaphor for the world.

19 *deep* "Persepolis: call'd also *Takht'i Jamshyd*—The THRONE OF JAMSHYD, 'King-Splendid,' of the mythical *Peeshdádian* Dynasty, and supposed (with Shah-náma Authority) to have been founded and built by him, though others refer it to the Work of the Genie King, Ján Ibn Jann, who also built the Pyramids before the time of Adam. It is also called *Chehl-minar—Forty-column*; which is Persian, probably, for *Column-countless*; the Hall they adorned or supported with their Lotus Base and taurine Capital indicating double that Number, though now counted down to less than half by Earthquake and other Inroad. By whomsoever built, unquestionably the Monument of a

XVIII

I sometimes think that never blows so red
The Rose as where some buried Cæsar bled;
That every Hyacinth[20] the Garden wears
Dropt in its Lap from some once lovely Head.

70

XIX

And this delightful Herb whose tender Green
Fledges the River's Lip on which we lean—
Ah, lean upon it lightly! for who knows
From what once lovely Lip it springs unseen!

75

XX

Ah, my Belovéd, fill the Cup that clears
To-day of past Regrets and future Fears—
To-morrow?—Why, To-morrow I may be
Myself with Yesterday's Sev'n Thousand Years.[21]

80

Notes

long extinguished Dynasty and Mythology; its Halls, Chambers and Galleries, inscribed with Arrow-head Characters, and sculptured with colossal, wing'd, half human Figures like those of Nimroud; Processions of Priests and Warriors—(doubtful if any where a Woman)—and Kings sitting on Thrones or in Chariots, Staff or Lotus-flower in hand, and the *Ferooher*—Symbol of Existence—with his wing'd Globe, common also to Assyria and Ægypt—over their heads. All this, together with Aqueduct and Cistern, and other Appurtenance of a Royal Palace, upon a Terrace-platform, ascended by a double Flight of Stairs that may be gallop'd up, and cut out of and into the Rock-side of the *Koh'i Ráhmet, Mountain of Mercy*, where the old Fire-worshiping Sovereigns are buried, and overlooking the Plain of Merdasht.

Persians, like some other People, it seems, love to write their own Names, with sometimes a Verse or two, on their Country's Monuments. Mr. Binning (from whose sensible Travels the foregoing Account is mainly condens't) found several such in Persepolis; in one Place a fine Line of Háfiz: in another 'an original, no doubt,' he says, 'by no great Poet,' however 'right in his Sentiment.' The Words somehow looked to us, and the 'halting metre' sounded, familiar; and on looking back at last among the 500 Rubáyiát of the Calcutta Omar MS.—*there* it is: old Omar quoted by *one* of his Countrymen, and here turned into hasty Rhyme, at any rate—

> This Palace that its Top to Heaven threw,
> And Kings their Forehead on its Threshold drew—
> I saw a Ring-dove sitting there alone,
> And 'Coo, Coo, Coo,' she cried, and 'Coo, Coo, Coo.'

So as it seems the Persian speaks the English Ring-dove's *Péhlevi*, which is also articulate Persian for 'Where?'

BAHRÁM GÚR—*Bahrám of the Wild Ass*, from his Fame in hunting it—a Sassanian Sovereign, had also his Seven Castles (like the King of Bohemia!) each of a different Colour; each with a Royal Mistress within side; each of whom recounts to Bahrám a Romance, according to one of the most famous Poems of Persia, written by Amír Khusraw: these Sevens also figuring (according to Eastern Mysticism) the Seven Heavens, and perhaps the Book itself that Eighth, into which the mystical Seven transcend, and within which they revolve. The Ruins of Three of these Towers are yet shown by the Peasantry; as also the Swamp in which Bahrám sunk, like the Master of Ravenswood, while pursuing his *Gúr*" [author's note].

FitzGerald draws on Binning (see n. 4) for his description of Persepolis, the capital city of Darius the Great and Xerxes of the Achaemenid Empire (*c.*550–330 BCE), north-east of Shiraz in modern Iran. FitzGerald refers to the vast archaeological site with its columns, terraces, stairs, rooms, and bas-relief sculptures, many of which are given the names he cites. Bahrám V, known also as Bahrám-Gur, was king of Persia from 421 to 438, best known for having repulsed the invasion of the Huns and for the legendary exploits that gathered around him. The king of Bohemia is Ludwig II of Bavaria (1845–64), the builder of many castles, including Neuschwanstein, and the patron of Richard Wagner. Ravenswood is both the name of a family and a castle in Walter Scott's *The Bride of Lammermoor* (1819) where the Master of Ravenswood dies in a pit of quicksand.

20 *Cæsar . . . Hyacinth* for Caesar see *Hamlet* 4. 1. 203–4, 213–14. In Greek mythology, the hyacinth is the flower that blooms from the blood of Hyacinthus who was accidentally killed by Apollo (see *Metamorphoses* 10. 162 ff.).

21 *Belovéd . . . years* "A Thousand Years to each Planet" [author's note]. The Belovéd here could be of either sex,

XXI

Lo! some we loved, the loveliest and best
That Time and Fate of all their Vintage prest,
    Have drunk their Cup a Round or two before,
And one by one crept silently to Rest.

XXII

And we, that now make merry in the Room   85
They left, and Summer dresses in new Bloom,
    Ourselves must we beneath the Couch of Earth
Descend, ourselves to make a Couch—for whom?

XXIII

Ah, make the most of what we yet may spend,
Before we too into the Dust descend;   90
    Dust into Dust, and under Dust, to lie,
Sans Wine, sans Song, sans Singer, and—sans End![22]

XXIV

Alike for those who for To-DAY prepare,
And those that after a To-MORROW stare,
    A Muezzín[23] from the Tower of Darkness cries   95
"Fools! your Reward is neither Here nor There!"

XXV

Why, all the Saints and Sages who discuss'd
Of the Two Worlds[24] so learnedly, are thrust
    Like foolish Prophets forth; their Words to Scorn
Are scatter'd, and their Mouths are stopt with Dust.   100

XXVI

Oh, come with old Khayyám, and leave the Wise
To talk; one thing is certain, that Life flies;
    One thing is certain, and the Rest is Lies;
The Flower that once has blown for ever dies.[25]

Notes

and the illustrated versions that proliferated after the 1890s make the beloved a female. But the implication throughout is that the beloved is male, as is also so in FitzGerald's Latin version. Similarly the *"sáki"* or wine-bearer in later texts is a male figure, as are all of the implications of quatrains XVII to XX.

[22] *Dust ... End* see the Burial Service in BCP: "earth to earth, ashes to ashes, dust to dust," echoing Genesis 3:19. For the repeated use of *"sans"* (Lat. without), see the speech in *As You Like It* on the stages of human life that begins: "All the

world's a stage" that ends with "Last scene of all, / That ends this strange eventful history, / Is second childishness and mere oblivion, / Sans teeth, sans eyes, sans taste, sans everything (2. 7. 143–70).

[23] *Muezzin* a mosque official who summons the faithful to prayer five times a day.

[24] *Worlds* this world and the afterlife.

[25] *dies* see Robert Herrick (1591–1674): "To the Virgins, to Make Much of Time" (1648: 1–4): "Gather ye rosebuds while ye may, / Old time is still a-flying; / And this same

XXVII

Myself when young did eagerly frequent   105
Doctor[26] and Saint, and heard great Argument
    About it and about: but evermore
Came out by the same Door as in I went.

XXVIII

With them the Seed of Wisdom did I sow,
And with my own hand labour'd it to grow: 110
    And this was all the Harvest that I reap'd—
I came like Water, and like Wind I go."

XXIX

Into this Universe, and *why* not knowing,
Nor *whence*, like Water willy-nilly flowing:
    And out of it, as Wind along the Waste,   115
I know not *whither*, willy-nilly blowing.

XXX

What, without asking, hither hurried *whence*?
And, without asking, *whither* hurried hence!
    Another and another Cup to drown
The Memory of this Impertinence!   120

XXXI

Up from Earth's Centre through the Seventh Gate
I rose, and on the Throne of Saturn sate,[27]
    And many Knots unravel'd by the Road;
But not the Knot of Human Death and Fate.

XXXII

There was a Door to which I found no Key: 125
There was a Veil[28] past which I could not see:
    Some little Talk awhile of ME and THEE
There seem'd—and then no more of THEE and ME.[29]

Notes

flower that smiles today, Tomorrow will be dying." An instance of the *carpe diem* (Lat. seize the day) motif.
[26] *Doctor* (Lat. teacher).
[27] *sate* "Saturn, Lord of the Seventh Heaven" [author's note].
[28] *Veil* see TENNYSON, IN MEMORIAM, SECTION LVI.

[29] ME "ME AND THEE; that is, some Dividual Existence or Personality apart from the Whole" [author's note]. In the first edition (1859), some of the author's footnotes were misnumbered, here numbers 29, 32, and 35. They have been put into their proper sequence here.

XXXIII

Then to the rolling Heav'n itself I cried,
Asking, "What Lamp had Destiny to guide   130
    Her little Children stumbling in the Dark?"
And—"A blind Understanding!" Heav'n replied.

XXXIV

Then to this earthen Bowl did I adjourn
My Lip the secret Well of Life[30] to learn:
    And Lip to Lip it murmur'd—"While you live   135
Drink!—for once dead you never shall return."

XXXV

I think the Vessel, that with fugitive
Articulation answer'd, once did live,
    And merry-make; and the cold Lip I kiss'd
How many Kisses might it take—and give!   140

XXXVI

For in the Market-place, one Dusk of Day,
I watch'd the Potter thumping his wet Clay:
    And with its all obliterated Tongue
It murmur'd—"Gently, Brother, gently, pray!"

XXXVII[31]

Ah, fill the Cup:—what boots it to repeat   145
How Time is slipping underneath our Feet:
    Unborn To-morrow, and dead Yesterday,
Why fret about them if To-day be sweet!

XXXVIII

One Moment in Annihilation's Waste,
One Moment, of the Well of Life to taste—   150
    The Stars are setting and the Caravan
Starts for the Dawn of Nothing—Oh, make haste![32]

Notes

[30] *Life* see Psalms 36: 9 and also *Paradise Lost* (II. 416).

[31] *XXXVII* this quatrain, as well as XLV, were completely omitted from subsequent revisions of the poem.

[32] *haste* "The Caravan travelling by Night (after their New Year's Day of the Vernal Equinox) by command of Mohammed, I believe" [author's note]. Night travel was enjoined because of the heat of the day.

XXXIX

How long, how long,[33] in infinite Pursuit
Of This and That endeavour and dispute?
    Better be merry[34] with the fruitful Grape   155
Than sadden after none, or bitter, Fruit.

XL

You know, my Friends, how long since in my House
For a new Marriage I did make Carouse:
    Divorced old barren Reason from my Bed,
And took the Daughter of the Vine to Spouse.   160

XLI

For "Is" and "Is-not" though *with* Rule and Line,
And "Up-and-down" *without*, I could define[35];
    I yet in all I only cared to know,
Was never deep in anything but—Wine.

XLII

And lately, by the Tavern Door agape,   165
Came stealing through the Dusk an Angel Shape
    Bearing a Vessel on his Shoulder; and
He bid me taste of it; and 'twas—the Grape!

XLIII

The Grape that can with Logic absolute
The Two-and-Seventy jarring Sects[36] confute: 170
    The subtle Alchemist that in a Trice
Life's leaden Metal into Gold transmute.

XLIV

The mighty Mahmúd, the victorious Lord,
That all the misbelieving and black Horde[37]
    Of Fears and Sorrows that infest the Soul   175
Scatter and slays with his enchanted Sword.

Notes

[33] *long* see Psalms 6: 3; 13: 1; and 94: 3–4.

[34] *merry* a biblical euphemism for being drunk, especially in the phrase "eat, drink, and be merry" (Ecclesiastes 8: 15; and Luke 12: 19), often conflated with "for tomorrow we die" (1 Corinthians 15: 32).

[35] *define* "A Laugh at his Mathematics perhaps"[author's note]. It is more likely that Omar is referring to the philosophical problems of being and non-being.

[36] *Sects* "The 72 Sects into which Islamism so soon split" [author's note]. The two major divisions of Islam are the Sunni and the Shia, within which are the proverbial seventy-two different sects or factions.

[37] *Horde* "This alludes to Mahmúd's Conquest of India and its swarthy Idolaters [author's note]. See n. 13. Mahmud invaded India in 1001, allegedly slaughtering 50,000 Hindus.

XLV[38]

But leave the Wise to wrangle, and with me
The Quarrel of the Universe let be:
　　And, in some corner of the Hubbub[39] couch,
Make Game of that which makes as much of Thee.　　　　180

XLVI

For in and out, above, about, below,
'Tis nothing but a Magic Shadow-show,
　　Play'd in a Box whose Candle is the Sun,
Round which we Phantom Figures come and go.[40]

XLVII

And if the Wine you drink, the Lip you press,　　　　185
End in the Nothing all Things end in—Yes—
　　Then fancy while Thou art, Thou art but what
Thou shalt be—Nothing—Thou shalt not be less.

XLVIII

While the Rose blows along the River Brink,
With old Khayyám the Ruby Vintage drink:　　　　190
　　And when the Angel[41] with his darker Draught
Draws up to Thee—take that, and do not shrink.

XLIX

'Tis all a Chequer-board[42] of Nights and Days
Where Destiny with Men for Pieces plays:
　　Hither and thither moves, and mates, and slays,　　　　195
And one by one back in the Closet lays.

L

The Ball no Question makes of Ayes and Noes,
But Right or Left as strikes the Player goes;
　　And He that toss'd Thee down into the Field,
He knows about it ALL—HE knows—HE knows![43]　　　　200

Notes

[38] *XLV* like XXXVII, quatrain was omitted from subsequent editions.

[39] *Hubbub* for Satan's hearing the "universal hubbub at the throne of Chaos," see *Paradise Lost* 2. 951–52.

[40] *go* "*Fanúsi khiyál*, a Magic-lanthorn still used in India; the cylindrical Interior being painted with various Figures, and so lightly poised and ventilated as to revolve round the Candle lighted within" [author's note].

[41] *Angel* in Islamic thought, the angel of death was called "Azräel."

[42] *Chequer-board* chess, played on a chequer board, was a commonplace metaphor, turning human life into a game, often depicted in medieval manuscripts as played between lovers In *The Tempest* Ferdinand and Miranda play chess. Often a living person plays against the figure of death. Chess was also a recreation for the elite, its rules seen as metaphors for living as in William Caxton's *The Game and Playe of Chesse* (1474). The metaphor was widely used in the nineteenth century, as in Browning's *Luria* (4. 1, 6–11; 1846), Kingsley's *A Saint's Tragedy* (4. 2. 32; 1848), Anne Brontë's *The Tenant of Wildfell Hall* (1848), and Lewis Carroll's *Through the Looking-Glass* (1872).

LI

The Moving Finger writes; and, having writ,
Moves on[44]; nor all thy Piety nor Wit
    Shall lure it back to cancel half a Line,
Nor all thy Tears wash out a Word of it.

LII

And that inverted Bowl we call The Sky,   205
Whereunder crawling coopt we live and die,
    Lift not thy hands to *It* for help—for It
Rolls impotently on as Thou or I.

LIII

With Earth's first Clay They did the Last Man's knead,
And then of the Last Harvest[45] sow'd the Seed: 210
    Yea, the first Morning of Creation wrote
What the Last Dawn of Reckoning shall read.

LIV

I tell Thee this—When, starting from the Goal,
Over the shoulders of the flaming Foal
    Of Heav'n Parwín and Mushtara they flung,[46]   215
In my predestin'd Plot of Dust and Soul

LV

The Vine had struck a Fibre[47]; which about
If clings my Being—let the Súfi flout[48];
    Of my Base Metal may be filed a Key,
That shall unlock the Door he howls without.   220

Notes

[43] *knows* "A very mysterious Line in the original;

    U dánad u dánad u dánad u—

breaking off something like our Wood-pigeon's Note, which she is said to take up just where she left off" [author's note]. (Persian: He knows he knows he knows he). The game referred to in this quatrain is polo, which originated in Persia in the fifth century BCE but did not become an established British sport until the founding of the Calcutta Polo Club (1862). FitzGerald knew of the sport from his reading of medieval Persian authors like Omar and Firdusi (see n. 12). In a letter to his friend Cowell he writes that these lines mean "Whither Destiny strikes the Ball must go—no use Grumbling: for he who strikes as he runs..." FitzGerald then quotes the Persian line above, meaning that "he who strikes as he runs, he knows where the ball goes." But the line also breaks off in uncertainty, just as the wood-pigeon's song does, only to be resumed at the same place.

[44] *on* human actions, on one level, once committed, cannot be undone; on another level, the inscription of human deeds in the book of life by God, once written, cannot be unwritten.

[45] *Clay ... Harvest* Adam (Heb. red, earth) in the Bible and the Koran is the first man, shaped from clay by God. In the Bible Christ is called the second Adam (1 Corinthians 15: 45); the Last Harvest is the Last Judgement (Revelation 14: 14–20).

[46] *flung* "Parwín and Mushtara—The Pleiads and Jupiter" [author's note]. In Omar's creation story, the stars of heaven are cast over the shoulders of the horse who draws the sun in his circuit, from the goal of the beginning of time, and marking it with the constellations of the Pleiades and the planet Jupiter, used astrologically to read one's fate, already determined in the stars. Omar, as FitzGerald says, was an astronomer but he also served as court astrologer.

[47] *Fibre* that is, it is my fate to be a drunkard, with a pun on "plot" as both a narrative or story and a burial ground.

[48] *flout* that is, let the Sufi jeer. The Sufi practised the mystical aspects of Islam, claiming that it derived from Mohammed and the Koran, a devotional style that became systematized about the year 1000.

LVI

And this I know: whether the one True Light,
Kindle to Love, or Wrath consume me quite,
    One Glimpse of It within the Tavern caught
Better than in the Temple lost outright.

LVII

Oh Thou, who didst with Pitfall and with Gin   225
Beset the Road I was to wander it,
    Thou wilt not with Predestination round
Enmesh me, and impute my Fall to Sin?

LVIII

Oh, Thou, who Man of baser Earth didst make,
And who with Eden didst devise the Snake;   230
    For all the Sin wherewith the Face of Man
Is blacken'd, Man's Forgiveness give—and take![49]

★ ★ ★ ★ ★ ★ ★ ★

KÚZA-NÁMA[50]

LIX

Listen again. One Evening at the Close
Of Ramazán, ere the better Moon arose,[51]
    In that old Potter's Shop I stood alone   235
With the clay Population round in Rows.

Notes

[49] *And this I know … take* FitzGerald translates these three quatrains that set out Omar's defiance to God's justice in terms of the contemporary debate in England about predestination and especially the literalist Anglican view of future punishment for present sins. The issue would come to a head with the publication of *Essays and Reviews* a year after the *Rubáiyát* (see RELIGION: RELIGIOUS FAITH; JOWETT (WEB p. 206)). Biblical language is used throughout these quatrains: "True Light" (John 1: 9); "Wrath consume" (Psalm 59: 13; Psalm 90: 7; and Ezekiel 22: 31); "Temple" (frequent), "Pitfall" (Lamentations 3: 47); "Gin" (a trap: Job 18: 8); and "Predestination" (Ephesians 1: 11 and elsewhere). "Fall" and "Sin" occur frequently. For Eden and the Snake, see Genesis 3.

[50] *Kúza-Náma* (Persian: Book of Pots), a section of the poem (LIX to LXVI) in which Omar visits a potter's shop in the evening, before the rising of the new moon during the fasting month of Ramadan. Seven of the pots speak to Omar, challenging both the authority and the skill of the potter, and demanding that Omar distinguish them from their maker. As an allegory for human beings made by

God, the Bible offers ample illustrations: Isaiah 45: 9; Jeremiah 18: 3–6; and Romans 9: 18–21. Browning wrote a reply to FitzGerald in his "Rabbi Ben Ezra" (1864) in which he takes a far more positive attitude to human life, including his section on the potter (XXVI and XXVII).

[51] *arose* "At the Close of the Fasting Month, Ramazán (which makes the Musulman unhealthy and unamiable), the first Glimpse of the New Moon (who rules their Division of the Year) is looked for with the utmost Anxiety, and hailed with all Acclamation. Then it is that the Porter's Knot may be heard toward the *Cellar*, perhaps. Old Omar has elsewhere a pretty Quatrain about this same Moon—

> Be of Good Cheer—the sullen Month will die,
> And a young Moon requite us by and bye:
>   Look how the Old one meagre, bent, and wan
> With Age and Fast, is fainting from the Sky!" [author's note].

Here and elsewhere FitzGerald shares in a general English (and western European) prejudice against both Persia and Islam. He writes in his letters to Cowell of the "effeminate Persian" and the decline of Persian culture and civilization

LX

And, strange to tell, among the Earthen Lot
Some could articulate, while others not:
    And suddenly one more impatient cried—
"Who *is* the Potter, pray, and who the Pot?"   240

LXI

Then said another—"Surely not in vain
My Substance from the common Earth was ta'en,
    That He who subtly wrought me into Shape
Should stamp me back to common Earth again."

LXII

Another said—"Why, ne'er a peevish Boy,   245
Would break the Bowl from which he drank in Joy;
    Shall He that *made* the Vessel in pure Love
And Fansy, in an after Rage destroy?"

LXIII

None answer'd this; but after Silence spake
A Vessel of a more ungainly Make: 250
    "They sneer at me for leaning all awry;
What! did the Hand then of the Potter shake?"

LXIV

Said one—"Folks of a surly Tapster tell,
And daub his Visage with the Smoke of Hell;
    They talk of some strict Testing of us—Pish!   255
He's a Good Fellow, and 'twill all be well."

LXV

Then said another with a long-drawn Sigh,
"My Clay with long oblivion is gone dry:
    But, fill me with the old familiar Juice,
Methinks I might recover by-and-bye!"   260

LXVI

So while the Vessels one by one were speaking,
One spied the little Crescent all were seeking:
    And then they jogg'd each other, "Brother! Brother!
Hark to the Porter's Shoulder-knot[52] a-creaking!"

* * * * * * * *

Notes

under the despotic rule of the Seljuk dynasty from the eleventh to the fourteenth centuries, despite the fact that the Seljuks adopted Persian culture and language.

[52] *Shoulder-knot* padded rope on which a carrier could rest his load.

LXVII

Ah, with the Grape my fading Life provide,   265
    And wash my Body whence the Life has died,
    And in a Windingsheet of Vine-leaf wrapt,
So bury me by some sweet Garden-side.

LXVIII

That ev'n my buried Ashes such a Snare
Of Perfume shall fling up into the Air,   270
    As not a True Believer passing by
But shall be overtaken unaware.

LXIX

Indeed the Idols I have loved so long
Have done my Credit in Men's Eye much wrong:
    Have drown'd my Honour in a shallow Cup,   275
And sold my Reputation for a Song.

LXX

Indeed, indeed, Repentance oft before
I swore—but was I sober when I swore?
    And then and then came Spring, and Rose-in-hand
My thread-bare Penitence apieces tore.   280

LXXI

And much as Wine has play'd the Infidel,
And robb'd me of my Robe of Honour—well,
    I often wonder what the Vintners buy
One half so precious as the Goods they sell.

LXXII

Alas, that Spring should vanish with the Rose!   285
That Youth's sweet-scented Manuscript should close!
    The Nightingale that in the Branches sang,
Ah, whence, and whither flown again, who knows!

LXXIII

Ah Love! could thou and I with Fate conspire
To grasp this sorry Scheme of Things entire,   290
    Would not we shatter it to bits—and then
Re-mould it nearer to the Heart's Desire!

LXXIV

Ah, Moon of my Delight who know'st no wane,
The Moon of Heav'n is rising once again:
How oft hereafter rising shall she look
Through this same Garden after me—in vain!

295

LXXV

And when Thyself with shining Foot shall pass
Among the Guests Star-scatter'd on the Grass,
And in thy joyous Errand reach the Spot
Where I made one—turn down an empty Glass!

300

TAMÁM SHUD[53]

Alfred Tennyson (1809–92)

Born in Somersby, Lincolnshire, to a clergyman father, George Clayton Tennyson (1778–1831) and Elizabeth Fytche (1781–1865), a clergyman's daughter, Tennyson was educated at home by his father who required him to recite in Latin the four books of Horace's *Odes* from memory before leaving for the grammar school at Louth. In 1828 he entered Trinity College, Cambridge, joining the Cambridge Apostles, a debating society whose members included Arthur Henry Hallam (1811–33), with whom he developed a close friendship. With his brother Charles Tennyson Turner (1808–79) he had published *Poems by Two Brothers* (1827), and two years later won the Chancellor's Gold Medal for the prize poem "Timbuctoo." On his father's death in 1831, he left Cambridge before taking his degree to help support his family. Hallam came to visit and became engaged to marry Tennyson's sister, Emily (1811–87). Tennyson published the poorly received *Poems* (title page dated 1833; published Dec. 1832) and in the same year Hallam died suddenly in Vienna of an aneurism. In 1837 Tennyson became engaged to marry Emily Sellwood

(1813–96), but he broke off the engagement until 1850 when he became financially secure. Over ten years Tennyson ruminated on Hallam's death and his own mortality, and in 1842 published *Poems*, two volumes of poems already published, but much revised, and new poems, winning considerable success. His Civil List pension (1842) and the publication of *The Princess: A Medley* (1847) prepared for the success of *In Memoriam* (1850), his long elegy on Hallam, and his appointment to succeed Wordsworth as Poet Laureate. In the following forty years Tennyson continued to gain honours and acclaim, including a peerage (1883). His numerous publications included the multiformed *Maud* (1855) and his blank-verse epic in twelve books, *The Idylls of the King*, a retelling of the King Arthur story published at intervals between 1859 and 1885. His domestic or English idylls included *Enoch Arden* (1864). Equally at home in classical metres and mythology as in medieval themes and contemporary issues, Tennyson is particularly noted for his extraordinary suppleness in versification, his adroit manipulation of the technical resources of rhetoric and

Notes ───────────────────────────────────

53 *Tamám Shud* (Persian: it is finished).

versification, and his ability to control and vary the sounds, rhythms, and metaphors of English diction. He epitomized many Victorian conflicts: between science and religion, faith and doubt, patriotism and political indignation, banality and sublimity, moralizing and inclusivity, and jingoism and the most evocative melancholy. He is buried in the Poets' Corner of Westminster Abbey, beside Robert Browning and T. S. Eliot. Standard edition: *The Poems of Tennyson*, ed. Christopher Ricks (3 vols, second edition 1987); *The Letters of Alfred Lord Tennyson*, eds Cecil Y. Lang and Edgar F. Shannon (3 vols, 1981–90); Leonee Ormond, *Alfred Tennyson: A Literary Life* (1993); Hallam, Lord Tennyson, *Alfred, Lord Tennyson: A Memoir* (2 vols, 1899). Tennyson's Arthurian poems: http://d.lib.rochester.edu/camelot/creator/alfred-tennyson; and Lord Alfred Tennyson, Biography and Works: http://www.online-litera-ture.com/tennyson. Our text: *The Works of Tennyson* (Eversley Edition, 9 vols, 1907–8), unless stated otherwise.

Mariana

"Mariana in the moated grange."
Measure for Measure.[1]

With blackest moss the flower-plots
    Were thickly crusted, one and all:
The rusted nails fell from the knots
    That held the pear to the gable-wall.
The broken sheds look'd sad and strange: 5
    Unlifted was the clinking latch;
    Weeded and worn the ancient thatch
Upon the lonely moated grange.
        She only said, "My life is dreary,
            He cometh not," she said;   10
        She said, "I am aweary, aweary,
            I would that I were dead!"

Her tears fell with the dews at even;
    Her tears fell ere the dews were dried;
She could not look on the sweet heaven,[2]   15
    Either at morn or eventide.
After the flitting of the bats,
    When thickest dark did trance[3] the sky,
    She drew her casement-curtain by,
And glanced athwart the glooming flats.   20
        She only said, "The night is dreary,
            He cometh not," she said;
        She said, "I am aweary, aweary,
            I would that I were dead!"

Notes ─────────────────────────────────────

ALFRED TENNYSON

[1] *title* the paraphrase is from 3. 1. 277. First published in *Poems Chiefly Lyrical* (1830).

[2] *heaven* possible echo of *Aeneid* 4. 451, for Dido's comment, "heaven's vault is a weariness to look on" (trans. Conington).

[3] *trance* cross.

Upon the middle of the night,[4]   25
    Waking she heard the night-fowl crow:
The cock sung out an hour ere light:
    From the dark fen the oxen's low
Came to her: without hope of change,
    In sleep she seem'd to walk forlorn,   30
    Till cold winds woke the gray-eyed morn
About the lonely moated grange.
    She only said, "The day is dreary,
        He cometh not," she said;
    She said, "I am aweary, aweary,   35
        I would that I were dead!"

About a stone-cast from the wall
    A sluice with blacken'd waters slept,
And o'er it many, round and small,
    The cluster'd marish-mosses[5] crept.   40
Hard by a poplar shook alway,
    All silver-green with gnarled bark:
    For leagues no other tree did mark
The level waste, the rounding gray.
    She only said, "My life is dreary,   45
        He cometh not," she said;
    She said, "I am aweary, aweary,
        I would that I were dead!"

And ever when the moon was low,
    And the shrill winds were up and away,   50
In the white curtain, to and fro,
    She saw the gusty shadow sway.
But when the moon was very low,
    And wild winds bound within their cell,
    The shadow of the poplar fell   55
Upon her bed, across her brow.
    She only said, "The night is dreary,
        He cometh not," she said;
    She said, "I am aweary, aweary,
        I would that I were dead!"   60

All day within the dreamy house,
    The doors upon their hinges creak'd;
The blue fly sung in the pane; the mouse
    Behind the mouldering wainscot shriek'd,
Or from the crevice peer'd about.   65
    Old faces glimmer'd thro' the doors,
    Old footsteps trod the upper floors,
Old voices called her from without.
    She only said, "My life is dreary,
        He cometh not," she said;   70

Notes

[4] *night* see *Romeo and Juliet* 2. 3. 1.   [5] *marish-mosses* marsh-mosses.

She said, "I am aweary, aweary,
    I would that I were dead!"

The sparrow's chirrup on the roof,
    The slow clock ticking, and the sound
Which to the wooing wind aloof   75
    The poplar made, did all confound
Her sense; but most she loathed the hour
    When the thick-moted sunbeam lay
Athwart the chambers, and the day
Was sloping toward his western bower.   80
        Then, said she, "I am very dreary,
           He will not come," she said;
        She wept, "I am aweary, aweary,

The Kraken[6]

Below the thunders of the upper deep;
Far, far beneath in the abysmal sea,
His ancient, dreamless, uninvaded sleep
The Kraken sleepeth: faintest sunlights flee
About his shadowy sides: above him swell   5
Huge sponges of millennial growth and height;
And far away into the sickly light,
From many a wondrous grot and secret cell
Unnumber'd and enormous polypi
Winnow with giant arms the slumbering green.   10
There hath he lain for ages and will lie
Battening upon huge seaworms in his sleep,
Until the latter fire shall heat the deep;
Then once by man and angels to be seen,
In roaring he shall rise and on the surface die.[7]   15

The Lady of Shalott[8]

Part I

On either side the river lie
Long fields of barley and of rye,
That clothe the wold and meet the sky;
And thro' the field the road runs by

Notes

[6] *title* the Kraken is a mythological Scandinavian sea monster based on Bishop Erik Pontoppidan's *History of Norway* (1752) and also used in Walter Scott's *Minstrelsy of the Scottish Border* (1802). It is identified with the sea-beast Leviathan (Job 41) in Hobbes's *Leviathan* (1651), where the image is a source of human pride to be curtailed by the ideal government, the commonwealth; and in *Paradise Lost* (1: 203–8; and 7: 411–16), where its size and power are

similes for Satan. The poem is often read as a Petrarchan (Italian) sonnet, though of fifteen lines. First published in *Poems Chiefly Lyrical* (1830).

[7] *fire … die* at the day of judgement, Leviathan will rise to be destroyed in fire (Isaiah 21: 1; Revelation 8: 8–9; 13: 1–10; and 16: 8–9).

[8] *title* derived from an Italian novelette, *La Donna di Scalotta* (It. The lady of Shalott; thirteenth century), rather than

To many-tower'd Camelot[9];   5
And up and down the people go,
Gazing where the lilies blow
Round an island there below,
    The island of Shalott.

Willows whiten, aspens quiver,   10
Little breezes dusk and shiver
Thro' the wave that runs for ever
By the island in the river
    Flowing down to Camelot.
Four gray walls, and four gray towers,   15
Overlook a space of flowers,
And the silent isle[10] imbowers
    The Lady of Shalott.

By the margin, willow-veil'd,
Slide the heavy barges trail'd   20
By slow horses; and unhail'd
The shallop flitteth silken-sail'd
    Skimming down to Camelot:
But who hath seen her wave her hand?
Or at the casement seen her stand?   25
Or is she known in all the land,
    The Lady of Shalott?

Only reapers, reaping early
In among the bearded barley,
Hear a song that echoes cheerly   30
From the river winding clearly,
    Down to tower'd Camelot:
And by the moon the reaper weary,
Piling sheaves in uplands airy,
Listening, whispers "'Tis the fairy   35
    Lady of Shalott."

Notes

from Thomas Malory (Caxton's edition, 1485, chs 18–20), where the lady who dies of grief for love of Lancelot is called Elaine. Tennyson invented the curse, the weaving, and the mirror. The poem is his earliest use of Arthurian legend, later to be the source of *The Idylls of the King* (1856–85); in *Elaine*, one of the first of Tennyson's *Idylls* (1859; later *Lancelot and Elaine*, 1870), Elaine is the "Lily-maid of Astolat"; Shalott and Astolat are the same place. First published *Poems* (1833; issued Dec. 1832); extensively revised in *Poems* (2 vols, 1842); our text: 1842. The poem was brilliantly parodied in both verse and imitation Pre-Raphaelite engravings by George du Maurier (1834–96) in "A Legend of Camelot" (*Punch*, Mar. 1866), beginning:

    Tall Braunighrindas left her bed
    At cock-crow with an aching head.
        O miserie!

    "I yearn to suffer and to do,"
    She cried, "ere sunset, something new!
        O miserie!
    To do and suffer, ere I die,
    I care not what. I know not why.
        O miserie!

[9] *Camelot* the legendary capital of Arthur's kingdom, sometimes identified with Tintagel or Camelford in Cornwall, is located in Wales by Caxton.

[10] *isle* the contrasts throughout between the silent island and the noisy town, the tower and the fields are emblematic of the poem's layers of oppositions, in many respects implicated by the condition of England question: isolated individual and community, rural and urban landscapes and social conditions, hand workers and machine workers, and the interrogation of conventional male and female roles.

Part II

There she weaves by night and day
A magic web with colours gay.
She has heard a whisper say,
A curse is on her if she stay   40
        To look down to Camelot.
She knows not what the curse may be,
And so she weaveth steadily,
And little other care hath she,
        The Lady of Shalott.   45

And moving thro' a mirror clear¹¹
That hangs before her all the year,
Shadows of the world appear.
There she sees the highway near
        Winding down to Camelot: 50
There the river eddy whirls,
And there the surly village-churls,
And the red cloaks of market girls,
        Pass onward from Shalott.

Sometimes a troop of damsels glad,   55
An abbot on an ambling pad,
Sometimes a curly shepherd-lad,
Or long-hair'd page in crimson clad,
        Goes by to tower'd Camelot;
And sometimes thro' the mirror blue   60
The knights come riding two and two:
She hath no loyal knight and true,
        The Lady of Shalott.

But in her web she still delights
To weave the mirror's magic sights,   65
For often thro' the silent nights
A funeral, with plumes and lights
        And music, went to Camelot:
Or when the moon was overhead,
Came two young lovers lately wed;   70
"I am half sick of shadows," said
        The Lady of Shalott.

Part III

A bow-shot from her bower-eaves,
He rode between the barley-sheaves,
The sun came dazzling thro' the leaves,   75
And flamed upon the brazen greaves

Notes

¹¹ *mirror clear* tapestry workers placed a mirror behind their work to see the finished pattern, an ironic displacement onto her of the plight of the cotton weavers of Manchester and the industrial north.

Of bold Sir Lancelot.[12]
A red-cross knight[13] for ever kneel'd
To a lady in his shield,
That sparkled on the yellow field, 80
    Beside remote Shalott.

The gemmy bridle[14] glitter'd free,
Like to some branch of stars we see
Hung in the golden Galaxy.
The bridle bells rang merrily 85
    As he rode down to Camelot:
And from his blazon'd baldric slung
A mighty silver bugle hung,
And as he rode his armour rung,
    Beside remote Shalott. 90

All in the blue unclouded weather
Thick-jewell'd shone the saddle-leather,
The helmet and the helmet-feather
Burn'd like one burning flame together,
    As he rode down to Camelot. 95
As often thro' the purple night,
Below the starry clusters bright,
Some bearded meteor, trailing light,
    Moves over still Shalott.

His broad clear brow in sunlight glow'd; 100
On burnish'd hooves his war-horse trode;
From underneath his helmet flow'd
His coal-black curls as on he rode,
    As he rode down to Camelot.
From the bank and from the river 105
He flash'd into the crystal mirror,
"Tirra lirra,"[15] by the river
    Sang Sir Lancelot.

She left the web, she left the loom,
She made three paces thro' the room,
She saw the water-lily bloom, 100
She saw the helmet and the plume,
    She look'd down to Camelot.
Out flew the web and floated wide;
The mirror crack'd from side to side; 115
"The curse is come upon me," cried
    The Lady of Shalott.

Notes

[12] *Lancelot* knight of the Round Table whose adultery with Arthur's queen, Guinevere, according to Tennyson, led to the breakup of the Round Table and the destruction of Arthur's kingdom; the tale is retold by Tennyson in *Idylls* as an allegory for the condition of Victorian England. See also MORRIS, "DEFENCE"; and FANE, "LANCELOT."

[13] *red-cross knight* see *Faerie Queene* 3. 2, where the knight is an allegory for the Tudor monarchy.

[14] *bridle* the knight's appearance is modelled on *Faerie Queene* I. 7. 29.

[15] *Tirra lirra* see *The Winter's Tale* 4. 3. 9.

Part IV

In the stormy east-wind straining,
The pale yellow woods were waning,
The broad stream in his banks complaining,   120
Heavily the low sky raining
        Over tower'd Camelot;
Down she came and found a boat
Beneath a willow left afloat,
And round about the prow she wrote   125
        The Lady of Shalott.

And down the river's dim expanse
Like some bold seër in a trance,
Seeing all his own mischance—
With a glassy countenance   130
        Did she look to Camelot.
And at the closing of the day
She loosed the chain, and down she lay;
The broad stream bore her far away,
        The Lady of Shalott.   135

Lying, robed in snowy white
That loosely flew to left and right—
The leaves upon her falling light—
Thro' the noises of the night
        She floated down to Camelot: 140
And as the boat-head wound along
The willowy hills and fields among,
They heard her singing her last song,
        The Lady of Shalott.

Heard a carol, mournful, holy,   145
Chanted loudly, chanted lowly,
Till her blood was frozen slowly,
And her eyes were darken'd wholly,
        Turn'd to tower'd Camelot.
For ere she reach'd upon the tide   150
The first house by the water-side,
Singing in her song she died,
        The Lady of Shalott.

Under tower and balcony,
By garden-wall and gallery,   155
A gleaming shape she floated by,
Dead-pale between the houses high,
        Silent into Camelot.
Out upon the wharfs they came,
Knight and burgher, lord and dame,   160
And round the prow they read her name,
        The Lady of Shalott.

Who is this? and what is here?
And in the lighted palace near
Died the sound of royal cheer; 165
And they cross'd themselves for fear,
  All the knights at Camelot:
But Lancelot mused a little space;
He said, "She has a lovely face;
God in his mercy lend her grace, 170
  The Lady of Shalott."

> **WEB p. 330**
>
> The Lotos-Eaters
> Choric Song

Ulysses[16]

It little profits that an idle king,
By this still hearth, among these barren crags,
Match'd with an aged wife, I mete and dole
Unequal laws unto a savage race,
That hoard, and sleep, and feed,[17] and know not me. 5

I cannot rest from travel: I will drink
Life to the lees: all times I have enjoy'd
Greatly, have suffer'd greatly, both with those
That loved me, and alone; on shore, and when
Thro' scudding drifts the rainy Hyades[18] 10
Vext the dim sea: I am become a name;
For always roaming with a hungry heart
Much have I seen and known; cities of men
And manners, climates, councils, governments,[19]
Myself not least, but honour'd of them all; 15
And drunk delight of battle with my peers,
Far on the ringing plains of windy Troy.[20]
I am a part of all that I have met;[21]

Notes

[16] *title* Ulysses is the Latin name of Odysseus. Some time after having returned home, after his ten-years' wandering following the Trojan War, Ulysses plans his last voyage; see *Odyssey* 11. 100–37. Exalting Ulysses' enthusiastic restlessness, Tennyson combines Homer with Dante's account in *Inferno* 26. 90 ff., where Ulysses, placed in Hell among the fraudulent advisors because of his advice in the Trojan War and because he challenges divine law, does not return home but exhorts his crew to undertake a voyage of exploration beyond the Strait of Gibraltar. This poem was written on 20 October 1833; Tennyson learned on 1 October 1833 that his friend Arthur Henry Hallam had died in Vienna on 15 September. First published in *Poems* (1842).

[17] *feed* see *Hamlet* 4. 4. 33–39.

[18] *Hyades* (Gk. from the verb *hyein*: "to rain"); a star cluster in the constellation Taurus. In Greek mythology the Hyades were the five daughters of Atlas who, weeping for the death of their brother Hyas, were transformed by Zeus into a cluster of stars whose appearance prefigures spring rains and autumn storms (see *Iliad* 18. 485–90; and *Aeneid* 1. 744).

[19] *governments* see *Odyssey* 1. 3–5; and Horace, *Epistles* 1. 2. 19–20.

[20] *windy Troy* Homeric epithet, as at *Iliad* 23. 34.

[21] *met* see *Aeneid* 2. 5–6.

Yet all experience is an arch wherethro'
Gleams that untravell'd world, whose margin fades   20
For ever and for ever when I move.
How dull it is to pause, to make an end,
To rust unburnish'd, not to shine in use!
As tho' to breathe were life. Life piled on life
Were all too little, and of one to me   25
Little remains: but every hour is saved
From that eternal silence, something more,
A bringer of new things; and vile it were
For some three suns to store and hoard myself,
And this gray spirit yearning in desire   30
To follow knowledge like a sinking star,
Beyond the utmost bound of human thought.

This is my son, mine own Telemachus,[22]
To whom I leave the sceptre and the isle—
Well-loved of me, discerning to fulfil   35
This labour, by slow prudence to make mild
A rugged people, and thro' soft degrees
Subdue them to the useful and the good.
Most blameless is he, centred in the sphere
Of common duties, decent not to fail   40
In offices of tenderness, and pay
Meet adoration to my household gods,
When I am gone. He works his work, I mine.

There lies the port; the vessel puffs her sail:
There gloom the dark broad seas. My mariners,   45
Souls that have toil'd, and wrought, and thought with me—
That ever with a frolic welcome took
The thunder and the sunshine, and opposed
Free hearts, free foreheads—you and I are old;
Old age hath yet his honour and his toil;   50
Death closes all: but something ere the end,
Some work of noble note, may yet be done,
Not unbecoming men that strove with Gods.
The lights begin to twinkle from the rocks:
The long day wanes: the slow moon climbs: the deep   55
Moans round with many voices. Come, my friends,
'Tis not too late to seek a newer world.
Push off, and sitting well in order smite
The sounding furrows[23]; for my purpose holds
To sail beyond the sunset, and the baths   60
Of all the western stars, until I die.[24]
It may be that the gulfs will wash us down:

Notes

[22] *Telemachus* the son of Ulysses and Penelope.
[23] *sounding furrows* Homeric epithet, as at *Odyssey* 4. 580.

[24] *western stars . . . die* classical cosmology perceived the earth as a disc surrounded by waters, so that the stars dipped into them when they set; see *Odyssey* 5. 270–75.

It may be we shall touch the Happy Isles,[25]
And see the great Achilles,[26] whom we knew.
Tho' much is taken, much abides; and tho'   65
We are not now that strength which in old days
Moved earth and heaven; that which we are, we are;
One equal temper of heroic hearts,
Made weak by time and fate, but strong in will
To strive, to seek, to find, and not to yield.   70

["Break, break, break"][27]

Break, break, break,
   On thy cold gray stones, O Sea!
And I would that my tongue could utter
   The thoughts that arise in me.

O, well for the fisherman's boy,   5
   That he shouts with his sister at play!
O, well for the sailor lad,
   That he sings in his boat on the bay!

And the stately ships go on
   To their haven under the hill;   10
But O for the touch of a vanish'd hand,
   And the sound of a voice that is still!

Break, break, break
   At the foot of thy crags, O Sea!
But the tender grace of a day that is dead   15
   Will never come back to me.

WEB p. 335

Locksley Hall
Songs from *The Princess*
   ["O Swallow, Swallow, flying, flying South]
   ["Tears, idle tears"]
   ["Now sleeps the crimson petal, now the white"]
   ["Come down, O maid"]
   ["Sweet and low"]
   ["The splendour falls on castle walls"]

Notes

[25] *Happy Isles* the Islands of the Blessed, beyond the Western Sea and the Pillars of Hercules (Gibraltar), where the dead heroes are blessed with immortality.

[26] *Achilles* leader of the Greeks during the Trojan War.

[27] *title* written in Lincolnshire before 1837 in memory of Arthur Hallam. First published in *Poems* (1842).

In Memoriam A. H. H.

Obiit MDCCCXXXIII

In Memoriam (Lat. to the memory of … ; *obiit* Lat. he died). Written between 1833 and 1850, the poem is in memory of Arthur Henry Hallam, who died at the age of 22 (15 Sept. 1833). The elegy, or series of elegies, is comprised of four-lined octosyllabic stanzas in 132 sections of varying length. Tennyson said about it: "

> It is founded on our friendship, on the engagement of Arthur Hallam to my sister [Emily, 1811–87], on his sudden death at Vienna, just before the time fixed for their marriage, and on his burial at Clevedon Church. The poem concludes with the marriage of my youngest sister Cecilia. It was meant to be a kind of *Divina Commedia*, ending with happiness. The sections were written at many different places, and as the phases of our intercourse came to my memory and suggested them. I did not write them with any view of weaving them into a whole, or for publication, until I found that I had written so many. The different moods of sorrow as in a drama are dramatically given, and my conviction that fear, doubts, and suffering will find answer and relief only through Faith in a God of Love. "I" is not always the author speaking of himself, but the voice of the human race speaking through him. After the Death of A. H. H., the divisions of the poem are made by First Xmas Eve (section xxviii), Second Xmas

(lxxviii), Third Xmas Eve (civ and cv etc.). (*Tennyson: A Memoir* 1. 304–5)

Hence, the poem can be divided into four parts: [Prologue]–XXVII; XXVIII–LXXVII; LXXVIII–CIII; and CIV–end. The poem recalls and celebrates the deep love that Tennyson had for Hallam, to some readers perhaps an expression of a suppressed homoerotic relationship, one that can be read in such sections as XIII with the metaphor of widowhood, or section XCIII: "Descend, and touch, and enter; hear / The wish too strong for words to name." Others emphasize the elegy as a chronicle of a profound male friendship, expressed in a dizzying array of generic conventions and literary allusions. The poem was a critical and popular success, speaking to Victorian doubt in the language of faith, while questioning knowledge. It invokes current issues in astronomy, geology, evolutionary biology, and their relation to theology. The poem challenges the traditional elegiac evasion of grief by celebrating nature, in that it interweaves Tennyson's personal grief with the concerns of his whole society, with nature, and finally with the cosmos itself. The original title of Tennyson's private edition was "Fragments of an Elegy." The public edition (1850) was published anonymously. Our text: 1850, except that we have included LIX ("O Sorrow, wilt thou live with me") that Tennyson added in 1851 and XXXIX ("Old warder of these buried bones") that Tennyson added in 1869, renumbering all of the subsequent sections, as have we, giving 131 numbered sections, plus a prologue and epilogue.

> Strong Son of God, immortal Love,[28]
> Whom we, that have not seen thy face,
> By faith, and faith alone, embrace,[29]
> Believing where we cannot prove;

Notes

[28] *Love* see 1 John 4–5. No edition published during Tennyson's lifetime had a title for the prologue or introductory stanzas. They were placed before the title and

date, and had the date of first printing in a trial edition, 1849, placed after them. Here and elsewhere throughout the poem Tennyson alludes to the double tradition of

Thine are these orbs of light and shade;   5
    Thou madest Life in man and brute;
    Thou madest Death; and lo, thy foot
Is on the skull which thou hast made.[30]

Thou wilt not leave us in the dust[31]:
    Thou madest man, he knows not why,   10
    He thinks he was not made to die;
And thou hast made him: thou art just.

Thou seemest human and divine,
    The highest, holiest manhood, thou:
    Our wills are ours, we know not how,   15
Our wills are ours, to make them thine.

Our little systems have their day;
    They have their day and cease to be[32]:
    They are but broken lights of thee,
And thou, O Lord, art more than they.   20

We have but faith: we cannot know;
    For knowledge is of things we see[33];
    And yet we trust it comes from thee,
A beam in darkness: let it grow.

Let knowledge grow from more to more,   25
    But more of reverence in us dwell;
    That mind and soul, according well,
May make one music as before,

But vaster. We are fools and slight;
    We mock thee when we do not fear: 30
    But help thy foolish ones to bear;
Help thy vain worlds to bear thy light.

Forgive what seem'd my sin in me;
    What seem'd my worth since I began;
    For merit lives from man to man,   35
And not from man, O Lord, to thee.

Forgive my grief for one removed,
    Thy creature, whom I found so fair.
    I trust he lives in thee, and there
I find him worthier to be loved.   40

Notes

the classical funeral elegy and the love elegy, as in the reference in stanza 2 to Propertius (c.50–15 BCE); other classical writers who used the genre of the love elegy are Catullus (84–54 BCE), Tibullus (55–19 BCE), and Ovid (43 BCE–18 CE).

[29] *embrace* see 1 Peter 1: 8.

[30] *made* see Propertius, *Ode* 1. 1. 4: "and Love ... stepped on my head with his foot."

[31] *Thou ... dust* see Psalms 16: 10; 22: 15; and 44: 26.

[32] *systems ... be* systems of knowledge, but also the solar system and the notion of cosmic decay; see n. 40.

[33] *faith ... knowledge* the conventional contrast between faith and knowledge and between wisdom and knowledge, with the wisdom of God invoked in the last stanza. See below, IN MEMORIAM, nn. 103 and CXXIV and 282; and TENNYSON, n. 29 (WEB p. 339).

Forgive these wild and wandering cries,
 Confusions of a wasted youth;
 Forgive them where they fail in truth,
And in thy wisdom make me wise.

1849

I

I held it truth, with him who sings[34]
 To one clear harp in divers tones,
 That men may rise on stepping-stones
Of their dead selves to higher things.

But who shall so forecast the years   5
 And find in loss a gain to match?
 Or reach a hand thro' time to catch
The far-off interest of tears?

Let Love clasp Grief lest both be drown'd,
 Let darkness keep her raven gloss: 10
 Ah, sweeter to be drunk with loss,
To dance with death, to beat the ground,

Than that the victor Hours[35] should scorn
 The long result of love, and boast,
 "Behold the man that loved and lost,   15
But all he was is overworn."

II

Old Yew,[36] which graspest at the stones
 That name the under-lying dead,
 Thy fibres net the dreamless head,
Thy roots are wrapt about the bones.

The seasons bring the flower again,   5
 And bring the firstling to the flock[37];
 And in the dusk of thee, the clock
Beats out the little lives of men.

O not for thee the glow, the bloom,
 Who changest not in any gale,   10
 Nor branding summer suns avail
To touch thy thousand years of gloom:

Notes

[34] *sings* Tennyson said he was referring to Goethe, though the reference has not been located.
[35] *Hours* the Horae (Lat. hours), the twelve daughters of Zeus and Themis (the goddess of the law of nature), who govern the unfolding of rightful order in time.

[36] *Yew* conventional long-lived graveyard tree that does not lose its foliage but is forever green; see Thomas Gray, "Elegy Written in a Country Churchyard" (1751: 13–16).
[37] *flock* see Genesis 4: 4.

And gazing on thee, sullen tree,
    Sick for thy stubborn hardihood,
    I seem to fail from out my blood   15
And grow incorporate into thee.

III

O Sorrow, cruel fellowship,
    O Priestess in the vaults of Death,[38]
    O sweet and bitter in a breath,
What whispers from thy lying lip?

"The stars," she whispers, "blindly run[39];   5
    A web is wov'n across the sky;
    From out waste places comes a cry,
And murmurs from the dying sun[40]:

"And all the phantom, Nature, stands—
    With all the music in her tone,   10
    A hollow echo of my own,—
A hollow form with empty hands."

And shall I take a thing so blind,
    Embrace her as my natural good;
    Or crush her, like a vice of blood,   15
Upon the threshold of the mind?

IV

To Sleep I give my powers away;
    My will is bondsman to the dark;
    I sit within a helmless bark,
And with my heart I muse and say:

O heart, how fares it with thee now,   5
    That thou should'st fail from thy desire,
    Who scarcely darest to inquire,
"What is it makes me beat so low?"

Something it is which thou hast lost,
    Some pleasure from thine early years.   10
    Break, thou deep vase of chilling tears,[41]
That grief hath shaken into frost!

Notes

[38] *Death* Catullus refers to the priestess's mingling of the sweet and bitter (Poem 68. 17–18).

[39] *run* blind stars do not influence the zodiac or human fortune; the impersonal universe runs mechanically rather than by benevolent divine design.

[40] *sun* suggestions of entropy – in physics, the increasing failure of a system to do work, and hence to run down – are based on the nebular theory of cosmology of Pierre-Simon Laplace's *Celestial Mechanics* (1799–1805). Laplace argued that the solar system had evolved from nebulae of incandescent gases. As they cooled while rotating around an axis, successive rings broke off the outer edge, finally

Such clouds of nameless trouble cross
   All night below the darken'd eyes;
   With morning wakes the will, and cries,   15
"Thou shalt not be the fool of loss."

V

I sometimes hold it half a sin
   To put in words the grief I feel;
   For words, like Nature, half reveal
And half conceal the Soul within.

But, for the unquiet heart and brain,   5
   A use in measured language lies;
   The sad mechanic exercise,
Like dull narcotics, numbing pain.

In words, like weeds,[42] I'll wrap me o'er,
   Like coarsest clothes against the cold: 10
   But that large grief which these enfold
Is given in outline and no more.

VI

One writes, that "Other friends remain,"
   That "Loss is common to the race"—
   And common is the commonplace,
And vacant chaff well meant for grain.

That loss is common would not make   5
   My own less bitter, rather more:
   Too common! Never morning wore
To evening, but some heart did break.[43]

O father, wheresoe'er thou be,
   Who pledgest[44] now thy gallant son;   10
   A shot, ere half thy draught be done,
Hath still'd the life that beat from thee.

O mother, praying God will save
   Thy sailor,—while thy head is bow'd,
   His heavy-shotted hammock-shroud[45]   15
Drops in his vast and wandering grave

Notes

condensing into planets, of which the "dying sun" is the last one remaining. William Whewell (1794–1866), English scientist and theologian, Tennyson's tutor at Cambridge, particularly stressed the certainty of stellar decay. See RELIGION: GEOLOGY, n. 1.

[41] *tears* lachrymal vases (Lat. *lacrima*, tear) were found in Roman tombs, once thought to contain the tears of mourners. They began to be used again in the Victorian era, with special stoppers that allowed the contents to evaporate, ending the period of mourning. Tennyson comments on how water in a vase, if jarred at the point of freezing, changes to ice.

[42] *weeds* mourning garments, as in the phrase "widow's weeds."

[43] *break* see Lucretius, *De rerum natura* (Lat. concerning the nature of things): 2. 578–80.

[44] *pledgest* toasts.

[45] *shroud* Tennyson imagines that Hallam's body is like that of a dead sailor shrouded in his hammock, weighted with cannon shot to make it sink.

Ye know no more than I who wrought
    At that last hour to please him well;
    Who mused on all I had to tell,
And something written, something thought;   20

Expecting still his advent home;
    And ever met him on his way
    With wishes, thinking, "here to-day,"
Or "here to-morrow will he come."

O somewhere, meek, unconscious dove,[46]   25
    That sittest ranging golden hair;
    And glad to find thyself so fair,
Poor child, that waitest for thy love!

For now her father's chimney glows
    In expectation of a guest;   30
    And thinking "this will please him best,"
She takes a riband or a rose;

For he will see them on to-night;
    And with the thought her colour burns;
    And, having left the glass, she turns   35
Once more to set a ringlet right;

And, even when she turn'd, the curse
    Had fallen, and her future Lord
    Was drown'd in passing thro' the ford,
Or kill'd in falling from his horse.   40

O what to her shall be the end?
    And what to me remains of good?
    To her, perpetual maidenhood,
And unto me no second friend.

VII

Dark house,[47] by which once more I stand
    Here in the long unlovely street,
    Doors, where my heart was used to beat
So quickly, waiting for a hand,

A hand that can be clasp'd no more—   5
    Behold me, for I cannot sleep,
    And like a guilty thing I creep
At earliest morning to the door.

Notes

[46] *dove* Emily Tennyson, to whom Hallam was engaged to be married.

[47] *house* Hallam's house at 67 Wimpole Street, London. Section VII conforms to the minor classical and troubadour genre of the excluded lover lamenting outside the door of the beloved (called the *paraclausithyron*; Gk. *para*, beside; *clausi*, closed; *thyron*, door), as in Tibullus 1. 2; Horace, *Odes* 3. 10; Propertius 1. 16; and Ovid, *Amores* 1. 6. See also Petrarch, *Sonnet* 53. Such an exclusion is a metaphor for the exclusion of the dead from those living, as in CXVII.

He is not here[48]; but far away
    The noise of life begins again,   10
    And ghastly thro' the drizzling rain
On the bald street breaks the blank day.

VIII

A happy lover who has come
    To look on her that loves him well,
    Who 'lights[49] and rings the gateway bell,
And learns her gone and far from home;

He saddens, all the magic light   5
    Dies off at once from bower and hall,
    And all the place is dark, and all
The chambers emptied of delight:

So find I every pleasant spot
    In which we two were wont to meet,   10
    The field, the chamber and the street,
For all is dark where thou art not.

Yet as that other, wandering there
    In those deserted walks, may find
    A flower beat with rain and wind,   15
Which once she foster'd up with care;

So seems it in my deep regret,
    O my forsaken heart, with thee
    And this poor flower of poesy
Which little cared for fades not yet.   20

But since it pleased a vanish'd eye,[50]
    I go to plant it on his tomb,
    That if it can it there may bloom,
Or dying, there at least may die.

IX

Fair ship, that from the Italian shore[51]
    Sailest the placid ocean-plains[52]
    With my lost Arthur's loved remains,
Spread thy full wings, and waft him o'er.

Notes

[48] *here* the angel's announcement that Jesus' tomb is empty and he had risen; see Luke 24: 6.

[49] *'lights* alights from a horse.

[50] *eye* in 1831 Hallam had favourably reviewed Tennyson's first volume *Poems, Chiefly Lyrical* (1830) in "On Some Characteristics of Modern Poetry" in *The Englishman's Magazine* (Aug. 1831).

[51] *shore* this is the first section of *In Memoriam* written, shortly after Tennyson learned about Hallam's death, on 1 October 1833. See above, n. 16. Sections IX to XVII comprise the prayerful invocation for a safe journey for a beloved traveller on his leave-taking, the genre of the classical Greek and Latin love elegy known as a *propemptikon* (Gk. *pro*, for, on; *pemptikos*, escorting, sending forth), as in Theocritus *Idylls* 7. 52–70; Tibullus 1. 3; Horace, *Odes* 1. 3; and Statius, *Silvae* 3. 2.

[52] *ocean-plains* (Lat. *placida aequora pontus*): see *Aeneid* 10. 103.

So draw him home to those that mourn 5
    In vain; a favourable speed
    Ruffle thy mirror'd mast, and lead
Thro' prosperous floods his holy urn.

All night no ruder air perplex
    Thy sliding keel, till Phosphor,[53] bright 10
    As our pure love, thro' early light
Shall glimmer on the dewy decks.

Sphere all your lights[54] around, above;
    Sleep, gentle heavens, before the prow;
    Sleep, gentle winds, as he sleeps now, 15
My friend, the brother of my love;

My Arthur, whom I shall not see
    Till all my widow'd race be run;
    Dear as the mother to the son,
More than my brothers are to me. 20

X

I hear the noise about thy keel;
    I hear the bell struck in the night:
    I see the cabin-window bright;
I see the sailor at the wheel.

Thou bring'st the sailor to his wife, 5
    And travell'd men from foreign lands;
    And letters unto trembling hands;
And, thy dark freight, a vanish'd life.

So bring him: we have idle dreams:
    This look of quiet flatters thus 10
    Our home-bred fancies: O to us,
The fools of habit, sweeter seems

To rest beneath the clover sod,
    That takes the sunshine and the rains,
    Or where the kneeling hamlet drains 15
The chalice of the grapes of God;

Than if with thee the roaring wells[55]
    Should gulf him fathom-deep in brine;
    And hands so often clasp'd in mine,
Should toss with tangle[56] and with shells. seaweed 20

Notes

[53] *Phosphor* (Gk. light-bringer); name given to Venus when the planet appears before dawn.
[54] *lights* common classical and biblical reference to the stars as the lights of heaven; see Genesis 1: 14; and Catullus, Poem 65. 59.
[55] *wells* whirlpools.
[56] *tangle* seaweed.

XI

Calm is the morn without a sound,[57]
   Calm as to suit a calmer grief,
   And only thro' the faded leaf
The chestnut pattering to the ground:

Calm and deep peace[58] on this high wold,   5
   And on these dews that drench the furze,
   And all the silvery gossamers
That twinkle into green and gold:

Calm and still light on yon great plain
   That sweeps with all its autumn bowers,   10
   And crowded farms and lessening towers,
To mingle with the bounding[59] main:

Calm and deep peace in this wide air,
   These leaves that redden to the fall;
   And in my heart, if calm at all,   15
If any calm, a calm despair:

Calm on the seas, and silver sleep,
   And waves that sway themselves in rest,
   And dead calm in that noble breast
Which heaves but with the heaving deep.   20

XII

Lo, as a dove when up she springs[60]
   To bear thro' Heaven a tale of woe,
   Some dolorous message knit below
The wild pulsation of her wings;

Like her I go; I cannot stay;   5
   I leave this mortal ark behind,
   A weight of nerves without a mind,
And leave the cliffs, and haste away

O'er ocean-mirrors rounded large,
   And reach the glow of southern skies,   10
   And see the sails at distance rise,
And linger weeping on the marge,

Notes

[57] *sound* section X paints a scene in the tradition of an eighteenth-century topographical genre, a prospect poem, involving the description of a particular landscape viewed from a high vantage point, like John Denham's *Cooper's Hill* (1642) and Thomas Gray's "Ode on a Distant Prospect of Eton College" (1747). The motif was also popular in seventeenth- and eighteenth-century landscape paintings, such as those by Claude Lorrain and Thomas Wilson. This section is a single sentence, as are sections XIV, LXIV, LXXXVI, CXXIX, and CXXXI.

[58] *calm ... peace* the figure of anaphora, the repetition of the same word at the beginning of a line or clause; see Horace, *Odes* 2. 16, where he begins a number of lines with the word *otium* (Lat. calm, peace) in a sailor's prayer for calm in a storm at sea.

[59] *bounding* limiting, setting boundaries.

[60] *springs* a long-standing classical tradition that at death the soul escapes the body and flies away (Gk. *psyche*, soul, butterfly); see also Genesis 8: 8–9.

And saying; "Comes he thus, my friend?
    Is this the end of all my care?"
    And circle moaning in the air: 15
"Is this the end? Is this the end?"

And forward dart again, and play
    About the prow, and back return
    To where the body sits, and learn
That I have been an hour away.   20

XIII

Tears of the widower, when he sees
    A late-lost form that sleep reveals,
    And moves his doubtful arms, and feels
Her place is empty,[61] fall like these;

Which weep a loss for ever new,   5
    A void where heart on heart reposed;
    And, where warm hands have prest and closed,
Silence, till I be silent too.

Which weep the comrade of my choice,
    An awful thought, a life removed,   10
    The human-hearted man I loved,
A Spirit, not a breathing voice.

Come Time, and teach me, many years,
    I do not suffer in a dream;
    For now so strange do these things seem,   15
Mine eyes have leisure for their tears;

My fancies time to rise on wing,
    And glance about the approaching sails,
    As tho' they brought but merchants' bales,
And not the burthen that they bring.   20

XIV

If one should bring me this report,[62]
    That thou hadst touch'd the land to-day,
    And I went down unto the quay,
And found thee lying in the port;

Notes

[61] *empty* Tennyson's domestic metaphor of the widower's loss and tears indicates the intimate relationship he had with Hallam and also allows him to elaborate the same theme derived from classical and English authors: see Ovid, *Heroides* 10. 9–12, where Ariadne reaches out in bed for the dead Theseus; and Milton's Sonnet 19, where he has a night-vision of his dead wife: "Methought I saw my late espoused saint, / Come to me like Alcestis from the grave."

[62] *report* section XIV conforms to the Greek and Latin classical genre of the welcome speech conferred on a returning traveller, hero, or famous person, known as

And standing, muffled round with woe,   5
 Should see thy passengers in rank
 Come stepping lightly down the plank,
And beckoning unto those they know;

And if along with these should come
 The man I held as half-divine;   10
 Should strike a sudden hand in mine,
And ask a thousand things of home;

And I should tell him all my pain,
 And how my life had droop'd of late,
 And he should sorrow o'er my state   15
And marvel what possess'd my brain;

And I perceived no touch of change,
 No hint of death in all his frame,
 But found him all in all the same,
I should not feel it to be strange.   20

XV

To-night the winds begin to rise
 And roar from yonder dropping day:
 The last red leaf is whirl'd away,
The rooks are blown about the skies;

The forest crack'd, the waters curl'd,   5
 The cattle huddled on the lea;
 And wildly dash'd on tower and tree
The sunbeam strikes along the world:

And but for fancies, which aver
 That all thy motions gently pass   10
 Athwart a plane of molten glass,
I scarce could brook the strain and stir

That makes the barren branches loud;
 And but for fear it is not so,
 The wild unrest that lives in woe   15
Would dote and pore on yonder cloud

That rises upward always higher,
 And onward drags a labouring breast,
 And topples round the dreary west,
A looming bastion fringed with fire.[63]   20

Notes

a *prosphonetikon* (Gk. *pros*, to; *phonetikos*, speaking < *phonein*, to speak). It is here addressed to the ship, but indirectly to Hallam through the ship. See Statius, *Silvae* 3. 2: 127–45; Theocritus, *Idylls* 12; Horace, *Odes* 1. 36; Catullus, Poem 9; Ovid, *Amores* 2: 37–56; Juvenal 12; and the *Argonautica* of Apollonius of Rhodes, 3. 253–74.

[63] *fire* see Arthur Hallam's sonnet "The Garden Trees": "The wild grey light that fronts yon massive cloud, / Or the half bow, rising like pillared fire?" (*Remains*, 1834).

XVI

What words are these have fall'n from me?
   Can calm despair and wild unrest
   Be tenants of a single breast,
Or sorrow such a changeling be?

Or doth she only seem to take   5
   The touch of change in calm or storm;
   But knows no more of transient form
In her deep self, than some dead lake

That holds the shadow of a lark
   Hung in the shadow of a heaven?   10
   Or has the shock, so harshly given,
Confused me like the unhappy bark

That strikes by night a craggy shelf,
   And staggers blindly ere she sink?
   And stunn'd me from my power to think   15
And all my knowledge of myself;

And made me that delirious man
   Whose fancy fuses old and new,
   And flashes into false and true,
And mingles all without a plan?   20

XVII

Thou comest, much wept for: such a breeze
   Compell'd thy canvas, and my prayer
   Was as the whisper of an air
To breathe thee over lonely seas.

For I in spirit saw thee move   5
   Thro' circles of the bounding sky,
   Week after week: the days go by:
Come quick, thou bringest all I love.

Henceforth, wherever thou may'st roam,
   My blessing, like a line of light,   10
   Is on the waters day and night,
And like a beacon guards thee home.

So may whatever tempest mars
   Mid-ocean, spare thee, sacred bark;
   And balmy drops in summer dark   15
Slide from the bosom of the stars.[64]

Notes

[64] *stars* a classical legend claims that the Milky Way was formed when the goddess Juno expressed the milk from her breasts, as in the painting by Tintoretto, *The Origin of the Milky Way* (1570); National Gallery, London.

So kind an office hath been done,
    Such precious relics brought by thee;
    The dust of him I shall not see
Till all my widow'd race be run.   20

XVIII

'Tis well; 'tis something; we may stand
    Where he in English earth is laid,[65]
    And from his ashes may be made
The violet[66] of his native land.

'Tis little; but it looks in truth   5
    As if the quiet bones[67] were blest
    Among familiar names to rest
And in the places of his youth.

Come then, pure hands, and bear the head
    That sleeps or wears the mask of sleep,   10
    And come, whatever loves to weep,
And hear the ritual of the dead.

Ah yet, ev'n yet, if this might be,
    I, falling on his faithful heart,
    Would breathing thro' his lips impart   15
The life that almost dies in me;

That dies not, but endures with pain,
    And slowly forms the firmer mind,
    Treasuring the look it cannot find,
The words that are not heard again.   20

XIX

The Danube to the Severn[68] gave
    The darken'd heart that beat no more;
    They laid him by the pleasant shore,
And in the hearing of the wave.

There twice a day the Severn fills;   5
    The salt sea-water passes by,
    And hushes half the babbling Wye,[69]
And makes a silence in the hills.

Notes

[65] *laid* Hallam was buried in the Elton family vault inside St Andrew's parish church, Clevedon in Somerset, on 3 January 1834. Sections XVIII–XXI deal with Hallam's burial. For the sea journey ending in the hope of burial in solid ground, see Ovid, *Tristia* 1. 2. 53–54.

[66] *violet* see *Hamlet* 5. 1. 232–34.

[67] *bones* (Lat. *ossa quieta*): classical commonplace, as in Ovid, *Amores* 3. 10. 67.

[68] *Danube … Severn* from Vienna to Clevedon. Tennyson imagines that Hallam arrived by sea at Bristol near Clevedon, although he arrived at Dover.

[69] *Wye* the river Wye (on which Tintern Abbey stands), flows into the Severn, whose mouth is tidal in the Bristol Channel; see "TEARS, IDLE TEARS" (WEB p. 342)

The Wye is hush'd nor moved along,
    And hush'd my deepest grief of all,   10
    When fill'd with tears that cannot fall,
I brim with sorrow drowning song.

The tide flows down, the wave again
    Is vocal in its wooded walls;
    My deeper anguish also falls,   15
And I can speak a little then.

XX

The lesser griefs that may be said,
    That breathe a thousand tender vows,
    Are but as servants in a house
Where lies the master newly dead;

Who speak their feeling as it is,   5
    And weep the fulness from the mind:
    "It will be hard," they say, "to find
Another service such as this."

My lighter moods are like to these,
    That out of words a comfort win;   10
    But there are other griefs within,
And tears that at their fountain freeze;

For by the hearth the children sit
    Cold in that atmosphere of Death,
    And scarce endure to draw the breath,   15
Or like to noiseless phantoms flit:

But open converse is there none,
    So much the vital spirits sink
    To see the vacant chair, and think,
"How good! how kind! and he is gone."   20

XXI

I sing to him that rests below,
    And, since the grasses round me wave,
    I take the grasses of the grave,
And make them pipes whereon to blow.⁷⁰

The traveller hears me now and then,   5
    And sometimes harshly will he speak:
    "This fellow would make weakness weak,
And melt the waxen hearts of men."

Notes ───────────────────────────

⁷⁰ *blow* pan-pipe or syrinx made from hollow reeds, a
common convention in classical poetry as in Virgil,
Eclogues 10. 64–65; see also XXIII and BARRETT BROWNING,
"A MUSICAL INSTRUMENT."

Another answers, "Let him be,
 He loves to make parade of pain   10
 That with his piping he may gain
The praise that comes to constancy."

A third is worth: "Is this an hour
 For private sorrow's barren song,
 When more and more the people throng   15
The chairs and thrones of civil power?"[71]

A time to sicken and to swoon,
 When Science reaches forth her arms
 To feel from world to world, and charms
Her secret from the latest moon?"[72]   20

Behold, ye speak an idle thing:
 Ye never knew the sacred dust:
 I do but sing because I must,
And pipe but as the linnets sing:

And one is glad; her note is gay,   25
 For now her little ones have ranged;
 And one is sad; her note is changed,
Because her brood is stol'n away.

XXII

The path[73] by which we twain did go,
 Which led by tracts that pleased us well,
 Thro' four sweet years arose and fell,
From flower to flower, from snow to snow:

And we with singing cheer'd the way,   5
 And, crown'd with all the season lent,
 From April on to April went,
And glad at heart from May to May:

But where the path we walk'd began
 To slant the fifth autumnal slope,   10
 As we descended following Hope,
There sat the Shadow[74] fear'd of man;

Notes

[71] *power* reference probably to both Chartism (50,000 attended a mass meeting at Kennington Common in London on 10 April 1848) and to the French Revolution; see Carlyle, *French Revolution,* 2. 1. 13: "Through every inlet of that National Amphitheatre ... floods-in the living throng.... It is as one more or less peopled Amphitheatre; which the eye grows dim with measuring.... Comes National Assembly, and takes seat under its Canopy; comes Royalty, and takes seat on a throne beside it."

[72] *moon* allusion to the telescope. On 23 September 1846 Neptune was discovered by calculating its position from the changes in the orbit of Uranus, and soon after, on 10 October 1846 its largest moon, Triton, was discovered by the English astronomer, William Lassell (1799–1880).

[73] *path* section XXII–XXVI develop the conventional image of the path of life traversed over the passing months and years, a review of the course of friendship travelled first together, and then by the mourner alone.

[74] *Shadow* Death.

Who broke our fair companionship,
   And spread his mantle dark and cold,
   And wrapt thee formless in the fold,   15
And dull'd the murmur on thy lip,

And bore thee where I could not see
   Nor follow, tho' I walk in haste,
   And think, that somewhere in the waste
The Shadow sits and waits for me.   20

XXIII

Now, sometimes in my sorrow shut,
   Or breaking into song by fits,
   Alone, alone, to where he sits,
The Shadow cloak'd from head to foot,

Who keeps the keys of all the creeds,   5
   I wander, often falling lame,
   And looking back to whence I came,
Or on to where the pathway leads;

And crying, How changed from where it ran
   Thro' lands where not a leaf was dumb;   10
   But all the lavish hills would hum
The murmur of a happy Pan[75]:

When each by turns was guide to each,
   And Fancy light from Fancy caught,
   And Thought leapt out to wed with Thought   15
Ere Thought could wed itself with Speech;

And all we met was fair and good,
   And all was good that Time could bring,
   And all the secret of the Spring
Moved in the chambers of the blood;   20

And many an old philosophy
   On Argive[76] heights divinely sang,
   And round us all the thicket rang
To many a flute of Arcady.[77]

Notes

[75] *Pan* in Greek mythology the god of shepherds, flocks, fields, and woodlands; a conventional figure in pastoral elegies from classical writers: Theocritus, *Idyll* 1; Moschus, and Virgil, *Eclogue* 10; through to Milton's *Epitaphium Damonis* (1639) and Elizabeth Barrett Browning's "The Dead Pan" (1844). Pan was also associated with Christ as the Good Shepherd in English poetry, as in Milton's "On the Morning of Christ's Nativity" (1629: 85–9).

[76] *Argive* related to the city of Argos in Greece; more generally, Greek, as in Virgil.

[77] *Arcady* Arcadia, remote and mountainous area of southern Greece; in mythology the locale of happy rustic shepherds leading an idyllic life that became a conventional setting of pastoral elegy; see Virgil, *Eclogue* 10. 8 and 31–33.

XXIV

And was the day of my delight
   As pure and perfect as I say?
   The very source and fount of Day
Is dash'd with wandering isles of night.

If all was good and fair we met,   5
   This earth had been the Paradise[78]
   It never look'd to human eyes
Since our first Sun arose and set.

And is it that the haze of grief
   Makes former gladness loom so great?   10
   The lowness of the present state,
That sets the past in this relief?

Or that the past will always win
   A glory from its being far;
   And orb into the perfect star[79]   15
We saw not, when we moved therein?

XXV

I know that this was Life,—the track
   Whereon with equal feet we fared;
   And then, as now, the day prepared
The daily burden for the back.

But this it was that made me move   5
   As light as carrier-birds in air;
   I loved the weight I had to bear,
Because it needed help of Love:

Nor could I weary, heart or limb,
   When mighty Love would cleave in twain   10
   The lading of a single pain,
And part it, giving half to him.

XXVI

Still onward winds the dreary way;
   I with it; for I long to prove
   No lapse of moons can canker Love,
Whatever fickle tongues may say.[80]

Notes

[78] *Paradise* Eden; see Genesis 1: 1–2: 17.

[79] *star* just as Earth is seen as an orb from a vantage point in space, so the relationship with Hallam is smoothed into a perfect shape with distance in time.

[80] *say* Catullus used the convention that love will endure, and will not rot or become infected with the passing of time, despite gossiping tongues. He maintained that the thousand kisses given to Lesbia will make the lovers impervious to the evil eye of the envious (Poem 5) and the evil tongues of the malevolent (Poem 7: 11–12).

And if that eye which watches guilt 5
   And goodness, and hath power to see
   Within the green the moulder'd tree,
And towers fall'n as soon as built—

Oh, if indeed that eye foresee
   Or see (in Him is no before)[81] 10
   In more of life true life no more
And Love the indifference to be,

Then might I find, ere yet the morn
   Breaks hither over Indian seas,
   That Shadow waiting with the keys, 15
To shroud me from my proper scorn.

XXVII

I envy not in any moods
   The captive void of noble rage,
   The linnet born within the cage,[82]
That never knew the summer woods:

I envy not the beast that takes 5
   His license in the field of time,
   Unfetter'd by the sense of crime,
To whom a conscience never wakes;

Nor, what may count itself as blest,
   The heart that never plighted troth 10
   But stagnates in the weeds of sloth;
Nor any want-begotten rest.

I hold it true, whate'er befall;
   I feel it, when I sorrow most;
   'Tis better to have loved and lost 15
Than never to have loved at all.

XXVIII

The time draws near the birth of Christ[83]:
   The moon is hid; the night is still;
   The Christmas bells from hill to hill
Answer each other in the mist.

Notes

[81] *foresee … before* God's characteristics of prescience (fore-knowledge), omniscience, and existence outside time.

[82] *cage* see Thomas Gray, "Ode on a Distant Prospect of Eton College" (1747: 27); and "Elegy Written in a Country Churchyard" (1751: 51).

[83] *Christ* the setting is Christmas Eve, 1833, at the Tennyson's family home in the village of Somersby in Lincolnshire, the beginning of the second part of the poem. Sections XXVIII—XXX deal with the first Christmas after Hallam's death.

Four voices of four hamlets round,   5
    From far and near, on mead and moor,
    Swell out and fail, as if a door
Were shut between me and the sound:

Each voice four changes[84] on the wind,
    That now dilate, and now decrease,   10
    Peace and goodwill, goodwill and peace,
Peace and goodwill, to all mankind.

This year I slept and woke with pain,
    I almost wish'd no more to wake,
    And that my hold on life would break   15
Before I heard those bells again:

But they my troubled spirit rule,
    For they controll'd me when a boy;
    They bring me sorrow touch'd with joy,
The merry merry bells of Yule.   20

XXIX

With such compelling cause to grieve
    As daily vexes household peace,
    And chains regret to his decease,
How dare we keep our Christmas-eve;

Which brings no more a welcome guest   5
    To enrich the threshold of the night
    With shower'd largess of delight
In dance and song and game and jest?

Yet go, and while the holly boughs
    Entwine the cold baptismal font,   10
    Make one wreath more for Use and Wont,[85]
That guard the portals of the house;

Old sisters of a day gone by,
    Gray nurses, loving nothing new;
    Why should they miss their yearly due   15
Before their time? They too will die.

Notes

[84] *changes* the ringing of church bells in elaborate sequences.

[85] *Use and Wont* old-fashioned legal term for customary and distinctive practice, often applied, as William Blackstone pointed out in his *Commentaries on the Laws of England* (1765–69), to the unwritten services or duties attached to rent and land-holding. The Tennyson family feared that they might have to leave Somersby on the death of Tennyson's father in 1831, but they were able to rent it for a further six years.

XXX

With trembling fingers did we weave
    The holly round the Christmas hearth;
    A rainy cloud possess'd the earth,
And sadly fell our Christmas-eve.

At our old pastimes in the hall   5
    We gambol'd, making vain pretence
    Of gladness, with an awful sense
Of one mute Shadow[86] watching all.

We paused: the winds were in the beech:
    We heard them sweep the winter land;   10
    And in a circle hand-in-hand
Sat silent, looking each at each.

Then echo-like our voices rang;
    We sung, tho' every eye was dim,
    A merry song we sang with him   15
Last year: impetuously we sang:

We ceased: a gentler feeling crept
    Upon us: surely rest is meet:
    "They rest," we said, "their sleep is sweet,"[87]
And silence follow'd, and we wept.   20

Our voices took a higher range;
    Once more we sang: "They do not die
    Nor lose their mortal sympathy,
Nor change to us, although they change;

Rapt from the fickle and the frail   25
    With gather'd power, yet the same,
    Pierces the keen seraphic flame
From orb to orb, from veil to veil."[88]

Rise, happy morn, rise, holy morn,
    Draw forth the cheerful day from night: 30
    O Father, touch the east, and light
The light that shone when Hope was born.

Notes

[86] *Shadow* not Death, but Hallam's spirit.

[87] *sweet* see Proverbs 3: 24.

[88] *veil* John Keble uses "orb after orb" ("Christmas Day") and develops the image of Moses on the top of Mount Sinai in the presence of God as the blessed spirits move about him: "Through gold and gems, a dazzling maze, / From veil to veil the vision led" ("Thirteenth Sunday after Trinity" in *The Christian Year*, 1827). For veil, see also n. 144. The notion of the progress of the soul through successive stages after death is an ancient one, summarized towards the end of the medieval period in *The Divine Comedy*, where Dante, aided by the guidance first of Virgil and then of Beatrice, moves in his visionary journey through the states of life after death. In the eighteenth century in England speculation about such progress was common in Church of England circles, as in Joseph Butler's *Analogy of Religion* (1736), where death is spoken of as perhaps initiating "great alterations" (I. 1. 2).

XXXI

When Lazarus[89] left his charnel-cave,
    And home to Mary's house return'd,
    Was this demanded—if he yearn'd
To hear her weeping by his grave?

"Where wert thou, brother, those four days?"   5
    There lives no record of reply,
    Which telling what it is to die
Had surely added praise to praise.

From every house the neighbours met,
    The streets were fill'd with joyful sound,   10
    A solemn gladness even crown'd
The purple brows of Olivet.[90]

Behold a man raised up by Christ!
    The rest remaineth unreveal'd;
    He told it not; or something seal'd   15
The lips of that Evangelist.

XXXII

Her eyes are homes of silent prayer,
    Nor other thought her mind admits
    But, he was dead, and there he sits,[91]
And he that brought him back is there.

Then one deep love doth supersede   5
    All other, when her ardent gaze
    Roves from the living brother's face,
And rests upon the Life indeed.

All subtle thought, all curious fears,
    Borne down by gladness so complete,   10
    She bows, she bathes the Saviour's feet
With costly spikenard and with tears.[92]

Thrice blest whose lives are faithful prayers,
    Whose loves in higher love endure;
    What souls possess themselves so pure,   15
Or is there blessedness like theirs?

Notes

[89] *Lazarus* brother of Martha and Mary of the village of Bethany, near Jerusalem; Lazarus is raised from the dead by Jesus; see John 11. Sections XXXI–XXXVI are concerned with love and immortality.

[90] *Olivet* Mount of Olives in Jerusalem, where Jesus prepared for the crucifixion.

[91] *sits* see John 12: 2.

[92] *tears* spikenard is costly ointment; a woman, traditionally identified with Mary Magdalen, washes Jesus' feet with her tears, and anoints them; see John 12: 3.

XXXIII

O thou[93] that after toil and storm
    Mayst seem to have reach'd a purer air,[94]
    Whose faith has centre everywhere,
Nor cares to fix itself to form,

Leave thou thy sister[95] when she prays,   5
    Her early Heaven, her happy views;
    Nor thou with shadow'd hint confuse
A life that leads melodious days.

Her faith thro' form is pure as thine,
    Her hands are quicker unto good: 10
    Oh, sacred be the flesh and blood
To which she links a truth divine!

See thou, that countest reason ripe
    In holding by the law within,
    Thou fail not in a world of sin,   15
And ev'n for want of such a type.[96]

XXXIV

My own dim life should teach me this,
    That life shall live for evermore,
    Else earth is darkness at the core,
And dust and ashes all that is;

This round of green, this orb of flame,   5
    Fantastic beauty; such as lurks
    In some wild Poet, when he works
Without a conscience or an aim.

What then were God to such as I?
    'Twere hardly worth my while to choose   10
    Of things all mortal, or to use
A little patience ere I die;

'Twere best at once to sink to peace,
    Like birds the charming serpent draws,
    To drop head-foremost in the jaws[97]   15
Of vacant darkness and to cease.

Notes

[93] *thou* Lazarus, continued from sections XXXI and XXXII; also, more generally, an abstract thinker or pantheist.

[94] *air* see *Purgatorio* I. 13–18, where Dante leaves the atmosphere of Hell for the purer air of Mount Purgatory.

[95] *sister* Mary in the Lazarus story; as well as a person whose childlike faith remains attached to human forms.

[96] *type* Tennyson here and elsewhere contrasts the individual with the "type." He uses type in two senses: a scientific term in biology (a class or division of plants or animals with similar characteristics, especially of structure); and as a mode of reading the Bible (typology), whereby earlier events foreshadow later ones (type and antitype; Moses and Jesus), in which Hallam becomes the type of later and higher human development. See sections LV and LVI.

[97] *jaws* rattlesnakes are discussed in Tennyson's copy of C. C. Clarke's *The Hundred Wonders of the World* (1821): Birds "are so frightened at the sight of their enemy, who fixes his

XXXV

Yet if some voice that man could trust
   Should murmur from the narrow house,
   "The cheeks drop in; the body bows;
Man dies: nor is there hope in dust":

Might I not say? "Yet even here,   5
   But for one hour, O Love, I strive
   To keep so sweet a thing alive":
But I should turn mine ears and hear

The moanings of the homeless sea,
   The sound of streams that swift or slow   10
   Draw down Æonian hills,[98] and sow
The dust of continents to be[99];

And Love would answer with a sigh,
   "The sound of that forgetful shore[100]
   Will change my sweetness more and more,   15
Half-dead to know that I shall die."

O me, what profits it to put
   An idle case? If Death were seen
   At first as Death, Love had not been,
Or been in narrowest working shut,   20

Mere fellowship of sluggish moods,
   Or in his coarsest Satyr-shape[101]
   Had bruised the herb and crush'd the grape,
And bask'd and batten'd in the woods.

Notes

lively piercing eyes upon one or other of them, that they have not the power to get away, but leap about from bough to bough, till they are quite tired, and at last falling to the ground, are snapped into his mouth" (479).

[98] *Æonian hills* everlasting hills (Gk. *aion*; Lat. *eon*, age, the ages, eternity).

[99] *streams . . . be* a reference to the transformation of landscapes by the action of water's eroding of banks and hills, and depositing of earth downstream. Such phenomena are discussed as part of the process of the uniformitarian evolution of the earth in chapters 10–13 of book 1 of Lyell's *The Principles of Geology* (1830–33) that Tennyson had read: "We shall begin, then, by describing the destroying and transporting power of running water, as exhibited by torrents and streams" In the frame poem ("The Epic") for "Morte d'Arthur" (1842), Tennyson alludes to Lyell's views that aroused controversy concerning the antiquity of the earth and conflicts with those who took literally the account of

creation in Genesis. The Uniformitarian theory is opposed to Catastrophism, a theory of Earth's changes resulting from violent earthquakes, volcanoes, and floods, as in Georges Cuvier's *Discourse on the Revolutionary Upheavals on the Surface of the Earth* (1825). See RELIGION: GEOLOGY; CHAMBERS.

[100] *shore* the shores of the River Lethe, the river of forgetfulness in Hades (*Aeneid* 6. 713–15). Dante also drinks from the River Lethe that he locates as one of the dual rivers of the Earthly Paradise at the top of Mount Purgatory (*Purgatorio* 28).

[101] *Satyr-shape* in Greek mythology, satyrs were the companions of Pan and Dionysus, the gods of fields, shepherds, and wine. They were depicted with a horse-tail and were symbols of sexuality and savage pleasure. In Roman mythology they were conflated with Faunus and had half-human and half-goat characteristics. They were also components of the pastoral elegy, as in Milton's *Lycidas* (33–34).

XXXVI

Tho' truths in manhood darkly join,
    Deep-seated in our mystic frame,
    We yield all blessing to the name
Of Him[102] that made them current coin;

For Wisdom dealt with mortal powers,   5
    Where truth in closest words shall fail,
    When truth embodied in a tale[103]
Shall enter in at lowly doors.[104]

And so the Word had breath,[105] and wrought
    With human hands the creed of creeds   10
    In loveliness of perfect deeds,
More strong than all poetic thought;

Which he may read that binds the sheaf,
    Or builds the house, or digs the grave,
    And those wild eyes that watch the wave   15
In roarings round the coral reef.[106]

XXXVII

Urania[107] speaks with darken'd brow:
    "Thou pratest here where thou art least;
    This faith has many a purer priest,
And many an abler voice than thou.

Go down beside thy native rill,   5
    On thy Parnassus[108] set thy feet,
    And hear thy laurel whisper sweet
About the ledges of the hill."

And my Melpomene[109] replies,
    A touch of shame upon her cheek: 10
    "I am not worthy ev'n to speak
Of thy prevailing mysteries;

Notes

[102] *Him* Christ.

[103] *Wisdom ... tale* divine wisdom (Gk. *sophia*; *logos*) or the Word as in the next stanza (see John 1) where the "Word" is the original ordering principle of the cosmos; the "tale" refers to the Gospels of the New Testament. See also TENNYSON, n. 29 (WEB p. 339).

[104] *doors* see John 10: 9.

[105] *breath* see John 1: 14.

[106] *reef* Darwin had observed reefs on the voyage of the *Beagle* and on his return to England read a paper to the Geological Society on their formation as the only continuous geological formations in time – all others being discontinuous; see above, section I, concerning humans being compared to geological formations, rising "on stepping stones of their dead selves." Darwin later published his argument

as *The Structure and Distribution of Coral Reefs* (1842) that had already caught the attention of Charles Lyell, William Whewell and other acquaintances of Tennyson. At the same time the passage has a double meaning, the "Word," "creed," "wild eyes," and "coral reef" also refer to the current missionary activity in the South Pacific islands.

[107] *Urania* muse of astronomy and also heavenly poetry, as in the invocation in *Paradise Lost* 7. 1 ff. For this section see Propertius, *Elegies* 3. 3, where Apollo rebukes the poet for attempting to write beyond his competence.

[108] *Parnassus* mountain in central Greece above Delphi, sacred to Apollo and the Muses. The laurel was the unfading leaf used to crown the victorious poet; see HEMANS, n. 17.

[109] *Melpomene* muse of tragedy and elegy; invoked by Horace, *Odes* 1. 24; and 4. 3.

For I am but an earthly Muse,
   And owning but a little art
   To lull with song an aching heart,   15
And render human love his dues;

But brooding on the dear one dead,
   And all he said of things divine,[110]
   (And dear to me as sacred wine
To dying lips is all he said),   20

I murmur'd, as I came along,
   Of comfort clasp'd in truth reveal'd;
   And loiter'd in the master's field,
And darken'd sanctities with song."

XXXVIII

With weary steps I loiter on,[111]
   Tho' always under alter'd skies
   The purple from the distance dies,
My prospect and horizon gone.

No joy the blowing season gives,   5
   The herald melodies of spring,
   But in the songs I love to sing
A doubtful gleam of solace lives.

If any care for what is here
   Survive in spirits render'd free,   10
   Then are these songs I sing of thee
Not all ungrateful to thine ear.

XXXIX

Old warder of these buried bones,[112]
   And answering now my random stroke
   With fruitful cloud and living smoke,[113]
Dark yew, that graspest at the stones

And dippest toward the dreamless head,   5
   To thee too comes the golden hour
   When flower is feeling after flower;
But Sorrow—fixt upon the dead,

Notes

[110] *divine* Hallam dealt with theology in *Theodicaea Novissima* (Lat. Newest theodicy) that he read to the Cambridge Apostles in 1831; it was printed at Tennyson's request in Hallam's *Remains* (1834). A theodicy is a philosophical enquiry into the nature of God.

[111] *loiter on* the first Spring of three in the poem; see sections LXXXVI and LXXXVIII for the second, and CXV–CXVI for the third.

[112] *bones* Tennyson added this section to the poem in the 1870 edition of *In Memoriam*, as a response to section II, renumbering the subsequent sections to give a total of 131 sections, with the addition also of section LIX.

[113] *smoke* yellow pollen from the yew-tree flowers.

And darkening the dark graves of men,—
    What whisper'd from her lying lips?   10
    Thy gloom is kindled at the tips,
And passes into gloom again.

XL

Could we forget the widow'd hour[114]
    And look on Spirits breathed away,
    As on a maiden in the day
When first she wears her orange-flower!

When crown'd with blessing she doth rise   5
    To take her latest leave of home,
    And hopes and light regrets that come
Make April of her tender eyes[115];

And doubtful joys the father move,
    And tears are on the mother's face,   10
    As parting with a long embrace
She enters other realms of love;

Her office there to rear, to teach,
    Becoming as is meet and fit
    A link among the days, to knit   15
The generations each with each;

And, doubtless, unto thee is given
    A life that bears immortal fruit
    In those great offices that suit
The full-grown energies of heaven.   20

Ay me, the difference I discern!
    How often shall her old fireside
    Be cheer'd with tidings of the bride,
How often she herself return,

And tell them all they would have told,   25
    And bring her babe, and make her boast,
    Till even those that miss'd her most
Shall count new things as dear as old:

But thou and I have shaken hands,
    Till growing winters lay me low;   30
    My paths are in the fields I know.
And thine in undiscover'd lands.[116]

Notes

[114] *hour* sections XL–XLVII continue the discussion raised in sections XXXI–XXXVI concerning love and immortality, asking whether reunion in the afterlife is possible.

[115] *eyes* see *Antony and Cleopatra* 3. 2. 43.
[116] *lands* see *Hamlet* 3. 1. 79–80.

XLI

Thy spirit ere our fatal loss
 Did ever rise from high to higher;
 As mounts the heavenward altar-fire,
As flies the lighter thro' the gross.

But thou art turn'd to something strange,   5
 And I have lost the links that bound
 Thy changes; here upon the ground,
No more partaker of thy change.

Deep folly! yet that this could be—
 That I could wing my will with might   10
 To leap the grades of life and light,
And flash at once, my friend, to thee.

For tho' my nature rarely yields
 To that vague fear implied in death;
 Nor shudders at the gulfs beneath,   15
The howlings from forgotten fields[117];

Yet oft when sundown skirts the moor
 An inner trouble I behold,
 A spectral doubt which makes me cold,
That I shall be thy mate no more,   20

Tho' following with an upward mind
 The wonders that have come to thee,
 Thro' all the secular[118] to-be,
But evermore a life behind.

XLII

I vex my heart with fancies dim:
 He still outstript me in the race;
 It was but unity of place
That made me dream I rank'd with him.

And so may Place retain us still,   5
 And he the much-beloved again,
 A lord of large experience, train
To riper growth the mind and will:

And what delights can equal those
 That stir the spirit's inner deeps,   10
 When one that loves but knows not, reaps
A truth from one that loves and knows?

Notes ——————————————

[117] *fields* see Deuteronomy 32: 10; more generally the under-world: see *Inferno* 3. 25–51; and *Measure for Measure* 3. 1. 27–29.

[118] *secular* the term is not merely opposed to a concept of sacred eternity, but also means an "age" (Lat. *saeculum*) or

XLIII

If Sleep and Death be truly one,[119]
    And every spirit's folded bloom
    Thro' all its intervital gloom
In some long trance should slumber on;

Unconscious of the sliding hour,   5
    Bare of the body, might it last,
    And silent traces of the past
Be all the colour of the flower:

So then were nothing lost to man;
    So that still garden of the souls   10
    In many a figured leaf enrolls
The total world since life began[120];

And love will last as pure and whole
    As when he loved me here in Time,
    And at the spiritual prime[121]   15
Rewaken with the dawning soul.

XLIV

How fares it with the happy dead?[122]
    For here the man is more and more;
    But he forgets the days before
God shut the doorways of his head.[123]

The days have vanish'd, tone and tint,   5
    And yet perhaps the hoarding sense[124]
    Gives out at times (he knows not whence)
A little flash, a mystic hint;

And in the long harmonious years
    (If Death so taste Lethean springs[125]),   10
    May some dim touch of earthly things
Surprise thee ranging with thy peers.

Notes

period of time, or even unbounded time. The term is used liturgically in the conclusion of each psalm in the Latin translation of the Book of Psalms, "throughout all ages, world without end" (Lat. *per omnia saecula saeculorum*).

[119] *one* see 1 Thessalonians 4: 13–17.

[120] *began* see J. P. Nichol's *Views of the Architecture of the Heavens* (1837): "May not some similar system and similar destiny characterise the System of Firmaments? Perhaps in the mean while these are also related, somehow as the stars in each cluster—slowly performing mighty revolutions, whose recurrence constitutes the greatest Annus Magnus of Creation, the highest unity of existing Time. Probably the elements of decay, or rather change, are also amid this mechanism—probably all is passing, in a silence next to motionless—quietly as

the leaf grows, toward some unknown consummation!" The book was in Tennyson's library.

[121] *prime* moment of origin, beginning of friendship; the spiritual awakening of the individual dead at the general resurrection.

[122] *happy dead* in classical mythology the blessed dead dwelt in the Elysian Fields in Hades; see, for instance, *Odyssey* 4. 563; and *Aeneid* 6. 541.

[123] *head* the closing of the sutures of the skull in infancy.

[124] *sense* memory; the suggestion is that the child in infancy, as in Wordsworth's "Ode: Intimations of Immortality" (sect. 5), may have flashing "recollections" of earlier experiences, or, in Plato, of an earlier life.

[125] *springs* see n. 100.

If such a dreamy touch should fall,
    O turn thee round, resolve the doubt;
    My guardian angel will speak out   15
In that high place, and tell thee all.

XLV

The baby new to earth and sky,
    What time his tender palm is prest
    Against the circle of the breast,
Has never thought that "this is I"[126]:

But as he grows he gathers much,   5
    And learns the use of "I," and "me,"
    And finds "I am not what I see,
And other than the things I touch."

So rounds he to a separate mind
    From whence clear memory may begin,   10
    As thro' the frame that binds him in
His isolation grows defined.

This use may lie in blood and breath,[127]
    Which else were fruitless of their due,
    Had man to learn himself anew   15
Beyond the second birth of Death.

XLVI

We ranging down this lower track,
    The path we came by, thorn and flower,[128]
    Is shadow'd by the growing hour,
Lest life should fail in looking back.

So be it: there no shade can last   5
    In that deep dawn behind the tomb,
    But clear from marge to marge shall bloom
The eternal landscape of the past;

A lifelong tract of time reveal'd;
    The fruitful hours of still increase;   10
    Days order'd in a wealthy peace,
And those five years[129] its richest field.

Notes

[126] *I* see Hallam's essay "On Sympathy": "The infant cannot separate the sensations of nourishment from the form of his nurse or mother."

[127] *breath* see Shakespeare, *King John* 4. 2. 246.

[128] *thorn and flower* see Hallam's poem, "On My Sister's Birth-Day" (in *Remains* 1834): "thy career / Is all before thee, thorn and flower."

[129] *five years* the duration of the friendship of Hallam and Tennyson.

O Love, thy province were not large,
    A bounded field, nor stretching far;
    Look also, Love, a brooding star,   15
A rosy warmth from marge to marge.

XLVII

That each, who seems a separate whole,
    Should move his rounds, and fusing all
    The skirts of self again, should fall
Remerging in the general Soul,[130]

Is faith as vague as all unsweet: 5
    Eternal form shall still divide
    The eternal soul from all beside;
And I shall know him when we meet:

And we shall sit at endless feast,
    Enjoying each the other's good: 10
    What vaster dream can hit the mood
Of Love on earth? He seeks at least

Upon the last and sharpest height,
    Before the spirits fade away,
    Some landing-place, to clasp and say,   15
"Farewell! We lose ourselves in light."

XLVIII

If these brief lays, of Sorrow born,
    Were taken to be such as closed
    Grave doubts and answers here proposed,
Then these were such as men might scorn:

Her care is not to part and prove;   5
    She takes, when harsher moods remit,
    What slender shade of doubt may flit,
And makes it vassal unto love:

And hence, indeed, she sports with words,
    But better serves a wholesome law,   10
    And holds it sin and shame to draw
The deepest measure from the chords:

Nor dare she trust a larger lay,
    But rather loosens from the lip
    Short swallow-flights of song, that dip   15
Their wings in tears, and skim away.

Notes

[130] *Soul* the theological issue is whether psychic and spiritual individuality and particular love and identity are lost, or are absorbed after death into the general soul, or are incorporated into the life of God.

XLIX

From art, from nature, from the schools,[131]
   Let random influences glance,
   Like light in many a shiver'd lance
That breaks about the dappled pools:

The lightest wave of thought shall lisp,   5
   The fancy's tenderest eddy wreathe,
   The slightest air of song shall breathe
To make the sullen surface crisp.

And look thy look, and go thy way,
   But blame not thou the winds that make   10
   The seeming-wanton ripple break,
The tender-pencil'd shadow play.

Beneath all fancied hopes and fears
   Ay me, the sorrow deepens down,
   Whose muffled motions blindly drown   15
The bases of my life in tears.

L

Be near me when my light is low,[132]
   When the blood creeps, and the nerves prick
   And tingle; and the heart is sick,
And all the wheels of Being slow.

Be near me when the sensuous frame   5
   Is rack'd with pangs that conquer trust;
   And Time, a maniac scattering dust,
And Life, a Fury slinging flame.

Be near me when my faith is dry,
   And men the flies of latter spring,   10
   That lay their eggs, and sting and sing
And weave their petty cells and die.

Be near me when I fade away,
   To point the term of human strife,
   And on the low dark verge of life   15
The twilight of eternal day.

Notes

[131] *schools* universities; more generally, philosophy.
[132] *low* possible echo of a stanza of the German hymn "O Sacred Head now wounded" by Paul Gerhardt (1607–76), translated from Bernard of Clairvaux (1090–1153): "Be near when I am dying, / O show thy cross to me."

Sections L–LVIII deal with the mourner's wish for present communion with the dead friend and with the interfering and distracting conditions of pain in the real world that raise doubts about the efficacy of love.

LI

Do we indeed desire the dead
    Should still be near us at our side?
    Is there no baseness we would hide?
No inner vileness that we dread?

Shall he for whose applause I strove,   5
    I had such reverence for his blame,
    See with clear eye some hidden shame
And I be lessen'd in his love?

I wrong the grave with fears untrue:
    Shall love be blamed for want of faith?   10
    There must be wisdom with great Death:
The dead shall look me thro' and thro'.

Be near us when we climb or fall:
    Ye watch, like God, the rolling hours
    With larger other eyes than ours,   15
To make allowance for us all.

LII

I cannot love thee as I ought,
    For love reflects the thing beloved;
    My words are only words, and moved
Upon the topmost froth of thought.

"Yet blame not thou thy plaintive song,"   5
    The Spirit of true love replied;
    "Thou canst not move me from thy side,
Nor human frailty do me wrong.

What keeps a spirit wholly true
    To that ideal which he bears?   10
    What record? not the sinless years
That breathed beneath the Syrian blue[133]:

So fret not, like an idle girl,
    That life is dash'd with flecks of sin.
    Abide: thy wealth is gather'd in,   15
When Time hath sunder'd shell from pearl."

LIII

How many a father have I seen,
    A sober man, among his boys,
    Whose youth was full of foolish noise,
Who wears his manhood hale and green:

Notes

[133] *sinless … blue* the life of Christ; Syria, north and east of
Palestine, was a Roman province from 64 BCE.

And dare we to this fancy give,   5
    That had the wild oat not been sown,
    The soil, left barren, scarce had grown
The grain by which a man may live?[134]

Or, if we held the doctrine sound
    For life outliving heats of youth,   10
    Yet who would preach it as a truth
To those that eddy round and round?

Hold thou the good: define it well[135]:
    For fear divine Philosophy[136]
    Should push beyond her mark, and be   15
Procuress to the Lords of Hell.

LIV

Oh yet we trust that somehow good
    Will be the final goal of ill,
    To pangs of nature, sins of will,
Defects of doubt, and taints of blood;

That nothing walks with aimless feet;   5
    That not one life shall be destroy'd,
    Or cast as rubbish to the void,
When God hath made the pile complete;

That not a worm is cloven in vain;
    That not a moth with vain desire   10
    Is shrivell'd in a fruitless fire,
Or but subserves another's gain.

Behold, we know not anything;
    I can but trust that good shall fall
    At last—far off—at last, to all,   15
And every winter change to spring.

So runs my dream: but what am I?
    An infant[137] crying in the night:
    An infant crying for the light:
And with no language but a cry.   20

LV

The wish, that of the living whole[138]
    No life may fail beyond the grave,
    Derives it not from what we have
The likest God within the soul?

Notes

[134] *live* see Matthew 4: 4.

[135] *well* see 1 Thessalonians 5: 21.

[136] *Philosophy* see Milton, *Comus* (1634: 476); and Marlowe, *Doctor Faustus* (1604, 1620): "Come, Mephistophilis, let us dispute again, / And argue of divine astrology" (6. 35–36).

[137] *infant* the Latin *infans* means both *child* and *unable to speak*. See Jeremiah 1: 6.

[138] *whole* sections LV and LVI are concerned with religious doubt raised by the new sciences of comparative anatomy, geology, and the relationship of species in natural history.

Are God and Nature then at strife,   5
    That Nature lends such evil dreams?
    So careful of the type she seems,
So careless of the single life[139];

That I, considering everywhere
    Her secret meaning in her deeds,   10
    And finding that of fifty seeds
She often brings but one to bear,

I falter where I firmly trod,
    And falling with my weight of cares
    Upon the great world's altar-stairs   15
That slope thro' darkness up to God,

I stretch lame hands of faith, and grope,
    And gather dust and chaff, and call
    To what I feel is Lord of all,
And faintly trust the larger hope.   20

LVI

"So careful of the type?" but no.
    From scarped cliff and quarried stone[140]
    She cries, "A thousand types are gone:
I care for nothing, all shall go.[141]

Notes

Comparative anatomy pointed to possible relationships between humans and birds and animals (especially the greater apes); in geology the fossil record questioned the accepted biblical account of the age of the earth; and in natural history there was new study of changes and developments within species. Each of these issues seemed to contradict the notion of the special creation of species once and for all, as recorded in Genesis. Tennyson was deeply interested in such scientific discoveries, having read Buffon's *Natural History* (1749–78) as a child, Lyell's *Principles of Geology* (1830–33) in 1837, and Chambers's *Vestiges of the Natural History of Creation* (1844) in the year of its publication. See RELIGION: GEOLOGY; CHAMBERS.

[139] *type … life* this section questions the supposed conflict between God's care of the individual and Nature's disinterest in individual welfare in favour of the general survival of the type or species, as well as the finite duration of species, evidenced by extinctions and the fossil record. These notions were widespread in scientific discussions after about 1830, as in the use of the epigraph from John Playfair's *Illustrations of the Huttonian Theory* (1802) on the title page of the second volume of Lyell's *The Principles of Geology*: "The inhabitants of the globe, like all the other parts of it, are subject to change. It is not only the individual that perishes, but whole species." Robert Chambers's *Vestiges of Creation* (1844) makes a similar point: "There is, as has been said, a remarkable persistency in national features and forms, insomuch that a single individual thrown

into a family different from himself is absorbed in it, and all trace of him lost after a few generations. … Nature has a power of producing new varieties, though this is only done rarely. Such novelties of type abound in the vegetable world, are seen more rarely in the animal circle, and perhaps are least frequent of occurrence in our own race" (ch. 16); "It is clear, moreover, from the whole scope of the natural laws, that the individual, as far as the present sphere of being is concerned, is to the Author of Nature a consideration of inferior moment. Everywhere we see the arrangements for the species perfect; the individual is left, as it were, to take his chance amidst the mêlée of the various laws affecting him" (ch. 18); see also n. 96.

[140] *stone* fossils found in cliffs and quarries; possibly also a suggestion of Perseus (humanity?) in the labyrinth, seeking both the Minotaur (knowledge? Nature?) and escape.

[141] *go* the concept of the extinction of species is derived from George Cuvier (1769–1832), French palaeontologist and zoologist, who in 1796 delivered two papers to the Institut de France and later published as *Mémoires sur les espèces d'éléphants vivants et fossiles* (Fr. Memorials on the living and fossil species of elephants, 1800). This ground-breaking work in comparative anatomy was the basis for the acceptance of the notion of extinction. Cuvier's study of living and fossil elephant-like creatures, including Indian and African elephants, the fossils of mammoths, and the recently found "Ohio animal" from North America that he would later name "mastodon," showed that the fossil

Thou makest thine appeal to me: 5
   I bring to life, I bring to death:
   The spirit does but mean the breath:
I know no more." And he, shall he,

Man, her last work, who seem'd so fair,
   Such splendid purpose in his eyes,   10
   Who roll'd the psalm to wintry skies,
Who built him fanes of fruitless prayer,

Who trusted God was love indeed
   And love Creation's final law—
   Tho' Nature, red in tooth and claw[142]   15
With ravine, shriek'd against his creed—

Who loved, who suffer'd countless ills,
   Who battled for the True, the Just,
   Be blown about the desert dust,
Or seal'd within the iron hills?[143]   20

No more? A monster then, a dream,
   A discord. Dragons[144] of the prime,
   That tare each other in their slime,
Were mellow music match'd with him.

O life as futile, then, as frail!   25
   O for thy voice to soothe and bless!
   What hope of answer, or redress?
Behind the veil, behind the veil.[145]

Notes

mammoth and mastodon are species distinct from the Indian and African elephants, and that the megatherium, a kind of giant sloth, is distinct from other sloth species. By means of comparative anatomy he demonstrated for the first time that species could become extinct, and that these fossils are from extinct species, unrelated to species still alive. See also SWINBURNE, n. 40 (WEB p. 430).

[142] *claw* this famous phrase concerning the violence of nature has many antecedents in scientific and other literatures, as for instance, in Erasmus Darwin's *The Temple of Nature; or, The Origin of Society* (1803):

> —Air, earth, and ocean, to astonish'd day
> One scene of blood, one mighty tomb display!
> From Hunger's arm the shafts of Death are hurl'd
> And one great Slaughter-house the warring world!

Though different from it, the notion is often related to Darwin's later concept of the struggle for existence: see RELIGION: GEOLOGY, n. 37; and DARWIN, n. 3.

[143] *desert dust ... iron hills* Lyell has a section of volume 2, chapter 14 of *The Principles of Geology* called "Imbedding of organic bodies and human remains in blown sand." Tennyson had also read Hugh Miller's *The Old Red Sandstone* (1841) in which the red sandstone hills of

Scotland are caused by iron oxide in the soil and which contain the fossils of fish and other sea animals that were "sealed" in the stone.

The seven relative clauses that modify the interrogative "Shall he?" (l. 8) ("who seem'd ... who roll'd ... who built ... who trusted ... who loved, who suffer'd ... who battled," and the concluding verbs, "be blown ... or seal'd") themselves encircle or bury syntactically the famous parenthetical image of nature's violence: "Tho' Nature, red in tooth and claw ... shriek'd against his creed."

[144] *Dragons ... tare* fossil dinosaurs; tare (arch. tear).

[145] *veil* see Hebrews 6: 19; the veil of the Holy of Holies of the Temple in Jerusalem. It shielded the Ark of the Covenant that contained the tablets of the Law given by God to Moses. Only the High Priest could pass into this sanctuary on certain religious festivals. The veiling of a sacred statue or person was a commonplace of Eastern mystery religions, as in the veiled statue of Truth at the temple at Sais, of which Hallam wrote in "After first meeting Emily Tennyson" (*Remains* 1834): "Art thou not She / Who in my Sais-temple was a light / Behind all veils of thought, and fantasy." See n. 88. See also FITZGERALD, *RUBÁIYÁT, XXXII*.

LVII

Peace; come away[146]: the song of woe
    Is after all an earthly song:
    Peace; come away: we do him wrong
To sing so wildly: let us go.

Come; let us go: your cheeks are pale;   5
    But half my life[147] I leave behind:
    Methinks my friend is richly shrined;
But I shall pass; my work will fail.

Yet in these ears, till hearing dies,
    One set slow bell will seem to toll   10
    The passing of the sweetest soul
That ever look'd with human eyes.

I hear it now, and o'er and o'er
    Eternal greetings to the dead;
    And "Ave, Ave, Ave,"[148] said,   15
"Adieu, adieu" for evermore.

LVIII

In those sad words I took farewell:
    Like echoes in sepulchral halls,
    As drop by drop the water falls
In vaults and catacombs, they fell;

And, falling, idly broke the peace   5
    Of hearts that beat from day to day,
    Half-conscious of their dying clay,
And those cold crypts where they shall cease

The high Muse[149] answer'd: "Wherefore grieve
    Thy brethren with a fruitless tear?   10
    Abide a little longer here,
And thou shalt take a nobler leave."

Notes

[146] *away* the addressee is Tennyson's sister Emily, Hallam's betrothed.

[147] *life* commonplace in Latin poetry, as in Horace's *propemptikon* for the safe arrival of his friend Virgil in Greece in *Odes* 1. 3 (see n. 51). The opening prayer ends by claiming Virgil as "half of my own life" (*animae dimidium meae* 1. 3. 8, quoted by St Augustine in *Confessions* 4. 6). Another variant is to call a friend "part of my soul" (*pars animae*) as in *Metamorphoses* 8. 406.

[148] *Ave* (Lat. hail); repeated in Catullus' elegiac ode on the death of his brother: *frater, ave atque vale* (Lat. Brother, hail and farewell; Poem 101. 10). The Latin phrase was used by Tennyson in his poem "Frater Ave atque Vale" on the death of his brother Charles in 1879 (see below).

[149] *Muse* Urania; see n. 102.

LIX

O Sorrow,[150] wilt thou live with me
    No casual mistress, but a wife,
    My bosom-friend and half of life[151];
As I confess it needs must be;

O Sorrow, wilt thou rule my blood,   5
    Be sometimes lovely like a bride,
    And put thy harsher moods aside,
If thou wilt have me wise and good.

My centred passion cannot move,
    Nor will it lessen from to-day;   10
    But I'll have leave at times to play
As with the creature of my love;

And set thee forth, for thou art mine,
    With so much hope for years to come,
    That, howsoe'er I know thee, some   15
Could hardly tell what name were thine.

LX

He past; a soul of nobler tone[152]:
    My spirit loved and loves him yet,
    Like some poor girl whose heart is set
On one whose rank exceeds her own.

He mixing with his proper sphere,   5
    She finds the baseness of her lot,
    Half jealous of she knows not what,
And envying all that meet him there.

The little village looks forlorn;
    She sighs amid her narrow days,   10
    Moving about the household ways,
In that dark house where she was born.

The foolish neighbours come and go,
    And tease her till the day draws by:
    At night she weeps, "How vain am I!   15
How should he love a thing so low?"

Notes

[150] *Sorrow* this section was added to the poem in the fourth edition (1851), as related to section III, to which this section is a partial answer.

[151] *life* see n. 147.
[152] *tone* sections LX–LXV voice the hope that Hallam will think of the speaker.

LXI

If, in thy second state sublime,[153]
   Thy ransom'd reason change replies
   With all the circle of the wise,[154]
The perfect flower of human time;

And if thou cast thine eyes below,   5
   How dimly character'd and slight,
   How dwarf'd a growth of cold and night,
How blanch'd with darkness must I grow!

Yet turn thee to the doubtful shore,
   Where thy first form was made a man;   10
   I loved thee, Spirit, and love, nor can
The soul of Shakspeare[155] love thee more.

LXII

Tho' if an eye that's downward cast
   Could make thee somewhat blench[156] or fail,
   Then be my love an idle tale,
And fading legend of the past;

And thou, as one that once declined,[157]   5
   When he was little more than boy,
   On some unworthy heart with joy,
But lives to wed an equal mind;

And breathes a novel world, the while
   His other passion wholly dies,   10
   Or in the light of deeper eyes
Is matter for a flying smile.

LXIII

Yet pity for a horse o'er-driven,
   And love in which my hound has part,
   Can hang no weight upon my heart
In its assumptions up to heaven;

Notes

[153] *state sublime* see Thomas Gray's "Ode to Music" (1769), where "Newton's self" bends from his "state sublime" in heaven. On the stages of life after death, see n. 88.

[154] *wise* the commonplace of the gathering of the great, especially the heroic dead, in Hades, Elysium, or Paradise occurs in *Odyssey* 11, *Aeneid* 6, and *Inferno* 4. 79–147.

[155] *Shakspeare* spelling promoted by Edmond Malone in his edition (1790); Hallam greatly admired Shakespeare, as his father asserted: "It was in Shakspeare alone that he found the fulness of soul which seemed to slake the thirst of his own rapidly expanding genius for an inexhaustible fountain of thought and emotion" (*Remains*, 1834, vii).

[156] *blench* flinch.

[157] *declined* stooped.

And I am so much more than these,   5
  As thou, perchance, art more than I,
  And yet I spare them sympathy,
And I would set their pains at ease.

So mayst thou watch me where I weep,
  As, unto vaster motions bound,[158]   10
  The circuits of thine orbit round
A higher height, a deeper deep.

LXIV

Dost thou look back on what hath been,[159]
  As some divinely gifted man,
  Whose life in low estate[160] began
And on a simple village green;

Who breaks his birth's invidious bar,   5
  And grasps the skirts of happy chance,
  And breasts the blows of circumstance,
And grapples with his evil star;

Who makes by force his merit known
  And lives to clutch the golden keys,   10
  To mould a mighty state's decrees,
And shape the whisper of the throne;

And moving up from high to higher,
  Becomes on Fortune's crowning slope
  The pillar of a people's hope,   15
The centre of a world's desire;

Yet feels, as in a pensive dream,
  When all his active powers are still,
  A distant dearness in the hill,
A secret sweetness in the stream,   20

The limit of his narrower fate,
  While yet beside its vocal springs
  He play'd at counsellors and kings,
With one that was his earliest mate;

Notes

[158] *bound* in medieval cosmology angelic spirits maintained the motion of the planets in their orbits; so Hallam's spirit may be relocated to another orbit larger than Earth's, as Isaac Taylor had suggested in *Physical Theory of Another Life* (1836): "If each sun be a place of assembly, and a home of immortality to the rational planetary tribes of its systems, the vast world around which all suns are supposed to be revolving, may be the home of a still higher order of life, and the theatre of a still more comprehensive convocation of the intellectual community" (234).

[159] *been* see n. 57; section LXIV is a single sentence.

[160] *estate* see Psalm 136: 23.

Who ploughs with pain his native lea   25
 And reaps the labour of his hands,
 Or in the furrow musing stands;
"Does my old friend remember me?"

LXV

Sweet soul, do with me as thou wilt;
 I lull a fancy trouble-tost
 With "Love's too precious to be lost,
A little grain shall not be spilt."[161]

And in that solace can I sing,   5
 Till out of painful phases wrought
 There flutters up a happy thought,
Self-balanced on a lightsome wing:

Since we deserved the name of friends,
 And thine effect so lives in me,   10
 A part of mine may live in thee
And move thee on to noble ends.

LXVI

You thought my heart too far diseased;
 You wonder when my fancies play
 To find me gay among the gay,
Like one with any trifle pleased.

The shade by which my life was crost,   5
 Which makes a desert in the mind,
 Has made me kindly with my kind,
And like to him whose sight is lost;

Whose feet are guided thro' the land,
 Whose jest among his friends is free,   10
 Who takes the children on his knee,
And winds their curls about his hand:

He plays with threads,[162] he beats his chair
 For pastime, dreaming of the sky;
 His inner day can never die,   15
His night of loss is always there.

Notes

[161] *spilt* see Amos 9: 9.   [162] *threads* cat's cradle.

LXVII

When on my bed the moonlight falls,[163]
 I know that in thy place of rest
 By that broad water of the west,[164]
There comes a glory on the walls;

Thy marble[165] bright in dark appears,   5
 As slowly steals a silver flame
 Along the letters of thy name,
And o'er the number of thy years.

The mystic glory swims away;
 From off my bed the moonlight dies;   10
 And closing eaves of wearied eyes
I sleep till dusk is dipt in gray:

And then I know the mist is drawn
 A lucid veil from coast to coast,
 And in the dark church like a ghost   15
Thy tablet glimmers[166] to the dawn.

LXVIII

When in the down I sink my head,
 Sleep, Death's twin-brother,[167] times my breath;
 Sleep, Death's twin-brother, knows not Death,
Nor can I dream of thee as dead:

I walk as ere I walk'd forlorn,   5
 When all our path was fresh with dew,
 And all the bugle breezes blew
Reveillée to the breaking morn.

But what is this? I turn about,
 I find a trouble in thine eye,   10
 Which makes me sad I know not why,
Nor can my dream resolve the doubt:

But ere the lark hath left the lea
 I wake, and I discern the truth;
 It is the trouble of my youth   15
That foolish sleep transfers to thee.

Notes

[163] *falls* sections LXVII–LXXI are linked by references to night, sleep, and dreams.
[164] *west* the Bristol Channel, overlooked on the eastern side by Clevedon parish church where Hallam is buried.
[165] *marble* tablet, Hallam's memorial in the south transept.

[166] *ghost . . . glimmers* see TENNYSON, "NOW SLEEPS THE CRIMSON PETAL, NOW THE WHITE" (5–6) (WEB p. 343).
[167] *twin-brother* Sleep is the brother of Death in *Iliad* 14. 231; see also *Aeneid* 6. 278.

LXIX

I dream'd there would be Spring no more,
    That Nature's ancient power was lost:
    The streets were black with smoke and frost,
They chatter'd trifles at the door:

I wander'd from the noisy town,   5
    I found a wood with thorny boughs:
    I took the thorns to bind my brows,
I wore them like a civic crown:

I met with scoffs, I met with scorns
    From youth and babe and hoary hairs: 10
    They call'd me in the public squares
The fool that wears a crown of thorns:[168]

They call'd me fool, they call'd me child:
    I found an angel of the night;
    The voice was low, the look was bright;   15
He look'd upon my crown and smiled:

He reach'd the glory of a hand,
    That seem'd to touch it into leaf:
    The voice was not the voice of grief,
The words were hard to understand.   20

LXX

I cannot see the features right,
    When on the gloom I strive to paint
    The face I know; the hues are faint
And mix with hollow masks of night;

Cloud-towers by ghostly masons wrought,   5
    A gulf that ever shuts and gapes,
    A hand that points, and palled shapes
In shadowy thoroughfares of thought;

And crowds that stream from yawning doors,
    And shoals of pucker'd faces drive;   10
    Dark bulks that tumble half alive,
And lazy lengths on boundless shores;[169]

Till all at once beyond the will
    I hear a wizard music roll,
    And thro' a lattice on the soul   15
Looks thy fair face and makes it still.

Notes

[168] *thorns* see John 19: 5.

[169] *shores* stanzas 2–3 recall the spirits waiting to cross the River Styx in Hades in *Aeneid* 6. 296–329; and Dante's vision of a similar scene in *Inferno* 3. 22–30.

LXXI

Sleep, kinsman thou to death and trance
   And madness, thou hast forged at last
   A night-long Present of the Past
In which we went thro' summer France.[170]

Hadst thou such credit with the soul?   5
   Then bring an opiate trebly strong,
   Drug down the blindfold sense of wrong
That so my pleasure may be whole;

While now we talk as once we talk'd
   Of men and minds, the dust of change,   10
   The days that grow to something strange,
In walking as of old we walk'd

Beside the river's wooded reach,
   The fortress, and the mountain ridge,
   The cataract flashing from the bridge,   15
The breaker breaking on the beach.

LXXII

Risest thou thus, dim dawn, again,[171]
   And howlest, issuing out of night,
   With blasts that blow the poplar white,
And lash with storm the streaming pane?

Day, when my crown'd estate begun   5
   To pine in that reverse of doom,
   Which sicken'd every living bloom,
And blurr'd the splendour of the sun;

Who usherest in the dolorous hour
   With thy quick tears that make the rose   10
   Pull sideways, and the daisy close
Her crimson fringes to the shower;

Who might'st have heaved a windless flame
   Up the deep East, or, whispering, play'd
   A chequer-work of beam and shade   15
Along the hills, yet look'd the same.

As wan, as chill, as wild as now;
   Day, mark'd as with some hideous crime,
   When the dark hand struck down thro' time,
And cancell'd nature's best: but thou,   20

Notes

[170] *France* during the summer of 1830 Tennyson and Hallam travelled through France to the Pyrenees.

[171] *again* the first anniversary of Hallam's death, 15 September 1834; paired with section XCIX, the second anniversary.

Lift as thou may'st thy burthen'd brows
 Thro' clouds that drench the morning star,
 And whirl the ungarner'd sheaf afar,
And sow the sky with flying boughs,

And up thy vault with roaring sound   25
 Climb thy thick noon, disastrous day;
 Touch thy dull goal of joyless gray,
And hide thy shame beneath the ground.

LXXIII

So many worlds, so much to do,[172]
 So little done, such things to be,
 How know I what had need of thee,
For thou wert strong as thou wert true?

The fame is quench'd that I foresaw,   5
 The head hath miss'd an earthly wreath:
 I curse not nature, no, nor death;
For nothing is that errs from law.

We pass; the path that each man trod
 Is dim, or will be dim, with weeds: 10
 What fame is left for human deeds
In endless age? It rests with God.

O hollow wraith of dying fame,
 Fade wholly, while the soul exults,
 And self-infolds the large results   15
Of force that would have forged a name.

LXXIV

As sometimes in a dead man's face,
 To those that watch it more and more,
 A likeness, hardly seen before,
Comes out—to some one of his race:

So, dearest, now thy brows are cold,   5
 I see thee what thou art, and know
 Thy likeness to the wise below,
Thy kindred with the great of old.

But there is more than I can see,
 And what I see I leave unsaid,   10
 Nor speak it, knowing Death has made
His darkness beautiful with thee.

Notes

[172] *do* sections LXXIII–LXXVII lament Hallam's lost fame, though his virtues will be recognized in the afterlife; in sections LXXV–LXXVII the goal of immortalizing Hallam, conferring fame through the poet's words, is futile; the poems only alleviate grief.

LXXV

I leave thy praises unexpress'd
   In verse that brings myself relief,
   And by the measure[173] of my grief
I leave thy greatness to be guess'd;

What practice howsoe'er expert   5
   In fitting aptest words to things,
   Or voice the richest-toned that sings,
Hath power to give thee as thou wert?

I care not in these fading days
   To raise a cry that lasts not long,   10
   And round thee with the breeze of song
To stir a little dust of praise.

Thy leaf has perish'd in the green,
   And, while we breathe beneath the sun,
   The world which credits what is done   15
Is cold to all that might have been.

So here shall silence guard thy fame;
   But somewhere, out of human view,
   Whate'er thy hands are set to do
Is wrought with tumult of acclaim.   20

LXXVI

Take wings of fancy, and ascend,[174]
   And in a moment set thy face[175]
   Where all the starry heavens of space
Are sharpen'd to a needle's end[176];

Take wings of foresight; lighten thro'   5
   The secular[177] abyss to come,
   And lo, thy deepest lays are dumb
Before the mouldering of a yew;

And if the matin songs,[178] that woke
   The darkness of our planet, last,   10
   Thine own shall wither in the vast,
Ere half the lifetime of an oak.

Notes

[173] *measure* pun on both amount and metre or writing of the poem.
[174] *ascend* sections LXXVI and LXXVII reverse the notion that the poet's monument endures longer than earthly fame, and so can immortalize the subject of art, known as the *exegi monumentum* trope (Lat. I have raised a monument), quoting from Horace's poem that begins with this phrase, "I have raised a monument more lasting than bronze" (*Ode* 3. 30); see also Shakespeare, Sonnet 55.
[175] *face* see Ezekiel 6: 2.
[176] *end* see *Cymbeline* I. 3.18–19.
[177] *secular* see n. 118.
[178] *matin songs* songs of early morning; Tennyson identified them as "the great early poets," perhaps classical poets or Chaucer.

Ere these have clothed their branchy bowers
    With fifty Mays, thy songs are vain;
    And what are they when these remain   15
The ruin'd shells of hollow towers?

LXXVII

What hope is here for modern rhyme
    To him, who turns a musing eye[179]
    On songs, and deeds, and lives, that lie
Foreshorten'd in the tract of time?

These mortal lullabies of pain   5
    May bind a book, may line a box,
    May serve to curl a maiden's locks;
Or when a thousand moons shall wane

A man upon a stall may find,
    And, passing, turn the page that tells   10
    A grief, then changed to something else.
Sung by a long-forgotten mind.

But what of that? My darken'd ways
    Shall ring with music all the same;
    To breathe my loss is more than fame,   15
To utter love more sweet than praise.

LXXVIII

Again at Christmas did we weave[180]
    The holly round the Christmas hearth;
    The silent snow possess'd the earth,
And calmly fell our Christmas-eve:

The yule-clog[181] sparkled keen with frost,   5
    No wing of wind the region swept,
    But over all things brooding slept
The quiet sense of something lost.

As in the winters left behind,
    Again our ancient games had place,   10
    The mimic picture's[182] breathing grace,
And dance and song and hoodman-blind.[183]

Notes

[179] *eye* see Shakespeare, Sonnet 83 (7–9).
[180] *weave* the second Christmas (1834) after the death of Hallam, the beginning of the third part of the poem. For the first Christmas, see above, sections XXVIII–XXX; for the third Christmas and New Year's Eve, see below, sections CIV–CVI.
[181] *yule-clog* Lincolnshire dialect for "yule-log."
[182] *mimic picture* a parlour game known as "*tableaux vivants*" (Fr. living pictures) in which some participants adopt poses from famous paintings, sculptures, the theatre, or literature while others guess their identities.
[183] *hoodman-blind* blind man's buff.

Who show'd a token of distress?
  No single tear, no mark of pain:
  O sorrow, then can sorrow wane?   15
O grief, can grief be changed to less?

O last regret, regret can die!
  No—mixt with all this mystic frame.
  Her deep relations are the same,
But with long use her tears are dry.   20

LXXIX

"More than my brothers are to me,"[184]—
  Let this not vex thee, noble heart!
  I know thee of what force thou art
To hold the costliest love in fee.[185]

But thou and I are one in kind,   5
  As moulded like in Nature's mint;
  And hill and wood and field did print
The same sweet forms in either mind.

For us the same cold streamlet curl'd
  Thro' all his eddying coves; the same   10
  All winds that roam the twilight came
In whispers of the beauteous world.

At one dear knee we proffer'd vows,
  One lesson from one book we learn'd,
  Ere childhood's flaxen ringlet turn'd   15
To black and brown on kindred brows.

And so my wealth resembles thine,
  But he was rich where I was poor,
  And he supplied my want the more
As his unlikeness fitted mine.   20

LXXX

If any vague desire should rise,
  That holy Death ere Arthur died
  Had moved me kindly from his side,
And dropt the dust on tearless eyes;

Notes

[184] *me* line repeated from IX. 20. Sections LXXIX–LXXXIX are chiefly occasional poems in which present life is enriched by the past, especially by the speaker's love for the dead. Tennyson said that section LXXIX is addressed to his favourite brother, Charles Tennyson Turner.

[185] *hold … in fee* "to hold as one's absolute and rightful possession" (*OED*).

Then fancy shapes, as fancy can, 5
    The grief my loss in him had wrought,
    A grief as deep as life or thought,
But stay'd[186] in peace with God and man.

I make a picture in the brain;
    I hear the sentence that he speaks; 10
    He bears the burthen of the weeks
But turns his burthen into gain.

His credit thus shall set me free;
    And, influence-rich to soothe and save,
    Unused example from the grave 15
Reach out dead hands to comfort me.

LXXXI

Could I have said while he was here,
    "My love shall now no further range;
    There cannot come a mellower change,
For now is love mature in ear."[187]

Love, then, had hope of richer store: 5
    What end is here to my complaint?
    This haunting whisper makes me faint,
"More years had made me love thee more."

But Death returns an answer sweet:
    "My sudden frost was sudden gain, 10
    And gave all ripeness to the grain,
It might have drawn from after-heat."

LXXXII

I wage not any feud with Death
    For changes wrought on form and face;
    No lower life that earth's embrace
May breed with him, can fright my faith.

Eternal process moving on, 5
    From state to state[188] the spirit walks;
    And these are but the shatter'd stalks,
Or ruin'd chrysalis of one.

Nor blame I Death, because he bare
    The use of virtue out of earth: 10
    I know transplanted human worth
Will bloom to profit, otherwhere.

Notes

[186] *stay'd* supported.
[187] *ear* of grain.
[188] *state* see n. 88.

For this alone on Death I wreak
    The wrath that garners in my heart;
    He put our lives so far apart   15
We cannot hear each other speak.

LXXXIII

Dip down upon the northern shore,
    O sweet new-year delaying long;
    Thou doest expectant nature wrong;
Delaying long, delay no more.

What stays thee from the clouded noons,   5
    Thy sweetness from its proper place?
    Can trouble live with April days,
Or sadness in the summer moons?

Bring orchis, bring the foxglove spire,
    The little speedwell's darling blue,   10
    Deep tulips dash'd with fiery dew,
Laburnums, dropping-wells of fire.

O thou, new-year, delaying long,
    Delayest the sorrow in my blood,
    That longs to burst a frozen bud   15
And flood a fresher throat with song.

LXXXIV

When I contemplate all alone
    The life that had been thine below,
    And fix my thoughts on all the glow
To which thy crescent would have grown;

I see thee sitting crown'd with good,   5
    A central warmth diffusing bliss
    In glance and smile, and clasp and kiss,
On all the branches of thy blood;

Thy blood, my friend, and partly mine;
    For now the day was drawing on,   10
    When thou should'st link thy life with one
Of mine own house,[189] and boys of thine

Had babbled "Uncle" on my knee;
    But that remorseless iron hour
    Made cypress of her orange flower,[190]   15
Despair of Hope, and earth of thee.

Notes

[189] *house* the projected marriage of Arthur Hallam with Tennyson's sister Emily.

[190] *cypress … orange flower* cypress trees are symbolic of death; orange flowers, of weddings.

I seem to meet their least desire,
    To clap their cheeks, to call them mine.
    I see their unborn faces shine
Beside the never-lighted fire.   20

I see myself an honour'd guest,
    Thy partner in the flowery walk
    Of letters, genial table-talk,
Or deep dispute, and graceful jest:

While now thy prosperous labour fills   25
    The lips of men with honest praise,
    And sun by sun the happy days
Descend below the golden hills

With promise of a morn as fair;
    And all the train of bounteous hours   30
    Conduct by paths of growing powers,
To reverence and the silver hair;

Till slowly worn her earthly robe,
    Her lavish mission richly wrought,
    Leaving great legacies of thought,   35
Thy spirit should fail from off the globe;

What time mine own might also flee,
    As link'd with thine in love and fate,
    And, hovering o'er the dolorous strait[191]
To the other shore, involved in thee,   40

Arrive at last the blessed goal,
    And He that died in Holy Land
    Would reach us out the shining hand,
And take us as a single soul.

What reed[192] was that on which I leant?   45
    Ah, backward fancy, wherefore wake
    The old bitterness again, and break
The low beginnings of content.

LXXXV

This truth came borne with bier and pall,
    I felt it, when I sorrow'd most,
    'Tis better to have loved and lost,
Than never to have loved at all[193]—

Notes

[191] *strait* the boundary or gulf between life and death; also the River Acheron, a branch of the Styx, in the classical underworld; see n. 169.

[192] *reed* see Isaiah 36: 6.

[193] *all* echo of XXVII. 3–16. This section is addressed to Edmund Lushington (1811–93), professor of Greek, Glasgow, who married Tennyson's sister Cecilia on 10 October 1842.

O true in word, and tried in deed, 5
    Demanding, so to bring relief
    To this which is our common grief,
What kind of life is that I lead;

And whether trust in things above
    Be dimm'd of sorrow, or sustain'd; 10
    And whether love for him have drain'd
My capabilities of love;

Your words have virtue such as draws
    A faithful answer from the breast,
    Thro' light reproaches, half exprest, 15
And loyal unto kindly laws.

My blood an even tenor kept,
    Till on mine ear this message falls,
    That in Vienna's fatal walls
God's finger[194] touch'd him, and he slept. 20

The great Intelligences[195] fair
    That range above our mortal state,
    In circle round the blessed gate,
Received and gave him welcome there;

And led him thro' the blissful climes, 25
    And show'd him in the fountain fresh[196]
    All knowledge that the sons of flesh
Shall gather in the cycled times.[197]

But I remain'd, whose hopes were dim,
    Whose life, whose thoughts were little worth, 30
    To wander on a darken'd earth,
Where all things round me breathed of him.

O friendship, equal-poised control,
    O heart, with kindliest motion warm,
    O sacred essence, other form, 35
O solemn ghost, O crowned soul!

Yet none could better know than I,
    How much of act at human hands
    The sense of human will demands
By which we dare to live or die. 40

Notes

[194] *finger* see Job 19: 21; the reverse of the creation of Adam by the finger of God in Michelangelo's Sistine ceiling.

[195] *Intelligences* angels, as in Dante's conflation of the traditional Christian understanding of the nine orders of angels with Aristotle's concept that the nine heavenly spheres or orbs are moved by divine intelligences; see Dante, *Convivio* (Lat. The banquet): 2. 2. 7; and 2. 4. 2.

[196] *fresh* see Revelation 22: 1.

[197] *times* see Milton's *Lycidas* (178–81). Stanzas six and seven constitute the genre of the *prosphonetikon* or welcome speech given to a traveller who arrives at a new destination, here part of conventional classical descriptions of the reception of the noble dead into the afterlife, as in Cicero's *Somnium Scipionis* (Lat. Dream of Scipio), the sixth book of his *De re publica* (Lat. On the commonwealth, 54–51 BCE); see n. 62.

Whatever way my days decline,
    I felt and feel, tho' left alone,
    His being working in mine own,
The footsteps of his life in mine;

A life that all the Muses deck'd   45
    With gifts of grace, that might express
    All-comprehensive tenderness,
All-subtilising intellect:

And so my passion hath not swerved
    To works of weakness, but I find   50
    An image comforting the mind,
And in my grief a strength reserved.

Likewise the imaginative woe,
    That loved to handle spiritual strife,
    Diffused the shock thro' all my life,   55
But in the present broke the blow.

My pulses therefore beat again
    For other friends that once I met;
    Nor can it suit me to forget
The mighty hopes that make us men.   60

I woo your love: I count it crime
    To mourn for any overmuch;
    I, the divided half of such
A friendship as had master'd Time;

Which masters Time indeed, and is   65
    Eternal, separate from fears:
    The all-assuming[198] months and years
Can take no part away from this:

But Summer on the steaming floods,
    And Spring that swells the narrow brooks,   70
    And Autumn, with a noise of rooks,
That gather in the waning woods,

And every pulse of wind and wave
    Recalls, in change of light or gloom,
    My old affection of the tomb,   75
And my prime passion in the grave:

My old affection of the tomb,
    A part of stillness, yearns to speak;
    "Arise, and get thee forth and seek
A friendship for the years to come.   80

Notes

[198] *all-assuming* all-consuming.

I watch thee from the quiet shore;
    Thy spirit up to mine can reach;
    But in dear words of human speech
We two communicate no more."

And I, "Can clouds of nature stain   85
    The starry clearness of the free?
    How is it? Canst thou feel for me
Some painless sympathy with pain?"

And lightly does the whisper fall;
    "'Tis hard for thee to fathom this;   90
    I triumph in conclusive bliss,
And that serene result of all."

So hold I commerce with the dead;
    Or so methinks the dead would say;
    Or so shall grief with symbols play   95
And pining life be fancy-fed.

Now looking to some settled end,
    That these things pass, and I shall prove
    A meeting somewhere, love with love,
I crave your pardon, O my friend;   100

If not so fresh, with love as true,
    I, clasping brother-hands, aver
    I could not, if I would, transfer
The whole I felt for him to you.

For which be they that hold apart   105
    The promise of the golden hours?
    First love, first friendship, equal powers,
That marry with the virgin heart.

Still mine, that cannot but deplore,
    That beats within a lonely place,   110
    That yet remembers his embrace,
But at his footstep leaps no more,

My heart, tho' widow'd, may not rest
    Quite in the love of what is gone,
    But seeks to beat in time with one   115
That warms another living breast.

Ah, take the imperfect gift I bring,
    Knowing the primrose yet is dear,
    The primrose of the later year,
As not unlike to that of Spring.   120

Alfred Tennyson

LXXXVI

Sweet after showers, ambrosial air,[199]
    That rollest from the gorgeous gloom
    Of evening over brake[200] and bloom
And meadow, slowly breathing bare

The round of space, and rapt below   5
    Thro' all the dewy-tassell'd wood,
    And shadowing down the horned flood[201]
In ripples, fan my brows and blow

The fever from my cheek, and sigh
    The full new life that feeds thy breath   10
    Throughout my frame, till Doubt and Death,
Ill brethren, let the fancy fly

From belt to belt of crimson seas
    On leagues of odour streaming far,
    To where in yonder orient star[202]   15
A hundred spirits whisper "Peace."

LXXXVII

I past beside the reverend walls
    In which of old I wore the gown;[203]
    I roved at random thro' the town,
And saw the tumult of the halls;

And heard once more in college fanes   5
    The storm their high-built organs make,
    And thunder-music, rolling, shake
The prophet blazon'd on the panes;[204]

And caught once more the distant shout,
    The measured pulse of racing oars   10
    Among the willows; paced the shores
And many a bridge, and all about

The same gray flats again, and felt
    The same, but not the same; and last
    Up that long walk of limes[205] I past   15
To see the rooms in which he dwelt.[206]

Notes

[199] *air* see *Purgatorio* 28. 6–9.

[200] *brake* bushes.

[201] *flood* see *Aeneid* 8. 77: *corniger ... fluvius* (Lat. horned floods); and *Paradise Lost*: "push'd by the horned flood" (11. 831).

[202] *star* Venus.

[203] *gown* academic gown; reference to Tennyson's time as an undergraduate at Cambridge.

[204] *And heard ... panes* see Milton's description of King's College, Cambridge in "Il Penseroso" (159–66), with prophets in the stained-glass windows.

[205] *limes* the row of lime trees at Trinity College.

[206] *dwelt* Hallam's rooms in New Court, Trinity College which he entered in October 1828. He left in January 1832, after taking his degree.

Another name was on the door;
　　I linger'd; all within was noise
　　Of songs, and clapping hands, and boys
That crash'd the glass and beat the floor;　　　　　　20

Where once we held debate, a band
　　Of youthful friends, on mind and art,
　　And labour, and the changing mart,
And all the framework of the land;

When one would aim an arrow fair,　　　　　　　　25
　　But send it slackly from the string;
　　And one would pierce an outer ring,
And one an inner, here and there;

And last the master-bowman, he,
　　Would cleave the mark. A willing ear　　　　　30
　　We lent him. Who, but hung to hear
The rapt oration flowing free

From point to point, with power and grace
　　And music in the bounds of law,
　　To those conclusions when we saw　　　　　　35
The God within him light his face,

And seem to lift the form, and glow
　　In azure orbits heavenly-wise;
　　And over those ethereal eyes
The bar of Michael Angelo.[207]　　　　　　　　40

LXXXVIII

Wild bird,[208] whose warble, liquid sweet,
　　Rings Eden thro' the budded quicks,[209]
　　O tell me where the senses mix,
O tell me where the passions meet,

Whence radiate: fierce extremes[210] employ　　　5
　　Thy spirits in the darkening leaf,
　　And in the midmost heart of grief
Thy passion clasps a secret joy:

And I—my harp would prelude woe—
　　I cannot all command the strings;　　　　　　10
　　The glory of the sum of things
Will flash along the chords and go.

Notes

[207] *Michael Angelo* the Florentine artist Michelangelo (1475–1564) was said by his apprentice and biographer Ascanio Condivi to have had a prominent forehead, taken to be an indicator of superior intellect.

[208] *bird* nightingale.

[209] *quicks* thorns.

[210] *fierce extremes* see Shakespeare, *King John* 5. 7. 13; *Paradise Lost* 2. 599 and 7. 272; and Wordsworth, *Ecclesiastical Sonnets* 3. 11. 12.

LXXXIX

Witch-elms that counterchange the floor
    Of this flat lawn with dusk and bright;
    And thou, with all thy breadth and height
Of foliage, towering sycamore;

How often, hither wandering down,   5
    My Arthur found your shadows fair,[211]
    And shook to all the liberal air
The dust and din and steam of town:[212]

He brought an eye for all he saw;
    He mixt in all our simple sports;   10
    They pleased him, fresh from brawling courts
And dusty purlieus of the law.[213]

O joy to him in this retreat,
    Immantled in ambrosial dark,
    To drink the cooler air, and mark   15
The landscape winking thro' the heat:

O sound to rout the brood of cares,
    The sweep of scythe in morning dew,
    The gust that round the garden flew,
And tumbled half the mellowing pears!   20

O bliss, when all in circle drawn
    About him, heart and ear were fed
    To hear him, as he lay and read
The Tuscan poets[214] on the lawn:

Or in the all-golden afternoon   25
    A guest, or happy sister, sung,
    Or here she brought the harp and flung
A ballad to the brightening moon:

Nor less it pleased in livelier moods,
    Beyond the bounding hill to stray,   30
    And break the livelong summer day
With banquet in the distant woods;[215]

Whereat we glanced from theme to theme,
    Discuss'd the books to love or hate,
    Or touch'd the changes of the state,   35
Or threaded some Socratic dream;[216]

Notes

[211] *fair* Hallam had made several visits to Somersby to visit Tennyson's sister Emily, to whom he had become engaged in 1832.

[212] *town* see Horace, *Odes* 3. 29. 12.

[213] *law* after graduating from Cambridge Hallam studied law and worked in a legal firm.

[214] *poets* Hallam's favourite poets were Dante and Petrarch.

[215] *woods* see Horace, *Odes* 2. 7. 6–7.

[216] *Socratic dream* Socrates (*c.*469–399 BCE), Greek philosopher, known for philosophical enquiry by means of ironic dialogue using a question and answer method. Tennyson had originally written "handled some Platonic dream."

But if I praised the busy town,
  He loved to rail against it still,
  For "ground in yonder social mill
We rub each other's angles down,   40

And merge" he said "in form and gloss
  The picturesque of man and man."
  We talk'd: the stream beneath us ran,
The wine-flask lying couch'd in moss,

Or cool'd within the glooming wave;   45
  And last, returning from afar,
  Before the crimson-circled star[217]
Had fall'n into her father's grave,[218]

And brushing ankle-deep in flowers,[219]
  We heard behind the woodbine veil   50
  The milk that bubbled in the pail,
And buzzings of the honied hours.

XC

He tasted love with half his mind,[220]
  Nor ever drank the inviolate spring
  Where nighest heaven, who first could fling
This bitter seed among mankind;

That could the dead, whose dying eyes   5
  Were closed with wail, resume their life,
  They would but find in child and wife
An iron welcome when they rise:

'Twas well, indeed, when warm with wine,
  To pledge them with a kindly tear,   10
  To talk them o'er, to wish them here,
To count their memories half divine;

But if they came who past away,
  Behold their brides in other hands;
  The hard heir strides about their lands,   15
And will not yield them for a day.

Yea, tho' their sons were none of these,
  Not less the yet-loved sire would make
  Confusion worse than death, and shake
The pillars of domestic peace.   20

Notes

[217] *star* Venus or Hesperus, the evening star that disappears at sunset.

[218] *grave* the fading of the stars at sunset and darkness; possibly also a reference to the nebular theory of cosmogony; see n. 40.

[219] *flowers* see Keats, *Hyperion* (1820): 3. 35.

[220] *mind* sections XC–XCV are a unit on the communion with the dead.

Ah dear, but come thou back to me:
 Whatever change the years have wrought,
 I find not yet one lonely thought
That cries against my wish for thee.

XCI

When rosy plumelets tuft the larch,
 And rarely pipes the mounted thrush;
 Or underneath the barren bush
Flits by the sea-blue bird[221] of March;

Come, wear the form by which I know   5
 Thy spirit in time among thy peers;
 The hope of unaccomplish'd years
Be large and lucid round thy brow.[222]

When summer's hourly-mellowing change
 May breathe, with many roses sweet,   10
 Upon the thousand waves of wheat,
That ripple round the lonely grange;

Come: not in watches of the night,
 But where the sunbeam broodeth warm,
 Come, beauteous in thine after form,   15
And like a finer light in light.

XCII

If any vision should reveal
 Thy likeness, I might count it vain
 As but the canker of the brain;
Yea, tho' it spake and made appeal.[223]

To chances where our lots were cast   5
 Together in the days behind,
 I might but say, I hear a wind
Of memory murmuring the past.

Yea, tho' it spake and bared to view
 A fact within the coming year;   10
 And tho' the months, revolving near,
Should prove the phantom-warning true,

They might not seem thy prophecies,
 But spiritual presentiments,
 And such refraction of events[224]   15
As often rises ere they rise.

Notes

[221] *bird* kingfisher.

[222] *brow* see *Aeneid*, 2. 681–84.

[223] *appeal* see *Hamlet* I. I (especially the repetition of "speak" throughout the scene).

[224] *events* Tennyson had read about refraction in Mary Somerville's *On the Connexion of the Physical Sciences* (1834); refraction in astronomy is the optical illusion from the atmosphere that stars are seen above the horizon

XCIII

I shall not see thee. Dare I say
   No spirit ever brake the band
   That stays him from the native land
Where first he walk'd when claspt in clay?

No visual shade of some one lost,   5
   But he, the Spirit himself, may come
   Where all the nerve of sense is numb;
Spirit to Spirit, Ghost to Ghost.

O, therefore from thy sightless range
   With gods in unconjectured bliss,   10
   O, from the distance of the abyss
Of tenfold-complicated[225] change,

Descend, and touch, and enter; hear
   The wish too strong for words to name;
   That in this blindness of the frame   15
My Ghost may feel that thine is near.

XCIV

How pure at heart and sound in head,
   With what divine affections bold
   Should be the man whose thought would hold
An hour's communion with the dead.

In vain shalt thou, or any, call   5
   The spirits from their golden day,
   Except, like them, thou too canst say,
My spirit is at peace with all.

They haunt the silence of the breast,
   Imaginations calm and fair,   10
   The memory like a cloudless air,
The conscience as a sea at rest:

But when the heart is full of din,
   And doubt beside the portal waits,
   They can but listen at the gates,   15
And hear the household jar within.

XCV

By night we linger'd on the lawn,
   For underfoot the herb was dry;
   And genial warmth; and o'er the sky
The silvery haze of summer drawn;

Notes

before they rise and after they set; the "likeness" in line 2 of this refraction is Hallam's spirit.

[225] *tenfold-complicated* see the ten levels of heaven in *Paradiso* 28.

And calm that let the tapers burn 5
    Unwavering: not a cricket chirr'd:
    The brook alone far-off was heard,
And on the board the fluttering urn:[226]

And bats went round in fragrant skies,
    And wheel'd or lit the filmy shapes 10
    That haunt the dusk, with ermine capes
And woolly breasts and beaded eyes;

While now we sang old songs that peal'd
    From knoll to knoll, where, couch'd at ease,
    The white kine glimmer'd, and the trees 15
Laid their dark arms about the field.

But when those others, one by one,
    Withdrew themselves from me and night,
    And in the house light after light
Went out, and I was all alone, 20

A hunger seized my heart; I read
    Of that glad year which once had been,
    In those fall'n leaves which kept their green,
The noble letters of the dead:

And strangely on the silence broke 25
    The silent-speaking words, and strange
    Was love's dumb cry defying change
To test his worth; and strangely spoke

The faith, the vigour, bold to dwell
    On doubts that drive the coward back, 30
    And keen thro' wordy snares to track
Suggestion to her inmost cell.[227]

So word by word, and line by line,[228]
    The dead man touch'd me from the past,
    And all at once it seem'd at last 35
The living soul was flash'd on mine,

And mine in this was wound, and whirl'd
    About empyreal heights of thought,
    And came on that which is,[229] and caught
The deep pulsations of the world, 40

Notes

[226] *urn* boiling teapot.

[227] *cell* see Shelley, *The Cenci* (1819): 5. 2. 187; and "Epipsychidon" (1821: 568–69).

[228] *line* see Isaiah 28: 13.

[229] *that which is* a translation (Gr. *to on*: that which is), meaning the being, the one, ultimate reality, or the supreme truth of all things that transcends human comprehension, as in Plato (*Phaedo* 65C, 75D; and *Symposium* 211C).

Æonian music²³⁰ measuring out
    The steps of Time—the shocks of Chance—
    The blows of Death.²³¹ At length my trance
Was cancell'd, stricken thro' with doubt.

Vague words! but ah, how hard to frame   45
    In matter-moulded forms of speech,
    Or ev'n for intellect to reach
Thro' memory that which I became:

Till now the doubtful dusk reveal'd
    The knolls once more where, couch'd at ease,   50
    The white kine²³² glimmer'd, and the trees
Laid their dark arms about the field:

And suck'd from out the distant gloom
    A breeze began to tremble o'er
    The large leaves of the sycamore,   55
And fluctuate all the still perfume,

And gathering freshlier overhead,
    Rock'd the full-foliaged elms, and swung
    The heavy-folded rose, and flung
The lilies to and fro, and said   60

"The dawn, the dawn," and died away;
    And East and West, without a breath,
    Mixt their dim lights, like life and death,
To broaden into boundless day.

XCVI

You say, but with no touch of scorn,
    Sweet-hearted, you, whose light-blue eyes
    Are tender over drowning flies,
You tell me, doubt is Devil-born.

I know not: one indeed I knew   5
    In many a subtle question versed,
    Who touch'd a jarring lyre at first,
But ever strove to make it true:

Perplext in faith, but pure in deeds,
    At last he beat his music out.²³³   10
    There lives more faith in honest doubt,
Believe me, than in half the creeds.²³⁴

Notes

²³⁰ *Æonian music* (Gk. *aeon*, age) eternal harmony, the music of the spheres.

²³¹ *Death* see Milton, "On Time" (1645: 22).

²³² *kine* cattle (archaic).

²³³ *out* among Hallam's poems on doubt are "Then What is Life?"; "Lines Written in Great Depression of Mind"; "A Meeting and a Farewell"; and "A Melancholy Thought"; all published in *Remains* (1834).

²³⁴ *creeds* see Philip James Bailey, *Festus* (1839), "A Country Town" (Sc. 5): "Who never doubted, never half believed. / Where doubt there truth is—'tis her shadow."

He fought his doubts and gather'd strength,
    He would not make his judgment blind,
    He faced the spectres of the mind   15
And laid them: thus he came at length

To find a stronger faith his own;
    And Power was with him in the night,
    Which makes the darkness and the light,
And dwells not in the light alone,   20

But in the darkness and the cloud,
    As over Sinaï's peaks of old,
    While Israel made their gods of gold,
Altho' the trumpet blew so loud.[235]

XCVII

My love has talk'd with rocks and trees;
    He finds on misty mountain-ground
    His own vast shadow glory-crown'd;
He sees himself in all he sees.

Two partners of a married life—   5
    I look'd on these and thought of thee
    In vastness and in mystery,
And of my spirit as of a wife.

These two—they dwelt with eye on eye,
    Their hearts of old have beat in tune,   10
    Their meetings made December June
Their every parting was to die.

Their love has never past away;
    The days she never can forget
    Are earnest that he loves her yet,
Whate'er the faithless people say.   15

Her life is lone, he sits apart,
    He loves her yet, she will not weep,
    Tho' rapt in matters dark and deep
He seems to slight her simple heart.   20

He thrids[236] the labyrinth of the mind,
    He reads the secret of the star,
    He seems so near and yet so far,
He looks so cold: she thinks him kind.

She keeps the gift of years before,   25
    A wither'd violet is her bliss:
    She knows not what his greatness is,
For that, for all, she loves him more.

Notes

[235] *loud* see Exodus 19: 16.   [236] *thrids* threads.

For him she plays, to him she sings
    Of early faith and plighted vows;   30
    She knows but matters of the house,
And he, he knows a thousand things.

Her faith is fixt and cannot move,
    She darkly feels him great and wise,
    She dwells on him with faithful eyes,   35
"I cannot understand: I love."

XCVIII

You leave us: you will see the Rhine,[237]
    And those fair hills I sail'd below,
    When I was there with him; and go
By summer belts of wheat and vine

To where he breathed his latest breath,   5
    That City. All her splendour seems
    No livelier than the wisp that gleams
On Lethe in the eyes of Death.

Let her great Danube rolling fair
    Enwind her isles, unmark'd of me: 10
    I have not seen, I will not see
Vienna; rather dream that there,

A treble darkness, Evil haunts
    The birth, the bridal; friend from friend
    Is oftener parted, fathers bend   15
Above more graves, a thousand wants

Gnarr at the heels of men, and prey
    By each cold hearth, and sadness flings
    Her shadow on the blaze of kings:
And yet myself have heard him say,   20

That not in any mother town
    With statelier progress to and fro
    The double tides of chariots flow
By park and suburb under brown

Of lustier leaves; nor more content,   25
    He told me, lives in any crowd,
    When all is gay with lamps, and loud
With sport and song, in booth and tent,

Imperial halls, or open plain;
    And wheels the circled dance, and breaks   30
    The rocket molten into flakes
Of crimson or in emerald rain.

Notes

[237] *Rhine* Tennyson's brother Charles married in 1836 and
travelled to Vienna for his honeymoon.

XCIX

Risest thou thus, dim dawn, again,[238]
 So loud with voices of the birds,
 So thick with lowings of the herds,
Day, when I lost the flower of men;

Who tremblest thro' thy darkling red   5
 On yon swoll'n brook that bubbles fast
 By meadows breathing of the past,
And woodlands holy to the dead;

Who murmurest in the foliaged eaves
 A song that slights the coming care,   10
 And Autumn laying here and there
A fiery finger on the leaves;

Who wakenest with thy balmy breath[239]
 To myriads on the genial earth,
 Memories of bridal, or of birth,   15
And unto myriads more, of death.

O wheresoever those may be,
 Betwixt the slumber of the poles,
 To-day they count as kindred souls;
They know me not, but mourn with me.   20

C

I climb the hill: from end to end
 Of all the landscape underneath,
 I find no place that does not breathe
Some gracious memory of my friend;

No gray old grange, or lonely fold,   5
 Or low morass and whispering reed,
 Or simple stile from mead to mead,
Or sheepwalk up the windy wold;

Nor hoary knoll of ash and haw
 That hears the latest linnet trill,   10
 Nor quarry trench'd along the hill
And haunted by the wrangling daw;

Nor runlet tinkling from the rock;
 Nor pastoral rivulet that swerves
 To left and right thro' meadowy curves, 15
That feed the mothers of the flock;

Notes —————————————————————————————————————

[238] *again* second anniversary of Arthur Hallam's death; see n. 171. [239] *breath* see *Othello* 5. 2. 16.

But each has pleased a kindred eye,
    And each reflects a kindlier day;
    And, leaving these, to pass away,
I think once more he seems to die.[240]   20

CI

Unwatch'd, the garden bough shall sway,
    The tender blossom flutter down,
    Unloved, that beech will gather brown,
This maple burn itself away;

Unloved, the sun-flower, shining fair,   5
    Ray round with flames her disk of seed,
    And many a rose-carnation feed
With summer spice the humming air;

Unloved, by many a sandy bar,
    The brook shall babble down the plain,   10
    At noon or when the lesser wain[241]
Is twisting round the polar star;

Uncared for, gird the windy grove,
    And flood the haunts of hern[242] and crake;
    Or into silver arrows break   15
The sailing moon in creek and cove;

Till from the garden and the wild
    A fresh association blow,
    And year by year the landscape grow
Familiar to the stranger's child;   20

As year by year the labourer tills
    His wonted glebe, or lops the glades;
    And year by year our memory fades
From all the circle of the hills.

CII

We leave the well-beloved place
    Where first we gazed upon the sky;
    The roofs, that heard our earliest cry,
Will shelter one of stranger race.

We go, but ere we go from home,   5
    As down the garden-walks I move,
    Two spirits of a diverse love
Contend for loving masterdom.

Notes

[240] *die* sections C–CIII treat the family's move from Tennyson's boyhood home; see n. 85.

[241] *wain* star constellation of Ursa Minor (Lat. the small bear) or the little dipper.

[242] *hern* heron.

One whispers, "Here thy boyhood sung
 Long since its matin song, and heard   10
 The low love-language of the bird
In native hazels tassel-hung."

The other answers, "Yea, but here
 Thy feet have stray'd in after hours
 With thy lost friend among the bowers,   15
And this hath made them trebly dear."

These two have striven half the day,
 And each prefers his separate claim,
 Poor rivals in a losing game,
That will not yield each other way.   20

I turn to go: my feet are set
 To leave the pleasant fields and farms;
 They mix in one another's arms
To one pure image of regret.

CIII

On that last night before we went
 From out the doors where I was bred,
 I dream'd a vision of the dead,
Which left my after-morn content.

Methought I dwelt within a hall,   5
 And maidens with me: distant hills
 From hidden summits fed with rills
A river sliding by the wall.

The hall with harp and carol rang.
 They sang of what is wise and good   10
 And graceful. In the centre stood
A statue veil'd, to which they sang;

And which, tho' veil'd, was known to me,
 The shape of him I loved, and love
 For ever: then flew in a dove   15
And brought a summons from the sea:

And when they learnt that I must go
 They wept and wail'd, but led the way
 To where a little shallop lay
At anchor in the flood below;   20

And on by many a level mead,
 And shadowing bluff that made the banks,
 We glided winding under ranks
Of iris, and the golden reed;

And still as vaster grew the shore   25
    And roll'd the floods in grander space,
    The maidens gather'd strength and grace
And presence, lordlier than before;

And I myself, who sat apart
    And watch'd them, wax'd in every limb;   30
    I felt the thews of Anakim,[243]
The pulses of a Titan's heart;

As one would sing the death of war,
    And one would chant the history
    Of that great race, which is to be,   35
And one the shaping of a star;

Until the forward-creeping tides
    Began to foam, and we to draw
    From deep to deep, to where we saw
A great ship lift her shining sides.   40

The man we loved was there on deck,
    But thrice as large as man he bent
    To greet us. Up the side I went,
And fell in silence on his neck:

Whereat those maidens with one mind   45
    Bewail'd their lot; I did them wrong:
    "We served thee here," they said, "so long,
And wilt thou leave us now behind?"

So rapt I was, they could not win
    An answer from my lips, but he   50
    Replying, "Enter likewise ye
And go with us": they enter'd in.

And while the wind began to sweep
    A music out of sheet and shroud,
    We steer'd her toward a crimson cloud   55
That landlike slept along the deep.

CIV

The time draws near the birth of Christ;[244]
    The moon is hid, the night is still;
    A single church below the hill
Is pealing, folded in the mist.

A single peal of bells below,   5
    That wakens at this hour of rest
    A single murmur in the breast,
That these are not the bells I know.

Notes

[243] *Anakim* giants in Deuteronomy 2: 10.

[244] *Christ* the third Christmas of the poem, and the beginning of the fourth section of the poem.

Like strangers' voices here they sound,
 In lands where not a memory strays,   10
 Nor landmark breathes of other days,
But all is new unhallow'd ground.

CV

To-night ungather'd let us leave
 This laurel, let this holly stand:
 We live within the stranger's land,
And strangely falls our Christmas-eve.

Our father's dust[245] is left alone   5
 And silent under other snows:
 There in due time the woodbine blows,
The violet comes, but we are gone.

No more shall wayward grief abuse
 The genial hour with mask and mime;   10
 For change of place, like growth of time,
Has broke the bond of dying use.

Let cares that petty shadows cast,
 By which our lives are chiefly proved,
 A little spare the night I loved,   15
And hold it solemn to the past.

But let no footstep beat the floor,
 Nor bowl of wassail mantle warm;
 For who would keep an ancient form
Thro' which the spirit breathes no more?   20

Be neither song, nor game, nor feast;
 Nor harp be touch'd, nor flute be blown;
 No dance, no motion, save alone
What lightens in the lucid east

Of rising worlds by yonder wood.   25
 Long sleeps the summer in the seed;
 Run out your measured arcs, and lead
The closing cycle rich in good.

CVI

Ring out, wild bells, to the wild sky,[246]
 The flying cloud, the frosty light:
 The year is dying in the night;
Ring out, wild bells, and let him die.

Notes

[245] *dust* George Clayton Tennyson (1778–1831) was buried at Somersby.

[246] *sky* the section is modelled on Philip John Bailey's *Festus* (1839: 75–82).

Ring out the old, ring in the new,   5
    Ring, happy bells, across the snow:
    The year is going, let him go;
Ring out the false, ring in the true.

Ring out the grief that saps the mind,
    For those that here we see no more;   10
    Ring out the feud of rich and poor,
Ring in redress to all mankind.

Ring out a slowly dying cause,
    And ancient forms of party strife;
    Ring in the nobler modes of life,   15
With sweeter manners, purer laws.

Ring out the want, the care, the sin,
    The faithless coldness of the times;
    Ring out, ring out my mournful rhymes,[247]
But ring the fuller minstrel in.   20

Ring out false pride in place and blood,
    The civic slander and the spite;
    Ring in the love of truth and right,
Ring in the common love of good.

Ring out old shapes of foul disease;   25
    Ring out the narrowing lust of gold;
    Ring out the thousand wars of old,
Ring in the thousand years[248] of peace.

Ring in the valiant man and free,
    The larger heart, the kindlier hand;   30
    Ring out the darkness of the land,
Ring in the Christ that is to be.

CVII

It is the day when he was born,[249]
    A bitter day that early sank
    Behind a purple-frosty bank
Of vapour, leaving night forlorn.

The time admits not flowers or leaves   5
    To deck the banquet. Fiercely flies
    The blast of North and East, and ice
Makes daggers at the sharpen'd eaves,

Notes

[247] *mournful rhymes* a possible reference to the Greek word for elegy, *elegeia*, perhaps derived from an Ionian dirge, a funeral lament, *e, lege e, lege*, woe, cry woe!, cry!

[248] *thousand years* the millennium; see Revelation 20: 2–4.

[249] *born* Hallam was born on 1 February 1811. This section begins almost as an inverse birthday celebration poem (the Greek genre, *genethliakon*, < *genethlios*, concerning a

And bristles all the brakes and thorns
    To yon hard crescent, as she hangs   10
    Above the wood which grides and clangs
Its leafless ribs and iron horns

Together, in the drifts that pass
    To darken on the rolling brine
    That breaks the coast. But fetch the wine,   15
Arrange the board and brim the glass;

Bring in great logs[250] and let them lie,
    To make a solid core of heat;
    Be cheerful-minded, talk and treat
Of all things ev'n as he were by;   20

We keep the day. With festal cheer,
    With books and music, surely we
    Will drink to him, whate'er he be,
And sing the songs he loved to hear.

CVIII

I will not shut me from my kind,
    And, lest I stiffen into stone,
    I will not eat my heart[251] alone,
Nor feed with sighs a passing wind:

What profit lies in barren faith,   5
    And vacant yearning, tho' with might
    To scale the heaven's highest height,
Or dive below the wells of Death?

What find I in the highest place,
    But mine own phantom chanting hymns?   10
    And on the depths of death there swims
The reflex of a human face.

I'll rather take what fruit may be
    Of sorrow under human skies:
    'Tis held that sorrow makes us wise,   15
Whatever wisdom sleep with thee.

Notes

birth, < *genea*, birth, origin, generation), outlining the reasons not to celebrate; then in stanza four the form becomes a traditional *genethliakon* with wine, feasting, and celebratory songs. For classical examples, see

Tibullus 2: 2 in honour of Cornutus Sulpicia; and Statius, *Silvae* 2: 7; and 4: 7.
[250] *wine . . . logs* see Horace, *Odes* 1. 9; and 3. 17.
[251] *eat my heart* see *Faerie Queen* 1. 2. 6.

CIX

Heart-affluence in discursive talk
    From household fountains never dry;[252]
    The critic[253] clearness of an eye,
That saw thro' all the Muses' walk;

Seraphic intellect and force   5
    To seize and throw the doubts of man;
    Impassion'd logic, which outran
The hearer in its fiery course;

High nature amorous of the good,
    But touch'd with no ascetic gloom;   10
    And passion pure in snowy bloom
Thro' all the years of April blood;

A love of freedom rarely felt,
    Of freedom in her regal seat
    Of England; not the schoolboy heat,   15
The blind hysterics of the Celt;

And manhood fused with female grace
    In such a sort, the child would twine
    A trustful hand, unask'd, in thine,
And find his comfort in thy face;   20

All these have been, and thee mine eyes
    Have look'd on: if they look'd in vain,
    My shame is greater who remain,
Nor let thy wisdom make me wise.

CX

Thy converse drew us with delight,
    The men of rathe and riper years:
    The feeble soul, a haunt of fears,
Forgot his weakness in thy sight.

On thee the loyal-hearted hung,5   5
    The proud was half disarm'd of pride,
    Nor cared the serpent at thy side
To flicker with his double tongue.

The stern were mild when thou wert by,
    The flippant put himself to school   10
    And heard thee, and the brazen fool
Was soften'd, and he knew not why;

Notes

[252] *dry* this section enumerates the idealized qualities of Hallam in a poem of praise, an *encomium* (Lat. < Gk. *encomion* expression of praise). For classical examples, see Propertius 2. 1.

[253] *critic* see n. 50.

While I, thy nearest, sat apart,
    And felt thy triumph was as mine;
    And loved them more, that they were thine,   15
The graceful tact, the Christian art;

Nor mine the sweetness or the skill,
    But mine the love that will not tire,
    And, born of love, the vague desire
That spurs an imitative will.   20

CXI

The churl in spirit, up or down
    Along the scale of ranks, thro' all,
    To him who grasps a golden ball,
By blood a king, at heart a clown;

The churl in spirit, howe'er he veil   5
    His want in forms for fashion's sake,
    Will let his coltish nature break
At seasons thro' the gilded pale:

For who can always act? but he,
    To whom a thousand memories call,   10
    Not being less but more than all
The gentleness he seem'd to be,

Best seem'd the thing he was, and join'd
    Each office of the social hour
    To noble manners, as the flower   15
And native growth of noble mind;

Nor ever narrowness or spite,
    Or villain fancy fleeting by,
    Drew in the expression of an eye,
Where God and Nature met in light;   20

And thus he bore without abuse
    The grand old name of gentleman,
    Defamed by every charlatan,
And soil'd with all ignoble use.

CXII

High wisdom holds my wisdom less,
    That I, who gaze with temperate eyes
    On glorious insufficiencies,
Set light by narrower perfectness.

But thou, that fillest all the room   5
    Of all my love, art reason why
    I seem to cast a careless eye
On souls, the lesser lords of doom.

For what wert thou? some novel power
    Sprang up for ever at a touch,   10
    And hope could never hope too much,
In watching thee from hour to hour,

Large elements in order brought,
    And tracts of calm from tempest made,[254]
    And world-wide fluctuation sway'd   15
In vassal tides that follow'd thought.

CXIII

'Tis held that sorrow makes us wise;
    Yet how much wisdom sleeps with thee
    Which not alone had guided me,
But served the seasons that may rise;

For can I doubt, who knew thee keen   5
    In intellect, with force and skill
    To strive, to fashion, to fulfil—
I doubt not what thou wouldst have been:

A life in civic action warm,
    A soul on highest mission sent,   10
    A potent voice[255] of Parliament,
A pillar steadfast in the storm,

Should licensed boldness gather force,
    Becoming, when the time has birth,
    A lever to uplift the earth   15
And roll it in another course,[256]

With thousand shocks[257] that come and go,
    With agonies, with energies,
    With overthrowings, and with cries,
And undulations to and fro.   20

CXIV

Who loves not Knowledge? Who shall rail
    Against her beauty? May she mix
    With men and prosper! Who shall fix
Her pillars?[258] Let her work prevail.

Notes

[254] *tempest made* see Hallam, "Lines for Ellen Hunt" (*Remains*, 1834), where he claims he has "faced / Himself the tempest, and can prize the calm" (11–12).

[255] *voice* see *Paradise Lost* 8. 100.

[256] *course* when demonstrating the principle of the lever, Archimedes (c.287–c.212 BCE) is reported to have said:

"Give me a place to stand, and I shall move the earth": Pappus of Alexandria, *Synagoge* (c.340 CE; bk. 8).

[257] *shocks* see *Hamlet* 3. 1. 62–63.

[258] *pillars* see Proverbs 9: 1, where Wisdom has built a house with seven pillars.

But on her forehead sits a fire: 5
    She sets her forward countenance
    And leaps into the future chance,
Submitting all things to desire.

Half-grown as yet, a child, and vain—
    She cannot fight the fear of death.   10
    What is she, cut from love and faith,
But some wild Pallas[259] from the brain

Of Demons? fiery-hot to burst
    All barriers in her onward race
    For power. Let her know her place;   15
She is the second, not the first.

A higher hand must make her mild,
    If all be not in vain; and guide
    Her footsteps, moving side by side
With wisdom, like the younger child: 20

For she is earthly of the mind,
    But Wisdom[260] heavenly of the soul.
    O, friend, who camest to thy goal
So early, leaving me behind,

I would the great world grew like thee,   25
    Who grewest not alone in power
    And knowledge, but by year and hour
In reverence and in charity.

CXV

Now fades the last long streak of snow,
    Now burgeons every maze[261] of quick
    About the flowering squares, and thick
By ashen roots the violets blow.

Now rings the woodland loud and long,   5
    The distance takes a lovelier hue,
    And drown'd in yonder living blue
The lark becomes a sightless song.

Now dance the lights on lawn and lea,
    The flocks are whiter down the vale,
    And milkier every milky sail   10
On winding stream or distant sea;

Notes ——————————————————————————

[259] *Pallas* Pallas Athene, Greek goddess of wisdom, sprang from the head of Zeus fully armed.

[260] *Wisdom* see TENNYSON, n. 29 (WEB p. 339).
[261] *maze* hedge.

Where now the seamew pipes, or dives
        In yonder greening gleam, and fly
        The happy birds, that change their sky   15
To build and brood; that live their lives

From land to land; and in my breast
        Spring wakens too; and my regret
        Becomes an April violet,
And buds and blossoms like the rest.   20

CXVI

Is it, then, regret for buried time[262]
        That keenlier in sweet April wakes,
        And meets the year, and gives and takes
The colours of the crescent prime?

Not all: the songs, the stirring air,   5
        The life re-orient out of dust,
        Cry thro' the sense to hearten trust
In that which made the world so fair.

Not all regret: the face will shine
        Upon me, while I muse alone;   10
        And that dear voice, I once have known,
Still speak to me of me and mine:

Yet less of sorrow lives in me
        For days of happy commune dead;
        Less yearning for the friendship fled,   15
Than some strong bond which is to be.

CXVII

O days and hours,[263] your work is this
        To hold me from my proper place,
        A little while from his embrace,
For fuller gain of after bliss:

That out of distance might ensue   5
        Desire of nearness doubly sweet;
        And unto meeting when we meet,
Delight a hundredfold accrue,

Notes

[262] *time* this and the next section are the third spring in the poem; for the first description, see section XXXVIII; for the second, sections LXXXVI and LXXXVIII.

[263] *days and hours* see Henry Vaughan, "The Evening-Watch: A Dialogue" (1650: 14).

For every grain of sand[264] that runs,
   And every span of shade that steals,   10
   And every kiss of toothed wheels,
And all the courses of the suns.[265]

CXVIII

Contemplate all this work of Time,
   The giant labouring in his youth;
   Nor dream of human love and truth,
As dying Nature's earth and lime;[266]

But trust that those we call the dead   5
   Are breathers of an ampler day
   For ever nobler ends. They say,
The solid earth whereon we tread

In tracts of fluent heat began,
   And grew to seeming-random forms,   10
   The seeming prey of cyclic storms,[267]
Till at the last arose the man;

Who throve and branch'd from clime to clime,
   The herald of a higher race,
   And of himself in higher place,   15
If so he type this work of time

Within himself, from more to more;[268]
   Or, crown'd with attributes of woe
   Like glories, move his course, and show
That life is not as idle ore,   20

But iron dug from central gloom,
   And heated hot with burning fears,
   And dipt in baths of hissing tears,
And batter'd with the shocks of doom

Notes

[264] *sand* see Catullus, Poem 7, where innumerable kisses are compared to grains of sand.

[265] *suns* see Shakespeare, Sonnet 59: 6; the stanza contains four ways of measuring time: sand, hourglass; shade, sundial; wheels, clock; and suns, stars.

[266] *earth and lime* chemical compounds in the material analysis of living matter.

[267] *storms* see nn. 40 and 99.

[268] *branch'd ... more* the concept of the diversification of human races and the development to higher forms was advanced by Chambers in *Vestiges of the Natural History of Creation* (1844): "It may have only been when a varied climate arose, that the originally few species branched off into the present extensive variety" (ch. 15). "As yet we have not seen very distinctly how the various branches of the family, as they parted off, and took up separate ground, became marked by external features so peculiar.... All of these phenomena appear, in a word, to be explicable on the ground of *development*" (ch. 16); "Who can tell what progress may be made, even in a single century, towards reversing the proportions of the perfect and imperfect types? and who can tell but that the time during which the mean types have lasted, long as it appears, may yet be thrown entirely into the shade by the time during which the best types will remain predominant?" (ch. 16). See also below, the concluding section [Epilogue]: lines 120–132, and n. 306.

To shape and use. Arise and fly   25
    The reeling Faun, the sensual feast;[269]
    Move upward, working out the beast,
And let the ape and tiger die.

CXIX

Doors,[270] where my heart was used to beat
    So quickly, not as one that weeps
    I come once more; the city sleeps;
I smell the meadow in the street;

I hear a chirp of birds; I see   5
    Betwixt the black fronts long-withdrawn
    A light-blue lane of early dawn,
And think of early days and thee,

And bless thee, for thy lips are bland,
    And bright the friendship of thine eye;   10
    And in my thoughts with scarce a sigh
I take the pressure of thine hand.

CXX

I trust I have not wasted breath:
    I think we are not wholly brain,
    Magnetic mockeries;[271] not in vain,
Like Paul with beasts, I fought with Death;[272]

Not only cunning casts in clay: 5
    Let Science prove we are, and then
    What matters Science unto men,
At least to me? I would not stay.[273]

Let him, the wiser man who springs
    Hereafter, up from childhood shape   10
    His action like the greater ape,
But I was *born* to other things.

Notes

[269] *feast* see Shakespeare, Sonnet 141:8.

[270] *Doors* another example of the *paraclausithyron*; see above, VII, n. 1.

[271] *mockeries* Fredrich Anton Mesmer (1733–1815), German physician, practised animal magnetism and hypnosis in Paris from 1778. His cures were later denounced as fraudulent. Animal magnetism assumed that the body could be controlled by magnetism and the forces of the planets, enacting miraculous cures. Mesmerism, animal magnetism, and electrobiology were topics in the British popular press from 1830 to 1850.

[272] *beasts … Death* see 1 Corinthians 15: 32.

[273] *not stay* see the opening sentence of Francis Bacon, "Of Truth" (1625) where "jesting Pilate … would not stay for an answer" to his question of Christ, "What is truth?" (see John 18: 38).

CXXI

Sad Hesper[274] o'er the buried sun
    And ready, thou, to die with him,
    Thou watchest all things ever dim
And dimmer, and a glory done:

The team is loosen'd from the wain,[275]   5
    The boat is drawn upon the shore;
    Thou listenest to the closing door,
And life is darken'd in the brain.

Bright Phosphor, fresher for the night,
    By thee the world's great work is heard   10
    Beginning, and the wakeful bird;
Behind thee comes the greater light:

The market boat is on the stream,
    And voices hail it from the brink;
    Thou hear'st the village hammer clink,   15
And see'st the moving of the team.

Sweet Hesper-Phosphor, double name[276]
    For what is one, the first, the last,[277]
    Thou, like my present and my past,
Thy place is changed; thou art the same.   20

CXXII

Oh, wast thou with me, dearest, then,
    While I rose up against my doom,
    And yearn'd to burst the folded gloom,
To bare the eternal Heavens again,

To feel once more, in placid awe,   5
    The strong imagination roll
    A sphere of stars about my soul,
In all her motion one with law;

If thou wert with me, and the grave
    Divide us not, be with me now,   10
    And enter in at breast and brow,
Till all my blood, a fuller wave,

Notes

[274] *Hesper* Venus or the evening star; thought by the ancients to be different from "Bright Phosphor" (line 9), the morning star.

[275] *wain* wagon, a reference to the unshackling of the chariot of the Apollo, the sun god in the evening. His chariot is the constellation of the Great Bear (big dipper); see *OED*, s.v. "wain"; see also n. 241.

[276] *double name* from the Hellenistic period (fourth century BCE), they were known to be the same planet, Venus.

[277] *first ... last* Alpha and Omega, first and last letters of Greek alphabet; see Revelation 1: 11.

Be quicken'd with a livelier breath,
　　And like an inconsiderate boy,
　　As in the former flash of joy,　　　　　　　　　　　15
I slip the thoughts of life and death;

And all the breeze of Fancy blows,
　　And every dew-drop paints a bow,[278]
　　The wizard lightnings deeply glow,
And every thought breaks out a rose.[279]　　　　　　20

CXXIII

There rolls the deep where grew the tree.[280]
　　O earth, what changes[281] hast thou seen!
　　There where the long street roars, hath been
The stillness of the central sea.

The hills are shadows, and they flow　　　　　　　　5
　　From form to form, and nothing stands;
　　They melt like mist, the solid lands,
Like clouds they shape themselves and go.

But in my spirit will I dwell,
　　And dream my dream, and hold it true;　　　　　10
　　For tho' my lips may breathe adieu,
I cannot think the thing farewell.

CXXIV

That which we dare invoke to bless;
　　Our dearest faith; our ghastliest doubt;
　　He, They, One, All; within, without;
The Power in darkness whom we guess;

I found Him not in world or sun,　　　　　　　　　5
　　Or eagle's wing, or insect's eye;
　　Nor thro' the questions men may try,
The petty cobwebs we have spun:[282]

Notes

[278] *bow* rainbow.

[279] *rose* art; specifically a poem.

[280] *tree* this section draws heavily upon geologists such as Charles Lyell, *Principles of Geology* (1830–33); see n. 99.

[281] *changes* see Ovid's description of the four elements, *Metamorphoses* 15. 229–85.

[282] *spun* Tennyson questions the widespread teleological argument for God's existence, the argument from design. William Paley (1743–1805) in *Natural Theology; or, Evidences of the Existence and Attributes of the Deity, Collected from the Appearances of Nature* (1802) discusses both the wings of birds and the eyes of animals, fishes, and insects as complex designs that point to an intelligent designer. Paley's famous analogy concerning complexity is based on a watch found on a heath. Its existence presumes a watchmaker, sufficient to design the order and complexity of the watch, and by analogy from the complexity of creation (as in the eye of an insect, for instance) to the notion of a creator. Further, while the purpose or "end" (Gk. *telos*) of the watch is to tell time, the purpose of creation to Paley is the general well-being in the order and harmony of the natural world and concord and happiness in the human social order. Here Tennyson relies instead on the validation of Christianity in human experience: "I have felt." See the distinction between knowledge and faith/wisdom that opens *In Memoriam* (Proem: "Strong Son of God"; n. 33). See also DARWIN, headnote; THOMSON, n. 13; and RELIGION: GEOLOGY, n. 51.

If e'er when faith had fall'n asleep,
    I heard a voice "believe no more"   10
    And heard an ever-breaking shore
That tumbled in the Godless deep;

A warmth within the breast would melt
    The freezing reason's colder part,
    And like a man in wrath the heart   15
Stood up and answer'd "I have felt."

No, like a child in doubt and fear:
    But that blind clamour made me wise;
    Then was I as a child that cries,
But, crying, knows his father near;   20

And what I am beheld again
    What is, and no man understands;
    And out of darkness came the hands
That reach thro' nature, moulding men.

CXXV

Whatever I have said or sung,
    Some bitter notes my harp would give,
    Yea, tho' there often seem'd to live
A contradiction on the tongue,

Yet Hope had never lost her youth;   5
    She did but look through dimmer eyes;
    Or Love but play'd with gracious lies,
Because he felt so fix'd in truth:

And if the song were full of care,
    He breathed the spirit of the song;   10
    And if the words were sweet and strong[283]
He set his royal signet there;

Abiding with me till I sail
    To seek thee on the mystic deeps,
    And this electric force,[284] that keeps   15
A thousand pulses dancing, fail.

CXXVI

Love is and was my Lord and King,
    And in his presence I attend
    To hear the tidings of my friend,
Which every hour his couriers bring.[285]

Notes

283 *sweet and strong* see Judges 14: 14.
284 *electric force* see n. 271.
285 *bring* see George Herbert, "The Holy Communion" (1633: 23–24).

Love is and was my King and Lord,   5
    And will be, tho' as yet I keep
    Within his court on earth, and sleep
Encompass'd by his faithful guard,

And hear at times a sentinel
    Who moves about from place to place,   10
    And whispers to the worlds of space,
In the deep night, that all is well.

CXXVII

And all is well, tho' faith and form
    Be sunder'd in the night of fear;
    Well roars the storm to those that hear
A deeper voice across the storm,[286]

Proclaiming social truth shall spread,   5
    And justice, ev'n tho' thrice again[287]
    The red fool-fury of the Seine
Should pile her barricades with dead.[288]

But ill for him that wears a crown,[289]
    And him, the lazar,[290] in his rags: 10
    They tremble, the sustaining crags;
The spires of ice are toppled down,

And molten up, and roar in flood;
    The fortress crashes from on high,
    The brute earth[291] lightens to the sky,   15
And the great Æon sinks in blood,[292]

And compass'd by the fires of Hell;
    While thou, dear spirit, happy star,
    O'erlook'st the tumult from afar,
And smilest, knowing all is well.   20

CXXVIII

The love that rose on stronger wings,
    Unpalsied when he met with Death,
    Is comrade of the lesser faith
That sees the course of human things.

Notes

[286] *storm* see Revelation 16: 17–18.
[287] *again* in a manuscript Tennyson wrote "once" for "thrice." France underwent revolutions in 1789, 1830, and 1848; although Tennyson wrote this section before 1848, he very likely altered it to allude to the revolution of 1848.
[288] *red ... Seine ... dead* The Seine is the river that runs through Paris; barricades probably refers to the massacres during the revolution of 1830; hence, the red river and the dead.
[289] *crown* see *2 Henry IV* 3. 1. 31.
[290] *lazer* leper, beggar.
[291] *brute earth* see Milton, *Comus* (1634: 707–79); see also Horace, *Odes* 1. 39. 9.
[292] *blood* apocalyptic changes; see Revelation 8: 7–8.

No doubt vast eddies in the flood 5
 Of onward time shall yet be made,
 And throned races may degrade;
Yet O ye mysteries of good,

Wild Hours that fly with Hope and Fear,
 If all your office had to do 10
 With old results that look like new;
If this were all your mission here,

To draw, to sheathe a useless sword,
 To fool the crowd with glorious lies,[293]
 To cleave a creed in sects and cries, 15
To change the bearing of a word,

To shift an arbitrary power,
 To cramp the student at his desk,
 To make old bareness picturesque
And tuft with grass a feudal tower; 20

Why then my scorn might well descend
 On you and yours. I see in part
 That all, as in some piece of art,
Is toil cöoperant to an end.

CXXIX

Dear friend, far off, my lost desire,
 So far, so near in woe and weal;
 O loved the most, when most I feel
There is a lower and a higher;

Known and unknown; human, divine; 5
 Sweet human hand and lips and eye;
 Dear heavenly friend that canst not die,
Mine, mine, for ever, ever mine;

Strange friend, past, present, and to be;
 Loved deeplier, darklier understood; 10
 Behold, I dream a dream of good,
And mingle all the world with thee.

CXXX

Thy voice is on the rolling air;
 I hear thee where the waters run;
 Thou standest in the rising sun,[294]
And in the setting thou art fair.

Notes

[293] lies see Horace, Odes 9. 3. 36; see also "noble lie" in Plato, Republic, 3. 414b–417b. [294] sun see Revelation 19: 17.

What art thou then? I cannot guess;   5
    But tho' I seem in star and flower
    To feel thee some diffusive power,
I do not therefore love thee less:

My love involves the love before;
    My love is vaster passion now;   10
    Tho' mix'd with God and Nature thou,
I seem to love thee more and more.

Far off thou art, but ever nigh;
    I have thee still, and I rejoice;
    I prosper, circled with thy voice;   15
I shall not lose thee tho' I die.

CXXXI

O living will[295] that shalt endure
    When all that seems shall suffer shock,
    Rise in the spiritual rock,[296]
Flow thro' our deeds and make them pure,

That we may lift from out of dust   5
    A voice as unto him that hears,[297]
    A cry above the conquer'd years
To one that with us works, and trust,

With faith that comes of self-control,
    The truths that never can be proved   10
    Until we close with all we loved,
And all we flow from, soul in soul.

O true and tried, so well and long,[298]
    Demand not thou a marriage lay;
    In that it is thy marriage day
Is music more than any song.

Nor have I felt so much of bliss   5
    Since first he told me that he loved
    A daughter of our house;[299] nor proved
Since that dark day a day like this;

Notes

295 *will* Tennyson claimed this force was not divine will, but human free will.

296 *rock* see 1 Corinthians 10: 4.

297 *hears* see Isaiah 29: 4.

298 *long* most modern editions entitle this section "Epilogue"; Tennyson did not give it a title. The section is modelled on the classical genre of the *epithalamion*, a poem celebrating a marriage (Gr. *epi* of, outside; *thalamos* bridal chamber). The most famous classical model is Catallus, Song 61, and among Elizabthan examples is Edmund Spenser's "Epithalamion" (1595). Tennyson dated this "Epilogue," as he had the "Prologue." The occasion for this section is the wedding of Tennyson's sister Cecilia to Edmund Lushington, 10 October 1842.

299 *house* Tennyson's sister, Emily, six years older than Cecilia; see n. 46.

Tho' I since then have number'd o'er
    Some thrice three years: they went and came,   10
    Remade the blood and changed the frame,
And yet is love not less, but more;

No longer caring to embalm
    In dying songs a dead regret,
    But like a statue solid-set,   15
And moulded in colossal calm.

Regret is dead, but love is more
    Than in the summers that are flown,
    For I myself with these have grown
To something greater than before;   20

Which makes appear the songs I made
    As echoes out of weaker times,
    As half but idle brawling rhymes,
The sport of random sun and shade.

But where is she, the bridal flower,   25
    That must be made a wife ere noon?[300]
    She enters, glowing like the moon
Of Eden on its bridal bower:

On me she bends her blissful eyes
    And then on thee; they meet thy look   30
    And brighten like the star that shook[301]
Betwixt the palms of paradise.

O when her life was yet in bud,
    He too foretold the perfect rose.
    For thee she grew, for thee she grows   35
For ever, and as fair as good.

And thou art worthy; full of power;
    As gentle; liberal-minded, great,
    Consistent; wearing all that weight
Of learning[302] lightly like a flower.   40

But now set out: the noon is near,
    And I must give away[303] the bride;
    She fears not, or with thee beside
And me behind her, will not fear.

Notes

[300] *noon* until 1886, for marriages to be legal they had to be celebrated between 8 a.m. and noon.

[301] *shook* when Jupiter approved of the marriage of Thetis and Peleus, the stars shook; see Pindar, *Isthmian* 8. 58.

[302] *learning* Lushington was professor of Greek at Glasgow (1838–75).

[303] *give away* Tennyson's father, George Clayton, had died in 1831.

For I that danced her on my knee,   45
    That watch'd her on her nurse's arm,
    That shielded all her life from harm
At last must part with her to thee;

Now waiting to be made a wife,
    Her feet, my darling, on the dead;   50
    Their pensive tablets round her head,
And the most living words of life

Breathed in her ear. The ring is on,
    The "wilt thou" answer'd, and again
    The "wilt thou" ask'd, till out of twain   55
Her sweet "I will" has made you one.

Now sign your names, which shall be read,
    Mute symbols of a joyful morn,
    By village eyes as yet unborn;
The names are sign'd, and overhead   60

Begins the clash and clang that tells
    The joy to every wandering breeze;
    The blind wall rocks, and on the trees
The dead leaf trembles to the bells.

O happy hour, and happier hours   65
    Await them. Many a merry face
    Salutes them—maidens of the place,
That pelt us in the porch with flowers.

O happy hour, behold the bride
    With him to whom her hand I gave.   70
    They leave the porch, they pass the grave
That has to-day its sunny side.

To-day the grave is bright for me,
    For them the light of life increased,
    Who stay to share the morning feast,   75
Who rest to-night beside the sea.

Let all my genial spirits advance
    To meet and greet a whiter sun;
    My drooping memory will not shun
The foaming grape of eastern France.   80

It circles round, and fancy plays,
    And hearts are warm'd and faces bloom,
    As drinking health to bride and groom
We wish them store of happy days.

Nor count me all to blame if I   85
    Conjecture of a stiller guest,
    Perchance, perchance, among the rest,
And, tho' in silence, wishing joy.

But they must go, the time draws on,
    And those white-favour'd horses wait;   90
    They rise, but linger; it is late;
Farewell, we kiss, and they are gone.

A shade falls on us like the dark
    From little cloudlets on the grass,
    But sweeps away as out we pass   95
To range the woods, to roam the park,

Discussing how their courtship grew,
    And talk of others that are wed,
    And how she look'd, and what he said,
And back we come at fall of dew.   100

Again the feast, the speech, the glee,
    The shade of passing thought, the wealth
    Of words and wit, the double health,
The crowning cup, the three-times-three,[304]

And last the dance;—till I retire: 105
    Dumb is that tower which spake so loud,
    And high in heaven the streaming cloud,
And on the downs a rising fire:

And rise, O moon, from yonder down,
    Till over down and over dale   110
    All night the shining vapour[305] sail
And pass the silent-lighted town,

The white-faced halls, the glancing rills,
    And catch at every mountain head,
    And o'er the friths that branch and spread   115
Their sleeping silver thro' the hills;

And touch with shade the bridal doors,
    With tender gloom the roof, the wall;
    And breaking let the splendour fall
To spangle all the happy shores   120

By which they rest, and ocean sounds,
    And, star and system rolling past,
    A soul shall draw from out the vast
And strike his being into bounds,

And, moved thro' life of lower phase,   125
    Result in man, be born and think,
    And act and love, a closer link
Betwixt us and the crowning race[306]

Notes

[304] *three-times-three* three cheers.
[305] *vapour* Aurora Borealis, the northern lights.

[306] *soul ... race* Chambers's *Vestiges of the Natural History of Creation* (1844) poses the question of later stages of

Of those that, eye to eye, shall look
    On knowledge; under whose command   130
    Is Earth and Earth's, and in their hand
Is Nature like an open book;[307]

No longer half-akin to brute,
    For all we thought and loved and did,
    And hoped, and suffer'd, is but seed   135
Of what in them is flower and fruit;

Whereof the man, that with me trod
    This planet, was a noble type
    Appearing ere the times were ripe,
That friend of mine who lives in God,   140

That God, which ever lives and loves,
    One God, one law, one element,
    And one far-off divine event,
To which the whole creation moves.

1842

The Eagle

FRAGMENT[308]

He clasps the crag with crooked hands;[309]
Close to the sun in lonely lands,
Ring'd with the azure world, he stands.
The wrinkled sea beneath him crawls;
He watches from his mountain walls,   5
And like a thunderbolt he falls.[310]

Notes

evolutionary development: "Is our race but the initial of the grand crowning type? Are there yet to be species superior to us in organization, purer in feeling, more powerful in device and act, and who shall take a rule over us! ... There may then be occasion for a nobler type of humanity, which shall complete the zoological circle on this planet, and realize some of the dreams of the purest spirits of the present race" (ch. 15). See also n. 268.

[307] *open book* the theory of the two books, that the book of God (the Bible) and the book of Nature were both written by God and are complementary. See also n. 282; and Bevington, n. 1. See also RELIGION: GEOLOGY, n. 24.

[308] *title* experiment in iambic tetrameter triplets with substituted troches that Tennyson had used earlier in "The Two Voices" (written 1833, published 1842) when Tennyson was trying to cope with the death of Arthur Hallam. This form had been used by Robert Herrick (1591–1674) in the six-line poem "Upon Julia's Clothes" (1648) and elsewhere. In 1863 and 1864 Tennyson published "Experiments in Quantity," attempts to render classical metres in English verse; see also the poems to Virgil and Catullus below. First published in *Poems*, seventh edition, 1851).

[309] *hands* see *Aeneid* 6. 360.

[310] *falls* see Milton, *Samson Agonistes* (1671: 1695–96).

The Charge of the Light Brigade[311]

I

Half a league, half a league,
  Half a league onward,
All in the valley of Death[312]
  Rode the six hundred.
"Forward, the Light Brigade!   5
Charge for the guns!" he said[313]:
Into the valley of Death
  Rode the six hundred.

II

"Forward, the Light Brigade!"
Was there a man dismay'd?   10
Not tho' the soldier knew
  Some one had blunder'd:
Their's not to make reply,
Their's not to reason why,
Their's but to do and die: 15
Into the valley of Death
  Rode the six hundred.

Notes

[311] *title* the Crimean War (1853–56) was fought between Russia and the allied armies of Britain, France, Turkey, and Sardinia over Russian expansion in the Middle East during the collapse of the Ottoman Empire. Much of it was fought over the control of the Black Sea and the Crimean Peninsula, defended by the Russian city of Sebastopol. Though marred with egregious incompetence, it was also one of the first modern wars, using the telegraph, war correspondents, and photographers to relay news immediately from the front to readers at home. The reports to *The Times* were written by correspondent William Howard Russell (1820–1907); see EMPIRE: IMPERIAL TRAVELLERS (WEB p. 258). The poem was written after Tennyson read the reports of the battle of Balaklava on 25 October 1854 (*The Times*, 14 Nov. 1854). In an editorial *The Times* claimed: "The British soldier will do his duty, even to certain death, and is not paralyzed by feeling that he is the victim of some hideous blunder" (13 Nov. 1854). The order to charge from army commander, Lord Raglan (1788–1855), and cavalry commander, Lord Lucan (1800–88), was misinterpreted, and the brigade set out under Lord Cardigan (1797–1868). The Light Brigade of the British cavalry charged straight into the fusillades of the entrenched Russian artillery for a 2.5 kilometres ("half a league"). Some 673 (Russell says 607) men started, but only 195 returned. The charge became a symbol of the courage but also the stupidity of warfare, especially of the military commanders. Raglan's command was disastrous, causing much suffering and sickness among the troops by denying them fires against the cold, as well as the military calamities at Balaklava and Inkerman. The immense popularity of Tennyson's poem extended to a privately printed sheet (1855) for circulation to troops in the Crimea. A number of recorded voices and other documents are related to this poem: see LITERATURE: RECORDING; TENNYSON; NIGHTINGALE; and LANDFREY (WEB p. 158); see also, in the same context, PHOTOGRAPHY; FENTON (WEB p. 172). For female perspectives, see CAMPBELL, "THE WINDMILL," "THE CRIMEAN WAR" and CAMPBELL, n. 26 (WEB p. 290) and SEACOLE (WEB p. 295). See also Plate 17: William Simpson, *One of the Wards ... at Scutari*. First published in *The Examiner* (9 Dec. 1854); collected in *Maud and Other Poems* (1855). Our text: 1854.

[312] *Death* see Psalm 23: Russell had used the phrase "arms of death" (*The Times*, 14 Nov. 1854).

[313] *said* Raglan's order for the charge was delivered to Lord Lucan by Captain Louis Edward Nolan (1818–54). In the charge, he rode across in front of Cardigan who was leading his troops – perhaps to indicate that their route was wrong – and was the first man killed in the assault.

III

Cannon to right of them,
Cannon to left of them,
Cannon in front of them   20
    Volley'd and thunder'd;
Storm'd at with shot and shell,
Boldly they rode and well,
Into the jaws of Death,
Into the mouth of Hell   25
    Rode the six hundred.

IV

Flash'd all their sabres bare,
Flash'd as they turn'd in air
Sabring the gunners there,
Charging an army, while   30
    All the world wonder'd:
Plunged in the battery-smoke
Right thro' the line they broke;
Cossack and Russian
Reel'd from the sabre-stroke   35
    Shatter'd and sunder'd.
Then they rode back, but not
    Not the six hundred.

V

Cannon to right of them,
Cannon to left of them,   40
Cannon behind them
    Volley'd and thunder'd;
Storm'd at with shot and shell,
While horse and hero fell,
They that had fought so well   45
Came thro' the jaws of Death,
Back from the mouth of Hell,
All that was left of them,
    Left of six hundred.

VI

When can their glory fade?   50
O the wild charge they made!
    All the world wonder'd.
Honour the charge they made!
Honour the Light Brigade,
    Noble six hundred!   55

WEB p. 345

The Higher Pantheism

To Virgil

Written at the Request of the Mantuans for the Nineteenth Centenary of Virgil's Death[314]

I

Roman Virgil, thou that singest Ilion's lofty temples robed in fire,
Ilion falling, Rome arising, wars, and filial faith, and Dido's pyre;[315]

II

Landscape-lover, lord of language more than he that sang the "Works and Days,"[316]
All the chosen coin of fancy flashing out from many a golden phrase;

III

Thou that singest wheat and woodland, tilth and vineyard, hive and horse and herd;[317]   5
All the charm of all the Muses often flowering in a lonely word;

IV

Poet of the happy Tityrus piping underneath his beechen bowers;[318]
Poet of the poet-satyr whom the laughing shepherd bound with flowers;[319]

V

Chanter of the Pollio,[320] glorying in the blissful years again to be,
Summers of the snakeless meadow, unlaborious earth and oarless sea;[321]   10

Notes

[314] *title* Virgil, the chief poet of the Augustan Age, was born on a farm near Mantua in 70 BCE and died in Brundisium in 19 BCE. Tennyson was requested to write a commemorative verse by the Virgilian Academy of Mantua. The trochaic lines suggest Virgil's Latin hexameters. First published in the *Nineteenth Century* (Sept. 1882); collected in *Tiresias and Other Poems* (1885). Our text 1882.

[315] *pyre* section I alludes to the burning and sacking of Troy, "Ilion" (*Aeneid* 2), the love of Queen Dido of Carthage and Aeneas, and Dido's suicide (*Aeneid* 4), and the meeting with the shade of his father Anchises in the Underworld, with his prophesy of Rome's rising glory (*Aeneid* 6. 680 ff.).

[316] *Days* Hesiod (eighth century BCE); Greek poet whose *Works and Days* (*c*.700 BCE) is a predecessor to Virgil's treatment of agricultural themes in *Georgics* (*c*.29 BCE).

[317] *herd* this line summarizes of the themes of *Georgics*, that Virgil sums up in *Georgics* I. 1–5.

[318] *bowers* echo of the opening of Virgil's *Eclogue* I. 1, where the shepherd Tityrus is addressed by name.

[319] *flowers* the poet-satyr is Silenus, the companion of the wine god Dionysus, who is bound with garlands of flowers in *Eclogue* 6. 19.

[320] *Pollio* Virgil's patron, Gaius Asinius Pollio (*c*.75 BCE–4 CE), mentioned in *Eclogue* 4, the so-called messianic eclogue that foretells a coming golden age, once taken as referring prophetically to the birth of Christ.

[321] *sea* this line echoes words and lines from *Eclogue* 4: no serpent is there (24), the earth is untilled (18–19), nor shall the mariner ply the sea (38).

VI

Thou that seëst Universal Nature moved by Universal Mind;[322]
Thou majestic in thy sadness at the doubtful doom of human kind;[323]

VII

Light among the vanish'd ages; star that gildest yet this phantom shore;
Golden branch[324] amid the shadows, kings and realms that pass to rise no more;

VIII

Now thy Forum roars no longer, fallen every purple Cæsar's dome[325]—   15
Tho' thine ocean-roll of rhythm sound forever of Imperial Rome—

IX

Now the Rome of slaves hath perish'd, and the Rome of freemen[326] holds her place,
I, from out the Northern Island sunder'd once from all the human race,[327]

X

I salute thee, Mantovano,[328] I that loved thee since my day began,
Wielder of the stateliest measure[329] ever moulded by the lips of man.   20

"Frater Ave atque Vale"[330]

Row us out from Desenzano,[331] to your Sirmione row!
So they row'd, and there we landed—'O venusta Sirmio!'[332]
There to me thro' all the groves of olive[333] in the summer glow,

Notes

[322] *Mind* a reference to Anchises' teaching Aeneas the control of all of the elements by the divine mind in *Aeneid* 6. 725–27.

[323] *kind* see *Aeneid* 1. 462: "here, too, there are tears for human fortune" (*sunt lacrimae rerum*), "and hearts that are touched by mortality" (trans. Conington).

[324] *Golden branch* just as Aeneas carried the Golden Bough from Venus to pass into the underworld (*Aeneid* 6. 208), so Virgil is praised for being a guide to the underworld, and as a light to other poets.

[325] *dome* for the purple of tyrants see Horace, *Odes* 1. 35. 12.

[326] *freemen* Tennyson is playing on slaves and freemen in Augustan Rome in comparison with Italy under the control of the Austrian Empire and the Vatican. While Italy had become a nation in 1861, Austria continued to control much of Italy until 1870.

[327] *race* see Virgil, *Eclogue* 1. 66–67: "The Britons, wholly sundered from the world" (trans. Fairclough).

[328] *Mantovano* Italian for "citizen of Mantua," the term used by Dante when Sordello greets Virgil in *Purgatorio*

6. 74, and hence, Tennyson, through Dante, pays tribute to Virgil.

[329] *measure* the Latin hexameter of Virgil's *Aeneid*.

[330] *title* (Lat. brother, hail and farewell); a citation from Catullus, Poem 101, an elegy for his dead brother. The poem is in memory of Tennyson's brother Charles, who had died in April 1879. Tennyson, then, combines his own grief with that of Catullus for his brother in this tribute poem to Catullus. Furthermore, Tennyson also draws on Catullus, Poem 31, his address to the peninsula of Sirmio on the southern shore of Lake Garda in northern Italy (Lombardy). Tennyson wrote the poem on a visit to Sirmio in June, 1880. See n. 148. First published in the *Nineteenth Century* (Mar. 1883); collected in *Tiresias and Other Poems* (1885). Our text 1883.

[331] *Desenzano* small town at the southern end of Lake Garda.

[332] *"O venusta Sirmio"* (Lat. O lovely Sirmio); from Catullus, Poem 31. 12.

[333] *olive* the peninsula is covered with olive groves, symbol of fecundity.

There beneath the Roman ruin[334] where the purple flowers grow,
Came that 'Ave atque Vale' of the Poet's hopeless woe,   5
Tenderest of Roman poets nineteen-hundred years ago,
'Frater Ave atque Vale'—as we wander'd to and fro
Gazing at the Lydian laughter[335] of the Garda Lake below
Sweet Catullus's all-but-island,[336] olive-silvery Sirmio![337]   10

Crossing the Bar[338]

Sunset and evening star,
        And one clear call[339] for me!
And may there be no moaning of the bar,[340]
        When I put out to sea,

But such a tide as moving seems asleep,   5
        Too full for sound and foam,
When that which drew from out the boundless deep
Turns again home.

Twilight and evening bell,
        And after that the dark!   10
And may there be no sadness of farewell,
        When I embark;

For tho' from out our bourne[341] of Time and Place
        The flood may bear me far,
I hope to see my Pilot face to face[342]   15
        When I have crost the bar.

Robert Browning (1812–89)

Born in Camberwell in south London, and raised in a middle-class family, Browning learned Latin and Greek from his bibliophile father, Robert Browning Sr (1782–1866), a Bank of England clerk, and music and religious piety from his nonconformist mother, Sarah Anna Wiedemann (1772–1849). He became an accomplished linguist in classical and modern languages, with

Notes

[334] *Roman ruin* at the end of the peninsula, as the travel guide Baedeker's *Northern Italy* (1889) said: "On the promontory are relics of a building extending into the lake, said to have been the country-house of Catullus, who wrote his poems here" (192).

[335] *Lydian laughter* echo of Catullus, Poem 31. 13–14. The pre-Roman inhabitants, the Etruscans, were supposed to be descended from the Lydians of Asia Minor.

[336] *all-but-island* a literal translation of "peninsula," and a translation of the opening words of Catullus, Poem 31: (Lat. *paene insularum, Sirmio, insularumque / ocelle:* of peninsulas, Sirmio, the bright eye of islands).

[337] *olive-silvery* the under-side of olive leaves are silvery.

[338] *title* Tennyson wrote this poem in twenty minutes in October 1889 when crossing the Solent, separating the English mainland from the Isle of Wight, where Tennyson had his home at Farringford. He died 6 October 1892, having stipulated that this poem should be placed last in editions of his works. First published in *Demeter and Other Poems* (1889), as the last poem. Our text: 1889.

[339] *call* marine term meaning a summons to duty.

[340] *bar* sandbank across a harbour mouth.

[341] *bourne* see *Hamlet* 3. 1. 79–80.

[342] *face* see 1 Corinthians 13: 12.

private tutors, a year at London University, and extensive reading in his father's large library. When a series of long poems failed to win public attention or critical acclaim, he turned to shorter dramatic lyrics that caught the attention of the best-known female poet of the day, Elizabeth Barrett. Their intense correspondence (1845–46) led to secret meetings almost weekly, and a clandestine marriage. Despite Barrett's ill-health, they eloped, and lived the rest of their lives in Italy. Browning published his most famous volume, *Men and Women* (1855), a gallery of fifty highly personalized figures from many walks of life – lovers, painters, vagabonds, and priests, each caught in a crisis of their own lives and their historical contexts. After Elizabeth Barrett's sudden death in 1861, Browning returned to England and continued to publish almost annually, including *Dramatis Personae* (1864) and his masterpiece, *The Ring and the Book* (1868–69), based on an obscure seventeenth-century Roman murder case. Browning established the dramatic monologue

as his own *tour de force* and as a dominant poetic form of the nineteenth century. In many of Browning's monologues a speaker inadvertently reveals his warts and blemishes with ironic self-justification to an invisible auditor. In an interplay of passion and philosophy, a speaker outlines a crisis of moral, intellectual, aesthetic, and social dimensions whose tortuous path is set out in idiosyncratic and often elliptical speech and complex dialogue. Browning is buried in Westminster Abbey beside Tennyson. Standard edition: *The Poetical Works of Robert Browning*, eds Ian Jack, Margaret Smith, and Robert Inglesfield (15 vols, 1981–); *The Brownings' Correspondence*, eds Philip Kelly and Ronald Hudson (19 vols, 1984–); William Irvine and Park Honan, *The Book, the Ring, and the Poet: A Biography of Robert Browning* (1974); Richard S. Kennedy and Donald Hair, *The Dramatic Imagination of Robert Browning: A Literary Life* (2007). The Browning Society: www.browningsociety.org. Our text: *Poetical Works* (1888–89).

Porphyria's Lover[1]

The rain set early in to-night,
    The sullen wind was soon awake,
It tore the elm-tops down for spite,
    And did its worst to vex the lake:
    I listened with heart fit to break.   5
When glided in Porphyria; straight
    She shut the cold out and the storm,
And kneeled and made the cheerless grate
    Blaze up, and all the cottage warm;

Notes

ROBERT BROWNING

[1] *title* porphyria (Gk. *porphyros*, purple) is a purple stone similar to marble; also a disease characterized by purple urine, extreme sensitivity to sunlight, delusions, and mental instability – the disease suffered by George III (1738–1820). Hence, the original title might refer to the medical condition of the speaker, rather than the name of the victim. The hero of John Keats's poem "The Eve of St. Agnes" (1820) is called Porphyro. First published (*Monthly Repository*, Jan. 1836) as "Porphyria"; reprinted in *Bells and Pomegranates, No. III* (Nov. 1842), a collection of sixteen poems entitled *Dramatic Lyrics*, before "Johannes Agricola in Meditation" under the title of "Madhouse Cells" with no other title, but numbered "II." *Bells and Pomegranates* was a series of eight pamphlets of poetry that Browning described as "an alternation, a mixture, of music with discoursing, sound with sense, poetry with thought." For the title of the series, see Exodus 28: 33. Present title of this poem in *Poetical Works*, 1863.

Which done, she rose, and from her form 10
Withdrew the dripping cloak and shawl,
    And laid her soiled gloves by, untied
Her hat and let the damp hair fall,
    And, last, she sat down by my side
    And called me. When no voice replied, 15
She put my arm about her waist,
    And made her smooth white shoulder bare,
And all her yellow hair displaced,
    And, stooping, made my cheek lie there,
    And spread, o'er all, her yellow hair, 20
Murmuring how she loved me—she
    Too weak, for all her heart's endeavour,
To set its struggling passion free
    From pride, and vainer ties dissever,
    And give herself to me for ever. 25
But passion sometimes would prevail,
    Nor could to-night's gay feast restrain
A sudden thought of one so pale
    For love of her, and all in vain:
    So, she was come through wind and rain. 30
Be sure I looked up at her eyes
    Happy and proud; at last I knew
Porphyria worshipped me; surprise
    Made my heart swell, and still it grew
    While I debated what to do. 35
That moment she was mine, mine, fair,
    Perfectly pure and good: I found
A thing to do, and all her hair
    In one long yellow string I wound
    Three times her little throat around, 40
And strangled her. No pain felt she;
    I am quite sure she felt no pain.
As a shut bud that holds a bee,
    I warily oped her lids: again
    Laughed the blue eyes without a stain. 45
And I untightened next the tress
    About her neck; her cheek once more
Blushed bright beneath my burning kiss:
    I propped her head up as before,
    Only, this time my shoulder bore 50
Her head, which droops upon it still:
    The smiling rosy little head,
So glad it has its utmost will,
    That all it scorned at once is fled,
    And I, its love, am gained instead! 55
Porphyria's love: she guessed not how
    Her darling one wish would be heard.
And thus we sit together now,
    And all night long we have not stirred,
    And yet God has not said a word! 60

From *Pippa Passes*[2]

Song

The year's at the spring
And day's at the morn;
Morning's at seven;
The hill-side's dew-pearled;
The lark's on the wing;   5
The snail's on the thorn:
God's in his heaven—
All's right with the world!

My Last Duchess[3]

FERRARA

That's my last Duchess painted on the wall,
Looking as if she were alive. I call
That piece a wonder, now: Frà Pandolf's[4] hands
Worked busily a day, and there she stands.
Will't please you sit and look at her? I said   5
'Frà Pandolf' by design, for never read
Strangers like you that pictured countenance,
The depth and passion of its earnest glance,
But to myself they turned (since none puts by
The curtain I have drawn for you, but I)   10
And seemed as they would ask me, if they durst,
How such a glance came there; so, not the first
Are you to turn and ask thus. Sir, 'twas not
Her husband's presence only, called that spot
Of joy into the Duchess' cheek: perhaps   15
Frà Pandolf chanced to say 'Her mantle laps
Over my Lady's wrist too much,' or 'Paint
Must never hope to reproduce the faint
Half-flush that dies along her throat'; such stuff
Was courtesy, she thought, and cause enough   20

Notes

[2] *title* this song recurs throughout *Pippa Passes*. Pippa, a young girl, works in a silk mill and passes through Asolo, an Italian town near Venice. Each scene involves characters in crisis; as Pippa passes by their houses, she sings her song, an ironic comment on each event, influencing it in ways she does not comprehend. The poem is sometimes misread as a statement of Browning's easy optimism. First published in the first number of *Bells and Pomegranates* (April 1841).

[3] *title* the duke is based on Alfonso II, duke of Ferrara (1533–97), who married 14-year-old Lucrezia, daughter of Cosimo I de'Medici (1519–74) of Florence in 1558. She died in 1561, possibly a victim of poisoning. The duke renegotiated a second marriage in 1565 with the niece of the Count of Tyrol (Barbara of Austria, 1539–72), using the count's emissary, Nikolaus Mardruz. First published in *Bells and Pomegranates, No. III* (Nov. 1842): *Dramatic Lyrics*. This poem was the first of a pair entitled "Italy and France," and was first titled "I. Italy"; in *Poems* (2 vols, 1849) it was given its present title. The other poem was "II. France," later titled "Count Gismond." Richard Howard (b. 1929), American poet and translator, published a sequel poem, "Nikolaus Mardruz to his Master Ferdinand, Count of Tyrol, 1565" (in *Trappings* 2000).

[4] *Pandolf* an imaginary painter and brother of a religious order.

For calling up that spot of joy. She had
A heart—how shall I say?—too soon made glad,
Too easily impressed; she liked whate'er
She looked on, and her looks went everywhere.
Sir, 'twas all one! My favour⁵ at her breast,   25
The dropping of the daylight in the West,
The bough of cherries some officious fool
Broke in the orchard for her, the white mule
She rode with round the terrace—all and each
Would draw from her alike the approving speech,   30
Or blush, at least. She thanked men,—good! but thanked
Somehow—I know not how—as if she ranked
My gift of a nine-hundred-years-old name
With anybody's gift. Who'd stoop to blame
This sort of trifling? Even had you skill   35
In speech—(which I have not)—to make your will
Quite clear to such an one, and say, 'Just this
Or that in you disgusts me; here you miss,
Or there exceed the mark'—and if she let
Herself be lessoned so, nor plainly set   40
Her wits to yours, forsooth, and made excuse,
—E'en then would be some stooping; and I choose
Never to stoop. Oh, sir, she smiled, no doubt,
Whene'er I passed her; but who passed without
Much the same smile? This grew; I gave commands;   45
Then all smiles stopped together. There she stands
As if alive. Will't please you rise? We'll meet
The company below, then. I repeat,
The Count your Master's known munificence
Is ample warrant that no just pretence   50
Of mine for dowry will be disallowed;
Though his fair daughter's self, as I avowed
At starting, is my object. Nay, we'll go
Together down, Sir! Notice Neptune,⁶ though,
Taming a sea-horse, thought a rarity,   55
Which Claus of Innsbruck⁷ cast in bronze for me.

Soliloquy of the Spanish Cloister⁸

I

Gr-r-r—there go, my heart's abhorrence!
   Water your damned flower-pots, do!
If hate killed men, Brother Lawrence,

Notes

⁵ *favour* token of special regard, such as a ribbon, necklace, or locket.
⁶ *Neptune* the Roman god of the sea (Gk. Poseidon), often depicted in a chariot drawn by sea-horses.
⁷ *Claus of Innsbruck* an imaginary sculptor. Innsbruck was the capitol of the Tyrol in Austria, where the most famous

bronze sculptures are full-life statues adorning the tomb of Emperor Maximilian I that Browning had visited in 1838.
⁸ *title* probably the cloister attached to the Church of Santa Maria Novella in Florence (1279–1360), a church of the Dominican order of friars, and hence the speaker would be a Dominican. The largest chapel in the cloister is the

God's blood, would not mine kill you!
   What? your myrtle-bush wants trimming?   5
    Oh, that rose has prior claims—
   Needs its leaden vase filled brimming?
    Hell dry you up with its flames!

II

At the meal we sit together:
   *Salve tibi!*⁹ I must hear   10
Wise talk of the kind of weather,
    Sort of season, time of year:
Not a plenteous cork-crop: scarcely
   *Dare we hope oak-galls,*¹⁰ *I doubt:*
*What's the Latin name for 'parsley'?*¹¹   15
   What's the Greek name for Swine's Snout?¹²

III

Whew! We'll have our platter burnished,
   Laid with care on our own shelf!
With a fire-new spoon we're furnished,
    And a goblet for ourself,   20
Rinsed like something sacrificial
   Ere 'tis fit to touch our chaps—
Marked with L. for our initial!
   (He-he! There his lily snaps!)

IV

*Saint,*¹³ forsooth! While brown Dolores   25
   Squats outside the Convent bank
With Sanchicha, telling stories,
    Steeping tresses in the tank,
Blue-black, lustrous, thick like horsehairs,
   —Can't I see his dead eye glow,   30
Bright as 'twere a Barbary corsair's?¹⁴
   (That is, if he'd let it show!)

Notes

Spanish Chapel, so named when Eleonora di Toledo (1522–62), wife of Cosimo I de'Medici (1519–74), assigned it to her Spanish courtiers. It was decorated with frescoes by Andrea de Bonaiuto (1343–77). First published in *Bells and Pomegranates, No. III* (Nov. 1842; see n. 1). This poem, called "II. Cloister (Spanish)," was originally part of a pair titled "Camp and Cloister" and was grouped with "I. Camp (French)," later retitled (1849) "Incident of the French Camp."

⁹ *Salve tibi* (Lat. greeting to you), conventional salutation used by monastics. The italics throughout indicate the words of Brother Lawrence.

¹⁰ *oak-galls* fungous growths on oak leaves whose tannin is used in dyeing and making ink.

¹¹ *parsley* the Latin for parsley is *petroselinem.*

¹² *snout* (Lat. *rostrum porcinum:* sow thistle): a member of the dandelion family; in Greek *leontodon:* tooth of the lion; see also Proverbs 11: 22.

¹³ *Saint* when the stem of the lily (a symbol for the Virgin Mary or purity; the symbol of Florence) breaks, Lawrence's brother-friar utters an oath, swearing by "Saint" somebody.

¹⁴ *Barbary corsair* the Barbary (Berber) west coast of North Africa; home to sea-going pirates from the time of the crusades until the nineteenth century.

V

When he finishes refection,
    Knife and fork he never lays
Cross-wise, to my recollection,   35
    As I do, in Jesu's praise.
I the Trinity illustrate,
    Drinking watered orange-pulp—
In three sips the Arian[15] frustrate:
    While he drains his at one gulp.   40

VI

Oh, those melons? If he's able
    We're to have a feast! so nice!
One goes to the Abbot's table,
    All of us get each a slice.
How go on your flowers? None double?   45
    Not one fruit-sort can you spy?
Strange!—And I, too, at such trouble,
    Keep them close-nipped on the sly!

VII

There's a great text in Galatians,[16]
    Once you trip on it, entails   50
Twenty-nine distinct damnations,
    One sure, if another fails:
If I trip him just a-dying,
    Sure of heaven as sure can be,
Spin him round and send him flying   55
    Off to hell, a Manichee?[17]

VIII

Or, my scrofulous French novel[18]
    On grey paper with blunt type!
Simply glance at it, you grovel
    Hand and foot in Belial's[19] gripe: 60

Notes

[15] *Arian* follower of fourth-century heretic Arius, who denied the Trinity by asserting that the Son was created by and was subordinate to the Father.

[16] *Galatians* see Galatians 5: 19–21, a list of seventeen sins (not twenty-nine).

[17] *Manichee* follower of third-century Persian prophet Manes, who held that the world was the site of the battle between equal forces of good and evil. The sect spread widely and was attacked by St Augustine in *Against the Manichees* (397); hence, a general term for heretic.

[18] *novel* sensationalism of some French novels when Browning was publishing, such as Théophile Gauthier's *Mademoiselle de Maupin* (1835). Here it is depicted as having salacious illustrations.

[19] *Belial* (Heb. worthless, wicked), a biblical demon (Deuteronomy 13: 13; and 2 Corinthians 6: 15), one of the princes of hell who seizes lost souls; last of the fallen angels who becomes one of the princes of hell in *Paradise Lost* (1. 490–505). Four such demons (see "Satan" in stanza IX) are painted on the altar wall in the Spanish Chapel, lamenting as Christ calls the dead from Limbo where they have been waiting for him.

If I double down its pages
   At the woeful sixteenth print,
When he gathers his greengages,
   Ope a sieve and slip it in't?

IX

Or, there's Satan!—one might venture   65
   Pledge one's soul to him, yet leave
Such a flaw in the indenture
   As he'd miss till, past retrieve,
Blasted lay that rose-acacia
   We're so proud of! *Hy, Zy, Hine*[20] ...   70
'St, there's Vespers! *Plena gratiâ*
   Ave, Virgo![21] Gr-r-r—you swine!

The Bishop Orders His Tomb at Saint Praxed's Church[22]

ROME, 15–

Vanity, saith the preacher, vanity![23]
Draw round my bed: is Anselm keeping back?
Nephews—sons[24] mine .. ah God, I know not! Well—
She, men would have to be your mother once,
Old Gandolf envied me, so fair she was!   5
What's done is done, and she is dead beside,
Dead long ago, and I am Bishop since,
And as she died so must we die ourselves,
And thence ye may perceive the world's a dream.
Life, how and what is it? As here I lie   10

Notes

[20] *Hy, Zy, Hine* meaning uncertain: perhaps the sound of vesper bells calling to evening prayer, or a medieval curse.

[21] *Virgo* the beginning of the "Hail Mary," the archangel Gabriel's greeting to Mary (Luke 1: 28). The poem's Latin means "full of grace, hail O Virgin," reversing the biblical order.

[22] *title* St Prassede (Lat. Praxedes) was a second-century virgin, the daughter of St Pudens, reputedly converted by St Paul. The basilica housing her remains was built by Pope St Paschal I (d. 824) in 822 on the site of St Praxed's home, according to Murray's nineteenth-century guidebook, a site of peace and security for persecuted martyrs (see lines 13–14). It is decorated with ninth-century mosaics. Although the tomb in the poem is not modelled on one existing tomb, three in the church have features that Browning's bishop orders: the wall-tomb of the Santacroce family (originally a floor tomb) has columns supporting an arch and bas-relief angels over a black basalt sarcophagus (53–54); the tomb of Cardinal Anchero (Pantaléon Anchier de Troyes, 1210–86), by Arnolfo di Cambio (*c.*1240–1310), depicts his recumbent effigy in marble, dressed in mass-vestments, lying on his sarcophagus, held up by seven columns at the front and one at the head and foot (27), covered with a sculpted shroud (89); and the sepulchre of Cardinal Alain Cetine de Taillebour is decorated with classical and Christian motifs, including a tabernacle with a relief of St Praxed (56–62). Browning visited the church in the autumn of 1844. First published in *Hood's Magazine* (Mar. 1845) as "The Tomb at St. Praxed's"; retitled in *Bells and Pomegranates No. VII: Dramatic Romances and Lyrics* (1849), and eventually placed in the second edition of *Men and Women* in *Poetical Works* (1863).

[23] *vanity* Ecclesiastes 1: 2; spoken like a text at the beginning of a sermon. Normally deathbed addresses are commendations, occasions of repentance, and exhortations to amended life, as in John Donne's "Death's Duell" (1631).

[24] *sons* clergy, including bishops, were supposed to be celibate, though many, including popes, had illegitimate children.

In this state-chamber, dying by degrees,
Hours and long hours in the dead night, I ask
'Do I live, am I dead?' Peace, peace seems all.
Saint Praxed's ever was the church for peace;
And so, about this tomb of mine. I fought   15
With tooth and nail to save my niche, ye know:
—Old Gandolf cozened me, despite my care;
Shrewd was that snatch from out the corner South
He graced his carrion with, God curse the same!
Yet still my niche is not so cramped but thence   20
One sees the pulpit o' the epistle-side,[25]
And somewhat of the choir,[26] those silent seats,
And up into the aery dome where live
The angels,[27] and a sunbeam's sure to lurk:
And I shall fill my slab of basalt there,   25
And 'neath my tabernacle[28] take my rest,
With those nine columns[29] round me, two and two,
The odd one at my feet where Anselm stands:
Peach-blossom marble[30] all, the rare, the ripe
As fresh-poured red wine of a mighty pulse.   30
—Old Gandolf with his paltry onion-stone,[31]
Put me where I may look at him! True peach,
Rosy and flawless: how I earned the prize![32]
Draw close: that conflagration of my church
—What then? So much was saved if aught were missed!   35
My sons, ye would not be my death? Go dig
The white-grape vineyard where the oil-press stood,
Drop water gently till the surface sink,
And if ye find .. Ah God, I know not, I! ..
Bedded in store of rotten fig-leaves soft,   40
And corded up in a tight olive-frail,[33]
Some lump, ah God, of *lapis lazuli*,[34]
Big as a Jew's head cut off at the nape,[35]
Blue as a vein o'er the Madonna's breast ..
Sons, all have I bequeathed you, villas, all,   45
That brave Frascati[36] villa with its bath,

Notes

[25] *epistle-side* right (south) side of the church where the epistles of the New Testament are read during Mass.

[26] *choir* chancel; area in a church at the east end of the nave, for the singers and clergy, and just outside the sanctuary housing the altar.

[27] *angels* in the chapel of St Zeno in St Prassede's, the golden ninth-century mosaics on the dome show four angels holding up an image of Christ.

[28] *tabernacle* stone canopy over a tomb. See n. 22.

[29] *columns* see Exodus 25–27. See n. 2.

[30] *marble* peach-blossom was a more expensive marble with coloured veins running through it, often used in columns in Renaissance churches for decorative purposes.

[31] *onion-stone* less expensive greenish marble that curls off in layers, called *cipollino*.

[32] *prize* see Philippians 3: 14.

[33] *olive-frail* rush basket for packing olives.

[34] *lapis lazuli* (Lat. *lapis*, stone and Persian for Lazvard, where it was originally mined in modern Afghanistan) deep blue semi-precious stone from which the word "azure" derives; used from ancient times for jewellery, decoration, an aphrodisiac, and ground for the blue colour, more costly than gold, in medieval manuscripts.

[35] *nape* possibly a reference to the severed head of John the Baptist; see Mark 6: 21–29.

[36] *Frascati* town in the Alban Hills fifteen miles south east of Rome; site of expensive villas.

So, let the blue lump poise between my knees,
Like God the Father's globe on both his hands
Ye worship in the Jesu Church[37] so gay,
For Gandolf shall not choose but see and burst!   50
Swift as a weaver's shuttle fleet our years:
Man goeth to the grave, and where is he?[38]
Did I say basalt for my slab, sons? Black—
'Twas ever antique-black[39] I meant! How else
Shall ye contrast my frieze to come beneath?   55
The bas-relief in bronze ye promised me,
Those Pans and Nymphs ye wot of, and perchance
Some tripod, thyrsus, with a vase[40] or so,
The Saviour at his sermon on the mount,[41]
Saint Praxed in a glory,[42] and one Pan   60
Ready to twitch the Nymph's last garment off,
And Moses with the tables[43] .. but I know
Ye mark me not! What do they whisper thee,
Child of my bowels,[44] Anselm? Ah, ye hope
To revel down my villas while I gasp   65
Bricked o'er with beggar's mouldy travertine[45]
Which Gandolf from his tomb-top chuckles at!
Nay, boys, ye love me—all of jasper,[46] then!
'Tis jasper ye stand pledged to, lest I grieve
My bath must needs be left behind, alas!   70
One block, pure green as a pistachio-nut,
There's plenty jasper somewhere in the world
And have I not Saint Praxed's ear to pray
Horses for ye, and brown Greek manuscripts,[47]
And mistresses with great smooth marbly limbs?   75
—That's if ye carve my epitaph aright,
Choice Latin, picked phrase, Tully's every word,
No gaudy ware like Gandolf's second line—
Tully, my masters? Ulpian[48] serves his need!
And then how I shall lie through centuries,   80
And hear the blessed mutter of the mass,

Notes

[37] *Church* Church of the Gesù is the mother church of the Jesuit Order in Rome, built 1568–84. Above the altar in the chapel of St Ignatius Loyola (1491–1556), founder of the Jesuits, is a sculpture of the Trinity by Andrea Pozzo (1642–1709), with a large lapis lazuli globe, reputed to be the largest in the world, between the Son and the Father.

[38] *Swift … he* see Job 7: 6; and Job 21: 13.

[39] *antique-black* (It. *nero antico*) blackest of all marbles, darker than black basalt that looks grey beside it, and hence more expensive.

[40] *Pans … vase* the bronze bas-relief is a flat sculpture in low or shallow detail, often used on tombs and their enclosures to depict the life of the person commemorated. Classical figures such as Pan, the god of the pastures, shepherds, and flocks and nymphs, minor deities of the forests – all erotic – were sometimes depicted on Roman sarcophagi. A tripod is a three-legged stool on which the

Oracle of Delphi sat to deliver prophesies; a thyrsus was a staff carried by followers of Dionysus, god of wine and fertility; vases, holding grain or wine, often depicted scenes from Greek mythology, and urns depict mortality. See n. 22.

[41] *mount* see Matthew 5–7.

[42] *glory* St Praxed is surrounded by an almond-shaped halo or vesica, a set of flames, called a mandorla.

[43] *tables* the Ten Commandments or decalogue; see Exodus 20: 2–17; Deuteronomy 5: 6–21.

[44] *bowels* see 2 Samuel 16: 11.

[45] *travertine* limestone.

[46] *jasper* kind of quartz; see Revelation 21: 18–21.

[47] *manuscripts* when Constantinople fell in 1453, many manuscripts of Greek authors on darkened vellum came into Italy, a major factor in the Renaissance recovery of Greek.

And see God made and eaten all day long,[49]
And feel the steady candle-flame, and taste
Good strong thick stupefying incense-smoke!
For as I lie here, hours of the dead night,   85
Dying in state and by such slow degrees,
I fold my arms as if they clasped a crook,[50]
And stretch my feet forth straight as stone can point,
And let the bedclothes, for a mortcloth,[51] drop
Into great laps and folds of sculptor's-work: 90
And as yon tapers dwindle, and strange thoughts
Grow, with a certain humming in my ears,
About the life before I lived this life,
And this life too, popes, cardinals and priests,
Saint Praxed at his sermon on the mount,[52]   95
Your tall pale mother with her talking eyes,
And new-found agate urns as fresh as day,
And marble's language, Latin pure, discreet,
—Aha, ELUSCEBAT[53] quoth our friend?
No Tully, said I, Ulpian at the best!   100
Evil and brief hath been my pilgrimage.[54]
All *lapis*, all, sons! Else I give the Pope
My villas! Will ye ever eat my heart?
Ever your eyes were as a lizard's quick,
They glitter like your mother's for my soul,   105
Or ye would heighten my impoverished frieze,
Piece out its starved design, and fill my vase
With grapes, and add a vizor and a Term,[55]
And to the tripod ye would tie a lynx[56]
That in his struggle throws the thyrsus down,   110
To comfort me on my entablature[57]
Whereon I am to lie till I must ask
'Do I live, am I dead?' There, leave me, there!
For ye have stabbed me with ingratitude
To death—ye wish it—God, ye wish it! Stone—   115
Gritstone,[58] a-crumble! Clammy squares which sweat
As if the corpse they keep were oozing through—
And no more *lapis* to delight the world!
Well go! I bless ye. Fewer tapers there,
But in a row: and, going, turn your backs   120

Notes

[48] *Tully ... Ulpian* Marcus Tullius Cicero (106–43 BCE), Latin orator and rhetorician, was considered by Renaissance thinkers to be the model of Latin eloquence; Ulpian, Domitius Ulpianus (*c.*170–228), Roman jurist and writer, was thought to be an inferior model of Latin prose.

[49] *God ... long* transubstantiation; the conversion of bread and wine into the body and blood of Christ.

[50] *crook* bishop's crozier or pastoral staff.

[51] *mortcloth* funeral pall spread over a coffin. See n. 22 for shroud.

[52] *mount* the bishop misidentifies Praxed for Jesus as the speaker, and refers to her as male ("his sermon"); see n. 42.

[53] ELUSCEBAT (Lat. he was illustrious): Ciceronian Latin ("Tully") would be *elucebat*. See n. 49.

[54] *pilgrimage* see Genesis 47: 9.

[55] *Term* square pillar with a bust of Terminus, Roman god of boundaries.

[56] *lynx* associated with Dionysus. See also n. 41.

[57] *entablature* part of the mouldings above columns in classical architecture that support the roof; the bishop means "entablement," a platform supporting a statue.

[58] *gritstone* inexpensive sandstone.

—Ay, like departing altar-ministrants,
And leave me in my church, the church for peace,
That I may watch at leisure if he leers—
Old Gandolf, at me, from his onion-stone,
As still he envied me, so fair she was!   125

Meeting at Night[59]

I

The grey sea and the long black land;
And the yellow half-moon large and low;
And the startled little waves that leap
In fiery ringlets from their sleep,
As I gain the cove with pushing prow,   5
And quench its speed i' the slushy sand.

II

Then a mile of warm sea-scented beach;
Three fields to cross till a farm appears;
A tap at the pane, the quick sharp scratch
And blue spurt of a lighted match,   10
And a voice less loud, thro' its joys and fears,
Than the two hearts beating each to each!

Parting at Morning

Round the cape of a sudden came the sea,
And the sun looked over the mountain's rim:
And straight was a path of gold for him,   15
And the need of a world of men for me.

Love Among the Ruins[60]

I

Where the quiet-coloured end of evening smiles,
      Miles and miles
On the solitary pastures where our sheep
      Half-asleep

Notes

[59] *title* first published in *Bells and Pomegranates No. VII: Dramatic Romances and Lyrics* (1849); the two parts of the poem were originally titled "I. Night" and "II. Morning"; retitled in *Poems* (1849).

[60] *title* first published as the opening poem of *Men and Women* (1855); it was printed as fourteen stanzas of six lines each; the stanzas were combined into seven stanzas of twelve lines each in *Poetical Works* (6 vols, 1868).

Tinkle homeward thro' the twilight, stray or stop 5
    As they crop—
Was the site once of a city great and gay,[61]
    (So they say)
Of our country's very capital, its prince
    Ages since 10
Held his court in, gathered councils, wielding far
    Peace or war.

II

Now—the country does not even boast a tree,
    As you see,
To distinguish slopes of verdure, certain rills 15
    From the hills
Intersect and give a name to, (else they run
    Into one)
Where the domed and daring palace shot its spires
    Up like fires 20
O'er the hundred-gated[62] circuit of a wall
    Bounding all
Made of marble, men might march on nor be prest
    Twelve abreast.

III

And such plenty and perfection, see, of grass 25
    Never was!
Such a carpet as, this summer-time, o'erspreads
    And embeds
Every vestige of the city, guessed alone,
    Stock or stone— 30
Where a multitude of men breathed joy and woe
    Long ago;
Lust of glory pricked their hearts up, dread of shame
    Struck them tame;
And that glory and that shame alike, the gold 35
    Bought and sold.

Notes

[61] *great and gay* see Spenser, *Ruines of Time* (1591): "All that in this world is great or gay, / Doth as a vapour vanish and decay" (55–56).

[62] *hundred-gated* Babylon and particularly Thebes in Egypt were reputed to have had 100 gates (see, for instance, *Iliad* 9: 391). The poem refers directly to the flat land of the Roman Campagna and to the ancient history of the Roman Empire. However, the references to gates, gold, warriors, kings, and capital cities suggest contemporary layers from other empires, especially those of Babylon and Assyria (capital at Nineveh). Nineveh was excavated by Sir Austen Henry Layard (1817–94) in 1845, and Babylon in 1849. Layard began to publish his archaeological records, *Nineveh and its Remains* (1848–49), and his treasures began to be placed in the British Museum.

IV

Now,—the single little turret that remains
    On the plains,
By the caper over-rooted, by the gourd
    Overscored,   40
While the patching houseleek's head of blossom winks
    Through the chinks—
Marks the basement whence a tower in ancient time
    Sprang sublime,
And a burning ring, all round, the chariots traced   45
    As they raced,
And the monarch and his minions and his dames
    Viewed the games.

V

And I know, while thus the quiet-coloured eve
    Smiles to leave   50
To their folding, all our many-tinkling fleece
    In such peace,
And the slopes and rills in undistinguished grey
    Melt away—
That a girl with eager eyes and yellow hair   55
    Waits me there
In the turret whence the charioteers caught soul
    For the goal,
When the king looked, where she looks now, breathless, dumb
    Till I come.   60

VI

But he looked upon the city, every side,
    Far and wide,
All the mountains topped with temples, all the glades'
    Colonnades,
All the causeys, bridges, aqueducts,—and then   65
    All the men!
When I do come, she will speak not, she will stand,
    Either hand
On my shoulder, give her eyes the first embrace
    Of my face,   70
Ere we rush, ere we extinguish sight and speech
    Each on each.

VII

In one year they sent a million fighters forth
    South and North,
And they built their gods a brazen pillar[63] high   75
    As the sky,

Notes —————————————————————————————

[63] *pillar* possibly the Tower of Babel (Genesis 11) in Babylon.

Yet reserved a thousand chariots in full force—
    Gold, of course.
Oh heart! oh blood that freezes, blood that burns!
    Earth's returns   80
For whole centuries of folly, noise and sin!
    Shut them in,
With their triumphs and their glories and the rest!
    Love is best.

Fra Lippo Lippi[64]

I am poor brother Lippo, by your leave!
You need not clap your torches to my face.
Zooks,[65] what's to blame? you think you see a monk!
What, 'tis past midnight, and you go the rounds,
And here you catch me at an alley's end   5
Where sportive ladies leave their doors ajar?
The Carmine's[66] my cloister: hunt it up,
Do,—harry out, if you must show your zeal,
Whatever rat, there, haps on his wrong hole,
And nip each softling of a wee white mouse,   10
Weke, weke, that's crept to keep him company!
Aha, you know your betters! Then, you'll take
Your hand away that's fiddling on my throat,
And please to know me likewise. Who am I?
Why, one, sir, who is lodging with a friend   15
Three streets off—he's a certain . . how d'ye call?
Master—a . . Cosimo of the Medici,[67]
I' the house[68] that caps the corner. Boh! you were best!
Remember and tell me, the day you're hanged,
How you affected such a gullet's-gripe!   20
But you, sir, it concerns you that your knaves
Pick up a manner nor discredit you:
Zooks, are we pilchards, that they sweep the streets
And count fair prize what comes into their net?
He's Judas[69] to a tittle, that man is!   25

Notes

[64] *title* Brother Filippo Lippi (*c*.1412–69) was a Florentine painter, whose life Browning had read in Georgio Vasari's *Lives of the Painters* (1550), using details noted below. Browning had a copy of the first edition in his library. Lippi has been out on a night's romantic escapade, and is intercepted by the night watch or guards, to whom he speaks. First published in *Men and Women* (1855).

[65] *Zooks* oath; abbreviation of "Gadzooks," a euphemism for swearing by "God's hooks" or the nails of the crucifixion.

[66] *Carmine* convent of Santa Maria del Carmine, home of the Carmelite friars in Florence where Lippi was housed from the age of 8. Its chapel was covered with frescoes by Masaccio (see lines 276–77) that Lippi helped to complete.

[67] *Medici* Cosimo de'Medici, the elder (1389–1464); wealthy banker and politician, founder of the Medici dynasty that ruled Florence until the seventeenth century, including Lorenzo the Magnificent (1449–92), grandson of Cosimo, and three popes (Leo X, Clement VII, and Leo XI). Without holding public office, Cosimo was the real ruler of Florence, and a patron of art and literature.

[68] *house* the Medici family lived in the Palazzo Medici, now the Palazzo Medici-Riccardi, built by Michelozzo between 1444 and 1460. Lippi painted the chapel's altarpiece, now in Berlin.

[69] *Judas* Judas Iscariot, apostle who betrayed Jesus (Matthew 26; and Luke 22).

Just such a face! Why, sir, you make amends.
Lord, I'm not angry! Bid your hang-dogs go
Drink out this quarter-florin[70] to the health
Of the munificent House[71] that harbours me
(And many more beside, lads! more beside!)   30
And all's come square again. I'd like his face—
His, elbowing on his comrade in the door
With the pike and lantern,—for the slave that holds
John Baptist's head[72] a-dangle by the hair
With one hand ('Look you, now,' as who should say)   35
And his weapon in the other, yet unwiped!
It's not your chance to have a bit of chalk,
A wood-coal or the like? or you should see!
Yes, I'm the painter, since you style me so.
What, brother Lippo's doings, up and down,   40
You know them and they take you? like enough!
I saw the proper twinkle in your eye—
'Tell you, I liked your looks at very first.
Let's sit and set things straight now, hip to haunch.
Here's spring come, and the nights one makes up bands   45
To roam the town and sing out carnival,[73]
And I've been three weeks shut within my mew,[74]
A-painting for the great man, saints and saints
And saints again. I could not paint all night—
Ouf! I leaned out of window for fresh air.   50
There came a hurry of feet and little feet,
A sweep of lute-strings, laughs, and whifts of song,—
Flower o' the broom,
Take away love, and our earth is a tomb!
Flower o' the quince,   55
I let Lisa go, and what good in life since?
Flower o' the thyme[75]—and so on. Round they went.
Scarce had they turned the corner when a titter
Like the skipping of rabbits by moonlight,—three slim shapes,
And a face that looked up .. zooks, sir, flesh and blood,   60
That's all I'm made of! Into shreds it went,
Curtain and counterpane and coverlet,
All the bed-furniture—a dozen knots,
There was a ladder! Down I let myself,
Hands and feet, scrambling somehow, and so dropped,   65

Notes

[70] *florin* gold coin minted at Florence (hence, the name) from 1252, becoming the basis of the banking economy of western Europe in which the Florentine bankers, especially the Medici, predominated. The coin showed the lily or *fleur de lys* of Florence on one side (see lines 350, 385) and on the other, Florence's patron saint, John the Baptist.

[71] *House* Lippi refers to the Medici family or dynasty and its entourage of which he was a part; see above n. 67.

[72] *head* Lippi painted a series of frescoes (1452–66) of the life of John the Baptist for Prato Cathedral, including a decapitation, for which Lippi in the poem suggests one of the guards was a model for a servant holding St John's head.

[73] *carnival* period of festivities of drinking and masquerades before Ash Wednesday and Lent. In Italy it lasted at least a month, and in some places from St Stephen's Day (Dec. 26), longer than the northern Mardi Gras or parades for Shrove Tuesday on the weekend before Lent begins.

[74] *mew* cage, confinement in the Medici palace.

[75] *thyme* popular Italian folk verse form called the *stornello*, consisting of a short line with the name of a flower, followed by a longer line of eleven syllables (ten in Browning).

And after them. I came up with the fun
Hard by Saint Laurence,[76] hail fellow, well met,—
Flower o' the rose,
If I've been merry, what matter who knows?
And so as I was stealing back again   70
To get to bed and have a bit of sleep
Ere I rise up to-morrow and go work
On Jerome[77] knocking at his poor old breast
With his great round stone to subdue the flesh,
You snap me of the sudden. Ah, I see!   75
Though your eye twinkles still, you shake your head—
Mine's shaved[78]—a monk, you say—the sting's in that!
If Master Cosimo announced himself,
Mum's the word naturally; but a monk!
Come, what am I a beast for? tell us, now!   80
I was a baby when my mother died
And father died and left me in the street.
I starved there, God knows how, a year or two
On fig-skins, melon-parings, rinds and shucks,
Refuse and rubbish. One fine frosty day,   85
My stomach being empty as your hat,
The wind doubled me up and down I went.
Old Aunt Lapaccia[79] trussed me with one hand,
(Its fellow was a stinger as I knew)
And so along the wall, over the bridge,   90
By the straight cut to the convent. Six words there,
While I stood munching my first bread that month:
'So, boy, you're minded,' quoth the good fat father
Wiping his own mouth, 'twas refection-time,[80]—
'To quit this very miserable world?   95
Will you renounce' .. 'the mouthful of bread?' thought I;
By no means! Brief, they made a monk of me;
I did renounce the world, its pride and greed,
Palace, farm, villa, shop and banking-house,
Trash, such as these poor devils of Medici   100
Have given their hearts to—all at eight years old.
Well, sir, I found in time, you may be sure,
'Twas not for nothing—the good bellyful,
The warm serge and the rope that goes all round,
And day-long blessed idleness beside!   105

Notes

[76] *Laurence* Church of San Lorenzo, near the Palazzo Medici, designed by Filippo Brunelleschi (1377–1446) and largely financed by the Medici family (1419–69).

[77] *Jerome* St Jerome (c.340–420), translator of the Bible and ascetic, often depicted as a cardinal. The painting referred to is probably the *Annalena Adoration of the Infant Jesus* (c.1450) that includes a kneeling St Jerome in penitence beating his breast with a stone. It was in the Academy in Florence when Browning lived there. Lippi also painted a number of other studies of Jerome.

[78] *shaved* the shaved dome of the head, known as a tonsure, was given to a monk or friar when they professed their vows of poverty, chastity, and obedience.

[79] *Lapaccia* according to Vasari, Lippi was left an orphan at 2 years of age and was raised by his aunt, Mona Lapaccia, his father's sister, to the age of 8, who then placed him with the Carmelite friars.

[80] *refection-time* meal time, taken in the refectory.

'Let's see what the urchin's fit for'—that came next.
Not overmuch their way, I must confess.
Such a to-do! They tried me with their books:
Lord, they'd have taught me Latin in pure waste!
Flower o' the clove.   110
All the Latin I construe is, 'amo' I love!
But, mind you, when a boy starves in the streets
Eight years together, as my fortune was,
Watching folk's faces to know who will fling
The bit of half-stripped grape-bunch he desires,   115
And who will curse or kick him for his pains,—
Which gentleman processional and fine,
Holding a candle to the Sacrament,[81]
Will wink and let him lift a plate and catch
The droppings of the wax to sell again,   120
Or holla for the Eight[82] and have him whipped,—
How say I?—nay, which dog bites, which lets drop
His bone from the heap of offal in the street,—
Why, soul and sense of him grow sharp alike,
He learns the look of things, and none the less   125
For admonition from the hunger-pinch.
I had a store of such remarks, be sure,
Which, after I found leisure, turned to use.
I drew men's faces on my copy-books,
Scrawled them within the antiphonary's marge,   130
Joined legs and arms to the long music-notes,[83]
Found eyes and nose and chin for A's and B's,
And made a string of pictures of the world
Betwixt the ins and outs of verb and noun,
On the wall, the bench, the door. The monks looked black.   135
'Nay,' quoth the Prior, 'turn him out, d'ye say?
In no wise. Lose a crow and catch a lark.
What if at last we get our man of parts,
We Carmelites, like those Camaldolese
And Preaching Friars,[84] to do our church up fine   140
And put the front on it that ought to be!'
And hereupon he bade me daub away.
Thank you! my head being crammed, the walls a blank,
Never was such prompt disemburdening.

Notes

[81] *Sacrament* some members of Florentine noble families joined charitable confraternities, such as the Confraternity of the Most Holy Sacrament, that carried the Eucharist in candlelit processions wearing special robes that concealed their identities.

[82] *Eight* the Council of Eight, a group of powerful magistrates responsible for security in Renaissance Florence.

[83] *music-notes* Lippi drew faces around the square music notation and in the openings in such letters as A and B, and in the margins of vellum manuscript books that contained the music for church chants, such as antiphons,

verses sung before and after psalms and other music in various monastic services.

[84] *Friars* two of the four orders of mendicant friars are mentioned here: the Carmelites or White Friars (white robes and cloak), and the Order of Friars Preachers (Dominicans) or Black Friars, named for their black cloaks over white robes (including Fra Angelico); missing are the Franciscans (Grey Friars) and the Augustinians (Austin Friars). The Camaldolese are an order of Benedictine monks, wearing black habits, that included Lorenzo Monaco (see lines 234–37 and nn. 95 and 96).

First, every sort of monk, the black and white,[85]   145
I drew them, fat and lean: then, folk at church,
From good old gossips waiting to confess
Their cribs[86] of barrel-droppings, candle-ends,—
To the breathless fellow at the altar-foot,
Fresh from his murder, safe[87] and sitting there   150
With the little children round him in a row
Of admiration, half for his beard and half
For that white anger of his victim's son
Shaking a fist at him with one fierce arm,
Signing[88] himself with the other because of Christ   155
(Whose sad face on the cross sees only this
After the passion of a thousand years)
Till some poor girl, her apron o'er her head,
(Which the intense eyes looked through) came at eve
On tiptoe, said a word, dropped in a loaf,   160
Her pair of earrings and a bunch of flowers
(The brute took growling), prayed, and so was gone.
I painted all, then cried ''Tis ask and have;
Choose, for more's ready!'—laid the ladder flat,
And showed my covered bit of cloister-wall.   165
The monks closed in a circle and praised loud
Till checked, taught what to see and not to see,
Being simple bodies,—'That's the very man!
Look at the boy who stoops to pat the dog!
That woman's like the Prior's niece[89] who comes   170
To care about his asthma: it's the life!'
But there my triumph's straw-fire flared and funked;[90]
Their betters took their turn to see and say:
The Prior and the learned pulled a face
And stopped all that in no time. 'How? what's here?   175
Quite from the mark of painting, bless us all!
Faces, arms, legs and bodies like the true
As much as pea and pea! it's devil's-game!
Your business is not to catch men with show,
With homage to the perishable clay,   180
But lift them over it, ignore it all,
Make them forget there's such a thing as flesh.
Your business is to paint the souls of men—
Man's soul, and it's a fire, smoke .. no, it's not..
It's vapour done up like a new-born babe—   185
(In that shape when you die it leaves your mouth)[91]
It's .. well, what matters talking, it's the soul!
Give us no more of body than shows soul!

Notes

[85] *black and white* Dominicans and Carmelite habits or robes.
[86] *cribs* petty thefts.
[87] *safe* churches offered sanctuary or safe haven from the civil law, including murderers.
[88] *signing* making the sign of the cross.
[89] *niece* a circumlocution for the Prior's mistress.

[90] *funked* smoked.
[91] *mouth* some medieval and early Renaissance paintings of death scenes show the soul leaving the body as a small baby, as in the fresco of *The Triumph of Death* (anonymous, thirteenth century) in the Camposanto at Pisa that Browning visited.

Here's Giotto,[92] with his Saint a-praising God,
That sets us praising,—why not stop with him?   190
Why put all thoughts of praise out of our head
With wonder at lines, colours, and what not?
Paint the soul, never mind the legs and arms!
Rub all out, try at it a second time.
Oh, that white smallish female with the breasts,   195
She's just my niece .. Herodias,[93] I would say,—
Who went and danced and got men's heads cut off!
Have it all out!' Now, is this sense, I ask?
A fine way to paint soul, by painting body
So ill, the eye can't stop there, must go further   200
And can't fare worse! Thus, yellow does for white
When what you put for yellow's simply black,
And any sort of meaning looks intense
When all beside itself means and looks nought.
Why can't a painter lift each foot in turn,   205
Left foot and right foot, go a double step,
Make his flesh liker and his soul more like,
Both in their order? Take the prettiest face,
The Prior's niece .. patron-saint—is it so pretty
You can't discover if it means hope, fear,   210
Sorrow or joy? won't beauty go with these?
Suppose I've made her eyes all right and blue,
Can't I take breath and try to add life's flash,
And then add soul and heighten them three-fold?
Or say there's beauty with no soul at all—   215
(I never saw it—put the case the same—)
If you get simple beauty and nought else,
You get about the best thing God invents:
That's somewhat: and you'll find the soul you have missed,
Within yourself, when you return him thanks.   220
'Rub all out!' Well, well, there's my life, in short,
And so the thing has gone on ever since.
I'm grown a man no doubt, I've broken bounds:
You should not take a fellow eight years old
And make him swear to never kiss the girls.   225
I'm my own master, paint now as I please—
Having a friend, you see, in the Corner-house!
Lord, it's fast holding by the rings in front—
Those great rings[94] serve more purposes than just

Notes

[92] *Giotto* Giotto di Bondone (*c.*1267–1337), Florentine painter and architect, who broke away from the dominant Byzantine stylizations and painted more realistically in such frescoes as St Francis's *Apparition at Arles* (1319–28), in the Church of Santa Croce, Florence, a possible model for the scene referred to.

[93] *Herodias* see Matthew 14. John the Baptist had preached against Herodias (*c.*15 BCE–39 CE) who had married her brother-in-law, Herod (Mark 6: 17). Her daughter, Salome, pleased Herod with her dancing and was granted the Baptist's head as a reward. Vasari mixes up the mother and daughter. Lippi painted frescoes of the life of St John the Baptist in the cathedral of Prato, including the *Feast of Herod*, with *The Dance of Salome* and *The Presentation of the Baptist's Head* (1460–64).

[94] *rings* still existing in the Palazzo Medici, they were also used for torture, and possibly for Lippi's escape from his house-confinement.

To plant a flag in, or tie up a horse!   230
And yet the old schooling sticks, the old grave eyes
Are peeping o'er my shoulder as I work,
The heads shake still—'It's art's decline, my son!
You're not of the true painters, great and old;
Brother Angelico's[95] the man, you'll find;   235
Brother Lorenzo[96] stands his single peer:
Fag[97] on at flesh, you'll never make the third!'
Flower o' the pine,
You keep your mistr . . manners, and I'll stick to mine!
I'm not the third, then: bless us, they must know!   240
Don't you think they're the likeliest to know,
They with their Latin? So, I swallow my rage,
Clench my teeth, suck my lips in tight, and paint
To please them—sometimes do and sometimes don't;
For, doing most, there's pretty sure to come   245
A turn, some warm eve finds me at my saints—
A laugh, a cry, the business of the world—
(*Flower o' the peach,*
Death for us all, and his own life for each!)
And my whole soul revolves, the cup runs over,[98]   250
The world and life's too big to pass for a dream,
And I do these wild things in sheer despite,
And play the fooleries you catch me at,
In pure rage! The old mill-horse, out at grass
After hard years, throws up his stiff heels so,   255
Although the miller does not preach to him
The only good of grass is to make chaff.[99]
What would men have? Do they like grass or no—
May they or mayn't they? all I want's the thing
Settled for ever one way. As it is,   260
You tell too many lies and hurt yourself:
You don't like what you only like too much,
You do like what, if given you at your word,
You find abundantly detestable.
For me, I think I speak as I was taught;   265
I always see the garden and God there
A-making man's wife: and, my lesson learned,
The value and significance of flesh,
I can't unlearn ten minutes afterwards.

You understand me: I'm a beast, I know.   270
But see, now—why, I see as certainly
As that the morning-star's about to shine,

Notes

[95] *Angelico* so named for the spiritual quality of his painting, Fra Giovanni de Fiesole (1387–1455), was a Dominican painter in Florence influenced by the International Gothic style but also embodying early Renaissance emphasis upon realistic moulding of the human body, unlike the even more realistic style of Lippi.

[96] *Lorenzo* Lorenzo Monaco (c.1370–1425) was a Florentine painter and Camaldolese monk (see n. 84); even more than Angelico, he painted in the International Gothic style.

[97] *fag* toil.

[98] *over* see Psalms 23: 5.

[99] *grass ... chaff* for grass, see 1 Peter 1: 24; for chaff, see Matthew 3: 12.

What will hap some day. We've a youngster here
Comes to our convent, studies what I do,
Slouches and stares and lets no atom drop: 275
His name is Guidi—he'll not mind the monks—
They call him Hulking Tom,[100] he lets them talk—
He picks my practice up—he'll paint apace.
I hope so—though I never live so long,
I know what's sure to follow. You be judge! 280
You speak no Latin more than I, belike;
However, you're my man, you've seen the world
—The beauty and the wonder and the power,
The shapes of things, their colours, lights and shades,
Changes, surprises,—and God made it all! 285
—For what? Do you feel thankful, ay or no,
For this fair town's face, yonder river's line,
The mountain round it and the sky above,
Much more the figures of man, woman, child,
These are the frame to? What's it all about? 290
To be passed over, despised? or dwelt upon,
Wondered at? oh, this last of course!—you say.
But why not do as well as say,—paint these
Just as they are, careless what comes of it?
God's works—paint any one, and count it crime 295
To let a truth slip. Don't object, 'His works
Are here already; nature is complete:
Suppose you reproduce her'—(which you can't)
'There's no advantage! you must beat her, then.'
For, don't you mark? we're made so that we love 300
First when we see them painted, things we have passed
Perhaps a hundred times nor cared to see;
And so they are better, painted—better to us,
Which is the same thing. Art was given for that;
God uses us to help each other so, 305
Lending our minds out. Have you noticed, now,
Your cullion's hanging face? A bit of chalk,
And trust me but you should, though! How much more,
If I drew higher things with the same truth!
That were to take the Prior's pulpit-place, 310
Interpret God to all of you! Oh, oh,
It makes me mad to see what men shall do
And we in our graves! This world's no blot for us,
Nor blank; it means intensely, and means good:
To find its meaning is my meat and drink. 315
'Ay, but you don't so instigate to prayer!'
Strikes in the Prior: 'when your meaning's plain
It does not say to folk—remember matins,
Or, mind you fast next Friday!' Why, for this

Notes

[100] *Tom* Tommaso Guidi, known as Masaccio (1401–28), was actually Lippi's teacher. His major works are the frescoes in the Brancacci chapel of the Carmine, on which Lippi was an assistant. Browning was following Vasari. In Italian the suffix "accio" signifies a large person: hence, the abbreviation of Tommasaccio to "Masaccio."

What need of art at all? A skull and bones,   320
Two bits of stick nailed crosswise, or, what's best,
A bell to chime the hour with, does as well.
I painted a Saint Laurence[101] six months since
At Prato, splashed the fresco in fine style:
'How looks my painting, now the scaffold's down?'   325
I ask a brother: 'Hugely,' he returns—
'Already not one phiz[102] of your three slaves
Who turn the Deacon off his toasted side,
But's scratched and prodded to our heart's content,
The pious people have so eased their own   330
With coming to say prayers there in a rage:
We get on fast to see the bricks beneath.
Expect another job this time next year,
For pity and religion grow i' the crowd—
Your painting serves its purpose!' Hang the fools!   335

    That is—you'll not mistake an idle word
Spoke in a huff by a poor monk, God wot,[103]
Tasting the air this spicy night which turns
The unaccustomed head like Chianti wine!
Oh, the church knows! don't misreport me, now!   340
It's natural a poor monk out of bounds
Should have his apt word to excuse himself:
And hearken how I plot to make amends.
I have bethought me: I shall paint a piece
. . There's for you! Give me six months, then go, see   345
Something in Sant' Ambrogio's![104] Bless the nuns!
They want a cast o' my office.[105] I shall paint
God in the midst, Madonna and her babe[106]
Ringed by a bowery flowery angel-brood,
Lilies and vestments and white faces, sweet   350
As puff on puff of grated orris-root[107]
When ladies crowd to Church at midsummer.
And then i' the front, of course a saint or two—
Saint John,[108] because he saves the Florentines,
Saint Ambrose,[109] who puts down in black and white   355

Notes

[101] *Laurence* St Laurence (*c.*225–58), deacon of Rome, was martyred by being burned on a gridiron. Legend has it he asked to be turned over (328). Although Lippi did at least two paintings of Laurence, they are not in Prato, a city in Tuscany, 23 km. from Florence. Instead, a painting of *The Martyrdom of St. Laurence* by Mario Balassi and Carlo Dolci (mid-seventeenth century) in the Cathedral at Prato does show him being roasted by three servants.

[102] *phiz* face.

[103] *wot* knows.

[104] *Ambrogio* convent in Florence. Lippi painted *Coronation of the Virgin* (1441–47) for the main altar of San Ambrogio. It was in the Academy in Florence when Browning was there; now in the Uffizi Gallery, Florence. See https://artsy.net/artwork/fra-filippo-lippi-coronation-of-the-virgin.

[105] *office* sample of my work.

[106] *babe* although Lippi painted many works of the Madonna, such as *Madonna and Child with Angels* (1457–65), there is no infant Jesus in the *Coronation*.

[107] *orris-root* from some species of the iris; used in perfumes.

[108] *John* John the Baptist, on the left margin of the painting, is the patron saint of Florence; the famous Baptistry outside the cathedral where all Florentine children were baptized is dedicated to him.

[109] *Ambrose* (*c.*338–97), patron of "Sant' Ambrogio's" (see above, line 346), one of the original four fathers of the church; standing on left side of the *Coronation*.

The convent's friends and gives them a long day,
And Job, I must have him there past mistake,
The man of Uz (and Us without the z,
Painters who need his patience).[110] Well, all these
Secured at their devotion, up shall come   360
Out of a corner when you least expect,
As one by a dark stair into a great light,
Music and talking, who but Lippo! I!—
Mazed, motionless and moonstruck—I'm the man!
Back I shrink—what is this I see and hear?   365
I, caught up with my monk's-things by mistake,
My old serge gown and rope that goes all round,
I, in this presence, this pure company!
Where's a hole, where's a corner for escape?
Then steps a sweet angelic slip[111] of a thing   370
Forward, puts out a soft palm—'Not so fast!'
—Addresses the celestial presence, 'nay—
He made you and devised you, after all,
Though he's none of you! Could Saint John there draw—
His camel-hair make up a painting-brush?[112]   375
We come to brother Lippo for all that,
Iste perfecit opus!'[113] So, all smile—
I shuffle sideways with my blushing face
Under the cover of a hundred wings
Thrown like a spread of kirtles[114] when you're gay   380
And play hot cockles,[115] all the doors being shut,
Till, wholly unexpected, in there pops
The hothead husband! Thus I scuttle off
To some safe bench behind, not letting go
The palm of her, the little lily thing   385
That spoke the good word for me in the nick,
Like the Prior's niece .. Saint Lucy,[116] I would say.
And so all's saved for me, and for the church
A pretty picture gained. Go, six months hence!
Your hand, sir, and good-bye: no lights, no lights!   390
The street's hushed, and I know my own way back,
Don't fear me! There's the grey beginning. Zooks!

Notes

[110] *Job ... Uz ... patience* see Job 1: 1; Job remains faithful to God despite being tested by Satan. Uz was the name of Job's city; Job is identified by name on the left of the kneeling bishop (St Martin) in the front row of Lippi's *Coronation*.

[111] *slip* perhaps the model for the angel standing with arm outstretched towards the Virgin in Lippi's *Coronation*; or, alternatively, for the figure of Theophista, seated and looking out of the painting, with her two children and husband, St Eustace.

[112] *brush* John the Baptist wore a camel-hair shirt (Matthew 3: 4); Lippi is here speaking again of the guard as a potential model (see lines 31–4). Camel-hair brushes, expensive and good quality, are actually made of other types of hair.

[113] *opus* (Lat. this man completed the work); in Lippi's *Coronation*, an angel is holding a scroll with this inscription in front of Canon Francesco Maringhi, who commissioned the painting ("this man enabled the work"). Browning mistakenly believed the figure represented the painter himself; in fact, Lippo is at the left of the painting, leaning on his elbow.

[114] *kirtles* skirts.

[115] *cockles* a double entendre, meaning both a game involving touching, played blindfolded, and, and a euphemism for sexual intercourse.

[116] *Lucy* St Lucy of Syracuse (283–304), virgin martyr, the patron saint of the blind and of sight. Lippi's *St. Lucy* (1472–74) is in the Cathedral Museum in Prato.

WEB p. 346

"Childe Roland to the Dark Tower Came"

Andrea del Sarto

(Called "The Faultless Painter")[117]

But do not let us quarrel any more,
No, my Lucrezia;[118] bear with me for once:
Sit down and all shall happen as you wish.
You turn your face, but does it bring your heart?
I'll work then for your friend's friend, never fear,   5
Treat his own subject after his own way,
Fix his own time, accept too his own price,
And shut the money into this small hand
When next it takes mine. Will it? tenderly?
Oh, I'll content him,—but to-morrow, Love!   10
I often am much wearier than you think,
This evening more than usual, and it seems
As if—forgive now—should you let me sit
Here by the window with your hand in mine
And look a half-hour forth on Fiesole,[119]   15
Both of one mind, as married people use,
Quietly, quietly the evening through,
I might get up to-morrow to my work
Cheerful and fresh as ever. Let us try.
To-morrow, how you shall be glad for this!   20
Your soft hand is a woman of itself,
And mine the man's bared breast she curls inside.
Don't count the time lost, neither; you must serve
For each of the five pictures we require:
It saves a model. So! keep looking so—   25
My serpentining beauty, rounds on rounds!
—How could you ever prick those perfect ears,

Notes

[117] *title* Andrea (1486–1531) was a Florentine painter, the son of a tailor, and hence his name "del Sarto." Giorgio Vasari (see n. 64), wrote that his figures are "entirely free from errors and perfect in all their proportions"; Anna Jameson, a friend of the Brownings, in *Memoirs of the Early Italian Painters* (1845), wrote, "He attained so much excellence that he was called in his own time 'Andrea senza errori,' that is, Andrea *the Faultless*." Browning follows Vasari in placing Andrea in the second rank of his contemporaries in the first quarter of the sixteenth century, after Leonardo da Vinci, Raphael, and Michelangelo. First printed in *Men and Women* (1855) where it was the first poem in the second volume. In the second edition of *Men and Women* (1863) it was paired with "Fra Lippo Lippi."

[118] *Lucrezia* Andrea married Lucrezia del Fede (*c.*1490–1570) in 1517. According to Vasari she was the model for all of his female portraits (see lines 23–25). The poem suggests that the quarrel was over Lucrezia's demand that Andrea refuse the request of Francis I (see n. 126) to return to paint in France. A painting in the Pitti Palace in Florence attributed to Andrea del Sarto in the nineteenth century (*Portrait of a Man and a Woman*) shows a woman holding a letter and gazing out of the canvas, while the man looks at her, puts his arm around her shoulder, and indicates the letter – perhaps prompting the poem. See http://www.florin.ms/AndreaSarto.html.

[119] *Fiesole* a small hill-town overlooking Florence.

Even to put the pearl there! oh, so sweet—
My face, my moon, my everybody's moon,[120]
Which everybody looks on and calls his,   30
And, I suppose, is looked on by in turn,
While she looks—no one's: very dear, no less.
You smile? why, there's my picture ready made,
There's what we painters call our harmony!
A common greyness silvers[121] everything,—   35
All in a twilight, you and I alike
—You, at the point of your first pride in me
(That's gone you know),—but I, at every point;
My youth, my hope, my art, being all toned down
To yonder sober pleasant Fiesole.   40
There's the bell clinking from the chapel-top;
That length of convent-wall[122] across the way
Holds the trees safer, huddled more inside;
The last monk leaves the garden; days decrease,
And autumn grows, autumn in everything.   45
Eh? the whole seems to fall into a shape
As if I saw alike my work and self
And all that I was born to be and do,
A twilight-piece.[123] Love, we are in God's hand.
How strange now, looks the life he makes us lead;   50
So free we seem, so fettered fast we are!
I feel he laid the fetter: let it lie!
This chamber for example—turn your head—
All that's behind us! You don't understand
Nor care to understand about my art,   55
But you can hear at least when people speak:
And that cartoon,[124] the second from the door
—It is the thing, Love! so such things should be—
Behold Madonna!—I am bold to say.
I can do with my pencil what I know,   60
What I see, what at bottom of my heart
I wish for, if I ever wish so deep—
Do easily, too—when I say, perfectly,
I do not boast, perhaps: yourself are judge,
Who listened to the Legate's[125] talk last week,   65

Notes

[120] *moon* possible echo of the description of Cleopatra in Dryden's *All for Love* (1678): "Your Cleopatra; / Dolabella's Cleopatra; Everyman's Cleopatra" (4. 1. 297–98).

[121] *silvers* some of Andrea's paintings show colours painted over a grey or silver ground to give them a shimmering look; possibly a reference to the theory of colour harmony in the nineteenth century, that grey provides a bridge between colours; also an ironic suggestion of spiritual inadequacy (see lines 88–89).

[122] *convent-wall* the convent for the Servite religious order attached to the Church of the Annunciation (1481) in Florence, across the street from Andrea's house. Andrea is buried in the church.

[123] *twilight-piece* genre or type of painting, sometimes called a "night piece," representing moonlight effects, or the light of a lantern.

[124] *cartoon* full-scale drawing for a painting, usually executed in charcoal or crayon. No particular drawing is specified, but perhaps he refers to a cartoon for the contemporary fresco of the *Madonna del Sacco* (1525) in the cloister of the Church of the Annunciation that Vasari praised.

[125] *Legate* papal emissary.

[126] *France* invited to the court of Francis I, king of France (1494–1547), a major patron of Italian Renaissance artists, Andrea spent a year there (1518–19), three years after Francis was crowned.

And just as much they used to say in France.[126]
At any rate 'tis easy, all of it!
No sketches first, no studies, that's long past:
I do what many dream of, all their lives,
—Dream? strive to do, and agonize to do,   70
And fail in doing. I could count twenty such
On twice your fingers, and not leave this town,
Who strive—you don't know how the others strive
To paint a little thing like that you smeared
Carelessly passing with your robes afloat,—   75
Yet do much less, so much less, Someone[127] says,
(I know his name, no matter)—so much less!
Well, less is more, Lucrezia: I am judged.
There burns a truer light of God in them,
In their vexed beating stuffed and stopped-up brain,   80
Heart, or whate'er else, than goes on to prompt
This low-pulsed forthright craftsman's hand of mine.
Their works drop groundward, but themselves, I know,
Reach many a time a heaven that's shut to me,
Enter and take their place there sure enough,   85
Though they come back and cannot tell the world.
My works are nearer heaven, but I sit here.
The sudden blood of these men! at a word—
Praise them, it boils, or blame them, it boils too.
I, painting from myself and to myself,   90
Know what I do, am unmoved by men's blame
Or their praise either. Somebody remarks
Morello's outline[128] there is wrongly traced,
His hue mistaken; what of that? or else,
Rightly traced and well ordered; what of that?   95
Speak as they please, what does the mountain care?
Ah, but a man's reach should exceed his grasp,
Or what's a heaven for? All is silver-grey
Placid and perfect with my art: the worse!
I know both what I want and what might gain,   100
And yet how profitless to know, to sigh
'Had I been two, another and myself,
Our head would have o'erlooked the world!' No doubt.
Yonder's a work now, of that famous youth
The Urbinate[129] who died five years ago.   105
('Tis copied, George Vasari[130] sent it me.)
Well, I can fancy how he did it all,
Pouring his soul, with kings and popes[131] to see,

Notes

[127] *Someone* Michelangelo (see n. 132).

[128] *outline* Morello is the highest mountain in the Appenine range, north of Florence, and visible from the city.

[129] *Urbinate* Raphael (1483–1520) was born in Urbino, near Florence. The reference to Raphael's death as "five years ago" dates the poem as taking place in 1525. The painting being discussed is possibly Raphael's *Pope Leo X with two Cardinals* (1518). His painting is in the Uffizi Gallery in Florence while the copy by Andrea (1525) is in the Museo di Capodimonte in Naples.

[130] *Vasari* Giorgio Vasari (1511–1574), author of the *Lives of the Artists*, was also a painter and architect (of the Uffizi and the Palazzo della Signoria in Florence), in the service of Cosimo de'Medici from 1555.

[131] *popes* Raphael's patrons were Popes Julius II (1443–1513) and Leo X (1475–1521) and Francis I (see n. 126).

Reaching, that heaven might so replenish him,
Above and through his art—for it gives way;   110
That arm is wrongly put—and there again—
A fault to pardon in the drawing's lines,
Its body, so to speak: its soul is right,
He means right—that, a child may understand.
Still, what an arm! and I could alter it: 115
But all the play, the insight and the stretch—
Out of me, out of me! And wherefore out?
Had you enjoined them on me, given me soul,
We might have risen to Rafael, I and you!
Nay, Love, you did give all I asked, I think—   120
More than I merit, yes, by many times.
But had you—oh, with the same perfect brow,
And perfect eyes, and more than perfect mouth,
And the low voice my soul hears, as a bird
The fowler's pipe, and follows to the snare—   125
Had you, with these the same, but brought a mind!
Some women do so. Had the mouth there urged
'God and the glory! never care for gain.
The present by the future, what is that?
Live for fame, side by side with Agnolo![132]   130
Rafael is waiting: up to God, all three!'
I might have done it for you. So it seems:
Perhaps not. All is as God over-rules.
Beside, incentives come from the soul's self;
The rest avail not. Why do I need you?   135
What wife had Rafael, or has Agnolo?
In this world, who can do a thing, will not;
And who would do it, cannot, I perceive:
Yet the will's somewhat—somewhat, too, the power—
And thus we half-men struggle. At the end,   140
God, I conclude, compensates, punishes.
'Tis safer for me, if the award be strict,
That I am something underrated here,
Poor this long while, despised, to speak the truth.
I dared not, do you know, leave home all day,   145
For fear of chancing on the Paris lords.[133]
The best is when they pass and look aside;
But they speak sometimes; I must bear it all.
Well may they speak! That Francis, that first time,
And that long festal year at Fontainebleau![134]   150
I surely then could sometimes leave the ground,
Put on the glory, Rafael's daily wear,

Notes

[132] *Agnolo* Michelangelo Buonarroti (1475–1564), painter, sculptor, and architect.

[133] *lords* according to Vasari, when, at the urging of his wife, Andrea left France in 1519, he was given a large sum of money by Francis I to obtain Florentine art for the king. He squandered the money on "building and pleasures."

[134] *Fontainebleau* Palace of Fontainebleau, west of Paris, famous for its art and gardens, was rebuilt by Francis I.

In that humane great monarch's golden look,—
One finger in his beard or twisted curl
Over his mouth's good mark that made the smile,   155
One arm about my shoulder, round my neck,
The jingle of his gold chain in my ear,
I painting proudly with his breath on me,
All his court round him, seeing with his eyes,
Such frank[135] French eyes, and such a fire of souls   160
Profuse, my hand kept plying by those hearts,—
And, best of all, this, this, this face beyond,
This in the background, waiting on my work,
To crown the issue with a last reward!
A good time, was it not, my kingly days?   165
And had you not grown restless .. but I know—
'Tis done and past: 'twas right, my instinct said;
Too live the life grew, golden and not grey,
And I'm the weak-eyed bat no sun should tempt
Out of the grange whose four walls make his world.   170
How could it end in any other way?
You called me, and I came home to your heart.
The triumph was—to reach and stay there; since
I reached it ere the triumph, what is lost?
Let my hands frame your face in your hair's gold,   175
You beautiful Lucrezia that are mine!
'Rafael did this, Andrea painted that;
The Roman's[136] is the better when you pray,
But still the other's Virgin was his wife—'
Men will excuse me. I am glad to judge   180
Both pictures in your presence; clearer grows
My better fortune, I resolve to think.
For, do you know, Lucrezia, as God lives,
Said one day Agnolo, his very self,
To Rafael .. I have known it all these years..   185
(When the young man was flaming out his thoughts
Upon a palace-wall for Rome to see,[137]
Too lifted up in heart because of it)
'Friend, there's a certain sorry little scrub
Goes up and down our Florence, none cares how,   190
Who, were he set to plan and execute
As you are, pricked on by your popes and kings,
Would bring the sweat into that brow of yours!'
To Rafael's!—And indeed the arm is wrong.
I hardly dare .. yet, only you to see,   195
Give the chalk here—quick, thus the line should go!
Ay, but the soul! he's Rafael! rub it out!

Notes

[135] *frank* pun; the Franks, a group of west German tribes first identified in the third century, gave their name to France.

[136] *Roman* Raphael moved to Rome in 1508 and remained there until his death in 1520.

[137] *see* Raphael painted seventeen frescos in the Stanze della Segnatura in the Vatican Palace (1508–11).

Still, all I care for, if he spoke the truth,
(What he? why, who but Michel Agnolo?
Do you forget already words like those?)   200
If really there was such a chance, so lost,—
Is, whether you're—not grateful—but more pleased.
Well, let me think so. And you smile indeed!
This hour has been an hour! Another smile?
If you would sit thus by me every night   205
I should work better, do you comprehend?
I mean that I should earn more, give you more.
See, it is settled dusk now; there's a star;
Morello's gone, the watch-lights show the wall,
The cue-owls[138] speak the name we call them by.   210
Come from the window, love,—come in, at last,
Inside the melancholy little house
We built[139] to be so gay with. God is just.
King Francis may forgive me: oft at nights
When I look up from painting, eyes tired out,   215
The walls become illumined, brick from brick
Distinct, instead of mortar, fierce bright gold,
That gold of his I did cement them with!
Let us but love each other. Must you go?
That Cousin[140] here again? he waits outside?   220
Must see you—you, and not with me? Those loans?
More gaming debts to pay? you smiled for that?
Well, let smiles buy me! have you more to spend?
While hand and eye and something of a heart
Are left me, work's my ware, and what's it worth?   225
I'll pay my fancy. Only let me sit
The grey remainder of the evening out,
Idle, you call it, and muse perfectly
How I could paint, were I but back in France,
One picture, just one more—the Virgin's face,   230
Not yours this time! I want you at my side
To hear them—that is, Michel Agnolo—
Judge all I do and tell you of its worth.
Will you? To-morrow, satisfy your friend.
I take the subjects for his corridor,   235
Finish the portrait out of hand—there, there,
And throw him in another thing or two
If he demurs; the whole should prove enough
To pay for this same Cousin's freak.[141] Beside,
What's better and what's all I care about,   240
Get you the thirteen scudi[142] for the ruff!

Notes

138 *cue-owls* small scops owls; their call, in Italian rendered as *chiu*, is anglicized by Browning to "cue."

139 *built* according to Vasari, a large part of the money Andrea expropriated from Francis was used to build the house for his wife at 22 Via Gino Capponi in Florence (see above, nn. 122 and 133).

140 *Cousin* euphemism for lover, a commonplace in Elizabethan and Stuart drama, as in Thomas Dekker's *Honest Whore* (1604): 1. 2. 117 and 3. 1. 143.

141 *freak* sudden arbitrary change of mind; whim (archaic).

142 *scudi* silver coins used throughout Italy until 1857.

Love, does that please you? Ah, but what does he,
The Cousin! what does he to please you more?

I am grown peaceful as old age to-night.
I regret little, I would change still less.   245
Since there my past life lies, why alter it?
The very wrong to Francis!—it is true
I took his coin, was tempted and complied,
And built this house and sinned, and all is said.
My father and my mother died of want.[143]   250
Well, had I riches of my own? you see
How one gets rich! Let each one bear his lot.
They were born poor, lived poor, and poor they died:
And I have laboured somewhat in my time
And not been paid profusely. Some good son   255
Paint my two hundred pictures—let him try!
No doubt, there's something strikes a balance. Yes,
You loved me quite enough, it seems to-night.
This must suffice me here. What would one have?
In heaven, perhaps, new chances, one more chance—   260
Four great walls in the New Jerusalem,
Meted on each side by the angel's reed,[144]
For Leonard,[145] Rafael, Agnolo and me
To cover—the three first without a wife,
While I have mine! So—still they overcome   265
Because there's still Lucrezia,—as I choose.

Again the Cousin's whistle! Go, my Love.

WEB p. 354

Caliban Upon Setebos; or, Natural Theology in the Island

From *Asolando*

Epilogue[146]

At the midnight in the silence of the sleep-time,
   When you set your fancies free,
Will they pass to where—by death, fools think, imprisoned—
Low he lies who once so loved you, whom you loved so,
    —Pity me?   5

Notes

143 *want* according to Vasari, Andrea abandoned his parents in favour of his wife's relatives.

144 *reed* see Revelation 21: 10–21.

145 *Leonard* Leonardo da Vinci (1452–1519), Florentine artist and polymath.

146 *title* last poem in Browning's final volume, *Asolando*, published on the day he died (12 December 1889), and traditionally printed last in collections of his poetry.

Oh to love so, be so loved, yet so mistaken!
    What had I on earth to do
With the slothful, with the mawkish, the unmanly?
Like the aimless, helpless, hopeless, did I drivel
    —Being—who?   10

One who never turned his back but marched breast forward,
    Never doubted clouds would break,
Never dreamed, though right were worsted, wrong would triumph,
Held we fall to rise, are baffled to fight better,
    Sleep to wake.   15

No, at noonday in the bustle of man's work-time
    Greet the unseen with a cheer!
Bid him forward, breast and back as either should be,
"Strive and thrive!" cry "Speed,—fight on, fare ever
    There as here!"   20

Edward Lear (1812–88)

Born in Highgate near London, Lear was the twentieth of twenty-one children, and was largely raised by his oldest sister Ann when his stockbroker father went bankrupt. Afflicted with epilepsy, asthma, and bouts of depression, he moved with Ann into London (1827) and helped support them by selling his drawings, some to the British Museum. By 1829 he was drawing at the newly opened Regent's Park Zoo and in 1830 began work on his *Illustrations of the Family of Psittacidæ or Parrots* (1830), the first ever elephant folio book of multicoloured lithographs it established his reputation at the age of 19 and was one of the greatest accomplishments of nineteenth-century publishing. Hired by Lord Stanley (1775–1851), heir to the earl of Derby, to record his menagerie at Knowsley near Liverpool, Lear was supported well and made connections that helped him for the rest of his life. For Stanley's children he wrote *A Book of Nonsense* (1846), a collection of limericks (he popularized the form) with clever illustrations. He often exploited rhymes that drew on working-class accents, as in Sparta / daughter (Sparter / dorter) and caricatures that developed metonymic associations (the nose for the whole person), or even cruel or violent eccentricities. In 1846 he gave drawing lessons to Queen Victoria, who had been impressed by his *Views in Rome and its Environs* (1841) and *Illustrated Excursions in Italy* (1846). After 1837 he left England to study art in Rome, returning only occasionally. He travelled widely – touring, not once, but a number of times, throughout Italy, Sicily, Malta, Corfu, Greece, Turkey, Egypt, Palestine as well as going to India and Ceylon (Sri Lanka) – and often dangerously, especially for a man in somewhat frail health. He kept careful journals, and recording his travels with numerous watercolours, until his death at San Remo in January, 1888. His original nonsense book went through several dozen editions, and as well he published *Nonsense Songs and Stories* (1871), *More Nonsense Songs, Pictures, &c.* (1872), *Laughable Lyrics* (1877), and *Nonsense Botany and Nonsense Alphabets*. Standard edition: *The Complete Verse and Other Nonsense*, ed. Vivien Noakes (2001); *Selected Letters*, ed. Vivien Noakes (1988); Peter Levi, *Edward Lear: A Biography* (1995). Nonsense books at the Baldwin

From *A Book of Nonsense*[1]

There was an Old Man of Nepaul,[2]
From his horse had a terrible fall;
But, though split quite in two, by some very strong glue,
They mended that Man of Nepaul.

There was a Young Lady whose nose,
Was so long that it reached to her toes;
So she hired an Old Lady, whose conduct was steady,
To carry that wonderful nose.

There was an Old Person of Sparta,[3]
Who had twenty-five sons and one daughter;
He fed them on snails, and weighed them in scales,
That wonderful person of Sparta.

There was a Young Lady of Dorking,[4]
Who bought a large bonnet for walking;
But its colour and size, so bedazzled her eyes,
That she very soon went back to Dorking.

There was an Old Man from Whitehaven,[5]
Who danced the quadrille with a raven,
They said, "It's absurd, to encourage that bird!"
So they smashed the old man from Whitehaven.

There was an Old Man, who said, "Well!
Will NOBODY answer this bell?[6]
I have pulled day and night, till my hair has grown white,
But nobody answers this bell!"

Notes

EDWARD LEAR

[1] *title* Lear's limericks were first published in *Book of Nonsense* (1846); the first four poems were in that edition; our text: 1871.

[2] *Nepaul* currently spelled Nepal.

[3] *Sparta* city in southern Greece.

[4] *Dorking* market town south of London.

[5] *Whitehaven* a coastal port on the north-west coast of England. This and the following limerick were added to the third edition of *A Book of Nonsense* in 1861.

[6] *bell* in large Victorian homes, bell pulls were available in most of the rooms to summon servants.

The Owl and the Pussy-Cat[7]

I

The Owl and the Pussy-Cat went to sea
    In a beautiful pea-green boat,
They took some honey, and plenty of money,
    Wrapped up in a five-pound note.
The Owl looked up to the stars above,   5
    And sang to a small guitar,
"O lovely Pussy! O Pussy, my love,
    What a beautiful Pussy you are,
        You are,
        You are!   10
    What a beautiful Pussy you are!"

II

Pussy said to the Owl, "You elegant fowl!
    How charmingly sweet you sing!
O let us be married! too long we have tarried:
    But what shall we do for a ring?"   15
They sailed away for a year and a day,
    To the land where the Bong-tree grows
And there in a wood a Piggy-wig stood
    With a ring at the end of his nose,
        His nose,   20
        His nose,
    With a ring at the end of his nose.

III

"Dear Pig, are you willing to sell for one shilling
    Your ring?" Said the Piggy, "I will."
So they took it away, and were married next day   25
    By the Turkey who lives on the hill.
They dined on mince, and slices of quince,
    Which they ate with a runcible[8] spoon;
And hand in hand, on the edge of the sand,
    They danced by the light of the moon,   30
        The moon,
        The moon,
    They danced by the light of the moon.

Notes

[7] *title* first published in *Our Young Folks* (Boston, Feb. 1870); republished in *Nonsense Songs, Stories, Botany and Alphabets* (1871; our text).

[8] *runcible* one of Lear's neologisms. Numerous readers have attempted to derive or define it, without consensus; see below, "HOW PLEASANT," stz. 5, line 4.

How Pleasant to Know Mr. Lear[9]

"How pleasant to know Mr. Lear!"
    Who has written such volumes of stuff!
Some think him ill-tempered and queer,[10]
    But a few think him pleasant enough.

His mind is concrete and fastidious,   5
    His nose is remarkably big;
His visage is more or less hideous,
    His beard it resembles a wig.

He has ears, and two eyes, and ten ingers,
    Leastways if you reckon two thumbs;   10
Long ago he was one of the singers,
    But now he is one of the dumbs.

He sits in a beautiful parlour,
    With hundreds of books on the wall;
He drinks a great deal of Marsala,[11]   15
    But never gets tipsy at all.

He has many friends, laymen and clerical,
    Old Foss is the name of his cat;[12]
His body is perfectly spherical,
    He weareth a runcible hat.   20

When he walks in a waterproof white,
    The children run after him so!
Calling out, "He's come out in his night-
    gown, that crazy old Englishman, oh!"

He weeps by the side of the ocean,   25
    He weeps on the top of the hill;
He purchases pancakes and lotion,
    And chocolate shrimps from the mill.

He reads, but he cannot speak, Spanish,
    He cannot abide ginger beer: 30
Ere the days of his pilgrimage vanish,
    How pleasant to know Mr. Lear!

Notes

[9] *title* first printed in *Nonsense Books* (Boston, 1888); reprinted in Lear, *Nonsense Songs and Stories* (1895; our text).
[10] *queer* odd.
[11] *Marsala* wine produced in Sicily.
[12] *Foss ... cat* Foss was Lear's cat from November 1872 and died in September 1887, four months before Lear. He figures in many of Lear's caricatures.

Samuel Smiles (1812–1904)

Born in Haddington, Scotland, into a family of Cameronians, a sect of strict Presbyterianism, Smiles studied medicine at the University of Edinburgh, worked as a physician, and turned to journalism in 1838, strongly supporting electoral reform and women's suffrage. Smiles is the author of exemplary, inspirational biographies, including *The Life of George Stephenson* (1857), *Lives of the Engineers* (3 vols, 1862), and *Men of Invention and Industry* (1884). In 1859 he published *Self-Help*, which would become one of the bestselling books of the century. He followed on that success with a number of similar inspirational tracts aimed at working-class and lower middle-class men: *Character* (1871), *Thrift* (1875), *Duty* (1880), and *Life and Labour* (1887). He advocated throughout a form of hero-worship, individual achievement through hard work, thrift, and perseverance; as he wrote in chapter 7 of *Self-Help*: "It is not even eminent talent that is required to ensure success in any pursuit, so much as purpose,—not merely the power to achieve, but the will to labour energetically and perseveringly." His character sketches and inspirational advice are similar to an American phenomenon, the fiction of Horatio Alger, Jr (1832–99). Modern critical edition: *Self-Help, with Illustrations of Character, Conduct, and Perseverance* [1859], ed. Peter W. Sinnema (2002); Adrian Jarvis, *Samuel Smiles and the Construction of Victorian Values* (1997). "Samuel Smiles": http://gerald-massey.org.uk/smiles/index.htm.

Self-Help: With Illustrations of Character and Conduct[1]

From Chapter 1: "Self-Help: National and Individual"

"Heaven helps those who help themselves,"[2] is a well-worn maxim, embodying in a small compass the results of vast human experience. The spirit of self-help is the root of all genuine growth in the individual; and, exhibited in the lives of many, it constitutes the true source of national vigour and strength. Help from without is often enfeebling in its effects, but help from within invariably invigorates. Whatever is done *for* men or classes, to a certain extent takes away the stimulus and necessity of doing for themselves; and where men are subjected to over-guidance and over-government, the inevitable tendency is to render them comparatively helpless.

Even the best institutions can give a man no active aid. Perhaps the utmost they can do is, to leave him *free* to develop himself and improve his individual condition. But in all

Notes

SAMUEL SMILES

[1] *title* as Smiles explains in his autobiography (1905), the book originated in a lecture to a mutual improvement society for working men in Leeds in March 1845; the lecture was later published as *The Education of the Working Classes: An Address given by Dr. Samuel Smiles to the Members and Friends of the Leeds Mutual Improvement Society* (1845). Smiles first submitted the manuscript to Routledge in 1856, but it was rejected; it was published by John Murray on 24 November 1859, the same day as Darwin's *Origin of Species*, and immediately became a runaway success, selling 20,000 copies in the first year; the *Origin* sold 3,800 in the first year. By the time of Smiles's death, *Self-Help* would sell over 250,000 copies and would be translated into over a dozen languages. The book consists of a number of short, inspirational biographies and can be compared to conduct books such as Lord Chesterfield's *Letters to His Son* (1774), Hannah More's *Strictures on the Modern System of Female Education* (1799) and *Hints Towards Forming the Character of a Young Princess* (1805), and other later self-improvement manuals like Baden-Powell's *Scouting for Boys* (1908) and Dale Carnegie's *How to Win Friends and Influence People* (1930).

[2] *themselves* a variation of "God helps those who help themselves," attributed to various writers, most famously Benjamin Franklin in *Poor Richard's Almanac* (1733).

times men have been prone to believe that their happiness and well-being were to be secured by means of institutions rather than by their own conduct. Hence the value of legislation as an agent in human advancement has always been greatly over-estimated. To constitute the millionth part of a Legislature, by voting for one or two men once in three or five years, however conscientiously this duty may be performed, can exercise but little active influence upon any man's life and character. Moreover, it is every day becoming more clearly understood, that the function of Government is negative and restrictive, rather than positive and active; being resolvable principally into protection—protection of life, liberty, and property.³ Hence the chief "reforms" of the last fifty years have consisted mainly in abolitions and disenactments. But there is no power of law that can make the idle man industrious, the thriftless provident, or the drunken sober; though every individual can be each and all of these if he will, by the exercise of his own free powers of action and self-denial. Indeed all experience serves to prove that the worth and strength of a State depend far less upon the form of its institutions than upon the character of its men. For the nation is only the aggregate of individual conditions, and civilization itself is but a question of personal improvement....

Biographies of great, but especially of good men, are, nevertheless, most instructive and useful, as helps, guides, and incentives to others. Some of the best are almost equivalent to Gospels—teaching high living, high thinking, and energetic action for their own and the world's good. British biography is studded over, as "with patines of bright gold,"⁴ with illustrious examples of the power of self-help, of patient purpose, resolute working, and steadfast integrity, issuing in the formation of truly noble and manly character; exhibiting in language not to be misunderstood, what it is in the power of each to accomplish for himself; and illustrating the efficacy of self-respect and self-reliance in enabling men of even the humblest rank to work out for themselves an honourable competency and a solid reputation.

From Chapter 2: "Leaders of Industry—Inventors and Producers" [James Watt]⁵

Watt was one of the most industrious of men. Whatever subject came under his notice in the course of his business, immediately became to him an object of study; and the story of his life proves, what all experience confirms, that it is not the man of the greatest natural vigour and capacity who achieves the highest results, but he who employs his powers with the greatest industry and the most carefully disciplined skill—the skill that comes by labour, application, and experience. Many men in his time knew far more than Watt, but none laboured so assiduously as he did to turn all that he did know to useful practical purposes. He was, above all things, most persevering in his pursuit of facts. He cultivated carefully that habit of active attention on which all the higher working qualities

Notes

³ *life . . . property* from John Locke, "Of Civil Government," (ch. 2). Smiles had been active in radical politics in the 1840s, advocating a utilitarian approach in his work as editor of the *Leeds Times*, supporting women's suffrage, the repeal of the Corn Laws, and better education for the working classes; however, by 1845 he became disillusioned with attempts to improve society by collective action and was repelled by the violence associated with the Chartists and the socialism of Robert Owens (1771–1858). In an epigraph to this chapter, Smiles quotes John Stuart Mill, *On Liberty*, published in February, 1859: "The worth of a State, in the long run, is the worth of the individuals composing it" (ch. 5).

⁴ *gold* see *Merchant of Venice*, 5. 1. 65.

⁵ *Producers* to exemplify the "spirit of industry" that characterizes "one of the most strongly-marked features of the English people," which has "laid the foundations and built up the industrial greatness of the empire," Smiles in this chapter gives short biographies of no less than fifteen inventors, including James Watt (1736–1819), Scottish inventor and mechanical engineer, best known for his work on the steam engine, an essential innovation for the Industrial Revolution.

of the mind mainly depend. Indeed, Mr. Edgworth[6] entertained the opinion, that many of the great differences of intellect which are found in men depend more upon the early cultivation of this *habit of attention*, than upon any great disparity between the powers of one individual and another.

Even when a boy, Watt found science in his toys. The quadrants[7] lying about his father's carpenter's shop led him to the study of optics and astronomy; his ill health induced him to pry into the secrets of physiology; and his solitary walks through the country attracted him to the study of botany, history, and antiquarianism. While carrying on the business of a mathematical instrument–maker, he received an order to build an organ; and, though without any ear for music, he undertook the study of harmonics, and successfully constructed the instrument. And, in like manner, when the little model of Newcomen's steam-engine,[8] belonging to the University of Glasgow, was placed in his hands for repair, he forthwith set himself to learn all that was then known about heat, evaporation, and condensation,—at the same time plodding his way in mechanics and the science of construction,—the results of which he at length embodied in the condensing steam-engine.

For ten years he went on contriving and inventing—with little hope to cheer him— with few friends to encourage him—struggling with difficulties, and earning but a slender living at his trade. Even when he had brought his engine into a practicable working condition, his difficulties seemed to be as far from an end as ever; and he could find no capitalist to join him in his great undertaking, and bring the invention to a successful practical issue. He went on, meanwhile, earning bread for his family by making and selling quadrants, making and mending fiddles, flutes, and other musical instruments; measuring mason work, surveying roads, superintending the construction of canals, or doing anything that turned up, and offered a prospect of honest gain. At length, Watt found a fit partner in another eminent leader of industry—Mathew Boulton,[9] of Birmingham; a skilful, energetic, and far-seeing man, who vigorously undertook the enterprise of introducing the condensing engine into general use as a working power; and his success is now a matter of history.

Charlotte Brontë (1816–55)

Like her sisters, Emily and Anne, and her brother, Branwell (1817–48), Charlotte was born at Thornton in Yorkshire and moved to Haworth in 1820, where her father, Patrick Brontë (1777– 1861), was secure but poor as the perpetual curate. Her mother, Maria Branwell, died the next year. Charlotte, like the others, was raised by her father and her aunt, Elizabeth Branwell (1776–1842). She attended the Clergy Daughters' School at Cowan Bridge, later

Notes

[6] *Edgworth* Richard Lowell Edgeworth (1744–1817, name misspelt by Smiles in the first edition); Anglo-Irish educational theorist, father of novelist Maria Edgeworth (1768–1849), friend of Watt: the two were members of the Lunar Society of Birmingham, an informal learning society that included Erasmus Darwin (1731–1802), Matthew Boulton (1728–1809), and Josiah Wedgwood (1730–95).

[7] *quadrants* instruments used to measure angles up to ninety degrees, used in optics and astronomy to measure altitude, and in maritime navigation to determine latitude.

[8] *steam-engine* Thomas Newcomen (1664–1729), ironmonger, invented the first steam-driven engine to pump water in 1710. The engine was inefficient, with a great deal of heat wasted; nevertheless, it remained the standard in use for about seventy-five years. In 1769 Watt patented a separate condenser, improving the engine with a more fuel-efficient system.

[9] *Birmingham* Matthew Boulton (1728–1809; first name misspelled in 1859), English manufacturer of ornamental metalware, went into partnership with Watt, forming the company of Boulton and Watt in 1775 that installed hundreds of steam engines in Britain and worldwide.

recreated as Lowood School in *Jane Eyre* (1847), but, like her sisters, she left to be home-schooled when typhoid fever broke out. With Emily and Anne, she invented the imaginary world of Angria, located in Africa, and influenced by Byron, Walter Scott, *The Arabian Nights*, and James Ridley's *Tales of the Genii* (1764). From 1831 to 1832 she attended Miss Wooler's school at Roe Head, later becoming a teacher there from 1835 to 1838. After two posts as a governess, she went to study languages in Brussels, where she fell in love with her teacher, M. Heger, who did not return her affection. The Brontë sisters published under androgynous pseudonyms *Poems by Currer, Ellis, and Acton Bell* (1846), containing twenty-one poems each by Emily and Anne (Ellis and Acton) and nineteen by Charlotte (Currer). The sisters paid for the publication. Of the 1,000 copies of *Poems* printed, only two copies were sold in the first year. When Smith, Elder and Company bought the remaining stock in 1848, thirty-nine had been sold; they reissued it the same year and it sold steadily with 556 copies remaining in 1856. After her sisters died of tuberculosis within a year, Charlotte published two of the novels of Emily and Anne, *Wuthering Heights and Agnes Grey* (1850), containing in the third volume a collection of additional poems from manuscripts of Emily and Anne, editing them heavily, and sometimes rewriting them, a matter of considerable textual and interpretive controversy to the present; see, for instance, Anne Brontë's "Last Lines." Because of these controversies, we have occasionally alluded to MS variants in the Brontë sisters' poems.

Charlotte is best known as a novelist: for *Jane Eyre* (1847), *Shirley* (1849), and *Villette* (1853). In June 1854 she married her father's curate. By the following March she was dead. Standard editions: *The Poems of Charlotte Brontë: A New Text and Commentary*, ed. Victor A. Neufeldt (1985); *Jane Eyre*, eds Jane Jack and Margaret Smith (1969); *Shirley*, eds Herbert Rosengarten and Margaret Smith (1979); *Villette*, eds Herbert Rosengarten and Margaret Smith (1985); The *Letters of Charlotte Brontë*, ed. Margaret Smith (2 vols, 2000); Elizabeth Gaskell, *The Life of Charlotte Brontë* (1857); Rebecca Fraser, *Charlotte Brontë: A Writer's Life* (2008); *The Oxford Companion to the Brontës*, eds Christine Alexander and Margaret Smith (2003). Charlotte Brontë's writings from the University of Adelaide: http://ebooks.adelaide.edu.au/b/bronte/charlotte. "The Brontës": www.thebrontes.net.

The Missionary[1]

Plough, vessel, plough the British main,
Seek the free ocean's wider plain;
Leave English scenes and English skies,
Unbind, dissever English ties;
Bear me to climes remote and strange,   5
Where altered life, fast-following change,
Hot action, never-ceasing toil,
Shall stir, turn, dig, the spirit's soil;
Fresh roots shall plant, fresh seed shall sow,
Till a new garden there shall grow,   10
Cleared of the weeds that fill it now,—

Notes

CHARLOTTE BRONTË

[1] *title* the ideas and expression of "The Missionary" anticipate the views of St John Rivers in Charlotte Brontë's *Jane Eyre* (1847), exploiting the missionary zeal contained in the biblical injunction at the end of the Gospel of Mark (16:15). First published in *Poems* (1846).

Mere human love, mere selfish yearning,
Which, cherished, would arrest me yet.
I grasp the plough, there's no returning,[2]
Let me, then, struggle to forget.   15

But England's shores are yet in view,
And England's skies of tender blue
Are arched above her guardian sea.
I cannot yet Remembrance flee;
I must again, then, firmly face   20
That task of anguish, to retrace.
Wedded to home—I home forsake,
Fearful of change—I changes make;
Too fond of ease—I plunge in toil;
Lover of calm—I seek turmoil: 25
Nature and hostile Destiny
Stir in my heart a conflict wild;
And long and fierce the war will be
Ere duty both has reconciled.

What other tie yet holds me fast   30
To the divorced, abandoned past?
Smouldering, on my heart's altar lies
The fire of some great sacrifice,
Not yet half quenched. The sacred steel
But lately struck my carnal will,   35
My life-long hope, first joy and last,
What I loved well, and clung to fast;
What I wished wildly to retain,
What I renounced with soul-felt pain;
What—when I saw it, axe-struck, perish—   40
Left me no joy on earth to cherish;
A man bereft—yet sternly now
I do confirm that Jephtha[3] vow:
Shall I retract, or fear, or flee?
Did Christ, when rose the fatal tree   45
Before him, on Mount Calvary?
'Twas a long fight, hard fought, but won,
And what I did was justly done.

Yet, Helen! from thy love I turned,
When my heart most for thy heart burned;   50
I dared thy tears, I dared thy scorn—
Easier the death-pang had been borne.
Helen! thou mightst not go with me,
I could not—dared not stay for thee!
I heard, afar, in bonds[4] complain   55

Notes

[2] *returning* see Luke 9: 62.
[3] *Jephta* see Judges 11: 30–40.

[4] *bonds* a reference to slavery. For an account of the anti-slavery movement in the 1830s and 1840s that the Brontë family supported, see MILL, n. 16 and NORTON, n. 9.

The savage from beyond the main;
And that wild sound rose o'er the cry
Wrung out by passion's agony;
And even when, with the bitterest tear
I ever shed, mine eyes were dim,   60
Still, with the spirit's vision clear,
I saw Hell's empire, vast and grim,
Spread on each Indian river's shore,
Each realm of Asia covering o'er.
There, the weak, trampled by the strong,   65
Live but to suffer—hopeless die;
There pagan-priests, whose creed is Wrong,
Extortion, Lust, and Cruelty,
Crush our lost race—and brimming fill
The bitter cup of human ill;   70
And I—who have the healing creed,
The faith benign of Mary's Son;
Shall I behold my brother's need
And, selfishly, to aid him shun?
I—who upon my mother's knees,   75
In childhood, read Christ's written word,
Received his legacy of peace,
His holy rule of action heard;
I—in whose heart the sacred sense
Of Jesus' love was early felt;   80
Of his pure full benevolence,
His pitying tenderness for guilt;
His shepherd-care for wandering sheep,⁵
For all weak, sorrowing, trembling things,
His mercy vast, his passion deep   85
Of anguish for man's sufferings;
I—schooled from childhood in such lore—
Dared I draw back or hesitate,
When called to heal the sickness sore
Of those far off and desolate?   90
Dark, in the realm and shades of Death,
Nations and tribes and empires lie,
But even to them the light of Faith
Is breaking on their sombre sky:
And be it mine to bid them raise   95
Their drooped heads to the kindling scene,
And know and hail the sunrise blaze
Which heralds Christ the Nazarene.⁶
I know how Hell the veil will spread
Over their brows and filmy eyes,   100
And earthward crush the lifted head
That would look up and seek the skies;
I know what war the fiend will wage

Notes

⁵ *sheep* see Matthew 18: 12–14 and Luke 15: 3–7.   ⁶ *Nazarene* title applied to Jesus of Nazareth, so named from his childhood home.

Against that soldier of the cross,
Who comes to dare his demon-rage,   105
And work his kingdom shame and loss.
Yes, hard and terrible the toil
Of him who steps on foreign soil,
Resolved to plant the gospel vine,⁷
Where tyrants rule and slaves repine;   110
Eager to lift Religion's light
Where thickest shades of mental night
Screen the false god and fiendish rite;
Reckless that missionary blood,
Shed in wild wilderness and wood,   115
Has left, upon the unblest air,
The man's deep moan—the martyr's prayer.
I know my lot—I only ask
Power to fulfil the glorious task;
Willing the spirit, may the flesh   120
Strength for the day receive afresh.
May burning sun or deadly wind
Prevail not o'er an earnest mind;
May torments strange or direst death
Nor trample truth, nor baffle faith.   125
Though such blood-drops should fall from me
As fell in old Gethsemane,⁸
Welcome the anguish, so it gave
More strength to work—more skill to save.
And, oh! if brief must be my time,   130
If hostile hand or fatal clime
Cut short my course—still o'er my grave,
Lord, may thy harvest whitening wave.⁹
So I the culture may begin,
Let others thrust the sickle in;   135
If but the seed will faster grow,
May my blood water what I sow!¹⁰

What! have I ever trembling stood,
And feared to give to God that blood?
What! has the coward love of life   140
Made me shrink from the righteous strife?
Have human passions, human fears
Severed me from those Pioneers,
Whose task is to march first, and trace
Paths for the progress of our race?   145
It has been so; but grant me, Lord,

Notes

⁷ *vine* see John 15: 1–5.
⁸ *Gethsemane* see Matthew 26: 36 and Mark 14: 32.
⁹ *wave* for fields ripe for the harvest, see John 4: 31–38; see also
Matthew 9: 37; Jesus often refers to the saving of souls in
the metaphor of the harvest (Matthew 9: 37–8; 13: 30; Mark
4: 29; and John 12: 24).

¹⁰ *sow* a reference to a famous statement of the early
Christian writer, Tertullian (c.160–c.220): "The blood
of the martyrs is the seed of the church" (*Apologeticus*,
ch. 50).

Now to stand steadfast by thy word!
Protected by salvation's helm,
Shielded by faith—with truth begirt,[11]
To smile when trials seek to whelm   150
And stand 'mid testing fires unhurt!
Hurling hell's strongest bulwarks down,
Even when the last pang thrills my breast,
When Death bestows the Martyr's crown,
And calls me into Jesus' rest.   155
Then for my ultimate reward—
Then for the world-rejoicing word—
The voice from Father—Spirit—Son:
"Servant of God, well hast thou done!"

"My feet they are sore, and my limbs they are weary"[12]

My feet they are sore, and my limbs they are weary;
    Long is the way, and the mountains are wild;
Soon will the twilight close moonless and dreary
    Over the path of the poor orphan child.

Why did they send me so far and so lonely,   5
    Up where the moors spread and grey rocks are piled?
Men are hard-hearted, and kind angels only
    Watch o'er the steps of a poor orphan child.

Yet distant and soft the night-breeze is blowing,
    Clouds there are none, and clear stars beam mild;   10
God, in His mercy, protection is showing,
    Comfort and hope to the poor orphan child.

Ev'n should I fall o'er the broken bridge passing,
    Or stray in the marshes, by false lights beguiled,
Still will my Father, with promise and blessing,   15
    Take to His bosom the poor orphan child.

There is a thought that for strength should avail me,
    Though both of shelter and kindred despoiled:
Heaven is a home, and a rest will not fail me;
    God is a friend to the poor orphan child.   20

Notes

[11] *Protected … begirt* see the whole armour of God in Ephesians 6: 11–13.

[12] *title* untitled when first printed in *Jane Eyre* (1847, ch. 3): "I had often heard the song before, and always with lively delight; for Bessie [the nurse-maid] had a sweet voice,—at least, I thought so. But now, though her voice was still sweet, I found in its melody an indescribable sadness. Sometimes, pre-occupied with her work, she sang the refrain very low, very lingeringly; 'A long time ago' came out like the saddest cadence of a funeral hymn. She passed into another ballad, this time a really doleful one. 'My feet they are sore, and my limbs they are weary'; [poem follows]." The theme of the orphan child's eventual home in heaven was conventional in ballad poetry, though this poem is not in ballad form.

Eventide ["The house was still, the room was still"][13]

The house was still, the room was still,
    'Twas eventide in June;
A caged canary to the sun
    Then setting, trilled a tune.

A free bird on that lilac bush   5
    Outside the lattice heard,
He listened long—there came a hush,
    He dropped an answering word.

Dec 24 [1848] [On the Death of Emily Brontë][14]

My darling, thou wilt never know
The° grinding agony of woe   °MS The / Such \
    That° we have borne° for thee.   °MS That / As \; °MS borne /felt known \
Thus may we consolation tear
    E'en from the depth of our despair   5
    And° wasting misery.   °MS &

The nightly anguish thou art spared
When all the crushing truth is bared
    To the awakening mind,
When° the galled heart is pierced with grief,   °MS When / And \   10
Till wildly it implores relief,
    But small relief can find.

Nor know'st thou what it is to lie
Looking forth with streaming eye[15]
    On life's lone wilderness.[16]   15
"Weary, weary, dark and° drear,   °MS &
How shall I the journey bear,
    The burden and distress?"

Notes

[13] *title* first published (eight lines) with the title "Eventide" (not in the MS) in *Brontë Poems* (1915, ed. Arthur C. Benson). After the eighth line, the MS adds: "The prisoner to the free replied."

[14] *title* first published with a facsimile of the MS and transcription in *The Woman at Home* (Dec. 1896), a journal edited by the suffragist and novelist Annie Shepherd Swan (1859–1943), titled "On the Death of Emily Brontë" (our text). In the MS in the Huntington Library the title reads: "Dec. 24 [1848]"; the year given in brackets may be in a different hand. The MS has no punctuation except for terminal punctuation at the end of each stanza, and a dash at the end of line 11. The MS shows a number of variant readings without any cancellations, as noted. Emily Jane Brontë died on 19 December 1848 and was buried on 22 December, less than three months after her brother Branwell died of the same disease, consumption or pulmonary tuberculosis. Emily had refused medical treatment and persisted in the routines of the Haworth parsonage until the day of her death.

[15] *eye* the first MS version reads: "Looking with streaming eye," and then "forth" is added: "Looking forth with streaming eye." Other MS variants follow: "Exploring / Beholding \ with tear dimmed eye."

[16] *wilderness* the first MS version of line 15 reads "On life's wilderness" and below is given the published reading.

Then° since thou art spared such pain,   °MS Then / O \
We will not wish thee here again,   20
    He that lives must mourn.
God help° us through our misery,   °MS help / relieve \
And give us rest and° joy with thee   °MS &
    When we reach our bourne!

June 21 1849 [On the Death of Anne Brontë][17]

There's little joy in life for me,
    And° little terror in the grave;   °MS &
I've lived the parting hour° to see   °MS parting hour \ lingering death /
    Of one I would have died to save.

Calmly to watch the failing breath,[18]   5
    Wishing each sigh might be the last;[19]
Longing to see the shade° of death   °MS cloud \ shade /
    O'er those beloved features cast.

The cloud, the stillness that must part
    The darling of my life from me.   10
And then to thank God from my heart,
    To thank Him well and° fervently!   °MS &

Although I knew that we had lost
    The hope and° glory of our life;   °MS &
And now, benighted, tempest-tossed,   15
    Must bear° alone the weary strife.   °MS ~~face~~ \bear / \meet /

Grace Aguilar (1816–47)

Educated chiefly by her Jewish parents of Spanish–Portuguese descent, Aguilar took an early interest in nature, history, and the literature of Europe, but her chief literary activity consisted in writing and publishing stories and theological studies of Judaism: a translation of Orobio de Castro's *Israel Defended* (1838); her own *The Spirit of Judaism* (1842); and The

Notes

[17] *title* first published with a facsimile of the MS and transcription in *The Woman at Home* (Dec. 1896) (see above, "Dec. 24 [1848]"). The title of the poem in *The Woman at Home* is "On the Death of Anne Brontë"; in the MS title reads: "June 21 1849" (our text). Like the poem on the death of Emily Brontë, the MS has no punctuation except for terminal punctuation at the end of each stanza and a comma at the end of lines 10 and 13. The MS shows a number of variant readings with only one cancellation in line 16, as noted. Lines 7 and 8 are run together. In the first publication the lines are indented as in the present version; in the MS they are all flush left. Our text: 1896.

    Less than two weeks after Emily Brontë's death, Anne Brontë was also diagnosed with tuberculosis. Despite medical treatment, her health declined, and in May she went with Charlotte and a family friend to the North Sea town of Scarborough in Yorkshire to take the sea-air cure, to no avail: she died on 28 May and was buried in Scarborough on 30 May.

[18] *breath* the first version of line 5 reads: "Calmly to watch each gasp of breath"; the second, with the variations written above it: "Calmly to watch struggling for breath"; the third version, written above the second: "Calmly to watch the failing breath"; in each variation the words "Calmly to watch" and "breath" are not repeated.

[19] *last the* MS reading of line 6 is "\Wishing / \Still hoping / \ [Still] wishing / each \ sigh/ would \might/ be the last."

Jewish Faith: its Spiritual Consolation, Moral Guidance, and Immortal Hope (1846); and other works and collections of essays. Her novels include Home Influence: A Tale for Mothers and Daughters (1847; published in almost thirty editions), The Vale of Cedars (1850), and The Days of Bruce (1852), the last two published posthumously. She also contributed to such periodicals as The Keepsake and La Belle Assemblée. She was as popular in the United States as she was in Britain. No standard edition. Rachel Beth Zion Lask Abrahams, "Grace Aguilar: A Centenary Tribute," in Transactions of the Jewish Historical Society of England 16 (1952): 137–45; Cynthia Scheinberg, Women's Poetry and Religion in Victorian England: Jewish Identity and Christian Culture (2002).

The Vision of Jerusalem[1]

While Listening to a Beautiful Organ in one of the Gentile Shrines

I saw thee, oh my fatherland, my beautiful, my own!
As if thy God had raised thee from the dust where thou art strewn,
His glory cast around thee, and thy children bound to Him,
In links so brightly woven, no sin their light could dim.

Methought the cymbal's sacred sound came softly on my ear,
The timbrel, and the psaltery,[2] and the harp's full notes were near;
And thousand voices chaunted, His glory to upraise,
More heavenly and thrillingly than e'en in David's days.

Methought the sons of Levi[3] were in holy garments there,
Th' anointed one[4] upon his throne, in holiness so fair,
That all who gazed on him might feel the promise be fulfill'd,
And sin, and all her baleful train, now he had come, were still'd.

And thousands of my people throng'd the pure and holy fane,
The curse removed from every brow, ne'er more to come again;
Th' Almighty hand from each, from all, had ta'en the scorching brand,
And Israel, forgiven, knelt within our own bright band!

My country! oh my country! was my soul enrapt in thee
One passing moment, that mine eyes might all thy glory see?
What magic power upheld me there?—alas! alas! it past,
And darkness o'er my aspiring soul the heavy present cast.

Notes

GRACE AGUILAR

[1] title first published in the Occident and American Jewish Advocate (Feb. 1844).

[2] timbrel . . . psaltery the timbrel is the ancient Hebrew version of the tambourine: see Job 21: 12; and Psalms 149: 3. A psaltery is a stringed instrument of the harp family: see Psalm 33: 2; 71: 22; and 150: 3.

[3] Levi in the Hebrew Bible, Levi, one of the twelve sons of Jacob, had three sons, Gershon, Kohath, and Merari (Genesis 46: 11). Kohath was the grandfather of Aaron,

Moses, and Miriam, and Aaron's descendants became the class of priests in Israel. The other descendants ministered in the Temple, served the priests, and had the special office of singing the psalms in the services in the Temple (Numbers 18: 2–6). In the prophets they are specially mentioned with the coming of the messenger of God, presaging the Messiah (Malachi 3: 1–3).

[4] anointed one (Heb. Mashiach, Messiah); see Psalm 47: 8.

I stood ALONE 'mid throning crowds who fill'd that stranger shrine,
For there were none who kept the faith I held so dearly mine:
An exile felt I, in that house, from Israel's native sod,—
An exile yearning for my *house*,—yet loved still by my God.

No exile from His love! No, no; tho' captive I may be,
And I must weep whene'er I think, my fatherland, on thee!
Jerusalem! my beautiful! my own! I feel thee still,
Though for our sins thy tainted sod the Moslem strangers⁵ fill.

Oh! that thy children all would feel what our sins have done.
And by our every action prove such guilt the exiles shun,
Until they seek their God in prayer, oh! will He turn to them,
And raise thee once again in life, my own Jerusalem!

"If they their own iniquity in humbleness confess,
And all their fathers' trespasses,—nor seek to make them less;
If they my judgments say are right, and penitently own
They reap the chastisement of sin, whose seeds long years have sown:⁶

Then will I all my vows recall, and from them take my hand,
My covenant remember, and have mercy on their land."⁷
So spake the Lord in boundless love to Israel his son;⁸
But can we, dare we say, these things we *do*, or we *have* done?

Alas, my country! thou must yet deserted rest and lone,
Thy glory, loveliness and life, a Father's gifts, are flown!
Oh that my prayers could raise thee radiant from the sod,
And turn from Judah's exiled sons their God's avenging rod!

And like an oak thou standest, of leaves and branches shorn;⁹
And we are like the wither'd leaves by autumn tempests torn¹⁰
From parent stems, and scatter'd wide o'er hill, and vale, and sea,
And known as Judah's ingrate race wherever we may be.

Oh! blessed was that vision'd light that flash'd before mine eye;
But, oh, the quick awakening check'd my soul's ecstatic sigh!
Yet still, still wilt thou rise again, my beautiful, my home,
Our God will bring thy children back, ne'er, ne'er again to roam!

Notes

⁵ *strangers* Jerusalem was generally under the control of the
Ottoman Turks from 1517 until 1917. As the Ottoman
Empire began to disintegrate in the nineteenth century,
Egypt under Muhammad Ali Pasha (1769–1849) attacked
Syria in October, 1831, then under the Ottoman Sultan
Mahmud II (1785–1839), and soon after annexed Jerusalem.
In 1840 the Ottoman Empire regained control of Jerusalem.
The population about the time when Aguilar was writing
remained in a state of rivalry, with about 7,000 Jews, 5,000
Muslims, 3,500 Christians, along with Turkish soldiers.

⁶ *sown* for biblical sources for this stanza, see Leviticus 26:
40–41.
⁷ *Then . . . land* for this couplet, see Leviticus 26: 42, 45.
⁸ *son* see Exodus 4: 22, 23.
⁹ *shorn* see Isaiah 1: 29, 30; and 6: 13.
¹⁰ *torn* the Jews of the Diaspora are like scattered leaves,
echoing Milton's description of the fallen angels in *Paradise
Lost*: "Thick as autumnal leaves that strew the brooks / In
Vallombrosa" (1. 302–3). See also HOUSMAN, n. 27.

Edwin Waugh (1817–90)

Born in Rochdale in Lancashire, the son of a shoemaker, Waugh attended school for five years, became a printer, taught himself further by wide reading, and became assistant secretary to the Lancashire Public School Association (1847–52) in Manchester. In 1847 he married Mary Ann Hill, but they separated in 1855. Waugh began publishing poetry in the *Manchester Examiner and Times* and gathered his poems together in *Sketches of Lancashire Life and Localities* (1855). Shortly thereafter he began to publish his dialect verse, which won him a wide audience and led to the publication of *Poems and Songs* (1859) and to his being able to live by his writing. He also published *Rambles in the Lake Country* (1861), a collection of stories, *Besom Ben* (1865), *Home Life of the Lancashire Factory Folk During the Cotton Famine, 1862* (1867), and numerous other travel books, collections of stories, and poems. Hailed as the spokesman for Lancashire working men in their own language, he was granted a civil list pension in 1882. No modern edition. Edwin Waugh, *Collected Works* (10 vols, 1881–83) with an eleventh volume of his collected poems (1889); Martha Vicinus, *The Ambiguities of Self-Help: Concerning the Life and Work of the Lancashire Dialect Writer, Edwin Waugh* (1984). Edwin Waugh Dialect Society: http://www.edwin-waughdialectsociety.com/page7.htm.]/ecp

Come Whoam° to Thy Childer° an' Me[1]

°Home °Children

Aw°'ve just mended th' fire wi' a cob;°   ° I ° lump of coal
   Owd Swaddle has brought thi new shoon;°   ° shoes
There's some nice bacon-collops° o'th' hob,   ° slices
   An' a quart o' ale-posset i'th' oon;°   ° oven
Aw've brought thi top-cwot,° does ta know,   ° top coat ° thou   5
   For the rain's comin' deawn very dree;°   ° wearily continuous
An' th' har'stone's° as white as new snow;   ° hearth stone
   Come whoam to thy childer an' me.

When aw put little Sally to bed,
   Hoo° cried 'cose her feyther weren't theer;   ° she ° father   10
So aw kiss'd th' little thing, an' aw said,
   At thae'd bring her a ribbin fro th' fair;
An' aw gav her her doll, an' some rags,
   An' a nice little white cotton bo',°   ° cotton ball
An' aw kissed her again; but hoo said   15
   At hoo wanted to kiss *thee* an' o'.°   ° as well

An' Dick, too, aw'd sich wark° wi' him,   ° work
   Afore aw could get him up th' stairs;
Thae towd him thae'd bring him a drum,

Notes

EDWIN WAUGH
[1] *title* Waugh's first dialect poem, a phonetic rendering in his Rochdale, Lancashire dialect. First published in the *Liverpool Mercury* (17 Sept. 1856; our text). Reprinted in the *Manchester Examiner* (1 Nov. 1856, often cited as first published here) and other newspapers, gaining in popularity. The poem was reprinted as a ballad-sheet and was publicized by Samuel Laycock, and in the south of England by Angela Burdett-Coutts (1814–1906); set to music by John Graham (*Songs of the North*, second edition, 1908); reprinted as "Come Whoam to Thi Childer an' Me" in *Lancashire Songs* (1866).

He said, when he're sayin' his prayers; 20
  Then he look'd i' my faze,° an' he said, °face
    "Has th' boggart° taen houd o' my dad?" °ghost, spectre
An' he cried whol his e'en° were quite red— °eyes
  He likes thee some weel, does yon lad!

At th' lung-length,° aw geet 'em laid still; °long length, at the end 25
  An' aw hearken't folk's feet at went by;
So aw iron't o' my clooas° reet weel,° °clothes °right well
  An' aw hanged 'em o' th' maiden² to dry;
When aw'd mended thi stockin's an' shirts,
  Aw sit deawn to knit i' my cheer, 30
An' aw rayley° did feel rather hurt— °really
  Mon,° aw'm *one-ly*° when theaw artn't theer. °man °lonely

"Aw've a drum an' a trumpet for Dick;
  Aw've a yard o' blue ribbon for Sal;
Aw've a book full o' babs;° an' a stick, °babies, pictures 35
  An' some 'bicco° an' pipes for mysel; °tobacco
Aw've brought thee some coffee an' tay;° °tea
  Iv thae'll *feel* i' my pocket, thae'll *see*;
An' aw've bought tho a new cap to-day—
  But, aw olez° bring summat° for *thee*! °always °something 40

God bless tho, my lass; aw'll go whoam,
  An' aw'll kiss thee an' th' childer o' reawnd;° °all round
Thae knows, at wheerever aw roam,
  Aw'm fain to get back to th' owd greawnd;° °old ground
Aw can do wi' o' crack° o'er a glass; °good talk or time 45
  Aw can do wi' a bit ov a spree;
But aw've no gradely° comfort, my lass, °right, proper
  Except wi' yon childer and thee."

Eawr Folk³

Eawr° Johnny gi's his mind to books; °our
  Eawr Abram studies plants,—
He caps the dule° for moss an' ferns, °beats the devil
  An' grooin' polyants;° °polyanthus, primroses
For aught abeawt° mechanickin', °about 5
  Eawr Ned's the very lad;
My uncle Jamie roots° i'th stars, °studies
  Enough to drive him mad.

Eawr Alick keeps a badger's° shop, °grocer's
  An' teyches Sunday schoo'; 10
Eawr Joseph's welly blynt,° poor lad; °well-nigh blind

Notes

² *maiden* (northern dial. clothes horse) drying rack.   ³ *title* published in *Lancashire Songs* (1866).

Eawr Timothy's—a foo';—
He's tried three different maks° o' trades,　　　　　°makes, kinds
　　An' olez missed his tip;°　　　　　　　　　　　°aim, goal
But, then, he's th' nicest whistler　　　　　　　　15
　　That ever cocked a lip!

Eawr Matty helps my mother, an'
　　Hoo sews, an' tents° eawr Joe;　　　　　°attends, cares for
At doin' sums, an' sich as that,
　　My feyther licks 'em o'!　　　　　　　　　　20
Eawr Charley,—eh, there connot be
　　Another pate° like his;　　　　　　　　　　°head
It's o' crom-full° o' ancientry,　　　　　　　°crammed full
　　An' Roman haw-pennies!°　　　　　°half-pennies, coins

Eawr Tummy's taen to preitchin',— °　　　°preaching　25
　　He's a topper at it, too!
But then,—what's th' use,—eawr Bill comes in
　　An' swears it winnut do:
When t'one's bin striven' o' he con°　°been striving all he can
　　To awter° wicked men,　　　　　　　°alter　30
Then t'other mays some marlocks,° an　°makes some pranks
　　Convarts 'em o'er again.

Eawr Abel's th' yung'st; an' next to Joe,
　　My mother likes him t' best;
Hoo gi's him brass,° aboon° his share,　　°money °above　35
　　To keep him nicely drest;—
He's gettin in wi' th' quality,°　　　°people of quality, class
　　An' when his clarkin's done,
He's olez oather° cricketin',　　　　　　　°either
　　Or shootin' wi' a gun.　　　　　　　　　40

My Uncle Sam's a fiddler; an'
　　Aw fain could yer° him play　　　　　　°hear
Fro' set o' sun till winter neet
　　Had melted into day;
For eh,—sich glee!—sich tenderness!　　　　45
　　Through every changin' part,
It's th' heart 'at stirs his fiddle,—
　　An' his fiddle stirs his heart.

When th' owd brid° touches th' tremblin' streng,　°bird
　　It knows his thowt so weel,　　　　　　50
It seawnds° as iv an angel tried　　　　　°sounds
　　To tell what angels feel;
An', sometimes, th' water in his e'en,
　　'At fun has made to flow,
Can hardly roll away, afore　　　　　　　　55
　　It's weet wi' drops o' woe.

Then, here's to Jone, an' Ab, an' Ned,
   An' Matty,—an' eaw Joe,—
My feyther, an' my mother; an'
   Eawr t'other lads an' o';
An' thee, too, owd musicianer,—   60
   Aw wish lung life to thee,—
A mon 'at plays a fiddle weel
   Should never awse to dee!°   °attempt to die

Emily Jane Brontë (1818–48)

Like her sisters, Emily was born at Thornton in Yorkshire (see CHARLOTTE BRONTË). After a brief stay at the Clergy Daughters' School at Cowan Bridge she returned home sick, to be taught at home by her father, Patrick Brontë (1777–1861), and aunt, Elizabeth Branwell (1776–1842). With her sisters and brother Branwell (1817–48) she began to create imaginary worlds adorned with characters, histories, and literatures: especially with Anne she created the world of Gondal (see n. 1). In 1837 she was a governess at Law Hill near Halifax, and in 1842 went to Brussels with Charlotte to study languages. Within nine months she returned to Haworth on the death of her aunt, who had largely raised the sisters. She remained at Haworth for the rest of her brief life. With her sisters she collaborated in the pseudonymous *Poems* (1846), including twenty-one of her own works (see CHARLOTTE BRONTË). The next year her only novel, *Wuthering Heights,* was published in two volumes, with Anne Brontë's *Agnes Grey* as the third. Emily's novel received mixed and puzzled reviews that condemned its "brutal cruelty" and violent emotions as "inexpressibly painful," while acknowledging its "great power." *Wuthering Heights* is acclaimed as one of the most important novels of the century, notable especially for its evocation of the Yorkshire moors, characters, and its elaborate framing narrative. Emily became sick in 1848, having caught a cold at her brother's funeral in September, and, refusing medical aid, died on 19 December.

In 1850 Charlotte republished *Wuthering Heights and Agnes Grey* under the authors' rightful names, and she included a number of new poems (see CHARLOTTE BRONTË), cited as *1850.* Emily Brontë's 200 poems are generally acknowledged as the most accomplished of the three sisters' verse, and an important development in nineteenth-century poetry. Standard editions: *The Poems of Emily Brontë,* eds Derek Roper and Edward Chitham (1995); *Wuthering Heights,* eds Ian Jack, Robert James, and Hilda Marsden (1976); Robert Barnard, *Emily Brontë* (2000); papers and diaries: http://academic. brooklyn.cuny.edu/english/melani/novel_19c/ wuthering/diary_papers.

Remembrance[1]

Cold in the earth[2]—and the deep snow piled above thee,
Far, far, removed, cold in the dreary grave!
Have I forgot, my only Love, to love thee,
Severed at last by Time's all-severing° wave?   °MS allwearing

Notes

EMILY JANE BRONTË
[1] *title* one of Emily Brontë's best-known poems, originally one of some sixty-seven "Gondal" poems. Gondal was an imaginary kingdom located in the north Pacific, with a climate like that of Yorkshire or Scotland, and made up of

Now, when alone, do my thoughts no longer hover
Over the mountains, on that northern° shore,　　　　　　°MS Angora's
Resting their wings where heath and fern-leaves cover
Thy noble heart for ever, ever more?

Cold in the earth—and fifteen wild Decembers,
From those brown hills, have melted into spring:　　　　　10
Faithful, indeed, is the spirit that remembers
After such years of change and suffering!

Sweet Love of youth, forgive, if I forget thee,
While the world's tide is bearing me along;
Other desires and other hopes beset me,[3]　　　　　　　　15
Hopes which obscure, but cannot do thee wrong!

No later light° has lightened up my heaven,　　　　　　°MS other sun
No second morn° has ever shone for me;　　　　　　　　°MS other star
All my life's bliss from thy dear life was given,
All my life's bliss is in the grave with thee.　　　　　　20

But, when the days of golden dreams had perished,
And even Despair was powerless to destroy;
Then did I learn how existence could be cherished,
Strengthened, and fed without the aid of joy.

Then did I check the tears of useless passion—　　　　　25
Weaned my young soul from yearning after thine;
Sternly denied its burning wish to hasten
Down to that tomb already more than mine.

And, even yet, I dare not let it languish,
Dare not indulge in memory's rapturous pain;　　　　　　30
Once drinking deep of that divinest° anguish,　　　　　°MS delightful
How could I seek the empty world again?

Song ["The Linnet in the rocky dells"][4]

The linnet in the rocky dells,
　　The moor-lark in the air,
The bee among the heather bells,
　　That hide my lady fair:

Notes

four kingdoms of warring dynasties. This poem is a lament by the ambitious, aristocratic Rosina Alcona for Julius Brenzaida of Angora, one of the kingdoms in Gondal. In the Brontë mythology, he had been imprisoned by her but later married her. Eventually Brenzaida became emperor of Gondal, ruling for some years before he was assassinated. Fifteen years later this elegy is spoken over his grave by Rosina. Some specific references to Gondal were removed when the poem was published with the title "Remembrance" in *Poems* (1846); in the MS there is no title but a heading concerning the speaker and occasion of the poem: "R Alcona to J Brenzaida" with the date "March 3d 1845," the date of composition. Our text: *Poems* (1846). We include important MS variants flush right or in footnotes.

[2] *earth* the opening phrase is used twice in Thomas Moore's *Irish Melodies* (1801–34), notably in the song "When cold in the earth lies the friend thou hast lov'd"; the book was known by the Brontës.

[3] *me* MS: "Sterner desires and darker Hopes beset me."

[4] *title* the MS is untitled and dated "May 1st 1844." This poem is another Gondal lament, in which the speaker is very likely Lord Eldred W., captain of the Queen's Guard,

The wild deer browse above her breast; 5
    The wild birds raise their brood;
And they, her smiles of love caressed,
    Have left her solitude!

I ween, that when the grave's dark wall
    Did first her form retain; 10
They thought their hearts could ne'er recall
    The light of joy again.

They thought the tide of grief would flow
    Unchecked through future years;
But where is all their anguish now, 15
    And where are all their tears?

Well, let them fight for honour's breath,
    Or pleasure's shade pursue—
The dweller in the land of death
    Is changed and careless too. 20

And, if their eyes should watch and weep
    Till sorrow's source were dry,
She would not, in her tranquil sleep,
    Return a single sigh!

Blow, west-wind, by the lonely mound: 25
    And murmur, summer-streams—
There is no need of other sound
    To soothe my lady's dreams.

To Imagination[5]

When weary with the long day's care,
    And earthly change from pain to pain,
And lost and ready to despair,
    Thy kind voice calls me back again:
Oh, my true friend! I am not lone, 5
    While thou canst speak with such a tone!

So hopeless is the world without;
    The world within I doubly prize;
Thy world, where guile, and hate, and doubt,

Notes

indicated in the MS by the initials at the end of the poem: "EW." In the Gondal epic, the lament is spoken over the grave of Augusta Geraldine Almeda, the queen of Gondal, murdered on Elmor Hill at the prompting of her step-daughter. Here Eldred, who earlier had found her body, laments the power of fate that granted her a peaceful grave after a passionate life with many treacheries and many lovers (whose short-lived grief is referred to). Our text: *Poems* (1846).

[5] *title* dated in the MS "September 3d 1844." In Romantic ideology, imagination is the creative source of poetic inspiration. Brontë draws on this tradition in setting out imagination as the true companion of the soul. Our text: *Poems* (1846).

Emily Jane Brontë

And cold suspicion never rise;   10
Where thou, and I, and Liberty,[6]
    Have undisputed sovereignty.

What matters it, that, all around,
    Danger, and guilt, and darkness lie,
If but within our bosom's bound   15
    We hold a bright, untroubled sky,
Warm with ten thousand mingled rays,
Of suns that know no winter days?

Reason, indeed, may oft complain
    For Nature's sad reality,   20
And tell the suffering heart, how vain
    Its cherished dreams must always be;
And Truth may rudely trample down
The flowers of Fancy, newly-blown:

But, thou art ever there, to bring   25
    The hovering vision back, and breathe
New glories o'er the blighted spring,
    And call a lovelier Life from Death,
And whisper, with a voice divine,
Of real worlds, as bright as thine.   30

I trust not to thy phantom bliss,
    Yet, still, in evening's quiet hour,
With never-failing thankfulness,
    I welcome thee, Benignant Power;
Sure solacer of human cares,   35
And sweeter hope, when hope despairs!

Plead for Me[7]

Oh, thy bright eyes must answer now,
When Reason, with a scornful brow,
Is mocking at my overthrow!
Oh thy sweet tongue must plead for me
And tell why I have chosen thee!   5

Stern Reason is to judgment come,
Arrayed in all her forms of gloom:

Notes

[6] *Liberty* David Hume (1711–76) in *A Treatise of Human Nature* (1739) argues for "the liberty of the imagination to transpose and change ideas" (sect. 3), an idea taken up at the end of the eighteenth century by many writers, including Jean-Jacques Rousseau in *Essay on the Origin of Language* (1781). To the Romantic poets liberty and freedom are abstract virtues deriving from the principles of the French Revolution (1789) and its "Declaration of the Rights of Man and of the Citizen" (1791), in which liberty is the first of the natural and universal human rights that is claimed for all citizens.

[7] *title* dated in the MS "October 14th 1844." The subject is imagination contrasted with reason. Our text: *Poems* (1846).

Wilt thou, my advocate, be dumb?
No, radiant angel, speak and say,
Why I did cast the world away.   10

Why I have persevered to shun
The common paths that others run,
And on a strange road journeyed on,
Heedless, alike, of wealth and power—
Of glory's wreath and pleasure's flower.   15

These, once, indeed, seemed Beings Divine;
And they, perchance, heard vows of mine,
And saw my offerings on their shrine;
But, careless gifts are seldom prized,
And *mine* were worthily despised.   20

So, with a ready heart I swore
To seek their altar-stone no more;
And gave my spirit to adore
Thee, ever-present, phantom thing;
My slave, my comrade, and my king,   25

A slave because I rule thee still;
Incline thee to my changeful will,
And make thy influence good or ill:
A comrade, for by day and night
Thou art my intimate delight,—   30

My darling pain that wounds and sears
And wrings a blessing out from tears
By deadening me to earthly cares;
And yet, a king, though Prudence well
Have taught thy subject to rebel.   35

And am I wrong to worship, where
Faith cannot doubt, nor hope despair,
Since my own soul can grant my prayer?
Speak, God of visions, plead for me,
And tell why I have chosen thee!   40

The Old Stoic[8]

Riches I hold in light esteem;
     And love I laugh to scorn;
And lust of fame was but a dream
     That vanished with the morn:

Notes ─────────────────────────────

[8] *title* dated in the MS "March 1st 1841." The speaker is possibly a character from the Gondal epic. Stoicism was a philosophical movement in Athens in the third century BCE, founded by Zeno of Citium. It held that the emotions of fear, envy, and other passions such as sexual love or hate, come from false judgements, and that calm of mind and

And if I pray, the only prayer   5
    That moves my lips for me
Is, "Leave the heart that now I bear,
    And give me liberty!"

Yes, as my swift days near their goal,
    'Tis all that I implore;   10
In life and death, a chainless soul,
    With courage to endure.

"Shall earth no more inspire thee?"[9]

Shall earth no more inspire thee,
    Thou lonely dreamer, now?
Since passion may not fire thee,
    Shall nature cease to bow?

Thy mind is ever moving,   5
    In regions dark to thee;
Recall its useless roving,
    Come back, and dwell with me.

I know my mountain breezes
    Enchant and soothe thee still;   10
I know my sunshine pleases,
    Despite thy wayward will.

When day with evening blending,
    Sinks from the summer sky,
I've seen thy spirit bending   15
    In fond idolotry.

I've watched thee every hour;
    I know my mighty sway:
I know my magic power
    To drive thy griefs away.   20

Few hearts to mortals given,
    On earth so wildly pine;
Yet few° would ask a heaven   °MS none
    More like this° earth than thine.   °MS the

Notes

the cultivation of virtue lead to happiness. Seneca the Younger (*c.*4 BCE–55 CE) and Epictetus (55–135) held such views in ancient Rome, arguing that abandoning passions would lead to true freedom. Stoic came to mean indifference to pleasure or pain, to joy or sorrow, or, more generally, to endure adversities with patience, but Brontë's ideas are more closely related to those of classical Greece and Rome. Our text: *Poems* (1846).

[9] *title* first printed in *1850* with Charlotte Brontë's note: "The following little piece has no title; but in it the Genius of a solitary region seems to address his wandering and wayward votary, and to recall within his influence the proud mind which rebelled at times even against what it most loved." Charlotte Brontë made the two alterations from the MS.

Then let my winds caress thee; 25
    Thy comrade let me be:
Since nought beside can bless thee,
    Return—and dwell with me.

"Ay—there it is! it wakes to-night"[10]

Ay—there it is! it wakes to-night
    Deep feelings I thought dead;°   °MS Sweet thoughts that will not die
Strong in the blast—quick gathering light°—   °MS And feeling's fires flash all as bright
    The heart's flame kindles red°.   °MS As in the years gone by!—

"Now° I can tell by thine altered cheek,   °MS "And 5
    And by thine eyes' full° gaze,   °MS thy kindled
And by the words thou scarce dost speak,
    How wildly fancy plays.

Yes—I could swear that glorious wind
    Has swept the world aside,   10
Has dashed its memory from thy mind
    Like foam-bells from the tide:

And thou art now a spirit pouring
    Thy presence into all:
The thunder° of the tempest's° roaring,   °MS essence; °MS Tempest 15
    The whisper of its° fall: °MS And of the Tempest's

An° universal influence,   °MS A
    From thine own influence free;
A principle of life—intense—
    Lost to mortality.   20

Thus truly, when that breast is cold,
    Thy prisoned soul shall rise;
The dungeon mingle with the mould—
    The captive with the skies.
Nature's deep being, thine shall hold,   25
    Her spirit all thy spirit fold,
    Her breath absorb thy sighs.
Mortal! though soon life's tale is told;
    Who once lives, never dies!"

Notes

[10] *title* first published *1850* with the prefatory remark: "In these stanzas a louder gale has roused the sleeper on her pillow: the wakened soul struggles to blend with the storm by which it is swayed." The MS was much revised, probably by Charlotte Brontë, for publication, including all of the poem after line 4 in quotation marks; in the MS there are no quotation marks, and almost no punctuation except dashes after lines 8, 12, 14, 16, 18, 20, 23, and 24. Lines 25–29 (not in the MS) are added to the last stanza in *1850*. The poem is dated in the MS: "July 6th 1841."

"No coward soul is mine"[11]

No coward soul is mine,
No trembler in the world's storm-troubled sphere:
   I see Heaven's glories shine,
And faith shines equal, arming me from fear.

   O God within my breast,   5
Almighty, ever-present Deity!
   Life—that in me has° rest,   °MS hast
As I—undying Life—have power in thee!

   Vain are the thousand creeds
That move men's hearts: unutterably vain,   10
   Worthless as withered weeds,
Or idlest froth amid the boundless main,

   To waken doubt in one
Holding so fast by thine° infinity;   °MS thy
   So surely anchored on   15
The steadfast rock of immortality.

   With wide-embracing love
Thy spirit animates eternal years,
   Pervades and broods above,
Changes, sustains, dissolves, creates, and rears.   20

   Though earth and man° were gone,   °MS moon
And suns and universes ceased to be,
   And Thou wert° left alone,   °MS were
Every existence would exist in Thee.

   There is not room for Death,   25
Nor atom that his might could render void:
   Thou—THOU° art Being and Breath,   °MS Since Thou
And what THOU art may never be destroyed.

Eliza Cook (1818–89)

The youngest of the eleven children of Joseph Cook, a Southwark tinsmith and brazier, Eliza was educated in her local Sunday school, but was largely self-taught. In 1827 her father retired to a farm in Sussex, near Horsham. In 1835 she published her first volume of verse, *Lays of a Wild Harp*, praised by William Jerdan (1782–1869) in his *Literary Gazette*. In 1837

Notes

[11] *title* first published *1850*, with the following prefatory comment: "The following are the last lines my sister Emily ever wrote." However, Emily Brontë did make additions to two unfinished poems. The MS. bears the date: "Jan 2d 1846." Emily Dickinson (1830–86), American poet, chose this poem to be read at her funeral.

she published her best-known poem "The Old Arm-Chair" in the radical newspaper the *Weekly Dispatch*, edited by William Johnson Fox (1786–1864), a friend of Robert Browning's. Her second volume, *Malaia, and Other Poems* (1838), was wildly popular: many of her poems were set to music. She also aroused some controversy from the reviewers who criticized her on the basis of her sex: gender norms specified that she should conform to womanly writing in subject-matter, themes, and diction, all of which she transgressed in such poems as "The Englishman" and "Old Times," and about which she defended herself in the preface to *Poems* (1845). She also supported the Chartist cause. In 1849 she established the popular *Eliza Cook's Journal* (selling between 50,000 and 60,000 copies at one penny) in which she appealed to women, working-class and artisan readers, and middle-class readership with such causes as women's education, women's property rights, dress reform, and sanitation. In 1863 she was granted a Civil List Petition of £100 a year, after which her publications included *New Echoes, and Other Poems* (1864) and *Diamond Dust* (1865). She had a lesbian relationship (1845–49) with the American actress Charlotte Cushman (1816–76). Like George Sand (1804–76) and others, Cook broke with accepted convention in wearing male clothing. Her ill health resulted in a sharp decline in writing, as she became a semi-reclusive invalid. No modern edition; *The Poetical Works of Eliza Cook: Complete Edition* (n. d. 1872?); no standard biography or editions of letters. See the Orlando Project: Women's Writing in the British Isles: http://orlando.cambridge.org/public/svPeople?person_id=cookel.

The Old Arm-Chair[1]

I love it, I love it; and who shall dare
To chide me for loving that old arm-chair?
I've treasured it long as a sainted prize,
I've bedew'd it with tears, and embalmed it with sighs;
'Tis bound by a thousand bands to my heart;   5
Not a tie will break, not a link will start.
Would ye learn the spell? a mother sat there,
And a sacred thing is that old arm-chair.

In childhood's hour I linger'd near
The hallow'd seat with list'ning ear;   10
And gentle words that mother would give,
To fit me to die and teach me to live.
She told me shame would never betide,
With truth for my creed and God for my guide;
She taught me to lisp my earliest prayer,   15
As I knelt beside that old arm-chair.

I sat and watch'd her many a day,
When her eye grew dim, and her locks were grey;
And I almost worshipp'd her when she smil'd
And turn'd from her Bible to bless her child.   20
Years roll'd on, but the last one sped—

Notes

Eliza Cook
[1] *title* first published *Weekly Dispatch* (May, 1837); republished in Cook's *Melaia, and Other Poems* (1838). Cook's best-known and most-loved poem among Victorian readers. Our text: *Melaia, and Other Poems* (1840).

My idol was shatter'd, my earth-star fled;
I learnt how much the heart can bear,
When I saw her die in that old arm-chair.

'Tis past! 'tis past! but I gaze on it now   25
With quivering breath and throbbing brow:
'Twas there she nursed me, 'twas there she died;
And memory flows with lava tide.
Say it is folly, and deem me weak,
While the scalding drops start down my cheek;   30
But I love it, I love it, and cannot tear
My soul from a mother's old arm-chair.

Arthur Hugh Clough (1819–61)

Born in Liverpool, the son of a cotton merchant, James Butler Clough (1784–1844), and Anne Perfect (d. 1860), Clough (rhymes with rough) emigrated to the United States, from 1822 to 1836. The family lived in Charleston, South Carolina, but Arthur was sent back to England for a year's schooling in Chester (1828) before entering Rugby School (1829–36). There he admired the headmaster Thomas Arnold and became friends with his sons, Matthew and Thomas. Winning numerous prizes, he entered Balliol College, Oxford (1837–42) and won a fellowship to Oriel College (1842–48) where John Henry Newman was also a fellow, then completing the *Tracts for the Times*. Balliol and Oriel Colleges were centres of Tractarian controversy that caught Clough up in religious questionings concerning his evangelical background and the historical basis of the Gospels, leading him to resign his fellowship. In 1847 Clough met Ralph Waldo Emerson (1803–82), American transcendentalist, and joined him in Paris to observe the French Revolution (1848). In the same year he went to Italy, where he witnessed the short-lived Italian Republic under Giuseppe Mazzini (1805–72). Clough published in flexible hexameters *The Bothie of Toper-na-Fuosich* (1848, changed later to *The Bothie of Tober-na-Vuolich*), a pastoral narrative poem set in the Scottish highlands. It was followed by a collection of poems coauthored with Thomas Burbidge (1816–92) entitled *Ambarvalia* (1849). He wrote three longer poems:

Amours de Voyage (1849; published 1858), based on his travel experiences in Rome; the unfinished Faustian poem *Dipsychus* (1850), concerning a youth of two minds about his future; and *Mari Magno, or Tales on Board* (1861). Earlier, he had been appointed in 1848 head of University Hall in the University of London, and Professor of English at University College. The following year he went with W. M. Thackeray to America, writing letters back to England to Carlyle and his future wife, Blanche Smith (1828–1904), whom he married in 1854. Finding congenial employment as an examiner for the Education Board, he also helped Florence Nightingale with her writing projects and campaigns for hospital reform. Because of poor health he took a leave from his employment and travelled to Greece, Constantinople, and the Pyrenees with the Tennysons, but he became much sicker and died in Florence. Matthew Arnold commemorated his lifelong friendship with Clough in the elegy, *Thyrsis* (1865). After Clough's death, his wife published *Poems* (1862), another edition that included *Dipsychus* (1865), and *Poems and Prose Remains of Arthur Hugh Clough* (2 vols, 1869). Standard edition: *The Poems of Arthur Hugh Clough*, ed. F. L. Mulhauser (second edition 1974); *The Correspondence of Arthur Hugh Clough*, ed. F. L. Mulhauser (2 vols, 1957); Anthony Kenny, *Arthur Hugh Clough: A Poet's Life* (2005). Clough at the Victorian Web: http://www.victorianweb.org/authors/clough/index.html.

Qui Laborat, Orat[1]

O only Source of all our light and life,
    Whom as our truth, our strength, we see and feel,
But whom the hours of mortal moral strife
    Alone aright reveal!

Mine inmost soul, before Thee inly brought,   5
    Thy presence owns ineffable, divine;
Chastised each rebel self-encentered thought,
    My will adoreth Thine.

With eye down-dropt, if then this earthly mind
    Speechless abide, or speechless e'en depart;   10
Nor seek to see—for what of earthly kind,
    Can see Thee as Thou art?[2]—

If sure-assured 'tis but profanely bold
    In thought's abstractest forms to seem to see,
It dare not dare the dread communion hold   15
    In ways unworthy Thee,

O not unowned, thou shalt unnamed forgive,
    In worldly walks the prayerless heart prepare;
And if in work its life it seem to live,
    Shalt make that work be prayer.   20

Nor times shall lack, when while the work it plies,
    Unsummoned powers the blinding film shall part,
And scarce by happy tears made dim, the eyes
    In recognition start.

As wills Thy will, or give or e'en forbear   25
    The beatific supersensual sight,
So, with Thy blessing blest, that humbler prayer
    Approach Thee morn and night.

"Duty—that's to say complying"[3]

Duty—that's to say complying
    With whate'er's expected here;

Notes

ARTHUR HUGH CLOUGH

[1] *title* the Latin phrase (who works, prays) is attributed to St Augustine of Hippo (354–430) and in a somewhat different version, was also used by St Bernard of Clairvaux (1090–1153): "He who prays and labours lifts his heart to God with his hands." The motto of Rugby School was "*Orando laborando*" (Lat. by praying, by working), a variant of the motto of the Benedictine monks, *laborare est orare* (Lat. to work is to pray), itself used in Carlyle's *Past and Present*

(1843) in the opening paragraph of chapter 12. Clough later questioned this injunction to work for the good of society and the soul. First published in *Ambarvalia* (1849); dated "Oxford, 1845" in *Poems* (1862).

[2] *art* see 1 Corinthians 13: 12: "For now we see through a glass darkly; but then face to face."

[3] *title* a bitter reflection on conventional Victorian morality that was extended from military obedience to rules and

On your unknown cousin's dying,
Straight be ready with the tear;
Upon etiquette relying,   5
Unto usage nought denying,
Lend your waist to be embraced,[4]
    Blush not even, never fear;
Claims of kith and kin connection,
    Claims of manners honour still,   10
Ready money of affection
    Pay, whoever drew the bill.
With the form conforming duly,
Senseless what it meaneth truly,
Go to church—the world require you,   15
    To balls—the world require you too,
And marry—papa and mamma desire you,
    And your sisters and schoolfellows do.
Duty—'tis to take on trust
What things are good, and right, and just;   20
    And whether indeed they be or be not,
    Try not, test not, feel not, see not:
    'Tis walk and dance, sit down and rise
    By leading, opening ne'er your eyes;
Stunt sturdy limbs that Nature gave,   25
And be drawn in a Bath chair[5] along to the grave.

    'Tis the stern and prompt suppressing,
        As an obvious deadly sin,
All the questing and the guessing
        Of the soul's own soul within: 30
'Tis the coward acquiescence
        In a destiny's behest,
To a shade by terror made,
Sacrificing, aye, the essence
        Of all that's truest, noblest, best: 35
'Tis the blind non-recognition
        Either of goodness, truth, or beauty,
Except by precept and submission;
        Moral blank, and moral void,
        Life at very birth destroyed,   40
Atrophy, exinanition![6]
Duty!——
Yea, by duty's prime condition
    Pure nonentity of duty!

Notes

orders to the whole of society with the injunction to "keep a stiff upper lip," not showing emotion, but also persevering in one's post. See also HEMANS, n. 1; and HOPKINS, "FELIX RANDAL." First published in *Ambarvalia* (1849).

[4] *embraced* this line was omitted in 1862 as indecorous.

[5] *chair* a three-wheeled chair with a collapsible hood for the disabled.

[6] *exinanition* the process of emptying or exhausting, or the condition of emptiness or exhaustion.

The Latest Decalogue[7]

Thou shalt have one God only; who
Would be at the expense of two?
No graven images may be
Worshipped except the currency;
Swear not at all; for, for thy curse   5
Thine enemy is none the worse:
At church on Sunday to attend
Will serve to keep the world thy friend:
Honour thy parents; that is, all
From whom advancement may befall: 10
Thou shalt not kill; but need'st not strive
Officiously to keep alive:
Do not adultery commit:
Advantage rarely comes of it:
Thou shalt not steal; an empty feat,   15
When it's so lucrative to cheat:
Bear not false witness; let the lie
Have time on its own wings to fly
Thou shalt not covet, but tradition
Approves all forms of competition.[8]   20

The Struggle[9]

Say not the struggle nought availeth,
    The labor and the wounds are vain,
The enemy faints not nor faileth,
    And as things have been, things remain.

If hopes were dupes, fears may be liars;   5
    It may be, in yon smoke concealed,
Your comrades chase e'en now the fliers—
    And, but for you, possess the field.[10]

Notes

[7] *title* the decalogue is the Ten Commandments (Exodus 20), here parodied to conform with mid-nineteenth-century social and moral expectations, conventions, and actual values. Two manuscripts of the poem exist: one in the British Library (the version given here), published in *Poems* (1862); the second version is based on the MS in the Houghton Library at Harvard; see *Poems* (ed. Mulhauser, 1974).

[8] *competition* the British Library MS contains four additional lines (excluded from the printed version) that ironically restate the summary of the decalogue given by Jesus when asked which is the greatest commandment in the law (see Matthew 22: 37–39): "The sum of all is, thou shalt love, / If any body, God above: / At any rate shall never labour / *More* than thyself to love thy neighbour."

[9] *title* written when Clough was in Rome in June, 1849, already discouraged by the collapse of the revolution of

1848 in France. He witnessed the siege of Rome by the French under General Charles Oudinot (1791–1863), who defeated the Italian Republican army under Giuseppe Garibaldi (1807–82). Manuscripts indicate that alternative titles were considered: "In Profundis" (Lat. in the depths), an adaptation of Psalm 130 (Lat. *De Profundis clamavi Domine:* out of the depths have I called unto thee, O Lord"); and "Dum Spiro" (Lat. while I breathe), the first words of the common motto, *Dum spiro, spero* (Lat. while I live I hope), from Cicero, *Ad Atticum* (Letters to Atticus 9.11). First published as "The Struggle" in the American art journal, *The Crayon* (1 Aug. 1855), our text; republished without a title in *Poems* (1862); and with the title of the first line in *Poems and Prose Remains* (1869).

[10] *field* for the confusion of armies fighting in smoke or darkness, even slaying their own comrades, see Thucydides' account of the battle of Epipolae in *The Peloponnesian War*

For while the tired waves vainly breaking,
    Seem here no painful inch to gain,   10
Far back through creeks and inlets making,
    Comes silent, flooding-in, the main.

And not by eastern windows only,
    When daylight comes, comes in the light,
In front the sun climbs slow, how slowly,   15
    But westward, look! the land is bright.

Ah! Yet Consider it Again![11]

"Old things need not be therefore true,"
O brother men, nor yet the new;
Ah! still awhile the old thought retain,
And yet consider it again!

The souls of now two thousand years,   5
Have laid up here[12] their toils and fears,
And all the earnings of their pain,—
Ah, yet consider it again!

We! what do we see? each a space
Of some few yards before his face;   10
Does that the whole wide plan explain?
Ah, yet consider it again!

Alas! the great world goes its way,
And takes its truth from each new day;
They do not quit, nor can retain,   15
Far less consider it again.

Epi-strauss-ium[13]

Matthew and Mark and Luke and holy John
Evanished all and gone!

Notes

7. 4., used also in Matthew Arnold's "Dover Beach" (see ARNOLD 35–37; and n. 67).

[11] *title* in his late essay, unpublished in his lifetime, and entitled by his wife as "Notes On the Religious Tradition," Clough writes, "Where then, since neither in Rationalism nor in Rome is our refuge, where then shall we seek for the Religious Tradition?

Everywhere; but above all in our own work: in life, in action, in submission, so far as action goes, in service, in experience, in patience, and in confidence. I would scarcely have any man dare say that he has found it, till that moment when death removes his power of telling it. Let no young man presume to talk to us vainly and confidently about it" (*Poems and Prose Remains*, 1869). First published in *Poems* (1862); the title was added in *Poems and Prose Remains* (1869).

[12] *here* in Christianity.

[13] *title* a pun on "epi-thalamium" (Gk. concerning the bridal chamber), used as a literary genre for the celebration of a wedding, as in Edmund Spenser's *Epithalamium* (1595). Clough turns it to a different celebration as "Concerning Strauss-ism," the advent of the thought of German biblical critics as represented by David Friedrich Strauss

Yea, he[14] that erst, his dusky curtains quitting,
Thro' Eastern pictured panes his level beams transmitting,
With gorgeous portraits blent,   5
On them his glories intercepted spent,
Southwestering now, thro' windows plainly glassed,
On the inside face his radiance keen hath cast,
And in the lustre lost, invisible and gone,
Are, say you, Matthew, Mark and Luke and holy John?   10
Lost, is it, lost, to be recovered never?
However,
The place of worship the meantime with light
Is, if less richly, more sincerely bright,
And in blue skies the Orb is manifest to sight.   15

John Ruskin (1819–1900)

The only child of a wealthy wine-importer father, John James Ruskin (1785–1864), and his mother, Margaret Cock (1781–1871), John Ruskin was born in London and was educated at home in the Bible (committing much to memory), evangelical Christianity, and the works of Shakespeare, Scott, and Byron. In travels with his father on business, he developed a taste for the English landscape, and with his family had protracted tours of France, Belgium, Germany, Switzerland, and Italy, becoming enamoured of the Alps and Venice. Throughout his life he kept detailed notebooks recording his reactions to scenery, atmospheric conditions, and colours, with descriptions, sketches, and measurements. He first studied art with a conventional teacher (Copley Fielding, 1787–1855), and then with a more adventuresome one (J. D. Harding, 1798–

1863). He began to publish poems and enrolled at Oxford (1836) at Christ Church where his tutor was Henry Liddell (1811–98, father of Alice of Wonderland fame). Ruskin's mother had moved to Oxford's High Street to guard his religion and morals, and his father visited on weekends. In 1839 Ruskin won the Newdigate Prize for poetry, but his health deteriorated and he left to recover, returning to graduate in 1842. During this period he wrote the fairy tale *The King of the Golden River* (written in 1841 for 12-year-old Effie Gray, whom he later married; published in Dec. 1850). Meanwhile he had met the painter J. M. W. Turner (1775–1851), whom he would champion in the five volumes of *Modern Painters* (1843–60). In 1845 he first travelled without his parents, studying the Alps, and art and architecture in Italy, especially in

Notes

(1808–74). Strauss published *Das Leben Jesu, kritisch bearbeitet* (1835–36), translated by George Eliot as *The Life of Jesus, Critically Examined* (3 vols, 1846). Strauss argued that the supernatural and miraculous elements in the Gospels should not be read as having a historical foundation but seen as part of the effort of the early church to understand the meaning of Jesus. Hence he proposes that these stories are "mythological" – that is, they embody truths seen in the light of Jewish history and tradition, whereby Jesus' life, teaching, and leadership as one who challenged the religious authorities attracted miraculous deeds after his death. These deeds, often set in parallel to other stories from the Hebrew Scriptures, indicated Jesus' Messianic

status in the early Christian communities in which the Gospels were written. Such views challenged the notions of the Bible's literal truth and proved enormously controversial, although the concept of textual analysis and the study of mythology in this sense gradually became conventional tools for biblical criticism throughout the nineteenth century. See RELIGION: RELIGIOUS FAITH; JOWETT, "INTERPRETATION" (WEB p. 206). While written in 1847, the poem was not published until *Poems and Prose Remains* (1869).

[14] *he* the sun, a conventional association between Christ and the sun, and as the light of the world (see Psalm 19: 5; and John 8: 12).

Lucca, Pisa, Florence, and Venice. His marriage in 1848 to Effie Gray (1828–97) was never consummated, ending in annulment (1854), after which she married John Millais (1829–96), the Pre-Raphaelite painter and friend of Ruskin's. In the 1850s he became the patron and advocate of the Pre-Raphaelites, praising them for their goal of painting (and writing) according to nature. Later in life he became the Slade Professor of Art at Oxford (1869–79; 1883–84). Ruskin suffered from a series of mental breakdowns from 1871, the first perhaps precipitated by his love for the young girl Rose la Touche (1848–75), including a rejected proposal when she was 18.

Ruskin established himself as a Victorian polymath, the arbiter of taste for the nineteenth century, making pronouncements on almost every topic, including painting, architecture, landscape, poetry, aesthetics, politics, and economics. After *Modern Painters*, other important works followed: *The Seven Lamps of Architecture* (1849), with its stress on the moral characteristics of both the builders and their buildings: sacrifice, truth, power, beauty, life, memory, and obedience. *The Stones of Venice* (3 vols, 1851–53) discussed the rise of Venetian architecture and included his famous essay on "The Nature of Gothic." True to the vocation of the Victorian sage, he also wrote on social issues, in *Unto this Last* (1860 in the *Cornhill Magazine*), challenging the laissez-faire economics of J. S. Mill. For thirteen years (1871–84) he published irregular letters to the "Workmen of England" entitled *Fors Clavigera*. His autobiography, *Praeterita* (Lat. concerning things past), was published in 1885–89. Standard works: *The Complete Works of John Ruskin*, eds E. T. Cook and Alexander Wedderburn (39 vols, 1903–12); *The Diaries of John Ruskin*, eds Joan Evans and John Howard Whitehouse (3 vols, 1956–59); Robert Hewison, *John Ruskin* (2007). Lancaster University Ruskin Library and Research Centre: http://www.lancs.ac.uk/depts/ruskinlib/Pages/Works.html.

Modern Painters[1]

In 1843 Ruskin published anonymously, as by "A Graduate of Oxford," the first volume of *Modern Painters*. Initially it was a response to the attack on J. M. W. Turner in a review by John Eagles (1783–1855), art critic of *Blackwood's Magazine* (Oct. 1836), who had called Turner's *Juliet and Her Nurse* (1836): "a strange jumble … a composition as from models of different parts of Venice, thrown higgledy-piggledy together, streaked blue and pink, and thrown into a flour tub." Eventually, by 1860, *Modern Painters* would expand to five huge volumes, an analysis of the ways in which contemporary painters, especially Turner, worked according to close observation of the "truth" of nature. Eventually Ruskin widened his scope to consider numerous aspects of meteorology, the human form in its mental, spiritual, and physical dimensions, and the varied techniques of the painter. For his work Ruskin proposed the title "Turner and the Ancients," changed at the publisher's suggestion to *Modern Painters*. Turner and the other "moderns" were set up as opposed to the classical landscape

Notes

JOHN RUSKIN

[1] *title* Ruskin's full title was *Modern Painters: Their Superiority in the Art of Landscape Painting to all the Ancient Masters, Proved by example of the True, the Beautiful, and the Intellectual from the Works of Modern Artists, especially from those of J. M. W. Turner*. In our notes we follow the traditional numbering of Ruskin's sections from Cook and Wedderburn.

When he published Volume II of *Modern Painters* in 1846, he also published a revised version of Volume I, trimming it of much of the description, reshaping, and, he felt, tightening his argument. He also inserted 100 pages of new material derived from his Italian travels and studies. Our text: 1843.

painters – a late manifestation of the seventeenth-century literary debate concerning the Ancients (of Greece and Rome) and the Moderns, known as the *Querelle des Anciens et des Modernes*. In France Nicolas Boileau (1636–1711) maintained that the classical writers should be imitated, while the case for the moderns was advocated by Charles Perrault (1628–1703): modern writers should be free of imitation, relying instead on genius and invention, and should be conformed by the prevailing cultural and social conditions of the day. In England a similar debate took place, finally satirized for the eighteenth century in Jonathan Swift's *Battle of the Books*, part of *A Tale of a Tub* (1704). But the debate continued in relation to the classical epic – Was Homer an "original genius" and should he be imitated (as the classicists maintained), or was he a primitive bard (as Thomas Blackwell, 1707–57, and others maintained)? Could Homer provide inspiration for other primitive epics, like those of Ossian? In France as well as in England this literary debate had profound historical, social, and cultural implications: the imitation of the ancient writers showed a respect for tradition and, above all, authority in cultural taste and religious belief – at a time when those conventions were being challenged by the new thinking of the Glorious Revolution (1688) and the challenges of the Deists. On the other hand, the advocates of the moderns aligned themselves with new developments in science that challenged religious authority – such as the achievements of Isaac Newton and the work of the French Encyclopedists. Through the Romantic movement, poetic tradition generally rejected the close imitation of ancient models and genres in favour of inspiration from nature; to the Victorians, the debate was revived by Ruskin and others as part of the battle over styles in painting, architecture, and literature (see LITERATURE: DEBATES; PUGIN, *CONTRASTS*).

Ruskin was going against the practices of traditionalist wealthy and titled collectors, who prized the work of the Old Masters like Raphael and Titian, and the classical landscape painters,

Nicholas Poussin (1594–1665), Claude Lorrain (1600–82), and Richard Wilson (1714–82). To Ruskin much of their work represented an adherence to the rules of beauty set down by Edmund Burke in *The Sublime and Beautiful* (1757). Ruskin held that such views were out-of-date, and had to be replaced with new notions of colour. The tradition of studio painting also had to be replaced by painting in the open air to capture "truth to nature," and the principles of design and order had to be imbued with the moral and spiritual meaning of clouds, storms, air, water, rocks, and vegetation.

In the first chapters of *Modern Painters* Ruskin lays the foundation for his work. The first volume is divided into two large parts. Part I sets out general principles and Part II is entitled "Of Truth." Within this complex organization, Ruskin also divides Part I into two sections and Part II into three sections as follows, showing where we have made our selections:

Part I   General Principles
   Section I   Of the Nature of the Ideas
          Conveyable by Art
     Chapter I   Introductory
     Chapter II   Definition of Greatness in
             Art
     Chapter III   Of Ideas of Power
     Chapter IV   Of Ideas of Imitation
     Chapter V   Of Ideas of Truth
     Chapter VI   Of Ideas of Beauty
             [extracted, see RUSKIN
             (WEB p. 361)]
     Chapter VII   Of Ideas of Relation
   Section II   Of Power
     Chapter I   General Principles
             respecting Ideas of Power
     Chapter II   Of Ideas of Power, as
             they are dependent upon
             Execution
     Chapter III   Of the Sublime

Part II   Of Truth
   Section I   General Principles Respecting
          Ideas of Truth (with separate
          chapters on truth of nature)

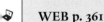

WEB p. 361

"Of Ideas of Beauty"

From "Of Water, as Painted by Turner"[2]

I believe it is a result of the experience of all artists, that it is the easiest thing in the world to give a certain degree of depth and transparency to water; but that it is next thing to impossible, to give a full impression of surface. If no reflection be given—a ripple being supposed—the water looks like lead: if reflection be given, it in nine cases out of ten looks *morbidly* clear and deep, so that we always go down *into* it, even when the artist most wishes us to glide *over* it. Now, this difficulty arises from the very same circumstance which occasions the frequent failure in effect of the best drawn foregrounds, noticed in Section II., Chapter III.,[3] the change, namely, of focus necessary in the eye in order to receive rays of light coming from different distances. Go to the edge of a pond, in a perfectly calm day, at some place where there is duckweed floating on the surface,—not thick, but a leaf here and there. Now, you may either see in the water the reflection of the sky, or you may see the duckweed; but you cannot, by any effort, see both together. If you look for the reflection, you will be sensible of a sudden change or effort in the eye, by which it adapts itself to the reception of the rays which have come all the way from the clouds, have struck on the water, and so been sent up again to the eye. The focus you adopt is one fit for great distance; and, accordingly, you will feel that you are looking down a great way under the water, while the leaves of the duckweed, though they lie upon the water at the very spot on which you are gazing so intently, are felt only as a vague, uncertain interruption, causing a little confusion in the image below, but entirely indistinguishable as leaves,—and even their colour unknown and unperceived. Unless you think of them, you will not even feel that anything interrupts your sight, so excessively slight is their effect. If, on the other hand, you make up your mind to look for the leaves of the duckweed, you will perceive an instantaneous change in the effort of the eye, by which it becomes adapted to receive near rays—those

Notes

---

[2] *title* from *Modern Painters* (1843; vol. I, pt. II, sect. V, ch. III).
[3] *III* on "Of the Truth of Chiaroscuro" (Ital. light/dark), that is, the effects of the treatment of light and dark, especially

areas of a painting that are illuminated and those that are shadowed.

which have only come from the surface of the pond. You will then see the delicate leaves of the duckweed with perfect clearness, and in vivid green; but while you do so, you will be able to perceive nothing of the reflections in the very water on which they float—nothing but a vague flashing and melting of light and dark hues, without form or meaning, which, to investigate, or find out what they mean or are, you must quit your hold of the duckweed, and plunge down.

Hence it appears, that whenever we see plain reflections of comparatively distant objects, in near water, we cannot possibly see the surface, and vice versa; so that when in a painting we give the reflections, with the same clearness with which they are visible in nature, we pre-suppose the effort of the eye to look under the surface, and, of course, destroy the surface, and make every body incline to cry out—the moment they come before the picture—"Dear me, what excessively *clear* water!" when, perhaps, in a lowland study, clearness is not a quality which the artist has particularly wished to attain, but which he has found himself forced into, by his reflections, in spite of himself. And the reason of this effect of clearness appearing preter-natural[4] is, that people are not in the habit of looking at water with the distant focus adapted to the reflections, unless by particular effort. We invariably, under ordinary circumstances, use the surface focus; and in consequence, receive nothing more than a vague and confused impression of the reflected colours and lines, however clearly, calmly, and vigorously all may be defined underneath, if we choose to look for them. We do not look for them, but glide along over the surface, catching only playing light and capricious colour, for evidence of reflection, except where we come to images of objects close to the surface, which the surface focus is of course adapted to receive; and these we see clearly, as of the weeds on the shore, or of sticks rising out of the water, &c. Hence, the right and natural effect of water is only to be rendered by giving the reflections of the *margin* clear and distinct (so clear they usually are in nature, that it is impossible to tell where the water begins); but the moment we touch the reflection of distant objects, as of high trees or clouds, that instant we must become vague and uncertain in drawing, and, though vivid in colour and light as the object itself, quite indistinct in form and feature. And now we see wherein the peculiar glory of Turner's water-drawing consists; for it is to him only that we can look for the rendering of such high and difficult truths. If we take such a piece of water as that in the foreground of his Chateau of Prince Albert,[5] the first impression from it is,—"What a wide *surface!*" We glide over it a quarter of a mile into the picture before we know where we are, and yet the water is as calm and crystalline as a mirror; but we are not allowed to tumble into it, and gasp for breath as we go down,—we are kept upon the surface, though that surface is flashing and radiant with every hue of cloud, and sun, and sky, and foliage. But the secret is in the drawing of these reflections. We cannot tell when we look *at* them and *for* them, what they mean. They have all character, and are evidently reflections of something definite and determined; but yet they are all uncertain and inexplicable; playing colour and palpitating shade, which, though we recognize in an instant for images of something, and feel that the water is bright, and lovely, and calm, we cannot penetrate nor interpret: we are not allowed to go down to them, and we repose, as we should in nature, upon the lustre of the level surface. It is in this power of saying everything, and yet saying nothing too plainly, that the perfection of art here, as in all other cases, consists.[6] . . .

Notes

[4] *preter-natural* (Lat. beyond nature); not a supernatural or divine occurrence but one without a natural explanation, sometimes considered magical or surreal.

[5] *Albert* Turner's oil, *Schloss Rosenau: Seat of H.R.H. Prince Albert of Coburg, near Coburg, Germany*, exhibited at the RA, 1841; Walker Art Gallery, Liverpool. *The Times* described

the painting as representing "nothing in nature beyond eggs and spinach. The lake is a composition in which salad oil abounds, and the art of cookery is more predominant than the art of painting" (4 May 1841).

[6] *consists* Ruskin discusses a large number of other paintings of Turner showing water, in England, Switzerland, France –

But, beyond dispute, the noblest sea that Turner has ever painted, and therefore the noblest ever painted by man, is that of the "Slave Ship,"[7] the chief Academy picture of the Exhibition of 1840. It is a sunset on the Atlantic, after prolonged storm; but the storm is partially lulled, and the torn and streaming rain-clouds are moving in scarlet lines to lose themselves in the hollow of the night. The whole surface of sea included in the picture is divided into two ridges of enormous swell, not high, nor local, but a low, broad heaving of the whole ocean, like the lifting of its bosom by deep drawn breath after the torture of the storm. Between these two ridges the fire of the sunset falls along the trough of the sea, dying[8] it with an awful, but glorious light, the intense and lurid splendour which burns like gold, and bathes like blood. Along this fiery path and valley, the tossing waves by which the swell of the sea is restlessly divided, lift themselves in dark, indefinite, fantastic forms, each casting a faint and ghastly shadow behind it along the illumined foam. They do not rise everywhere, but three or four together in wild groups, fitfully and furiously, as the under strength of the swell compels or permits them; leaving between them treacherous spaces of level and whirling water, now lighted with green and lamp-like fire, now flashing back the gold of the declining sun, now fearfully dyed from above with the indistinguishable images of the burning clouds, which fall upon them in flakes of crimson and scarlet, and give to the reckless waves the added motion of their own fiery

Notes

lakes, rivers, waterfalls, ships in harbour and in storms – indicating how he represents "the surface of calm or the *force* of agitated water." His concern throughout is, as he had argued indirectly in the preceding paragraphs, that the conventional expectation of critics and viewers was that a painting should direct a viewer's gaze from outside the painting; that its subject matter should be able to be described in clear and welcoming terms to make it a part of the viewer's world and values (a potential conflict between the visual and the verbal, the technical and the literary, the personal and the social); that its perspective should be stable when seen perpendicular to the centre of the painting at a distance of about ten feet; and that its single central image should be defined by even illumination of highlights and medium tones, bringing the subject out of peripheral shadows into immediate comprehension. Hence the conventions of line, perspective, and chiaroscuro control the viewer's eye, making the painting's meaning comprehensible, and translatable into verbal description, underlined often by literary titles. Ruskin challenged these positions in two respects: first, by showing how Turner destabilizes the control of the viewer's eye, by placing the viewer within the painting, destroying perspective (the inability to see both sky and water, reflection and reality, surface and deep volumes, near and far at the same time), shifting the expected balance of chiaroscuro, and challenging the easy association of a literary title with a technically virtuosic use of colour. Second, Ruskin takes up the conventional role of Victorian critics who saw their task as giving a verbal description of the *content* of a painting under review. Turning the tables on the negative critics of Turner who saw only indecipherable content and messy brushwork, Ruskin shows how their actual content is what their title and a viewer's close observation can identify – a content that rightly read has a meaning beyond content: the destabilizing of a viewer's placement outside the painting, while engaging with its col-

ours and perspective, thereby enabling new perceptions about the aesthetics and meaning of the paintings.

[7] *Ship* Turner's *Slavers Throwing Overboard the Dead and Dying—Typhon Coming On* shows a slave ship in a storm where victims who are sick or have died are being thrown overboard at sunset, a common practice to collect insurance money. The painting was exhibited at the RA (1840) with the following lines in the catalogue from Turner's unpublished poem, *The Fallacies of Hope*: "Aloft all hands, strike the top-masts and belay; / Yon angry setting sun and fierce-edged clouds / Declare the Typhon's coming. / Before it sweep your decks, throw overboard / The dead and dying—ne'er heed their chains. / Hope, Hope, fallacious Hope! / Where is thy market now?"

The exhibition coincided with a meeting of the Anti-Slavery Society at which Prince Albert was to speak, and perhaps influenced the passing of the 1843 Act that increased pressure on other nations to end the traffic in slavery. Contemporary critics ridiculed the painting, as did Thackeray, describing it as "flakes of white laid on with a trowel; bladders of vermilion madly spirted here and there" with the fish resembling "huge, slimy, poached eggs" ("Pictorial Rhapsody," *Fraser's Magazine*, 1840). Mark Twain discusses how his eyes were opened by Ruskin's description to move from thinking of the painting what a Boston reporter was alleged to have said, "a tortoise-shell cat having a fit in a platter of tomatoes"—but after Ruskin, Twain sees "sunset glories" (*A Tramp Abroad*, 1880: 1. 24). There were also literary sources: James Thomson's *Summer* (1727: 980–1025) with its "mighty tempest" around a slave ship. The painting was given to Ruskin by his father as a New Year's present, 1844. It was in Ruskin's collection until 1872 when he decided to sell it, having decided it was "too painful to live with." It is now in the Museum of Fine Arts in Boston. See Plate 19.

[8] *dying* corrected in later editions to "dyeing."

flying. Purple and blue, the lurid shadows of the hollow breakers are cast upon the mist of the night, which gathers cold and low, advancing like the shadow of death upon the guilty[9] ship as it labours amidst the lightning of the sea, its thin masts written upon the sky in lines of blood, girded with condemnation in that fearful hue, which signs the sky with horror, and mixes its flaming flood with the sunlight,—and cast far along the desolate heave of the sepulchral waves, incarnadines the multitudinous sea.[10]

I believe, if I were reduced to rest Turner's immortality upon any single work, I should choose this. Its daring conception—ideal in the highest sense of the word, is based on the purest truth, and wrought out with the concentrated knowledge of a life; its colour is absolutely perfect, not one false or morbid hue in any part or line, and so modulated that every square inch of canvas is a perfect composition; its drawing as accurate as fearless; the ship buoyant, bending, and full of motion; its tones as true as they are wonderful;[11]; and the whole picture dedicated to the most sublime of subjects and impressions—(completing thus the perfect system of all truth, which we have shown to be formed by Turner's works)—the power, majesty, and deathfulness of the open, deep, illimitable sea.

From "Of Pathetic Fallacy"[12]

We may go on at our ease to examine the point in question,—namely, the difference between the ordinary, proper, and true appearances of things to us; and the extraordinary, or false appearances, when we are under the influence of emotion, or contemplative fancy; false appearances, I say, as being entirely unconnected with any real power or character in the object, and only imputed to it by us.

> For instance—
> The spendthrift crocus, bursting through the mould
> Naked and shivering, with his cup of gold.[13]

This is very beautiful, and yet very untrue. The crocus is not a spendthrift, but a hardy plant; its yellow is not gold, but saffron. How is it that we enjoy so much the having it put into our heads that it is anything else than a plain crocus?

It is an important question. For, throughout our past reasonings about art, we have always found that nothing could be good or useful, or ultimately pleasurable, which was untrue. But here is something pleasurable in written poetry which is nevertheless *untrue*.

Notes

9 *guilty* "She is a slaver, throwing her slaves overboard to escape. The near sea is encumbered with corpses" [author's note]. Also a transferred epithet, the application of a modifier to an object with which it is not usually associated. See also "Pathetic Fallacy," n. 12.

10 *sea* see *Macbeth* 2. 2. 60; incarnadine: make red.

11 *wonderful* Ruskin inserts a long footnote here comparing Turner favourably to Willem Van de Velde the Younger (1633–1707), a Flemish sea painter popular in England.

12 *fallacy* Ruskin moves away from the problems of representing truth by means of realism in art to the parallel problems in literature. Pathetic here does not mean feeble or weak but relative to the emotions (Gk. *pathos*), namely that quality which a writer confers upon descriptions of an object or perception, and also the distortion (the fallacy) that might result. Tennyson and others thought that Ruskin was unfair and too rigorous in

pointing up the fallacy. Pathetic fallacy came to be applied to the drawing of equivalence between nature and human emotions: animate or human characteristics, especially moods or passions, are attributed to inanimate nature; hence, a special kind of personification, such as the famous opening of Edward Bulwer-Lytton's *Paul Clifford* (1830) where the mood of nature echoes the mood of the characters: "It was a dark and stormy night." Ruskin himself uses it; see his "guilty ship" in discussing the *Slave Ship* above, n. 9. For an application of pathetic fallacy in his discussion of the Pre-Raphaelites, see LITERATURE: PRE-RAPHAELITISM, n. 35. From *Modern Painters*, Volume III (1856; pt. IV, ch. XII).

13 *gold* "Holmes (Oliver Wendell), quoted by Miss Mitford in her *Recollections of a Literary Life*" [author's note]. The quotation is from "Astræa" (1850) by Oliver Wendell Holmes (1841–1935), American poet.

And what is more, if we think over our favourite poetry, we shall find it full of this kind of fallacy, and that we like it all the more for being so.

It will appear also, on consideration of the matter, that this fallacy is of two principal kinds. Either, as in this case of the crocus, it is the fallacy of wilful fancy, which involves no real expectation that it will be believed; or else it is a fallacy caused by an excited state of the feelings, making us, for the time, more or less irrational. Of the cheating of the fancy we shall have to speak presently; but, in this chapter, I want to examine the nature of the other error, that which the mind admits when affected strongly by emotion. Thus, for instance, in Alton Locke,—

> They rowed her in across the rolling foam—
> The cruel, crawling foam.[14]

The foam is not cruel, neither does it crawl. The state of mind which attributes to it these characters of a living creature is one in which the reason is unhinged by grief. All violent feelings have the same effect. They produce in us a falseness in all our impressions of external things, which I would generally characterize as the "Pathetic fallacy."

Now we are in the habit of considering this fallacy as eminently a character of poetical description, and the temper of mind in which we allow it, as one eminently poetical, because passionate. But, I believe, if we look well into the matter, that we shall find the greatest poets do not often admit this kind of falseness—that it is only the second order of poets who much delight in it.[15]

Thus, when Dante describes the spirits falling from the bank of Acheron "as dead leaves flutter from a bough,"[16] he gives the most perfect image possible of their utter lightness, feebleness, passiveness, and scattering agony of despair, without, however, for an instant losing his own clear perception that *these* are souls, and *those* are leaves; he makes no confusion of one with the other. But when Coleridge speaks of

> The one red leaf, the last of its clan,
> That dances as often as dance it can,[17]

he has a morbid, that is to say, a so far false, idea about the leaf: he fancies a life in it, and will, which there are not; confuses its powerlessness with choice, its fading death with merriment, and the wind that shakes it with music. Here, however, there is some beauty,

Notes

[14] *foam* from Charles Kingsley *Alton Locke* (1850: ch. 26).

[15] *it* "I admit two orders of poets, but no third; and by these two orders I mean the Creative (Shakspere, Homer, Dante), and Reflective or Perceptive (Wordsworth, Keats, Tennyson). But both of these must be *first*-rate in their range, though their range is different; and with poetry second-rate in *quality* no one ought to be allowed to trouble mankind. There is quite enough of the best,—much more than we can ever read or enjoy in the length of a life; and it is a literal wrong or sin in any person to encumber us with inferior work. I have no patience with apologies made by young pseudo-poets, 'that they believe there is *some* good in what they have written: that they hope to do better in time,' &c. *Some* good! If there is not *all* good, there is no good. If they ever hope to do better, why do they trouble us now? Let them rather courageously burn all they have done, and wait for the better days. There are few men, ordinarily educated, who in moments of strong feeling could not strike out a poetical thought, and afterwards polish it so as to be presentable. But men of sense know better than so to waste their time; and those who sincerely love poetry, know the touch of the master's hand on the chords too well to fumble among them after him. Nay, more than this; all inferior poetry is an injury to the good, inasmuch as it takes away the freshness of rhymes, blunders upon and gives a wretched commonalty to good thoughts; and, in general, adds to the weight of human weariness in a most woful and culpable manner. There are few thoughts likely to come across ordinary men, which have not already been expressed by greater men in the best possible way; and it is a wiser, more generous, more noble thing to remember and point out the perfect words, than to invent poorer ones, wherewith to encumber temporarily the world" [author's note].

[16] *bough* see *Inferno* 3. 112; the Acheron is one of the rivers of Hades.

[17] *Ulysses … can* from S. T. Coleridge, *Christabel* (1816: 49–50).

even in the morbid passage; but take an instance in Homer and Pope. Without the knowledge of Ulysses, Elpenor, his youngest follower, has fallen from an upper chamber in the Circean palace, and has been left dead, unmissed by his leader, or companions, in the haste of their departure. They cross the sea to the Cimmerian land; and Ulysses summons the shades from Tartarus.[18] The first which appears is that of the lost Elpenor. Ulysses, amazed, and in exactly the spirit of bitter and terrified lightness which is seen in Hamlet,[19] addresses the spirit with the simple, startled words:—

> Elpenor! How camest thou under the shadowy darkness? Hast thou come faster
> on foot than I in my black ship?[20]

Which Pope renders thus:—

> O, say, what angry power Elpenor led
> To glide in shades, and wander with the dead?
> How could thy soul, by realms and seas disjoined,
> Outfly the nimble sail, and leave the lagging wind?[21]

I sincerely hope the reader finds no pleasure here, either in the nimbleness of the sail, or the laziness of the wind! And yet how is it that these conceits[22] are so painful now, when they have been pleasant to us in the other instances?

For a very simple reason. They are not a *pathetic* fallacy at all, for they are put into the mouth of the wrong passion—a passion which never could possibly have spoken them—agonized curiosity. Ulysses wants to know the facts of the matter; and the very last thing his mind could do at the moment would be to pause, or suggest in anywise what was *not* a fact. The delay in the first three lines, and conceit in the last, jar upon us instantly, like the most frightful discord in music. No poet of true imaginative power could possibly have written the passage.[23]

Therefore, we see that the spirit of truth must guide us in some sort, even in our enjoyment of fallacy. Coleridge's fallacy has no discord in it, but Pope's has set our teeth on edge. Without farther questioning, I will endeavour to state the main bearings of this matter. . . .

So, then, we have the three ranks: the man who perceives rightly, because he does not feel, and to whom the primrose is very accurately the primrose, because he does not love it. Then, secondly, the man who perceives wrongly, because he feels, and to whom the primrose is anything else than a primrose: a star, or a sun, or a fairy's shield, or a forsaken maiden. And then, lastly, there is the man who perceives rightly in spite of his feelings, and to whom the primrose is for ever nothing else than itself—a little flower, apprehended in the very plain and leafy fact of it, whatever and how many soever the associations and passions may be, that crowd around it. And, in general, these three classes may be rated in comparative order, as the men who are not poets at all, and the poets of the second order, and the poets of the first; only however great a man may be, there are always some subjects which *ought* to throw him off his balance; some, by

Notes

[18] *Tartarus* Circe, in Greek mythology, was a beautiful sorceress who lived on the island of Aeæa where she transformed Odysseus' companions into pigs (see *Odyssey* 10); Cimmerian peoples lived, according to Homer (*Odyssey* 11, 14), at the margin of the world near the entrance to Hades. Tartarus is the lowest region of the classical underworld.

[19] *Hamlet* "Well said, old mole! can'st work i' the ground so fast!" [author's note]. See *Hamlet* 1. 5. 162.

[20] *Ship* see *Odyssey* 11. 51.

[21] *wind* from Alexander Pope's translation of the *Odyssey* (1715–20).

[22] *conceits* extended rhetorical flourishes.

[23] *passage* "It is worth while comparing the way a similar question is put by the exquisite sincerity of Keats:—

> He wept, and his bright tears
> Went trickling down the golden bow he held. [. . .]
> "How cam'st thou over the unfooted sea?"

[author's note]. From John Keats, *Hyperion* (1820: 3. 42–50).

which his poor human capacity of thought should be conquered, and brought into the inaccurate and vague state of perception, so that the language of the highest inspiration becomes broken, obscure, and wild in metaphor, resembling that of the weaker man, overborne by weaker things.

And thus, in full, there are four classes: the men who feel nothing, and therefore see truly; the men who feel strongly, think weakly, and see untruly (second order of poets); the men who feel strongly, think strongly, and see truly (first order of poets); and the men who, strong as human creatures can be, are yet submitted to influences stronger than they, and see in a sort untruly, because what they see is inconceivably above them. This last is the usual condition of prophetic inspiration.

I separate these classes, in order that their character may be clearly understood; but of course they are united each to the other by imperceptible transitions, and the same mind, according to the influences to which it is subjected, passes at different times into the various states. Still, the difference between the great and less man is, on the whole, chiefly in this point of *alterability*. That is to say, the one knows too much, and perceives and feels too much of the past and future, and of all things beside and around that which immediately affects him, to be in any wise shaken by it. His mind is made up; his thoughts have an accustomed current; his ways are steadfast; it is not this or that new sight which will at once unbalance him. He is tender to impression at the surface, like a rock with deep moss upon it; but there is too much mass of him to be moved. The smaller man, with the same degree of sensibility, is at once carried off his feet; he wants to do something he did not want to do before; he views all the universe in a new light through his tears; he is gay or enthusiastic, melancholy or passionate, as things come and go to him. Therefore the high creative poet might even be thought, to a great extent, impassive (as shallow people think Dante stern), receiving indeed all feelings to the full, but having a great centre of reflection and knowledge in which he stands serene, and watches the feeling, as it were, from afar off.

Dante, in his most intense moods, has entire command of himself, and can look around calmly, at all moments, for the image or the word that will best tell what he sees to the upper or lower world. But Keats and Tennyson, and the poets of the second order, are generally themselves subdued by the feelings under which they write, or, at least, write as choosing to be so, and therefore admit certain expressions and modes of thought which are in some sort diseased or false.

The Stones of Venice

Ruskin intended The Stones of Venice to take its place with the Seven Lamps of Architecture (1849) as his major works on architecture; in that sense, as Ruskin says, "If I should succeed, as I hope, in making the Stones of Venice touchstones," he would show not only the glories of Venetian architecture but also the reasons for its decline and neglect. To that end he used the first volume to set out the "Foundations" of architecture – walls, roofs, apertures, various kinds of columns and shafts, arches over apertures, and ornaments. In Volume II he deals with two periods. The first is the Byzantine, in which the chief monument is St Mark's Basilica in Venice. He also looks at the earlier churches on the Venetian islands of Torcello and Murano. The second period is the Gothic, with the first of three chapters on "The Nature of Gothic," the second on Gothic Palaces, and the third on the Doge's Palace in Venice, his ideal of Gothic: "It is the central building of the world." The third volume deals with what Ruskin considers the decline and fall of Venice during the period of the Renaissance: the early Renaissance, the Roman Renaissance, and the Grotesque Renaissance: "I date the commencement of the Fall of Venice from the death of Carlo Zeno, 8th May 1418.... Foscari became doge five years later, and in his reign the first marked signs appear in architecture of that mighty change ...

to which London owes St. Paul's, Rome St. Peter's, Venice and Vicenza the edifices commonly supposed to be their noblest, and Europe in general the degradation of every art she has since practised" (vol. I, chap I, sect. V, XXXIV). Zeno (1333–1418) had been a heroic admiral and military leader in the wars of Venice with Genoa; after his death the republic declined, shifting from aristocratic to oligarchic rule. According to Ruskin, with the ascension of Francesco Foscari (1373–1457) as doge (1423), the decline was marked in architecture with the rebuilding of the Doge's Palace, a shift from Gothic to Renaissance style. Later in the same volume he wrote even more caustically about the Renaissance: "Instant degradation followed in every direction, —a flood of folly and hypocrisy. Mythologies ill understood at first, then perverted into feeble sensualities, take the place of the representations of Christian subjects, which had become blasphemous under the treatment of men like the Caracci. Gods without power, satyrs without rusticity, nymphs without innocence, men without humanity, gather into idiot groups upon the polluted canvas, and scenic affectations encumber the streets with preposterous marble. Lower and lower declines the level of abused intellect; the base school of landscape gradually usurps the place of the historical painting, which had sunk into prurient pedantry ... the confectionery idealities of Claude, the dull manufacture of Gaspar [Poussin, a pupil of Nicolas Poussin] and Canaletto, south of the Alps, and on the north the patient devotion of besotted lives to delineation of bricks and fogs, fat cattle and ditchwater. And thus, Christianity and morality, courage, and intellect, and art all crumbling together in one wreck, we are hurried on to the fall of Italy, the revolution in France, and the condition of art in England" (*Stones of Venice*, 1853; vol. I, chap. I, sect. XXXVII: "The Quarry").

Ruskin reads Venice as a book: "Never had city a more glorious Bible .... The skill and the treasures of the East had gilded every letter, and illumined every page, till the Book-Temple shone from afar off like the star of the Magi" (vol. II, chap. IV, sect. LXXI); the "great series of capitals" on the arcade of the Doge's Palace "might be read, like the pages of a book, by those... who habitually walked beneath"; and again, "The whole edifice [of St Mark's] is to be regarded less as a temple wherein to pray, than as itself a Book of Common Prayer, a vast illuminated missal, bound with alabaster instead of parchment, studded with porphyry pillars instead of jewels, and written within and without in letters of enamel and gold" (sect. XLVI). But Ruskin also read Venice as a feminized and eroticized body, an architectural maiden alluring in her innocence, and a courtesan seductive in her fall: "The bright hues of the early architecture of Venice were no sign of gaiety of heart, and that the investiture with the mantle of many colours by which she is known above all other cities of Italy and of Europe, was not granted to her in the fever of her festivity, but in the solemnity of her early and earnest religion. She became in after times the revel of the earth, the masque of Italy [Byron, *Childe Harold* 4. 3]; and *therefore* is she now desolate; but her glorious robe of gold and purple was given her when first she rose a vestal from the sea, not when she became drunk with the wine of her fornication" (chap. V, sect. XXXV). In 1877 Ruskin joined with notable Italians and with William Morris and the Society for the Preservation of Ancient Buildings to put a stop to the ruinous restoration (instead of preservation) of St Mark's. As part of that project, Ruskin commissioned for £500 the architectural artist John Wharlton Bunney (1828–82) to paint a large view of the west front of St Mark's, that remains in the Ruskin collections – showing the colours as he knew them.

 WEB p. 364

From "St. Mark's"

From "The Nature of Gothic"[24]

I shall endeavour therefore to give the reader in this chapter an idea, at once broad and definite, of the true nature of *Gothic* architecture, properly so called; not of that of Venice only, but of universal Gothic: for it will be one of the most interesting parts of our subsequent inquiry, to find out how far Venetian architecture reached the universal or perfect type of Gothic, and how far it either fell short of it, or assumed foreign and independent forms.

The principal difficulty in doing this arises from the fact that every building of the Gothic period differs in some important respect from every other; and many include features which, if they occurred in other buildings, would not be considered Gothic at all; so that all we have to reason upon is merely, if I may be allowed so to express it, a greater or less degree of *Gothicness* in each building we examine. And it is this Gothicness,— the character which, according as it is found more or less in a building, makes it more or less Gothic,—of which I want to define the nature. . . .

The Gothic character submitted to our analysis, just as the rough mineral is submitted to that of the chemist, entangled with many other foreign substances, itself perhaps in no place pure, or ever to be obtained or seen in purity for more than an instant; but nevertheless a thing of definite and separate nature, however inextricable or confused in appearance. Now observe: the chemist defines his mineral by two separate kinds of character; one external, its crystalline form, hardness, lustre, &c., the other internal, the proportions and nature of its constituent atoms. Exactly in the same manner, we shall find that Gothic architecture has external forms, and internal elements. Its elements are certain mental tendencies of the builders, legibly expressed in it; as fancifulness, love of variety, love of richness, and such others. Its external forms are pointed arches, vaulted roofs,[25] &c. And unless both the elements and the forms are there, we have no right to call the style Gothic. It is not enough that it has the Form, if it have not also the power and life. It is not enough that it has the Power, if it have not the form. . . .

I believe, then, that the characteristic or moral elements of Gothic are the following, placed in the order of their importance:

Notes

[24] *title* Ruskin's Gothic in *Stones* is almost entirely Italian, a neglect of French and English Gothic with which many of his readers would disagree. He praised the Gothic for both its "savageness" and also its "naturalism" – its imaginative creativity and its reverence for nature and the natural forms of nature. He articulated for the nineteenth century the relationship between art and craft, the monument and the worker's skill, arguing that Gothic buildings were the free and untrammelled expression of an artisan's imaginative thought, brought to bear on the materials with which he worked. This notion was later encapsulated by William Morris's claim that the worker should have joy in his labour, and that the worker should find his ideal in a community or brotherhood of workers. Finally, Ruskin saw a historical, social, and cultural continuity between workers and their guilds, and more widely, between workers and their social communities and their environments, and between the monuments that they built and the continuities of historical institutions – all done for the glory of God. Morris called this chapter "one of the very few necessary and inevitable utterances of the century." Our text: 1853 (vol. II, ch. VI).

[25] *forms . . . roofs* other definitions of the external forms of Gothic architecture have added flying buttresses (lateral extensions that help hold up the walls and vaults) to the definition; Abbot Suger at St Denis outside Paris wrote that he intended his new (Gothic) rebuilding of the Abbey (1144) to have it suffused with light, and to make the walls transparent – a more spiritual, aesthetic, and metaphysical set of aims – accomplished by huge windows, ribbed vaulting, and buttresses; others emphasized the stress on vertical elements and soaring height, including the ribbed columns and piers, as well as the symbolic decoration; or the idea of a Gothic cathedral as a unified body of all of its parts into a total knowledge (a *summa* or summary, summation). Ruskin, however, devotes comparatively little attention to French Gothic architecture, drawing his few French examples largely from Normandy, and speaking disparagingly of Chartres, Rouen, and Rheims; English Gothic he describes as "our own rude cathedrals." Ruskin's Gothic is Italian, and so his stress is on walls, not windows or buttresses, on pointed roofs, not ribbed vaulting, on polychrome marble overlays not sculptural programmes, on differentiated details not overall structural design or *summa*.

1. Savageness.
2. Changefulness.
3. Naturalism.
4. Grotesqueness.
5. Rigidity.
6. Redundance.

These characters are here expressed as belonging to the building; as belonging to the builder, they would be expressed thus:—1. Savageness, or Rudeness. 2. Love of Change. 3. Love of Nature. 4. Disturbed Imagination. 5. Obstinacy. 6. Generosity. And I repeat, that the withdrawal of any one, or any two will not at once destroy the Gothic character of a building, but the removal of a majority of them will. I shall proceed to examine them in their order.

1. SAVAGENESS. I am not sure when the word "Gothic" was first generically applied to the architecture of the North; but I presume that, whatever the date of its original usage, it was intended to imply reproach, and express the barbaric character of the nations among whom that architecture arose. It never implied that they were literally of Gothic lineage, far less that their architecture had been originally invented by the Goths[26] themselves; but it did imply that they and their buildings together exhibited a degree of sternness and rudeness, which, in contradistinction to the character of Southern and Eastern nations, appeared like a perpetual reflection of the contrast between the Goth and the Roman in their first encounter. And when that fallen Roman, in the utmost impotence of his luxury, and insolence of his guilt, became the model for the imitation of civilized Europe,[27] at the close of the so-called Dark ages, the word Gothic became a term of unmitigated contempt, not unmixed with aversion.[28] From that contempt, by the exertion of the antiquaries and architects of this century, Gothic architecture has been sufficiently vindicated; and perhaps some among us, in our admiration of the magnificent science of its structure, and sacredness of its expression, might desire that the term of ancient reproach should be withdrawn, and some other, of more apparent honourableness, adopted in its place. There is no chance, as there is no need, of such a substitution. As far as the epithet was used scornfully, it was used falsely; but there is no reproach in the word, rightly understood; on the contrary, there is a profound truth, which the instinct of mankind almost unconsciously recognizes. It is true, greatly and deeply true, that the architecture of the North is rude and wild; but it is not true, that, for this reason, we are to condemn it, or despise. Far otherwise: I believe it is in this very character that it deserves our profoundest reverence.

The charts of the world which have been drawn up by modern science have thrown into a narrow space the expression of a vast amount of knowledge, but I have never yet

Notes

[26] *Goths* East Germanic people who settled on the lower Danube River in the third century, eventually controlling the area of Eastern Europe from the Black Sea to the Baltic Sea. The western branch, the Visigoths under their leader Alaric (370–410), sacked Rome in 410, and defeated the Huns under Attila in 451. The eastern Goths, the Ostrogoths, under Theodoric the Great (471–526) took control of Ravenna and northern Italy and most of the south by 526 and converted to Arianism, a heretical form of Christianity. They had their own mostly portable art forms, but were not the originators of what came to be known as Gothic art and architecture.

[27] *Europe* a reference to the Renaissance rediscovery of the classical world of literature, sculpture, and architecture –

all disliked by Ruskin as too ornate and deriving from states that were politically and spiritually corrupt. In *Stones* he sought to demonstrate that "the Gothic architecture of Venice had risen out of … a state of pure national faith and domestic virtue; and that its Renaissance architecture had arisen out of … a state of concealed national infidelity and domestic corruption" (*The Crown of Wild Olive*, sect. 65).

[28] *aversion* Giorgio Vasari, the Florentine author of *The Lives of the Most Excellent Painters, Sculptors, and Architects* (1550), and others, had described as rude and barbaric the German architecture forced on Europe by the Goths and their successors that preceded the beginnings of Renaissance architecture from about 1430.

seen any one pictorial enough to enable the spectator to imagine the kind of contrast in physical character which exists between Northern and Southern countries. We know the differences in detail, but we have not that broad glance and grasp which would enable us to feel them in their fulness. We know that gentians grow on the Alps, and olives on the Apennines;[29] but we do not enough conceive for ourselves that variegated mosaic of the world's surface which a bird sees in its migration, that difference between the district of the gentian and of the olive which the stork and the swallow see far off, as they lean upon the sirocco[30] wind. Let us, for a moment, try to raise ourselves even above the level of their flight, and imagine the Mediterranean lying beneath us like an irregular lake, and all its ancient promontories sleeping in the sun: here and there an angry spot of thunder, a grey stain of storm, moving upon the burning field; and here and there a fixed wreath of white volcano smoke, surrounded by its circle of ashes; but for the most part a great peacefulness of light, Syria and Greece, Italy and Spain, laid like pieces of a golden pavement into the sea-blue, chased, as we stoop nearer to them, with bossy[31] beaten work of mountain chains, and glowing softly with terraced gardens, and flowers heavy with frankincense, mixed among masses of laurel, and orange, and plumy palm, that abate with their grey-green shadows the burning of the marble rocks, and of the ledges of porphyry[32] sloping under lucent sand. Then let us pass farther towards the north, until we see the orient colours change gradually into a vast belt of rainy green, where the pastures of Switzerland, and poplar valleys of France, and dark forests of the Danube and Carpathians stretch from the mouths of the Loire to those of the Volga,[33] seen through clefts in grey swirls of rain-cloud and flaky veils of the mist of the brooks, spreading low along the pasture lands: and then, farther north still, to see the earth heave into mighty masses of leaden rock and heathy moor, bordering with a broad waste of gloomy purple that belt of field and wood, and splintering into irregular and grisly islands amidst the northern seas, beaten by storm, and chilled by ice-drift, and tormented by furious pulses of contending tide, until the roots of the last forests fail from among the hill ravines, and the hunger of the north wind bites their peaks into barrenness; and, at last, the wall of ice, durable like iron, sets, deathlike, its white teeth against us out of the polar twilight. And, having once traversed in thought this gradation of the zoned iris of the earth in all its material vastness, let us go down nearer to it, and watch the parallel change in the belt of animal life; the multitudes of swift and brilliant creatures that glance in the air and sea, or tread the sands of the southern zone; striped zebras and spotted leopards, glistening serpents, and birds arrayed in purple and scarlet. Let us contrast their delicacy and brilliancy of colour and swiftness of motion, with the frost-cramped strength, and shaggy covering, and dusky plumage of the northern tribes; contrast the Arabian horse with the Shetland, the tiger and leopard with the wolf and bear, the antelope with the elk, the bird of paradise with the osprey: and then, submissively acknowledging the great laws by which the earth and all that it bears are ruled throughout their being, let us not condemn, but rejoice in the expression by man of his own rest in the statutes of the lands that gave him birth. Let us watch him with reverence as he sets side by side the burning gems, and smooths with soft sculpture the jasper[34] pillars, that are to reflect a ceaseless

Notes

[29] *Apennines* mountain range that extends the length of Italy.

[30] *sirocco* Mediterranean wind that blows across Italy and Greece, arising in the Sahara and North Africa.

[31] *bossy* decorated with embossed ornament.

[32] *porphyry* deep purple crystalline rock.

[33] *Volga* Ruskin imagines the view of the rivers, forests, and mountain ranges of France and central Europe before moving north: hence in France, the River Loire, and the Danube from Germany through Austria, Slovakia, Hungary, Serbia, and other countries to empty into the Black Sea. The Carpathian Mountains arch across central and Eastern Europe around the Black Sea.

[34] *jasper* an opaque rock, usually of red, yellow, or green colours, used in gemstones or decoration because of its ability to be highly polished and carved.

sunshine, and rise into a cloudless sky: but not with less reverence let us stand by him, when, with rough strength and hurried stroke, he smites an uncouth animation out of the rocks which he has torn from among the moss of the moorland, and heaves into the darkened air of the pile of iron buttress and rugged wall, instinct[35] with a work of an imagination as wild and wayward as the northern sea; creations of ungainly shape and rigid limb, but full of wolfish life; fierce as the winds that beat, and changeful as the clouds that shade them.

There is, I repeat, no degradation, no reproach in this, but all dignity and honourableness: and we should err grievously in refusing either to recognize as an essential character of the existing architecture of the North, or to admit as a desirable character in that which it yet may be, this wildness of thought, and roughness of work; this look of mountain brotherhood between the cathedral and the Alp; this magnificence of sturdy power, put forth only the more energetically because the fine finger-touch was chilled away by the frosty wind, and the eye dimmed by the moor-mist, or blinded by the hail; this out-speaking of the strong spirit of men who may not gather redundant fruitage from the earth, nor bask in dreamy benignity of sunshine, but must break the rock for bread, and cleave the forest for fire, and show, even in what they did for their delight, some of the hard habits of the arm and heart that grew on them as they swung the axe or pressed the plough.

If, however, the savageness of Gothic architecture, merely as an expression of its origin among Northern nations, may be considered, in some sort, a noble character, it possesses a higher nobility still, when considered as an index, not of climate, but of religious principle.

In the 13th and 14th paragraphs of Chapter XXI. of the first volume of this work,[36] it was noticed that the systems of architectural ornament, properly so called, might be divided into three:—1. Servile ornament, in which the execution or power of the inferior workman is entirely subjected to the intellect of the higher:—2. Constitutional ornament, in which the executive inferior power is, to a certain point, emancipated and independent, having a will of its own, yet confessing its inferiority and rendering obedience to higher powers;—and 3. Revolutionary ornament, in which no executive inferiority is admitted at all. I must here explain the nature of these divisions at somewhat greater length.

Of Servile ornament, the principal schools are the Greek, Ninevite,[37] and Egyptian; but their servility is of different kinds. … The Greek gave to the lower workman no subject which he could not perfectly execute. The Assyrian gave him subjects which he could only execute imperfectly, but fixed a legal *standard* for his imperfection. The workman was, in both systems, a slave.[38]

But in the mediæval, or especially Christian, system of ornament, this slavery is done away with altogether; Christianity having recognized, in small things as well as great, the individual value of every soul. But it not only recognizes its value; it confesses its imperfection, in only bestowing dignity upon the acknowledgment of unworthiness. That admission of lost power and fallen nature, which the Greek or Ninevite felt to be intensely painful, and, as far as might be, altogether refused, the Christian makes daily

Notes

[35] *instinct* filled with or animated by.

[36] *work* a discussion of "The Treatment of Ornament."

[37] *Ninevite* related to the Neo-Assyrian Kingdom (934–605 BCE) with its capital at Nineveh on the Tigris River in modern Iraq.

[38] *slave* "The third kind of ornament, the Renaissance, is that in which the inferior detail becomes principal, the execu-tor of every minor portion being required to exhibit skill and possess knowledge as great as that which is possessed by the master of the design; and in the endeavour to endow him with this skill and knowledge, his own original power is overwhelmed, and the whole building becomes a wearisome exhibition of well-educated imbecility. We must fully inquire into the nature of this form of error, when we arrive at the examination of the Renaissance schools" [author's note].

and hourly, contemplating the fact of it without fear, as tending, in the end, to God's greater glory. Therefore, to every spirit which Christianity summons to her service, her exhortation is: Do what you can, and confess frankly what you are unable to do; neither let your effort be shortened for fear of failure, nor your confession silenced for fear of shame. And it is, perhaps, the principal admirableness of the Gothic schools of architecture, that they thus receive the results of the labour of inferior minds; and out of fragments full of imperfection, and betraying that imperfection in every touch, indulgently raise up a stately and unaccusable whole.

But the modern English mind has this much in common with that of the Greek, that it intensely desires, in all things, the utmost completion or perfection[39] compatible with their nature. This is a noble character in the abstract, but becomes ignoble when it causes us to forget the relative dignities of that nature itself, and to prefer the perfectness of the lower nature to the imperfection of the higher; not considering that as, judged by such a rule, all the brute animals would be preferable to man, because more perfect in their functions and kind, and yet are always held inferior to him, so also in the works of man, those which are more perfect in their kind are always inferior to those which are, in their nature, liable to more faults and shortcomings. For the finer the nature, the more flaws it will show through the clearness of it; and it is a law of this universe, that the best things shall be seldomest seen in their best form. ... Now, in the make and nature of every man, however rude or simple, whom we employ in manual labour, there are some powers for better things: some tardy imagination, torpid capacity of emotion, tottering steps of thought, there are, even at the worst; and in most cases it is all our own fault that they *are* tardy or torpid. But they cannot be strengthened, unless we are content to take them in their feebleness, and unless we prize and honour them in their imperfection above the best and most perfect manual skill. And this is what we have to do with all our labourers; to look for the *thoughtful* part of them, and get that out of them, whatever we lose for it, whatever faults and errors we are obliged to take with it. For the best that is in them cannot manifest itself, but in company with much error. Understand this clearly: You can teach a man to draw a straight line, and to cut one; to strike a curved line, and to carve it; and to copy and carve any number of given lines or forms, with admirable speed and perfect precision; and you find his work perfect of its kind: but if you ask him to think about any of those forms, to consider if he cannot find any better in his own head, he stops; his execution becomes hesitating; he thinks, and ten to one he thinks wrong; ten to one he makes a mistake in the first touch he gives to his work as a thinking being. But you have made a man of him for all that. He was only a machine before, an animated tool.

And observe, you are put to stern choice in this matter. You must either made a tool of the creature, or a man of him. You cannot make both. ... Let him but begin to imagine, to think, to try to do anything worth doing; and the engine-turned precision is lost at once. Out come all his roughness, all his dulness, all his incapability; shame upon shame, failure upon failure, pause after pause: but out comes the whole majesty of him also; and we know the height of it only, when we see the clouds settling upon him. And, whether the clouds be bright or dark, there will be transfiguration behind and within them.

Notes

[39] *perfection* Ruskin's concept of perfection here does not mean an idealized faultlessness, expertness, or excellence. Instead it means completeness with all of something's potential fulfilled, the state of being finished to the final and utmost degree. This notion became a topic of discussion in the years following the publication of *Stones*. For instance, Browning's "Old Pictures in Florence" (from *Men and Women*, 1855) proposes that it is incompletion that suggests and inspires, while perfection has achieved and leaves nothing still to be aspired for – symbolized for Browning in Giotto's incomplete masterpiece, the campanile in Florence (1359), a building that Ruskin too considered (with the Doge's Palace in Venice) as one of the two most beautiful buildings in the world. To Ruskin it was "the central type of beautiful edifice yet existing in the world."

And now, reader, look round this English room of yours, about which you have been proud so often, because the work of it was so good and strong, and the ornaments of it so finished. Examine again all those accurate mouldings, and perfect polishings, and unerring adjustments of the seasoned wood and tempered steel. Many a time you have exulted over them, and thought how great England was, because her slightest work was done so thoroughly.[40] Alas! if read rightly, these perfectnesses are signs of a slavery in our England a thousand times more bitter and more degrading than that of the scourged African, or helot[41] Greek. Men may be beaten, chained, tormented, yoked like cattle, slaughtered like summer flies, and yet remain in one sense, and the best sense, free. But to smother their souls within them, to blight and hew into rotting pollards[42] the suckling branches of their human intelligence, to make the flesh and skin which, after the worm's work on it, is to see God,[43] into leathern thongs to yoke machinery with,—this it is to be slave-masters indeed; and there might be more freedom in England, though her feudal lords' lightest words were worth men's lives, and though the blood of the vexed husband-man dropped in the furrows of her fields, than there is while the animation of her multitudes is sent like fuel to feed the factory smoke, and the strength of them is given daily to be wasted into the fineness of a web, or racked into the exactness of a line.

And, on the other hand, go forth again to gaze upon the old cathedral front, where you have smiled so often at the fantastic[44] ignorance of the old sculptors: examine once more those ugly goblins, and formless monsters, and stern statues, anatomiless and rigid; but do not mock at them, for they are signs of the life and liberty of every workman who struck the stone; a freedom of thought, and rank in scale of being, such as no laws, no charters, no charities can secure; but which it must be the first aim of all Europe at this day to regain for her children. . . .

We have much studied and much perfected, of late, the great civilized invention of the division of labour;[45] only we give it a false name. It is not, truly speaking, the labour that is divided; but the men:—Divided into mere segments of men—broken into small fragments and crumbs of life; so that all the little piece of intelligence that is left in a man is not enough to make a pin, or a nail, but exhausts itself in making the point of a pin, or the head of a nail. Now it is a good and desirable thing,[46] truly, to make many pins in a day; but if we could only see with what crystal sand their points were polished,—sand of human soul, much to be magnified before it can be discerned for what it is,—we should think there might be some loss in it also. And the great cry that rises from all our manufacturing cities, louder than their furnace blast, is all in very deed for this,—that we manufacture everything there except men; we blanch cotton, and strengthen steel, and refine sugar, and shape pottery; but to brighten, to strengthen, to refine, or to form a single living spirit, never enters into our estimate of advantages. And all the evil to which that cry is urging our myriads can be met only in one way: not by teaching nor preaching, for to teach them is but to show them their misery, and to preach to them, if we do nothing more than preach, is to mock at it. It can be met only by a right understanding, on the part of all classes, of what kinds of labour are good for men, raising them, and making them happy; by a determined sacrifice of such convenience, or beauty, or cheapness as is to be

Notes

[40] *thoroughly* see LITERATURE: PRE-RAPHAELITISM; RUSKIN, "PRÆ-RAPHAELITES" on *The Awakening Conscience*" (Plate 10).

[41] *helot* a slave or serf; historically a slave in ancient Sparta.

[42] *pollards* trees that are cropped or pruned two or three metres from the ground, having their crown cut off. Such a practice produces new branching growth from a rounded head or mass, the new growth being cut in subsequent years to provide fodder from twigs and leaves for sheep and cattle grazing on the common land. William

Morris wrote a series of letters to the *Daily Chronicle* in 1895 defending the use of pollarding in Epping Forest.

[43] *God* see Job 19: 26.

[44] *fantastic* see *OED* (meaning 4): "of persons . . . having a lively imagination, imaginative, fanciful."

[45] *labour* the division of labour is mentioned in the first sentence of Adam Smith's *Wealth of Nations* (1776) concerning the manufacture of pins.

[46] *thing* see Proverbs 8: 11.

Plate 1 J. M. W. Turner (1775–1851), *The Burning of the Houses of Lords and Commons, October 16, 1834* (1834–35). Oil on canvas. 92.1 × 123.2 cm. Source: Philadelphia Museum of Art: The John Howard McFadden Collection 1928. Widely reported in the press and diaries of the time, and recorded in engravings and paintings, the spectacular burning of the medieval Houses of Parliament was painted by Turner in numerous watercolours and two completed oil paintings, this one and an other in Cleveland. This painting shows the fire from the south bank of the Thames, with Westminster Bridge on the right, crowded with spectators, as is the foreground. Boats dot the Thames and illuminated by the fire is St Stephen's Chapel with the twin towers of Westminster Abbey in the background, where British sovereigns have been crowned for a thousand years. Turner, familiar with radical politics, may have been aware that Parliament had been debating the Poor Law, against which there was popular opposition, perhaps reflected in the "No" on a placard in the foreground. The painting documents a moment of great historical and stylistic transformation: the forces of nature, and the fire and its reflection in the river, mark the consuming of the medieval institutions. The courts and libraries of British government, built incrementally from the thirteenth century, were destroyed, laying way for the new building begun in 1840 to designs by Sir Charles Barry and A. N. W. Pugin. This painting – far from the conventional drawing-room genre painting of the day like much of Turner's later work, is a revolutionary exploitation of light and colour in the immense power of nature and the insignificance of humans before it. First exhibited at the British Institution (February 1835). A month later the Select Committee first met to consider rebuilding the Houses of Parliament. See INTRODUCTION.

Victorian Literature: An Anthology, First Edition. Edited by Victor Shea and William Whitla.
© 2015 John Wiley & Sons, Ltd. Published 2015 by John Wiley & Sons, Ltd.

Plate 2 "Scientific Progress" in *Her Majesty's Glorious Jubilee 1897: The Record Number of a Record Reign.*
Plate 11. [Diamond Jubilee Special Number of the *Illustrated London News*, issued on Jubilee Day, 21
June 1897; with a text by Sir Walter Besant]. Coloured Lithograph. 40.5 × 30.7 cm. Source: courtesy
of the Robarts Library, University of Toronto. Contrasting "Scientific Progress During Sixty Years:
Locomotion by Land and Sea in 1837 and in 1897; [and] Street Scenes in 1837 and in 1897." The two
top illustrations are by W. L. Wyllie (1851–1931), marine painter and etcher, the one on the left por-
traying the *Great Western*, an oak-hulled steam-paddle transatlantic steamer designed by Isambard
Kingdom Brunel (1806–59) launched in 1837 and sailing on her maiden voyage to New York in 1838.
The other ship is very likely the propellor-driven *Lucania*, built in Scotland (1893) for the Cunard Line,
and the largest passenger ship afloat when she was launched, with 2,000 passengers and 424 crew. The
second level shows a coach-and-four stage and opposite an engine and passenger cars of the Midland
Railway (founded 1844), running between the Midlands and London (St Pancras); telegraph lines are
beside the tracks. The lower level, probably the work of Charles Paul Renouard (1845–1924) who
signed his pictures P.R. and worked for *The Graphic* from 1884 with Wyllie, shows a London street
scene lit by gas in 1837 and Fleet Street in 1897 lit by electric arc lamps. The portraits moving clockwise
from the upper left are British scientists and engineers: Charles Darwin, George Stevenson, Robert
Stevenson, Charles Lyell, Lord Kelvin, Isambard Brunel, Sir William Siemens, Rowland Hill, John
Rennie the Younger, Thomas Huxley, John Tyndall, Michael Faraday, and Herbert Spencer.

Plate 3 Sir Luke Fildes (1844–1927), *Applicants for Admission to a Casual Ward* (1874). Oil on canvas. 137.1 × 243.7 cm. Source: Royal Holloway College, University of London / The Bridgeman Art Library. On 4 December 1869 Fildes published a woodcut engraving, *Houseless and Hungry*, in the first issue of *The Graphic*. The basis for the later painting's composition, the engraving carried a commentary: "It is by virtue of that Act [The Houseless Poor Act, 1864] that the group before us will obtain food and shelter tonight.... They present themselves at a police station and ask for a ticket for admission to the casual ward of a workhouse. This is always given them.... The figures in the picture before us are portraits of real people who received the necessary order for admission on a recent evening." When it was exhibited at the RA the painting had to be railed off with a policeman posted to protect it from the press of the crowds. Advertisements on posters in the background offer rewards of £20 for a Pug Dog, £2 for a missing child, £50 for a murderer, and £100 fo~ an absconder. A similar scene is treated by Gustave Doré and Blanchard Jerrold in "Refuge—Applying for Admittance" in *London: A Pilgrimage* (1872). See CONDITION: SOCIAL FORMATION (WEB p. 27).

Plate 4 Sir Edwin Landseer (1802–73), *Windsor Castle in Modern Times* (1841–43). Oil on canvas. 113.4 × 144.3 cm. Source: Royal Collection Trust/© Her Majesty Queen Elizabeth II 2013. Commissioned by Queen Victoria and set in a corner of the White Drawing Room of Windsor Castle, this painting depicts Victoria entering the room dressed in a white evening gown trimmed with lace and carrying a nosegay to greet Albert, who has just returned from hunting. The spoils are improbably displayed on the carpet and a small stool; no sportsman would so display them in the drawing room. Victoria the Princess Royal (1840–1901), under a huge classical alabaster, plays with one of the dead birds, a kingfisher. Albert pats his favourite greyhound, Eos, and the other dogs, Dandie, Islay, and Cairnach, pose nearby. The other birds can be identified beside Albert's shooting bag. Outside is part of the East Terrace, where Victoria's mother is being wheeled in a chair. The painting is full of domestic details – suggesting bourgeois affinities but distanced from them by the sumptuous interior and the high finish of the picture. These associations are held in tension by the poses of the royal family: incongruously Albert, as the husband, sits while Victoria, as the wife, stands. Traditionally, however, no one sits while the queen stands, though her head is higher than his, dominating the diagonal of the composition. "Modern Times' in the title signifies the realignment of home and gender within the generic convention of the royal "conversation piece," portraits of the family in a domestic or casual setting, conversing about the objects before them. See GENDER: INTRODUCTION.

Plate 5 Ford Madox Brown (1821–93), *Work* (1852–65). Oil on canvas. 137 × 197.5 cm. Source: Manchester Art Gallery/The Bridgeman Art Library. An allegory of Victorian society, ostensibly under the guise of various kinds of work, physical and mental, and of those out of work or living on the periphery of society (like the girl with three children in the foreground and the beggar with herbs at the front left) or those leisured (like the society women in the middle left, or the two wealthy riders in the middle background). The navvy, elevated as a fit subject for heroic art, and his digging companions, are working on an extension to the water system on Heath Street in Hampstead, a well-to-do London suburb. To the right of the painting are the thinkers who inspired the painting: Frederick Denison Maurice, the founder of the 'Working Mens' College, and to his right, Thomas Carlyle, whose *Past and Present* (1843) and *Latter-Day Pamphlets* (1850) with their gospel of work underlie the painting. Four biblical quotations are inscribed on the frame. First exhibited at a special exhibition (1865) with Brown's catalogue; for Brown's commentary, see CONDITION: PROGRESS (WEB p. 32).

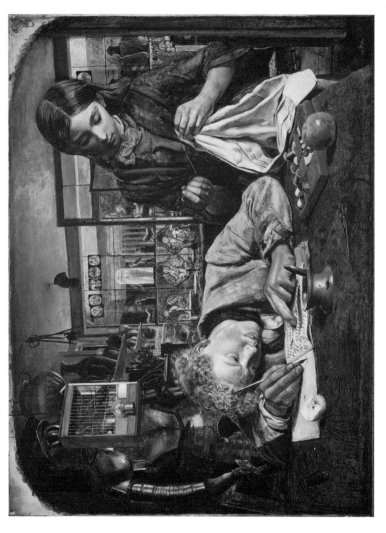

Plate 8 Robert Braithwaite Martineau (1826–69), *Kit's Writing Lesson* (1852). Oil on canvas. 52.1 × 70.5 cm. Source: © Tate, London 2013. The painting is based on the scene in chapter 3 of Dickens's *The Old Curiosity Shop* (1840–41), when Little Nell teaches her friend Kit Nubbles to write. The scene had been illustrated in the first extra-illustrated edition by Thomas Sibson (1817–44). The acquiring of literacy by the working class is often represented as a moment of liberation, as in William Dodd's *A Narrative*. Robert Lowe in a speech on the Second Reform Bill (1867) sarcastically claimed that the ruling classes must "prevail on our future masters to learn their letters." Martineau retains the setting inside the shop with its curios: two suits of armour, pieces of stained glass showing the symbols of the Evangelists, various pots, vases, candlesticks, chess pieces, and an angel figure under glass. The Gothic objects of the Middle Ages contrast with the modern action in the room, the acquiring of literacy and its concomitant empowerment of the working classes by copying cursive letters. The painting was bought by Charles Edward Mudie (1818–90), the founder of Mudie's Lending Library, which had such an impact on the reading public in the nineteenth century. See LITERATURE: INTRODUCTION and DODD: A NARRATIVE (WEB p. 291).

Plate 9 Alfred Concanen (1835–86), *Modern Advertising: A Railway Station in 1874* (1874). Frontispiece to Henry Sampson, *A History of Advertising from the Earliest Times* (1874). Chromo-lithograph. 15.5 × 31 cm. Source: author's collection. A passenger train with a steam locomotive built by the Vulcan Foundry at Newton-le-Willows in Lancashire, named on the boiler, is in the station; passengers are embarking and disembarking, and there is a multitude of activities on the platform. The walls are covered with advertisements for periodicals and newspapers, products (patent medicines and newspapers), travel (Cook's Tours and steamships), and entertainment (minstrels and barmaid contest). The kiosk of W. H. Smith, a pioneer in railway novels, is selling books, magazines, and newspapers. The degree of literacy increased greatly after the Education Act of 1870. The railway station as a site of social and cultural exchange became an iconic object of art as in William Powell Frith's painting *The Railway Station* (1862); see also Plate 18.

Plate 10 William Holman Hunt (1827–1910), *The Awakening Conscience* (1853–54). Oil on canvas. 76. × 55.9 cm. Source: © Tate, London 2013. The frame is inscribed with the text from Proverbs 25: 20, and when it was exhibited at the RA (1854), the catalogue gave two further biblical texts, Ecclesiastes 14:18 and Isaiah 35: 3–4a. All illustrated the modern moral subject of the kept woman's conscience suddenly awakening. It was exhibited with *The Light of the World* as a thematic pair: see Ruskin's letter to *The Times* (25 May 1854; LITERATURE: PRE-RAPHAELITISM), where he elaborates its complex moral allegory. The topic of the fallen woman was important among the Pre-Raphaelites, and in literary representations of both the independence and vulnerability of women in a patriarchal culture. Examples include Dante Rossetti's "Jenny" and his painting *Found* (see Plate 15), as well as Webster's "The Castaway" and Levy's "Magdalen"; prostitution was also a topic in several novels, such as Gaskell's *Ruth* (1853), Collins's *The New Magdalen* (1873), and Hardy's *Tess of the D'Urbervilles* (1891).

Plate 11 William Holman Hunt (1827–1910), *The Light of the World* (1851–53). Oil on canvas. 125.5 × 59.8 cm. Source: Keble College, Oxford / The Bridgeman Art Library. Inscribed on the frame is a text from Revelation 3: 20, signifying Christ knocking in the night on a door long closed and choked with weeds. Under the frame at the top is inscribed *Me non prætermisso Domine!* (Lat. Do not pass me by, Lord!), invisible to viewers. Carlyle called the painting "mere papistical phantasy... empty make-believe." Ruskin interpreted it in *The Times* (5 May 1854): "On the left-hand side of the picture is seen this door of the human soul. It is fast barred, its bars and nails are rusty.... Christ approaches in the night-time.... The lantern carried in Christ's left hand is this light of conscience. Its fire is red and fierce; it falls only on the closed door, upon the weeds which encumber it, and on an apple shaken from one of the trees of the orchard, thus marking... hereditary guilt." It was exhibited with its companion piece *The Awakening Conscience* at the RA in 1854, was engraved, and later copied by Hunt in a larger form (now in St Paul's Cathedral, London, after having been exhibited throughout England and the Commonwealth), and was reproduced everywhere, becoming the icon of British Imperial Protestantism and perhaps the best-known Victorian painting. It was purchased by Thomas Combe (1796–1872), printer to Oxford University, whose widow presented it to Keble College. See LITERATURE: PRE-RAPHAELITISM; DICKENS; see also RELIGION: RELIGIOUS FAITH; RUSKIN (WEB p. 202).

Plate 12 John Everett Millais (1829–96), *Christ in the House of His Parents* (1850). Oil on canvas. 86.4 × 139.7 cm. Source: © Tate, London 2013. When first shown at the RA in 1850 it had no title except the Biblical text, Zechariah 13:6 ("And one shall say unto him, What are those wounds in thine hands? Then he shall answer, Those with which I was wounded in the house of my friends"), an allusion to the typological reading that dominates the symbolism. Christ has injured his hand with a nail, and is comforted by the Virgin Mary and St Joseph. John the Baptist brings water to wash the wound (prefiguring Christ's baptism), the Virgin's mother St Anne and another worker look on. Hugely controversial, in part because of Dickens's negative review in *Household Words* (15 June 1850; see LITERATURE; PRE-RAPHAELITISM), and by its realism in depicting the carpenter's workshop with shavings, dirt, and wounds instead of the idealized, a-temporal, soft-contoured, conventional depictions of the Holy Family. The painting is, in many ways, a religious counterpart to Madox Brown's *Work* (see Plate 5).

Plate 13 Dante Gabriel Rossetti (1828–82), *The Girlhood of Mary Virgin* (1849). Oil on canvas. 83.2 × 65.4 cm. Source: © Tate, London 2013. A double work of art, Rossetti attached his two sonnets on the picture to the frame (see ROSSETTI) when it was first exhibited at the Free Exhibition, the first picture shown by the PRB and signed with their initials. The Virgin Mary embroiders a lily from the life, exemplifying the PRB rule of truth to nature; see LITERATURE: PRE-RAPHAELITISM; WILLIAM MICHAEL ROSSETTI. Her mother, St Anne, supervises in a teaching role while St Joachim (her father) prunes a symbolic vine. Other symbols include the books labelled with the names of the virtues, the palm branch and briar rose standing for the passion of Christ, the lilies for the Virgin's purity, and the dove for the Holy Spirit. His first completed oil, Rossetti used his family for the portraits. Painted on a white ground, its clarity of colour and outline, and its narrow perspective, as well as the naive religious sentiment, are typical of the PRB. The reviewer in the *Athenaeum* (Solomon Hart) praised its naturalism invested with symbolic accessories to give a "dignified and intellectual purpose."

Plate 14 Dante Gabriel Rossetti (1828–82), *The Blessed Damozel* (1871–78). Oil on canvas. 136.8 × 96.5 cm; Predella (lower panel) 35.2 × 96.2 cm. Source: courtesy of the Harvard Art Museums/Fogg Museum, Bequest of Grenville L. Winthrop, 1943.202 © President and Fellows of Harvard College. The gilded oak frame was designed by Rossetti with the first four stanzas of the poem inscribed on the lower border. Rossetti's most famous painting, the damozel (the model was Alexa Wilding, c. 1845–84) leans on the bar of heaven in Paradise, gazing down from the midst of eleven embracing couples under spreading branches; underneath are three haloed angels showing head and shoulders; beneath in the lower panel (the predella) the lover still on earth rests under a tree beside a river, gazing upwards. For the symbols, see ROSSETTI, "THE BLESSED DAMOZEL." The theme of the yearning relationship between the idealized beloved in Paradise, like Dante's Beatrice, and the earth-bound lover, is derived from both Dante's *Paradiso* and *Vita Nuova* (that Rossetti translated); it was also a common Victorian motif. Exhibited RA (1883) and Manchester (1887).

Plate 15 Dante Gabriel Rossetti (1828–82), *Found* (1854–81). Oil on canvas. 76.2 × 88.9 cm. Unfinished. Source: Delaware Art Museum, Wilmington; Samuel and Mary R Bancroft Memorial / The Bridgeman Art Library. Rossetti described the painting to Holman Hunt as a kind of pendant or complementary painting to Hunt's *The Awakening Conscience*: "The picture represents a London street at dawn, with the lamps still lighted along a bridge which forms the distant background. A drover has left his cart (in which a calf stands baaing, tied on its way to market) standing in the middle of the road, and has run a little way after a girl who has passed him, wandering in the streets. He has just come up with her and she, recognising him, has sunk under her shame upon her knees, against the wall of a raised churchyard in the foreground, while he stands holding her hands as he seized them, half in bewilderment and half guarding her from doing herself a hurt." Rossetti's sister Maria found a motto from Jeremiah: "I remember Thee; the kindness of thy youth, the love of thy betrothal" (2: 2). The theme of prostitution interested the PRB (see Plate 10; and ROSSETTI, "JENNY," n. 25), and was a major topic of verse and prose as well as contemporary social activism. This painting was Dante Rossetti's only treatment of a contemporary subject in oils. Rossetti's mistress Fanny Cornforth (*c.*1835–*c.*1906) was the model for the girl, Ford Madox Brown for the drover. Exhibited RA (1883); see the companion poem, "FOUND."

Plate 16 William Morris (1834–96), *La Belle Iseult* (1858). Oil on canvas. 71.8 × 51.2 cm. Source: © Tate, London 2013. Morris's only easel painting shows Jane Burden, whom he married in 1859, as Iseult mourning the absent Tristan banished from the court of King Mark of Cornwall. In *Le Morte d'Arthur* (c.1470), Thomas Malory writes that "the queen had always a little brachet [bitch-hound] with her that Sir Tristram gave her the first time that ever she came into Cornwall, and never would that brachet depart from her but if Sir Tristram was nigh" (9.20). She wears rosemary (remembrance) in her hair; "Dolours" (grief) is inscribed on her mirror. The intricate patterning is characteristic of Morris's later designs and the illuminated book prefigures his own work in the medium. The painting also captures the intense colour and claustrophobic medievalism of the Pre-Raphaelites; see Figure 7; and LITERATURE: INTRODUCTION.

Plate 17 William Simpson (1823–99), *One of the Wards of the Hospital at Scutari* in George
Brackenbury, *The Campaign in the Crimea: An Historical Sketch Illustrated by Forty Plates, Second Series;
From drawings Taken on the Spot by William Simpson* (1856). Plate 34. Coloured lithograph by
E. Walker after the watercolour by Simpson. 73 × 38.8 cm. Source: courtesy of Massey College,
University of Toronto. The lithograph shows Florence Nightingale during the Crimean War
(1853–56) holding a planning sheet while talking to an officer; three others sit around a stove
reading newspapers; another nurse helps feed a solder, one of five in bed. The Barrack Hospital had
long corridors, over two miles in total length, with beds 2½ feet apart lining one side of the
corridors for wounded or sick enlisted men, giving no privacy or air. By contrast, the wards leading
off them, for officers and supplies, were spacious, heated, and well ventilated, as in the illustration.
Brackenbury writes: "One figure which the artist has introduced into it will be recognised with
feelings of unutterable admiration and respect by many now in England, who beheld the original
engaged in her brave and devoted labour of love. They will recall her as they saw her in the days
gone by, when her presence cheered the bed of pain and sickness, and made its light penetrate even
the thick darkness of the valley of the shadow of death; when men, wasted by disease and fevered
with wounds, watched for her gentle ministrations and her words of consolation, even as they who
watch for the morning: when she walked in the beauty of the holiest charity and love through
scenes of horror and of anguish which thrilled hearts for which battle had no terrors, and when
the rough soldier in his untaught but noble chivalry kissed her shadow on the wall as she passed
along. Long may England possess such daughters to tend such sons!" See NIGHTINGALE; see also
see TENNYSON, n. 311; for the Crimean War, see LITERATURE: NEW TECHNOLOGIES; RECORDINGS
(WEB p. 158).

Plate 18 Axel Herman Haig (1835–1921), *The Great Indian Peninsula Railway Terminus: Victoria Station, Bombay* (1878). Watercolour on paper. 91.4 × 157.5 cm. Source: India Office Library, London/The Bridgeman Art Library. Frederick William Stevens (1848–1900), the architect of the Victoria Terminus, commissioned Haig's watercolour based on his design, as an interpretation of his masterpiece building which would not be completed until 1887 in time for Victoria's Jubilee. The Anglo-Indian architecture is a conflation of Indian, Saracenic, Venetian Gothic, Florentine Renaissance, and English neo-Gothic styles. It is particularly indebted to Gilbert Scott's St Pancras Station, London (1868). The train shed to the left of the picture is faced with a Gothic colonnade and tower, flying the Union Jack, beneath which marches a platoon of British Army soldiers, almost the only British figures represented – Indian groups walk on the pathways shielded with umbrellas held by servants, while water carriers surround the fountains. In the distance supply carts move toward the station, where a carriage with important travellers and their liveried footmen enter the gates. See EMPIRE: INTRODUCTION.

Plate 19 J. M. W. Turner (1775–1851), *Slavers Throwing Overboard the Dead and Dying – Typhoon Coming On* (1840). Oil on canvas. 91 × 122 cm. Source: © Boston Museum of Fine Arts. Turner was inspired in this canvas by reading *The History and Abolition of the Slave Trade* by Thomas Clarkson (1760–1846), about the slave ship *Zong*, which in 1781 threw 133 slaves overboard to collect insurance. First exhibited at the RA in 1840 during the World Anti-Slavery Convention that Prince Albert, its president, was to address. The Anti-Slavery Society, having succeeded in abolishing slavery in the British Dominions with the Slavery Abolition Act of 1833, was re-formed in 1839 as the British and Foreign Anti-Slavery Society to abolish worldwide slavery. The painting shows a ship in a treacherous sea with a flaming sunset illuminating the bodies in the sea, some legs still chained in the foreground, surrounded by sea monsters. See RUSKIN, n. 7.

Plate 20 James Abbott McNeill Whistler (1834–1903), *Symphony in White No. 2: The Little White Girl* (1864). Oil on canvas.76.0 × 51.0 cm. Source: © Tate, London 2013. One of a group of "White Girl" paintings, this canvas shows Whistler's mistress, Joanna (Jo) Heffernan (*c.*1843–*c.*1903), first shown in *Symphony in White No. 1* (1862). The woman in the painting became identified with Wilkie Collins's heroine in *The Woman in White* (1859–60). The French poet Théophile Gautier (1811–72) had published the poem "Symphonie en Blanc Majeur" in 1852, a crossover poem between literature and music, as is Whistler's painting with music. In addition, when it was exhibited at the RA (1865) Whistler attached Swinburne's stanzas (see SWINBURNE, "BEFORE THE MIRROR") to the frame printed on gold leaf. The painting embodies a number of elements of the principles of the aesthetes: a young woman dressed in a white muslin gown leans languidly against a mantle with her left arm (her hand showing a wedding band), while her face is three-quarters reflected in the mirror behind. On the mantle are an oriental blue-and-white Nankin vase and a small red Japanese lacquer jar. She holds a Japanese fan in her right hand and at the bottom and side of the painting is a spray of mauve, pink, and white azaleas, all details that allude to the cult of Orientalism. See LITERATURE: PRE-RAPHAELITISM; WHISTLER.

got only by the degradation of the workman; and by equally determined demand for the products and results of healthy and ennobling labour....

It seems a fantastic paradox, but it is nevertheless a most important truth, that no architecture can be truly noble which is *not* imperfect.[47] And this is easily demonstrable. For since the architect, whom we will suppose capable of doing all in perfection, cannot execute the whole with his own hands, he must either make slaves of his workmen in the old Greek, and present English fashion, and level his work to a slave's capacities, which is to degrade it; or else he must take his workmen as he finds them, and let them show their weaknesses together with their strength, which will involve the Gothic imperfection, but render the whole work as noble as the intellect of the age can make it.

But the principle may be stated more broadly still. I have confined the illustration of it to architecture, but I must not leave it as if true of architecture only. Hitherto I have used the words imperfect and perfect merely to distinguish between work grossly unskilful, and work executed with average precision and science; and I have been pleading that any degree of unskilfulness should be admitted, so only that the labourer's mind had room for expression. But, accurately speaking, no good work whatever can be perfect, and *the demand for perfection is always a sign of a misunderstanding of the ends of art.*[48]

The second mental element above named was CHANGEFULNESS, or Variety.

I have already enforced the allowing independent operation to the inferior workman, simply as a duty *to him,* and as ennobling the architecture by rendering it more Christian. We have now to consider what reward we obtain for the performance of this duty, namely, the perpetual variety of every feature of the building.

Wherever the workman is utterly enslaved, the parts of the building must of course be absolutely like each other; for the perfection of his execution can only be reached by exercising him in doing one thing, and giving him nothing else to do. The degree in which the workman is degraded may be thus known at a glance, by observing whether the several[49] parts of the building are similar or not; and if, as in Greek work, all the capitals are alike, and all the mouldings unvaried, then the degradation is complete; if, as in Egyptian or Ninevite work, though the manner of executing certain figures is always the same, the order of design is perpetually varied, the degradation less total; if, as in Gothic work, there is perpetual change both in design and execution, the workman must have been altogether set free.

How much the beholder gains from the liberty if the labourer may perhaps be questioned in England, where one of the strongest instincts in nearly every mind is that Love of Order which makes us desire that our house windows should pair like our carriage horses, and allows us to yield our faith unhesitatingly to architectural theories which fix a form for everything, and forbid variation from it. I would not impeach love of order: it is

Notes

[47] *imperfect* see n. 39.

[48] *art* Ruskin argues that this principle holds for two reasons: first, "that no great man ever stops working [towards perfection] till he has reached his point of failure"; and, second, because "imperfection is in some sort essential to all that we know of life." He adds: "I believe there has only been one man who would not acknowledge this necessity, and strove always to reach perfection, Leonardo; the end of his vain effort being merely that he would take ten years to a picture, and leave it unfinished. And therefore, if we are to have great men working at all, or less men doing their best, the work will be imperfect, however beautiful. . . . And in all things that live there are certain irregularities and deficiencies which are not only signs of life, but sources of beauty. No human face is exactly the same in its lines on each side, no leaf perfect in its lobes, no branch in its symmetry. All admit irregularity as they imply change; and to banish imperfection is to destroy expression, to check exertion, to paralyse vitality. All things are literally better, lovelier, and more beloved for the imperfections which have been divinely appointed, that the law of human life may be Effort, and the law of human judgment, Mercy. Accept this then for a universal law, that neither architecture nor any other noble work of man can be good unless it be imperfect" (*Stones of Venice,* vol. II, ch. VI, sect. 24, 25).

[49] *several* different.

one of the most useful elements of the English mind; it helps us in our commerce and in all purely practical matters; and it is in many cases one of the foundation stones of morality. Only do not let us suppose that love of order is love of art. It is true that order, in its highest sense, is one of the necessities of art, just as time is a necessity of music; but love of order has no more to do with our right enjoyment of architecture or painting, than love of punctuality with the appreciation of an opera. Experience, I fear, teaches us that accurate and methodical habits in daily life are seldom characteristic of those who either quickly perceive, or richly possess, the creative powers of art; there is, however, nothing inconsistent between the two instincts, and nothing to hinder us from retaining our business habits, and yet fully allowing and enjoying the noblest gifts of Invention. We already do so, in every other branch of art except architecture, and we only do *not* so there because we have been taught that it would be wrong. Our architects gravely inform us that, as there are four rules of arithmetic, there are five orders of architecture;[50] we, in our simplicity, think that this sounds consistent, and believe them. They inform us also that there is one proper form for Corinthian capitals, another for Doric, and another for Ionic. We, considering that there is also a proper form for the letters A, B, and C, think that this also sounds consistent, and accept the proposition. Understanding, therefore, that one form of the said capitals is proper, and no other, and having a conscientious horror of all impropriety, we allow the architect to provide us with the said capitals, of the proper form, in such and such a quantity, and in all other points to take care that the legal forms are observed; which having done, we rest in forced confidence that we are well housed. . . .

The third constituent element of the Gothic mind was stated to be NATURALISM; that is to say, the love of natural objects for their own sake, and the effort to represent them frankly, unconstrained by artistical laws.

This characteristic of the style partly follows in necessary connexion with those named above. For, so soon as the workman is left free to represent what subjects he chooses, he must look to the nature that is round him for material, and will endeavour to represent it as he sees it, with more or less accuracy according to the skill he possesses, and with much play of fancy, but with small respect for law. . . .

There is, however, one direction in which the Naturalism of the Gothic workmen is peculiarly manifested; and this direction is even more characteristic of the school than the Naturalism itself; I mean their peculiar fondness for the forms of Vegetation. . . . To the Gothic workman the living foliage became a subject of intense affection, and he struggled to render all its characters with as much accuracy as was compatible with the laws of his design and the nature of his material not unfrequently tempted in his enthusiasm to transgress the one and disguise the other.

There is a peculiar significance in this, indicative both of higher civilization and gentler temperament, than had before been manifested in architecture. Rudeness, and the love of change, which we have insisted upon as the first elements of Gothic, are also elements common to all healthy schools. But here is a softer element mingled with them, peculiar to the Gothic itself. The rudeness or ignorance which would have been painfully exposed in the treatment of the human form, are still not so great as to prevent the successful rendering of the wayside herbage; and the love of change, which becomes morbid and feverish in following the haste of the hunter, and the rage of the combatant, is at once soothed and satisfied

Notes

[50] *architecture* the four rules of arithmetic are those of addition, subtraction, multiplication, and division; the five orders of architecture are particular styles from the classical world, recognizable from the design of the columns: three Greek orders: Doric, Ionic, and Corinthian; and two Roman orders: Tuscan and Composite. The Roman architect Vitruvius (c.80–c.15 BCE) had set out the general concept in his *De Architectura* (*Ten Books on Architecture*, c.15 BCE) and Giacomo Barozzi da Vignola codified these orders for Renaissance and later architects in *The Five Orders of Architecture* (1562).

as it watches the wandering of the tendril, and the budding of the flower. Nor is this all: the new direction of mental interest marks an infinite change in the means and the habits of life. The nations whose chief support was in the chase, whose chief interest was in the battle, whose chief pleasure was in the banquet, would take small care respecting the shapes of leaves and flowers; and notice little in the forms of the forest trees which sheltered them, except the signs indicative of the wood which would make the toughest lance, the closest roof, or the clearest fire. The affectionate observation of the grace and outward character of vegetation is the sure sign of a more tranquil and gentle existence, sustained by the gifts, and gladdened by the splendour, of the earth. In that careful distinction of species, and richness of delicate and undisturbed organization, which characterize the Gothic design, there is the history of rural and thoughtful life, influenced by habitual tenderness, and devoted to subtle inquiry; and every discriminating and delicate touch of the chisel, as it rounds the petal or guides the branch, is a prophecy of the developement of the entire body of the natural sciences, beginning with that of medicine, of the recovery of literature, and the establishment of the most necessary principles of domestic wisdom and national peace....

The fourth essential element of the Gothic mind was above stated to be the sense of the GROTESQUE; but I shall defer the endeavour to define this most curious and subtle character until we have occasion to examine one of the divisions of the Renaissance schools, which was morbidly influenced by it.[51] It is the less necessary to insist upon it here, because every reader familiar with Gothic architecture must understand what I mean, and will, I believe, have no hesitation in admitting that the tendency to delight in fantastic and ludicrous, as well as in sublime, images, is a universal instinct of the Gothic imagination.

The fifth element above named was RIGIDITY; and this character I must endeavour carefully to define, for neither the word I have used, nor any other that I can think of, will express it accurately. For I mean, not merely stable, but *active* rigidity; the peculiar energy which gives tension to movement, and stiffness to resistance, which makes the fiercest lightning forked rather than curved, and the stoutest oak-branch angular rather than bending, and is as much seen in the quivering of the lance as in the glittering of the icicle....

Last, because the least essential, of the constituent elements of this noble school, was placed that of REDUNDANCE,—the uncalculating bestowal of the wealth of its labour. There is, indeed, much Gothic, and that of the best period, in which this element is hardly traceable, and which depends for its effect almost exclusively on loveliness of simple design and grace of uninvolved proportion: still, in the most characteristic buildings, a certain portion of their effect depends upon accumulation of ornament; and many of those which have most influence on the minds of men, have attained it by means of this attribute alone. And although, by careful study of the school, it is possible to arrive at a condition of taste which shall be better contented by a few perfect lines than by a whole façade covered with fretwork, the building which only satisfies such a taste is not to be considered the best. For the very first requirement of Gothic architecture being, as we saw above, that it shall both admit the aid, and appeal to the admiration, of the rudest as well as the most refined minds, the richness of the work is, paradoxical as the statement may appear, a part of its humility. No architecture is so haughty as that which is simple; which refuses to address the eye, except in a few clear and forceful lines; which implies, in offering so little to our regards, that all it has offered is perfect; and disdains, either by the complexity or the attractiveness of its features, to embarrass our investigation, or betray us into delight. That humility, which is the very life of the Gothic school, is shown not only in the imperfection, but in the accumulation, of ornament. The inferior rank of the workman is often shown as much in the richness, as the roughness, of his work; and if the

Notes

51 *it* Ruskin discusses the grotesque later in *The Stones of Venice* (vol. III, chap III).

co-operation of every hand, and the sympathy of every heart, are to be received, we must be content to allow the redundance which disguises the failure of the feeble, and wins the regard of the inattentive. There are, however, far nobler interests mingling, in the Gothic heart, with the rude love of decorative accumulation: a magnificent enthusiasm, which feels as if it never could do enough to reach the fulness of its ideal; an unselfishness of sacrifice, which would rather cast fruitless labour before the altar than stand idle in the market;[52] and, finally, a profound sympathy with the fulness and wealth of the material universe, rising out of that Naturalism whose operation we have already endeavoured to define. The sculptor who sought for his models among the forest leaves, could not but quickly and deeply feel that complexity need not involve the loss of grace, nor richness that of repose; and every hour which he spent in the study of the minute and various work of Nature, made him feel more forcibly the barrenness of what was best in that of man: nor is it to be wondered at, that, seeing her perfect and exquisite creations poured forth in a profusion which conception could not grasp nor calculation sum, he should think that it ill became him to be niggardly of his own rude craftsmanship; and where he saw throughout the universe a faultless beauty lavished on measureless spaces of broidered field and blooming mountain, to grudge his poor and imperfect labour to the few stones that he had raised one upon another, for habitation or memorial. The years of his life passed away before his task was accomplished; but generation succeeded generation with unwearied enthusiasm, and the cathedral front was at last lost in the tapestry of its traceries, like a rock among the thickets and herbage of spring....

We have now, I believe, obtained a sufficiently accurate knowledge both of the spirit and form of Gothic architecture; but it may, perhaps, be useful to the general reader, if, in conclusion, I set down a few plain and practical rules for determining, in every instance, whether a given building be good[53] Gothic or not, and, if not Gothic, whether its architecture is of a kind which will probably reward the pains of careful examination.

First. Look if the roof rises in a steep gable, high above the walls. If it does not do this, there is something wrong; the building is not quite pure Gothic, or has been altered.

Secondly. Look if the principal windows and doors have pointed arches with gables over them. If not pointed arches, the building is not Gothic; if they have not any gables over them, it is either not pure, or not first-rate.

If, however, it has the steep roof, the pointed arch, and gable all united, it is nearly certain to be a Gothic building of a very fine time.

Thirdly. Look if the arches are cusped, or apertures foliated. If the building has met the first two conditions, it is sure to be foliated somewhere; but, if not everywhere, the parts

Notes

[52] *market* see Matthew 20: 3.

[53] *good* Ruskin has set up a hierarchy of Gothic in this and the following paragraphs in which he refers to his preferred kind as "good," "fine," or "first-rate." The names for the various subdivisions of Gothic architecture were being formulated and normalized at the time Ruskin was writing. The four most common terms for English Gothic were coined by Thomas Rickman (1776–1841) in his *An Attempt to Discriminate the Styles of English Architecture from the Conquest to the Reformation* (1817): 1. Norman (c.1070–1180), a pre-Gothic style, marked by the round arch and barrel vaults; 2. Early English (c.1180–1250/75) with pointed arches, lancet windows (often grouped in twos or threes), rib vaults (such as the nave and transepts of Salisbury and Wells); 3. Decorated (c.1250/75–1350), traditionally subdivided into (a) Geometric Style (1250–90); and (b) Curvilinear Style (1290–1350), both marked by elaborate window tracery; and finally, Perpendicular (c.1350–1530), marked by very elaborate rib-vaulting or fan-vaulting, and wide windows. In Italy, France, and Germany the terms were in flux. Earlier in *Stones* Ruskin wrote, "Now, all Gothic may be divided into two vast schools, one early, the other late; of which the former, noble, inventive, and progressive, uses the element of foliation [vegetable or plant decoration] moderately, that of floral and figure-sculpture decoration profusely; the latter, ignoble, uninventive, and declining, uses foliation immoderately, floral and figure-sculpture subordinately." The former he dates as earlier than about 1300–50, the latter after it, though the dates varied in different regions. Such dating by means of a single detail is not now followed. In general Ruskin is claiming that the best Gothic periods are those of what are now called Early Gothic (c.1140–1200) and High Gothic (thirteenth century)

are unfoliated are imperfect unless they are large bearing arches, or small and sharp arches in groups, forming a kind of foliation by their own multiplicity, and relieved by sculpture and rich mouldings. The upper windows, for instance, in the east end of Westminster Abbey are imperfect for want of foliation. If there be no foliation anywhere, the building is assuredly imperfect Gothic.

Fourthly. If the building meets all the first three conditions, look if its arches in general, whether of windows and doors, or of minor ornamentation, are carried on *true shafts with bases and capitals*. If they are, then the building is assuredly of the finest Gothic style. It may still, perhaps, be an imitation, a feeble copy, or a bad example, of a noble style; but the manner of it, having met all these four conditions, is assuredly first-rate....

This is all that is necessary to determine whether the building be of a fine Gothic style. The next tests to be applied are in order to discover whether it be good architecture or not: for it may be very impure Gothic, and yet very noble architecture; or it may be very pure Gothic, and yet, if a copy, or originally raised by an ungifted builder, very bad architecture.

If it belong to any of the great schools of colour, its criticism becomes as complicated, and needs as much care, as that of a piece of music, and no general rules for it can be given; but if not—

First. See if it looks as if it had been built by strong men; if it has the sort of roughness, and largeness, and nonchalance, mixed in places with the exquisite tenderness which seems always to be the sign-manual of the broad vision, and massy power of men who can see *past* the work they are doing, and betray here and there something like disdain for it. If the building has this character, it is much already in its favour; it will go hard but it proves a noble one. If it has not this, but is altogether accurate, minute, and scrupulous in its workmanship, it must belong to either the very best or the very worst of schools: the very best, in which exquisite design is wrought out with untiring and conscientious care, as in thc Giottesque Gothic;[54] or the very worst, in which mechanism has taken the place of design. It is more likely, in general, that it should belong to the worst than the best: so that, on the whole, very accurate workmanship is to be esteemed a bad sign; and if there is nothing remarkable about the building but its precision, it may be passed at once with contempt.

Secondly. Observe if it be irregular, its different parts fitting themselves to different purposes, no one caring what becomes of them, so that they do their work. If one part always answers accurately to another part, it is sure to be a bad building; and the greater and more conspicuous the irregularities, the greater the chances are that it is a good one. For instance, in the Ducal Palace . . .[55] the general idea is sternly symmetrical; but two windows are lower than the rest of the six; and if the reader will count the arches of the small arcade as far as to the great balcony, he will find it is not in the centre but set to the right-hand side by the whole width of one of those arches. We may be pretty sure that the building is a good one; none but a master of his craft would have ventured to do this.

Thirdly. Observe if all the traceries, capitals, and other ornaments are of perpetually varied design. If not, the work is assuredly bad.

Lastly. *Read* the sculpture. Preparatory to reading it, you will have to discover whether it is legible (and, if legible, it is nearly certain to be worth reading). On a good building, the sculpture is *always* so set, and on such a scale, that at the ordinary distance from which

Notes

[54] *Gothic* Giotto (1266–1337), Italian painter and architect, whose masterpiece in fresco painting is the Scrovegni Chapel in Padua with cycles of the life of Christ and of the Virgin Mary, and in architecture the bell-tower or campanile in Florence (see n. 39).

[55] *Palace* usually called the Doge's Palace in Venice (1340–1442), to which Ruskin pays much attention throughout *The Stones of Venice*.

the edifice is seen, the sculpture shall be thoroughly intelligible and interesting. In order to accomplish this, the uppermost statues will be ten or twelve feet high, and the upper ornamentation will be colossal, increasing in fineness as it descends, till on the foundation it will often be wrought as if for a precious cabinet in a king's chamber; but the spectator will not notice that the upper sculptures are colossal. He will merely feel that he can see them plainly, and make them all out at his ease.

And having ascertained this, let him set himself to read them. Thenceforward the criticism of the building is to be conducted precisely on the same principles as that of a book; and it must depend on the knowledge, feeling, and not a little on the industry and perseverance of the reader, whether, even in the case of the best works, he either perceive them to be great, or feel them to be entertaining.

Queen Victoria (1819–1901)

Daughter of Prince Edward, Duke of Kent (1767–1820), fourth son of George III, and Princess Victoria of Saxe-Coburg-Saalfield (1786–1861), Victoria was raised to be queen in a strict household after her father and his three brothers died without legitimate heirs. She ascended the throne in 1837 and soon after (1840) married Prince Albert of Saxe-Coburg and Gotha (1819–61), known as the Prince Consort, in what was a happy marriage. She had nine children and thirty-four grandchildren, almost all of them marrying into the noble or royal families of Europe, so that Victoria was, in a real sense, the grandmother of Europe, able to cement liasons and diplomatic relationships throughout the continent on the basis of family loyalty. She retired to Windsor as "the Widow of Windsor" after the devastating blow of the sudden death of Albert in 1861 but was persuaded to emerge in 1872 to increasing popularity, culminating in her being declared Empress of India (1876) and celebrating her golden (1887) and diamond (1897) jubilees in festivities of national pomp and imperial rejoicing. No standard editions of her letters or diaries, but large sections have been published: *The Letters of Queen Victoria,* eds A. C. Benson and Viscount Esher (3 vols, 1907); Second series, ed. George Earle Buckle (1926); Third Series, ed. George Earle Buckle (1930); Elizabeth Longford, *Victoria R. I.* (1964); Christopher Hibbert, *Queen Victoria: A Personal History* (2000); British Monarchy Website: http://www.royal.gov.uk/historyofthemonarchy/kingsandqueensoftheunitedkingdom/thehanoverians/victoria.aspx.

Speech to Parliament 8 August 1851[1]

Prorogation of Parliament by Her Majesty in Person

My Lords and Gentlemen,

I am glad to be able to release you from your attendance in Parliament, and I thank you for the diligence with which you have performed your laborious duties.

Notes

Queen Victoria

[1] *title* Written by the Whig government of Lord John Russell (1792–1878), Victoria delivered the speech in the new Palace of Westminster (see Plate 1), in the House of Lords (completed in 1847). The House of Commons would not be completed until 1852. Such parliamentary speeches were formal public orations marking a ceremonial occasion,

I continue to maintain the most friendly relations with foreign Powers.

I am happy to be able to congratulate you on the very considerable diminution which has taken place in the African and Brazilian Slave Trade. The exertions of my squadrons on the coasts of Africa and Brazil, assisted by the vigilance of the cruisers of France and of the United States, and aided by the co-operation of the Brazilian Government, have mainly contributed to this result.[2]

Gentlemen of the House of Commons,

I thank you for the readiness with which you have granted the supplies necessary for the service of the year.[3]

My Lords and Gentlemen,

It is satisfactory to observe that, notwithstanding very large reductions of taxes the revenue for the past year considerably exceeded the public expenditure for the same period.

I am rejoiced to find that you have thereby been enabled to relieve my people from an impost which restricted the enjoyment of light and air in their dwellings. I trust that this enactment,[4] with others to which your attention has been and will be directed, will contribute to the health and comfort of my subjects.

I thank you for the assiduity with which you have applied yourselves to the consideration of a measure framed for the purpose of checking the undue assumption of ecclesiastical titles conferred by a foreign Power.[5]

It gives me the highest satisfaction to find that, while repelling unfounded claims, you have maintained inviolate the great principles of religious liberty so happily established among us.

The attention you have bestowed on the administration of justice in the courts of law and equity will, I trust, prove beneficial, and lead to further improvements.

I have willingly given my consent to a Bill relating to the administration of the land revenues of the Crown, which will, I hope, conduce to the better management of that department, and at the same time tend to the promotion of works of public utility.

It has been very gratifying to me, on an occasion[6] which has brought many foreigners to this country, to observe the spirit of kindness and good-will which so generally prevailed.

Notes

outlining the government's achievements in office, and looking forward to future legislation. Slightly more personally, Victoria alludes to the recent events associated with her opening of the Great Exhibition on 1 May 1851 in which Prince Albert had been deeply involved. From *The Queen's Speeches in Parliament* (ed. S. Sidney Ensor, 1882).

[2] *result* in the Act for the Abolition of the Slave Trade (the Slave Trade Act, 1807), Britain had imposed heavy fines for any slave found on a British ship but had not abolished slavery itself that remained legal until the Slavery Abolition (1833); see EMPIRE: CELEBRATION, n. 1 and DARWIN, n. 9. The West Africa Squadron of the Royal Navy (established 1808 and based at Portsmouth) patrolled the west coast of Africa in an effort to suppress the Atlantic slave trade. Among other settlements, the Webster–Ashburton Treaty (1842) between Britain and the United States made the United States a formal partner in the suppression of the Atlantic slave trade. Under the terms of the Treaty of Paris (1815) France agreed to abolish the slave trade by 1819, although it was not repudiated until 1848 when, at the instigation of Victor Schoelcher (1804–1893), the French government banned it in all French colonies. Under continuous pressure from the British South American Squadron that seized ships carrying slaves from Africa, the Brazilian government in 1850 had decided to implement legislation to end the trade in African slaves.

[3] *year* it is the right of the House of Commons to "grant supplies" or funds necessary for the operation of government and for all public service, usually part of the budget brought forward by the Chancellor of the Exchequer.

[4] *enactment* a window tax was introduced in England under William III in 1696 and remained in effect until its repeal in 1851. It consisted of a flat tax, and an extra tax (during the nineteenth century) on more than seven windows in a house. It was often called a tax on light and air.

[5] *Power* the foreign power was the Vatican State of the Roman Catholic Church. Laws which had restricted the civil liberties of Roman Catholics including the Acts of Uniformity (1549–62) and the Test Acts (1661–78) were repealed in 1829 with the Catholic Relief Act. In 1850, amidst anti-Catholic riots calling for "no popery," Pius IX (1792–1878) established a Roman Catholic hierarchy in England and Wales. The British Parliament responded with the Ecclesiastical Titles Act (1851) that made it a criminal offence for anyone outside the "united Church of England and Ireland" to use in a bishop's title the name "of any city, town or place, or of any territory or district (under any designation or description whatsoever), in the United Kingdom."

[6] *occasion* the opening of the Great Exhibition by Victoria and Prince Albert on 1 May, 1851. See CONDITION: PROGRESS; ALBERT (WEB p. 26).

It is my anxious desire to promote among nations the cultivation of all those arts which are fostered by peace, and which, in their turn, contribute to maintain the peace of the world.

In closing the present session, it is with feelings of gratitude to Almighty God that I acknowledge the general spirit of loyalty and willing obedience to the law which animates my people. Such a spirit is the best security at once for the progress and the stability of our free and happy institutions.

From *Leaves from the Journal of Our Life in the Highlands from 1848 to 1861*[7]

Love for Balmoral[8]

October 13, 1856.

Every year my heart becomes more fixed in this dear Paradise, and so much more so now, that *all* has become my dear Albert's *own* creation, own work, own building, own laying out, as at *Osborne*; and his great taste, and the impress of his dear hand, have been stamped everywhere.[9] He was very busy to-day, settling and arranging many things for next year.

Visits to the Old Women

Saturday, September 26, 1857.

Albert went out with Alfred for the day, and I walked out with the two girls and Lady Churchill,[10] stopped at the shop and made some purchases for poor people and others; drove a little way, got out and walked up the hill to *Balnacroft*,[11] Mrs. P. Farquharson's, and she walked round with us to some of the cottages to show me where the poor people lived, and to tell them who I was. Before we went into any we met an old woman, who, Mrs. Farquharson said, was very poor, eighty-eight years old, and mother to the former distiller. I gave her a warm petticoat, and the tears rolled down her old cheeks, and she shook my hands, and prayed God to bless me: it was very touching.

Notes

[7] *title* Victoria and Albert first went to Scotland in 1842, visiting Edinburgh, Perth, and Stirling; they returned in 1844 and 1847. In 1848 they first went to Balmoral to their newly leased personal property, and Victoria immediately fell in love with it. She spent most late summers and early autumns there until the end of her reign. From *Our Life in the Highlands*, ed. Arthur Helps (1868). Helps (1813–75) was the Clerk of the Privy Council. The book was a bestseller. It was extensively reviewed and quoted, including some of the extracts given here, in the *London Quarterly Review* (Jan. 1868), and elsewhere.

[8] *Balmoral* estate and castle in Aberdeenshire in Scotland near the village of Crathie, east of Ballater. Victoria and Albert purchased it in 1852 as the private property of the monarchy, as it remains. The existing house, described in this letter, was too small and was torn down to be replaced by Balmoral Castle (Scottish architect William Smith,

1817–91, modified by Prince Albert) in Scots Baronial style (1853–56). Over the years, the property was greatly enlarged from the original 17,400 to just over 50,000 acres.

[9] *Osborne ... everywhere* reference to Albert's design of Osborne House (1845–51; constructed by Thomas Cubitt, 1788–1855), a royal summer residence at East Cowes, Isle of Wight, off the south coast of England, as well as to Albert's modifications of the architecture of Balmoral (see n 8) and his laying out of its walkways, landscaping, and gardens. Osborne was in the Italian Renaissance style of a palazzo; Victoria would die at Osborne in 1901.

[10] *Churchill* Jane Spencer, Baroness Churchill (1826–1900), became Lady of the Bedchamber in 1854, serving until her death on Christmas Day, 1900.

[11] *Balnacroft* a village near Braemar in Aberdeenshire.

I went into a small cabin of old Kitty Kear's,[12] who is eighty-six years old—quite erect, and who welcomed us with a great air of dignity. She sat down and spun. I gave her, also, a warm petticoat; she said, "May the Lord ever attend ye and yours, here and hereafter; and may the Lord be a guide to ye, and keep ye from all harm." She was quite surprised at Vicky's height; great interest is taken in her. We went on to a cottage (formerly Jean Gordon's), to visit old widow Symons, who is "past fourscore," with a nice rosy face, but was bent quite double; she was most friendly, shaking hands with us all, asking which was I, and repeating many kind blessings: "May the Lord attend ye with mirth and with joy; may He ever be with ye in this world, and when ye leave it." To Vicky,[13] when told she was going to be married, she said, "May the Lord be a guide to ye in your future, and may every happiness attend ye." She was very talkative; and when I said I hoped to see her again, she expressed an expectation that "she should be called any day," and so did Kitty Kears. We went into three other cottages: to Mrs. Symons's (daughter-in-law to the old widow living next door), who had an "unwell boy"; then across a little burn to another old woman's; and afterwards peeped into Blair the fiddler's. We drove back, and got out again to visit old Mrs. Grant (Grant's mother), who is so tidy and clean, and to whom I gave a dress and handkerchief and she said, "You're too kind to me, you're over kind to me, ye give me more every year, and I get older every year." After talking some time with her, she said, "I am happy to see ye looking so nice." She had tears in her eyes, and speaking of Vicky's going, said, "I'm very sorry, and I think she is sorry hersel'"; and, having said she feared she would not see her (the Princess) again, said: "I am very sorry I said that, but I meant no harm; I always say just what I think, not what is fut" (fit). Dear old lady; she is such a pleasant person.

Really the affection of these good people, who are so hearty and so happy to see you, taking interest in everything, is very touching and gratifying.

George Eliot (1819–80)

Mary Ann (Marian) Evans was the third child of Robert Evans (1773–1849) and Christiana Pearson (1788–1836), having an older sister (Christina) and brother (Isaac), and a half-brother and half-sister. Born in the estate of Arbury Hall in Warwickshire, and raised in the hamlet of Griff, she attended three different schools and was given free access of Arbury Hall's library, which combined to give her a good education, especially in Greek literature. After her mother's death the family moved near to Coventry where she met the family of Charles and Cara Bray, and through them such radicals as Harriet Martineau, Robert Owen, Herbert Spencer, and Ralph Waldo Emerson. Her first work was a translation of the *Life of Jesus* (1846) by the German liberal theologian, David Friedrich Strauss (1808–74). After her father's death and a year in Switzerland, she moved to London and became assistant editor of the *Westminster Review* (1851). In 1854 she began her twenty-year relationship with the already married George Henry Lewes (1817–78), English journalist and Positivist philosopher. Our selection here is from her poetry, but, of course, she is best known as one of the foremost Victorian novelists. She wrote three short stories centred on rural life, the setting for most of her novels, published as *Scenes of Clerical Life* (1857), for the first time using her pseudonym,

Notes

[12] *Kear* "She died in Jan. 1865" [editor's note].
[13] *Vicky* Victoria the Princess Royal (1840–1901), the eldest of Queen Victoria's children, who married Prince William Frederick of Prussia in 1858, erected a "purchase" cairn (stone monument) in 1878 to commemorate the purchase of the Ballochbui forest in the Balmoral estate.

George Eliot. Other novels include *Adam Bede* (1859), *The Mill on the Floss* (1860), *Silas Marner* (1863), *Felix Holt, the Radical* (1866), and *Middlemarch* (1871–72). Her poetry included *The Spanish Gypsy* (1868) and *The Legend of Jubal and Other Poems* (1874). In May of 1880 Eliot married John Walter Cross (1840–1924), an English banker twenty years younger than she. She died in December of that year. Standard edition: *The Complete Shorter Poetry of George Eliot*, ed. Antonie Gerard van den Broek (2 vols, 2005); *The Clarendon Edition of the Novels of George Eliot* (various editors, 1980–); *The George Eliot Letters*, ed. Gordon S. Haight (9 vols, 1954–78); Gordon S. Haight, *George Eliot: A Biography* (1968). George Eliot at the Victorian Web: http://www.victorianweb.org/authors/eliot/index.html.

"O May I Join the Choir Invisible"[1]

Longum illud tempus, quum non ero, magis me movet, quam hoc exiguum. (Cicero, *ad Att.*, xii. 18[2])

O may I join the choir invisible
Of those immortal dead who live again
In minds made better by their presence: live
In pulses stirred to generosity,
In deeds of daring rectitude, in scorn   5
For miserable aims that end with self,
In thoughts sublime that pierce the night like stars,
And with their mild persistence urge man's search
To vaster issues.
          So to live is heaven:
To make undying music in the world,   10
Breathing as beauteous order that controls
With growing sway the growing life of man.
So we inherit that sweet purity
For which we struggled, failed, and agonised
With widening retrospect that bred despair.   15
Rebellious flesh that would not be subdued,
A vicious parent shaming still its child
Poor anxious penitence, is quick dissolved;[3]
Its discords, quenched by meeting harmonies,

Notes

George Eliot

[1] *title* the view here of immortality and reverence for the achievements of the past is reflective of Eliot's Positivist humanism. The poem was written in August 1867 while Eliot was travelling in Germany with Lewes while working again (she had left it in 1864) on her long poem, *The Spanish Gypsy* (1868). In the Plaça scene of that poem a similar passage occurs:

> When lo! With sound
> Stupendous throbbing, solemn as a voice
> Sent by the invisible choir of all the dead,
> Tolls the great passing bell that calls to prayer
> For souls departed...
> Religious silence and holy sign
> Of everlasting memories (1447–55).

First printed in *The Legend of Jubal and Other Poems* (1874), where the date is given at the end of the poem.

[2] *18* see Cicero, *Epistola Ad Atticum* (Lat. Letter to Atticus): "I am more concerned about the long ages, when I shall not be here, than about my short day" (trans. E. O. Winstedt, 1913). Titus Pomponius Atticus (*c.*109–*c.*32 BCE), a banker and literary patron, was a friend of Cicero's with whom there is a voluminous correspondence. Letter 12 (of 11 Mar. 45 BCE) concerns Cicero's effort to escape painful memories.

[3] *Rebellious ... dissolved* see 2 Corinthians 5: 1–2; Philippians 1: 21–24; and *Hamlet* 1. 2. 129–37; and 3. 4. 83–88.

Die in the large and charitable air.   20
And all our rarer, better, truer self,
That sobbed religiously in yearning song,
That watched to ease the burthen of the world,
Laboriously tracing what must be,
And what may yet be better—saw within   25
A worthier image for the sanctuary,
And shaped it forth before the multitude
Divinely human, raising worship so
To higher reverence more mixed with love—
That better self shall live till human Time   30
Shall fold its eyelids, and the human sky
Be gathered like a scroll within the tomb
Unread forever.
            This is life to come,
Which martyred men have made more glorious   35
For us who strive to follow. May I reach
That purest heaven, be to other souls
The cup of strength in some great agony,
Enkindle generous ardour, feed pure love,
Beget the smiles that have no cruelty—   40
Be the sweet presence of a good diffused,
And in diffusion ever more intense.
So shall I join the choir invisible
Whose music is the gladness of the world.

1867

Anne Brontë (1820–49)

The youngest of the Brontë family, Anne moved at the age of three months to Haworth in 1820 (see CHARLOTTE BRONTË). She was educated largely at home by her father, Patrick Brontë (1777–1861), and her aunt, Elizabeth Branwell (1776–1842), her mother having died when Anne was just over 1½ years old. Anne was closest to Emily, with whom she invented the exotic imaginary world of Gondal, writing its chronicles and literatures (see EMILY BRONTË, n. 1). She accompanied Charlotte to Roe Head School from 1836 to 1837, where Charlotte was a teacher and Anne a student. After six years as a governess, especially with the Robinson family at Thorp Green Hall near York (1841–45), she and her sisters published *Poems* (1846; see CHARLOTTE BRONTË). Twenty-one of her poems were included under the pseudonym Acton Bell. The same pseudonym was used for her first novel, *Agnes Grey* (1847), a vivid depiction of the life of a governess. It was published with *Wuthering Heights* by her sister (see EMILY BRONTË). Her second novel, *The Tenant of Wildfell Hall* (1848), was controversial for its frank depiction of a marriage doomed by alcoholism and adultery (see GENDER: CONSTRUCTING GENDERS; BRONTË, (WEB p. 72)). When it was published, she was already sick with tuberculosis, dying the following year. As with Emily, Charlotte added some further poems by Anne in a new edition of *Wuthering Heights and Agnes Grey* (1850), indicated as *1850* below, heavily edited by Charlotte. Standard editions: *The Poems of Anne Brontë,* ed. Edward Chitham (1979); *Agnes Grey,* eds R. Inglesfield and Hilda Marsden (1988); *The Tenant of Wildfell Hall,* ed. Herbert Rosengarten (1992); Edward Chitham, *A Life of Anne Brontë* (1991); "The Brontës": www.thebrontes.net; "The Brontë Parsonage Museum and Brontë Society": http://www.bronte.info/index.php?option=com_frontpage&Itemid=26.

Appeal[1]

Oh, I am very weary,
    Though tears no longer flow;
My eyes are tired of weeping,
    My heart is sick of woe;

My life is very lonely,   5
    My days pass heavily,
I'm weary of repining,
    Wilt thou not come to me?

Oh didst thou know my longings
    For thee, from day to day,   10
My hopes so often blighted,
    Thou wouldst not thus delay!

The Captive Dove[2]

Poor restless dove,[3] I pity thee;
And when I hear thy plaintive moan,
I mourn for thy captivity,
And in thy woes forget mine own.

To see thee stand prepared to fly,   5
And flap those useless wings of thine,
And gaze into the distant sky,
Would melt a harder heart than mine.

In vain—in vain! Thou canst not rise:
Thy prison roof confines thee there,   10
Its slender wires delude thine eyes,
And quench thy longings with despair.

Oh, thou wert made to wander free
In sunny mead and shady grove,
And, far beyond the rolling sea,   15
In distant climes, at will to rove!

Yet, hadst thou but one gentle mate
Thy little drooping heart to cheer,
And share with thee thy captive state,
Thou couldst be happy even there.   20

Notes

ANNE BRONTË
[1] title MS title: "Lines Written at Thorp Green" and dated "August 28th 1840." Our text: *Poems* (1846).
[2] title MS date: "October 31st 1843"; MS author's note: "Mostly written in the spring of 1842" when Anne was a governess at Thorp Green Hall. The identification of the lot of a governess with a caged bird is a commonplace of Victorian literature and art, an identification enunciated in Charlotte Brontë's *Jane Eyre* (1847) when Mr Rochester says to Jane: "I see at intervals the glance of a curious sort of bird through the close-set bars of a cage: a vivid, restless, resolute captive is there; were it but free, it would soar cloud-high" (pt. 4, ch. 14). Our text: *Poems* (1846). See Plate 7, Redgrave, *The Governess* (1844).
[3] *dove* see P. B. Shelley's caged nightingale in "Epipsychidion" (1817): "Poor captive bird! who, from thy narrow cage, / Pourest such music" (5–6).

Yes, even there, if, listening by,
One faithful dear companion stood,
While gazing on her full bright eye,
Thou mightst forget thy native wood.

But thou, poor solitary dove,   25
Must make, unheard, thy joyless moan;
The heart, that Nature formed to love,
Must pine, neglected, and alone.

"O, they have robbed me of the hope"[4]

O, they have robbed me of the hope
    My spirit held so dear;
They will not let me hear that voice
    My soul delights to hear.

They will not let me see that face   5
    I so delight to see;
And they have taken all thy smiles,
    And all thy love from me.

Well, let them seize on all they can;—
    One treasure still is mine,—   10
A heart that loves to think on thee,
    And feels the worth of thine.

Domestic Peace[5]

Why should such gloomy silence reign,
    And why is all the house so drear,
When neither danger, sickness, pain,
    Nor death, nor want have entered here?

We are as many as we were   5
    That other night,[6] when all were gay
And full of hope, and free from care;
    Yet, is there something gone away.

Notes

[4] *title* first published without a title in *Agnes Grey* (1847; ch. 17). Agnes is a governess in the upper-middle-class Murray family. She was developing a secret love for the new curate, Edward Weston, but she was prevented from seeing him by her charges, especially the vain 18-year-old Rosalie Murray, on the verge of marriage, and who, with her sister, tells lies about Agnes to Edward. Agnes expresses her unhappiness and longing, her "passion of grief," in the poem.

[5] *title* MS title: "Monday Night May 11th 1846"; published *1850* under title "Domestic Peace"; our text. Instead of the version

of stanza 7 that Charlotte Brontë published, the MS reads: "Sweet child of Heaven, and joy of earth! / O, when will Man thy value learn? / We rudely drove thee from our hearth, / And vainly sigh for thy return." In May 1846, when the poem was written, family dissension was caused by her brother Branwell's disruptions and serious drinking after his abortive affair with the wife, Mrs Robinson, of his employer at Thorp Green when he was a tutor there.

[6] *night* a possible reference to the last time the family gathered, given their travel and work as governesses, in May, 1835.

The moon without, as pure and calm,
    Is shining, as that night she shone;   10
But now, to us, she brings no balm,
    For something from our hearts is gone.

Something whose absence leaves a void—
    A cheerless want in every heart;
Each feels the bliss of all destroyed,   15
    And mourns the change—but each apart.

The fire is burning in the grate
    As redly as it used to burn;
But still the hearth is desolate,
    Till mirth, and love, and *peace* return.   20

'T was *peace* that flowed from heart to heart,
    With looks and smiles that spoke of heaven,
And gave us language to impart
    The blissful thoughts itself had given.

Domestic peace! best joy of earth,   25
    When shall we all thy value learn?
White angel—to our sorrowing hearth,
    Return—oh, graciously return!

[Last Lines] "I hoped that I was brave and strong"[7]

I hoped, that with° the brave and strong,   °MS amid
    My portioned task might lie;
To toil amid the busy° throng,   °MS labouring
    With purpose pure and high.[8]

Notes

[7] *title* Anne's last poem, sometimes entitled "Last Lines," has a complicated publishing history. The text of *1850* had been considerably shortened and changed, probably by Charlotte Brontë, who added at the beginning: "I have given the last memento of my sister Emily; this is the last of my sister Anne:—[eight stanzas of the poem]" and at the end: "These lines written, the desk was closed, the pen laid aside, for ever." The MS date is given as "January 7th [1849] & January 28th 1849."

In *1850* Charlotte Brontë published the eight stanzas given above that actually constituted stanzas 5–7, 10, and 13–16 of the complete poem. In *Brontë Poems* (ed. A. C. Benson, 1915), two further stanzas were added: the final stanzas 1 and 9 were added after stanza 6, the whole entitled "Last Lines." C. K. Shorter added two more stanzas (1920; 12 stanzas: Benson's order with stanzas 11 and 12 added after stanza 10). The full poem was first published in *Bronte Society Transactions* 42 (1932). Our text 1915.

When Anne learned in the first week of January 1849 that she too was suffering from tuberculosis, she began on January 7 to write her last poem, completing it at the end of the month. She died on 28 May (see CHARLOTTE BRONTË, "JUNE 21 1849"). Charlotte's cutting of the poem in half and her emendations change Anne's religious doubts and confusion into a resigned religious faith. The omitted stanzas, numbered by the present editors for convenience in reading the complete poem, are given here:

1 A dreadful darkness closes in
    On my bewildered mind;
O let me suffer and not sin,
    Be tortured yet resigned.

2 Through all this world of whelming° mist   °alt. MS reading: blinding
    Still let me look to Thee,
And give me courage to resist
    The Tempter, till he flee.

3 Weary I am—O give me strength,
    And leave me not to faint:
Say thou wilt comfort me at length
    And pity my complaint.

4 I've begged to serve thee heart and soul,
    To sacrifice to Thee
No niggard portion, but the whole
    Of my identity.

But God° has fixed another part   °MS Thou   5
    And He° has fixed it well;   °MS Thou
I said so with my bleeding heart,
    When first the anguish fell.

Thou, God,° hast taken our delight,   °MS For Thou
    Our treasured hope° away: °MS And hope of life   10
Thou bid'st us now weep through the° night   °MS And bid me watch the painful
    And sorrow through the day.

These weary hours will not be lost,
    These days of misery,°⁹   °MS of passive misery
These nights of darkness, anguish-tost,   15
    Can I but turn to° Thee.   °MS If I can fix my heart on

With° secret labour to sustain   °MS That
    In° humble patience every blow;   °MS With
To gather fortitude from pain,
    And hope and holiness from woe.   20

Thus let me serve Thee from my heart,
    Whate'er may° be my written fate: °MS Whatever
Whether thus early to depart,
    Or yet a while to wait.

If Thou shouldst bring me back to life,   25
    More humbled I should be;
More wise—more strengthened for the strife—
    More apt to lean on Thee.

Should death° be standing at the gate   °MS Death
    Thus should I keep my vow: 30
But, Lord! whatever be my° fate,   °MS whate'er my future
    Oh,° let me serve Thee now!   °MS So

Notes

8 The hope and the delight were thine:
    I bless thee for their loan;
  I gave thee while I deemed them mine
    Too little thanks, I own.

9 Shall I with joy thy blessings share
    And not endure their loss;
  Or hope the martyr's crown to wear
    And cast away the cross?

11 Weak and weary though I lie
    Crushed with sorrow, worn with pain,
  Still I may° lift to Heaven mine eyes   °MS Still I may
    And strive and labour not in vain;

12 That inward strife against the sins
    That ever wait on suffering
  To strike wherever° first begins   °alt. MS To watch and strike where
    Each ill° that would corruption bring,   °alt. MS deed

⁸ *high* the metre of each stanza is in Common Metre in the tradition of the hymns of Isaac Watts (1674–1748) and Charles Wesley (1707–88).

⁹ *misery* in the MS. version, the metre changes in this stanza from alternating iambic tetrameter and trimeter to iambic tetrameter verses throughout. In her edited version for 1850, Charlotte Brontë changed the metre to conform with the rest of the poem.

Jean Ingelow (1820–97)

Born in Boston in Lincolnshire and educated at home, Ingelow with her family was forced to move to Ipswich and then to London when her father's shipping and banking interest failed in 1845. As a child she contributed poetry and stories to magazines; her first volume of poetry, *A Rhyming Chronicle of Incidents and Feelings* (1850), was published anonymously. Her *Poems* (1863) was an enormous success in both Britain and the United States, eventually achieving thirty editions. Other volumes followed: *A Story of Doom and other Poems* (1867), and her popular children's story, *Mopsa the Fairy* (1869). She also published novels: *Off the Skelligs* (1872), *Fated to be Free* (1876), and *Sarah de Beringer* (1879). As part of the London artistic and literary scene, she had a number of poet friends, including Dora Greenwell, Adelaide Procter, Christina Rossetti, Alfred Tennyson, and Robert Browning. Standard edition: *Poetical Works* (1898); Maureen Peters, *Jean Ingelow: Victorian Poetess* (1972); "Jean Ingelow": http://gerald-massey.org.uk/ingelow/index.htm.

Remonstrance[1]

Daughters of Eve! your mother did not well:
    She laid the apple in your father's hand,[2]
And we have read, O wonder! what befel—
    The man was not deceived, nor yet could stand;
He chose to lose, for love of her, his throne—   5
With her could die, but could not live alone.

Daughters of Eve! he did not fall so low,
    Nor fall so far, as that sweet woman fell;
For something better, than as gods to know,
    That husband in that home left off to dwell: 10
For this, till love be reckoned, less than lore,
Shall man be first and best for evermore.

Daughters of Eve! it was for your dear sake
    The world's first hero died an uncrown'd king;
But God's great pity touched the grand mistake,   15
    And made his married love a sacred thing:
For yet his nobler sons, if aught be true,
Find the lost Eden in their love to you.

Notes

JEAN INGELOW

[1] *title* first published in *A Story of Doom, and Other Poems* (1867).   [2] *hand* see Genesis 3: 1–7.

Like a Laverock in the Lift[3]

I

It's we two, it's we two, it's we two for aye,
All the world and we two, and Heaven be our stay.
Like a laverock in the lift, sing, O bonny bride!
All the world was Adam once, with Eve by his side.

II

What's the world, my lass, my love!—what can it do?   5
I am thine, and thou art mine; life is sweet and new.
If the world have missed the mark, let it stand by,
For we two have gotten leave, and once more we'll try.

III

Like a laverock in the lift, sing, O bonny bride!
It's we two, it's we two, happy side by side.   10
Take a kiss from me thy man; now the song begins:
"All is made afresh for us, and the brave heart wins."

IV

When the darker days come, and no sun will shine,
Thou shalt dry my tears, lass, and I'll dry thine.
It's we two, it's we two, while the world's away,   15
Sitting by the golden sheaves on our wedding-day.

On the Borders of Cannock Chase[4]

A cottager leaned whispering by her hives,
    Telling the bees some news, as they lit down,
    And entered one by one their waxen town.
Larks passioning hung o'er their brooding wives,
And all the sunny hills where heather thrives   5
    Lay satisfied with peace. A stately crown
    Of trees enringed the upper headland brown,
And reedy pools, wherein the moor-hen dives,
Glittered and gleamed.
               A resting-place for light,

Notes ————————————————————————————————

[3] *title* laverock (Scots. skylark); lift (Scots. sky, uprising current of air); first published in Ingelow's popular children's story, *Mopsa the Fairy* (ch. 11, 1869).

[4] *title* Cannock Chase is an area of natural beauty in Staffordshire in the west Midlands of England between Lichfield and Stafford; first published in *The Monitions of the Unseen, and Poems of Love and Childhood* (1870).

They that were bred here love it; but they say,   10
    "We shall not have it long; in three years' time
A hundred pits[5] will cast out fires by night,
Down yon still glen their smoke shall trail its way,
And the white ash lie thick in lieu of rime."[6]

Florence Nightingale (1820–1910)

Born in Florence, Italy into a wealthy British family, Nightingale was educated by her intellectual father, William Nightingale (1781–1874) and mother, Frances Smith (1789–1880). The Smiths were a family of abolitionists. Florence learned the classical languages and literatures, science, modern languages, philosophy, and mathematics. Early in her life, in 1837 she received a call from God to devote herself to service. Until the 1850s her family blocked any chance to pursue a vocation. She only realized her call in 1853 when she became the superintendent of a hospital for "Sick Gentlewomen" in London. In the meantime she had informed her family of her wish to become a nurse in 1844 – much against their wishes, given that nurses were generally working-class women, supposedly given to drunkenness and debauchery. She undertook some training at an institution for training deaconesses in Germany. With the outbreak of the Crimean War in 1853 she was horrified at the reports in The Times of the suffering of soldiers in the hospitals there, and she gained permission from her friend Sidney Herbert (1810–61), Secretary at War, to travel to the Crimea in October 1854 with thirty-eight volunteer nurses (see also SEACOLE (WEB p. 295)). She found the hygiene, diet, and medical treatment at Scutari in Turkey appalling and reported these grievances to The Times, gaining among many other improvements a Sanitary Commission that cleared the sewers. Nevertheless the death rates remained high because of infections of typhoid and cholera, as well as other diseases. Known as "the lady with the lamp," (see Plate 17) she could command action when she returned, spending the remaining fifty-five years of her life campaigning for the better training of nurses, the reform of hospital sanitation, the reform of drainage and water treatment in India, and writing thousands of letters to ensure that her projects were effected. In fact, she established nursing as a respectable and necessary medical profession and pioneered the care of the sick in hospitals and home settings. She also kept up-to-date with advances in medical science and specialized in her numerous reports to parliament and royal commissions in the statistical analysis of data by means of graphs, particularly pie-charts, then almost unheard of. Nightingale spent many years after her return from the Crimea suffering from what was very likely brucellosis or Crimean fever, an infectious disease from unpasteurized milk, cheese, or meat that causes muscular weakness, very likely the cause of her years of being largely bedridden. Brucellosis was first known to the medical profession in the 1850s. Her disease is often discounted because it is alleged that she became a hypochondriac. Among some scholars her biography remains a site of some controversy, especially concerning the effectiveness of her work in the Crimea in reducing deaths and her acceptance of the germ theory (see n. 13). However,

Notes

5 *pits* coal had been extracted from the area from the Middle Ages, but in the nineteenth century numerous pits were dug, some to considerable depth, especially in the period from 1850 to 1870. The collieries at Brereton were the most extensive and important.

6 *rime* hoarfrost.

the range, organization, and administrative skill of her work remains unquestioned, as does her position as one of the most popular of all Victorian women. Scholarly editions: *Collected Works of Florence Nightingale*, ed. Lynn McDonald (16 vols, 2001–); *Ever Yours, Florence Nightingale: Selected Letters*, eds Martha Vicinus and Bea Nergaard (1990); *Notes on Nursing*, ed. Victor Skretkowicz (2010); Mark Bostridge, *Florence Nightingale: The Woman and Her Legend* (2008). Collected Works site at the University of Guelph: http://www.uoguelph.ca/~cwfn.

Notes on Nursing: What It Is, and What It Is Not[1]

Preface

The following notes are by no means intended as a rule of thought by which nurses can teach themselves to nurse, still less as a manual to teach nurses to nurse. They are meant simply to give hints for thought to women who have personal charge of the health of others. Every woman, or at least almost every woman, in England has, at one time or another of her life, charge of the personal health of somebody, whether child or invalid,—in other words, every woman is a nurse. Every day sanitary knowledge, or the knowledge of nursing, or in other words, of how to put the constitution in such a state as that it will have no disease, or that it can recover from disease, takes a higher place. It is recognized as the knowledge which every one ought to have—distinct from medical knowledge, which only a profession can have.

If, then, every woman must at some time or other of her life, become a nurse, *i.e.*, have charge of somebody's health, how immense and how valuable would be the produce of her united experience if every woman would think how to nurse.

I do not pretend to teach her how, I ask her to teach herself, and for this purpose I venture to give her some hints.

[Introduction][2]

Shall we begin by taking it as a general principle—that all disease, at some period or other of its course, is more or less a reparative process, not necessarily accompanied with suffering: an effort of nature to remedy a process of poisoning or of decay, which has taken place weeks, months, sometimes years beforehand, unnoticed, the termination of the disease being then, while the antecedent process was going on, determined?

Notes ───────────────────────

FLORENCE NIGHTINGALE

[1] *title* the book was primarily written for home-care nursing, stressing sanitary procedures; fresh air; nourishing food and drink; light, comfortable, and clean beds and bedding; and close observation of the sick. It was published in different versions. The first, was a short tract of seventy-nine pages, published in January 1860 (undated, but announced in December 1859), selling for two shillings. It was frequently republished into the twentieth century in Britain, North America, and by translations widely in Europe. Republished versions were often much cheaper, enabling the book to be purchased across the classes. However, by July 1860 Nightingale published another edition, "revised and enlarged," that she called the "Library Standard" edition, with new preliminary pages, marginal topic headings, and 224 pages of text, selling for an expensive five or six shillings (depending on the binding). The third version was aimed at a particular audience, *Notes on Nursing for the Labouring Classes* (April 1861), ninety-six pages selling at sixpence, with as a new chapter, "Minding Baby." The type of this third version was reset in 1868, and it was republished for forty-one years, claiming 74,000 copies by 1898. She had already published two earlier essays as *Notes on Hospitals* (1859) aimed at government committees responsible for public health; the new Nightingale Training School at St Thomas' Hospital, London opened on 9 July 1860. Our text: January 1860.

[2] *[Introduction]* this opening section is printed as an introduction, before chapter 1 on "Ventilation and Warming." See Plate 17.

If we accept this as a general principle, we shall be immediately met with anecdotes and instances to prove the contrary. Just so if we were to take, as a principle—all the climates of the earth are meant to be made habitable for man, by the efforts of man—the objection would be immediately raised,—Will the top of Mount Blanc[3] ever be made habitable? Our answer would be, it will be many thousands of years before we have reached the bottom of Mount Blanc in making the earth healthy. Wait till we have reached the bottom before we discuss the top.

In watching diseases, both in private houses and in public hospitals, the thing which strikes the experienced observer most forcibly is this, that the symptoms or the sufferings generally considered to be inevitable and incident to the disease are very often not symptoms of the disease at all, but of something quite different—of the want of fresh air, or of light, or of warmth, or of quiet, or of cleanliness, or of punctuality and care in the administration of diet, of each or of all of these. And this quite as much in private as in hospital nursing.

The reparative process which Nature has instituted and which we call disease, has been hindered by some want of knowledge or attention, in one or in all of these things, and pain, suffering, or interruption of the whole process sets in.

If a patient is cold, if a patient is feverish, if a patient is faint, if he is sick after taking food, if he has a bed-sore, it is generally the fault not of the disease, but of the nursing.

I use the word nursing for want of a better. It has been limited to signify little more than the administration of medicines and the application of poultices. It ought to signify the proper use of fresh air, light, warmth, cleanliness, quiet, and the proper selection and administration of diet—all at the least expense of vital power to the patient.

It has been said and written scores of times, that every woman makes a good nurse. I believe, on the contrary, that the very elements of nursing are all but unknown.

By this I do not mean that the nurse is always to blame. Bad sanitary, bad architectural, and bad administrative arrangements often make it impossible to nurse. But the art of nursing ought to include such arrangements as alone make what I understand by nursing, possible.

The art of nursing, as now practised, seems to be expressly constituted to unmake what God had made disease to be, viz., a reparative process.

To recur to the first objection. If we are asked, Is such or such a disease a reparative process? Can such an illness be unaccompanied with suffering? Will any care prevent such a patient from suffering this or that?—I humbly say, I do not know. But when you have done away with all that pain and suffering, which in patients are the symptoms not of their disease, but of the absence of one or all of the above-mentioned essentials to the success of Nature's reparative processes, we shall then know what are the symptoms of and the sufferings inseparable from the disease.

Another and the commonest exclamation which will be instantly made is—Would you do nothing, then, in cholera, fever, &c.?—so deep-rooted and universal is the conviction that to give medicine is to be doing something, or rather everything; to give air, warmth, cleanliness, &c., is to do nothing. The reply is, that in these and many other similar diseases the exact value of particular remedies and modes of treatment is by no means ascertained, while there is universal experience as to the extreme importance of careful nursing in determining the issue of disease.

Notes

[3] *Blanc* the highest mountain in the Swiss Alps. Thanks in part to Shelley's ode "Mont Blanc: Lines Written in the Vale of Chamouni" (1817) and Book VI of Wordsworth's *The Prelude* (1850) it became an analogue for the human imagination.

II. The very elements of what constitutes good nursing are as little understood for the well as for the sick. The same laws of health or of nursing, for they are in reality the same, obtain among the well as among the sick. The breaking of them produces only a less violent consequence among the former than among the latter,—and this sometimes, not always.

It is constantly objected,—"But how can I obtain this medical knowledge? I am not a doctor. I must leave this to doctors."

Oh, mothers of families! You who say this, do you know that one in every seven infants in this civilized land of England perishes before it is one year old? That, in London, two in every five die before they are five years old? And, in the other great cities of England, nearly one out of two?[4] "The life duration of tender babies" (as some Saturn,[5] turned analytical chemist, says) "is the most delicate test" of sanitary conditions. Is all this premature suffering and death necessary? Or did Nature intend mothers to be always accompanied by doctors? Or is it better to learn the piano-forte than to learn the laws which subserve the preservation of offspring?

Macaulay somewhere says, that it is extraordinary that, whereas the laws of the motions of the heavenly bodies, far removed as they are from us, are perfectly well understood, the laws of the human mind, which are under our observation all day and every day, are no better understood than they were two thousand years ago.[6]

But how much more extraordinary is it that, whereas what we might call the coxcombries of education—*e.g.*, the elements of astronomy—are now taught to every schoolgirl, neither mothers of families of any class, nor school-mistresses of any class, nor nurses of children, nor nurses of hospitals, are taught anything about those laws which God has assigned to the relations of our bodies with the world in which He has put them. In other words, the laws which make these bodies, into which He has put our minds, healthy or unhealthy organs of those minds, are all but unlearnt. Not but that these laws—the laws of life—are in a certain measure understood, but not even mothers think it worth their while to study them—to study how to give their children healthy existences. They call it medical or physiological knowledge, fit only for doctors.

Another objection.

We are constantly told,—"But the circumstances which govern our children's healths are beyond our control. What can we do with winds? There is the east wind. Most people can tell before they get up in the morning whether the wind is in the east."

Notes

[4] *two* "Upon this fact the most wonderful deductions have been strung. For a long time an announcement something like the following has been going the round of the papers:—'More than 25,000 children die every year in London under 10 years of age; therefore we want a Children's Hospital.' This spring there was a prospectus issued, and divers other means taken to this effect:—'There is a great want of sanitary knowledge in women; therefore we want a Women's Hospital.' Now, both the above facts are too sadly true. But what is the deduction? The causes of the enormous child mortality are perfectly well known; they are chiefly want of cleanliness, want of ventilation, want of whitewashing; in one word, defective *household* hygiene. The remedies are just as well known; and among them is certainly not the establishment of a Child's Hospital. This may be a want; just as there may be a want of hospital room for adults. But the Registrar-General would certainly never think of giving us as a cause for the high rate of child mortality in (say) Liverpool that there was not sufficient hospital room for children; nor would he urge upon us, as a remedy, to found a hospital for them.

Again, women, and the best women, are wofully deficient in sanitary knowledge; although it is to women that we must look, first and last, for its application, as far as *household* hygiene is concerned. But who would ever think of citing the institution of a Women's Hospital as the way to cure this want?

We have it, indeed, upon very high authority that there is some fear lest hospitals, as they have been *hitherto*, may not have generally increased, rather than diminished, the rate of mortality—especially of child mortality" [author's note].

[5] *Saturn* in Roman mythology sometimes identified with the Titan Cronos, who, in some versions, ate one of his children upon learning that it was prophesied that he would be overthrown by them.

To this one can answer with more certainty than to the former objections. Who is it who knows when the wind is in the east? Not the Highland drover, certainly, exposed to the east wind, but the young lady who is worn out with the want of exposure to fresh air, to sunlight, &c. Put the latter under as good sanitary circumstances as the former, and she too will not know when the wind is in the east.

"Note Upon Some Errors in Novels": From *Notes on Nursing* ("Library Standard Edition" 1860)[7]

Novels do much to spread and stereotype popular errors and ignorances, forming, as they do now, so large a proportion of the reading of women of all classes. A few of the most common errors in novels are these:—

1.   The joys of convalescence.—People must have had very different constitutions when they could rush back to life in the way recounted in fiction.[8] In these days, for people of middle age, in the large towns of highly civilized communities, recovery (?) from severe illness is seldom recovery at all—is often delayed by relapse,—and is never anything but a struggle, slow and by no means "joyful." The assisting and encouraging, instead of over-whelming, convalescence is one of the most difficult and important duties of the nurse. Taking for granted that the patient is in a state of enjoyment, or even ease, is folly. Often, when he has no engrossing interest or affection, he is regretting the being called back to life which has then no zest for him. Or when these instantly re-seize their hold on him, he is making a painful effort to fulfil duties for which he feels himself totally unequal.

2.   The loves of cousins are a favourite topic. The authors never think how they are assisting to thwart the plan of God for the human race.[9]

3.   Sick-beds and death-beds are painted with colours and descriptions which not only the novelist never could have seen, but which no one ever did see. There is perhaps but one novel-writer who is an exception to this.[10]

Notes

[6] *Macaulay* in Thomas Babington Macaulay's "Sir James Mackintosh," a review of Mackintosh's *History of the Revolution in England in 1688* (1834) in the *Edinburgh Review* (July 1835), Macaulay in fact says the opposite of what Nightingale claims. In a long paragraph praising England as the most progressive state in the world, he asserts that the English "have carried the science of healing, the means of locomotion and correspondence, every mechanical art, every manufacture, everything that promotes the convenience of life, to a perfection which our ancestors would have thought magical, have produced a literature which may boast of works not inferior to the noblest which Greece has bequeathed to us, have discovered the laws which regulate the motions of the heavenly bodies, have speculated with exquisite subtilty on the opera-tions of the human mind, have been the acknowledged leaders of the human race in the career of political improvement."

[7] *title* added to the Library Standard edition of May/July 1860. Omitted from the *Notes on Nursing for the Labouring Classes* (April 1861). This section on novels follows a section on "Children in London" on the care of babies and chil-dren (expanded into "Minding Baby" in *Notes on Nursing for the Labouring Classes*) and is followed by "Method of Polishing Floors."

[8] *fiction* Charles Lamb (1775–1834) had outlined the situation in his essay "The Convalescent" in *Last Essays of Elia* (1833). In *Pendennis* (1848–50) Thackeray refers to "the joys of con-valescence" (ch. 53).

[9] *race* the marriage of cousins is not prohibited in the "Table of Kindred and Affinity"of the BCP, which lists those persons who may not marry in the Church of England. For instance, Charles Darwin married his cousin Emma Wedgwood and Victoria married her cousin Albert. However, it was also a topic of some controversy in the nineteenth century, even though such provisions were a major means of consolidating property and wealth within families. Jane Eyre discovers that St John Rivers, an object of her romantic interest before she is reunited with Rochester, is her first cousin (*Jane Eyre*, 1847); other cousin relationships occur in Thackeray's *History of Henry Esmond* (1852) and Elizabeth Barrett Browning's *Aurora Leigh* (1856).

[10] *this* possibly Nightingale's friend, Harriet Martineau. She had written about her own experience of illness in *Life in the Sick Room: Essays by an Invalid* (1844). Her novel *Deerbrook* (1839) involves the story of a small community doctor, Edward Hope, whose medical practice is deci-mated by rumours spread by a malicious Mrs Rowland. His reputation, however, is made unimpeachable when he performs heroically through a fever epidemic.

In England, of all human experience, sickness and death have met with the least faithful observation. The materials of course are there, but the careful study is altogether wanting. The "death-bed" of almost every one of our novels is as mere a piece of stage-effect as is the singing-death of a PRIMA DONNA in an opera.[11] One would think death did not exist in reality. Shakespeare is the only author who has ever touched the subject with truth, and his truth is only on the side of art.

4.   In novels, lives are saved by "*strong* jelly!" (what does *strong* jelly mean?) and by other things equally absurd.[12]

5.   The heroine always braves "contagion"; and then dies of it with her whole family or charge. More shame for her if they do!

Now, it is a question whether disease and death should be made matters of fiction at all. But if authors choose to write about such grave interests, surely it is not too much to ask that they will at least take the trouble to observe before they describe. Why should they encourage serious and even fatal mistakes? Why should they not inform themselves, for instance, as to what "infection" is, and make their heroine prevent it for others and herself, not partake in it, if such is to be the scene of her labours?

The true definition of infection is, that it is a means of spreading disease, which, when it exists, proves neglect or ignorance on the part of somebody, doctor, nurse, or relative; or that the place where it occurs is not fit for habitation, either by sick or by well.[13]

Notes

[11] *opera* the most famous death bed scene in Victorian fiction is the death of Little Nell in Dickens's *The Old Curiosity Shop* (1840–41), followed closely by the death of Paul Dombey in *Dombey and Son* (1846–48), and Colonel Newcome in Thackeray's *The Newcomes* (1855). Others include the death of John Barton in Elizabeth Gaskell's *Mary Barton* (1848) and of Robert Dempster in "Janet's Repentance" in George Eliot's *Scenes of Clerical Life* (1857). Such scenes are melodramatic spectacles, an occasion for the gathering of family and friends at the bedside for last farewells, final words, with Christian resignation to meet God, or with Stoic courage to meet suffering, the pious with prayer, the sinners with agony. A singing death occurs in numerous operas, including, among Victorian favourites, Giuseppe Verdi's *La Traviata* (1853), where Violetta the heroine dies of tuberculosis in the hero's arms; Verdi's *Rigoletto* (1851), where the heroine Gilda is stabbed; Gaetano Donizetti's *Lucia di Lammermoor* (1835), where the heroine goes mad and dies having murdered her hated husband on her wedding night; Vincenzo Bellini's *Norma* (1831), where the heroine is consumed by fire on her sacrificial pyre; and Gounod's *Faust* (1859), in which the heroine Marguerite, having been seduced by Faust, gives birth to an illegitimate child, is imprisoned for killing her child, but is saved in a chorus of angels.

[12] *absurd* strong broth and jelly are conventions in nineteenth-century Scottish cooking. Mrs Beeton in *Household Management* begins the ingredients for "invalid's jelly" with "12 shanks of mutton, 3 quarts of water," herbs, onion, spices, and "1lb. of lean beef" – all cooked for five hours and left to gel. Her recipe for "Beef tea" adds the comment: "Miss Nightingale says, one of the most common errors among nurses, with respect to sick diet, is the belief that beef tea is the most nutritive of all articles.... Nevertheless, there is a certain reparative quality in it."

[13] *well* in 1860 Nightingale held the predominating view of diseases, that they were caused by miasma, bad or polluting air or mist – recognized by a foul smell (hence her requirement in *Notes on Nursing* for good ventilation), and that they were equally contaminating to all who were in the presence of a miasma: indeed, a miasma caused multiple diseases. Opposed to this notion was the emerging germ theory, that each specific disease was caused by a specific micro-organism, a particular bacillus, cholera by one, typhus by another, and so on, and the spread of disease was by contact with an infected individual or contaminated object, such as bedclothes. Nightingale opposed isolation or quarantine to avoid contact for infected patients, believing that patients needed company to help recovery. John Snow (1813–58), English physician, demonstrated that the cholera outbreak in Soho in 1854 was the result of contaminated drinking water, not miasma. His views were dismissed until Joseph Lister (1827–1912), British surgeon, showed the value of antiseptic in surgery (1867). Robert Koch (1843–1910), German physician, furthered the germ theory with his paper on "Traumatic Infectious Diseases" in 1879. By 1873 some early germ theory was being taught at the Nightingale School, and by 1885 Nightingale came to accept the idea of germs as the cause of disease, but she continued to think of disease as something which could eventually be entirely eradicated by sanitation. She eventually advocated the use of antiseptics to prevent the spread of micro-organisms as well as germ theory in hygiene in India.

From *Cassandra*[14]

I

"The voice of one crying in the" crowd, "Prepare ye the way of the Lord."[15]

One often comes to be thus wandering alone in the bitterness of life without. It might be that such an one might be tempted to seek an escape in the hope of a more congenial sphere. Yet, perhaps, if prematurely we dismiss ourselves from this world, all may even have to be suffered through again—the premature birth may not contribute to the production of another being, which must be begun again from the beginning.

Such an one longs to replunge into the happy unconscious sleep of the rest of the race![16] they slumber in one another's arms—they are not yet awake. To them evil and suffering are not, for they are not conscious of evil. While one alone, awake and prematurely alive to it, must wander out in silence and solitude—such an one has awakened too early, has risen up too soon, has rejected the companionship of the race, unlinked to any human being. Such an one sees the evil they do not see, and yet has no power to discover the remedy for it.

Notes

[14] *title* this feminist essay was written between 1850 and 1852, revised in 1859 as a possible draft for a projected novel for a working-class audience and was printed privately in 1860 in the second volume of her religious–philosophical treatise *Suggestions for Thought to Searchers after Truth among the Artizans of England* (3 vols). Nightingale's extended lament on the limited opportunities for and restrictions on women in Victorian England may be compared to several other such laments, such as Augusta Webster's "The Castaway" (see especially WEBSTER nn. 23 and 29), whose heroine makes the same claims from the position of a prostitute who would rather remain as such than return to the conventional restrictions that Nightingale outlines. Nightingale sent the text to J. S. Mill and Benjamin Jowett (1817–93), theologian and master of Balliol College, Oxford, and to four others, seeking their advice about publication. Mill urged publication; in *On the Subjection of Women* (1869) Mill alludes to her directly: "A celebrated woman, in a work which I hope will some day be published, remarks truly that everything a woman does is done at odd times" (ch. 3). Jowett warned of possible attacks but thought Nightingale should proceed by revising to make it as "forcible as possible." In one of the most important texts of first-wave feminism, Virginia Woolf would write, "If a woman wrote she would have to write in the common sitting-room. And, as Miss Nightingale was so vehemently to complain,—'Women never have half an hour .. that they can call their own'— she was always interrupted." Nightingale's phrase "call their own" prefigures Woolf's *A Room of One's Own* (1929). Newly discovered manuscript material shows that Nightingale drafted two different versions: in one, as a novel, the protagonists are clever daughters of a well-to-do upper-middle-class English family who discuss religion, family, and marriage; in another version, the single woman Nofariari, who will die young, is confined by the constraints of family conventions and seeks to break loose; in a night of insomnia she begins the reflective meditation on the unhappy condition of women that she later discusses with her sympathetic brother. In the version revised and published as *Cassandra* (given here) the names are removed and the narrative is distanced to third-person. In the MS in a passage at the end of our section III, the heroine cries out: "Oh! Call me no more Nofariari, call me Cassandra. For I have preached and prophesied in vain. I have gone about crying all these many years. Woe to the people! And no one has listened or believed. And now I cry, Woe to myself!" The printed text is divided into seven numbered sections; we include extracts from sections I, II, III, V, and VI. In Greek mythology, Cassandra was the daughter of Priam and Hecuba of Troy, blessed by Apollo with the gift of prophesy, but, when she did not return his love, cursed by him never to be believed. The first public edition of *Cassandra* was in an appendix in Ray Strachey's *"The Cause": A Short History of the Women's Movement in Great Britain* (1928); our text.

[15] *Lord* the epigraph is adapted by substituting "crowd" for "wilderness" from the words of John the Baptist in Matthew 3: 3; Mark 1: 3; Luke 3: 4; and John 1: 23: "The voice of one crying in the wilderness, prepare ye the way of the Lord, make his paths straight." The embedded quotation is from Isaiah 40: 3: "The voice of him that crieth in the wilderness, Prepare ye the way of the Lord, make straight in the desert a highway for our God." Nightingale is implicitly comparing her feminist message of "good news" to that of John the Baptist greeting Christ, to which she returns at the end of the essay.

[16] *race* that is, the unconscious sleep of those who have not awakened to the plight of women in Victorian society. In the next sentences it is "Cassandra" who is awake but ignored (see n. 14).

Why have women passion, intellect, moral activity—these three—and a place in society where no one of the three can be exercised? Men say that God punishes for complaining. No, but men are angry with misery. They are irritated with women for not being happy. They take it as a personal offence. To God alone may women complain without insulting Him!

And women, who are afraid, while in words they acknowledge that God's work is good, to say, Thy will be *not* done[17] (declaring another order of society from that which He has made), go about maudling to each other and teaching to their daughters that "women have no passions." In the conventional society, which men have made for women, and women have accepted, they *must* have none, they *must* act the farce of hypocrisy, the lie that they are without passion—and therefore what else can they say to their daughters, without giving the lie to themselves?

Suffering, sad "female "humanity!"[18] What are these feelings which they are taught to consider as disgraceful, to deny to themselves? What form do the Chinese feet assume when denied their proper development?[19] If the young girls of the "higher classes," who never commit a false step, whose justly earned reputations were never sullied even by the stain which the fruit of mere "knowledge of good and evil"[20] leaves behind, were to speak, and say what are their thoughts employed upon, their *thoughts*, which alone are free, what would they say?...

What are the thoughts of these young girls while one is singing Schubert, another is reading the *Review*, and a third is busy embroidering?[21] Is not one fancying herself the nurse of some new friend in sickness; another engaging in romantic dangers with him, such as call out the character and afford more food for sympathy than the monotonous events of domestic society; another undergoing unheard-of trials under the observation of someone whom she has chosen as the companion of her dream; another having a loving and loved companion in the life she is living, which many do not want to change?[22]...

What are novels?[23] What is the secret of a charm of every romance that ever was written? The first thing in a good novel is to place the persons together in circumstances which naturally call out the high feelings and thoughts of the character, which afford food for sympathy between them on these points—romantic events they are called. The second is that the heroine has *generally* no family ties (almost *invariably* no mother), or, if she has, these do not interfere with her entire independence.

These two things constitute the main charm of reading novels. Now, in as far as these are good and not spurious interests, let us see what we have to correspond with them in

Notes

[17] *done* see "The Lord's Prayer": "Thy will be done / On earth ..." (Matthew 6: 9–13; and Luke 11: 2–4).

[18] *humanity* see Henry Wadsworth Longfellow's "The Goblet of Life" (1841, stz. 11); and William Wordsworth, "Tintern Abbey" (1798: 92): "The still sad music of humanity."

[19] *development* the binding of small girls' feet in China to prevent growth originated in the Sung (or Song) dynasty (960–1279) and continued until the twentieth century. Ostensibly a mark of beauty since it resulted in a swaying walk, foot-binding posited an ideal foot length of 7 centimetres, obtained by binding the toes so tightly into the sole of the foot that the toes and the arch are broken and permanently constricted. The practice was known to the Victorians through George Tradescant Lay's *The Chinese as They Are* (1841), with notices in *Chambers's Edinburgh Journal* (24 Apr. 1841) on "Artificial Deformities" and mention by Nightingale's friend Harriet Martineau in the *Westminster Review* (Apr. 1858).

[20] *evil* see Genesis 2: 17. The tree of knowledge of good and evil in Eden, the eating of whose fruit caused the fall, or the "stain" referred to.

[21] *Schubert ... embroidering* conventional pastimes for girls: learning to play the piano and sing German *lieder* (songs) by such composers as Franz Schubert (1797–1828); reading the *Saturday Review* (founded in 1855) or one of the quarterlies, the *Edinburgh*, the *Quarterly*, or the *Westminster*; and embroidering or doing other needlework.

[22] *change* Nightingale argues that subduing such "perpetual day-dreaming" is equivalent to the ascetic work of a Trappist monk, the moral preparation of a Greek hero of mythology, or the training of a Mohican warrior in the novels of the American James Fenimore Cooper (1789–1851) – a required social preparation for the conventions of courtship and marriage, symbolized in the idealized love in romantic fiction.

[23] *novels* see above, "Errors in Novels."

real life. Can high sympathies be set upon the opera, the exhibitions, the gossip of the House of Commons, and the political caricature?[24] If, together, man and woman approach any of the high questions of social, political, or religious life, they are said (and justly—under our present disqualifications) to be going "too far." That such things can be!

"Is it Thou, Lord?" and He said, "It is I." Let our hearts be still.[25]

II

"Yet I would spare no pang,
Would wish no torture less,
The more that anguish racks,
The earlier it will bless."[26]

Give us back our suffering, we cry to Heaven in our hearts—suffering rather than indifferentism; for out of nothing comes nothing.[27] But out of suffering may come the cure. Better have pain than paralysis! A hundred struggle and drown in the breakers. One discovers the new world. But rather, ten times rather, die in the surf, heralding the way to that new world, than stand idly on the shore!

Passion, intellect, moral activity—these three have never been satisfied in a woman. In this cold and oppressive conventional atmosphere, they cannot be satisfied. To say more on this subject would be to enter into the whole history of society, of the present state of civilisation. . . .

Is man's time more valuable than woman's? or is the difference between man and woman this, that woman has confessedly nothing to do?

Women are never supposed to have any occupation of sufficient importance *not* to be interrupted, except "suckling their fools";[28] and women themselves have accepted this, have written books to support it, and have trained themselves so as to consider whatever they do as *not* of such value to the world or to others, but that they can throw it up at the first "claim of social life." They have accustomed themselves to consider intellectual occupation as a merely selfish amusement, which it is their "duty" to give up for every trifler more selfish than themselves. . . .

How do we explain then the many cases of women who have distinguished themselves in classics, mathematics, even in politics?[29]

Widowhood, ill-health, or want of bread, these three explanations or excuses are supposed to justify a woman taking up an occupation. In some cases, no doubt, an indomitable force of character will suffice without any of these three, but such are rare. . . .

A married woman was heard to wish that she could break a limb that she might have a little time to herself. Many take advantage of the fear of "infection" to do the same.[30]

It is a thing *so* accepted among women that they have nothing to do, that one woman has not the least scruple in saying to another, "I will come and spend the morning with you." And you would be thought quite surly and absurd, if you were to refuse it on the

Notes

[24] *caricature* in her MS version, Nightingale makes clear that she was referring to "the political character in *Punch*."

[25] *It is I . . . still* see Matthew 14: 25–28; and Mark 4: 39.

[26] *bless* see Emily Brontë, "The Prisoner," stz. 14.

[27] *nothing* (Lat. *ex nihilo nihil fit*: out of nothing, nothing comes), from Lucretius, *De Rerum Natura* I. 149–59; see also *King Lear* I. I. 93: "Nothing will come of nothing."

[28] *fools* in *Othello* Iago says that women have no use except "To suckle fools and chronicle small beer" (2. I.

160), that is, bear children and keep track of household provisions.

[29] *politics* see, for instance, CONDITION: EDUCATION; RIGBY; and GENDER: CONSTRUCTING GENDERS: MARTINEAU, "BOYS" (WEB p. 73).

[30] *same* the symptoms of brucellosis, from which Nightingale very likely suffered for the rest of her life following her return from Crimea, are depression, severe to moderate weakness and pain, anaemia, and intermittent fever.

plea of occupation. Nay, it is thought a mark of amiability and affection, if you are "on such terms" that you can "come in" "any morning you please."...

Women have no means given them, whereby they *can* resist the "claims of social life." They are taught from their infancy upwards that it is wrong, ill-tempered, and a misunderstanding of "woman's mission" (with a great M)[31] if they do not allow themselves *willingly* to be interrupted at all hours. If a woman has once put in a claim to be treated as a man by some work of science or art or literature, which she can *show* as the "fruit of her leisure,"[32] then she will be considered justified in *having* leisure (hardly, perhaps, even then). But if not, not. If she has nothing to show, she must resign herself to her fate.

III

... Women often strive to live by intellect. The clear, brilliant, sharp radiance of intellect's moonlight rising above such an expanse of snow is dreary, it is true, but some love its solemn desolation, its silence, its solitude—if they are but *allowed* to live in it; if they are not perpetually baulked or disappointed. But a woman cannot live in the light of intellect. Society forbids it. Those conventional frivolities, which are called her "duties," forbid it. Her "domestic duties,"[33] high-sounding words, which, for the most part, are bad habits (which she has not the courage to enfranchise herself from, the strength to break through) forbid it. What are these duties (or bad habits)?—Answering a multitude of letters which lead to nothing, from her so-called friends, keeping herself up to the level of the world that she may furnish her quota of amusement at the breakfast-table; driving out her company in the carriage. And all these things are exacted from her by her family which, if she is good and affectionate, will have more influence with her than the world.

What wonder, if, wearied out, sick at heart with hope deferred, the springs of will broken, not seeing clearly *where* her duty lies, she abandons intellect as a vocation and takes it only, as we use the moon, by glimpses through her tight-closed window-shutters?

The family? It is too narrow a field for the development of an immortal spirit, be that spirit male or female. The chances are a thousand to one that, in that small sphere, the task for which that immortal spirit is destined by the qualities and the gifts which its Creator has placed within it, will not be found.

The family uses people, *not* for what they are, nor for what they are intended to be, but for what it wants them for—its own uses. It thinks of them not as what God has made them, but as the something which it has arranged that they shall be. If it wants someone to sit in the drawing-room, *that* someone is supplied by the family, though that member may be destined for science, or for education, or for active superintendence by God, *i.e.* by the gifts within.

This system dooms some minds to incurable infancy, others to silent misery....

Notes

[31] *mission* ... M George Elgar Hicks (1824–1914), British painter, exhibited "Woman's Mission" at the RA in 1863; the work, a triptych (three-part picture), consisted of "Guide of Childhood," "Companion of Manhood," and "Comfort of Old Age," that is, woman as mother, wife, and daughter. *The Times* described the work as representing "woman in three phases of her duties as ministering angel." *The Times* had used the same phrase to describe Nightingale nursing the soldiers in Crimea: "She is a ministering angel without any exaggeration in these hospitals, and as her slender form glides quietly along each corridor, every poor fellow's face softens with gratitude at the sight of her. When all the medical officers have retired for the night and silence and darkness have settled down upon those miles of prostrate sick, she may be observed alone, with a little lamp in her hand, making her solitary rounds." Great M is "Mission" with a capital letter. See Plate 17. See also GENDER: CONSTRUCTING GENDER, n. 6.

[32] *leisure* see Proverbs 31: 31; Nightingale has substituted "leisure" for "labour."

[33] *duties* Mrs William (Frances) Parkes (1786–1842) wrote a conduct book, *Domestic Duties, or, Instructions to Young Married Ladies, on the Management of their Households, and the Regulation of their Conduct in the Various Relations and Duties of Married Life* (1825).

In every dream of the life of intelligence or that of activity, women are accompanied by a phantom—the phantom of sympathy guiding, lighting the way—even if they do not marry. Some few sacrifice marriage, because they sacrifice all other life if they accept that. That man and woman have an equality of duties and rights is accepted by woman even less than by man. Behind *his* destiny woman must annihilate herself, must be only his complement. A woman dedicates herself to the vocation of her husband; she fills up and performs the subordinate parts in it. But if she has any destiny, any vocation of her own, she must renounce it, in nine cases out of ten. Some few, like Mrs Somerville, Mrs Chisholm, Mrs Fry, have not done so; but these are exceptions.[34] The fact is that woman has so seldom any vocation of her own, that it does not much signify; she has none to renounce. A man gains everything by marriage: he gains a "helpmate,"[35] but a woman does not....

V

The more complete a woman's organisation, the more she will feel it, till at last there shall arise a woman, who will resume, in her own soul, all the sufferings of her race, and that woman will be the Saviour of her race.[36]

Jesus Christ raised women above the condition of mere slaves, mere ministers to the passions of the man, raised them by His sympathy, to be Ministers of God. He gave them moral activity. But the Age, the World, Humanity, must give them the means to exercise this moral activity, must give them intellectual cultivation, spheres of action....

VI

We live in the world, it is said, and must walk in its ways.

Was Christ called a complainer against the world?...

Christ, if He had been a woman, might have been nothing but a great complainer....

The next Christ will perhaps be a female Christ. But do we see one woman who looks like a female Christ? or even like "the messenger before" her "face," to go before her and prepare the hearts and minds for her?[37]

WEB p. 366

Dion Boucicault (1820–90)
The Octoroon; or Life in Louisiana. A Play in Four Acts
From Act 3 [The Auction]
From Act 4 [The Trial]

Notes

[34] *Somerville ... exceptions* Mary Fairfax Somerville (1780–1872), British scientist, author of *The Mechanisms of Heaven* (1831) and *On the Connexion of the Physical Sciences* (1834), was the first female member of the Royal Astronomical Society (1835); Caroline Chisholm (1808–77), British social reformer, was known primarily for her work with immigrant women in Australia; and Elizabeth Fry (1780–1845) was a British prison reformer and philanthropist.

[35] *helpmate* see Genesis 2: 18–20.

[36] *race* possibly an echo of the fourth-century hymn attributed to Ambrose of Milan (330–97), *Veni Redemptor gentium* (Lat. come, Saviour of our race); translated by John Mason Neale (1818–66) as: "O come Redeemer of the earth."

[37] *her* an allusion to John the Baptist as the forerunner to Christ: see Isaiah 40: 3; Malachi 3: 1; Matthew 11: 10; Mark 1: 2; and Luke 1: 17. Nightingale had herself been portrayed as a Christ figure when in the Crimea, both in serious praise and in the satirical pages of *Punch*; the analogy was further extended by the links between her as "the lady with the lamp" and Holman Hunt's painting of *The Light of the World* (1852). The heterodox theological convention of a female saviour had long been used by women writers, from Julian of Norwich (c.1342–c.1416) and Hildegard of Bingen (1098–1179) in the Middle Ages, and was recurrent in nineteenth-century millenarian circles.

WEB p. 375

Bill the Navvy (b. 1820?)
From "Autobiography of a Navvy"

Dora Greenwell (1821–82)

Dorothy (Dora) Greenwell was born into a landed family in Lanchester, Durham, where she was educated by a governess. She taught herself five languages and read widely in politics, theology, and philosophy. Declared bankrupt, the family moved in with her clergyman brother in Northumberland in 1847. After her father's death (1854), Greenwell cared for her mother until her death in 1871. She published *Poems* (1848) and two important collections, *Poems* (1861) and *Poems* (1867). Collections of religious verse followed: *Carmina Crucis* (1869) and *Camera Obscura* (1876); with Jean Ingelow she published a collection of poetry for children, *Home Thoughts and Home Scenes* (1865). She became involved in various social issues through her friendship with social reformer Josephine Butler (1828–1906), including work against the Contagious Diseases Acts (1864–69). She also worked against slavery and vivisection, and on behalf of women's education, work, and the franchise. She collected her writings in *Essays* (1866). Her most famous work is the essay "Our Single Women" (*North British Review*, Feb. 1864), an argument for women's education. No standard edition. William Dowling, *Memoirs of Dora Greenwell* (1885); Henry Bell, *Dora Greenwell* (1950); "Dora Greenwell": http://orlando.cambridge.org/public/svPeople?person_id=greedo

A Scherzo[1]

(A Shy Person's Wishes)

With the wasp at the innermost heart of a peach,
On a sunny wall out of tip-toe reach,
With the trout in the darkest summer pool,
With the fern-seed clinging behind its cool
Smooth frond, in the chink of an aged tree,   5
In the woodbine's horn[2] with the drunken bee,
With the mouse in its nest in a furrow old,
With the chrysalis wrapt in its gauzy fold;
With things that are hidden, and safe, and bold,
With things that are timid, and shy, and free,   10
Wishing to be;

Notes

DORA GREENWELL
[1] *title* a scherzo (It. joke) is the third movement in the classical symphony, string quartet, or sonata, a quickly moving and playful composition. In form it is ternary, with an A section followed by a contrasting B section and then a return to the A section. The poem was first published in *Poems* (1867).

[2] *horn* one of the flowerlets on a species of sweet-smelling honeysuckle.

With the nut in its shell, with the seed in its pod,
With the corn as it sprouts in the kindly clod,
Far down where the secret of beauty shows
In the bulb of the tulip, before it blows;   15
With things that are rooted, and firm, and deep,
Quiet to lie, and dreamless to sleep;
With things that are chainless, and tameless, and proud,
With the fire in the jagged thunder-cloud,
With the wind in its sleep, with the wind in its waking,   20
With the drops that go to the rainbow's making,
Wishing to be with the light leaves shaking,
Or stones on some desolate highway breaking;
Far up on the hills, where no foot surprises
The dew as it falls, or the dust as it rises;   25
To be couched with the beast in its torrid lair,
Or drifting on ice with the polar bear,
With the weaver at work at his quiet loom;
Anywhere, anywhere, out of this room!

To Elizabeth Barrett Browning in 1851[3]

I lose myself within thy mind—from room
    To goodly room[4] thou leadest me, and still
    Dost show me of thy glory more, until
My soul like Sheba's Queen faints, overcome,
And all my spirit dies within me, numb,[5]   5
    Sucked in by thine, a larger star, at will;
    And hasting like thy bee, my hive to fill,
I "swoon for very joy"[6] amid thy bloom;
Till—not like that poor bird (as poets feign)
    That tried against the Lutanist's her skill,[7]   10
    Crowding her thick precipitate notes, until
Her weak heart brake above the contest vain—
    Did not thy strength a nobler thought instil,
I feel as if I ne'er could sing again!

Notes

[3] *title* first published as "To Elizabeth Barrett Browning" in *Poems* (1861). When republished in *Poems* (1867), it was retitled. Our text: 1867.

[4] *room* it was a convention for learned sonneteers aware of the tradition of Petrarch and Dante to use the room metaphor for another's poems ("room" in Italian is *stanza*) . See John Donne, "The Canonization" (1633: 32 "We'll build in sonnets pretty rooms." Elizabeth Barrett Browning's *Poems* (2 vols, 1850) included her sonnet sequence of forty-four love poems to Robert Browning, *Sonnets from the Portuguese.*

[5] *numb* when the Queen of Sheba visited King Solomon, she was in awe at the splendour of his court and "there was no more spirit in her" (1 Kings 10: 5).

[6] *joy* see Robert Browning, *Paracelsus* (1835: 51): "shivering for very joy."

[7] *skill* the nightingale was a common symbol of love, lyric poetry, and poetic inspiration, from William Byrd's "The Nightingale so pleasant and so gay" (1589) to Keats's "Ode to a Nightingale"(1820). The contest between the lute player and the nightingale derives from the Italian writer Famiano Strada (1572–1649) in *Prolusiones academicæ* (Lat. academic prolusions; 1617) and was used in Jacobean and Caroline plays and poems. Various female writers, including Anne Finch (1661–1720), had redefined the nightingale-poet as a female subject.

To Elizabeth Barrett Browning in 1861[8]

I praised thee not while living; what to thee
    Was praise of mine? I mourned thee not when dead;
    I only loved thee,—love thee! oh thou fled
Fair spirit, free at last where all are free,
I only love thee, bless thee, that to me   5
    For ever thou hast made the rose more red,
    More sweet each word by olden singers said
In sadness, or by children in their glee;
    Once, only once in life I heard thee speak,[9]
    Once, only once I kissed thee on the cheek,   10
And met thy kiss and blessing; scarce I knew
Thy smile, I only loved thee, only grew,
    Through wealth, through strength of thine, less poor, less weak;
Oh what hath death with souls like thine to do?

To Christina Rossetti[10]

Thou hast fill'd me a golden cup[11]
With a drink Divine that glows,
With the bloom that is shining up
From the heart of the folded rose.

The grapes in their amber glow,   5
And the strength of the blood-red wine
All mingle, and change, and flow
In this golden cup of thine.

With the scent of the curling wine,
With the balm of the rose's breath,—   10
For the voice of love is thine,
And thine is the Song of Death!

Notes

[8] *title* first published in *Poems* (1867); the volume was "Dedicated to the Memory of Elizabeth Barrett Browning," who had died in Florence in 1861.

[9] *speak* the encounter occurred very likely in 1851 when the Brownings made their single return visit to England from Italy where they had lived after their marriage. Writing to a friend in 1851, Greenwell says: "Mrs. Browning (I hear) is in the town, and *impending*."

[10] *title* the MS includes an epigraph: "'I have mingled my grapes and my wine.' (*The Song of Songs*)." The citation is not found in the KJV, but see Proverb 9: 5. The poem is also dated "Sept. 17th, 1875." Greenwell and Rossetti had met on a number of occasions and carried on a correspondence. Rossetti had sent her sonnet "Autumn Violets" (*Macmillan's Magazine*, 1868) to Greenwell with the inscription: "With love, and in the hope of our meeting ere long." First published in William Dowling, *Memoirs of Dora Greenwell* (1885).

[11] *cup* see Jeremiah 51: 7.

Matthew Arnold (1822–88)

Born in Laleham, son of Thomas Arnold (1795–1842), famous headmaster of Rugby School and educational reformer, and Mary Penrose (1791–1873), Arnold won a scholarship from Rugby to Balliol College, Oxford in 1840. He renewed there his friendship from Rugby with Arthur Hugh Clough (1819–61). Arnold won the Newdigate Prize for poetry in 1843 and a fellowship to Oriel in 1845. In 1851, the year of his marriage to Francis Lucy Wightman (1825–1901), he became a school inspector, a job he maintained for thirty-five years, during which he championed the expansion of public education. He was Oxford Professor of Poetry for ten years from 1857. Arnold is among the nineteenth century's pre-eminent poets and cultural and social critics. In 1849 he published anonymously *The Strayed Reveller, and Other Poems*, followed by *Empedocles on Etna, and Other Poems* (1852). For *Poems* (1853) he wrote the famous "Preface," in which he condemns poetry which presents life as "a continuous state of mental distress." He promotes a classical ideal of timeless and universal values as a corrective to what he saw as the sickness of his own society; in his poetry, the unattainability of these ideals is often expressed as alienation and despair, projecting a contemporary world in which religious belief and cultural values have been lost. His literary and cultural criticism was gathered into two volumes, *Essays in Criticism* (1865) and *Essays in Criticism: Second Series* (1888). His most famous work of cultural criticism, *Culture and Anarchy* (1869), condemns cultural sterility of the three classes, "Barbarians" (the aristocracy), the "Philistines" (the middle classes), and the "Populace" (the working classes), and warns of the need to educate the working class, who, in light of the Reform Bill of 1867, are destined to become the new masters of the country. For many years Arnold's ideal of liberal education was a model; however, since the 1960s this model has been sharply criticized as elitist, patriarchal, and Eurocentric. Recently some critics have begun to defend Arnold from such attacks. From the 1870s, he wrote on religious topics in *St. Paul and Protestantism* (1870), *Literature and Dogma* (1873), and *God and the Bible* (1875), for which he was sharply criticized for what were perceived to be attacks on orthodoxy. Standard edition: *Arnold: The Complete Poems*, ed. Miriam Allott (second edition, 1979); *The Complete Prose Works of Matthew Arnold*, ed. R. H. Super (11 vols, 1960–77); *The Letters of Matthew Arnold*, ed. Cecil Y. Lang (6 vols, 1996–2001), available at http://rotunda.upress.virginia.edu/arnold; Nicholas Murray, *A Life of Matthew Arnold* (1997); "Matthew Arnold on The Victorian Web": http://www.victorianweb.org/authors/arnold/index.html

The Forsaken Merman[1]

Come, dear children, let us away;
Down and away below.
Now my brothers call from the bay;
Now the great winds shorewards blow;

Notes

MATTHEW ARNOLD

[1] *title* based on a Danish ballad and folktale about a merman who charms a young girl to come to live with him in the ocean, as in Mary Howitt's translation of Hans Christian Andersen's *The True Story of My Life* (1847), and, more fully, in a review by George Borrow (1803–81) in *Universal Review* 2 (1825) of a collection of Danish folktales. First published in *The Strayed Reveller, and Other Poems* (1849). In *Poems* (1853) Arnold made a few verbal changes, removed almost all of the indentations, changed the punctuation, and introduced many exclamation points.

Now the salt tides seawards flow;   5
Now the wild white horses play,
Champ and chafe and toss in the spray.
    Children dear, let us away.
        This way, this way.

Call her once before you go.   10
    Call once yet.
In a voice that she will know:
    "Margaret! Margaret!"
Children's voices should be dear
(Call once more) to a mother's ear: 15
Children's voices, wild with pain.
    Surely she will come again.
Call her once and come away.
        This way, this way.
"Mother dear, we cannot stay."   20
The wild white horses foam and fret.
    Margaret! Margaret!

Come, dear children, come away down.
      Call no more.
One last look at the white-wall'd town,   25
And the little grey church on the windy shore.
      Then come down.
She will not come though you call all day.
    Come away, come away.

Children dear, was it yesterday   30
We heard the sweet bells over the bay?
    In the caverns where we lay,
    Through the surf and through the swell
The far-off sound of a silver bell?
Sand-strewn caverns, cool and deep,   35
Where the winds are all asleep;
Where the spent lights quiver and gleam;
Where the salt weed sways in the stream;
Where the sea-beasts rang'd all round
Feed in the ooze of their pasture-ground;   40
Where the sea-snakes coil and twine,
Dry their mail and bask in the brine;
Where great whales come sailing by,
Sail and sail, with unshut eye,
Round the world for ever and aye;   45
    When did music come this way?
    Children dear, was it yesterday?

    Children dear, was it yesterday
    (Call yet once) that she went away?
    Once she sate with you and me,   50
    On a red gold throne in the heart of the sea,
    And the youngest sate on her knee.

She comb'd its bright hair, and she tended it well,
When down swung the sound of a far-off bell.
She sigh'd, she look'd up through the clear green sea. 55
She said; "I must go, for my kinsfolk pray
In the little grey church on the shore to-day.
'Twill be Easter-time in the world—ah me!
And I lose my poor soul,[2] Merman, here with thee."
I said; "Go up, dear heart, through the waves. 60
Say thy prayer, and come back to the kind sea-caves."
    She smil'd, she went up through the surf in the bay.
        Children dear, was it yesterday?

        Children dear, were we long alone?
"The sea grows stormy, the little ones moan. 65
Long prayers," I said, "in the world they say.
Come," I said, and we rose through the surf in the bay.
We went up the beach, by the sandy down
Where the sea-stocks bloom, to the white-wall'd town.
Through the narrow pav'd streets, where all was still, 70
To the little grey church on the windy hill.
From the church came a murmur of folk at their prayers,
But we stood without in the cold blowing airs.
We climb'd on the graves, on the stones, worn with rains,
And we gaz'd up the aisle through the small leaded panes. 75
    She sate by the pillar; we saw her clear:
    "Margaret, hist! come quick, we are here.
    Dear heart," I said, "we are long alone.
    The sea grows stormy, the little ones moan."
But, ah, she gave me never a look, 80
For her eyes were seal'd to the holy book.
    "Loud prays the priest; shut stands the door."
Come away, children, call no more.
Come away, come down, call no more.

        Down, down, down. 85
        Down to the depths of the sea.
She sits at her wheel in the humming town,
        Singing most joyfully.
Hark, what she sings; "O joy, o joy,
For the humming street, and the child with its toy. 90
For the priest, and the bell, and the holy well.
        For the wheel where I spun,
        And the blessed light of the sun."
    And so she sings her fill,
    Singing most joyfully, 95
    Till the shuttle drops from her hand,
    And the whizzing wheel stands still.
She steals to the window, and looks at the sand;
        And over the sand at the sea;

Notes

[2] *soul* popular superstition held that those who went to live
with mermen or mermaids lost their souls.

And her eyes are set in a stare;   100
And anon there breaks a sigh,
And anon there drops a tear,
From a sorrow-clouded eye,
And a heart sorrow-laden,
    A long, long sigh.   105
For the cold strange eyes of a little Mermaiden
   And the gleam of her golden hair.

Come away, away children.
Come children, come down.
The salt tide rolls seaward.[3]   110
Lights shine in the town.
She will start from her slumber
When gusts shake the door;
She will hear the winds howling,
Will hear the waves roar.   115
We shall see, while above us
The waves roar and whirl,
A ceiling of amber,
A pavement of pearl.[4]
Singing, "Here came a mortal,   120
But faithless was she.
And alone dwell for ever
The kings of the sea."

But, children, at midnight,
When soft the winds blow;   125
When clear falls the moonlight;
When spring-tides are low:
When sweet airs come seaward
From heaths starr'd with broom;
And high rocks throw mildly   130
On the blanch'd sands a gloom:
Up the still, glistening beaches,
Up the creeks we will hie;
Over banks of bright seaweed
The ebb-tide leaves dry.   135
We will gaze, from the sand-hills,
At the white, sleeping town;
At the church on the hill-side—
    And then come back down.
Singing, "There dwells a lov'd one,   140
But cruel is she.
She left lonely for ever
The kings of the sea."

Notes

3 *The salt … seaward* line omitted 1853; substituted with "The hoarse wind blows coldly;"

4 *she … pearl* lines 112–19 imitate Byron, *Manfred* 1. 1. 76–87.

Matthew Arnold

Memorial Verses

April 27, 1850[5]

Goethe[6] in Weimar sleeps, and Greece,
Long since, saw Byron's[7] struggle cease.
But one such death remain'd to come.
The last poetic voice is dumb.
We stand to-day at Wordsworth's tomb.   5

When Byron's eyes were shut in death,
We bow'd our heads and held our breath.
He taught us little;[8] but our soul
Had *felt* him like the thunder's roll.
With shivering heart the strife we saw   10
Of Passion with eternal Law,
And yet with reverential awe
We watch'd the fount of fiery life
Which flow'd for that Titanic strife.

When Goethe pass'd away, we said,—   15
"Sunk, then, is Europe's sagest head.
Physician of the iron age,
Goethe has done his pilgrimage."
He took the suffering human race,
He scanned each wound, each weakness, near,   20
And struck his finger on the place,
And said, "Thou ailest here, and here."
He look'd on Europe's dying hour
Of fitful dream and feverish power,
His eye plunged down the seething strife,   25
The turmoil of expiring life:
He said, "The end is everywhere;
Art still has truth; take refuge there!"
And he was happy, if to know
Causes of things,[9] and far below   30

Notes

[5] *title* Wordsworth died on 23 April 1850 and was buried at Grasmere on 27 April. Arnold wrote at the request of his neighbour, Edward Quillinan (1791–1851), Wordsworth's son-in-law, who described it as "*very classical, … a triple Epicede on … Wordsworth and Goethe, and on Byron.*" See also Arnold's essay on Wordsworth published first as an introduction to his edition of the poems of Wordsworth (1879) and then in *Essays in Criticism, Second Series* (1888). An *epicedion* is a form of elegy that describes the feelings of the mourners at the tomb, concluding with a wish for the peaceful rest of the dead. For examples of this form, see TENNYSON, IN MEMORIAM, SECTIONS II, XXXIX, LVII, LXVII; and Catullus, Poem 101. Arnold published the poem in *Fraser's Magazine* in June, 1850. In *Poems* (1850) the subtitle reads APRIL, 1850.

[6] *Goethe* Johann Wolfgang von Goethe (1749–1832), German poet, dramatist, novelist, and critic with a vast European reputation, was buried in Weimar, one of the cultural centres of Germany.

[7] *Byron* George Gordon, Lord Byron (1788–1824) fought for Greek independence against the Ottoman Empire but contracted a fever and died at Messolonghi in Greece; his heart was buried there, the rest of his remains at the family church near Newstead Abbey, Nottingham.

[8] *little* denigrating Byron as a teacher in favour of Goethe had been a commonplace since Carlyle commanded in "The Everlasting Yea" in *Sartor Resartus* (1833–34): "Close thy *Byron*; open thy *Goethe*."

[9] *things* see Virgil, *Georgics* 2. 490–92: "happy is the one who is able to know the causes of things."

His feet to see the lurid flow
Of terror, and insane distress,
And headlong fate, be happiness.

And Wordsworth! Ah, pale Ghosts, rejoice!
For never has such soothing voice   35
Been to your shadowy world convey'd
Since erst, at morn, some wandering shade
Heard the clear song of Orpheus come
Through Hades, and the mournful gloom.[10]
Wordsworth is gone from us—and Ye,   40
Ah, may ye feel his voice as we!
He too upon a wintry clime
Was fallen, on the iron time.[11]
He found us when the age had bound
Our spirits in a brazen round:[12]   45
He spoke, and loos'd our heart in tears.
He tore us from the prison-cell
Of festering thoughts and personal fears,
Where we had long been doom'd to dwell.[13]
He laid, us as we lay at birth,   50
On the cool flowery lap of earth:
Smiles broke from us, and we had ease.
The hills were round us, and the breeze
Went o'er the sun-lit fields again:
Our foreheads felt the wind and rain: 55
Our youth came back; for there was shed
On spirits that had long been dead,
Spirits deep-crush'd, and closely furl'd,
The freshness of the early world.

Ah! since dark days still bring to light   60
Man's prudence and man's fiery might,
Time may restore us, in his course,
Goethe's sage mind, and Byron's force;
But where shall Europe's latter hour
Again find Wordsworth's healing power?   65
Others will teach us how to dare,
And against fear our breast to steel;
Others will strengthen us to bear—

[10] *gloom* see *Aeneid* 6. 119–20, where Virgil mentions Orpheus, the mythological poet and musician whose music so charmed Pluto, ruler of the Underworld or Tartarus, and Prosperine his queen. Proserpine, the daughter of Ceres, goddess of agriculture and fertility, was abducted by Pluto as she played near Mount Etna (Enna) and became his wife. Each spring she returned to Sicily, causing the flowers to bloom; she knew the Greek or Dorian modes of music. These rulers were so charmed with the music of Orpheus that they allowed him to take back his wife Eurydice from the dead, provided he not look upon her in the journey to the land of the living. But he did, and she slipped back among the dead; Arnold uses the details of this myth in his elegy for Clough, "Thyrsis" (85–97); see also Theocritus, "Lament for Bion" (123–24); Virgil, *Georgics* (4. 454–503); and Horace *Odes* (1. 24. 13–14); *Metamorphoses* 10. 1–105; and 11: 1–66; and *Paradise Lost* 4. 268–71.

[11] *time* in *Poems* (1852), Arnold added the following line here: "Of doubts, disputes, distractions, fears."

[12] *Our ... round* in *Poems* (1852): "Our souls in its benumbing round."

[13] *He tore ... to dwell* lines omitted in *Poems* (1852).

But who, ah who, will make us feel?
The cloud of mortal destiny, 70
Others will front it fearlessly—
But who, like him, will put it by?

Keep fresh the grass upon his grave,
O Rotha,[14] with thy living wave.
Sing him thy best; for few or none 75
Hears thy voice right, now he is gone.

[Isolation] To Marguerite[15]

We were apart: yet, day by day,
I bade my heart more constant be;
I bade it keep the world away,
And grow a home for only thee:
Nor fear'd but thy love likewise grew, 5
Like mine, each day more tried, more true.

The fault was grave: I might have known,
What far too soon, alas, I learn'd—
The heart can bind itself alone,
And faith is often unreturn'd.— 10
    Self-sway'd our feelings ebb and swell:
Thou lov'st no more: Farewell! Farewell!

Farewell! and thou, thou lonely heart,
Which never yet without remorse
Even for a moment did'st depart 15
From thy remote and sphered course
To haunt the place where passions reign,
Back to thy solitude again!

Back, with the conscious thrill of shame
Which Luna[16] felt, that summer night, 20
Flash through her pure immortal frame,
When she forsook the starry height
To hang over Endymion's sleep
Upon the pine-grown Latmian steep;[17]—

Notes

[14] *Rotha* river that flows by Wordsworth's grave in Grasmere churchyard.

[15] *title* "Marguerite" was either an unidentified French woman whom Arnold had met in 1848 at Thun in the Swiss Alps, or perhaps an alias for Mary Sophia Claude (1820–1912), of a French family, who resided in England from early childhood. First published in *Poems* (third edition 1857) as "VI. To Marguerite," the sixth poem of the sequence entitled "Switzerland," this poem printed before "To Marguerite—Continued" (see n. 18); reprinted as "Isolation. To Marguerite" (1869). Our text, 1857.

[16] *Luna* (Lat.) or Silene (Gk.) was one of the Titans, the daughter of Hyperion and Terra, and the brother of Helion, the god of the sun. In Greek mythology she was goddess of the moon, later conflated with Diana, who fell in love with the shepherd Endymion who persuaded Zeus to cause him to fall asleep ageless in a cave on Mount Latmos where she, descending from the night sky behind the mountain, could gaze upon him and renew her nightly tryst with him (Theocritus, *Idylls* 20. 37–39; and Apollonius of Rhodes, *Argonautica* 4. 57 ff.).

[17] *steep* Mount Latmus is on the western coast of Turkey, the site of the cave of Endymion.

Yet she, chaste queen, had never prov'd   25
How vain a thing is mortal love,
Wandering in Heaven, far remov'd.
But thou hast long had place to prove
This truth—to prove, and make thine own—
    Thou hast been, shalt be, art, alone.   30

Or, if not quite alone, yet they
Which touch thee are unmating things—
Ocean, and clouds, and night, and day;
Lorn autumns and triumphant springs;
And life, and others' joy and pain,   35
And love, if love, of happier men.

Of happier men—for they, at least,
Have *dream'd* two human hearts might blend
In one, and were through faith releas'd
From isolation withou t end   40
Prolong'd; nor knew, although not less
Alone than thou, their loneliness.

To Marguerite, in Returning a Volume of the Letters of Ortis[18]

Yes: in the sea of life enisl'd,
With echoing straits between us thrown,
Dotting the shoreless watery wild,
We mortal millions live *alone.*
    The islands feel the enclasping flow,   5
And then their endless bounds they know.

But when the moon their hollows lights
And they are swept by balms of spring,
And in their glens, on starry nights,
The nightingales divinely sing;   10
And lovely notes, from shore to shore,
Across the sounds and channels pour;

Oh then a longing like despair
Is to their farthest caverns sent;
—For surely once, they feel, we were   15
Parts of a single continent.

Notes

[18] *title* Ugo Foscolo (1778–1827) published a novel about a young man's coming of age and later committing suicide, *Ultime Lettere di Jacopo Ortis* (Ital. last letters of Jacopo Ortis) in 1798, revised 1802, and translated into French in 1839 by Alexandre Dumas—presumably the version Arnold used. First published in *Empedocles on Etna, and Other Poems* (1852). In *Poems* (1853) the poem was retitled as "To Marguerite." The poem was later grouped with a sequence of poems entitled "Switzerland"; it was printed with the title "Isolation" (*Poems* third ed. 1857); and with title: "To Marguerite—Continued" in 1869, when the title "Isolation" was transferred to the previous poem. Our text 1852. Subsequently, the poems have been printed as a pair. See above, title-note to "To Marguerite," n.1.

Now round us spreads the watery plain—
Oh might our marges meet again!

Who order'd, that their longing's fire
Should be, as soon as kindled, cool'd?   20
Who renders vain their deep desire?
    A God, a God their severance rul'd;
And bade betwixt their shores to be
The unplumb'd, salt, estranging sea.[19]

The Buried Life[20]

    Light flows our war of mocking words, and yet,
Behold, with tears my eyes are wet.
I feel a nameless sadness o'er me roll.
    Yes, yes, we know that we can jest,
We know, we know that we can smile;   5
But there's a something in this breast
To which thy light words bring no rest,
And thy gay smiles no anodyne.
    Give me thy hand, and hush awhile,
And turn those limpid eyes on mine,   10
And let me read there, love, thy inmost soul.

    Alas, is even Love too weak
To unlock the heart, and let it speak?
Are even lovers powerless to reveal
To one another what indeed they feel?   15
I knew the mass of men conceal'd
Their thoughts, for fear that if reveal'd
They would by other men be met
With blank indifference, or with blame reprov'd:
I knew they liv'd and mov'd   20
Trick'd in disguises, alien to the rest
Of men, and alien to themselves—and yet
The same heart beats in every human breast.

    But we, my love—doth a like spell benumb
Our hearts—our voices?—must we too be dumb?   25

Notes

[19] *God ... sea* in *Epode* 14. 6, Horace repeats *deus* (Lat. god) and in *Ode* 1. 3. 21–23, he refers to the *Oceano dissociabili* that had been translated at Rugby school by A. C. Tait as "with the estranging main."

[20] *title* Arnold expands a metaphor of a Greek philosopher, Epicurus (341–270 BCE), who urged his followers to "live a hidden life" based on ethical self-restraint to gain peace of mind and avoid anxiety. Arnold also explores the analogy of Greek philosopher, Heracleitus (c.535–475 BCE) of life to a river into which we can step only once because of its continual change. Heracleitus also argued that fire is the universal principle of the cosmos – also referred to by Arnold. Such goals are complicated in Arnold's melancholic meditation concerning the invisibility of the hidden self, only occasionally glimpsed in a moment of recognition through a loved hand, eye, or voice. First published in *Empedocles on Etna, and Other Poems* (1852). Our text *Poems* (second series, 1855).

Ah, well for us, if even we,
Even for a moment, can get free
Our heart, and have our lips unchain'd:
For that which seals them hath been deep-ordain'd.

Fate, which foresaw   30
How frivolous a baby man would be,
By what distractions he would be possess'd,
How he would pour himself in every strife,
And well-nigh change his own identity;
That it might keep from his capricious play   35
His genuine self, and force him to obey,
Even in his own despite, his being's law,
Bade through the deep recesses of our breast
The unregarded River of our Life
Pursue with indiscernible flow its way;   40
And that we should not see
The buried stream, and seem to be
Eddying about in blind uncertainty,
Though driving on with it eternally.

But often, in the world's most crowded streets,   45
But often, in the din of strife,
There rises an unspeakable desire
After the knowledge of our buried life,[21]
A thirst to spend our fire and restless force
In tracking out our true, original course;   50
A longing to inquire
Into the mystery of this heart that beats
So wild, so deep in us, to know
Whence our thoughts come and where they go.
And many a man in his own breast then delves,   55
But deep enough, alas, none ever mines:
And we have been on many thousand lines,
And we have shown on each talent and power,
But hardly have we, for one little hour,
Been on our own line, have we been ourselves;   60
Hardly had skill to utter one of all
The nameless feelings that course through our breast,
But they course on for ever unexpress'd.
And long we try in vain to speak and act
Our hidden self, and what we say and do   65
Is eloquent, is well—but 'tis not true:
    And then we will no more be rack'd
With inward striving, and demand
Of all the thousand nothings of the hour
Their stupefying power;   70

Notes

[21] *But often ... life* see Wordsworth, "Tintern Abbey" (25–27).

Ah yes, and they benumb us at our call:
Yet still, from time to time, vague and forlorn,
From the soul's subterranean depth upborne
As from an infinitely distant land,
Come airs, and floating echoes, and convey   75
A melancholy into all our day.

     Only—but this is rare—
When a beloved hand is laid in ours,
When, jaded with the rush and glare
Of the interminable hours,   80
Our eyes can in another's eyes read clear,
When our world-deafen'd ear
Is by the tones of a lov'd voice caress'd,—
     A bolt is shot back somewhere in our breast
And a lost pulse of feeling stirs again: 85
The eye sinks inward, and the heart lies plain,
And what we mean, we say, and what we would, we know.
A man becomes aware of his life's flow,
And hears its winding murmur, and he sees
The meadows where it glides, the sun, the breeze.   90

     And there arrives a lull in the hot race
Wherein he doth for ever chase
That flying and elusive shadow, Rest.
An air of coolness plays upon his face,
And an unwonted calm pervades his breast.   95
     And then he thinks he knows
The Hills where his life rose,
And the Sea where it goes.

Lines Written in Kensington Gardens[22]

In this lone open glade I lie,
Screen'd by dark trees on either hand;
And at its end, to stay the eye,
Those black-top'd, red-bol'd pine-trees stand.

The clouded sky is still and grey,   5
Through silken rifts soft peers the sun.
Like the green-foliag'd chestnuts play,
The darker elms stand grave and dun[23]

The birds sing sweetly in these trees,
Across the girdling city's hum.   10
How green under the boughs it is!
How thick the tremulous sheep-cries[24] come!

Notes

[22] *title* a park in central London, a continuation of Hyde Park to the west. First published in *Empedocles on Etna, and Other Poems* (1852).

[23] *The clouded sky ... dun* stanza omitted in *New Poems* (1867) and subsequently.

[24] *sheep-cries* sheep were occasionally grazed in London parks to crop the grass.

Sometimes a child will cross the glade
To take his nurse his broken toy:
Sometimes a thrush flit overhead 15
Deep in her unknown day's employ.

Here at my feet what wonders pass,
What endless, active life is here!
What blowing daisies, fragrant grass!
An air-stirr'd forest, fresh and clear. 20

Scarce fresher is the mountain sod
Where the tired angler lies, stretch'd out,
And, eased of basket and of rod,
Counts his day's spoil, the spotted trout.[25]

I, on men's impious uproar hurl'd, 25
Think sometimes, as I hear them rave,
That peace has left the upper world,
And now keeps only in the grave.

Yet here is peace for ever new.
When I, who watch them, am away, 30
Still all things in this glade go through
The changes of their quiet day.

Then to their happy rest they pass.
The flowers close, the birds are fed;
The night comes down upon the grass; 35
The child sleeps warmly in his bed.

Calm Soul of all things![26] make it mine
To feel, amid the city's jar,
That there abides a peace of thine,
Man did not make, and cannot mar. 40

The will to neither strive nor cry,
The power to feel with others give.
Calm, calm me more; nor let me die
Before I have begun to live.

Notes

[25] *trout* stanza added here in 1867:
  "In the huge world which roars hard by / Be others happy,
  if they can! / But in my helpless cradle I / Was breathed
  on by the rural Pan."
[26] *Soul ... things* the world-soul (Lat. *anima mundi*) of ancient
  philosophy that was supposed to subsist in and animate all
things (Plato, *Timaeus* 29/30), later appropriated by philosophers like Baruch Spinoza (1632–77) and Friedrich
Schelling (1775–1854), as well as the Romantic poets, as in
Wordsworth's *The Excursion* (1814): 9. 13–15.

Philomela[27]

Hark! ah, the Nightingale!
The tawny-throated!
Hark! from that moonlit cedar what a burst!
What triumph! hark—what pain![28]

O Wanderer from a Grecian shore,　　　　　　　　　　5
Still, after many years, in distant lands,
Still nourishing in thy bewilder'd brain
That wild, unquench'd, deep-sunken, old-world pain—
　　Say, will it never heal?
And can this fragrant lawn　　　　　　　　　　　　10
With its cool trees, and night,
And the sweet, tranquil Thames,
And moonshine, and the dew,
To thy rack'd heart and brain
　　Afford no balm?　　　　　　　　　　　　　　15

　　Dost thou to-night behold
Here, through the moonlight on this English grass,
The unfriendly palace in the Thracian wild?
　　Dost thou again peruse
With hot cheeks and sear'd eyes　　　　　　　　　20
The too clear web,[29] and thy dumb sister's shame?
　　Dost thou once more assay
Thy flight, and feel come over thee,
Poor Fugitive, the feathery change
Once more, and once more seem to make resound　　25
With love and hate, triumph and agony,
Lone Daulis,[30] and the high Cephissian vale?
　　Listen, Eugenia[31]—
How thick the bursts come crowding through the leaves!
　　Again—thou hearest!　　　　　　　　　　30
Eternal Passion!
Eternal Pain!

[27] *title* according to Greek mythology (retold in *Metamorphoses* 6. 430–721), Procne married Tereus, King of Thrace. When Tereus saw Procne's sister, Philomela, he fell in love with her and raped her, cutting out her tongue so that she could not tell of it. However, she embroidered a tapestry telling of her woes, and sent it to her sister. In revenge, Procne killed her son Itys and served him as a banquet to his father Tereus. All were changed into birds, Tereus into a hoopoe, Procne into a nightingale, and Philomela into a swallow. The Roman mythographers reverse the latter two. Arnold adopts the Roman version to have Philomela as a nightingale. First published in *Poems* (1853).

[28] *triumph ... pain* associated with poetic creation; see the conclusion to the poem; see also "The Strayed Reveller" (207–11).

[29] *web* the embroidered picture.

[30] *Daulis* a town in Phocis in central Greece, on the Gulf of Corinth, part of the realm of Tereus. The River Cephisus runs through it.

[31] *Eugenia* (Gk. nobility, excellence); unknown listener.

Requiescat[32]

Strew on her roses, roses,
    And never a spray of yew.
In quiet she reposes:
    Ah! would that I did too.

Her mirth the world required: 5
    She bath'd it in smiles of glee.
But her heart was tired, tired,
    And now they let her be.

Her life was turning, turning,
    In mazes of heat and sound.   10
But for peace her soul was yearning,
    And now peace laps her round.

Her cabin'd, ample Spirit,
    It flutter'd and fail'd for breath.
To-night it doth inherit   15
    The vasty Hall of Death.

Stanzas from the Grande Chartreuse[33]

Through Alpine meadows, soft suffus'd
    With rain, where thick the crocus blows,
Past the dark forges, long disus'd,
    The mule-track from Saint Laurent[34] goes:
The bridge is cross'd, and slow we ride,   5
Through forest, up the mountain side.

The autumnal evening darkens round,
    The wind is up, and drives the rain;
While, hark! far down, with strangled sound
    Doth the Dead Guiers' stream complain,   10
Where that wet smoke, among the woods,
Over his boiling cauldrons broods.

Swift rush the spectral vapours white
    Past limestone scars with ragged pines,
Shewing—then blotting from our sight.—   15

Notes

[32] *title* part of the prayer for the dead, *requiescat in pacem* (Lat. may he/she rest in peace), here a poem for an unknown lady. First published in *Poems* (1853).

[33] *title* the Grande Chartreuse, chief monastery of the Carthusian religious order (founded 1084) is in the remote Alps north of Grenoble in south-eastern France. Carthusians combine strict silence with isolation from the world. Arnold visited the Grande Chartreuse on 7 October 1851 while on his honeymoon. First published in *Fraser's Magazine* (Apr. 1855); collected in *New Poems* (1867).

[34] *Saint Laurent* St Laurent du Pont is a village near the Grande Chartreuse, and is its point of access. It is situated on a small stream, the Guiers Mort (Arnold's Dead Guiers), that rises near the monastery.

Halt! through the cloud-drift something shines!
High in the valley, wet and drear,
The huts of Courrerie[35] appear.

Strike leftward, cries our guide; and higher
   Mounts up the stony forest way.   20
At last the encircling trees retire:
   Look! through the showery twilight grey
What pointed roofs are these advance?—
A palace of the Kings of France?

Approach, for what we seek is here.   25
   Alight, and sparely sup, and wait
For rest in this outbuilding near;
   Then cross the sward, and reach that gate;
Knock; pass the wicket: thou art come
To the Carthusians' world-fam'd home.   30

The silent courts, where, night and day,
   Into their stone-carv'd basins cold
The splashing icy fountains play—
   The humid corridors behold,
Where, ghostlike in the deepening night,   35
Cowl'd forms brush by in gleaming white:[36]

The chapel, where no organ's peal
   Invests the stern and naked prayer;
With penitential cries they kneel
   And wrestle; rising then, with bare   40
And white uplifted faces stand,
Passing the Host[37] from hand to hand—

Each takes; and then his visage wan
   Is buried in his cowl once more:—
The Cells—The suffering Son of Man[38]   45
   Upon the wall; the knee-worn floor;
And, where they sleep, that wooden bed,
Which shall their coffin be, when dead.[39]

The Library, where tract and tome
   Not to feed priestly pride are there,   50

Notes

[35] *Courrerie* or La Correrie is the fifteenth-century lower house or monastery of the Grande Chartreuse, where lay brothers lived in cells or "huts."

[36] *white* the Carthusian habit is made of white serge with a cowl or hood.

[37] *chapel ... Host* this stanza addresses the liturgical worship of the monks, without instruments, using Gregorian chant. The Host is the consecrated wafer signifying the body of Jesus at the Mass, but it is not passed "from hand to hand." Instead Arnold is referring to the Pax, an exchange of peace by kissing and passing a small plaque carved with an image of the crucifixion.

[38] *Man* biblical synonym for man or ideal man, and often applied to the prophet Ezekiel (see Ezekiel 2: 1); in the Gospels it is used many times by Jesus to refer to himself; here a crucifix.

[39] *dead* it was a popular belief that monks were buried in the coffins in which they slept throughout their lives; the Carthusians, however, bury monks in their habits on a wooden plank.

To hymn the conquering march of Rome—
   Nor yet to amuse, as ours are.
They paint of souls the inner strife,
Their drops of blood, their death in life.

The Garden, overgrown—yet mild   55
   Those fragrant herbs are flowering there,
Strong children of the Alpine wild
   Whose culture is the Brethren's care;[40]
Of human tasks their only one,
And cheerful works beneath the sun.   60

Those Halls too, destin'd to contain
   Each its own pilgrim host[41] of old,
From England, Germany, or Spain—
   All are before me;—I behold
The House, the Brotherhood austere:—   65
And what am I, that I am here?

For rigorous Teachers[42] seiz'd my youth,
   And prun'd its faith, and quench'd its fire,
Shew'd me the pale cold star of Truth,
   There bade me gaze, and there aspire.   70
Even now their whispers pierce the gloom—
What dost thou in this living tomb?

Forgive me, Masters of the Mind!
   At whose behest I long ago
So much unlearnt, so much resign'd:—   75
   I come not here to be your foe.
I seek these Anchorites, not in ruth,
To curse and to deny your truth:

Not as their friend, or child, I speak:
   But as, on some far northern strand,   80
Thinking of his own Gods, a Greek
   In pity and mournful awe might stand
Before some fallen Runic stone:[43]
For both were faiths, and both are gone.

Wandering between two worlds, one dead,   85
   The other powerless to be born,
With nowhere yet to rest my head,[44]
   Like these on earth I wait forlorn.
Their faith, my tears, the world deride:

Notes

[40] *care* the distilling of Chartreuse liqueur according to a secret seventeenth-century recipe.

[41] *pilgrim host* the monastery had guest houses within the walls, not for visitors but for the priors and their entourages from various countries.

[42] *Teachers* such as Carlyle, Goethe, and Spinoza.

[43] *Runic stone* runes were alphabets of early Norse used in northern Europe between 150 and 1000 CE before the introduction of the Latin alphabet. Arnold uses Bishop Percy's translation of Paul Henri Mallet's *Northern Antiquities*, edited by I. A. Blackwell (1847).

[44] *head* see Matthew 8: 20.

I come to shed them at their side.   90
Oh hide me in your gloom profound
    Ye solemn seats of holy pain!
Invest me, steep me, fold me round,
    Till I possess my soul again;
Till free my thoughts before me roll,   95
Not chaf'd by hourly false controul.

For the World cries your faith is now
    But a dead time's exploded dream;
My melancholy, Sciolists say,
    Is a pass'd mode, an outworn theme: 100
As if the World had *ever* had
A faith, or Sciolists been sad.

Ah, if it *be* pass'd, take away,
    At least, the restlessness—the pain—
Be man henceforth no more a prey   105
    To these out-dated stings again:
The nobleness of grief is gone—
Ah, leave us not the pang alone.

But, if you cannot give us ease,
    Last of the race of them who grieve   110
Here leave us to die out with these
    Last of the people who believe.
Silent, while years engrave the brow;
Silent—the best are silent now.

Achilles[45] ponders in his tent,   115
    The kings of modern thought[46] are dumb;
Silent they are, though not content,
    And wait to see the Future come.
They have the grief men had of yore,
But they contend and cry no more.   120

Their fathers[47] water'd with their tears
    This Sea of Time whereon we sail;
Their voices were in all men's ears
    Who pass'd within their puissant hail.
Still the same Ocean round us raves,   125

Notes

[45] *Achilles* in *Iliad* 1–19 Achilles sulks in his tent at Troy and will not fight until the death of his friend Patroclus rouses him to arm himself and lead the Greeks. Arnold also alludes to the trial of John Henry Newman, who was charged with libel for attacking Dr Giovanni Giacinto Achilli (1803–60), a defrocked Dominican monk and priest accused of sexual misconduct in the rape of a young girl. He then became a virulent anti-Catholic propagandist, went to England, and was denounced by Cardinal Wiseman (1802–65). Newman used Wiseman's allegations of further seductions in his lectures on *The Present Position of Catholics in England* (1851) and was brought to trial by Achilli in 1851–52. See NEWMAN, *IDEA*, headnote.

[46] *thought* see Shelley, *Adonais* (430–31).

[47] *fathers* Arnold's predecessors among the Romantic poets, including Wordsworth, Keats, and Byron.

[48] *waves* possibly a contrast to King Canute (d. 1035) at Bosham in West Sussex, who, according to the twelfth-century chronicler Henry of Huntingdon, commanded the waves and tide to stop at his command and not wet his feet, in order to show his too deferential courtiers that his powers were limited.

But they stand mute, and watch the waves.[48]
For what avail'd it, all the noise
　　　And outcry of the former men?
Say, have their sons achieved more joys?
　　　Say, is life lighter now than then?　　　　　　130
The Sufferers died, they left their pain;
The pangs which tortur'd them remain.

What helps it now, that Byron[49] bore,
　　　With haughty scorn which mock'd the smart,
Through Europe to the Ætolian shore[50]　　　　135
　　　The pageant of his bleeding heart?
That thousands counted every groan,
And Europe made his woe her own?

What boots it, Shelley, that the breeze
　　　Carried thy lovely wail away　　　　　　　140
Musical through Italian trees
　　　That fringe thy dark-blue Spezzian bay?[51]
Inheritors of thy distress
Have restless hearts one throb the less?

Or are we easier, to have read,　　　　　　　145
　　　O Obermann,[52] the sad, stern page,
Which tells us how thou hidd'st thy head
　　　From the fierce tempest of thine age
In the lone brakes of Fontainebleau,
Or chalets near the Alpine snow?—　　　　　150

They slumber in their silent grave.
　　　The World, which for an idle day
Grace to your mood of sadness gave,
Long since hath thrown her weeds away.
The Eternal Trifler breaks their spell:　　　　155
But we—we learnt their lore too well.

Notes

[49] *Byron* the Romantic poets, Byron in this stanza and Shelley in the next, were close friends; the references are echoes of Carlyle's *Characteristics* (1831): "Behold a Byron, in melodious tones, 'cursing his day' . . . . Hear a Shelley filling the earth with inarticulate wail; like the infinite, inarticulate grief of forsaken infants."

[50] *Ætolian shore* Aetolia is a mountainous region of Greece on the north coast of the Gulf of Corinth, the location of Messolonghi where Byron died in 1824, fighting in the Greek War of Independence against the Ottoman Empire. His death caused a sensation in Europe, especially in Britain, where he was idealized as a hero concealing a secret, dark past while remaining a passionate rebel against social conventions. See n. 7.

[51] *breeze . . . bay* Shelley drowned on 8 July 1822 in the Bay of Spezzia. His body washed ashore near Viareggio, further south, where it was burned on the beach with his friends Edward Trelawny (1792–1881), Leigh Hunt (1784–1859), and Byron attending or nearby. Trelawny snatched Shelley's heart from the flames and it was kept by Mary Shelley (1897–1851) until her death. It was buried beside her in Bournemouth, England.

[52] *Obermann* Étienne Pivert de Senancour (1770–1846), French writer, published *Obermann* (1804), a series of letters from a melancholy and solitary man living the forest of Fontainbleau and in a remote Swiss valley in the Jura Mountains north east of the Grande Chartreuse. See also Arnold's "Stanzas in Memory of the Author of 'Obermann'" (1852) and "Obermann Once More" (1867).

There may, perhaps, yet dawn an age,
 More fortunate, alas, than we,
Which without hardness will be sage,
 And gay without frivolity.   160
Sons of the World, oh, haste those years:
But, till they rise, allow our tears.

Allow them:—We admire, with awe,
 The exulting thunder of your race:
You give the universe your law;   165
 You triumph over time and space.
Your pride of life, your tireless powers,
They awe us, but they are not ours.

We are like children, rear'd in shade
 Beneath some old-world abbey wall,   170
Forgotten in a forest glade,
 And secret from the eyes of all.
Deep, deep the greenwood round them waves,
Their abbey, and its close of graves.

But, where the road runs near the stream, 175
 Oft through the trees they catch a glance
Of passing troops in the sun's beam—
 Pennon, and plume, and flashing lance.
Forth to the mighty world they fare,
To life, to cities, and to war!   180

And through the woods, another way,
 Faint bugle-notes from far are borne
Where hunters gather, staghounds bay,
 Round some old forest lodge at morn.
Gay dames are there in sylvan green,   185
Laughter and cries—those notes between.

The banners flashing through the trees
 Make their blood dance and chain their eyes;
That bugle-music on the breeze
 Arrests them with a charm'd surprise. 190
Banner, by turns, and bugle woo—
Ye shy recluses, follow too!

O children, what do ye reply?—
 Action and Pleasure, will ye roam
Through these secluded dells to cry   195
 And call us? but too late ye come.
Too late for us your call ye blow,
Whose bent was taken long ago.

Long since we pace this shadow'd nave;
   We watch those yellow tapers shine,   200
Emblems of light above the grave,
   In the high altar's depth divine:—
The organ[53] carries to our ear
Its accents of another sphere.

Fenc'd early in this cloistral round   205
   Of reverie, of shade, of prayer,
How should we grow in other ground?
   How should we flower in foreign air?
Pass, banners, pass, and bugles, cease!
And leave our forest[54] to its peace.   210

East London[55]

'Twas August, and the fierce sun overhead
Smote on the squalid streets of Bethnal Green,
And the pale weaver, through his windows seen
In Spitalfields,[56] look'd thrice dispirited;

I met a preacher[57] there I knew, and said: 5
"Ill and o'erwork'd, how fare you in this scene?"
"Bravely!" said he; "for I of late have been
Much cheer'd with thoughts of Christ, *the living bread.*"[58]

O human soul! as long as thou canst so
Set up a mark of everlasting light,   10
Above the howling senses' ebb and flow,

To cheer thee, and to right thee if thou roam,
Not with lost toil thou labourest through the night!
Thou mak'st the heaven thou hop'st indeed thy home.

Notes

[53] *organ* there is no organ at the Grande Chartreuse.

[54] *forest* changed in *New Poems* (1867) to "desert"; the valley where the Grande Chartreuse is located is named "Le desert de Chartreuse." Traditionally Carthusian monasteries were located in what was known as "deserts," sustaining the link with the monasticism of the early desert hermits in North Africa.

[55] *title* East London was a working-class area of the city, including the London Docks. First published in *New Poems* (1867).

[56] *Bethnall Green ... Spitalfields* are areas in East London. Huguenots or French Protestants fled from the effect of the Edict of Nantes (1685) and settled in Spitalfields with their traditions of silk weaving, augmented in the eighteenth century by Irish weavers displaced from the linen trade and in the nineteenth century by Jewish workers and tailors in the textile industry. By the mid-nineteenth century the weaving trade had been greatly reduced and the area become one of London's worst slums.

[57] *preacher* identified by Arnold as the Rev. William Tyler (1812–90), pastor of Hanbury Street Congregational Church, Spitalfields, whom Arnold met when he was inspecting schools in London's East End.

[58] *bread* see John 6: 51.

West London[59]

Crouch'd on the pavement close by Belgrave Square,[60]
A tramp I saw, ill, moody, and tongue-tied;
A babe was in her arms, and at her side
A girl; their clothes were rags, their feet were bare.

Some labouring men, whose work lay somewhere there,   5
Pass'd opposite; she touch'd her girl, who hied
Across, and begg'd and came back satisfied.
The rich she had let pass with frozen stare.

Thought I: Above her state this spirit towers;
She will not ask of aliens, but of friends,   10
Of sharers in a common human fate.

She turns from that cold succour, which attends
The unknown little from the unknowing great,
And points us to a better time than ours.

Dover Beach[61]

The sea is calm to-night,
The tide is full, the moon lies fair
Upon the Straits;—on the French coast, the light
Gleams, and is gone; the cliffs of England stand,
Glimmering and vast, out in the tranquil bay.   5
Come to the window, sweet is the night air!
Only, from the long line of spray
Where the ebb meets the moon-blanch'd sand,
Listen! you hear the grating roar
Of pebbles which the waves suck back, and fling,   10
At their return, up the high strand,
Begin, and cease, and then again begin,
With tremulous cadence slow, and bring
The eternal note of sadness in.

Sophocles[62] long ago   15
Heard it on the Ægæan,[63] and it brought
Into his mind the turbid ebb and flow

Notes

[59] *title* West London includes the areas of Belgravia, Knightsbridge, and, further west, Kensington, and Chelsea, all wealthy districts. The sonnet was set to music in a song by the American composer, Charles Ives (1874–54), published in *Songs* (1922). First published in *New Poems* (1867).

[60] *Belgrave Square* was laid out by Thomas Cubitt in the 1820s for Earl Grosvenor, later the Marquess of Westminster and Viscount Belgrave, who owned much of the area of West London. Until World War Two it was occupied by the aristocracy.

[61] *title* Dover is on the English Channel, well known for its high chalk cliffs, facing Calais on the French coast. The poem is both parodied and extended in "The Dover Bitch," published during the centenary of Arnold's poem in 1967 by US Poet Laureate, Anthony Hecht (1923–2004). First published in *New Poems* (1867).

[62] *Sophocles* in *Antigone* (583–92), by Sophocles, Arnold's favourite Greek dramatist, the Chorus compares the threat of ruin to the dynastic house of Atreus with the angry sea. See also Sophocles' *Trachiniae* (112–19) and *Oedipus at Colonus* (1239–48).

[63] *Ægæan* part of the Mediterranean that lies between Greece and Turkey.

Of human misery; we
Find also in the sound a thought,
Hearing it by this distant northern sea.[64]   20

The sea of faith
Was once, too, at the full, and round earth's shore
Lay like the folds of a bright girdle furl'd;
But now I only hear
Its melancholy, long, withdrawing roar,   25
Retreating to the breath
Of the night-wind down the vast edges drear
And naked shingles of the world.[65]

Ah, love, let us be true
To one another! for the world, which seems   30
To lie before us[66] like a land of dreams,
So various, so beautiful, so new,
Hath really neither joy, nor love, nor light,
Nor certitude, nor peace, nor help for pain;
And we are here as on a darkling plain   35
Swept with confused alarms of struggle and flight,
Where ignorant armies clash by night.[67]

Growing Old[68]

What is it to grow old?
Is it to lose the glory of the form,
The lustre of the eye?
Is it for beauty to forego her wreath?
Yes, but not this alone.   5

Is it to feel our strength—
Not our bloom only, but our strength—decay?
Is it to feel each limb
Grow stiffer, every function less exact,
Each nerve more weakly strung?   10

Notes

[64] *northern sea* English Channel.

[65] *at the full ... world* the governing analogy of the cycles of time compares the movement of the tides to the ebb and flow of faith. Bright girdle is an encircling garment; shingles are loose water-worn pebbles pushed up on the beach by the waves and tides.

[66] *world ... before us* see *Paradise Lost* (12. 646).

[67] *darkling plain ... night* see Thucydides' description of the night-battle of Epipolae (413 BCE) in which the Athenians became confused, mistaking their comrades for enemies, and enemies for friends, and so slaughtered their own comrades, or thought they saw them in flight (*History of the Peloponnesian War* bk. 7. chs 43–44). Thomas Arnold, Matthew's father, made this passage familiar to students at Rugby, and edited the whole of Thucydides' *History* (1830–35). Clough also used the passage in *The Bothie* (9. 51–54) and "The Struggle" (5–8).

[68] *title* possibly a response to Browning's "Rabbi Ben Ezra" (1864; 1–3): "Grow old along with me / The best is yet to be, / The last of life, for which the first was made." First published in *New Poems* (1867).

Yes, this, and more! but not,
Ah, 'tis not what in youth we dream'd 'twould be!
'Tis not to have our life
Mellow'd and soften'd as with sunset glow,
A golden day's decline!   15

'Tis not to see the world
As from a height, with rapt prophetic eyes,
And heart profoundly stirr'd;
And weep, and feel the fulness of the past,
The years that are no more!⁶⁹   20

It is to spend long days
And not once feel that we were ever young.
It is to add, immured
In the hot prison of the present, month
To month with weary pain.   25

It is to suffer this,
And feel but half, and feebly, what we feel.
Deep in our hidden heart
Festers the dull remembrance of a change,
But no emotion—none.   30

It is—last stage of all⁷⁰—
When we are frozen up within, and quite
The phantom of ourselves,
To hear the world applaud the hollow ghost
Which blamed the living man.   35

WEB p. 379

Rugby Chapel

Preface to *Poems* (1853)⁷¹

In two small volumes of Poems, published anonymously, one in 1849, the other in 1852, many of the Poems which compose the present volume have already appeared. The rest are now published for the first time.

Notes

⁶⁹ *no more* see TENNYSON, SONGS FROM *THE PRINCESS*, "TEARS, IDLE TEARS" (3–5) (WEB p. 342).

⁷⁰ *all* see *As You Like It* 2. 7. 163–65.

⁷¹ *title* Arnold combined two previous volumes of poetry, *The Strayed Reveller, and Other Poems* (1849) and *Empedocles on Etna, and Other Poems* (1852) in the volume of 1853, adding this preface. This preface has been taken by many critics to be a statement of Arnold's general theory of poetry, although in actuality, his aim was more limited, to explain why he eliminated the major poem of the second volume (see n. 72). Despite the wide range of Arnold's allusions to European literature and culture from the classics to the

present, this preface, to a great extent, focuses upon two recent reviews of poetry in succeeding months, without mentioning either by name. The first is David Masson's "Theories of Poetry and a New Poet" (*North British Review* Aug. 1853), a review of E. S. Dallas's *An Essay on Poetry* (1852) and *A Life Drama and Other Poems* (1853) by Alexander Smith. The second is A. H. Clough's "Recent English Poetry" (*North American Review*, July 1853), a review of Smith's *A Life-Drama* (1853), Arnold's *The Strayed Reveller and Other Poems* (1849) and *Empedocles on Etna, and Other Poems* (1852), and other writers. Much of Arnold's condemnation of the condition of poetry in contemporary

I have, in the present collection, omitted the Poem from which the volume published in 1852 took its title.[72] I have done so, not because the subject of it was a Sicilian Greek born between two and three thousand years ago, although many persons would think this a sufficient reason. Neither have I done so because I had, in my own opinion, failed in the delineation which I intended to effect. I intended to delineate the feelings of one of the last of the Greek religious philosophers, one of the family of Orpheus and Musæus,[73] having survived his fellows, living on into a time when the habits of Greek thought and feeling had begun fast to change, character to dwindle, the influence of the Sophists[74] to prevail. Into the feelings of a man so situated there entered much that we are accustomed to consider as exclusively modern; how much, the fragments of Empedocles himself which remain to us are sufficient at least to indicate.[75] What those who are familiar only with the great monuments of early Greek genius suppose to be its exclusive characteristics, have disappeared; the calm, the cheerfulness, the disinterested objectivity have disappeared: the dialogue of the mind with itself has commenced; modern problems have presented themselves; we hear already the doubts, we witness the discouragement, of Hamlet and of Faust.

The representation of such a man's feelings must be interesting, if consistently drawn. We all naturally take pleasure, says Aristotle,[76] in any imitation or representation whatever: this is the basis of our love of Poetry: and we take pleasure in them, he adds, because all knowledge is naturally agreeable to us; not to the philosopher only, but to mankind at large. Every representation therefore which is consistently drawn may be supposed to be interesting, inasmuch as it gratifies this natural interest in knowledge of all kinds. What is *not* interesting, is that which does not add to our knowledge of any kind; that which is vaguely conceived and loosely drawn; a representation which is general, indeterminate, and faint, instead of being particular, precise, and firm.

Any accurate representation may therefore be expected to be interesting; but, if the representation be a poetical one, more than this is demanded. It is demanded, not only that it shall interest, but also that it shall inspirit and rejoice the reader: that it shall convey a charm, and infuse delight. For the Muses, as Hesiod says, were born that they might be "a forgetfulness of evils, and a truce from cares":[77] and it is not enough that the Poet should add to the knowledge of men, it is required of him also that he should add to their happiness. "All Art," says Schiller, "is dedicated to Joy, and there is no

Notes

England is narrowed to the "Spasmodic School" of poetry, in particularly one poet, Alexander Smith (1830–67). Arnold distances himself from such Spasmodic followers of Keats as Smith, Sydney Thompson Dobell (1824–74), and Philip James Bailey (1816–1902). Clough and other reviewers attack Smith for piling up images, stressing subjectivity and sensation, and elaborating metaphors. For Spasmodic School, see SYDNEY DOBELL, headnote.

[72] title Arnold omitted *Empedocles on Etna* because of its "morbid" and "painful" tone. According to legend, Empedocles (c.490–430 BCE), Greek pre-Socratic philosopher, committed suicide by throwing himself into Mt Etna in Sicily. Arnold continued to omit the poem from collections until 1867, when he republished it at the request of Robert Browning.

[73] Orpheus … Musæus in Greek mythology Orpheus was renowned as a singer, musician (the lyre), and poet,

famous for charming the kingdom of the dead to lead his wife Eurydice back to life. Musæus was a pupil of Orpheus, the legendary founder of the Orphic religion.

[74] Sophists (Gr. *sophia* wisdom), teachers of rhetoric in ancient Greece attacked by Plato in his dialogues as false philosophers, using rhetoric to deceive.

[75] *indicate* Empedocles wrote treatises on medicine and science in verse. Fragments of only two poems, *Purifications* and *On Nature*, survive. His work is chiefly known from quotations in other classical authors, such as Aristotle, Lucretius, and Plutarch.

[76] *Aristotle* see *Poetics* 1, 2, 4, 7, and 14; especially 4: 2–5.

[77] *cares* see *Theogony* 52–6. Hesiod (seventh century BCE), Greek oral poet, wrote on mythology, astronomy, and farming; *Theogony* is a narrative poem synthesizing Greek mythology and cosmology.

higher and no more serious problem, than how to make men happy. The right Art is that alone, which creates the highest enjoyment."[78]

A poetical work, therefore, is not yet justified when it has been shown to be an accurate, and therefore interesting representation; it has to be shown also that it is a representation from which men can derive enjoyment. In presence of the most tragic circumstances, represented in a work of Art, the feeling of enjoyment, as is well known, may still subsist: the representation of the most utter calamity, of the liveliest anguish, is not sufficient to destroy it: the more tragic the situation, the deeper becomes the enjoyment; and the situation is more tragic in proportion as it becomes more terrible.

What then are the situations, from the representation of which, though accurate, no poetical enjoyment can be derived? They are those in which the suffering finds no vent in action; in which a continuous state of mental distress is prolonged, unrelieved by incident, hope, or resistance; in which there is everything to be endured, nothing to be done. In such situations there is inevitably something morbid, in the description of them something monotonous. When they occur in actual life, they are painful, not tragic; the representation of them in poetry is painful also.

To this class of situations, poetically faulty as it appears to me, that of Empedocles, as I have endeavoured to represent him, belongs; and I have therefore excluded the Poem from the present collection.

And why, it may be asked, have I entered into this explanation respecting a matter so unimportant as the admission or exclusion of the Poem in question? I have done so, because I was anxious to avow that the sole reason for its exclusion was that which has been stated above; and that it has not been excluded in deference to the opinion which many critics of the present day appear to entertain against subjects chosen from distant times and countries: against the choice, in short, of any subjects but modern ones.

"The Poet," it is said, and by an apparently intelligent critic, "the Poet who would really fix the public attention must leave the exhausted past, and draw his subjects from matters of present import, and *therefore* both of interest and novelty."[79]

Now this view I believe to be completely false. It is worth examining, inasmuch as it is a fair sample of a class of critical dicta everywhere current at the present day, having a philosophical form and air, but no real basis in fact; and which are calculated to vitiate the judgment of readers of poetry, while they exert, so far as they are adopted, a misleading influence on the practice of those who write it.

What are the eternal objects of Poetry, among all nations, and at all times? They are actions; human actions; possessing an inherent interest in themselves, and which are to be communicated in an interesting manner by the art of the Poet.[80] Vainly will the latter imagine that he has everything in his own power; that he can make an intrinsically inferior action equally delightful with a more excellent one by his treatment of it: he may indeed compel us to admire his skill, but his work will possess, within itself, an incurable defect.

The Poet, then, has in the first place to select an excellent action; and what actions are the most excellent? Those, certainly, which most powerfully appeal to the great primary human affections: to those elementary feelings which subsist permanently in the race,

Notes

[78] *enjoyment* J. C. F. Schiller (1759–1805), German poet, philosopher, and historian; the quotation is from the preface to *The Bride of Messina* (1803), a tragedy on the life of Joan of Arc. To Arnold, "joy" is an antidote to the continuing Romantic condition of melancholy, as in Coleridge's "Dejection: An Ode" (1802). On the other hand, Schiller's "Ode to Joy" (1786) praises joy as the "daughter of Elysium," under which

"all men become brothers," a text used by Beethoven as part of the final movement of the ninth symphony (1824).

[79] *novelty* in a reprinting a year later, Arnold added in a note: "In the *Spectator* of April 2, 1853. The words quoted were not used with reference to poems of mine." The critic was the editor of the *Spectator*, Robert S. Rintoul (1787–1858).

[80] *Poet* see *Poetics* 6.

and which are independent of time. These feelings are permanent and the same; that which interests them is permanent and the same also. The modernness or antiquity of an action, therefore, has nothing to do with its fitness for poetical representation; this depends upon its inherent qualities. To the elementary part of our nature, to our passions, that which is great and passionate is eternally interesting; and interesting solely in proportion to its greatness and to its passion. A great human action of a thousand years ago is more interesting to it than a smaller human action of to-day, even though upon the representation of this last the most consummate skill may have been expended, and though it has the advantage of appealing by its modern language, familiar manners, and contemporary allusions, to all our transient feelings and interests. These, however, have no right to demand of a poetical work that it shall satisfy them; their claims are to be directed elsewhere. Poetical works belong to the domain of our permanent passions: let them interest these, and the voice of all subordinate claims upon them is at once silenced.

Achilles, Prometheus, Clytemnestra, Dido[81]—what modern poem presents personages as interesting, even to us moderns, as these personages of an "exhausted past"? We have the domestic epic[82] dealing with the details of modern life which pass daily under our eyes; we have poems representing modern personages in contact with the problems of modern life, moral, intellectual, and social; these works have been produced by poets the most distinguished of their nation and time; yet I fearlessly assert that *Hermann and Dorothea, Childe Harold, Jocelyn, The Excursion*,[83] leave the reader cold in comparison with the effect produced upon him by the latter books of the *Iliad*, by the *Oresteia*, or by the episode of Dido.[84] And why is this? Simply because in the three latter cases the action is greater, the personages nobler, the situations more intense: and this is the true basis of the interest in a poetical work, and this alone.

It may be urged, however, that past actions may be interesting in themselves, but that they are not to be adopted by the modern Poet, because it is impossible for him to have them clearly present to his own mind, and he cannot therefore feel them deeply, nor represent them forcibly. But this is not necessarily the case. The externals of a past action, indeed, he cannot know with the precision of a contemporary; but his business is with its essentials. The outward man of Œdipus or of Macbeth, the houses in which they lived, the ceremonies of their courts, he cannot accurately figure to himself; but neither do they essentially concern him. His business is with their inward man;[85] with their feelings and behaviour in certain tragic situations, which engage their passions as men; these have in them nothing local and casual; they are as accessible to the modern Poet as to a contemporary.

The date of an action, then, signifies nothing: the action itself, its selection and construction, this is what is all-important. This the Greeks understood far more clearly than we do. The radical difference between their poetical theory and ours consists, as it appears to me, in this: that, with them, the poetical character of the action in itself, and the

Notes

[81] *Achilles … Dido* tragic heroes and heroines in *Iliad*; Aeschylus, *Prometheus Unbound*; Aeschylus, *Agamemnon*; and *Aeneid*; see n. 14 below.

[82] *epic* a code word for Spasmodic poetry, and in particular Alexander Smith's *A Life-Drama and Other Poems* (1853). Tennyson had published *English Idylls and Other Poems* (1842), which contained domestic poems such as "Audley Court" and "Edwin Morris." Tennyson's much longer poem on a modern theme, women's education, was *The Princess* (1850).

[83] *Dorothea … Excursion* long poems by, respectively, Goethe (1797), Byron (1818), Lamartine (1836), and Wordsworth (1814).

[84] *Iliad* the latter books of the *Iliad* deal with the battle between Hector and Achilles, Hector's death, and the funeral games mourning him. The *Oresteia* by Aeschylus comprises *Agamemnon, The Libation Bearers*, and the *Eumenides*, that tell of the return of Agamemnon from Troy and the results of his murder by his wife Clytemnestra and the consequent fall of the house of Atreus. Dido, the Queen of Carthage in *Aeneid* 4, loves Aeneas but kills herself when he leaves her to found Rome.

[85] *outward man … inward man* see 2 Corinthians 4: 16.

conduct of it, was the first consideration; with us, attention is fixed mainly on the value of the separate thoughts and images which occur in the treatment of an action. They regarded the whole; we regard the parts. With them, the action predominated over the expression of it; with us, the expression predominates over the action. Not that they failed in expression, or were inattentive to it; on the contrary, they are the highest models of expression, the unapproached masters of the *grand style*: but their expression is so excellent because it is so admirably kept in its right degree of prominence; because it is so simple and so well subordinated; because it draws its force directly from the pregnancy of the matter which it conveys. For what reason was the Greek tragic poet confined to so limited a range of subjects? Because there are so few actions which unite in themselves, in the highest degree, the conditions of excellence: and it was not thought that on any but an excellent subject could an excellent Poem be constructed. A few actions, therefore, eminently adapted for tragedy, maintained almost exclusive possession of the Greek tragic stage; their significance appeared inexhaustible; they were as permanent problems, perpetually offered to the genius of every fresh poet. This too is the reason of what appears to us moderns a certain baldness of expression in Greek tragedy; of the triviality with which we often reproach the remarks of the chorus, where it takes part in the dialogue: that the action itself, the situation of Orestes, or Merope, or Alcmæon,[86] was to stand the central point of interest, unforgotten, absorbing, principal; that no accessories were for a moment to distract the spectator's attention from this; that the tone of the parts was to be perpetually kept down, in order not to impair the grandiose effect of the whole. The terrible old mythic story on which the drama was founded stood, before he entered the theatre, traced in its bare outlines upon the spectator's mind; it stood in his memory, as a group of statuary, faintly seen, at the end of a long and dark vista: then came the Poet, embodying outlines, developing situations, not a word wasted, not a sentiment capriciously thrown in: stroke upon stroke, the drama proceeded: the light deepened upon the group; more and more it revealed itself to the rivetted gaze of the spectator: until at last, when the final words were spoken, it stood before him in broad sunlight, a model of immortal beauty.

This was what a Greek critic demanded; this was what a Greek poet endeavoured to effect. It signified nothing to what time an action belonged; we do not find that the *Persæ*[87] occupied a particularly high rank among the dramas of Æschylus, because it represented a matter of contemporary interest: this was not what a cultivated Athenian required; he required that the permanent elements of his nature should be moved; and dramas of which the action, though taken from a long-distant mythic time, yet was calculated to accomplish this in a higher degree than that of the *Persæ*, stood higher in his estimation accordingly. The Greeks felt, no doubt, with their exquisite sagacity of taste, that an action of present times was too near them, too much mixed up with what was accidental and passing, to form a sufficiently grand, detached, and self-subsistent object for a tragic poem: such objects belonged to the domain of the comic poet, and of the lighter kinds of poetry. For the more serious kinds, for *pragmatic* poetry, to use an excellent expression of Polybius,[88] they were more difficult and severe in the range of subjects which they

Notes

[86] *Orestes* character in Aeschylus's *The Libation Bearers* (458 BCE), Sophocles' *Electra* (c.410 BCE), Euripides' *Orestes* (408 BCE), and elsewhere, where he and his sister Electra plot and carry out – and suffer the aftermath of – their revenge against Clytemnestra for the murder of Agamemnon; Merope, Queen of Messenia is the heroine of a story of political intrigue and murder within a royal family, told by Hyginus in *Fables* 137 and in a lost play of Euripides, *Cresphontes* (fifth century BCE), also the subject of a drama by Arnold, *Merope* (1858). Alcmaeon is one of the heroes who attacked Thebes and in subsequent narratives murdered his mother in vengeance for his father's death and was pursued by the Furies – the subject of a number of lost Greek plays.

[87] *Persae* Aeschylus' drama, *The Persians*, was performed in 472 BCE, shortly after Xerxes' invasion of Greece and defeat in the Battle of Salamis (480 BCE).

[88] *Polybius* Greek historian (c.200–118 BCE).

permitted. But for all kinds of poetry alike there was one point on which they were rigidly exacting; the adaptability of the subject to the kind of poetry selected, and the careful construction of the poem. Their theory and practice alike, the admirable treatise of Aristotle, and the unrivalled works of their poets, exclaim with a thousand tongues—"All depends upon the subject; choose a fitting action, penetrate yourself with the feeling of its situations; this done, everything else will follow."[89]

How different a way of thinking from this is ours! We can hardly at the present day understand what Menander meant, when he told a man who enquired as to the progress of his comedy that he had finished it, not having yet written a single line, because he had constructed the action of it in his mind.[90] A modern critic would have assured him that the merit of his piece depended on the brilliant things which arose under his pen as he went along. We have poems which seem to exist merely for the sake of single lines and passages; not for the sake of producing any total-impression. We have critics who seem to direct their attention merely to detached expressions, to the language about the action, not to the action itself. I verily think that the majority of them do not in their hearts believe that there is such a thing as a total-impression to be derived from a poem at all, or to be demanded from a poet; they think the term a commonplace of metaphysical criticism. They will permit the Poet to select any action he pleases, and to suffer that action to go as it will, provided he gratifies them with occasional bursts of fine writing, and with a shower of isolated thoughts and images. That is, they permit him to leave their poetical sense ungratified, provided that he gratifies their rhetorical sense and their curiosity. Of his neglecting to gratify these, there is little danger; he needs rather to be warned against the danger of attempting to gratify these alone; he needs rather to be perpetually reminded to prefer his action to everything else; so to treat this, as to permit its inherent excellences to develope themselves, without interruption from the intrusion of his personal peculiarities: most fortunate, when he most entirely succeeds in effacing himself, and in enabling a noble action to subsist as it did in nature.

But the modern critic not only permits a false practice; he absolutely prescribes false aims.—"A true allegory of the state of one's own mind in a representative history," the Poet is told, "is perhaps the highest thing that one can attempt in the way of poetry."[91]— And accordingly he attempts it. An allegory of the state of one's own mind, the highest problem of an art which imitates actions! No assuredly, it is not, it never can be so: no great poetical work has ever been produced with such an aim. Faust itself, in which something of the kind is attempted, wonderful passages as it contains, and in spite of the unsurpassed beauty of the scenes which relate to Margaret, Faust itself, judged as a whole, and judged strictly as a poetical work, is defective: its illustrious author, the greatest poet of modern times, the greatest critic of all times, would have been the first to acknowledge it; he only defended his work, indeed, by asserting it to be "something incommensurable."[92]

The confusion of the present times is great, the multitude of voices counselling different things bewildering, the number of existing works capable of attracting a young writer's attention and of becoming his models, immense: what he wants is a

Notes

[89] *follow* Aristotle discusses the relation of plot (Arnold's "subject") and action in *Poetics* 7–14, and especially chapter 17: "The poet should place the scene, as far as possible, before his eyes. In this way, seeing everything with the utmost vividness, as if he were a spectator of the action, he will discover what is in keeping with it" (trans. S. H. Butcher). Arnold, however, is not quoting Aristotle, but is subjecting him to a Romantic

reinterpretation concerning imaginative sympathy or "penetration."

[90] *mind* Menander (342–292 BCE), Greek writer of comedies, about whom the story is told in Plutarch, *Moralia* 347 E–F.

[91] *poetry* Arnold quotes with some modifications Masson's review (332); see n. 71.

[92] *incommensurable* Arnold quotes Goethe: see *Conversations of Goethe with Eckermann* (3 Jan. 1830).

hand to guide him through the confusion, a voice to prescribe to him the aim which he should keep in view, and to explain to him that the value of the literary works which offer themselves to his attention is relative to their power of helping him forward on his road towards this aim. Such a guide the English writer at the present day will nowhere find. Failing this, all that can be looked for, all indeed that can be desired, is, that his attention should be fixed on excellent models; that he may reproduce, at any rate, something of their excellence, by penetrating himself with their works and by catching their spirit, if he cannot be taught to produce what is excellent independently.

Foremost among these models for the English writer stands Shakspeare:[93] a name the greatest perhaps of all poetical names; a name never to be mentioned without reverence. I will venture, however, to express a doubt, whether the influence of his works, excellent and fruitful for the readers of poetry, for the great majority, has been of unmixed advantage to the writers of it. Shakspeare indeed chose excellent subjects; the world could afford no better than Macbeth, or Romeo and Juliet, or Othello: he had no theory respecting the necessity of choosing subjects of present import, or the paramount interest attaching to allegories of the state of one's own mind; like all great poets, he knew well what constituted a poetical action; like them, wherever he found such an action, he took it; like them, too, he found his best in past times. But to these general characteristics of all great poets he added a special one of his own; a gift, namely, of happy, abundant, and ingenious expression, eminent and unrivalled: so eminent as irresistibly to strike the attention first in him, and even to throw into comparative shade his other excellences as a poet. Here has been the mischief. These other excellences were his fundamental excellences *as a poet*; what distinguishes the artist from the mere amateur, says Goethe, is *Architectonicé*[94] in the highest sense ; that power of execution, which creates, forms, and constitutes: not the profoundness of single thoughts, not the richness of imagery, not the abundance of illustration. But these attractive accessories of a poetical work being more easily seized than the spirit of the whole, and their accessories being possessed by Shakspeare in an unequal degree, a young writer having recourse to Shakspeare as his model runs great risk of being vanquished and absorbed by them, and, in consequence, of reproducing, according to the measure of his power, these, and these alone. Of this preponderating quality of Shakspeare's genius, accordingly, almost the whole of modern English poetry has, it appears to me, felt the influence. To the exclusive attention on the part of his imitators to this it is in a great degree owing, that of the majority of modern poetical works the details alone are valuable, the composition worthless. In reading them one is perpetually reminded of that terrible sentence on a modern French poet—*il dit tout ce qu'il veut, mais malheureusement il n'a rien à dire.*[95]

Let me give an instance of what I mean. I will take it from the works of the very chief among those who seem to have been formed in the school of Shakspeare: of one whose exquisite genius and pathetic death render him for ever interesting. I will take the poem of *Isabella, or the Pot of Basil*, by Keats. I choose this rather than the *Endymion*, because the latter work, (which a modern critic has classed with the *Fairy Queen!*) although undoubtedly there blows through it the breath of genius, is yet as a whole so utterly incoherent,

Notes

[93] *Shakspeare* Arnold's spelling was conventional among some Victorians from Edmond Malone's edition (1790). The general discussion in this paragraph is based on Goethe's *Conversations* (25 Dec. 1825).

[94] *Architectonicé* Arnold's transliteration of Goethe's German, meaning the overall structure of a thing. Arnold quotes his own unpublished translation from Goethe's "Concerning So-Called Dilettantism" (1799).

[95] *dire* (Fr. he says all that he wishes to, but unfortunately he has nothing to say), alleged to be from a review of Théophile Gauthier's poems, *Émaux et Camées* ("Enamels and Cameos," 1852).

as not strictly to merit the name of a poem at all.[96] The poem of *Isabella*, then, is a perfect treasure-house of graceful and felicitous words and images: almost in every stanza there occurs one of those vivid and picturesque turns of expression, by which the object is made to flash upon the eye of the mind, and which thrill the reader with a sudden delight. This one short poem contains, perhaps, a greater number of happy single expressions which one could quote than all the extant tragedies of Sophocles.[97] But the action, the story? The action in itself is an excellent one; but so feebly is it conceived by the Poet, so loosely constructed, that the effect produced by it, in and for itself, is absolutely null. Let the reader, after he has finished the poem of Keats, turn to the same story in the *Decameron*:[98] he will then feel how pregnant and interesting the same action has become in the hands of a great artist, who above all things delineates his object; who subordinates expression to that which it is designed to express.

I have said that the imitators of Shakspeare, fixing their attention on his wonderful gift of expression, have directed their imitation to this, neglecting his other excellences. These excellences, the fundamental excellences of poetical art, Shakspeare no doubt possessed them—possessed many of them in a splendid degree; but it may perhaps be doubted whether even he himself did not sometimes give scope to his faculty of expression to the prejudice of a higher poetical duty. For we must never forget that Shakspeare is the great poet he is from his skill in discerning and firmly conceiving an excellent action, from his power of intensely feeling a situation, of intimately associating himself with a character; not from his gift of expression, which rather even leads him astray, degenerating some-times into a fondness for curiosity of expression, into an irritability of fancy, which seems to make it impossible for him to say a thing plainly, even when the press of the action demands the very directest language, or its level character the very simplest. Mr. Hallam,[99] than whom it is impossible to find a saner and more judicious critic, has had the courage (for at the present day it needs courage) to remark, how extremely and faultily difficult Shakspeare's language often is. It is so: you may find main scenes in some of his greatest tragedies, *King Lear* for instance, where the language is so artificial, so curiously tortured, and so difficult, that every speech has to be read two or three times before its meaning can be comprehended. This over-curiousness of expression is indeed but the excessive employment of a wonderful gift—of the power of saying a thing in a happier way than any other man; nevertheless, it is carried so far that one understands what M. Guizot[100] meant, when he said that Shakspeare appears in his language to have tried all styles except that of simplicity. He has not the severe and scrupulous self-restraint of the ancients, partly no doubt, because he had a far less cultivated and exacting audience: he has indeed a far wider range than they had, a far richer fertility of thought; in this respect he rises above them: in his strong conception of his subject, in the genuine way in which he is penetrated with it, he resembles them, and is unlike the moderns: but in the accurate

Notes

[96] *all* see Keats's "Isabella, or the Pot of Basil" (1818); Keats's "Endymion" (1817); and Spenser's *Faerie Queene* (1590–96). Arnold's paragraph is indebted to Clough's review (see n. 71): "The antecedents of the Life-Drama, the one long poem which occupies almost the whole of his volume, are to be found in the Princess, in parts of Mrs. Browning, in the love of Keats, and the *habit* of Shakspeare.... We have before us ... the latest disciple of the school of Keats.... Alexander Smith ... has given us, so to say, his Endymion; it is certainly as imperfect, and as mere a promise of some-thing wholly different as was that of the master he has followed." Arnold also uses Masson's review (see n. 71), in which Mason draws a comparison between Keats and Spenser (332), and on the whole reviews Smith favourably:

"We think Mr. Smith a true poet, and a poet of no com-mon order. We place him on the slope of Parnassus within sight of Keats and Tennyson as our two latest and best of preceding poets."

[97] *Sophocles* Greek dramatist (496–406 BCE), wrote 123 plays, seven of which have survived.

[98] *Decameron* collection of novellas (1353) by Giovanni Boccaccio: the story is the fifth novel of the fourth day.

[99] *Hallam* Henry Hallam (1777–1859), English historian, dis-cusses Shakespeare in *Introduction to the Literature of Europe in the Fifteenth, Sixteenth, and Seventeenth Centuries* (1854 2:175–85).

[100] *Guizot* François Pierre Guillaume Guizot (1787–1874), French historian and statesman, in *Shakspeare et son temps* (1852).

limitation of it, the conscientious rejection of superfluities, the simple and rigorous development of it from the first line of his work to the last, he falls below them, and comes nearer to the moderns. In his chief works, besides what he has of his own, he has the elementary soundness of the ancients; he has their important action and their large and broad manner: but he has not their purity of method. He is therefore a less safe model; for what he has of his own is personal, and inseparable from his own rich nature; it may be imitated and exaggerated, it cannot be learned or applied as an art; he is above all suggestive; more valuable, therefore, to young writers as men than as artists. But clearness of arrangement, rigour of development, simplicity of style—these may to a certain extent be learned: and these may, I am convinced, be learned best from the ancients, who although infinitely less suggestive than Shakspeare, are thus, to the artist, more instructive.

What then, it will be asked, are the ancients to be our sole models? the ancients with their comparatively narrow range of experience, and their widely different circumstances? Not, certainly, that which is narrow in the ancients, nor that in which we can no longer sympathize. An action like the action of the *Antigone* of Sophocles,[101] which turns upon the conflict between the heroine's duty to her brother's corpse and that to the laws of her country, is no longer one in which it is possible that we should feel a deep interest. I am speaking too, it will be remembered, not of the best sources of intellectual stimulus for the general reader, but of the best models of instruction for the individual writer. This last may certainly learn of the ancients, better than anywhere else, three things which it is vitally important for him to know:—the all-importance of the choice of a subject; the necessity of accurate construction; and the subordinate character of expression. He will learn from them how unspeakably superior is the effect of the one moral impression left by a great action treated as a whole, to the effect produced by the most striking single thought or by the happiest image. As he penetrates into the spirit of the great classical works, as he becomes gradually aware of their intense significance, their noble simplicity, and their calm pathos, he will be convinced that it is this effect, unity and profoundness of moral impression, at which the ancient Poets aimed; that it is this which constitutes the grandeur of their works, and which makes them immortal. He will desire to direct his own efforts towards producing the same effect. Above all, he will deliver himself from the jargon of modern criticism, and escape the danger of producing poetical works conceived in the spirit of the passing time, and which partake of its transitoriness.

The present age makes great claims upon us: we owe it service, it will not be satisfied without our admiration. I know not how it is, but their commerce with the ancients appears to me to produce, in those who constantly practise it, a steadying and composing effect upon their judgment, not of literary works only, but of men and events in general. They are like persons who have had a very weighty and impressive experience: they are more truly than others under the empire of facts, and more independent of the language current among those with whom they live. They wish neither to applaud nor to revile their age: they wish to know what it is, what it can give them, and whether this is what they want. What they want, they know very well; they want to educe and cultivate what is best and noblest in themselves: they know, too, that this is no easy task—χαλεπὸν, as Pittacus said, χαλεπὸν ἐσθλὸν ἔμμεναι[102]—and they ask themselves sincerely whether their age and its literature can assist them in the attempt. If they are endeavouring to practise any art, they remember the plain and simple proceedings of the old artists, who

Notes ————————————————————————————————

[101] *Sophocles* in *Antigone* (*c.*442 BCE) the heroine attempts to bury her brother, Polyneices, against the laws of Creon and the state of Thebes.

[102] ἔμμεναι (Gk. it is hard to be good), attributed by Plato in *Protagoras* (343C) to Pittacus of Mytelene (*c.*640–568 BCE), military commander and politician.

attained their grand results by penetrating themselves with some noble and significant action, not by inflating themselves with a belief in the preeminent importance and greatness of their own times. They do not talk of their mission, nor of interpreting their age, nor of the coming Poet; all this, they know, is the mere delirium of vanity; their business is not to praise their age, but to afford to the men who live in it the highest pleasure which they are capable of feeling.[103] If asked to afford this by means of subjects drawn from the age itself, they ask what special fitness the present age has for supplying them: they are told that it is an era of progress, an age commissioned to carry out the great ideas of industrial development and social amelioration. They reply that with all this they can do nothing; that the elements they need for the exercise of their art are great actions, calculated powerfully and delightfully to affect what is permanent in the human soul; that so far as the present age can supply such actions, they will gladly make use of them; but that an age wanting in moral grandeur can with difficulty supply such, and an age of spiritual discomfort with difficulty be powerfully and delightfully affected by them. A host of voices will indignantly rejoin that the present age is inferior to the past neither in moral grandeur nor in spiritual health. He who possesses the discipline I speak of will content himself with remembering the judgments passed upon the present age, in this respect, by the men of strongest head and widest culture whom it has produced; by Goethe and by Niebuhr.[104] It will be sufficient for him that he knows the opinions held by these two great men respecting the present age and its literature; and that he feels assured in his own mind that their aims and demands upon life were such as he would wish, at any rate, his own to be; and their judgment as to what is impeding and disabling such as he may safely follow. He will not, however, maintain a hostile attitude towards the false pretensions of his age; he will content himself with not being overwhelmed by them. He will esteem himself fortunate if he can succeed in banishing from his mind all feelings of contradiction, and irritation, and impatience; in order to delight himself with the contemplation of some noble action of a heroic time, and to enable others, through his representation of it, to delight in it also.

I am far indeed from making any claim, for myself, that I possess this discipline; or for the following Poems, that they breathe its spirit. But I say, that in the sincere endeavour to learn and practise, amid the bewildering confusion of our times, what is sound and true in poetical art, I seemed to myself to find the only sure guidance, the only solid footing, among the ancients. They, at any rate, knew what they wanted in Art, and we do not. It is this uncertainty which is disheartening, and not hostile criticism. How often have I felt this when reading words of disparagement or of cavil: that it is the uncertainty as to what is really to be aimed at which makes our difficulty, not the dissatisfaction of the critic, who himself suffers from the same uncertainty. *Non me tua turbida terrent Dicta: Dii me terrent, et Jupiter hostis.*[105]

Two kinds of *dilettanti*, says Goethe, there are in poetry: he who neglects the indispensable mechanical part and thinks he has done enough if he shows spirituality and feeling;

Notes

[103] *feeling* Arnold takes a view opposite to that of Smith in *A Life-Drama*: "My Friend! a Poet must ere long arise / And with a regal song sub-crown this age, ... / A mighty Poet whom this age shall choose / To be its Spokesman to all coming times" (Sc. 2), a passage quoted by Masson (see n. 71). Masson, after quoting these and other lines, praises their "sentimental fervour" but condemns their "intellectual crudeness" (333).

[104] *Goethe and Niebuhr* for instance, on 29 January 1826 Goethe in conversation said, "Our present time is retrograde, for it is subjective: we see this not merely in poetry, but also in painting and in much besides. Every healthy effort, on the contrary, is directed from the inward to the outward world." See *Conversations of Goethe with Eckermann and Soret* (trans. John Oxenham, 1850, vol. 1, 125–26). Barthold Georg Niebuhr (1776–1831), German historian and statesman, whose *Life and Letters of Barthold Georg Niebuhr*, containing many critical comments on contemporary life and literature, was published in English translation (1852).

[105] *hostis* see *Aeneid* 12. 894–95: "Thy fierce words dismay me not, insolent! the gods dismay me, and Jupiter's enmity" (trans. Mackail).

and he who seeks to arrive at poetry merely by mechanism, in which he can acquire an artisan's readiness, and is without soul and matter.[106] And he adds, that the first does most harm to Art, and the last to himself. If we must be *dilettanti*: if it is impossible for us, under the circumstances amidst which we live, to think clearly, to feel nobly, and to delineate firmly: if we cannot attain to the mastery of the great artists—let us, at least, have so much respect for our Art as to prefer it to ourselves: let us not bewilder our successors: let us transmit to them the practice of Poetry, with its boundaries and wholesome regulative laws, under which excellent works may again, perhaps, at some future time, be produced, not yet fallen into oblivion through our neglect, not yet condemned and cancelled by the influence of their eternal enemy, Caprice.

WEB p. 384

From "The Function of Criticism at the Present Time"
Culture and Anarchy
    From [Chapter 1: "Sweetness and Light"]
    From [Chapter 2: "Doing as One Likes"]
    From [Chapter 4: "Hebraism and Hellenism"]

Coventry Patmore (1823–96)

Coventry Kersey Dighton Patmore was the eldest child of Eliza Anne Robertson (1798–1851) and Peter George Patmore (1786–1855), an author and friend of the Romantic essayists Leigh Hunt (1784–1859), Charles Lamb (1775–1834), and William Hazlitt (1778–1830). Within this privileged literary background, Patmore was privately educated in his native Essex and in France. He published *Poems* in 1844, winning him both an attack in *Blackwood's*, famous for such broadsides, and the friendship of Dante Rossetti and other members of the fledgling PRB. His father's financial losses compelled him to earn his own living, chiefly in writing periodical essays, eventually more than three hundred. Through Swinburne's literary patron and the parliamen-

tarian, Richard Monckton Milnes (1809–85), Patmore became assistant librarian at the British Museum and was also able to continue his poetic career with *Tamerton Church Tower and Other Poems* (1853). He married Emily Andrews in 1847, the inspiration for his most famous literary work, *The Angel in the House* (1854–63), whose complicated history eventually involved four parts and multiple reprintings, each with extensive revisions, appearing together first in 1863 after the death of his first wife a year earlier. Patmore converted to Roman Catholicism and married a second time, to a wealthy Catholic convert, Marianne Byles. After her death in 1880, he married a third time, to Harriet Robson. In 1868 he had published a collection of elegies as *Odes*, later

Notes

---

[106] *matter* in the summer of 1799 Goethe and Schiller carried out a project on the subject of dilettantism (apprenticeship, parody, being a taster rather than a doer of the arts, trivializing, and amateurism) that was published in 1833 in Goethe's *Collected Works*. Carlyle also carried out a discussion on the subject with Goethe and J. S. Mill in letters, and included a chapter on "The Gospel of Dilettantism" in *Past and Present* (3. 3).

gathered with others as *The Unknown Eros* (1877), esteemed by many as his best work; the volume also contains his reactionary denunciation of the 1867 Reform Bill (see CONDITION: PROGRESS (WEB p. 38)). It is for *The Angel in the House*, however, that he is best known. It presents a feminine ideal that is seen as quintessentially Victorian, a glorification of wedded bliss, and of the role of a wife in the domestic sphere. Standard edition: *The Poems of Coventry Patmore*, ed. Frederick Page (1949); Basil Champneys, *Memoirs and Correspondence of Coventry Patmore* (2 vols, 1900); and Ian Anstruther, *Coventry Patmore's Angel* (1992). "Victorian Web": http://www.victorianweb. org/authors/patmore/index.html.

From *The Angel in the House*[1]

Book I: The Prologue[2]

"Mine is no winged horse[3] to gain
   The region of the spheral chime:
He does but drag a rumbling wain,[4]
   Cheer'd by the silver bells of rhyme:
And if, at Fame's bewitching note,   5
   My homely Pegasus pricks an ear,
The world's cart-collar hugs his throat,
   And he's too wise to kick or rear."

Notes

COVENTRY PATMORE

[1] *title* after a slow beginning, Patmore's poem quickly became a Victorian bestseller, as well as a widespread cliché for one ideal of Victorian womanhood, the submissive and devoted wife, charming, consoling, graceful, self-sacrificing, and self deprecating, running her home flawlessly, raising her children appropriately, and supporting her husband unquestioningly. However, the word "submissive" does not appear, and its cognates only twice. Margaret Oliphant pointed out that the real subject of the poem was not so much the conforming wife as epitomized in the cliché but the spirit of married love and domestic bliss, a somewhat neglected theme in Victorian poetry, making Patmore "the laureate of the tea-table" as Edmund Gosse called him. Virginia Woolf criticized both the clichéd image and the ideal: "Had I not killed her she would have killed me. She would have plucked the heart out of my writing.... Killing the Angel in the House was part of the occupation of a woman writer" ("Professions for Women," 1931).

The first two books narrate the story of the young poet Felix Vaughan and his beloved, Honoria Churchill, their courtship and marriage, told largely in the man's voice, as a kind of epithalamium or marriage song, but also, to some extent, as an artist's coming-of-age poem (*Künstlergedicht*), a variant of the coming-of-age novel (*Bildungsroman*). The second two books focus more on the married life of another couple. Frederick, Honoria's cousin, had been rejected by Honoria as a possible suitor, and he thereupon marries another friend, Jane, whom he struggles to love with the same ardour with which he had loved Honoria. Their conflicted feelings and doubts, and eventual devotion to each other, are told through a series of poetic letters to their respective mothers and others, in which the female voices predominate.

Patmore reworked the poem extensively, reprinting revisions, and adding to and re-arranging the poem many times, so that it has one of the most complex textual histories of any nineteenth-century poem. He retained, however, his original elaborate structure of four books: Book I: "The Betrothal" (1854); Book II: "The Espousals" (1856) – these two books eventually constituting Part I of the poem; Book III "Faithful for Ever" (1860); and Book IV "The Victories of Love: (1862/3) – the final two books constituting Part II. Within each book are numbered cantos, each with "The Accompaniments" (1854; called "Preludes" from the second edition, 1856, on) consisting of between two and six titled subsections, meditations on the theme of the canto, followed in each case by a numbered Idyl (1854; replaced from the second edition by a narrative in the lover's voice). The first two books have prologues and epilogues. The second two books are epistolary poems. Our text, 1854.

[2] *Prologue* in the second edition (1856) the prologue was divided into five numbered sections of unequal length; the prologue as given here is complete, in the version of the first edition (1854).

[3] *horse* Pegasus is a white-winged horse of Greek mythology whose hooves originated the spring called "Hippocrene" on Mount Helicon, sacred to the Muses, whose water generated poetic inspiration.

[4] *wain* (arch. wagon).

Thus ever answer'd Vaughan his wife,
    Who, more than he, desired his fame;   10
But secretly his thoughts were rife
    How for her sake to earn a name.
With College laurels three times crown'd,[5]
    And other annual honours won,
If he but chose to be renown'd,   15
    He might, he had little doubt, she none:
And, in a loftier phrase, he talk'd
    With her upon their Wedding-Day,
While thro' the new-mown meads they walk'd,
    Their children shouting by the way: 20
"Not careless of the gift of song,
    Nor out of love with noble fame,
I, meditating much and long
    What I should sing, how win a name,
Considering well what theme unsung,   25
    What reason worth the cost of rhyme,
Remains to loose the Poet's tongue
    In these last days, the dregs of time,
Learn that to me, though born so late,
    There does, beyond desert, befall   30
(May my great fortune make me great!)
    The first of themes sung last of all.
In green and undiscover'd ground,
    Yet near where many others sing,
I have the very well-head found   35
    Whence gushes the Pierian Spring."[6]
Then she: "What is it, Dear? The Life
    Of Arthur, or Jerusalem's Fall?"[7]
"Neither: your gentle self, my wife,
    Yourself, and love that's all in all.   40
And if I faithfully proclaim
    Of these the exceeding worthiness,
Surely, the sweetest wreath of Fame
    Shall, to your hope, my brows caress;
And if, by virtue of my choice   45
    Of the most bosom-touching theme
That ever tuned a poet's voice,
    I live, as now I dare to dream,
To be delight to future days,
    And into silence only cease   50

Notes

[5] *crown'd* for laurel, see HEMANS, n. 17.

[6] *Spring* sacred to the Muses in Greek mythology, and the source of inspiration in the arts, the spring is located in Macedonia, in north-east Greece; see Alexander Pope: "A little learning is a dangerous thing. / Drink deep, or taste not the Pierian Spring" ("Essay on Criticism" 1711; pt II, 215–16).

[7] *Arthur ... Fall* the wife refers to well-known subjects for long poems, such as the legends of King Arthur drawn from Malory (Tennyson had published "Morte d'Arthur" in 1842 and republished it as a revised book in *The Idylls of the King* in 1869) and the siege of Jerusalem in 1099 at the end of the First Crusade, as retold by Torquato Tasso in *La Gerusalemme liberata* (Ital. Jerusalem delivered, 1580).

With those great Bards who shared their bays
    With Laura and with Beatrice,[8]
Imagine, Love, how learned men
    Will deep-conceived devices find,
Beyond the purpose and the ken   55
    Of the old Poet's simple mind!
You, Sweet, his Mistress, Wife, and Muse,
    Were you for mortal Woman meant?
Your praises give a hundred clues
    To mythological intent!   60
And, severing thus the truth from trope,
    In you the Commentators see,
Some Faith, some Charity, some Hope,[9]
    Some, wiser, think you all the three.
I press your arm! These are the meads   65
    In which we pass our peaceful days;
There Avon[10] runs, now hid with reeds,
    Now brightly brimming pebbly bays;
Those are our children's songs that come
    With bells and bleatings of the sheep;   70
And there, in yonder happy home,
    We thrive on mortal food and sleep."
She laugh'd. How proud she always was
    To see how proud he was of her!
Then, arguing high artistic laws,   75
    Long did they o'er the plan confer.
'Twas fix'd, with much on both sides said,
    The Song should have no incidents,
They are so dull, and pall, twice read:
    Its scope should be the heart's events: 80
Their Salisbury, for the verse unfit,
    They settled last should Sarum[11] be;
And, not to wake their neighbour's wit,
    He Felix, and Honoria she.

His purpose with performance crown'd,   85
    To her, kind critic, he rehears'd,
When next their Wedding-Day came round,
    His leisure's labour, "Book the First."

Notes

[8] *Laura ... Beatrice* the beloved women and the poetic muses of the most famous Italian poets: Laura (d. 1338) was the muse of Petrarch (1304–74) in *Il Canzoniere* (Ital. the song-book) consisting mostly of sonnets and canzones in praise of Laura; Beatrice Portinari (1266–90) was the love and muse of Dante (1265–1321) in *The Divine Comedy* (Dante's guide in the third book, *Paradiso*). In *La Vita Nuova* (Ital. the new life) Dante writes sonnets and canzones in praise of her.

[9] *Faith ... Hope* see 1 Corinthians 13: 13.

[10] *Avon* the River Avon in south-west England runs through Bath and Bristol into the English Channel; not the River Avon that runs through Stratford, the birthplace of Shakespeare.

[11] *Salisbury ... Sarum* the couple lived in the cathedral city of Salisbury in Wiltshire in the west of England. Sarum is the old name for Salisbury where much of the story takes place. See n. 25.

III Honoria: The Accompaniments[12]

1 The Lover

I

When ripen'd time and chasten'd will
    Have stretch'd and tuned for love's accords   90
The five-string'd lyre[13] of life, until
    It vibrates with the wind of words;
And "Woman," "Lady," "She," and "Her"
    Are names for perfect Good and Fair,
And unknown maidens, talk'd of, stir   95
    His thoughts with reverential care;
He meets, by heavenly chance express,
    His destined wife: some hidden hand
Unveils to him that loveliness
    Which others cannot understand.   100
No songs of love, no summer dreams
    Did e'er his longing fancy fire
With vision like to this: she seems
    In all things better than desire.
His merits in her presence grow,   105
    To match the promise in her eyes,
And round her happy footsteps blow
    The authentic airs of Paradise.
For love of her he cannot sleep;
    Her beauty haunts him all the night;   110
It melts his heart, it makes him weep
    For wonder, worship, and delight.

2

To her account does he transfer
    His pride, a base and barren root
In him, but, grafted into her,   115
    The bearer of Hesperian[14] fruit.
He dresses, dances well: he knows
    A small weight turns a heavy scale:
Who'd have her care for him, and shows
    Himself no care, deserves to fail: 120

Notes

[12] *Accompaniment* changed to "Preludes" in later versions (see n. 1). This lyric was the first poem addressed specifically to his betrothed, Honoria.

[13] *lyre* the Aeolian harp or wind harp (named after Aeolus, the god of winds in Greek mythology), hung in an open window allowing the strings to vibrate when wind passes through, producing musical sounds; a metaphor for both love songs and poetic inspiration. See also S. T. Coleridge, "Effusion XXXV" (1796) and the better known later version, "The Eolian Harp" (1817). See also FIELD, "AN AEOLIAN HARP."

[14] *Hesperian* the Hesperides, three daughters of the evening, are the guardians of the garden of Hera in the extreme west of the world of Greek mythology, near the Atlas Mountains, where they, along with a dragon, guard the tree that bears the golden apples of immortality.

The least is well, yet nothing's light
    In all the lover does; for he
Who pitches hope at such a height
    Will do all things with dignity.
She is so perfect, true and pure,   125
    Her virtue all virtue so endears,
That, often, when he thinks of her,
    Life's meanness fills his eyes with tears.
She's far too lovely to be wrong:
    Black, if she pleases, shall be white: 130
Prerogative ties cavil's tongue:
    Being a Queen her wrong is right:
Defect super-perfection is:
    Her great perfections make him grieve,
Refusing him the bliss of bliss,   135
    Which is to give, and not receive.[15]
Her graces make him rich, and ask
    No guerdon: this imperial style
Affronts him: he disdains to bask,
    The pensioner of her priceless smile.   140
He prays for some hard thing to do,
    Some work of fame and labour immense,
To stretch the languid bulk and thew
    Of love's fresh-born magnipotence.

3

O, paradox of love, he longs,   145
    Most humble when he most aspires,
To suffer scorn and cruel wrongs
    From her he worships and desires:
And yet his passion, if need be,
    Would spend all on a single kiss,   150
And call it great economy,
    Counting the honour, not the bliss:
A trifle serves for his relief,
    A trifle turns him sick and pale;
And yet his pleasure and his grief   155
    Are both on a majestic scale.
No smallest boon were bought too dear,
    Though barter'd for his love-sick life;
Yet trusts he, with undaunted cheer,
    To vanquish heaven and call her wife.   160
He notes how Queens of sweetness still
    Neglect their crowns and stoop to mate:
How, self-consign'd with lavish will,
    They ask but love proportionate;
How swift pursuit by small degrees,   165

Notes

[15] *receive* see Acts 20: 35.

Love's tactic, works like miracle;
　How valour, clothed in courtesies,
　　Brings down the haughtiest citadel;[16]
And therefore, though he merits not
　　To kiss the braid upon her skirt,　　　　　　170
His hope, discouraged ne'er a jot,
　　Out-soars all possible desert:
Resistance only makes him gay:
　　The fiercer fight the fairer she:
In vain her distance says him nay:　　　　　　175
　　Hope, desperate grown, feigns certainty.

Book II: "The Espousals"

X The Epitaph: The Accompaniments

3 The Foreign Land

A woman is a foreign land,[17]
　　Of which, though there he settle young,
A man will ne'er quite understand
　　The customs, politics, and tongue.　　　　　180
The foolish hie them post-haste through,
　　See fashions odd, and prospects fair,
Learn of the language, "How d'ye do,"
　　And go and brag that they've been there.
The most for leave to trade apply,　　　　　185
　　For once, at Empire's seat, her heart,
Then get what knowledge ear and eye
　　Glean chancewise in the life-long mart.
And certain others, few and fit,
　　Attach them to the Court, and see　　　　　190
The Country's best, its accent hit,
　　And partly sound its polity.

XI The Departure: The Accompaniments

1 Womanhood[18]

Be man's hard virtues highly wrought,
　　But let my gentle Mistress be,
In every look, word, deed, and thought,

Notes

16 *citadel* the siege of the castle or citadel of love, an allegory of the lover's pursuit of the aloof beloved, was a theme in carved ivories of the fourteenth century; several are in the Victoria and Albert Museum, London.

17 *land* poem added in 1858 as one of the Preludes in Canto X. Our text, 1858. Patmore uses a common convention of comparing a beloved woman to a geographical exploration, as in John Donne's lines "O, my America, my New-foundland, / My kingdom, safest when with one man mann'd" from "Elegy XX: To His Mistress Going to Bed" (1633).

18 *Womanhood* the first poem after the wedding of Felix and Honoria in the 1856 edition. See also nn. 1 and 11.

Nothing but sweet and womanly! 195
    Her virtues please my virtuous mood,
        But what at all times I admire
Is, not that she is wise or good,
        But just the thing which I desire.
With versatility to bring 200
        Her mental tone to any strain,
If oft'nest she is anything,
        Be it thoughtless, talkative, and vain.
That seems in her supremest grace
        Which, virtue or not, apprises me 205
That my familiar arms embrace
        Unfathomable mystery.

Idyl XI: The Departure[19]

I

Life smitten with a feverish chill,
    The brain too tired to understand,
In apathy of heart and will, 210
    I took the woman from the hand
Of him who stood for God, and heard
    Of Christ, and of the Church his Bride;
The Feast, by presence of the Lord
    And his first Wonder, beautified;[20] 215
The mystic sense to Christian men;
    The bonds in innocency made,
And gravely to be enter'd then
    For children, godliness, and aid,[21]
And honour'd, and kept free from smirch; 220
    And how a man must love his wife
No less than Christ did love his Church,
    If need be, giving her his life:
And, vowing then the mutual vow,
    The tongue spake, but intention slept. 225

Notes

[19] *Departure* in 1856 the first of three lyrics in "The Idyl" of "The Departure," as the couple are about to depart for their honeymoon.

[20] *Bride ... beautified* echoes of the BCP from the opening exhortation of the wedding liturgy or "The Form of Solemnization of Matrimony": "Dearly beloved, we are gathered together here in the sight of God, and in the face of this congregation, to join together this Man and this Woman in holy Matrimony; which is an honourable estate, instituted of God in the time of man's innocency, signifying unto us the mystical union that is betwixt Christ and his Church; which holy estate Christ adorned and beautified with his presence, and first miracle that he wrought, in Cana of Galilee; [John 2: 1–12] and is commended of Saint Paul to be honourable among all men: and therefore is not by any to be enterprised, nor taken in hand, unadvisedly, lightly, or wantonly, to satisfy men's carnal lusts and appetites, like brute beasts that have no understanding; but reverently, discreetly, advisedly, soberly, and in the fear of God."

[21] *aid* the BCP sets out "the causes for which Matrimony was ordained. First, It was ordained for the procreation of children, to be brought up in the fear and nurture of the Lord, and to the praise of his holy Name. Secondly, It was ordained for a remedy against sin, and to avoid fornication; that such persons as have not the gift of continency might marry, and keep themselves undefiled members of Christ's body. Thirdly, It was ordained for the mutual society, help, and comfort, that the one ought to have of the other, both in prosperity and adversity."

Ah, well for us Heav'n asks not how
Such oaths are sworn, but how they're kept!

The Epilogue[22]

"I did not call you 'Dear' or 'Love,'
I think, till after Frank was born."
That fault I cannot well remove;   230
"The rhymes"—but Frank now blew his horn,
And Walter bark'd, on hands and knees,
At Baby in the mignionette,[23]
And all made, full-cry, for the trees
Where Felix and his wife were set.   235
Again disturb'd, (crickets have cares!)
True to their annual use they rose,
To offer thanks at Evening Prayers
In three times sacred Sarum Close.[24]

Sydney Dobell (1824–74)

Sydney Thompson Dobell was born in Cranbrook in Kent where his father, John Dobell, was a wine merchant. His mother, Julietta Thompson, was the daughter of Samuel Thompson (1766–1837), religious reformer. In 1836 Dobell moved with his family to Cheltenham, where he was educated at home. He admired Byron, especially *Manfred* (1817), and held that poetry could engage Romantic self-consciousness, social engagement, and religious individualism. He married Emily Fordham (1844) and took over part of his father's wine business. He met advocates of Italian unification, leading to his popular first publication, a long poem, *The Roman* (1850), under the pseudonym Sydney Yendys. He became friends with the leading writers of the day, including Robert Browning, Alfred Tennyson, Thomas Carlyle, John Ruskin, and George MacDonald. A number of poems followed, including a long epic, *Balder* (1854), which showed he had identified with the so-called Spasmodic school of Philip Bailey (1816–1902). The Spasmodic poets, including among them Bailey, Alexander Smith (1830–67), and George Gilfillan (1813–78), tended to write long poems with mythic heroes who were lonely and isolated, disillusioned and alienated from the world but still aspiring after lofty though unattainable goals. Their intense self-scrutiny and morbid psychologizing was expressed in an ornate and obscure style with extravagant use of metaphors and intricate nature imagery, often overcast with pathetic fallacy. Dobell's association with the Spasmodics was made clear when the critic William Edmondstoune Aytoun (1813–65) in his drama *Firmilian* (1854) parodied Dobell's *Balder* for its sensationalism, formless plot, and extravagant metaphors. Dobell moved to Scotland for several years; with Alexander Smith he published

Notes

[22] *Epilogue* first part of five short lyrics in the epilogue (1856).

[23] *mignionette* a kind of delicate, narrow lace popular from the sixteenth to the first half of the nineteenth century, made in Arras and other lace centres in France, here used to trim the baby's garment or cap.

[24] *Close* the cathedral precinct, enclosed with a wall since the fourteenth century.

Sonnets on the War (1855), and by himself, England in Time of War (1856). As his health began to fail in the 1860s, he sought more comforting climates, travelling and residing in France, Spain, and Italy, until he injured himself in a fall in 1865 and returned to spend the rest of his life at home. Standard edition:

The Poetical Works of Sydney Dobell, ed. John Nichol (2 vols, 1875); Thoughts on Art, Philosophy and Religion, ed. John Nichol (1876); E. Jolly, The Life and Letters of Sydney Dobell (2 vols, 1878); and Martha Westwater, The Spasmodic Career of Sydney Dobell (1992).

To the Authoress of "Aurora Leigh"[1]

Were Shakspeare born a twin, his lunar twin
(Not of the golden but the silver bow)
Should be like thee: so, with such eyes and brow,
Sweeten his looks, so, with her dear sex in
His voice, (a king's words writ out by the queen,)   5
Unman his bearded English, and, with flow
Of breastfull robes about her female snow,
Present the lordly brother. Oh Last-of-kin,
There be ambitious women here on earth
Who will not thank thee to have sung so well!   10
Apollo and Diana are one birth,[2]
Pollux and Helen break a single shell.[3]
Who now may hope? While Adam was alone
Eve was to come. She came; God's work was done.

Two Sonnets on the Death of Prince Albert[4]

I

In a great house by the wide Sea I sat,
And down slow fleets and waves that never cease
Looked back to the first keels of War and Peace;
I saw the Ark, what time the shoreless flat

Notes

SYNDEY DOBELL

[1] *title* a poem in honour of Elizabeth Barrett Browning, written in 1860, a year before her death. Both Barrett Browning and Dobell were both strong supporters of Italian unification, and in 1860, after fighting broke out in 1859, she had published *Poems Before Congress* celebrating the Italian cause. The volume caused a sensation in England where she was attacked by conservative reviews in *Blackwoods* and the *Saturday Review* as ranting with a misplaced patriotism. In her preface she claimed to "love truth and justice . . . more even than Shakespeare and Shakespeare's country." Our text: *Poetical Works* (1875).

[2] *birth* Leto was one of the daughters of the Titans in Greek mythology. Wooed by Zeus, she gave birth to the twins Apollo and Artemis, the Roman Diana. Apollo was the god of the sun, medicine, and the arts; Artemis the goddess of the moon, virginity, and the hunt.

[3] *shell* in Greek mythology, Leda was the wife of King Tyndareus of Sparta. She was raped by Zeus in the form of a swan on the same night that she made love to Tyndareus, later giving birth to two eggs: from one hatched Helen (later of Troy) and Cassandra, and from the other the *Dioscuri* (Gk. twins; Lat. *Gemini*) Castor and Pollux. Ancient sources were divided about which was divine, which mortal, and even which pair came from the same egg. Here Pollux is deemed to be immortal.

[4] *title* Albert died 14 December 1861. The poem was written in 1861; published first in *Poetical Works* (1875).

Began to rock to rising Ararat;[5]   5
Or Argo,[6] surging home, with templed Greece
To leeward, while, mast-high, the lurching fleece
Swung morn from deep to deep.
Then in a plat of tamarisk a bird called me. When again
My soul looked forth I ponder'd not the main   10
Of waters but of time; and from our fast
Sure Now, with Pagan joy, beheld the pain
Of tossing heroes on the triremed Past
Obtest the festive Gods and silent stars in vain.

II

And as I mused on all we call our own,
And (in the words their passionate hope had taught
Expressing this late world for which they fought
And prayed) said, lifting up my head to the sun,
"Ne quibus diis immortalibus,"[7]—one   5
Ran with fear's feet, and lo! a voice distraught
"The Prince" and "Dead." And at the sound methought
The bulwark of my great house thunder'd down.
And, for an instant,—as some spell were sapping
All place—the hilly billows and billowy hills   10
Heaved through my breast the lapping wave that kills
The heart; around me the floor rises and falls
And jabbling stones of the unsteady walls
Ebb and flow together, lapping, lapping.

William Topaz McGonagall
(1825–1902)

McGonagall, a Scottish weaver, was, by his own definition, a "poet and tragedian," and by that of others, "the worst poet in the world." He was born in Edinburgh, the son of an Irish cotton weaver; McGonagall's family moved to Dundee where he became a handloom weaver and amateur actor, specializing in *Macbeth*, combining the Scottish history that he venerated, and Shakespearean English, at which he aimed, but missed. In 1877 he wrote, "I discovered myself to be a poet," soon thereafter gaining notoriety with "The Tay Bridge Disaster," his best-known

Notes

[5] *Ararat* Noah's ark comes to rest after the great flood on Mount Ararat; see Genesis 8: 4.

[6] *Argo* in Greek mythology the ship on which Jason and his companions, the Argonauts, sailed in search of the Golden Fleece, as recounted in the *Argonautica* by Apollonius of Rhodes (third century BCE), and retold later by William Morris in *The Life and Death of Jason* (1867).

[7] *Ne ... immortalibus* (Lat. not for him for the immortal gods), an echo of Cicero's "Oration in favour of the Manilian Law" (c.66 BCE).

work. After leaving Dundee, he settled in Perth (1894), where he claimed to have received a letter from King Thibaw Min (1859–1916) of Burma who had decorated him as Sir Topaz, Knight of the White Elephant of Burmah, a title he adopted. McGonagall specialized in epic narratives of public triumphs and disasters and the deaths of the famous, presented with an endearing naïvety and utter disregard for metrics. He began publishing in local papers (the *Weekly News* of Dundee) and began collecting his work from 1878, published by his friends as *Poetic Gems* (1890) and *Poetic Gems Second Series* (1891) to assist him in financial hardship. Although well known and often mocked in Scotland, he could not gain success in publishing or music hall performances in either London or New York. Blending the rhetoric of popular melodrama, Scottish patriotism, love of royalty, especially Victoria herself (whom he sought as a patron – she refused – and to whom he sent his volumes), and the chaotic metre of street broadsheets, he gained a cult following. His work has been satirized by a number of twentieth-century comedians including Peter Sellers (1925–80) and Spike Milligan (1918–2002); nevertheless, his work was popular among his contemporaries. Standard editions: *William McGonagall: Collected Poems*, ed. Chris Hunt (2006); *The Complete McGonagall* (1992); "The Autobiography of Sir William Topaz McGonagall, Poet and Tragedian" in *Poetic Gems Second Series* (1891); "McGonagall Online": www.mcgonagall-online.org.uk.

The Tay Bridge Disaster[1]

Beautiful Railway Bridge of the Silv'ry Tay!
Alas! I am very sorry to say
That ninety lives have been taken away
On the last Sabbath day of 1879,
Which will be remember'd for a very long time.   5

'Twas about seven o'clock at night,
And the wind it blew with all its might,
And the rain came pouring down,
And the dark clouds seem'd to frown,
And the Demon of the air seem'd to say—   10
"I'll blow down the Bridge of Tay."

When the train left Edinburgh
The passengers' hearts were light and felt no sorrow,
But Boreas[2] blew a terrific gale,

Notes

WILLIAM TOPAZ MCGONAGALL

[1] *title* on 28 December 1879 twelve of the highest cast iron columns of the Tay Bridge (3.5 km, over the Firth of Tay), running from Dundee (north shore) to the small town of Wormit (south) on the North British Railway in Scotland, collapsed during a gale when a train was passing over it. Although McGonagall claims that ninety lives were lost, modern historians calculate that the death toll was about seventy-five. The bridge was designed by Sir Thomas Bouch (1822–80), whose reputation was destroyed by the official enquiry that found that the bridge was "badly designed, badly built and badly maintained." The bridge had been opened by Queen Victoria on 1 June 1878 when she crossed it in a train. Our text: *Poetic Gems* (1890).

[2] *Boreas* the north wind.

Which made their hearts for to quail,   15
And many of the passengers with fear did say-
"I hope God will send us safe across the Bridge of Tay."

But when the train came near to Wormit Bay,
Boreas he did loud and angry bray,
And shook the central girders of the Bridge of Tay   20
On the last Sabbath day of 1879,
Which will be remember'd for a very long time.

So the train sped on with all its might,
And Bonnie Dundee soon hove in sight,
And the passengers' hearts felt light,   25
Thinking they would enjoy themselves on the New Year,
With their friends at home they lov'd most dear,
And wish them all a happy New Year.

So the train mov'd slowly along the Bridge of Tay,
Until it was about midway,   30
Then the central girders with a crash gave way,
And down went the train and passengers into the Tay!
The Storm Fiend did loudly bray,
Because ninety lives had been taken away,
On the last Sabbath day of 1879,   35
Which will be remember'd for a very long time.

As soon as the catastrophe came to be known
The alarm from mouth to mouth was blown,
And the cry rang out all o'er the town,
Good Heavens! the Tay Bridge is blown down,   40
And a passenger train from Edinburgh,
Which fill'd all the peoples hearts with sorrow,
And made them for to turn pale,
Because none of the passengers were sav'd to tell the tale
How the disaster happen'd on the last Sabbath day of 1879,   45
Which will be remember'd for a very long time.

It must have been an awful sight,
To witness in the dusky moonlight,
While the Storm Fiend did laugh, and angry did bray,
Along the Railway Bridge of the Silv'ry Tay.   50
Oh! ill-fated Bridge of the Silv'ry Tay,
I must now conclude my lay
By telling the world fearlessly without the least dismay,
That your central girders would not have given way,
At least many sensible men do say,   55
Had they been supported on each side with buttresses,
At least many sensible men confesses,
For the stronger we our houses do build,
The less chance we have of being killed.

The Death of the Queen[3]

William Topaz McGonagall

Alas! our noble and generous Queen Victoria is dead,
And I hope her soul to Heaven has fled,
To sing and rejoice with saints above,
Where all is joy, peace, and love.

'Twas on January 22, 1901, in the evening she died at 6.30 o'clock,   5
Which to the civilised world has been a great shock;
She was surrounded by her children and grandchildren dear,
And for the motherly, pious Queen they shed many a tear.

She has been a model and faithful Queen,
Very few like her have been;   10
She has acted virtuously during her long reign,
And I'm afraid the world will never see her like again.

And during her reign she was beloved by the high and the low,
And through her decease the people's hearts are full of woe,
Because she was kind to her subjects at home and abroad,   15
And now she's receiving her reward from the Eternal God.

And during her reign in this world of trouble and strife
Several attempts were made to take her life;
Maclean[4] he tried to shoot her, but he did fail,
But he was arrested and sent to an asylum, which made him bewail.   20

Victoria was a noble Queen, the people must confess,
She was most charitable to them while in distress;
And in her disposition she wasn't proud nor vain,
And tears for her loss will fall as plentiful as rain.

The people around Balmoral[5] will shed many tears   25
Owing to her visits amongst them for many years;
She was very kind to the old, infirm women there,
By giving them provisions and occasionally a prayer.

Notes

[3] *title* McGonagall had written a number of poems in honour of Queen Victoria, including "Ode to the Queen on her Jubilee Year" (1887). He published at least three other poems on Victoria, this one being one of his last poems. He died the following year. Our text: *More Poetic Gems* (1962).

[4] *Maclean* Roderick Maclean attempted to shoot Queen Victoria when she was leaving Windsor railway station in her carriage on 2 March 1882. Maclean was angry with Victoria for her secretary's brief reply to his letter enclosing his poetry. He was declared insane and lived until 9 June 1921 at Broadmoor Asylum. McGonagall himself commemorated the event in "Attempted Assassination of the Queen" (*Poetic Gems*, 1890).

[5] *Balmoral* Balmoral Castle, west of Aberdeen in Scotland, was purchased by Albert for Victoria and became a summer royal residence in 1852, undergoing extensive architectural extensions. McGonagall walked from Dundee to Balmoral (99 km) in 1878, through rain and over mountains, to read to Victoria, but he was refused entrance.

And while at Balmoral she found work for men unemployed,
Which made the hearts of the poor men feel overjoyed;   30
And for Her Majesty they would have laid down their lives,
Because sometimes she saved them from starving, and their wives.

Many happy days she spent at Balmoral,
Viewing the blooming heather and the bonnie Highland floral,
Along with Prince Albert, her husband dear,   35
But alas! when he died[6] she shed many a tear.

She was very charitable, as everybody knows,
But the loss of her husband caused her many woes,
Because he cheered her at Balmoral as they the heather trod,
But I hope she has met him now at the Throne of God.   40

They ascended the Hill of Morven[7] when she was in her fortieth year,
And Her Majesty was delighted as she viewed the Highland deer;
Also dark Lochnagar,[8] which is most beautiful to see,
Not far from Balmoral and the dark River Dee.

I hope they are walking in Heaven together as they did in life   45
In the beautiful celestial regions, free from all strife,
Where God's family together continually meet,
Where the streets are paved with gold, and everything complete.

Alas! for the loss of Queen Victoria the people will mourn,
But she unto them can never return;   50
Therefore to mourn for her is all in vain,
Knowing that she can never return again.

Therefore, good people, one and all,
Let us be prepared for death when God does on us call,
Like the good and noble Queen Victoria of renown,   55
The greatest and most virtuous Queen that ever wore a crown.

Thomas Henry Huxley (1825–1895)

Born in Ealing, now a suburb of London, the son of a mathematics teacher, George Huxley (1780–1853), and his wife, Rachel Withers (1785–1852), Huxley had only two years at school. He determined to educate himself, beginning by reading Carlyle and James Hutton's *Theory of the Earth* (1788), while turning away from his mother's Anglicanism and his school's evangelicalism. He taught himself Latin and Greek, learned French from his sister, and applied himself to algebra, geometry, history, physics, physiology, and chemistry. He

Notes ———

[6] *died* Albert, Prince Consort (1819–61), husband of Queen Victoria; they were married 10 February 1840. After his death on 14 December 1861, Victoria wore mourning black for the rest of her life.

[7] *Morven* (Gael. great mountain) in Aberdeenshire near Ballater, climbed by Victoria in 1859.

[8] *Lochnagar* mountain in the Grampian range south of the River Dee and part of the Royal Estate of Balmoral.

began to study medicine at the private Sydenham College (1841), winning the prize in botany and a silver medal from the Society of Apothecaries' competition (1842). He then transferred to Charing Cross Hospital to continue his medical studies. Having won more prizes, he joined the navy to pay debts, and went as assistant surgeon on the four-year voyage of *The Rattlesnake* (1846–50), whose main goal was the charting of New Guinea, Australia, and the Great Barrier Reef. Huxley wrote numerous papers on his studies of sea invertebrates, jellyfish, sea nettles, and sea anemones, reorganizing their classification in Cuvier's system. Acclaimed on his return, he published an account of his researches on the voyage, *The Oceanic Hydrozoa* (1859), was elected to the Royal Society at the age of 25, and joined the free-thinking circle around the *Westminster Review*, becoming one of its columnists. He lectured on natural history at both the Royal School of Mines and the London Institution and became the naturalist for the Geological Survey – and with enough to live on, he could finally marry (1855) Henrietta (Nettie) Ann Heathorn (1825–1914), whom he had met and

proposed to in Australia in 1847. His interests and activities expanded quickly – raising a family, teaching at the Working Men's College, and examining at London University. From 1860 to 1870 he earned the name of "Darwin's Bulldog" for his defence of evolution, most publically in the debate with Bishop Samuel Wilberforce at the Oxford Union in 1860 (see RELIGION: GEOLOGY; OXFORD DEBATE (WEB p. 182)). He helped to found the journal *Nature* (1869) and advocated for reform in education in science throughout the schools' curricula at every level. He coined the term "agnostic." As a public intellectual, Huxley served on eight Royal Commissions, was secretary and president of the Royal Society and of the Geological Society, and won numerous national and international medals and awards. *Collected Essays* (9 vols, 1893–94); Leonard Huxley, *The Life and Letters of Thomas Henry Huxley* (2 vols, 1900); *The Thomas Henry Huxley Family Correspondence*, ed. Adrian Desmond (4 vols, forthcoming); Adrian Desmond, *Huxley: From Devil's Disciple to Evolution's High Priest* (1997). The Huxley File: http://aleph0.clarku.edu/huxley.

From "'On a Piece of Chalk.' A Lecture to Working Men" in *Macmillan's Magazine* (Sept. 1868)[1]

A great chapter of the history of the world is written in the chalk. Few passages in the history of man can be supported by such an overwhelming mass of direct and indirect evidence as that which testifies to the truth of the fragment of the history of the globe, which I hope to enable you to read with your own eyes to-night.

Let me add, that few chapters of human history have a more profound significance for ourselves. I weigh my words well when I assert, that the man who should know the true history of the bit of chalk which every carpenter carries about in his breeches-pocket, though ignorant of all other history, is likely, if he will think his knowledge out to its ultimate results, to have a truer, and therefore a better, conception of this wonderful universe, and of man's relation to it, than the most learned student who is deep-read in the records of humanity and ignorant of those of Nature.

Notes

THOMAS HUXLEY
[1] *title* "Delivered during the Meeting of the British Association at Norwich" [author's note]. The lecture was delivered on the evening of 26 August 1868 to working men in Norwich when the British Association for the Advancement of Science was holding its annual meetings.

The language of the chalk is not hard to learn, not nearly so hard as Latin, if you only want to get at the broad features of the story it has to tell; and I propose that we now set to work to spell that story out together....

Let us try another method of making the chalk tell us its own history. To the unassisted eye chalk looks simply like a very loose and open kind of stone. But it is possible to grind a slice of chalk down so thin that you can see through it—until it is thin enough, in fact, to be examined with any magnifying power that may be thought desirable. A thin slice of the fur[2] of a kettle might be made in the same way. If it were examined microscopically, it would show itself to be a more or less distinctly laminated mineral substance, and nothing more.

But the slice of chalk presents a totally different appearance when placed under the microscope. The general mass of it is made up of very minute granules; but imbedded in this matrix are innumerable bodies, some smaller and some larger, but, on a rough average not more than a hundredth of an inch in diameter, having a well-defined shape and structure. A cubic inch of some specimens of chalk may contain hundreds of thousands of these bodies, compacted together with incalculable millions of the granules....

It may be worth while briefly to consider a few of these collateral proofs that the chalk was deposited at the bottom of the sea. The great mass of the chalk is composed, as we have seen, of the skeletons of *Globigerinæ*,[3] and other simple organisms, imbedded in granular matter. Here and there, however, this hardened mud of the ancient sea reveals the remains of higher animals which have lived and died, and left their hard parts in the mud, just as the oysters die and leave their shells behind them in the mud of the present seas....

Thus, not only is it certain that the chalk is the mud of an ancient sea-bottom; but it is no less certain that the chalk sea existed during an extremely long period, though we may not be prepared to give a precise estimate of the length of that period in years. The relative duration is clear, though the absolute duration may not be definable. The attempt to affix any precise date to the period at which the chalk sea began, or ended, its existence, is baffled by difficulties of the same kind. But the relative age of the cretaceous[4] epoch may be determined with as great ease and certainty as the long duration of that epoch....

Thus there is a writing upon the wall of cliffs at Cromer,[5] and whoso runs may read it. It tells us, with an authority which cannot be impeached, that the ancient sea-bed of the chalk sea was raised up and remained dry land until it was covered with forest, stocked with the great game the spoils of which have rejoiced your geologists.[6] How long it remained in that condition cannot be said; but "the whirligig of time brought its revenges"[7] in those days as in these. That dry land, with the bones and teeth of generations of long-lived elephants hidden away among the gnarled roots and dry leaves of its ancient trees, sank gradually to the bottom of the icy sea, which covered it with huge masses of drift and boulder clay. Sea-beasts, such as the walrus now restricted to the extreme north, paddled about where birds had twittered among the topmost twigs of the fir-trees. How long

Notes

[2] *fur* "crust formed by the deposit of carbonate of lime on the interior surface of a kettle" (*OED* 6. c.).

[3] *Globigerinæ* microscopic animals with many-celled shells found fossilized in chalk formations, formerly alive near the surface of seas where dead shells fall to the bottom.

[4] *cretaceous* (>Lat. *creta*, chalk); a period following the Jurassic epoch, roughly 145 to 65 million years ago.

[5] *Cromer* town on the coast of the North Sea in the county of Norfolk.

[6] *geologists* Cromer Ridge is a terminal moraine (the huge amount of accumulated debris deposited at the end of a glacial advance) behind the town of Cromer, as well as the cliffs, formed during the last ice age when the material was heaved up from the North Sea, covering the forest bed. It is the site of numerous fossil discoveries, including many small animals, as well as deer antlers. In 1995 the almost complete skeleton of a gigantic mammoth four metres high was discovered nearby at West Runton, Norfolk.

[7] *revenges* see *Twelfth Night* 5. 1. 395.

this state of things endured we know not, but at length it came to an end. The upheaved glacial mud hardened into the soil of modern Norfolk. Forests grew once more, the wolf and the beaver replaced the reindeer and the elephant; and at length what we call the history of England dawned.

Thus you have within the limits of your own county, proof that the chalk can justly claim a very much greater antiquity than even the oldest physical traces of mankind. But we may go further, and demonstrate, by evidence of the same authority as that which testifies to the existence of the father of men, that the chalk is vastly older than Adam himself.[8]

The Book of Genesis informs us that Adam, immediately upon his creation, and before the appearance of Eve, was placed in the Garden of Eden. The problem of the geographical position of Eden has greatly vexed the spirits of the learned in such matters, but there is one point respecting which, so far as I know, no commentator has ever raised a doubt. This is, that of the four rivers which are said to run out of it, Euphrates and Hiddekel are identical with the rivers now known by the names of Euphrates and Tigris.[9]

But the whole country in which these mighty rivers take their origin, and through which they run, is composed of rocks which are either of the same age as the chalk, or of later date. So that the chalk must not only have been formed, but after its formation the time required for the deposit of these later rocks and for their upheaval into dry land must have elapsed, before the smallest brook which feeds the swift stream of "the great river, the river of Babylon,"[10] began to flow.

Thus evidence which cannot be rebutted, and which need not be strengthened, though if time permitted I might indefinitely increase its quantity, compels you to believe that the earth, from the time of the chalk to the present day, has been the theatre of a series of changes as vast in their amount, as they were slow in their progress. The area on which we stand has been first sea and then land, for at least four alternations, and has remained in each of these conditions for a period of great length....

Taking the many changes of any given spot of the earth's surface, from sea to land and from land to sea, as an established fact, we cannot refrain from asking ourselves how these changes have occurred. And when we have explained them—as they must be explained—by the alternate slow movements of elevation and depression which have affected the crust of the earth, we go still further back, and ask, Why these movements?

I am not certain that any one can give you a satisfactory answer to that question. Assuredly I cannot. All that can be said for certain is, that such movements are part of the ordinary course of nature, inasmuch as they are going on at the present time. Direct proof may be given that some parts of the land of the northern hemisphere are at this moment insensibly rising and others insensibly sinking; and there is indirect but perfectly satisfactory proof, that an enormous area now covered by the Pacific has been deepened thousands of feet since the present inhabitants of that sea came into existence.

Thus there is not a shadow of a reason for believing that the physical changes of the globe in past times have been effected by other than natural causes.

Is there any more reason for believing that the concomitant modifications in the forms of the living inhabitants of the globe have been brought about in other ways?

Before attempting to answer this question, let us try to form a distinct mental picture of what has happened in some special case.

Notes

[8] *himself* Huxley refers to the dating by James Ussher of biblical creation as in the year 4004 BCE – a claim wholly repudiated by geologists and palaeontologists. See RELIGION: GEOLOGY, n. 1; RELIGION, GEOLOGY, n. 52; and HOWITT, n. 3.

[9] *Tigris* the two great rivers on either side of the plain of Mesopotamia. The other two rivers of Eden are Pishon and Gihon, neither clearly identifiable. See Genesis 2: 14.

[10] *Babylon* see Genesis 15: 18.

The crocodiles are animals which, as a group, have a very vast antiquity. They abounded ages before the chalk was deposited; they throng the rivers in warm climates at the present day. There is a difference in the form of the joints of the back-bone, and in some minor particulars, between the crocodiles of the present epoch and those which lived before the chalk; but, in the cretaceous epoch, as I have already mentioned, the crocodiles had assumed the modern type of structure. Notwithstanding this, the crocodiles of the chalk are not identically the same as those which lived in the times called "older tertiary," which succeeded the cretaceous epoch; and the crocodiles of the older tertiaries are not identical with those of the newer tertiaries, nor are these identical with existing forms. (I leave open the question whether particular species may have lived on from epoch to epoch). But each epoch has had its peculiar crocodiles, though all since the chalk have belonged to the modern type, and differ simply in their proportions, and in such structural particulars as are discernible only to trained eyes.

How is the existence of this long succession of different species of crocodiles to be accounted for?

Only two suppositions seem to be open to us—Either each species of crocodile has been specially created, or it has arisen out of some pre-existing form by the operation of natural causes.[11]

Choose your hypothesis; I have chosen mine. I can find no warranty for believing in the distinct creation of a score of successive species of crocodiles in the course of countless ages of time. Science gives no countenance to such a wild fancy; nor can even the perverse ingenuity of a commentator pretend to discover this sense, in the simple words in which the writer of Genesis records the proceedings of the fifth and sixth days of the Creation.[12]

On the other hand, I see no good reason for doubting the necessary alternative, that all these varied species have been evolved from pre-existing crocodilian forms by the operation of causes as completely a part of the common order of nature as those which have effected the changes of the inorganic world.

Few will venture to affirm that the reasoning which applies to crocodiles loses its force among other animals, or among plants. If one series of species has come into existence by the operation of natural causes, it seems folly to deny that all may have arisen in the same way.

A small beginning has led us to a great ending. If I were to put the bit of chalk with which we started into the hot but obscure flame of burning hydrogen, it would presently shine like the sun. It seems to me that this physical metamorphosis is no false image of what has been the result of our subjecting it to a jet of fervent though nowise brilliant thought to-night. It has become luminous, and its clear rays, penetrating the abyss of the remote past, have brought within our ken some stages of the evolution of the earth. And in the shifting "without haste, but without rest"[13] of the land and sea, as in the endless variation of the forms assumed by living beings, we have observed nothing but the natural product of the forces originally possessed by the substance of the universe.

Notes

[11] *specially created ... causes* on the special creation of species and the invariability of species that Huxley is rejecting here, as well as the operation of evolution, see RELIGION: GEOLOGY; WALLACE, "TENDENCY"; and RELIGION: GEOLOGY, n. 36.

[12] *Creation* see Genesis 1: 20–31; see also RELIGION: GEOLOGY, n. 3.

[13] *rest* see Goethe's poem, *Zahme Xenien* II (1820: Ger. gentle reminders): *Wie das Gestirn, / Ohne Hast. / Aber ohne Rast / Drehe sich jeder / Um die eige Last* (Ger. As the stars, without haste, without rest, turn each to one's own load). Huxley wrote to his sister that the passage was "my favourite motto."

Adelaide Anne Procter (1825–64)

Daughter of Anne Benson Skepper (1800–88) and Bryan Waller Procter (1787–1874), a London lawyer and poet who used the pseudonym "Barry Cornwall," Procter was part of the London literary scene from an early age. Educated in languages, literature, mathematics, and music, she was widely published and enormously popular, both in Britain and the United States. She was active in reform movements and on behalf of women's education, work, and rights. She converted to Roman Catholicism in 1851. Under the pseudonym "Miss Mary Berwick" she began publishing in Dickens's *Household Words* in 1853 and later in *All the Year Round*. Her *Legends and Lyrics* (1858; later edition in 1866 with an introduction by Dickens) was dedicated to the social activist Matilda Hays (c.1820–97), with whom it is now thought she had a love affair.

Proctor and Hays, along with Bessie Parkes (1829–1925) and Emily Faithfull (1835–95), started the Victoria Press (1860) for women to print the *English Woman's Journal*. For that press Procter edited a collection of women writers, *Victoria Regia* (1861). Shortly after, she died from tuberculosis. Queen Victoria's favourite poet, she often wrote sentimental and pious verse but also could use ironic questioning of commonplaces, often for social and political ends on behalf of the poor and homeless, or against the doctrine of separate spheres for men and women. No standard edition. *Poems: Complete Edition* (1858; with an introduction by Dickens); Gill Gregory, *The Life and Work of Adelaide Procter: Poetry, Feminism, and Fathers* (1998). "Adelaide Anne Proctor": http://gerald-massey.org.uk/procter/index.htm.

Envy[1]

He was the first always: Fortune
   Shone bright in his face.
I fought for years; with no effort
   He conquer'd the place:
We ran; my feet were all bleeding,   5
   But he won the race.

Spite of his many successes,
   Men loved him the same;
My one pale ray of good-fortune
   Met scoffing and blame;   10
When we err'd, they gave him pity,
   But me—only shame.

My home was still in the shadow,
   His lay in the sun:
I long'd in vain: what he ask'd for   15
   It straightway was done.

Notes

ADELAIDE ANNE PROCTER
[1] *title* first printed in *Household Words* (12 Mar. 1859); reprinted in *Legends and Lyrics: Second Volume* (1866).

Once I staked all my heart's treasure,
　　We played—and he won.

Yes, and just now I have seen him,
　　Cold, smiling, and blest,　　　　　　　　　　　　　　20
Laid in his coffin. God help me!
　　While he is at rest,
I am cursed still to live:—even
　　Death loved him the best.

A Woman's Question[2]

Before I trust my fate to thee,
　　Or place my hand in thine,
Before I let thy future give
　　Colour and form to mine,—
Before I peril all for thee, question thy soul to-night, for me.　　　　　5

I break all slighter bonds, nor feel
　　One shadow of regret:
Is there one link within the past
　　That holds thy spirit yet?
Or is thy faith as clear and free as that which I can pledge to thee?　　　10

Does there within thy dimmest dreams
　　A possible future shine,
Wherein thy life could henceforth breathe,
　　Untouched, unshared by mine?
If so, at any pain or cost, O tell me before all is lost!　　　　　15

Look deeper still. If thou canst feel,
　　Within thy inmost soul
That thou hast kept a portion back,
　　While I have staked the whole,
Let no false pity spare the blow, but, in true mercy, tell me so.　　　20

Is there within thy heart a need
　　That mine cannot fulfil?
One chord that any other hand
　　Could better wake or still?
Speak now, lest at some future day, my whole life wither and decay.　　　25

Notes

[2] *title* first published anonymously in *Household Words* (6 Feb. 1858); reprinted *Legends and Lyrics: A Book of Verses* (1858), with an additional final stanza:

Nay, answer not—I dare not hear,
　　The words would come too late;

Yet I would spare thee all remorse,
　　So, comfort thee, my Fate;—

Whatever on my heart may fall,—remember,
　　I *would* risk it all!

Lives there, within thy nature hid,
    The demon-spirit, Change,
Shedding a passing glory still
    On all things new and strange?
It may not be thy fault alone, but shield my heart against thy own.   30

Couldst thou withdraw thy hand one day
    And answer to my claim
That fate, and that to-day's mistake,
    Not thou, had been to blame?
Some soothe their conscience thus; but thou—O surely thou, wilt warn me now!   35

A Woman's Answer[3]

I will not let you say a Woman's part
Must be to give exclusive love alone;
Dearest, although I love you so, my heart
Answers a thousand claims beside your own.

I love—what do I not love? earth and air   5
Find space within my heart, and myriad things
You would not deign to heed, are cherished there,
And vibrate on its very inmost strings.

I love the summer with her ebb and flow
Of light, and warmth, and music that have nurst   10
Her tender buds to blossoms .. and you know
It was in summer that I saw you first.

I love the winter dearly too, .. but then
I owe it so much; on a winter's day,
Bleak, cold, and stormy, you returned again,   15
When you had been those weary months away.

I love the Stars like friends; so many nights
I gazed at them, when you were far from me,
Till I grew blind with tears .. those far-off lights
Could watch you, whom I longed in vain to see.   20

I love the Flowers; happy hours lie
Shut up within their petals close and fast:
You have forgotten, dear: but they and I
Keep every fragment of the golden Past.

Notes

[3] *title* first published in *Legends and Lyrics: A Book of Verses: Second Volume* (1861).

I love, too, to be loved; all loving praise   25
Seems like a crown upon my Life,—to make
It better worth the giving, and to raise
Still nearer to your own the heart you take.

I love all good and noble souls;—I heard
One speak of you but lately, and for days   30
Only to think of it, my soul was stirred
In tender memory of such generous praise.

I love all those who love you; all who owe
Comfort to you: and I can find regret
Even for those poorer hearts who once could know,   35
And once could love you, and can now forget.

Well, is my heart so narrow—I, who spare
Love for all these? Do I not even hold
My favourite books in special tender care,
And prize them as a miser does his gold?   40

The Poets that you used to read to me
While summer twilights faded in the sky;
But most of all I think Aurora Leigh,[4]
Because—because—do you remember why?

Will you be jealous? Did you guess before   45
I loved so many things?—Still you the best:—
Dearest, remember that I love you more,
Oh, more a thousand times than all the rest!

A Lost Cord[5]

Seated one day at the Organ
      I was weary, and ill at ease,
And my fingers wandered idly
      Over the noisy keys.

I do not know what I was playing,   5
      Or what I was dreaming then,
But I struck one chord of music,
      Like the sound of a great Amen.

Notes

[4] *Leigh* novel-length poem by Elizabeth Barrett Browning (1856).

[5] *title* a very popular poem, it was set to music as "The Lost Chord" (1877) by Sir Arthur Sullivan (1842–1900), composed at the bedside of his dying brother Frederic, an actor and singer. A recording of Sullivan's song by Enrico Caruso (1873–1921) was made at the Metropolitan Opera in New York on 29 April 1912. That evening he sang it again at a benefit for the families of the *Titanic*, which sank on 15 April 1912: http://www.youtube.com/watch?v=O9I1R8TK-yc&list=RD03MeXhXM7_lro. See LITERATURE: NEW TECHNOLOGIES, AURAL CULTURE (WEB p. 160). First published in the *English Woman's Journal* (1 Mar. 1860), signed "A. A. P"; republished in *Legends and Lyrics: A Book of Verses: Second Volume* (1861).

It flooded the crimson twilight
    Like the close of an Angel's Psalm,   10
And it lay on my fevered spirit
    With a touch of infinite calm.

It quieted pain and sorrow
    Like love overcoming strife;
It seemed the harmonious echo   15
    From our discordant life.

It linked all perplexèd meanings
    Into one perfect peace,
And trembled away into silence,
    As if it were loth to cease.   20

I have sought, and I seek it vainly,
    That one lost chord divine,
That came from the soul of the Organ
    And entered into mine.

It may be that Death's bright Angel   25
    Will speak in that chord again—
It may be that only in Heaven,
    I shall hear that grand Amen.

A Woman's Last Word[6]

Well—the links are broken,
    All is past;
This farewell, when spoken,
    Is the last.
I have tried and striven   5
    All in vain;
Such bonds must be riven,
    Spite of pain,
And never, never, never
    Knit again.   10

So I tell you plainly,
    It must be:
I shall try, not vainly,
    To be free;
Truer, happier chances   15
    Wait me yet,
While you, through fresh fancies,
    Can forget;—
And life has nobler uses
    Than Regret.   20

Notes

[6] *title* a response to Robert Browning's "A Woman's Last Word" from *Men and Women* (1855), in the same metre, though Procter extends his quatrains to ten-line stanzas. First published in *Legends and Lyrics: Second Volume* (1861).

All past words retracing,
    One by one,
Does not help effacing
    What is done.
Let it be. O, stronger   25
    Links can break!
Had we dreamed still longer
    We could wake,—
Yet let us part in kindness
    For Love's sake.   30

Bitterness and sorrow
    Will at last,
In some bright to-morrow,
    Heal their past
But future hearts will never   35
    Be as true
As mine was—is ever,
    Dear, for you..
.. Then must we part, when loving
    As we do?   40

Eliza Harriet Keary (1827–1918)

Born in Yorkshire into a clergy family, Keary was the daughter of William Keary (d. 1856), rector of Bilton, and his wife Lucy Plumer (d. 1869). She lived in Nunnington, Yorkshire, and later in Clifton, near Bristol. Keary collaborated with her older sister, Anna Maria, (1825–79) in publishing children's stories such as *The Heroes of Asgard* (1857) and *Little Wanderlin and Other Fairy Tales* (1865). The sisters travelled to Egypt in 1858, and after returning to London helped run a home for young unemployed female servants. In her collection *Little Seal-Skin and Other Poems* (1874) she experimented in many genres, becoming an expert in the sonnet and dramatic monologue. She also published three volumes of Bible selections and various stories for children, including *The Magic Valley* (1877), *Pets and Playmates* (1887), and, with her niece, Maud Keary, *Enchanted Tulips and Other Verses for Children* (1914). No standard edition.

Disenchanted[1]

I took my heart up in my hand,
    I climbed the hill,
That superb height on which you stand;
    And my strung will
Found only sweet   5
The labour that it was to reach your feet.

Notes ———————————————————————

Eliza Harriet Keary
[1] title from *Little Seal-Skin and Other Poems* (1874).

I poured my life out at your feet;
    I almost ceased
To breathe or be; my heart scarce beat;
    No flutter teased   10
My calm; strength fast
Struck through my soul, that worshipped, loved, at last.

But then I looked up at your face,
    And your self spoke;
My stung soul shuddered from its place   15
    As my love broke
Wild from its chain,
And rebegotten in the womb of pain.

I dragged my life up from the ground,
    And went forth bare,   20
(I had not found, I had not found)
    Through sharp, stern air
Alone I went,
Alone I go, through vast abandonment.

Renunciation[2]

Away, little tender heart from me, away!
I will not keep
Thee fluttering in the cage I made so strong,
My love, that should have held thee long!
Thee, aye!   5
Thou didst lie quietly once, asleep;
Awake, dost beat
Against the golden wires.
Oh! stay, panting dear pain upon my passion—fires
That scare thee so.   10
Lo! they shall part and free thee, sweet.
One life's-drop on thy wing—
A sting?—Yes, that might break so frail a thing—
No, no; no, no;—fly free!
See, I can bear the smart for thee;   15
Will thee no ill.
Little trembling heart, from me away!

A Mother's Call[3]

Come back, sons, over the sea!
Strong limbs I bore,
Ye are mine still!

Notes

[2] title from *Little Seal-Skin and Other Poems* (1874).   [3] title from *Little Seal-Skin and Other Poems* (1874).

Do you rise, do you move to me?
Do you hear there, across the tossing brine,   5
Sons?—for the great seas swell;
I smell the breath of them, I hear the roar of them,
Leaping, tossing, toppling over one another,
Lapping up to the shore,
Lashing the rock—furies,   10
What do they come for?
Sires of yours, yearsfull agonies—
Home with a wild lament?
Seas, is it this you bear?
No. But the times that come,   15
And the thunders I hear,
And the rent wide apart in her garment
That covered us, blinded us, wound us—
Chains ground that bound us,
That gyved us, sword that drank at our heart!   20
Leap to the rock, waves!
Leap to the land, sons, O braves!
Over graves, upon blood-trodden graves
Plant your feet!
Come, times, God-revenge,   25
Slow, sure, complete!

Old Age[4]

Such a wizened creature,
    Sitting alone;
    Every kind of ugliness thrown
Into each feature.

"I wasn't always so,"   5
    Said the wizened
    One; "sweet motions unimprisoned
Were mine long ago."

And again, "I shall be—
    At least something   10
    Out of this outside me, shall wing
Itself fair and free."

A Portrait[5]

A face tender and wise,
God, what power to bless in the pure eyes!
All that perfect grace,

Notes

[4] title from *Little Seal-Skin and Other Poems* (1874).   [5] title from *Little Seal-Skin and Other Poems* (1874).

With no place for "I" or for "mine";
But a look straight out   5
On us weak, strewn all about;
A desire to bear, and to bear, and to bear,
A fire kept steady, and strong, and clear;
A prayer to be let near
Unto distress most dire.   10
Arm, O so weak, that would wield
A sword for the world, or a shield—
Would embrace the whole world from harm.
Little arm, ah! but one caress,
To bless me, sweet face, but one charm!   15

Samuel Laycock (1826–93)

Born near Marsden in Yorkshire, the third child of John Laycock (1791–1861), a handloom weaver, and his wife, Sarah France (1791–1860), Laycock was educated only at the Sunday School of the local Independent Chapel. He began working in a woollen mill at age 9, and continued in a cotton mill at Stalybridge, to where the family had moved in 1837. His first wife, Martha Broadbent, died after only two year's of marriage (1852), and in 1858 he married again, to Hannah Woolley. He had already begun to write and publish poetry in 1855 in broadsheets. In the cotton famine during the American Civil War (1861–65), he became unemployed, and turned increasingly to publishing dialect poetry about ordinary lives: *Lancashire Rhymes or, Homely Pictures of the People* (1864) and *Lancashire Songs* (1866). Laycock's wife died in 1863 and he married again in 1864 to Eliza Pontefract. He became the librarian at Stalybridge Mechanics' Institute (1865–67) and then at Whitworth Institute, Fleetwood. His last career was as a photographer. His final collection was *Warblin's fro' an Owd Songster* (1893), published just before his death. No standard edition. See *The Collected Writings of John Laycock*, ed. George Milner (second edition 1908); *Selected Poems: Samuel Laycock*, ed. Glyn Hughes (1991). Samuel Laycock site at Gerald Massey page: http://gerald-massey.org.uk/laycock/index.htm.

To My Owd Friend, Thomas Kenworthy[1]

These strokes come thick an' heavy, mon;°   °man
But bear 'em bravely iv° tha con,   °if
    Brother Bard.
Tha's° had thi share o' grief, aw° know,   °thou has °I

Notes

SAMUEL LAYCOCK

[1] *title* Thomas Kenworthy (d. 1869) was known as the Dukinfield Poet. Dukinfield is a small town about 9.5 km east of Manchester. It was heavily industrialized in the nineteenth century with the excavation of coal, and later with fourteen cotton mills; it was also a centre of Chartist agitation. A little further to the east is Stalybridge, and it was there, about 1866 in the Mechanics' Institute, that there was a benefit for Kenworthy at which John Critchly Prince (1808–66), Ben Brierley (1825–96), and Edwin Waugh (1817–90) read poems and Laycock, librarian at the Mechanics' Institute, read this tribute. From *Warblin's Fro' an Owd Songster* (1893) reprinted in *Collected Writings* (1908), our text.

An' fowt° loife's° battles here below 5 °fought °life's
    Long an' hard.

That yead° o' thine is gettin' gray; °head
Aw see it's lateish on i' th' day
    Wi' thee, lad.
But come, cheer up, mon, things ull mend, 10
Aw dunno loike to see a friend
    Lookin' sad.

One's had their cares as weel as thee;
Tha's noan° had mony° moor nor me, °no one °many
    That awm sure. 15
But, then, tha knows there's nob'dy beawt,° °without
So th' ills we conno get witheawt
    Let's endure.

O sickness, death, want, grief, an' care,
There's some foalks get a biggish share— 20
    Moor than's sweet.
It's noan so pleasant kissin' th' rod;²
But come, mon, put thi trust i' God,
    He'll do reet.° °right

Tha's noan so fur° to tramp, owd° friend, 25 °far °old
Tha's welly° reach'd thi journey's end; °almost
    Trudge along.
Thi fiddle's mony a toime bin strung,
An' aw've noa deawt bo° what tha's sung °doubt but
    Mony a song. 30

But neaw,° owd mon, thi days are few, °now
So iv there's owt° tha has to do, °aught, anything
    Do it soon;
An' th' bit o' toime tha has to stop,
Get ready for another shop° 35 °place
    Up aboon.° °above

John Bull an' His Tricks!³

Oh, forshame on thi, John! forshame on thi, John!
    Tha murderin' owd thief 'at theaw art:
Tha'rt a burnin' disgrace to humanity, mon,

Notes

² *rod* before and/or after corporal punishment by whipping with a birch rod, Victorian school children were often required to "kiss the rod," a sign of submission to authority.

³ *title* the poem is addressed to John Bull, a personification of Britain, first introduced in 1712 by John Arbuthnot (1667–1735), British satirist and friend of Pope and Swift. John Bull came to be regarded as a country squire, dressed in a Union Jack waistcoat, top hat and tails and white breeches, fond of beer and conservative politics. Here "John" is attacked for his hypocrisy and exploitation in various efforts to promote resettlement schemes in the

Tho' theaw thinks thisel'° clever an' smart. °thyself
Tha'rt a beggar° for sendin' eawt° Bibles an' beer, 5 °bugger °out
    An' co-in° it "Civilisation";[4] °calling
While thee an' thi dear christian countrymen here,
    Are chettin'° an' lyin' like station.[5] °cheating

Thee tak' my advoice, John, an' get a good brush,
    An' sweep well abeawt thi own door; 10
An' put th' bit o' th' lond at tha's stown° to some use, °stolen
    'Ere theaw offers to steal ony moor.
An' let th' heathens a-be; for tha's no need to fear
    'At they're loikely to get into hell:[6]
My opinion is this, if there's onyone near 15
    A place o' that mack,° it's thisel'. °kind

It's thee 'at aw meon,° John, theaw hypocrite, theaw; °mean
    Wi' thi Sundayfied, sanctified looks!
Doesta think 'at o° th' milk comes fro' th' paps o' thy ceaw!° °all °cow
    Is o th' wisdom beawnd° up i' thy books! 20 °bound
An' what abeawt th' mixture o' cotton an' clay,[7]
    'At theaw thrusts on thi unwillin' neighbours?
Eh John, tha'rt a "Cure,"[8] but tha'll catch it some day,
    When tha's ended these damnable labours.

Tha may weel tell the Lord what a wretch theaw art, John, 25
    For tha poos° a long face on a Sunday; °pulls
An', to prove what tha says, tha does o 'at° tha con °all that
    To rob thi poor neighbours on th' Monday.
What business has theaw to go battin' thi wings.
    An' crowin' on other folks middin?° 30 °dung-heap
Doesta think thi black brothers sich mean cringin' things
    As to give up the'r whoams° at thy biddin'? °homes

Notes

British Colonies. One of the most active promoters was Edward Gibbon Wakefield (1796–1862), who promoted settlement in New Zealand (1838–39), Australia, and Canada (through the Durham Report of 1839, of which he was a partial architect, and which became a model for British colonial policy). The Indian Mutiny (1857–58) had resulted in the British taking over from the East India Company in India (1858). In 1862 J. S. Mill published "Of the Government of Dependencies by a Free State." The poem seems to have been written when the context of "the cure" was in vogue (see n. 8). Published in *Warblin's Fro' an Owd Songster* (1893) and reprinted in *The Collected Writings of Samuel Laycock* (1908), our text.

[4] *civilisation* Laycock mentions all three "Cs" that were part of the imperial mission of British colonial expansion in the nineteenth century: "Civilisation," Christianity ("Bibles"), and commerce ("beer").

[5] *like station* (Lancashire dial. as hard or as fast as he could).

[6] *Hell* Laycock takes a liberal Christian viewpoint here, that pagans who have not heard the Christian message do not go to Hell as most Christian missionaries taught. Laycock takes the same position in other poems, such as "Th' Pulpit an' th' Pews" (1893): "An' this is th' greawnd wheer th' parson stands! / An' th' trash is sent to foreign lands!"

[7] *clay* cotton goods from the mills of Manchester and the Midlands, and clay made into pottery and hard-fired bricks for building, as well as glass products from similar kilns from such centres as Bristol, were major nineteenth-century exports.

[8] *cure* a pun on medical remedy for a disease, especially syphilis, which British soldiers and sailors were believed to have exported to the colonies in the 1860s (see GENDER: WOMAN QUESTION; MARTINEAU, "MANIFESTO"). The other meaning of "cure" is a slang abbreviation for "curious" or "curiosity," hence "an odd or eccentric person; a funny fellow" (*OED*): "It appears to have obtained vogue largely from a Music Hall song [by F. C. Perry] with the chorus 'The cure, the cure, the perfect cure' ... popular in 1862" (*OED*).

An' tha's th' cheek to thank God, when tha meets wi' success,
    As iv° He stooped to sanction sich wark!°   °if °work
Neaw one would ha' thowt 'at tha couldn't ha' done less   35
    Than to keep sich loike actions i' th' dark.
Iv tha meons° to go on wi' committin' these sins—   °means
    Sins tha'll ne'er get weshed eawt or forgiven,—
Tha should try to keep matters as quiet as tha con,
    An' ne'er let em' know up i' heaven.   40

Tha wur allus a bull-yead,° i' thi best o' thi days;   °bull-headed
    An' this o thi neighbours must know;
An', tho' tha seems pious, an' pulls a long face,
    They con manage to see through it o.°   °all
But when tha goes sneakin' an' tries to che't° God,   45 °cheat
    It strikes me tha'rt goin' to' far.
Aw'm noan mitch surprised at thi impudence, John;
    Aw'm only surprised heaw tha dar'!°   °dare

What business has theaw to be sendin' eawt thieves,
    To steal slices off other folks' bread?   50
It would look better on thi to rowl up thi sleeves,
    An' work for thi livin' instead.
Aw' tell thi what, John—an' tak' notice o' this—
    Tha ne'er knew a nation to thrive,
Wheer th' bees preferred feightin' to good honest wark;—   55
    They're like drones stealin' honey fro' th' hive!

Iv tha's th' sense ov a jackass tha'll tarry awhoam,
    An' keep th' own garden i' fettle;
But tha'd rather be eawt wi' thi Bible an' gun,
    An' robbin' some other mon's kettle.°   60 °cattle
Neaw drop these mean tricks, this contemptible wrong,
    An' behave a bit more loike a mon;
Or aw'll gie thee another warm dose before long,
    For aw'm gradely° ashamed on thi, John!   °thoroughly

Emily Pfeiffer (1827–90)

Daughter of Thomas Richard Davis, an ex-army officer, and the well-to-do Emily Tilsey of Montgomeryshire, Wales, Emily Jane Davis shared in the family's sudden poverty when the bank holding her father's investments failed. Denied formal education, she set out on a programme of self-education, despite her frequent bouts of insomnia and depression. She later took up the cause of women's rights, education, and work in essays for the *Cornhill Magazine* and the *Contemporary Review*, many gathered in *Women and Work* (1888). After a tour of Europe, she married (1850) Jurgen Edward Pfeiffer (d. 1889), a wealthy German-English banker who encouraged her writing and dedication to social reform. In the endowments made after their deaths she was able to establish an orphanage, a drama school, and a residence for university women in Wales, as well as provide other gifts for women's education. After *Gerard's Monument* (1873), she published a book every several years, including poetry

(*Poems*, 1876; *Sonnets and Songs*, 1880; *Flowers of the Night*, 1889), novels in verse (*The Wynnes of Wynhavod*, 1881), travel writing, and papers on social reform. She travelled widely in Eastern Europe, Asia, and North America, writing about her experiences in *Flying Leaves from East and West* (1884). No standard edition; "Orlando Women's Writing Project": http://orlando.cambridge.org/public/svPeople?person_id=pfeiem.

Peace to the Odalisque [I][1]

Peace to the odalisque, the facile slave,
Who uninvidious love rewards the brave,
Or cherishes the coward; she who yields
Her lord the fief of waste, uncultur'd fields
To perish in non-using: she whose hour   5
Is measur'd by her beauties' transient flower;
Who lives in him, as he in God, and dies
The death of parasites, no more to rise.
Graceful ephemera! Fair morning dream
   Of the young world! In vain would women's hearts   10
In love with sacrifice, withstand the stream
   Of human progress; other spheres, new parts
Await them. God be with them in their quest—
Our brave, sad working-women of the west!

[Peace to the Odalisque II]

Peace to the odalisque, whose morning glory
Is vanishing, to live alone in story.
Firm in her place, a dull-rob'd figure stands
With wistful eyes, and earnest, grappling hands:
The working-woman, she whose soul and brain—   5
Her tardy right—is bought with honest pain.
Oh woman! sacrifice may still be thine—
More fruitful than the souls ye did resign
To sated masters; from your lives, so real,
Shall shape itself a pure and high ideal,   10
That ye shall seek with sad, wide-open eyes,
Till, finding nowhere, baffled love shall rise
To higher planes, where passion may look pale,
But charity's white light shall never fail.

Notes

EMILY PFEIFFER
[1] *title* an odalisque (Turkish *Odalik*, chambermaid) was a servant to the concubines and wives in the imperial harem of the Ottoman Empire. In the later eighteenth- and nineteenth-century cult of Orientalism, harem topics became popular, as in Mozart's opera *The Abduction from the Seraglio* (1782), and such paintings of voluptuous nudes as *La Grande Odalisque* (1814) by Auguste Dominique Ingres (1780–1867). See MILL, "n. 24; see also CONDITION: SOCIAL FORMATION, n. 5. By the end of the nineteenth century the term was beginning to refer to the kept mistress of a wealthy philanderer. Here her exotic image of luxuriant surroundings and indolent composure is contrasted with the working woman. First published in *Gerard's Monument and Other Poems* (1873).

Emily Pfeiffer

Any Husband to Many a Wife[2]

I scarcely know my worthless picture,
  As seen in those soft eyes and clear;
But oh, dear heart, I know the stricture fear
  You pass on it when none are near.

Deep eyes that smiling give denial   5
  To tears that you have shed in vain;
Fond heart that summoned on my trial,
  Upbraids the witness of its pain

Eyes, tender eyes, betray me never!
  Still hold the flattered image fast   10
Whereby I shape the fond endeavour
  To justify your faith at last.

Studies from the Antique

Kassandra I[3]

Virgin of Troy,[4] the days were well with thee
  When wandering singing by the singing streams
  Of Ilion, thou beheld'st the golden gleams
Of the bold sun that might not facèd be,
Come murmuring to thy feet caressingly;   5
  But best that day when, steeped in noontide dreams,
  The young Apollo wrapped thee in his beams,
And quenched his love in thine as in a sea!
And later, in thy tower[5] 'twas sweet to teach
  The loveless night the joys high day had known;   10
To dream, to wake—and find thy love impeach
  Late sleep with kisses, and thy spirit flown
To his, and at the ivory gates[6] of speech
  Breaking in[7] words as burning as his own.

Notes

[2] *title* a riposte to Robert Browning's "Any Wife to Any Husband" (in *Men and Women*, 1855), as would be, much later, Adrienne Rich's "Any Husband to Any Wife" (1965). The poem is one of many Victorian "mirror" poems in which a speaker looks into a mirror or its equivalent (here, another's eyes) to (mis-)read character, motive, or response; see, for instance, TENNYSON, "THE LADY OF SHALOTT"; and DANTE ROSSETTI, "WILLOWWOOD" sonnets (WEB p. 412). First published in *Flowers of the Night* (1889).

[3] *title* Kassandra (English spelling, Cassandra), daughter of Priam and Hecuba of Troy, was loved by Apollo, god of the sun, who granted her the gift of prophecy. But when she spurned him, he cursed her so that she would never be believed. Hence she fruitlessly predicts the danger of

the Trojan horse in the Greek defeat of Troy and the death of Agamemnon on the heroes' return to Mycenae after the Trojan War (retold in Aeschylus's *Agamemnon*). The first three of these sonnets were printed in *Quarterman's Grace and Other Poems* (1879); the fourth sonnet was added to them in *Songs and Sonnets* (1880), our text.

[4] *Troy* the capital city in north-west Anatolia (Hisarlik in modern Turkey) known as Troja (in the region of Troas), or Ilium or Ilion, from which Homer derives the name of his epic, the *Iliad*.

[5] *tower* in which Cassandra was imprisoned by Apollo.

[6] *gates* teeth.

[7] *in* into.

Emily Pfeiffer

Kassandra II[8]

How far from Ilion, and how far from joy,
    Captive[9] Kassandra, wert thou, when in sight
    Of conquering Greece thou satest on thy height
Of shame—a waif from out the wreck of Troy!
Thine still the burning word, but slave's employ   5
    Had from thy trembling lips effacèd quite
    The kisses of the god, and heaven's light
Now shone upon thee only to destroy.
For thee, sun-stricken one, th' abysmal sties
    Of sin lay open as the secret grave—   10
Things of which speech seemed madness—while thy cries
    On wronged Apollo lost the way to save;
Till at the last, the faith of upturned eyes
    Brought him to right, as death to free the slave.

Klytemnestra I[10]

Daughter of gods and men, great ruling will,
    Seething in oily rage within the sphere
    Which gods and men assign the woman here,
'Till, stricken where the wound[11] approved thee still
Mother and mortal, all the tide of ill   5
    Rushed through the gap, and nothing more seemed dear
    But power to wreak high ruin, nothing clear
But the long dream you waited to fulfil.
Mother and spouse—queen of the king of men[12]—
    What fury[13] brought Ægysthus to thy side—   10
That bearded semblant, man to outward ken,
    But else mere mawworm,[14] made to fret man's pride;
Woman, thy foot was on thy tyrant then—
    Mother, thou wert avenged for love defied !

Notes

[8] title first printed in *Quarterman's Grace and Other Poems* (1879); see n. 3.

[9] Cassandra was part of Agamemnon's spoils of war, and he took her with him back to Greece and Mycenae, where she predicted his murder and urged him not to enter his palace to his death, but her prophecy was not believed.

[10] title Klytemnestra (Eng. Clytemnestra) was the daughter of Zeus and Leda and the wife of Agamemnon, the commander of the Greeks in the Trojan War. When Agamemnon left, he was informed by the soothsayer Calchas that Artemis demanded he sacrifice his daughter Iphigeneia to secure favourable winds to sail to Troy; meanwhile Clytemnestra took her husband's cousin Aegisthus as her partner, and when Agamemnon returned after ten years, Clytemnestra and Aegisthus murdered him.

[11] wound the sacrifice of her daughter, Iphigeneia.

[12] king of men Homer's epithet for Agamemnon.

[13] fury in Greek mythology, the Furies (Gk. *Erinyes*, the angry ones) were godesses of vengeance for patricide and matricide; in Aeschylus' *Eumenides* (458 BCE; his plays underlie these four sonnets), they pursue Orestes to avenge the death of his father, Agamemnon, at the hands of his mother, Clytemnestra, by killing her. The Furies continue to pursue Orestes to Athens where he invokes Athene, who calls in Athenian citizens to judge between the claims of Orestes and the Erinyes. The tie vote goes to Orestes, and the Furies are appeased and renamed Eumenides (Gk. the kindly ones). Virgil (*Aeneid* 6. 250) gave three of them names and functions: Alecto (unremitting); Megaera (jealous or grudging), and Tisiphone (the avenger of murder).

[14] mawworm a parasitic intestinal worm, derived from a character in *The Hypocrite* (1769) by Isaac Bickerstaffe (1733–1812), Irish playwright.

Klytemnestra II[15]

Woman and Greek—so doubly trained in art!—
    Spreading the purple[16] for the conqueror's tread,
    Bowing with feline grace thy royal head—
How perfect whelp-robbed lioness thy part!
One wrong the more to wring the ancient smart,   5
    Then three swift strokes, and the slow hope blooms red,
    Who shamed the hero lays him with the dead,
Where nevermore his word may vex her heart.
Bold queen, what were to thee the gods of Greece?
    What had been any god of any name,   10
More than the lion-heart you made to cease,
    Or the live dog[17] to all your humours tame?—
The very furies left your soul in peace
    Until Orestes' sword drave home their claim.

Ellen Johnston (c.1827–74)

According to her autobiography, Johnston was born in Hamilton, Lanarkshire, Scotland, a village just outside Dundee, the daughter of a stonemason, James Johnston, and his wife, Mary Bilsland. She entered Monteith's muslin mill at Anderston, at the age of 11 to learn power-loom weaving, and continued to work in various mills in Glasgow, Belfast (1857–59), Manchester (1859), and Dundee (c.1861–67). She became well known as Scotch Nell, "The Factory Girl," through her poetic contributions to working-class newspapers such as the Glasgow *Penny Post*, gathering them into her collections with her short autobiography in 1867. Ill health and consequent loss of work led to parish outdoor relief and occasional time in the workhouse, despite £50 from the Royal Bounty Fund, and a personal gift of £5 from Queen Victoria (1868). Her death is recorded in the Barony Poorhouse in Glasgow as "Helen" Johnston on 20 April 1874. Unlike many working-class writers, Johnston often praises mills and factory work, and contradictorily writes both patriotic and radical verse, and as well uses conventional sentimentality and class and gender inversion of literary roles; her dialect verse is often poignant, savagely satiric, and witty. In Johnston's lowland Scots dialect, *ae, au,* and *a* in dialect words usually signify a short *o*. No standard edition: *Autobiography, Poems, and Songs of Ellen Johnston, the "Factory Girl"* (1867; second edition 1869); Florence Boos, "The 'Queen' of the 'Far-Famed Penny Post': 'The Factory Girl Poet' and Her Audience," *Women's Writing* 10:3 (2003): 503–26; H. Gustav Klaus, *Factory Girl: Ellen Johnston and Working-Class Poetry in Victorian Scotland* (1998); H. Gustav Klaus, "New Light on Ellen Johnston" *Notes and Queries* 55 (Dec. 2008): 430–33.

Notes

[15] *title* first published in *Songs and Sonnets* (1880), our text; see n. 3.
[16] *purple* in Aeschylus' *Agamemnon* (458 BCE) purple carpets are spread for the return of Agamemnon, and Cassandra urges Agamemnon not to walk on them, but in an act of hubris, he does so.
[17] *dog* Aegisthus.

The Working Man

The spring is come at last, my freens,° cheer up, you sons of toil,   °friends
Let the seeds of independence be sown in labour's soil,
And tho' the nipping blast of care should blight your wee bit° crop,   °food
Oh dinna° let your spirits sink, cling closer aye° to hope.   °do not °always

If youth and health be on your side, you ha'e a richer boon   5
Than him that's dressed in royal robes and wears a diamond crown;
Nae widow's curse lies in your cup, you bear nae orphan's blame;
Nae guilty conscience haunts your dreams wi' visions of the slain.

Tho' light your purse, and worn your coat the darkest hour of night,
Is whiles the very ane° that is before it dawns daylight;   °one   10
And tho' your lot looks unco° hard, your future prospects drear,   °very
Hope's sun may burst through sorrow's cloud, your sinking soul to cheer.

The summer's drawing near, my freens, cheer up ye sons of toil,
Let the sun of independence aye greet ye wi' a smile;
His genial beams will light your hearth when it is mirk° wi' care,   °dark   15
When ye ha'e little for to spend, and far less for to spare.

Let him that ne'er kent° labour's yoke but come to Glasgow toon,   °knew
And let him take a cannie° walk her bonny buildings roon,   °careful, slow
And let him wi' his lady hands, his cheeks sae° pale and wan,   °so
Stand face to face, without a blush, before the Working Man.   20

But the man who wins fair fortune wi' labour's anxious pain,
He is the man who's justly earned her favour and her fame;
And may he aye keep flourishing wherever he may gang,°   °go
And ne'er forget the days that gane when but a Working Man.

The harvest soon will be, my freens, cheer up, you sons of toil,   25
And the fu'some hand of plenty will store your domicile;
Ye are the sons of nature's art, aye forming some new plan,
Oh what would bonny Scotland do without the Working Man?

The Last Sark[1]

Written in 1859

Gude° guide me, are you hame° again, an' ha'e ye got nae wark,   °good [God] °home
We've naething noo tae put awa'° unless yer auld blue sark;   °now to pawn
My head is rinnin' roon about far lichter° than a flee—   °lighter
What care some gentry if they're weel though a' the puir wad dee!   °poor would die

Notes

ELLEN JOHNSTON
[1] *title* a dramatic monologue in which only the man's blue
  working shirt (sark) is left to sell for food.

Our merchants an' mill masters they wad never want° a meal,   °lack 5
Though a'° the banks in Scotland wad for a twelvemonth fail;   °all
For some o' them have far mair goud° than ony ane° can see—   °more gold °any one
What care some gentry if they're weel though a' the puir wad dee!

This is a funny warld, John, for it's no divided fair,
And whiles° I think some o' the rich have got the puir folk's share,   °sometimes 10
Tae see us starving here the nicht° wi' no ae bless'd bawbee° —   °tonight °Scottish ha'penny
What care some gentry if they're weel though a' the puir wad dee!

Oor hoose ance° bean an' cosey, John; oor beds ance snug an warm   °once
Feels unco° cauld an' dismal noo, an' empty as a barn;   °extremely
The weans° sit greeting° in oor face, and we ha'e noucht° to gie—   °wee ones °crying 15
What care some gentry if they're weel though a' the puir wad dee!   [°have nothing

It is the puir man's hard-won toil that fills the rich man's purse;
I'm sure his gouden° coffers they are het° wi' mony a curse;   °golden °hot
Were it no for the working men what wad the rich men be?
What care some gentry if they're weel though a' the puir wad dee!   20

My head is licht, my heart is weak, my een° are growing blin';   °eyes
The bairn° is faen' aff° my knee—oh! John, catch haud o' him,   °child °fallen off
You ken° I hinna° tasted meat for days far mair than three;   °know °have not
Were it no for my helpless bairns I wadna care to dee.

Nelly's Lament for the Pirnhouse Cat,

Killed by the Elevator, C—e Factory, Dundee[2]

Oh! fare-ye-weel my bonnie cat,
Nae mair I'll smooth yer skin sae black.
Mony a time I stroked yer back,
    Puir wee creator;
Ye've gane yer last lang sleep tae tak'.   5
    The Elevator

Has sent ye aff tae your lang hame,
Whaur hunger ne'er will jag yer wame,°   °jog your belly
Whaur ye shall ne'er put in a claim
    For meal or milk;   10
Yer in the "pond,"[3] free frae a'° blame,   °from all
    Boiled like a whelk.

Notes

[2] *title* a pirn is a bobbin on which the yarn is first wound and then is placed in the shuttle for weaving. The pirnhouse is the building where the bobbins are wound. The C—e Factory is Chapelshade Mill, where Johnston worked for three and a half years before she published her collection in 1867. The elegy, very probably for her own cat, since Johnston was called "Nell" by her co-workers, is in the tradition of Burns's "To a Mouse" (1785), using the same metre, as well as Thomas Gray's "Ode on the Death of a Favourite Cat Drowned in a Tub of Goldfishes" (1748).

[3] *pond* one of the hot ponds used in dyeing at the mill.

Puir hapless beast, what was't that took
Ye hunting into yon dark nook?
Whaur "Death" sat cooring° wi' his hook   °covering   15
       Tae nip yer neck.
I'll think upon yer deein' look
       Wi' sad respect.

My very brain ran roon about
When I saw Archie tak' ye oot,   20
Wi' scalped° pow and bluidy snoot.°   °skinned °nose
       Heigh, when I think,
A stane° tied roon yer neck, nae doot   °stone
       Tae gar° ye sink.   °make

Jist yesterday, my bonnie beast,
I held ye close unto my breast;   25
When, ye as proud as ony priest,
       Did cock yer lug;°   °ear
Syne° aff ye ran tae get a feast   °then
       Frae yer milk mug.   30

But noo nae mair in oor pirnhouse
Ye'll hunt the rats, nor catch a moose,
Nor on the counter sit fu' douse,°   °fully beat
       And mew and yell,
And shoot yer humph° sae prude° and spruce   °please your coal-black °proud 35
       At rhyming Nell.

Your race upon the earth was ran,
Puir puss, ere it was weel began;
Ye've gane whaur beastie, boy, and man
       Are doomed tae go.   40
Omnipotence in His vast plan
       Ordained it so.

There's nane° has deign'd tae mourn ye here,   °no one
Unless mysel' wi' grief sincere;
Though but a cat I'll still revere   45
       Thy worth wi' pity,
And ower yer memory drap a tear,
       Puir we cheetie.°   °cat

Wanted, a Man[4]

Mr. Editor,

I hae a canty° wee housie,   °cheerful
   I've got a' thing, frae pat° to pan;   °pot
And I'm a dainty wee lassie
   Jist wanting a coothie° wee man.   °friendly

Notes

[4] *title* the poem purports to be both an advertisement in the classified ads section of a newspaper, as well as an epistle addressed to the editor of the Glasgow *Penny Post*, where Johnston often published.

Maybe ye winna° believe me,   °will not 5
    But I live a fell° irksome life;   °harsh
Indeed I ne'er will deceive ye,
    I think I wad mak' a guid wife.

I'm guid at making and mending,
    And I can baith bake an' brew: 10
Some think me better at lending
    A han' for tae drink it, I trew.°   °believe

I ken a lad they ca' Johnnie,
    I think, has a notion o' me;
He says I'm wonnerfu' bonnie,   15
    And blythe as a midsummer bee.

That my cheeks are like twa roses,
    That my e'en are a bonnie blue,
Like violets amang sweet posies,
    When kissed wi' the morning dew.   20

When I was just about twenty—
    Last June I was neat° twenty-nine—   °exactly
I could get braw° wooers plenty,   °fine
    But few could I get to my mind.°   °that I liked

Ilk ane° had fauts but Jamie,   °every one 25
    But Jamie saw sad fauts in me;
When he won my puir heart frae me
    He then took a notion tae dee.°   °die

I vowed I'd ne'er coort° anither,   °court
    I'd ne'er be a living man's wife;   30
Noo I jist think it's a haver°   °proper role
    Tae live sae a eerisome° life.   °strange, dismal

Gin° I could get a bit manie°   °if °man-struck
    Aye to welcome hame frae his wark,
And sing him a nice love sangie°   °song 35
    When I wad be clouting° his sark.   °mending

I ken I could mak' him happy,
    If happy he wanted to be;
And whiles gie him a wee drappie°   °drop (of liquor)
    Ilk noo and then in his tea.   40

Folk ca's me a wonnerfu' body,
    Jist as smart as a Pepper ghost;[5]
A drap o' rum punch gars me study
    My muse for the famed Penny Post.[6]

Notes

[5] *ghost* John Henry Pepper (1821–1900), educationist and illusionist, taught popular science at London's Royal Polytechnic from 1847 and at the South Kensington Museum. In 1862 he used an apparatus of mirrors and a

Noo gin ye will send me some chielie°　　　　　　　°young fellow　45
　　Ye think a fit marrow° for me,　　　　　　　　°companion, match
In your poet's corner I'll feel aye
　　Most happy your servant tae be.

The Last Lay of "The Factory Girl"[7]

(Written under severe bodily and mental affliction at Glasgow, in January, 1868)

Farewell, my loved one, fare thee well for ever;[8]
　　I come, my love, to sing thee my last lay;
King Death, ere long, life's silver links will sever,
　　And leave me slumbering in the silent clay.

My heart is fraught with many a secret sorrow—　　　　　　　5
　　With many a care the world may never know;
I sleep to dream of joy, then comes the morrow,
　　With hope deferred, wrapped in wreaths of snow.

I cannot longer live to look upon thee;
　　Still doubting, I may not hope thy heart to gain;　　　　　10
In sad despair, my love, I hasten from thee—
　　We part; oh, Heaven! have I thus loved in vain?

Once I loved thee only as a daughter—
　　Ah! thou wert more than father unto me;
But now, the boundless depths of Lethe's water[9]　　　　　　15
　　Can never quench my boundless love for thee.

Oh! couldst thou know the war that's wildly raging
　　Within this heart that longs thine own to press,
Whilst those bright eyes of thine are still engaging
　　Every pulse with throbs of heavenly bliss.　　　　　　　20

Notes

hidden stage to give an illusion known as "Pepper's ghost" in a presentation of Dickens's *The Haunted Man* (1848) to enormous success; the device was soon incorporated into the machinery of theatres in London, Paris, and New York.

[6] *Post* the Glasgow paper was run from 1860 to 1868 by the radical Alexander Campbell (1796–1870). Johnston often contributed to it under the pseudonym of "The Factory Girl." Campbell also published Johnston's *Autobiography, Poems, and Songs* (1867).

[7] *title* the poem is addressed to her daughter Mary; first published with subtitle at the end of the second edition of her collection (1869). In 1868, when Johnston was still in Glasgow, her daughter, at the age of 16, married a shoemaker, Robert Thomson, in Dundee. The witness of the marriage was the Rev. George Gilfillan (1813–78), writer and Spasmodic poet, who had written a testimonial for

Johnston's collection of 1867. After writing this poem, perhaps her last, Johnston's health and fortunes declined. By 1871 Mary and her husband lived in Glasgow, and her mother lived with them, eventually seeking poor relief in 1873 and 1874, the year of her death. Our text: 1869.

[8] *ever* possible echo of Byron's "Fare Thee Well" (1816), beginning "Fare thee well! and if for ever, / Still for ever, fare thee well," a poem addressed to Annabella (Anne Isabella) Milbanke (1792–1860) whom he had married a year earlier, and by whom he had a child, Augusta Ada. Byron wrote the poem at the time of his formal separation from his wife on 25 April 1816 before leaving England, never to return.

[9] *water* Lethe (Gk. forgetfulness) is one of the rivers of the classical Greek underworld whose waters the dead drank to forget their earthly lives.

Ellen Johnston

'Tis heaven to know that thou didst never doubt me—
　　To dream thou think'st it is for thee I sigh;
'Tis worse than hell, alas! to live without thee;
　　I go, my loved one, far from thee to die.

No other star shall ever light my heaven—　　　　　　　　　25
　　No higher heaven ever shall be mine—
Save thy dear self, till life's last links are riven,
　　And Death his iron chains around me twine.

Thy name shines like a beacon, ever sparkling
　　Radiant beams where mystery sits unveil'd;　　　　　　30
Where Truth lights Error through its waters darkling—
　　Where Persecution thy great aim assail'd.

I go, my loved one, and I leave behind me
　　This gay, green world of splendour, rich and rare;
It hath no other charm but thee to bind me—　　　　　　35
　　I've lived and loved, thy name alone to bear.

Some pitying angel may descend to cheer thee,
　　When thou may'st think I loved thee so to die;
Perchance my spirit still may linger near thee,
　　To guard and guide thee whenever danger's nigh.　　　40

Ah! Scotland's minstrels never more shall hear me
　　Wail forth my woes in page of "Penny Post";[10]
No more her heartless Mammonites[11] shall fear me,
　　Whose gold could never pay the love I've lost.

When this frail form is in the earth reposing,　　　　　　45
　　Live on, still undisturb'd by thoughts of me,
Whilst to the world this requiem is disclosing
　　The worth of one who lived and died for thee.

I go, my loved one, but I leave no token,
　　As I would have done, had fortune smiled on me;　　　50
The sad remembrance of a heart that's broken
　　Is all, my loved one, I can leave to thee.

Stay; I will leave my fame's-crown in thy keeping;
　　Its gems may cheer thee at some future day.
Adieu, my loved one, when I'm calmly sleeping,　　　　　55
　　Sing to the world—'The Factory Girl's Last Lay.'

Notes

[10] *Post* see n. 6.
[11] *Mammonites* worshippers of Mammon, the god of wealth,
　a term of abuse popularized by Carlyle for greedy
　entrepreneurs; see CARLYLE, n. 6.

WEB p. 399

From "Autobiography of Ellen Johnston, 'The Factory Girl'"

George Meredith (1828–1909)

Born in Plymouth, Meredith suffered deprivation when his father, a tailor, declared bankruptcy and had his son made a ward of Chancery to protect a meagre inheritance. At the age of 14 he was sent abroad to Germany for two years; returning to England, he had no further formal education. He was apprenticed to a solicitor but did not practice law, turning to poetry and journalism. In 1849 he married Mary Ellen Nicolls, the widowed daughter of the novelist Thomas Love Peacock (1785–1866). In 1856 Meredith modelled for a painting, *The Death of Chatterton* by the Pre-Raphaelite artist, Henry Wallis (1830–1916). Two years later Meredith's wife ran off with Wallis, dying

three years later. Meredith's unhappy marriage provides a backdrop to his novel *The Ordeal of Richard Feverel* (1859) and his sequence of modified sonnets, *Modern Love* (1862). He married Marie Vulliamy in 1864 and continued writing poetry and novels, notably *The Egoist* (1879) and *Diana of the Crossways* (1885), as well as the influential *Essay on Comedy* (1877). Standard Editions: *The Works of George Meredith* (27 vols, 1911); *The Poems of George Meredith*, ed. Phyllis B. Bartlett (2 vols, 1978); *The Letters of George Meredith*, ed. C. L. Cline, (3 vols, 1970); "George Meredith": http://www.victorianweb.org/authors/meredith/index.html.

WEB p. 402

Modern Love
  Sonnets I–VI
  Sonnet XVII
  Sonnet XXXIII
  Sonnets XLIX–L

Lucifer in Starlight[1]

On a starred night Prince Lucifer uprose.
Tired of his dark dominion swung the fiend
Above the rolling ball[2] in cloud part screened,
Where sinners hugged their spectre of repose.

Notes

GEORGE MEREDITH

[1] *title* Lucifer (Lat. light bearer); the identification of Lucifer with Satan depends upon an interpretation of Isaiah 4: 3–20, an account of the Morning Star as "Lucifer" falling from heaven (see also Isaiah 14: 12–17; Luke 10: 18; and Revelation12: 7–10). The passages from Isaiah were transferred from being a title of the kings of Babylon to Satan,

using the New Testament authorities, in the early Christian writings of Tertullian and Origen in the second century CE. In *Paradise Lost* Milton only rarely refers to Satan as Lucifer. See also Meredith's novel *The Ordeal of Richard Feverel* (1859; revised 1878): When Richard Feverel realizes that his love, Lucy Desborough (Lucy: Lat. light; see above,

Poor prey to his hot fit of pride were those.   5
And now upon his western wing he leaned,
Now his huge bulk o'er Africa careened,
Now the black planet shadowed Arctic snows.
Soaring through wider zones that pricked his scars
With memory of the old revolt from Awe,[3]   10
He reached a middle height, and at the stars,[4]
Which are the brain of heaven, he looked, and sank.
Around the ancient track marched, rank on rank,
The army of unalterable law.

Dante Gabriel Rossetti (1828–82)

Rossetti was born in London into an intensely political and literary family that included his sister, the poet Christina, and his civil-servant brother, William Michael (1829–1919), a writer and editor. His father was Gabriele Pasquale Rossetti (1783–1854) and his mother, Frances Marie Levina Polidori (1800–86). Leaving school at 13, he studied art, first in a prep school, and then at the Academy Schools (1845–48). In 1848 he was a founder of the Pre-Raphaelite Brotherhood (PRB) that redirected the course of English painting. He exhibited *The Girlhood of Mary Virgin* (1849; Plate 13) and his painting of the Annunciation, *Ecce Ancilla Domini* (Lat. Behold the handmaid of the Lord, 1850), both severely criticized by establishment critics until lavishly defended by John Ruskin. Thereafter he used both Dantean and Arthurian themes in both his paintings and poetry. He also paired paintings and poems. He published his first verse, including "The Blessed Damozel," in the PRB journal, *The Germ* in 1850.

In the same year he met Elizabeth Siddal (1829–62) and used her as a frequent model. For ten years they lived together, and finally they married in 1860. Their daughter was stillborn; in 1862 Siddal died of a laudanum overdose. Rossetti had other relationships: with Fanny Cornforth (1835–1906) and also with Jane Morris (1839–1914), whom William Morris had married in 1859. Rossetti's first major publication was an important set of translations, *The Early Italian Poets … Together with Dante's Vita Nuova* (1861), still a useful Dante resource. All of his family published on Dante or made detailed reference to him, including Rossetti's father, Gabriele, who published a neo-Platonic commentary on Dante.

On Siddal's death, Rossetti impulsively buried his manuscript notebook of poems in her hair. The manuscript was recovered when her coffin

Notes

Lucifer) from a neighbouring farm, has been sent away to school at his father's orders to keep her from him he cannot accept the fact that she is gone. Meredith introduces a citation from a cynical dissection of womanhood that Richard's father had written, *The Pilgrim's Scrip*: 'For the tenacity of true passion is terrible' says THE PILGRIM'S SCRIP: 'it will stand against the hosts of heaven, God's great array of Facts, rather than surrender its aim, and must be crushed before it will succumb—sent to the lowest pit!' He knew she was not there; she was gone. But the power of a will strained to madness fought at it, kept it down, conjured forth her ghost, and would have it as he dictated. Poor

youth! the great array of facts was in due order of march" (ch. 23). The poem was first published in *Poems and Lyrics of the Joy of Earth* (1883).

[2] *ball* at the end of Book 2 of *Paradise Lost* Satan sees the earth "hanging in a golden Chain / This pendant world in bigness as a Starr" (2. 1051–52).

[3] *Awe* God; Satan's rebellion against God, out of pride instead of awe, depicted in the apocryphal 2 Enoch 29: 4; and 31: 4; and Revelation 12: 7–9; and in *Paradise Lost*.

[4] *stars* for the creation of the stars and their function as heavenly luminaries and ordered courses through the heavens, see *Paradise Lost* 7: 339–86.

was exhumed (5 Oct. 1869). These events led to Rossetti's serious depressions, insomnia, and addiction to chloral, but he continued to write, publishing *Poems* (1870) to great success – and virulent attack from Robert Buchanan. After his intense relationship with Jane Morris ended in 1874 his remaining seven years were dominated by sickness, guilt, manias, and addictions, but he continued to paint, and less frequently, to write, finally publishing two volumes in 1881. The first *Ballads and Sonnets* contained his masterpiece, *The House of Life* (doubled in size from 1870), and the second, a revised and expanded *Poems*. Standard edition: *Collected Poetry and Prose*, ed. Jerome McGann (2003); *The Correspondence of Dante Gabriel Rossetti*, ed. William E. Fredeman (7 vols, 2002–07); Oswald Doughty, *A Victorian Romantic: Dante Gabriel Rossetti* (second edition 1960); Alicia Craig Faxon, *Dante Gabriel Rossetti* (1989); Alison Chapman and Joanna Meacock, *A Rossetti Family Chronology* (2007); *The Complete Writings and Pictures of Dante Gabriel Rossetti: A Hypermedia Research Archive*, ed. Jerome McGann: www.rossetti-archive.org.

WEB p. 407

Songs of One Household. No. 1. My Sister's Sleep

The Girlhood of Mary Virgin[1]

[I]

This is that blessed Mary, pre-elect
   God's virgin. Gone is a great while, and she
   Dwelt thus[2] in Nazareth of Galilee;
Her kin she cherished with[3] devout respect:
A profound simpleness of intellect   5
   Was hers, and supreme patience. From the knee[4]

Notes

DANTE GABRIEL ROSSETTI

[1] *title* written on 21 November 1848 when Rossetti was working on his painting *The Girlhood of Mary Virgin* (Plate 13) and his first exercise in a double work of art, painting and poem. The sonnet was first published in the *Catalogue of the Association for Promoting the Free Exhibition of Modern Art* (1849), our text, to accompany the painting, shown at the exhibition. Although no title is given to the poem, it is placed immediately beneath the title of the painting. This sonnet and the following one were both available to viewers of the painting in the *Catalogue*, and perhaps both were printed on gold foil. Just as the painting is a manifesto of the values, subject matter, and execution of the PRB (the first painting was the first to bear their initials) that imitates painters like Giotto (1266–1337) in its clarity and flatness of tone and simplicity of outline rather than the popular light and shadow (chiaroscuro) of much

contemporary art, so the sonnet uses anachronistic verbal description to imitate the picture as an ekphrasis. In opposition to contemporary emotional and affective verse, the two poems are programmatic for Pre-Raphaelite theory: they describe and summarize with allusion and symbol, using details for aesthetic rather than religious purposes. Subsequently Rossetti published it in *Poems* (1870), titled "Mary's Girlhood" with a subtitle: "(For a Picture)." It was subsequently collected in *Poems* (1881).
[2] *thus* reads "young" in *Poems* (1870).
[3] *Her kin ... with* reads "Unto God's will she brought" in *Poems* (1870).
[4] *A profound ... knee* these lines in *Poems* (1870) read: "A profound simplicity of intellect, / And supreme patience. From her mother's knee." Line 5 was revised again for *Poems* (1881): "Her gifts were simpleness of intellect."

Faithful and hopeful; wise in charity;
Strong in grave peace; in duty[5] circumspect.[6]
Thus[7] held she through her girlhood; as it were
An angel-watered lily, that near God   10
Grows, and is quiet. Till one dawn, at home,
She woke in her white bed, and had no fear
At all,—yet wept till sunshine, and felt awed;
Because the fulness of the time was come.[8]

[II][9]

These are the symbols. On that cloth of red
I' the centre is the Tripoint:[10] perfect each,
Except the second of its points, to teach
That Christ is not yet born. The books—whose head
Is golden Charity, as Paul hath said—   5
Those virtues[11] are wherein the soul is rich:
Therefore on them the lily standeth, which
Is Innocence, being interpreted.

The seven-thorn'd briar and the palm[12] seven-leaved
Are her great sorrow and her great reward.   10
Until the end be full, the Holy One
Abides without. She soon shall have achieved
Her perfect purity: yea, God the Lord
Shall soon vouchsafe His Son to be her Son.

The Blessed Damozel[13]

The blessed Damozel leaned out
From the gold bar of Heaven:
Her blue grave eyes were deeper much

Notes

[5] *duty* reads "pity" in *Poems* (1870 and 1881).

[6] *circumspect* Mary's virtues are those inscribed on the books that hold the vase of lilies: patience (Lat. *temperentia*, temperance), the three Christian virtues: faith (Lat. *fides*), hope (Lat. *spes*), and charity (Lat. *caritas*, love) (see 1 Corinthians 13: 13), strength (Lat. *fortitudo*) and being circumspect (Lat. *prudentia*), three of the four classical virtues, justice being absent.

[7] *Thus* reads "So" in *Poems* (1870).

[8] *come* see Galatians 4: 4, here representing the Annunciation of the angel to Mary (Luke 1: 26–39) to which the sestet refers, as well as to the subsequent painting, *Ecce Ancilla Domini* (Lat. behold the handmaid of the Lord).

[9] *title* this second poem on Rossetti's painting *The Girlhood of Mary Virgin* (Plate 13) was originally written early in 1849 when he was readying the painting for the summer exhibition of that year (see n. 1). It was there printed, as some Rossetti experts maintain, on a slip of gilded paper fastened to the frame, along with the first sonnet. When it was repainted and reframed in 1864, the sonnets were written on the frame. The poem was first published in a widely accessible form in William Sharp's *Dante Gabriel Rossetti: A Record and a Study* (1882) and was reprinted in William Michael Rossetti's edition of his brother's *Collected Works* (1886).

[10] *Tripoint* a traditional symbol of the Trinity.

[11] *said . . . virtues* see 1 Corinthians 13: 13 and n. 6.

[12] *briar . . . palm* the seven sorrows of Mary are the prophecy of Simeon (Luke 2: 34–35), the flight into Egypt (Matthew 2:13), Jesus as a child lost in Jerusalem (Luke 2: 43–45), Mary's meeting of Jesus on the way to Calvary (no scriptural reference), the death of Jesus on the Cross (John 19: 25), Mary's receiving Jesus in her arms (Matthew 27: 57–59), and the placing of Jesus in the tomb (John 19: 40–42). The palm symbolizes Mary's glorification.

[13] *title* (OFr. *demoiselle*, damsel); the first of many medievalisms in the poem. Rossetti also completed a painting entitled *The Blessed Damozel* (1871–76, Fogg Museum, Harvard; see Plate 14), depicting the Damozel leaning out

Than a deep water, even.[14]
  She had three lilies in her hand,   5
    And the stars in her hair were seven.[15]

Her robe, ungirt from clasp to hem,
  No wrought flowers did adorn,
But a white rose of Mary's gift
  On the neck meetly worn;   10
And her hair, lying down her back,
  Was yellow like ripe corn.[16]

Herseemed she scarce had been a day
  One of God's choristers;
The wonder was not yet quite gone   15
  From that still look of hers;
Albeit to them she left, her day
  Had counted as ten years.[17]

(To *one*[18] it is ten years of years:
  .. Yet now, here in this place,   20
Surely she leaned o'er me,—her hair
  Fell all about my face..

Notes

over a golden bar or parapet of heaven, surrounded by roses, and holding lilies, while in the background numerous reunited lovers embrace in paradise under a great tree. Below the Damozel are the heads of three young angels. The Damozel gazes out of the painting towards the predella (the smaller, lower panel), showing the lover reclining on earth gazing upwards in a dream vision.

Both the poem and the painting derive from Rossetti's study of and writing about Dante, especially *La Vita Nuova* (Ital. the new life; 1295) telling of Dante's love for Beatrice (Ital. blessed) Portinari, especially his canzone "Donne ch'avete intelletto d'amore" (Ital. "Ladies that have intelligence in love"). Rossetti translated *La Vita Nuova* and published it together with translations of other twelfth- and thirteenth-century Italian poetry in *The Early Italian Poets* (1861). Rossetti's painting operates on two levels, earth and heaven, but the poem adds a third, the lover's reflection or musing on the dream vision of his beloved whom he imagines as looking down on him (set out in parentheses in the poem). To his friend Hall Caine (1853–1931), Rossetti said: "I saw that what [Edgar Allen] Poe [in "The Raven" 1845] had done the utmost it was possible to do with the grief of the lover on earth, and so I determined to reverse the condition, and give utterance to the yearning of the loved one in heaven."

Written in 1846–47, the ballad was first printed in the Pre-Raphaelite journal, *The Germ* (No. 2; Feb. 1850), our text, and thereafter underwent numerous changes in subsequent reprints: in *The Oxford and Cambridge Magazine*, the journal edited by William Morris for the so-called second Pre-Raphaelite brotherhood (1856), Rossetti's *Poems* (1870), and *Poems* (1881). Some stanzas were excluded, others included,

and some were changed substantially. We give a number of these changes from *Poems* (1870) in the notes.

[14] *even* see *Paradiso* 3: 11–12. These two lines were revised to read: "Her eyes were deeper than the depth / Of waters stilled at even" (1870).

[15] *three ... seven* symbolic numbers and objects, three suggesting the Trinity, and lilies for purity (often portrayed as carried by Gabriel at the Annunciation); the seven stars are the constellation Pleiades, auguring fair weather and auspicious events. Seven is also the perfect number, composed of the earthly four (four winds, four directions, four elements, etc.) and the heavenly three. In Rossetti's painting there are only six stars in the Damozel's hair, so she herself is the invisible Pleiade (one star in the constellation is invisible to the naked eye). See also Revelation 1: 16, 20; and 12: 1. See TENNYSON n. 21 (WEB p. 335).

[16] *corn* wheat.

[17] *ten years* it was conventional to mark off anniversaries in courtly love poetry of the Italian *dolce stil nuovo* (Ital. sweet new style), Dante's term for twelfth- and thirteenth-century Tuscan vernacular verse based on Provençal and Sicilian models, especially the sonnet, ballade, and canzone, in which idealized love and the beloved are exalted. Rossetti draws on this tradition. Dante first met with Beatrice Portinari at the age of 9 (she was 8) when he fell in love with her at first sight. He next met her again nine years later, the second of their two meetings. Beatrice died in 1290, and Dante in the *Purgatorio* imagines an encounter with her again ten years later, in 1300. Rossetti's poem follows Dante in specifying an interval of ten years.

[18] *one* the parentheses indicate that the lover on earth is imagining his beloved Damozel in paradise.

Nothing: the Autumn-fall of leaves.[19]
    The whole year sets apace.)

It was the terrace[20] of God's house   25
    That she was standing on,—
By God built over the sheer depth
    In which Space is begun;
So high, that looking downward thence,
    She could scarce see the sun.   30 .

It lies from Heaven across the flood
    Of ether, as a bridge.
Beneath, the tides of day and night
    With flame and blackness ridge
The void, as low as where this earth   35
    Spins like a fretful midge.[21]

But in those tracts, with her, it was
    The peace of utter light
And silence. For no breeze may stir
    Along the steady flight   40
Of seraphim; no echo there,
    Beyond all depth or height.[22]

Heard hardly, some of her new friends,
    Playing at holy games,
Spake, gentle-mouthed,[23] among themselves,   45
    Their virginal chaste names;[24]
And the souls, mounting up to God,
    Went by her like thin flames.[25]

And still she bowed herself, and stooped
    Into the vast waste calm;   50
Till her bosom's pressure must have made
    The bar she leaned on warm,
And the lilies lay as if asleep
    Along her bended arm.

Notes

[19] *leaves* see *Aeneid* 6: 309, describing the shades: "Thick as the leaves in autumn strow the woods" (trans. Dryden, 1697), crowding on the shore of the River Styx to await Charon to ferry them across into the underworld.

[20] *terrace* rampart (1870).

[21] *house ... midge* the details of the vast space between heaven and earth seen by the Damozel recall Satan's vision of the cosmos at the end of Book 2 of *Paradise Lost* (1021–55); see also *Paradiso* 22: 133 ff.; and especially *Paradiso* 27, where Beatrice asks Dante to look down from the Empyrean Heaven towards earth across space (76–90).

[22] *height* stanza omitted from subsequent editions.

[23] *gentle-mouthed* gentle here means courteous or noble (Ital. *gentile*) as in Chaucer and the Elizabethan poets, as well as Shakespeare. Dante used the word frequently in referring to Beatrice in *La Vita Nuova*, as in the sonnet "*Tanto gentile e tanto onesta pare*" (Ital. My lady looks so gentle and so pure; ch. 26).

[24] *names* in the first edition of *Poems* (1870), the first four lines of this stanza were revised to read: "Around her, lovers, newly met / In joy no sorrow claims, / Spoke evermore among themselves / Their rapturous new names." In the sixth edition (1873) of *Poems* (1870) the first four lines of this stanza were revised further to read: "Around her, lovers, newly met / 'Mid deathless love's acclaims, / Spoke evermore among themselves / Their heart-remembered names."

[25] *flames* in his translation of Dante's *La Vita Nuova* in *The Early Italian Poets* (1861), Rossetti translates Dante's canzone: "Ladies that have intelligence in love" with the

From the fixt lull of heaven, she saw   55
    Time, like a pulse, shake fierce
Through all the worlds. Her gaze still strove,
    In that steep gulph, to pierce
The swarm: and then she spake, as when
    The stars sang in their spheres.[26]   60

"I wish that he were come to me,
    For he will come," she said.
"Have I not prayed in solemn heaven?
    On earth, has he not prayed?
Are not two prayers a perfect strength?[27]   65
    And shall I feel afraid?

When round his head the aureole[28] clings,
    And he is clothed in white,[29]
I'll take his hand, and go with him
    To the deep wells of light,   70
And we will step down as to a stream[30]
    And bathe there in God's sight.

We two will stand beside that shrine,
    Occult, withheld, untrod,
Whose lamps tremble continually   75
    With prayer sent up to God;
And where each need, revealed, expects
    Its patient period.[31]

We two will lie i' the shadow of
    That living mystic tree[32]   80

Notes

lines: "Whatever her sweet eyes are turned upon, / Spirits of love do issue thence in flame, / Which through their eyes who then may look on them / Pierce to the heart's deep chamber every one" (ch. 19: 51–54). Rossetti also completed a drawing of *La Donna della Fiamma* (Ital. The lady of the flame) showing a woman gazing at the palm of her hand whence a flaming spirit rises. So also in the *Paradiso* the spirits of the blessed rise like flames to circle around the presence of God (for instance, Canto 12: 1–6; and 23: 118–26).

[26] *spheres* an allusion to the Pythagorean and medieval notion of the music of the spheres in which an angelic spirit for each of the planets sang a particular note to create the heavenly harmony, only able to be heard in the Ptolemaic and poetic universe above the moon; in the sublunary world only the music of earth, a faint echo of the heavenly music, can be heard. See Cicero, *The Dream of Scipio*; and *The Merchant of Venice* (5.1.58–65). In *Paradiso* 21 and 22, Peter Damian (1007–72), saint and Doctor of the Church, explains such concepts to Dante. In *Poems* (1870) and subsequent editions Rossetti added two stanzas here:

    The sun was gone now; the curled moon
        Was like a little feather
    Fluttering far down the gulf; and now
        She spoke through the still weather.
    Her voice was like the voice the stars
        Had when they sang together.

    (Ah sweet! Even now, in that bird's song,
        Strove not her accents there,
    Fain to be hearkened? When those bells
        Possessed the mid-day air,
    Strove not her steps to reach my side
        Down all the echoing stair?)

[27] *strength* see Matthew 18: 19.

[28] *aureole* (Lat. *aureus*, gold) golden halo or nimbus around the head of a saint, a word known in Rossetti's Pre-Raphaelite circle through its use by Anna Jameson (1794–1860) to describe Renaissance paintings in *Sacred and Legendary Art* (1848), and by Robert Browning as the term of honour and endearment, as well as the proper name, of the main character in *Paracelsus* (1835).

[29] *white* like the purified saints in Revelation (7: 14; and 22: 14).

[30] *light ... stream* see Revelation 22: 1; and *Paradiso* 30: 49–51; and 61–64.

[31] *period* for this stanza, see Revelation 4: 4; 5: 8; and 8: 3.

[32] *tree* see Revelation 22: 2.

Within whose secret growth the Dove[33]
  Sometimes is felt to be,
While every leaf that His plumes touch
  Saith His name audibly.

And I myself will teach to him—   85
  I myself, lying so,—
The songs I sing here; which his mouth
  Shall pause in, hushed and slow,
Finding some knowledge at each pause
  And some new thing to know."[34]   90

(Alas! to *her* wise simple mind[35]
  These things were all but known
Before: they trembled on her sense,—
  Her voice had caught their tone.
Alas for lonely Heaven! Alas   95
  For life wrung out alone!

Alas, and though the end were reached?..
  Was *thy* part understood
Or borne in trust? And for her sake
  Shall this too be found good?—   100
May the close lips that knew not prayer
  Praise ever, though they would?)

"We two," she said, "will seek the groves
  Where the lady Mary is,[36]
With her five handmaidens, whose names   105
  Are five sweet symphonies[37]:—
Cecily, Gertrude, Magdalen,
  Margaret, and Rosalys.[38]

Notes

[33] *Dove* the Holy Spirit (see Mark 1: 10).

[34] *songs … know* see *Paradiso* 8: 16–30; and 9: 73–78, where Beatrice shows Dante the songs of the blessed in the sphere of Venus.

[35] *mind* this and the following stanzas were omitted from subsequent reprintings. From *Poems* (1870) the following stanza replaced them: "(Alas! We two, we two, thou say'st! / Yea, one wast thou with me / That once of old. But shall God lift / To endless unity / The soul whose likeness with thy soul / Was but its love for thee?)."

[36] *is* for the first two lines of this stanza, see Rossetti's translation of Dante's sonnet, "Era venuta nella mente mia" in *La Vita Nuova* (ch. 35): "That lady of all gentle memories / Had lighted on my soul;—whose new abode / Lies now, as it was well ordained of God, / Among the poor in heart, where Mary is."

[37] *symphonies* harmonies or concords of words or music (*OED*: obs. or arch.; Gk. *symphonia*, agreement of sound).

[38] *Cecilia … Rosalys* the first four names are female saints: Cecilia was a Roman martyr of the second or third century and the patron saint of sacred music; Gertrude (626–59), a daughter of Pepin the Elder (d. 640), became the abbess of a convent in Belgium and is the patron saint of travellers; Magdalen is Mary of Magdala, a companion of Jesus as narrated in the Gospels (Luke 8: 2; Mark 15: 40; Mark 16: 1; and John 20: 1); a legend says that she journeyed by sea with Martha and Lazarus, other friends of Jesus, to the south of France were her body was venerated at Aix-en-Provence; Margaret of Antioch, a martyr in the Diocletian persecutions of 303 and later, and the patron saint of women in labour; Rosalys is a saint of Rossetti's invention, combining the rose (Lat.*rosa*) of love and beauty with the lily (Fr. *lys*) of chastity.

Circle-wise sit they, with bound locks
    And bosoms covered;[39]   110
Into the fine cloth, white like flame,
    Weaving the golden thread,
To fashion the birth-robes for them
    Who are just born, being dead.

He shall fear haply, and be dumb.   115
    Then I will lay my cheek
To his, and tell about our love,
    Not once abashed or weak:
And the dear Mother[40] will approve
    My pride, and let me speak.   120

Herself shall bring us, hand in hand,
    To Him round whom all souls
Kneel—the unnumber'd solemn heads
    Bowed with their aureoles:
And Angels, meeting us, shall sing   125
    To their citherns and citoles.[41]

There will I ask of Christ the Lord
    Thus much for him and me:—
To have more blessing than on earth
    In nowise; but to be   130
As then we were,—being as then
    At peace. Yea, verily.[42]

Yea, verily; when he is come
    We will do thus and thus:
Till this my vigil seem quite strange   135
    And almost fabulous;
We two will live at once, one life;
    And peace shall be with us."[43]

She gazed, and listened, and then said,
    Less sad of speech than mild: 140
"All this is when he comes." She ceased:
    The light thrilled past her,[44] filled
With Angels, in strong level lapse.
    Her eyes prayed, and she smiled.

Notes

[39] *covered* "foreheads garlanded" (1870).

[40] *Mother* Mary, the mother of Jesus.

[41] *citherns … citoles* archaisms: a cithern (or cittern) is a metal-stringed musical instrument, popular in the Renaissance, with a flat back and a pear-shaped body, somewhat like a mandolin, played by strumming or plucking. A citole was a medieval stringed instrument, probably with four strings and a holly-leaf shape.

[42] *verily* in *Poems* (1870) the last four lines of this stanza read: "Only to live as once on earth / With Love,—only to be, / As then awhile, for ever now / Together, I and he."

[43] *us* this stanza omitted in *Poems* (1870) and subsequently.

[44] *her* see Rossetti's translation of the sonnet by Guido Cavalcanti (*c.*1250–1300), "A Rapture concerning his Lady": "Who is she coming, whom all gaze upon, / Who makes the air all tremulous with light / And at whose side is Love himself?" (*The Early Italian Poets*, 1861).

(I saw her smile.) But soon their flight 145
    Was vague 'mid the poised spheres.
And then she cast her arms along
    The golden barriers,
And laid her face between her hands,
    And wept. (I heard her tears.)[45] 150

The Woodspurge[46]

The wind flapped loose, the wind was still,
Shaken out dead from tree and hill:
I had walked on at the wind's will,—
I sat now, for the wind was still.

Between my knees my forehead was,— 5
My lips, drawn in, said not Alas!
My hair was over in the grass,
My naked ears heard the day pass.

My eyes, wide open, had the run
Of some ten weeds to fix upon; 10
Among those few, out of the sun,
The woodspurge flowered, three cups in one.

From perfect grief there need not be
Wisdom or even memory:
One thing then learnt remains to me,— 15
The woodspurge has a cup of three.

Jenny[47]

"Vengeance of Jenny's case! Fie on her! Never name her, child!"   (Mrs. Quickly.)[48]

Lazy laughing languid Jenny,
Fond of a kiss and fond of a guinea,[49]
Whose head upon my knee to-night
Rests for a while, as if grown light

Notes

[45] *tears* for this stanza see *Paradiso* 31: 64–70; and 91–2: "'Where is she' all sudden I exclaimed ... without answering I lifted up mine eyes and saw her ... from that region which thundereth most high, no mortal eye is so far distant ... there from Beatrice was my sight ... for her image descended to me not mingled with any medium.... So did I pray; and she, so distant as she seemed, smiled and looked on me, then turned her to the eternal fountain" (trans. Howell and Wicksteed).

[46] *title* in *Poems* (1870; our text) this poem was placed with the section called "Songs" in a longer work, "Sonnets and Songs, Towards a Work to be Called The House of Life." In *Poems and Ballads* (1881) the poem was placed in a section headed "Lyrics." The woodspurge is a greenish-yellow flowering woodland plant.

[47] *title* the poem was vehemently attacked by Robert Buchanan in "The Fleshly School of Poetry" to which Rossetti responded with "The Stealthy School of Criticism" (see LITERATURE: PRE-RAPHAELITISM (WEB p. 131)). For a monologue on a prostitute from a woman's point of view, see WEBSTER, "A CASTAWAY" and LEVY, "MAGDALEN." For Victorian prostitution, see GENDER: SEX; GREG (WEB p. 87). See also Plates 10 and 15. See also CHRISTINA ROSSETTI, "GOBLIN MARKET," n. 5. First published in *Poems* (1870).

[48] *Quickly* from *The Merry Wives of Windsor* (4. 1.62); Rossetti omits the last clause of this citation: "if she be a whore."

With all our dances and the sound   5
To which the wild tunes spun you round:
Fair Jenny mine, the thoughtless queen
Of kisses which the blush between
Could hardly make much daintier;
Whose eyes are as blue skies, whose hair   10
Is countless gold incomparable:
Fresh flower, scarce touched with signs that tell
Of Love's exuberant hotbed:⁵⁰—Nay,
Poor flower left torn since yesterday
Until to-morrow leave you bare;   15
Poor handful of bright spring-water
Flung in the whirlpool's shrieking face;
Poor shameful Jenny, full of grace⁵¹
Thus with your head upon my knee;—
Whose person or whose purse⁵² may be   20
The lodestar of your reverie?
    This room of yours, my Jenny, looks
A change from mine so full of books,
Whose serried ranks hold fast, forsooth,
So many captive hours of youth,—   25
The hours they thieve from day and night
To make one's cherished work come right,
And leave it wrong for all their theft,
Even as to-night my work was left:
Until I vowed that since my brain   30
And eyes of dancing seemed so fain,
My feet should have some dancing too:—
And thus it was I met with you.
Well, I suppose 'twas hard to part,
For here I am. And now, sweetheart,   35
You seem too tired to get to bed.
    It was a careless life I led
When rooms like this were scarce so strange
Not long ago. What breeds the change,—
The many aims or the few years?   40
Because to-night it all appears
Something I do not know again.
    The cloud's not danced out of my brain,—
The cloud that made it turn and swim
While hour by hour the books grew dim.   45
Why, Jenny, as I watch you there,—
For all your wealth of loosened hair,⁵³

Notes

⁴⁹ *guinea* gold coin worth one pound one shilling (twenty-one shillings). Though not minted after 1813, the price of professional fees (as, ironically, here), horse racing, and luxury items was still given in guineas until decimalization in 1971.

⁵⁰ *hotbed* a pun, conflating Jenny's bed and the florist's greenhouse.

⁵¹ *grace* ironic echo of the *Ave Maria*; see Luke 1: 28.

⁵² *purse* the phrase "person ... purse" was cited by Buchanan as a "wretched pun."

⁵³ *hair* possible allusion to the golden-haired Rapunzel story as told by the Brothers Grimm (1812). William Morris had included a poem "Rapunzel" in his *Defence of Guenevere and Other Poems* (1858). Rossetti had retrieved the MS of "Jenny" from Elizabeth Siddal's coffin where it was buried within her golden hair.

Your silk ungirdled and unlac'd
And warm sweets open to the waist,
All golden in the lamplight's gleam,—   50
You know not what a book you seem,
Half-read by lightning in a dream!
How should you know, my Jenny? Nay,
And I should be ashamed to say:—
Poor beauty, so well worth a kiss!   55
But while my thought runs on like this
With wasteful whims more than enough,
I wonder what you're thinking of.

  If of myself you think at all,
What is the thought?—conjectural   60
On sorry matters best unsolved?—
Or inly is each grace revolved
To fit me with a lure?—or (sad
To think!) perhaps you're merely glad
That I'm not drunk or ruffianly   65
And let you rest upon my knee.

  For sometimes, were the truth confess'd,
You're thankful for a little rest,—
Glad from the crush to rest within,
From the heart-sickness and the din   70
Where envy's voice at virtue's pitch
Mocks you because your gown is rich;
And from the pale girl's dumb rebuke,
Whose ill-clad grace and toil-worn look
Proclaim the strength that keeps her weak   75
And other nights than yours bespeak;
And from the wise unchildish elf,
To schoolmate lesser than himself
Pointing you out, what thing you are:—
Yes, from the daily jeer and jar,   80
From shame and shame's outbraving too,
Is rest not sometimes sweet to you?—
But most from the hatefulness of man
Who spares not to end what he began,
Whose acts are ill and his speech ill,   85
Who, having used you at his will,
Thrusts you aside, as when I dine
I serve the dishes and the wine.

  Well, handsome Jenny mine, sit up,
I've filled our glasses, let us sup,   90
And do not let me think of you,
Lest shame of yours suffice for two.
What, still so tired? Well, well then, keep
Your head there, so you do not sleep;
But that the weariness may pass   95
And leave you merry, take this glass.
Ah! lazy lily hand, more bless'd
If ne'er in rings it had been dress'd
Nor ever by a glove conceal'd!
  Behold the lilies of the field,   100

They toil not neither do they spin;[54]
(So doth the ancient text begin,—
Not of such rest as one of these
Can share.) Another rest and ease   105
Along each summer-sated path
From its new lord the garden hath,
Than that whose spring in blessings ran
Which praised the bounteous husbandman,
Ere yet, in days of hankering breath,
The lilies sickened unto death.   110
    What, Jenny, are your lilies dead?
Aye, and the snow-white leaves are spread
Like winter on the garden-bed.
But you had roses left in May,—
They were not gone too. Jenny, nay,   115
But must your roses die, and those
Their purfled[55] buds that should unclose?
Even so; the leaves are curled apart,
Still red as from the broken heart,
And here's the naked stem of thorns.[56]   120
    Nay, nay, mere words. Here nothing warns
As yet of winter. Sickness here
Or want alone could waken fear,—
Nothing but passion wrings a tear.
Except when there may rise unsought   125
Haply at times a passing thought
Of the old days which seem to be
Much older than any history
That is written in any book;
When she would lie in fields and look   130
Along the ground through the blown grass,
And wonder where the city was,
Far out of sight, whose broil and bale
They told her then for a child's tale.
    Jenny, you know the city now.   135
A child can tell the tale there, how
Some things which are not yet enroll'd
In market-lists are bought and sold
Even till the early Sunday light,
When Saturday night is market-night   140
Everywhere, be it dry or wet,
And market-night in the Haymarket.[57]
Our learned London children know,
Poor Jenny, all your mirth and woe;

Notes

[54] *spin* see Matthew 6: 28. Lilies are traditional symbols of virginity: the archangel Gabriel often is depicted as carrying one in paintings of the Annunciation to the Virgin Mary. Rossetti had the Virgin embroidering them in his painting "The Girlhood of Mary Virgin" (1850). See Plate 13.

[55] *purfled* decorated, embroidered with a border of flowers.
[56] *thorns* ironic allusions to traditional religious images of the Sacred Heart of Jesus and the Crucifixion.
[57] *Haymarket* a street in the Westminster district of London, part of the theatre district, and in the nineteenth century popular with prostitutes and their clients.

Have seen your lifted silken skirt   145
Advertize dainties through the dirt;
Have seen your coach-wheels splash rebuke
On virtue; and have learned your look
When, wealth and health slipped past, you stare
Along the streets alone, and there,   150
Round the long park, across the bridge,
The cold lamps at the pavement's edge
Wind on together and apart,
A fiery serpent for your heart.
    Let the thoughts pass, an empty cloud!   155
Suppose I were to think aloud,—
What if to her all this were said?
Why, as a volume seldom read
Being opened halfway shuts again,
So might the pages of her brain   160
Be parted at such words, and thence
Close back upon the dusty sense.
For is there hue or shape defin'd
In Jenny's desecrated mind,
Where all contagious currents meet,   165
A Lethe⁵⁸ of the middle street?
Nay, it reflects not any face,
Nor sound is in its sluggish pace,
But as they coil those eddies clot,
And night and day remember not.   170
    Why, Jenny, you're asleep at last!—
Asleep, poor Jenny, hard and fast,—
So young and soft and tired; so fair,
With chin thus nestled in your hair,
Mouth quiet, eyelids almost blue   175
As if some sky of dreams shone through!
    Just as another woman sleeps!
Enough to throw one's thoughts in heaps
Of doubt and horror,—what to say
Or think,—this awful secret sway,   180
The potter's power over the clay!⁵⁹
Of the same lump (it has been said)
For honour and dishonour made,
Two sister vessels.⁶⁰ Here is one.
    My cousin Nell is fond of fun,   185
And fond of dress, and change, and praise,
So mere a woman in her ways:
And if her sweet eyes rich in youth
Are like her lips that tell the truth,

Notes

⁵⁸ *Lethe* river of forgetfulness in the underworld, according to Greek mythology; here an open sewer in the street.
⁵⁹ *clay* see Romans 9: 21.
⁶⁰ *sister vessels* drawn from the passage in Romans (see n. 59); the image is a conventional contrast between the Virgin Mary / Nell / the whore / Venus / and Jenny. Rossetti's paintings such as *Venus Verticordia* (1864–68) and *Found* (1853–81; unfinished; Plate 15) display similar oppositions.

My cousin Nell is fond of love.   190
And she's the girl I'm proudest of.
Who does not prize her, guard her well?
The love of change, in cousin Nell,
Shall find the best and hold it dear:
The unconquered mirth turn quieter   195
Not through her own, through others' woe:
The conscious pride of beauty glow
Beside another's pride in her,
One little part of all they share.
For Love himself shall ripen these   200
In a kind soil to just increase
Through years of fertilizing peace.
 Of the same lump (as it is said)
For honour and dishonour made,
Two sister vessels. Here is one.   205
  It makes a goblin of the sun.
  So pure,—so fall'n! How dare to think
Of the first common kindred link?
Yet, Jenny, till the world shall burn[61]
It seems that all things take their turn;   210
And who shall say but this fair tree
May need, in changes that may be,
Your children's children's charity?
Scorned then, no doubt, as you are scorn'd!
Shall no man hold his pride forewarn'd   215
Till in the end, the Day of Days,
At Judgment, one of his own race,
As frail and lost as you, shall rise,—
His daughter, with his mother's eyes?
 How Jenny's clock ticks on the shelf!   220
Might not the dial scorn itself
That has such hours to register?
Yet as to me, even so to her
Are golden sun and silver moon,
In daily largesse of earth's boon,   225
Counted for life-coins to one tune.
And if, as blindfold fates are toss'd,
Through some one man this life be lost,
Shall soul not somehow pay for soul?[62]
 Fair shines the gilded aureole[63]   230
In which our highest painters place
Some living woman's simple face.
And the stilled features thus descried
As Jenny's long throat droops aside,—
The shadows where the cheeks are thin,   235

Notes

[61] *burn* at the Last Judgement: see Matthew 13: 40–43; and Revelation 8: 7–9.

[62] *through some ... soul* a reference to the "ransom" theory of the atonement in Christianity, whereby Christ died to pay back the debt or to pay a ransom to Satan who properly could claim human souls as a result of sin: see Mark 10: 45; and 1 Timothy 2: 5–6.

[63] *aureole* see n. 28.

And pure wide curve from ear to chin,—
With Raffael's or Da Vinci's hand[64]
To show them to men's souls, might stand,
Whole ages long, the whole world through,
For preachings of what God can do. 240
What has man done here? How atone,
Great God, for this which man has done?
And for the body and soul which by
Man's pitiless doom must now comply
With lifelong hell, what lullaby 245
Of sweet forgetful second birth
Remains? All dark. No sign on earth
What measure of God's rest endows
The many mansions of his house.[65]
　　If but a woman's heart might see 250
Such erring heart unerringly
For once! But that can never be.
　　Like a rose shut in a book
In which pure women may not look,
For its base pages claim control 255
To crush the flower within the soul;
Where through each dead rose-leaf that clings,
Pale as transparent psyche-wings,[66]
To the vile text, are traced such things
As might make lady's cheek indeed 260
More than a living rose to read;
So nought save foolish foulness may
Watch with hard eyes the sure decay;
And so the life-blood of this rose,
Puddled with shameful knowledge, flows 265
Through leaves no chaste hand may unclose:
　　Yet still it keeps such faded show
Of when 'twas gathered long ago,
That the crushed petals' lovely grain,
The sweetness of the sanguine stain, 270
Seen of a woman's eyes, must make
Her pitiful heart, so prone to ache,
Love roses better for its sake:—
Only that this can never be:—
Even so unto her sex is she. 275
　　Yet, Jenny, looking long at you,
The woman almost fades from view.
A cipher[67] of man's changeless sum
Of lust, past, present, and to come,
Is left. A riddle that one shrinks 280

Notes

[64] *hand* Raphael Sanzio (1483–1520) and Leonardo Da Vinci (1452–1519), major artists of the High Renaissance, painted numerous Madonnas and saints.

[65] *house* see John 14: 2.

[66] *psyche-wings* in Greek and Roman mythology, Psyche (Gk. spirit, soul, butterfly) was beloved by Cupid.

[67] *cipher* zero; secret writing.

To challenge from the scornful sphinx.[68]
　　Like a toad within a stone[69]
Seated while Time crumbles on;
Which sits there since the earth was curs'd
For Man's transgression at the first;[70]　　　　　285
Which, living through all centuries,
Not once has seen the sun arise;
Whose life, to its cold circle charmed,
The earth's whole summers have not warmed;
Which always—whitherso the stone　　　　　290
Be flung—sits there, deaf, blind, alone;—
Aye, and shall not be driven out
Till that which shuts him round about
Break at the very Master's stroke,
And the dust thereof vanish as smoke,　　　　　295
And the seed of Man vanish as dust:—
Even so within this world is Lust.
　　Come, come, what use in thoughts like this?
Poor little Jenny, good to kiss,—
You'd not believe by what strange roads　　　　　300
Thought travels, when your beauty goads
A man to-night to think of toads!
Jenny, wake up … Why, there's the dawn!
　　And there's an early waggon drawn
To market, and some sheep that jog　　　　　305
Bleating before a barking dog;
And the old streets come peering through
Another night that London knew;
And all as ghostlike as the lamps.[71]
　　So on the wings of day decamps　　　　　310
My last night's frolic. Glooms begin
To shiver off as lights creep in
Past the gauze curtains half drawn-to,
And the lamp's doubled shade grows blue,—
Your lamp, my Jenny, kept alight,　　　　　315
Like a wise virgin's,[72] all one night!
And in the alcove coolly spread
Glimmers with dawn your empty bed;
And yonder your fair face I see
Reflected lying on my knee,　　　　　320
Where teems with first foreshadowings

Notes

[68] *sphinx* to the riddle of the sphinx – what walks with four legs in the morning, two legs at noon, and three legs in the evening – the answer is a human being, crawling as a child, walking upright, and walking with a cane. The riddle was solved by Oedipus. Rossetti did a finished pencil drawing of the subject entitled "The Question" (1875).

[69] *stone* fossilized toads and frogs have been found in widely dispersed locations across the globe. However, this entire paragraph bears inverse relationship to the idealized green world of the Forest of Arden in *As You Like It* where the

Duke describes the absence of the penalty of Adam, a jewel in the head of a toad, and sermons in stones (2. 1. 1–17).

[70] *first* the Fall: see Genesis 3.

[71] *lamps* the subject matter of this paragraph used in Rossetti's unfinished painting *Found*, begun in 1854, depicts a shepherd who has brought a calf to market in London. As he crosses Blackfriars Bridge he sees his former country girlfriend, now a prostitute. For the poem "Found," see below; for the painting, see Plate 15.

[72] *virgin's* see Matthew 25: 1–13.

Your pier-glass scrawled with diamond rings.[73]
　　And now without, as if some word
Had called upon them that they heard,
The London sparrows[74] far and nigh　　　　　　　　325
Clamour together suddenly;
And Jenny's cage-bird grown awake
Here in their song his part must take,
Because here too the day doth break.
　　And somehow in myself the dawn　　　　　　　　330
Among stirred clouds and veils withdrawn
Strikes greyly on her. Let her sleep.
But will it wake her if I heap
These cushions thus beneath her head
Where my knee was? No,—there's your bed,　　　335
My Jenny, while you dream. And there
I lay among your golden hair
Perhaps the subject of your dreams,
These golden coins.[75]
　　For still one deems　　　　　　　　　　　　340
That Jenny's flattering sleep confers
New magic on the magic purse,—
Grim web, how clogged with shrivelled flies!
Between the threads fine fumes arise
And shape their pictures in the brain.　　　　　　345
There roll no streets in glare and rain,
Nor flagrant man-swine whets his tusk;
But delicately sighs in musk
The homage of the dim boudoir;
Or like a palpitating star　　　　　　　　　　350
Thrilled into song, the opera-night
Breathes faint in the quick pulse of light;
Or at the carriage-window shine
Rich wares for choice; or, free to dine,
Whirls through its hour of health (divine　　　　355
For her) the concourse of the Park.[76]
And though in the discounted dark
Her functions there and here are one,
Beneath the lamps and in the sun
There reigns at least the acknowledged belle　　360
Apparelled beyond parallel.
Ah Jenny, yes, we know your dreams.

Notes

[73] *rings* mirror hung between two windows scratched with lovers' names. The following lines were added here in *Poems and Ballads* (1881): "And on your bosom all night worn / Yesterday's rose now droops forlorn / But dies not yet this summer morn."

[74] *sparrows* symbol of lust and promiscuity, as in *Measure for Measure* (3. 2. 169).

[75] *coins* suggestion of the Greek myth of Danaë with whom Zeus had intercourse by coming to her in a shower of gold. See n. 79.

[76] *Park* probably St James's Park, a well-known haunt for prostitutes and their clients.

[77] *Venus* the goddess of love in Roman mythology (the Greek Aphrodite) whose temple in the city of Paphos on the island of Crete marks the site where Venus was born or near where she rose from the sea.

[78] *Priapus* in Greek and Roman mythology, a rustic fertility god, protector of livestock, gardens, and male genitals. He usually carries a huge erection that Rossetti conjectures would be hidden by the sacrificial offerings brought to

For even the Paphian Venus[77] seems
A goddess o'er the realms of love,
When silver-shrined in shadowy grove: 365
Aye, or let offerings nicely placed
But hide Priapus[78] to the waist,
And whoso looks on him shall see
An eligible deity.
    Why, Jenny, waking here alone 370
May help you to remember one,
Though all the memory's long outworn
Of many a double-pillowed morn.
I think I see you when you wake,
And rub your eyes for me, and shake 375
My gold, in rising, from your hair,
A Danaë[79] for a moment there.
    Jenny, my love rang true! for still
Love at first sight is vague, until
That tinkling makes him audible. 380
    And must I mock you to the last,
Ashamed of my own shame,—aghast
Because some thoughts not born amiss
Rose at a poor fair face like this?
Well, of such thoughts so much I know: 385
In my life, as in hers, they show,
By a far gleam which I may near,
A dark path I can strive to clear.
    Only one kiss. Goodbye, my dear.

The Ballad of Dead Ladies

Translation from François Villon, 1450[80]

Tell me now in what hidden way is
    Lady Flora the lovely Roman?
Where's Hipparchia, and where is Thais,
    Neither of them the fairer woman?
Where is Echo,[81] beheld of no man, 5

Notes

him and to Venus by love's devotees. See LITERATURE, PRE-RAPHAELITISM, n. 37 (WEB p. 138).

[79] *Danaë* see n. 75.

[80] *title* first of three poems in a section of *Poems* (1870) entitled "Three Translations from François Villon, 1450." François Villon (1431–c.1463), medieval French poet, wrote *Ballade*, later retitled *Ballade des dames du temps jadis* (1533; Fr. Ballade of the ladies of bygone times). It had the refrain: *Où sont les neiges d'antan?* (Fr. Where are the snows of other times?), a variant of the *"ubi sunt"* motif (Lat. *ubi sunt qui ante nos fuerunt?*: where are those who were before us?).

[81] *Flora ... Echo* the list of famous lovers of times past begins with Flora, a wealthy Roman courtesan who left her fortune to the people of Rome who set up a festival

in her honour, and hence she is also associated with the Flora, the goddess of spring and flowers; Rossetti substituted Hipparchia for Villon's Archipiada (the mistress of Alcibiades, an Athenian friend of Socrates): Hipparchia was a wealthy Athenian who married the Cynic philosopher, Crates (fourth century BCE), and lived with him in poverty on the streets of Athens. Thais was either the mistress of Alexander the Great (336–323 BCE), famous as a witty courtesan, or St Thais of Alexandria (fourth century), a converted courtesan who devoted herself to Christian asceticism in the Egyptian desert. Echo was a nymph beloved by Zeus who aroused Hera's anger, leading to her punishment by repeating the last words of others (see *Metamorphoses* 3: 339 ff.).

Only heard on river and mere,—
    She whose beauty was more than human? ..
But where are the snows of yester-year?

Where's Héloise, the learned nun,
    For whose sake Abeillard,[82] I ween,
Lost manhood and put priesthood on?
    (From Love he won such dule and teen!)
    And where, I pray you, is the Queen
Who willed that Buridan[83] should steer
    Sewed in a sack's mouth down the Seine? ..
But where are the snows of yester-year? 15

White Queen Blanche, like a queen of lilies,
    With a voice like any mermaiden,—
Bertha Broadfoot, Beatrice, Alice,[84]
    And Ermengarde the lady of Maine,— 20
    And that good Joan[85] whom Englishmen
At Rouen doomed and burned her there,—
    Mother of God, where are they then? ..
But where are the snows of yester-year?

Nay, never ask this week, fair lord,[86] 25
    Where they are gone, nor yet this year,
Except with this for an overword,—
    But where are the snows of yester-year?

Notes

[82] *Abeillard* Peter Abelard (1079–1142) was one of the pre-eminent philosophers and theologians of the twelfth century, becoming the head of the school at Notre Dame in Paris, where he fell in love with Heloise d'Argenteuil (1090–1164), the niece of one of the canons of Notre Dame. Abelard seduced her, she became pregnant, and her uncle had Abelard castrated. Thereafter, she became an abbess and he resumed his teaching amidst persecution, while acting as her faithful adviser. Their story is told Abelard's *History of My Misfortunes* (Lat. *Historia Calamitatum*) and in their letters.

[83] *Buridan* Jean Buridan (*c.*1300–58) was a French philosopher who was alleged to have had an affair with Queen Jeanne de Navarre (1528–72). She entertained students over several days with food, drink, and lovemaking, only

to have each thrown in a sack into the River Seine, but he anticipated this result and prepared an escape.

[84] *Blanche ... Alice* Blanche is very likely Blanche de Bourgogne (1296–1326), wife of Charles IV and imprisoned for adultery; the others are characters in the twelfth-century *chanson de geste* entitled *Hervis de Metz*.

[85] *Ermengarde ... Joan* Ermengarde was countess of Maine (d. 1126), mother of Geoffrey V, Count of Anjou, later king of Jerusalem. Joan is Joan of Arc (*c.*1412–31), who led the French army to defeat the English at Orléans (1428–29); subsequently she was betrayed into English hands, was tried, and was condemned and burned for witchcraft.

[86] *lord* the concluding four lines are a traditional "envoi" (Fr. a send-off or farewell), an address to the poet's patron.

Sunset Wings[87]

To-night this sunset spreads two golden wings
    Cleaving the western sky;
Winged too with wind it is, and winnowings
Of birds; as if the day's last hour in rings
    Of strenuous flight must die.   5

Sun-steeped in fire, the homeward pinions sway
    Above the dovecote-tops;
And clouds of starlings, ere they rest with day,
Sink, clamorous like mill-waters, at wild play,
    By turns in every copse: 10

Each tree heart-deep the wrangling rout receives,—
    But for the whirr within,
You could not tell the starlings from the leaves;
Then one great puff of wings, and the swarm heaves
    Away with all its din.   15

Even thus Hope's hours, in ever-eddying flight,
    To many a refuge tend;
With the first light she laughed, and the last light
Glows round her still; who natheless in the night
    At length must make an end.   20

Notes

[87] title first printed, Athenæum (24 May 1873); signed "Dante
G. Rossetti."; collected in Ballads and Sonnets (1881).

And now the mustering rooks innumerable
　　Together sail and soar,
While for the day's death, like a tolling knell,
Unto the heart they seem to cry, Farewell,
　　No more, farewell, no more!　　　　　　　　　　　25

Is Hope not plumed, as 'twere a fiery dart?
　　And oh thou dying day,
Even as thou goest must she too depart,
And Sorrow fold such pinions on the heart
　　As will not fly away?　　　　　　　　　　　　　30

"Found"[88]

(FOR A PICTURE)

"There is a budding morrow in midnight:"[89]—
　　So sang our Keats, our English nightingale.
　　And here, as lamps across the bridge turn pale
In London's smokeless resurrection-light,
Dark breaks to dawn. But o'er the deadly blight　　　5
　　Of love deflowered and sorrow of none avail
　　Which makes this man gasp and this woman quail,
Can day from darkness ever again take flight?

Ah! gave not these two hearts their mutual pledge,
Under one mantle sheltered 'neath the hedge　　　　10
　　In gloaming courtship? And O God! to-day
He only knows he holds her;—but what part
Can life now take? She cries in her locked heart,—
　　"Leave me—I do not know you—go away!"

Spheral Change[90]

In this new shade of Death, the show
　　Passes me still of form and face;
Some bent, some gazing as they go,
　　Some swiftly, some at a dull pace,
　　Not one that speaks in any case.　　　　　　　　5

Notes

[88] *title* a companion sonnet to the painting *Found* (begun 1853
and left unfinished at Rossetti's death: see Plate 15), representing a rural shepherd who has come to London to sell
his calf, tied in a net in his cart, but he has found his old
sweetheart, now a prostitute, who turns from him. See
n. 71. The poem was printed in *Ballads and Sonnets* (1881).

[89] *midnight* cited from Keats's "To Homer" (1848: 11).

[90] *title* echoing the shades in Dante' *Inferno* in the circle
of the lustful in Canto 5, such as Paolo and Francesca
(73–242), and the longing for Beatrice in the last cantos
of the *Purgatorio* (as in 33: 27–46). The title also suggests the changes in the spheres of the blessed in the
Paradiso. The poem was first published in *Ballads and
Sonnets* (1881).

If only one might speak!—the one
    Who never waits till I come near;
But always seated all alone
    As listening to the sunken air,
    Is gone before I come to her.   10

O dearest! while we lived and died
    A living death in every day,
Some hours we still were side by side,
    When where I was you too might stay
    And rest and n eed not go away.   15

O nearest, furthest! Can there be
    At length some hard-earned heart-won home,
Where,—exile changed for sanctuary,—
    Our lot may fill indeed its sum,
    And you may wait and I may come?   20

Proserpina[91]

(FOR A PICTURE)

Afar away the light that brings cold cheer
    Unto this wall,—one instant and no more
    Admitted at my distant palace-door:
Afar the flowers of Enna[92] from this drear
Cold fruit,[93] which, tasted once, must thrall me here: 5
    Afar those skies from this Tartarean[94] grey
    That chills me: and afar, how far away,
The nights that shall be from the days that were.

Afar from mine own self I seem, and wing
    Strange ways in thought, and listen for a sign: 10

Notes

[91] *title* Proserpina (Gk. Persephone) was the daughter of Jupiter and Ceres, the goddess of the harvest and fertility. She was abducted by Pluto to be his queen in Hades for the winter months, returning to earth in the spring. See SWIN-BURNE, n. 1 (WEB p. 425). Rossetti first wrote a version of the poem in Italian and published it preceding the version in English. He also completed a painting of *Proserpina* (1874: Tate Britain, London) with the Italian version of the poem in the upper right corner. He explained its symbolism to the purchaser of one of the versions, W. A. Turner: "The figure represents Proserpine as Empress of Hades. After she was conveyed by Pluto to his realm, and became his bride, her mother Ceres importuned Jupiter for her return to earth, and he was prevailed on to consent to this, provided only she had not partaken any of the fruits of Hades. It was found, however, that she had eaten one grain of a pomegranate, and this enchained her to her new empire and destiny. She is represented in a gloomy corridor of her palace, with the fatal fruit in her hand. As she passes, a gleam strikes on the wall behind her from some inlet suddenly opened, and admitting for a moment the light of the upper world; and she glances furtively toward it, immersed in thought. The incense-burner stands behind her as the attribute of a goddess. The ivy-branch in the background (a decorative appendage to the sonnet inscribed on the label) may be taken as a symbol of clinging memory." The figure of Proserpina is modelled on Jane Morris, the wife of William Morris. First published under the title, "Sonnets for Pictures" in the *Athenæum* (28 Aug. 1875), along with another poem, "La Bella Mano" in both English and Italian; republished in *Ballads and Sonnets* (1881).

[92] *Enna* the city and region in the centre of Sicily was famous in classical times for the worship of Ceres (Demeter) and Proserpine who according to legend came from the area.

[93] *fruit* pomegranate; see n. 91. In 1881 the phrase was changed from "Cold fruit" to "Dire fruit."

[94] *Tartarean* from Tartarus, a dark pit far beneath the underworld (Hades) in Greek and Roman mythology.

And still some heart unto some soul doth pine,—
(Whose sounds mine inner sense is fain to bring,
Continually together murmuring),—
"Woe's me for thee, unhappy Proserpine!"⁹⁵

Gerald Massey (1828–1907)

The son of a canal boatman, Massey was forced to go to work at an early age, first in a silk mill at Tring, then as a straw plaiter, then as a London errand boy. After teaching himself to read and write, he published his first volume, (1848), and wrote and edited the newspaper *Spirit of Freedom* (1849), published in Uxbridge. He published his verse in radical papers like *Cooper's Journal* and *The Red Banner*. Joining the Christian Socialists, he published *Voices of Freedom and Lyrics of Love* (1851) and *The Ballad of Babe Christabel* (1854) to critical approval, winning him a place in Samuel Smiles's *Self-Help* (1859) as an example of a self-made success. After five more volumes of poetry, he turned to reviewing for the *Athenæum* and other journals, including an article on Shakespeare's sonnets (*Quarterly Review*, April 1864). In 1863 he received a civil-list pension of £70. Subsequently he lectured in North America, Australia, and New Zealand on poetry, art, spiritualism, and mesmerism; from the 1880s he studied ancient Egypt, on which he published voluminously. No standard edition. David Shaw, *Gerald Massey: Chartist, Poet, Radical and Freethinker* (1995); David Shaw and Ian Pettigrew, *Gerald Massey: Poet, Author and Evolutionist: Centenary* (CD-ROM, 2007); "Gerald Massey": http://www.gerald-massey.org.uk/massey/index.htm.

The Cry of the Unemployed¹

'Tis hard! 'tis hard! to wander on through this bright world of ours,—
Beneath a sky of smiling blue,—on velvet paths of flowers:
With music in the woods, as there were nought but pleasure known,
Or angels walked earth's solitudes:—and yet with want to groan!
To see no beauty in the stars, nor in the sun's glad smile;   5
To wail and wander misery-cursed! willing, but cannot toil!
There's burning sickness at my heart: I sink down famished:
God of the wretched, hear my prayer! I would that I were dead!

Heaven droppeth down with manna still in many a golden shower,²
And feeds the leaves with fragrant breath, with silver dew, the flower: 10

Notes

⁹⁵ *Proserpine* possibly the speaker's own cry of despair at lost or imperilled love (see line 11); often read as a reference to Rossetti's long-standing relationship with Jane Morris that had intensified when he and William Morris took joint tenancy of Kelmscott Manor in rural Oxfordshire in 1871 – when Morris left for a prolonged trip to Iceland leaving Rossetti and Jane Morris together.

GERALD MASSEY
¹ *title* first published in *Cooper's Journal: or, Unfettered Thinker and Plain Speaker for Truth, Freedom, and Progress* (Feb. 1850).
² *manna ... shower* manna was the sweet bread from heaven that fed the Israelites in the wilderness in their wandering from Egypt to Canaan: see Exodus 14. In Greek mythology Zeus appeared to Danaë in a shower of gold, impregnating her with the hero Perseus, a common topic for Renaissance paintings, such as Titian's *Danaë* (1553–56); see also DANTE ROSSETTI, nn. 75 and 79.

There's honeyed fruit for bee and bird, with bloom laughs out the tree;
There's food for all God's happy things; but none gives food to me!
Earth decked with Plenty's garland-crown, smiles on my aching eye:
The purse-proud, swathed in luxury, disdainful pass me by:
I've eager hands—I've earnest heart—but may not work for bread: 15
God of the wretched, hear my prayer! I would that I were dead!

Gold art thou not a blessed thing? A charm above all other,
To shut up hearts to nature's cry, when brother pleads with *brother*?
Hast thou a music sweeter than the loving voice of kindness?
No, curse thee, thou'rt a mist twixt God and men in outer blindness!   20
"Father, come back!" My children cry! Their voices once so sweet,
Now quiver—lance-like, in my bleeding heart! I cannot meet!
The looks that make the brain go mad, of dear ones asking bread!
God of the wretched hear my prayer! I would that I were dead!

Lord, what right have the poor to wed? Love's for the gilded great!   25
Are they not formed of nobler clay who dine off golden plate?
'Tis the worst curse of poverty to have a feeling heart:
Why can I not, with iron grasp, thrust out the tender part?
I cannot slave in yon Bastile!³ Ah, no! 'twere bitterer pain—
I'd wear the pauper's iron within, than clank the convict's chain!   30
To work but cannot—starve, I may—but will not beg for bread:
God of the wretched, hear my prayer! I would that I were dead!

The Red Banner⁴

Fling out the Red Banner! o'er mountain and valley,
    Let earth feel the tread of the Free, once again;
Now, Soldiers of Freedom, for love of God, rally—
    Old Earth yearns to know that her children are men;
We are nerved by a million wrongs burning and bleeding,   5
    Bold thoughts leap to birth, but, the bold deeds must come,
And, wherever humanity's yearning and pleading,
    One battle for liberty strike ye heart-home!

Notes

³ *Bastile* poor-house; so named after the Bastille, the state prison in Paris stormed on 14 June 1789, inaugurating the French Revolution. Carlyle would use the term "Workhouse Bastilles" and "Poor-Law Bastilles" throughout *Past and Present* (1843); see CONDITION: SOCIAL FORMATION, n. 19.

⁴ *title* a red banner had long been a symbol for popular revolution, even before its use in the French Revolution of 1789–92. It was used again in the June Rebellion (1832) in Paris, an unsuccessful republican revolt to undo the results of the July Revolution (1830) that had placed Louis-Philippe (1773–1850) on the French throne; it was used by anti-monarchist and socialist groups throughout Europe to represent the blood of the people who had died fighting repression. The poem first appeared in the "Poetry of the People" column of the first number of *The Red Republican* (22 June 1850). Massey's poem "Song of the Red Republican," beginning "Ay, tyrants, build your bulwarks! forge your fetters! link your chains!" appeared on the first page of the same issue. The paper was published in London by George Julian Harney (1817–97), political activist and journalist. Harney, like Massey, had become a socialist after the 1848 revolutions in Europe. In November 1850, *The Red Republican* published the first English translation of *The Communist Manifesto* by Karl Marx (1818–83) and Frederick Engels (1820–95). Massey's poem was republished under the title "Our Symbol" in his *Voices of Freedom and Lyrics of Love* (1851).

Fling out the Red Banner! its fiery front under,
    Come, gather ye, gather ye! Champions of Right! 10
And roll round the world with the voice of God's thunder
    The wrongs we've to reckon—oppressors to smite;
They deem that we strike no more like the old hero-band—
    Martyrdom's own battle-hearted and brave;
Blood of Christ! brothers mine, it were sweet, but to see ye stand 15
    Triumph or tomb! welcome! glory or grave!

Fling out the Red Banner! achievements immortal
    Have yet to be won by the hands labour-brown,
And few, few may enter the proud promise-portal,
    Yet, wear it in thought, boys! the glorious crown! 20
And, oh! joy of the conflict! sound trumpet! array us!
    True hearts would leap up, were all hell in our path,
Up! up! from the slave land! who stirreth to stay us
    Shall fall as of old in the Red Sea⁵ of wrath!

Fling out the Red Banner! and range ye around, 25
    Young spirits, abiding to burst into wings,
We stand, by the coming events, shadow-crowned,
    There's a grim hush in heaven! and the Bird of Storm⁶ sings:
"All's well!" saith the Sentry on Tyranny's tower,
    "Even Hope by their watch-fire is grey and tear-blind." 30
Aye, all's well! Freedom's altar burns hour by hour—
    Live brands for the fire-damps⁷ with which ye are mined.

Fling out the Red Banner! the patriots perish!
    But where their bones moulder the seed taketh root⁸—
Their heart's-life ran red the great harvest to cherish, 35
    Then gather ye Reapers, and garner the fruit.
Victory! victory! Tyrants are quaking,
    The Titan of Toil from the bloody thrall starts,
The Slaves are awaking! the dawnlight is breaking!
    The footfall of Freedom beats quick at our hearts! 40

The Awakening of the People⁹

O sweet is the fair face of Nature, when Spring
    With living flower-rainbow in glory hath spann'd
Hill and dale; and the music of birds on the wing

Notes

5 *slave land ... Red Sea* the exodus of Israel from slavery in Egypt, a common metaphor for republican overthrow of indentured labour and political tyranny; see Exodus 13–14.

6 *Storm* storm or stormy petrel, which in sea-lore is said to warn of coming storms.

7 *fire-damps* flammable gas in coal mines; here gas that would ignite by the flaming torches of the republicans.

8 *root* see Tertullian, *Apologeticus* (*c.*197 CE): "The blood of the martyrs is the seed of the Church" (ch. 50). See also CHARLOTTE BRONTË, "THE MISSIONARY," n. 10.

9 *title* published in *The Ballad of Babe Christabel: With Other Lyrical Poems* (1854); our text 1855 (third edition).

Makes earth seem a beautiful færy land!
And dear is our first-love's young spirit-wed bride,   5
    With her meek eyes just sheathing in tender eclipse,
When the sound of our voice calls her heart's ruddy tide,
    Uprushing in beauty to melt on her lips.
But Earth has no sight half so glorious to see,
As a People up-girding its might to be free.   10

To see men awake from the slumber of ages,
    With brows grim from labour, and hands hard and tan,
Start up living heroes, the dreamt-of by Sages!
    And smite with strong arm the oppressors of man:
To see them come dauntless forth 'mid the world's warring,   15
    Slaves of the midnight-mine! serfs of the sod!
Show how the Eternal within them is stirring,
    And never more bend to a crowned clod:
Dear God! 'tis a sight for Immortals to see,—
A People up-girding its might to be free.   20

Battle on bravely, O sons of humanity!
    Dash down the cup from your lips, O ye Toilers!
Too long hath the world bled for Tyrants' insanity—
    Too long our weakness been strength to our spoilers.
For Freedom and Right, gallant hearts, wrestle ever,   25
    And speak ye to others the proud words that won ye:
Your rights conquer'd once, shall be wrung from you never;
    O battle on bravely; the world's eyes are on ye;
And Earth hath no sight half so glorious to see,
As a People up-girding its might to be free!   30

Elizabeth Siddal (1829–62)

Born in the London district of Holborn, Elizabeth Eleanor Siddal was spotted as a "stunner" (as the Pre-Raphaelite brothers called beautiful women) while working in a milliner's shop. She modelled for Walter Deverell (1827–54), D. G. Rossetti (1828–82), J. E. Millais (1829–96, sitting for *Ophelia*, 1852), and William Holman Hunt (1827–1910). After becoming Rossetti's mistress, she started painting and writing poetry under his instruction, and came under the patronage and support of John Ruskin. She became sick and travelled to Paris and Nice to recover. The engagement to Rossetti was broken (1858); however, they married in 1860 and she had a stillborn child. In February 1862 she died, probably suicidally, from an overdose of laudanum. Rossetti buried his only copy of his manuscript poems in her coffin, only to recover it at her exhumation (1869). William Michael Rossetti, her brother-in-law, had published fifteen of her poems by 1906. Standard edition: *Poems and Drawings of Elizabeth Siddal*, eds Roger C. Lewis and Mark Samuels Lasner (1978); Jan Marsh, *The Legend of Elizabeth Siddal* (1989); "Exploring Lizzie Siddal": http://lizziesiddal.com/portal/?p=25.

Dead Love[1]

Oh never weep for love that's dead,
    Since love is seldom true,
But changes his fashion from blue to red,
    From brightest red to blue,
And love was born to an early death
    And is so seldom true.

Then harbour no smile on your loving face
    To win the deepest sigh;
The fairest words on truest lips
    Pass off and surely die;
And you will stand alone, my dear,
    When wintry winds draw nigh.

Sweet, never weep for what cannot be,
    For this God has not given:
If the merest dream of love were true,
    Then, sweet, we should be in heaven;
And this is only earth, my dear,
    Where true love is not given.

Love and Hate[2]

Ope not thy lips, thou foolish one,
    Nor turn to me thy face:
The blasts of heaven shall strike me down
    Ere I will give thee grace.

Take thou thy shadow from my path,
    Nor turn to me and pray:
The wild, wild winds thy dirge may sing
    Ere I will bid thee stay.

Lift up thy false brow from the dust,
    Nor wild thine hands entwine
Among the golden summer-leaves
    To mock the gay sunshine.

And turn away thy false dark eyes,
    Nor gaze into my face:
Great love I bore thee; now great hate
    Sits grimly in its place.

Notes

ELIZABETH SIDDAL

[1] title according to William Michael Rossetti, perhaps written in 1859, this poem was said to be Christina Rossetti's favourite poem of Siddal's. First published in *Ruskin, Rossetti, Pre-Raphaelitism*, ed. William Michael Rossetti (1899).

[2] title first published in W. M. Rossetti, *Some Reminiscences* (2 vols, 1906). In the edition of Lewis and Lasner (1978), the third stanza is omitted.

All changes pass me like a dream,
    I neither sing nor pray;
And thou art like the poisonous tree
    That stole my life away.

Lord, May I Come?[3]

Life and night are falling from me,
Death and day are opening on me.
Wherever my footsteps come and go
Life is a stony way of woe.
    Lord, have I long to go?

Hollow hearts are ever near me,
Soulless eyes have ceased to cheer me:
    Lord, may I come to Thee?

Life and youth and summer weather
To my heart no joy can gather:
Lord, lift me from life's stony way.
Loved eyes, long closed in death, watch o'er me—
Holy Death is waiting for me—
    Lord, may I come to-day?

My outward life feels sad and still,
Like lilies in a frozen rill.
I am gazing upwards to the sun,
Lord, Lord, remembering my lost one.[4]
    O Lord, remember me!

How is it in the unknown land?
Do the dead wander hand in hand?
Do we clasp dead hands, and quiver
With an endless joy for ever?
Is the air filled with the sound[5]
Of spirits circling round and round?
Are there lakes, of endless song,
To rest our tirèd eyes upon?
Do tall white angels gaze and wend
Along the banks where lilies bend?
Lord, we know not how this may be;
Good Lord, we put our faith in Thee—
    O God, remember me.

Notes

[3] *title* probably written early in 1862, and said to have been found by Dante Rossetti near Elizabeth Siddal when she was dying. First published in W. M. Rossetti, *Some Reminiscences* (2 vols, 1906).

[4] *one* William Michael Rossetti adds the following note: "I do not know of any 'lost one,' unless the reference is to the still-born infant (1861). I learned however of late years from Mr. James Siddal (brother of Lizzie) that, shortly before her acquaintance with Dante Rossetti, she had been in lengthened and very exhausting attendance on the sick-bed of another much-loved brother [Charles], whose illness ended in death. Possibly this is the allusion—as also in the line 'Loved eyes' etc."

[5] *sound* this line and the following three are omitted by Lewis and Lasner (1978).

Christina Rossetti (1830–94)

Born in London into a family of Italian exiles, Christina Georgina Rossetti was the youngest of four children of Gabriele Rossetti (1783–1854), an Italian nationalist, forced to flee his home country in 1821 for his political views, and interpreter of Dante in the light of arcane mystical readings in religious and political movements of his day. He was professor of Italian at King's College, London. His wife, Frances Polidori (1800–86), was the sister of Byron's physician, John Polidori (1795–1821). Christina's family was renowned: Maria Francesca (1827–76), Dante Gabriel (1828–82), and William Michael (1829–1919). Maria wrote on Dante, as did both of the brothers. The family home became a centre for Italian political exiles and Italian culture and literature. Christina along with her mother and sister were devout High Church Anglicans, attending Christ Church, Albany Street, Maria Francesca becoming a nun with the Society of All Saints. Christina was educated at home in literature and the classics, as well as religion, and benefited from the numerous visiting Italian emigrés. Engaged for a short while to another member of the PRB, James Collinson (1825–81), she broke it off in 1850 when he reconverted to Roman Catholicism. Religious differences lay at the heart of at least one other potential romance, that in 1856 with the agnostic linguist Charles Bagot Cayley (1823–83) – though Rossetti and Cayley remained the best of friends, and she became his literary executor on his death. Dante Rossetti painted her as the Virgin Mary in The Girlhood of Mary Virgin (1850; Plate 13) and did many other portraits. Using the pseudonym "Ellen Alleyn" she published in the Pre-Raphaelite journal, The Germ (1850), and in the Athenæum and Macmillan's, and succeeded Elizabeth Barrett Browning as the leading female poet in England with the publication of Goblin Market and Other Poems (1862). Subsequent volumes included The Prince's Progress and Other Poems (1866), Speaking Likenesses (1874), Sing-Song: A Nursery Rhyme Book (1875), and New Poems (posthumous, 1896). William Michael issued her Collected Poetry in 1904. Her prose included a number of volumes of devotional writing: Called to be Saints (1881), Time Flies: A Reading Diary (1885), and The Face of the Deep (1893), a commentary on the Revelation of St John. From 1871 she suffered from Grave's disease (a thyroid condition), and two years before her death she was operated on for breast cancer. Praised during her lifetime in her Pre-Raphaelite circle and amongst other women poets, her reputation declined in the first half of the twentieth century, despite praise of her by Virginia Woolf. Her revival began with the advent of feminist criticism in the later twentieth century. Standard editions: The Complete Poems of Christina Rossetti, ed. R. W. Crump (3 vols, 1979–90); Christina Rossetti: The Complete Poems, ed. R. W. Crump; notes by Betty S. Flower (2001); Selected Prose of Christina Rossetti, eds David A. Kent and P. G. Stanwood (1998); Christina Rossetti: Poems and Prose, ed. Simon Humphries (2008); The Letters of Christina Rossetti, ed. Antony H. Harrison (4 vols, 1997–2004); Diane D'Amico, Christina Rossetti: Faith, Gender, and Time (1999). See Orlando Project: http://orlando.cambridge.org.

Sappho[1]

I sigh at day-dawn, and I sigh
When the dull day is passing by.
I sigh at evening, and again
I sigh[2] when night brings sleep to men.
Oh! it were better far to die   5
Than thus for ever mourn and sigh,
And in death's dreamless sleep to be
Unconscious that none weep for me;
Eased from my weight of heaviness,
Forgetful of forgetfulness,   10
Resting from pain and care and sorrow
Through the long night that knows no morrow;[3]
Living unloved, to die unknown,
Unwept, untended and alone.[4]

Goblin Market[5]

Morning and evening
Maids heard the goblins cry:
"Come buy our orchard fruits,

Notes

CHRISTINA ROSSETTI

[1] *title* for Sappho as a model for the poet, especially the female poet, and her dying for love, see LANDON, n. 1; and HEMANS, n. 14. Rossetti also wrote another poem, in 1848, on Sappho: "What Sappho Would Have Said Had Her Leap Cured Instead of Killing Her" (1904). First printed privately in *Verses: Dedicated to Her Mother* (1847).

[2] *sigh ... sigh ... sigh ... sigh* the sighing poet, continuing into line 6, is a constant in the poems on Sappho by both Landon and Hemans. Landon writes: "Poison hath been upon thy sigh" (3) and Hemans: "my weary soul hath sought / In vain one echoing sigh" (9–10).

[3] *morrow* see Robert Burns's "Raving Winds Around Her Blowing" (1788): "Cheerless night that knows no morrow" (8).

[4] *unknown ... alone* see HEMANS, "LAST SONG": "And I— unsought, unwatch'd for" (36); for *alone*: "its own ceaseless cry—'Alone, alone!'" (4).

[5] *title* underlying the poem is the idea of the forbidden fruit of the Garden of Eden (see Genesis 2: 16–17; and Revelation 18: 14–15) in the face of lavish plenty. As well, there are allusions to Bunyan's *Pilgrim's Progress* (1678), especially the rhetorical repetitions and the allegory of Beelzebub's Orchard whose fruit poisons Matthew, the eldest son of Christiana: "Then said Samuel, Mother, Mother. . . You know that there was an Orchard on the left hand, on the other side of the wall, some of the trees hung over the wall, and my Brother did plash and did eat.... [Physician Skill:] I knew he had eaten something that was not wholesome food, and that food, to wit, that Fruit, is even the most hurtful of all. It is the Fruit of Beelzebub's Orchard. I do marvel that none did warn you of it; many have died thereof.... When Mr Skill had seen that that Purge was too weak, he made him one to the pur-

pose.... It caused him to purge, it caused him to sleep and rest quietly, it put him into a fine heat and breathing sweat, and did quite rid him of his Gripes" (pt. 2, ch. 5). This temptation poem is also a seduction poem, since Laura succumbed to the goblin men, and bought their tempting fruit with her golden curl. As a result, like the unfortunate Jeanie (147–60; 364), she dwindled to come near to death. The intervention of Lizzie to save her sister Laura's life raises the poem's theme of self-sacrifice, a kind of sisterly heroism that was read typologically through the Eucharistic language and imagery as a reinscription of Christ's sacrifice for the sins of others in the crucifixion. Such redemptive aims were conventional in the Magdalen hospitals to reclaim prostitutes; see WEBSTER, nn. 1 and 20. Rossetti volunteered at St Mary Magdalen Home for Fallen Women on Highgate Hill from about 1859 to 1865. The poem has been read for its questioning of economic exchange and the perils of consumerism and also as a representation of lesbian desire and of the ravages of tubercular consumption. In a letter to Edmund Gosse (1849–1928), Rossetti claimed, "In my own intention Goblin Market was no allegory at all, so it does not surprise me that it is inexplicable in detail." The poem was first published in *Goblin Market and Other Poems* (1862), with a cover and *frontispiece* designed by her brother Dante. The title page was also signed by the engraver, W. J. Linton (1812–97), and the frontispiece bears the initials also of the firm of Morris, Marshall, Faulkner & Co. (founded by William Morris in 1861). In 1893 Rossetti wrote an inscription in a copy of *Goblin Market* that included the following: "'Goblin Market' ... in M.S. was inscribed to my dear only sister Maria Francesca Rossetti herself long afterwards the author of 'A Shadow of Dante.'"

Come buy, come buy:[6]
Apples and quinces,   5
Lemons and oranges,
Plump unpecked cherries,
Melons and raspberries,
Bloom-down-cheeked peaches,
Swart-headed[7] mulberries,   10
Wild free-born cranberries,
Crab-apples, dewberries,
Pine-apples, blackberries,
Apricots, strawberries;—
All ripe together   15
In summer weather,—
Morns that pass by,
Fair eves that fly;
Come buy, come buy:
Our grapes fresh from the vine,   20
Pomegranates full and fine,
Dates and sharp bullaces,
Rare pears and greengages,
Damsons[8] and bilberries,
Taste them and try: 25
Currants and gooseberries,
Bright-fire-like barberries,
Figs to fill your mouth,
Citrons from the South,
Sweet to tongue and sound to eye;[9]   30
Come buy, come buy."

Evening by evening
Among the brookside rushes,
Laura bowed her head to hear,
Lizzie[10] veiled her blushes: 35
Crouching close together
In the cooling weather,
With clasping arms and cautioning lips,
With tingling cheeks and fingertips.
"Lie close," Laura said,   40
Pricking up her golden head:
"We must not look at goblin men,

Notes

[6] *buy* see Isaiah 55: 1.

[7] *swart-headed* black-headed, the dark purple colour of mulberries.

[8] *bullaces … Damsons* varieties of plums: wild, green, and purple.

[9] *apples … sound to eye* a conventional epic catalogue, like Homer's catalogue of the ships that sailed to Troy in *Iliad* (2.494–759), and, more appropriately, the catalogue of the peers of Lucifer in *Paradise Lost* (1. 361–75). Here the catalogue of fruits most closely resembles what the Redcrosse knight takes to be "a shady grove" and a "faire harbour," but that instead is "the wandring wood, this *Errours* den" in Spenser's *Faerie Queene,* where the trees are catalogued (1.1.9, 69–81.) These trees, like Rossetti's fruit that is "sound to the eye," seem "inward sound."

[10] *Laura … Lizzie* Laura is associated in Rossetti's poetry with Petrarch's beloved and muse (as in *Monna Innominata,* below); according to some critics, Lizzie is associated with St Elizabeth of Hungary (1207–31), depicted in such Pre-Raphaelite paintings as James Collinson's *An Incident in the Life of St. Elizabeth of Hungary* (1850), illustrating Charles Kingsley's *A Saint's Tragedy* (1848).

We must not buy their fruits:
Who knows upon what soil they fed
Their hungry thirsty roots?"   45
"Come buy," call the goblins
Hobbling down the glen.
"Oh," cried Lizzie, "Laura, Laura,
You should not peep at goblin men."
Lizzie covered up her eyes,   50
Covered close lest they should look;
Laura reared her glossy head,
And whispered like the restless brook:
"Look, Lizzie, look, Lizzie,
Down the glen tramp little men.   55
One hauls a basket,
One bears a plate,
One lugs a golden dish
Of many pounds weight.
How fair the vine must grow   60
Whose grapes are so luscious;
How warm the wind must blow
Through those fruit bushes."
"No," said Lizzie: "No, no, no;
Their offers should not charm us,   65
Their evil gifts[11] would harm us."
She thrust a dimpled finger
In each ear, shut eyes and ran:[12]
Curious Laura chose to linger
Wondering at each merchant man.   70
One had a cat's face,
One whisked a tail,
One tramped at a rat's pace,
One crawled like a snail,
One like a wombat prowled obtuse and furry,   75
One like a ratel[13] tumbled hurry skurry.
She heard a voice like voice of doves
Cooing all together:
They sounded kind and full of loves
In the pleasant weather.   80

    Laura stretched her gleaming neck
Like a rush-imbedded swan,
Like a lily from the beck,
Like a moonlit poplar branch,
Like a vessel at the launch   85
When its last restraint is gone.

Notes

[11] *gifts* Lizzie calls the fruit "gifts" here; and at line 149 the "gifts" were taken by Jeanie to terrible effect – though the goblins said, "Come buy." See also line 439 where the proffered coins are rejected.

[12] *She ... ran* see *Pilgrim's Progress* where Pilgrim puts his fingers in his ears as he flees the City of Destruction and runs towards the wicket-gate and the shining light, to block his wife and children's calling him back (ch. 1: "The First Stage").

[13] *wombat ... ratel* a wombat is a South Australian burrowing marsupial; a ratel is a honey badger, native to Africa and India. Dante Rossetti eventually had one of each in his menagerie.

Backwards up the mossy glen
Turned and trooped the goblin men,
With their shrill repeated cry,
"Come buy, come buy." 90
When they reached where Laura was
They stood stock still upon the moss,
Leering at each other,
Brother with queer brother;
Signalling each other, 95
Brother with sly brother.
One set his basket down,
One reared his plate;
One began to weave a crown
Of tendrils, leaves, and rough nuts brown 100
(Men sell not such in any town);
One heaved the golden weight
Of dish and fruit to offer her:
"Come buy, come buy," was still their cry.
Laura stared but did not stir, 105
Longed but had no money:
The whisk-tailed merchant bade her taste
In tones as smooth as honey,
The cat-faced purr'd,
The rat-paced spoke a word 110
Of welcome, and the snail-paced even was heard;
One parrot-voiced and jolly
Cried "Pretty Goblin" still for "Pretty Polly";
One whistled like a bird.

But sweet-tooth Laura spoke in haste: 115
"Good folk, I have no coin;
To take were to purloin:
I have no copper in my purse,
I have no silver either,
And all my gold is on the furze 120
That shakes in windy weather
Above the rusty heather."
"You have much gold upon your head,"
They answered altogether:
"Buy from us with a golden curl."[14] 125
She clipped a precious golden lock,[15]
She dropped a tear more rare than pearl,
Then sucked their fruit globes fair or red:
Sweeter than honey from the rock,[16]
Stronger than man-rejoicing wine, 130

Notes

[14] *curl* line used by Dante Rossetti to illustrate the frontispiece to the volume.

[15] *lock* see Alexander Pope, *The Rape of the Lock* (1714): "The meeting points the sacred hair dissever / From the fair head, for ever, and for ever!" (3. 153–54).

[16] *rock* see Deuteronomy 32: 13; and Psalm 81: 16.

Clearer than water flowed that juice;
She never tasted such before,
How should it cloy with length of use?
She sucked and sucked and sucked the more
Fruits which that unknown orchard[17] bore;   135
She sucked until her lips were sore;
Then flung the emptied rinds away
But gathered up one kernel stone,
And knew not was it night or day
As she turned home alone.   140

    Lizzie met her at the gate
Full of wise upbraidings:
"Dear, you should not stay so late,
Twilight is not good for maidens;
Should not loiter in the glen   145
In the haunts of goblin men.
Do you not remember Jeanie,[18]
How she met them in the moonlight,
Took their gifts both choice and many,
Ate their fruits and wore their flowers   150
Plucked from bowers
Where summer ripens at all hours?
But ever in the noonlight
She pined and pined away;
Sought them by night and day,   155
Found them no more but dwindled and grew gray;
Then fell with the first snow,
While to this day no grass will grow
Where she lies low:
I planted daisies there a year ago   160
That never blow.
You should not loiter so."
"Nay, hush," said Laura:
"Nay, hush, my sister:
I ate and ate my fill,   165
Yet my mouth waters still;
To-morrow night I will
Buy more": and kissed her:
"Have done with sorrow;
I'll bring you plums to-morrow   170
Fresh on their mother twigs,
Cherries worth getting;
You cannot think what figs
My teeth have met in,

Notes

[17] *orchard* concerning the "Fruit of Beelzebub's Orchard" in *Pilgrim's Progress*, see n. 5.

[18] *Jeanie* her name rhymes with "many" two lines on, and therefore might be associated with Dante Rossetti's "Jenny," a poem about a prostitute (see DANTE ROSSETTI).

Although first published in 1870, Dante Rossetti had been working on "Jenny" in 1847–48, and had revised it further in 1859–60. Christina Rossetti doubtlessly would have known her brother's poem as it progressed.

What melons icy-cold 175
Piled on a dish of gold
Too huge for me to hold,
What peaches with a velvet nap,
Pellucid grapes without one seed:
Odorous indeed must be the mead 180
Whereon they grow, and pure the wave they drink
With lilies at the brink,
And sugar-sweet their sap."

    Golden head by golden head,[19]
Like two pigeons in one nest 185
Folded in each other's wings,
They lay down in their curtained bed:
Like two blossoms on one stem,
Like two flakes of new-fall'n snow,
Like two wands of ivory 190
Tipped with gold for awful kings.
Moon and stars gazed in at them,
Wind sang to them lullaby,
Lumbering owls forbore to fly,
Not a bat flapped to and fro 195
Round their rest:
Cheek to cheek and breast to breast
Locked together in one nest.

    Early in the morning
When the first cock crowed his warning, 200
Neat like bees, as sweet and busy,
Laura rose with Lizzie:
Fetched in honey, milked the cows,
Aired and set to rights the house,
Kneaded cakes of whitest wheat, 205
Cakes for dainty mouths to eat,
Next churned butter, whipped up cream,
Fed their poultry, sat and sewed;
Talked as modest maidens should:
Lizzie with an open heart, 210
Laura in an absent dream,
One content, one sick in part;
One warbling for the mere bright day's delight,
One longing for the night.

    At length slow evening came: 215
They went with pitchers to the reedy brook;
Lizzie most placid in her look,
Laura most like a leaping flame.

Notes

[19] *head* the line that Dante Rossetti chose to illustrate in his title-page illustration. Sisters often slept together in Victorian and later times.

They drew the gurgling water from its deep;
Lizzie plucked purple and rich golden flags,[20]   220
Then turning homeward said: "The sunset flushes
Those furthest loftiest crags;
Come, Laura, not another maiden lags,
No wilful squirrel wags,
The beasts and birds are fast asleep."   225
But Laura loitered still among the rushes
And said the bank was steep.

And said the hour was early still,
The dew not fall'n, the wind not chill:
Listening ever, but not catching   230
The customary cry,
"Come buy, come buy,"
With its iterated jingle
Of sugar-baited words:
Not for all her watching   235
Once discerning even one goblin
Racing, whisking, tumbling, hobbling;
Let alone the herds
That used to tramp along the glen,
In groups or single,   240
Of brisk fruit-merchant men.[21]
Till Lizzie urged, "O Laura, come;
I hear the fruit-call but I dare not look:
You should not loiter longer at this brook:
Come with me home.   245
The stars rise, the moon bends her arc,
Each glowworm winks her spark,
Let us get home before the night grows dark:
For clouds may gather
Though this is summer weather,   250
Put out the lights and drench us through;
Then if we lost our way what should we do?"

Laura turned cold as stone
To find her sister heard that cry alone,
That goblin cry,   255
"Come buy our fruits, come buy."
Must she then buy no more such dainty fruit?
Must she no more such succous pasture[22] find,
Gone deaf and blind?
Her tree of life[23] drooped from the root: 260
She said not one word in her heart's sore ache;

Notes

[20] *flags* water-iris.
[21] *men* "Mr. Brisk" also appears in *Pilgrim's Progress* (pt. 2), just before the passage concerning Beelzebub's Orchard (see n. 5).
[22] *succous pasture* succous means juicy (<Lat. *succosus*, juicy < *succus*, juice; Ital. *succoso*), with an etymology related to suck. Pasture signifies food but also spiritual food (*OED*, 2: obs.), a possible echo of Malbecco's "pasture poysonous" in Spenser, *Faerie Queene* (3. 10. 59).
[23] *life* see especially Proverbs 13: 12; see also Genesis 2: 9; and 3: 22; and Revelation 2: 7; 22: 2; and 22: 19.

But peering thro' the dimness, nought discerning,
Trudged home, her pitcher dripping all the way;
So crept to bed, and lay
Silent till Lizzie slept;   265
Then sat up in a passionate yearning,
And gnashed her teeth for baulked desire, and wept
As if her heart would break.

    Day after day, night after night,
Laura kept watch in vain   270
In sullen silence of exceeding pain.
She never caught again the goblin cry:
"Come buy, come buy";—
She never spied the goblin men
Hawking their fruits along the glen: 275
But when the noon waxed bright
Her hair grew thin and gray;
She dwindled, as the fair full moon doth turn
To swift decay and burn
Her fire away.   280

    One day remembering her kernel-stone
She set it by a wall that faced the south;
Dewed it with tears, hoped for a root,
Watched for a waxing shoot,
But there came none;   285
It never saw the sun,
It never felt the trickling moisture run:
While with sunk eyes and faded mouth
She dreamed of melons, as a traveller sees
False waves in desert drouth   290
With shade of leaf-crowned trees,
And burns the thirstier in the sandful breeze.
    She no more swept the house,
Tended the fowls or cows,
Fetched honey, kneaded cakes of wheat,   295
Brought water from the brook:
But sat down listless in the chimney-nook
And would not eat.

    Tender Lizzie could not bear
To watch her sister's cankerous care   300
Yet not to share.
She night and morning
Caught the goblins' cry:
"Come buy our orchard fruits,
Come buy, come buy":—   305
Beside the brook, along the glen
She heard the tramp of goblin men,
The voice and stir
Poor Laura could not hear;
Longed to buy fruit to comfort her,   310
But feared to pay too dear.

She thought of Jeanie in her grave,
Who should have been a bride;
But who for joys[24] brides hope to have
Fell sick and died   315
In her gay prime,
In earliest Winter time,
With the first glazing rime,[25]
With the first snow-fall of crisp Winter time.

 Till Laura dwindling   320
Seemed knocking at Death's door:
Then Lizzie weighed no more
Better and worse;
But put a silver penny in her purse,
Kissed Laura, crossed the heath with clumps of furze 325
At twilight, halted by the brook:
And for the first time in her life
Began to listen and look.

 Laughed every goblin
When they spied her peeping: 330
Came towards her hobbling,
Flying, running, leaping,
Puffing and blowing,
Chuckling, clapping, crowing,
Clucking and gobbling,   335
Mopping and mowing,[26]
Full of airs and graces,[27]
Pulling wry faces,
Demure grimaces,
Cat-like and rat-like,   340
Ratel- and wombat-like,
Snail-paced in a hurry,
Parrot-voiced and whistler,
Helter skelter, hurry skurry,
Chattering like magpies,   345
Fluttering like pigeons,
Gliding like fishes,—
Hugged her and kissed her:
Squeezed and caressed her:
Stretched up their dishes,   350
Panniers, and plates:
"Look at our apples
Russet and dun,[28]

Notes

[24] *for joys* a much-disputed line. "For" could mean forsaking all bridal joys, the joys of married life; or it could mean desiring, yearning for bridal joys.

[25] *rime* freezing mist.

[26] *mopping and mowing* (< "mock and mow," to jeer and grimace, *OED*); see Shelley, *Peter Bell, the Third* ([1819] 1839: 6. 20); see also Byron, *The Island* (1823: 6. 7).

[27] *graces* see *The Tempest*: "the isle is full of noises, / Sounds and sweet airs" (3. 2. 1533–34).

[28] *dun* reddish and dull brown.

Bob at our cherries,
Bite at our peaches,   355
Citrons and dates,
Grapes for the asking,
Pears red with basking
Out in the sun,
Plums on their twigs;   360
Pluck them and suck them,
Pomegranates, figs."—

    "Good folk," said Lizzie,
Mindful of Jeanie,
"Give me much and many":—   365
Held out her apron,
Tossed them her penny.
"Nay, take a seat with us,
Honour and eat with us,"
They answered grinning: 370
"Our feast is but beginning.
Night yet is early,
Warm and dew-pearly,
Wakeful and starry:
Such fruits as these   375
No man can carry;
Half their bloom would fly,
Half their dew would dry,
Half their flavour would pass by.
Sit down and feast with us,   380
Be welcome guest with us,
Cheer you and rest with us."—
"Thank you," said Lizzie: "But one waits
At home alone for me:
So without further parleying,[29]   385
If you will not sell me any
Of your fruits though much and many,
Give me back my silver penny
I tossed you for a fee."—
They began to scratch their pates,[30]   390
No longer wagging, purring,
But visibly demurring,
Grunting and snarling.
One called her proud,
Cross-grained, uncivil;   395
Their tones waxed loud,
Their looks were evil.
Lashing their tails
They trod and hustled her,
Elbowed and jostled her,   400

Notes

[29] *parleying* discussion, conversation.   [30] *pates* heads.

Clawed with their nails,
Barking, mewing, hissing, mocking,
Tore her gown and soiled her stocking,
Twitched her hair out by the roots,
Stamped upon her tender feet,   405
Held her hands and squeezed their fruits
Against her mouth to make her eat.

 White and golden Lizzie stood,
Like a lily in a flood,—
Like a rock of blue-veined stone   410
Lashed by tides obstreperously,—
Like a beacon left alone
In a hoary roaring sea,
Sending up a golden fire,—
Like a fruit-crowned orange-tree   415
White with blossoms honey-sweet[31]
Sore beset by wasp and bee,—
Like a royal virgin town[32]
Topped with gilded dome and spire
Close beleaguered by a fleet   420
Mad to tug her standard down.

 One may lead a horse to water,
Twenty cannot make him drink.[33]
Though the goblins cuffed and caught her,
Coaxed and fought her,   425
Bullied and besought her,
Scratched her, pinched her black as ink,
Kicked and knocked her,
Mauled and mocked her,
Lizzie uttered not a word;[34]   430
Would not open lip from lip
Lest they should cram a mouthful in:
But laughed in heart to feel the drip
Of juice that syrupped all her face,
And lodged in dimples of her chin,   435
And streaked her neck which quaked like curd.
At last the evil people
Worn out by her resistance
Flung back her penny, kicked their fruit
Along whichever road they took,   440

Notes

[31] *honey-sweet* fragrant orange blossoms were often carried by brides from the early nineteenth century in a custom originating in China and brought to Europe at the time of the crusades. They were symbolic of fruitfulness because blossoms and fruit occur at the same time.

[32] *town* a town never besieged and taken; analogous to the medieval and Renaissance concept of the assault on the castle of chastity or love, as in various ivories in the British Museum and the Victoria and Albert Museum; see also Milton, *Comus* (1634), a masque in honour of chastity. For the besieged town, see n. 96; see also PATMORE n. 16.

[33] *drink* proverbial.

[34] *word* like Christ's silence before his accusers before his mocking and scourging: see Matthew 27: 12–14, 29; Mark 15; Luke 23; and John 19.

Not leaving root or stone or shoot;
Some writhed into the ground,
Some dived into the brook
With ring and ripple,
Some scudded on the gale without a sound,　445
Some vanished in the distance.

In a smart, ache, tingle,
Lizzie went her way;
Knew not was it night or day;
Sprang up the bank, tore thro' the furze,　450
Threaded copse and dingle,
And heard her penny jingle
Bouncing in her purse,—
Its bounce was music to her ear.
She ran and ran　455
As if she feared some goblin man
Dogged her with gibe or curse
Or something worse:
But not one goblin skurried after,
Nor was she pricked by fear;　460
The kind heart made her windy-paced
That urged her home quite out of breath with haste
And inward laughter.

She cried "Laura," up the garden,[35]
"Did you miss me?　465
Come and kiss me.
Never mind my bruises,
Hug me, kiss me, suck my juices
Squeezed from goblin fruits for you,
Goblin pulp and goblin dew.　470
Eat me, drink me, love me;[36]
Laura, make much of me:
For your sake I have braved the glen
And had to do with goblin merchant men."

Laura started from her chair,　475
Flung her arms up in the air,
Clutched her hair:
"Lizzie, Lizzie, have you tasted
For my sake the fruit forbidden?[37]
Must your light like mine be hidden,[38]　480
Your young life like mine be wasted,
Undone in mine undoing

Notes

[35] *garden* see Genesis 2.
[36] *me* echo of Jesus' words at the Last Supper (see Luke 22: 18–20; 1 Corinthians 11: 23–29; and BCP, Holy Communion, Prayer of Consecration).
[37] *forbidden* see Genesis 2: 16–17; see also Beelzebub's Orchard, n. 5.
[38] *hidden* see Matthew 5: 15–16.

And ruined in my ruin,
Thirsty, cankered, goblin-ridden?"—
She clung about her sister,   485
Kissed and kissed and kissed her:
Tears once again
Refreshed her shrunken eyes,
Dropping like rain
After long sultry drouth;   490
Shaking with aguish[39] fear, and pain,
She kissed and kissed her with a hungry mouth.

    Her lips began to scorch,
That juice was wormwood[40] to her tongue,
She loathed the feast: 495
Writhing as one possessed she leaped and sung,
Rent all her robe, and wrung
Her hands in lamentable haste,
And beat her breast.
Her locks streamed like the torch   500
Borne by a racer at full speed,
Or like the mane of horses in their flight,
Or like an eagle when she stems the light[41]
Straight toward the sun,
Or like a caged thing freed,   505
Or like a flying flag when armies run.

    Swift fire spread through her veins, knocked at her heart,
Met the fire smouldering there
And overbore its lesser flame,[42]
She gorged on bitterness without a name: 510
Ah! fool, to choose such part
Of soul-consuming care!
Sense failed in the mortal strife:
Like the watch-tower of a town
Which an earthquake shatters down,   515
Like a lightning-stricken mast,
Like a wind-uprooted tree
Spun about,
Like a foam-topped water spout
Cast down headlong in the sea,   520
She fell at last;
Pleasure past and anguish past,
Is it death or is it life?

Notes

[39] *aguish* like the ague or fever.

[40] *wormwood* bitter-tasting plant (see Proverbs 5: 4) from which the liqueur absinthe was made. See SYMONS, n. 2.

[41] *light* the myth that the eagle could gaze directly into the sun without being hurt is found in two first-century texts: Lucan, *Pharsalia* (6. 799–800) and Pliny, *Natural History* (10. 3–6), as well as in medieval bestiaries.

[42] *flame* see George Herbert (1593–1633), two sonnets called "Love" (1633), asking that God's "greater flame" of the "Immortall Heat" enkindle "true desires."

Life out of death.
That night long Lizzie watched by her,   525
Counted her pulse's flagging stir,
Felt for her breath,
Held water to her lips, and cooled her face
With tears and fanning leaves:
But when the first birds chirped about their eaves,   530
And early reapers plodded to the place
Of golden sheaves,
And dew-wet grass
Bowed in the morning winds so brisk to pass,
And new buds with new day   535
Opened of cup-like lilies on the stream,
Laura awoke as from a dream,
Laughed in the innocent old way,
Hugged Lizzie but not twice or thrice;
Her gleaming locks showed not one thread of gray,   540
Her breath was sweet as May
And light danced in her eyes.

    Days, weeks, months, years
Afterwards, when both were wives
With children of their own;   545
Their mother-hearts beset with fears,
Their lives bound up in tender lives;
Laura would call the little ones
And tell them of her early prime,
Those pleasant days long gone   550
Of not-returning time:
Would talk about the haunted glen,
The wicked, quaint fruit-merchant men,
Their fruits like honey to the throat
But poison in the blood;   555
(Men sell not such in any town):
Would tell them how her sister stood
In deadly peril to do her good,
And win the fiery antidote:
Then joining hands to little hands   560
Would bid them cling together,
"For there is no friend like a sister[43]
In calm or stormy weather;
To cheer one on the tedious way,
To fetch one if one goes astray,   565
To lift one if one totters down,
To strengthen whilst one stands."

Notes

[43] *sister* see the inscription to "my dear only sister," above, n. 5.

A Birthday[44]

My heart is like a singing bird
    Whose nest is in a watered shoot;
My heart is like an appletree
    Whose boughs are bent with thickset fruit;
My heart is like a rainbow shell   5
    That paddles in a halcyon[45] sea;
My heart is gladder than all these,
    Because my love is come to me.

Raise me a dais of silk and down;
    Hang it with vair[46] and purple dyes;   10
Carve it in doves, and pomegranates,
    And peacocks with a hundred eyes;
Work it in gold and silver grapes,
    In leaves, and silver fleurs-de-lys;[47]
Because the birthday of my life   15
    Is come, my love is come to me.

Remember[48]

Sonnet

Remember me[49] when I am gone away,
    Gone far away into the silent land;
    When you can no more hold me by the hand,
Nor I half turn to go yet turning stay.
Remember me when no more day by day   5
    You tell me of our future that you planned:
    Only remember me; you understand
It will be late to counsel then or pray.

Notes

[44] *title* see Song of Solomon 2: 8–13. The Song of Solomon (or Song of Songs) was often read allegorically as referring to the loving relationship between God and Israel, or typologically as the relationship between Christ (the bridegroom) and the church (the bride), or between Christ and the individual Christian, interpretations that go back to the commentaries of early Christian theologians like Hippolytus of Rome (170–235) and Origen (184–254). This and the following poems down to "Up-Hill" are selected from the order in which they were printed in *Goblin Market and Other Poems* (1862). First published *Macmillan's Magazine* (Apr. 1861); republished *Goblin Market and Other Poems* (1862), our text.

[45] *halcyon* see *OED*: "A bird of which the ancients fabled that it bred about the time of the winter solstice in a nest floating on the sea, and that it charmed the wind and waves so that the sea was specially calm during the period."

[46] *vair* heraldic fur from ermine (arch.) or black and white squirrel.

[47] *fleurs-de-lys* heraldic lily of France.

[48] *title* see Shakespeare, Sonnet 71: "No longer mourn for me when I am dead." The sonnet makes some use of the *memento mori* (Lat. remember you must die) topos often inscribed on graves as an epitaph to urge readers to remember the dead within the tomb because they too will die. Here Rossetti perhaps alludes to the controversial advocacy by the Tractarians for prayers for the dead, as in Newman's *Tract 72* (1833) on Archbishop James Ussher (1581–1656) and Prayers for the Dead. Such practices were followed at Rossetti's parish church, Christ Church, Albany Street. From *Goblin Market and Other Poems* (1862).

[49] *me* for "remember me," see Judges 16: 28; Psalm 106: 4; Jeremiah 15: 15; Nehemiah 5: 19; and Luke 23: 42. See also Dido's lament from Naham Tate's libretto to Henry Purcell's *Dido and Aeneas* (1688): "When I am laid, am laid

Yet if you should forget me for a while
    And afterwards remember, do not grieve: 10
    For if the darkness and corruption leave
    A vestige of the thoughts that once I had,
Better by far you should forget and smile
    Than that you should remember and be sad.

After Death[50]

Sonnet

The curtains were half drawn, the floor was swept
    And strewn with rushes, rosemary and may[51].
    Lay thick upon the bed on which I lay,
Where through the lattice ivy-shadows crept.
He leaned above me, thinking that I slept   5
    And could not hear him; but I heard him say:
    "Poor child, poor child": and as he turned away
Came a deep silence, and I knew he wept.
He did not touch the shroud, or raise the fold
    That hid my face, or take my hand in his,   10
        Or ruffle the smooth pillows for my head:
        He did not love me living; but once dead
    He pitied me; and very sweet it is
To know he still is warm though I am cold.

An Apple Gathering[52]

I plucked pink blossoms from mine apple tree
    And wore them all that evening in my hair:
Then in due season when I went to see
    I found no apples there.

With dangling basket all along the grass   5
    As I had come I went the selfsame track:
My neighbours mocked me while they saw me pass
    So empty-handed back.

Lilian and Lilias smiled in trudging by,
    Their heaped-up basket teazed me like a jeer;   10
Sweet-voiced they sang beneath the sunset sky,
    Their mother's home was near.

Notes

in earth, / May my wrongs create / No trouble, no trouble in thy breast; / Remember me, remember me, but ah! forget my fate. / Remember me, but ah! forget my fate."
[50] *title* from *Goblin Market and Other Poems* (1862).

[51] *rosemary . . . may* for rosemary, see *Hamlet* 4. 5. 172; the may is the blossom of the hawthorne.
[52] *title* first published in *Macmillan's Magazine* (Aug. 1861); republished in *Goblin Market and Other Poems* (1862), our text.

Plump Gertrude passed me with her basket full,
    A stronger hand than hers helped it along;
A voice talked with her through the shadows cool   15
    More sweet to me than song.

Ah Willie, Willie, was my love less worth
    Than apples with their green leaves piled above?
I counted rosiest apples on the earth
    Of far less worth than love.   20

So once it was with me you stooped to talk
    Laughing and listening in this very lane:
To think that by this way we used to walk
    We shall not walk again!

I let my neighbours pass me, ones and twos   25
    And groups; the latest said the night grew chill,
And hastened: but I loitered, while the dews
    Fell fast I loitered still.

Echo[53]

Come to me in the silence of the night;
    Come in the speaking silence of a dream;
Come with soft rounded cheeks and eyes as bright
    As sunlight on a stream;
        Come back in tears,   5
O memory, hope, love of finished years.

Oh dream how sweet, too sweet, too bitter sweet,
    Whose wakening should have been in Paradise,
Where souls brimfull of love abide and meet;
    Where thirsting longing eyes   10
        Watch the slow door
That opening, letting in, lets out no more.

Yet come to me in dreams, that I may live
    My very life again though cold in death:
Come back to me in dreams, that I may give   15
    Pulse for pulse, breath for breath:
        Speak low, lean low,
As long ago, my love, how long ago!

Notes

[53] *title* from *Goblin Market and Other Poems* (1862).

My Secret[54]

I tell my secret? No indeed, not I:
Perhaps some day, who knows?
But not to-day; it froze, and blows, and snows,
And you're too curious: fie!
You want to hear it? well: 5
Only, my secret's mine, and I won't tell.

  Or, after all, perhaps there's none:
Suppose there is no secret after all,
But only just my fun.
To-day's a nipping day, a biting day;   10
In which one wants a shawl,
A veil, a cloak, and other wraps:
I cannot ope to every one who taps,
And let the draughts come whistling through my hall;
Come bounding and surrounding me,   15
Come buffeting, astounding me,
Nipping and clipping through my wraps and all.
I wear my mask for warmth: who ever shows
His nose to Russian snows
To be pecked at by every wind that blows?   20
You would not peck? I thank you for good will,
Believe, but leave that truth untested still.

  Spring's an expansive time: yet I don't trust
March with its peck of dust,
Nor April with its rainbow-crowned brief showers,   25
Nor even May, whose flowers
One frost may wither through the sunless hours.

  Perhaps some languid summer day,
When drowsy birds sing less and less,
And golden fruit is ripening to excess,   30
If there's not too much sun nor too much cloud,
And the warm wind is neither still nor loud,
Perhaps my secret I may say,
Or you may guess.

Notes

[54] *title* a counter-attack on the Romantic convention that a lyric reveals the poet's self, that the act of writing invites others into authorial experience. At the same time, the poem sends up the close associations between poem, biography, and autobiography – that the latter two can be read from the lyric. Robert Browning explored the same issue in "Memorabilia" (1855): "Ah, did you once see Shelley plain, / And did he stop and speak to you?"; and a late poem "House," and its companion poem "Shop" (1876). The title in Rossetti MS notebook was originally "Nonsense"; changed to "Winter: My Secret" in 1875, the title by which the poem is now best known; from *Goblin Market and Other Poems* (1862).

"No, Thank You, John"[55]

I never said I loved you, John:
    Why will you teaze me day by day,
And wax a weariness to think upon
    With always "do" and "pray?"

You know I never loved you, John;   5
    No fault of mine made me your toast:
Why will you haunt me with a face as wan
    As shows an hour-old ghost?

I dare say Meg or Moll would take
    Pity upon you, if you'd ask: 10
And pray don't remain single for my sake
    Who can't perform that task.

I have no heart?—Perhaps I have not;
    But then you're mad to take offence
That I don't give you what I have not got: 15
    Use your own common sense.

Let bygones be bygones:
    Don't call me false, who owed not to be true:
I'd rather answer "No" to fifty Johns
    Than answer "Yes" to you.   20

Let's mar our pleasant days no more,
    Song-birds of passage, days of youth:
Catch at to-day,[56] forget the days before:
    I'll wink at your untruth.

Let us strike hands as hearty friends;   25
    No more, no less; and friendship's good:
Only don't keep in view ulterior ends,
    And points not understood

In open treaty. Rise above
    Quibbles and shuffling off and on: 30
Here's friendship for you if you like; but love,—
    No, thank you, John.

Notes

[55] *title* the poem echoes the seventeenth-century hunting song, "Oh, No, John." Although Rossetti wrote to Dante Gabriel that "no such person existed or exists," some critics have read this poem biographically, as alluding to Rossetti's rejection of the marriage proposal of the painter John Brett (1831–1902). William Michael Rossetti seems to be the source, saying in his edition of *Family Letters* (1908) that Brett was "somewhat smitten by Christina." From *Goblin Market and Other Poems* (1862).

[56] *to-day* the *carpe diem* (Lat. seize the day) motif over lines 21–3, because time is flying; see HOUSMAN, n. 7.

Song[57]

When I am dead, my dearest,
    Sing no sad songs for me;
Plant thou no roses at my head,
    Nor shady cypress tree:[58]
Be the green grass above me   5
    With showers and dewdrops wet;[59]
And if thou wilt, remember,
    And if thou wilt, forget.

I shall not see the shadows,
    I shall not feel the rain;   10
I shall not hear the nightingale
    Sing on, as if in pain:
And dreaming through the twilight
    That doth not rise nor set,
Haply I may remember,[60]   15
    And haply may forget.

Up-Hill[61]

Does the road wind up-hill all the way?
    Yes, to the very end.
Will the day's journey take the whole long day?
    From morn to night, my friend.

But is there for the night a resting-place?   5
    A roof for when the slow dark hours begin.
May not the darkness hide it from my face?
    You cannot miss that inn.

Shall I meet other wayfarers at night?
    Those who have gone before.   10
Then must I knock, or call when just in sight?
    They will not keep you standing at that door.

Shall I find comfort, travel-sore and weak?
    Of labour you shall find the sum.
Will there be beds for me and all who seek?   15
    Yea, beds for all who come.

Notes

[57] *title* from *Goblin Market and Other Poems* (1862).

[58] *tree* like the yew, a common graveyard tree, symbolic because if once cut down it will not grow again.

[59] *wet* that is, wet with nature's moisture, not with grieving tears.

[60] *haply* (arch. perhaps); the lines leave ambiguous the state of the knowledge of the soul after death in the mid-nineteenth century; Dante has no such concern in having Beatrice recognize him in *Paradiso*. See also n. 48.

[61] *title* see George Herbert, "The Pilgrimage" from *The Temple* (1633): "I travell'd on, seeing the hill, where lay / my expectation" (1–2); see also the foot of the Hill Difficulty in *Pilgrim's Progress* (sect. 3). First printed in *Macmillan's Magazine* (Feb. 1861); reprinted in *Goblin Market and Other Poems* (1862), our text.

A Better Resurrection[62]

I have no wit, no words, no tears;
    My heart within me like a stone
Is numbed too much for hopes or fears;
    Look right, look left, I dwell alone;
I lift mine eyes,[63] but dimmed with grief   5
    No everlasting hills[64] I see;
My life is in the falling leaf:[65]
    O Jesus, quicken me.

My life is like a faded leaf,
    My harvest dwindled to a husk: 10
Truly my life is void and brief
    And tedious in the barren dusk;
My life is like a frozen thing,
    No bud nor greenness can I see:
Yet rise it shall—the sap of Spring;   15
    O Jesus, rise in me.

My life is like a broken bowl,[66]
    A broken bowl that cannot hold
One drop of water for my soul
    Or cordial in the searching cold;   20
Cast in the fire the perished thing,
    Melt and remould it, till it be
A royal cup for Him my King:
    O Jesus, drink of me.

L. E. L.[67]

"Whose heart was breaking for a little love."[68]
        E. B. Browning

Downstairs I laugh, I sport and jest with all:
    But in my solitary room above
I turn my face in silence to the wall;[69]
    My heart is breaking for a little love.
        Tho' winter frosts are done,   5
        And birds pair every one,
And leaves peep out, for springtide is begun.

Notes

[62] *title* see Hebrews 11: 35; from *Goblin Market and Other Poems* (1862) in a section of sixteen poems called "Devotional Pieces."

[63] *eyes* see Psalm 121: 1.

[64] *hills* see Genesis 49: 26.

[65] *leaf* see Isaiah 64: 6; see also *Macbeth* 5. 3. 27–28.

[66] *bowl* see Ecclesiastes 12: 6.

[67] *title* the initials of this tribute poem stand for Letitia Elizabeth Landon who had died on 15 October 1838. First published in *The Victoria Magazine* (May, 1863); republished in *The Prince's Progress and Other Poems* (1866), our text.

[68] *love* the epigraph misquotes or echoes Elizabeth Barrett's tribute to Landon; see BARRETT BROWNING, n. 13.

[69] *wall* see 2 Kings 20: 2; and Isaiah 38: 2: a reference to King Hezekiah, who was told by the prophet Amos that he was about to die. See n. 104.

I feel no spring, while spring is wellnigh blown,
   I find no nest, while nests are in the grove:
Woe's me for mine own heart that dwells alone,   10
   My heart that breaketh for a little love.
     While golden in the sun
     Rivulets rise and run,
While lilies bud, for springtide is begun.

All love, are loved, save only I; their hearts   15
   Beat warm with love and joy, beat full thereof:
They cannot guess, who play the pleasant parts,
   My heart is breaking for a little love.
     While beehives wake and whirr,
     And rabbit thins his fur,   20
In living spring that sets the world astir.

I deck myself with silks and jewelry,
   I plume myself like any mated dove:
They praise my rustling show, and never see
   My heart is breaking for a little love.   25
     While sprouts green lavender
     With rosemary and myrrh,
For in quick spring the sap is all astir.

Perhaps some saints in glory guess the truth,
   Perhaps some angels read it as they move,   30
And cry one to another full of ruth,
   "Her heart is breaking for a little love."
     Tho' other things have birth,
     And leap and sing for mirth,
When springtime wakes and clothes and feeds the earth.   35

Yet saith a saint: "Take patience for thy scathe";
   Yet saith an angel: "Wait, for thou shalt prove
True best is last, true life is born of death,
   O thou, heart-broken for a little love.
     Then love shall fill thy girth,   40
     And love make fat thy dearth,
When new spring builds new heaven and clean new earth."

From *Sing-Song: A Nursery Rhyme Book*[70]

If a pig wore a wig,
   What could we say?
Treat him as a gentleman,
   And say "Good day."

Notes ————————————————————————

[70] *title* this popular book of whimsical verse, illustrated by Arthur Hughes (1832–1915), Pre-Raphaelite painter, was one of the era's most popular illustrated books for children. First published as *Sing-Song: A Nursery Rhyme Book* (1872); an enlarged edition was published in 1893.

If his tail chanced to fail,   5
   What could we do?—
Send him to the tailoress
   To get one new.

★ ★ ★ ★ ★

A pin has a head, but has no hair;
A clock has a face, but no mouth there;
Needles have eyes, but they cannot see;
A fly has a trunk without lock or key;
A timepiece may lose, but cannot win;   5
A corn-field dimples without a chin;
A hill has no leg, but has a foot;
A wine-glass a stem, but not a root;
A watch has hands, but no thumb or finger;
A boot has a tongue, but is no singer;   10
Rivers run, though they have no feet;
A saw has teeth, but it does not eat;
Ash-trees have keys, yet never a lock;
And baby crows, without being a cock

★ ★ ★ ★ ★

When fishes set umbrellas up
   If the rain-drops run,
Lizards will want their parasols
   To shade them from the sun.

★ ★ ★ ★ ★

The peacock has a score of eyes,
   With which he cannot see;
The cod-fish has a silent sound,
   However that may be;

No dandelions tell the time,   5
   Although they turn to clocks;
Cat's-cradle does not hold the cat,
   Nor foxglove fit the fox.

★ ★ ★ ★ ★

When the cows come home the milk is coming,
Honey's made while the bees are humming;
Duck and drake on the rushy lake,
And the deer live safe in the breezy brake;
And timid, funny, brisk little bunny,   5
Winks his nose and sits all sunny.

★ ★ ★ ★ ★

Who has seen the wind?
   Neither I nor you:
But when the leaves hang trembling
   The wind is passing thro'.

Who has seen the wind?   5
    Neither you nor I:
But when the trees bow down their heads
    The wind is passing by.

★ ★ ★ ★ ★

An emerald is as green as grass;
    A ruby red as blood;
A sapphire shines as blue as heaven;
    A flint lies in the mud.

A diamond is a brilliant stone,   5
    To catch the world's desire;
An opal holds a fiery spark;
    But a flint holds fire.

Monna Innominata[71]

A Sonnet of Sonnets

Beatrice,[72] immortalized by "altissimo poeta . . cotanto amante";[73] and Laura,[74] celebrated by a great though an inferior bard,—have alike paid the exceptional penalty of exceptional honour, and have come down to us resplendent with charms, but (at least, to my apprehension) scant of attractiveness.

Notes

[71] *title* (Ital. unnamed lady). In her preface Rossetti places her fourteen sonnets, one sonnet standing analogously for each of the lines of a sonnet (hence, "a sonnet of sonnets"), within a long poetic tradition of courtly love poetry. She writes against that tradition in challenging conventional gender roles: instead of a male poet's writing about a desired but unattainable lady, the lady herself speaks and writes. After alluding to the tradition of Dante and Petrarch (by giving pre-eminence to the women as muses, the *donne nominata* – named ladies – rather than their poets in first paragraph) and to the troubadours and others in Provence (in the second), Rossetti refers in the last paragraph to her contemporary model in Elizabeth Barrett Browning. The sequence turns at Sonnet 9 (the ninth line of a Petrarchan sonnet was called the *volta* or turn in which the direction of thought shifted) from "all that was and all / That might have been" in the relationship between poet as persona and the beloved, to what "now can never be" – and the aftermath of such a "now." The *volta*, Sonnet 9, also uses a citation from the second part of Petrarch's poems, "Laura in Death." At the same time, following the sonnet sequence convention, each sonnet with its epigraphs engages the reader in a complex intertextual confrontation with other poems, with other poets, and with the writing of poetry itself. For instance, each of the Dante epigraphs is from the *Divine Comedy* and refers to other poets or to Apollo, the god of poetry; and eight of the fourteen epigraphs from Petrarch's *Rime*

sparse (Ital. scattered rhymes) or *Il Canzoniere* (Ital. the songbook) refer explicitly or indirectly to the writing of poetry (in Sonnets 2, 5, 7, 8, 9, 10, 13, and 14). Rossetti insisted to her publishers that the whole sequence be printed together, and not be extracted. She published six sonnet sequences, and another was published posthumously. As well as *Monna Innominata*, she published "Later Life: A Double Sonnet of Sonnets," consisting of twenty-eight sonnets in the same volume. *Monna Innominata* was first published in "A Pageant" and Other *Poems* (1881). For another instance of the reversal of gender roles in a sonnet sequence, see BARRETT BROWNING, n. 13 (WEB p. 306).

[72] *Beatrice* Beatrice Portinari (1267?–1290; her name is a derivative of the Lat. *beatus*, blessed), Dante's beloved who becomes his guide in the *Paradise* section of the *Divine Comedy* and who is his muse in *La Vita Nuova* (Ital. the new life); Dante Rossetti published a translation of *The New Life* in 1861 as *The Early Italian Poets*. See DANTE ROSSETTI, n. 13.

[73] *altissimo . . . amante* the first phrase (Ital. the highest poet) is an accolade given to Virgil by other poets in *Inferno* 4. 80; the second phrase (Ital. with such a lover) is a reference to Lancelot in the Paolo and Francesca story in *Inferno* 5. 134.

[74] *Laura* the beloved muse of Francesco Petrarca (1304–74), now identified as probably Laura de Noves from Avignon (1310–48), whom Petrarch met on Good Friday, 6 April 1327.

These heroines of world-wide fame were preceded by a bevy of unnamed ladies "donne innominate" sung by a school of less conspicuous poets; and in that land and that period which gave simultaneous birth to Catholics, to Albigenses, and to Troubadours,[75] one can imagine many a lady as sharing her lover's poetic aptitude, while the barrier between them might be one held sacred by both, yet not such as to render mutual love incompatible with mutual honour.

Had such a lady spoken for herself, the portrait left us might have appeared more tender, if less dignified, than any drawn even by a devoted friend. Or had the Great Poetess[76] of our own day and nation only been unhappy instead of happy, her circumstances would have invited her to bequeath to us, in lieu of the "Portuguese Sonnets" an inimitable "donna innominata" drawn not from fancy but from feeling, and worthy to occupy a niche beside Beatrice and Laura.

1

"Lo dì che han detto a' dolci amici addio."
DANTE

"Amor, con quanto sforzo oggi mi vinci!"
PETRARCA[77]

Come back to me, who wait and watch for you:—
    Or come not yet, for it is over then,
    And long it is before you come again,
So far between my pleasures are and few.
While, when you come not, what I do I do   5
    Thinking "Now when he comes," my sweetest "when":
    For one man is my world of all the men
This wide world holds; O love, my world is you.
Howbeit, to meet you grows almost a pang
    Because the pang of parting comes so soon;   10
    My hope hangs waning, waxing, like a moon
        Between the heavenly days on which we meet:
Ah me, but where are now the songs I sang
        When life was sweet because you called them sweet?

Notes

[75] *land ... Troubadours* Provence and Languedoc in southern France in the twelfth and thirteenth centuries were the site of the heresy of the Albigenses (named after their city of Albi). Sometimes called Catharism (Gk. pure), this sect raised women to a high level, as in the tradition of courtly love with its poetic conventions of the abject lover and the exalted married woman. The Cathars were put down by the Albigensian Crusade (1209–55) inaugurated by Pope Innocent III (1160–1216). The troubadours were twelfth-century Provençal minstrel poets who also exalted women. All of these were used by Rossetti's father, Gabriele Rossetti (1873–54), in his *Disquisition on the Antipapal Spirit* (1834), explicating Dante and twelfth-century thought.

[76] *Poetess* Elizabeth Barrett Browning; see BARRETT BROWNING, "SONNETS FROM THE PORTUGUESE" (WEB p. 306).

[77] *epigraphs* William Michael in *The Poetical Works of Christina Georgina Rossetti* (1904) translated the epigraphs, given below for each sonnet; the sources in Dante and Petrarch have been added, using the following abbreviations: *Inferno* (*Inf.*) *Purgatory* (*Purg.*), *Paradise* (*Par.*); and for Petrarch, *Rime*.

"The day that they have said adieu to their sweet friends" (*Purg.* 8. 3).

"Love, with how great a stress dost thou vanquish me today!" (*Rime* 85. 12).

The epigraphs of Sonnets 1, 2, and 8 are all drawn from the same 12 lines of the *Purgatorio* (8: 1–12). Sonnets 1 and 2 also allude to the thirteenth-century Lombard troubadour Sordello who had made himself known to Dante's guide Virgil earlier in the poem since both Virgil and Sordello were from Mantua (*Purg.* 6: 49–75). See Robert Browning, *Sordello* (1840).

2

"Era già 1'ora che volge il desio."
DANTE

"Ricorro al tempo ch'io vi vidi prima."
PETRARCA[78]

I wish I could remember that first day,
    First hour, first moment of your meeting me,[79]
    If bright or dim the season, it might be
Summer or Winter for aught I can say;
So unrecorded did it slip away,   5
    So blind was I to see and to foresee,
    So dull to mark the budding of my tree
That would not blossom yet for many a May.
If only I could recollect it, such
    A day of days! I let it come and go   10
    As traceless as a thaw of bygone snow;
It seemed to mean so little, meant so much;
If only now I could recall that touch,
    First touch of hand in hand—Did one but know!

3

"O ombre vane, fuor che ne l'aspetto!"
DANTE

"Immaginata guida la conduce."
PETRARCA[80]

I dream of you to wake: would that I might
    Dream of you and not wake but slumber on;
    Nor find with dreams the dear companion gone,
As Summer ended Summer birds take flight.
In happy dreams I hold you full in sight,   5
    I blush again who waking look so wan;
    Brighter than sunniest day that ever shone,
In happy dreams your smile makes day of night.
Thus only in a dream we are at one,
    Thus only in a dream we give and take   10
        The faith that maketh rich who take or give;

Notes

[78] *epigraphs* "It was already the hour which turns back the desire" (*Purg.* 8. 1). / "I recur to the time when I first saw thee" (*Rime* 20. 3). In the Dante passage, the souls in Purgatory are singing their evening hymn, *Te lucis ante terminum* (Lat. before the ending of the light) by St Ambrose (c.330–97), bishop of Milan.

[79] *me* a lost memory of first meeting, totally unlike Dante's unforgettable remembrance of first meeting Beatrice, or of Petrarch's meeting Laura.

[80] *epigraphs* "Oh shades, empty save in semblance!" (*Purg.* 2. 79). / "An imaginary guide conducts her" (*Rime* 277. 9). Dante seeks to embrace the shade of Casella, a fellow poet and old friend, but cannot because he is an insubstantial shade. Laura in heaven will now lead the wandering and lost Petrarch.

If thus to sleep is sweeter than to wake,
  To die were surely sweeter than to live,
 Though there be nothing new beneath the sun.[81]

4

  "Poca favilla gran fiamma seconda."
DANTE

  "Ogni altra cosa, ogni pensier va fore,
  E sol ivi con voi rimansi amore."
PETRARCA[82]

I loved you first: but afterwards your love
  Outsoaring mine, sang such a loftier song
As drowned the friendly cooings of my dove.
  Which owes the other most? my love was long,
  And yours one moment seemed to wax more strong;   5
I loved and guessed at you, you construed me
And loved me for what might or might not be—
  Nay, weights and measures do us both a wrong.
For verily love knows not "mine" or "thine";
  With separate "I" and "thou" free love has done,   10
  For one is both and both are one in love:
Rich love knows nought of "thine that is not mine";
  Both have the strength and both the length thereof,
Both of us, of the love which makes us one.

5

  "Amor che a nulla amato amar perdona."
DANTE

  "Amor m'addusse in sì gioiosa spene."
PETRARCA[83]

O my heart's heart, and you who are to me
  More than myself myself, God be with you,
  Keep you in strong obedience leal[84] and true
To Him whose noble service setteth free,[85]

Notes

[81] *sun* see Ecclesiastes 1: 9.

[82] *epigraphs* "A small spark fosters a great flame" (*Par.* 1. 34). / "Every other thing, every thought, goes off, and love alone remains there with you" (*Rime* 72. 44–45). At the beginning of the *Paradiso* Dante's invocation for inspiration is to Apollo. The great flame springing from a little spark is a conventional way of speaking of passionate love (see also James 3: 5).

[83] *epigraphs* "Love, who exempts no loved one from loving" (*Inf.* 5. 103). / "Love led me into such joyous hope" (*Rime* 56. 11). Dante's passage is part of the famous address to him from his contemporary Francesca da Rimini concerning her love for Paolo Malatesta, brought to its culmination and their death – and doom in the Circle of the Lustful in *Inferno* – when they read together the romance of Lancelot and Guenevere and committed adultery. The story of Paolo and Francesca was enormously popular in the nineteenth century where it was idealized as a narrative of tragic love, as in Leigh Hunt's *The Story of Rimini* (1816), numerous plays and operas, and especially Dante Rossetti's watercolour *Francesca da Rimini* (1855).

[84] *leal* loyal.

[85] *free* see BCP, the second collect for peace in the Order for Morning Prayer, beginning: "O God, who art the author of peace and lover of concord, in knowledge of whom standeth our eternal life, whose service is perfect freedom: Defend us thy humble servants in all assaults of our enemies."

Give you all good we see or can foresee,   5
    Make your joys many and your sorrows few,
    Bless you in what you bear and what you do,
Yea, perfect you as He would have you be.[86]
So much for you; but what for me, dear friend?
    To love you without stint and all I can   10
To-day, to-morrow, world without an end;[87]
    To love you much and yet to love you more,
    As Jordan[88] at his flood sweeps either shore;
Since woman is the helpmeet made for man.[89]

6

    "Or puoi la quantitate
Comprender de l'amor che a te mi scalda."
                     Dante

    Non vo'che da tal nodo amor mi scioglia."
                  Petrarca[90]

Trust me, I have not earned your dear rebuke,
    I love, as you would have me, God the most;
    Would lose not Him, but you, must one be lost,
Nor with Lot's wife cast back a faithless look[91]
Unready to forego what I forsook;   5
    This say I, having counted up the cost,
    This, though I be the feeblest of God's host,
The sorriest sheep Christ shepherds with His crook.
Yet[92] while I love my God the most, I deem
    That I can never love you overmuch;   10
    I love Him more, so let me love you too;
Yea, as I apprehend it, love is such
I cannot love you if I love not Him,
    I cannot love Him if I love not you.[93]

Notes

[86] *be* see Matthew 5: 48.

[87] *end* echo of the liturgical conclusion of the psalms and canticles in the BCP: "As it was in the beginning, is now, and ever shall be, world without end. Amen."

[88] *Jordan* see Joshua 3 and 4.

[89] *man* see Genesis 2: 18.

[90] *epigraphs* "Now canst thou comprehend the quantity of the love which glows in me towards thee" (*Purg.* 21. 133–34). / "I do not choose that Love should release me from such a tie" (*Rime* 59. 17). The Dante quotation cites the first-century Roman poet Statius, who finds out that Virgil is his interlocutor. He tries to embrace Virgil's feet, forgetting that they are both shades—again one poet venerating another as in Rossetti's sequence.

[91] *look* see Genesis 19: 26; see also the backward glance of Orpheus towards Eurydice as he was leading her from the underworld, thereby losing her. This episode is referred to again in Sonnet 11.

[92] *Yet* the *volta* of the sonnet; see John Donne, "Valediction: Forbidding Mourning" (1633) for a similar use of "yet" (30).

[93] *you* see Edmund Spenser, *Amoretti* 68 (1595): "So let us love, dear love, like as we aught / Love is the lesson which the Lord us taught" (13–14); see also George Herbert, "Affliction (I)" (1633): "Let me not love thee, if I love thee not" (66).

7

"Qui primavera sempre ed ogni frutto."

"Qui primavera sempre ed ogni frutto."
                                        DANTE
"Ragionando con meco ed io con lui."
                                        PETRARCA[94]

"Love me, for I love you"—and answer me,
   "Love me, for I love you"—so shall we stand
   As happy equals in the flowering land
Of love, that knows not a dividing sea.[95]
Love builds the house on rock and not on sand,[96]   5
   Love laughs what while[97] the winds rave desperately;
   And who hath found love's citadel unmanned?
   And who hath held in bonds love's liberty?
My heart's a coward though my words are brave—
   We meet so seldom, yet we surely part   10
   So often; there's a problem for your art!
      Still I find comfort in his Book, who saith,
Though jealousy be cruel as the grave,
   And death be strong, yet love is strong as death.[98]

8

"Come dicesse a Dio: D'altro non calme."
                                        DANTE

"Spero trovar pietà non che perdono."
                                        PETRARCA[99]

"I, if I perish, perish"—Esther[100] spake:
   And bride of life or death she made her fair
   In all the lustre of her perfumed hair
And smiles that kindle longing but to slake.
She put on pomp of loveliness,[101] to take   5
   Her husband through his eyes at unaware;
   She spread abroad her beauty for a snare,
Harmless as doves and subtle as a snake.[102]
She trapped him with one mesh of silken hair,
   She vanquished him by wisdom of her wit,   10

Notes

[94] *epigraphs* "Here always Spring and every fruit." (*Purg.* 28. 143). / "Conversing with me, and I with him" (*Rime* 35. 14).

[95] *sea* in the same canto as the epigraph for this sonnet, Dante alludes to the myth of Hero and Leander, tragic lovers separated by the Hellespont.

[96] *sand* see Matthew 7: 24–27. The assault and siege of the castle of love is a common conceit in Renaissance love poetry: see Petrarch, *Rime* 274; Philip Sidney, *Astrophel and Stella* (1591): Sonnets 12 and 36; and Edmund Spenser, *Amoretti* (1595): Sonnet 14; see n. 32. For love in bonds and loss of liberty, see Petrarch 89; Sidney 2 and 29; and Barnabe Barnes, *Parthenophil and Parthenope* (1593): Sonnet 65.

[97] *while* when.

[98] *death* see Song of Songs 8: 6.

[99] *epigraphs* "As if he were to say to God, 'I care for nought else.'" (*Purg.* 8. 12). / "I hope to find pity, and not only pardon" (*Rime* 1. 8).

[100] *Esther* she was the Jewish wife of the Persian king, Ahasuerus, identified as possibly Xerxes I (519–465 BCE) or Artaxerses (d. 401 BCE); see Esther 4: 16.

[101] *loveliness* see Esther 5: 1–2.

[102] *snake* see Matthew 10: 16.

And built her people's house that it should stand:—
　　If I might take my life so in my hand,
　　And for my love to Love put up my prayer,
And for love's sake by Love be granted it!

9

"O dignitosa coscienza e netta!"
　　　　　　　　　　DANTE

"Spirto più acceso di virtuti ardenti."
　　　　　　　　　　PETRARCA[103]

Thinking of you, and all that was, and all
　　That might have been and now can never be,
　　I feel your honoured excellence, and see
Myself unworthy of the happier call:
For woe is me who walk so apt to fall,　　　　　　　　　5
　　So apt to shrink afraid, so apt to flee,
　　Apt to lie down and die (ah, woe is me!)
Faithless and hopeless turning to the wall.[104]
And yet not hopeless quite nor faithless quite,
Because not loveless; love may toil all night,[105]　　　10
　　But take at morning; wrestle[106] till the break
　　　Of day, but then wield power with God and man:—
　　So take I heart of grace as best I can,
Ready to spend and be spent for your sake.[107]

10

"Con miglior corso e con migliore stella."
　　　　　　　　　　DANTE

"La vita fugge e non s'arresta un' ora."
　　　　　　　　　　PETRARCA[108]

Time flies, hope flags, life plies a wearied wing;
　　Death following hard on life gains ground apace;
　　Faith runs with each and rears an eager face,
Outruns the rest, makes light of everything,
Spurns earth, and still finds breath to pray and sing;　　　5
　　While love ahead of all uplifts his praise,
　　Still asks for grace and still gives thanks for grace,
Content with all day brings and night will bring.
Life wanes; and when love folds his wings above

Notes

103 *epigraphs* "O dignified and pure conscience!" (*Purg.* 3. 8). /
　"Spirit more lit with burning virtues" (*Rime* 283. 3).
104 *wall* see 2 Kings 20: 2; and Isaiah 38: 2; see also above,
　"L. E. L.," n. 3.
105 *night* see Luke 5: 4–6.

106 *wrestle* see Jacob's wrestling with the angel in Genesis
　32: 24.
107 *sake* see 2 Corinthians 12: 15.
108 *epigraphs* "With better course and with better star"
　(*Par.* 1. 40). / "Life flees, and stays not an hour" (*Rime* 272. 1).

Tired hope, and less we feel his conscious pulse,   10
    Let us go fall asleep, dear friend, in peace:
    A little while, and age and sorrow cease;
A little while, and life reborn annuls
Loss and decay and death, and all is love.

11

"Vien dietro a me e lascia dir le genti."
                                    DANTE

"Contando i casi della vita nostra."
                                    PETRARCA[109]

Many in aftertimes will say of you
    "He loved her"—while of me what will they say?
    Not that I loved you more than just in play,
For fashion's sake as idle women do.
Even let them prate; who know not what we knew   5
    Of love and parting in exceeding pain,
    Of parting hopeless here to meet again,
Hopeless on earth, and heaven is out of view.
But by my heart of love laid bare to you,
    My love that you can make not void nor vain,   10
Love that foregoes you but to claim anew
        Beyond this passage of the gate of death,
    I charge you at the Judgment make it plain
        My love of you was life and not a breath.

12

"Amor, che ne la mente mi ragiona."
                                    DANTE

"Amor vien nel bel viso di costei."
                                    PETRARCA[110]

If there be any one can take my place
    And make you happy whom I grieve to grieve,
    Think not that I can grudge it, but believe
I do commend you to that nobler grace,
That readier wit than mine, that sweeter face;   5
    Yea, since your riches make me rich, conceive
    I too am crowned, while bridal crowns I weave,
And thread the bridal dance with jocund pace.
For if I did not love you, it might be
    That I should grudge you some one dear delight;   10

Notes

[109] *epigraphs* "Come after me, and leave folk to talk" (*Purg.* 5.
13). / "Relating the casualties of our life" (*Rime* 285. 12).

[110] *epigraphs* "Love, who speaks within my mind" (*Purg.* 2.
112). / "Love comes in the beautiful face of this lady"
(*Rime* 13. 2).

But since the heart is yours that was mine own,
    Your pleasure is my pleasure, right my right,
    Your honourable freedom makes me free,
        And you companioned I am not alone.

13

"E drizzeremo gli occhi al Primo Amore."
              DANTE

"Ma trovo peso non da le mie braccia."
              PETRARCA[III]

If I could trust mine own self with your fate,
    Shall I not rather trust it in God's hand?
    Without Whose Will one lily doth not stand,[112]
Nor sparrow fall at his appointed date;[113]
    Who numbereth the innumerable sand,[114]   5
Who weighs the wind and water with a weight,[115]
To Whom the world is neither small nor great,
    Whose knowledge foreknew every plan we planned.
Searching my heart for all that touches you,
    I find there only love and love's goodwill   10
Helpless to help and impotent to do,
    Of understanding dull, of sight most dim;
    And therefore I commend you back to Him
Whose love your love's capacity can fill.

14

"E la Sua Volontade è nostra pace."
              DANTE

"Sol con questi pensier, con altre chiome."
              PETRARCA[116]

Youth gone, and beauty gone if ever there
    Dwelt beauty in so poor a face as this;
    Youth gone and beauty, what remains of bliss?

Notes

[III] *epigraphs* "And we will direct our eyes to the Primal Love" (*Par.* 32. 142). / "But I find a burden to which my arms suffice not" (*Rime* 20. 5). In the Dante citation, St. Bernard is directing Dante's gaze to the "Primal Love," just as the speaker in Sonnet 13 strives to "commend you back to Him."

[112] *stand* see Luke 12: 27.

[113] *date* see Matthew 10: 29.

[114] *sand* see Psalm 139: 18; and Ecclesiasticus 1: 2.

[115] *weight* see Job 28: 25.

[116] *epigraphs* "And His will is our peace" (*Par.* 3. 85). / "Only with these thoughts, with different locks" (*Rime* 30. 32). Dante's citation is the summary of the theology of the *Divine Comedy* in the words of Piccarda, the sister of Dante's wife, who was referred to along with Beatrice at the opening of *Paradiso* 3. Piccarda had been forced to break a religious vow to marry, and Dante, despite his love for the unattainable Beatrice, had also married. Here Piccarda raises Dante's vision to the spiritual ground for love beyond earth's passion, as she speaks this citation, and sings the *Ave Maria*, vanishing into song. Petrarch's second sestina (*Rime* 30) alludes to hair or locks (Ital. *chiome*), (Rossetti's "hair," line 4) and to the myth of Apollo and Daphne, whereby Daphne is turned into a laurel tree, allowing Petrarch's verbal play on the "Laura-laurel" theme, the leaves of the poem, the laurel for the poet's crown, the breeze (Ital. *l'aura*; Rossetti's "blow," line 8) and gold (Ital. *l'auro*). Rossetti, alluding to these connotations in Dante and Petrarch, has her poet refuse roses (not laurels), and accept autumnal flowers growing with wheat (corn) ready for

I will not bind fresh roses in my hair,
To shame a cheek at best but little fair,— 5
   Leave youth his roses, who can bear a thorn,—
I will not seek for blossoms anywhere,
   Except such common flowers as blow with corn.
Youth gone and beauty gone, what doth remain?
   The longing of a heart pent up forlorn, 10
     A silent heart whose silence loves and longs
     The silence of a heart which sang its songs
   While youth and beauty made a summer morn,
Silence of love that cannot sing again.

A Life's Parallels[117]

Never on this side of the grave again,
  On this side of the river,
On this side of the garner of the grain,
    Never,—

Ever while time flows on and on and on, 5
  That narrow noiseless river,
Ever while corn bows heavy-headed, wan,
    Ever,—

Never despairing, often fainting, ruing,
  But looking back, ah never! 10
Faint yet pursuing, faint yet still pursuing[118]
    Ever.

"For Thine Own Sake, O My God"[119]

Wearied of sinning, wearied of repentance,
  Wearied of self, I turn, my God, to Thee;[120]
To Thee, my Judge, on Whose all-righteous sentence
    Hangs mine eternity:
I turn to Thee, I plead Thyself with Thee,[121]— 5
    Be pitiful to me.

Wearied I loathe myself, I loathe my sinning,
  My stains, my festering sores, my misery:
Thou the Beginning, Thou ere my beginning

Notes

harvest (Matthew 13: 30), her songs lapsing into silence as she writes her last words. For laurel, see also HEMANS, "LAST SONG OF SAPPHO," n. 4.

[117] title from "A Pageant" and Other Poems (1881).

[118] pursuing see Judges 8: 4. Gideon's army crossed the Jordan, pursuing the Midianites, "faint, yet pursuing them" an idea that became a metaphor for the soul's or the saints' passing from death to eternal life; see also Deuteronomy 3: 25; and Joshua 3: 14–17.

[119] title see Daniel 9: 19. From "A Pageant" and Other Poems (1881).

[120] Thee see the popular hymn by Sarah Adams (1805–48), "Nearer My God to Thee."

[121] Thee see Christina Rossetti, "Sooner or Later: Yet at Last" (33).

Didst see and didst foresee   10
Me miserable, me sinful, ruined me,—
I plead Thyself with Thee.

I plead Thyself with Thee Who art my Maker,
Regard Thy handiwork that cries to Thee;
I plead Thyself with Thee Who wast partaker   15
Of mine infirmity,
Love made Thee what Thou art, the love of me,—
I plead Thyself with Thee.

Birchington Churchyard[122]

A lowly hill which overlooks a flat,
Half sea, half country side;
A flat-shored sea of low-voiced creeping tide
Over a chalky, weedy mat.

A hill of hillocks, flowery and kept green   5
Round Crosses raised for hope,
With many-tinted sunsets where the slope
Faces the lingering western sheen.

A lowly hope, a height that is but low,
While Time sets solemnly,   10
While the tide rises of Eternity,
Silent and neither swift nor slow.

Cobwebs[123]

It is a land with neither night nor day,
Nor heat nor cold, nor any wind nor rain,
Nor hills nor valleys: but one even plain
Stretches through long unbroken miles away,
While through the sluggish air a twilight grey   5
Broodeth: no moons or seasons wax and wane,
No ebb and flow are there along the main,
No bud-time, no leaf-falling, there for aye,
No ripple on the sea,[124] no shifting sand,
No beat of wings to stir the stagnant space: 10

Notes

[122] *title* first published in *Athenæum* (29 Apr. 1882) and added to *Poems* (1888). Dante Rossetti had died on 9 April 1882 and was buried at Birchington-on-Sea, Kent, on the southeast coast of England.

[123] *title* see E. A. Poe's "The City in the Sea" (1846) for a city under the rule of Death; see also THOMSON, "CITY OF DREADFUL

NIGHT" (especially sect. I, stz. 1). From *New Poems*, ed. William Michael Rossetti (1896), to which he added the probable date of composition, as also in the following three poems.

[124] *main ... sea* see Poe, "The City in the Sea": "The melancholy waters lie" (11); and "For no ripples curl, alas! / Along that wilderness of glass—" (36–37).

No pulse of life through all the loveless land
And loveless sea; no trace of days before,
   No guarded home, no time-worn resting-place,
No future hope, no fear forevermore.[125]

October 1855

In an Artist's Studio[126]

One face looks out from all his canvases,
   One selfsame figure sits or walks or leans:
   We found her hidden just behind those screens,
That mirror gave back all her loveliness.
A queen in opal or in ruby dress,   5
   A nameless girl in freshest summer-greens,
   A saint, an angel—every canvas means
The same one meaning, neither more nor less.
He feeds upon her face by day and night,
   And she with true kind eyes looks back on him,   10
Fair as the moon and joyful as the light:
   Not wan with waiting, not with sorrow dim;
Not as she is, but was when hope shone bright;
   Not as she is, but as she fills his dream.

24 December 1856

An Echo from Willow-Wood[127]

"O ye, all ye that walk in willow-wood."
          D. G. ROSSETTI

Two gazed into a pool, he gazed and she,
   Not hand in hand, yet heart in heart, I think,
   Pale and reluctant on the water's brink,
As on the brink of parting which must be.
Each eyed the other's aspect, she and he,   5
   Each felt one hungering heart leap up and sink,

Notes

[125] *forevermore* the word is used by Thomson in "City of Dreadful Night" (VI, stz. 16); see also the terminal rhyme used repeatedly in Poe's "The Raven" (1846).

[126] *title* William Michael Rossetti says: "The reference is apparently to our brother's studio, and to his constantly-repeated heads of the lady whom he afterwards married, Miss Siddal." See ELIZABETH SIDDAL. From *New Poems*, ed. W. M. Rossetti (1896).

[127] *title* William Michael Rossetti commented: "The title indicates that this sonnet by Christina is based on those sonnets by our brother, named *Willow-wood*, which were first published in 1869. I incline to think that Christina's

sonnet is intended to refer to the love and marriage of my brother and Miss Siddal, and to her early death in 1862." In a later edition (1904), he adds: "or it may (which I think far more probable) be intended for a wholly different train of events," perhaps alluding to the prolonged affair of Rossetti with Jane Morris, the wife of his friend William Morris, that became particularly intense from 1869 to 1872. See DANTE GABRIEL ROSSETTI, "HOUSE OF LIFE," SONNETS XXIV–XXVII (WEB p. 412). The epigraph is the first line of the third of these sonnets. First published in *Magazine of Art* (Sept. 1890); republished in *New Poems*, ed. William Michael Rossetti (1896), our text.

Each tasted bitterness which both must drink,
There on the brink of life's dividing sea.
Lilies upon the surface, deep below
    Two wistful faces craving each for each,   10
        Resolute and reluctant without speech:—
A sudden ripple made the faces flow,
    One moment joined, to vanish out of reach:
        So those hearts joined, and ah were parted so.

circa 1870

Sleeping at Last[128]

Sleeping at last, the trouble and tumult over,
    Sleeping at last, the struggle and horror past,
Cold and white, out of sight of friend and of lover,
    Sleeping at last.

    No more a tired heart downcast or overcast,   5
No more pangs that wring or shifting fears that hover,
    Sleeping at last in a dreamless sleep locked fast.

Fast asleep. Singing birds in their leafy cover
    Cannot wake her, nor shake her the gusty blast.   10
Under the purple thyme and the purple clover
    Sleeping at last.

circa 1893

WEB p. 419

Charles Stuart Calverley (1831–84)
    The Cock and the Bull

Notes

[128] *title* William Michael Rossetti wrote on the back of the
MS: "The verses must I think be the last that C. ever
wrote—perhaps late in 1893 or early in 94." From *New
Poems*, ed. William Michael Rossetti (1896).

Lewis Carroll [Charles Lutwidge Dodgson] (1832–98)

The third child of Charles Dodgson (1800–68), a mathematician and Anglican clergyman, and his first cousin, Frances Jane Lutwidge (1804–51), Dodgson, like all eleven children in the family, was schooled at home in rural Cheshire. After three years at Rugby School he went on to Christ Church College, Oxford, excelling as a brilliant student with a first-class degree in mathematics and classics (1854). He was elected a fellow of the college (1855), was ordained deacon in the Anglican Church (he chose not to become a priest), and remained at Christ Church teaching mathematics for the rest of his life. Shy, with a stammer, he took the pseudonym of Lewis Carroll (Lewis, an English version of the Ludovicus, the Latin for his middle name, Lutwidge; and Carroll derived from Carolus, Latin for Charles). He became an accomplished photographer, taking portraits of many Oxford notables, children, and his friends in the Pre-Raphaelite circle, including the Rossetti family. Among his friends was the dean of Christ Church, Henry Liddell, and his family, which included the three Liddell children. He entertained them with stories, magic, and boating trips, where *Alice's Adventures Underground* (as it was first called on 4 July 1862, when it occurred) first took oral – and in 1864, handwritten – form. Published as *Alice's Adventures in Wonderland* (1865) with illustrations by John Tenniel (1820–1914), chief political cartoonist for *Punch*, the book was a runaway bestseller. Late in 1871 Carroll published the sequel, *Through the Looking-Glass and What Alice Found There* (December 1871, title page dated 1872), again with illustrations by Tenniel. The first book is partly based on a deck of cards that comes to life, and the second on a game of chess that functions backwards, appropriate to a looking-glass world – both full of transformations of animals and people, as well as things, that challenge the stability of Victorian morality, social conventions, and the fixity of species. As a Menippean satire, it alternates varying literary styles and narrative voices, presenting an encyclopedia of Victorian life and mental and moral attitudes. He also published a long nonsense narrative poem, *The Hunting of the Snark* (1876), and, late in life, two novels, *Sylvie and Bruno* (1889) and *Bruno Concluded* (1893), whose complex plots did not win widespread popularity. He also invented a number of games and made respected contributions to mathematics (*Curiosa Mathematica: A New Theory of Parallels*, 1888, and several other books on algebra and geometry), as well as to logic (*Symbolic Logic*, 1896).

Carroll has remained a beloved Victorian author, with a continuing influence in popular culture in music (including opera, ballet, and rock musicals) and films, such as *Alice in Wonderland* by Walt Disney (1951) and Tim Burton (2010). At the same time, his life has also been a matter of controversy around the "Victorian Child Cult." Carroll's biographers and critics have tended to align either with the conventional view that Carroll's fascination with prepubescent girls was a sign of his repressed sexuality (Morton Cohen and Martin Gardner) or with those such as Karoline Leach and Hugues Lebailly who attack this "Carroll myth" by stressing alternative Victorian conventions that viewed child nudity as a sign of innocence and who also point to Carroll's varied relationships with a number of older women. Standard Edition: *The Complete Works of Lewis Carroll*, intro. Alexander Woollcott (1939); *The Annotated Alice*, ed. Martin Gardner (1970); *The Pamphlets of Lewis Carroll*, eds Edward Guiliano and Stan Marx (6 vols, 1993–); *The Letters of Lewis Carroll*, ed. Morton N. Cohen (2 vols, 1979); *The Diaries of Lewis Carroll*, ed. Edward Wakeling (10 vols, 1993–2005). Morton N. Cohen, *Lewis Carroll: A Biography*

(1995); Karoline Leach, *In the Shadow of the Dreamchild: A New Understanding of Lewis Carroll* (1999); and Hugues Lebailly, "C. L. Dodgson and the Victorian Cult of the Child," *The Carrollian* (Autumn, 1999). For a large collection of Carroll texts online, see Lewis Carroll Society of North America: http://www.lewiscarroll.org/carroll/texts; see also "Contrariwise: The Association for New Lewis Carroll Studies": contrariwise.wild-reality.net.

From *Alice's Adventures in Wonderland* (1865)

[Prefatory Poem]¹

All in the golden afternoon
    Full leisurely we glide;
For both our oars, with little² skill,
    By little arms are plied,
While little hands make vain pretense   5
    Our wanderings to guide.

Ah, cruel Three!³ In such an hour,
    Beneath such dreamy weather,
To beg a tale of breath too weak
    To stir the tiniest feather!⁴   10
Yet what can one poor voice avail
    Against three tongues together?

Imperious Prima flashes forth
    Her edict to "begin it"—
In gentler tones Secunda hopes   15
    "There will be nonsense in it"—
While Tertia interrupts the tale
    Not *more* than once a minute.

Anon, to sudden silence won,
    In fancy they pursue   20
The dream-child moving through a land

Notes

LEWIS CARROLL

¹ *title* this untitled poem is prefatory to the first chapter of *Alice*. It recounts the origin of the tale – or the coalescing of it, as Alice Liddell described it – when Dodgson (Carroll) with his friend Robinson Duckworth (1834–1911) and the three Liddell sisters rowed up the Isis River (the name of the Thames at Oxford) from Folly Bridge in Oxford to the village of Godstow, a distance of about 5 kilometres, where they picnicked before rowing back. Carroll had been rowing with the children from about 1857, and very likely had told a number of the episodes of the first *Alice* book before the trip of 4 July 1862, the occasion for the poem. He later (1887) helped elaborate the grounds for myth that it was all told for the first time, complete, on this afternoon. First published in *Alice's Adventures in Wonderland* (1865) with Lewis Carroll's name as author.

² *little* a pun: in this line and each of the following two lines, one for each "little" (Liddell) girl.

³ *Three* the three Liddell sisters, all daughters of the Dean of Christ Church, Oxford, Henry Liddell (1811–98): the eldest, Lorina Charlotte (b. 1839: *Prima*; Lat. the first; age 13); the middle one, Alice Pleasance (1852–1934: *Secunda*, Lat. second; age 10); and the youngest, Edith Mary (b. 1854: *Tertia*, Lat. the third; age 8). The modifier "cruel" and the capital letter for "Three" suggests that the girls are comic versions of the *Moirai* (Lat. *Parcae* or Fates) of Greek and Roman mythology: Clotho (who spins the thread of life), Lachesis (who allots a determined length), and Atropos (the unturnable one, who cuts the thread).

⁴ *feather* a pun: both the feather of a bird, and also the turning of the oar when it is out of the water to avoid

Of wonders wild and new,
In friendly chat with bird or beast—
And half believe it true.

And ever, as the story drained   25
    The wells of fancy dry,
And faintly strove that weary one
    To put the subject by,
"The rest next time"—"It *is* next time!"
    The happy voices cry.   30

Thus grew the tale of Wonderland:
    Thus slowly, one by one,
Its quaint events were hammered out—
    And now the tale is done,
And home we steer, a merry crew,   35
    Beneath the setting sun.

Alice! a childish story take,
    And with a gentle hand
Lay it where Childhood's dreams are twined
    In Memory's mystic band,   40
Like pilgrim's withered wreath of flowers[5]
    Plucked in a far-off land.

From *Through the Looking-Glass* (1871).

[Prefatory Poem][6]

Child[7] of the pure unclouded brow
    And dreaming eyes of wonder!
Though time be fleet, and I and thou
    Are half a life asunder,[8]
Thy loving smile will surely hail   5
The love-gift of a fairy-tale.

I have not seen thy sunny face,
    Nor heard thy silver laughter;
No thought of me shall find a place
    In thy young life's hereafter—   10
Enough that now thou wilt not fail
To listen to my fairy-tale.

Notes

being caught in the air – a problem Alice will have when rowing in *Through the Looking-Glass* ("Wool and Water," ch. 5).
[5] *flowers* in the Middle Ages pilgrims often wore flower
garlands on their pilgrimage.

[6] *title* this prefatory poem is untitled.
[7] *Child* Alice Pleasance Liddell; see n. 3.
[8] *asunder* when *Looking-Glass* was published Alice Liddell
was 18; Carroll was 36, twice her age.

> A tale begun in other days,[9]
>> When summer suns were glowing—
> A simple chime, that served to time   15
>> The rhythm of our rowing—
> Whose echoes live in memory yet,
> Though envious years would say "forget."

> Come, hearken then, ere voice of dread,
>> With bitter tidings laden,   20
> Shall summon to unwelcome bed
>> A melancholy maiden!
> We are but older children, dear,
> Who fret to find our bedtime near.

> Without, the frost, the blinding snow,   25
>> The storm-wind's moody madness—
> Within, the firelight's ruddy glow,
>> And childhood's nest of gladness.
> The magic words shall hold thee fast:
> Thou shalt not heed the raving blast.   30

> And, though the shadow of a sigh
>> May tremble through the story,
> For "happy summer days"[10] gone by,
>> And vanish'd summer glory—
> It shall not touch with breath of bale,   35
> The pleasance[11] of our fairy-tale.

Jabberwocky[12]

> 'Twas brillig, and the slithy toves
>> Did gyre and gimble in the wabe;
> All mimsy were the borogoves,
>> And the mome raths outgrabe.[13]

Notes

[9] *days* the first novel, *Wonderland*, begins on 4 May, Alice's birthday; *Looking-Glass*, the second volume of Alice's adventures, is set exactly six months after *Wonderland*, on 4 November: hence, the contrast in seasons.

[10] *days* the last phrase of *Wonderland*.

[11] *pleasance* Alice Liddell's middle name; also a secluded and enclosed garden, "with shady walks, trees and shrubs, statuary, and ornamental water" (*OED*), a metaphor for the private world shared by Alice and Carroll.

[12] *title* at the end of chapter 1 Alice finds a book that she tries to read, only finding that it is written "all in some language I don't understand." Then it occurs to her that it is "a Looking-glass book" and so is written backwards: "ɈɅBBᴙɘɯϙϾꓘɅ" with the first stanza following in a mirror font. Upon holding it up to a mirror it appears in a legible if incomprehensible format and language. The poem is acclaimed as one of the best and best-known nonsense poems in English – or pseudo-English. Carroll uses nonce words (words coined for the occasion, often by adding to an existing word to make a logatome, a nonsense word that sounds like and functions syntactically as a meaningful word), and portmanteau words (words that combine meanings as he explains; see n. 13). In chapter 6 of *Through the Looking-Glass* Humpty Dumpty interprets the poem with his own idiosyncratic meanings. The narrative is a version of the romance tale of a hero's slaying of a deadly dragon, as in the story of St George (eleventh century), Sigurd in the *Volsunga Saga* (thirteenth century), Siegfried's slaying of Fafnir in the *Nibelingenlied* (thirteenth century), and Richard Wagner's opera *Siegfried* (1876).

"Beware the Jabberwock, my son!   5
 The jaws that bite, the claws that catch!
Beware the Jubjub bird, and shun
 The frumious Bandersnatch!"[14]

He took his vorpal sword in hand:
 Long time the manxome foe he sought—   10
So rested he by the Tumtum tree,
 And stood awhile in thought.[15]

And as in uffish thought he stood,
 The Jabberwock, with eyes of flame,
Came whiffling through the tulgey wood,   15
 And burbled[16] as it came!

One, two! One, two! and through and through
 The vorpal blade went snicker-snack!
He left it dead, and with its head
 He went galumphing back.   20

"And hast thou slain the Jabberwock?
 Come to my arms, my beamish boy!
O frabjous day! Callooh! Callay!"
 He chortled in his joy.

Notes

[13] *outgrabe* the first stanza was printed in Carroll's handwritten family periodical, *Mischmasch* in 1855 (republished in *The Rectory Umbrella and Mischmasch*, 1932), described as a "Stanza of Anglo-Saxon Poetry" in supposedly Old English characters (including the definite article "yᵉ" for "the"). Then Carroll gave a series of whimsical explanations of the words:

BRYLLYG (derived from the verb to BRYL or BROIL), "the time of broiling dinner, i.e. the close of the afternoon."

SLYTHY (compounded of SLIMY and LITHE). "Smooth and active."

TOVE. A species of Badger. They had smooth white hair, long hind legs, and short horns like a stag; lived chiefly on cheese.

GYRE, verb (derived from GYAOUR or GIAOUR, "a dog"). To scratch like a dog.

GYMBLE (whence GIMBLET). "To screw out holes in anything."

WABE (derived from the verb to SWAB or SOAK). "The side of a hill" (from its being soaked by the rain).

MIMSY (whence MIMSERABLE and MISERABLE). "Unhappy."

BOROGOVE An extinct kind of Parrot. They had no wings, beaks turned up, and made their nests under sundials: lived on veal.

MOME (hence SOLEMOME, SOLEMONE, and SOLEMN). "Grave."

RATH. A species of land turtle. Head erect: mouth like a shark: forelegs curved out so that the animal walked on its knees: smooth green body: lived on swallows and oysters.

OUTGRABE, past tense of the verb to OUTGRIBE. (It is connected with old verb to GRIKE, or SHRIKE, from which are derived "shriek" and "creak"). "Squeaked."

Hence the literal English of the passage is: "It was evening, and the smooth active badgers were scratching and boring holes in the hill-side; all unhappy were the parrots; and the grave turtles squeaked out."

There were probably sundials on the top of the hill, and the "borogoves" were afraid that their nests would be undermined. The hill was probably full of the nests of "raths," which ran out, squeaking with fear, on hearing the "toves" scratching outside. This is an obscure, but yet deeply-affecting, relic of ancient Poetry.

The *OED*, not published when Carroll was writing, provides additional information: slithy (obs. < sleathy = slovenly); gyre = to turn, whirl; gimble (<gimbals = balancing rings, as for a ship's compass); mimsy (<mimsey = prim, pridish); mome (obs. fool, buffoon); rath (Irish: enclosure, walled fort); chortle is a combination of chuckle and snort; galumphing is a combination of gallop and triumph; tulgey is perhaps a combination of thick and bulgey.

[14] *Jabberwock ... Bandersnatch* in a letter Carroll says that jabber means "excited and voluble discussion" and wock derives from OE wocer / wocor, meaning "offspring" or "fruit"; in fact the OE means an increase. The Jubjub bird (Carroll said it was "too rare to illustrate") is explained in greater detail in Carroll's nonsense poem "The Hunting of the Snark" (1876), which contains eight of the nonsense words that occur in "Jabberwocky": mimsy, borogoves, outgrabe, Jubjub, frumious, Bandersnatch, uffish, and beamish. "Frumious" is a combination of fuming and furious. Beamish means radiant, shining brightly with glowing beams. The Bandersnatch is a creature with a long neck and snapping jaws.

[15] *vorpal ... tree* vorpal is perhaps a combination of verbal and lethal; manxone is related to the Isle of Man where the language is Manx; a tum-tum is a colloquial diminutive for a child's stomach or tummy; also the sound of plucking on a stringed instrument.

[16] *burbled* Carroll explained: "If you take the three verbs 'bleat,' 'murmur,' and 'warble,' and select the bits I have underlined, it certainly makes 'burble': though I am afraid I can't distinctly remember having made it that way."

'Twas brillig, and the slithy toves   25
      Did gyre and gimble in the wabe;
All mimsy were the borogoves,
      And the mome raths outgrabe.

The Walrus and the Carpenter[17]

The sun was shining on the sea,
      Shining with all his might:
He did his very best to make
      The billows smooth and bright—
And this was odd, because it was   5
      The middle of the night.

The moon was shining sulkily,
      Because she thought the sun
Had got no business to be there
      After the day was done—   10
"It's very rude of him," she said,
      "To come and spoil the fun!"

The sea was wet as wet could be,
      The sands were dry as dry.
You could not see a cloud, because   15
      No cloud was in the sky:
No birds were flying overhead—
      There were no birds to fly.

The Walrus and the Carpenter
      Were walking close at hand;   20
They wept like anything to see
      Such quantities of sand:
"If this were only cleared away,"
      They said, "it would be grand!"

"If seven maids with seven mops   25
      Swept it for half a year,
Do you suppose," the Walrus said,
      "That they could get it clear?"
"I doubt it," said the Carpenter,
      And shed a bitter tear.   30

Notes

[17] *title* a poem recited by Tweedledee because it "is the longest" (ch. 4). In the nineteenth century oysters were widely consumed by all classes – cooked as cheap food by the working classes, and raw on the half-shell by the middle and upper classes. In his illustrations John Tenniel clothes these characters as working-class. The poem parodies the conventional beast fable as in Aesop; instead of driving home a moral lesson, subverts it.

"O Oysters, come and walk with us!"
  The Walrus did beseech.
"A pleasant walk, a pleasant talk,
  Along the briny beach:
We cannot do with more than four,   35
  To give a hand to each."

The eldest Oyster looked at him,
  But never a word he said:
The eldest Oyster winked his eye,
  And shook his heavy head—   40
Meaning to say he did not choose
  To leave the oyster-bed.

But four young Oysters hurried up,
  All eager for the treat:
Their coats were brushed, their faces washed,   45
  Their shoes were clean and neat—
And this was odd, because, you know,
  They hadn't any feet.

Four other Oysters followed them,
  And yet another four;   50
And thick and fast they came at last,
  And more, and more, and more—
All hopping through the frothy waves,
  And scrambling to the shore.

The Walrus and the Carpenter   55
  Walked on a mile or so,
And then they rested on a rock
  Conveniently low:
And all the little Oysters stood
  And waited in a row.   60

"The time has come," the Walrus said,
  "To talk of many things:
Of shoes—and ships—and sealing-wax—
  Of cabbages—and kings—
And why the sea is boiling hot—   65
  And whether pigs have wings."

"But wait a bit," the Oysters cried,
  "Before we have our chat;
For some of us are out of breath,
  And all of us are fat!"   70
"No hurry!" said the Carpenter.
  They thanked him much for that.

"A loaf of bread," the Walrus said,
  "Is what we chiefly need:
Pepper and vinegar besides   75

Are very good indeed—
Now if you're ready, Oysters dear,
    We can begin to feed."

"But not on us!" the Oysters cried,
    Turning a little blue.   80
"After such kindness, that would be
    A dismal thing to do!"
"The night is fine," the Walrus said.
    "Do you admire the view?

It was so kind of you to come!   85
    And you are very nice!"
The Carpenter said nothing but
    "Cut us another slice:
I wish you were not quite so deaf—
    I've had to ask you twice!"   90

"It seems a shame," the Walrus said,
    "To play them such a trick,
After we've brought them out so far,
    And made them trot so quick!"
The Carpenter said nothing but   95
    "The butter's spread too thick!"

"I weep for you," the Walrus said:
    "I deeply sympathize."
With sobs and tears he sorted out
    Those of the largest size,   100
Holding his pocket-handkerchief
    Before his streaming eyes.

"O Oysters," said the Carpenter,
    "You've had a pleasant run!
Shall we be trotting home again?"   105
    But answer came there none—
And this was scarcely odd, because
    They'd eaten every one.

[Concluding Poem][18]

A boat, beneath a sunny sky,
Lingering onward dreamily
In an evening of July—

Notes

[18] *title* the untitled poem functions as an *envoi* or commission-ing of the poem (and book) to the world, in terms that recall the themes of the cycles of summer and winter, life and death in the novel. An acrostic, the first letter of each line spells Alice's name. Some critics have seen the concluding poem as the final song of the White Knight as he bids fare-well to Alice as she leaves Looking-glass land to return to the real world, possibly a cypher for Carroll's own adieu to Alice.

Children three that nestle near,
Eager eye and willing ear,   5
Pleased a simple tale to hear—

Long has paled that sunny sky:
Echoes fade and memories die:
Autumn frosts have slain July.

Still she haunts me, phantomwise,   10
Alice moving under skies
Never seen by waking eyes.

Children yet, the tale to hear,
Eager eye and willing ear,
Lovingly shall nestle near.   15

In a Wonderland they lie,
Dreaming[19] as the days go by,
Dreaming as the summers die:

Ever drifting down the stream—
Lingering in the golden gleam—   20
Life, what is it but a dream?[20]

William Morris (1834–96)

Morris described himself as born in the "suburban village" of Walthamstow, now part of London, in a well-to-do family of a London financier, William Morris (1797–1847), and his wife, Emma Shelton (1805–94). Morris began reading Walter Scott at 4 and completed him at 7; his father's death when he was 13 left him wealthy, with stocks in Devon copper mines. He went to Marlborough College, then in turmoil, and on to Exeter College (1852), where he met his lifelong friend, the painter Edward Burne-Jones. Abandoning study for the Anglican priesthood, he became an architect, working in the firm of George Street, one of the leading Gothic revival architects, and undertook a series of walking tours to visit the churches of northern France. He met D. G. Rossetti, and with him and other Pre-Raphaelite artists he painted the Oxford Union murals (1857–59). He also edited and paid for a new journal, the *Oxford and Cambridge Magazine* (1856), in which the Pre-Raphaelites, including himself, first published, and he published his own first book of poetry, *The Defence of Guenevere and Other Poems* (1858). In 1859 he married Jane Burden (1839–1914), whose beauty became a Pre-Raphaelite ideal. Morris established a firm (1861; later called Morris & Co.) to undertake interior decorating, eventually to supply wallpapers, tapestries, furniture, carpets, and stained

Notes

[19] *Dreaming* see *Looking-Glass*: "'So I wasn't dreaming, after all,' she said to herself, 'unless—unless we're all part of the same dream. Only I hope it's *my* dream.... I don't like belonging to another person's dream,' she went on in a rather complaining tone" (ch. 8).

[20] *stream ... dream* echo of the popular children's song, "Row, row, row your boat."

glass, much designed by him to conform to his maxim that homes should only contain what you "know to be useful or believe to be beautiful," a foundational principle for the Arts and Crafts movement of which he was a founder. He also continued to publish prolifically: *The Life and Death of Jason* (1866), *The Earthly Paradise* (1868–70), an extensive series of translations from the Norse sagas, a retelling of the *Volsungasaga* as *The Story of Sigurd the Volsung* (1877), as well as translations of the *Aeneid* (1876) and the *Odyssey* (1887). He wrote a series of prose romances later in his life, and his well-known utopian vision, *News from Nowhere* (1890). During the 1870s he taught himself calligraphy, mastering a series of different italic and roman hands based on Renaissance calligraphy handbooks, eventually producing several thousands of pages filled with gold and coloured illuminations, including a complete Horace and an almost complete *Aeneid*. From the 1870s he became involved in political activities, first for the liberals in the Eastern Question Association, and then, to the end of his life, with various socialist organizations, travelling all over England and Scotland, delivering upwards of 500 lectures on well over 100 texts. He was deeply interested in ecology and the preservation of heritage sites, and founded (1877) the Society for the Protection of Ancient Buildings. He established the Kelmscott Press to produce finely printed books (see Figure 7), inaugurating the private press movement and reform of typography, and also became a notable collector of manuscripts and early printed books. Standard edition: *Collected Works of William Morris*, ed. May Morris (24 vols, 1910–15); *The Collected Letters of William Morris*, ed. Norman Kelvin (4 vols in 5, 1984–96); May Morris, *William Morris: Artist, Writer, Socialist* (2 vols, 1936); E. P. Thompson, *William Morris: Romantic to Revolutionary* (1977); Fiona MacCarthy, *William Morris: A Life for Our Times* (1995). The William Morris Society: www.williammorrissociety.org; Morris Online edition from the University of Iowa: http://morrisedition.lib.uiowa.edu/index.html.

Riding Together[1]

For many, many days together
    The wind blew steady from the East;
For many days hot grew the weather,
    About the time of our Lady's Feast.[2]

For many days we rode together,   5
    Yet met we neither friend nor foe;
Hotter and clearer grew the weather,
    Steadily did the East wind blow.

Notes

WILLIAM MORRIS

[1] title the poem is set in the seventh crusade of Louis IX (St Louis, 1214–70), king of France. The crusade lasted from 1248 to 1250, and was focussed on the seizure of the port of Damietta in the Nile delta. Gaining control of that city, as well as Cairo further up the Nile, would enable attacks on Turkish-Muslim-controlled Palestine. The story of the crusade is told by Jean de Joinville (1224–1317), seneschal of Champagne, in his *Life of Saint Louis* (1309). It is most likely that Morris knew the version translated from the French by Thomas Johnes (1807), widely available in Bohn's Antiquarian Library as part of *Chronicles of the Crusades* (1848), edited by Margaret Renée Bryers Shaw. Morris had used material from the first crusade in his first public poem, his submission of "The Mosque Rising in the Place of the Temple of Solomon" for the Newdigate Prize Poem competition at Oxford in 1855. First published in the *Oxford and Cambridge Magazine* (May 1856; our text) that Morris edited; republished in an extensively revised form in *The Defence of Guenevere and Other Poems* (1858).

[2] Feast March 25, the feast of the Annunciation, also known as "Lady Day" (for the Virgin Mary) in the Anglican and Roman Catholic Churches.

We saw the trees in the hot, bright weather,
　　Clear-cut, with shadows very black,　　　　　　　　　10
As freely we rode on together
　　With helms unlaced and bridles slack.

And often, as we rode together,
　　We, looking down the green-bank'd stream,³
Saw flowers in the sunny weather,　　　　　　　　　　　15
　　And saw the bubble-making bream.

And in the night lay down together,
　　And hung above our heads the rood,⁴
Or watch'd night-long⁵ in the dewy weather,
　　The while the moon did watch the wood.　　　　　　　20

Our spears stood bright and thick together,
　　Straight out the banners stream'd behind,
As we gallop'd on in the sunny weather,
　　With faces turn'd towards the wind.

Down sank our three-score spears together,　　　　　　　25
　　As thick we saw the pagans ride;⁶
His eager face in the clear fresh weather
　　Shone out that last time by my side.

Up the sweep of the bridge we dash'd together,
　　It rock'd to the crash of the meeting spears,⁷　　　　　30
Down rain'd the buds of the dear spring weather,
　　The elm-tree flowers fell like tears.

There, as we roll'd and writhed together,
　　I threw my arms above my head,
For close by my side, in the lovely weather,　　　　　　　35
　　I saw him reel and fall back dead.

Notes

³ *stream* Joinville records the march of the crusaders through Egypt along the various rivers of the Nile Delta.

⁴ *rood* the cross of Christ.

⁵ *night-long* concerning the night attacks in 1249, Joinville wrote: "I must inform you that the sultan gave for every head of a Christian that was brought to him a besant of gold; and these Saracen traitors entered our camp during the night, and wherever they found any asleep they cut off their heads" (398).

⁶ *ride* part of Joinville's account of the battle of Al Mansurah (1249) describes the river and the arms: "As we thus gained the river, following its course downward between it and the road, we observed that the king had ascended it, and that the Turks were sending fresh troops after him. Both armies now met on the banks, and the event was miserably unfortunate; for the weaker part of our army thought to cross over to the division of the duke of Burgundy, but that was impossible from their horses being worn down, and the extreme heat of the weather. As we descended the river, we saw it covered with lances, pikes, shields, men and horses, unable to save themselves from death" (415).

⁷ *spears* during the defence of the bridge at Mansura (Feb. 1250) so many bodies filled the river that they could not pass the small bridge that had been defended at such great cost of lives (415–18): "These bodies floated down the river until they came to the small bridge that communicated with each part of our army; and the arch was so low it almost touched the water, and prevented the bodies passing underneath. The river was covered with them from bank to bank, so that the water could not be seen a good stone's throw from the bridge upward. The king hired one hundred labourers, who were full eight days in separating the bodies of the Christians from the Saracens, which were easily distinguishable: the Saracen bodies they thrust under the bridge by main force, and floated them down to the sea; but the Christians were buried in deep graves, one over the other" (432). The battle of Fariskur (6 Apr. 1250) ended the crusade with the total defeat of the French armies, and the seizure of Louis and thousands of prisoners, eventually freed by paying an enormous ransom.

I and the slayer met together,
    He waited the death-stroke there in his place,
With thoughts of death, in the lovely weather,
    Gapingly mazed[8] at my madden'd face.   40

Madly I fought as we fought together;
    In vain: the little Christian band
The pagans drown'd, as in stormy weather,
    The river drowns low-lying land.[9]

They bound my blood-stain'd hands together,   45
    They bound his corpse to nod by my side:
Then on we rode, in the bright March weather,
    With clash of cymbals did we ride.

We ride no more, no more together;
    My prison-bars are thick and strong,   50
I take no heed of any weather,
    The sweet Saints grant I live not long.

The Defence of Guenevere[10]

But, knowing now that they would have her speak,
She threw her wet hair[11] backward from her brow,
Her hand close to her mouth touching her cheek,

As though she had had there a shameful blow,
And feeling it shameful to feel ought but shame   5
All through her heart, yet felt her cheek burned so,

Notes

[8] *mazed* amazed.

[9] *land* Joinville gave attention to the flooding of the Nile and the resulting fertilization of the land: "When arrived in Egypt, it spreads its waters over the country. About the period of St. Remy's day [St Remigius, d. 13 Jan. 533], it expands itself into seven branches, and thence flows over the plains" (401).

[10] *title* although Arthur was alleged to be a British leader at the time of the Roman withdrawal from Britain, about 410 and later, he and his knights came to be identified with chivalric deeds of the twelfth and thirteenth centuries in England and France in a series of romances. Morris's poem is drawn chiefly from two passages in Sir Thomas Malory's *Le Morte d'Arthur*, printed by William Caxton (1485). He used an edition with an introduction and notes by Robert Southey (2 vols, 1817, from which we quote below). He drew on book 19 (Caxton), chapters 1–5 concerning Mellyagraunce and Guenevere (in the poem: 167–222); and the major part of the plot, book 20 (Caxton), chapters 1–4, concerning the plot by Mordred and Agravayne (Gawaine's brother) to entrap Lancelot as Guenevere's guilty lover. Lancelot had been discovered in Guenevere's room, and subsequently slew Agravayne and twelve other knights, and wounded Mordred—for which Arthur condemns Guenevere to be burned, as complicit in adultery. Because of Lancelot's inadvertent slaying of Gawaine's two other brothers, Gareth and Gaherys, Gawaine abandons his fierce defence of Lancelot and Guenevere for a fatal enmity – all this being the frame for the main narrative, a dramatic monologue, in which Guenevere defends herself. Lancelot was first called "Lancelot-du-lac" in *Le Chevalier de la Charette* (Fr. the knight of the cart) by Chrétien de Troyes (late twelfth century), a French poet of the court of Marie de Champagne (1145–98). In the *Vulgate Cycle* of the Arthurian materials (especially the *Prose Lancelot*, largely thirteenth century), Lancelot's story is considerably extended: the son of King Ban of Benwick, he was raised by the Lady of the Lake to become the most heroic of Arthur's knights. After sleeping with Elaine of Corbenic, he became the father of Galahad. The adultery of Lancelot and Guenevere was the prime cause of the collapse of Arthur's realm and the Round Table. Guenevere became a nun, and eventually abbess; Lancelot became a hermit, joined by his kin, and eventually a priest, dying shortly after Guenevere, and his kin returned to his lands in France, and eventually went to the Holy Land. Morris had intended to write a complete cycle of Arthurian poems, as did Tennyson in *The Idylls of the King*, but he completed only four in *The Defence of Guenevere and Other*

She must a little touch it; like one lame
She walked away from Gauwaine,[12] with her head
Still lifted up; and on her cheek of flame

The tears dried quick; she stopped at last and said: 10
"O knights and lords, it seems but little skill°   °use, help
To talk of well-known things past now and dead.

God wot I ought to say, I have done ill,
And pray you all forgiveness heartily!
Because you must be right such great lords—still   15

Listen, suppose your time were come to die,
And you were quite alone and very weak;
Yea, laid a dying while very mightily

The wind was ruffling up the narrow streak
Of river through your broad lands running well: 20
Suppose a hush should come, then some one speak:

'One of these cloths is heaven, and one is hell,[13]
Now choose one cloth for ever; which they be,
I will not tell you, you must somehow tell

Notes

Poems: the title poem, "King Arthur's Tomb," "Sir Galahad,
A Christmas Mystery," and "The Chapel in Lyoness." The
"Defence" is written in *terza rima* (Ital. third rhyme), three-
line stanzas with a chained rhyme scheme (aba, bcb, cdc,
etc.), as in Dante's *Divine Comedy* (1300), Shelley's "Ode to
the West Wind" (1820), and Browning's "The Statue and the
Bust" (1855), the latter of which Morris had praised in his
review as "rhythm so wonderfully suited to the story"
(1856). For another version of the narrative, see FANE,
"LANCELOT AND GUINEVERE." First published in *The Defence
of Guenevere and Other Poems* (1858), a volume with a
dedication: "*To my friend, / Dante Gabriel Rossetti, / Painter, /
I dedicate these poems.*"

In 1910 Morris's daughter May Morris printed twenty-six
lines from Morris's manuscript that had formed the opening
to the poem. She claimed that he had "discarded it for the
abrupt and dramatic opening of the published poem"
(*Collected Works* 1. xx). Others, however, have suggested that
the printer accidentally omitted the manuscript's first page:

That summer morning out in the green fields
Along the Itchen,° sat King Arthur's knights   °river in Hampshire
Long robed and solemn, their brave battle shields

Hung in the canopies, to see such sights
As might be seen that morning, and to hear
Such strange grim words fiercer than many fights,

That on that morn 'twixt anger and great fear
Brave lips and beautiful might writhe to say.
High up in wooden galleries anear

That solemn court of judgment dames sat—gay
With many coloured kirtles, yea, but some
Were sick and white with much fear on that day;

For now take notice, Launcelot was not come;
The lordly minstrel Tristram,° nigh to death   °hero of *Tristan
                                                            and Iseult*
From King Mark's° glaive,° sat brooding at his home;   °King Mark of
                                                            Cornwall slew
                                                            Tristram °blade at the
                                                            end of a pole

Gareth was riding fearful of men's breath
Since he was Gawaine's brother; through the trees
And over many a mountain and bare heath

The questing beast,° wings spread out to the breeze,   °the Beast
                                                            Glatisant, a monster
                                 •   of Arthurian romances
Trailed Palomydes, wearied feet and sore,
And ever Lawaine° was at Launcelot's knees,   °Arthurian knight,
                                                            brother of Elaine
                                                            of Astolat.

So he was missed too; ever more and more
Grew Gawaine's nets round Guenevere the Queen.
Look round about what knights were there that wore

Sir Launcelot's colours, the great snake of green
That twisted on the quartered white and red—

[11] *hair* wet hair because perhaps she had undergone an
ordeal by cold water, being submerged by judges at the
sworn statements of her accusers, from which she has
obviously survived. Such a trial does not occur in Malory.
See also n. 52.
[12] *Gauwaine* King Arthur's nephew and a knight of the
Round Table – as well as Guenevere's accuser: see n. 10.
[13] *hell* the example of the choosing cloths is Morris's invention, not drawn from any known literary source.

Of your own strength and mightiness; here, see!'
Yea, yea, my lord, and you to ope your eyes,
At foot of your familiar bed to see   25

A great God's angel standing, with such dyes,
Not known on earth, on his great wings, and hands,
Held out two ways, light from the inner skies   30

Showing him well, and making his commands
Seem to be God's commands, moreover, too,
Holding within his hands the cloths on wands;

And one of these strange choosing cloths was blue,
Wavy and long, and one cut short and red;   35
No man could tell the better of the two.

After a shivering half-hour you said:
'God help! heaven's colour, the blue'; and he said, 'hell.'
Perhaps you then would roll upon your bed,

And cry to all good men that loved you well,   40
'Ah Christ! if only I had known, known, known';
Launcelot went away, then I could tell,

Like wisest man how all things would be, moan,
And roll and hurt myself, and long to die,
And yet fear much to die for what was sown.   45

Nevertheless you, O Sir Gauwaine, lie,[14]
Whatever may have happened through these years,
God knows I speak truth, saying that you lie."

Notes

[14] *lie* presumably the lie is the accusation of Guenevere's adultery with Launcelot; however, worded so that she can denounce it as a lie. Earlier, Agravayne had plotted against Launcelot and Guenevere, planning to catch him in the queen's chambers in the act of adultery (bk. 20, ch. 2). Launcelot goes there unarmed. However, Malory carefully avoids saying that they had intercourse: "And soo he past tyl he came to the quenes chamber, and thenne sir launcelot was ly3tely putte in to the chamber. And thenne as the Frensshe book sayth the quene and Launcelot were to gyders. And whether they were a bedde or at other maner of disportes, me lyst not herof make no mencyon, for loue that tyme was not as is now a dayes" (bk. 20, ch. 4; punctuation added here and in following citations). Nevertheless, Agravayne accuses Lancelot of being a traitor, but says nothing about Guenevere: "And euer stode sir Agrauayn and sir Mordred cryenge traytoure knyghte come oute of the quenes chamber. Leue your noyse sayd syr launcelot vnto sir Agrauayne. For wete yow wel sir Agrauayne ye shall not prysone me this nyghte.... I shal as to morne appiere afore yow alle before the kyng, and thenne lete it be sene whiche of yow all outher els ye all that wille accuse me of treason, and there I shal ansuer yow as a knyghte shold that hydder I cam to the quene for no maner of male engyne and that wyl I preue and make hit good vpon yow with my handes. Fy on the traytour sayd sir Agrauayn and sir Mordred. We wylle haue the maulgre thy hede, and slee the yf we lyste, for we lete the wete we haue the choyse of kynge Arthur to saue the or to slee the. A sirs sayd sir launcelot, is there none other grace with you, thenne kepe your self. Soo thenne sir Launcelot set al open the chamber dore and myghtely and knyghtely he strode in amongest them and anone at the fyrst buffet, he slewe sir Agrauayne and twelue of his felawes" (bk. 20, ch. 4). Although Malory has Gauwaine defend the honour of both Launcelot and Guenevere at this point in his narrative, only when Launcelot rescues Guenevere from the fire and slays many knights, including Gauwaine's brothers Gareth and Gaheris, does Gauwaine denounce Launcelot and Guenevere. (bk. 20, ch. 8–9). Morris compresses these events.

Her voice was low at first, being full of tears,
But as it cleared, it grew full loud and shrill,   50
Growing a windy shriek in all men's ears,

A ringing in their startled brains, until
She said that Gauwaine lied, then her voice sunk,
And her great eyes began again to fill,

Though still she stood right up, and never shrunk,   55
But spoke on bravely, glorious lady fair!
Whatever tears her full lips may have drunk,

She stood, and seemed to think, and wrung her hair,
Spoke out at last with no more trace of shame,
With passionate twisting of her body there: 60

"It chanced upon a day that Launcelot came
To dwell at Arthur's court: at Christmas-time
This happened; when the heralds sung his name,

'Son of King Ban of Benwick,'[15] seemed to chime
Along with all the bells that rang that day,   65
O'er the white roofs, with little change of rhyme.

Christmas and whitened winter passed away,
And over me the April sunshine came,
Made very awful with black hail-clouds, yea

And in the Summer I grew white with flame,   70
And bowed my head down—Autumn, and the sick
Sure knowledge things would never be the same,

However often Spring might be most thick
Of blossoms and buds, smote° on me, and I grew   °shone
Careless of most things, let the clock tick, tick,[16]   75

To my unhappy pulse, that beat right through
My eager body; while I laughed out loud,
And let my lips curl up at false or true,

Seemed cold and shallow without any cloud.
Behold my judges, then the cloths were brought: 80
While I was dizzied thus, old thoughts would crowd,

Notes

[15] *Benwick* Launcelot does not identify his father in Malory, but in the French *Vulgate Cycle's Lancelot Propre* (*c.*1210) he is so named as the King of Brittany.

[16] *tick* a clock is not an anachronism in light of the dating of the thirteenth-century development of the Arthurian cycle of romances. Mechanical clocks were used in a number of places in Europe in the early thirteenth century and the cathedral clock of Salisbury (1386) still functions.

Belonging to the time ere I was bought
By Arthur's great name and his little love,
Must I give up for ever then, I thought,

That which I deemed would ever round me move   85
Glorifying all things; for a little word,[17]
Scarce ever meant at all, must I now prove

Stone-cold for ever? Pray you, does the Lord
Will that all folks should be quite happy and good?
I love God now a little, if this cord[18]   90

Were broken, once for all what striving could
Make me love anything in earth or heaven.
So day by day it grew, as if one should

Slip slowly down some path worn smooth and even,
Down to a cool sea on a summer day;   95
Yet still in slipping was there some small leaven

Of stretched hands catching small stones by the way,
Until one surely reached the sea at last,
And felt strange new joy as the worn head lay

Back, with the hair like sea-weed; yea all past   100
Sweat of the forehead, dryness of the lips,
Washed utterly out by the dear waves o'ercast

In the lone sea, far off from any ships!
Do I not know now of a day in Spring?
No minute of the wild day ever slips   105

From out my memory; I hear thrushes sing,
And wheresoever I may be, straightway
Thoughts of it all come up with most fresh sting;

I was half mad with beauty on that day,
And went without my ladies all alone,   110
In a quiet garden walled round every way;[19]

I was right joyful of that wall of stone,
That shut the flowers and trees up with the sky,
And trebled all the beauty: to the bone,

Notes

[17] *word* Guenevere's marriage vow to Arthur.

[18] *cord* both the cords restraining her and the love-bond with
Launcelot.

[19] *way* the enclosed or walled-in garden (Lat. *hortus conclusus*)
was a symbol of virginity, and is here ironic, part of
Guenevere's plea for innocence. See Genesis 1–2 and
Mark 14: 32. The protected garden was an emblematic
representation of the Virgin Mary, widely alluded to in
medieval literature (as in the *Romance of the Rose*) and in
Renaissance art (as in Fra Angelico's *Annunciation*
(1442–43). Morris knew the enclosed garden in the *Roman
de la Rose* from his days in Oxford when he and his friend
Edward Burne-Jones examined such illuminated MSS in
the Bodleian Library as Bodley MS e Mus 65 f. 1r and 7r and
Douce 371, f. 4v. He later printed the *Roman* in the *Works
of Chaucer* (1896); see Figure 7. See also Song of Solomon
4: 12: "A garden enclosed is my sister, my spouse; a garden
enclosed, a fountain sealed up." See also n. 61.

Yea right through to my heart, grown very shy   115
With weary thoughts, it pierced, and made me glad;
Exceedingly glad, and I knew verily,

A little thing just then had made me mad;
I dared not think, as I was wont° to do,   °accustomed
Sometimes, upon my beauty; if I had   120

Held out my long hand up against the blue,
And, looking on the tenderly darken'd fingers,
Thought that by rights one ought to see quite through,

There, see you, where the soft still light yet lingers,
Round by the edges; what should I have done,   125
If this had joined with yellow spotted singers,[20]

And startling green drawn upward by the sun?
But shouting, loosed out, see now! all my hair,
And trancedly stood watching the west wind run

With faintest half-heard breathing sound: why there   130
I lose my head e'en now in doing this;
But shortly listen—In that garden fair

Came Launcelot walking; this is true, the kiss[21]
Wherewith we kissed in meeting that spring day,
I scarce dare talk of the remember'd bliss,   135

When both our mouths went wandering in one way,
And aching sorely, met among the leaves;
Our hands being left behind strained far away.

Never within a yard of my bright sleeves
Had Launcelot come before—and now so nigh!   140
After that day why is it Guenevere grieves?

Nevertheless you, O Sir Gauwaine, lie,
Whatever happened on through all those years,
God knows I speak truth, saying that you lie.

Being such a lady could I weep these tears   145
If this were true? A great queen such as I
Having sinn'd this way, straight her conscience sears;

Notes

[20] *singers* songbirds, possibly the yellowhammer bunting or the song thrush.

[21] *kiss* this key moment in the narrative is not included in Malory, but in the Lancelot part of the *Vulgate Cycle*. The episode was well known from its occurrence in the story of the lovers Paulo and Francesca, who have a copy of the Lancelot romance open when they have their own first kiss (*Inferno* 5, 127 ff.), a passage that Dante Rossetti illustrated in a watercolour in 1855.

And afterwards she liveth hatefully,
Slaying and poisoning,[22] certes[23] never weeps,—
Gauwaine be friends now, speak° me lovingly.   °address 150

Do I not see how God's dear pity creeps
All through your frame, and trembles in your mouth?
Remember in what grave your mother sleeps,[24]

Buried in some place far down in the south,
Men are forgetting as I speak to you;   155
By her head sever'd in that awful drouth°   °drought

Of pity that drew Agravaine's fell blow,
I pray your pity! let me not scream out
For ever after, when the shrill winds blow

Through half your castle-locks!° let me not shout   °keyholes 160
For ever after in the winter night
When you ride out alone! in battle-rout°   °battle-turmoil

Let not my rusting tears[25] make your sword light!
Ah! God of mercy how he turns away!
So, ever must I dress me[26] to the fight,   165

So—let God's justice work! Gauwaine, I say,
See me hew down your proofs: yea all men know
Even as you said how Mellyagraunce[27] one day,

One bitter day in *la Fausse Garde*,[28] for so
All good knights held it after, saw—   170
Yea, sirs, by cursed unknightly outrage; though

Notes

[22] *poisoning* in an earlier episode, when Guenevere had sent Launcelot away, she invited twenty-four knights to dinner, and one knight, Sir Patryce of Ireland, was poisoned by eating an apple prepared by Sir Pynel for Sir Gauwaine. At first the queen was accused, but later was exonerated (bk. 18, ch. 3–4).

[23] *certes* (ME < OFr. < Lat. *certus*, certain) certainly.

[24] *sleeps* the accusation of adultery that Guenevere defends herself against is analogous to the charge for which Gauwaine's mother was executed. Malory records that Gauwaine's mother, Queen Margawse of the Orkneys, was discovered by Gauwaine's brother, Gaheris, making love with Sir Lamorak; Gaheris thereupon struck off her head (bk. 10, ch. 24). Morris lays the blame on another brother, Agravaine.

[25] *tears* rusting is either an instrumental usage (on the analogy of the Latin case of the instrumental ablative) or a transferred epithet: it is the sword that would be rusting; or her tears would make his sword weak.

[26] *dress me* address myself, prepare, arm. Malory uses a similar phrase in the trial of combat between Launcelot and Mellyagraunce: "And whanne the kynge and the quene and al the lordes knewe of the treason of sir Mellyagraunce, they were alle ashamed on his behalfe. Thenne was quene Gueneuer sente for, and sette by the kynge in grete truste of her champyon. And thenne there was no more els to say, but syr Launcelot and sire Mellyagraunce dressid them vnto bataille, and took their speres, and soo they came to gyders as thonder and there sir launcelot bare hym doune quyte ouer his hors croupe. And thenne sire Launcelot alyghte and dressid his sheld on his sholder with his suerd in his hand. And sir Mellyagraunce in the same wyse dressid hym vnto hym, and there they smote many grete strokes to gyders, and at the laste sire Launcelot smote hym suche a buffet vpon the helmet that he felle on the one syde to the erthe" (bk. 19, ch. 9).

[27] *Mellyagraunce* in lines 168–221 Morris gives the story of Guenevere and Mellyagraunce. Malory recounts how Mellyagraunce had long lusted for Guenevere, and so he kidnapped her after wounding the knights with her, taking her to his castle. Launcelot broke the bars on her window to gain access to her, thereby cutting himself. Mellyagraunce discovered the blood on the queen's sheets the next morning, and blamed a wounded knight for having violated her, and her of adultery. Eight days later, in an ordeal by combat, whereby the winner's victory would be accepted as the judgement of God, Launcelot killed Mellyagraunce, thereby vindicating Guenevere again (bk. 19, ch.1–9).

[28] *Garde* (Fr. the false keep, castle), the name of Mellyagraunce's castle. Launcelot's castle was first called

You, Gauwaine, held his word without a flaw,
This Mellyagraunce saw blood upon my bed—
Whose blood then pray you? is there any law

To make a queen say why some spots of red   175
Lie on her coverlet? or will you say,
'Your hands are white, lady, as when you wed,

Where did you bleed?' and must I stammer out—'Nay,
I blush indeed, fair lord, only to rend
My sleeve up to my shoulder, where there lay   180

A knife-point last night': so must I defend
The honour of the Lady Guenevere?
Not so, fair lords, even if the world should end

This very day, and you were judges here
Instead of God. Did you see Mellyagraunce   185
When Launcelot stood by him? what white fear

Curdled his blood, and how his teeth did dance,
His side sink in? as my knight cried and said,
'Slayer of unarm'd men, here is a chance!

Setter of traps, I pray you guard your head,   190
By God I am so glad to fight with you,
Stripper of ladies,[29] that my hand feels lead

For driving weight; hurrah now! draw and do,
For all my wounds are moving in my breast,
And I am getting mad[30] with waiting so.'   195

He struck his hands together o'er the beast,
Who fell down flat, and grovell'd at his feet,
And groan'd at being slain so young—'At least,'

My knight said, 'Rise you, sir, who are so fleet
At catching ladies, half-arm'd will I fight,   200
My left side all uncovered!'[31] then I weet,[32]

Notes

"La Douleureuse Garde" (Fr. the castle of sorrow), until
he was given the challenge by Arthur of taking it from the
evil knights who held it; he did so and renamed it "La
Joyous Garde."

[29] *men … traps … ladies* in lines 189–92 the three accusations
against Mellyagraunce refer to the details in Malory: first,
he attacked and wounded (he did not slay) the knights but
slew the attendant yeomen who accompanied Guenevere
on her Maying ride when she was captured (bk. 19, ch. 2);
second, when showing his castle to Launcelot,
Mellyagraunce had him fall through a trap door to

imprison him (bk. 19, ch. 7); and third, the ladies who
accompanied the knights were also required to go to
Mellyagraunce's castle (bk. 19, ch. 3).

[30] *mad* not angry but deranged.

[31] *uncovered* unarmoured: from Malory: "I shalle profer yow
large profers sayd sir Launcelot, that is for to say, I shall
vnarme my hede & my lyfte quarter of my body alle that
may be vnarmed & lete bynde my lyfte hande behynde
me, soo that it shalle not helpe me and ryghte so I shall
doo bataille with yow" (bk 19, ch. 9).

[32] *weet* (arch. < OE *witan* < ME *witen* to know) know.

Up sprang Sir Mellyagraunce with great delight
Upon his knave's face; not until just then
Did I quite hate him, as I saw my knight

Along the lists look to my stake and pen[33]   205
With such a joyous smile, it made me sigh
From agony beneath my waist-chain, when

The fight began, and to me they drew nigh;
Ever Sir Launcelot kept him on the right,
And traversed warily, and ever high   210

And fast leapt caitiff's° sword, until my knight   °cowardly villain
Sudden threw up his sword to his left hand,
Caught it, and swung it; that was all the fight.[34]

Except a spout of blood on the hot land;
For it was hottest summer; and I know   215
I wonder'd how the fire, while I should stand,

And burn, against the heat, would quiver so,
Yards above my head; thus these matters went;
Which things were only warnings of the woe

That fell on me. Yet Mellyagraunce was shent,[35]   220
For Mellyagraunce had fought against the Lord;
Therefore, my lords, take heed lest you be blent[36]

With all this wickedness; say no rash word
Against me, being so beautiful; my eyes,
Wept all away to grey, may bring some sword   225

To drown you in your blood; see my breast rise,
Like waves of purple sea, as here I stand;
And how my arms are moved in wonderful wise,

Yea also at my full heart's strong command,
See through my long throat how the words go up   230
In ripples to my mouth; how in my hand

Notes

[33] *pen* lists are the spaces for tilting, particularly the barriers separating jousting knights in a tournament. The pen confined Guenevere and the stake (to which she was chained – see line 207) was where she was to be burned for treason (that is, adultery) against King Arthur: "And speke we of Quene Gueneuer, that was broughte to a fyre to be brent" (bk. 19, ch. 9).

[34] *fight* Malory writes: "Thenne syre Mellyagraunce came with his suerd all on hygh, and sire launcelot shewed him openly his bare hede and the bare lyfte syde. And whan he wende to haue smyten hym vpon the bare hede, thenne lyghtly he auoyded the lyfte legge & the lyfte syde, & put his ryght hand and his suerd to that stroke, and soo putte it on syde with grete sleyghte, and thenne with grete force syr launcelot smote hym on the helmet suche a buffet that the stroke kerued the hede in two partyes, thenne there was no more to doo" (bk. 19, ch. 9).

[35] *shent* (arch. < OE *shendan* < ME *shend*) shamed, ruined, destroyed.

[36] *blent* blinded by, contaminated by.

The shadow lies like wine within a cup
Of marvellously colour'd gold; yea now
This little wind is rising, look you up,

And wonder how the light is falling so   235
Within my moving tresses: will you dare,
When you have looked a little on my brow,

To say this thing is vile? or will you care
For any plausible lies of cunning woof,°   °weaving
When you can see my face with no lie there   240

For ever? am I not a gracious proof—
'But in your chamber Launcelot was found'—[37]
Is there a good knight then would stand aloof,

When a queen says with gentle queenly sound:
'O true as steel come now and talk with me,   245
I love to see your step upon the ground

Unwavering, also well I love to see
That gracious smile light up your face, and hear
Your wonderful words, that all mean verily

The thing they seem to mean: good friend, so dear   250
To me in everything, come here to-night,
Or else the hours will pass most dull and drear;

If you come not, I fear this time I might
Get thinking over much of times gone by,
When I was young, and green hope was in sight;   255

For no man cares now to know why I sigh;
And no man comes to sing me pleasant songs,
Nor any brings me the sweet flowers that lie

So thick in the gardens; therefore one so longs
To see you, Launcelot;[38] that we may be   260
Like children once again, free from all wrongs

Just for one night.' Did he not come to me?
What thing could keep true Launcelot away
If I said, 'come?' there was one less than three

In my quiet room that night, and we were gay;   265
Till sudden I rose up, weak, pale, and sick,
Because a bawling broke our dream up, yea

Notes —————————————————————————————————

[37] *found* see n. 14.
[38] *Launcelot* these arguments are advanced by Gauwaine in
   Malory (bk. 20, ch. 7).

I looked at Launcelot's face and could not speak,
For he looked helpless[39] too, for a little while;
Then I remember how I tried to shriek,   270

And could not, but fell down; from tile to tile
The stones they threw up rattled o'er my head,
And made me dizzier; till within a while

My maids were all about me, and my head
On Launcelot's breast was being soothed away   275
From its white chattering, until Launcelot said—

By God! I will not tell you more to-day,
Judge any way you will—what matters it?
You know quite well the story of that fray,

How Launcelot still'd their bawling, the mad fit[40]   280
That caught up Gauwaine—all, all, verily,
But just that which would save me; these things flit.

Nevertheless you, O Sir Gauwaine, lie,
Whatever may have happen'd these long years,
God knows I speak truth, saying that you lie!   285

All I have said is truth, by Christ's dear tears."
She would not speak another word, but stood
Turn'd sideways; listening, like a man who hears

His brother's trumpet sounding through the wood
Of his foes' lances. She lean'd eagerly,   290
And gave a slight spring sometimes, as she could

At last hear something really; joyfully
Her cheek grew crimson, as the headlong speed
Of the roan charger° drew all men to see,   °horse of mixed colours
The knight who came was Launcelot at good need.[41]   295

Notes

[39] *helpless* at her entreaty, Launcelot had come to Guenevere's chambers without his armour, only bearing his sword: "Soo sir Launcelot departed and took his swerd vnder his arme and soo in his mantel that noble knyghte putte hym self in grete jeopardy and soo he past tyl he came to the quenes chamber" (bk. 20, ch. 3); see n. 14.

[40] *fit* Gauwaine's fit occurs in Malory after the killing of his brothers Gaheris and Gareth: "Allas sayd sire Gawayne now is my Joye gone and thenne he felle doune and swouned, and long he lay there as he had ben dede" (bk. 20, ch. 10).

[41] *need* just in time. When fighting with the knights who ambushed him in Guenevere's chambers (see n. 14), Malory reports the following exchange between them: "And thenne syre launcelot retorned ageyne vnto the Quene and sayd madame, now wete yow wel all oure true loue is brought to an ende. . . . I shalle saue yow from alle manere aduentures daungerous. that is not best sayd the quene. . . . And yf ye see that as to morne they wylle put me vnto the dethe, thenne may ye rescowe me as ye thynke best. I wyll wel sayd sir launcelot, for haue ye no doubte whyle I am lyuynge, I shalle rescowe yow" (bk. 20, ch. 4). The rescue by Launcelot occurs as Guenevere is about to be burned: "Thenne was ther one that sire Launcelot had sente vnto that place for to aspye what tyme the quene sold goo vnto her dethe. And anone as he sawe the quene despoylled in to her smok, and soo shryuen. Thenne he gaf sir launcelot warnynge, thenne was there but sporynge and pluckynge vp of horses and ryghte so they cam to the fyre. And who that stood ageynste them there were they slayne. . . . Thenne he rode streyghte vnto dame Gueneuer and maade a kyrtyl and a gowne to be cast vpon her, and thenne he made her to be sette behynde hym and prayd her to be of good chere.

The Haystack in the Floods[42]

Had she come all the way for this,
To part at last without a kiss?
Yea, had she borne the dirt and rain
That her own eyes might see him slain
Beside the haystack in the floods?   5

Along the dripping leafless woods,
The stirrup touching either shoe,
She rode astride[43] as troopers do;
With kirtle kilted to her knee,[44]
To which the mud splash'd wretchedly;   10
And the wet dripp'd from every tree
Upon her head and heavy hair,
And on her eyelids broad and fair;
The tears and rain ran down her face.

By fits and starts they rode apace,   15
And very often was his place
Far off from her; he had to ride
Ahead, to see what might betide
When the roads cross'd; and sometimes, when
There rose a murmuring from his men,   20
Had to turn back with promises;
Ah me! she had but little ease;
And often for pure doubt and dread
She sobb'd, made giddy in the head
By the swift riding; while, for cold,   25
Her slender fingers scarce could hold
The wet reins; yea, and scarcely, too,
She felt the foot within her shoe
Against the stirrup: all for this,
To part at last without a kiss   30
Beside the haystack in the floods.

For when they near'd that old soak'd hay,
They saw across the only way

Notes

Wete yow wel, the Quene was gladde that she was escaped from the dethe, and thenne she thanked god and sir Launcelot, and soo he rode his way with the Quene as the Frensshe book saith vnto Joyous gard" (bk. 20, ch. 8).

[42] *title* this poem is one of ten or more in Morris's first volume of poems that are drawn from the *Chroniques de France* (Fr. chronicles of France) by Jean Froissart (*c.*1337–*c.*1405). The *Chronicles* cover the years 1322 to 1400, including the first half of the Hundred Years' War between England and France, the historical context for the poem. Morris used the translation by John Bourchier, Lord Berners (1467–1532), published in two volumes (1523–25) that he had in Rivington's edition of 1812 (2 vols); later in his life he collected the first edition in English (1525) as well as the Paris edition in French (1530). The lovers, an English knight, Sir Robert de Marny (see n. 47) and Jehane, his French mistress, are trying to escape to English-held Gascony after the English defeated the French at the Battle of Poitiers (see n. 48). First published in *The Defence of Guenevere and Other Poems* (1858).

[43] *astride* in Morris's day and in the Middle Ages it was customary for women to ride side-saddle to maintain propriety because of their long skirts. Troopers are mounted soldiers, cavalry.

[44] *knee* long gown hitched up. See Walter Scott, "The Young Tamlane" in *The Minstrelsy of the Scottish Border* (1802–03).

That Judas, Godmar, and the three
Red running lions[45] dismally   35
Grinn'd from his pennon, under which,
In one straight line along the ditch,
They counted thirty heads.
                              So then,
While Robert turn'd round to his men,
She saw at once the wretched end,   40
And, stooping down, tried hard to rend
Her coif[46] the wrong way from her head,
And hid her eyes; while Robert[47] said:
"Nay, love, 'tis scarcely two to one,
At Poictiers[48] where we made them run   45
So fast—why, sweet my love, good cheer,
The Gascon frontier[49] is so near,
Nought after this."

                        But, "O," she said,
"My God! my God! I have to tread
The long way back without you; then   50
The court at Paris; those six men;
The gratings of the Chatelet;[50]
The swift Seine[51] on some rainy day
Like this, and people standing by,
And laughing, while my weak hands try   55
To recollect how strong men swim.[52]
All this, or else a life with him,
For which I should be damned at last,
Would God that this next hour were past!"

He answer'd not, but cried his cry,   60
"St. George for Marny!"[53] cheerily;

Notes

[45] *Godmar … lions* possibly Godmar du Fay, a French knight accused of treachery by the French king, Philip VI (1293–1350), who blamed him for supposedly losing the Battle of Crécy (1346), according to Froissart (bk. 1, ch. 134); see also Morris's poem, "The Eve of Crecy" in *Defence of Guenevere* (1858). At Crécy the vastly superior French numbers were defeated by the power of the English longbows and by better battle tactics. Here Godmar is French and fighting for the French but luring the lovers into supposed safety by bearing the arms of England, three lions *passant* (with one paw raised) – hence traitorous, a Judas, the betrayer of Jesus.

[46] *coif* close-fitting cap that covered the hair and the back and sides of the head. Because Jehane had to hold the reins, she tried to pull it down unsuccessfully, instead of taking it off.

[47] *Robert* Robert de Marny was either an English knight (c.1340–94) at the court of Edward III (1312–77) or a French knight caught in circumstances somewhat like those in Morris, recounted in Froissart (bk. 1, ch. 29–30).

[48] *Poictiers* the battle of Poitiers (19 Sept. 1356) where, like Crécy and the later Agincourt, Edward the Black Prince (1330–76, who had fought at Crécy) defeated the far more numerous French by means of the English longbows and superior tactics.

[49] *frontier* area in southwest France, bordering Spain, that was held by England throughout the Hundred Years' War (1337–1453) – and so a safe haven for the lovers.

[50] *Chatelet* Le Grand Châtelet was both the infamous prison and court at Paris where the "six men" would be her judges.

[51] *Seine* river flowing through Paris, on the bank of which was the Châtelet.

[52] *swim* Jehane fears that her judges will impose the trial by cold water (see n. 11), usually reserved for the trial of witches at this time. Their powers supposedly enabled them to float, even when their limbs were bound and a millstone was attached to them – and they would then be found guilty and be burned. If they sank they either drowned (and went to heaven as innocent) or were rescued (by an attached rope). This last alternative is not mentioned by Morris: Jehane faces death in Paris by drowning or burning, or suicide with Godmar.

[53] *Marny* Robert's battle cry. St George is the patron saint of England, a third-century soldier in the army of Diocletian (244–311) who was martyred on 23 April 303 in the

And laid his hand upon her rein.
Alas! no man of all his train
Gave back that cheery cry again;
And, while for rage his thumb beat fast   65
Upon his sword-hilts, some one cast
About his neck a kerchief long,
And bound him.

        Then they went along
To Godmar; who said: "Now, Jehane,[54]
Your lover's life is on the wane   70
So fast, that, if this very hour
You yield not as my paramour,
He will not see the rain leave off—
Nay, keep your tongue from gibe and scoff,
Sir Robert, or I slay you now."   75

She laid her hand upon her brow,
Then gazed upon the palm, as though
She thought her forehead bled, and—"No."
She said, and turn'd her head away,
As there were nothing else to say,   80
And everything were settled: red
Grew Godmar's face from chin to head:
"Jehane, on yonder hill there stands
My castle, guarding well my lands:
What hinders me from taking you,   85
And doing that I list to do
To your fair wilful body, while
Your knight lies dead?"

        A wicked smile
Wrinkled her face, her lips grew thin,
A long way out she thrust her chin: 90
"You know that I should strangle you
While you were sleeping; or bite through
Your throat, by God's help—ah!" she said,
"Lord Jesus, pity your poor maid!
For in such wise they hem me in,   95
I cannot choose but sin and sin,
Whatever happens: yet I think
They could not make me eat or drink,
And so should I just reach my rest."

"Nay, if you do not my behest,   100
O Jehane! though I love you well,"
Said Godmar, "would I fail to tell

Notes

persecutions of Christians. Among the legends concerning
him is his slaying of the dragon, as recorded in *The Golden
Legend* by Jacobus de Voragine (1230–98).

[54] *Jehane* medieval spelling of Jane.

All that I know." "Foul lies," she said.
"Eh? lies my Jehane? by God's head,
At Paris folks would deem them true!　　　　　　　105
Do you know, Jehane, they cry for you,
'Jehane the brown! Jehane the brown!⁵⁵
Give us Jehane to burn or drown!'—
Eh—gag me, Robert!—sweet my friend,
This were indeed a piteous end　　　　　　　110
For those long fingers, and long feet,
And long neck, and smooth shoulders sweet;
An end that few men would forget
That saw it—So, an hour yet:
Consider, Jehane, which to take　　　　　　　115
Of life or death!'

　　　　　　　So, scarce awake,
Dismounting, did she leave that place,
And totter some yards: with her face
Turn'd upward to the sky she lay,
Her head on a wet heap of hay,　　　　　　　120
And fell asleep: and while she slept,
And did not dream, the minutes crept
Round to the twelve again; but she,
Being waked at last, sigh'd quietly,
And strangely childlike came, and said:　　　　　　　125
"I will not." Straightway Godmar's head,
As though it hung on strong wires, turn'd
Most sharply round, and his face burn'd.

For Robert—both his eyes were dry,
He could not weep, but gloomily　　　　　　　130
He seem'd to watch the rain; yea, too,
His lips were firm; he tried once more
To touch her lips; she reach'd out, sore
And vain desire so tortured them,
The poor grey lips, and now the hem　　　　　　　135
Of his sleeve brush'd them.

　　　　　　　With a start
Up Godmar rose, thrust them apart;
From Robert's throat he loosed the bands
Of silk and mail; with empty hands
Held out, she stood and gazed, and saw,　　　　　　　140
The long bright blade without a flaw

Notes

⁵⁵ *brown* Jehane is a brunette, like Jane Burden, who was discovered as a model by Dante Rossetti for the figure of Queen Guenevere in the painting of the Oxford Union murals in 1857, in which William Morris also took part. Morris painted her as *La Belle Iseult* (1858: see Plate 16) in the same year that he published *The Defence of Guenevere and Other Poems*, and married her in 1859. Rossetti continued to paint her and they had a prolonged love affair. Her hair became a hallmark of Pre-Raphaelite beauty. Jehane is one of two brown-haired women in Morris's volume, the other being the one spoken of in "Praise of My Lady": "Heavy to make the pale face sad, / And dark, but dead as though it had / Been forged by God most wonderfully / Beata mea Domina!—" (Lat. my blessed lady).

Glide out from Godmar's sheath, his hand
In Robert's hair; she saw him bend
Back Robert's head; she saw him send
The thin steel down; the blow told well,   145
Right backward the knight Robert fell,
And moan'd as dogs do, being half dead,
Unwitting, as I deem: so then
Godmar turn'd grinning to his men,
Who ran, some five or six, and beat   150
His head to pieces at their feet.

Then Godmar turn'd again and said:
"So, Jehane, the first fitte[56] is read!
Take note, my lady, that your way
Lies backward to the Chatelet!"   155
She shook her head and gazed awhile
At her cold hands with a rueful smile,
As though this thing had made her mad.

This was the parting that they had
Beside the haystack in the floods.   160

In Prison[57]

Wearily, drearily,
Half the day long,
Flap the great banners
High over the stone;
Strangely and eerily   5
Sounds the wind's song,
Bending the banner-poles.

While, all alone,
Watching the loophole's spark,
Lie I, with life all dark,   10
Feet tether'd, hands fetter'd
Fast to the stone,
The grim walls, square-letter'd
With prison'd men's groan.

Still strain the banner-poles   15
Through the wind's song,
Westward the banner rolls
Over my wrong.

Notes

[56] *fitte* (arch. and obs. < OE *fitt* < ME *fyt*[te] section of a poem: *OED*), a term used for a canto or other division in medieval metrical romances like *The Romance of Sir Degravant* (that Morris printed at his Kelmscott Press in 1896) or ballads, like "Chevy Chase" (fifteenth century). It was later used to divide the long poem by Lewis Carroll, *The Hunting of the Snark (An Agony in 8 Fits)*, 1876.

[57] *title* this short poem is chiefly written in dactylic dimeter lines. Two-stress lines, a comparative rarity, were sometimes used by Ben Jonson ("A Hymn to God the

From *The Earthly Paradise*[58]

An Apology

Of Heaven or Hell I have no power to sing,[59]
I cannot ease the burden of your fears,
Or make quick-coming death a little thing,
Or bring again the pleasure of past years,
Nor for my words shall ye forget your tears,   5
Or hope again for aught that I can say,[60]
The idle singer of an empty day.[61]

But rather, when aweary of your mirth,
From full hearts still unsatisfied ye sigh,
And, feeling kindly unto all the earth,   10
Grudge every minute[62] as it passes by,
Made the more mindful that the sweet days die—
—Remember me a little then I pray,
The idle singer of an empty day.

The heavy trouble, the bewildering care   15
That weighs us down who live and earn our bread,

Notes

Father," 1640) and by Robert Herrick ("Upon His Departure Hence," 1648); however both Jonson and Herrick use iambic feet. Morris greatly complicates the rhythm, and also adds internal rhymes, alliteration, and assonance. Generically the poem is a complaint on the theme of unjust imprisonment. First printed without a title as a song sung by Mabel and overheard by her life-long but rejected lover in Morris's story, "Frank's Sealed Letter" in his magazine, *The Oxford and Cambridge Magazine* (Apr. 1856), our text. It was given its present title and was reprinted as the last poem in *The Defence of Guenevere and Other Poems* (1858).

[58] *title* one of the longest poems in the English language, *The Earthly Paradise* (1868–70) is preceded by "An Apology" and an opening frame poem, "Prologue—The Wanderers." It tells how Norwegian sailors of the fourteenth century find a remote island inhabited by descendants of ancient Greeks, with whom they exchange their traditional stories. Norse and Greek tales alternate for each month, and each pair of tales is introduced with a lyric on the month in which they are set. The epic concludes with an "Epilogue," followed by "L'Envoi," mirroring "An Apology." Apology is here used not as an expression of regret or demurral, but as a defence of an ideological position: the epic poet is claiming his right as a teller of tales. In part this position is claimed by Morris's verse form, rime royal, named after James I of Scotland's *The Kingis Quair* (1423), and identified with Chaucer's *Troilus and Criseyde* (1385), four of the *Canterbury Tales* (c.1400), Shakespeare's *The Rape of Lucrece* (1594), and Spenser's *Fowre Hymnes* (1596). The opening poem to Morris's epic is printed in italics without a title, but in the "Table of Contents" it is listed as "An Apology."

[59] *sing* Morris turns from the conventional invocation of the poetic muse in epic in order to enumerate the topics that he will not cover. They include no treatment of heaven and hell as in Dante or Milton.

[60] *say* each line of this stanza sets out Morris's abnegation of the conventional tasks of the poet: the easing of fear, the evasion of death, nostalgia for the past, the healing of grief, and the restoration of hope, each associated with well-established genres.

[61] *day* Morris uses the word "idle" not in the sense of wasting time, but as it was used in one of his favourite books, *Le Roman de la Rose* by Guillaume de Lorris (c.1230) and Jean de Meun (c.1275). He had several copies of it in his library, including a French printing of 1526. He also printed Chaucer's translation of it in *The Works of Geoffrey Chaucer* (Kelmscott Press, 1896; see Figure 7). In the *Roman*, Dame Oiseuse (OFr. idleness, ease, leisure), the first allegorical character met, leads the lovers into an enclosed garden, a *hortus delicarum* (Lat. garden of pleasure) where Mirth is lord: "Lo, sir, my name is Ydelnesse … Ful myghty and ful riche am I, / And that of oon thyng namely / For I entende to nothyng / But to my joye and my pleying (593 ff.). The lovers are not there either for study or worship, but for entertainment in learning the arts of love. Hence, Ydelnesse invokes that time of both anticipation and promise that will fill the "empty" day when the duties and responsibilities of the working day are set aside. More generally, this "idle singer" is leading the way for readers into the "earthly paradise" of the poem.

[62] *minute* the following tales, then, are a means of meeting the *carpe diem* (Lat. seize the day) figure – they are a means of catching or stopping time to enjoy the present.

These idle verses have no power to bear;
So let me sing of names remembered,
Because they, living not, can ne'er be dead,
Or long time take their memory quite away   20
From us poor singers of an empty day.

   Dreamer of dreams, born out of my due time,
Why should I strive to set the crooked straight?[63]
Let it suffice me that my murmuring rhyme
Beats with light wing against the ivory gate,[64]   25
Telling a tale not too importunate
To those who in the sleepy region stay,
Lulled by the singer of an empty day.

   Folk say, a wizard[65] to a northern king
At Christmas-tide such wondrous things did show,   30
That through one window men beheld the spring,
And through another saw the summer glow,
And through a third the fruited vines a-row,
While still, unheard, but in its wonted way,
Piped the drear wind of that December day.   35

   So with this Earthly Paradise it is,
If ye will read aright, and pardon me,
Who strive to build a shadowy isle of bliss[66]
Midmost the beating of the steely sea,
Where tossed about all hearts of men must be;   40
Whose ravening monsters mighty men shall slay,
Not the poor singer of an empty day.[67]

WEB p. 421

From "How I became a Socialist".

Notes

[63] *straight* see Isaiah 40: 4; 45: 2; and Luke 3: 5, where the same verses are applied to John the Baptist as a prophet. In a letter of 1856 from Oxford, where he was studying, Morris wrote to his friend Cormell Price: "I can't enter into politico-social subjects with any interest, for on the whole I see that things are in a muddle, and I have no power or vocation to set them right in ever so little a degree. My work is the embodiment of dreams in one form or another" (July 1856).

[64] *gate* the ivory gate is the gate of false or deceitful dreams in *Odyssey* 19: 560–69, as opposed to the gate of horn whence true or prophetic dreams come. The same point is made by Virgil in *Aeneid* 6: 893–98. Here Morris suggests that his tales are imaginative or fictive.

[65] *wizard* late in his life Morris claimed that the idea of the wizard's opening a window on the four seasons came from the Faustus story – either Marlowe's *Dr. Faustus* (1604 / 1616) or the prose *Damnable History* (1592), when Faust opens a casement window in January to give summer grapes to the Duchess of Vanholt. The wizard's four seasons anticipate the fourfold grouping of the tales into three-month sections.

[66] *bliss* a possible echo of the "Bower of Blisse" in Spenser's *Faerie Queene* (1590: bk. II canto XII).

[67] *day* at the end of *The Earthly Paradise* Morris has an "Epilogue" followed by seventeen rime royal stanzas of "L'Envoi," beginning:

> Here are we for the last time face to face,
> Thou and I, Book, before I bid thee speed
> Upon thy perilous journey to that place
> For which I have done on thee pilgrim's weed,
> Striving to get thee all things for thy need—
> —I love thee, whatso time or men may say
> Of the poor singer of an empty day.

This traditional author's farewell to the reader is like the one that Chaucer uses at the end of *Troilus and Criseyde*: "Go, litel bok, go, litel myn tragedye" (V. 1786; *c*.1380); and, like Chaucer's dedication of *Troilus* to "moral [John] Gower," so does Morris dedicate his poem to "a friend, / Of whom for love I may not be afeard … My Master, GEOFFRY CHAUCER."

James Thomson [B. V.] (1834–82)

Born in Port Glasgow in Scotland into a family that followed the millennialist teachings of Edward Irving (the "Irvingites"), Thomson's father James Thomson (1806–53), a merchant sailor, suffered a stroke and was disabled, so the family moved to London. His mother, Sarah Kennedy (1798–1843) had him placed at the age of 8 in the Royal Caledonian Asylum (a school for Scottish children orphaned in the Napoleonic wars) where he was educated (to 1848), as well as at the Royal Military Academy at Chelsea (to 1854). He had already been nominated as a student-teacher in Ireland in 1851, where he met Charles Bradlaugh (1833–91), later the radical MP, and also developed an affection for a young girl, Matilda Weller, who died young in 1853. After eight years as an army schoolteacher, he settled in London as a journalist from 1863, using the pseudonym "B. V." (standing for Bysshe Vanolis, in honour of Shelley and Novalis, the latter as an anagram). He published a great deal in Bradlaugh's paper, the *National Reformer* – reviews, poems, articles on secularism (to which he had become partly committed), politics, and translations. His pessimistic masterpiece *The City of Dreadful Night* came out in four instalments in the *Reformer* in 1874 and was welcomed by George Eliot and George Meredith. His friend Bertram Dobell (1842–1914), British bookseller, helped him to publish *The City of Dreadful Night and Other Poems* (1880), *Vane's Story, Weddah and Om-el-Bonain and Other Poems* (1881), and a prose collection, *Essays and Phantasies* (1881). His chronic alcoholism pulled him into one boarding house after another, only rescued by friends at the point of death. Standard Edition: *Poems and Some Letters of James Thomson*, ed. Ann Ridler (1963); James Thomson, *The Speedy Extinction of Evil and Misery: Selected Prose*, ed. W. D. Schaefer (1967); Tom Leonard, *Places of the Mind: The Life and Work of James Thomson ("B. V.")* (1993). The James Thomson Poetry Works: vasthead.com/Thomson.

The City of Dreadful Night[1]

This poem is a fundamental document for representing the Victorian city, London allegorized, as a scene of psychological dystopia, of hopelessness and despair, without light, God, or possible redemption. The poem is in the literary tradition of blighted communities, stretching from Dante's *Inferno* to Oliver Goldsmith's *The Deserted Village* (1770), 100 years before Thomson, concerning the end of the English peasantry during enclosure – the conversion of agricultural land into grazing land for sheep under the industrial revolution. It is an inversion of *The Castle of Indolence* (1748), a long poem in Spenserian stanzas in which the life of pleasure and luxury enervates soul and body, by

Notes

JAMES THOMSON

[1] *title* the poem has two epigraphs, one from Dante and the other from Giacomo Leopardi (1798–1837), Italian poet, whom Thomson had been translating. The Dante passage, the first line of Canto 3 of *Inferno*, is part of the inscription on the gate of hell: "Through me lies the way to the city of pain." The Leopardi passages are from *Canti* 23 (Ital. songs) and "Coro di Morti" from *Operetti Morali* (Ital. Chorus of the Dead from the Little moral works, 1825), the first, about how the cycles of the heavens show neither purpose nor gain, and the second, on the denial of happiness to the living and the dead. In the MS. notebooks in the British Library and the Pierpont Morgan Library in New York City a quotation from Job is written above the title of the poem: "A land of darkness, as darkness itself; and of the shadow of death, without any order, and where the light is as darkness" (Job 10: 22). First published anonymously in the *National Reformer* (issues of 22 Mar., 12 Apr., 26 Apr., and 17 May, 1874); republished in *The City of Dreadful Night and Other Poems* (1880), our text.

James Thomson (1700–48), Thomson's eighteenth-century Scottish namesake. It also anticipates T. S. Eliot's dark Modernist vision in *The Waste Land* (1922). There was a parallel in various histories of the collapse of empires and the recording of their antiquities, as in Giovanni Battista Piranesi's *Vedute di Roma* (It. views of Rome, 1743) and *Carceri* (It. prisons, 1750); Robert Wood's *Ruins of Palmyra* (1753) and *Balbeck* (1757), Edward Gibbon's *Decline and Fall of the Roman Empire* (1776), C. F. Volney's *Les Ruines* (Fr. Ruins of Empires, 1791), and James Stuart's *Antiquities of Athens* (1825–30). Rudyard Kipling would publish a collection of essays about Calcutta called *City of Dreadful Night* (1899). Chronologically situated between Henry Mayhew's *London Labour and the London Poor* (1851) and William Booth's *In Darkest England and the Way Out* (1890) and Charles Booth's *Life and Labour of the People in London* (2 vols, 1889–91; 9 vols, 1892–97), Thomson's poem is contemporaneous with *London: A Pilgrimage* (1872), with 180 engravings by Gustave Doré (1832–83) and a text by William Blanchard Jerrold (1826–84). But while Jerrold and Doré comment on and illustrate London's seamy side, they also illustrate the rich and their occupations and entertainments. Not so in Thomson: his gloom is unremitting. Where Dante had Virgil as a companion through the circles of suffering to explain and console (and Beatrice to lead him through Paradise), the poet-traveller through the City of Night is almost alone with only a few ineffectual and transient conversations with shadowy figures in a world where spiritual values are turned into materialist ruins. The Whig notion of historical progress, or the biological principle through Darwin of an evolution towards better survival and greater fitness for succeeding progeny, are both condemned (see below, SECT. XIV: 55–60). The city is a "necropolis," a city filled with "great ruins of an unremembered past," with "rangèd mansions dark and still as tombs," through which "worn faces … Each wrapt in his own doom, they wander, wander" with no respite, harbouring only "dead Faith, dead Love, dead Hope." The poem takes on the theme that Matthew Arnold felt he had improperly addressed in *Empedocles on Etna* (1852) as unsuitable for poetic treatment, "in which a continuous state of mental distress is prolonged, unrelieved by incident, hope, or resistance, in which there is everything to be endured, nothing to be done" ("Preface" to *Poems* of 1853). Divided into twenty-one sections of varying lengths, the poem uses a number of stanzaic forms: triplets, six-line *Venus and Adonis* stanzas with variations, seven-line, eight-line, and nine-line stanzas with considerable metrical variation. The odd-numbered sections, commentaries on the dream-sequences, are all in the same seven-line stanzas, and are all in the past tense, recounting the narrator's past in the city. The even-numbered sections, containing the dream sequences, use a variety of different metres, sometimes altering them in the same section, and are all in the present tense, describing the narrator's direct encounters with the parts of the city and its inhabitants. The poem culminates with a detailed poetic analysis of the engraving called *Melencholia I* by Albrecht Dürer (1471–1528), an ekphrasis or representation in one medium (here poetry) of another art form (here an engraving), in this case emblematic of the melancholic reflection upon the ruins of time.

Proem[2]

Lo, thus, as prostrate, "In the dust I write   <1–42>
    My heart's deep languor and my soul's sad tears."[3]
Yet why evoke the spectres of black night

Notes ──

[2] *Proem* (Lat. *proœmium* < Gk. *prooimion* a before-song): prelude, preface.

[3] *tears* see *Titus Andronicus* (1594): 3. 1. 12–13: "For these, these, tribunes, in the dust I write / My heart's deep languor and my soul's sad tears."

To blot the sunshine of exultant years?
Why disinter dead faith from mouldering hidden?
Why break the seals of mute despair unbidden,
    And wail life's discords into careless ears?

Because a cold rage seizes one at whiles
    To show the bitter old and wrinkled truth
Stripped naked of all vesture that beguiles,
    False dreams, false hopes, false masks and modes of youth;
Because it gives some sense of power and passion
In helpless innocence to try to fashion
    Our woe in living words howe'er uncouth.

Surely I write not for the hopeful young,
    Or those who deem their happiness of worth,
Or such as pasture and grow fat among
    The shows of life and feel nor doubt nor dearth,
Or pious spirits with a God above them
To sanctify and glorify and love them,
    Or sages who foresee a heaven on earth.

For none of these I write, and none of these
    Could read the writing if they deigned to try:
So may they flourish, in their due degrees,[4]
    On our sweet earth and in their unplaced sky.
If any cares for the weak words here written,
It must be some one desolate, Fate-smitten,
    Whose faith and hope are dead, and who would die.

Yes, here and there some weary wanderer
    In that same city of tremendous night,
Will understand the speech, and feel a stir
    Of fellowship in all-disastrous fight;
"I suffer mute and lonely, yet another
Uplifts his voice to let me know a brother
    Travels the same wild paths though out of sight."

O sad Fraternity,[5] do I unfold
    Your dolorous mysteries shrouded from of yore?
Nay, be assured; no secret can be told
    To any who divined it not before:
None uninitiate by many a presage
Will comprehend the language of the message,
    Although proclaimed aloud for evermore.

Notes

[4] *degrees* status according to class or social rank.
[5] *Fraternity* religious brotherhood or association, one of the very few references in the poem to a social collective or community. The word also has associations with the republican slogan of the French Revolution, *"Liberté, Égalité, Fraternité,"* still the French national motto.

I⁶

The City is of Night; perchance of Death   <1–21>
     But certainly of Night; for never there
Can come the lucid morning's fragrant breath
     After the dewy dawning's cold grey air;
The moon and stars may shine with scorn or pity;
The sun has never visited that city,
     For it dissolveth in the daylight fair.

Dissolveth like a dream of night away;
     Though present in distempered gloom of thought
And deadly weariness of heart all day.
     But when a dream night after night is brought
Throughout a week, and such weeks few or many
Recur each year for several years, can any
     Discern that dream from real life in aught?

For life is but a dream whose shapes return,⁷
     Some frequently, some seldom, some by night
And some by day, some night and day: we learn,
     The while all change and many vanish quite,
In their recurrence with recurrent changes
A certain seeming order; where this ranges
     We count things real; such is memory's might....

The street-lamps burn amid the baleful glooms,   <43–56>
     Amidst the soundless solitudes immense
Of rangèd mansions dark and still as tombs.
     The silence which benumbs or strains the sense
Fulfils with awe the soul's despair unweeping:
Myriads of habitants are ever sleeping,
     Or dead, or fled from nameless pestilence!

Yet as in some necropolis you find
     Perchance one mourner to a thousand dead,
So there; worn faces that look deaf and blind
     Like tragic masks of stone. With weary tread,
Each wrapt in his own doom, they wander, wander,
Or sit foredone and desolately ponder
     Through sleepless hours with heavy drooping head....

They leave all hope behind who enter there:⁸   <78–84>
     One certitude while sane they cannot leave,
One anodyne⁹ for torture and despair;

Notes

⁶ *title* the first section gives a general description of the city, as a physical location and then as a psychological account of the isolation and despair of its sleepless inhabitants, tormented with inner demons and external suffering. We have included six out of twelve stanzas (stz. 1–3, 6, 11–12).

⁷ *return* see LEWIS CARROLL: "LIFE, WHAT IS IT BUT A DREAM?" (*LOOKING-GLASS*, [CONCLUDING POEM]). See also William

Wordsworth "Ode: Intimations of Immortality" (1807): "Our birth is but a sleep and a forgetting."

⁸ *there* last words inscribed above the gate of hell in *Inferno* 3. 9: "Abandon hope, all ye who enter here" (trans. H. F. Cary); repeated below with variations, see n. 15.

⁹ *anodyne* (Gk. *an* without; *odynos* pain), medicine to alleviate pain, often an opiate.

The certitude of Death, which no reprieve
Can put off long; and which, divinely tender,
But waits the outstretched hand to promptly render
    That draught whose slumber nothing can bereave.[10]

II[11]

Because he seemed to walk with an intent   <1–6>
    I followed him; who, shadowlike and frail,
Unswervingly though slowly onward went,
    Regardless, wrapt in thought as in a veil:
Thus step for step with lonely sounding feet
We travelled many a long dim silent street....

When he had spoken thus, before he stirred,   <25–36>
    I spoke, perplexed by something in the signs
Of desolation I had seen and heard
    In this drear pilgrimage to ruined shrines:
Where Faith and Love and Hope[12] are dead indeed,
Can Life still live? By what doth it proceed?

As whom his one intense thought overpowers,
    He answered coldly, Take a watch,[13] erase
The signs and figures of the circling hours,
    Detach the hands, remove the dial-face;
The works proceed until run down; although
Bereft of purpose, void of use, still go....

VI

I sat forlornly by the river-side,   <1–63>
    And watched the bridge-lamps glow like golden stars
Above the blackness of the swelling tide,
    Down which they struck rough gold in ruddier bars;
And heard the heave and plashing of the flow
Against the wall a dozen feet below.

Large elm-trees stood along that river-walk;
    And under one, a few steps from my seat,
I heard strange voices join in stranger talk,

Notes

[10] *bereave* "Though the Garden of thy Life be wholly waste, the sweet flowers withered, the fruit-trees barren, over its wall hang ever the rich dark clusters of the Vine of Death, within easy reach of thy hand, which may pluck of them when it will." [author's note]. See FITZGERALD, RUBÁIYÁT, STZ. XXXVIII.

[11] *title* in the eight stanzas of II (we give three) the poet encounters a figure who proceeds through the city turning right three time to trace a circle to three locales where faith, love, and hope died.

[12] *Hope* for the three Gospel virtues, see 1 Corinthians 13: 13. As presented in Thomson, they are the inversion of the life-giving power in either the Corinthians passage or in Spenser's *Faerie Queene* as Redcrosse is educated in the House of Holiness (bk. 1, canto 10) by Fidenza (faith), Speranza (hope), and Charissa (charity or love).

[13] *watch* an allusion to a watch found on a heath by which Paley draws an analogy to his argument from design (see TENNYSON, n. 282).

Although I had not heard approaching feet:
These bodiless voices in my waking dream
Flowed dark words blending with sombre stream:—

And you have after all come back; come back.[14]
I was about to follow on your track.
And you have failed: our spark of hope is black.

That I have failed is proved by my return:
The spark is quenched, nor ever more will burn.
But listen; and the story you shall learn.

I reached the portal common spirits fear,
And read the words above it, dark yet clear,
"Leave hope behind, all ye who enter here":[15]

And would have passed in, gratified to gain
That positive eternity of pain,
Instead of this insufferable inane.

A demon warder clutched me, Not so fast;
First leave your hopes behind!—But years have passed
Since I left all behind me, to the last:

You cannot count for hope, with all your wit,
This bleak despair that drives me to the Pit:[16]
How could I seek to enter void of it?

He snarled, What thing is this which apes a soul,
And would find entrance to our gulf of dole
Without the payment of the settled toll?[17]

Outside the gate he showed an open chest:
Here pay their entrance fees the souls unblest;
Cast in some hope, you enter with the rest.

Notes

[14] *back* the "strange voices" of this section engage in a dialogue in rhyming triplets, like Dante's *terza rima* in *Inferno*, but without the middle rhyme providing the initial rhyme for the next stanza (aba, bcb, cdc, etc.). The whole of this section alludes to Canto 3 of *Inferno*, but particularly in such lines as "these are they who in death have no hope" (3. 46) on the gate of hell (see n. 8). But the scene could equally be played out between estranged lovers as one goes onto Waterloo Bridge contemplating suicide (see nn. 17, 44, and XIX, 52).

[15] *here* see n. 8. This line from *Inferno* echoes throughout this section, as, for instance, at lines 26, 36, and 49–50.

[16] *Pit* hell; see *Inferno*, 18. 5: a pit both wide and deep; and 32. 16: a cloudy pit.

[17] *toll* Charon's obol, the coin (a silver coin, called an *obolos*) or sop, usually a silver coin placed in the mouth of the dead, paid to Charon, the ferryman over the River Styx (Propertius, *Elegies* 4: 11; see also *Aeneid* 6:

298 ff. and *Inferno* 3. 111). Here the payment is the last shred of hope. Waterloo Bridge required a toll of a halfpenny paid to a warder to cross. See George Augustus Sala's *Twice Round the Clock, or The Hours of the Day and Night in London* (1859). In the penultimate chapter, representing London at 2:00 a.m. and "The Turnstile of Waterloo Bridge," that he calls "'The Bridge of Sighs,'" Sala writes, "The sharp, clicking turnstile revolves; the ever-wakeful tollman is there, with his preternaturally keen apron. I call this man Charon, and the river which his standing ferry bridges over might well be the Styx. Impossible, immobile, indifferent, the gate-keeper's creed is summed up in one word —'A halfpenny!' Love, hope, happiness, misery, despair, and death—what are they to him? 'A halfpenny for the bridge' is all he asks! but 'a halfpenny for the bridge' he must have." See DANTE ROSSETTI, n. 4 (WEB p. 410); FIELD, n. 38; WATSON, n. 14.

This is Pandora's box;[18] whose lid shall shut,
And Hell-gate too, when hopes have filled it; but
They are so thin that it will never glut.

I stood a few steps backwards, desolate;
And watched the spirits pass me to their fate,
And fling off hope, and enter at the gate.

When one casts off a load he springs upright,
Squares back his shoulders, breathes will all his might,
And briskly paces forward strong and light:

But these, as if they took some burden, bowed;
The whole frame sank; however strong and proud
Before, they crept in quite infirm and cowed.

And as they passed me, earnestly from each
A morsel of his hope I did beseech,
To pay my entrance;[19] but all mocked my speech.

No one would cede a tittle of his store,
Though knowing that in instants three or four
He must resign the whole for evermore.

So I returned. Our destiny is fell;
For in this Limbo[20] we must ever dwell,
Shut out alike from Heaven and Earth and Hell.

The other sighed back, Yea; but if we grope
With care through all this Limbo's dreary scope,
We yet may pick up some minute lost hope;

And, sharing it between us, entrance win,
In spite of fiends so jealous for gross sin:
Let us without delay our search begin.

VII

Some say that phantoms haunt those shadowy streets,   <1–21>
 And mingle freely there with sparse mankind;
And tell of ancient woes and black defeats,
 And murmur mysteries in the grave enshrined:
But others think them visions of illusion,
Or even men gone far in self-confusion;
 No man there being wholly sane in mind.

Notes

[18] *box* Pandora (Gk. *pan* < *pas* all; *doron* gift; hence, the all-gifted), the first woman created out of clay by the Greek god Hephaestus was presented with gifts by the gods, including a box (a later mistranslation) or jar which she opened, allowing all of the evils to escape, only hope being left inside when it was closed again (Hesiod, *Works and Days*, 60–105).

[19] *morsel . . . entrance* see n. 17.

[20] *Limbo* according to Dante, limbo is on the edge of hell as the first circle, where the ancient Greeks and Romans are

And yet a man who raves, however mad,
    Who bares his heart and tells of his own fall,
Reserves some inmost secret good or bad:
    The phantoms have no reticence at all:
The nudity of flesh will blush though tameless
The extreme nudity of bone grins shameless,
    The unsexed skeleton mocks shroud and pall.

I have seen phantoms there that were as men
    And men that were as phantoms flit and roam;
Marked shapes that were not living to my ken,
    Caught breathings acrid as with Dead Sea[21] foam:
The City rests for man so weird and awful,
That his intrusion there might seem unlawful,
    And phantoms there may have their proper home.

IX

It is full strange to him who hears and feels,   <1–21>
    When wandering there in some deserted street,
The booming and the jar of ponderous wheels,
    The trampling clash of heavy ironshod feet:
Who in this Venice of the Black Sea[22] rideth?
Who in this city of the stars abideth
    To buy or sell as those in daylight sweet?

The rolling thunder seems to fill the sky
    As it comes on; the horses snort and strain,
The harness jingles, as it passes by;[23]
    The hugeness of an overburthened wain:[24]
A man sits nodding on the shaft or trudges
Three parts asleep beside his fellow-drudges:
    And so it rolls into the night again.

Notes

to be found; to medieval theologians, however, it also contained the souls of the Patriarchs of the Hebrew Scriptures until Christ "descended among the dead" to rescue them in what was known in the English mystery plays as "the Harrowing of Hell."

[21] *Sea* a highly saline sea bordering modern Jordan and Israel in which almost no organisms can live.

[22] *Venice ... Sea* Venice of the Black Sea is a conflation of cities on the sea, such as Venice and Constantinople. This is possibly an allusion to an area of London in Paddington area called "Little Venice" at the junction of the Grand Union and Regent's Canals where in the later nineteenth century were decaying genteel villas fronting the canals, with warehouse-workers and bargemen living on the canal boats. Byron had compared Venice to London as poetical sites: "There would be nothing to make the canal of Venice more poetical than that of Paddington, were it

not for the artificial adjuncts above-mentioned" – namely, the Grand Canal, the Bridge of Sighs, the Rialto, and the stone palaces and churches (*Edinburgh Review*, May 1831). See also RUSKIN, STONES OF VENICE, where he not only describes the architectural glories of medieval and Renaissance Venice but also uses his analysis of the workers' joy to critique modern industrialization.

[23] *by* see HOUSMAN, A SHROPSHIRE LAD (1896) XXVII. 3: "And hear the harness jingle."

[24] *wain* wagon used for hauling heavy loads – a haywain piled high as in Hieronymous Bosch's triptych (three-panel painting in the Prado in Madrid, 1490–1510?) entitled *The Haywain*, well known through prints. The left panel shows the Fall in the Garden of Eden; the central panel depicts the world as an enormous haywain with people committing all kinds of sins as various horrible beasts haul it off into hell, depicted on the right panel.

What merchandise? whence, whither, and for whom?
　　Perchance it is a Fate-appointed hearse,
Bearing away to some mysterious tomb
　　Or Limbo of the scornful universe
The joy, the peace, the life-hope, the abortions
Of all things good which should have been our portions,
　　But have been strangled by that City's curse.

XIII[25]

Of all things human which are strange and wild　　　　　　　　　　<1–42>
　　This is perchance the wildest and most strange,
And showeth man most utterly beguiled,
　　To those who haunt that sunless City's range;
That he bemoans himself for aye,[26] repeating
How Time is deadly swift, how life is fleeting,[27]
　　How naught is constant on the earth but change.

The hours are heavy on him and the days;
　　The burden of the months he scarce can bear;
And often in his secret soul he prays
　　To sleep through barren periods unaware,
Arousing at some longed-for date of pleasure;
Which having passed and yielded him small treasure,
　　He would outsleep another term of care.

Yet in his marvellous fancy he must make
　　Quick wings for Time, and see it fly from us;
This Time which crawleth like a monstrous snake,[28]
　　Wounded and slow and very venomous;
Which creeps blindwormlike round the earth and ocean,
Distilling poison at each painful motion,
　　And seems condemned to circle ever thus.

And since he cannot spend and use aright
　　The little time here given him in trust,
But wasteth it in weary undelight
　　Of foolish toil and trouble, strife and lust,
He naturally claimeth to inherit
The everlasting Future, that his merit
　　May have full scope; as surely is most just.

Notes

25 *title* in XII the wanderer had entered the stone cathedral, giving as his password the ills of the human race and in this section meditates on the spiritual barrenness of those within.
26 *aye* ever.
27 *fleeting* possible echo of half of the Greek aphorism of Hippocrates, "Life is short, art is long (often translated into Latin as *vita brevis, ars longa*); see also Ecclesiastes 9: 11; and Shelley's fragment, "Yes! all is past—swift time has fled away" (1839).

28 *wings . . . snake* see Virgil, *Georgics* 3. 284–85: time irretrievably flees: (Lat. *tempus fugit*), often inscribed on sundials. For snake, see Alexander Pope's comment on his verse form, particularly the six-foot or hexameter line that slows the tempo: "A needless alexandrine ends the song / That like a wounded snake, drags its slow length along" (*Essay on Criticism*, 1711: 2. 156).

O length of the intolerable hours,
    O nights that are as æons[29] of slow pain,
O Time, too ample for our vital powers,
    O Life, whose woeful vanities remain
Immutable for all of all our legions
Through all the centuries and in all the regions,
    Not of your speed and variance *we* complain.

We do not ask a longer term of strife,
    Weakness and weariness and nameless woes;
We do not claim renewed and endless life
    When this which is our torment here shall close,
An everlasting conscious inanition![30]
We yearn for speedy death in full fruition,
    Dateless oblivion and divine repose.

XIV[31]

Large glooms were gathered in the mighty fane,[32]   <1–90>
    With tinted moongleams slanting here and there;
And all was hush: no swelling organ-strain,
    No chant, no voice or murmuring of prayer;
No priests came forth, no tinkling censers fumed,
And the high altar space was unillumed.

Around the pillars and against the walls
    Leaned men and shadows; others seemed to brood
Bent or recumbent in secluded stalls.
    Perchance they were not a great multitude
Save in that city of so lonely streets
Where one may count up every face he meets.

All patiently awaited the event
    Without a stir or sound, as if no less
Self-occupied, doomstricken, while attent.[33]
    And then we heard a voice of solemn stress
From the dark pulpit, and our gaze there met
Two eyes which burned as never eyes burned yet:

Two steadfast and intolerable eyes
    Burning beneath a broad and rugged brow;
The head behind it of enormous size.

Notes

[29] *æons* (Gk. ages, eternity); in Homer the word means the lifespan of a person, but later usage has it mean an indefinite but almost boundless time span. In geology the term was used in the nineteenth century to describe what Darwin called "enormous intervals of time" (*Origin*, ch. 10), namely the intervals between the great geological periods, as between the Paleozoic and Mesozoic periods.

[30] *inanition* emptiness, lethargy, exhaustion.

[31] *title* in XIV, the moral and narrative nadir of the poem, the preacher to the lost souls delivers his gloomy message of despair: no purpose in life or death; no divine laws to lead or follow; no purpose in the cause-and-effect pattern of pain and suffering; and no reason for life.

[32] *fane* temple.

[33] *attent* attentive.

And as black fir-groves in a large wind bow,
Our rooted congregation, gloom-arrayed,
By that great sad voice deep and full were swayed:—

O melancholy[34] Brothers, dark, dark, dark![35]
O battling in black floods without an ark![36]
 O spectral wanderers of unholy Night!
My soul hath bled for you these sunless years,
With bitter blood-drops running down like tears:
 Oh, dark, dark, dark, withdrawn from joy and light!

My heart is sick with anguish for your bale;
Your woe hath been my anguish; yea, I quail
 And perish in your perishing unblest.
And I have searched the highths and depths, the scope
Of all our universe, with desperate hope
 To find some solace for your wild unrest.

And now at last authentic word I bring,
Witnessed by every dead and living thing;
 Good tidings of great joy for you, for all: [37]
There is no God; no Fiend with names divine
Made us and tortures us; if we must pine,
 It is to satiate no Being's gall.

It was the dark delusion of a dream,
That living Person[38] conscious and supreme,
 Whom we must curse for cursing us with life;[39]
Whom we must curse because the life He gave
Could not be buried in the quiet grave,
 Could not be killed by poison or by knife.

This little life is all we must endure,
The grave's most holy peace is ever sure,[40]
 We fall asleep and never wake again;
Nothing is of us but the mouldering flesh,

Notes

[34] *melancholy* the first appearance of the word that becomes so important in the last section of the poem. While the word in modern usage is a psychological or emotional state of sadness or depression, its historical meaning from Hippocrates (460–370 BCE) and Galen (131–200) identifies it as one of the four "humours" or basic bodily fluids: sanguine (blood – active and pleasure-seeking), phlegmatic (phlegm – relaxed, calm, even lethargic), choleric (yellow bile – decisive, aggressive, even angry), and melancholic (black bile – reclusive). An individual whose humours were properly balanced was healthy but an imbalance lead to dysfunction and disease. Robert Burton's *The Anatomy of Melancholy* (1621) is an exhaustive treatment of its topic as an index to human emotion and cultural analysis.

[35] *dark* see Milton's *Samson Agonistes* (1671), a drama about Samson (see Judges 13–16) after he has been blinded and forced to turn the millstones in the workhouse-prison in Gaza: "O dark, dark, dark, amid the blaze of noon, / Irrecoverably dark, total eclipse / Without all hope of day!" (80–82).

[36] *ark* a reference to the story of Noah in Genesis 6: 9; the ark, a symbol of salvation, here represents typologically the church, the main body of which is called a "nave" (<Lat. *navis*, ship).

[37] *all* an ironic allusion to the message of the angels to the shepherds concerning the birth of Jesus (Luke 2: 10).

[38] *Person* that is, Christ; see also Genesis 2: 7.

[39] *life* see Job 3: 1–3.

[40] *sure* see Andrew Marvel "To His Coy Mistress" (1681): "The grave's a fine and private place, / But none, I think, do there embrace" (31–32).

Whose elements dissolve and merge afresh
   In earth, air, water, plants, and other men.

We finish thus; and all our wretched race
Shall finish with its cycle, and give place
   To other beings with their own time-doom:
Infinite æons ere our kind began;
Infinite æons after the last man[41]
   Has joined the mammoth in earth's tomb and womb.

We bow down to the universal laws,
Which never had for man a special clause
   Of cruelty or kindness, love or hate:
If toads and vultures are obscene to sight,
If tigers burn with beauty and with might,[42]
   Is it by favour or by wrath of Fate?

All substance lives and struggles evermore[43]
Through countless shapes continually at war,
   By countless interactions interknit:
If one is born a certain day on earth,
All times and forces tended to that birth,
   Not all the world could change or hinder it.

I find no hint throughout the Universe
Of good or ill, of blessing or of curse;
   I find alone Necessity Supreme;[44]
With infinite Mystery, abysmal, dark,
Unlighted ever by the faintest spark
   For us the flitting shadows of a dream.

O Brothers of sad lives! they are so brief;
A few short years must bring us all relief:
   Can we not bear these years of labouring breath?
But if you would not this poor life fulfil,
Lo, you are free to end it when you will,[45]
   Without the fear of waking after death.—

Notes

[41] *man* Thomson inverts the Darwinian notion of evolution into the devolution of the human race, using Darwin's idea of the extinction of species. Mary Shelley and other Romantics had capitalized on the concept of the end of the human race in various dystopias. Her novel of 1826 was entitled *The Last Man*, about a future world at the end of the twenty-first century in which a single man has survived a devastating plague. See also Thomas Campbell's poem, "The Last Man" (1823); and Thomas Hood's "The Last Man" (1826).

[42] *might* see William Blake, "The Tyger" in *Songs of Innocence and of Experience* (1795): "Tyger! Tyger! burning bright / In the forests of the night."

[43] *struggles evermore* see n. 50. The word evermore occurs three times in the complete poem, each time at the end of

a line, and twice at the end of a stanza. For struggle, see the complete title of Darwin's *The Origin of Species by Means of Natural Selection, or the Preservation of Favoured Races in the Struggle for Life* (1859).

[44] *Supreme* for Necessity Supreme, see John Stuart Mill on "philosophical necessity" (MILL, n. 2).

[45] *will* the freedom to end life given in the preacher's last words is in ironic contrast to the principle of "Necessity Supreme" that is declared to be the governing principle of the city two stanzas earlier. To take one's own life had been prohibited by the common and canon law of the church from the early Middle Ages, and continued in England until 1961. The law included denial of burial rites in consecrated ground, allowing instead burial at night at a crossroads, with a stake driven through the

The organ-like vibrations of his voice
      Thrilled through the vaulted aisles and died away;
The yearning of the tones which bade rejoice
      Was sad and tender as a requiem lay:
Our shadowy congregation rested still
As brooding on that "End it when you will."

XVI

Our shadowy congregation rested still,   <1–54>
      As musing on that message we had heard
And brooding on that "End it when you will";
      Perchance awaiting yet some other word;
When keen as lightning through a muffled sky
Sprang forth a shrill and lamentable cry:—

The man speaks sooth, alas! the man speaks sooth:[46]
      We have no personal life beyond the grave;
There is no God; Fate knows nor wrath nor ruth:[47]
      Can I find here the comfort which I crave?

In all eternity I had one chance,
      One few years' term of gracious human life:[48]
The splendours of the intellect's advance,
      The sweetness of the home with babes and wife;

The social pleasures with their genial wit:
      The fascination of the worlds of art,
The glories of the worlds of nature, lit
      By large imagination's glowing heart;

The rapture of mere being, full of health;
      The careless childhood and the ardent youth,
The strenuous manhood winning various wealth,
      The reverend age serene with life's long truth:

Notes

corpse and the forfeit of lands and goods (Blackstone, *Commentaries on the Laws of England* 4. 190). In 1823 this practice was abolished in favour of burial in churchyards at night, but without the funeral service or other religious rites. Attempted suicide and aiding or abetting suicide were also crimes. Suicide after financial failure was common in life as in literature (as John Sadleir, MP, in 1856; and Mr Murdle in Dickens's *Little Dorrit*, 1855–57). In London the places of choice were jumping off the Monument to the Great Fire, or off Waterloo or another bridge into the Thames. See n. 52; see also HOOD, "BRIDGE."

[46] *sooth* truth. The following quatrains, changing the verse forms in this section, contain the response of one anonymous congregant to the sermon preached in the

dark cathedral, continuing until the six-line stanzas resume at the end of the section. Section XVI perhaps echoes *Inferno* (10. 28–103) when Dante and Virgil have entered the city of Dis in the circle of the heretics, and from one of the arches or tombs comes the voice of Farinata degli Uberti (1212–64) who says that he recalls the past only dimly, and concerning the present, his intellect is empty, void (see especially line 28, "blank and dumb").

[47] *ruth* pity, compassion.

[48] *life* the following three stanzas set out conventional bourgeois middle-class aspirations – and expectations – as "prerogatives" or rights, one of the few moments in the poem that concede anything to such ideals, only to have them taken away in the stanzas that follow.

All the sublime prerogatives of Man;
  The storied memories of the times of old,
The patient tracking of the world's great plan
  Through sequences and changes myriadfold.[49]

This chance was never offered me before;
  For me this infinite Past is blank and dumb:
This chance recurreth never, nevermore;[50]
  Blank, blank for me the infinite To-come.

And this sole chance was frustrate from my birth,
  A mockery, a delusion; and my breath
Of noble human life upon this earth
  So racks me that I sigh for senseless death.

My wine of life is poison mixed with gall,[51]
  My noonday passes in a nightmare dream,
I worse than lose the years which are my all:
  What can console me for the loss supreme?

Speak not of comfort where no comfort is,
  Speak not at all: can words make foul things fair?
Our life's a cheat, our death a black abyss:
  Hush and be mute envisaging despair.—

This vehement voice came from the northern aisle
  Rapid and shrill to its abrupt harsh close;
And none gave answer for a certain while,
  For words must shrink from these most wordless woes;
At last the pulpit speaker simply said,
With humid eyes and thoughtful drooping head:—

My Brother, my poor Brothers, it is thus;
This life itself holds nothing good for us,
  But ends soon and nevermore can be;
And we knew nothing of it ere our birth,
And shall know nothing when consigned to earth:
  I ponder these thoughts and they comfort me.

XIX

The mighty river flowing dark and deep,   <1–35>
  With ebb and flood from the remote sea-tides
Vague-sounding through the City's sleepless sleep,
  Is named the River of the Suicides;[52]
For night by night some lorn wretch overweary,

Notes

[49] *myriadfold* numberless, countless.

[50] *never, nevermore* the word "nevermore" (and its cognate, "evermore – see n. 43) echoes throughout the poem, alluding, as is emphasized by the repetition of "never," to the repeated refrain of Edgar Allen Poe's "The Raven" (1845). See also n. 68.

[51] *gall* see Matthew 27: 34.Gall is a bitter liquid stored in the gall bladder of animals.

[52] *Suicides* both the River Thames in London and that in *Inferno*, where the river of violence in the seventh circle of hell is called "Phlegethon," the river of boiling blood and

James Thomson [B. V.]

And shuddering from the future yet more dreary,
　Within its cold secure oblivion hides.

One plunges from a bridge's parapet,[53]
　As by some blind and sudden frenzy hurled;
Another wades in slow with purpose set
　Until the waters are above him furled;
Another in a boat with dreamlike motion
Glides drifting down into the desert ocean,
　To starve or sink from out the desert world.

They perish from their suffering surely thus,
　For none beholding them attempts to save,
The while each thinks how soon, solicitous,
　He may seek refuge in the self-same wave;
Some hour when tired of ever-vain endurance
Impatience will forerun the sweet assurance
　Of perfect peace[54] eventual in the grave.

When this poor tragic-farce has palled us long,
　Why actors and spectators do we stay?—
To fill our so-short *rôles* out right or wrong;
　To see what shifts are yet in the dull play[55]
For our illusion; to refrain from grieving
Dear foolish friends by our untimely leaving:
　But those asleep at home, how blest are they!

Yet it is but for one night after all:
　What matters one brief night of dreary pain?
When after it the weary eyelids fall
　Upon the weary eyes and wasted brain;
And all sad scenes and thoughts and feelings vanish
In that sweet sleep no power can ever banish,
　That one best sleep which never wakes again.[56]

Notes

fire. In the middle ring of this circle are the suicides (violent against themselves) who are in the form of dense thorny bushes, representative of the tortured state of their minds when they took their own lives. See n. 45; see also HOOD, "BRIDGE."

[53] *parapet* the scene of the parapet or the vault beneath it on Waterloo Bridge was common in Victorian literature and art, especially for female suicides, as in Charles Knight's *London* (1841–44): "How many unfortunates have stood shivering in those very recesses [of Waterloo Bridge], taking their last farewell of the world in which they had experienced so much misery"; "The River" (1850), an illustration by Hablôt Knight Brown ("Phiz") to Dickens's *David Copperfield* as Martha considers suicide (ch. 47); Dante Rossetti's *Found* (1854–81); and Augustus Egg's triptych *Past and Present* (1858), with the third painting of a

woman under the Adelphi arches of the Hungerford Bridge; see HOOD, "BRIDGE"; see also n. 17.

[54] *peace* see Isaiah 26: 3.

[55] *play* see Jaques's speech in *As You Like It* (1623): "All the world's a stage / And all the men and women merely players" (2. 7. 142–69); see also the fragment of Petronius Arbiter: *quod fere totus mundus exerceat histrionem* (Lat. because almost the whole world are players), said to have been inscribed above the door of Shakespeare's Globe theatre.

[56] *again* this stanza alludes to, and inverts, the last lines of John Donne's "Holy Sonnet: 'Death Be Not Proud'": "One short sleep past, we wake eternally, / And death shall be no more; Death, thou shalt die." It is also a general parody of the "Choric Song" of "The Lotos-Eaters" (see TENNYSON (WEB p. 331)).

XX

I sat me weary on a pillar's base,[57]   <1–48>
  And leaned against the shaft; for broad moonlight
O'erflowed the peacefulness of cloistered space,
  A shore of shadow slanting from the right:
The great cathedral's western front stood there,
A wave-worn rock in that calm sea of air.

Before it, opposite my place of rest,
  Two figures faced each other, large, austere;
A couchant sphinx[58] in shadow to the breast,
  An angel standing in the moonlight clear;
So mighty by magnificence of form,
They were not dwarfed beneath that mass enorm.[59]

Upon the cross-hilt of a naked sword
  The angel's hands, as prompt to smite, were held;
His vigilant, intense regard was poured
  Upon the creature placidly unquelled,
Whose front was set at level gaze which took
No heed of aught, a solemn trance-like look.

And as I pondered these opposèd shapes
  My eyelids sank in stupor, that dull swoon
Which drugs and with a leaden mantle drapes
  The outworn to worse weariness. But soon
A sharp and clashing noise the stillness broke,
And from the evil lethargy I woke.

The angel's wings had fallen, stone on stone,
  And lay there shattered; hence the sudden sound:
A warrior leaning on his sword alone
  Now watched the sphinx with that regard profound;
The sphinx unchanged looked forthright, as aware
Of nothing in the vast abyss of air.

Notes

[57] *base* an allusion to a Victorian commonplace, Macaulay's "New Zealander." In 1840 in a review of von Ranke's *The Ecclesiastical and Political History of the Popes* in the *Edinburgh Review* (Oct. 1840) Macaulay imagines a dystopian future, with a Maori New Zealander, in a London in ruins, sitting on a broken pillar of London Bridge to sketch the ruins of St Paul's Cathedral. The same image is the final illustration by Gustave Doré in Blanchard and Doré's *London: A Pilgrimage* (1872).

[58] *sphinx* mythical beast with the body of a lion and the head of a human, usually a woman. It was a sphinx who interviewed Oedipus, testing him with the riddle of what walks on four legs, two legs, and three (answer: a human or man, as a child, adult, and aged person with a cane). See also Dante Rossetti, "The Burden of Nineveh" (1856, 1870), about a sphinx-like winged bull from Nineveh being brought into the British Museum. A sphinx and angel are near each other in the gardens at Blenheim Palace, near Oxford. Thomson might also have drawn on Winwood Reade's *The Martyrdom of Man* (1872), popular among Thomson's secularist friends, and reviewed at length in the *National Reformer* to which Thomson contributed reviews and articles. Reade wrote, "Egypt was no longer a nation, but an assemblage of torpid castes.... No longer a body animated by the same heart ... but an automaton neatly pieced together, of which the head was the priesthood, the arms the army, and the feet the working class. In quiescence it was a perfect image of the living form, but a touch came from without and the arms broke asunder at the joints and fell upon the ground."

[59] *enorm* enormous.

Again I sank in that repose unsweet,
    Again a clashing noise my slumber rent;
The warrior's sword lay broken at his feet:
    An unarmed man with raised hands impotent
Now stood before the sphinx, which ever kept
Such mien[60] as if with open eyes it slept.

My eyelids sank in spite of wonder grown;
    A louder crash upstartled me in dread:
The man had fallen forward, stone on stone,
    And lay there shattered, with his trunkless head
Between the monster's large quiescent paws,
Beneath its grand front changeless as life's laws.[61]

The moon had circled westward full and bright,
    And made the temple-front a mystic dream,
And bathed the whole enclosure with its light,
    The sworded angel's wrecks, the sphinx supreme:
I pondered long that cold majestic face
Whose vision seemed of infinite void space.

XXI

Anear the centre of that northern crest   <1–84>
    Stands out a level upland bleak and bare,
From which the city east and south and west
    Sinks gently in lon g waves; and thronèd there
An Image sits, stupendous, superhuman,
The bronze colossus of a wingèd Woman,[62]
    Upon a graded granite base foursquare.

Low-seated she leans forward massively,
    With cheek on clenched left hand, the forearm's might
Erect, its elbow on her rounded knee;
    Across a clasped book in her lap the right
Upholds a pair of compasses; she gazes
With full set eyes, but wandering in thick mazes
    Of sombre thought beholds no outward sight.

Words cannot picture her;[63] but all men know
    That solemn sketch the pure sad artist wrought
Three centuries and threescore years ago,[64]

Notes

[60] *mien* deportment, bearing. The word used by Poe to describe the Raven's bearing as it enters the room "with mien of lord or lady"; see n. 50. The word is also used in the second-to-last stanza of the poem (see below).

[61] *laws* see Shelley, "Ozymandias" (1817).

[62] *Woman* Melencholia; see below, nn. 64 and 66.

[63] *her* the narrator demurs that description is possible, a typical trope that begins an ekphrasis or representation of a picture in words.

[64] *artist … ago* the artist was Albrecht Dürer (1471–1528), German painter, engraver, and mathematician; Dürer's engraving, the subject of the following stanzas, is *Melencolia I*, dated 1514 in the print, exactly 360 years before Thomson's poem. Thomson owned a copy of the print. See also PATER n. 9 (WEB p. 431). For an illustration of Dürer's print, see http://www.princeton.edu/~his291/Durer_Melancolia.html.

With phantasies of his peculiar thought:
The instruments of carpentry and science
Scattered about her feet, in strange alliance
    With the keen wolf-hound sleeping undistraught;

Scales, hour-glass, bell, and magic-square above;[65]
    The grave and solid infant perched beside,
With open winglets that might bear a dove,
    Intent upon its tablets, heavy-eyed;
Her folded wings as of a mighty eagle,
But all too impotent to lift the regal
    Robustness of her earth-born strength and pride;

And with those wings, and that light wreath which seems
    To mock her grand head and the knotted frown
Of forehead charged with baleful thoughts and dreams,
    The household bunch of keys, the housewife's gown
Voluminous, indented, and yet rigid
As if a shell of burnished metal frigid,
    The feet thick-shod to tread all weakness down;

The comet hanging o'er the waste dark seas,
    The massy rainbow curved in front of it
Beyond the village with the masts and trees;
    The snaky imp, dog-headed, from the Pit,
Bearing upon its batlike leathern pinions
Her name unfolded in the sun's dominions,
    The "MELENCHOLIA" that transcends all wit.[66]

Thus has the artist copied her, and thus
    Surrounded to expound her form sublime,
Her fate heroic and calamitous;
    Fronting the dreadful mysteries of Time,
Unvanquished in defeat and desolation,
Undaunted in the hopeless conflagration
    Of the day setting on her baffled prime.

Baffled and beaten back she works on still,
    Weary and sick of soul she works the more,
Sustained by her indomitable will:

Notes

[65] *magic-square above* in the print, the diagram above Melencholia's head with smaller squares in which the numbers always add up the same (34), whether read horizontally, vertically, or diagonally, or the four quadrants, or the central four. Thomson refers to a number of symbolic references in the print – Melencholia's book and compasses, the instruments of carpentry, the wolf-hound, scales, hour-glass, all based on late medieval and Renaissance theories of Melancholy and alchemy.

[66] *wit* there is some disagreement about why Dürer entitles the print *Melencolia I*: first, possibly a reference to the first of three kinds of melancholy identified by Cornelius Agrippa (1486–1535), German alchemist and author of *De Occulta Philosophia* (Lat. on occult philosophy, 1509–10): (1) *melencolia imaginativa* that inspires poets and artists, as opposed to (2) *malencholia rationalis* (Lat. melancholia of knowledge) and (3) *melancholia mentalis* (Lat. melancholia of the mind); second, possibly, the first of a series on the four humours or temperaments (see n. 34). For "transcends all wit," see Philippians 4: 7; and *Paradiso* 30. 42. Thomson had left in MS a poem entitled "The Melencolia of Albrecht Dürer" that was not printed until 1963.

The hands shall fashion and the brain shall pore,
And all her sorrow shall be turned to labour,
Till Death the friend-foe piercing with his sabre
    That mighty heart of hearts ends bitter war.

But as if blacker night could dawn on night,[67]
    With tenfold gloom on moonless night unstarred,
A sense more tragic than defeat and blight,
    More desperate than strife with hope debarred,
More fatal than the adamantine Never[68]
Encompassing her passionate endeavour,
    Dawns glooming in her tenebrous regard:

To sense that every struggle brings defeat
    Because Fate holds no prize to crown success;
That all the oracles are dumb[69] or cheat
    Because they have no secret to express;
That none can pierce the vast black veil uncertain
Because there is no light beyond the curtain;[70]
    That all is vanity[71] and nothingness.

Titanic[72] from her high throne in the north,
    That City's sombre Patroness and Queen,
In bronze sublimity she gazes forth
    Over her Capital of teen and throne,[73]
Over the river with its isles and bridges,
The marsh and moorland, to the stern rock-ridges,
    Confronting them with a coëval mien.

The moving moon and stars from east to west[74]
    Circle before her in the sea of air;
Shadows and gleams glide round her solemn rest.
    Her subjects often gaze up to her there:
The strong to drink new strength of iron endurance,
The weak new terrors; all, renewed assurance
    And confirmation of the old despair.

Notes

[67] *night* see *Paradiso* 1. 61–62.

[68] *adamantine Never* for adamantine, see *Paradise Lost* 1. 48: "Adamantine Chains"; for Never, see n. 50.

[69] *dumb* see Milton, "Ode on the Morning of Christ's Nativity" (1629): "The oracles are dumb" (173).

[70] *curtain* see TENNYSON, IN MEMORIAM: "Behind the veil, behind the veil" (LVI. 26).

[71] *vanity* see Ecclesiastes 1: 2.

[72] *Titanic* a reference to the figure of Melancholia in the Dürer engraving.

[73] *teen and threne* woe and lamentation.

[74] *west* inversion or parody of the last lines of *Paradiso*: "I . . . would fain / Measure the circle . . . and trace out the form, / How to the circle fitted . . . like a wheel / In even motion, by the Love impell'd , / That moves the sun in heav'n and all the stars" (33. 134–45; tr. H. F. Cary).

E. B. B.[75]

1861

I

The white-rose garland at her feet,
    The crown of laurel at her head,[76]
Her noble life on earth complete,
    Lay her in the last low bed
For the slumber calm and deep:
"He giveth His belovèd sleep."[77]

II

Soldiers find their fittest grave
    In the field whereon they died;
So her spirit pure and brave
    Leaves the clay it glorified
To the land for which she fought
With such grand impassioned thought.[78]

III

Keats and Shelley sleep at Rome,[79]
    She in well-loved Tuscan[80] earth;
Finding all their death's long home
    Far from their old home of birth.
Italy, you hold in trust
Very sacred English dust.

IV

Therefore this one prayer I breathe,—
    That you yet may worthy prove
Of the heirlooms they bequeath
    Who have loved you with such love:
Fairest land while land of slaves
Yields their free souls no fit graves.

Notes

[75] *title* tribute poem to Elizabeth Barrett Browning on her death in Florence on 29 June 1861. First published in the *National Reformer* as "Elizabeth Barrett Browning" (29 Nov. 1862); republished as "E. B. B." in *City of Dreadful Night and Other Poems*, 1880 (our text).

[76] *head* Henry James has recorded that the Brownings' friend, William Wetmore Story (1819–95), an American sculptor and writer, placed wreathes of white roses and laurel or bay leaves on Barrett Browning's coffin at her burial in the English Cemetery in Florence (*William Wetmore Story and His Friends*, 1903). For laurel, see also HEMANS, n. 17.

[77] *sleep* see Psalm 127: 2; and Barrett Browning's poem "The Sleep" (1838).

[78] *thought* Barrett Browning was a strong supporter of Italian unification and published a collection of poems on the topic, *Poems Before Congress* (1860), that provoked a negative reaction in England from such conservative journals as *Blackwoods Magazine*.

[79] *Rome* Keats died in Rome on 23 February 1821. Shelley was drowned on 8 July 1822; when his body was recovered, it was burned on the shore at Viareggio. Keats's body and Shelley's ashes are both interred in Rome's Protestant cemetery.

[80] *Tuscan* of Tuscany, a region of central Italy that included Florence (see above, nn. 75 and 76).

William Schwenck Gilbert (1836–1911)

Born in London, he was the son of a naval surgeon, William Gilbert (1804–90) and Ann Mary Bye Morris (1812–88); his father gave up his medical practice and the family travelled widely. Educated in France, and later at schools in London, Gilbert graduated from King's College London, and having tried the military, the civil service, and the law, he settled down as a writer. He wrote over seventy-five plays and libretti, the most famous being the fourteen in which he collaborated with Sir Arthur Sullivan (1842–1900), including *H.M.S. Pinafore* (1878), *The Pirates of Penzance* (1879), and *The Mikado* (1885). Their collaboration was ensured by the theatrical impresario Richard D'Oyly Carte (1844–1901), who established the D'Oyly Carte Opera Company to perform their works, later called the "Savoy Operas" after the theatre Carte built to perform them (1881). Their joint work was also marred by frequent quarrels. Gilbert also wrote libretti for other composers, serious drama, pastiches, and pantomimes, reviews, stories, and comic poems (collected as *Bab Ballads*, 1872, with his own illustrations). In 1867 Gilbert married Lucy Agnes Turner. He was knighted in 1907, the first dramatist to receive that honour for his plays alone. Standard edition: *The Complete Annotated Gilbert and Sullivan*, ed. Ian Bradley (1996); Michael Ainger, *Gilbert and Sullivan—A Dual Biography* (2002); Jane W. Stedman, *W. S. Gilbert, A Classic Victorian and His Theatre* (1996). The Gilbert and Sullivan Archive: http://diamond.boisestate.edu/gas.

From *Patience*[1]

Bunthorne's Recitative and Song [Act 1]

> Am I alone,
> And unobserved? I am!
> Then let me own

Notes

WILLIAM SCHWENCK GILBERT

[1] *title* the sixth collaboration of Gilbert and Sullivan, *Patience, or Bunthorne's Bride* opened at the Opera Comique in London on 23 April 1881, and on 10 October transferred to the new Savoy Theatre, the first in the world lit entirely by electricity. Running for 578 performances, it satirized the aesthetic movement of the 1870s and 1880s. Bunthorne, who in his Act I recitative and solo ("Am I alone?") outlines his beliefs, was identified as a "fleshly poet" in the cast of characters; see LITERATURE: PRE-RAPHAELITISM; BUCHANAN (WEB p. 128). Bunthorne is thought to be a composite of several Pre-Raphaelite aesthetes, particularly Swinburne, Whistler, and Wilde – and perhaps Pater. The D'Oyly Carte tradition was to dress Bunthorne after the manner of Whistler (see LITERATURE: PRE-RAPHAELITISM; WHISTLER). A first-night reviewer in *The Times* thought that the role was based on Swinburne, who was also attacked by Buchanan. The metres and words of Bunthorne's songs "O Hollow" and "Heart Foam" resemble Swinburne's "To Victor Hugo" (1874) and " *Satia Te Sanguine*" (1866). The contributions of Wilde to the Bunthorne image include his practice of posing with a large lily in his hand, just as Bunthorne speaks later of "walking down Piccadilly with a poppy or a lily in his mediæval hand..." (see also n. 2). Wilde was already becoming known for his blue-and-white pottery and love of Japanese artifacts; D'Oyly Carte was to send Wilde to tour North America to promote *Patience* in 1882. The costume and makeup of George Grossmith (1847–1912), who created Bunthorne's role, included the lock of white hair and the monocle that were Whistler's hallmarks, a velvet coat of the kind worn by Pre-Raphaelite Walter Crane (1845–1915), a designer and engraver, and dirty-green velvet breeches much like Wilde's. Archibald Grosvenor, described as an "Idyllic Poet" in the cast of characters, is not a caricature of Tennyson but of William Morris, and to some degree Coventry Patmore, whose *Angel in the House* contained "Idylls." Grosvenor was played by the stocky Rutland Barrington in the original production, with a mane of curly hair like Morris. Grosvenor's devotion to beauty and simplicity also reflect Morris's ideals in his lectures on art. The solo is from Act I and the duet is from Act 2. The separate libretto was not published until 1882 by Chappell, our text.

I'm an æsthetic sham!

This air severe   5

Is but a mere

Veneer!

This cynic smile

Is but a wile

Of guile!   10

This costume chaste

Is but good taste

Misplaced!

Let me confess!

A languid love for lilies[2] does *not* blight me!   15

Lank limbs and haggard cheeks[3] do *not* delight me!

I do *not* care for dirty greens[4]

By any means.

I do *not* long for all one sees

That's Japanese.[5]   20

I am *not* fond of uttering platitudes

In stained-glass attitudes.[6]

In short, my mediævalism's affectation,

Born of a morbid love of admiration!

Song

If you're anxious for to shine in the high æsthetic line as a man of culture rare,   25
You must get up all the germs[7] of the transcendental terms, and plant them everywhere.
You must lie upon the daisies and discourse in novel phrases of your complicated state of mind,
The meaning doesn't matter if it's only idle chatter of a transcendental kind.

Notes

[2] *lilies* the lily craze was possibly the result of several well-known paintings by the PRB, especially Dante Rossetti's *The Girlhood of Mary Virgin* (1849), in which an angel holds a lily resting on a pile of books as a model for the Virgin Mary's embroidering it on a piece of red cloth (see Plate 13); and *The Blessed Damozel* (1875–78; see Plate 14), in which the Damozel looks out from heaven, with her arms on a ledge decked with lilies. The word "Damozel" occurs in the libretto of *Patience*. Wilde had come to London in 1879 and had developed an admiration for the society beauty, actress, and eventual mistress of Edward VII, then Prince of Wales, Lillie Langtry (1853–1929), known as "The Jersey Lily" (from her birthplace, the island of Jersey). Her diary records that Wilde on several occasions purchased a "Jersey Lily" (*Amaryllis belladonna*) at Covent Garden and carried it through Piccadilly to give to her (see DOYLE, n. 21 (WEB p. 488)). The lily was often contrasted with the sunflower, also ubiquitous in caricatures of the Pre-Raphaelites and Wilde, in both England and North America.

[3] *cheeks* pallid looks, limp wrists, slack knees were all trademarks of the aesthetes of the 1880s in parodies and pastiches in such magazines as *Punch*.

[4] *greens* dirty green or leafy vegetables, here used to foreground the colour green as an aesthetic colour, made popular by the Green Dining Room with green walls and Pre-Raphaelite decoration at the South Kensington Museum (now the Victoria and Albert Museum, London), designed by William Morris and Philip Webb (1831–1915) and their firm, Morris and Co. (1866–68); see also n. 6.

[5] *Japanese* a later comic opera, *The Mikado* (1885), by Gilbert and Sullivan capitalized on the Japanese vogue that was exploited with the Japanese Village set up for two years in Knightsbridge in London from January 1885. But even earlier, Japanese objects had been exhibited in London at the International Exhibition (1862) and from 1875 were imported and sold in large quantities at Liberty's store in London. Dante Rossetti, Whistler, and Wilde collected Japanese "blue and white" porcelain and Japanese prints; collecting such porcelain became a fad in the aesthetic movement of the 1870s and 1880s (see Plate 20: Whistler's *Symphony in White No. 2, The Little White Girl*).

[6] *attitudes* the stained glass of Morris and Co. (see n. 4) was very popular among High Church Anglican parishes that were either being built or restored, depicting biblical and Arthurian topics. The figures in the windows were frequently depicted with raised arms and hands, or in an attitude capturing a moment in a religious event.

[7] *germs* reference to the Pre-Raphaelite journal, *The Germ* (1850); see LITERATURE: PRE-RAPHAELITISM, n. 1.

And every one will say,
As you walk your mystic way,   30
"If this young man expresses himself in terms too deep for *me*,
Why, what a very singularly deep young man this deep young man must be!"

Be eloquent in praise of the very dull old days which have long since passed away,
And convince 'em, if you can, that the reign of good Queen Anne[8] was Culture's palmiest day.
Of course you will pooh-pooh whatever's fresh and new, and declare it's crude and mean,   35
For Art stopped short in the cultivated court of the Empress Josephine.[9]
And every one will say,
As you walk your mystic way,
"If that's not good enough for him which is good enough for *me*,
Why, what a very cultivated kind of youth this kind of youth must be!"   40

Then a sentimental passion of a vegetable fashion must excite your languid spleen,
An attachment *à la* Plato for a bashful young potato, or a not-too-French French bean![10]
Though the Philistines may jostle, you will rank as an apostle in the high æsthetic band,
If you walk down Piccadilly with a poppy or a lily in your mediæval hand.[11]
And every one will say,
As you walk your flowery way,   45
"If he's content with a vegetable love which would certainly not suit *me*,
Why, what a most particularly pure young man this pure young man must be!"

Bunthorne and Grosvenor's Duet: "When I go out of door" [Act II]

BUNTHORNE: When I go out of door,
               Of damozels[12] a score,
                   (All sighing and burning,
                   And clinging and yearning)
               Will follow me as before.   5
               I shall, with cultured taste,

Notes

[8] *Anne* queen of Great Britain (1665–1714). The culture of her reign involved a rejection of both neo-Gothic and neo-Classical style in favour of the neo-Baroque "Queen Anne Style," increasingly espoused by the aesthetes, especially in architecture. For example, the style was revived in England in the second half of the nineteenth century, after Thackeray's *Henry Esmond* (1852), in the architecture of Norman Shaw (1831–1912). The "Culture" is a contemporary reference to Arnold's *Culture and Anarchy* (see n. 11).

[9] *Josephine* Josephine de Beauharnais (1763–1814), first wife of Napoleon Bonaparte, and crowned by him Empress of the French in 1804. Her brilliant court in Paris became the cultural and social capital of Europe. But the "Art stopped short" when Napoleon divorced her in 1809, in part because she did not provide a male heir.

[10] *spleen . . . Plato. . . bean* in medieval and Renaissance theory of humours or temperaments, the spleen was the source of anger and melancholy, the latter operative here. In Platonic love, a chaste love based on Plato's *Symposium* (*c.*380 BCE), the beautiful and the lovable in the object of desire (here, a potato or a French bean) lead the mind to aspire for a spiritual ascent to unite with the ideal or even the divine. In this close relationship sexual passion is suppressed or sublimated. A French bean is a kidney bean.

[11] *Philistines . . . hand* a series of references to contemporary cultural topics associated with the aesthetes: Philistines is a reference to Arnold's designation of the well-to-do but uncultured middle classes in *Culture and Anarchy* (1869); an Apostle is one of the twelve followers of Jesus, but in the nineteenth century, the name of a Cambridge undergraduate discussion society that had included Tennyson, Hallam, Maurice, and in the 1880s, the art critic Roger Fry (1866–1934) and the philosopher A. N. Whitehead (1861–1947). Piccadilly is a London street running from Hyde Park to Piccadilly Circus on which a number of famous houses were located, including Devonshire House and Burlington House (the RA) – a locale for promenades. Both the poppy and lily are associated with the Pre-Raphaelite painters (see n. 2). The mediæval hand refers both to the many contorted hands in the Pre-Raphaelite medievalizing paintings like Dante Rossetti's *Proserpine* (1880) or Holman Hunt's *Lady of Shalott* (1857–1905), as well as to medieval handwriting in illuminated manuscripts in Pre-Raphaelite paintings, such as Charles Collins's *Convent Thoughts* (1851) or Morris's *La Belle Iseult* (1858).

[12] *damozels* a medievalizing term for damsels used by the Pre-Raphaelite poets and painters, especially by DANTE ROSSETTI (see n. 2).

Distinguish gems from paste,[13]
And "High diddle diddle"
Will rank as an idyll,
If I pronounce it chaste![14]　　　　　　　　　　10
A most intense young man,
A soulful-eyed young man,
An ultra-poetical, super-aesthetical,
Out of the way young man

BOTH:　　　A most intense young man, &c.　　　　15

GROSVENOR:　Conceive me, if you can,
An every-day young man:
A commonplace type,
With a stick[15] and a pipe,
And a half-bred black-and-tan;[16]　　　　　20
Who thinks suburban "hops"
More fun than "Monday Pops."[17]
Who's fond of his dinner,
And doesn't get thinner
On bottled beer and chops.　　　　　　25
A common-place young man—
A matter-of-fact young man—
A steady and stolid-y, jolly Bank-holiday[18]
Every-day young man!

BOTH:　　　A common-place young man—　　　30
A matter-of-fact young man—
A steady and stolid-y, jolly Bank-holiday
Every-day young man!

BUNTHORNE:　A Japanese young man—
A blue and white young man[19]—　　　　35
Francesca di Rimini, miminy, piminy,
Je-ne-sais-quoi young man.[20]

Notes

[13] *paste* genuine gemstones are contrasted with cut lead-glass imitations of gems, known as "paste," often highly decorative in the Victorian era; good literature (that is, aesthetic) contrasted with bad.

[14] *diddle … idyll … chaste* from the English nursery rhyme "High diddle diddle, the cat and the fiddle" (c.1765). The comparison with an idyll invokes Tennyson's twelve blank-verse *Idylls of the King* (1856–85), his elegiac story of King Arthur and the adventures of his knights of the Round Table, an allegory of Britain in the nineteenth century. Chaste is the opposite of "fleshly" or impure (see n. 1).

[15] *stick* in contrast to the aesthetes who used a cane as an accessory of fashionable attire, the working man of Grosvenor's stanza carried a stick, and is followed by a dog.

[16] *black-and-tan* a Manchester terrier, so coloured; "half-bred" signifies mixed parentage.

[17] *hops … pops* weekly dances held in the suburbs of London on Saturday nights and Monday Populars – classical music concerts, held at St James's Hall by Samuel Arthur

Chappell (1834–1904) from 1858 until the end of the century.

[18] *Bank-holiday* the type of person who attended the Hampstead Heath August Bank Holiday Fair. The holiday, the first Monday in August, as well as Easter Monday, Whit Monday, and Boxing Day, was established by the Bank Holidays Act of 1871.

[19] *Japanese … blue and white* see n. 5.

[20] *Rimini … piminy … quoi* Francesca da Rimini (1255–85) was the beloved of Paulo Malatesta (c.1246–1285), both killed for their adultery by Paulo's brother, to whom Francesca was married. They were placed by Dante in the circle of the lustful in the *Inferno* (Canto 5). In the nineteenth century their love story inspired many artists and numerous plays, operas, and incidental music throughout Europe, including pieces by Tchaikovsky and Rossini. Miminy piminy (originally "a niminy-piminy lisp" in the *Monthly Review*, 1801) means excessively foppish or affected. *Je ne sais quoi* (Fr. I don't know what).

GROSVENOR:	A Chancery Lane young man—	
	A Somerset House young man—	
	A very delectable, highly respectable,	40
	Threepenny-bus[21] young man!	

BUNTHORNE: A pallid and thin young man—
A haggard and lank young man—
A greenery-yallery, Grosvenor Gallery,[22]
Foot-in-the-grave young man!   45

GROSVENOR: A Sewell and Cross young man—
A Howell and James young man—
A pushing young particle what's the next article—
Waterloo House[23] young man!

[*Bunthorne and Grosvenor Ensemble*]

BUNTHORNE: Conceive me, if you can,   50
A crotchetty, cracked young man,
An ultra-poetical, super-aesthetical,
Out-of-the-way young man!

GROSVENOR: Conceive me, if you can,
A matter-of-fact young man,   55
An alphabetical, arithmetical,
Every-day young man!

From *Iolanthe*[24]

Lord Mountararat's Solo: "When Britain really ruled the waves" [Act 2]

LORD MOUNTARARAT: When Britain really ruled the waves –
(In good Queen Bess's[25] time)

Notes

[21] *Lane ... House ... bus* a highly respectable lawyer's clerk working in the centre of the Law Courts and offices; a respectable public servant working in the office of the Registrar General at Somerset House, where were kept the records of births, deaths, wills, testaments, and so on. Fare wars amongst rival omnibus companies forced fares down from sixpence or more (depending on distance) to a universal threepenny (pronounced "thrippenny") fare.

[22] *Gallery* green and yellow were favourite colours of the aesthete painters (see also n. 1). Grosvenor Gallery (which gave the character Grosvenor his name) was founded by Sir Coutts Lindsay in 1877 at a fashionable address in New Bond Street, where it regularly exhibited paintings by Whistler, including his *Nocturne in Black and Gold* (1877) that sparked the controversy with Ruskin (see LITERATURE, PRE-RAPHAELITISM, WHISTLER, n. 1).

[23] *Cross ... James ... article ... House* all three were fashionable drapers or clothing stores in London; an enterprising London salesman would ask: "What's the next article I can show you?" William Morris also had his fashionable store, "Morris & Co." in London on Oxford Street.

[24] *title* this seventh collaboration (1882) between Gilbert and Sullivan sets a company of clever and immortal fairies against both the law and the aristocracy, taking particular aim at the Lord Chancellor (who had had an affair with Iolanthe, one of the Fairies, twenty-five years before) and at the House of Lords (as privileged, inept, and slow-witted) – as Lord Mountararat explains in this patriotic song from Act 2. Other patriotic songs in Gilbert and Sullivan operas include "For he is an Englishman" from *H. M. S. Pinafore* (1878) (see http://www.youtube.com/watch?v=KY4S0237Ql4); see also EMPIRE: CELEBRATION; BENSON, "LAND OF HOPE AND GLORY." Lord Mountararat's name refers to the mountain on which the ark of Noah is said to have come to rest after the great flood in Genesis 8: 4. The separate libretto was not published until 1882/3 by Chappell: our text.

[25] *Bess's* Elizabeth I (1533–1603), queen of England. The glories of her reign included the defeat of the Spanish Armada (1588) under Sir Francis Drake (1540–96); the literary and cultural revival, the English Renaissance; and Drake's circumnavigation of the globe (1581).

The House of Peers made no pretence
To intellectual eminence,
    Or scholarship sublime;   5
Yet Britain won her proudest bays[26]
In good Queen Bess's glorious days!

CHORUS: Yes Britain won her proudest bays
            In good Queen Bess's glorious days!

LORD MOUNTARARAT: When Wellington thrashed Bonaparte,[27]   10
         As every child can tell,
The House of Peers, throughout the war,
Did nothing in particular,
       And did it very well:
Yet Britain set the world ablaze   15
In good King George's[28] glorious days!

CHORUS: Yes, Britain set the world ablaze
           In good King George's glorious days!

LORD MOUNTARARAT: And while the House of Peers withholds
        Its legislative hand,   20
And noble statesmen do not itch
To interfere with matters which
       They do not understand,
As bright will shine Great Britain's rays
As in King George's glorious days!

CHORUS: As bright will shine Great Britain's rays
           As in King George's glorious days!   25

From *The Gondoliers* (1889)[29]

Quartet: "Then one of us will be a Queen" [Act 1]

GIANETTA: Then one of us will be a Queen,
         And sit on a golden throne,
           With a crown instead
           Of a hat on her head,
         And diamonds all her own!   5
        With a beautiful robe of gold and green,

Notes

[26] *bays* laurels, crowns of victory.
[27] *Bonaparte* Arthur Wellesley, Duke of Wellington (1769–1852), leading the English and Allied armies, together with the Prussians, defeated the French armies under Napoleon Bonaparte (1769–1821) at the Battle of Waterloo (18 June 1815).
[28] *George's* George III of the United Kingdom (1738–1820), who ruled throughout the period of the French Revolution and the ensuing Napoleonic wars.
[29] *title* the twelfth comic opera of Gilbert and Sullivan ran for a record 554 performances and was given a command performance before Victoria at Windsor Castle in March 1891, the first entertainment given at Windsor since the death of Albert in 1861. The opera concerns an heir to the throne of Barataria, entrusted to the care of a drunken gondolier in Venice who mixed him up with his own son. They then have to rule jointly, along with their new brides as queens. The real bride (betrothed formerly to the infant heir) arrives to find her betrothed(s?) married, allowing for diverse satire of class, monarchy, and public and private social roles. This quartet occurs as part of the finale to Act 1. See http://www.youtube.com/watch?v=_LqfR36xqXM. The separate libretto was not published by Chappell until 1890, our text.

I've always understood;
    I wonder whether
    She'd wear a feather?
I rather think she should!   10

ALL: Oh, 'tis a glorious thing, I ween,
To be a regular[30] Royal Queen!
No half-and-half affair, I mean,
No half-and-half affair,
But a right-down regular,   15
    Regular, regular,
Regular Royal Queen!

MARCO: She'll drive about in a carriage and pair,[31]
    With the King on her left-hand side,
      And a milk-white horse,   20
      As a matter of course,
    Whenever she wants to ride!
With beautiful silver shoes to wear
    Upon her dainty feet;
      With endless stocks   25
      Of beautiful frocks
And as much as she wants to eat!

ALL: Oh, 'tis a glorious thing, I ween,
To be a regular Royal Queen!
No half-and-half affair, I mean,   30
No half-and-half affair,
But a right-down regular,
    Regular, regular,
Regular Royal Queen!

TESSA: Whenever she condescends to walk,   35
    Be sure she'll shine at that,
      With her haughty stare
      And her nose in the air,
    Like a well-born aristocrat!
At elegant high society talk   40
    She'll bear away the bell,[32]
      With her "How de do?"
      And her "How are you?"
And "I trust I see you well!"

ALL: Oh, 'tis a glorious thing, I ween,   45
To be a regular Royal Queen!

Notes

[30] *regular* a nineteenth-century colloquialism: "thorough, complete, absolute, perfect" (*OED*).

[31] *pair* matched horses: the king would be mounted separately on his own horse.

[32] *bell* take the prize, from the custom of giving a small gold bell to the winner of a horse race.

No half-and-half affair, I mean,
No half-and-half affair,
But a right-down regular,
    Regular, regular,   50
Regular Royal Queen!

GIUSEPPE: And noble lords will scrape and bow,
    And double themselves in two,
      And open their eyes
      In blank surprise   55
    At whatever she likes to do.
And everybody will roundly vow
    She's fair as flowers in May,
      And say, "How clever!"
      At whatsoever   60
    She condescends to say!

ALL: Oh, 'tis a glorious thing, I ween,
To be a regular Royal Queen!
No half-and-half affair, I mean,
No half-and-half affair,   65
But a right-down regular,
    Regular, regular,
Regular Royal Queen!
Oh, 'tis a glorious thing, I ween,
To be a regular Royal Queen,   70
A right-down regular Royal Queen! ...

Giuseppe's Solo: "Rising early in the morning" [Act 2][33]

GIUSEPPE: Rising early in the morning,
    We proceed to light the fire,[34]
Then our Majesty adorning
In its workaday attire,
    We embark without delay   5
    On the duties of the day.

First, we polish off some batches
Of political despatches,[35]
    And foreign politicians circumvent;
Then, if business isn't heavy,   10
We may hold a Royal levee,
    Or ratify some Acts of Parliament.[36]

Notes

[33] *title* this song occurs near the beginning of Act 2, when the two gondoliers, now joint working monarchs, contemplate their duties in a classless realm / republic where "all shall equal be."

[34] *fire* all class roles are reversed, and here one of the monarchs, crowned and robed, undertakes the first daily task of one of the lowest-ranking servants, lighting the fires.

[35] *despatches* government acts, memoranda, and reports were sent to Victoria in official despatch boxes.

[36] *levee ... Parliament* a levee is a formal court reception of visitors or state guests held in the morning. An act of the British Parliament only became law when signed by the monarch.

Then we probably review the household troops—
With the usual "Shalloo humps!" and "Shalloo hoops!"[37]
Or receive with ceremonial and state   15
An interesting Eastern potentate.
   After that we generally
   Go and dress our private valet—
(It's a rather nervous duty—he's a touchy little man)—
   Write some letters literary   20
   For our private secretary—
He is shaky in his spelling, so we help him if we can.
   Then, in view of cravings inner,
   We go down and order dinner;
Then we polish the Regalia and the Coronation Plate—[38]   25
   Spend an hour in titivating[39]
   All our Gentlemen-in-Waiting;
Or we run on little errands for the Ministers of State.

   Oh, philosophers[40] may sing
   Of the troubles of a King;   30
Yet the duties are delightful, and the privileges great;
   But the privilege and pleasure
   That we treasure beyond measure
Is to run on little errands for the Ministers of State.

CHORUS: Oh, philosophers may sing   35
   Of the troubles of a King;
Yet the duties are delightful, and the privileges great;
   But the privilege and pleasure
   That we treasure beyond measure
Is to run on little errands for the Ministers of State.   40

GIUSEPPE: After luncheon (making merry
On a bun and glass of sherry),
   If we've nothing in particular to do,
We may make a Proclamation,
Or receive a deputation —   45
   Then we possibly create a Peer or two.
Then we help a fellow-creature on his path
With the Garter or the Thistle or the Bath,[41]
Or we dress and toddle off in semi-state[42]
To a festival, a function, or a fete.   50
   Then we go and stand as sentry

Notes

[37] *hoops* parodies of a drill sergeant's military parade ground command, "Shoulder arms."

[38] *Plate* the royal regalia, the Crown Jewels kept in the Tower of London. To refer to them as plate (that is, silver plate, usually brass or another base metal covered with silver) is ironic.

[39] *titivating* smartening up.

[40] *philosophers* there are numerous examples, from Plato's rejection of tyranny in *Republic* (*c.*380 BCE), to Niccolò Machiavelli's *The Prince* (1532), and Thomas Paine's *Rights of Man* (1791). Britain had passed the Treason Felony Act (1848) that made republicanism a crime with the punishment of transportation to Australia.

[41] *Garter . . . Bath* the three highest orders of British chivalry, the Order of the Garter (founded 1348), of the Thistle (1687), and of the Bath (1399).

[42] *semi-state* court dress for ordinary ceremonial occasions, that is, without robes and crowns.

At the Palace (private entry),
Marching hither, marching thither, up and down and to and fro,
While the warrior on duty
Goes in search of beer and beauty   55
(And it generally happens that he hasn't far to go).
He relieves us, if he's able,
Just in time to lay the table,
Then we dine and serve the coffee, and at half-past twelve or one,
With a pleasure that's emphatic,   60
We retire to our attic
With the gratifying feeling that our duty has been done!

Oh, philosophers may sing
Of the troubles of a King,
But of pleasures there are many and of troubles[43] there are none;   65
And the culminating pleasure
That we treasure beyond measure
Is the gratifying feeling that our duty has been done!

CHORUS: Oh, philosophers may sing
Of the troubles of a King,   70
But of pleasures there are many and of worries there are none;
And the culminating pleasure
That we treasure beyond measure
Is the gratifying feeling that our duty[44] has been done!

Augusta Webster (1837–94)

Born at Poole in Dorsetshire, Julia Augusta Davies was the daughter of Vice-Admiral George Davies (1800–76) and Julia Hume (1803–97), one of six children. They were educated first at home – that is, on board his ship, *The Griper*, stationed at Chichester, and later at Banff in Scotland and Penzance in Cornwall. Her grandfather on her mother's side was a friend of Charles Lamb (1775–1834), William Hazlitt (1778–1830), and William Godwin (1756–1836). She learned Greek and Latin and helped teach them to her brother. After her father became the chief magistrate for Cambridgeshire in 1851, she attended the Cambridge School of Art and later the South Kensington School of

Art. She married Thomas Webster, a fellow and lecturer in law of Trinity College, Cambridge, in 1863, and they had one child, Margaret. Augusta would write a sonnet sequence about her relationship with her child, the posthumous and unfinished *Mother and Daughter* (1895). In the 1860s the family moved to London where Webster met John Stuart Mill and Frances Power Cobbe and became active in the women's suffrage movement. Webster's publications include two translations from Greek, *The Prometheus Bound of Aeschylus* (1866) and *The Medea of Euripides* (1868), as well as several other plays: *The Auspicious Day* (1874), *Disguises* (1879), *In a Day* (1882), and her

Notes

[43] *troubles* changed to "worries" in the third edition of the libretto.
[44] *duty* one of the chief Victorian public virtues. For instance, Samuel Smiles extols it in *Duty: With Illustrations of*

Courage, Patience, and Endurance (1880). It was also the subject of derision; see, for instance, CLOUGH, "DUTY."

most praised drama, *The Sentence* (1887). She published poetry, *Blanche Lisle and Other Poems* (1860) and *Lilian Gray, A Poem* (1864), as well as a novel, *Lesley's Guardians* (1864), all under the pseudonym Cecil Home. For ten years she was the poetry reviewer for the *Athenæum* (1884–94), and contributed articles to the *Examiner* from 1874, many on women's rights, women's education, the rearing of children, and the running of an efficient household, collected as *A Housewife's Opinions* (1879). She was the first woman writer elected to public office, the London School Board (1879, 1885). She published two collections of monologues, *Dramatic Studies* (1866) and *Portraits* (1870),

elaborate and intimate portrayals of women's psychology, setting historical, mythological, and contemporary women in situations of sexual complexity. Her dramatic monologues, unlike those of Tennyson and Browning, are without an implied silent listener. Other collections are *A Woman Sold and Other Poems* (1867) and *A Book of Rhymes* (1881). Scholarly edition: *Augusta Webster: Portraits and Other Poems*, ed. Christine Sutphin (2000). Patricia Rigg, *Julia Augusta Webster: Victorian Aestheticism and the Woman Writer* (2009). Victorian Women's Writers' Project: Webster: http://webappl.dlib.indiana.edu/vwwp/browse.do?type=creator&filter=A.

A Castaway[1]

Poor little diary, with its simple thoughts,
its good resolves, its "Studied French an hour,"
"Read Modern History," "Trimmed up my grey hat,"
"Darned stockings," "Tatted,"[2] "Practised my new song,"
"Went to the daily service," "Took Bess[3] soup,"   5
"Went out to tea." Poor simple diary!
and did *I* write it? Was I this good girl,
this budding colourless young rose of home?
did I so live content in such a life,
seeing no larger scope, nor asking it,   10
than this small constant round—old clothes to mend,
new clothes to make, then go and say my prayers,
or carry soup, or take a little walk
and pick the ragged-robins[4] in the hedge?
Then for ambition, (was there ever life   15

Notes

AUGUSTA WEBSTER

[1] *title* a dramatic monologue spoken by a middle-class fallen woman named Eulalie who has come across her youthful diary and reflects on her life, and her family, and especially her relationship with her brother Edward (later called "Clement" in 1893). "Castaway" was a commonly used term for prostitutes in Victorian England, drawing on the Bible: see 1 Corinthians 9: 27: "But I keep under my body, and bring it into subjection: lest that by any means, when I have preached to others, I myself should be a castaway"; the last half of this verse is the text quoted at the beginning of Webster's monologue "A Preacher" in *Dramatic Studies* (1866). For Victorian prostitution, see GENDER: SEX; GREG, "PROSTITUTION" (WEB p. 87). Unlike Dante Rossetti's "Jenny" of the same year (1870), this monologuist speaks her own thoughts, and is not ventriloquized by her male lover;

for another poem on prostitution from a woman's point of view, see LEVY, "MAGDALEN." The great increase in prostitution was partly the result of many thousands of women unable to obtain work, the context for both poems and a number of paintings, such as Augustus Egg's *Past and Present* triptych (1858) and Dante Rossetti's *Found* (1858–81; see Plate 15). By the mid-1860s concerns about venereal diseases led to the passing of the Contagious Diseases Acts (1864–69); see GENDER: WOMAN QUESTION; MARTINEAU, "MANIFESTO." First published in *Portraits* (1870); when it was republished (1893), the first words in enjambed lines were capitalized.

[2] *tatted* knotted cotton or linen thread into lace-like patterns.

[3] *Bess* common name for a household servant.

[4] *ragged-robins* common English wayside flower.

that could forego that?) to improve my mind
and know French better and sing harder songs;
for gaiety, to go, in my best white
well washed and starched and freshened with new bows,
and take tea out to meet the clergyman.   20
No wishes and no cares, almost no hopes,
only the young girl's hazed and golden dreams
that veil the Future from her.

               So long since:
and now it seems a jest to talk of me
as if I could be one with her, of me   25
who am .. me.

            And what is that? My looking-glass
answers it passably; a woman sure,
no fiend, no slimy thing out of the pools,
a woman with a ripe and smiling lip
that has no venom in its touch I think,   30
with a white brow on which there is no brand;
a woman none dare call not beautiful,
not womanly in every woman's grace.

    Aye let me feed upon my beauty thus,
be glad in it like painters when they see   35
at last the face they dreamed but could not find
look from their canvass on them, triumph in it,
the dearest thing I have. Why, 'tis my all,
let me make much of it: is it not this,
this beauty, my own curse at once and tool   40
to snare men's souls—(I know what the good say
of beauty in such creatures)—is it not this
that makes me feel myself a woman still,
some little pride, some little—

              Here's a jest!
what word will fit the sense but modesty?   45
A wanton I but modest!

          Modest, true;
I'm not drunk in the streets, ply not for hire
at infamous corners with my likenesses
of the humbler kind;⁵ yes, modesty's my word—
'twould shape my mouth well too, I think I'll try: 50
"Sir, Mr What-you-will, Lord Who-knows-what,
my present lover or my next to come,
value me at my worth, fill your purse full,
for I am modest; yes, and honour me

Notes ──

⁵ *kind* common prostitutes.

as though your schoolgirl sister or your wife   55
could let her skirts brush mine or talk of me;
for I am modest."

                Well, I flout myself:
but yet, but yet—

                Fie, poor fantastic fool,
why do I play the hypocrite alone,
who am no hypocrite with others by?   60
where should be my "But yet"? I am that thing
called half a dozen dainty names, and none
dainty enough to serve the turn and hide
the one coarse English worst[6] that lurks beneath:
just that, no worse, no better.

                And, for me,   65
I say let no one be above her trade;
I own my kindredship with any drab[7]
who sells herself as I, although she crouch
in fetid garrets and I have a home
all velvet and marqueterie and pastilles,[8]   70
although she hide her skeleton in rags
and I set fashions and wear cobweb lace:
the difference lies but in my choicer ware,
that I sell beauty and she ugliness;
our traffic's one—I'm no sweet slaver-tongue   75
to gloze[9] upon it and explain myself
a sort of fractious angel misconceived—
our traffic's one: I own it. And what then?
I know of worse that are called honourable.
Our lawyers, who, with noble eloquence   80
and virtuous outbursts, lie to hang a man,
or lie to save him, which way goes the fee:
our preachers, gloating on your future hell
for not believing what they doubt themselves:
our doctors, who sort poisons out by chance,   85
and wonder how they'll answer, and grow rich:
our journalists, whose business is to fib
and juggle truths and falsehoods to and fro:
our tradesmen,[10] who must keep unspotted names
and cheat the least like stealing that they can: 90
our— all of them, the virtuous worthy men

Notes

[6] *dainty ... worst* the lurking worst word is probably "whore."

[7] *drab* prostitute.

[8] *pastilles* inlaid mosaic wood veneer; expensive medicinal cough drops, or aromatic paste to be burnt as incense.

[9] *gloze* flattering tongue to explain, or discourse.

[10] *lawyers ... tradesmen* in *Unto This Last*, "The Roots of Honour" (1860) Ruskin gives his list of favoured professions: "Five great intellectual professions, relating to daily necessities of life, have hitherto existed—three exist necessarily, in every civilized nation: The Soldier's profession is to *defend* it. / The Pastor's to *teach* it. / The Physician's to *keep it in health*. / The Lawyer's to *enforce justice* in it. / The Merchant's to *provide* for it."

who feed on the world's follies, vices, wants,
and do their businesses of lies and shams
honestly, reputably, while the world
claps hands and cries "good luck," which of their trades,   95
their honourable trades, barefaced like mine,
all secrets brazened out, would shew more white?

    And whom do I hurt more than they? as much?
The wives? Poor fools, what do I take from them
worth crying for or keeping? If they knew   100
what their fine husbands look like seen by eyes
that may perceive there are more men than one!
But, if they can, let them just take the pains
to keep them: 'tis not such a mighty task
to pin an idiot to your apron-string;   105
and wives have an advantage over us,
(the good and blind ones have), the smile or pout
leaves them no secret nausea at odd times.
Oh they could keep their husbands if they cared,
but 'tis an easier life to let them go,   110
and whimper at it for morality.

    Oh! those shrill carping virtues, safely housed
from reach of even a smile that should put red
on a decorous cheek, who rail at us
with such a spiteful scorn and rancourousness,   115
(which maybe is half envy at the heart),
and boast themselves so measurelessly good
and us so measurelessly unlike them,
what is their wondrous merit that they stay
in comfortable homes whence not a soul   120
has ever thought of tempting them, and wear
no kisses but a husband's upon lips
there is no other man desires to kiss—
refrain in fact from sin impossible?
How dare they hate us so? what have they done,   125
what borne, to prove them other than we are?
What right have they to scorn us—glass-case saints,
Dianas[11] under lock and key—what right
more than the well-fed helpless barn-door fowl
to scorn the larcenous wild-birds?[12]

Notes ───

[11] *glass-cased … Dianas* the bodies of some saints were kept under glass to be exposed to the faithful, like St Clare in Assisi or St Rita of Cascia, both in Italy; Victorian rooms were sometimes decorated with stuffed birds preserved under glass domes. Diana was the Roman goddess of chastity, as well as the moon, and the hunt.

[12] *wild-birds* the magpie is known to steal shiny objects; see also "The Jackdaw of Rheims" in *The Ingoldsby Legends* (1837) by Richard Harris Barham (1788–1845).

Pshaw, let be!   130

Scorn or no scorn, what matter for their scorn?
I have outfaced my own—that's harder work.
Aye let their virtuous malice dribble on—
mock snowstorms on the stage—I'm proof long since:
I have looked coolly on my what and why,   135
and I accept myself.

                  Oh I'll endorse
the shamefullest revilings mouthed at me,
cry "True! Oh perfect picture! Yes, that's I!"
and add a telling blackness here and there,
and then dare swear you, every nine of ten,   140
my judges and accusers, I'd not change
my conscience against yours, you who tread out
your devil's pilgrimage along the roads
that take in church and chapel, and arrange
a roundabout and decent way to hell.   145

      Well, mine's a short way and a merry one:[13]
so says my pious hash of ohs and ahs,
choice texts and choicer threats, appropriate names,
(Rahabs and Jezebels), some fierce Tartuffe[14]
hurled at me through the post. We had rare fun   150
over that tract[15] digested with champagne.
Where is it? where's my rich repertory
of insults biblical?[16] *'I prey on souls'*—
only my men have oftenest none I think:
'I snare the simple ones'—but in these days   155
there seem to be none simple and none snared,
and most men have their favourite sinnings planned
to do them civilly and sensibly:
'I braid my hair'—but braids are out of date:
'I paint my cheeks'—I always wear them pale: 160
'I—'

      Pshaw! the trash is savourless to-day:
one cannot laugh alone. There, let it burn.
What, does the windy dullard think one needs
his wisdom dove-tailed on to Solomon's,[17]

Notes

[13] *one* motto attributed to the seventeenth-century Welsh pirate, Bartholomew Roberts (1682–1722), known as "Black Bart," who claimed: "a merry life and a short one shall be my motto."

[14] *Rahab … Tartuffe* Rahab was a prostitute who was important for the Israelites in the siege of Jericho: she hid their spies in her house, thereby saving her family (see Joshua 6: 17–25). For Jezebel, wife of Ahab, king of Israel, accused of murders and sexual profligacy, see 1 Kings 16–21; and 2 Kings 9: 7–10; and 30–37; because she painted her face her name is associated with elaborately made-up women and with cruelty. Tartuffe is the eponymous name of the hypocritical hero of Molière's play of 1664, a byword for pretensions to religious piety.

[15] *tract* short religious or political pamphlet.

[16] *biblical … cheeks* for the cited passages, see in order: prey: Ezekiel 22: 25; snare: Ecclesiastes 7: 26; braid: 1 Timothy 2: 9; and cheeks: 2 Kings 9: 30.

[17] *Solomon* the son of King David who became the king of Israel, famed for his wisdom (see 1 Kings 3: 4–9; 11–12; see also the Judgement of Solomon, 1 Kings 3: 16–28).

his threats out-threatening God's, to teach the news 165
that those who need not sin have safer souls?
We know it, but we've bodies to save too;
and so we earn our living.

               Well lit, tract!
at least you've made me a good leaping blaze.
Up, up, how the flame shoots! and now 'tis dead. 170
Oh proper finish, preaching to the last—
no such bad omen either; sudden end,
and no sad withering horrible old age.
How one would clutch at youth to hold it tight!
and then to know it gone, to see it gone, 175
be taught its absence by harsh careless looks,
to live forgotten, solitary, old
the cruellest word that ever woman learns.
Old—that's to be nothing, or to be at best
a blurred memorial that in better days 180
there was a woman once with such a name.
No, no, I could not bear it: death itself
shews kinder promise .. even death itself,
since it must come one day—

               Oh this grey gloom!
This rain, rain, rain, what wretched thoughts it brings! 185
Death: I'll not think of it.

               Will no one come?
'Tis dreary work alone.

             Why did I read
that silly diary? Now, sing song, ding dong,
come the old vexing echoes back again,
church bells and nursery good-books,[18] back again 190
upon my shrinking ears that had forgotten—
I hate the useless memories: 'tis fools' work
singing the hacknied dirge of 'better days':
best take Now kindly, give the past good-bye,
whether it were a better or a worse. 195

    Yes, yes, I listened to the echoes once,
the echoes and the thoughts from the old days.
The worse for me: I lost my richest friend,
and that was all the difference. For the world

Notes

[18] *sing-song ... good-books* a long line of moral verse for children included Isaac Watts's *Divine Songs for Children* (1715) and *Divine and Moral Songs for Children* (1720). It continued throughout the eighteenth and nineteenth centuries to such journals as *Aunt Judy's Magazine* beginning in 1866. Christina Rossetti was about to publish *Sing-Song: A Nursery Rhyme Book* in 1872. See also STEVENSON, n. 4. Lewis Carroll in *Alice in Wonderland* (1865) exploits the same genre in "How doth the Little Crocodile" (ch. 2, a parody of Watts's "Against Idleness and Mischief") and the song of the Lobster, "'Tis the voice of the Lobster" (ch. 10, a parody of Watts's "The Sluggard").

I would not have that flight known. How they'd roar: 200
"What! Eulalie,[19] when she refused us all,
'ill' and 'away,' was doing Magdalene,
tears, ashes, and her Bible, and then off
to hide her in a Refuge[20] .. for a week!"

A wild whim that, to fancy I could change 205
my new self for my old, because I wished!
since then, when in my languid days there comes
that craving, like homesickness, to go back
to the good days, the dear old stupid days,
to the quiet and the innocence, I know 210
'tis a sick fancy and try palliatives.

What is it? You go back to the old home,
and 'tis not *your* home, has no place for you,
and, if it had, you could not fit you in it.
And could I fit me to my former self? 215
If I had had the wit, like some of us,
to sow my wild-oats into three per cents,[21]
could I not find me shelter in the peace
of some far nook where none of them would come,
nor whisper travel from this scurrilous world, 220
that gloats and moralizes through its leers,
to blast me with my fashionable shame?
There I might—oh my castle in the clouds!
and where's its rent?—but there, were there a there,
I might again live the grave blameless life 225
among such simple pleasures, simple cares:
but could they be my pleasures, be my cares?
The blameless life, but never the content—
never. How could I henceforth be content
in any life but one that sets the brain 230
in a hot merry fever with its stir?
what would there be in quiet rustic days,
each like the other, full of time to think,
to keep one bold enough to live at all?
Quiet is hell, I say—as if a woman 235
could bear to sit alone, quiet all day,
and loathe herself, and sicken on her thoughts.

They tried it at the Refuge, and I failed:
I could not bear it. Dreary hideous room,

Notes

[19] *Eulalie* (Gk. *Eulalia* sweetly speaking); also the title of a poem, "Eulalie—A Song" (1845) by Edgar Allan Poe (1809–49).
[20] *Magdalen ... Refuge* tradition holds that Mary Magdalen was a repentant prostitute (see Luke 7: 37–44). Magdalen was a name given to those who gave up prostitution by entering a refuge or rescue home such as Urania Cottage established by Charles Dickens (1812–70) and Angela Burdett-Coutts (1814–1906). Wilkie Collins would publish his novel *The New Magdalen* in 1873 on the fallen woman Mercy Merrick and her reclamation. See DANTE ROSSETTI, n. 47 and CHRISTINA ROSSETTI, n. 5.
[21] *three per cents* common name for British government stocks that offered 3% interest annually.

coarse pittance, prison rules, one might bear these   240
and keep one's purpose; but so much alone,
and then made faint and weak and fanciful
by change from pampering to half-famishing—
good God, what thoughts come! Only one week more
and 'twould have ended: but in one day more   245
I must have killed myself. And I loathe death,
the dreadful foul corruption, with who knows
what future after it.

               Well, I came back,
Back to my slough.[22] Who says I had my choice?
Could I stay there to die of some mad death?   250
and if I rambled out into the world,
sinless but penniless, what else were that
but slower death, slow pining shivering death
by misery and hunger? Choice! what choice
of living well or ill? could I have that?   255
And who would give it me? I think indeed
some kind hand, a woman's—I hate men—
had stretched itself to help me to firm ground,
taken a chance and risked my falling back,
I could have gone my way not falling back: 260
but, let her be all brave, all charitable,
how could she do it? Such a trifling boon,
little work to live by, 'tis not much,
and I might have found will enough to last:
but where's the work? More sempstresses than shirts;   265
and defter hands at white work than are mine
drop starved at last: dressmakers, milliners,[23]
too many too they say; and then their trades
need skill, apprenticeship. And who so bold
as hire me for their humblest drudgery?   270
not even for scullery slut;[24] not even, I think,
for governess, although they'd get me cheap.
And after all it would be something hard,
with the marts for decent women overfull,
if I could elbow in and snatch a chance   275

Notes

[22] *slough* bog or swamp; here a moral state of depravity, made famous by John Bunyan's "Slough of Despond" in *Pilgrim's Progress* (1678), where Pilgrim sinks under the "scum and filth that attends conviction for sin."

[23] *white ... milliners* along with the governess (see n. 29), being a seamstress would be one of the few sources of livelihood available to unmarried women. Eulalie refers to various kinds of needlework. This occupation is idealized in Dante Rossetti's painting of *The Girlhood of Mary Virgin* (1849); for its economic conditions and consequences, see HOOD, especially n. 1. White work is the embroidery on white cotton or linen, such as pillowslips or handkerchiefs; sempstresses or seamstresses sewed shirts by hand, as in

the paintings by Richard Redgrave *The Sempstress* (1846) and Anna Blunden *The Sempstress* (1854); dressmakers sewed made-to-order dresses almost overnight at what was known as "slop" work; milliners made hats to order following the most recent styles. Various commissions reported on the state of distressed sempstresses, such as the 1843 report on *Children's Employment, Trade and Manufactures*; see also CONDITION: PROGRESS; KINGSLEY, "CLOTHES" (WEB p. 31).

[24] *slut* the scullery maid had the lowest job in the hierarchy of the middle-class Victorian household. Simultaneously the word denoted a woman of low or loose character. See GENDER: SEX; CULLWICK, *DIARIES* (WEB p. 89) and n. 1.

and oust some good girl so, who then perforce
must come and snatch her chance among our crowd.

Why, if the worthy men who think all's done
if we'll but come where we can hear them preach,
could bring us all, or any half of us,   280
into their fold, teach all us wandering sheep,
or only half of us, to stand in rows
and baa them hymns and moral songs, good lack,
what would they do with us? what could they do?
Just think! with were't but half of us on hand   285
to find work for .. or husbands. Would they try
to ship us to the colonies for wives?[25]

Well, well, I know the wise ones talk and talk:
"Here's cause, here's cure"[26]: "No, here it is and here":
and find society to blame, or law,   290
the Church, the men, the women, too few schools,
too many schools, too much, too little taught:
somewhere or somehow someone is to blame:
but I say all the fault's with God himself
who puts too many women in the world.   295
We ought to die off reasonably and leave
as many as the men want, none to waste.
Here's cause; the woman's superfluity:
and for the cure, why, if it were the law,
say, every year, in due percentages,   300
balancing them with men as the times need,
to kill off female infants, 'twould make room;
and some of us would not have lost too much,
losing life ere we know what it *can* mean.

The other day I saw a woman weep   305
beside her dead child's bed: the little thing
lay smiling, and the mother wailed half mad,
shrieking to God to give it back again.
I could have laughed aloud: the little girl
living had but her mother's life to live;   310
there she lay smiling, and her mother wept
to know her gone!

        My mother would have wept.

Notes

[25] *wives* in 1849 Sir Sidney Herbert (1810–61) established the Fund for Promoting Female Emigration on the basis that 500,000 women from England and Wales be shipped to the colonies to meet the need for an equivalent number there. He was relying on the sensational letters in the *Morning Chronicle* (Nov.–Dec. 1849) by Henry Mayhew on the problems of sweated labour in the needlework industry, especially that many women supplemented their income with occasional prostitution.

[26] *cause ... cure* the campaign against the Contagious Diseases Acts was known as "The Cause" (see n. 1). The Magdalen hospitals (see n. 20) were supposedly able to offer a cure.

Oh mother, mother, did you ever dream,
you good grave simple mother, you pure soul
no evil could come nigh, did you once dream   315
in all your dying cares for your lone girl
left to fight out her fortune all alone
that there would be *this* danger?—for *your* girl,
taught by you, lapped in a sweet ignorance,
scarcely more wise of what things sin could be   320
than some young child a summer six months old,
where in the north the summer makes a day,
of what is darkness .. darkness that will come
to-morrow suddenly. Thank God at least
for this much of my life, that when you died,   325
that when you kissed me dying, not a thought
of this made sorrow for you, that I too
was pure of even fear.

               Oh yes, I thought,
still new in my insipid treadmill life,
(my father so late dead), and hopeful still   330
there might be something pleasant somewhere in it,
some sudden fairy come, no doubt, to turn
my pumpkin to a chariot,[27] I thought then
that I might plod, and plod, and drum the sounds
of useless facts into unwilling ears,   335
tease children with dull questions half the day,
then con[28] dull answers in my room at night
ready for next day's questions,[29] mend quill pens
and cut my fingers, add up sums done wrong
and never get them right; teach, teach, and teach—   340
what I half knew, or not at all—teach, teach
for years, a lifetime—I!

              And yet, who knows?
it might have been, for I was patient once,
and willing, and meant well; it might have been
had I but still clung on in my first place—   345
a safe dull place, where mostly there were smiles
but never merry-makings; where all days
jogged on sedately busy, with no haste;

Notes

[27] *chariot* a reference to the Cinderella story in Charles Perrault's *Histoires ou contes du temps passé* (Fr. Stories or tales of olden time, 1697).

[28] *con* (<OE *cunnan* to know) study, learn.

[29] *questions* probably a reference to the standard book of pedagogy for governesses throughout the nineteenth century, *Mangnall's Questions*, a catechism of questions and answers to be memorized by children by Richmal Mangnall (1769–1821), English schoolmistress, with the full title, *Historical and Miscellaneous Questions for the Use of Young People* (1800). There were eighty-four editions by 1851; it was published with a "new and revised edition" in 1859 to account for numerous "political changes ... and the progress of discoveries." Sequels were published by Julia Corner (1798–1875) and adaptations by Ingram Cobbin (1777–1851) and others. Like the seamstress, the governess was one of the few means of livelihood for unmarried woman; see also CONDITION: EDUCATION, nn. 33, 34, and 35; GENDER: CONSTRUCTING GENDER; MARTINEAU, "MIDDLE-CLASS ... GIRLS" (WEB p. 75). See also Plate 7: Redgrave, *The Governess*.

where all seemed measured out, but margins broad:
a dull home but a peaceful, where I felt   350
my pupils would be dear young sisters soon,
and felt their mother take me to her heart,
motherly to all lonely harmless things.
But I must have a conscience, must blurt out
my great discovery of my ignorance!   355
And who required it of me? And who gained?
What did it matter for a more or less
the girls learnt in their schoolbooks, to forget
in their first season?[30] We did well together:
they loved me and I them: but I went off   360
to housemaid's pay, six crossgrained brats to teach,
wrangles and jangles, doubts, disgrace .. then this;
and they had a perfection[31] found for them,
who has all ladies' learning in her head
abridged and scheduled, speaks five languages,   365
knows botany and conchology and globes,[32]
draws, paints, plays, sings, embroiders, teaches all
on a patent method never known to fail:
and now they're finished and, I hear, poor things,
are the worst dancers and worst dressers out.[33]   370
And where's their profit of those prison years
all gone to make them wise in lesson books?
who wants his wife to know weeds' Latin names?
who ever chose a girl for saying dates?
or asked if she had learned to trace a map?   375

  Well, well, the silly rules this silly world
makes about women! This is one of them.
Why must there be pretence of teaching them
what no one ever cares that they should know,
what, grown out of the schoolroom, they cast off   380
like the schoolroom pinafore, no better fit
for any use of real grown-up life,
for any use to her who seeks or waits
the husband and the home, for any use,
for any shallowest pretence of use,   385
to her who has them? Do I not know this,
I like my betters, that a woman's life,
her natural life, her good life, her one life,
is in her husband, God on earth to her,
and what she knows and what she can and is   390
is only good as it brings good to him?

Notes

[30] *season* during the London social season, covering the sitting of Parliament from late January until mid-July or early August, landowners left their country estates for their London houses for rounds of political meetings as well as balls and entertainments. See INTRODUCTION, p. 7.

[31] *perfection* new governess.

[32] *conchology ... globes* study of shells and molluscs; geography.

[33] *out* to come out meant for a woman to be presented in society, especially to be presented at court to the sovereign, a signal that she was eligible to marry.

Oh God, do I not know it? I the thing
of shame and rottenness, the animal
that feed men's lusts and prey on them, I, I,
who should not dare to take the name of wife   395
on my polluted lips, who in the word
hear but my own reviling, I know that.
I could have lived by the rule, how content:
my pleasure to make him some pleasure, pride
to be as he would have me, duty, care,   400
to fit all to his taste, rule my small sphere
to his intention; then to lean on him,
be guided, tutored, loved—no not that word,
that *loved* which between men and women means
all selfishness, all putrid talk, all lust,   405
all vanity, all idiocy—not loved
but cared for. I've been loved myself, I think,
some once or twice since my poor mother died,
but *cared for*, never:—that a word for homes,
kind homes, good homes, where simple children come   410
and ask their mother is this right or wrong,
because they know she's perfect, cannot err;
their father told them so, and he knows all,
being so wise and good and wonderful,
even enough to scold even her at times   415
and tell her everything she does not know.
Ah the sweet nursery logic!

                Fool! thrice fool!
do I hanker after that too? Fancy me
infallible[34] nursery saint, live code of law!
me preaching! teaching innocence to be good!   420
a mother!

         Yet the baby thing that woke
and wailed an hour or two, and then was dead,
was mine, and had he lived .. why then my name
would have been mother. But 'twas well he died:
I could have been no mother, I, lost then   425
beyond his saving. Had he come before
and lived, come to me in the doubtful days
when shame and boldness had not grown one sense,
for his sake, with the courage come of him,
I might have struggled back.

             But how? But how?   430
His father would not then have let me go:

Notes

[34] *infallible* in the First Vatican Council of 1869–70, in a highly controversial and much discussed debate, the pope was declared to be infallible when making a pronouncement on faith and morals as the teacher of the universal church. The word took on a special meaning in the light of this dogmatic pronouncement, and was applied in all sorts of situations, as here, contemporaneous with the Vatican's definition.

his time had not yet come to make an end
of my 'for ever' with a hireling's fee
and civil light dismissal. None but him
to claim a bit of bread of if I went,   435
child or no child: would he have given it me?
He! no; he had not done with me. No help,
no help, no help. Some ways can be trodden back,
but never our way, we who one wild day
have given goodbye to what in our deep hearts   440
the lowest woman still holds best in life,
good name—good name though given by the world
that mouths and garbles with its decent prate,
and wraps it in respectable grave shams,
and patches conscience partly by the rule   445
of what one's neighbour thinks but something more
by what his eyes are sharp enough to see.
How I could scorn it with its Pharisees,[35]
if it could not scorn me: but yet, but yet—
oh God, if I could look it in the face!   450

    Oh I am wild, am ill, I think, to night:
will no one come and laugh with me? No feast,
no merriment to-night. So long alone!
Will no one come?

            At least there's a new dress
to try, and grumble at—they never fit   455
to one's ideal. Yes, a new rich dress,
with lace like this too, that's a soothing balm
for any fretting woman, cannot fail,
I've heard men say it .. and they know so well
what's in all women's hearts, especially   460
women like me.

            No help! no help! no help!
How could it be? It was too late long since—
even at the first too late. Whose blame is that?
there are some kindly people in the world,
but what can they do? If one hurls oneself   465
into a quicksand, what can be the end,
but that one sinks and sinks? Cry out for help?
Ah yes, and, if it came, who is so strong
to strain from the firm ground and lift one out?
And how, so firmly clutching the stretched hand,   470
as death's pursuing terror bids, even so,
how can one reach firm land, having to foot
the treacherous crumbling soil that slides and gives

Notes

35 *Pharisees* Jewish sect who held to the written law of Moses, and who in the Christian scriptures are the opponents of Jesus, who calls them hypocrites for exalting religious conformity over love, justice, and mercy. See Matthew 15: 1–20; and Mark 2: 1–11.

and sucks one in again? Impossible path!
No, why waste struggles, I or any one?   475
what is must be. What then? I, where I am,
sinking and sinking; let the wise pass by
and keep their wisdom for an apter use,
let me sink merrily as I best may.

    Only, I think, my brother—I forgot   480
he stopped his brotherhood some years ago—
but if he had been just so much less good
as to remember mercy. Did he think
how once I was his sister, prizing him
as sisters do, content to learn for him   485
the lesson girls with brothers all must learn,
to do without?

              I have heard girls lament
that doing so without all things one would,
but I saw never aught to murmur at,
for men must be made ready for their work,   490
and women all have more or less their chance
of husbands to work for them, keep them safe
like summer roses in soft greenhouse air
that never guess 'tis winter out of doors:
no, I saw never aught to murmur at,   495
content with stinted fare and shabby clothes
and cloistered silent life to save expense,
teaching myself out of my borrowed books,
while he for some one pastime, (needful true
to keep him of his rank, 'twas not his fault),   500
spent in a month what could have given me
my teachers for a year.

             'Twas no one's fault:
for could he be launched forth on the rude sea
of this contentious world and left to find
oars and the boatman's skill by some good chance?   505
'Twas no one's fault: yet still he might have thought
of our so different youths, and owned at least
'tis pitiful when a mere nerveless girl,
untutored, must put forth upon that sea,
not in the woman's true place, the wife's place,   510
to trust a husband and be borne along,
but impotent blind pilot to herself.

    Merciless, merciless—like the prudent world
that will not have the flawed soul prank[36] itself
with a hoped second virtue, will not have   515

Notes

[36] *prank* dress up pretentiously; flaunt oneself.

the woman fallen once lift up herself ..
lest she should fall again. Oh how his taunts,
his loathing fierce reproaches, scarred and seared,
like branding iron hissing in a wound!
And it was true—*that* killed me: and I felt   520
a hideous hopeless shame kill out my heart,
and knew myself for ever that he said,
that which I was—Oh it was true, true, true.

No, not true then. I was not all that then.
Oh, I have drifted on before mad winds   525
and made ignoble shipwreck, not to-day
could any breeze of heaven prosper me
into the track again, nor any hand
snatch me out of the whirlpool I have reached;
but then?

Nay he judged very well: he knew   530
repentance was too dear a luxury
for a beggar's buying, knew it earns no bread—
and knew me a too base and nerveless thing
to bear my first fault's sequel and just die.
And how could he have helped me? Held my hand,   535
owned me for his, fronted the angry world
clothed with my ignominy? Or maybe
taken me to his home to damn him worse?
What did I look for? for what less would serve
that he could do, a man without a purse?   540
He meant me well, he sent me that five pounds,
much to him then; and, if he bade me work
and never vex him more with news of me,
we both knew him too poor for pensioners.
I see he did his best; I could wish now   545
sending it back I had professed some thanks.

But there! I was too wretched to be meek:
it seemed to me as if he, every one,
the whole great world, were guilty of my guilt,
abettors and avengers: in my heart   550
I gibed them back their gibings; I was wild.

I see clear now and know one has one's life
in hand at first to spend or spare or give
like any other coin; spend it or give
or drop it in the mire, can the world see   555
you get your value for it, or bar back
the hurrying of its marts to grope it up
and give it back to you for better use?
And if you spend or give that is your choice;
and if you let it slip that's your choice too,   560
you should have held it firmer. Yours the blame,
and not another's, not the indifferent world's
which goes on steadily, statistically,

and count by censuses not separate souls—
and if it somehow needs to its worst use   565
so many lives of women, useless else,
it buys us of ourselves, we could hold back,
free all of us to starve, and some of us,
(those who have done no ill and are in luck),
to slave their lives out and have food and clothes   570
until they grow unserviceably old.

      Oh I blame no one—scarcely even myself.
It was to be: the very good in me
has always turned to hurt; all I thought right
at the hot moment, judged of afterwards,   575
shows reckless.

            Why, look at it, had I taken
the pay my dead child's father offered me
for having been its mother, I could then
have kept life in me, (many have to do it,
that swarm in the back alleys, on no more,   580
cold sometimes, mostly hungry, but they live);
I could have gained a respite trying it,
and maybe found at last some humble work
to eke the pittance out. Not I, forsooth,
I must have spirit, must have womanly pride,   585
must dash back his contemptuous wages, I,
who had not scorned to earn them, dash them back
the fiercer that he dared to count our boy
in my appraising: and yet now I think
I might have taken it for my dead boy's sake;   590
it would have been *his* gift.

               But I went forth
with my fine scorn, and whither did it lead?
Money's the root of evil[37] do they say?
money is virtue, strength: money to me
would then have been repentance: could I live   595
upon my idiot's pride?

          Well, it fell soon.
I had prayed Edward[38] might believe me dead,
and yet I begged of him—That's like me too,
beg of him and then send him back his alms!
What if he gave as to a whining wretch   600
that holds her hand and lies? I am less to him
than such a one; her rags do him no wrong,
but I, I, wrong him merely that I live,

Notes

[37] *evil* see 1 Timothy 6: 10. The text is alluded to ironically for the Pardoner's homily in Chaucer's "Prologue to the Pardoner's Tale" in the *Canterbury Tales* (c.1400).

[38] *Edward* the brother's name is changed to "Clement" (<Lat. *clemens*, merciful) in the republication in 1893.

being his sister. Could I not at least
have still let him forget me? But 'tis past: 605
and naturally he may hope I am long dead.

     Good God! to think that we were what we were
one to the other .. and now!

               He has done well;
married a sort of heiress, I have heard,
a dapper little madam, dimple cheeked 610
and dimple brained, who makes him a good wife—
No doubt she'd never own but just to him,
and in a whisper, she can even suspect
that we exist, we other women things:
what would she say if she could learn one day 615
she has a sister-in-law! So he and I
must stand apart till doomsday.

             But the jest,
to think how she would look!—Her fright, poor thing!
The notion!—I could laugh outright .. or else,
for I feel near it, roll on the ground and sob. 620

     Well, after all, there's not much difference
between the two sometimes.

            Was that the bell?
Some one at last, thank goodness. There's a voice,
and that's a pleasure. Whose though? Ah I know.
Why did she come alone, the cackling goose? 625
why not have brought her sister?—she tells more
and titters less. No matter; half a loaf
is better than no bread.
          Oh, is it you?
Most welcome, dear: one gets so moped alone.

Algernon Charles Swinburne
(1837–1909)

Born into a well-to-do and well-connected family, Swinburne was the eldest child of Admiral Charles Henry Swinburne (1797–1877) and Lady Jane Henrietta (1809–96), daughter of the third Earl of Ashburnham. He grew up at East Dene on the Isle of Wight, attended Eton and Balliol College, Oxford (1856–60), where he wrote poetry, memorized the poetry of his contemporaries, espoused republican and heterodox causes, and became a friend of Dante Rossetti, William Morris and other Pre-Raphaelites. His first volume was a classical drama, *Atalanta in Calydon* (1865), followed by the notorious *Poems and Ballads* (1866) that aroused the ire (with accusations of blasphemy and obscenity) of numerous critics, including, most famously, Robert Buchanan's attack in *The Fleshly School of Poetry*. Numerous volumes of poetry followed, including *Songs Before Sunrise* (1871), a second series of *Poems and Ballads* (1878), and *Tristram of Lyonesse* (1882). He also wrote novels: *Love's Cross-Currents* (1905), first serialized in the *Tatler* (1877) as *A Year's Letters*, and *Lesbia Brandon* (1952); a number of plays including a trilogy on Mary, Queen of Scots; and a series of brilliant parodies. He was a correspondent of Victor Hugo (1802–85) and Charles Baudelaire (1821–67), and a promoter of Walt Whitman (1819–92). Suffering from alcoholism, he was taken in 1879 by Theodore Watts-Dunton (1832–1914) to live in Putney in London, becoming a revered member of the literary establishment. A master of rhetorical flourishes and prosodic assonance and alliteration, he was also experimental in a wide variety of English and French verse forms. He exploited themes drawn from a broad reading in medieval, Renaissance, and modern literatures – using classical literature and religion to subvert pious Victorian Christianity and medieval and modern literature to confront the conventional post-Romantic language of love, romance, and marriage. Swinburne offers special bibliographic challenges as the canon is compromised by his editors Edmund Gosse and T. J. Wise (1859–1937), the latter exposed as a forger. Standard edition: *The Poems of Algernon Charles Swinburne* (6 vols, 1904); *The Tragedies of Algernon Charles Swinburne* (5 vols, 1905); both of these sets were prepared by Swinburne. *The Complete Works of Algernon Charles Swinburne*, ed. Edmund Gosse and Thomas James Wise (20 vols, 1925–27; textually unreliable); *The Swinburne Letters*, ed. Cecil Y. Lang (6 vols, 1959–62); *Uncollected Letters of Algernon Charles Swinburne*, ed. Terry L. Meyers (3 vols, 2005); Rikky Rooksby, *A. C. Swinburne: A Poet's Life* (1997). The Swinburne Project: http://swinburneproject.indiana.edu/swinburne/.

From *Atalanta in Calydon*[1]

Chorus ["When the hounds of spring are on winter's traces"][2]

When the hounds of spring are on winter's traces,
   The mother of months[3] in meadow or plain
Fills the shadows and windy places
   With lisp of leaves and ripple of rain;

Notes

ALGERNON CHARLES SWINBURNE

[1] *title* Swinburne writes a Victorian imitation of a classical Greek drama in *Atalanta in Calydon* (1865) as others had done before him, going back to the reforms in opera by Christoph Willibald Gluck (1747–87), who used Euripides in his *Alceste* (1767) and *Iphigeneia in Aulis* (1774, through the French play by Jean Racine). The tradition included Shelley's rewriting of Aeschylus in *Prometheus Unbound* (1820) and after Swinburne, Browning's "transcript" of Aeschylus in *Agamemnon* (1877). In his edition of the play (1865), Swinburne provided the "Argument": "Althæa, daughter of Thestius and Eurythemis, queen of Calydon, being with child of Meleager her first-born son, dreamed that she brought forth a brand burning; and upon his birth came the three Fates and prophesied of him three things, namely these; that he should have great strength of his hands, and good fortune in this life, and that he should live no longer when the brand then in the fire were consumed: wherefore his mother plucked it forth and kept it by her.

And the child being a man grown sailed with Jason after the fleece of gold, and won himself great praise of all men living; and when the tribes of the north and west made war upon Ætolia, he fought against their army and scattered it. But Artemis, having at the first stirred up these tribes to war against Œneus king of Calydon, because he had offered sacrifice to all the gods saving her alone, but her he had forgotten to honour, was yet more wroth because of the destruction of this army, and sent upon the land of Calydon a wild boar which slew many and wasted all their increase, but him could none slay, and many went against him and perished. Then were all the chief men of Greece gathered together, and among them Atalanta daughter of Iasius the Arcadian, a virgin; for whose sake Artemis let slay the boar, seeing she favoured the maiden greatly; and Meleager having despatched it gave the spoil thereof to Atalanta, as one beyond measure enamoured of her; but the brethren of Althæa his mother, Toxeus and Plexippus,

And the brown bright[4] nightingale amorous 5
    Is half assuaged for Itylus,
For the Thracian ships and the foreign faces,
    The tongueless vigil, and all the pain.[5]

Come with bows bent and with emptying of quivers,[6]
    Maiden most perfect, lady of light, 10
With a noise of winds and many rivers,
    With a clamour of waters, and with might;
Bind on thy sandals, O thou most fleet,
Over the splendour and speed of thy feet;[7]
For the faint east quickens, the wan west shivers, 15
    Round the feet of the day and the feet of the night.

Where shall we find her, how shall we sing to her,
    Fold our hands round her knees, and cling?
O that man's heart were as fire and could spring to her,
    Fire, or the strength of the streams that spring! 20
For the stars and the winds are unto her
As raiment, as songs of the harp-player;
For the risen stars and the fallen cling to her,
    And the southwest-wind and the west-wind sing.

Notes

with such others as misliked that she only should bear off the praise whereas many had borne the labour, laid wait for her to take away her spoil; but Meleager fought against them and slew them: whom when Althæa their sister beheld and knew to be slain of her son, she waxed for wrath and sorrow like as one mad, and taking the brand whereby the measure of her son's life was meted to him, she cast it upon a fire; and with the wasting thereof his life likewise wasted away, that being brought back to his father's house he died in a brief space; and his mother also endured not long after for very sorrow; and this was his end, and the end of that hunting." Swinburne's sources included *Iliad* 9. 529–99; Apollodorus, *Library* 1.7.7–8.322; and especially Ovid's *Metamorphoses* 8. 11–273; amongst others. The limited-edition publication of about 500 copies, published by Edward Moxon and Co., was originally subsidized by Swinburne's father in 1865 and later in the same year it was issued as a commercial success by Chatto and Windus (our text).

2 *traces* this chorus (lines 65–120 of the text) corresponds to the *parados* or choric ode of ancient Greek drama in which the chorus enters after the prologue (1–64 in Swinburne's play), singing and dancing, here in praise of the goddess Artemis. In the first line, as the hounds representing spring are bounding forward, they are held back by the traces or reins of winter. These lines and this chorus also introduce the major theme of the chase, the boar hunt, and the final tragedy as preordained – a human recreation as a transferred motif applied to the inexorable pursuit of the seasons.

3 *months* Artemis, in Greek mythology, Diana in Roman mythology, goddess the moon (hence "months"), chastity, and hunting. She is so named by Shelley in several places, including *Prometheus Unbound* (4. 207).

4 *brown bright* Swinburne's translation of *xoutha* (Gk.) as used in Aeschylus' *Agamemnon*: "Like some brown nightingale / Insatiable of noise" (1142; trans. Robert Browning). This second quatrain of the first stanza tells the story of Procne and Philomela in *Metamorphoses* 6. Procne, the wife of Tereus, king of Thrace, lusts after his wife's sister, Philomela, rapes her, cuts out her tongue, and confines her. After she weaves her story in a tapestry for Procne, they kill Itylus, son of Tereus and Procne, and cook him for Tereus to eat. He pursues them, but the gods turn Philomela into a nightingale and Procne to a swallow (though in Greek mythology Procne becomes the nightingale). See also ARNOLD, "PHILOMELA."

5 *Itylus . . . pain* Itylus was the son of Aedon in Greek mythology. She mistakenly kills him and is relieved of her grief by Zeus who changes her into a nightingale. She cries in grief every night; see *Odyssey* 19. 519–24. For another nightingale myth, see ARNOLD, "PHILOMELA." The Thracians were an Indo-European people who lived in what is now Thracia in north-eastern Greece; Homer refers to their ships in his catalogue of the ships in *Iliad* 2. 494–759. For pain, see *Paradise Lost* 4. 271.

6 *quivers* Artemis as the huntress is often depicted with a bow and arrows, as in the *Homeric Hymn to Artemis* (seventh century BCE) and in *Diana of Versailles*, a Roman copy of a Greek statue by Leochares (*c.*325 BCE), now in the Louvre.

7 *sandals . . . feet* see Homer's description of Pallas Athene: "So she spoke, and bound beneath her feet her beautiful sandals, immortal, golden, which were wont to bear her both over the waters of the sea and over the boundless land swift as the blasts of the wind" (*Odyssey* 1. 95–99; trans. A. T. Murray, 1919).

For winter's rains and ruins are over,   25
    And all the season of snows and sins;
The days dividing lover and lover,
    The light that loses, the night that wins;
And time remembered is grief forgotten,
And frosts are slain and flowers begotten,   30
And in green underwood and cover
    Blossom by blossom the spring begins.

The full streams feed on flower of rushes,
    Ripe grasses trammel a travelling foot,
The faint fresh flame of the young year flushes   35
    From leaf to flower and flower to fruit;
And fruit and leaf are as gold and fire,
And the oat is heard above the lyre,[8]
And the hoofèd heel of a satyr[9] crushes
    The chestnut-husk at the chestnut-root.   40

And Pan by noon and Bacchus[10] by night,
    Fleeter of foot than the fleet-foot kid,
Follows with dancing and fills with delight
    The Mænad and the Bassarid;[11]
And soft as lips that laugh and hide   45
The laughing leaves of the trees divide,
And screen from seeing and leave in sight
    The god pursuing, the maiden hid.

The ivy falls with the Bacchanal's hair[12]
    Over her eyebrows hiding her eyes;   50
The wild vine slipping down leaves bare
    Her bright breast shortening into sighs;
The wild vine slips with the weight of its leaves,
But the berried ivy catches and cleaves
To the limbs that glitter, the feet that scare   55
    The wolf that follows, the fawn that flies.

Chorus ["Before the beginning of years"][13]

Before the beginning of years
    There came to the making of man[14]
Time, with a gift of tears;

Notes

[8] *lyre* a stress on the rural and rustic associations of Artemis, as the goddess of the wilderness and protector of wild animals (oat pipes) rather than the lyre, the cultivated instrument of her brother, Apollo. See Milton, *Lycidas* (32–34; 88).

[9] *satyr* part man and, from the waist down, the legs of a goat; followers of Pan and Dionysus, associated with sexual desire.

[10] *Pan ... Bacchus* Pan is the god of shepherds, flocks, and rustic music; Bacchus is the Roman name for Dionysus, the god of the grape harvest, wine, and the theatre.

[11] *Mænad ... Bassarid* female followers of Dionysus who joined in his worship with ecstatic dances; also called "Bassarids."

[12] *Bacchanal* the Roman term for the Maenads was "Bacchantes," the devotees of Bacchus, the god of wine. The ivy was sacred to Bacchus, often worn around the hair of his followers, supposedly to ward off the effects of drinking wine.

[13] *years* this chorus (314–61 of the complete text) corresponds to the first *stasimon* in an ancient Greek drama, the stationary ode sung by the chorus following the first episode in the play.

[14] *man* perhaps an allusion to the Prometheus myth wherein Prometheus shaped humans out of clay and Athena breathed life into them. Prometheus stole fire from the

Grief, with a glass[15] that ran;
   Pleasure, with pain for leaven;   5
      Summer, with flowers that fell;
Remembrance fallen from heaven,
      And madness risen from hell;
Strength without hands to smite;
      Love that endures for a breath;   10
Night, the shadow of light,
      And life, the shadow of death.

And the high gods[16] took in hand
      Fire,[17] and the falling of tears,
And a measure of sliding sand   15
      From under the feet of the years;[18]
And froth and drift of the sea;
      And dust of the labouring earth;
And bodies of things to be
      In the houses of death and of birth;   20
And wrought with weeping and laughter,
      And fashioned with loathing and love,
With life before and after
      And death beneath and above,[19]
For a day and a night and a morrow,   25
      That his strength might endure for a span
With travail and heavy sorrow,
      The holy spirit of man.

From the winds of the north and the south
      They gathered as unto strife;   30
They breathed upon his mouth,[20]
      They filled his body with life;
Eyesight and speech they wrought
      For the veils of the soul therein,
A time for labour and thought,[21]   35
      A time to serve and to sin;
They gave him light in his ways,
      And love, and a space for delight,
And beauty and length of days,

Notes

gods and gave it to humans. For this offense, Zeus chained Prometheus to a rock, an eagle devouring his liver every day, only to have it regrow overnight, the subject of Aeschylus play, *Prometheus Bound*. See the last stanza of Goethe's *Prometheus* (1789): "Here I sit, forming men, / In my image, a race to be like me / To suffer, to weep." Shelley recounts Prometheus' escape from the bondage imposed by Zeus in *Prometheus Unbound* (1820); see also HEMANS, n. 15.

[15] *glass* hourglass.

[16] *high gods* Olympians, Zeus and his family.

[17] *Fire* the many references to fire (see n. 14) throughout *Atalanta* are linked to the prophecy that Atalanta's son,

Meleager, will live only as long as the brand in the flames at his birth was not consumed, so Atalanta pulled it from the flames and kept it. In the previous scene she had a dream concerning being consumed by fire: "All my sleep is turned into a fire, / And all my dreams to stuff that kindles it" (146–47); "I dreamed that out of this my womb had sprung / Fire and a firebrand" (233–34).

[18] *years* see FITZGERALD, RUBÁIYÁT, STZ. XXXVII: "—what boots it to repeat / How Time is slipping underneath our Feet."

[19] *above* see Shelley, "Death" (1824: 3–4): "All around, within, beneath. / Above is death."

[20] *mouth* see Genesis 2: 7.

[21] *thought* see Ecclesiastes 3: 1–8.

And night, and sleep in the night.   40
His speech is a burning fire;[22]
    With his lips he travaileth,
In his heart is a blind desire,
    In his eyes foreknowledge of death;
He weaves, and is clothed with derision;[23]   45
    Sows, and he shall not reap;[24]
His life is a watch or a vision
    Between a sleep and a sleep.

WEB p. 425

Hymn to Proserpine

The Leper[25]

Nothing is better, I well think,
    Than love; the hidden well-water
Is not so delicate to drink:
    This was well seen of me and her.

I served her in a royal house;   5
    I served her wine and curious meat.
For will to kiss between her brows
    I had no heart to sleep or eat.

Mere scorn God knows she had of me;
    A poor scribe, nowise great or fair,   10
Who plucked his clerk's hood back to see
    Her curled-up lips and amorous hair.

I vex my head with thinking this.
    Yea, though God always hated me,
And hates me now that I can kiss   15
    Her eyes, plait up her hair to see

Notes

[22] *fire* see Proverbs 16: 27; see also n. 17.

[23] *derision* see Ezekiel 7: 27 and 23: 32.

[24] *reap* see Matthew 6: 26.

[25] *title* like a number of other poems in Swinburne's 1866 volume, "The Leper" was also condemned as "foul stuff" that "no critics can speak worse of than" it deserves (*Spectator* 22 Sept. 1866) and concerning which "nothing can be more horribly impure, more utterly loathsome, than the story of the unclean priest and his leprous mistress" (*Athenæum*, 3 Nov. 1866). Swinburne claimed to have taken his date and place (see n. 29) from the *Annales et Chroniques de France* by Maistre Nicole Gilles, published with various dates (1533–49) and variations of title, in which is recorded the death of Philip IV, the Fair (1285–1314), *estant à Fontainebellant, en Gastinois* (as occurs at the end of his invented account). He also drew on *Amis and Amiloun* (late thirteenth-century English metrical romance) that he read in the second volume of Henry Weber's *Metrical Romances* (3 vols, 1810), which remained in his library at his death. From this story he drew specific details concerning the repudiation of lepers by family and friends, the care given to lepers, and the faithfulness of some towards lepers. First published in *Poems and Ballads* (1866); our text: 1866 (second edition).

How she then wore it on the brows,
    Yet am I glad to have her dead
Here in this wretched wattled house
    Where I can kiss her eyes and head.   20

Nothing is better, I well know,
    Than love; no amber in cold sea
Or gathered berries under snow:
    That is well seen of her and me.

Three thoughts I make my pleasure of: 25
    First I take heart and think of this:
That knight's gold hair she chose to love,
    His mouth she had such will to kiss.

Then I remember that sundawn
    I brought him by a privy way   30
Out at her lattice, and thereon
    What gracious words she found to say.

(Cold rushes for such little feet—
    Both feet could lie into my hand.
A marvel was it of my sweet   35
    Her upright body could so stand.)

"Sweet friend, God give you thank and grace;
    Now am I clean and whole of shame,
Nor shall men burn me in the face
    For my sweet fault that scandals them."   40

I tell you over word by word.
    She, sitting edgewise on her bed,
Holding her feet, said thus. The third,
    A sweeter thing than these, I said.

God, that makes time and ruins it,   45
    And alters not, abiding God,
Changed with disease her body sweet,
    The body of love wherein she abode.

Love is more sweet and comelier
    Than a dove's throat strained out to sing.   50
All they spat out and cursed at her[26]
    And cast her forth for a base thing.

Notes

[26] *cursed* in one of Swinburne's sources, *Amis and Amiloun,* the family of the leper-husband curses him and casts him out; he is subsequently cared for by the child Owaines (later called Amourant).

They cursed her, seeing how God had wrought
    This curse to plague her, a curse of his.
Fools were they surely, seeing not   55
    How sweeter than all sweet she is.

He that had held her by the hair,
    With kissing lips blinding her eyes,
Felt her bright bosom, strained and bare,
    Sigh under him, with short mad cries   60

Out of her throat and sobbing mouth
    And body broken up with love,
With sweet hot tears his lips were loth
    Her own should taste the savour of,

Yea, he inside whose grasp all night   65
    Her fervent body leapt or lay,
Stained with sharp kisses red and white,
    Found her a plague to spurn away.

I hid her in this wattled house,
    I served her water and poor bread.[27]   70
For joy to kiss between her brows
    Time upon time I was nigh dead.

Bread failed; we got but well-water
    And gathered grass with dropping seed.
I had such joy of kissing her,   75
    I had small care to sleep or feed.

Sometimes when service made me glad
    The sharp tears leapt between my lids,
Falling on her, such joy I had
    To do the service God forbids.   80

"I pray you let me be at peace,
    Get hence, make room for me to die."
She said that: her poor lip would cease,
    Put up to mine, and turn to cry.

I said, "Bethink yourself how love   85
    Fared in us twain, what either did;
Shall I unclothe my soul thereof?
    That I should do this, God forbid."

Notes

[27] *bread* see the Middle English romance, *Amis and Amiloun* (see n. 29): "And grete logge [lodging] he let make / Both of lym [lime, mortar] and stoon. / Thereyn was the lady ladde [led] / And with bred and water was she fed, / Tyl her lyvedays were goon" (2477–81).

Yea, though God hateth us, he knows
    That hardly in a little thing   90
Love faileth of the work it does
    Till it grow ripe for gathering.

Six months,[28] and now my sweet is dead
    A trouble takes me; I know not
If all were done well, all well said,   95
    No word or tender deed forgot.

Too sweet, for the least part in her,
    To have shed life out by fragments; yet,
Could the close mouth catch breath and stir,
    I might see something I forget.   100

Six months, and I sit still and hold
    In two cold palms her cold two feet.
Her hair, half grey half ruined gold,
    Thrills me and burns me in kissing it.

Love bites and stings me through, to see   105
    Her keen face made of sunken bones.
Her worn-off eyelids madden me,
    That were shot through with purple once.

She said, "Be good with me; I grow
    So tired for shame's sake, I shall die   110
If you say nothing": even so.
    And she is dead now, and shame put by.

Yea, and the scorn she had of me
    In the old time, doubtless vexed her then.
I never should have kissed her. See   115
    What fools God's anger makes of men!

She might have loved me a little too,
    Had I been humbler for her sake.
But that new shame could make love new
    She saw not—yet her shame did make.   120

I took too much upon my love,
    Having for such mean service done
Her beauty and all the ways thereof,
    Her face and all the sweet thereon.

Yea, all this while I tended her,   125
    I know the old love held fast his part:
I know the old scorn waxed heavier,
    Mixed with sad wonder, in her heart.

Notes

[28] *months* twelve months in *Amis and Amiloun*.

It may be all my love went wrong—
    A scribe's work writ awry and blurred,   130
Scrawled after the blind evensong—
    Spoilt music with no perfect word.

But surely I would fain have done
    All things the best I could. Perchance
Because I failed, came short of one,   135
    She kept at heart that other man's.

I am grown blind with all these things:
    It may be now she hath in sight
Some better knowledge; still there clings
    The old question. Will not God do right?[29]   140

Before the Mirror[30]

(VERSES WRITTEN UNDER A PICTURE)
INSCRIBED TO J. A. WHISTLER

I

White rose in red rose-garden
    Is not so white;
Snowdrops that plead for pardon
    And pine for fright
Because the hard East blows   5

Notes

[29] *right* En ce temps-là estoyt dans ce pays grand nombre de ladres et de meseaulx, ce dont le roy eut grand desplaisir, veu que Dieu dust en estre moult griefvement courroucé. Ores il advint qu'une noble damoyselle appelée Yolande de Sallières estant atteincte et touste guastée de ce vilain mal, tous ses amys et ses parens ayant devant leurs yeux la paour de Dieu la firent issir fors de leurs maisons et oncques ne voulurent recepvoir ni reconforter chose mauldicte de Dieu et à tous les hommes puante et abhominable. Ceste dame avoyt esté moult belle et gracieuse de formes, et de son corps elle estoyt large et de vie lascive. Pourtant nul des amans qui l'avoyent souventesfois accollée et baisée moult tendrement ne voulust plus héberger si laide femme et si détestable pescheresse. Ung seul clerc qui feut premièrement son lacquays et son entremetteur en matière d'amour la reçut chez luy et la récéla dans une petite cabane. Là mourut la meschinette de grande misère et de male mort: et après elle décéda ledist clerc qui pour grand amour l'avoyt six mois durant soignée, lavée, habillée et deshabillée tous les jours de ses mains propres. Mesme dist-on que ce meschant homme et mauldict clerc se remémourant de la grande beauté passée et guastée de ceste femme se délectoyt maintesfois à la baiser sur sa bouche orde et lépreuse et l'accoller doulcement de ses mains amoureuses. Aussy est-il mort de ceste mesme maladie abhominable. Cecy advint près Fontaine-bellant en Gastinois. Et quand ouyt le roy Philippe ceste adventure moult en estoyt esmerveillé. —*Grandes Chroniques de France*, 1505 [author's note].

Swinburne invented both the source and the text, in his own version of medieval French. It may be translated as follows: At that time, there was in this country a great number of unclean people and lepers because of which the king was greatly displeased, seeing that because of them God must be most grievously angered. Now it came to pass that a noble damsel called Yolande de Sallières was afflicted and totally wasted by this shameful disease; all her friends and her relatives, having before their eyes the fear of God, sent her forth from their houses, determining never to receive or comfort a thing so cursed of God, and to all men foul smelling and abominable. In former times, this lady had been most beautiful and gracious of form, and of her body she was generous and of her life, lascivious. However, none of those lovers who had oftentimes embraced her and kissed her most tenderly would give shelter to so repugnant a woman and so detestable a sinner. One clerk [cleric] alone who was formerly her servant and intermediary in affairs of love took her into his place and concealed her in a little hut. There the wretched woman died a terrible death in great misery. And after she

Over their maiden rows
    Grow not as this face grows from pale to bright.

Behind the veil,[31] forbidden,
    Shut up from sight,
Love, is there sorrow hidden,   10
    Is there delight?
Is joy thy dower or grief,
White rose of weary leaf,
    Late rose whose life is brief, whose loves are light?

Soft snows that hard winds harden   15
    Till each flake bite
Fill all the flowerless garden
    Whose flowers took flight
Long since when summer ceased,
And men rose up from feast,   20
    And warm west wind grew east, and warm day night.

II

"Come snow, come wind or thunder[32]
    High up in air,
I watch my face, and wonder
    At my bright hair;   25
Nought else exalts or grieves
The rose at heart, that heaves
    With love of her own leaves and lips that pair.

She knows not loves that kissed her
    She knows not where,   30
Art thou the ghost, my sister,
    White sister there,
Am I the ghost, who knows?
My hand, a fallen rose,
    Lies snow-white on white snows, and takes no care.   35

Notes

died, the aforementioned clerk died, who for the great love he bore for her, cared for her for six months, bathing her, dressing and undressing her every day with his own hands. They even say that this wicked man and accursed cleric, remembering the great beauty in past time of this wasted woman, often delighted himself by kissing her on her filthy and leprous mouth and embracing her tenderly with his loving hands. So he also died of this same abominable sickness. This came about near Fontainebellant in Gastinois. And when King Philippe heard of this event, he was greatly amazed by it.—*Great Chronicles of France*, 1505.

[30] *title* the painting by J. A. McNeill Whistler (1834–1903) was *Symphony in White, No. 2: The Little White Girl* (1864, Tate Gallery; see Plate 20). When the painting was exhibited at the summer exhibition of the RA in 1865, the fourth and sixth stanzas of Swinburne's poem were printed in the catalogue. The entire poem was printed on gold paper and was fastened to the frame at the Academy show. Whistler's title emphasizes his art-for-art's-sake philosophy (see PATER, n. 32; and LITERATURE: PRE-RAPHAELITISM; WHISTLER, "TEN O'CLOCK") that the elements of the composition were important, not the subject matter or any narrative content. Further, the title of the painting stressed the analogy with music, the synesthesia of using colours to invoke sound, and the interrelationships of painting, literature, and music. Swinburne exploits similar interrelationships through his melodic stanzas, colours and flowers, and the implied and stated rhetorical questions. First published on that occasion in 1865; reprinted in *Poems and Ballads* (1866). Our text: *Poems and Ballads* (1866, second edition).

[31] *veil* see TENNYSON, *IN MEMORIAM*, LVI. 28; see also Hebrews 6: 19.

I cannot see what pleasures
Or what pains were;
What pale new loves and treasures
New years will bear;
What beam will fall, what shower,   40
What grief or joy for dower;
But one thing knows the flower; the flower is fair."

III

Glad, but not flushed with gladness,
Since joys go by;
Sad, but not bent with sadness,   45
Since sorrows die;
Deep in the gleaming glass[33]
She sees all past things pass,
And all sweet life that was lie down and lie.

There glowing ghosts of flowers   50
Draw down, draw nigh;
And wings of swift spent hours
Take flight and fly;
She sees by formless gleams,
She hears across cold streams,   55
Dead mouths of many dreams that sing and sigh.

Face fallen and white throat lifted,
With sleepless eye
She sees old loves that drifted,
She knew not why,   60
Old loves and faded fears
Float down a stream that hears
The flowing of all men's tears beneath the sky.

WEB p. 429

The Higher Pantheism in a Nutshell

Nephelidia[34]

From the depth of the dreamy decline of the dawn through a notable nimbus of
nebulous noonshine,
Pallid and pink as the palm of the flag-flower[35] that flickers with fear of the flies as
they float,

Notes

[32] *thunder* see John Bunyan, "He who would valiant be, / Let
him come hither; / One here will constant be, / Come
wind, come weather" (original version in *The Pilgrim's
Progress* (1678).

[33] *glass* mirror.

[34] *title* a self-parody or amphigouri (meaningless or nonsen-
sical writing) of Swinburne's own style and a gathering
together of his themes (erotic love, time, death, night,
memory, necrophilia, blood, bosom, and malevolent God).
His chief rhetorical device is alliteration. The title word has

Are they looks of our lovers that lustrously lean from a marvel of mystic miraculous
    moonshine,
These that we feel in the blood of our blushes that thicken and threaten with
    throbs through the throat?
Thicken and thrill as a theatre thronged at appeal of an actor's appalled agitation,   5
Fainter with fear of the fires of the future than pale with the promise of pride in
    the past;
Flushed with the famishing fullness of fever that reddens with radiance of rathe[36]
    recreation,
Gaunt as the ghastliest of glimpses that gleam through the gloom of the gloaming
    when ghosts go aghast?
Nay, for the nick of the tick of the time is a tremulous touch on the temples of
    terror,
Strained as the sinews yet strenuous with strife of the dead who is dumb as the
    dust-heaps of death: 10
Surely no soul is it, sweet as the spasm of erotic emotional exquisite error,
Bathed in the balms of beatified bliss, beatific itself by beatitude's breath.
Surely no spirit or sense of a soul that was soft to the spirit and soul of
    our senses
Sweetens the stress of suspiring suspicion that sobs in the semblance and sound
    of a sigh;
Only this oracle opens Olympian, in mystical moods and triangular tenses—   15
"Life is the lust of a lamp for the light that is dark till the dawn of the day when
    we die."
Mild is the mirk and monotonous music of memory, melodiously mute as
    it may be,
While the hope in the heart of a hero is bruised by the breach of men's rapiers,
    resigned to the rod;
Made meek as a mother whose bosom-beats bound with the bliss-bringing bulk
    of a balm-breathing baby,
As they grope through the grave-yard of creeds, under skies growing green
    at a groan for the grimness of God.   20
Blank is the book of his bounty beholden of old, and its binding is blacker
    than bluer:
Out of blue into black is the scheme of the skies, and their dews are the wine
    of the bloodshed of things;
Till the darkling desire of delight shall be free as a fawn that is freed from the
    fangs that pursue her,
Till the heart-beats of hell shall be hushed by a hymn from the hunt that has
    harried the kennel of kings.

Notes

a Greek root *nephelo* (concerning clouds); hence, little clouds or cloud study, with perhaps a reference to "Of Truth of Clouds" in Ruskin's *Modern Painters* (1846). See also Aristophanes, *The Clouds* (Gk. *Nephelai*, 423 BCE), perhaps alluding to Socrates' speeches in the play concerning cloud-thought (263–66) and the responses of the Chorus of Clouds throughout, and especially in their comments on

moonshine (584–626). For another parody of Swinburne, see HILTON, "OCTOPUS." For an example of his parody of Tennyson, see SWINBURNE, "HIGHER PANTHEISM" (WEB p. 429). From *Specimens of Modern Poets: Heptalogia, or the Seven Against Sense. A Cap with Seven Bells* (1880); our text.
[35] *flag-flower* iris.
[36] *rathe* fervent, rapid.

From "A Sequence of Sonnets on the Death of Robert Browning"[37]

I

The clearest eyes in all the world they read
    With sense more keen and spirit of sight more true
    Than burns and thrills in sunrise, when the dew
Flames, and absorbs the glory round it shed,
As they the light of ages quick and dead,
    Closed now, forsake us: yet the shaft that slew
    Can slay not one of all the works we knew,
Nor death discrown that many-laurelled head.

The works of words whose life seems lightning wrought,
And moulded of unconquerable thought,
    And quickened with imperishable flame,
Stand fast and shine and smile, assured that nought
    May fade of all their myriad-moulded fame,
    Nor England's memory clasp not Browning's name.

Dec. 12th 1889

Walter Horatio Pater (1839–94)

Born in Stepney in East London to a physician, Richard Glode Pater (1797?–1842), and Maria Hill (1803–54), the third of four children, Pater and his family moved around London several times. Eventually Pater attended Enfield Grammar School for one year before moving to Kent and attending King's School, Canterbury (1853–58). He studied classics at Queen's College, Oxford (1858–62), where one of his tutors was the noted Platonist and religious radical, Benjamin Jowett; thereafter he became a tutor (1863) and a non-clerical fellow in classics (1864–83) of Brasenose College, Oxford. In January 1864 Pater broke with conventional Christianity (though he seems to have returned to it in his later years) in his *Westminster Review* essay on Coleridge and developed an interest in male friendship, modelled to some degree on his studies of ancient Greek culture, as evidenced in his essay on the eighteenth-century classicist Johann Joachin Winckelmann (1717–68). He exploited coded homoerotic and homosocial analyses of other times and cultures in subsequent essays. Gerard Manley Hopkins was a student of his, and friends included Mark (1813–84) and Emilia (1840–1904) Pattison and the Platonist Ingram Bywater (1840–1914). In 1865 he travelled to Italy for the first time, with his student Charles Shadwell (1840–1919), the first of a number of visits, and later

Notes

37 *title* Browning died in Venice on 12 December 1889. From his undergraduate days when he had memorized long passages of *Sordello* and *Paracelsus*, Swinburne had greatly admired Browning. Despite Swinburne's brilliant parody of him in "John Jones" (see Swinburne, n. 35 (WEB p. 429), the two remained good friends. The complete sequence of seven sonnets was published in the *Fortnightly Review* (Jan. 1890).

lived in Rome in 1882–83. He began to publish widely in periodicals such as the *Westminster* and the *Fortnightly*, gathering the essays so published together, re-editing them, and assembling them in a published volume – a practice first attempted with remarkable success in *Studies in the History of the Renaissance* (1873). In the "Preface" Pater changed Matthew Arnold's stress on the perception of the object to the perceiver's perception of himself, and in the "Conclusion," in the famous phrase, claimed that success in life was to burn with "a hard, gem-like flame." Pater freed the Renaissance as a period from its chronological tardiness in the sixteenth century to turn it into a synchronic and transhistorical moment in many cultures, including his own. As an aesthete, he developed an interest in the Pre-Raphaelites, including a friendship with Swinburne from 1869. Pater developed the genre of the "imaginary portrait" from the biographies in *The Renaissance*, using such figures to interrogate and epitomize their age, continued with the more fictionalized study, "The Child in the House" (*Macmillan's*

Magazine, 1878). In 1885 he published the first of his novels, *Marius the Epicurean* (2 vols, 1885), and the second, unfinished, *Gaston de Latour*, with six chapters was published in 1888–89. Further works included *Imaginary Portraits* (1887), *Appreciations* (1889), *Plato and Platonism* (1893), and others after his death: *Greek Studies* and *Miscellaneous Studies*, both edited in 1895 by his executor, Shadwell, and three more collections followed. He lived with his sisters in Oxford and then later in London (1885–93), returning to Oxford for his last year, 1893–94, where he died of a heart attack. Standard editions: *New Library Edition of the Works of Walter Pater* (10 vols, 1910); *Studies in the History of the Renaissance* [1873]. ed. Matthew Beaumont (2010); *The Renaissance: Studies in Art and Poetry: The 1893 Text*, ed. Donald L. Hill (1980); *Letters of Walter Pater*, ed. Lawrence Evans (1970); Thomas Wright, *The Life of Walter Pater* (2 vols, 1907); Michael Levey, *The Case of Walter Pater* (1978). Pater Newsletter: paternewsletter.org.

Studies in the History of the Renaissance[1]

Walter Pater's *Studies in the History of the Renaissance* (1873; our text) has a complicated publishing history. It was revised as *The Renaissance: Studies in Art and Poetry* (1877, 1888, 1891). Of the eight essays in the first edition, five had already been published in the *Fortnightly Review* and the *Westminster Review*.

The first edition had a "Preface" and a "Conclusion" (for details, see n. 18). The "Conclusion" was omitted from the second edition (1877) but was restored in the third (1888) and subsequent editions. To give another example, "The School of Giorgione" was sent to the publishers but was withdrawn by Pater for

Notes

WALTER HORATIO PATER

[1] *title* in her review of Pater in the *Westminster Review* (Apr. 1873), Francis Pattison (author of *The Renaissance of Art in France*, 2 vols, 1879) challenged Pater's title as "misleading": "Instead of approaching his subject, whether in Art or Literature, by the true scientific method, through the life of the time of which it was an outcome, Mr. Pater prefers in each instance to detach it wholly from its surroundings, to suspend it isolated before him. . . . Mr. Pater writes of the Renaissance as if it were a kind of sentimental revolution having no relation to the conditions of the actual world. . . . He can detect with singular subtlety the shades of tremulous variation which have been embodied in throbbing

pulsations of colour, in doubtful turns of line, in veiled words; he can not only do this, but he can match them for us in words, in the choice of which he is often so brilliantly accurate that they gleam upon the paper with the radiance of jewels. In this respect these studies of the Renaissance have a real critical value. But they are not history." Perhaps it was in the light of such trenchant comment that Pater changed his title for all subsequent editions to *The Renaissance: Studies in Art and Poetry*. It was the original edition, however, that Oscar Wilde read in his first term at Oxford in 1874: "Mr. Pater's essays became to me 'the golden book of spirit and sense, the holy writ of beauty.' They are still this to me."

further revisions (printed in the *Fortnightly Review*, Oct. 1877, and in the 1888 edition after "Leonardo da Vinci"). The volume was dedicated to Charles Lancelot Shadwell; the title page carried an engraved illustration of a young man from the school of Leonardo in the Louvre.

In the first essay, "Aucassin and Nicolette," Pater defines his period: "The word *Renaissance* indeed is now generally used to denote not merely that revival of classical antiquity which took place in the fifteenth century, and to which the word was first applied, but a whole complex movement, of which that revival of classical antiquity was but one element or symptom." Although the French art historian Seroux d'Agincourt (1730–1814) is credited with first using "Renaissance" in *Histoire de l'art* (Fr. 6 vols, 1823; Eng. 1847) to signal a break between the medieval and the modern, it was the French historian Jules Michelet (1798–1874) who had invented the word as an application to a specific historical period (the fifteenth century in France) in a positive sense in his seventh volume (1855) of the *History of France*. He was imitating the Italian *rinascita* used in the fourteenth century to refer to the revival of classical learning, and by Giorgio Vasari in *Lives of the Painters* (1550) to refer to the revival of the visual arts in Italy in the fourteenth and fifteenth centuries.

This usage went against the tradition that disparaged such revivals as marking social, cultural, and artistic decline, as in Victor Hugo's *Notre-Dame de Paris* (1831), in which the printing press replaces the cathedral as social memory:

> *The Book will kill the Edifice.* The invention of printing is the greatest event in history. It is the mother of all revolutions.... Thus we see that, starting from the discovery of printing, architecture has gradually become withered, atrophied, and denuded.... In the fifteenth century the press is still too weak, and can do no more than draw away from powerful architecture a superabundance of life.

But, from the sixteenth century the sickness of architecture is visible; it is not any more the essential expression of society.... This is the decadence that we call the Renaissance. (ch. 2)

A second attack came from Alexis-François Rio (1797–1874) in his *De la poésie chrétienne* (1836) and *De l'art chrétien* (1851), published together in London as *History of Christian Art* (1854), in which he praises the work of Giotto (1266–1337) as the end of great art and the patronage and art done in Florence under the Medici in the fifteenth century as the coming of decadence. Third, came the attack on the Renaissance by John Ruskin, who had read Rio in 1843, and who alone amongst the art historians found the moment of the Renaissance and its decay in Venice – in 1418 (see RUSKIN, STONES, headnote). In Rome Ruskin dated the decline of culture to Raphael's painting of *The School of Athens* in 1509 (*Architecture and Painting*, 1854).

On the other hand, the collecting practice of the National Gallery in London made it a policy to fill in gaps with the Renaissance old masters. Furthermore, an important series of studies of the Renaissance was published, pre-eminent amongst which was first guidebook by Jacob Burckhardt (1818–97), *Cicerone* (1855), followed by his *Culture of the Renaissance in Italy* (1860), though it had at first a small circulation and was not translated from German into English until 1878. But in the literature of the 1850s and 1860s the Renaissance was a popular theme: Robert Browning had published a number of poems on Renaissance subjects from 1849 to 1869; Charles Reade published his fifteenth-century story of religious upheavals in early modern Europe in *The Cloister and the Hearth* (1861), and George Eliot wrote of late fifteenth-century Florence in *Romola* (1863). The Pre-Raphaelite painters and poets were modelling their work on the artists and writers before Raphael (1483–1520), and John Addington Symonds (1840–93) was preparing to write his seven-volume *The Renaissance in Italy* (1875–86), a cultural history for English readers.

Pater continued with his definition of the Renaissance in "Aucassin and Nicolette" by shifting the weight of historical definition to contemporary application: "

> For us, the Renaissance is the name of a many-sided but yet united movement, in which the love of the things of the intellect and the imagination for their own sake, the desire for a more liberal and comely way of conceiving life, make themselves felt, prompting those who experience this desire to seek first one and then another means of intellectual or imaginative enjoyment, and directing them not merely to the discovery of old and forgotten sources of this enjoyment, but to divine new sources of it, new experiences, new subjects of poetry, new forms of art.

Pater was not concerned with the date when Venice fell, as is Ruskin, nor with its historiographical periodization, but with specific "moments" – in Pico (1463–94) or Botticelli (1445–1510), or Leonardo (1452–1519) – in which these past moments can be read as representing a present experience for a modern viewer/reader. The affective and reiterated words whereby Pater configures the Renaissance in this definition are important: love, desire (twice), liberal, comeliness, life, feeling, experience (twice), enjoyment, discovery, not-forgetfulness, sources (twice), and newness (four times) – all of them suggesting the renewal that was already a hallmark of the Renaissance but doing so as a sign of individualistic romanticism, revelling in the self, already engaged in the experience of itself in the moment of perception.

Preface[2]

Many attempts have been made by writers on art and poetry to define beauty in the abstract, to express it in the most general terms, to find a universal formula for it.[3] The value of these attempts has most often been in the suggestive and penetrating things said by the way. Such discussions help us very little to enjoy what has been well done in art or poetry, to discriminate between what is more and what is less excellent in them, or to use words like beauty, excellence, art, poetry, with a more meaning than they would otherwise have. Beauty, like all other qualities presented to human experience, is relative;[4] and the definition of it becomes unmeaning and useless in proportion to its abstractness. To define beauty not in the most abstract, but in the most concrete terms possible, not to find a universal formula for it, but the formula which expresses most adequately this or that special manifestation of it, is the aim of the true student of æsthetics.

Notes

[2] *Preface* Pater's assertion of the place of condensed impressions in the perception of beauty and the function of the aesthetic critic challenge the dominant views of the time, represented first by Ruskin's notion of the emotional response to art as presenting the greatest number of ideas, and of the moral qualities of art (such as sacrifice, power, truth, beauty, life, memory, and obedience in *Seven Lamps of Architecture*, 1849); and second, by Matthew Arnold's tradition of the best that can be known and thought in the world (see ARNOLD, (WEB p. 384)).

[3] *it* see RUSKIN, n. 1 (WEB p. 361).

[4] *relative* against Ruskin's notion of beauty as a moral virtue and as an absolute that is a typological manifestation of God, Pater argues that Coleridge's struggle to apprehend the absolute was "against the relative spirit" as a mark of modern thought, and that all knowledge is relative because

it is perceived under qualifying and changing conditions: "Modern thought is distinguished from ancient by its cultivation of the 'relative' spirit in place of the 'absolute.' ... To the modern spirit nothing is, or can be rightly known, except relatively and under conditions. The philosophical conception of the relative has been developed in modern times through the influence of the sciences of observation. Those sciences reveal types of life evanescing into each other by inexpressible refinements of change. Things pass into their opposites by accumulation of undefinable quantities.... The faculty for truth is recognised as a power of distinguishing and fixing delicate and fugitive detail. The moral world is ever in contact with the physical, and the relative spirit has invaded moral philosophy from the ground of the inductive sciences." ("Coleridge," *Westminster Review* Jan. 1866).

"To see the object as in itself it really is,"[5] has been justly said to be the aim of all true criticism whatever; and in æsthetic criticism the first step towards seeing one's object as it really is, is to know one's own impression as it really is, to discriminate it, to realise it distinctly. The objects with which æsthetic criticism deals, music, poetry, artistic and accomplished forms of human life, are indeed receptacles of so many powers or forces; they possess, like natural elements, so many virtues or qualities. What is this song or picture, this engaging personality presented in life or in a book, to *me*? What effect does it really produce on me? Does it give me pleasure? and if so, what sort or degree of pleasure? How is my nature modified by its presence and under its influence? The answers to these questions are the original facts with which the æsthetic critic has to do; and, as in the study of light, of morals, of number, one must realise such primary data for oneself or not at all. And he who experiences these impressions strongly, and drives directly at the discrimination of them, need not trouble himself with the abstract question what beauty is in itself, or its exact relation to truth or experience,—metaphysical questions, as unprofitable as metaphysical questions elsewhere. He may pass them all by as being, answerable or not, of no interest to him.

The æsthetic critic, then, regards all the objects with which he has to do, all works of art and the fairer forms of nature and human life, as powers or forces, producing pleasurable sensations, each of a more or less peculiar and unique kind. This influence he feels, and wishes to explain, analysing it and reducing it to its elements. To him, the picture, the landscape, the engaging personality in life or in a book, La Gioconda, the hills of Carrara, Pico of Mirandula,[6] are valuable for their virtues, as we say in speaking of a herb, a wine, a gem; for the property each has of affecting one with a special, unique impression of pleasure. Education grows in proportion as one's susceptibility to these impressions increases in depth and variety. And the function of the æsthetic critic is to distinguish, analyse, and separate from its adjuncts, the virtue by which a picture, a landscape, a fair personality in life or in a book, produces this special impression of beauty or pleasure, to indicate what the source of that impression is, and under what conditions it is experienced. His end is reached when he has disengaged that virtue, and noted it, as a chemist notes some natural element, for himself and others; and the rule for those who would reach this end is stated with great exactness in the words of a recent critic of Sainte-Beuve: "De se borner à connaître de près les belles choses, et à s'en nourrir en exquis amateurs, en humanistes accomplis."[7]

Notes

[5] is a citation from Matthew Arnold's *On Translating Homer* (1861): "Of the literature of France and Germany, as of the intellect of Europe in general, the main effort, for now many years, has been a critical effort; the endeavour … to see the object as in itself it really is"; this entire passage was repeated in the opening paragraph of "The Function of Criticism at the Present Time" (see ARNOLD, n. 12 (WEB p. 385)). Pater then uses an Oxford common-room rhetorical trick of saying the opposite by using metonymy as one set of words substitutes for another. He both undermines and extends Arnold's position by shifting "criticism" to "æsthetic criticism" and moving from "object" in an external world to "impression" in a subjective observer. "Æsthetic" in Pater carries the meaning of its Greek root (Gk. *aisthetikos* sensitive, sensing, perceiving > *aisthetes* the one who perceives < *aisthanomai* I perceive); hence this meaning bears on the remarks on Coleridge (see n. 4). Pater suggests in the next paragraph that aesthetic criticism is modern criticism, just as aesthetic poetry is modern poetry.

[6] *Gioconda … Mirandula* La Gioconda is the name given to Leonardo's *Mona Lisa* (1506); Carrara, a city north-west of Florence, is the site of the major marble quarries for the sculptors of the Renaissance. Giovanni Pico (1463–94) of Mirandola ("Mirandula," changed in later editions to "Mirandola") was an Italian Neoplatonist philosopher, and author of *Oration on the Dignity of Man* (1486). All are discussed later in *The Renaissance*.

[7] *critic … accomplis* "critic" is used in the sense of "critique" or criticism by Sainte-Beuve. The French citation (Fr. to restrict oneself to knowing beautiful things intimately and to nourish oneself on these things, as discriminating amateurs and accomplished humanists do) is from a review of the writings of Joachim du Bellay by Charles Augustin Sainte-Beuve (1804–69), French literary critic, in *Nouveaux lundis* (vol. 13, 1873). Sainte-Beuve comments on what it was to be part of a literary circle in the Renaissance. Du Bellay (1522–60) was a French poet and critic, the subject of the seventh essay in Pater's *Renaissance*. He was the joint author of the manifesto of the *Pléiade*, a literary group, *The Defense and Illustration of the French Language* (1549), and a sonnet sequence, *L'Olive* (1549).

What is important, then, is not that the critic should possess a correct abstract defini-tion of beauty for the intellect, but a certain kind of temperament, the power of being deeply moved by the presence of beautiful objects. He will remember always that beauty exists in many forms. To him all periods, types, schools of taste, are in themselves equal. In all ages there have been some excellent workmen and some excellent work done. The question he asks is always, In whom did the stir, the genius, the sentiment of the period find itself? who was the receptacle of its refinement, its elevation, its taste? "The ages are all equal," says William Blake, "but genius is always above its age."[8]

Often it will require great nicety to disengage this virtue from the commoner elements with which it may be found in combination. Few artists, not Goethe or Byron even,[9] work quite cleanly, casting off all debris, and leaving us only what the heat of their imagination has wholly fused and transformed. Take for instance the writings of Wordsworth. The heat of his genius, entering into the substance of his work, has crystallised a part, but only a part, of it; and in that great mass of verse there is much which might well be forgotten. But scattered up and down it, sometimes fusing and transforming entire compositions, like the Stanzas on "Resolution and Independence" and the Ode on the "Recollections of Childhood,"[10] sometimes, as if at random, turning a fine crystal here and there, in a mat-ter it does not wholly search through and transform, we trace the action of his unique incommunicable faculty, that strange mystical sense of a life in natural things, and of man's life as a part of nature, drawing strength and colour and character from local influ-ences, from the hills and streams and from natural sights and sounds. Well! that is the *virtue*, the active principle in Wordsworth's poetry; and then the function of the critic of Wordsworth[11] is to trace that active principle, to disengage it, to mark the degree in which it penetrates his verse.

The subjects of the following studies are taken from the history of the Renaissance, and touch what I think the chief points in that complex, many-sided movement. I have explained in the first of them[12] what I understand by the word, giving it a much wider scope than was intended by those who originally used it to denote only that revival of classical antiquity in the fifteenth century which was but one of many results of a general stimulus and enlightening of the human mind, of which the great aim and achievements of what, as Christian art, is often falsely opposed to the Renaissance, were another result. This outbreak of the human spirit may be traced far into the middle age itself, with its qualities already clearly pronounced, the care for physical beauty, the worship of the body, the breaking down of those limits which the religious system of the middle age imposed on the heart and the imagination.[13] I have taken as an example of this movement,

Notes

[8] *periods ... age* in this paragraph Pater stresses temperament rather than taste or intellect, a sympathetic consciousness on the part of the aesthetic critic that can trace the mental life rather than the external world or personal detail of his Renaissance gallery. Further, in rejecting his contemporaries' interest in determining historical periods and applying a categorical value scale, "all periods ... are in themselves equal." The citation from William Blake is one of his annotations to *The Works of Joshua Reynolds* (vol. 1, 1798); cited in Alexander Gilchrist's *Life of William Blake* (vol. 1, 1863) that Dante Rossetti had helped Mrs Gilchrist bring to publication.

[9] *even* Johann Wolfgang von Goethe (1749–1832) German philosopher, playwright, and novelist of the Enlightenment and Romantic eras; Lord Byron (1788–1824), English Romantic poet.

[10] *Resolution ... Childhood* see Wordsworth's "Resolution and Independence" (1807) and "Ode: Intimations of Immortality from Recollections of Early Childhood" (1807).

[11] *Wordsworth* Pater's essay "Wordsworth" was printed in the *Fortnightly Review* (Apr. 1874); reprinted in *Appreciations* (1889).

[12] *them* Pater outlines his chapters, first mentioning "Aucassin et Nicolette," a late twelfth-century French romance in prose and verse.

[13] *imagination* a phrase of Matthew Arnold's to describe medieval religious sentiment from his Oxford lecture, "Pagan and Christian Religious Sentiment" (*Cornhill Magazine* Apr. 1864), reprinted as "Pagan and Mediaeval Religious Sentiment." Arnold contrasts it unfavourably with what he calls "Hellenism" in *Culture and Anarchy*, for "its appeal to the senses and the understanding." Again Pater qualifies Arnold's contrast.

this earlier Renaissance within the middle age itself, and as an expression of its qualities, a little composition in early French; not because it is the best possible expression of them, but because it helps the unity of my series, inasmuch as the Renaissance ends also in France, in French poetry, in a phase of which the writings of Joachim du Bellay[14] are in many ways the most perfect illustration; the Renaissance thus putting forth in France an aftermath, a wonderful later growth, the products of which have to the full the subtle and delicate sweetness which belong to a refined and comely decadence; just as its earliest phases have the freshness which belongs to all periods of growth in art, the charm of *ascesis*,[15] of the austere and serious girding of the loins in youth.

But it is in Italy, in the fifteenth century, that the interest of the Renaissance mainly lies, in that solemn fifteenth century which can hardly be studied too much, not merely for its positive results in the things of the intellect and the imagination, its concrete works of art, its special and prominent personalities, with their profound æsthetic charm, but for its general spirit and character, for the ethical qualities of which it is a consummate type.

The various forms of intellectual activity which together make up the culture of an age, move for the most part from different starting points and by unconnected roads. As products of the same generation they partake indeed of a common character and unconsciously illustrate each other; but of the producers themselves, each group is solitary, gaining what advantage or disadvantage there may be in intellectual isolation. Art and poetry, philosophy and the religious life, and that other life of refined pleasure and action in the open places of the world, are each of them confined to its own circle of ideas, and those who prosecute either of them are generally little curious of the thoughts of others. There come however from time to time eras of more favourable conditions, in which the thoughts of men draw nearer together than is their wont, and the many interests of the intellectual world combine in one complete type of general culture. The fifteenth century in Italy is one of these happier eras; and what is sometimes said of the age of Pericles is true of that of Lorenzo[16] —it is an age productive in personalities, many-sided, centralised, complete. Here, artists and philosophers and those whom the action of the world has elevated and made keen, do not live in isolation, but breathe a common air and catch light and heat from each other's thoughts. There is a spirit of general elevation and enlightenment in which all alike communicate. It is the unity of this spirit which gives unity to all the various products of the Renaissance, and it is to this intimate alliance with mind, this participation in the best thoughts which that age produced, that the art of Italy in the fifteenth century owes much of its grave dignity and influence.

I have added an essay on Winckelmann,[17] as not incongruous with the studies which precede it, because Winckelmann, coming in the eighteenth century, really belongs in spirit to an earlier age. By his enthusiasm for the things of the intellect and the imagination for their own sake, by his Hellenism, his life-long struggle to attain to the Greek spirit, he is in sympathy with the humanists of an earlier century. He is the last fruit of the Renaissance, and explains in a striking way its motive and tendencies.

Notes

[14] *du Bellay* see n. 6.

[15] *ascesis* (Gk. exercise): the training of the body and mind of Greek athletes, and later applied to the spiritual and physical discipline (that is, asceticism) of the desert saints and hermits. In his essay "Style" (1888) Pater defines it as "self-restraint, a skilful economy of means … that too has a beauty of its own." Hence *ascesis* is not sublimation, but self-curtailment, a concept central to Epicureanism. Pico (see n. 6) is seeking a kind of Lucretian vision of truth in appearances, of mind as a flow of sensory patterns, and moral good as directly related to pleasurable sensations.

[16] *Pericles … Lorenzo* Pericles (c.495–29 BCE) was an Athenian statesman at the time of the Golden Age of Greece, of which he was an eminent patron; Lorenzo de' Medici (1449–1492), called "Lorenzo the Magnificent," was a statesman and patron of Florentine art.

[17] *Winckelmann* Johann Joachim Winckelmann (1717–68), German archaeologist and the author of *History of Ancient Art* (1764), is the subject of the eighth and last of Pater's essays in *The Renaissance*.

> **WEB p. 430**
>
> From "Leonardo da Vinci"
> From "The School of Giorgione"

Conclusion[18]

Λέγει που Ἡράκλειτςο ὅτι πάντα χωρεῖ καὶ οὐδὲν μένει[19]

To regard all things and principles of things as inconstant modes or fashions has more and more become the tendency of modern thought.[20] Let us begin with that which is without—our physical life. Fix upon it in one of its more exquisite intervals, the moment,[21] for instance, of delicious recoil from the flood of water in summer heat. What is the whole physical life in that moment but a combination of natural elements to which science gives their names? But these elements, phosphorus and lime and delicate fibres, are present not in the human body alone: we detect them in places most remote from it. Our physical life is a perpetual motion of them—the passage of the blood, the wasting and repairing of the lenses of the eye, the modification of the tissues of the brain by every ray of light and sound—processes which science reduces to simpler and more elementary forces. Like the elements of which we are composed, the action of these forces extends beyond us; it rusts iron and ripens corn. Far out on every side of us these elements are broadcast, driven by many forces; and birth and gesture and death and the springing of violets from the grave[22] are but a few out of ten thousand resultant combinations. That clear perpetual outline of face and limb is but an image of ours under which we group

Notes

[18] *title* first published as the last one-quarter of an unsigned review (six of the final seven paragraphs) of the poems of William Morris (*The Defense of Guenevere*, 1858; *The Life and Death of Jason*, 1867; and *The Earthly Paradise* (1868–70) in the *Westminster Review* (Oct. 1868). In the third edition (1888), when Pater restored the "Conclusion" omitted from the second edition (1877), he added the following note: "This brief 'Conclusion' was omitted in the second edition of this book, as I conceived it might possibly mislead some of those young men into whose hands it might fall. On the whole, I have thought it best to reprint it here, with some slight changes which bring it closer to my original meaning. I have dealt more fully in *Marius the Epicurean* with the thoughts suggested by it." See also Pater's novel, *Marius the Epicurean* (1885). The first part of the review of Morris's poems was later reprinted by Pater as "Æsthetic Poetry" in Pater's *Appreciations* (1889), but it was omitted from the 1890 and later editions. See LITERATURE: PRE-RAPHAELITISM; PATER, "POEMS OF WILLIAM MORRIS."

[19] *μένει* (Gk. "Heracleitus is supposed to say that all things are in motion and nothing at rest"; trans. Benjamin Jowett). The epigraph is a citation from Plato's *Cratylus* (402A) of about 360 BCE; Heracleitus was a Greek philosopher (c.500 BCE). This quotation was not included in the review of Morris's poems.

[20] *thought* for "modern thought" see n. 4.

[21] *moment* Pater's concept of the moment is drawn from the phenomenalism of David Hume (1711–76) and John Stuart Mill (1806–73). To Hume the self is a bundle of sensations or impressions and objects are collections of properties or relations: the mind, then, is a collection of impressions united or joined by specific relations between these impressions. Substances, accordingly, are relations between such ideas known by the mind by frequent associations. To Mill, the "permanent possibility of sensations" makes these impressions of substances continue to exist. So in Pater, the capturing of the impression or sensation is of the utmost importance, since it is fleeting almost before it is. Pater had been reading Johann Gottlieb Fichte's *Die Bestimmung des Menschen* (Ger. *The Vocation of Man*, 2 vols, 1800: trans. William Smith, 1848–49): "Nature pursues her course of ceaseless change, and while I yet speak of the moment which I sought to detain before me it is gone, and all is changed; and in like manner, before I had fixed my observation upon it, all was otherwise." Yet the coming of an impression in a moment may be multiplied and their impact may be made more vivid by perceiving them with passion, with heightened sensations. Finally, the perception of the impression or sensation is an insight into moral knowledge because it conveys a unified personality. Two important concepts of the moment, James Joyce's "epiphany" and Virginia Woolf's "moments of being," can be traced back to this notion of Pater.

[22] *grave* see *Hamlet* 5. 1. 232–4.

them—a design in a web, the actual threads of which pass out beyond it. This at least of flame-like our life has, that it is but the concurrence, renewed from moment to moment, of forces parting sooner or later on their ways.

Or if we begin with the inward world of thought and feeling, the whirlpool is still more rapid, the flame more eager and devouring. There it is no longer the gradual darkening of the eye and fading of colour from the wall,—the movement of the shore-side, where the water flows down indeed, though in apparent rest,—but the race of the mid-stream, a drift of momentary acts of sight and passion and thought. At first sight experience seems to bury us under a flood of external objects, pressing upon us with a sharp importunate reality, calling us out of ourselves in a thousand forms of action. But when reflexion begins to act upon those objects they are dissipated under its influence; the cohesive force is suspended like a trick of magic; each object is loosed into a group of impressions,— colour, odour, texture,—in the mind of the observer. And if we continue to dwell on this world, not of objects in the solidity with which language invests them, but of impressions unstable, flickering, inconsistent, which burn and are extinguished with our consciousness of them, it contracts still further; the whole scope of observation is dwarfed to the narrow chamber of the individual mind. Experience, already reduced to a swarm of impressions, is ringed round for each one of us by that thick wall of personality through which no real voice has ever pierced on its way to us, or from us to that which we can only conjecture to be without. Every one of those impressions is the impression of the individual in his isolation, each mind keeping as a solitary prisoner its own dream of a world.

Analysis goes a step further still, and tells us that those impressions of the individual to which, for each one of us, experience dwindles down, are in perpetual flight; that each of them is limited by time, and that as time is infinitely divisible,[23] each of them is infinitely divisible also; all that is actual in it being a single moment, gone while we try to apprehend it, of which it may ever be more truly said that it has ceased to be than that it is. To such a tremulous wisp constantly reforming itself on the stream, to a single sharp impression, with a sense in it, a relic more or less fleeting, of such moments gone by, what is *real* in our life fines itself down. It is with the movement, the passage and dissolution of impressions, images, sensations, that analysis leaves off,—that continual vanishing away, that strange perpetual weaving and unweaving of ourselves.

Philosophiren, says Novalis, *ist dephlegmatisiren, vivificiren*.[24] The service of philosophy, and of religion and culture as well, to the human spirit, is to startle it into a sharp and eager observation. Every moment some form grows perfect in hand or face; some tone on the hills or sea is choicer than the rest; some mood of passion or insight or intellectual excitement is irresistibly real and attractive for us,—for that moment only. Not the fruit of experience, but experience itself is the end. A counted number of pulses only is given to us of a variegated dramatic life. How may we see in them all that is to be seen in them by the finest senses? How shall we pass most swiftly from point to point, and be present always at the focus where the greatest number of vital forces unite in their purest energy?

To burn always with this hard gem-like flame,[25] to maintain this ecstasy, is success in life. Failure is to form habits; for habit is relative to a stereo-typed world; meantime it is

Notes

[23] *divisible* Hume in *A Treatise of Human Nature* (1739) devoted two chapters to "Of the Infinite Divisibility of Our Ideas of Space and Time" and "Of the Infinite Divisibility of Space and Time" (bk. 1, pt. 2, sect. 1 and 2). Both chapters set out to show that time was not infinitely divisible; its indivisibility of moment-by-moment alone allows progression.

[24] *Philosophiren ... vivificiren* (Ger. to philosophize is to cast off apathy, to come to life); from *Fragment 15* (1798).

Novalis was the pseudonym of the German poet and novelist Friedrich von Hardenberg (1772–1801).

[25] *flame* a recent critic, Billie Andrew Inman, has proposed that this metaphor for intense life could have been suggested by John Tyndall's article "On the Relations of Heat to Chemical Constitution, Colour, Texture" (*Fortnightly Review*, Feb. 1866). Such passages as the following outline Tyndall's experiment: "The oxyhydrogen flame ... is scarcely visible in the air of this room, and it

only the roughness of the eye that makes any two persons, things, situations, seem alike. While all melts under our feet, we may well catch at any exquisite passion, or any contribution to knowledge that seems, by a lifted horizon, to set the spirit free for a moment, or any stirring of the senses, strange dyes, strange flowers, and curious odours, or work of the artist's hands, or the face of one's friend. Not to discriminate every moment some passionate attitude in those about us, and in the brilliance of their gifts some tragic dividing of forces on their ways is, on this short day of frost and sun, to sleep before evening. With this sense of the splendour of our experience and of its awful brevity, gathering all we are into one desperate effort to see and touch, we shall hardly have time to make theories about the things we see and touch. What we have to do is to be for ever curiously testing new opinions and courting new impressions, never acquiescing in a facile orthodoxy of Comte or of Hegel,[26] or of our own. Theories, religious or philosophical ideas, as points of view, instruments of criticism, may help us to gather up what might otherwise pass unregarded by us. *La Philosophie, c'est la microscope de la pensée.*[27] The theory, or idea, or system, which requires of us the sacrifice of any part of this experience, in consideration of some interest into which we cannot enter, or some abstract morality we have not identified with ourselves, or what is only conventional, has no real claim upon us.

One of the most beautiful places in the writings of Rousseau is that in the sixth book of the "Confessions,"[28] where he describes the awakening in him of the literary sense. An undefinable taint of death had always clung about him, and now in early manhood he believed himself stricken by mortal disease. He asked himself how he might make as much as possible of the interval that remained; and he was not biassed by anything in his previous life when he decided that it must be by intellectual excitement, which he found in the clear, fresh writings of Voltaire. Well, we are all *condamnés*, as Victor Hugo says: *les hommes sont tous condamnés à mort avec des sursis indéfinis*:[29] we have an interval, and then our place knows us no more. Some spend this interval in listlessness, some in high passions, the wisest[30] in art and song. For our one chance is in expanding that interval, in getting as many pulsations as possible into the given time. High passions give one this quickened sense of life, ecstasy and sorrow of love, political or religious enthusiasm, or the "enthusiasm of humanity."[31] Only, be sure it is passion, that it does yield you this fruit of a quickened,

Notes

would be still less visible if we could burn the gas in a clean atmosphere. But the atmosphere … is dirty; … and the burning dirt gives to this flame the greater portion of its present light. But the heat of the flame is enormous.… A piece of platinum is heated to vivid redness, at a distance of two inches beyond the visible termination of the flame. The vapour which produces incandescence is here absolutely dark. In the flame itself the platinum is raised to dazzling whiteness, and is even pierced by the flame. When this flame impinges on a piece of lime, we have the dazzling Drummond light." Drummond light was the adaptation of the burning of quick-lime by gas to heat it to very high temperatures to give off a crystal brightness, compared with a diamond, the gem to which Pater refers. Thomas Drummond (1797–1840) used the qualities of such brilliance in theatre footlights (where they were called "lime-lights"; hence, being in the limelight), first used at Covent Garden Theatre in 1837.

[26] *Comte … Hegel* Auguste Comte (1798–1857), French philosopher and the founder of Positivism; for Hegel, see PATER, n. 34 (WEB p. 435).

[27] *pensée* (Fr. "Philosophy is the microscope of thought"). The quotation (properly reading *"le microscope"*) is from Victor Hugo, *Les Miserables* (1862; pt. 5, bk. 2, ch. 2).

[28] *Confessions* Jean-Jacques Rousseau (1712–78), Swiss philosopher and writer, published his *Confessions*, his autobiography up to 1765, in 1782. Rousseau does not mention Voltaire in book 6.

[29] *indéfinis* from Victor Hugo's *Le Dernier Jour d'un condamné* (Fr. the last day of a condemned man, 1832). In the third edition of *The Renaissance* (1888), Pater gave a translation: "we are all under sentence of death but with a sort of indefinite reprieve."

[30] *wisest* from 1873 Pater added after "wisest" "at least among the 'children of this world,'" citing Luke 16: 8.

[31] *humanity* this sentence was amended in the third edition (1888) and later to read: "Great passions may give us this quickened sense of life, ecstasy and sorrow of love, the various forms of enthusiastic activity, disinterested or otherwise, which come naturally to many of us." "Enthusiasm of humanity" is a Comtean phrase used by J. R. Seeley in his controversial theological work, *Ecce Homo: A Survey of the Life and Work of Jesus Christ* (1866), where it is the title for chapter 14.

multiplied consciousness. Of this wisdom, the poetic passion, the desire of beauty, the love of art for art's sake,[32] has most; for art comes to you professing frankly to give nothing but the highest quality to your moments as they pass, and simply for those moments' sake.

Thomas Hardy (1840–1928)

Living mostly in Dorset, part of south-west England that he called "Wessex" in his novels and poems, Hardy was best known in the nineteenth century and later for his novels, chiefly *Far from the Madding Crowd* (1874), *The Return of the Native* (1878), *The Mayor of Casterbridge* (1886), and *Tess of the d'Urbervilles* (1891). They depict the conflict between traditional rural life and contemporary agricultural and social problems. After *Jude the Obscure* (1896) was severely attacked on religious and moral grounds, Hardy published only one more novel, *The Well-Beloved* (1897), written before *Jude*, and thereafter published only poetry. His poems, often presenting a deeply pessimistic philosophy, religious doubt, and elegiac melancholy, include *Wessex Poems* (1898), *The Dynasts* (1904–8) on the Napoleonic Wars, and *Satires of Circumstance* (1914). His ashes are buried in Westminster Abbey. We have followed Hardy's ordering of the poems. Modern edition: *The Complete Poems of Thomas Hardy*, ed. James Gibson (1976); *The Complete Poetical Works of Thomas Hardy*, ed. Samuel Hynes (5 vols, 1982–95); *The Collected Letters of Thomas Hardy*, eds Richard Little Purdy and Michael Millgate (7 vols, 1978–88); Michael Millgate, *Thomas Hardy: A Biography* (1982) and *Thomas Hardy: A Biography Revisited* (2004); "Thomas Hardy Association": thethomashardyassociation.org.

Hap[1]

If but some vengeful god would call to me
    From up the sky, and laugh: "Thou suffering thing,
Know that thy sorrow is my ecstasy,
    That thy love's loss is my hate's profiting!"

Then would I bear, and clench myself, and die,   5
    Steeled by the sense of ire unmerited;
Half-eased[2] in that a Powerfuller than I
    Had willed and meted me the tears I shed.

Notes

[32] *sake* this famous phrase that was made ever more popular by the aesthetes and decadents of the 1880s and 1890s, was changed in the fourth edition (1891) to "the love of art for its own sake." See the preface to Théophile Gautier's *Mademoiselle de Maupin* (1835): "Only those things that are altogether useless can be truly beautiful; anything that is useful is ugly, for it is the expression of some need, and the needs of man are base and disgusting, as his nature is weak and poor." Swinburne had used the phrase in 1866 in *William Blake: A Critical Essay* (1866): "Art for art's sake first of all, and afterwards we may suppose all the rest shall be added to her." See also SWINBURNE, n. 30.

THOMAS HARDY
[1] *title* chance, casualty; written in 1866, the MS title was "Chance." On one level the poem is a lament for lost love, and on another a claim that the universe, while not executing arbitrary vengeance remains indifferent to human life. Hardy had read Darwin's *On the Origin of Species* (1859) and understood Darwin's evolutionary scheme as arbitrary and governed by chance; however, Darwin explicitly rejects this interpretation in the final paragraph with the famous "tangled bank" metaphor. See RELIGION: GEOLOGY, nn. 60 and 61. First published in *Wessex Poems* (1898).
[2] *Half-eased* see Keats, "Ode to a Nightingale" (1819: 51–52): "Darkling I listen; and, for many a time / I have been half in love with easeful Death."

But not so. How arrives it joy lies slain,
    And why unblooms[3] the best hope ever sown?   10
—Crass Casualty[4] obstructs the sun and rain,
    And dicing[5] Time for gladness casts a moan ..
       These purblind Doomsters[6] had as readily strown
Blisses about my pilgrimage as pain.

Neutral Tones[7]

We stood by a pond that winter day,
And the sun was white, as though chidden[8] of God,
And a few leaves lay on the starving sod;
   —They had fallen from an ash, and were gray.

Your eyes on me were as eyes that rove   5
Over tedious riddles solved years ago;
And some words played between us to and fro—
    On which lost the more by our love.

The smile on your mouth was the deadest thing
Alive enough to have strength to die;   10
And a grin of bitterness swept thereby
    Like an ominous bird a-wing ..

Since then, keen lessons that love deceives,
And wrings with wrong, have shaped to me
Your face, and the God curst sun, and a tree,   15
    And a pond edged with grayish leaves.

Nature's Questioning[9]

When I look forth at dawning, pool,
    Field, flock, and lonely tree,
    All seem to look at me
Like chastened children sitting silent in a school;

    Their faces dulled, constrained, and worn,   5
      As though the master's ways
      Through the long teaching days
Their first terrestrial zest had chilled and overborne.

Notes

[3] *unblooms* in elegies a common metaphor compares the death of a youth to the failure of nature's flowers to bloom, as in *Lycidas* (1638: 42–9); and Shelley's *Adonais* (1821: 52–53): "The bloom, whose petals nipp'd before they blew / Died on the promise of the fruit, is waste."

[4] *Casualty* glossed by Hardy as "insensible" change. There is also a possible implication of malignant causality.

[5] *dicing* throwing dice, gambling.

[6] *purblind Doomsters* half-blind judges or Fates.

[7] *title* the metaphor in the title is drawn from painting, where neutral tones or grays mute or neutralize the primary and secondary colours; it is here applied to a landscape emblematic of a terminated human relationship. First published in *Wessex Poems* (1898).

[8] *chidden* rebuked, scolded.

[9] *title* first published in *Wessex Poems* (1898), with an illustration of a broken door key, a traditional symbol for human inability to unlock the secret of life, and in Hardy's west country, an omen of death.

Upon them stirs, in lippings mere[10]
    (As if once clear in call,   10
    But now scarce breathed at all)—
"We wonder, ever wonder, why we find us here!

    Has some Vast Imbecility,
        Mighty to build and blend,
        But impotent to tend,   15
Framed us in jest, and left us now to hazardry?"[11]

    Or come we of an Automaton
        Unconscious of our pains?[12] ..
        Or are we live remains
Of Godhead dying downwards, brain and eye now gone?[13]   20

    Or is it that some high Plan betides,
        As yet not understood,
        Of Evil stormed by Good,
We the Forlorn Hope over which Achievement strides?"[14]

    Thus things around. No answerer I ..   25
        Meanwhile the winds, and rains,
        And Earth's old glooms and pains
Are still the same, and gladdest Life Death neighbours nigh.

A Christmas Ghost-Story[15]

South of the Line, inland from far Durban,
A mouldering soldier lies—your countryman.
Awry and doubled up are his gray bones,[16]

Notes

[10] *lippings mere* barely spoken words; or perhaps rote repetitions.

[11] *hazardry* questions follow concerning the author of creation: first is the mechanistic god of the deists who created the world in all of its complex order but has left it to run on its own without further divine intervention. Deism as a religious system began with Lord Herbert of Cherbury (1583–1648), who set out his views in *De Veritate* (Lat. Concerning truth, 1624), flourishing for about 100 years, to Matthew Tindal's *Christianity as Old as the Creation* (1730). The deists' argument on design was restated by the English theologian and philosopher William Paley, who in *Natural Theology* (1802) presented the analogy of the watch and the watchmaker (see TENNYSON, n. 282).

[12] *pains* this theological and philosophical question asks whether the deity is an unconscious automaton (Gk. acting on your own will), a self-operating machine that is driven by the power of will but is unconscious of its actions, somewhat similar to the views of the pessimistic German philosopher Arthur Schopenhauer (1788–1860) in *The World as Will and Idea* (1818, trans. 1883), which Hardy had been reading by 1886.

[13] *gone* the shrinking deity of the image of nature's god and the Christian God shrinking into a transcendental Idea (as in Carlyle), or as a dying god, was a commonplace of late nineteenth-century religious sceptics; see, for instance, SWINBURNE, "HYMN TO PROSERPINE" (1866) (WEB p. 425).

[14] *strides* one of the questions raised by evolution is whether it is purposive or teleological. To Tennyson (see TENNYSON, IN MEMORIAM, SECTIONS LV, LVI, CXVIII, and [EPILOGUE]) the struggle of good with evil, and its ultimate triumph, is a mark of the human role in evolution.

[15] *title* first published *Westminster Gazette* (23 Dec. 1899). Collected in *Poems of the Past and the Present* (1901), our text, where Hardy placed this poem before "Drummer Hodge," although the latter was published about a month before. In the *Westminster Gazette* the poem consisted of only the first eight lines; the remaining four were added in 1901. Other changes are noted below.

The Second Boer War had begun on 11 October 1899 between the British from the Cape Colony and the Boers from the Orange Free State. In what was known as "Black Week" (10–17 Dec.) the British had suffered three serious defeats, at the battles of Stormberg, Magersfontein, and

And on the breeze his puzzled phantom moans
Nightly to clear Canopus:[17] "I would know   5
By whom and when the All-Earth-gladdening Law
Of Peace,[18] brought in by that Man Crucified,
Was ruled to be inept, and set aside?

And what of logic or of truth appears
In tacking 'Anno Domini'[19] to the years?   10
Near twenty-hundred liveried[20] thus have hied,
But tarries yet the Cause for which He died."

Christmas-eve, 1899

The Dead Drummer [Drummer Hodge][21]

I

They throw in Drummer Hodge, to rest
    Uncoffined—just as found:
His landmark is a kopje-crest[22]
    That breaks the veldt[23] around;
And foreign constellations west[24]   5
    Each night above his mound.

II

Young Hodge the Drummer never knew—
    Fresh from his Wessex home—
The meaning of the broad Karoo,[25]
    The Bush,[26] the dusty loam,

Notes

Colenso. The defeats and loss of life by British soldiers demoralized public opinion in Britain. Hardy's poem was criticized as unpatriotic. A lead article in the Morning Chronicle (25 Dec. 1899) said Hardy "has pictured the soul of a dead soldier in Natal contemplating the battlefield, and wondering where is that peace on earth which is the Christian ideal of Christmastide. A fine conception, but we fear that soldier is Mr. Hardy's soldier, and not one of the Dublin Fusiliers who cried amidst the storm of bullets at Tugela, 'Let us make a name for ourselves!'" Hardy defended himself with a long letter to the same paper (published 28 Dec.), claiming that the soldier's views are "no longer local ... [but] Universal.... Neither British nor Boer, but a composite, typical phantom, may consistently be made to regret on or about Christmas Eve (when even the beasts of the field kneel, according to a tradition of my childhood) the battles of his life and war in general."

[16] *Durban ... bones* Durban is a port city in the north-east of South Africa. The "Line" is both the line of battle stretching over the northern part of the Cape Colony, with the British on the south, the Boers on the north, as well as a reference to soldiers "of the line" or foot soldiers. In the *Westminster Gazette* ll. 2–3 read: "There lies—be he or not your country-man— / A fellow-mortal. Riddles are his bones."

[17] *Canopus* second brightest star in the southern hemisphere, in the constellation of Carina, named after the pilot of

Menelaus' ship that sailed to Troy to start the Trojan War. In the *Westminster Gazette* the soldier's ghost muses in the third person: for *Canopus ... know* the *Gazette* reads "Canopus—fain to know."

[18] *All-Earth ... Peace* see Luke 2: 14.

[19] *Anno Domini* (Lat. the year of the Lord; AD).

[20] *liveried* livery is the distinctive clothing or insignia a servant wears as provided by a master; here, a military uniform. Its symbolism applies both to all the soldiers dead in wars over twenty centuries as metonym, as well as to the years themselves as "liveried," referring to the number of years that have passed since the birth of Christ.

[21] *title* Hodge is an English rural form of Roger, applied to an agricultural labourer or rustic, here a teenager serving in the Boer War (1899–1902). When first published in *Literature* (25 Nov. 1899), our text, the poem was entitled "The Dead Drummer," followed by "One of the Drummers killed was a native of a village near Casterbridge." Casterbridge is Hardy's name for Dorchester. Collected in *Poems of the Past and the Present* (1901).

[22] *kopje-crest* (Africaans or South African Dutch, small hill).

[23] *veldt* (Africaans, grassy plain).

[24] *west* circle to westward.

[25] *Karoo* (Hottentot, dry, elevated plateau).

[26] *Bush* British colonial term for uncleared land.

And why uprose to nightly view 10
    Strange stars amid the gloom.

III

Yet portion of that unknown plain
    Will Hodge for ever be;
His homely Northern breast and brain
    Grow up a Southern tree, 15
And strange-eyed constellations reign
    His stars eternally.

The Darkling Thrush[27]

I leant upon a coppice gate[28]
    When Frost was spectre-gray,
And Winter's dregs made desolate
    The weakening eye of day.
The tangled bine-stems[29] scored the sky 5
    Like strings from broken lyres,
And all mankind that haunted nigh
    Had sought their household fires.

The land's sharp features seemed to be
    The Century's corpse outleant, 10
His crypt the cloudy canopy,
    The wind his death-lament.
The ancient pulse of germ and birth[30]
    Was shrunken hard and dry,
And every spirit upon earth 15
    Seemed fervourless as I.

At once a voice outburst among
    The bleak twigs overhead
In a full-hearted evensong[31]
    Of joy illimited; 20

Notes

[27] *title* darkling means obscured by darkness. On its use with birds, see the invocation of book 3 of *Paradise Lost* (1667: 37–40) where Milton compares inspiration to the song of the nightingale: "as the wakeful Bird / Sings darkling, and in shadiest Covert hid / Tunes her nocturnal Note"; see also Keats, "Ode to a Nightingale" (1820: 51–52): "Darkling I listen; and, for many a time / I have been half in love with easeful Death." See also ARNOLD, "DOVER BEACH" (1867), where Matthew Arnold, like Hardy, regrets the loss of the "Sea of Faith" replaced by scientific questions and religious doubts: "And we are here as on a darkling plain." When first published to commemorate the end of the Victorian century in *The Graphic* (29 Dec. 1900), the poem was entitled "By the Century's Deathbed." It was later dated 31 December 1900. Our text: *Poems of the Past and the Present* (1901).

[28] *gate* entrance into the wood of small trees, as a metaphor for leaving an old and entering a new century.

[29] *bine-stems* dried out stems of the bindweed, a kind of climbing plant of the morning glory family, suggesting the loss of inspiration by the broken strings of Orpheus' lyre (see LANDON, "SAPPHO'S SONG") or the Aeolian harp: see also PATMORE, n. 13.

[30] *birth* for this line and the three following, see TENNYSON, IN MEMORIAM, LXXXV.

[31] *evensong* metaphor alluding to the singing of Evening Prayer or Evensong in the Church of England.

An aged thrush, frail, gaunt, and small,
 In blast-beruffled plume,
Had chosen thus to fling his soul
 Upon the growing gloom.

So little cause for carolings   25
 Of such ecstatic sound
Was written on terrestrial things
 Afar or nigh around,
That I could think there trembled through
 His happy good-night air   30
Some blessed Hope, whereof he knew
 And I was unaware.

December 1900

The Ruined Maid[32]

"O 'Melia,[33] my dear, this does everything crown!
Who could have supposed I should meet you in Town?
And whence such fair garments, such prosperi-ty?"—
"O didn't you know I'd been ruined?" said she.

— "You left us in tatters, without shoes or socks,   5
Tired of digging potatoes, and spudding up docks;[34]
And now you've gay bracelets and bright feathers three!"—
"Yes: that's how we dress when we're ruined," said she.

— "At home in the barton[35] you said 'thee' and 'thou,'
And 'thik oon,' and 'theäs oon,' and 't'other';[36] but now 10
Your talking quite fits 'ee for high compa-ny!" —
"Some polish is gained with one's ruin," said she.

—"Your hands were like paws then, your face blue and bleak
But now I'm bewitched by your delicate cheek,
And your little gloves fit as on any la-dy!"—   15
"We never do work when we're ruined," said she.

—"You used to call home-life a hag-ridden dream,
And you'd sigh, and you'd sock;[37] but at present you seem
To know not of megrims[38] or melancho-ly!"—
"True. There's an advantage in ruin," said she.   20

Notes

[32] *title* Hardy wrote this poem when the campaign against the Contagious Diseases Acts was gathering momentum (the Second Act was passed in 1866) and when prostitution was a growing social concern: see GENDER: WOMAN QUESTION; MARTINEAU ET AL. First published in *Poems of the Past and the Present* (1901).

[33] *'Melia* Amelia.

[34] *spudding up docks* digging thick-rooted weeds with a spade.

[35] *barton* farm.

[36] *thik oon ... t'other* Dorset dialect for "that one," this one," and "the other."

[37] *sock* sigh.

[38] *megrims* low spirits.

—"I wish I had feathers, a fine sweeping gown,
And a delicate face, and could strut about Town!"—
"My dear—a raw country girl, such as you be,
Isn't equal to that. You ain't ruined," said she.

Westbourne Park Villas 1866

De Profundis [In Tenebris]³⁹

I

"Percussus sum sicut foenum, et aruit cor meum."
Ps. ci.⁴⁰

> Wintertime nighs;
> But my bereavement-pain
> It cannot bring again:
> Twice no one dies.⁴¹

> Flower-petals flee;   5
> But, since it once hath been,
> No more that severing scene
> Can harrow me.

> Birds faint in dread:
> I shall not lose old strength   10
> In the lone frost's black length:
> Strength long since fled!

> Leaves freeze to dun;
> But friends can not turn cold
> This season as of old   15
> For him with none.

> Tempests may scath;⁴²
> But love can not make smart
> Again this year his heart
> Who no heart hath.   20

> Black is night's cope;⁴³
> But death will not appal
> One who, past doubtings all,
> Waits in unhope.

Notes

³⁹ *title* (Lat. out of the depths); see BCP, Psalm 130: "Out of the deep have I called unto thee O Lord." First published in *Poems of the Past and the Present* (1901), our text; title changed in later editions to *In Tenebris* (Lat. in darkness); see Psalm 143: 3 (Vulgate version 142: 3): "For the enemy hath persecuted my soul . . . he hath made me to dwell in darkness, as those that have been long dead." The Vulgate is the name given to the Latin version of the Bible translated by St Jerome (*c*.347–420); the Psalms are numbered differently in the Greek and the Hebrew versions, with the Roman Catholic version following the Greek tradition.

⁴⁰ *Percussus . . . ci* (Lat. I am beaten like hay, and my heart is dried up; Vulgate 101: 4); KJV version: "My heart is smitten, and withered like grass." (Psalm 102: 4).

⁴¹ *dies* see Jude 1: 12.

⁴² *scath* damage, injure.

⁴³ *cope* liturgical vestment in the form of a full-length cloak.

De Profundis [In Tenebris][44]

II

"Considerabam ad dexteram, et videbam; et non erat qui cognosceret me .. Non est qui requirat animam meam."

Ps. cxli[45]

When the clouds' swoln bosoms echo back the shouts of the many and strong
That things are all as they best may be, save a few to be right ere long,
And my eyes have not the vision in them to discern demonstrations so clear,
The blot seems straightway in me alone; one better he were not here.

The stout upstanders say, All's well with us: ruers have nought to rue!　　　　　5
And what the potent say so oft, can it fail to be somewhat true?
Breezily go they, breezily come; their dust smokes around their career,
Till I think I am one born out of due time,[46] who has no calling here.

Their dawns bring lusty joys, it seems; their eves exultance sweet;
Our times are blessed times, they cry: Life shapes it as is most meet,　　　　　10
And nothing is much the matter; there are many smiles to a tear;
Then what is the matter is I, I say. Why should such an one be here? ..

Let him to whose ears the low-voiced Best seems stilled by the clash of the First,
Who holds that if way to the Better there be, it exacts a full look at the Worst,[47]
Who feels that delight is a delicate growth cramped by crookedness, custom, and fear,　15
Get him up and be gone as one shaped awry; he disturbs the order here.

Mathilde Blind (1841–96)

The daughter of a German banker, Jacob Abraham Cohen, who died when she was an infant, Mathilde Cohen was born in Mannheim, Germany, her name being changed in 1849 when her widowed mother, Friederike Ettlinger, married Karl Blind (1826–1907), a political agitator who helped lead the Baden insurrection for a unified Germany in 1848–49. Expelled from Germany, France, and Belgium, the family sought asylum in England in 1851 and settled in the St John's Wood area of London, where radical European exiles joined their intellectual circle. There Blind met such European leaders as Giuseppe Garibaldi (1807–82), Karl Marx (1818–83), and Joseph Mazzini (1805–72), to whom, in 1867, she dedicated *Poems* under her pseudonym, Claude Lake. She also was an associate of the Pre-Raphaelites, including Ford Madox Brown, with whose family she lived for some years in Manchester. She was influenced by the English Romantics, Wordsworth, Coleridge, and especially Shelley, as well as German philosophers and writers like Goethe, Kant, Hegel, and Schiller. She also joined the group of women writers around Vernon Lee, Amy Levy, and Augusta Webster. Blind published

Notes

[44] *title* see n. 39.

[45] *Considerabam ... cxli* (Lat. "I looked on my right hand, and beheld, but there was no man that would know me; ... no man cared for my soul," Vulgate Psalm 141: 4); KJV version, Psalm 142: 4.

[46] *one ... time* see 1 Corinthians 15: 8.

[47] *Who holds ... Worst* doctrine of meliorism or improvement mitigated by a pessimistic realism.

seven volumes of poetry, a novel, the first biography of George Eliot (1883), as well as biographies of Shelley (1872) and Madame Roland (1886), translations, and essays (including a long essay on Shelley for the *Westminster Review*, July 1870), and was a reviewer for both the *Athenæum* and *The Examiner*. Blind confronted Victorian complacencies about the cruel Highland Clearances of the 1830s in *The Heather on Fire* (1886); she also reimagined Darwinian evolution in *The Ascent of Man* (1889); and she exposed anti-female prejudices and discrimination in *Dramas in Miniature* (1891). She left her fortune, inherited from her stepbrother, to Newnham College, Cambridge,

to further women's higher education. Although well received in her day, and the subject of a *Selection* (1897), edited by Arthur Symons, Blind was almost completely forgotten until the revival of Victorian women writers late in the twentieth century. Standard edition: *The Poetical Works of Mathilde Blind*, ed. Arthur Symons (1900); James Diedrick, *Exile in Bohemia: Mathilde Blind and the Culture of Late-Victorian London* (forthcoming); see "Mathilde Blind" at the Victorian Women Writers' Project: http://webapp1.dlib.indiana.edu/vwwp/welcome.do and http://www.nipissingu.ca/faculty/annbg/myweb/mathilde_blind.htm.

Winter[1]

How hushed the world is: how the sea-like sound
Of multitudinous streets, that shriek and swell
With life, is muffled, save for some lone bell
Making the sunless silence more profound.
The awful whiteness, spread along the ground,   5
Of the inviolate snow, seems to compel
The flames of fire to flash with visible
Increase of radiance, by drear norlight[2] bound.

Thou, too, O heart, sore beat by roar and flow
Of heavy-weltering, clamorous-tongued desires,   10
Liest hush'd, as yon shrill streets smooth'd by the snow,
Each louder wish 'neath fresh-fallen peace expires;
Yet all the intenser throb thought's quenchless fires,
Wan Memory rims with tears and years of woe.

The Dead[3]

The Dead abide with us! Though stark and cold
Earth seems to grip them, they are with us still:
They have forged our chains of being for good or ill:

Notes

MATHILDE BLIND
[1] *title* Blind had been publishing in the Oxford journal *The Dark Blue* since June, 1871 when her review of a medieval Icelandic poem translated by Eiríkr Magnússon (1833–1913) was printed. He was a collaborator with William Morris in translating Icelandic sagas, and some of Morris's translations also appeared in *The Dark Blue*. It was a radical journal where a number of her Pre-Raphaelite friends also published. An earlier poem, "The Song of the Willi," was

issued in August 1871. "Winter," her first published sonnet, appeared in *The Dark Blue* in January 1872, followed by "Nocturne" (Mar. 1872).
[2] *norlight* not in the *OED*; probably the northern lights, from *nor*, sailor's slang for north, northern.
[3] *title* first published in the *Athenæum* (2 Apr. 1881); republished in *The Prophecy of Saint Oran and Other Poems* (1881).

And their invisible hands these hands yet hold.
Our perishable bodies are the mould 5
In which their strong, imperishable will,
Mortality's deep yearning to fulfil,
Hath grown incorporate through dim time untold.

Vibrations infinite of life in death,
As a star's travelling light survives its star! 10
So let us hold our lives that when we are
The fate of those who then will draw this breath,
They shall not drag us to their judgment bar
And curse the heritage which we bequeath.

Manchester by Night[4]

O'er this huge town, rife with intestine wars,[5]
Whence as from monstrous sacrificial shrines
Pillars of smoke climb heavenward, Night inclines
Black brows majestical with glimmering stars.
Her dewy silence soothes life's angry jars: 5
And like a mother's wan white face, who pines
Above her children's turbulent ways, so shines
The moon athwart the narrow cloudy bars.

Now toiling multitudes that hustling crush
Each other in the fateful strife for breath, 10
And, hounded on by diverse hungers, rush
Across the prostrate ones that groan beneath,
Are swathed within the universal hush,
As life exchanges semblances with death.

The Red Sunsets, 1883 [I][6]

The boding sky was charactered with cloud,
    The scripture of the storm—but high in air,
    Where the unfathomed zenith still was bare,
A pure expanse of rose-flushed violet glowed
And, kindling into crimson light, o'erflowed 5

Notes

4 *title* Blind lived for some time with Ford Madox Ford and his family in Manchester. From *The Prophecy of Saint Oran and Other Poems* (1881).
5 *wars* usually internal discord or civil wars; here referring to the clashes between the working classes and their industrial masters in Manchester, often taken as the English archetypal industrial with such conflicts, as in Dickens's Coketown (Manchester or Preston) in *Hard Times* (1854) or Gaskell's *Mary Barton* (1848) set in Manchester or *North and South* (1855) set in the north of England town of Milton. See also CONDITION: SOCIAL FORMATION; ENGELS, *CONDITION*

(WEB p. 6); and CONDITION: SOCIAL FORMATION; GASKELL, *MARY BARTON* (WEB p. 8).
6 *title* after the eruption of the volcanic island Krakatoa in the Dutch East Indies (modern Indonesia) in August 1883, with huge destruction, large loss of life, and the loudest sound in modern history, fine particles carried in the high atmosphere around the earth caused flaming sunsets. These sonnets with identical titles, here numbered I and II, were published in *The Ascent of Man* (1889). In *Songs and Sonnets* (1895) the order of the poems was reversed.

The hurrying wrack with such a blood-red glare,
That heaven, igniting, wildly seemed to flare
On the dazed eyes of many an awe-struck crowd.

And in far lands folk presaged with blanched lips
Disastrous wars, earthquakes, and foundering ships,   10
    Such whelming floods as never dykes could stem,
Or some proud empire's ruin and eclipse:
    Lo, such a sky, they cried, as burned o'er them
Once lit the sacking of Jerusalem![7]

The Red Sunsets, 1883 [II]

The twilight heavens are flushed with gathering light,
    And o'er wet roofs and huddling streets below
    Hang with a strange Apocalyptic glow
On the black fringes of the wintry night.
Such bursts of glory may have rapt the sight   5
    Of him to whom on Patmos[8] long ago
    The visionary angel came to show
That heavenly city built of chrysolite.[9]

And lo, three factory hands begrimed with soot,
    Aflame with the red splendour, marvelling stand,   10
And gaze with lifted faces awed and mute.
    Starved of earth's beauty by Man's grudging hand,
O toilers, robbed of labour's golden fruit,
    Ye, too, may feast in Nature's fairyland.

Violet Fane (pseudonym of Mary Montgomerie Lamb, Lady Currie) (1843–1905)

The daughter of Charles J. H. Lamb (1816–56) and Charlotte Gray (1824–80) of Beauport Park in Sussex, Fane had a well-to-do but unconventional upbringing, her young father having adopted Turkish dress and customs. He also introduced her to his literary friends, especially George Borrow (1803–81), Edward FitzGerald (1809–83), and Edward Bulwer-Lytton

Notes

[7] *Jerusalem* the sacking of Jerusalem occurred in the year 70 CE, during the Jewish-Roman war by the Roman army under Titus (39–81), later Roman emperor from 79 to 81. The Second Temple was destroyed and its treasures carried off. Christians read it as a fulfilment of Jesus' prediction in Luke 19: 41–44. See also Josephus, *Wars of the Jews* (*c.*75; bks. 5 and 6). Jerusalem was also sacked during the First Crusade in July 1099.

[8] *Patmos* a Greek island in the Aegean sea where St John the Divine is supposed to have written the Book of Revelation, also known as the Apocalypse (Gk. lifting of the veil, revelation), at the bidding of an angel (see Revelation 1).

[9] *chrysolite* also known as chrysoberyl or peridot, a green or yellow precious gemstone that forms the seventh foundation stone of the heavenly Jerusalem: see Revelation 21: 20.

(1803–73). On her mother's desertion and her father's death in 1856, she was raised by a relative, Lady Sophia Eglinton (1840–86), and learned the social graces that later made the society beauty a brilliant conversationalist, as portrayed as Mrs. Sinclair in W. H. Mallock's *roman-à-clef* and satire, *The New Republic* (1877). She first married Henry Singleton (1818/19–93) and raised a family of four children; after Singleton's death in 1893, she married the diplomat Sir Philip, later Baron, Currie (1834–1906), ambassador to the Ottoman Empire, residing in Constantinople; however, her life was the occasion of gossip because of a number of affairs, including one with Currie's cousin, the poet Wilfrid Scawen Blunt (1840–1922). Her pseudonym was derived from a character in Disraeli's *Vivian Gray* (1826–27). Her first book of poetry was *From Dawn to Noon* (1872), followed by five others, including her controversial novel in verse, *Denzil Place* (1875), concerning marriage and adultery, all of them popular and often elegant. Her London literary circle included Oscar Wilde, Robert Browning, Algernon Swinburne, and James McNeill Whistler. As well as three prose novels, *Sophy* (1881), *Thro' Love and War* (1886), and *The Story of Helen Davenant* (1889), she published widely in such periodicals as *The World, Pall Mall Magazine,* and *Ladies Realm,* her essays being collected as *Moods of a Man* (1901) and *Collected Essays* (1902). No standard edition. *Poems* (2 vols, 1892); Violet Fane, *The Feast of Kebobs* (1904), an autobiographical essay.

Lancelot and Guinevere[1]

"Oh! read to me some other lay,"
    She cried to one about to read;
"I love to hear of tourney[2] gay,
    Of feats of arms and daring deed,

Yet read to-day some simple rhyme,   5
    Or else some tender ballad sing,
And let me hear another time
    The Idylls of the blameless king."[3]

Her husband did not seem to hear,
    Or, if he heard, he heeded not,   10
And so he read of Guinevere
    And of her love for Lancelot.

Notes —————————————————————————————

VIOLET FANE

[1] *title* Arthurian material was highly popular in the nineteenth century, especially the adulterous love affair between Sir Lancelot and Guenevere, Arthur's queen. William Morris had published "The Defence of Guenevere" in 1858 (see MORRIS). Tennyson had published his *Idylls of the King* over a number of years (1856–85), including "Guinevere" in 1859 and "The Last Tournament," telling of the disastrous battles of Arthur's knights, in the *Contemporary Review* the year before Fane's poem, in 1871. The poem sets up a comparison between the complicated love triangles of Lancelot, Arthur, Guinevere, and Elaine, and compares them with the contemporary reader and listener of the tales. First published in *From Dawn to Noon: Poems* (1872). In the Table of Contents to the volume, this poem's title is spelled differently: "Launcelot and Guinevere." For a parody of Arthurian verse, see TENNYSON, n. 8.

[2] *tourney* tournament. Violet Fane's relative Archibald Montgomerie (1812–61), thirteenth Earl of Eglinton, organized the celebrated Eglinton Tournament of 30 August 1839, attended by more than 100,000 people (and costing more than £40,000), at which various knights on horseback in medieval armour jousted for the honour of the "Queen of Beauty," Georgiana Sheridan (1809–84), wife of the Duke of Somerset (Edward Seymour, 1804–85) and sister of Caroline Norton. It was the most extravagant performance of the Gothic revival of the nineteenth century.

[3] *king* a reference to Tennyson's *Idylls of the King*; see n. 1.

He read how first the rumour grew,
    Unheard by him it harm'd the most,
And how the courtiers link'd their two   15
    Unwedded names in song and toast;

And how, "love-loyal" to her will,
    The great knight sought within her eyes
Her wishes when her lips were still,
    Ere striving for the diamond prize,   20

And how he did not read them right—
    The lady sadden'd at each word:
"Alas," she sigh'd, "how true the knight!
    How fair the queen! how great her lord!"

She turn'd away and sigh'd anew   25
    As in each act his love was seen,
And thought, "Ah! I had loved him too
    Were he my knight, were I his queen."

But when the poet told of how
    His guilty love had darken'd o'er,   30
And marr'd the beauty of his brow
    (Such love makes some men smile the more),

And how he did not lightly wear
    The prize of which he made no boast,
'Twas then she deem'd him doubly fair,   35
    'Twas then she felt she loved him most.

And when she heard of fair Elaine,[4]
    "Alas! it seemeth hard," she sigh'd,
"That he should let her love in vain
    The hopeless love whereof she died.   40

But ah! how loyal to his queen!
    How warm the heart that seem'd so cold!
Hath ever knight so faithful been
    Since he of whom the poet told?"

Notes

[4] *Elaine* in the story told by Sir Thomas Malory (*c.*1405–71) in his Arthurian compilation, usually called *Le Morte d'Arthur* (1485), Elaine is the "lily-maid of Astolat" that Tennyson had written about in "The Lady of Shalott" (1833–42) and in Idyll 7 of the *Idylls*, "Lancelot and Elaine." Having won eight of nine diamonds in tournaments, Lancelot, after numerous complications, enters the lists for the ninth in disguise supplied by the Lord of Astolat, wearing Astolat's daughter's token. He wins the joust, and Elaine falls in love with him. When Lancelot rejects her, she pines and dies and is sent in a barge to Camelot, just as Lancelot presents the nine diamonds to Guinevere. In a jealous rage she hurls them out the window into the river, and they slip from Elaine's barge into the water. As Guinevere seeks forgiveness, Lancelot compares the love of Guinevere and Elaine.

And when she heard how Elaine died,   45
    And floated to him on her bier,
She turn'd away her head to hide
    The falling of a passing tear.

But when Sir Lancelot had sought
    The little reedy river cove,   50
And, all remorseful, sigh'd and thought
    The *maiden's* was the tend'rer love;

Then throbb'd the heart of her who heard,
    As though the spirit of the queen
Within her bosom lived and stirr'd,   55
    And made of her what *she* had been:

And wildly to herself she said,
    "The *woman's* love! the queen's! my own!
Ah! could he covet in its stead
    What but a love-sick girl has shown?   60

The sneering word, the tarnish'd name,
    The galling mask for him she bore;
She heeded not her loss of fame,
    And risk'd the queenly crown she wore:

For him she did not scorn to lie   65
    To one[5] whose very life was truth;
She put her robes and sceptre by,
    And crown'd him king of all her youth.

That simple maiden could but prove
    The love she bore him by her death;   70
Give me to *live* for him I love,
    To yield him heart and soul and breath!

Give me the risk, the shame, the sin,
    The love that can have nought to gain,
Save the fond hope one day to win   75
    A dearer link to clasp the chain!

But read no more!" she cried aloud;
    Her cheek was flush'd and wild her eye,
Whilst on her brow the gath'ring cloud
    Told of the tempest passing by.   80

"Ah! read no more," she said again,
    "My ears are weary of the sound!"
And half in anger, half in pain,
    She flung the book upon the ground.

Notes

[5] *one* King Arthur.

"Alas, for lawless love!" she sigh'd,   85
    "I share the cross of Guinevere;
Like her my guilty secret hide,
    Like her I earn the doom I fear.

To see one day his passion fade,
    Or hear him say *mine* pales beside   90
The love of some such lily maid
    As she who floated down the tide.

For *me* to steel my heart at need,
    Nor let that live that makes love's curse,
Then can I all unheeding read   95
    The tender tales of poet's verse."

She bent her head and seem'd to pray,
    Then, starting, listen'd to a sound,
Push'd back her hair, and dash'd away
    The tears in which her eyes were drown'd.   100

With mantling cheeks and lips apart,
    She waits and strains her anxious sight;
And all the pulses of her heart
    Seem quicken'd by some near delight.

Her lord stepp'd down upon the grass   105
    And vanish'd in the twilight dim;
Her guardian angel moan'd "Alas!
    Alas for her! alas for him!"

Alas! for erring woman's pray'r!
    Reader and book alike forgot;   110
She trembles, hearing on the stair
    The coming step of Lancelot.

Gerard Manley Hopkins (1844–89)

Hopkins was born in Stratford, in east London, into a well-read and talented family of nine children. His father, Manley Hopkins (1818–1897), was a marine insurance adjuster and poet, and his mother, Catherine Smith (1821–1920), came from a medical family. He was educated at Highgate School and Balliol College, Oxford (1863–67) where his tutors included Benjamin Jowett and Walter Pater. Hopkins converted from Anglicanism to Roman Catholicism at Oxford (1866) under Newman's guidance. He went on to take a first-class degree in classics.

His lifelong friendship with the poet and classicist Robert Bridges (1844–1930) involved sending him copies of his verse. In 1867 Hopkins taught classics at the Oratory School in Birmingham (founded by John Henry Newman in 1859). While there, he decided to join the Jesuits, beginning his novitiate at Roehampton (1868). Soon after, he burnt all of his poetry as he "resolved to write no more, as not belonging to my profession, unless by the wishes of my superiors." At St Beuno's College in north Wales he continued his philosophical studies and first vows of poverty, chastity, and obedience (1870), and his theological studies (which he failed), final vows, and ordination (1877). While there he broke his seven-year self-imposed abstinence from writing poetry with "The Wreck of the Deutschland," using his revolution in English prosody, sprung rhythm (see below, "WRECK," headnote). As well as the classical Greek and Latin he had studied at Oxford, he was well-versed in languages, in Hebrew, French, and Welsh. He served in a number of parishes in Oxford, Manchester, Liverpool, and Dublin, with varying success. He became professor of Greek at University College, Dublin (1884), where he was isolated and unwell, with failing eyesight, and distressed at the increasingly difficult political situation between England and Ireland. His work during these years came to be called the "terrible sonnets." He died of typhoid fever, having, in his view, failed in so many aspects of his life, including as a poet, almost without publication. His friend Bridges, to whom he had entrusted his poetic manuscripts as they were composed, held off publication for almost thirty years, until 1918, partly from a timid fear that his work would be misunderstood, berated, or completely rejected. Even then Bridges in the "Preface to Notes" (1918) declared that the

poems could be "arraigned for errors," for "faults of taste," "purely artistic wantonness," "faults of style," absence of "literary decorum," as well as for "Oddity and Obscurity" – all criticisms that were paraded through the reviews until the tide changed after the second edition in 1930, and when Herbert Read in 1938 acclaimed Hopkins, saying that he was "amongst the most vital poets of our time, and his influence will reach far into the future of English poetry." Much of Hopkins's difficulty is mitigated when the poetry is read aloud. Like Joyce's *Finnegans Wake* (1939), it makes sense at the aural level. Standard edition: *The Poetical Works of Gerard Manley Hopkins,* ed. Norman H. MacKenzie (1990); *The Poems of Gerard Manley Hopkins,* ed. Robert Bridges (1918), our text; *The Collected Works of Gerard Manley Hopkins* (7 vols, 2006–); *The Letters of Gerard Manley Hopkins to Robert Bridges,* ed. C. C. Abbott (1955); *The Letters of Gerard Manley Hopkins to Richard Watson Dixon,* ed. C. C. Abbott (1955); Robert Barnard Martin, *Gerard Manley Hopkins: A Very Private Life* (1991). Poems of Hopkins: http://www.bartleby.com/122/index1.html; Gerard Manley Hopkins Society Archive: http://www.gerardmanleyhopkins.org/archive/overview.html.

The Wreck of the Deutschland[1]

In 1873 Otto von Bismarck (1815–98), chancellor of Germany, adopted a policy of anti-Catholic *Kulturkampf* (Ger. cultural struggle) and passed the Falk Laws, named after the minister responsible, Adalbert Falk (1827–1900). Amongst the many effects of these discriminatory laws, five Franciscan sisters were exiled from their convent at Salzkotten in Germany, setting sail for the United States from Bremerhaven on 4 December 1875 on board the

German ship *Deutschland.* It was swept off course in a storm in the English Channel, becoming stuck on the Kentish Knock, a sandbank in the Thames estuary, where the lifeboats were swept away and their signals for rescue lost in the storm. After twenty-eight hours some help came and about 155 passengers and crew were rescued, while clinging to the rigging, but the nuns remained in the first-class saloon that filled with water, and they, and about fifty-five

Notes ──────────────────────────────

GERARD MANLEY HOPKINS

[1] *title* throughout Hopkins refers to or echoes the Douay-Rheims Roman Catholic translation of the Bible (1582–1609).

The poem remained unpublished until Robert Bridges's edition of 1918.

others who were swept from the decks and rigging, were drowned. The shipwreck was widely reported in the press, and the telegraph circulated the news around the world. At St Beuno's Hopkins had access to *The Times* (8–15 Dec. 1875) and the *Illustrated London News* (18 Dec. 1875), and his parents mailed him other newspaper clippings. He later wrote about seeking permission to end his seven years of poetic silence: "I was affected by the account and happening to say so to my rector he said that he wished someone would write a poem on the subject. On this hint I set to work and, though my hand was out at first, produced one."

The poem is in the tradition of the Pindaric ode with its constellation of images around a theme (such as water in the Great Flood of Noah as the type of Baptism, and hence, God's power and mercy), but it also has connections with other great elegies, including Milton's *Lycidas* (1638), Shelley's *Adonais* (1821), and Tennyson's *In Memoriam* (1850). Like them it positions God in nature, and also wrestles with the problems of loss and faith. The "Wreck" does so, however, from a position of a struggle of understanding and faith, not of belief. Hence, it invokes both the doctrine of the Incarnation (Christ, the Word of God became flesh, as in John 1: 1–18) and of the Passion (the suffering and death of Christ on the cross). The poem considers the problem of evil in a divinely ordered universe, along with the role of redemptive suffering as it might impact those far removed from the suffering itself. There are also conflicts between the omniscience, benevolence, and omnipotence of God, and the occurrence of disasters in human affairs. External events involving the shipwreck, the many drownings, especially of the five Franciscan Sisters, and their destiny in the scheme of salvation, are set in the context of an internal spiritual struggle concerning theological doctrine and personal belief.

The poem is complex in its structure. Clearly divided into two parts, the first part is composed of stanzas 1 to 10, the second of stanzas 11 to 35, but less clear is the internal organization within the poem. Hopkins told Robert Bridges (21 Aug. 1877) that he began with the narrative section of the voyage and the wreck (stanzas 12 to 19, with Hopkins's response to the nun's cry interposed at stanzas 17–18), perhaps the easiest part of the poem to comprehend. The first part (stanzas 1–10) sets out the parallel between the storm/wreck and the crisis in the poet's spiritual life – whether that of his final preparation after many years for ordination as a priest or the crisis brought on by the apparent conflict between the benevolent providence of God and the seemingly arbitrary deaths of God's servants; or, put another way, the conflict between benign and malignant nature, both the creation of God. The second part begins with an introduction (stanza 11) and the dramatic narrative section (stanzas 12–19) of the sailing from Germany and the wreck, up to the tall nun's cry to Christ and its questioning at mid-poem (stanzas 18–19). Then follows the discussion of the motives and circumstances of the tall nun as both prophet and visionary (stanzas 20 to 31, with the climax occurring at stanza 28). The conclusion of the poem (stanzas 32–35) returns to the themes of the first part but on a higher level, as the spiritual crisis culminates in both a reconciliation of the problem of evil and a hymn of adoration and prayer for the conversion of Britain back to Roman Catholicism.

The poem reacts strongly against the traditions of Romantic and Victorian poetic content (theological), narrative (non-linear or sequential), prosody (disrupted syntax, alliteration, assonance, and internal rhymes), diction (many coinings, dialect words, and unusual double formations), and puns used for serious purposes (analogies between the natural, emotional, and spiritual worlds). A wide range of literary and biblical citations occurs throughout the ode, as noted in fully annotated scholarly texts, but only a selection can be included here. Most important are his two poetic innovations, inscape/instress and sprung rhythm. Inscape is Hopkins's word for the make-up of the inner nature of a thing, its inherent pattern as a paradigm, as a creation of God. Indeed, to Hopkins, the whole purpose of poetry is to capture the inscape of human speech. It is a concept resembling Wordsworth's "spots of time," or the "epiphany" of James Joyce. Instress is the means by which this inscape is unified or by which its effect is perceived. Hopkins invented a revolutionary new "sprung rhythm," whereby syllabic count is abandoned in favour of a sequence of stressed words. As he explained: "I had long had haunting my ear the echo of a new rhythm which now I realised on paper. To speak shortly, it consists in scanning by accents or stresses along, without any account of the number of syllables, so that a foot may be one strong syllable or it may be many light and one strong." Hence a line can have almost any number of syllables, but its "length" is governed by the number of stressed words that Hopkins marked in many copies of his manuscripts. Accordingly, in each stanza of the "Wreck" the first line has two stresses (three stresses in part two); the second line has three stresses, the third line has four, the fourth line has three, the fifth line has five, the sixth line has five, the seventh line has four, and the eighth line has six. Hopkins relates his metrics and diction to traditional Welsh verse forms: "Certain chimes suggested by the Welsh poetry I had been reading (what they call *cynghanedd*) and a great many more oddnesses could not but dismay an editor's eye." The Welsh poetic device of *cynghanedd* (Welsh: harmony) is a system of alliteration and internal rhyme, whereby one of its forms involves the repetition in the second half of a line of the consonants from the first half, with different vowels. Hopkins experiments throughout the "Wreck" with different versions of this device.

To the
happy memory of five Franciscan Nuns
exiles by the Falk Laws
drowned between midnight and morning of
Dec. 7th, 1875

PART THE FIRST

I

Thou mastering me
God! giver of breath and bread;
World's strand, sway of the sea;
Lord of living and dead;
Thou hast bound bones and veins in me, fastened me flesh,   5
And after it almost unmade, what with dread,
Thy doing: and dost thou touch me afresh?
Over again I feel thy finger and find thee.²

Notes

² *thee* stanza 1 is both the traditional invocation of the muse in an epic or ode and an acclamation of the power of God in nature to create and destroy. As well, the power of God forms humans in the divine image and gives them breath and inspiration (see Genesis 1: 27; 2: 7; Job 10: 9–11; and Psalm 139). The gerund "mastering" carries many meanings: first, God's power over the poet; second, divine inspiration; third, Christ as "master" (Luke 5: 5; and Matthew 8: 23–27); and fourth, the *Deutschland*'s "Master," who was unable to master the ship; see also *The Tempest* 1. 1. 1. Hence, God is the master of shore (earth) and wave (water). The strand is the sandy shore or the bank that the ship struck. For living and dead, see Romans 14: 9; fastened me flesh implies both the fashioning of my flesh as well as fashioning your flesh for me, both in the Incarnation and the Eucharist (John 1: 14; and 1 Corinthians 11: 23–33). Finger is metonymic for the power of God (Luke 11: 20).

2

I did say yes
O at lightning and lashed rod;
Thou heardst me truer than tongue confess   10
Thy terror, O Christ, O God;
Thou knowest the walls, altar and hour and night:[3]
The swoon of a heart that the sweep and the hurl of thee trod
Hard down with a horror of height: 15
And the midriff astrain with leaning of, laced with fire of stress.

3

The frown of his face
Before me, the hurtle° of hell   °assault
Behind,° where, where was a, where was a place?   °following
I whirled out wings that spell°   °in that bout   20
And fled with a fling of the heart to the heart of the Host.[4]
My heart, but you were dovewinged, I can tell,
Carrier-witted,[5] I am bold to boast,
To flash from the flame to the flame then, tower° from the grace
to the grace.[6]   °soar

4

I am soft sift°   °sifted sand   25
In an hourglass—at the wall
Fast, but mined with a motion, a drift,
And it crowds and it combs[7] to the fall;
I steady as a water in a well, to a poise, to a pane,
But roped with, always, all the way down from the tall   30
Fells or flanks of the voel, a vein
Of the gospel proffer, a pressure, a principle, Christ's gift.[8]

5

I kiss my hand
To the stars, lovely-asunder
Starlight, wafting him out of it; and   35
Glow, glory in thunder;

Notes

[3] *yes … night* the poet's "yes" is multiple: to God's grace, to conversion to Roman Catholicism (1866), becoming a Jesuit (and especially his encounter with the *Spiritual Exercises* of St Ignatius Loyola, 1491–1556, the founder of the Jesuits, during his long retreat in his novitiate and after, 1868–70), and seeking ordination (1877); to illumination ("lightning") and correction ("rod") – and the correction of the storm. The *Spiritual Exercises* provided a method of meditation on human experience as a means of understanding Christ. For truer than tongue, see 1 John 3: 18. The poet's preparatory retreats at the "altar and hour and night" refer to his, as well as to the nuns', retreats and vigils, like medieval squires preparing for knighthood, as St Ignatius did, to which the poet's experience is paralleled.

[4] *Host* both the hospitable inn- or house-keeper and the body of Christ in the Eucharist.
[5] *Carrier-witted* like the carrier-pigeon, the dove's instinct for seeking home (see Psalm 55: 3–8).
[6] *grace* flash on wings from the flames of hell to the fire of love in the welcoming Host's heart; from one level of grace to another (see John 1: 16).
[7] *hourglass … combs* for hourglass and the poet's dust, see George Herbert, "Church Monuments" from *The Temple* (1633: 19–24); combs are crests or breaks of a bank or waves toppling over.
[8] *Fells … voel … gift* fells (north British: high moorlands, mountains); voel (Welsh: bare high hill, pronounced *foil*): the ropes or coils of water flowing down the hills as a type of baptismal water (see Jeremiah 17: 13, Douay): "the Lord the vein of living waters." Gift is the grace given in baptism.

Kiss my hand to the dappled-with-damson[9] west:
Since, tho' he is under the world's splendour and wonder,
   His mystery must be instressed,[10] stressed;
For I greet him the days I meet him, and bless when I understand.   40

6

    Not out of his bliss°   °heavenly blessedness
   Springs the stress felt
  Nor first from heaven (and few know this)
   Swings the stroke dealt—
Stroke and a stress that stars and storms deliver,   45
That guilt is hushed by, hearts are flushed by and melt—
  But it rides time like riding a river
(And here the faithful waver, the faithless fable and miss).

7

    It dates from day
  Of his going in Galilee;[11]   50
Warm-laid grave of a womb-life grey;
   Manger, maiden's knee;
The dense and the driven Passion, and frightful sweat;[12]
Thence the discharge of it, there its swelling to be,
  Though felt before, though in high flood yet—   55
What none would have known of it, only the heart, being hard at bay,[13]

8

    Is out with it!° Oh,   °(dial.) utters
  We lash° with the best or worst   °cry out
  Word last! How a lush-kept plush-capped sloe°   °fruit of blackthorn
   Will, mouthed to flesh-burst,   60
Gush!—flush the man, the being with it, sour or sweet,
Brim, in a flash, full!—Hither then, last or first,
  To hero of Calvary, Christ,'s feet—
Never ask if meaning it, wanting it, warned of it—men go.

9

    Be adored among men,   65
  God, three-numberèd form;
Wring thy rebel, dogged in den,

Notes

[9] *kiss ... damson* to honour or adore the Gods, the Romans kissed their right hand in a gesture towards them (Lat. *ad* to; *oro, orare* to pray; but with a popular etymology *ad* + *os, oris* mouth); see Pliny, *Natural History* 28. 25; damson is a deep purple colour, as of damson plums, or of preserves made from them.

[10] *instressed* instress is the shaping force that impresses on a thing its character, its inscape – and that, when "caught" or perceived, is then comprehended by the beholder as inscape, an inherent pattern in the order of nature, bestowed by sublime power; a divine mystery, from the sublimity of "lightning and lashed rod" to the intimate colour of cottage jam ("dappled-with-damson").

[11] *Galilee* Christ's ascension (see Luke 24: 49–51).

[12] *Manger ... sweat* events in Christ's life, from the nativity ("manger") to the suffering on the cross ("Passion"), with the preparation for it in the garden of Gethsemane (Luke 22: 39–54); for Jesus' bloody sweat, see Luke 22: 44.

[13] *bay* in the following lines these events release a spiritual flood of grace (1 Corinthians 10: 4), unrecognized until the heart (hart) is under stress in a spiritual crisis (or the deer at bay before hounds); see also *Julius Caesar* 3. 1. 204–5: "Here wast thou bay'd, brave hart / Here didst thou fall." See also *OED*, s.v.: "bay": "position of the hunted animal ... at or to one's last extremity."

Man's malice, with wrecking and storm.
Beyond saying sweet, past telling of tongue,
Thou art lightning and love,[14] I found it, a winter and warm;   70
Father and fondler of heart thou hast wrung:
Hast thy dark descending and most art merciful then.

10

With an anvil-ding
And with fire in him forge thy will[15]
Or rather, rather then, stealing as Spring   75
Through him, melt him but master him still:
Whether at once, as once at a crash Paul,
Or as Austin,[16] a lingering-out sweet skíll,
Make mercy in all of us, out of us all
Mastery, but be adored, but be adored King.   80

PART THE SECOND

11

"Some find me a sword; some
The flange and the rail; flame,
Fang, or flood" goes Death on drum,
And storms bugle his fame.[17]
But wé dream we are rooted in earth—Dust!   85
Flesh falls within sight of us, we, though our flower the same,
Wave with the meadow,[18] forget that there must
The sour scythe[19] cringe, and the blear share° come.   °ploughshare

12

On Saturday sailed from Bremen,
American-outward-bound,   90
Take settler and seamen, tell men with women,
Two hundred souls[20] in the round—
O Father, not under thy feathers[21] nor ever as guessing
The goal was a shoal, of a fourth the doom to be drowned;
Yet did the dark side of the bay of thy blessing   95
Not vault° them, the million of rounds of thy mercy not reeve°
even them in? °entomb
                                                                    °gather

---

Notes

[14] *dens … love* see Wisdom 17: 2–6 (Douay).

[15] *will* for the metaphor of the smith at the forge, see Ecclesiasticus 38: 28.

[16] *Paul … Austin* for Paul (formerly called Saul) and his conversion, see Acts 9: 1–18; Austin is a common English abbreviation for St Augustine of Hippo (354–430). See his *Confessions*: "Thou, O Lord, little by little with most tender and most merciful touching and composing my heart, didst persuade me … 'That Thou art … and that the government of human beings belongs to Thee'" (trans. E. B. Pusey, 1838).

[17] *sword … fame* the harvest of Death begins the second part, as in the medieval/Renaissance versions of the "Triumph or Dance of Death" (as in Holbein's engravings; see FIELD,

n. 12). Here Death's conventional instruments include the sword (see Revelation 6: 8), the railway, fire, wild beasts, drowning, and battle, with Death beating the drum and playing the bugle.

[18] *flesh … meadow* Job 14: 1–2; Psalm 103: 14–16; Isaiah 40: 6; Jeremiah 9: 22; and 1 Peter 1: 24. Wave has a double meaning, both the ocean wave and the waving flowers.

[19] *scythe* for Time as the grim reaper or mower, see James Shirley, "Death the Leveller" (1659).

[20] *Bremen … souls* Bremerhaven is the port of Bremen; for souls, see Paul's shipwreck, Acts 27, especially 27: 37. This is the first stanza of the poem that Hopkins wrote.

[21] *feathers* see BCP, Psalm 91: 4.

13

Into the snows she sweeps,
Hurling the haven behind,
The Deutschland, on Sunday; and so the sky keeps,
For the infinite air²² is unkind, 100
And the sea flint-flake, black-backed in the regular²³ blow,
Sitting Eastnortheast, in cursed quarter, the wind;
Wiry and white-fiery and whirlwind-swivellèd snow
Spins to the widow-making unchilding²⁴ unfathering deeps.

14

She drove in the dark to leeward,²⁵ 105
She struck—not a reef or a rock
But the combs of a smother of sand: night drew her
Dead to the Kentish Knock;
And she beat the bank down with her bows and the ride of her keel:
The breakers rolled on her beam with ruinous shock; 110
And canvass and compass, the whorl²⁶ and the wheel
Idle for ever to waft her or wind° her with, these she endured. °turn (naut., *OED*)

15

Hope had grown grey hairs,
Hope had mourning on,
Trenched with tears, carved with cares, 115
Hope was twelve hours gone;
And frightful a nightfall folded rueful a day
Nor rescue, only rocket and lightship,²⁷ shone,
And lives at last were washing away:
To the shrouds²⁸ they took,—they shook in the hurling and horrible airs. 120

16

One stirred from the rigging to save
The wild woman-kind below,
With a rope's end round the man, handy and brave—
He was pitched to his death at a blow,
For all his dreadnought breast and braids of thew: 125
They could tell²⁹ him for hours, dandled the to and fro
Through the cobbled foam-fleece. What could he do
With the burl° of the fountains of air, buck and the flood of the wave? °knot in wood;

Notes

²² *air* see *Iliad* 8. 558.
²³ *regular* (Victorian colloq. complete, thorough); see GILBERT, n. 30.
²⁴ *unchilding* see *Coriolanus* 5. 6. 15.
²⁵ *leeward* pronounced "lured" (naut.), rhyming with "drew her / D" (ead) two lines later. For combs, see n. 7.
²⁶ *whorl* propeller; the single propeller had been sheared off when the engines reversed, trying to avoid the breakers on the sandbank.
²⁷ *rocket and lightship* at first distress rockets were not seen in the storm. Later they became visible and eventually were seen at Harwich and a rescue ship was dispatched. The lightship, with warning lights about the sandbank, was 4 kilometres away, but it was anchored and could not help.
²⁸ *shrouds* rigging that supported the masts, with horizontal ropes up which the captain ordered as many passengers as could climb; also the sheet to wrap the dead before burial.
²⁹ *tell* use him to count the hours as he was swinging like a pendulum. This stanza depends on the account in *The Times* (11 Dec. 1875).

17

They fought with God's cold—[30]

And they could not and fell to the deck   130

(Crushed them) or water (and drowned them) or rolled

With the sea-romp over the wreck.

Night roared, with the heart-break hearing a heart-broke rabble,

The woman's wailing, the crying of child without check—

Till a lioness[31] arose breasting the babble,   135

A prophetess towered in the tumult, a virginal tongue told.[32]

18

Ah, touched in your bower of bone

Are you! turned for an exquisite smart,

Have you! make words break from me here all alone,

Do you!—mother of being in me, heart.   140

O unteachably after evil,[33] but uttering truth,

Why, tears! is it? tears; such a melting, a madrigal start!

Never-eldering revel and river of youth,

What can it be, this glee?[34] the good you have there of your own?

19

Sister, a sister calling   145

A master,[35] her master and mine!—

And the inboard seas run swirling and hawling;

The rash smart° sloggering brine   °reckless stinging

Blinds her; but she that weather sees[36] one thing, one;

Has one fetch° in her: she rears herself to divine   °to reach by tacking (naut.) 150

Ears, and the call of the tall nun

To the men in the tops and the tackle[37] rode over the storm's brawling.

20

She was first of a five and came

Of a coifèd sisterhood.

(O Deutschland, double a desperate name![38]   155

O world wide of its good!

Notes

[30] *cold* see Psalm 147: 16–17.

[31] *lioness* see Isaiah 21: 8; and Ezekiel 19: 1–2 (Douay); as well as *The Times* (13 Dec. 1875).

[32] *prophetess ... told* a prophetess here is one who proclaims the word of God, not predicting the future. Told is also "tolled" as she continued her cry.

[33] *words break ... evil* the poet breaks his seven-year self-imposed silence; for the heart's resisting evil, see Genesis 8: 21.

[34] *madrigal ... revel ... glee* three musical forms current from the Renaissance to the Baroque: the tall nun's cry as a love-song with its repeated refrain as a high art form (madrigal); as a festive celebration (revel); and as a popular folk song (glee), whose refrain the audience can pick up – and so appealing to all.

[35] *master* see n. 2.

[36] *blinds ... sees* an oxymoron: blind-sight.

[37] *tall nun ... tops and the tackle* a double meaning, since a tall nun is also the name of a maritime buoy (naut.); tops and tackle are the rigging.

[38] *first ... coifèd ... name* Hopkins took the tall nun as the leader, following *The Times* (11 Dec. 1875), although the leader of the group was Sr M. Henrica Fassbaender, 28 years old. The sisters wore a coif, a close-fitting cap, with a wimple that covered the cheeks and neck, and a veil over all except their faces, as well as a long flowing habit –clothing which, like that of other women, made survival in the water almost impossible. *Deutschland* is both the name of the ship and the new German empire.

But Gertrude, lily, and Luther, are two of a town,[39]
Christ's lily and beast of the waste wood:
From life's dawn it is drawn down,
Abel is Cain's brother and breasts they have sucked the same.)[40]   160

21

Loathed for a love men knew in them,
Banned by the land of their birth,
Rhine refused them, Thames would ruin them;
Surf, snow, river and earth
Gnashed: but thou art above, thou Orion[41] of light;   165
Thy unchancelling poising palms were weighing the worth,
Thou martyr-master:[42] in thy sight
Storm flakes were scroll-leaved flowers, lily showers—sweet heaven
was astrew° in them.   °strewn

22

Five! the finding and sake
And cipher[43] of suffering Christ.   170
Mark, the mark is of man's make
And the word of it Sacrificed.
But he scores° it in scarlet himself on his own bespoken,   °imprints
Before-time-taken, dearest prizèd and priced—
Stigma, signal, cinquefoil token   175
For lettering of the lamb's fleece, ruddying[44] of the rose-flake.

23

Joy fall to thee, father Francis,[45]
Drawn to the Life[46] that died;
With the gnarls of the nails in thee, niche of the lance, his

Notes

[39] Gertrude … town St Gertrude the Great (1256–c.1302), German mystic and theologian, was born at Eisleben in Saxony or nearby at Helfta where, as a small child, she was presented to the convent of St Mary. Gertrude wrote The Herald of Divine Love and Spiritual Exercises, devoted to nuptial mysticism with the author/reader as the bride of Christ. Martin Luther (1843–1546), German theologian and church reformer, was also born in Eisleben. His posting on the church door at Wittenberg in 1517 of ninety-five theses for theological debate about doctrine is often taken as the beginning of the Protestant Reformation.

[40] lily … same a contrast between the lily (symbol for purity) and Luther as a beast laying waste to the Catholic Church in the Reformation (see Psalm 80: 13; Douay Psalm 79: 14; see also Jeremiah 5: 6; Douay). Just as Germany and the church gave birth to and nurtured the opposites Gertrude and Luther; so did Eve suckle both Cain and Abel.

[41] Orion constellation of the Hunter, Orion and his dogs, which traditionally was the cause of storms (see Job 9: 8–9; and Amos 5: 8), manifesting God's power.

[42] unchancelling … martyr-master the nuns were exiled from the safety of their chancels (the choir-part of the church)

by the Falk Laws and are now exposed to the world's dangers; for poising palm, see Isaiah 40: 12 (Douay): the nuns' hands were clasped together as they were found drowned (The Times 11 Dec. 1875); martyr-master is both the tall nun as leader ("master") and Christ as the master of martyrs.

[43] Five … cipher stanza 22 stresses the interplay of Christ's suffering and the death of martyrs: the five are both the nuns and the five wounds of Christ. Cipher is a symbol with hidden meaning; for instance, in De Musica (c.390) St Augustine applies number symbolism based on Wisdom 11: 21 (Douay).

[44] mark … ruddying for mark, see Galatians 6: 17: the signs of Christ's passion and the mark of baptism. Scarlet is the colour of blood, of martyrdom. Stigma is sign of rejection; also the stigmata or marks of Christ's passion (see below, stz. 23). A cinquefoil is a five-leaved flower, and also the five-arches around a window in Gothic architecture. Ruddying is the marking of a sheep's fleece for ownership, as Christ marks his flock.

[45] Francis Francis of Assisi (1181/2–1226), religious leader and founder (1210) of Franciscan order to which the five nuns

Lovescape crucified   180
And seal of his seraph-arrival! and these thy daughters
And five-livèd and leavèd favour and pride,
    Are sisterly sealed in wild waters,
To bathe in his fall-gold mercies, to breathe in his all-fire glances.

24

Away in the loveable west,[47]   185
    On a pastoral forehead of Wales,
I was under a roof here, I was at rest,
    And they the prey of the gales;
She to the black-about air, to the breaker, the thickly
Falling flakes, to the throng that catches and quails   190
    Was calling[48] "O Christ, Christ, come quickly":
The cross to her she calls Christ to her, christens her wild-worst Best.

25

The majesty! what did she mean?
    Breathe, arch and original Breath.[49]
Is it love in her of the being as her lover had been?   195
    Breathe, body of lovely Death.
They were else-minded then, altogether, the men
Woke thee with a *We are perishing* in the weather of Gennesareth.[50]
    Or ís it that she cried for the crown then,
The keener to come at the comfort for feeling the combating keen?°
                                          °eagerness; also wailing lament   200

26

For how to the heart's cheering
    The down-dugged ground-hugged grey
Hovers off, the jay-blue heavens appearing
    Of pied and peeled May!
Blue-beating and hoary-glow height; or night, still higher,   205
With belled fire and the moth-soft Milky Way,
    What by your measure is the heaven of desire,
The treasure never eyesight got, nor was ever guessed what for the hearing?[51]

Notes

belonged. In 1224 while praying he was visited by a seraph (six-winged angel) who gave him the stigmata, the five marks of Christ's wounds as described in the following lines.

[46] *Life* drawn to Christ's life (see John 12: 32–33).

[47] *west* at St Beuno's College in Wales where Hopkins was finishing his studies and preparing for ordination, and where he wrote this poem.

[48] *calling* different reports of the shipwreck give the tall nun different words, in both German and English translation. The cry as given was reported in *The Times* (11 Dec. 1875). See also Revelation 3: 11; and 22: 7, 12, and 20.

[49] *Breath* the Holy Spirit (Gk. *pneuma*). Stanzas 25 to 29 discuss the possible motives for the nuns' martyrdom.

[50] *lovely Death ... Gennesareth* the body of lovely death is Christ crucified; possibly an echo of J. S. Bach's *Komm, süsser Tod* (Ger. come sweet death, 1736), an extremely well-known aria in Germany, in which every verse begins with the same line. See also Shakespeare's *King John* (3. 4. 28): "Death, death: O, amiable lovely death!" For perishing, see Luke 8: 22–25, where the disciples awaken Jesus who is sleeping in the boat on the Sea of Galilee in a storm in the area of Gennesareth.

[51] *hearing* see 1 Corinthians 2: 9, quoting Isaiah 64: 4.

27

No, but it was not these.
  The jading° and jar of the cart,   °tiring of horses 210
   Time's tasking, it is fathers that asking for ease
    Of the sodden-with-its-sorrowing heart,
  Not danger, electrical horror; then further it finds
   The appealing of the Passion is tenderer in prayer apart:
    Other, I gather, in measure her mind's   215
Burden, in wind's burly and beat of endragonèd seas.[52]

28

  But how shall I .. make me room there:
   Reach me a .. Fancy, come faster—
  Strike you the sight of it? look at it loom there,
    Thing[53] that she .. there then! the Master,   220
Ipse,° the only one, Christ, King, Head: °(Lat. he himself)
  He was to cure the extremity where he had cast her;
   Do, deal, lord it with living and dead;
Let him ride, her pride, in his triumph,[54] despatch and have done
  with his doom there.

29

  Ah! there was a heart right!   225
   There was single eye![55]
  Read the unshapeable shock night
    And knew the who and the why;
  Wording it how but by him that present and past,
   Heaven and earth are word of, worded by?—   230
    The Simon Peter[56] of a soul! to the blast
Tarpeian-fast,[57] but a blown beacon of light.

30

  Jesu, heart's light,
   Jesu, maid's son,
  What was the feast followed the night   235
    Thou hadst glory of this nun?—
  Feast of the one woman without stain.
   For so conceivèd, so to conceive thee is done;
    But here was heart-throe, birth of a brain,[58]
Word, that heard and kept thee and uttered thee outright.   240

Notes

[52] *seas* see Psalm 148: 7–8.

[53] *Thing* see Matthew 14: 26 (Douay): "And they seeing him walk upon the sea, were troubled, saying: It is an apparition. And they cried out for fear."

[54] *triumph* exultation as in a victory procession; the tall nun sees nature as Christ's riding in triumph on the horses of the waves, which overwhelm her to claim her as Christ's own.

[55] *eye* see Luke 11: 34. The tall nun reads all of nature, including the violence of the storm and the chaos of the shipwreck, as part of the creation by the Word: Genesis 1: 1–3; and John 1: 1–5.

[56] *Peter* see Peter's confession of Christ's messiahship (Matthew 16: 16), and his standing up after Pentecost to preach (Acts 2: 2, 14).

[57] *Tarpeian-fast* part of the Capitoline Hill in Rome, from which traitors were thrown to their deaths. See *Paradise Regained* 4. 44–50. See also CONDITION, PROGRESS, nn. 109 and 112 (WEB p. 40–41), where the allusion relates to the rioters over the Reform Bill of 1867.

[58] *night. . . brain* the feast of the Immaculate Conception of the Virgin Mary (8 December), inaugurated 1854 by Pius IX, decreed that the Virgin Mary was herself conceived

31

Well, she has thee for the pain, for the
    Patience; but pity of the rest of them!
Heart, go and bleed at a bitterer vein for the
    Comfortless unconfessed of them—
No not uncomforted: lovely-felicitous Providence   245
Finger of a tender of, O of a feathery delicacy, the breast of the
    Maiden could obey so, be a bell to, ring of it, and
Startle the poor sheep back! is the shipwrack then a harvest, does tempest
    carry the grain for thee?

32

I admire thee, master of the tides,
    Of the Yore-flood,[59] of the year's fall;   250
The recurb and the recovery of the gulf's sides,
    The girth of it and the wharf of it and the wall;
Staunching, quenching ocean of a motionable mind;
Ground of being, and granite of it: past all
    Grasp God, throned behind   255
Death with a sovereignty that heeds but hides, bodes but abides;

33

With a mercy that outrides
    The all of water, an ark
For the listener; for the lingerer with a love glides
    Lower than death and the dark;   260
A vein for the visiting of the past-prayer, pent in prison,
The-last-breath penitent spirits—the uttermost mark
    Our passion-plungèd giant risen,[60]
The Christ of the Father compassionate, fetched in the storm of his strides.

34

Now burn, new born to the world,   265
    Doubled-naturèd name,[61]
The heaven-flung, heart-fleshed, maiden-furled
    Miracle-in-Mary-of-flame,[62]
Mid-numbered He in three of the thunder-throne!

Notes

"exempt from all stain of original sin." Birth of a brain could mean birth from a brain, suggesting the birth of Pallas Athene, the goddess of wisdom in Greek mythology, from the head of Zeus. Hopkins draws a parallel between the Virgin Mary's giving birth to Jesus and the tall nun's "heart-throe" (labour) to give the spiritual birth of Christ the Word from her brain and heart.

[59] *Yore-flood* Noah's flood (*yore* ME, long ago, of old); see Genesis 6–8. Noah's flood was a frequent subject in Romantic and Victorian painting of the "apocalyptic sublime" as in John Martin's *The Deluge* (1834) and *The Great Day of his Wrath* (1853), J. M. W. Turner's *Disaster at Sea* (1835), and Francis Danby's *The Deluge* (1837–40). See also RUSKIN, MODERN, "OF WATER." See also Plate 19: Turner's *Slavers Throwing Overboard the Dead and Dying* (1840).

[60] *ark … giant risen* Noah's ark, the type or prefiguration of Christ and the Church (see Isaiah 54: 9–11; and 2 Peter 2: 5). Those who are "past-prayer" or in "prison" are perhaps references to Christ's "Descent into Hell" to rescue the souls who died before his coming (Apostles' Creed); see 1 Peter 3: 19. Giant-risen refers to Christ's passion, with a suggestion of rising from the dead.

[61] *name* Christ as having two natures, human and divine.

[62] *flame* many paintings of the annunciation of the angel's message to the Virgin Mary show her or the angel in a flame, as in Carlo Crivelli's *Annunciation* (1486) and D. G. Rossetti's *Ecce Ancilla Domini* (1850, Lat. "Behold the handmaid of the Lord"; see Luke 1: 38).

Not a dooms-day dazzle in his coming nor dark as he came;   270
  Kind, but royally reclaiming his own;
A released shower, let flash to the shire, not a lightning of fire hard-hurled.

35

  Dame, at our door
  Drowned, and among our shoals,
  Remember us in the roads, the heaven-haven of the Reward: 275
    Our Kíng back, Oh, upon English souls!
  Let him easter in us, be a dayspring to the dimness of us, be a
    crimson-cresseted east,
  More brightening her, rare-dear Britain, as his reign rolls,
    Pride, rose, prince, hero of us, high-priest,[63]
Our hearts' charity's hearth's fire, our thoughts' chivalry's throng's Lord.   280

God's Grandeur

The world is charged with the grandeur of God.
  It will flame out, like shining from shook foil;
  It gathers to a greatness, like the ooze of oil
Crushed.[64] Why do men then now not reck[65] his rod?
Generations have trod, have trod, have trod;   5
  And all is seared with trade; Bleared, smeared with toil;
  And wears man's smudge and shares man's smell: the soil
Is bare now, nor can foot feel, being shod.

And for all° this, nature is never spent;   °despite all
  There lives the dearest freshness deep down things;   10
And though the last lights off the black West went
  Oh, morning, at the brown brink eastward, springs—
Because the Holy Ghost over the bent
  World broods with warm breast and with ah! bright wings.[66]

The Starlight Night

Look[67] at the stars! Look, look up at the skies!
  O look at all the fire-folk sitting in the air!
  The bright boroughs, the circle-citadels[68] there!

Notes

[63] easter... dayspring... high-priest the last stanza culminates with the translation of the shipwreck into an inscape or vision of Britain's conversion to the Roman Catholic Church. Easter is used as a verb meaning to rise; for dayspring, see Luke 1: 78; and Malachi 4: 2. Crimson-cresseted suggests the east as a beacon (with an outdated etymology that had a cresset-beacon surmounted with a cross): hence, the easter/eastern Christian/Catholic religion, now in the light of these martyrdoms, is enlightening Britain. For high-priest, see Hebrews 4: 14–15.

[64] foil... crushed sheets of gold foil that when shaken refract light brilliantly; olive oil is a biblical mark of God's plenty; see Ezra 6: 9; 7: 22; Ezekiel 32: 14; and Micah 6: 7, 15. The

garden of Christ's agony was called Gethsemane (Heb. oil press); oil was used for illumination (lamps) and for the consecration of sacred persons and objects, as continued in church rituals in the nineteenth century. This sonnet was written on 23 February 1877.

[65] reck heed. See Hamlet 1. 3. 51.

[66] wings see Genesis 1: 2: a marginal reading in the Revised Version (1885) reads: "And the spirit of God was brooding upon the face of the waters."

[67] look in the Spiritual Exercises (1548) of Ignatius Loyola, which Hopkins knew intimately and made detailed notes on, the first act in meditation is to see in the imagination the setting in Palestine in which a biblical passage is set, to

Down in dim woods the diamond delves! the elves'-eyes!
The grey lawns cold where gold, where quickgold lies!   5
    Wind-beat whitebeam! Airy abeles[69] set on a flare!
    Flake-doves sent floating forth at a farmyard scare!—
Ah well! It is all a purchase, all is a prize.

Buy then! Bid then!—What?—Prayer, patience, alms, vows.
Look, look: a May-mess,[70] like on orchard boughs!   10
    Look! March-bloom, like on mealed-with-yellow sallows![71]
These are indeed the barn; withindoors house
The shocks. This piece-bright paling[72] shuts the spouse
    Christ home, Christ and his mother and all his hallows.°   °saints

Spring

Nothing is so beautiful as Spring—
    When weeds, in wheels, shoot long and lovely and lush;
    Thrush's eggs[73] look little low heavens, and thrush
Through the echoing timber does so rinse and wring
The ear, it strikes like lightnings to hear him sing;   5
    The glassy peartree leaves and blooms, they brush
    The descending blue; that blue is all in a rush
With richness; the racing lambs too have fair their fling.

What is all this juice and all this joy?
    A strain of the earth's sweet being in the beginning   10
In Eden garden.—Have, get, before it cloy,
    Before it cloud, Christ, lord, and sour with sinning,
Innocent mind and Mayday in girl and boy,
    Most, O maid's child, thy choice and worthy the winning.

The Windhover[74]

To Christ our Lord

I caught this morning morning's minion, king-
    dom of daylight's dauphin,[75] dapple-dawn-drawn Falcon, in his riding

Notes ————————————————————————————

visualize it as concretely as possible, perceiving its meanings and relationships, and then to proceed through the
other senses (Third Contemplation). Intense and imaginative looking helped one see the inscape of the stars (see n.
10). This sonnet was written on 24 February 1877.
[68] *circle-citadels* the watch-fires burning around the walls of
Troy (*Iliad* 8. 553 ff.).
[69] *whitebeam ... abeles* trees whose leaves have white
undersides.
[70] *May-mess* see *Timon of Athens* 4. 3. 423–4.
[71] *sallows* goat willow (or pussy willow or great sallow) with
yellow catkins.
[72] *barn ... hallows* a barn sided with paling boards with knot-
holes, through which the traditional feast for the harvesters

at the end of the reaping can be seen glowing from outside:
an analogy to the messianic banquet of Christ with his
saints, perhaps at All Hallows (*i.e.* All Saints, 1 Nov.).
[73] *eggs* pale blue. This sonnet was written in May 1877.
[74] *title* a small falcon, the European kestrel, hovers in the lower
winds but does not rise to great heights or catch its prey in
diving. Instead, it hunts small creatures on the ground, riding the winds up to 12 metres above the earth to cover its
territory. This sonnet is dated by Hopkins 30 May 1877. The
ascription "To Christ our Lord" was added in 1884.
[75] *minion ... dauphin* (Fr. *mignon*: favourite, darling); *dauphin*
the title of the king of France's eldest son, and heir to the
throne, suitable for the attributes of a princely knight that
are to be applied to the windhover. See *Henry V*: 3. 7. 15–25.

Of the rolling level underneath him steady air, and striding
High there, how he rung upon the rein of a wimpling° wing   °rippling
In his ecstasy! then off, off forth on swing,   5
    As a skate's heel sweeps smooth on a bow-bend: the hurl and gliding
    Rebuffed the big wind. My heart in hiding
Stirred for a bird,—the achieve of, the mastery of the thing!

Brute beauty and valour and act, oh, air, pride, plume, here
    Buckle![76] AND the fire that breaks from thee then, a billion   10
Times told lovelier, more dangerous, O my chevalier!°   °(Fr.) knight

    No wonder of it: shéer plód makes plough down sillion[77]
Shine, and blue-bleak embers, ah my dear,
    Fall, gall themselves, and gash gold-vermilion.[78]

Pied Beauty[79]

Glory be to God for dappled things—
    For skies of couple-colour as a brinded° cow;   °streaked, spotted
        For rose-moles[80] all in stipple upon trout that swim;
Fresh-firecoal chestnut-falls; finches' wings;
    Landscape plotted and pieced—fold,° fallow, and plough;   °high pasture   5
        And áll trádes, their gear and tackle and trim.

All things counter,° original, spare, strange;   °contrary, non-conforming
    Whatever is fickle, freckled (who knows how?)
        With swíft, slow; sweet, sour; adazzle, dím;
He fathers-forth whose beauty is past change: 10
        Praise hím.

Hurrahing in Harvest[81]

Summer ends now; now, barbarous in beauty, the stooks° rise   °sheaves
    Around; up above, what wind-walks! what lovely behaviour
    Of silk-sack clouds! has wilder, wilful-wavier
Meal-drift moulded ever and melted across skies?

Notes

[76] *Buckle* the word is much disputed: join together? or collapse – of the world of natural beauty simultaneous with the breaking through of the spiritual beauty in Christ ("thee").

[77] *sillion* part of a field jointly owned and worked by a tenant farmer. Humble duty done shines, as does a rusty ploughshare brought into use, or a turned furrow (see Matthew 5: 16; and Virgil, *Georgics* I. 43–46).

[78] *gall ... vermilion* for gall as bitterness at Christ's passion, see Matthew 27: 34; here also to inflame. Hopkins's metaphor is of seemingly dead embers falling in the grate only to flame up again, an analogy for the death of Christ flaming up into the glory of the resurrection. See Milton *Samson Agonistes* (1671: 1687–1707); and Shakespeare, Sonnet 73 (1609: 8–14).

[79] *title* Hopkins called this form a "curtal sonnet," that is, three-quarters of a Petrarchan sonnet in which the octave is reduced to a sestet, and the sestet is reduced to a quatrain plus a half-line (see n. 111). Dated by Hopkins, Summer, 1877.

[80] *rose-moles* rose-coloured spots on a live trout that disappear when it dies.

[81] *title* Dated by Hopkins 1 September 1877.

I walk, I lift up, I lift up heart, eyes,   5
    Down all that glory in the heavens to glean our Saviour;
    And, éyes, heárt, what looks, what lips yet gave you a
Rapturous love's greeting of realer, of rounder replies?

And the azurous hung hills are his world-wielding shoulder
    Majestic—as a stallion stalwart, very-violet-sweet! —   10
These things, these things were here and but the beholder
    Wanting; which two when they once meet,
The heart rears wings bold and bolder
    And hurls for him, O half hurls earth for him off under his feet.

Binsey Poplars[82]

felled 1879

My aspens dear, whose airy cages quelled,
Quelled or quenched in leaves the leaping sun,
All felled, felled, are all felled;
    Of a fresh and following folded rank
        Not spared, not one   5
        That dandled a sandalled
    Shadow that swam or sank
On meadow and river and wind-wandering weed-winding bank.

    O if we but knew what we do
        When we delve or hew—   10
    Hack and rack the growing green!
        Since country is so tender
    To touch, her being só slender,
    That, like this sleek and seeing ball°
    But a prick will make no eye at all,   15
    Where we, even where we mean
        To mend her we end her,
    When we hew or delve:
After-comers cannot guess the beauty been.
    Ten or twelve, only ten or twelve   20
    Strokes of havoc únselve[83]
        The sweet especial scene,
    Rural scene, a rural scene,
    Sweet especial rural scene.

Notes

[82] *title* Binsey is a small village near Oxford on the banks of the River Thames. Hopkins laments the destruction of the poplars or aspens that lined the bank. They were almost immediately replanted. See also CONDITION: POLLUTION (WEB p. 61). Dated by Hopkins 13 March 1879.

[83] *únselve* remove or ruin the essence of the rural scene, destroy the self-hood or inscape of it; for inscape, see n. 10.

Duns Scotus's Oxford[84]

Towery city and branchy between towers;
Cuckoo-echoing, bell-swarmèd,[85] lark-charmèd, rook racked, river-rounded;
The dapple-eared lily below thee; that country and town did
Once encounter in, here coped and poisèd powers;

Thou hast a base and brickish skirt[86] there, sours   5
That neighbour-nature thy grey beauty is grounded
Best in; graceless growth, thou hast confounded
Rural, rural keeping—folk, flocks, and flowers.

Yet ah! this air I gather and I release
He lived on; these weeds and waters, these walls are what   10
He haunted who of all men most sways my spirits to peace;

Of realty[87] the rarest-veinèd unraveller; a not
Rivalled insight, be rival Italy or Greece;
Who fired France for Mary without spot.[88]

Felix Randal[89]

Felix Randal the farrier, O he is dead then? my duty[90] all ended,
Who have watched his mould of man, big-boned and hardy-handsome

Notes

[84] *title* the Franciscan monk John Duns Scotus (1266–1308) lectured at Oxford from 1300 to 1304, and later at Paris, on the *Sentences* of Peter Lombard, taking philosophical and theological positions somewhat different from the thought of Thomas Aquinas (1225–74), especially that the Incarnation of Christ was not simply the rebalancing of divine justice caused by the Fall of Adam but that it was the culmination of creation, in the mind of God from the beginning. Hence all aspects of creation manifest not only their own individuality (what Scotus called *haecceitas*, Lat. the this-ness of a thing – related to Hopkins's inscape; see n. 10) but also allude to their creation by the Word (John 1: 1). Hopkins enthusiastically read Scotus's Oxford lectures in Latin, finding him a liberating influence as opposed to accepted Jesuit theology, embodied in Aquinas as interpreted by the Spaniard Francisco Suárez (1548–1617). Since Hopkins was devouring Duns Scotus before his final examinations, his deviations from the Jesuit's conventional theology may have caused Hopkins's failure. Dated by Hopkins at Oxford, March 1879.

[85] *bell-swarmèd* several Oxford colleges ring bells on the quarter hour, many ring them before services, and several also have a peal of bells that rings elaborate changes.

[86] *skirt* from the 1860s' worker's houses made of yellow brick were extended into Oxford's suburbs, amidst complaints from John Ruskin and William Morris.

[87] *realty* the realism of Duns Scotus's metaphysics (see n. 84) that Hopkins found compatible. Scotus held that "universals" (abstract qualities such as the colour blue, or female-ness, or a moral quality like goodness, or a species, like human, or lily, or falcon) exist, and, further, that they are individuated in the form of a specific thing, having its "this-ness," or *haecceitas* (see nn. 1 and 84).

[88] *Italy . . . spot* Scotus is the "unraveller" of the doctrine of the Immaculate Conception (see n. 58) that he is reputed to have defended in debate at the University of Paris (and in his text "On the fittingness of the Immaculate Conception," *c.*1306) against the continuing theological tradition and debates of the Greeks and Italians, that is, about Greek realism from Plato on, concerning the existence of universal categories like colours or qualities (such as purity), and the Italian Aristotelians, like Thomas Aquinas.

[89] *title* Felix Spencer was one of Hopkins's parishioners in the Liverpool slums. He died of tuberculosis at the age of 31 on 21 April 1880. A farrier is a blacksmith – Randal (Hopkins changes his name) had to be exceptionally strong to shoe the huge Clydesdale horses that pulled wagons loaded with barrels of beer. George Orwell said the poem was perhaps "the best short poem in the language." Hopkins dated the poem at Liverpool, 28 April 1880.

[90] *duty* a virtue greatly esteemed in the Victorian moral hierarchy, but here also referring to his priestly duty to care for the sick and dying. In his first sermon in Liverpool, Hopkins redefined duty, saying *"Duty is love . . . There is nothing higher than duty* in creatures or in God." In the same year Samuel Smiles published *Duty*. For duty, see also HEMANS, n. 1; and CLOUGH, "DUTY."

Pining, pining, till time when reason rambled in it and some
Fatal four disorders, fleshed there, all contended?

Sickness broke him. Impatient he cursed at first, but mended   5
Being anointed and all; though a heavenlier heart began some
Months earlier, since I had our sweet reprieve and ransom[91]
Tendered to him. Ah well, God rest him all road° ever he offended!   °(dial.) all ways

This seeing the sick endears them to us, us too it endears.
My tongue had taught thee comfort, touch had quenched thy tears,   10
Thy tears that touched my heart, child, Felix, poor Felix Randal;

How far from then forethought of, all thy more boisterous years,
When thou at the random grim forge, powerful amidst peers,
Didst fettle° for the great grey drayhorse his bright and battering sandal!   °(dial.) shape

Spring and Fall:[92]

to a young child

Márgarét, áre you gríeving
Over Goldengrove[93] unleaving?
Leáves, líke the things of man, you
With your fresh thoughts care for, can you?
Áh! ás the heart grows older   5
It will come to such sights colder
By and by, nor spare a sigh
Though worlds of wanwood[94] leafmeal lie;
And yet you wíll weep and know why.
Now no matter, child, the name: 10
Sórrow's spríngs áre the same.
Nor mouth had, no nor mind, expressed[95]
What heart heard of, ghost guessed:
It ís the blight man was born for,[96]
It is Margaret you mourn for.   15

"As kingfishers catch fire, dragonflies dráw fláme"[97]

As kingfishers catch fire, dragonflies dráw fláme;
As tumbled over rim in roundy wells
Stones ring; like each tucked° string tells, each hung bell's   °(dial.) plucked

Notes

[91] *anointed … ransom* the last rites for the dying, confession, anointing and holy communion.

[92] *title* the seasons become metaphoric points of contrast in human life between innocence and experience, life and death. The poem is dated by Hopkins at Lydiate, Lancashire, 7 September 1880. It was first published in *The Spirit of Man*, edited by Robert Bridges (1915), omitting lines 3 and 4.

[93] *Goldengrove* both an idyllic paradise, Arcadia, or Eden, and a grove where perpetual spring in the Golden Age suc-

cumbs to the fall of leaves, analogous to the Fall in Genesis 3: 16–19.

[94] *wanwood* pale wood, decaying wood, where leaves drop one at a time, piecemeal; also a suggestion of wan as pale from sorrow.

[95] *expressed* see 1 Corinthians 2: 9–10.

[96] *for* see Job 5: 7.

[97] *title* the poem sets out Hopkins's theory of inscape indebted to the theology of John Duns Scotus (see nn. 10

Bow swung finds tongue to fling out broad its name;
Each mortal thing does one thing and the same:　　　　　　　5
Deals out that being indoors each one dwells;
Selves—goes itself; *myself* it speaks and spells,
Crying *Whát I do is me: for that I came.*

Í say móre: the just man justices;
Kéeps gráce: thát keeps all his goings graces;　　　　　　　10
Acts in God's eye what in God's eye he is—
Chríst—for Christ plays in ten thousand places,
Lovely in limbs, and lovely in eyes not his
To the Father through the features of men's faces.

[Carrion Comfort]⁹⁸

Not, I'll not, carrion comfort, Despair, not feast on thee;
Not untwist—slack they may be—these last strands of man
In me ór, most weary, cry *I can no more.*⁹⁹ I can;
Can something, hope, wish day come, not choose not to be.
But ah, but O thou terrible, why wouldst thou rude° on me　　5　　°violently
Thy wring-world right foot rock? lay a lionlimb¹⁰⁰ against me? scan
With darksome devouring eyes my bruisèd bones? and fan,¹⁰¹
O in turns of tempest, me heaped there; me frantic to avoid thee and flee?

Why? That my chaff might fly; my grain lie, sheer and clear.
Nay in all that toil, that coil, since (seems) I kissed the rod,　　　　10
Hand rather, my heart lo! lapped strength,¹⁰² stole joy, would laugh, chéer.
Cheer whom though? the hero whose heaven-handling flung me, fóot tród
Me? or me that fought him? O which one? is it each one? That night, that year
Of now done darkness I wretch lay wrestling with (my God!) my God.¹⁰³

Notes

and 84). To medieval scholastic philosophers, the prodigality of nature represents the infinite degrees of goodness and beauty in the creator, and each singular item in nature realizes its individual potentiality by act – that is, by being precisely what it is. So Kingfishers, the most brilliant of British birds with blue backs and wings, and rosy breast, flash like fire, and dragonflies suggest the blue part of a flame. In *Poems* (1918) Bridges placed this poem with other poems of 1881–82 (an order we have followed), but the poem has now been redated in *Poetical Works* (1990) as March or April, 1877.

⁹⁸ *title* Bridges called the sonnets of 1887 to 1889 the "melancholy sonnets" and the "terrible sonnets," while others called them the "sonnets of desolation" or the "dark sonnets." Critics are not agreed about what poems to include, and the number varies from six or seven to eleven or twelve. Most include "Carrion Comfort." The metaphor is a wounded person on a battlefield becoming carrion comfort for vultures. Despair is both "carrion" (rotting flesh) and "comfort" (strengthening consolation: Lat. *cum*, with + *fors, fortis*, strength), so the phrase is an oxymoron,

in that despair receives its own comfort by wallowing in the rottenness of the spiritual state – or even the false comfort of doing nothing. Hopkins wrote on the topic in his commentary on the *Spiritual Exercises*: "the mind gnawing and feeding on its own most miserable self." The poem perhaps dates from August 1885 and was revised about September 1887.

⁹⁹ *more* see *Purgatory* 9. 139 (Ital. *Più non posso*: I can no more); and *Antony and Cleopatra* 4. 15. 59.

¹⁰⁰ *terrible ... lionlimb* an early draft of lines 5–6 reads: "Yet why, thou terrible, wouldst thou rock rude on me / With Thy wring-earth tread; launch lion-foot on me?" For "terrible," see Genesis 28: 17 (Douay); and Nehemiah 9: 32; for "wring-world," see Isaiah 66: 1; for "lionlimb," see Isaiah 38: 13–17; and Revelation 5: 5.

¹⁰¹ *eyes ... fan* for "eyes," see Revelation 1: 14; and 2: 18. The metaphor of the winnowing fan continues into the sestet as retribution and purification: see Jeremiah 15: 7; Matthew 3: 12; and Luke 3: 16–17.

¹⁰² *rod ... strength* accepted discipline – perhaps of becoming a priest and Jesuit. For "lapped," see Judges 7: 5–7.

Tom's Garland[104]

Upon the Unemployed

Tom—garlanded with squat° and surly steel	°hidden
Tom; then Tom's fallowbootfellow[105] piles pick	
By him and rips out rockfire° homeforth—sturdy Dick;	°casting sparks from rocks
Tom Heart-at-ease, Tom Navvy: he is all for his meal	
Sure, 's bed now. Low be it: lustily he his low lot (feel	5
That ne'er need hunger, Tom; Tom seldom sick,	
Seldomer heartsore; that treads through, prickproof, thick	
Thousands of thorns, thoughts) swings though. Commonweal	
Little I reck° ho! lacklevel in, if all had bread:	°(arch.) care
What! Country is honour enough in all us—lordly head,	10

Notes

[103] *wrestling … God* for "wrestling," see Genesis 32: 24–30; for "my God," see Jesus' cry from the cross, Matthew 27: 46.

[104] *title* a sonnet with two sestets, the second caudate (expanded form; see n. 111), with half-lines. Hopkins wrote to Bridges: "Dublin, Feb. 10, '88:…It means then that, as St. Paul and Plato and Hobbes and everybody says, the commonwealth or well-ordered human society is like one man; a body with many members and each its function; some higher, some lower, but all honourable, from the honour which belongs to the whole. The head is the sovereign, who has no superior but God and from heaven receives his or her authority: we must then imagine this head as bare (see St. Paul much on this) and covered, so to say, only with the sun and stars, of which the crown is a symbol, which is an ornament but not a covering; it has an enormous hat or skullcap, the vault of heaven. The foot is the day-labourer, and this is armed with hobnail boots, because it has to wear and be worn by the ground; which again is symbolical; for it is navvies or day-labourers who, on the great scale or in gangs and millions, mainly trench, tunnel, blast, and in other ways disfigure, 'mammock' the earth and, on a small scale, singly, and superficially stamp it with their footprints. And the 'garlands' of nails they wear are therefore the visible badge of the place they fill, the lowest in the commonwealth. But this place still shares the common honour, and if it wants [lacks] one advantage, glory or public fame, makes up for it by another, ease of mind, absence of care; and these things are symbolised by the gold and the iron garlands. (O, once explained, how clear it all is!) Therefore the scene of the poem is laid at evening, when they are giving over work and one after another pile their picks, with which they earn their living, and swing off home, knocking sparks out of mother earth not now by labour and of choice but by the mere footing, being strongshod and making no hardship of hardness, taking all easy. And so to supper and bed. Here comes a violent but effective hyperbaton or suspension, in which the action of the mind mimics that of the labourer—surveys his lot, low but free from care; then by a sudden strong act throws it over the shoulder or tosses it away as a light matter. The witnessing of which lightheartedness makes me indignant with the fools of Radical Levellers. But presently I remember that this is all very well for those who are in, however low in, the Commonwealth and share in any way the common weal; but that the curse of our times is that many do not share it, that they are outcasts from it and have neither security nor splendour; that they share care with the high and obscurity with the low, but wealth or comfort with neither. And this state of things, I say, is the origin of Loafers, Tramps, Cornerboys, Roughs, Socialists and other pests of society. And I think that it is a very pregnant sonnet, and in point of execution very highly wrought, too much so, I am afraid."

"Tom" is the first of the proverbial names for everyman, Tom, Dick, and Harry (see "HARRY PLOUGHMAN," below). The navvy, as the bottom of the British hierarchy, does not even appear in Cruikshank's etching of "The British Beehive" (see CONDITION: SOCIAL FORMATION; CRUIKSHANK), but he figures prominently in Ford Madox Brown's painting, *Work* (1865) and in his accompanying sonnet that Hopkins copied into his commonplace book in February 1865 (see CONDITION: PROGRESS; BROWN, "WORK" (WEB p. 32)). For the analogy of the body and the church as a commonwealth in which each part has a function, see 1 Corinthians 12. See also Plato, *Republic* 324; and Thomas Hobbes, *Leviathan* (1651, chap. 22). After the severe economic depression and widespread unemployment of 1886, numerous riots occurred throughout the country during Victoria's jubilee year, culminating in Bloody Sunday (13 February, 1887) in Trafalgar Square. The poem was written between September and December, 1887. Instead of the king or general's gold garland of victory, Tom's circular garland of hobnails driven into the soles of his boots are his hero's mark.

[105] *fallowbootfellow* "fallow" is both the reddish brown leather of boots and unworking (as an unseeded, unploughed field): their workday is over. The fellow is his workmate.

[106] *title* like "As Kingfishers," this sonnet specifies a significant role for each part of creation – here a body-part, each func-

With heaven's lights high hung round, or, mother-ground
That mammocks,° mighty foot. But no way sped,   °(dial.) breaks up
Nor mind nor mainstrength; gold go garlanded
With, perilous, O nó; nor yet plod safe shod sound;
         Undenizened,° beyond bound   °homeless outcast   15
Of earth's glory, earth's ease, all; no one, nowhere,
In wide the world's weal; rare gold, bold steel, bare
         In both; care, but share care—
This, by Despair, bred Hangdog dull; by Rage,
Manwolf, worse; and their packs infest the age.   20

Harry Ploughman[106]

Hard as hurdle[107] arms, with a broth of goldish flue[108]
Breathed round; the rack of ribs; the scooped flank; lank
Rope-over thigh; knee-nave;° and barrelled shank—   °knee cap
         Head and foot, shoulder and shank—
By a grey eye's heed steered well, one crew, fall to;[109]   5
Stand at stress. Each limb's barrowy brawn, his thew
That onewhere curded,° onewhere sucked or sank—   °one place bulged
         Soared or sank—,
Though as a beechbole° firm, finds his, as at a roll-call, rank   °beech tree trunk
And features, in flesh, what deed he each must do—   10
         His sinew-service where do.

He leans to it, Harry bends, look. Back, elbow, and liquid waist
In him, all quail to the wallowing o' the plough: 's cheek crimsons; curls
Wag or crossbridle, in a wind lifted, windlaced—
         See his wind-lilylocks-laced;   15
Churlsgrace, too, child of Amansstrength, how it hangs or hurls
Them—broad in bluff hide his frowning feet lashed! raced
With, along them, cragiron under and cold furls—
         With-a-fountain's shining-shot furls.[110]

Notes

tioning metonymically to represent its place in the whole, each perfect in its way, and each necessary for the functioning of the whole – like the "commonweal" in "Tom's Garland." The "octave" (eleven lines) outlines each part's potentiality, in the mediaeval scholastics' terms, only realized in the act of ploughing in the "sestet" (12–19). Hopkins himself had tried ploughing when in Dromore in Ireland in September 1887 when the poem was written. See LITERATURE: PHOTOGRAPHERS, EMERSON (WEB p. 172).

[107] *hurdle* flexible, strong wood like willow or ash, used in making hurdles for horse-jumping or wattle-gates or frames – here also an extension of the wooden handles of the plough.

[108] *flue* golden downy hair on the arms.

[109] *to* in lines 1–5 the body of the ploughman and the plough are seen as one, and are compared with a ship.

[110] *furls* the glistening furrows curled over one another.

[111] *title* in his experiments with the form of the sonnet, Hopkins tried shortening the form to 10 ½ lines (a curtal sonnet) with the same proportions as the Petrarchan (see n. 79). He also expanded it by adding an additional sestet as in "Tom's Garland" and "Harry Ploughman" in what he and Bridges called a caudate sonnet (Lat. *cauda*, tail), as here, using the model of Milton's "On the New Forcers of Conscience Under the Long Parliament" (1673). The sprung rhythm is in Alexandrines, with vertical lines marking the

That Nature is a Heraclitean Fire and of the Comfort of the Resurrection[111]

Cloud-puffball, torn tufts, tossed pillows | flaunt forth, then chevy° on an air-   °race
Built thoroughfare: heaven-roysterers, in gay-gangs | they throng; they glitter in marches.
Down roughcast, down dazzling whitewash, | wherever an elm arches,
Shivelights and shadowtackle[112] in long | lashes lace, lance, and pair.
Delightfully the bright wind boisterous | ropes, wrestles, beats earth bare   5
Of yestertempest's creases; in pool and rut peel parches
Squandering ooze to squeezed | dough, crust, dust; stanches, starches
Squadroned masks and manmarks° | treadmire toil there   °footprints
Footfretted in it. Million-fuelèd, | nature's bonfire burns on.
But quench her bonniest, dearest | to her, her clearest-selvèd spark[113]   10
Man, how fast his firedint, | his mark on mind, is gone!
Both are in an unfathomable, all is in an enormous dark
Drowned. O pity and indig | nation! Manshape, that shone
Sheer off, disseveral,° a star, | death blots black out; nor mark   °cut off
    Is any of him at all so stark   15
But vastness blurs and time | beats level. Enough! the Resurrection,[114]
A heart's-clarion! Away grief's gasping, | joyless days, dejection.
    Across my foundering deck shone
A beacon, an eternal beam. | Flesh fade, and mortal trash
Fall to the residuary worm; | world's wildfire, leave but ash: 20
    In a flash, at a trumpet crash,
I am all at once what Christ is, | since he was what I am, and
This Jack, joke, poor potsherd, | patch, matchwood, immortal diamond,[115]
    Is immortal diamond.

["Thou art indeed just, Lord"]

Justus quidem tu es, Domine, si disputem tecum: verumtamen justa loquar ad te: Quare via impiorum prosperatur? &c.[116]

Thou art indeed just, Lord, if I contend
With thee; but, sir, so what I plead is just.
Why do sinners' ways prosper? and why must

Notes

caesura as in Bridges's edition. Heraclitus (*c.*535–475 BCE) was a Greek philosopher who held that fire is the essential and underlying element of the cosmos, and that all things are changeable, in a state of flux. The first nine lines trace the upward movement Hopkins perceives after the storm, from clouds and brilliant light, from earth to dust and air. In the following six and a half lines, humankind follows a downward pattern, from sparks to nothingness. Then comes the "turn" (Ital. *volta*) with the resurrection. Hopkins dated the poem: in Dublin, 26 July 1888.

[112] *roughcast ... shivelights ... shadowtackle* roughcast is a plaster made of gravel and lime for covering house walls; a shive is a splinter (northern England dial.), hence splinters of light; shadowtackle is shadows of branches on the walls suggesting ships' rigging.

[113] *spark* see Wisdom 2: 2–4. To Heraclitus the stars were pure fire, and the human soul is a spark from the stars.

[114] *Resurrection* behind lines 16 to 24 lie 1 Corinthians 15: 20–27; and 35–55.

[115] *Jack ... diamond* a Jack is a common fellow; a laughable creation; a potsherd is a broken piece of pottery that the pot maker has discarded (Isaiah 45: 9), a fool; matchwood is a burnt match-stick; a diamond captures light and was supposedly indestructible by fire.

[116] *epigraph* see Jeremiah 12: 1: Lat. from the Vulgate version: "Righteous art thou, O Lord, when I plead with thee: yet let me talk with thee of thy judgments: Wherefore doth the way of the wicked prosper?" Hopkins dated the poem 17 March 1889; it is untitled.

Disappointment all I endeavour end?
    Wert thou my enemy, O thou my friend,   5
How wouldst thou worse, I wonder, than thou dost
Defeat, thwart me? Oh, the sots and thralls of lust
Do in spare hours more thrive than I that spend,
Sir, life upon thy cause. See, banks and brakes°   °thickets
Now leavèd how thick! lacèd they are again   10
With fretty° chervil,[117] look, and fresh wind shakes   °lacy, fretted
Them; birds build—but not I build; no, but strain,
Time's eunuch,[118] and not breed one work that wakes.
Mine, O thou lord of life, send my roots rain.

Louisa Sarah Bevington (1845–95)

The eldest of eight children in a Quaker family from Battersea in Surrey, Bevington was educated at home, developing an interest in natural science. In 1876 she published privately her first book of poetry, *Key Notes,* under the pseudonym Arbor Leigh (indebted to Elizabeth Barrett Browning's heroine, Aurora Leigh), republishing it under her own name in 1879. In the early 1880s she wrote articles in the *Nineteenth Century* and the *Fortnightly Review* on such subjects as ethics, atheism, morality, and evolution, including one in the latter journal on "The Moral Colour of Rationalism" (Aug. 1881), solicited by Herbert Spencer (1820–1903), English philosopher and sociologist. Her second volume was *Poems, Lyrics and Sonnets* (1882). On a trip to Germany in 1883 she met and married a Munich artist, Ignatz Guggenberger, but the marriage did not last and she returned to London alone in 1890. Lecturing on politics and social issues, she joined the anarchist and communist groups around Peter Kropotkin (1842–1921), Russian anarchist. In 1895 she helped establish the Anarchist Communist Alliance and published its *Manifesto* (1895). Bevington contributed articles and poetry on human rights and child-sexual abuse to such anarchist journals as James Tochatti's *Liberty,* Charlotte Wilson's *Freedom,* and William Morris's *Commonweal.* No standard edition. Hermia Oliver, *The International Anarchist Movement in Late Victorian London* (1983); "Louisa Sarah Bevington":

http://www.mantex.co.uk/2009/12/03/victorian-women-writers-07.

Morning[1]

What's the text to-day for reading
Nature[2] and its being by?
There is effort all the morning
Through the windy sea and sky.

Notes

[117] *chervil* cow parsley, Queen Anne's lace.
[118] *eunuch* see Matthew 19: 12.

LOUISA SARAH BEVINGTON
[1] *title* by reading the sequential times of a day against the order of nature (as in Genesis 1), set against a vast expanse of geological time, the poem adopts the tradi-

All, intent in earnest grapple,   5
    That the All may let it be:
Force, in unity, at variance
    With its own diversity.

Force, prevailing unto action:
    Force, persistent to restrain: 10
In a twofold, one-souled wrestle,
    Forging Being's freedom chain.

Frolic! say you—when the billow
    Tosses back a mane of spray?
No; but haste of earnest effort;   15
    Nature works in guise of play.

Till the balance shall be even
    Swings the to and fro of strife;
Till an awful equilibrium
    Stills it, beats the Heart of Life.   20

What's the text to-day for reading
    Nature and its being by?
Effort, effort all the morning,
    Through the sea and windy sky.

Afternoon

Purple headland over yonder,
    Fleecy, sun-extinguished moon,
I am here alone, and ponder
    On the theme of Afternoon.

Past has made a groove for Present,   5
    And what fits it *is*: no more.
Waves before the wind are weighty;
    Strongest sea-beats shape the shore.

Notes

tional metaphor of the two books, reading the book of nature with or against the book of the Bible. This view had been advanced by Richard Hooker (1554–1600), English theologian, and especially by Francis Bacon in *The Advancement of Learning* (1605; 1. 1. 3): "Let no man ... think ... [he can] be too well studied in the book of God's word, or in the book of God's works" – a passage cited by Darwin, whom Bevington had read, opposite the title page in *On the Origin of Species* (1859). The poem uses Darwin's notion of the struggle of existence (using such terms as grapple, force, effort) to achieve variation in species and change in the natural environment (see RELIGION: GEOLOGY; DARWIN, ORIGIN). The poem contains an implied parody of Keble's poems "Morning" and "Septuagesima" in *The Christian Year* (1827). First published in *Key-Notes* (1876). At the suggestion of her friend Herbert Spencer, these four poems on evolution were republished under her own name as "Teachings of a Day" in *Popular Science Monthly* (Jan. 1878); republished without the "Teachings of a Day" title in *Key-Notes* (1879). Our text: 1878.

2 *Nature* a pun working on at least three levels: the text of a homily in which a biblical citation sets the theme, a text that is useful in understanding nature, such as Darwin's *Origin of Species*, and a text for reading nature as in the metaphor of the two books (see n. 1).

Just what is is just what can be,
And the Possible is free;   10
'Tis by being, not by effort,
That the firm cliff juts to sea.

With an uncontentious calmness
Drifts the Fact before the "Law";
So we name the ordered sequence   15
We, remembering, foresaw.[3]

And a law is mere procession
Of the forcible and fit;
Calm of uncontested Being,
And our thought that comes of it.   20

In the mellow shining daylight
Lies the Afternoon at ease,
Little willing ripples answer
To a drift of casual breeze.

Purple headland to the westward!   25
Ebbing tide and fleecy moon!
In the "line of least resistance"[4]
Flows the life of Afternoon.

Twilight

Gray the sky, and growing dimmer,
And the twilight lulls the sea;
Half in vagueness, half in glimmer,
Nature shrouds her mystery.

What have all the hours been spent for?   5
Why the on and on of things?
Why eternity's procession
Of the days and evenings?

Hours of sunshine, hours of gloaming,
Wing their unexplaining flight,   10
With a measured punctuation
Of unconsciousness, at night.

Notes

[3] *foresaw* the model of inevitable change allows facts to be set in a specific order and so to be read in a system of causation and called a "law." The fallacy that because "x" comes after "y," "y" can be said to have caused "x," known as the *post hoc ergo propter hoc* (Lat. after this, therefore because of this) fallacy, does not take into account the almost infinite multiplicity of causes, immediate and remote – though the argument here concerns the effective causes in the struggle for existence and the survival of the fittest that can be ordered into a progressive sequence.

[4] *resistance* the principle of least effort and least action may be traced back to Euclid's showing that reflected light follows the shortest path and least time. Its modern formulation is credited to the French mathematician Pierre-Louis de Maupertuis in 1744: "The path of least action is the same as the path of shortest distance and the path of briefest time"; and "The laws of movement and of rest deduced from this principle [of least action] being the same as those observed in nature, we can admire the application of it to all phenomena."

Just at sunset was translucence,
    When the west was all aflame;
So I asked the sea a question,   15
    And an answer nearly came.

Is there nothing but Occurrence?
    Though each detail seem an Act,
Is that whole we deem so pregnant,
    But unemphasizèd Fact?   20

Or, when dusk is in the hollows
    Of the hill-side and the wave,
Are things just so much in earnest
    That they cannot but be grave?

Nay, the lesson of the Twilight   25
    Is as simple as 'tis deep;
Acquiescence, acquiescence,
    And the coming on of sleep.

Midnight

There are sea and sky about me,
    And yet nothing sense can mark;
For a mist fills all the midnight,
    Adding blindness to its dark.

There is not the faintest echo   5
    From the life of yesterday:
Not the vaguest stir foretelling
    Of a morrow on the way.

'Tis negation's hour of triumph,
    In the absence of the sun;   10
'Tis the hour of endings, finished,
    Of beginnings unbegun.

Yet the voice of awful silence
    Bids my waiting spirit hark;
There is action in the stillness,   15
    There is progress in the dark.

In the drift of things and forces,
    Comes the better from the worse,
Swings the whole of Nature upward,
    Wakes, and thinks—a universe.[5]   20

Notes

[5] *universe* the argument in these stanzas is that evolution is to some degree progressive, leading to better or better-adapted organisms, forms, or systems, a view known as "orthogenesis." The view of Theodor Eimer (1843–98), German zoologist, was that life forms evolve or even progress in a discernable linear way because of a driving force – often seen as an attack on Darwin's view of natural selection. This notion, when applied in a sociological way to human culture, was much debated in the nineteenth century and later, concerning whether or not evolution were progressive, that is, teleological, having a goal.

There will be *more* life to-morrow,
    And of life, more life that *knows*;
Though the sum of Force be constant,
    Yet the Living ever grows.

So we sing of Evolution,   25
    And step strongly on our ways,
And we live through nights in patience,
    And we learn the worth of days.

In the silence of murk midnight
    Is revealed to me this thing: 30
Nothing hinders, all enables
    Nature's vast awakening.

Marion Bernstein (1846–1906)

Very little is known about the life of Marion Bernstein. She was born in London into the family of Theodore Bernstein, a professor of languages, and Lydia Pulsford. By 1874, the family had moved to Glasgow, where she was a piano teacher, advertising in several newspapers as "Miss Marion Bernstein." She published poetry in a number of local newspapers: the *Glasgow Weekly Mail*, the *Glasgow Weekly Herald*, the *People's Journal*, and the *Helensburgh and Garloch Times*. The editor of the *Mail* gave her the name "Mirren." In 1876 she privately published *Mirren's Musings* (our text), a collection of her verse, and her only published volume. In the preface to the volume she explains that the poems were written during a long period of sickness and convalescence when she was confined to her home, possibly suffering from the results of infantile paralysis. Her autobiographical poem "Mirren's Autobiography" was published in E. H. Edwards's *One Hundred Modern Scottish Poets*

(1880). Her themes include radical support for the anti-slavery movement, temperance, and women's rights, including suffrage and especially opposition to domestic violence. She also wrote on religious topics, shipwrecks, and in support of Scots cleared from their lands by hereditary owners. Some of her poetry, such as "The Star of Bethlehem" in *The Christian Leader*, displays Christian themes, and she became associated later in her life with the Seventh Day Adventist congregation in Glasgow. No standard edition. *Working-Class Women Poets in Victorian Britain: An Anthology*, ed. Florence Boos (2008); *Radical Renfrew: Poetry from the French Revolution to the First World War*, ed. Tom Leonard (1990); Edward Cohen and Linda Fleming, "Mirren's Autobiography: The Life and Poetry of Marion Bernstein (1846-1906)" in *Scottish Literary Review* (2010): 59–76. A dozen of Bernstein's uncollected poems: http://www.nines.org/exhibits/A_Scottish_Dozen?page=14.

Woman's Rights and Wrongs[1]

I may be wrong in opinion, but still to my mind it seems
As if Parliament, Council, or Congress could never be womanly themes.—
Touching the so-called Woman's Rights, such discussion belongs
To the tender and true in a less degree than the subject of Woman's Wrongs.

                                          Jessie Russell[2]

Pray, in what way is wrong redressed,
       But by conceding right?
And Woman Suffrage is the best
       For which our sex can fight.

You'd give the lash to wifebeaters,   5
       But surely you should know,
If women legislated, they'd
       Have had it long ago.

You speak of women's wages
       Being scandalously small;   10
Believe me, Woman Suffrage
       Soon would find a cure for all.

Our claims are oft misunderstood;
       We would but share with man
The human right of doing good   15
       In any way we can.

Why should we put our trust in men,
       Who oft betray our cause?
Let women vote away their wrongs,
       And vote for righteous laws.   20

A Rule to Work Both Ways[3]

Suggested by a "Wife-beater's" Letter

If beating can reform a wife
       It might reform a husband too,
Since such are the effects of strife–
       My sisters, I advise that you

Notes

MARION BERNSTEIN

[1] *title* this poem, like others of Bernstein's, supports the campaign for women's rights from the 1860s and 1870s, especially advocating for female suffrage and against domestic abuse. For other poems of Bernstein, on ecology and animal rights, see CONDITION: POLLUTION (WEB p. 66).

[2] *Russell* Jennie Russell (1850–80) was another Glasgow working-class poet; the citation is from "Women's Rights *Versus* Women's Wrongs" (lines 1–4), published in *The Blinkin' O' the Fire* (1877); Russell did not support women's suffrage in her poem, prompting this response from Bernstein. In turn, Bernstein's poem convinced Russell to convert to the cause. Russell's later poem "A Recantation" has the following epigraph: "Dedicated to Miss Marion Bernstein, who wrote to me that "Woman's Suffrage" was the true antidote for all the evils complained of in *Woman's Rights v. Woman's Wrongs.*" It is a two-stanza poem, the last reading: "And if you'll do the

eloquent / (As Moses said to Aaron), / and plead our cause with Parliament, / I'll vote for none but 'Marion.'"

[3] *title* under the Aggravated Assaults Act (1853), often called the Women's Protection Act, imprisonment was increased to a maximum of six months hard labour and fines to £20 for assaults on women and children. Comparably, stealing a lamb could result in transportation for ten years. But the act was not a deterrent, and magistrates resisted imposing lengthy imprisonment because families would then be without provision. Adding flogging to the possible punishment for wife-battery was much debated, and was renewed in demands throughout the century from judges, magistrates, and MPs, but the provision was not added to the statute. Flogging in the army and navy, using the cat o'nine tails, had fallen into disuse after about 1870. Many cases of wife-beating were brought before magistrates in

Should try it, not with fists—Oh, no!   5
    For that would seem like some weak joker;
In husband-curing let each blow
    Be given with the kitchen poker!

When flagellating, let them see
    That you are not afraid to try   10
The very worst "extremity";
    Then they must yield, lest they should die.

And if you cannot cure them, "kill!"
    As cooly teaches the Wife-beater;
In widowhood, no doubt you will   15
    Find your existence somewhat sweeter.

When thus bad husbands cure bad wives,
    And wives cure brutes to whom they're mated,
Soon will the plagues of many lives
    Be safely buried, or cremated.   20

A wife or husband "in the way"
    You need but beat to death, or smother;
And then you may at any day
    Find better fortune with another.

Wanted A Husband[4]

Baking and cooking, scrubbing and dressing—
Accomplishments grand, well worth the possessing;
Economy too, with wisdom discrete,
    My wife must practise to make all ends meet.

                     Eleve[5]

Wanted a husband who doesn't suppose,
That all earthly employments one feminine knows,—
That she'll scrub, do the cleaning, and cooking, and baking,
And plain needlework, hats and caps, and dressmaking.
Do the family washing, yet always look neat,   5
Mind the bairns, with a temper unchangeably sweet,
Be a cheerful companion, whenever desired,
And contentedly toil day and night, if required.
Men expecting as much, one may easily see,
But they're not what is wanted, at least, not by me.   10

Notes

Glasgow in the 1870s, provoking agitation to have wife-beaters flogged. For instance, on 31 October 1874, a column in the *Glasgow Weekly Herald* cautioned against the use of the lash because it might "have the effect of hardening and self-abasing many of the men to whom it was employed," and urged that the existing law be applied with imprisonment required in grievous cases. The Home Office issued a report on the widespread occurrences of wife-assault (1875).

4 *title* imitating the many want-ads and advertisements in the newspapers for which Bernstein wrote. See ABDY, "A GOVERNESS WANTED."

Wanted a husband who's tender and true,
Who will stick to his duty, and never get "fou,"[6]
But when all his day's work he has blithely gone through,
Help his wife, "set to rights," till her work is done too;
Who will not absurdly, and helplessly go,   15
And trouble the wife about "buttons to sew,"
On his shirt, or his gloves, or his coat, or his vest,
But will sew them himself, and not think he's oppressed.
Now, if such a lad you should happen to see,
He's wanted by many, but yet—not by me!   20

Human Rights

Man holds so exquisitively tight
To everything he deems his right;
If woman wants a share, to fight
She has, and strive with all her might.

But we are nothing like so jealous   5
As any of you surly fellows;
Give us our rights and we'll not care
To cheat our brothers of their share.

Above such selfish *man-like* fright,
We'd give fair play, let come what might,   10
To he or she folk, black or white,
And haste the reign of Human Right.

A Dream[7]

I dreamt that the nineteenth century
    Had entirely passed away,
And had given place to a more advanced
    And very much brighter day.

For Woman's Rights were established quite,   5
    And man could the fact discern
That he'd long been teaching his grandmamma
    What she didn't require to learn.[8]

Notes

5 *Eleve* (Fr. a student, pupil), the pen name of another, uni-
    dentified, writer.
6 *fou* (Scots. full, drunk).
7 *title* Bernstein's best-known poem, using the dream-vision
    to imagine a future of sexual equality and utopian
    happiness.

8 *learn* a reference to the proverbial admonition not to teach
    your grandmother to suck eggs (*Brewer's Dictionary of
    Phrase and Fable*, s.v. eggs); also useless but conventional
    female accomplishments, such as painting on velvet; see
    CONDITION: EDUCATION, n. 33. See also Plate 7: Redgrave, *The
    Governess*.

There were female chiefs in the Cabinet,
    (Much better than males I'm sure!)   10
And the Commons were three-parts feminine,
    While the Lords were seen no more!⁹

And right well did the ladies legislate,
    They determined to "keep the peace,"
So well they managed the affairs of State,   15
    That the science of war might cease.

Now no man could venture to beat his wife,
    For the women had settled by law
That whoever did so should lose his life,
    Then he'd never do so any more.   20

There were no more physicians of either sex,
    For the schools were required to teach
The science of healing to every child
    As well as the parts of speech.

There were no more lawyers—all children learned   25
    The code of their country's laws;
There were female judges, and truth became
    The fashion in every cause,

All the churches attended a conference
    At which every sect agreed   30
That an erring opinion was not so bad
    As a false word or wicked deed.

At this I felt sure there was some mistake,
    It seemed such a *strange* idea!
My eyes opened wide, and that made me wake,   35
    Now wasn't the vision queer?

Married and "Settled"¹⁰

Oh! I have sighed to read
    The trials of this season;
Wife-murder seems, indeed,
    An every-day transgression.

Too oft the marriage bond   5
    Is one of fear and pain;
Affection true and fond
    Should link that sacred chain.

Notes

⁹ *more* the abolition of the hereditary and appointed House of Lords, representing the aristocracy, and the church's bishops and archbishops, was part of Bernstein's radical democratic agenda. Such appeals were common among the radicals; for instance, eight years later, during the Lords' refusal to pass the Franchise Bill in 1884, John Morley (1838–1923), Liberal MP for Newcastle, would say the Lords should be "mended or ended."

¹⁰ *title* a pun on "settled," meaning settled down into married life after bachelorhood (*OED* 8a), as well as "rendered staid, steadfast, or sober" (*OED* 1b).

Can home appear "sweet home"[11]
    When "husband" means a foe   10
And "wife" a slave?—for some
    Submit to have it so.

It seems to me such wives
    Act rashly, at the least,
Like men who risk their lives   15
    In taming a wild beast.

Beast-taming[12] seems to be
    Not quite a woman's mission;
The brutes might stay for me,
    In bachelor condition.   20

But, since you choose to wed
    And risk your limbs and lives,
Consider what I've said
    All ye unhappy wives.

Exert your common sense   25
    And form a combination[13]
For mutual defence
    Against assassination.

Michael Field [Katharine Harris Bradley (1846–1914) and Edith Cooper (1862–1913)]

Michael Field was a pseudonym for Katharine Bradley and her niece, Edith Cooper. Bradley was born in Birmingham, daughter of Charles Bradley (1810–48), a tobacco manufacturer, and Emma Harris (1812–68). Her father died of cancer when Bradley was 2, and thereafter she was home-schooled with tutors, in 1868 spent a year at the Collège de France, and then attended Newnham College, Cambridge, studying classics, especially Greek. Bradley and her widowed mother moved in with Katharine's older married sister, Emma, who had married James Robert Cooper in 1860 and who had a daughter, Edith, in 1862. When Emma Cooper became an invalid, Katharine took over the care of her niece, assuming responsibility for her

Notes

[11] *home* a reference to the popular song "Home, Sweet Home" (1823) beginning "Mid pleasures and palaces ... there's no place like home" with lyrics by John Howard Payne (1791–1852), American actor and dramatist, and music by English composer, Henry Bishop (1786–1855).

[12] *Beast-taming* wife-beaters were commonly called "brutes" (see above, "A RULE") and beasts in convictions for wife-assault in the Glasgow newspapers in the 1860s and 1870s.

The most famous beast-tamer of the nineteenth century was Isaac van Amburgh (1811–65), known as "the Lion King." He was painted amongst his animals in *Isaac van Amburgh with his Animals* (1839) by Edwin Landseer (1802–73), commissioned by Queen Victoria; see www.wga.hu/frames-e.html?/html/l/landseer/amburgh.html.

[13] *combination* a labour union or society to further the interests of equality and fair working conditions in marriage.

education as her ward. After a move to Bristol in 1878, both Bradley and Cooper attended University College; Cooper got first-class honours in philosophy. Bradley published *The New Minnesinger* (1875) under the pseudonym Arran Leigh; in 1881 they jointly published *Bellerophôn* with the name Arran and Isla Leigh. Two verse volumes followed in 1884, *Callirrhoë* and *Fair Rosamund*, for the first time using the name by which they would be known, "Michael Field," and being greeted as a strong new voice in poetry. Bradley was known in her circle of friends as Michael, and Cooper as Field or Henry. From about 1885 they shared an intense sexual relationship and intellectual collaboration. Bradley had been independently wealthy since the death of her father; when Cooper's father died in 1897, they had enough money to set up independently in Richmond. Together they published twenty-seven verse tragedies, and eight volumes of lyric poetry. Extracts from the twenty-nine volumes of their diaries were published by T. Sturge Moore as *Works and Days* (1933). The volumes of poetry were *Long Ago* (1889), based on Sappho's fragments, *Sight and Song* (1892), *Underneath the Bough* (1893), *Wild Honey from Various Thyme* (1908), *Poems of Adoration* (by Edith Cooper, 1912), *Mystic Trees* (by Katharine Bradley, 1913), *Whym Chow: Flame of Love* (1914), *Dedicated* (early poems by Edith Cooper, 1914), and *The Wattlefold:*

Unpublished Poems (1930). In Richmond they entertained and exchanged visits with the leading poets and artists of the day, including Algernon Swinburne, Robert Browning, the art critic Bernard Berenson (1865–1959), J. A. Symonds, Walter Pater, Oscar Wilde, and the artists and printers, Charles Shannon (1863–1937) and Charles Ricketts (1866–1931), like them, life-partners. Other admirers included George Meredith and W. B. Yeats. Both women converted to Roman Catholicism in 1907. They died within nine months of each other, in 1913 and 1914, and were buried in the same grave. No standard or scholarly edition. Selected poems: *Michael Field, the Poet: Published and Manuscript Materials*, eds Marion Thain and Ana Parejo Vadillo (2009); *In Leash to the Stranger: A Shorter Shîrazâd* (1999), *Music and Silence* (2000), and *Uncertain Rain*, ed. Ivor C. Treby (3 vols, 2002; annotated selected verse; 250 copies); *The Fowl and the Pussycat: Love Letters of Michael Field*, ed. Sharon Bickle (2008); Emma Donoghue, *We Are Michael Field* (1998); *Michael Field and Their World*, eds, Margaret D. Stetz and Cheryl A. Wilson (2007). Michael Field at the Orlando Project: Women's Writing in the British Isles (access through university library subscription): http://orlando.cambridge.org.ezproxy.library; see also the Michael Field journal, *The Michaelian*: www.oscholars.com/Field.

An Æolian Harp[1]

Dost thou not hear? Amid dun, lonely hills
Far off a melancholy music shrills
As for a joy that no fruition fills.

Who dwell in that far country of the wind?
The unclaimed hopes, the powers but half-defin'd,[2]   5
The shy, heroic passions of mankind.

Notes

MICHAEL FIELD

[1] *title* for Æolian harp, see PATMORE, "ANGEL," n. 13. The harp was often read as the poet with the wind of inspiration blowing through it to make poetic harmonies. First published in the *Contemporary Review* (Mar. 1889); republished with significant changes in *Underneath the Bough* (1893).

[2] *half-defin'd* the *Contemporary Review* reads "half-defin," here corrected; in *Underneath the Bough* the phrase was changed to "half-divined."

All, all are young in those reverberant bands;
None marshals them, no mellow voice commands,
They whirl and eddy as the shifting sands.

Ah, there is ruin and no ivy clings;   10
There pass the mourners for untimely things;
There breaks the stricken cry of crownless kings.

There sounds the shepherd's pipe—a jarring strain[3]
Of migratory, restless, baffled pain,
As in the sunshine he had never lain.   15

And ever and anon there spreads a boom
Of wonder through the air, arraigning doom
With ineffectual plaint as from a tomb.

But through the moving currents, more remote
Than the lark's twinkling wings, a bell-like note   20
Clear through the muffled turbulence doth float:

And there methinks that healing spirits live,
Gracious, benignant creatures, who can give
Welcome to errant thought and fugitive.

XIV [My Darling]

Τό μέλημα τοὐμόν[4]

Atthis,[5] my darling, thou did'st stray
A few feet to the rushy bed,
When a great fear and passion shook
My heart lest haply thou wert dead;
It grew so still about the brook,   5
As if a soul were drawn away.

Anon thy clear eyes, silver-blue,
Shone through the tamarisk-branches fine;
To pluck me iris thou had'st sprung
Through galingale and celandine;[6]   10
Away, away, the flowers I flung
And thee down to my breast I drew.

Notes ───

3 *strain* when the poem was reprinted in 1893, this and the final two stanzas of the 1889 poem were omitted.

4 *title* in *Long Ago* the poem is numbered but has no title. The epigraph (Gk. my darling) which we have also used as a title, is from a fragment of the seventh-century BCE poet, Sappho. The volume consisted of a short preface, sixty-eight numbered poems, each with an epigraph from Sappho, and a final unnumbered poem. The volume printed all of the epigraphs in gold, the poems in black ink. Field used a new edition of Sappho, Henry Wharton's *Sappho: Memoir, Test, Selected Renderings* (1885), and expanded his numbered fragments into individual lyrics.

Poem XIV cites Wharton's Fragment 126. For other Victorian poems on Sappho, see HEMANS, "LAST SONG"; LANDON, "SAPPHO'S SONG"; and NORTON, "THE PICTURE OF SAPPHO." From *Long Ago* (1889).

5 *Atthis* the addressee of a fragmentary poem by Sappho, "It was you, O Atthis." She was probably one of Sappho's students or associates.

6 *tamarisk ... celandine* exotic and aromatic flowering shrubs: tamarisk is a fragrant evergreen imported to the south of England from southern Europe; galingale, an English sedge; celandine, a yellow meadow flower.

My darling! Nay, our very breath
Nor light nor darkness shall divide;
Queen Dawn shall find us on one bed,   15
Nor must thou flutter from my side
An instant, lest I feel the dread,
Atthis, the immanence of death.

XXXV ["Come, Gorgo, put the rug in place"]

Ἄλλα, μὴ μεγαλύνεο δακτυλίω πέρι[7]

Come, Gorgo,[8] put the rug in place,
    And passionate recline;
I love to see thee in thy grace,
    Dark, virulent, divine.
But wherefore thus thy proud eyes fix   5
    Upon a jewelled band?
Art thou so glad the sardonyx[9]
    Becomes thy shapely hand?

Bethink thee! 'Tis for such as thou
    Zeus leaves his lofty seat;[10]   10
'Tis at thy beauty's bidding how
    Man's mortal life shall fleet;
Those fairest hands —dost thou forget
    Their power to thrill and cling?
O foolish woman, dost thou set   15
    Thy pride upon a ring?

["O free me, for I take the leap"]

Μνάσασθαι τινά φαμι καὶ ὕστερον ἄμμεων[11]

O free me, for I take the leap,
Apollo, from thy snowy steep!
Song did'st thou give me, and there fell
O'er Hellas an enchanter's spell;
I heard young lovers catch the strain: 5
For me there is the hoary main;
I would not hear my words again.

Notes

[7] *title* for the Sappho citation, see n. 1. The epigraph (Gk. foolish woman, pride not thyself on a ring) is Wharton's Fragment 35. From *Long Ago* (1889), untitled.

[8] *Gorgo* a wealthy woman in Sappho's circle.

[9] *sardonyx* or onyx, a precious stone of chalcedony, striped white and other colours, usually brown and flesh colours, traditionally carved into cameos.

[10] *seat* in Greek mythology, Zeus, the "Father of Gods and men" (Hesiod), left his throne on Mount Olympus in Greece to make love to beautiful women.

[11] *title* the epigraph (Gk. men I think will remember us even hereafter) is Wharton's Fragment 32. The poem is Field's version of the death of Sappho by plunging into the sea from the Leucadian Cliffs, having sung this hymn to Apollo, the god of lyric poetry. The poem is the last in *Long Ago* (1889), untitled.

Ah, lord of speech, well dost thou know
The incommunicable woe
Finds not in lyric cry release,   10
Finds but in Hades' bosom peace;
And therefore on thy temple-ground
Thou pointest lovers to the mound
Set high above the billows' sound.

Though in unfathomed seas I sink,   15
Men will remember me, I think,
Remember me, my King, as thine;
And must I take a shape divine
As thine immortal, let me be
A dumb sea-bird with breast love-free,   20
And feel the waves fall over me.

Praise of Thanatos[12]

Thanatos, thy praise I sing,
Thou immortal, youthful[13] king!
Glorious offerings I will bring;
For, men say, thou hast no shrine,
And I find thou art divine   5
As no other god: thy rage
Doth preserve the Golden Age.[14]
What we blame is thy delay—
Cut the flowers ere they decay!

Come, we would not derogate,   10
Age and nipping pains we hate;
Take us at our best estate![15]
While the head burns with the crown,
In the battle, strike us down!
At the bride-feast do not think   15
From thy summons we should shrink;
We would give our latest kiss
To a life still warm with bliss.

Come, and take us to the train
Of dead maidens on the plain   20

Notes

[12] *title* in Greek mythology, according to Hesiod, Thanatos (Death) was the twin of Hypnos (Sleep), sons of Nyx (Night) and Erebos (Darkness). This poem is a variant on the Flemish tradition of the *Danse Macabre* or Dance of Death, depicted, for example, in the etchings of Holbein (1538). First printed in *The Academy* (9 May 1891); reprinted with minor changes in punctuation in *Underneath the Bough* (1898), without a title.

[13] *youthful* a transferred epithet, because Thanatos preserved the youth of those slain young.

[14] *Age* the Golden Age in Greek mythology was the first age of human life marked by peace and innocence, prosperity and social harmony, when humans and animals lived in nature with accord and simplicity. Characteristic motifs include elements of the pastoral tradition: shepherds and nymphs tending bountiful flocks in an idealized rustic landscape.

[15] *estate* condition, in our prime of life.

Michael Field

Where white lilies have no stain;
Take us to the youths that thou
Lov'st to choose, of fervid brow,
Unto whom thy dreaded name
Hath been simply known as Fame: 25
With these unpolluted things
Be our endless revellings!

In Memoriam

Robert Browning[16]

Slowly we disarray,
  Our leaves grow few,
Few on the bough, and many on the sod:
Round him no ruining autumn tempest blew,
  Gathered on genial day,   5
  He fills, fresh as Apollo's bay,
  The hand of God.

Mona Lisa—Leonardo da Vinci (*The Louvre*)[17]

Historic, sidelong, implicating eyes;
Smile on the velvet cushion of the cheek[18]
Calm lips the smile leads upward; hand that lies
Glowing and soft, the patience in its rest
Of cruelty that waits and doth not seek   5
For prey; a dusky forehead and a breast
Where twilight touches ripeness amorously:
Behind her, crystal rocks, a sea and skies
Of evanescent blue on cloud and creek;
Landscape that shines suppressive of its zest   10
For those vicissitudes by which men die.

Notes

[16] *title* Browning died on 12 December 1889 in Venice. He had been a good friend of Bradley and Cooper, calling them his "two dear, Greek women," reading some of their poems before publication, and exchanging visits. He praised the volume of Sapphics entitled *Long Ago* (1889) and "prophesied they would make their mark." Printed in *The Academy and Literature* (21 Dec. 1889).

[17] *title* the *Mona Lisa* (1503–6) by Leonardo da Vinci (1452–1519) in the Louvre in Paris is the portrait was Mona (Madonna) Lisa Gherardini (1479–1550), the wife of a Florentine merchant, Francesco del Giocondo (b. 1465). During the 1880s and later, the poets travelled widely in Europe, visiting art galleries. They had attended lectures on art history and criticism in London and had the eminent Renaissance art critic Bernard Berenson as a guide and later as a friend. In the "Preface" to the 1892 volume, they write that they aimed "to translate into verse what the lines and colours of certain chosen pictures sing in themselves; to express not so much what these pictures are to the poet, but rather what poetry they objectively incarnate." That is, by following the doctrine of *ut pictura poesis* from Horace, that the poem should embody the picture in words, they were following the doctrine set forth by John Ruskin in the *Modern Painters* (vol. 3, 1856). The collection of thirty-one poems makes use of the trope of ekphrasis, the representation of a work or theory of art in one medium in another medium, alluding to a different painting in each poem. Bradley and Cooper were influenced by Pater's account of the painting: see PATER, "LEONARDO DA VINCI" (WEB p. 430). The poem was first published in *The Academy* (13 June 1891); reprinted as "La Gioconda" in *Sight and Song* (1892).

[18] *cheek* this line was revised in 1892 as "A smile of velvet's lustre on the cheek."

To Correggio's Holy Sebastian (*Dresden*)[19]

Bound by the hands, but with respect unto thine eyes how free—
Fixed on Madonna, seeing all that they were born to see!
    The Child thine upward face hath sighted,
        Still and delighted;
Oh, bliss when with mute rites two souls are plighted!   5

As the young aspen-leaves rejoice, though to the stem held tight,
In the soft visit of the air, the current of the light,
    Thou hast the peril of a captive's chances,
        Thy spirit dances,
Caught in the play of Heaven's divine advances.   10

While cherubs straggle on the clouds of luminous, curled fire,
The Babe looks through them, far below, on thee with soft desire.
    Most clear of bond must they be reckoned—
        No joy is second
To their's whose eyes by other eyes are beckoned.   15

Though arrows rain on breast and throat they have no power to hurt,
While thy tenacious face they fail an instant to avert.
    Oh might my eyes, so without measure,
        Feed on their treasure,
The world with thong and dart might do its pleasure!   20

Cupid's Visit ["I lay sick in a foreign land"][20]

    I lay sick in a foreign land;
    And by me on the right,
    A little Love had taken stand
    Who held up to my sight
    A vessel full of injured things,—   5
    His shivered bow, his bleeding wings;
    And underneath the pretty strew
    Of glistening feathers, half in view,
    A broken heart: he held them up
    Within the silver-lighted cup   10

Notes

[19] *title* Antonio Allegri da Correggio (1489–1534) was the chief Renaissance painter in Parma in Italy. His *Madonna with Saint Sebastian* (1523–24) also includes St Geminianus (d. *c.*397), bishop of Modena, and St Roch (d. 1327), who cared for victims of the plague, and who himself became a victim, though he recovered. The painting was commissioned for the cathedral at Modena. St Sebastian was a Christian martyr (*c.*288) during the persecutions by the Emperor Diocletian (244–311). Renaissance painters usually depict him as almost naked, bound to a tree or pillar, being shot with arrows. As a protector from the Black Death he was also associated with Apollo and was the patron saint of athletes. He was associated in the nineteenth century with muscular Christianity, masochism, and homosexuality. First printed in *The Academy* (19 Mar. 1892); reprinted as "Saint Sebastian / CORREGGIO / The Dresden Gallery" in *Sight and Song* (1892).

[20] *title* for Cupid, see n. 26. First printed in *The Academy* (23 April 1892); reprinted without a title in *Underneath the Bough* (1893), the second and fourth lines only being indented.

That I might mark each one; thven pressed
His little cheek against my chest,
And fell to singing in such wise
He shook the vision from my eyes.

The Birth of Venus

SANDRO BOTTICELLI

The Uffizi[21]

Frills of brimming wavelets lap
Round a shell that is a boat;
Roses fly like birds and float
Down the crisp air; garments flap:
Midmost of the breeze, with locks   5
In possession of the wind,
Coiling hair in loosened shocks,
Sways a girl who seeks to bind
New-born beauty with a tress
Gold about her nakedness.   10

And her chilled, wan body sweet
Greets the ruffled cloak of rose,
Daisy-stitched, that Flora[22] throws
Toward her ere she set her feet
On the green verge of the world: 15
Flora, with the corn-flower dressed,
Round her neck a rose-spray curled
Flowerless, wild-rose at her breast,
To her goddess hastes to bring
The wide chiton[23] of the spring.   20

While from ocean, breathing hard,
With sole pressure toward the bay,—
Olive raiment, pinions grey
By clipt rose-stems thinly starred,
Zephyrus and Boreas[24] pass,   25
One in wonder, one desire:
And the cool sea's dawnlit mass

Notes

[21] *title* Sandro Botticelli (*c.*1445–1510) was an Early Renaissance Florentine painter under the patronage of the Medici family. His *Primavera* (The Allegory of Spring, 1482) and *Birth of Venus* (1485) are among the most famous paintings of the Renaissance; by the end of the fifteenth century, both paintings were at the villa of Lorenzo di Pierfrancesco de' Medici at Castello near Florence. *The Birth of Venus* depicts the birth of Venus fully formed from the sea, blown by the winds towards the shore of Cyprus, about to be clothed by Flora. The poem was first published in *Sight and Song* (1892). See http://www.virtualuffizi.com/birth-of-venus.html.

[22] *Flora* Roman goddess of flowers.

[23] *chiton* loose garment of different lengths, gathered at the waist, worn by both women and men in ancient Greece.

[24] *Zephyrus ... Boreas* in Greek mythology the personifications of the west wind and the north wind.

Boreas' foot has lifted higher,
As he blows the shell to land,
Where the reed invades the sand.   30

She who treads the rocking shell—
Tearful shadow in her eyes
Of reluctant sympathies.
On her mouth a pause, a spell,
Candour far too lone to speak   35
And no knowledge on her brows;
Virgin stranger, come to seek
Covert of strong orange-boughs
By the sea-wind scarcely moved,—
She is Love that hath not loved.   40

["Sometimes I do dispatch my heart"]²⁵

Sometimes I do despatch my heart
Among the graves to dwell apart:
On some the tablets are erased,
Some earthquake-tumbled, some defaced,
And some that have forgotten lain   5
A fall of tears makes green again;
And my brave heart can overtread
Her brood of hopes, her infant dead,
And pass with quickened footsteps by
The headstone of hoar memory,   10
     Till she hath found
     One swelling mound
With just her name writ and *beloved*;
From that she cannot be removed.

["Ah, Eros doth not always smite"]²⁶

Ah, Eros doth not always smite
     With cruel, shining dart,
Whose bitter point with sudden might
     Rends the unhappy heart—
Not thus forever purple-stained,   5
     And sore with steely touch,

Notes

²⁵ *title* the poem has no title, like those that follow, with first lines enclosed in quotation marks and brackets. The title of the volume *Underneath the Bough* (first edition 1893) is a quotation from Edward FitzGerald's *The Rubáiyát of Omar Khayaám* (stz. 11, first edition 1859; present wording, stz. 12, third and fourth editions. 1872, 1879). FitzGerald's stanza is printed as an epigraph to the volume. Field's first edition was limited to 150 copies and consisted of 126 poems, arranged in four books of songs. The second unlimited edition (1893) reduced the number of poems to 72; the third edition (American, 1898) contained 100 poems, including 30 new ones.

²⁶ *title* Eros (Lat. Cupid) is the child of Aphrodite (Lat. Venus) in Greek mythology, adorned with wings and carrying a bow whose golden or lead arrows arouse love or cause indifference in the hearts they pierce. From *Underneath the Bough* (1893), where the poem is untitled.

Else were its living fountain drained
    Too oft and overmuch.
O'er it sometimes the boy will deign
    Sweep the shaft's feathered end;   10
And friendship rises without pain
    Where the white plumes descend.

Cyclamens[27]

    They are terribly white:
    There is snow on the ground,
And a moon on the snow at night;
The sky is cut by the winter light;
Yet I, who have all these things in ken,[28]   5
Am struck to the heart by the chiselled white
Of this handful of cyclamen.

["Already to mine eyelids' shore"][29]

Already to mine eyelids' shore
    The gathering waters swell,
For thinking of the grief in store
    When thou wilt say "Farewell."
I dare not let thee leave me, sweet,   5
    Lest it should be for ever;
Tears dew my kisses ere we meet,
    Foreboding we must sever:
Since we can neither meet nor part,
Methinks the moral is, sweetheart,   10
    That we must dwell together.

["A Girl"][30]

A girl,
Her soul a deep-wave pearl
Dim, lucent of all lovely mysteries;
A face flowered for heart's ease,[31]
A brow's grace soft as seas   5

Notes

[27] *title* cyclamens are tubrous plants with patterned leaves and elegant flowers whose petals turn upwards, in various colours, from intense snow-white to pinks and purples. From *Underneath the Bough* (1893).

[28] *ken* view, sight or knowledge.

[29] *title* see Robert Burns's "Ae Fond Kiss" (1792): "Ae fond kiss, and then we sever! / Ae farewell, and then forever! / Deep in heart-wrung tears I'll pledge thee, / Warring sighs and groans I'll wage thee." From *Underneath the Bough* (1893), untitled.

[30] *title* from *Underneath the Bough* (1893), untitled.

[31] *heart's ease* a pun referring simultaneously to the beauty of the face and to a common wildflower, also known as the wild pansy, used in herbal medicine for a number of maladies, including respiratory and chest ailments. In the language of flowers from the Renaissance through the nineteenth century, it was associated with thought (through the French name, *pensée*). A reference to the same flower occurs in the last line of the last poem Bradley wrote in May, 1914: ["What shall I do for Thee to-day?"].

Seen through faint forest-trees:
    A mouth, the lips apart,
Like aspen-leaflets trembling in the breeze
    From her tempestuous heart.
    Such: and our souls so knit,   10
    I leave a page half-writ—
The work begun
    Will be to heaven's conception done,
If she come to it.

[“I sing thee with a stock-dove's throat”][32]

I sing thee with the stock-dove's throat,
Warm, crooning, superstitious note,
That on its dearie so doth dote
    It falls to sorrow,
And from the fair, white swans[33] afloat   5
    A dirge must borrow.

In thee I have such deep content,
I can but murmur a lament;
It is as though my heart were rent
    By thy perfection,   10
And all my passion's torrent spent
    In recollection.

Unbosoming[34]

    The love that breeds
    In my heart for thee!
As the iris is full, brimful of seeds,
And all that it flowered for among the reeds
Is packed in a thousand vermilion-beads   5
That push, and riot, and squeeze, and clip,
Till they burst the sides of the silver scrip,
    And at last we see
What the bloom, with its tremulous, bowery fold
Of zephyr-petal[35] at heart did hold: 10
    So my breast is rent
With the burthen and strain of its great content;
For the summer of fragrance and sighs is dead,

Notes

[32] *title* the stock-dove or pigeon is usually grey with iridescent green or purple feathers on the neck. From *Underneath the Bough* (1893), untitled.

[33] *swans* a reference to the legend dating from Aeschylus' *Agamemnon* (458 BCE) that mute swans at their death are granted one final beautiful song: hence, swansong. Tennyson had used the myth in "Morte d'Arthur"

(1842): "like some full-breasted swan / That, fluting a wild carol ere her death / Ruffles her pure cold plume, and takes the flood / With swarthy webs."

[34] *title* from *Underneath the Bough* (1893).

[35] *zephyr-petal* flowering plant of the Amaryllis family with slender waving stems.

The harvest-secret is burning red,
And I would give thee, after my kind,   15
The final issues of heart and mind.

["It was deep April"]³⁶

It was deep April, and the morn
    Shakspere was born;³⁷
The world was on us, pressing sore;
My Love and I took hands and swore,
    Against the world, to be   5
Poets and lovers evermore,
To laugh and dream on Lethe's shore,
To sing to Charon in his boat,³⁸
Heartening the timid souls afloat;
Of judgment never to take heed,   10
But to those fast-locked souls to speed,
Who never from Apollo³⁹ fled,
Who spent no hour among the dead;
        Continually
            With them to dwell,   15
Indifferent to heaven and hell.

["Solitary Death, make me thine own"]⁴⁰

    Solitary Death, make me thine own,
And let us wander the bare fields together;
Yea, thou and I alone,
Roving in unembittered unison forever.

    I will not harry thy treasure-graves,   5
I do not ask at thy still hands a lover;
My heart within me craves
To travel till we twain Time's wilderness discover.

    To sojourn with thee my soul was bred,
And I, the courtly sights of life refusing,   10
To the wide shadows fled,
And mused upon thee often as I fell a-musing.

Notes

³⁶ *title* from *Underneath the Bough* (1893), untitled.
³⁷ *born* Shakespeare's traditional birthday (1564) and day of death (1616) is 23 April, St George's Day.
³⁸ *Lethe ... Charon* in Greek mythology Lethe is the river of forgetfulness in the underworld, Hades, over which the boatman, Charon, ferried the shades of the dead; see DANTE ROSSETTI, n. 4 (WEB p. 410); WATSON, n. 14; and THOMSON, n. 17.
³⁹ *Apollo* in Greek mythology, the god of music, healing, prophecy, and poetry, the leader of the Muses on Mount Parnassus.
⁴⁰ *title* from *Underneath the Bough* (1893), untitled.

Walter Pater

(July 30, 1894)[41]

The freshness of the light, its secrecy,
Spices, or honey from sweet-smelling bower,
The harmony of time, love's trembling hour
Struck on thee with a new felicity.
Standing, a child, by a red hawthorne-tree,[42]   5
Its perishing, small petals' flame had power
To fill with masses of soft, ruddy flower
A certain roadside in thy memory:
And haply when the tragic clouds of night
Were slowly wrapping round thee, in the cold   10
Of which men always die, a sense renewed
Of the things sweet to touch and breath and sight,
That thou didst touch and breathe and see of old
Stole on thee with the warmth of gratitude.

Constancy[43]

"I am pure! I am pure! I am pure!"[44]

I love her with the seasons, with the winds,
As the stars worship, as anemones
Shudder in secret for the sun, as bees
Buzz round an open flower: in all kinds
My love is perfect, and in each she finds   5
Herself the goal: then why, intent to teaze
And rob her delicate spirit of its ease,
Hastes she to range[45] me with inconstant minds?
If she should die, if I were left at large
On earth without her—I, on earth, the same   10
Quick mortal with a thousand cries, her spell
She fears would break. And I confront the charge
As sorrowing, and as careless of my fame
As Christ intact before the infidel.[46]

Notes

[41] *title* the date is Pater's death. The poem evokes multiple sensations, including the five senses, appropriate to Pater's stress on capturing "the splendour of our experience and of its awful brevity" in the "Conclusion" to *The Renaissance* (1873); see PATER. From *The Academy* (11 Aug. 1894).

[42] *hawthorne-tree* see Pater's "Child in the House" (1878): "It happened that, as he walked one evening, a garden gate, usually closed, stood open; and lo! within, a great red hawthorn in full flower, embossing heavily the bleached and twisted trunk and branches, so aged that there were but few green leaves thereon—a plumage of tender, crimson fire out of the heart of the dry wood.... Always afterwards, summer by summer, as the flowers came on, the blossom of the red hawthorn still seemed to him absolutely the reddest of all things; and the goodly crimson, still alive in the works of old Venetian masters or old Flemish tapestries, called out always from afar the recollection of the flame in those perishing little petals, as it pulsed gradually out of them, kept long in the drawers of an old cabinet."

[43] *title* first printed in *Underneath the Bough* (second edition 1898); reprinted in *Wild Honey from Various Thyme* (1908).

[44] *pure* from the Tibetan *Book of the Dead*; omitted from the reprinting of the poem.

[45] *range* classify.

[46] *infidel* Christ's constancy in confronting the charges against him in the mockery (Luke 22: 63–65) and trials

To Christina Rossetti[47]

Lady, we would behold thee moving bright
As Beatrice or Matilda[48] 'mid the trees,
Alas! thy moan was as a moan for ease
And passage through cool shadows to the night:
Fleeing from love, hadst thou not poet's right   5
To slip into the universe? The seas
Are fathomless to rivers drowned in these,
And sorrow is secure in leafy light.
Ah, had this secret touched thee, in a tomb
Thou hadst not buried thy enchanting self,   10
As happy Syrinx[49] murmuring with the wind,
Or Daphne,[50] thrilled through all her mystic bloom,
From safe recess as genius or as elf,
Thou hadst breathed joy in earth and in thy kind.

Penetration[51]

I love thee; never dream that I am dumb:
By day, by night, my tongue besiegeth thee,
As a bat's voice, set in too fine a key,
Too tender in its circumstance to come
To ears beset by havoc and harsh hum   5
Of the arraigning world; yet secretly
I may attain: lo, even a dead bee[52]
Dropt sudden from thy open hand by some
Too careless wind is laid among thy flowers,
Dear to thee as the bees that sing and roam: 10
Thou watchest when the angry moon drops foam;
Thou answerest the faun's soft-footed stare;
No influence, but thou feelest it is there,
And drawest it, profound, into thy hours.

Notes

(Matthew 26: 59–68; 27: 14); and remaining intact when the others crucified with him had their legs broken (John 19: 33–36).

[47] title Rossetti died on 29 December 1894. She had been a particularly skilled practitioner of the Italian (or Petrarchan) sonnet, paid tribute to in this example; see CHRISTINA ROSSETTI, MONNA INNOMINATA, especially n. 71. First published in *The Academy and Literature* (4 April 1896).

[48] *Matilda* Beatrice, named after Beatrice Portinari (1266–90), Dante's love and muse, is a character representing love in *The Divine Comedy*, guiding Dante through Paradise. Matilda meets Dante at the top of Mount Purgatory, introducing an allegorical masque (*Purgatory*, Canto 29) that prepares Dante to meet Beatrice and enter Paradise after his cleansing in the River Lethe from his memory of past sins.

[49] *Syrinx* to escape the amorous advances of Pan, the nymph Syrinx, a follower of Artemis, the goddess of chastity, was transformed into a bed of reeds. From those reeds, Pan fashioned his pipe, known as "syrinx." The story is told in *Metamorphoses* 689 ff. See BARRETT BROWNING, "A MUSICAL INSTRUMENT."

[50] *Daphne* pursued by Apollo, the nymph Daphne asked for help from the gods and was transformed into a laurel tree. The laurel, as an evergreen, was the customary crown of poets. See *Metamorphoses* I. 452 ff. For laurel, see HEMANS, n. 17.

[51] title from *Wild Honey from Various Thyme* (1908).

[52] *bee* Charles Ricketts had given Bradley and Cooper a bouquet of flowers in which he had put a dead bee. The cover of the *Wild Honey* volume was designed by him, featuring golden line drawings of bees in a honeycomb design on dark green silk.

To the Winter Aphrodite[53]

O Winter Aphrodite! (O acute,
Ice-eating pains, thine arrows!) shivering
By thy cold altar-stones, to thee I bring
Thy myrtle with its Erebus-black[54] fruit,
Locked up, provocative, profoundly mute,   5
Muter than snow or any melting thing,
Muter than fall'n winds, or bird's dead wing,
Secret as music of a fresh-struck lute
Laid by a little while and yet for aye—
By all that jealously thou dost enwomb,   10
By Sappho's words[55] hid of thee in a tomb,
Pondered of thee where no man passeth by,
Use thou my heart awhile for Love's own room,
O Winter Aphrodite, ere I die!

"I love you with my life"[56]

I love you with my life—'tis so I love you;
        I give you as a ring
The cycle of my days till death:
        I worship with the breath
That keeps me in the world with you and spring: 5
And God may dwell behind, but not above you.

Mine, in the dark, before the world's beginning:
        The claim of every sense,
        Secret and source of every need;
        The goal to which I speed,   10
And at my heart a vigour more immense
Than will itself to urge me to its winning.

A Palimpsest[57]

.. The rest
Of our life must be palimpsest—
The old writing written there the best.

Notes

[53] *title* Aphrodite, the Greek goddess of love, fell in love with the beautiful, youthful hunter Adonis, arousing the jealousy of Ares, the god of war. Ares assumed the guise of a wild boar and killed Adonis who was hunting him. Aphrodite turned the drops of blood from his wounds into anemone flowers, as Aphrodite prevailed upon Zeus to release Adonis for half of the year from the underworld, signalling the return of spring and summer before he returns to Hades for winter after the harvest. Hence Aphrodite and Adonis in winter are in mourning for the loss their beloved. See *Metamorphoses* 10. From *Wild Honey from Various Thyme* (1908).

[54] *Erebus-black* myrtle, an evergreen shrub with white flowers and dark blue-black berries, was sacred to Aphrodite. Oil from the leaves and berries is used medicinally. Erebus is part of the underworld in Greek mythology, a place of darkness through which the dead pass after dying.

[55] *words* possibly Sappho's fragment 62 (Wharton numbering): "Delicate Adonis is dying, Cytherea, what shall we do? / Beat your breasts, maidens, and rend your tunics" (trans. H. T. Wharton). For Sappho, see n. 4.

[56] *title* from *Wild Honey from Various Thyme* (1908).

[57] *title* a palimpsest is a manuscript or parchment that has been overwritten, the first writing having been erased or

In parchment hoary
Lies a golden story,   5
As 'mid secret feather of a dove,
As 'mid moonbeams shifted through a cloud:
Let us write it over,
O my lover,
For the far Time to discover,   10
As 'mid secret feathers of a dove,
As 'mid moonbeams shifted through a cloud!

"Beloved, my glory in thee is not ceased"[58]

Beloved, my glory in thee is not ceased,
Whereas, as thou art waning, forests wane:
Unmoved, as by the victim is the priest,
I pass the world's great altitudes of pain.
But when the stars are gathered for a feast,   5
Or shadows threaten on a radiant plain,
Or many golden cornfields wave amain,
Oh then, as one from a filled shuttle weaves,
    My spirit grieves.

"Lo, my loved is dying"[59]

Lo, my loved is dying, and the call
Is come that I must die,[60]
All the leaves are dying, all
Dying, drifting by.
Every leaf is lonely in its fall,   5
Every flower has its speck and stain;
The birds from hedge and tree
Lisp mournfully,
And the great reconciliation of this pain
Lies in the full, soft rain.   10

Composed Oct. 1913

Alice Meynell (1847–1922)

Born in London, one of two daughters of Thomas James Thompson (1809–81) and Christiana Jane Weller (1825–1910), Alice Christiana Gertrude Thompson Meynell was well educated at home by her father. Meynell's sister was to become Elizabeth, Lady Butler (1846–1943), an important painter of war subjects. After travelling widely in France, Switzerland, and especially Italy,

Notes

scraped away; a possible allusion to the author's turning from their earlier lives by converting to Roman Catholicism. From *Wild Honey from Various Thyme* (1908).

[58] *title* first published in *Mystic Trees* (1913).

[59] *title* by Edith Cooper, who died two months later; published in *The Wattlefold: Unpublished Poems by Michael Field* (1930).

[60] *die* Katherine Bradley's own cancer had been diagnosed.

the family settled in London in 1864. In 1868 Meynell became a Roman Catholic and met Wilfrid Meynell, a journalist and publisher. They were married (1877), and together they edited and published *Pen: A Journal of Literature* (1880), followed by the successful *Weekly Register* (1881–99), and *Merry England* (1883–95). Meynell published a collection of poems, *Preludes* (1875), and other volumes: *Poems* (1893), *Other Poems* (1896), *Later Poems* (1902), and *A Father of Women* (1917). Meanwhile, she had been very busy in publishing essays and reviews in the *Spectator*, the *Tablet*, the *Saturday Review*, the *World*, and the *Scots Observer*. Her first volume of essays was *The Rhythm of Life* (1893), followed by many others, as well as monographs on William Holman Hunt (1893) and John Ruskin (1899). One of her children, Francis Meynell (1891–1975), became a noted typographer and the founder of the Nonesuch Press. Standard edition: *The Poems of Alice Meynell: Complete Edition* (1923); June Badeni, *The Slender Tree: A Life of Alice Meynell* (1981). "Essays by Alice Meynell": http://essays. quotidiana.org/meynell/; "The Poems of Alice Meynell": http://poetry.elcore.net/CatholicPoets/ Meynell/index.html.

Renouncement[1]

I must not think of thee; and, tired yet strong,
   I shun the thought that lurks in all delight—
   The thought of thee—and in the blue Heaven's height,
And in the sweetest passage of a song.

Oh, just beyond the fairest thoughts that throng   5
   This breast, the thought of thee waits, hidden yet bright;
   But it must never, never come in sight;
I must stop short of thee the whole day long.

But when sleep comes to close each difficult day,
   When night gives pause to the long watch I keep,   10
   And all my bonds I needs must loose apart,

Must doff my will as raiment laid away,—
   With the first dream that comes with the first sleep
   I run, I run, I am gathered to thy heart.

Unlinked[2]

If I should quit thee, sacrifice, forswear,
   To what, my art, shall I give thee in keeping?
   To the long winds of heaven? Shall these come sweeping
My songs forgone against my face and hair?

Or shall the mountain streams my lost joys bear,   5
   My past poetic pain in rain be weeping?
   No, I shall live a poet waking, sleeping,
   And I shall die a poet unaware.

Notes

ALICE MEYNELL

[1] *title* probably written after Meynell was received by Father Augustus Dignam into the Roman Catholic Church on 20 July 1868 and reflecting her attachment to him. First published in *Preludes* (1875). Our text: *Collected Poems* (1913).

[2] *title* first published *Poems* (1893); our text: *Collected Poems* (1913).

From me, my art, thou canst not pass away;
　　And I, a singer though I cease to sing,
　　　Shall own thee without joy in thee or woe. 　　　　　10

Through my indifferent words of every day,
　　Scattered and all unlinked the rhymes shall ring,
　　　And make my poem; and I shall not know.

Parentage³

*"When Augustus Cæsar legislated against the unmarried citizens of Rome, he declared
them to be, in some sort, slayers of the people."⁴*

　　Ah! no, not these!
These, who were childless, are not they who gave
So many dead unto the journeying wave,
The helpless nurslings of the cradling seas;
Not they who doomed by infallible decrees 　　　　　5
Unnumbered man to the innumerable grave.

　　But those who slay
Are fathers. Theirs are armies. Death is theirs,
The death of innocences and despairs;
The dying of the golden and the grey. 　　　　　10
The sentence, when these speak it, has no Nay.
And she who slays is she who bears, who bears.

Maternity⁵

One wept whose only child was dead,
　　New-born, ten years ago.
"Weep not; he is in bliss," they said.
　　She answered, "Even so.

"Ten years ago was born in pain 　　　　　5
　　A child, not now forlorn.
But oh, ten years ago, in vain,
　　A mother, a mother was born."

WEB p. 437

Lucy Luck (1848–1922)
　From "A Little of My Life"

Notes

³ *title* from *Later Poems* (1901).
⁴ *people* the epigraph refers to an edict of Augustus of the year 9 requiring people to have children to populate the Roman legions. An analogue to this poem is *Elegy* 2. 7 of Propertius, writing just after the repeal of the edict of Augustus, concerning his refusal to beget children to be

soldiers. The poem perplexed early reviewers who could not comprehend Meynell's lack of patriotism at the time of the Boer War (1899–1902).
⁵ *title* first published in *Poetry Magazine* (Mar. 1913); later published in *Collected Poems* (1913), our text.

William Hurrell Mallock (1849–1923)

Born in Devon into an Anglican clerical and literary family (his mother was the sister of Richard Hurrell Froude, a leader of the Oxford Movement, and James Anthony Froude, Carlyle's biographer), Mallock was educated at home before going to Balliol College, Oxford in 1869 where he obtained a second-class degree. He won the Newdigate Prize for English poetry in 1871, writing on the set topic "The Isthmus of Suez." Benjamin Jowett was his tutor (whom he disliked), and he met Swinburne, Browning, Ruskin, and Carlyle. In 1872, when the Fleshly School controversy was at its height (see LITERATURE: PRE-RAPHAELITISM (WEB p. 128)) he published *Every Man His Own Poet: or, The Inspired Singer's Recipe Book*, a recipe book imitating Isabella Beeton's on how to write a poem in the style of the leading poets of the age, listing the ingredients and procedures for preparing each poetical dish. In 1877 he published *The New Republic*, an instant success. A shorter version was published in *Belgravia* (Mar. 1876 to Feb. 1877) and as an expanded book the same year, both anonymously. It is a satiric account of the English intelligentsia, located at a country-house party where the only action is learned discussion on religion and morality, modelled on Plato's *Symposium*. To his contemporaries it was an amusing *roman à clef* (Fr. novel with a key; novel in which actual people are disguised as fictitional characters), with characters that could be identified as Benjamin Jowett (Dr Jenkinson), Walter Pater (Mr Rose), Thomas Henry Huxley (Mr Storks), Matthew Arnold (Mr Luke), John Ruskin (Mr Herbert), and so on. He also wrote a satire on Positivism, *The New Paul and Virginia* (1878). In the last decades of the century he wrote other novels, dealing with religion, social morality, and romantic love: *A Romance of the Nineteenth Century* (1881), *The Old Order Changes* (1886), *A Human Document* (1892), *The Individualist* (1899), and others. Writing a number of articles for the Conservative periodical the *National Review*, he attacked religious liberalism, agnosticism, Positivism, and Socialism (in *Social Equality*, 1882), while defending traditional Conservative values and religious dogmatism (*Doctrine and Doctrinal Disruption*, 1900). He published a volume of *Poems* (1880), and translations of Lucretius. Scholarly edition: *The New Republic*, ed. J. Max Patrick (1950); W. H. Mallock, *Memoirs of Life and Literature* (1920).

Christmas Thoughts, by a Modern Thinker[1]

(After Mr. Matthew Arnold)

The windows of the church are bright;
'Tis Christmas Eve; a low wind breathes;
And girls with happy eyes to-night
Are hanging up the Christmas wreaths;

Notes

WILLIAM HURRELL MALLOCK

[1] *title* in the later nineteenth century Modern Thinker usually referred to a person with agnostic or atheistic religious views. Mallock challenged conventional and liberal religious beliefs and institutions in his own writings, urging clear dogma and creeds as the proper basis for religion in *Is Life Worth Living?* (1879) and *Doctrine and Doctrinal Disruption* (1900). The poem is a general parody of the poetry of Matthew Arnold, especially of "Stanzas from the Grande Chartreuse" and the poems on Obermann (see n. 4). Republished, allegedly from *The World: A Journal for Men and Women* (unlocated), probably by piracy, in *Parodies of the Works of English and American Authors*, ed. Walter Hamilton (vol. 6, 1889); republished in *Verses* (1893), our text.

And village voices by-and-by
    Will reach my windows through the trees,
With wild, sweet music: "Praise on high
    To God: on earth, good-will and peace."[2]   5

Oh, happy girls, that hang the wreaths
    Oh, village fiddlers, happy ye!   10
Christmas to you still truly breathes
    Good-will and peace; but not to me.

Yes, gladness is your simple rôle,
Ye foolish girls, ye labouring poor;
    But joy would ill beseem my soul—   15
    To sigh, my part is, and endure.

For once as Rousseau[3] stood, I stand
    Apart, made picturesque by grief—
One of a small world-weary band,
    The orphans of a dead belief.   20

Through graveyards lone we love to stray,
    And sadly the sad tombs explore,
And contradict the texts which say
    That we shall rise once more.

Our faith is dead, of course; and grief   25
    Fills its room up; and Christmas pie
And turkey cannot bring relief
    To such as Obermann[4] and I.

Ah,[5] Obermann, and might I pass
    This English Christmas-tide with thee,   30
Far by those inland waves whose glass
    Brightens and breaks by Meillerie;[6]

Notes

[2] *peace* a hymn-like version of the "Gloria"; see BCP, "Holy Communion"; and Luke 2: 14.

[3] *Rousseau* Jean-Jacques Rousseau (1712–78), French philosopher, advocated changes in education and social policy to return to the natural innocence of the "noble savage." Rousseau is here substituting for Sophocles in Arnold's "Dover Beach" (see ARNOLD) who "long ago heard "the ebb and flow of human misery" on the Aegean Sea, which Arnold parallels to the English Channel.

[4] *Obermann* Étienne de Senancour (1770–1846) wrote *Obermann* (1804), an epistolary novel from Switzerland. Arnold wrote two poems on him: "Stanzas in Memory of the Author of 'Obermann'" (1852) and "Obermann Once More" (1867). Arnold added a note to the first poem in 1862: "The author of *Obermann* ... has little celebrity in France, his own country; and out of France he is almost unknown. But the profound inwardness, the austere sincerity, of his principal work, *Obermann*, the delicate feeling for nature which it exhibits, and the melancholy eloquence of many passages of it, have attracted and charmed some of the most remarkable spirits of this century, such as George Sand and Sainte-Beuve, and will probably always find a certain number of spirits whom they touch and interest.... The influence of Rousseau, and certain affinities with more famous and fortunate authors of his own day,—Chateaubriand and Madame de Staël,—are everywhere visible in Senancour." Arnold also wrote a review of *Obermann* in *The Academy* (9 Oct. 1869).

[5] *Ah* a common interjection in Arnold's verse, occurring, for instance, four times in "Rugby Chapel."

[6] *Meillerie* a commune in Eastern France on the south shore of Lake Geneva. The "Rock of Jean-Jacques Rousseau," mentioned in letter 17 of his *Julie, ou La Nouvelle Héloïse* (1761), is located near the village.

Or else amongst the sternest dells
    Alp shags with pine, we'd mix our sighs,
Mourn at the sound of Christmas bells,   35
    Sniff at the smell of Christmas pies.

But thou art dead; and long, dank grass
    And wet mould cool thy tired, hot brain;
Thou art lain down, and now, alas!
    Of course you won't get up again.   40

Yet, Obermann, 'tis better so;
    For if, sad slumberer, after all
You were to re-arise, you know
    'Twould make us feel so very small.

Best bear our grief this manlier way,   45
    And make our grief be balm to grief;
For if in faith sweet comfort lay,
    There lurks sweet pride in unbelief.

Wherefore, remembering this, once more
    Unto my childhood's church I'll go,   50
And bow my head at that low door
    I passed through standing, long ago.

I'll sit in the accustomed place,
    And make, while all the unlearnèd stare,
A mournful, atheistic face   55
    At their vain[7] noise of unheard prayer.

Then, while they hymn the heavenly birth
    And angel voices from the skies,
My thoughts shall go where Weimar's earth
    For ever darkens Goethe's[8] eyes;   60

Till sweet girls' glances from their books
    Shall steal towards me, and they sigh:
"How intellectual he looks,
    And yet how wistful! And his eye

Has that vain look of baffled prayer!"   65
    And then when church is o'er I'll run,
Comb misery into all my hair,
    And go and get my portrait done.

Notes

7 *vain* another common Arnoldian word (three times in "Rugby Chapel").

8 *Goethe's* Johann Wolfgang von Goethe (1749–1832), German philosopher, poet, and dramatist, lived in Weimar from 1775. Weimar was the capital of the duchy of Saxe-Weimar and a major cultural centre in Germany. Arnold's writing often refers to Goethe; for instance, his "Memorial Verses" (1850) begins: "Goethe in Weimar sleeps" (see ARNOLD).

William Ernest Henley (1849–1903)

Born in Gloucester as the eldest of five sons of the struggling bookseller William Henley (1826–68) and his wife, Emma Morgan (1828–88), Henley was well-enough educated to attend the Crypt Grammar School (1861–67) and eventually to pass the Oxford Local Schools Examination (1867). He had spent long periods in hospital with tuberculosis of the bone, requiring amputation of part of his left leg. When his right foot was threatened, he entered the Royal Infirmary in Edinburgh (1873–75) under the care of Dr Joseph Lister (1827–1912), and his foot was saved. While there Henley met Robert Louis Stevenson, who modelled Long John Silver in *Treasure Island* (1883) on him, as well as his future wife, Hannah (Anna) Johnson Boyle (1855–1925), whom he married in 1878. His friendship with Stevenson resulted in collaboration in four plays, none a stage success, and ended with a prolonged quarrel between 1888 and 1890. Henley was a journalist, writing for and then editing the short-lived journal, *London* (1877–79), while contributing to many other periodicals, such as the *Athenæum*, the *Saturday Review*, the *Pall Mall Gazette*, and *St. James's Gazette*. In 1889 he became editor of the conservative and imperialist weekly, the *Scots* (later the *National*) *Observer*, whose writers included W. B. Yeats, J. M. Barrie, G. B. Shaw, Thomas Hardy, Rudyard Kipling, and many others. He published *A Book of Verses* (1888); *The Song of the Sword and Other Verses* (1892), retitled *London Voluntaries* (1893), all revised and collected as *Poems* (1898). Other volumes followed: *For England's Sake: Verses and Songs in Time of War* (1900); *Hawthorn and Lavender* (1901); and *A Song of Speed* (1903). He also edited Robert Burns (4 vols, 1896–97), *A Dictionary of Slang* (1890–1904), and the series of *Tudor Translations* (1892–1903). No scholarly edition. *The Works of W. E. Henley* (7 vols, 1908); *Selected Letters*, ed. Damian Atkinson (2000); *The Letters of William Ernest Henley to Robert Louis Stevenson*, ed. Damian Atkinson (2008); John Connell, *W. E. Henley* (1949). A collection of 137 of his poems at Poetry Archive: http://www.sanjeev.net/poetry/henley-william-ernest/index.html.

From *In Hospital*[1]

I   Enter Patient

The morning mists still haunt the stony street;
The northern summer air is shrill and cold;
And lo, the Hospital, grey, quiet, old,
Where Life and Death like friendly chafferers meet.
Thro' the loud spaciousness and draughty gloom   5
A small, strange child—so agèd yet so young!—
Her little arm besplinted and beslung,

Notes

WILLIAM ERNEST HENLEY

[1] *title* written during the long period Henley spent in the Royal Infirmary in Edinburgh (1873–75). Originally a sonnet sequence (nine sketches; nine portraits) first published under the title *Hospital Outlines: Sketches and Portraits* in the *Cornhill Magazine* (July 1875), the poems were signed with Henley's name and his address at "The Royal Infirmary, Edinburgh." Republished as *In Hospital* in *Poems* (1898) with different verse forms; our text: 1898.

Precedes me gravely to the waiting-room.
I limp behind, my confidence all gone.
The grey-haired soldier-porter waves me on,   10
And on I crawl, and still my spirits fail:
A tragic meanness seems so to environ
These corridors and stairs of stone and iron,
Cold, naked, clean—half-workhouse and half-jail.

II   Waiting

A square, squat room (a cellar on promotion),   5
　　Drab to the soul, drab to the very daylight;
　　Plasters astray in unnatural-looking tinware;
　　Scissors and lint and apothecary's jars.

Here, on a bench a skeleton would writhe from,
　　Angry and sore, I wait to be admitted: 10
　　Wait till my heart is lead upon my stomach,
　　While at their ease two dressers do their chores.

One has a probe—it feels to me a crowbar.
　　A small boy sniffs and shudders after bluestone.
　　A poor old tramp explains his poor old ulcers.   15
　　Life is (I think) a blunder and a shame.

XIV   Ave, Caesar![2]

From the winter's grey despair,
From the summer's golden languor,
Death, the lover of Life,
Frees us for ever.   5

Inevitable, silent, unseen,
Everywhere always,
Shadow by night and as light in the day,
Signs she at last to her chosen;
And, as she waves them forth,   10
Sorrow and Joy
Lay by their looks and their voices,
Set down their hopes, and are made
One in the dim Forever.

Into the winter's grey delight,   15
Into the summer's golden dream,
Holy and high and impartial,
Death, the mother of Life,
Mingles all men for ever.

Notes

[2] *Caesar* from the traditional greeting supposedly given to the emperor by gladiators about to battle to the death in the Roman amphitheatres (*Ave Caesar, morituri te salutamus;* Lat. "Hail, Caesar, we who are about to die salute you"), quoted in *The Lives of the Twelve Caesars* (*c.*121) of Suetonius (*c.*69–122).

IV To R. T. H. B. [Invictus]³

Out of the night that covers me,
    Black as the pit from pole to pole,
I thank whatever gods may be
    For my unconquerable soul.

In the fell clutch of circumstance   5
    I have not winced nor cried aloud.
Under the bludgeonings of chance
    My head is bloody, but unbowed.

Beyond this place of wrath and tears
    Looms but the Horror of the shade,   10
And yet the menace of the years
    Finds and shall find me unafraid.

It matters not how strait the gate,
    How charged with punishments the scroll,
I am the master of my fate: 15
    I am the captain of my soul.

1875

We Shall Surely Die⁴

We shall surely die:
Must we needs grow old?
Grow old and cold,
And we know not why?
O, the By-and-By,   5
And the tale that's told!
We shall surely die:
Must we needs grow old?

Grow old and sigh,
Grudge and withhold,   10
Resent and scold? ..
Not you and I?
We shall surely die!

Notes

³ *title* written in 1875 as part of "In Hospital," the poem was published in *A Book of Verses* (1888) as the fourth poem of a series called "Life and Death (Echoes)" with the date following the poem. The dedicatee was Robert Thomas Hamilton Bruce, a Scottish merchant and Henley's literary patron. In subsequent editions after 1899, it was retitled "I. M. [In Memoriam] / R.T. Hamilton Bruce (1846–99)." The title "Invictus" (Lat. unconquered) first appeared in the reprinting in *Oxford Book of Verse* (1902), edited by Arthur Quiller-Couch. Our text *A Book of Verses* (1888).

⁴ *title* published in *Echoes of Life and Death* (1888).

⁵ *title* published in *Echoes of Life and Death* (1888).

When You Are Old[5]

When you are old, and I am passed away—
Passed, and your face, your golden face, is gray—
I think, whate'er the end, this dream of mine,
Comforting you, a friendly star will shine
Down the dim slope where still you stumble and stray.   5
So may it be: that so dead Yesterday,
No sad-eyed ghost but generous and gay,
May serve you memories like almighty wine,
           When you are old!

Dear Heart, it shall be so. Under the sway   10
Of death the past's enormous disarray
Lies hushed and dark. Yet though there come no sign,
Live on well pleased: immortal and divine
Love shall still tend you, as God's angels may,
           When you are old.   15

Double Ballade of Life and Fate[6]

Fools may pine, and sots may swill,
Cynics gibe, and prophets rail,
Moralists may scourge and drill,
Preachers prose, and fainthearts quail.
Let them whine, or threat, or wail!   5
Till the touch of Circumstance
Down to darkness sink the scale,
Fate's a fiddler, Life's a dance.

What if skies be wan and chill?
What if winds be harsh and stale?   10
Presently the east will thrill,
And the sad and shrunken sail
Bellying with a kindly gale,
Bear you sunwards, while your chance
Sends you back the hopeful hail:—   15
"Fate's a fiddler, Life's a dance."

Idle shot or coming bill,
Hapless love or broken bail,
Gulp it (never chew your pill!),
And, if Burgundy should fail,   20
Try the humbler pot of ale!
Over all is heaven's expanse.
Gold's to find among the shale,
Fate's a fiddler, Life's a dance.

Notes

[6] *title* a double ballade is a French form, consisting of six eight-line stanzas rhyming a b a b b c b c (with the last line as a refrain), and a four-line envoi. First published in *Bric-à-Brac* (1888). See DANTE ROSSETTI, "BALLAD" n. 80.

Dull Sir Joskin sleeps his fill,   25
Good Sir Galahad seeks the Grail,
Proud Sir Pertinax flaunts his frill,
Hard Sir Æger[7] dints his mail;
And the while by hill and dale
Tristram's braveries[8] gleam and glance,   30
And his blithe horn tells its tale:—
"Fate's a fiddler, Life's a dance."

Araminta's grand and shrill,
Delia's passionate and frail,
Doris drives an earnest quill,   35
Athanasia takes the veil:
Wiser Phyllis[9] o'er her pail,
At the heart of all romance
Reading, sings to Strephon's flail:—
"Fate's a fiddler, Life's a dance."   40

Every Jack must have his Jill
(Even Johnson[10] had his Thrale!):
Forward, couples—with a will!
This, the world, is not a jail.
Hear the music, sprat and whale!   45
Hands across, retire, advance!
Though the doomsman's on your trail,
Fate's a fiddler, Life's a dance.

Envoy

Boys and girls, at slug and snail   50
And their kindred look askance.
Pay your footing on the nail:
Fate's a fiddler, Life's a dance.

Notes

[7] *Joskin ... Æger* Joskin is thieves' slang for a yokel, here sleeping off a meal; Galahad is the hero of the quest for the Holy Grail in both Sir Thomas Malory's *Morte D'Arthur* and Tennyson's *Idylls of the King* (see WATSON, n. 8). Sir Pertinax Surly is a character in Ben Jonson's *The Alchemist* (1610) who adopts the disguise of a Spaniard. Æger is the god of the stormy sea in Teutonic mythology, as recorded in the *Prose Edda* (thirteenth century).

[8] *braveries* Tristram or Tristan in Celtic mythology is the hero of both an Anglo-Norman tradition (Thomas of Britain) and a German one (Gottfried von Strassburg), as well as other prose and verse romances, especially by Béroul, all telling of his love for Iseult or Isolde. His story was turned into an opera by Richard Wagner, *Tristan and Isolde* (1865).

[9] *Araminta ... Phyllis* a collection of romantic heroines of various kinds: Araminta was a character in *The Old Bachelor* (1693), a comedy by William Congreve (1670–1729); Samuel Daniel (1562–1619) wrote a sonnet sequence entitled *Delia* (1592); Doris is possibly a reference to a poem "Doris: A Pastoral" (1865) by Arthur Joseph Munby; "Athanasia" (1879) is the title of a poem by Oscar Wilde about an athanasia plant grown from a seed in the hand of an Egyptian mummified girl. Phyllis and Strephon are the rustic lovers in Gilbert and Sullivan's opera *Iolanthe* (1882).

[10] *Johnson* Samuel Johnson (1709–84), one of the eighteenth-century's defining literary figures who became a good friend of Hester Thrale (1741–1821) and her husband, Henry Thrale (1724–71), staying with them for some seventeen years. Mrs Thrale recorded the details of Johnson's life in her letters and diaries.

Remonstrance[11]

Hitch, blunder, check—
    Each is *a new disaster*,
And it is who shall bleat and scrawl
    The feebler the faster.
Where is our ancient pride of heart?   5
    Our faith in blood and star?
Who but would marvel how we came
    If this is all we are?

Ours is the race
    That tore the Spaniard's ruff,   10
That flung the Dutchman by the breech,
    The Frenchman by the scruff;[12]
Through his diurnal round of dawns
    Our drum-tap squires the sun;
And yet, an old mad burgher-man[13]   15
    Can put us on the run!

Rise, England, rise!
    But in that calm of pride,
That hardy and high serenity,
    That none may dare abide;   20
So front the realms, your point abashed;
    So mark them chafe and foam;
And, if they challenge, so, by God,
    Strike, England, and strike home!

Pro Rege Nostro[14]

What have I done for you,
    England, my England?
What is there I would not do,
    England, my own?

Notes

[11] title from *For England's Sake: Verses and Songs in Time of War* (1900), with the poem dated "December 1899."

[12] *Spaniards ... scruff* a list of England's victories over various enemies: Sir Francis Drake's defeat of the Spanish Armada at the battle of Gravelines in Flanders (1588); the defeat of the Dutch in the first Anglo-Dutch War (1652–54), when the English navy won a series of battles to gain control of the seas around Britain; the defeat of the French under Napoleon (1769–1821) at Waterloo (1815) in Belgium by the allied forces of Britain and Prussia under Arthur Wellesley, Duke of Wellington (1769–1852) in the culminating event of the Napoleonic Wars.

[13] *burgher-man* derogatory term for the Boers then engaged in a war with Britain in the Second Anglo-Boer War (1899–1902).

[14] title (Lat. for our sovereign); the motto was allegedly first used when the Empress Maria Theresa (1717–80) appealed in Latin to the Hungarians in Pressburg against the seizure of Silesia (1740), by Frederick the Great (1712–86) when they replied, "*Moriamur pro rege nostro*, Maria Theresa" (Lat. we shall die for our sovereign, Maria Theresa). The phrase *pro rege nostro* was also long included in the Eucharistic prayer in Latin in the Roman Catholic Mass as a prayer for the sovereign. This story was repeated and undermined in Thomas Carlyle's *History of Frederick II of Prussia* (1869). Printed in *For England's Sake: Verses and Songs in Time of War* (1900), with the poem dated "January 1892."

With your glorious eyes austere,   5
As the Lord were walking near,
Whispering terrible things and dear
    As the Song on your bugles blown,
      England—
    Round the world on your bugles blown!   10

Where shall the watchful Sun,
    England, my England,
Match the master-work you've done,
    England, my own?
When shall he rejoice agen   15
Such a breed of mighty men
As come forward, one to ten,
    To the Song on your bugles blown,
      England—
    Down the years on your bugles blown?   20

Ever the faith endures,
England, my England:—
"Take and break us: we are yours,
England, my own!
Life is good, and joy runs high   25
Between English earth and sky:
Death is death; but we shall die
    To the Song on your bugles blown,
      England—
    To the stars on your bugles blown!"   30

They call you proud and hard,
    England, my England:
You with worlds to watch and ward,
    England, my own!
You whose mailed hand keeps the keys   35
Of such teeming destinies,
You could know nor dread nor ease,
    Were the Song on your bugles blown,
      England—
    Round the Pit on your bugles blown!   40

Mother of Ships whose might,
    England, my England,
Is the fierce old Sea's delight,
    England, my own,
Chosen daughter of the Lord,[15]   45
Spouse-in-Chief of the ancient Sword,
There's the menace of the Word
    In the Song on your bugles blown,
      England—
    Out of heaven on your bugles blown!   50

Notes

[15] *daughter ... Lord* references to Queen Victoria, with echoes of the legendary sword Excalibur of King Arthur.

Robert Louis Stevenson (1850–94)

The Scottish novelist and travel writer was born in Edinburgh into a Presbyterian family. His father, Thomas Stevenson (1818–87), an engineer, designed over thirty lighthouses around Scotland and made important advances in meteorology; his mother, Margaret Isabella Balfour (1829–97), was the daughter of a Presbyterian minister. At an early age Stevenson developed the breathing problems that afflicted his mother's family, and hence spent much of his youth at home, taught by private tutors. He entered Edinburgh University (1867) to study engineering, but he gave that up, eventually in 1871 informing his father that he would be a writer. To have a profession, he again studied at Edinburgh, this time law. In 1871 he went to London, met a wide circle of literary people (including Sidney Colvin, 1845–1927, later his literary executor), and began writing for the *Cornhill Magazine*. He had recuperative trips to France and Belgium, meeting Fanny Osbourne (1840–1914) and her three children. He followed her to California where she obtained a divorce from her estranged husband. On the several occasions when the impoverished Stevenson almost died from malnutrition and privation, Fanny nursed him back to health; she married him, and they returned to England (1880). He had already produced *Travels with a Donkey* (1879) and would write about his American experiences in *The Silverado Squatters* (1883). By 1888 he had produced most of his best-known work: *Treasure Island* (1883), *Kidnapped* (1886), *The Strange Case of Dr. Jekyll and Mr. Hyde* (1886), and *The Black Arrow* (1888). His volumes of verse included *A Child's Garden of Verses* (1885) and *Underwoods* (1887). In 1888 Stevenson and his family sailed to the Pacific and travelled from Hawaii to Samoa. Eventually he settled in Samoa (1890) and continued to write: *The Master of Ballantrae* (1889) and his final unfinished novel, *The Weir of Hermiston* (1896). He is buried in Samoa. Standard edition: *New Edinburgh Edition of the Collected Works of Robert Louis Stevenson*, eds Stephen Arata, Richard Drury, Penny Fielding, and Anthony Mandal (38 vols, 2012–); *The Collected Poems of Robert Louis Stevenson*, ed. Roger C. Lewis (2004); *The Letters of Robert Louis Stevenson*, eds Bradford A. Booth and Ernest Mehew (1994); Philip Callow, *A Life of Robert Louis Stevenson* (2001). Stevenson site at Edinburgh's "Scottish Writing in the Nineteenth Century": www.robert-louis-stevenson.org.

From *Treasure Island*

To the Hesitating Purchaser[1]

If sailor tales to sailor tunes,
  Storm and adventure, heat and cold,
If schooners, islands, and maroons,[2]
  And Buccaneers, and buried Gold,

Notes

ROBERT LOUIS STEVENSON

[1] *title* prefatory poem to *Treasure Island* (1883). The novel (without the prefatory poem) was serialized in the children's journal *Young Folks* (1881–82) with the title *Treasure Island; or, the Mutiny of the Hispaniola*, under the pseudonym Captain George North. Our text: 1883.

[2] *maroons* (<Sp. *Cimarron* mountain-top dwellers); runaway slaves who formed mountain communities in the Caribbean, especially Jamaica, where they gained a peace treaty with Britain in 1737. Later, the word refers to those put ashore on deserted islands with scant supplies, like the

And all the old romance, retold   5
    Exactly in the ancient way,
Can please, as me they pleased of old,
    The wiser youngsters of to-day:

—So be it, and fall on! If not,
    If studious youth no longer crave,   10
His ancient appetites forgot,
    Kingston, or Ballantyne the brave,
Or Cooper³ of the wood and wave:
    So be it, also! And may I
And all my pirates share the grave   15
    Where these and their creations lie!

A Child's Garden of Verses⁴

[From the first section]

I   Bed in Summer⁵

In winter I get up at night
And dress by yellow candle-light.
In summer, quite the other way,
I have to go to bed by day.

Notes

character Ben Gunn in *Treasure Island*. Buccaneers were the adventurers, loosely affiliated with one of the sea-trading nations, France, Spain, or England, who operated for plunder outside the law. Their name comes from a West Indian word for dried meat roasted over the campfire, "boucan," giving rise to the French *bucaniers*.

³ *Kingston ... Cooper* three authors of boys' adventure fiction: William Henry Giles Kingston (1814–80), author of a long list of boys' adventure stories, including *The Cruise of the Frolic* (1860) and *The Three Midshipmen* (1873); Robert Michael Ballantyne (1825–94), well known for *The Coral Island* (1857), *The Pirate City* (1874), and *The Settler and the Savage* (1877); and James Fenimore Cooper (1789–1851), who wrote the *Leatherstocking Tales*, with a famous frontiersman, Natty Bumpus, a series that included *The Last of the Mohicans* (1826) and *The Deerslayer* (1841).

⁴ *title* Stevenson experimented with a variety of titles for his collection of children's verse, and settled on *Penny Whistles* for a trial printing (1883), later revised to the present title with the content also revised. Stevenson sent copies to his friends Sidney Colvin (1845–1927) and William Ernest Henley, who responded marking numerous poems for deletion and adding comments, often biting and dismissive, such as, "junky metre," "priggish," "I don't like this one at all," "I've read almost the same lines on Christmas crackers," and "commonplace." Stevenson had heard that one of the books by Kate Greenaway (1846–1901), children's author and illustrator, had sold over 150,000 copies, and thought

children's verse would be a good idea for him. Despite Colvin and Henley's strictures, Stevenson stood his ground, and with its variety of rhythm and verse forms, the volume became enormously popular to the Victorians and Edwardians, attracting numerous famous illustrators, and has continued to please children and their parents. Like Stevenson himself, the supposed child-speaker in the poems is often confined to bed with illness, and looks back on his childhood with both nostalgia and imaginative sympathy for creative play and perceptions of innocent pastimes and natural observations. *A Child's Garden of Verses* (1885) follows in the tradition of Blake's *Songs of Innocence* (1789) and Christina Rossetti's *Sing-Song* (1872), but without their politics on the one hand, and their pointing of a moral on the other; with their innocence they are often undercut by the mingling of bourgeois conventions and the anxieties of class differences. Stevenson's notion of garden also connotes the safe middle-class space for the cultivation of flowers and lawns as well as the children's playground for games. In the Collected (Vailima) Edition (1922), Stevenson's wife wrote in a preface: "My husband drew upon his memory for The Sick Child [poem in *Underwoods*, 1887] who lay awake hoping for the dawn, and listening for the sound of the morning carts that proved the weary night was almost over. Indeed, every poem in The Child's Garden was a bit out of his own childhood.... In spite of the many days and nights passed in the 'Land of Counterpane,' and shining, perhaps, all the brighter by comparison, there

I have to go to bed and see   5
The birds still hopping on the tree,
Or hear the grown-up people's feet
Still going past me in the street.

And does it not seem hard to you,
When all the sky is clear and blue,   10
And I should like so much to play,
To have to go to bed by day?

V   Whole Duty of Children[6]

A child should always say what's true
And speak when he is spoken to,
And behave mannerly at table:
At least as far as he is able.

XXVIII   Foreign Children

Little Indian, Sioux, or Crow,[7]
Little frosty Eskimo,
Little Turk or Japanee,[8]
O! don't you wish that you were me?

You have seen the scarlet trees   5
And the lions over seas;
You have eaten ostrich eggs,
And turned the turtles off their legs.

Such a life is very fine,
But it's not so nice as mine: 10
You must often, as you trod,
Have wearied *not* to be abroad.

You have curious things to eat,
I am fed on proper meat;
You must dwell upon the foam,   15
But I am safe and live at home.

Notes

were brilliant episodes of play that remained clearer in my husband's memory than almost any other part of his life" (vol. 8). The volume had four sections: first, forty-one poems in an unnamed section, nine in a section titled "The Child Alone," eight in "Garden Days," and six in "Envoys." Poems I through XXXV are all from the first section. From *A Child's Garden of Verses* (1885).

[5] *Summer* the first poem in the collection, after the dedicatory poem to Stevenson's childhood nurse, Alison Cunningham (1822–1913), known as "Cummy," with whom he corresponded all his life.

[6] *title* an echo of Ecclesiastes 12: 13; also the title of an anonymous book of Anglican piety, *The Whole Duty of Man* (1658), that retained its important place for 200 years, setting out a programme for spiritual observances and moral improvement.

[7] *Sioux … Crow* indigenous or American Indian groups of peoples in the plains of the American and Canadian Midwest. Both were either exterminated or forced onto reservations by 1890.

[8] *Japanee* colonial slang for Japanese.

Little Indian, Sioux or Crow,
Little frosty Eskimo,
Little Turk or Japanee,
O! don't you wish that you were me?   20

From *Underwoods* (1887)

XXI   Requiem[9]

Under the wide and starry sky,
Dig the grave and let me lie.
Glad did I live and gladly die,
        And I laid me down with a will.

This be the verse you grave for me: 5
Here he lies where he longed to be;
Home is the sailor, home from sea,[10]
        And the hunter home from the hill.

"A Plea for Gas Lamps"[11]

Cities given, the problem was to light them. How to conduct individual citizens about the burgess-warren,[12] when once heaven had withdrawn its leading luminary? or—since we live in a scientific age—when once our spinning planet has turned its back upon the sun? The moon, from time to time, was doubtless very helpful; the stars had a cheery look among the chimney-pots; and a cresset here and there, on church or citadel, produced a fine pictorial effect and, in places where the ground lay unevenly, held out the right hand of conduct to the benighted. But sun, moon, and stars abstracted or concealed, the night-faring inhabitant had to fall back—we speak on the authority of old prints—upon stable lanthorns two stories in height. Many holes, drilled in the conical turret-roof of this vagabond Pharos,[13] let up spouts of dazzlement into the bearer's eyes; and as he paced forth in

Notes

[9] *title* (Lat. rest). The poem is part of the bronze panel on Stevenson's tomb near his home at Vailima in Samoa. A. E. Housman published a three-stanza poem entitled "R.L.S." in the *Academy* (3 Dec. 1894) beginning: "Home is the sailor, home from the sea: / Her far-borne canvas furled / The ship pours shining on the quay / The plunder of the world." From *Underwoods* (1887).

[10] *sea* often misquoted as "Home is the sailor, home from the sea."

[11] *title* gas lamps using coal gas were first used in lighting a home by William Murdoch (1754–1839) in Cornwall in 1792, and for street lighting in Pall Mall in London in 1807. Within fifteen years, coal-gas street lamps were in use in many cities in England, and by 1859 it was used everywhere. Lamplighters traversed the streets with a short ladder. Gas was used to light the theatre stage at the Lyceum (1804) in London, and soon after other theatres followed, before long lighting the whole amphitheatre, and changing the cost of theatre operation (much cheaper and safer than

candles) and acting style (brighter illumination made expansive gestures unnecessary). Gas began to be replaced with the steady and still brighter illumination of incandescent lamps, so that the Savoy Theatre, London was first lit with them in 1881. It is against such lighting, with widely reported experiments and patents from 1878, that Stevenson is reacting in favour of the softer glow of gas. First published in the journal *London* (27 Apr. 1878); republished in *Virginibus Puerisque and Other Papers* (1881); our text, 1881.

[12] *burgess-warren* the "warren" or den of tunnels and nest of burrowing animals, like rabbits – here applied to a city, presided over by the burgesses or city officials, originally the inhabitants in the Scots that Stevenson was familiar with.

[13] *Pharos* the light-house tower built in ancient Alexandria, one of the seven wonders of the world. The name was also given to Roman and later lighthouses in England; here a lantern with nail-holes pierced through the metal and a conical top.

the ghostly darkness, carrying his own sun by a ring about his finger, day and night swung to and fro and up and down about his footsteps. Blackness haunted his path; he was beleaguered by goblins as he went; and, curfew being struck, he found no light but that he travelled in throughout the township.

Closely following on this epoch of migratory lanthorns in a world of extinction, came the era of oil-lights, hard to kindle, easy to extinguish, pale and wavering in the hour of their endurance. Rudely puffed the winds of heaven; roguishly clomb up the all-destructive urchin; and, lo! in a moment night re-established her void empire, and the cit[14] groped along the wall, suppered but bedless, occult from guidance, and sorrily wading in the kennels. As if gamesome winds and gamesome youths were not sufficient, it was the habit to sling these feeble luminaries from house to house above the fairway. There, on invisible cordage, let them swing! And suppose some crane-necked general to go speeding by on a tall charger, spurring the destiny of nations, red-hot in expedition, there would indubitably be some effusion of military blood, and oaths, and a certain crash of glass; and while the chieftain rode forward with a purple coxcomb, the street would be left to original darkness, unpiloted, unvoyageable, a province of the desert night.

The conservative, looking before and after, draws from each contemplation the matter for content. Out of the age of gas lamps he glances back slightingly at the mirk and glimmer in which his ancestors wandered; his heart waxes jocund at the contrast; nor do his lips refrain from a stave, in the highest style of poetry, lauding progress and the golden mean.[15] When gas first spread along a city, mapping it forth about evenfall for the eye of observant birds, a new age had begun for sociality and corporate pleasure-seeking, and begun with proper circumstance, becoming its own birthright. The work of Prometheus[16] had advanced with another stride. Mankind and its supper parties were no longer at the mercy of a few miles of sea-fog; sundown no longer emptied the promenade; and the day was lengthened out to every man's fancy. The city-folk had stars of their own; biddable, domesticated stars.

It is true that these were not so steady, nor yet so clear, as their originals; nor indeed was their lustre so elegant as that of the best wax candles. But then the gas stars, being nearer at hand, were more practically efficacious than Jupiter himself.[17] It is true, again, that they did not unfold their rays with the appropriate spontaneity of the planets, coming out along the firmament one after another, as the need arises. But the lamplighters took to their heels every evening, and ran with a good heart. It was pretty to see man thus emulating the punctuality of heaven's orbs; and though perfection was not absolutely reached, and now and then an individual may have been knocked on the head by the ladder of the flying functionary, yet people commended his zeal in a proverb, and taught their children to say, "God bless the lamplighter!" And since his passage was a piece of the day's programme, the children were well pleased to repeat the benediction, not, of course, in so many words, which would have been improper, but in some chaste circumlocution, suitable for infant lips.

God bless him, indeed! For the term of his twilight diligence is near at hand; and for not much longer shall we watch him speeding up the street and, at measured intervals, knocking another luminous hole into the dusk. The Greeks would have made a noble myth of such an one; how he distributed starlight, and, as soon as the need was over,

Notes

[14] *cit* see *OED* (arch. short for citizen: "usually applied more or less contemptuously to a townsman or 'Cockney' as distinguished from a countryman, or to a tradesman or shopkeeper as distinguished from a gentleman").

[15] *mean* mid-point between two extremes.

[16] *Prometheus* in Greek mythology, Prometheus first stole fire from the gods as a gift for human beings; see HEMANS, n. 15.

[17] *himself* Jupiter's ability to illuminate by hurling lightning bolts.

re-collected it; and the little bull's-eye, which was his instrument, and held enough fire to kindle a whole parish, would have been fitly commemorated in the legend. Now, like all heroic tasks, his labours draw towards apotheosis, and in the light of victory himself shall disappear. For another advance has been effected. Our tame stars are to come out in future, not one by one, but all in a body and at once. A sedate electrician somewhere in a back office touches a spring—and behold! from one end to another of the city, from east to west, from the Alexandra to the Crystal Palace,[18] there is light! *Fiat Lux*,[19] says the sedate electrician. What a spectacle, on some clear, dark nightfall, from the edge of Hampstead Hill,[20] when in a moment, in the twinkling of an eye,[21] the design of the monstrous city flashes into vision—a glittering hieroglyph many square miles in extent; and when, to borrow and debase an image, all the evening street-lamps burst together into song![22] Such is the spectacle of the future, preluded the other day by the experiment in Pall Mall.[23] Star-rise by electricity, the most romantic flight of civilization; the compensatory benefit for an innumerable array of factories and bankers' clerks. To the artistic spirit exercised about Thirlmere,[24] here is a crumb of consolation; consolatory, at least, to such of them as look out upon the world through seeing eyes, and contentedly accept beauty where it comes.

But the conservative, while lauding progress, is ever timid of innovation; his is the hand upheld to counsel pause; his is the signal advising slow advance. The word *electricity* now sounds the note of danger. In Paris, at the mouth of the Passage des Princes, in the place before the Opera portico, and in the Rue Drouot at the *Figaro* office, a new sort of urban star now shines out nightly, horrible, unearthly, obnoxious to the human eye; a lamp for a nightmare![25] Such a light as this should shine only on murders and public crime, or along the corridors of lunatic asylums, a horror to heighten horror. To look at it only once is to fall in love with gas, which gives a warm domestic radiance fit to eat by. Mankind, you would have thought, might have remained content with what Prometheus stole for them and not gone fishing the profound heaven with kites to catch and domesticate the wildfire of the storm. Yet here we have the levin brand[26] at our doors, and it is proposed that we should henceforward take our walks abroad in the glare of permanent lightning. A man need not be very superstitious if he scruple to follow his pleasures by the light of the Terror that Flieth,[27] nor very epicurean if he prefer to see the face of beauty more becomingly displayed. That ugly blinding glare may not improperly advertise the home of slanderous *Figaro*, which is a back-shop to the infernal regions; but where soft joys prevail, where people are convoked to pleasure and the philosopher looks on smiling and silent, where love and laughter and deifying wine abound, there, at least, let the old mild lustre shine upon the ways of man.

Notes

[18] *Palace* that is, across the whole of London, from the Alexandra Palace (opened 1873; destroyed by fire the same year, and reopened 1875) at Muswell Hill, 10 kilometres north of London (reached by the Great Northern Railway), to the Crystal Palace (built by Joseph Paxton for the Great Exhibition of 1851, re-erected at Sydenham Hill in South London in 1854). The Crystal Palace would be destroyed by fire in 1936.

[19] *lux* (Lat. let there be light); see Genesis 1: 3.

[20] *Hill* Parliament Hill, on the south-east part of Hampstead Heath, has a wide view over the whole of London.

[21] *eye* see 1 Corinthians 15: 52. The passage continues "at the last trumpet. For the trumpet will sound, and the dead will be raised imperishable, and we shall be changed," at the last judgement – to which Stevenson is comparing the instantaneous illumination of the whole city of London.

[22] *song* see Job 38: 7; Isaiah 52: 9.

[23] *Mall* gas-lighting in Pall Mall in 1807; see n. 11.

[24] *Thirlmere* a water reservoir in Cumbria in the English Lake District to supply water to Manchester was projected in the 1870s, but it was met with fierce opposition from the Thirlmere Defence Association in 1878 because the dam and ensuing lake would submerge scenic cliffs.

[25] *nightmare* in February 1878 during the Paris Exhibition, the Avenue de l'Opéra was illuminated by the "electric candle" using arc-lamps invented by Pavel Yablochkov (1847–94), Russian electrical engineer. *Le Figaro* (founded 1826) was the leading Paris newspaper, originally satiric but sometimes sensational during the later nineteenth century.

[26] *levin brand* levin or leven: lightning.

[27] *Flieth* see Psalm 91: 5.

Arthur Clement Hilton (1851–77)

Hilton was educated at Marlborough College and St John's College, Cambridge, where he published *The Light Green* (1872), a collection of verse parodies. He was ordained deacon on 1 March 1874 and became curate of St Clement and St Mary, Sandwich. He was ordained priest in 1875 and took his MA at Cambridge in 1876.

His early death left him greatly mourned by his parishioners and the admirers of his talents for parodic invention. Standard edition: *The Works of Arthur Clement Hilton (Of Marlborough & Cambridge) Author of "The Light Green" Together with his Life and Letters,* ed. Robert P. Edgcumbe (1902).

Octopus

by Algernon Charles Sin-Burn[1]

Strange beauty, eight-limbed and eight-handed,
    Whence camest to dazzle our eyes?
With thy bosom bespangled and banded
    With the hues of the seas and the skies;
Is thy home European or Asian,   5
    O mystical monster marine?
Part molluscous and partly crustacean,
    Betwixt and between.

Wast thou born to the sound of sea trumpets?
    Hast thou eaten and drunk to excess   10
Of the sponges—thy muffins and crumpets,[2]
    Of the seaweed—thy mustard and cress?[3]
Wast thou nurtured in caverns of coral,
    Remote from reproof or restraint?
Art thou innocent, art thou immoral,   15
    Sinburnian or Saint?

Notes

ARTHUR CLEMENT HILTON
[1] *title* "Written at the Crystal Palace Aquarium" [author's note]. First published in *The Light Green* (May 1872), a Cambridge undergraduate journal of parodies (itself parodying Oxford's *The Dark Blue*). The poem is a parody of Swinburne's "Dolores" that first appeared in his *Poems and Ballads* (1866), consisting of fifty-five stanzas, of which the following are stanzas one and four:

> Cold eyelids that hide like a jewel
> Hard eyes that grow soft for an hour;
> The heavy white limbs, and the cruel
> Red mouth like a venomous flower;
> When these are gone by with their glories,
> What shall rest of thee then, what remain,
> O mystic and sombre Dolores,
> Our Lady of Pain?...

> O lips full of lust and of laughter,
> Curled snakes that are fed from my breast,
> Bite hard, lest remembrance come after

> And press with new lips where you pressed.
> For my heart too springs up at the pressure,
> Mine eyelids too moisten and burn;
> Ah, feed me and fill me with pleasure,
> Ere pain come in turn.

[2] *muffins ... crumpets* breakfast or tea breads, cooked on a griddle. English muffins are made with dough with yeast and flour and are cooked on both sides. on a griddle. English muffins are made with dough with yeast and flour, as are crumpets, though "more like batter than dough," as Mrs Beeton says in her *Book of Household Management* (1861). After they are cooked on both sides they may be toasted using a toasting fork "before a very clear fire." Both are served hot with butter, jams, and marmalade.

[3] *mustard and cress* a peppery herb, usually a sprout with a white stem and small green leaves at the top, used in society sandwiches and in decoration for salads.

Lithe limbs, curling free, as a creeper
    That creeps in a desolate place,
To enroll and envelop the sleeper
    In a silent and stealthy embrace,   20
Cruel beak craning forward to bite us,
    Our juices to drain and to drink,
Or to whelm us in waves of Cocytus,
    Indelible ink!

O breast, that 'twere rapture to writhe on!   25
    O arms 'twere delicious to feel
Clinging close with the crush of the Python,
    When she maketh her murderous meal!
In thy eight-fold embraces enfolden,
    Let our empty existence escape,   30
Give us death that is glorious and golden,
    Crushed all out of shape!

Ah! thy red lips, lascivious and luscious,
    With death in their amorous kiss,
Cling round us, and clasp us, and crush us,   35
    With bitings of agonised bliss;
We are sick with the poison of pleasure,
    Dispense us the potion of pain;
Ope thy mouth to its uttermost measure
    And bite us again!   40

Cold eyelids that hide like a jewel
    Hard eyes that grow soft for an hour;
The heavy white limbs, and the cruel
    Red mouth like a venomous flower;
When these are gone by with their glories,   45
    What shall rest of thee then, what remain,
O mystic and sombre Dolores,
    Our Lady of Pain?..

O lips full of lust and of laughter,
    Curled snakes that are fed from my breast,   50
Bite hard, lest remembrance come after
    And press with new lips where you pressed.
For my heart too springs up at the pressure,
    Mine eyelids too moisten and burn;
Ah, feed me and fill me with pleasure   55
    Ere pain come in turn.

Oscar Wilde (1854–1900)

The second of three children of Sir William Wilde (1815–76), a Dublin surgeon and Jane Francesca Elgee (1821–96), a poet and Irish nationalist (writing under the pseudonym of Speranza), Oscar Fingal O'Flahertie Wills Wilde was educated at Trinity College, Dublin and Oxford. He was a principle figure in the aesthetic movement. Known for his dazzling wit, he was a poet, novelist (*The Picture of Dorian Gray* 1891), essayist (*The Critic as Artist* 1890 and *The Soul of Man under Socialism* 1891), and playwright (*Lady Windermere's Fan* 1892 and *The Importance of Being Earnest* 1895). In 1895 he became entangled in a libel case with the father of his lover, Lord Alfred Douglas (1870–1945); subsequently, after two criminal trials, he was sentenced to two years' imprisonment in Reading Gaol for homosexual acts. He died in exile in Paris. Standard edition: *Collected Edition*, ed. Robert Ross (14 vols, 1908); *The Complete Works of Oscar Wilde*, eds Russell Jackson and Ian Small (4 vols, 2000–7); Richard Ellman, *Oscar Wilde* (1987). "The Trials of Oscar Wilde": http://law2.umkc.edu/faculty/projects/ftrials/wilde/wilde.htm; "Oscar Wilde on The Victorian Web": http://www.victorianweb.org/authors/wilde/index.html.

Requiescat[1]

Tread lightly, she is near
    Under the snow,
Speak gently, she can hear
    The daisies grow.

All her bright golden hair   5
    Tarnished with rust,
She that was young and fair
    Fallen to dust.

Lily-like, white as snow,
    She hardly knew   10
She was a woman, so
    Sweetly she grew.

Coffin-board, heavy stone,
    Lie on her breast,
I vex my heart alone   15
    She is at rest.

Peace, Peace, she cannot hear
    Lyre or sonnet,
All my life's buried here,
    Heap earth upon it.   20

Avignon

Notes

Oscar Wilde

[1] *title* (Lat. may he/she rest), as in *requiescat in pace* (may he/she rest in peace). This poem memorializes Wilde's sister, Isola Francesca, who died on 23 February 1867, aged 9. Wilde probably wrote the poem at Oxford about 1875, revising it at Avignon in southern France while on his Italian tour in June of the same year. The final line recalls *Hamlet* 5. 1. 251. First published in *Poems* (1881).

Impression du Matin[2]

The Thames nocturne of blue and gold
    Changed to a Harmony in grey:[3]
    A barge with ochre-coloured hay
Dropt from the wharf: and chill and cold

The yellow fog came creeping down   5
    The bridges, till the houses' walls
    Seemed changed to shadows, and S. Paul's
Loomed like a bubble o'er the town.[4]

Then suddenly arose the clang
    Of waking life; the streets were stirred   10
    With country waggons: and a bird
Flew to the glistening roofs and sang.

But one pale woman all alone,
    The daylight kissing her wan hair,
    Loitered beneath the gas lamps' flare,   15
With lips of flame and heart of stone.

Helas![5]

To driftwith every passion till my soul
Is a stringed lute[6] on which all winds can play,
Is it for this that I have given away
Mine ancient wisdom, and austere control?—
Methinks my life is a twice-written scroll   5
Scrawled over on some boyish holiday
With idle songs for pipe and virelay
Which do but mar the secret of the whole.
Surely there was a time I might have trod
The sunlit heights, and from life's dissonance   10

Notes

[2] *title* (Fr. impression of the morning). "Impressionist" was originally a derisive term for the Paris exhibition of 1874 that included Claude Monet's *Impression—Sunrise* (1873). To the Impressionists reality was perceived not as collections of solid objects but as fragments of colour bathed in light, unified in the act of perception. In England at the same time the Aesthetic Movement was interested in a return to nature, decorative arts and crafts, Japonism, a stress on line and colour, and on surface patterns. As Lady Bracknell says in *The Importance of Being Earnest*, "We live, I regret to say, in an age of surfaces." In *Poems* (1881) Wilde published a number of poems entitled "Impression"; "Impressions: I Les Silhouettes"; "II La Fuite de la Lune"; "Impression de Voyage"; five poems under the heading "Impressions du Théâtre"; and "Impression: La Reveillon." First published in *The World* (2 Mar. 1881); reprinted in *Poems* (1881): our text.

[3] *nocturne ... Harmony* James McNeill Whistler's paintings used such musical terms as "nocturne" and "harmony" with colours as titles; formerly friends, Whistler and Wilde quarrelled in the 1890s. See Plate 20: Whistler's *Symphony in White*; see also LITERATURE: PRE-RAPHAELITISM; WHISTLER.

[4] *S. Paul's ... town* dome of St Paul's Cathedral, London; Wilde echoed line 8 later in *Lord Arthur Savile's Crime*: "The huge dome of St. Paul's loomed like a bubble through the dusky air" (end of ch. V).

[5] *title* (Fr. alas). This sonnet was the first poem in Wilde's first volume, *Poems* (1881).

[6] *drift ... lute* an echo of Walter Pater's "Conclusion" to Studies in the History of the Renaissance (1873): "A drift of momentary acts of sight and passion and thought"; see PATER. For wind on the stringed lute, see Coleridge "Eolian Harp" (1796).

Struck one clear chord to reach the ears of God:
Is that time dead? lo! with a little rod
I did but touch the honey[7] of romance—
And must I lose a soul's inheritance?

Impressions[8]

I   Le Jardin[9]

The lily's withered chalice falls
    Around its rod of dusty gold,
    And from the beech trees on the wold
The last wood-pigeon coos and calls.

The gaudy leonine sunflower[10]   5
    Hangs black and barren on its stalk,
    And down the windy garden walk
The dead leaves scatter,— hour by hour.

Pale privet-petals white as milk
    Are blown into a snowy mass;   10
    The roses lie upon the grass,
Like little shreds of crimson silk.

II   La Mer[11]

A white mist drifts across the shrouds,[12]
    A wild moon in this wintry sky
    Gleams like an angry lion's eye   15
Out of a mane of tawny clouds.

The muffled steersman at the wheel
    Is but a shadow in the gloom;—
    And in the throbbing engine room
Leap the long rods of polished steel.   20

Notes

[7] *rod ... honey* see 1 Samuel 14: 43; quoted by Pater in his essay on Winckelmann in *The Renaissance*.

[8] *title Impressions* probably the French pronunciation, alluding to the French Impressionist school of painters, depicting two of their most popular subjects, gardens and the seaside. In the dialogue between two art critics in "The Decay of Lying" (1889), Wilde writes, "Where, if not from the Impressionists, do we get those wonderful brown fogs that come creeping down our streets, blurring the gas-lamps and changing the houses into monstrous shadows? To whom, if not to them and their master, do we owe the lovely silver mists that brood over our river, and turn to faint forms of fading grace curved bridge and swaying barge? The extraordinary change that has taken place in the climate of London during the last ten years is entirely due to a particular school of Art.... That white quivering sunlight that one sees now in France, with its strange blotches of mauve, and its restless violet shadows, is her latest fancy, and, on the whole, Nature reproduces it quite admirably. Where she used to give us Corots and Daubignys, she gives us now exquisite Monets and entrancing Pisaros." See also above, n. 2. The poems were first published together in the Philadelphia weekly, *Our Continent* (15 Feb. 1882); our text, *Poems* (1908).

[9] *Jardin* (Fr. the garden).

[10] *lily ... sunflower* the two symbolic flowers of the Aesthetic Movement.

[11] *Mer* (Fr. the sea).

[12] *shrouds* rope rigging supporting a ship's mast.

The shattered storm has left its trace
    Upon this huge and heaving dome,   10
For the thin threads of yellow foam
    Float on the waves like ravelled lace.

Symphony in Yellow[13]

An omnibus across the bridge
    Crawls like a yellow butterfly,
    And, here and there a passer-by
Shows like a little restless midge.

Big barges full of yellow hay   5
    Are moored against the shadowy wharf,
    And, like a yellow silken scarf,
The thick fog hangs along the quay.

The yellow leaves begin to fade
    And flutter from the Temple[14] elms,   10
    And at my feet the pale green Thames
Lies like a rod of rippled jade.

The Harlot's House[15]

We caught the tread of dancing feet,
We loitered down the moonlit street,
And stopped beneath the Harlot's house.

Inside, above the din and fray,
We heard the loud musicians play   5
The 'Treues Liebes Herz' of Strauss.

Like strange mechanical grotesques,
Making fantastic arabesques,
The shadows raced across the blind.

We watched the ghostly dancers spin   10
To sound of horn and violin,
Like black leaves wheeling in the wind.

Notes

[13] *title* James McNeill Whistler (1834–1903), American Impressionist painter, painted a series of "symphony" paintings in different colours, though not in yellow. Yellow was associated with the sensationalist press ("yellow press" and French yellow-back novels), as Wilde indicated the following year in *The Picture of Dorian Gray* (1890), when Lord Henry sends "a yellow book" to Dorian, very likely the decadent novel *À Rebours* (Fr. Against nature, 1884) by Joris-Karl Huysmans (1848–1907), in yellow paper. Yellow was also associated with the aesthetes and the sunflower, as in Gilbert and Sullivan's *Patience* (1881). The yellow butterfly became a symbol for the aesthete artist in the 1890s, as did the journal *The Yellow Book* (1894–97). First published in Australia in the *Centennial Magazine* (5 Feb. 1889); our text, *Poems* (1908).

[14] *Temple* part of the Inns of Court, centre of the legal profession in London, whose parks adjoin the Thames.

[15] *title* see Joshua 2: 1. First published in *The Dramatic Review* (11 Apr. 1885); our text, *Poems* (1908).

Like wire-pulled automatons,
Slim silhouetted skeletons
Went sidling through the slow quadrille.   15

Then took each other by the hand,
And danced a stately saraband;[16]
Their laughter echoed thin and shrill.

Sometimes a clock-work puppet pressed
A phantom lover to her breast,   20
Sometimes they seemed to try and sing.

Sometimes a horrible Marionette
Came out, and smoked its cigarette
Upon the steps like a live thing.

Then, turning to my love I said,   25
'The dead are dancing with the dead,
The dust is whirling with the dust.'

But she, she heard the violin,
And left my side, and entered in;
Love passed into the house of Lust.   30

Then suddenly the tune went false,
The shadows wearied of the waltz,
The shadows ceased to wheel and whirl,

And down the long and silent street,
The dawn with silver-sandalled feet,   35
Crept like a frightened girl.

A Preface to *The Picture of Dorian Gray*[17]

The artist is the creator of beautiful things.
     To reveal art and conceal the artist is art's aim.
The critic is he who can translate into another manner or a new material his impression
of beautiful things.
     The highest as the lowest form of criticism is a mode of autobiography.

Notes

[16] *Strauss...arabesque...quadrille ... saraband* under the inspiration of the music, the dances and postures mentioned, which vary in their formality, all become part of the frenetic movement; (*Treues Liebes Herz*: Ger. "The Heart of True Love"), a waltz by Johann Strauss (1825–1899); for arabesque and saraband see *The Picture of Dorian Gray* (ch. 16) and *The Ballad of Reading Gaol* (1898; ll. 297—99).

[17] *title* the preface's art-for-art's-sake position draws on Théophile Gauthier's preface to *Mademoiselle de Maupin* (1835). Wilde's novel was published in *Lippincott's Monthly Magazine* (July 1890). Responding to charges of immorality, Wilde published "A Preface" in The *Fortnightly Review* (Mar. 1891), extending and adding to it in a revised version of the novel published a month later. Wilde separated each aphorism with three spaced asterisks and signed it "Oscar Wilde."

Those who find ugly meanings in beautiful things are corrupt without being charming. This is a fault.

> Those who find beautiful meanings in beautiful things are the cultivated. For these there is hope.

They are the elect to whom beautiful things mean only Beauty.

> There is no such thing as a moral or an immoral book. Books are well written, or badly written. That is all.[18]

The nineteenth century dislike of Realism is the rage of Caliban[19] seeing his own face in a glass. The nineteenth century dislike of Romanticism is the rage of Caliban not seeing his own face in a glass.

> The moral life of man forms part of the subject-matter of the artist, but the morality of art consists in the perfect use of an imperfect medium.

No artist desires to prove anything. Even things that are true can be proved.

> No artist has ethical sympathies. An ethical sympathy in an artist is an unpardonable mannerism of style.

Thought and language are to the artist instruments of an art.

Vice and virtue are to the artist materials of his art.

From the point of view of Form, the type of all the arts is the art of the musician. From the point of view of Feeling the actor's craft is the type.

> All art is at once surface and symbol.

Those who go beneath the surface do so at their peril.

Those who read the symbol do so also at their peril.

It is the spectator, and not life, that art really mirrors.

> Diversity of opinion about a work of art shows that the work is new, complex, and vital.

> When critics disagree the artist is in accord with himself.

We can forgive a man for making a useful thing as long as he does not admire it. The only excuse for making a useless thing is that one admires it inordinately.

> All art is quite useless.[20]

WEB p. 440

The Importance of Being Earnest

Notes

[18] *all* an echo of Pater's essay on Wordsworth in *Appreciations* (1890): "The office of the poet is not that of the moralist, and the first aim of Wordsworth's poetry is to give the reader a particular kind of pleasure." Wilde also echoes Pater later in the "Preface," as when he uses Pater's "The School of Giorgione" (*Fortnightly Review*, 1877), added to *The Renaissance* (third edition 1888): "All art aspires to the condition of music"; see PATER (WEB p. 435).

[19] *Caliban* the monster in *The Tempest* (1610/11) and in BROWNING "CALIBAN UPON SETEBOS" (WEB p. 354) .

[20] *useless* Wilde aligns value with uselessness, subverting both Utilitarianism and conventional aesthetics about art's moral good. He probably derived this paradox from Taoism while reviewing Herbert Giles's translation of Chuang Tsu in *The Speaker* (Feb. 1890). In "The Critic as Artist" (1890/91) he praises Chuang for | "preaching . . . the uselessness of all things."

John Davidson (1857–1909)

Born in the town of Barrhead in the west of Scotland, into the Evangelical Union Church (a breakaway Presbyterian church) of his father, Alexander Davidson, and mother, Helen Crockett, Davidson was educated at the Highlanders' Academy in Greenock to where the family had moved. After further training as a chemist, he returned there in 1872 as a pupil-teacher, and spent a year at Edinburgh University (1876–77), thereafter teaching in a number of Scottish schools. In 1889 he went with his new wife, Margaret Cameron McArthur, to London to pursue a literary career, joining the Rhymers' Club of 1890–95 (a literary group that included W. B. Yeats, Arthur Symons, Richard Le Gallienne, Lionel Johnson, Ernest Dowson, and others). Davidson published a number of plays: *Diabolus amans* (1885); *Bruce* (1886); *Smith: A Tragic Farce* (1888); *An Unhistorical Pastoral* (1889); and *Scaramouche in Naxos* (1890). He worked as a journalist, writing for various periodicals, including *The Speaker*, *The Star*, the *Glasgow Herald*, and *The Yellow Book*. His verse included *In a Music Hall and Other Poems* (1891), two series of *Fleet Street Eclogues* (1893; 1896), *Ballads and Songs* (1894), *New Ballads* (1897), *The Last Ballad and Other Poems* (1899), and *Holiday and Other Poems* (1906). His novels included *The North Wall* (1891); *Perfervid: The Career of Ninian Jamieson* (1890); and *A Full and True Account … of Earl Lavender* (1895), a pastiche of 1890s' fiction with a frontispiece by the English illustrator Aubrey Beardsley (1872–98) showing flagellation. He also completed five blank-verse *Testaments* published between 1901 and 1908, and the unfinished trilogy of plays *God and Mammon* (1907–8). He suffered a breakdown in 1896, moved to Cornwall, and probably took his own life by drowning during a coastal walk. Standard edition of his poetry: *The Poems of John Davidson*, ed. Andrew Turnbull (2 vols, 1973); John Sloan, *John Davidson: First of the Moderns: A Literary Biography* (1995).

Thirty Bob a Week[1]

I couldn't touch a stop and turn a screw,[2]
    And set the blooming world a-work for me,
Like such as cut their teeth—I hope, like you—
    On the handle of a skeleton[3] gold key;
I cut mine on leek, which I eat it every week: 5
    I'm a clerk at thirty bob, as you can see.

Notes

JOHN DAVIDSON

[1] *title* a "bob" is London slang for a shilling; hence thirty shillings, or £ 1. 10s. or £78 a year; in current rates, about the equivalent of US$10,000 a year. The speaker is a clerk, possibly legal, banking, or accounting, earning what is almost a starvation wage, though not doing menial labour but skilled work, and so is poor but respectable. The poem was influential on modernism, for instance, on E. M. Forster's *Howards End* (1910) for the lower middle-class insurance clerk Leonard Bast who is treated with derision by the upper middle-class. Forster describes him as on "the extreme verge of gentility … not in the abyss." The poem also had a direct influence on T. S. Eliot's "Prufrock" (1915)

and "The Waste Land" (1922): Eliot wrote: "The personage Davidson created in this poem, has haunted me all my life, and the poem is to me a great poem for ever." First published in *The Yellow Book* (vol. 2, July 1894); republished in *Ballads and Songs* (1894).

[2] *stop … screw* the phrases are Victorian underworld and Cockney slang: to touch a stop is to rob a policeman (*stop* or *stopper* is rhyming slang for cop or copper); a screw is a skeleton key (see n. 3); hence, rob a house or shop.

[3] *skeleton* key that opens all locks, and hence golden to thieves.

But I don't allow it's luck and all a toss;[4]
    There's no such thing as being starred and crossed;[5]
It's just the power of some to be a boss,
    And the bally[6] power of others to be bossed: 10
I face the music,[7] sir; you bet I ain't a cur!
    Strike me lucky if I don't believe I'm lost!

For like a mole I journey in the dark,
    A-travelling along the underground[8]
From my Pillar'd Halls and broad suburban Park,[9]   15
    To come the daily dull official round;
And home again at night with my pipe all alight,
    A-scheming how to count ten bob a pound.[10]

And it's often very cold and very wet;
    And my missis stitches towels for a hunks;[11]   20
And the Pillar'd Halls is half of it to let[12] —
    Three rooms about the size of travelling trunks.
And we cough, the wife and I, to dislocate a sigh,
    When the noisy little kids are in their bunks.

But you'll never hear *her* do a growl, or whine,   25
    For she's made of flint and roses very odd;
And I've got to cut my meaning rather fine[13]
    Or I'd blubber, for *I'm* made of greens and sod:[14]
So p'rhaps we are in hell for all that I can tell,
    And lost and damned and served up hot to God.   30

I ain't blaspheming, Mr. Silvertongue;
    I'm saying things a bit beyond your art:
Of all the rummy starts[15] you ever sprung
    Thirty bob a week's the rummiest start!
With your science and your books and your the'ries about spooks,   35
    Did you ever hear of looking in your heart?

I didn't mean your pocket, Mr.; no!
    I mean that having children and a wife
With thirty bob on which to come and go
    Isn't dancing to the tabor and the fife![16]   40
When it doesn't make you drink, by Heaven, it makes you think,
    And notice curious items about life!

Notes

[4] *toss* game of chance, flip of a coin.
[5] *crossed* doomed by the stars; see, for instance, *Romeo and Juliet*, Prologue.
[6] *bally* bloody.
[7] *music* face adversity.
[8] *underground* subway, tube. The speaker is likened to a mole in its burrow; although moles are not blind: they have small eyes though very poor eyesight.
[9] *Halls … Park* hyperbole of the Grecian country estate for the clerk's suburban dwelling. Suburban changed to Suburbean in *Ballads and Songs* (1894), with perhaps a pun on "bean" meaning a coin.

[10] *pound* plotting how to squeeze ten shillings into a pound (twenty shillings).
[11] *hunks* grumbling misers; for the plight of seamstresses fifty years earlier, see HOOD, "SONG OF A SHIRT."
[12] *let* half of his dwelling must be rented ("to let") to pay for his own space.
[13] *fine* control his meaning and emotions carefully.
[14] *greens and sod* vegetables and earth.
[15] *rummy starts* bad happenings.
[16] *tabor … fife* small drum and fife, as in an Irish marching band.

I step into my heart and there I meet
    A god-almighty devil singing small,
Who would like to shout and whistle in the street,   45
    And squelch the passers flat against the wall;
If the whole world was a cake he had the power to take,
    He would take it, ask for more, and eat it all.

And I meet a sort of simpleton beside—
    The kind that life is always giving beans;[17]   50
With thirty bob a week to keep a bride
    He fell in love and married in his teens;
At thirty bob he stuck, but he knows it isn't luck;
    He knows the seas are deeper than tureens.

And the god-almighty devil and the fool[18]   55
    That meet me in the High Street on the strike,[19]
When I walk about my heart a-gathering wool,[20]
    Are my good and evil angels if you like;
And both of them together in every kind of weather
    Ride me like a double-seated "bike."[21]   60

That's rough a bit and needs its meaning curled;
    But I have a high old hot un[22] in my mind—
A most engrugious[23] notion of the world
    That leaves your lightning 'rithmetic behind:
I give it at a glance when I say "There ain't no chance,   65
    Nor nothing of the lucky-lottery kind."

And it's this way that I make it out to be:
    No fathers, mothers, countries, climates—none!—
Not Adam was responsible for me;
    Nor society, nor systems, nary one![24]   70
A little sleeping seed, I woke—I did indeed—
    A million years before the blooming sun.

I woke because I thought the time had come;
    Beyond my will there was no other cause:
And everywhere I found myself at home   75
Because I chose to be the thing I was;
    And in whatever shape, of mollusc, or of ape,[25]
I always went according to the laws.

Notes

[17] *beans* things of no value (see n. 9).
[18] *devil ... fool* two conflicting inner voices; see, for instance, the two angels competing for Faustus' soul in Christopher Marlowe's *Doctor Faustus* (1604).
[19] *strike* to make money.
[20] *wool* day-dreaming.

[21] *bike* "a bicycle built for two," as in the last words of "Daisy Bell" (1892), a popular musical hall song by Harry Dacre (1860–1922).
[22] *un* one, a good tip or prospect for making money.
[23] *engrugious* malapropism for egregious.
[24] *one* not a one.
[25] *mollusc ... ape* a dig at evolution and the descent of man from the sea-shells or the ape.

I was the love that chose my mother out;
 I joined two lives and from the union burst;   80
My weakness and my strength without a doubt
 Are mine alone for ever from the first.
It's just the very same with a difference in the name
 As "Thy will be done."²⁶ You say it if you durst!

They say it daily up and down the land   85
 As easy as you take a drink, it's true;
But the difficultest go²⁷ to understand,
 And the difficultest job a man can do,
Is to come it brave and meek with thirty bob a week,
 And feel that that's the proper thing for you.   90

It's a naked child against a hungry wolf;
 It's playing bowls upon a splitting wreck;²⁸
It's walking on a string across a gulf
 With millstones fore-and-aft about your neck:
But the thing is daily done by many and many a one ..   95
 And we fall, face forward, fighting, on the deck.

A Northern Suburb²⁹

Nature selects the longest way,
 And winds about in tortuous grooves;
A thousand years the oaks decay;
 The wrinkled glacier hardly moves.

But here the whetted fangs of change   5
 Daily devour the old demesne—
The busy farm, the quiet grange,
 The wayside inn, the village green.

In gaudy yellow brick and red,
 With rooting pipes, like creepers rank,   10
The shoddy terraces o'erspread
 Meadow, and garth, and daisied bank.

With shelves for rooms the houses crowd,
 Like draughty cupboards in a row—
Ice-chests when wintry winds are loud,   15
 Ovens when summer breezes blow.

Roused by the fee'd policeman's knock,
 And sad that day should come again,
Under the stars the workmen flock
 In haste to reach the workmen's train.   20

Notes

²⁶ *done* from the Lord's Prayer (Luke 11: 2).
²⁷ *go* thing, work, task.

²⁸ *bowls. . . wreck* lawn bowling upon a shipwreck that is splitting up; an impossible task.
²⁹ *title* from *New Ballads* (1897).

For here dwell those who must fulfil
    Dull tasks in uncongenial spheres,
Who toil through dread of coming ill,
    And not with hope of happier years,—

The lowly folk who scarcely dare   25
    Conceive themselves perhaps misplaced,
Whose prize for unremitting care
    Is only not to be disgraced.

Battle[30]

The war of words is done;
    The red-lipped cannon speak;
The battle has begun.

The web your speeches spun
    Tears and blood shall streak;   5
The war of words is done.

Smoke enshrouds the sun;
    Earth staggers at the shriek
Of battle new begun.

Poltroons and braggarts run: 10
    Woe to the poor, the meek!
The war of words is done.

"And hope not now to shun
    The doom that dogs the weak,"
Thunders every gun;   15

"Victory must be won."
    When the red-lipped cannon speak,
The war of words is done,
The slaughter has begun.

Constance Naden (1858–89)

Born in a suburb of Birmingham to her architect father, Thomas Naden (fl. 1848–78) and his wife, Caroline Anne Woodhill, who died two weeks after her daughter's birth, Constance Caroline Woodhill Naden was raised by her maternal grandparents, was educated in a Unitarian school and later studied botany, sciences, art, and languages at the Birmingham and Midland Institute and then continued with zoology and physics at Mason College of Science, under the influence of the writings of Herbert Spencer (1820–1903). Using an

Notes

[30] title from *The Last Ballad and Other Poems* (1899).

inheritance, she travelled widely in Asia and the Middle East, returning in 1887. Continuing her interests in philosophy, the theory and practice of science, and in women's rights, she helped establish the Hospital for Women in London, meeting the medical and political activist Elizabeth Garrett Anderson (1836–1917), with whom she joined forces in the cause for female suffrage. She published two volumes of poetry, *Songs and Sonnets of Springtime* (1881) and *A Modern Apostle, The Elixir of Life, and Other Poems* (1887). Her essays were published as *What is Religion: A Vindication of Free Thought* (1883), *Induction and Deduction and Other Essays* (1890), and *Further Reliques of Constance Naden* (1894), the last two issued posthumously. Standard edition: *The Complete Poetical Works of Constance Naden* (1894); William R. Hughes, *Constance Naden: A Memoir* (1890). "Victorian Women Writers Project": http://webapp1.dlib.indiana.edu/vwwp/view?docId=VAB7115

The Lady Doctor[1]

Saw ye that spinster gaunt and grey,
Whose aspect stern[2] might well dismay
   A bombardier stout-hearted?
The golden hair, the blooming face,
And all a maiden's tender grace   5
   Long, long from her have parted.

A Doctor she—her sole delight
To order draughts as black as night,
   Powders, and pills, and lotions;
Her very glance might cast a spell   10
Transmuting Sherry and Moselle[3]
   To chill and acrid potions.

Yet if some rash presumptuous man
Her early life should dare to scan
   Strange things he might discover;   15
For in the bloom of sweet seventeen
She wandered through the meadows green
   To meet a boyish lover.

She did not give him Jesuit's bark,[4]
To brighten up his vital spark,   20
   Nor ipecacuanha,
Nor chlorodyne, nor camomile,[5]

Notes

Constance Naden
[1] title from *Songs and Sonnets of Springtime* (1881).
[2] stern see Gilbert and Sullivan, *The Mikado* (1885), where the phrase would appear in the finale to Act I: "With aspect stern, / And gloomy stride / We come to learn / How you decide."
[3] *Moselle* white wine from southern Germany, named after the river of the region.
[4] bark the bark of a Peruvian tropical shrub, cinchona or quina, used by Jesuit missionaries, and eventually in the seventeenth century throughout Europe, against malaria, for which it is efficacious because it contained quinine, later isolated and named for it.
[5] *ipecacuanha ... camomile* ipecacuanha is a flowering plant from South America whose root is used as an emetic and expectorant, especially in poisoning; chlorodyne is a British patent medicine containing laudanum (opium in an alcohol solution), cannabis, and chloroform, invented by Dr John Collis Browne (1819–84) for the treatment of cholera and diarrhea; and camomile, from a plant of that name, is made into a tea to induce sleep.

But blushing looks, and many a smile,
   And kisses sweet as manna.[6]

But ah! the maiden's heart grew cold,   25
Perhaps she thought the youth too bold,
   Perhaps his views had shocked her;
In anger, scorn, caprice, or pride,
She left her old companion's side
   To be a Lady Doctor.   30

She threw away the faded flowers,
Gathered amid the woodland bowers,
   Her lover's parting token:
If suffering bodies we relieve,
What need for wounded souls to grieve?   35
   Why mourn, though hearts be broken?

She cared not, though with frequent moan
He wandered through the woods alone
   Dreaming of past affection:
She valued at the lowest price   40
Men neither patients for advice
   Nor subjects for dissection.

She studied hard for her degree;
At length the coveted M. D.
   Was to her name appended;   45
Joy to that Doctor, young and fair,
With rosy cheeks and golden hair,
   Learning with beauty blended.

Diseases man can scarce endure
A lady's glance may quickly cure,   50
   E'en though the pains be chronic;
Where'er that maiden bright was seen
Her eye surpassed the best quinine,[7]
   Her smile became a tonic.

But soon, too soon, the hand of care   55
Sprinkled with snow her golden hair,
   Her face grew worn and jaded;
Forgotten was each maiden wile,
She scarce remembered how to smile,
   Her roses all were faded.   60

And now, she looks so grim and stern,
We wonder any heart could burn
   For one so uninviting;

Notes

[6] *manna* the heaven-sent food that could be made into bread that fed the Israelites in the wilderness; see Exodus 16.   [7] *quinine* sometimes prescribed for eye twitches.

No gentle sympathy she shows,
She seems a man in woman's clothes,   65
   All female graces slighting.

Yet blame her not, for she has known
The woe of living all alone,
   In friendless, dreary sadness;
She longs for what she once disdained,   70
And sighs to think she might have gained
   A home of love and gladness.

MORAL

Fair maid, if thine unfettered heart
Yearn for some busy, toilsome part,
   Let that engross thee only;   75
But oh! if bound by love's light chain,
Leave not thy fond and faithful swain
   Disconsolate and lonely.

Love *Versus* Learning[8]

Alas, for the blight of my fancies!
   Alas, for the fall of my pride!
I planned, in my girlish romances,
   To be a philosopher's bride.

I pictured him learned and witty,   5
   The sage and the lover combined,
Not scorning to say I was pretty,
   Nor only adoring my *mind*.

No elderly, spectacled Mentor,
   But one who would worship and woo;   10
Perhaps I might take an inventor,
   Or even a poet would do.

And tender and gay and well-favoured,
   My fate overtook me at last:
I saw, and I heard, and I wavered,[9]   15
   I smiled, and my freedom was past.

He promised to love me for ever,
   He pleaded, and what could I say?
I thought he must surely be clever,
   For he is an Oxford M. A.[10]   20

Notes

[8] title from *Songs and Sonnets of Springtime* (1881).

[9] *wavered* parodic echo of a saying attributed to Julius Caesar, informing the Roman senate of his victory over Pharnaces of Pontus in 47 BCE: "*Veni, vidi, vici*" (Lat. I came, I saw, I conquered).

[10] *M. A.* an ironic comment, since the Oxford MA is available to any holder of an Oxford BA who pays a fee after a statutory period.

But now, I begin to discover
    My visions are fatally marred;
Perfection itself as a lover,
    He's neither a sage nor a bard.

He's mastered the usual knowledge,   25
    And says it's a terrible bore;
He formed his opinions at college,
    Then why should he think any more?

My logic he sets at defiance,
    Declares that my Latin's no use,   30
And when I begin to talk Science
    He calls me a dear little goose.

He says that my lips are too rosy
    To speak in a language that's dead,
And all that is dismal and prosy   35
    Should fly from so sunny a head.

He scoffs at each grave occupation,
    Turns everything off with a pun;
And says that his sole calculation
    Is how to make two into one.   40

He says Mathematics may vary,
    Geometry cease to be true,
But scorning the slightest vagary[11]
    He still will continue to woo.

He says that the sun may stop action,   45
    But he will not swerve from his course;
For love is his law of attraction,
    A smile his centripetal force.

His levity's truly terrific,[12]
    And often I think we must part,   50
But compliments so scientific
    Recapture my fluttering heart.

Yet sometimes 'tis very confusing,
    This conflict of love and of lore—
But hark! I must cease from my musing,   55
    For that is his knock at the door!

Notes

[11] *vagary* divergence from propriety: hence caprice; the emphasis in pronunciation on the second syllable is similar to that used by Gilbert and Sullivan in their comic verse.

[12] *terrific* pun: both great and terrifying.

To Amy, On Receiving Her Photograph[13]

When of some lovely landscape unforgot
    A shadowy sketch I see, my thought divines
    Clear sunshine gleaming through the pencilled lines,
And cool green shade, where seems a shapeless blot:
I know how morning pierced that sheltered grot,   5
    How noonday glowed between the tufted pines;
    And even so, your cold grey portrait shines
With tints unseen by those who know you not.

They cannot see the apple-blossom cheek,
    The eyes of midnight blue, the sun-lit hair;   10
Grave are the lips, and will not smile or speak:
    And yet to me the pictured face is fair:
I conned that May-tide bloom when last we met,
And all the eye saw then, the heart sees yet.

The New Orthodoxy[14]

So, dear Fred, you're not content
Though I quote the books you lent,
And I've kept that spray you sent
    Of the milk-white heather;
For you fear I'm too "advanced"   5
To remember all that chanced
In the old days, when we danced,
    Walked, and rode together.

Trust me, Fred, beneath the curls
Of the most "advanced" of girls,   10
Many a foolish fancy whirls,
    Bidding Fact defiance,
And the simplest village maid
Needs not to be much afraid
Of her sister, sage and staid,   15
    Bachelor of Science.

Ah! while yet our hope was new
Guardians thought 'twould never do
That Sir Frederick's heir should woo
    Little Amy Merton:[15]   20
So the budding joy they snatched
From our hearts, so meetly matched,

Notes

[13] title from *Songs and Sonnets of Springtime* (1881).

[14] title reversing the conventional Victorian trope of the simple girl's faith balking at the advanced unorthodoxy of the male suitor, this woman assured her doubting lover of her reliability. From *A Modern Apostle; The Elixir of Life; The Story of Clarice; and Other Poems* (1887), in a section called "Evolutional Erotics."

[15] *Merton* class and money politics are invoked to keep the lovers apart. Amy Merton is possibly so-named after Thomas Day's bestselling moralizing tales, *The History of*

You to Oxford they despatched,
    Me they sent to Girton.[16]

Were the vows all writ in dust?   25
No—you're one-and-twenty—just—
And you write—"We will, we must
    Now, at once, be married!"
Nay, you plan the wedding trip!
Softly, sir! there's many a slip   30
Ere the goblet to the lip[17]
    Finally is carried.

Oh, the wicked tales I hear!
Not that you at Ruskin jeer,
Nor that at Carlyle[18] you sneer,   35
    With his growls dyspeptic:
But that, having read in vain
Huxley, Tyndall, Clifford, Bain,[19]
All the scientific train—
    You're a hardened sceptic!   40

Things with fin, and claw, and hoof
Join to give us perfect proof
That our being's warp and woof
    We from near and far win;
Yet your flippant doubts you vaunt,   45
And—to please a maiden aunt—
You've been heard to say you can't
    Pin your faith to Darwin!

Then you jest, because Laplace[20]
Said this Earth was nought but gas   50
Till the vast rotating mass
    Denser grew and denser:
Something worse they whisper too,
But I'm sure it *can't* be true—
For they tell me, Fred, that you   55
    Scoff at Herbert Spencer![21]

Notes

Sandford and Merton (3 vols, 1783–89), telling of the rise of Tommy Merton from a spoiled and advantaged child to a virtuous gentleman.

[16] *Girton* while Fred goes to Oxford, Amy goes to Girton College for girls in Cambridge, recently founded by Emily Davies (1830–1921) in 1869; women could not take degrees at Cambridge until 1947; see CONDITION: EDUCATION; EAST-LAKE, "ENGLISHWOMAN."

[17] *lip* variant of the English proverb, "There's many a slip twixt the cup and the lip."

[18] *Ruskin … Carlyle* two of the Victorian sages: John Ruskin and Thomas Carlyle; Carlyle suffered from a well-known gastric illness from his time at Edinburgh University (1818) to the end of his life.

[19] *Huxley … Bain* leading scientists of the day: Thomas Henry Huxley (1825–95), British biologist and advocate of Charles Darwin; John Tyndall (1820–93), physicist; William Kingdon Clifford (1845–79), mathematician and philosopher; and Alexander Bain (1818–1903), psychologist, philosopher, and advocate of educational reform.

[20] *Laplace* French mathematician and astronomer Pierre Simon, Marquis de Laplace (1749–1827) was the author of *Mécanique Céleste* (Fr. Celestial mechanics, 5 vols, 1799–1825) that earned him the name of "the French Newton." He reformulated the "nebular hypothesis" concerning the origin of the solar system from gaseous clouds or *nebulae* that rotate, collapse, and over millennia form planets.

[21] *Spencer* British biologist, philosopher, and sociologist, and strong advocate of evolution, extending it to apply to

Write—or telegraph—or call!
Come yourself and tell me all:
No fond hope shall me enthrall,
    No regret shall sway me: 60
Yet—until the worst is said,
Till I know your faith is dead,
I remain, dear doubting Fred,
    Your believing
          AMY.

Natural Selection[22]

I had found out a gift for my fair,
    I had found where the cave-men were laid;
Skull, femur, and pelvis were there,
    And spears, that of silex[23] they made.

But he ne'er could be true, she averred,   5
    Who would dig up an ancestor's grave[24]—
And I loved her the more when I heard
    Such filial regard for the Cave.[25]

My shelves, they are furnished with stones
    All sorted and labelled with care,   10
And a splendid collection of bones,
    Each one of them ancient and rare;

One would think she might like to retire
    To my study—she calls it a "hole!"
Not a fossil I heard her admire,   15
    But I begged it, or borrowed, or stole.

But there comes an idealess lad,
    With a strut, and a stare, and a smirk;
And I watch, scientific though sad,
    The Law of Selection[26] at work.   20

Notes

social organization and human development. Naden was a follower of Spencer's views.

[22] *title* the term is from Darwin's *On the Origin of Species* (1859). From *A Modern Apostle; The Elixir of Life; The Story of Clarice; and Other Poems* (1887), in a section called "Evolutional Erotics."

[23] *silex* flint, used for tools, axes, and spear heads in the Stone Age.

[24] *grave* this palaeontologist is excavating to discover proto-human remains, alleging they are ancestors of modern humans, following on from Darwin's *The Descent of Man* (1871).

[25] *Cave* the most famous nineteenth-century fossil cave was Kirkdale Cave in Yorkshire, discovered in 1821, and analysed by the paleontologist, William Buckland (1784–1856).

[26] *Selection* Darwin's full title is *On the Origin of Species by Means of Natural Selection, or The Preservation of Favoured Races in the Struggle for Life* (1859). He devotes all of chapter 4 to the subject, specifying the principle or law: "This preservation of favourable variations and the rejection of injurious variations, I call Natural Selection." See RELIGION: GEOLOGY; DARWIN, ORIGIN.

Of Science he hasn't a trace,
He seeks not the How and the Why,
But he sings with an amateur's grace,
And he dances much better than I.

And we know the more dandified males   25
By dance and by song win their wives—
'Tis a law that with *Aves* prevails,
And even in *Homo*[27] survives.

Shall I rage as they whirl in the valse?[28]
Shall I sneer as they carol and coo?   30
Ah no! for since Chloe is false,
I'm certain that Darwin is true!

A. E. Housman (1859–1936)

Alfred Edward Housman was born near Bromsgrove in Worcestershire, the son of a rural solicitor, Edward Housman (1831–94), and Sarah Jane Williams (1828–71). His brother (and literary executor) Laurence (1865–1959) and his sister Clemence (1861–55) were noted book illustrators, writers, and activists for women's suffrage. Housman won a scholarship to St John's College, Oxford, forming a lifelong unrequited love for Moses Jackson (c.1858–1923), his roommate. Although he began with a first-class in his first examinations, he failed his finals for several reasons: his father's bankruptcy, his neglect of studying the history and philosophy parts of his requirements, his obsessive concentration on the text of the Roman elegiac poet Sextus Propertius (c.50–15 BCE), and possibly Jackson's rejection. He eventually graduated with a pass degree, qualified in the civil service examinations and took a job (1881) at the Patent Office where Jackson also worked. For ten years he worked in the evenings at the British Museum Library, completing an unpublished edition of Sextus Propertius and twenty-five articles in scholarly journals, mostly on the textual editing of classical authors. He won the chair of Latin at University College, London (1892) and stayed for nineteen years, publishing editions of Ovid (1894) and Juvenal (1905). In the first five months of 1895 he wrote much of *A Shropshire Lad* (1896), his best-known poem. In 1911 he was appointed professor of Latin at Cambridge, lectured on textual criticism, and published editions of Lucan (1926) and the final four of five volumes of Manilius (1930). He also published *Last Poems* (1922). His brother Laurence published other collections posthumously: *More Poems* (1936), and "Additional Poems" in Laurence Housman's *A.E.H: Some Poems, Some Letters and a Personal Memoir* (1937). Standard Edition: *The Poems of A. E. Housman*, ed. Archie Burnett (1997); *Collected Poems and Selected Prose*, ed. Christopher Ricks (1988); *The Letters of A. E. Housman*, ed. Archie Burnett (2 vols, 2007); Norman Page, *A. E. Housman: A Critical Biography* (1983). The Housman Society: www.housman-society.co.uk.

Notes

[27] *Aves ... Homo* (Lat. birds, plural of *avis*); *homo* (Lat. man). Darwin had conducted many of his researches on the finches of the Galapagos Islands during the voyage of *H.M.S. Beagle*, and he used them in *On the Origin of Species*.

Here Naden draws an analogy between the mating practices of birds and humans in relation to the evolution of humans.

[28] *valse* (Fr. waltz).

A Shropshire Lad

Originally called *Poems by Terence Hearsay*, giving a fictitious name to the supposed author, an ordinary Shropshire lad, but changed at the urging of his friend A. W. Pollard (1859–1944), British bibliographer, *A Shropshire Lad* was published at Housman's own expense in1896, having been rejected by the publisher Macmillan. It gradually was acclaimed for the vibrancy of its rustic narrator, timely cynicism, and its themes. Housman demythologized the conventions of the pastoral elegy as represented by Matthew Arnold's "Scholar Gypsy" and "Thyrsis": mutability, an idealized English countryside, the fickleness of love, the brevity of youth, the ravages of war, and the inexorability of death. The collection is structured as follows: it begins with an introductory occasional poem for Victoria's golden jubilee that begins in celebration and ends in cynicism about the deaths of soldiers in the Shropshire regiment in her "little wars." Then follows the first section (II to XXXI), set in Shropshire as a world of youthful love and beauty whose early innocence shifts (in XIII) to loss of innocence and awareness of death. The bridge section consists of various journey metaphors (six lyrics from XXXII to XXXVII), and finally, a third section (XXXVIII to LXI), based largely in London, looks back to Shropshire as a land of dreams. The final two lyrics (LXII and LXIII) are a kind of poetic credo, first in a dialogue between the Shropshire Lad and "Terence," and finally in the last lyric with its ambiguous metaphor of flowers and seeds – whether of love or poetry – or something else. The poem employs a variety of metrical forms, precision of phrasing, sharp observation, and echoes of the border ballads and the seeming simplicity of the songs in Shakespeare's plays.

I   1887[1]

From Clee[2] to heaven the beacon burns,
　　The shires have seen it plain,
From north and south the sign returns
　　And beacons burn again.

Look left, look right, the hills are bright,　　　　　　　5
　　The dales are light between,
Because 'tis fifty years to-night
　　That God has saved the Queen.[3]

Now, when the flame they watch not towers
　　About the soil they trod,　　　　　　　　　　　　　　10
Lads, we'll remember friends of ours
　　Who shared the work with God.

Notes

A. E. HOUSMAN

[1] *title* the date of Queen Victoria's Golden Jubilee was 28 June 1887, when beacon fires were lit on high points across England. It is the introductory poem to the volume, and is unique in being almost the only one referring to a specific occasion (but see below XLV, n. 1).

[2] *Clee* a range of hills in Shropshire between the west Midlands and Wales. Housman's sister records that "on Jubilee night, 1887... we saw the bonfires burning right round the counties from the Malvern Hills to the Wrekin, and farther."

[3] *Queen* see the opening of the British national anthem, "God save our gracious Queen."

To skies that knit their heartstrings right,
　　To fields that bred them brave,
The saviours come not home to-night:　　　　　　　　　15
　　Themselves they could not save.[4]

It dawns in Asia, tombstones show
　　And Shropshire names are read;
And the Nile spills his overflow
　　Beside the Severn's[5] dead.　　　　　　　　　　　20

We pledge in peace by farm and town
　　The Queen they served in war,
And fire the beacons up and down
　　The land they perished for.

"God save the Queen" we living sing,　　　　　　　　25
　　From height to height 'tis heard;
And with the rest your voices ring,
　　Lads of the Fifty-third.[6]

Oh, God will save her, fear you not:
　　Be you the men you've been,　　　　　　　　　　30
Get you the sons your fathers got,
　　And God will save the Queen.

II

Loveliest of trees, the cherry now[7]
Is hung with bloom along the bough,[8]
And stands about the woodland ride
Wearing white for Eastertide.[9]

Now, of my threescore years and ten,[10]　　　　　　5
Twenty will not come again,
And take from seventy springs a score,
It only leaves me fifty more.

Notes

[4] *save* see Matthew 27: 42; and Mark 15: 31.

[5] *Asia … Severn* Britain fought wars in Asia throughout the nineteenth century, including the second Afghan War (1878–81) and the third Anglo-Burmese War (1885–86). The Nile is a reference to the death on 26 January 1885 of General Charles Gordon (1833–85), British military leader, at Khartoum on the Nile, or, more generally, to the Sudan campaign against the Mahdi Muhammad Ahmad (1845–85), religious and military leader in the Sudan. The Severn is the longest river in Britain, flowing through Shropshire and emptying into the Bristol Channel. Mentioning the River Severn in relation to those who died abroad, here those in colonial wars, also alludes to the death of Arthur Hallam and the Severn (see TENNYSON, IN MEMORIAM, SECTION XIX).

[6] *Fifty-third* Shropshire regiment of infantry.

[7] *now* some 160 composers have set Housman's lyrics to music including a number of the "Shropshire Lad" lyrics as a song cycle. In 1911–12, George Butterworth (1885–1916) wrote settings for baritone and piano of eleven of Housman's poems. Butterworth died in the trenches in World War I. The first six songs from "A Shropshire Lad" were also set for string quartet, tenor and piano by Ralph Vaughan Williams (1872–1958), and altogether he set fifteen Housman lyrics. See also the parody of this poem by the American Dorothy Parker (1893–1967) entitled "Cherry White": "I never see the prettiest thing— / A cherry bough gone white with Spring— / But what I think, 'How gay 'twould be / To hang me from a flowering tree" (from *Death and Taxes*, 1931).

[8] *bough* see *The Tempest* 5. 1. 94.

[9] *Eastertide* white is the liturgical colour for vestments during the church season of Easter.

[10] *ten* see Psalm 90: 10.

And since to look at things in bloom
Fifty springs are little room,   10
About the woodlands I will go
To see the cherry hung with snow.

XIII

When I was one-and-twenty
    I heard a wise man say,
"Give crowns and pounds and guineas[11]
    But not your heart away;
Give pearls away and rubies   5
    But keep your fancy free."
But I was one-and-twenty,
    No use to talk to me.

When I was one-and-twenty
    I heard him say again,   10
"The heart out of the bosom
    Was never given in vain;
'Tis paid with sighs a plenty
    And sold for endless rue."
And I am two-and-twenty   15
    And oh, 'tis true, 'tis true.

XIX   To an Athlete Dying Young[12]

The time you won your town the race
We chaired you through the market-place;
Man and boy stood cheering by,
And home we brought you shoulder-high.

To-day, the road all runners come,[13]   5
Shoulder-high we bring you home,
And set you at your threshold down,
Townsman of a stiller town.[14]

Notes

11 *guineas* English coinage: a crown was a large coin worth five shillings; a pound was twenty shillings; a guinea was twenty-one shillings.

12 *title* a version of the *carpe diem* (Lat. seize the day) theme; the swift flight of time in carrying off the young in their glory is a common theme in the classical poets, as in Virgil, *Odes* 2. 14: "Alas, they fly by, Postumus, Postumus, the fleeting years, and piety will not slow wrinkles, the onward march of old age, nor indomitable death"; and Horace *Odes* 1. 11: "Now, while we're talking, grudging time is flying: seize the day, put as little faith in tomorrow as possible." See also Christopher Marlowe's "Passionate Shepherd To His Love" (1599), Robert Herrick's "To the Ladies to Make Much of Time" (1648), with its thematic *carpe diem* first line: "Gather ye rosebuds, while ye may," and Andrew Marvell's "To His Coy Mistress" (1681).
    See also FITZGERALD, *RUBÁIYÁT*, XXVI and n. 25.

13 *come* see Propertius, *Elegies* 3. 18. 21–22: "But yet, all come here, first and last ... and that road must be run by all." Housman spent many years on an edition of Propertius.

14 *town* see the painting by French artist Jacques-Louis David (1748–1825), *The Lictors Bring to Brutus the Bodies of His Sons* (1789); and Tennyson's "Home they brought her warrior dead," a lyric added to *The Princess* (third edition 1850).

Smart lad, to slip betimes away
From fields where glory does not stay 10
And early though the laurel grows
It withers quicker than the rose.

Eyes the shady night has shut
Cannot see the record cut,[15]
And silence sounds no worse than cheers 15
After earth has stopped the ears:[16]

Now you will not swell the rout
Of lads that wore their honours out,
Runners whom renown outran
And the name died before the man. 20

So set, before its echoes fade,
The fleet foot on the sill of shade,
And hold to the low lintel up
The still-defended challenge-cup.

And round that early-laurelled head 25
Will flock to gaze the strengthless dead[17]
And find unwithered on its curls
The garland briefer than a girl's.[18]

XXVII[19]

"Is my team ploughing,
    That I was used to drive
And hear the harness jingle[20]
    When I was man alive?"

Ay, the horses trample, 5
    The harness jingles now;
No change though you lie under
    The land you used to plough.[21]

"Is football playing
    Along the river shore, 10
With lads to chase the leather,
    Now I stand up no more?"

Notes

[15] *cut* reduced (*OED*, v. 21).

[16] *ears* see Matthew Arnold's elegy on the Brontës, "Haworth Churchyard" (1855): "The Muse / Gains not an earth-deafen'd ear" (37–38); "Her ear / Is deaf … a little earth / Stops it for ever to praise" (81–85).

[17] *dead* see *Odyssey* 11. 29, 49; and *Aeneid* 10. 636. For laurel, see HEMANS, n. 17.

[18] *girl's* see Matthew Arnold, *Merope* (1858): "Thy head drooped softly, and the golden curls / Clustering o'er thy white forehead, like a girl's" (1161–62).

[19] *title* Housman wrote to Houston Martin (1914–94), American bibliophile, that Florence Hardy (1871–1937) told him that XXVII was Thomas Hardy's favourite. Housman said: "it may be the best, though it is not the most perfect."

[20] *jingle* see THOMSON, THE CITY OF DREADFUL NIGHT, IX: 10.

[21] *plough* see Tennyson, "The Ancient Sage" (1885): "The ploughman passes, bent with pain, / To mix with what he ploughed" (144–15).

Ay, the ball is flying,
    The lads play heart and soul;[22]
The goal stands up, the keeper   15
    Stands up to keep the goal.

"Is my girl happy,
    That I thought hard to leave,
And has she tired of weeping
    As she lies down at eve?"   20

Ay, she lies down lightly,
    She lies not down to weep:
Your girl is well contented.
    Be still, my lad, and sleep.

"Is my friend hearty,   25
    Now I am thin and pine,
And has he found to sleep in
    A better bed than mine?"

Yes, lad, I lie easy,
    I lie as lads would choose;   30
I cheer a dead man's sweetheart,
    Never ask me whose.

XXX[23]

Others, I am not the first,
Have willed more mischief than they durst:
If in the breathless night I too
Shiver now, 'tis nothing new.

More than I, if truth were told,   5
Have stood and sweated hot and cold,
And through their reins in ice and fire[24]
Fear contended with desire.

Notes

[22] *soul* see Deuteronomy 6: 5; and Luke 10: 27; see also Browning, "Saul" (1842): "How good is man's life, the mere living! how fit to employ / All the heart and soul and the senses, for ever in joy!" (11–12).

[23] *title* this poem is one of the few in which Housman expressed conflicted sexual emotions. Housman had been angered by the treatment given to Oscar Wilde in the trials that led to his prison sentence – when he had been writing *A Shropshire Lad* in London in 1893–95. He sent Wilde an autographed copy when he was released from Reading prison. See also poem XLV (below). Others such conflicted poems include XXII, XXIII, XLII, XLVII ("The Carpenter's Son"), and LXIII. In a lyric published posthumously in *More Poems* (1936), Housman's attraction to Moses Jackson was made explicit: "Because I like

you better / Than suits a man to say / It irked you, and I promised / To throw the thought away." In 1942 his brother Laurence gave to the British Library an essay on Housman with the condition that it not be printed for twenty-five years. When it was published in *Encounter* (Oct. 1967) it openly discussed his lifelong sexual attraction to Jackson. From *More Poems*. See also n. 62.

[24] *reins … fire* for "reins" see *OED*: loins, sexual impulses; for the conventional descriptions of lovers as fire and ice, see Petrarch, *Canzoniere*, 134 [sometimes given as 104]: "*Pace non trovo*" (Ital. "I find no peace, and all my war is done; I fear and hope; I burn and freeze like ice"; trans. Sir Thomas Wyatt, 1557); Edmund Spenser knew Wyatt's translation and drew heavily on Petrarch's *Canzoniere*, as in *Amoretti* (1595), Sonnet 30: "My love is like to ice, and I to fire."

Agued once like me were they,
But I like them shall win my way   10
Lastly to the bed of mould
Where there's neither heat nor cold.

But from my grave across my brow
Plays no wind of healing now,
And fire and ice within me fight   15
Beneath the suffocating night.

XXXI[25]

On Wenlock Edge[26] the wood's in trouble,
    His forest fleece the Wrekin[27] heaves;
The gale, it plies the saplings double,
    And thick on Severn snow the leaves.[28]

'Twould blow like this through holt and hanger[29]   5
    When Uricon[30] the city stood:
'Tis the old wind in the old anger,
    But then it threshed another wood.

Then, 'twas before my time, the Roman
    At yonder heaving hill would stare: 10
The blood that warms an English yeoman,
    The thoughts that hurt him, they were there.

There, like the wind through woods in riot,
    Through him the gale of life blew high;
The tree of man was never quiet: 15
    Then 'twas the Roman, now 'tis I.

The gale, it plies the saplings double,
    It blows so hard, 'twill soon be gone:
To-day the Roman and his trouble
    Are ashes under Uricon.   20

XXXV[31]

On the idle hill of summer,
    Sleepy with the flow of streams,[32]
Far I hear the steady drummer
    Drumming like a noise in dreams.

Notes

[25] *title* Housman gave permission to Walter Raleigh (1861–1922), regius professor of English Literature at Oxford, to print this poem in one of *The Times Broadsheets* for troops in the trenches in 1915.

[26] *Edge* a limestone escarpment in Shropshire. Ralph Vaughan Williams (1872–1958) wrote a song on this poem (1909).

[27] *Wrekin* a hill in east Shropshire at the top of which is a large iron-age fort.

[28] *leaves* see *Paradise Lost* 1. 302–3. See also AGUILAR, n. 10.

[29] *holt and hanger* copse and wooded bank.

[30] *Uricon* Roman settlement near Shrewsbury, Viroconium (or Uriconium), the chief settlement of the Roman XIVth legion, *c.*55 to 88, with a population of 15,000.

[31] *title* like XXXI (see above, n. 25), Housman allowed this lyric to be printed in a *Times Broadsheet*.

[32] *streams* see Swinburne, "The Garden of Proserpine" (1866): "A sleepy world of streams" (8).

Far and near and low and louder 5
    On the roads of earth go by,
Dear to friends and food for powder,[33]
    Soldiers marching, all to die.

East and west on fields forgotten
    Bleach the bones of comrades slain, 10
Lovely lads and dead and rotten;[34]
    None that go return again.[35]

Far the calling bugles hollo,
    High the screaming fife replies,
Gay the files of scarlet[36] follow: 15
    Woman bore me,[37] I will rise.

XLV[38]

If by chance your eye offend you,[39]
    Pluck it out, lad, and be sound:
'Twill hurt, but here are salves to friend you,
    And many a balsam grows on ground.

And if your hand or foot offend you,[40] 5
    Cut it off, lad, and be whole;
But play the man,[41] stand up and end you,
    When your sickness is your soul[42]

LIV

With rue my heart is laden
    For golden friends I had,[43]
For many a rose-lipt maiden[44]
    And many a lightfoot lad.

Notes

[33] *powder* see 1 Henry IV 4. 2. 64–67.

[34] *rotten* see *Love's Labour's Lost* 5. 2. 654–56.

[35] *again* see Proverbs 2: 18–19.

[36] *scarlet* the colour of the tunics worn in the British army.

[37] *me* see Job 14: 1–2; and Ecclesiasticus 10: 18.

[38] *title* this poem and XLIV propose suicide by shooting oneself as a means of escaping what Housman calls "the soul that should not have been born" and "your sickness is your soul," coded words for homosexuality. Housman's brother found a newspaper clipping (*The Standard*, 10 Aug. 1895) inserted in the poet's copy of *A Shropshire Lad* between poems XLIV and XLV concerning the suicide with a revolver of an 18-year-old Woolwich naval cadet, Henry Clarkson Maclean, on 6 August whose letter to the coroner explained his reason as having "no earthly hope of obtaining" what would "make me thoroughly happy," so suicide is "better than a long series

of sorrows and disgraces." Lyric XLIV ends: "Oh soon, and better so than later / After long disgrace and scorn, / You shot dead the household traitor, / The soul that should not have been born." See also poem XXII.

[39] *you* see Matthew 5: 29; and Mark 9: 47.

[40] *you* see Matthew 18: 8; and Mark 9: 43.

[41] *man* a famous cry by Hugh Latimer (*c.*1470–1555), bishop of Worcester, to his friend Nicholas Ridley (1500–55), bishop of London, as they were being burned as heretics outside Balliol College, Oxford (16 October 1555): "Be of good comfort, Master Ridley, and play the man! We shall this day light such a candle, by God's grace, in England, as I trust shall never be put out" (*Foxe's Book of Martyrs*, 1563).

[42] *soul* see Wisdom 17: 8.

[43] *had* see *Cymbeline* 4. 2. 263–64.

[44] *maiden* see *Othello* 4. 2. 65.

By brooks too broad for leaping   5
The lightfoot boys are laid;
The rose-lipt girls are sleeping
In fields where roses fade.

LXII[45]

"Terence,[46] this is stupid stuff:
You eat your victuals fast enough;
There can't be much amiss, 'tis clear,
To see the rate you drink your beer.
But oh, good Lord, the verse you make,   5
It gives a chap the belly-ache.
The cow, the old cow, she is dead;[47]
It sleeps well, the horned head:
We poor lads, 'tis our turn now
To hear such tunes as killed the cow.[48]   10
Pretty friendship 'tis to rhyme
Your friends to death before their time
Moping melancholy mad:[49]
Come, pipe a tune to dance to, lad."

Why, if 'tis dancing you would be,   15
There's brisker pipes than poetry.
Say, for what were hop-yards meant,
Or why was Burton built on Trent?
Oh many a peer[50] of England brews
Livelier liquor than the Muse,   20
And malt does more than Milton can
To justify God's ways to man.[51]
Ale, man, ale's the stuff to drink
For fellows whom it hurts to think:
Look into the pewter pot   25
To see the world as the world's not.
And faith, 'tis pleasant till 'tis past:
The mischief is that 'twill not last.

Notes

[45] *title* the second-to-last poem in the cycle. Housman gave permission to have this poem printed in *The Times Broadsheets*; see n. 25.

[46] *Terence* the collection was first titled "The Poems of Terence Hearsay." It is not a reference to the Roman dramatist but to the supposed author of the entire cycle, Terence Hearsay (see headnote).

[47] *dead* echo of a traditional song, "There was an old man and he had an old cow/ But he had no fodder to give her, /So he took up his fiddle and played her the tune: /'Consider, good cow, consider.'"

[48] *cow* see n. 47.

[49] *mad* see *Paradise Lost* when Adam is first shown Death: "Demonic frenzy, moping melancholy / and moon-struck madness, pining atrophy . . ." (11. 484–85).

[50] *Burton . . . peer* Burton-on-Trent was a famous brewing city; in 1880 there were thirty breweries in Burton. The water of the River Trent contained dissolved salts that improved flavour and preservation, allowing its India Pale Ale to be shipped to India and the rest of the empire. Michael Bass (first Baron Burton, 1837–1909) was a local brewer and MP for Burton who was made a peer in 1886; Edward Cecil Guinness (1847–1927) was made a baron in 1891.

[51] *man* see *Paradise Lost* 1. 26.

Oh I have been to Ludlow[52] fair
And left my necktie God knows where,[53]   30
And carried half-way home, or near,
Pints and quarts of Ludlow beer:
Then the world seemed none so bad,
And I myself a sterling lad;
And down in lovely muck I've lain,   35
Happy till I woke again.
Then I saw the morning sky:
Heigho, the tale was all a lie;
The world, it was the old world yet,
I was I, my things were wet,   40
And nothing now remained to do
But begin the game anew.

    Therefore, since the world has still
Much good, but much less good than ill,
And while the sun and moon endure[54]   45
Luck's a chance, but trouble's sure,
I'd face it as a wise man would,
And train for ill and not for good.[55]
'Tis true, the stuff I bring for sale
Is not so brisk a brew as ale: 50
Out of a stem that scored the hand
I wrung it in a weary land.[56]
But take it: if the smack is sour,
The better for the embittered hour;
It should do good to heart and head   55
When your soul is in my soul's stead;[57]
And I will friend you, if I may,
In the dark and cloudy day.[58]

    There was a king reigned in the East:[59]
There, when kings will sit to feast,   60
They get their fill before they think
With poisoned meat and poisoned drink.
He gathered all that springs to birth
From the many-venomed earth;
First a little, thence to more,   65
He sampled all her killing store;
And easy, smiling, seasoned sound,
Sate the king when healths went round.

Notes

[52] *Ludlow* market town in south Shropshire where its local fair had been a tradition from the late Middle Ages.

[53] *where* see Rudyard Kipling, "Cells" (1890): "I left my cap in a public-house, my boots in the public road, / And Lord knows where—and I don't care—my belt and my tunic goed" (17–18).

[54] *endure* see Psalm 72: 5.

[55] *good* see Jeremiah 21: 10; 39: 16; and 44: 27. See also Amos 9: 4.

[56] *land* see Isaiah 32: 2.

[57] *stead* see Job 16: 4–5.

[58] *day* see Ezekiel 34: 12.

[59] *East* Mithridates VI (c.131–63 BCE), king of Pontus in Asia Minor, was fearful of being poisoned, and so developed his immunity by taking poison in small doses. For this line, see Robert Burns, "John Barleycorn": "There was three kings into the east."

They put arsenic in his meat
And stared aghast to watch him eat;   70
They poured strychnine in his cup
And shook to see him drink it up:
They shook, they stared as white's their shirt:[60]
Them it was their poison hurt.
—I tell the tale that I heard told.   75
Mithridates, he died old.

Additional Poems[61]

XVIII[62]

Oh who is that young sinner with the handcuffs on his wrists?
And what has he been after that they groan and shake their fists?
And wherefore is he wearing such a conscience-stricken air?
Oh they're taking him to prison for the colour of his hair.[63]

'Tis a shame to human nature, such a head of hair as his;   5
In the good old time 'twas hanging for the colour that it is;[64]
Though hanging isn't bad enough and flaying would be fair
For the nameless and abominable[65] colour of his hair.

Oh a deal of pains he's taken and a pretty price he's paid
To hide his poll or dye it of a mentionable shade;   10
But they've pulled the beggar's hat off for the world to see and stare,
And they're haling him to justice for the colour of his hair.

Now 'tis oakum for his fingers and the treadmill for his feet[66]
And the quarry-gang on Portland[67] in the cold and in the heat,
And between his spells of labour in the time he has to spare   15
He can curse the God that made him for the colour of his hair.

Notes

[60] *shirt* see *Hamlet* 2. 1. 82.

[61] *Poems* first published by Laurence Housman in *A.E.H.: Some Poems, Some Letters and a Personal Memoir* (1937).

[62] *title* this poem was conceived just after Wilde's conviction in May, 1895, and perhaps was written some five years later. When *A Shropshire Lad* was published, Housman sent a copy to Wilde when he was released from prison in Reading. Robert Ross, a friend of Wilde's had memorized some of the poems, and had recited them to Wilde in prison. Housman owned a copy of Wilde's *A Ballad of Reading Gaol* (1898). See n. 24.

[63] *hair* see the song of the Irish nationalists, "The Wearing of the Green": "They are hanging men and women / For the wearing of the green!"

[64] *is hanging* for homosexual practices was abolished in 1861. See GENDER: SEX; LABOUCHÈRE (WEB p. 102). See also the associations with Judas and the tradition that he had red hair, Matthew 27: 3–9.

[65] *nameless ... abominable* Wilde had referred in his trial to Lord Alfred Douglas's poem "Two Loves" with the line:

"the love that dare not speak its name" (see WILDE, n. 45 (WEB p. 451); see also GENDER: SEX; DOUGLAS (WEB p. 109 l. 74)). "Abominable" was the adjective usually used to describe sodomy in acts from Henry VIII to Victoria, including the "Offences Against the Persons Act," 1861.

[66] *feet* prisoners were expected to pick oakum. Oakum was disused tarred ropes formerly used by the navy, cut into pieces that had to be unravelled and picked apart into its constituent strands to be reused in packing the spaces between timbers on wooden and steel sheeting in iron-clad ships where it expanded when wet to seal the joints. Picking oakum was the most common prison and workhouse occupation. Treadmills, which used many prisoners to turn the same huge weighted wheel, was another prison occupation in Victorian England. Wilde was required to pick oakum. His health had deteriorated so he could not walk the treadmill.

[67] *Portland* the Isle of Portland is a limestone island in the English Channel of Dorset where Portland stone is quarried. It was used in the building of St Paul's Cathedral and Buckingham Palace in London.

WEB p. 482

Arthur Conan Doyle (1859–1930)
    A Scandal in Bohemia

Francis Thompson (1859–1907)

Born in Preston in Lancashire, the second son of a Roman Catholic doctor, Charles Thompson (1819–96) and Mary Turner Morton (1822–80), Francis Thompson was educated at Ushaw College near Durham to train for the Roman Catholic priesthood. There he began his habit of keeping notebooks, eventually over 100, the first showing early love for Tennyson and the Pre-Raphaelite poets, especially Dante Rossetti. Abandoning his vocation but not his faith, he then studied medicine at Owens College in Manchester (1877) but never practised. After family disputes following the death of his mother, he resolved to be a writer and moved to London (1885) in great poverty, reduced to selling matches in the streets. He also became addicted to laudanum, a product of opium then cheaply available. As an invalid for the rest of his life, he was on the verge of suicide but was rescued the first time by a vision of the Romantic boy-poet Thomas Chatterton (1752–70, who did commit suicide and was the subject of a famous painting by Henry Wallis, 1856) and the second time by a prostitute who took him in (1887). After he sent poems to the Roman Catholic journal *Merry England*, the editors Wilfrid (1852–1948) and Alice Meynell (1847–1922) rescued and housed him. They facilitated his recovery from opium at a monastic priory in Storrington in Sussex (1888) where he wrote two of his most important poems, "Ode to the Setting Sun" and "The Hound of Heaven." Another period of rest and recovery occurred when he went to a Franciscan friary in Wales (1892), allowing him to complete a quantity of writing. The Meynells published his first collection, *Poems* (1893), gaining the attention of Coventry Patmore (in the *Fortnightly Review*, Jan. 1894) and others. He also published *Sister Songs* (1895), *New Poems* (1897), and numerous reviews and prose studies, including *Health and Holiness* (1905) and "Shelley" (1909). Thompson's use of opium increased later in his life to alleviate the symptoms of his declining health, not from tuberculosis but from beriberi, as he conjectured, and has been confirmed posthumously. After his death, Thompson's poetry and prose (3 vols, 1913) were edited with numerous omissions, alterations, and deletions by Wilfrid Meynell from manuscripts found in a trunk in his rooms, almost his only possession. Scholarly edition: *The Poems of Francis Thompson*, ed. Brigid M. Boardman (2001); *The Letters of Francis Thompson*, ed. John Evangelist Walsh (1969); Brigid M. Boardman, *Between Heaven and Charing Cross: The Life of Francis Thompson* (1988).

The Hound of Heaven[1]

I fled Him, down the nights and down the days;
    I fled Him, down the arches of the years;
I fled Him, down the labyrinthine ways[2]
        Of my own mind; and in the mist of tears
    I hid from Him, and under running laughter.   5

Up vistaed hopes I sped;
And shot, precipitated
Adown Titanic glooms of chasmed fears,
From those strong Feet that followed, followed after.
But with unhurrying chase,   10
And unperturbèd pace,
Deliberate speed, majestic instancy,
They beat—and a Voice beat
More instant than the Feet—
"All things betray thee, who betrayest Me."   15

I pleaded, outlaw-wise,
By many a hearted casement, curtained red,
Trellised with intertwining charities;[3]
(For, though I knew His love Who followèd,
Yet was I sore adread   20
Lest, having Him, I must have naught beside)
But, if one little casement parted wide,
The gust of His approach would clash it to.
Fear wist not to evade, as Love wist to pursue.
Across the margent of the world I fled,   25
And troubled the gold gateways of the stars,
Fretted to dulcet jars[4]
And silvern clatter the pale ports o' the moon.
I said to dawn: Be sudden—to eve: Be soon;
With thy young skiey blossoms heap me over   30

Notes

FRANCIS THOMPSON

[1] *title* the basic metaphor is the hound chasing the hare with unremitting patience, as God pursues the fleeing heart and soul resistant to giving up worldly blandishments. Thompson wrote the poem when he was working on his essay on Shelley, whose *Prometheus Unbound* (1820) has two relevant lines: "Once the hungry hours were hounds/ Which chased the day like a bleeding deer" (4. 73–74). But there is another level: the Dominican Order of friars (founded 1216) were also knows as God's Hounds from a pun on their names in Latin (Lat. *Domini* of the Lord; *canes* dogs). The Dominicans wore black cloaks over their white habits and are depicted with dogs in some late medieval and early Renaissance paintings, such as those by Andrea di Bonaiuto (*c.*1368) in the Spanish Chapel in Santa Maria Novella in Florence, where numerous black and white hounds guard sheep. Dante, too, in the first canto of *Inferno* refers to the great Hound who will usher in a new world: "until the Greyhound come, … who will feed on wisdom, love, and human virtue" (1. 101–4). In form the poem is an irregular or Cowleyian Ode (named after the *Pindarique Odes* of Abraham Cowley of 1656), exalted in theme and diction with variable length and number of lines to a stanza, using an arsenal of figures, such as alliteration, anaphora, metaphor, personification, and so on. The poem was first published in *Merry England* (July 1890); reprinted in Thompson's first volume of *Poems* (1893); out text. It was included in *The Oxford Book of English Mystical Verse* (1917).

[2] *ways* "labyrinthine" is a favourite word of Shelley's, occurring twice in *Prometheus Unbound* (1820), and with the same collocation as Thompson's in the four-line fragment "Love the Universe Today" (1839): "And who feels discord now or sorrow? / Love is the universe to-day—/ These are the slaves of dim to-morrow, / Darkening Life's labyrinthine way."

[3] *hearted casement … charities* stone window, perhaps filled with stained glass symbols in the shape of a heart; see Shelley, "Ode to Psyche" (1820, stz. 5): "A bright torch, and a casement ope at night, / To let the warm love in." In Greek mythology, the Charities (Gk. *kharites*, Graces) are attendants of Aphrodite, the goddess of love: Aglaea (brilliance, radiance, glory, beauty), Thalia (flowering, festivity, and charm: the muse of comedy and pastoral poetry), and Euphrosyne (delight, joy, and mirth), as in Hesiod's *Theogony*; or the three Christian virtues, faith, hope, and love; see 1 Corinthians 13: 13.

[4] *stars … clatter* one line (27), "Smiting for shelter on their changèd bars," was either omitted in the first publication in *Merry England* after "stars," or was added in the publication in *Poems* (1893). In later editions "changèd" (1890) was altered to "clangèd"; that is, the outlaw fears being locked out. Dulcet jars signifies the harmonious or pleasant turning of rhetorical phrases or the tuning of sweet tones as in the harmony of the spheres. "Clatter" (1890) was changed to "Chatter" (1893).

From this tremendous Lover!
Float thy vague veil about me, lest He see!
 I tempted all His servitors, but to find
My own betrayal in their constancy,
In faith to Him their fickleness to me,   35
 Their traitorous trueness, and their loyal deceit.[5]
To all swift things for swiftness did I sue;
 Clung to the whistling mane of every wind.
 But whether they swept, smoothly fleet,
 The long savannahs of the blue;[6]   40
 Or whether, Thunder-driven,
 They clanged His chariot 'thwart a heaven,
Plashy with flying lightnings round the spurn o' their feet:—
 Fear wist not to evade as Love wist to pursue.
 Still with unhurrying chase,   45
 And unperturbèd pace,
 Deliberate speed, majestic instancy,
 Came on the following Feet,
 And a Voice above their beat—
 "Naught shelters thee, who wilt not shelter Me."[7]   50

I sought no more that, after which I strayed,
 In face of man or maid;
But still within the little children's eyes
 Seems something, something that replies,
They at least are for me, surely for me!   55
I turned me to them very wistfully;
But just as their young eyes grew sudden fair
 With dawning answers there,
Their angel plucked them from me by the hair.
"Come then, ye other children, Nature's—share   60
With me" (said I) "your delicate fellowship;
 Let me greet you lip to lip,
 Let me twine with you caresses,
 Wantoning
 With our Lady-Mother's[8] vagrant tresses,   65
 Banqueting
 With her in her wind-walled palace,
 Underneath her azured daïs,[9]
 Quaffing, as your taintless way is,
 From a chalice   70
Lucent-weeping out of the dayspring."[10]

Notes

[5] *deceit* a series of oxymorons; also at line 98: "they speak by silences."

[6] *savannahs … blue* for "savannahs" (plains) see Robert Southey, "Madoc" (1805, pt. 2, canto 1): "Slowly he sees them rise, and wind along / Through wide savannahs up the silver stream"; perhaps also an allusion to the vast blue painting by John Martin (1789–1854), *The Plains of Heaven* (1851–53), the second in his apocalyptic series on the Last Judgement that toured England after Martin's death.

[7] *Me* see Matthew 25: 34–46.

[8] *Lady-Mother* Nature.

[9] *daïs* raised platform at the end of a banqueting or other hall where the honoured guests sit. Here the halls of heaven, the blue sky.

[10] *dayspring* that is, overflowing with tears at the light of the dawn; see also Job 38: 12; and Luke 1: 78.

So it was done:
I in their delicate fellowship was one—
Drew the bolt of Nature's secrecies.
    I knew all the swift importings   75
    On the wilful face of skies;
    I knew how the clouds arise
    Spumèd of the wild sea-snortings;
        All that's born or dies
    Rose and drooped with—make them shapers   80
Of mine own moods, or wailful or divine—
      With them joyed and was bereaven.
      I was heavy with the even,
      When she lit her glimmering tapers
      Round the day's dead sanctities.   85
      I laughed in the morning's eyes.
I triumphed and I saddened with all weather,
      Heaven and I wept together,
And its sweet tears were salt with mortal mine;
Against the red throb of its sunset-heart   90
      I laid my own to beat,
      And share commingling heat;
But not by that, by that, was eased my human smart.
In vain my tears were wet on Heaven's grey cheek.
For ah! we know not what each other says,   95
      These things and I; in sound *I* speak—
Their sound it but their stir, they speak by silences.
Nature, poor stepdame,[II] cannot slake my drouth;
      Let her, if she would owe me,
Drop yon blue bosom-veil of sky, and show me   100
      The breasts o' her tenderness:
Never did any milk of hers once bless
        My thirsting mouth.
      Nigh and nigh draws the chase,
      With unperturbèd pace,   105
    Deliberate speed, majestic instancy,
      And past those noisèd Feet
      A Voice comes yet more fleet—
    "Lo! naught contents thee, who content'st not Me."

Naked I wait Thy love's uplifted stroke!   110
My harness piece by piece Thou hast hewn from me,
      And smitten me to my knee;
      I am defenceless utterly.
      I slept, methinks, and woke,
And, slowly gazing, find me stripped in sleep.   115
In the rash lustihead of my young powers

Notes

[II] *stepdame* nature is seen as a cruel stepmother (God is the true parent) to humans because of the arbitrary destruction by nature in the cycles of death and life. See Sir Philip Sidney's "Seventh Song" (1598): "Whose senses in so evil consort their stepdame Nature lies."

I shook the pillaring hours
And pulled my life upon me;[12] grimed with smears,
I stand amid the dust o' the mounded years—
My mangled youth lies dead beneath the heap.　　　　120
My days have crackled and gone up in smoke,
Have puffed and burst as sun-starts on a stream.
　　　Yea, faileth now even dream
The dreamer, and the lute the lutanist;
Even the linked fantasies, in whose blossomy twist　　125
I swung the earth a trinket at my wrist,[13]
Are yielding; what availeth they ever? I grazed
Too closely Thy blue window as I gazed,
Jutted a careless elbow through clear Heaven
And gashed me with the splinters—see, I bleed.　　　130
　　　Ah! is Thy love indeed
A weed, albeit an amaranthine[14] weed,
Suffering no flowers except its own to mount?
　　　Ah! must—
　　　　　Designer infinite!—　　　　　135
Ah! must Thou char the wood ere Thou canst limn with it?
My freshness spent its wavering shower i' the dust;
And now my heart is as a broken fount,
Wherein tear-drippings stagnate, spilt down ever
　　　From the dank thoughts that shiver　　　140
Upon the sighful branches of my mind.
　　　Such is; what is to be?
The pulp so bitter, how shall taste the rind?
I dimly guess what Time in mists confounds;
Yet ever and anon a trumpet sounds[15]　　　145
From the hid battlements of Eternity,
Those shaken mists a space unsettle, then
Round the half-glimpsèd turrets slowly wash again;
　　　But not ere him who summoneth[16]
　　　I first have seen, enwound　　　150

Notes

[12] *lustihead … me* (arch. lusty). For Samson's pulling the pillars of the temple upon himself and the Philistines, see Judges 16.

[13] *wrist* the following four lines (1890) are replaced by two lines in *Poems* (1893): "Are yielding; cords of all too weak account./ For earth with heavy griefs so overplussed./ Ah! is Thy love...."

[14] *amaranthine* (Gk. *amarantos*, unwithering), an allusion to the amaranthus flower that, according to legend, does not fade and so signifies immortality; see *Paradise Lost*: "Immortal amarant, a flower which once / In paradise, fast by the tree of life, / Began to bloom; but soon for man's offence / To heaven removed, where first it grew, there grows, / And flowers aloft, shading the fount of life" (3. 353–57).

[15] *sounds* see Revelation 8: 2–6; and 11: 15–19. See also the third vision ("The Vision of Sudden Death") of Thomas De Quincey's "The English Mail Coach" (1849): "In horror I rose at the thought; but then also, in horror at the thought, rose one that was sculptured on the bas-relief—a Dying Trumpeter. Solemnly from the field of battle he rose to his feet; and, unslinging his stony trumpet, carried it, in his dying anguish, to his stony lips—sounding once, and yet once again; proclamation that, in *thy* ears ... spoke from the battlements of death.... The hoofs of our horses, the rattling of our harness, alarmed the graves no more. By horror the bas-relief had been unlocked into life. By horror we, that were so full of life, we men and our horses, with their fiery fore-legs rising in mid air to their everlasting gallop, were frozen to a bas-relief. Then a third time the trumpet sounded; the seals were taken off all pulses; life, and the frenzy of life, tore into their channels again." (*Blackwoods Magazine*, Dec. 1849).

[16] *summoneth* Death, and death into life, as the following lines make clear.

With glooming robes purpureal, cypress-crowned;[17]
His name I know, and what his trumpet saith.
Whether man's heart or life it be which yields
    Thee harvest, must Thy harvest fields
    Be dunged with rotten death?   155
        Now of that long pursuit
        Comes on at hand the bruit;
    That Voice is round me like a bursting sea:
        "And is thy earth so marred,
        Shattered in shard on shard?   160
Lo, all things fly thee, for thou fliest Me!

    Strange, piteous, futile thing!
Wherefore should any set thee love apart?[18]
Seeing none but I makes much of naught" (He said),
"And human love needs human meriting: 165
    How hast thou merited—
Of all man's clotted clay the dingiest clot?
    Alack, thou knowest not
How little worthy of any love thou art!
Whom wilt thou find to love ignoble thee,   170
    Save Me, save only Me?
All which I took from thee I did but take,
    Not for thy harms,
But just that thou might'st seek it in My arms.
    All which thy child's mistake   175
Fancies as lost, I have stored for thee at home:
    Rise, clasp My hand, and come."

    Halts by me that footfall:
    Is my gloom, after all,
Shade of His hand, outstretched caressingly?   180
    "Ah, fondest, blindest, weakest,
    I am He Whom thou seekest![19]
Thou drovest love from thee, who drovest[20] Me."

Rosamund Marriott Watson (1860–1911)

Born Rosamund Ball in London and educated at the home of her bibliophile-accountant father, Watson first married the Australian George Armytage (1853–1921), had two daughters, and later separated. She eloped with the painter Arthur Graham Tomson (1859–1905) and,

Notes

[17] *cypress-crowned* the evergreen cypress tree is associated with graveyards and death because once cut, the branch does not grow back; see the story of the death of Cyparissus in *Metamorphoses* 10. 106–42; and the song in *Twelfth Night*: "Come away, come away, death, / And in sad cypress let me be laid" (2. 4. 50–51).

[18] *apart* that is, why should anyone set apart any love for you?

[19] *hand ... seekest* for "Shade of His hand," see Isaiah 49: 2; and Psalm 121: 5. For "weakest ... seekest," see Shelley, *Epipsychidion* (1821): "When a voice said:—'O thou of hearts the weakest, / The phantom is beside thee whom thou seekest.'"

[20] *fondest ... drovest* "fondest" is archaic for "most foolish." In *Poems* (1893) the two occurrences of "drovest" are changed to read "dravest" (arch.) for "you drove."

after Armytage divorced her, married him (1887), and had a son. She took the pen-name Graham R. Tomson (1887–94). Her husband divorced her in 1895 because of her affair with H. B. Marriott Watson (1863–1921), a friend of J. M. Barrie (1860–1973) and a writer for W. E. Henley's *National Observer*. From 1894 she wrote under her married name, Rosamund Marriott Watson.

A great beauty and wit, she moved in the fashionable aesthetic, decadent, and literary circles of Oscar Wilde, Henley, Andrew Lang (1844–1912), Bernard Shaw (1856–1950), Austin Dobson (1840–1921), Elizabeth Pennell (1855–1936), Katharine Tynan (1859–1931), and Alice Meynell. Poetry critic for the *Academy* and art critic for the *Morning Leader*, she also published in the *Pall Mall Gazette*, *The Athenæum*, and *The Yellow Book*. She published six volumes of poetry: *Tares* (1884, published anonymously); *The Bird-Bride: A Volume of Ballads and Sonnets* (1889); *A Summer Night, and Other Poems* (1891); *Vespertilia, and Other Verses* (1895); *After Sunset* (1904); and *The Lamp and the Lute* (1912, posthumous), as well as books on interior decoration (*The Art of the House*, 1897) and gardening (1906). No modern edition: *The Poems of Rosamund Marriott Watson* (1912); Linda K. Hughes, *Graham R.: Rosamund Marriott Watson, Woman of Letters* (2005); Ana Parejo Vadillo, *Women Poets and Urban Aestheticism* (2005); poetry online at Texas Christian University: http://www.rmwpoems.tcu.edu/index2.htm.

Scythe Song[1]

Stalwart mowers, brown and lithe,
    Over summer meads abloom,
Wielding fast the whispering Scythe,
    Where is all the old perfume?
Breathes it yet in tender gloom,   5
    Soft through Hades' twilight air?
Where hath Summer-tide her tomb?
    Hush, the Scythe says, *where, ah where*!

Comes the long blade gleaming cold
    Where the garden-ground is spread—   10
Rays of pearl on crowns of gold,
    Dainty daisies, white and red!
Dames that o'er them once would tread,
    Damsels blithe and debonair,

Notes

Rosamund Marriott Watson
[1] *title* the rhetorical convention used in the poem is the *ubi sunt* motif; see Dante Rossetti, n. 80. The poem was first printed with the pseudonym "B." in Andrew Lang's regular column, "At the Sign of the Ship" in *Longman's Magazine* (Sept. 1887). In his column Andrew Lang followed "Scythe Song" with his own two imitative verses, republished as "Scythe Song" in Lang's *Grass of Parnassus: Rhymes Old and New* (1888). Lang's stanzas read as follows:

Mowers, weary and brown, and blithe,
    What is the word methinks ye know,
Endless over-word that the Scythe
    Sings to the blades of the grass below?
Scythes that swing in the grass and clover,

Something, still, they say as they pass;
What is the word that, over and over,
    Sings the Scythe to the flowers and grass?

Hush, ah hush, the Scythes are saying,
    Hush, and heed not, and fall asleep,
Hush, they say to the grasses swaying,
    Hush, they sing to the clover deep!
Hush—'tis the lullaby Time is singing—
    Hush, and heed not, for all things pass,
Hush, ah hush! and the Scythes are swinging
    Over the clover, over the grass!

Watson's poem was republished in *The Bird-Bride: A Volume of Ballads and Sonnets* (1889), in the section called "Verses." See also Henley, double ballade, p. 839.

Where is all your sweetness fled?   15
    Hush, the Scythe says, where, ah where!

Time! who tak'st and giv'st again
    All things bitter, some things sweet,
Must we follow, all in vain
    Follow still those phantom feet?   20
Is there not some grass-grown street,
    Some old, yew-begirt parterre,
Where our Dreams and we may meet?
    Hush, the Scythe says, where, ah where!

Triolet[2]

The roses are dead,
    And swallows are flying:
White, golden, and red,
The roses are dead ;
Yet tenderly tread   5
    Where their petals are lying.
The roses are dead,
    And swallows are flying.

Omar Khayyám[3]

TO A. L.[4]

Sayer of sooth, and Searcher of dim skies![5]
    Lover of Song, and Sun, and Summertide,
    For whom so many roses bloomed and died ;
Tender Interpreter, most sadly wise,
Of earth's dumb, inarticulated cries!   5
    Time's self cannot estrange us, nor divide;
    Thy hand still beckons from the garden-side,
Through green vine-garlands, when the Winter dies.

Notes

[2] *title* a triolet is an old French form of eight lines in which there are only two rhymes and two repeated refrains. First published (among a variety of continental verse forms) with the title "Triolet" in *Ballades and Rondeaus*, ed. Gleeson White (1887) and signed Graham R. Tomson; it is one of five triolets by her in the volume in which she also published two ballades, one rondeau, one villanelle, and two Sicilian octaves. The volume was the largest collection of French and Italian verse forms in the late nineteenth century and included a large number of the major poets of the era, from Austin Dobson to Swinburne. Republished with the title "Les Roses Mortes" (Fr. The dead roses) in *The Bird-Bride: A Volume*

of *Ballads and Sonnets* (1889) as the last poem in the volume.

[3] *title* for Omar Khayyám, see FITZGERALD. From *The Bird-Bride: A Volume of Ballads and Sonnets* (1889) in the section called "Sonnets."

[4] A. L. Watson's friend, Andrew Lang (1844–1912), classicist, anthropologist, and folklorist, devoted much of his life to collecting and studying folktales, publishing twelve collections, beginning with the *Blue Fairy Book* (1889). He was also an important poet in *The Ballads and Lyrics of Old France* (1872), anticipating the vogue for old French verse forms like the rondeau and triolet in the 1880s and 1890s.

[5] *sooth . . . skies* (arch. truth); Omar was an astronomer.

Thy calm lips smile on us, thine eyes are wet;
　　The nightingale's full song[6] sobs all through thine,　　10
　　And thine in hers,—part human, part divine!
Among the deathless gods thy place is set,
　　All-wise, but drowsy with Life's mingled Wine,
Laughter and Learning, Passion and Regret.

Dead Poets[7]

Where be they that once would sing,
　　Poets passed from wood and dale?
Faintly, now, we touch the string,
　　Faithless, now, we seek the Grail:[8]
　　Shakspeare, Spenser, nought avail,　　5
Herrick, England's Oberon,
　　Sidney, smitten through his mail,[9]
Souls of Poets dead and gone!

Ronsard's Roses[10] blossoming
　　Long are faded, long are frail;
Gathered to the heart of Spring　　10
　　He that sang the breezy flail.[11]
　　Ah! could prayer at all prevail,
These should shine where once they shone,
　　These should 'scape the shadowy pale—　　15
Souls of Poets dead and gone!

Notes

[6] *song* throughout Watson echoes both Omar Khayyám's *Rubáiyát* and John Keats's "Ode to a Nightingale" (1819).

[7] *title* like "Scythe Song," a variant of the *ubi sunt* motif. The poem's repeated rhyme scheme in each stanza, the refrain, and the four-line "envoi" identify the form as a ballade. From *The Bird-Bride: A Volume of Ballads and Sonnets* (1889) in the section called "New Words to Old Tunes."

[8] *Grail* the legendary cup from Jesus' Last Supper was the sacred goal of the search of Arthur's knights of the Round Table in numerous sources from the twelfth century on, and in the nineteenth century in paintings by Dante Rossetti (1874), tapestries designed by Burne-Jones, Tennyson's poem by the same name (1870), and Wagner's opera *Parsifal* (1882). Hence, as here, it is the search for the sacred goal and its achievement – as of poetry for its authentic voice.

[9] *Shakespeare ... mail* poets of England's Elizabethan Renaissance are invoked like saints, but to no avail: William Shakespeare (1564–1616); Edmund Spenser (1552–99); Robert Herrick (1591–1674) wrote a series of poems (1648) on the king of the fairies, Oberon, a medieval and Renaissance mythological figure; and, Philip Sidney (1554–86) wrote the first great English sonnet sequence, *Astrophel and Stella* (1591); he died from a gunshot wound suffered in the siege

of Zulphen in the Netherlands, fighting against the Spanish.

[10] *Roses* Pierre de Ronsard (1524–85), French poet, published his first book of *Odes* (1550) in which was "Mignonne, allons voir si la rose" (Fr. Mignonne, let's go see if the rose) and the sonnet "Roses," both of which say that beauty and life fade like the rose, so it is best to love now. Both were translated by Andrew Lang in *Ballads and Lyrics of Old France* (1872). With du Bellay, Ronsard and five other poets were members of the group known as the Pléiade (named after the seven visible stars in the cluster constellation Taurus), whose purpose was to reform French poetry.

[11] *flail* "Joachim du Bellay" [author's note]: du Bellay (1522–60), French poet, was a friend of Ronsard's (see n. 10). His poem "D'un vanneur de blé, aux vents" (Fr. From a winnower of wheat, to the winds, 1550), also translated by Andrew Lang (see n. 10), alludes to the jointed wooden flails that were used to beat the seeds of wheat to separate the grains from the chaff. Walter Pater had quoted this poem in his *Studies in the History of the Renaissance* in his essay on "Joachim du Bellay" (1873). See also S. T. Coleridge, "Kubla Khan" (1816: 22): "Or chaffy grain beneath the thresher's flail."

What clear air knows Dante's wing?
　　What new seas doth Homer sail?
By what waters wandering
　　　Tells Theocritus[12] his tale?　　　　　　　　　　　　20
　　　Still, when cries the Nightingale,[13]
Singing, sobbing, on and on,
　　　Her brown feathers seem to veil
Souls of Poets dead and gone!

Charon, when my ghost doth hail　　　　　　　　　　　　25
　　　O'er Cocytus'[14] waters wan,
Land me where no storms assail
　　　Souls of Poets dead and gone!

In the Rain[15]

Rain in the glimmering street—
Murmurous, rhythmical beat;[16]
Shadows that flicker and fly;
Blue of wet road, of wet sky
(Grey in the depths and the heights);　　　　　　　　　　5
Orange of numberless lights,
Shapes fleeting on, going by.

Figures, fantastical, grim—
Figures, prosaical, tame,
Each with chameleon-stain,[17]　　　　　　　　　　　　10
Dun in the crepuscle[18] dim,
Red in the nimbus[19]of flame—
Glance through the veil of the rain.

Rosamund Mar

Notes

[12] *Dante ... Theocritus* three different kinds of poetry are alluded to here: Dante's *Commedia*, a religious allegory ending happily; Homer's classical epics; and the pastorals of Theocritus.

[13] *Nightingale* a reference to the violent story of Philomela and Procne (see ARNOLD, n. 27), and the nightingale's song as a symbol for poets and poetry, and the bird itself as the muse of poetry, now lamenting the poets "dead and gone." See also Keats, "Ode to a Nightingale" (1818).

[14] *Charon ... Cocytus* the ferryman of the dead in Greek mythology who rowed their shades across the river Styx to take them to Hades. Cocytus (the river of lamentation) is another of the five rivers at the entrance to Hades: Cocytus, Styx, Phlegethon (river of fire), Lethe (river of forgetfulness), and Acheron (river of hatred). See DANTE ROSSETTI, n. 4 (WEB p. 410); FIELD, n. 38; THOMSON, n. 17.

[15] *title* a series of quick impressions suggested by the broken phrases of one fleeting image and colour after another links this poem to French and English Impressionist paintings of landscapes and cityscapes with their shafts of light, speed, and sounds, as in J. M. W. Turner's painting *Rain, Steam, and Speed: the Great Western Railway* (1844) and the various paintings of urban London by John McNeill Whistler, and of Paris by Pierre-August Renoir, such as *Les Parapluies* (Fr. the umbrellas, 1881–87). Watson's second husband, Arthur Tomson, was a member of the New English Art Club (founded 1885), established to bring the principles of French Impressionism into English art. Watson also wrote art reviews for the *Morning Leader* and the *Art Weekly*. When this poem was republished in *A London Garland Selected from Five Centuries of English Verse*, ed. W. E. Henley (1895), it was illustrated with a moody night-picture by J. Chadwell Smith (fl. 1890s), showing a woman with an umbrella and others in a London square illuminated by gas lamps as a carriage rolls by. First published in the *Scots Observer* (24 May 1890), our text; republished in *A Summer Night* (1891).

[16] *beat* dactylic trimeter lines, with the last foot truncated, a possible imitation of the horses' hooves pulling the omnibus.

[17] *chameleon-stain* chameleon lizards can adapt themselves to their environment by changing colour.

[18] *crepuscule* twilight. Whistler painted *Crepuscule in Flesh Colour and Green: Valparaiso* in 1866.

[19] *nimbus* halo; a transferred epithet displacing a saint's halo onto the gas lamps.

Rain in the measureless street—
Vistas of orange and blue;   15
Music of echoing feet,
Pausing, and pacing anew.

Rain, and the clamour of wheels,
Splendour, and shadow, and sound;
Coloured confusion that reels   20
Lost in the twilight around.

   . . . .

When I lie hid from the light,
Stark, with the turf overhead,
Still, on a rainy Spring night,
I shall come back from the dead.[20]   25

Turn then and look for me here
Stealing the shadows along;
Look for me—I shall be near,
Deep in the heart of the throng:

Here, where the current runs rife,   30
Careless, and doleful, and gay,
Moving, and motley, and strong,
Good in its sport, in its strife.

   . . . .

Ah, might I be—might I stay—
Only for ever and aye,   35
Living and looking on Life!

A Summer Night[21]

"Le vent qui vient à travers la montagne
Me rendra fou."[22]

    The linden leaves are wet,
    The gas-lights flare—
    Deep yellow jewels set
    In dusky air,
    In dim air subtly sweet,   5
    With vanished rain.

Notes

[20] *dead* a revenant, usually a visible female ghost of one who returns to former locales from the dead, a female vampirish monster. Watson published a poem with the title "Revenant" in *The Lamp and the Lute* (1912).

[21] *title* the poem echoes John Keats's "Ode to a Nightingale" (1819: 66, 80: "The voice I hear this passing night ... Do I wake or sleep?"); and Matthew Arnold's "A Summer Night"

(1852: 24: "the same vainly throbbing heart"). First published as the title poem in *A Summer Night, and Other Poems* (1891).

[22] *Le ... fou* (Fr. the wind that comes across the mountain makes me crazy): the epigraph is the refrain from Victor Hugo's poem "Guitare" (1840).

Hush!—from the distant street[23]
Again—again—
Life's music swells and falls,
Despairing—light—
Beyond my garden walls[24]   10
This summer night.

Where do you call me, where?
O voice that cries!
O murky evening air,   15
What Paradise,
Unsought, unfound, unknown,
Inviteth me,
With faint night-odours blown?
With murmurous plea?   20

Future art thou, or Past?
Hope, or Regret?
My heart throbs thick and fast,[25]
Mine eyes are wet,
For well and well I know   25
Thou hast no share,
Nor hence, not long ago
Nor anywhere.

Chimæra[26]

The yellow light of an opal
    On the white-walled houses dies;
The roadway beyond my garden
    It glimmers with golden eyes.

Alone in the faint Spring twilight,   5
    The crepuscle[27] vague and blue,
Every beat of my pulses
    Is quickened by dreams of you.

Notes

[23] *street* Tomson lived at 20 St John's Wood Road. The St John's Wood area in London was well known for the residences of a number of poets and artists, but also for the homes of kept mistresses and prostitutes of the well-to-do, as well as lower-class prostitutes, some streets given over almost completely to them.

[24] *walls* see the Song of Songs 4: 12; and a long tradition of the *hortus conclusus* motif (Lat. enclosed garden) as in the *Roman de la Rose*; *Romeo and Juliet* (3. 5); and Andrew Marvell's "The Garden." See also MORRIS, n. 19.

[25] *fast* see n. 23.

[26] *title* a hybrid, female, fire-breathing animal from Lycia in Greek mythology, consisting of a lion's body, with a goat's neck and head protruding from the spine, and a tail ending in a snake's head; also an illusion or figment of the imagination. The Chimaera, like the Sphinx (the Chimaera's offspring), was a common figure of female desire in the painting and poetry of the Decadence. Desire is here captured as sexual tension and possibly violent fulfilment in the line of asterisks. The Chimaera was finally killed by Bellerophon, shooting the monster from the sky while riding on the winged horse, Pegasus. William Morris had devoted one of his tales to Bellerophon in *The Earthly Paradise* (1868–70). Oscar Wilde's depicts such exploits in the dialogue between the Sphinx and the Chimaera in "The Decay of Lying" (1891) in relation to Gustave Flaubert's *La Tentation de Saint Antoine* (pt. 7). In Wilde's "The Sphynx" (1894) the suggestion of violent and illicit copulation is explicit: "And from the brick-built Lycian tomb what horrible Chimera came / With fearful heads and fearful flame to breed new wonders from your womb?" The Chimaera also appears in Théophile Gauthier's *Mademoiselle de Maupin* (1835), in Flaubert's *Tentation de Saint Antoine* (Fr. Temptation of Saint Anthony, 1874), and in Joris-Karl Huysmans' *A Rebours* (Fr. Against the grain, 1884). First published in the *National Observer* (14 Mar. 1891); republished in *A Summer Night* (1891).

[27] *crepuscule* see n. 16.

You, whom I know and know not,
    You come as you came before;
Here, in the misty quiet,
    I greet you again once more.

            10

Welcome, O best beloved
    Life of my life—for lo!
All that I ask you promise,
    All that I seek you know.

            15

The dim grass stirs with your footstep,
    The blue dusk throbs with your smile;
I and the world of glory
    Are one for a little while.

            20

★ ★ ★ ★ ★

The Spring sun shows me your shadow,
    The Spring wind bears me your breath;
You are mine for a passing moment
    But I am yours to the death.

Mary Elizabeth Coleridge (1861–1907)

Coleridge was born into a famous literary family (Samuel Taylor Coleridge was her great-great uncle). Her father, Arthur Duke Coleridge (1830–1913), was an eminent lawyer; her mother was Mary Ann Jameson (d. 1898). Her literary and musical upbringing involved visits from Tennyson, Browning, Millais, Holman Hunt, Ruskin, and the singer Jenny Lind (1820–87). She early mastered Greek and Hebrew, as well as modern European languages, French, German, and Italian, and also became well-read in Elizabethan and Jacobean drama. She taught at the College for Working Women and at King's College for Women. She first published short articles in *Theatre*, and in 1893 published her first, little-noticed novel, *The Seven Sleepers of Ephesus*, followed by the successful *The King with Two Faces* (1897), and the most popular of her five novels, *The Lady on the Drawingroom Floor* (1906). Her contributions to periodicals included the *Contemporary Review*, the *National Review*, and the *Cornhill*. She had published some poems from the 1880s in *Merry England* and the *Monthly Packet*, later collecting forty-eight of them into a volume that Robert Bridges helped her revise and publish with the semi-private Daniel Press in Oxford as *Fancy's Following* (1896) under the pseudonym "Anodos" (Gk. wanderer), named after a character in George MacDonald's novel *Phantastes* (1858). It was republished commercially with additional poems as *Fancy's Guerdon* (1897). Other poems appeared in *The Spectator* and *The Pilot*, and articles in *The Guardian* and reviews in *The Times Literary Supplement*. She collected some of her essays on art and literature in *Non Sequitur* (1900). At the time of her death she was working on a biography, *Holman Hunt* (1908). Her friend Henry Newbolt edited her *Poems* (1908). Standard edition: *The Collected Poems of Mary Coleridge*, ed. Theresa Whistler (1954); *Gathered Leaves from the Prose of Mary E. Coleridge*, ed. Edith Sichel (1910); Jean R. Halladay, *Eight Late Victorian Poets Shaping the Artistic Sensibility of An Age* (1993); "The Victorian Web": http://www.victorianweb.org/authors/coleridge/index.html; and Orlando Women's Writing Project: orlando.cambridge.org.

Gone[1]

About the little chambers of my heart
Friends have been coming—going—many a year.
    The doors stand open there.
Some, lightly stepping, enter; some depart.

Freely they come and freely go, at will.   5
The walls give back their laughter; all day long
    They fill the house with song.
One door alone is shut, one chamber still.

The Other Side of a Mirror[2]

I sat before my glass one day,
And conjured up a vision bare,
Unlike the aspects glad and gay,
That erst were found reflected there—
The vision of a woman, wild   5
With more than womanly despair.

Her hair stood back on either side
A face bereft of loveliness.
It had no envy now to hide
What once no man on earth could guess.   10
It formed the thorny aureole[3]
Of hard, unsanctified distress.

Her lips were open—not a sound
Came through the parted lines of red.
Whate'er it was, the hideous wound   15
In silence and in secret bled.
No sigh relieved her speechless woe,
She had no voice to speak her dread.

Mary Elizabeth

Notes

MARY ELIZABETH COLERIDGE
[1] title from *Fancy's Following* (1896).

[2] title the mirror was a conventional image of pride (Lat. *vanitas*) in medieval accounts of the seven deadly sins, holding up a mirror to nature, to reality, reflecting beauty, the flaws of humanity, and the onset of age or even mortality. One conceit was that the beauty gazing into the mirror saw not herself but a skeletal head, the image of death: woman (like Eve) as the bringer of death is often read from the point of view of male sexuality that holds *vanitas* to be a sexually desirable attribute of availability in a woman; another significance is that the woman looking into the mirror is an image of fecundity – of sexuality, beauty, or plenty. During the Victorian era a mirror had continued as a device to extol beauty and fecundity, or, as here ambiguously, beauty faded and departed, while also distorting reality, reflecting external appearance not internal truth. As such the mirror can exploit spatial and moral transgressions and reversals, as in Tennyson's "Lady of Shalott" (1842) and Holman Hunt's engraving (1857) and painting (1886–1905), Lewis Carroll's *Through the Looking-Glass* (1871), Whistler's painting, *Symphony in White No. 2: The Little White Girl* (1864; see Plate 20), exhibited with stanzas by Swinburne, "Before the Mirror" (1866), D. G. Rossetti's *Lady Lilith* (1868), and W. B. Yeats's "The Two Trees" (1893). The convention of painting a woman, especially Venus, before a mirror, was long established in European art, as in Titian's *Vanitas or Woman with Two Mirrors* (1515, Louvre). Published in *Fancy's Following* (1896); reprinted in *Fancy's Guerdon* (1897) and in Elkin Mathews' *Garland of New Poetry* (vol. 2 1899).

And in her lurid eyes there shone
The dying flame of life's desire,   20
Made mad because its hope was gone,
And kindled at the leaping fire
Of jealousy and fierce revenge,
And strength that could not change nor tire.

Shade of a shadow in the glass,   25
O set the crystal surface free!
Pass—as the fairer visions pass—
Not ever more to return, to be
The ghost of a distracted hour,
That hear me whisper:—"I am she!"   30

Mortal Combat[4]

It is because you were my friend,
    I fought you as the devil fights.
Whatever fortune God may send,
    For once I set the world to rights.

And that was when I thrust you down,   5
    And stabbed you twice and twice again,
Because you dared take off your crown,
    And be a man like other men.

The Witch[5]

I have walked a great while over the snow,
And I am not tall nor strong.
My clothes are wet, and my teeth are set,
And the way was hard and long.
I have wandered over the fruitful earth,   5
But I never came here before.
Oh, lift me over the threshold, and let me in at the door!

The cutting wind is a cruel foe.
I dare not stand in the blast.
My hands are stone, and my voice a groan,   10

Notes

[3] *aureole* see DANTE ROSSETTI, n. 28 and Plate 14. Here the image is also used to suggest Christ's crown of thorns (see Matthew 27: 29; Mark 15: 17; and John 19: 2, 5).

[4] *title* published in *Fancy's Following* (1896).

[5] *title* this short lyric is a kind of response to and echo of *Christabel* (1816) by S. T. Coleridge, in which a strange ghost or witch-like figure named Geraldine claims to have been abducted and begs for help: "Stretch forth thy hand (thus ended she) / And help a wretched maid to flee" (100–101). Christabel offers help: "The lady sank, belike through pain, / And Christabel with might and main / Lifted her up, a weary weight, / Over the threshold of the gate" (124–27), and as they pass the hearth in the hall, the dead fire bursts out: "A tongue of light, a fit of flame." (155). Geraldine lies with Christabel for ghostly vengeance or as a demon lover, resulting in sexual and moral contamination. The poem is unfinished. Mary Coleridge's poem contains verbal echoes as well as moral and sexual ambiguities and reversals. It was a tradition for a husband to carry a new bride over the threshold into the new home. First published in *Fancy's Following* (1896).

And the worst of death is past.
I am but a little maiden still,
My little white feet are sore.
Oh, lift me over the threshold, and let me in at the door!

Her voice was the voice that women have,   15
Who plead for their heart's desire.
She came—she came—and the quivering flame
Sank and died in the fire.
It never was lit again on my hearth
Since I hurried across the floor,   20
To lift her over the threshold, and let her in at the door.

Marriage[6]

No more alone sleeping, no more alone waking,
　　Thy dreams divided, thy prayers in twain;
Thy merry sisters to-night forsaking,
　　Never shall we see thee, maiden, again.

Never shall we see thee, thine eyes glancing,   5
　　Flashing with laughter and wild in glee,
Under the mistletoe[7] kissing and dancing,
　　Wantonly free.

There shall come a matron walking sedately,
　　Low-voiced, gentle, wise in reply.   10
Tell me, O tell me, can I love her greatly?
　　All for her sake must the maiden die!

The White Women[8]

Where dwell the lovely, wild white women folk,
　　Mortal to man?
They never bowed their necks beneath the yoke,[9]
They dwelt alone when the first morning broke
　　And Time began.   5

Notes

6 *title* the poem treats ironically the metaphor of two becoming one in the marriage service in the BCP; see also Genesis 2: 24: "Therefore shall a man leave his father and his mother, and shall cleave unto his wife: and they shall be one flesh." Coleridge exploits three meanings of "cleave": to hold closely, to remain faithful, and to divide. From *The Garland* (1898), in which Coleridge published eleven poems along with a number of other poets.

7 *mistletoe* any girl standing beneath mistletoe, hung above a doorway at Christmas, may be kissed.

8 *title* "From a legend of Malay told by Hugh Clifford" [author's note]. Hugh Clifford (1866–1947), writer and traveller, lived in Malay from 1888 to 1903, writing many works on Malay culture and a Malay dictionary. He was a friend of Rudyard Kipling and Joseph Conrad. This community of warrior women is paralleled by the Amazons in Greek mythology, also living beyond the borders of civilization but with their own sophisticated culture. Clifford recounts this legend in *In Court and Kampong, Being Tales & Sketches of Native Life in the Malay Peninsula* (1897): "Beyond that great peak, in the depths of the silent forest places, there lives a tribe of women, fair of face and form, taller than men, paler in colour, stronger, bolder. This is the tribe that is to avenge us upon those who have won our

Taller are they than man, and very fair,
    Their cheeks are pale,
At sight of them the tiger in his lair,
The falcon hanging in the azure air,
    The eagles quail.   10

The deadly shafts their nervous hands let fly
    Are stronger than our strongest—in their form
Larger, more beauteous, carved amazingly,
And when they fight, the wild white women cry
    The war-cry of the storm.   15

Their words are not as ours. If man might go
    Among the waves of Ocean when they break
And hear them—hear the language of the snow
Falling on torrents—he might also know
    The tongue they speak.   20

Pure are they as the light; they never sinned,
    But when the rays of the eternal fire
Kindle the West,[10] their tresses they unbind
And fling their girdles to the Western wind,[11]
    Swept by desire.   25

Lo, maidens to the maidens then are born,
    Strong children of the maidens and the breeze,
Dreams are not—in the glory of the morn,
Seen through the gates of ivory and horn[12]—
    More fair than these.   30

And none may find their dwelling. In the shade
    Primeval of the forest oaks they hide.
One of our race, lost in an awful glade,
Saw with his human eyes a wild white maid,
    And gazing, died.   35

Notes

hunting grounds. These women know not men; but when the moon is at the full they dance naked, in the grassy places near the salt-licks, where the passing to-and-fro of much game has thinned the forest. The Evening Wind is their only spouse, and through Him they conceive and bear children. Yearly are born to them offspring, mostly women-folk whom they cherish even as we do our young; but if, perchance, they bear a manchild, the mother slays it ere it is well-nigh born. Thus live they, and thrive they, ever increasing and multiplying, and their bows and blow-pipes are sometimes found by us in the deep hollows of the woods. Larger are they than those we use, more beautifully carved, and, moreover, they are of a truer aim. But woe to the man who meets these women, or who dares to penetrate into the woods in which they dwell, for he will surely die unless the ghosts give speed to his flight. Of all this tribe, I alone have seen these women, and that when I was a young hunter, many many moons agone. I and two others, my brothers, when hunting through the forest … heard a loud, threatening cry in a strange tongue. Then I, looking up, beheld a gigantic form, as of a pale-skinned woman, breaking through the jungle, some two hundred elbow-lengths away, and, at the same moment, my elder brother fell pierced by an arrow. I stayed to see no more, but ran" (Ch. 14: "In the Camp of the Sĕmangs"). First published in *Poems* (1908).

[9] *yoke* of marriage.

[10] *West* sunset.

[11] *wind* Zephyrus is the western wind in Greek mythology, which is inter-mixed with Malay myths throughout Clifford; see n. 8.

[12] *horn* dreams that pass through the Gate of Ivory are false (Gk. *elephas*, ivory, < *elephairo*, to deceive or to cheat with empty hopes). Those that will come true pass through the Gate of Horn (Gk. *keras*, horn < *karanoo*, to fulfill or to accomplish); see *Odyssey* 19. 560–69; and *Aeneid* 6. 893–98.

Death and the Lady[13]

Turn in, my lord, turn in, she said;
    As it were the Father of Sin
I have hated the Father of the Dead,
    The slayer of my kin;
By the Father of the Living led,   5
    Turn in, my lord, turn in.

We were foes of old; thy touch was cold,
    But mine is warm as life;
I have struggled and made thee loose thy hold,
    I have turned aside the knife.   10
Despair itself in me was bold,
    I have striven, and won the strife.
But that which conquered thee and rose
    Again to earth descends;
For the last time we have come to blows,   15
    And the long combat ends.
The worst and secretest of foes,
    Be now my friend of friends.

Amy Levy (1861–89)

Born in Clapham in London, and raised in Brighton, in 1879 Levy was the first Jewish woman to be admitted to Newnham College, Cambridge, though she left part way through her second year. Her first volume of poetry was *Xantippe and Other Verse* (1881), in which the title poem revisions the misogyny of centuries that reads the wife of Socrates as a shrew, at the same time commenting on the new wave of women's education at Oxford and Cambridge in the establishment of colleges for women (see GENDER: EDUCATION; RIGBY, "ENGLISHWOMAN"). She continued to publish in various periodicals, as well as in *A Minor Poet and Other Verse* (1884). Her circle of friends included Clementina Black (1854–1922), Eleanor Marx (1855–98), and Olive Schreiner (1855–1920). After visiting Italy with Black in 1886, where she also met and had a romantic attraction to Vernon Lee, she became secretary for the Beaumont Trust (working for women's education in East London). She continued to publish: the novels *Romance of a Shop* (1888), *Reuben Sachs* (1888), and *Miss Meredith* (1889); articles on Jewish culture in the *Jewish Chronicle*; and *A London Plane-Tree* (1889), her last book of poetry. Subject to depression, she took her own life. Standard edition: *The Complete Novels and Selected Writings of Amy Levy*, ed. Melvyn New (1993); Linda Hunt Beckman, *Amy Levy: Her Life and Letters* (2000); poems of Amy Levy at the Victorian Women Writers Project: http://webapp1.dlib.indiana.edu/vwwp/browse.do?type=creator&filter=L.

Notes

[13] *title* perhaps an echo of one of the most famous *Lieder* (Ger. songs) and quartets of Franz Schubert (1797–1828), *Death and the Maiden* (Ger. *Der Tod und das Mädchen*). The song was written in 1817, to a poem by the German poet, Matthias Claudius (1740–1815). First published in *Poems* (1908).

Felo De Se[1]

With Apologies to Mr. Swinburne

For repose I have sighed and have struggled; have sigh'd and have struggled in vain;
I am held in the Circle of Being and caught in the Circle of Pain.
I was wan and weary with life; my sick soul yearned for death;
I was weary of women and war and the sea and the wind's wild breath;[2]
I cull'd sweet poppies[3] and crush'd them, the blood ran rich and red:— 5
And I cast it in crystal chalice and drank of it till I was dead.
And the mould of the man was mute, pulseless in ev'ry part,
The long limbs lay on the sand with an eagle eating the heart.[4]
Repose for the rotting head and peace for the putrid breast,
But for that which is "I" indeed the gods have decreed no rest; 10
No rest but an endless aching, a sorrow which grows amain:—
I am caught in the Circle of Being and held in the Circle of Pain.
Bitter indeed is Life, and bitter of Life the breath,
But give me life and its ways and its men, if this be Death.
Wearied I once of the Sun and the voices which clamour'd around: 15
Give them me back—in the sightless depths there is neither light nor sound.
Sick is my soul, and sad and feeble and faint as it felt
When (far, dim day) in the fair flesh-fane of the body it dwelt.
But then I could run to the shore, weeping and weary[5] and weak;
See the waves' blue sheen and feel the breath of the breeze on my cheek: 20
Could wail with the wailing wind; strike sharply the hands in despair;
Could shriek with the shrieking blast, grow frenzied and tear the hair;
Could fight fierce fights with the foe or clutch at a human hand;
And weary could lie at length on the soft, sweet, saffron sand ..
I have neither a voice nor hands, nor any friend nor a foe; 25
I am I—just a Pulse of Pain—I am I, that is all I know.
For Life, and the sickness of Life, and Death and desire to die;—
They have passed away like the smoke, here is nothing but Pain and I.

Notes

Amy Levy

[1] title (Sp. crime against oneself; suicide). A tribute to one of her admired poets, this poem also parodies both Swinburne's versification (rhyming anapestic hexameters, as in his "Hymn to Proserpine") as well as his diction, with its exaggerated alliteration, assonance, and repetitions. The theme is the Sapphic loss of poetic voice when she hurls herself into the sea. First published in *Xantippe and Other Verse* (1881). Our text: *A London Plane-Tree and Other Verse* (1889).

[2] Pain ... breath each of the nine circles of the damned in Dante's *Inferno* is dedicated to the particular sin committed; see SWINBURNE, "HYMN TO PROSERPINE" (10–12) (WEB p. 425) for the same metrics and rhyme scheme: pain, breath, death.

[3] poppies symbols of forgetfulness because of their use in making opium. See SWINBURNE, "HYMN TO PROSERPINE": "poppies are sweet" (97) (WEB p. 429). They are often depicted in Pre-Raphaelite painting, as in Dante Rossetti's *Beata Beatrix* (1872), *Lady Lilith* (1868), and *Sibylla Palmifera* (1866–70).

[4] heart according to the legend, for stealing fire from the gods to give to man, Prometheus was chained by Zeus to a rock where an eagle ate his liver every night, only to have it grow back by the following night.

[5] weary see Swinburne, "Anactoria" (1866): "And weeping of the weary Pleiads seven" (169).

Magdalen[6]

All things I can endure, save one.
The bare, blank room where is no sun;
The parcelled hours; the pallet hard;
The dreary faces here within;
The outer women's cold regard;   5
The Pastor's iterated "sin";—
These things could I endure, and count
No overstrain'd, unjust amount;
No undue payment for such bliss—
Yea, all things bear, save only this: 10
That you, who knew what thing would be,
Have wrought this evil unto me.
It is so strange to think on still—
That you, that *you* should do me ill!
Not as one ignorant or blind,   15
But seeing clearly in your mind
How this must be which now has been,
Nothing aghast at what was seen.
Now that the tale is told and done,
It is so strange to think upon.   20

You were so tender with me, too!
One summer's night a cold blast blew,
Closer about my throat you drew
The half-slipt shawl of dusky blue.
And once my hand, on a summer's morn,   25
I stretched to pluck a rose; a thorn
Struck through the flesh and made it bleed
(A little drop of blood indeed!)
Pale grew your cheek; you stoopt and bound
Your handkerchief about the wound;   30
Your voice came with a broken sound;
With the deep breath your breast was riven;
I wonder, did God laugh in Heaven?

How strange, that *you* should work my woe!
How strange! I wonder, do you know   35
How gladly, gladly I had died
(And life was very sweet that tide)

Notes

[6] *title* the conventional respectable name for a prostitute in Victorian England. Magdalen Houses were refuges for them. Pope Gregory the Great in 591 was the first to identify Mary Madgalen with a fallen woman in saying that the seven demons that were cast from her (Luke 8: 1–3) were "forbidden acts." She is also sometimes identified with the unnamed woman of the anointing whose hair is loosened (sometimes a mark of an unchaste woman): see Matthew 26; Mark 14; Luke 7; and John 12. For Victorian prostitution, see GENDER: SEX; GREG, "PROSTITUTION" (WEB p. 87); for other poems on prostitutes, see WEBSTER, "A CASTAWAY" and DANTE ROSSETTI "JENNY"; see also Plate 10: Hunt, *Awakening Conscience*; and Plate 15: Rossetti, *Found*. Here Levy assesses the impact of seduction upon a fallen woman's psyche and body, rather than projecting opinions and feeling upon her from a male perspective as in Rossetti's monologue. Published in *A Minor Poet and Other Verse* (1884). Our text: second edition (1891).

To save you from the least, light ill?
How gladly I had borne your pain.
With one great pulse we seem'd to thrill,— 40
Nay, but we thrill'd with pulses twain.

Even if one had told me this,
"A poison lurks within your kiss,
Gall that shall turn to night his day":
Thereon I straight had turned away— 45
Ay, tho' my heart had crack'd with pain—
And never kiss'd your lips again.

At night, or when the daylight nears,
I hear the other women weep;
My own heart's anguish lies too deep 50
For the soft rain and pain of tears.
I think my heart has turn'd to stone,
A dull, dead weight that hurts my breast;
Here, on my pallet-bed alone,
I keep apart from all the rest. 55
Wide-eyed I lie upon my bed,
I often cannot sleep all night;
The future and the past are dead,
There is no thought can bring delight.
All night I lie and think and think; 60
If my heart were not made of stone,
But flesh and blood, it needs must shrink
Before such thoughts. Was ever known
A woman with a heart of stone?[7]

The doctor says that I shall die.[8] 65
It may be so, yet what care I?
Endless reposing from the strife?
Death do I trust no more than life.
For one thing is like one arrayed,
And there is neither false nor true; 70
But in a hideous masquerade
All things dance on, the ages through.
And good is evil, evil good;
Nothing is known or understood
Save only Pain. I have no faith 75
In God, or Devil, Life or Death.

The doctor says that I shall die.
You, that I knew in days gone by,
I fain would see your face once more,
Con well its features o'er and o'er; 80

Notes ───────────────────────────────────────

[7] *stone* see Ezekiel 36: 26.
[8] *die* the woman is probably dying of a venereal disease;
    see GENDER: WOMAN QUESTION: MARTINEAU, "MANIFESTO."

And touch your hand and feel your kiss,
Look in your eyes and tell you this:
That all is done, that I am free;
That you, through all eternity,
Have neither part nor lot in me.   85

A Wallflower[9]

I lounge in the doorway and languish in vain
While Tom, Dick and Harry are dancing with Jane

My spirit rises to the music's beat;
There is a leaden fiend lurks in my feet!
To move unto your motion, Love, were sweet.   5
Somewhere, I think, some other where, not here,
In other ages, on another sphere,
I danced with you, and you with me, my dear.

In perfect motion did our bodies sway,
To perfect music that was heard alway;   10
Woe's me, that am so dull of foot to-day!

To move unto your motion, Love, were sweet;
My spirit rises to the music's beat—
But, ah, the leaden demon in my feet!

The First Extra[10]

A WALTZ SONG

O sway, and swing, and sway,
    And swing, and sway, and swing!
Ah me, what bliss like unto this,
    Can days and daylight bring?

A rose beneath your feet   5
    Has fallen from my head;
Its odour rises sweet,
    All crushed it lies, and dead.

O Love is like a rose,
    Fair-hued, of fragrant breath;   10
A tender flow'r that lives an hour,
    And is most sweet in death.

Notes

[9] *title* this was the first poem in a group entitled "Odds and Ends" in *A London Plane-Tree, and Other Verse* (1889; our text). First published in *Woman's World* (1889).

[10] *title* see *OED* (s.v. extra): "An extra item in a program, as a dance" – that is, after the scheduled dances for which one filled out a dance card with specified partners. The second poem in the group of "Odds and Ends" (see n. 10).

O swing, and sway, and swing,
    And rise, and sink, and fall!
There is no bliss like unto this,   15
    This is the best of all.

At a Dinner Party[11]

With fruit and flowers the board[12] is deckt,
    The wine and laughter flow;
I'll not complain—could one expect
    So dull a world to know?

You look across the fruit and flowers,   5
    My glance your glances find.—
It is our secret, only ours,
    Since all the world is blind.

A Ballad of Religion and Marriage[13]

Swept into limbo[14] is the host
        Of heavenly angels, row on row;
The Father, Son, and Holy Ghost,
        Pale and defeated, rise and go.
The great Jehovah is laid low,   5
        Vanished his burning bush and rod[15]—
Say, are we doomed to deeper woe?
        Shall marriage go the way of God?

Monogamous, still at our post,
        Reluctantly we undergo   10
Domestic round of boiled and roast,
        Yet deem the whole proceeding slow.
Daily the secret murmurs grow;
        We are no more content to plod
Along the beaten paths—and so   15
        Marriage must go the way of God.

Soon, before all men, each shall toast
        The seven strings unto his bow,[16]
Like beacon fires along the coast,

Notes

[11] *title* the third poem in the group of "Odds and Ends"
(see above, "A Wallflower," n. 1).

[12] *board* formal dinner table.

[13] *title* twelve copies of this poem were printed posthumously "for private circulation" by Clement Shorter
(1857–1926), British editor. The British Library's copy is
dated 1915. The phrase "way of God" in the refrain
occurs numerous times in the Bible; see, for instance,
Acts 18.

[14] *limbo* the place assigned to the souls of the just who died
before Christ's ascension and both infants and adults free
from grievous sin who had died unbaptized; see Dante's
version in *Inferno* (the first circle, Canto 4).

[15] *Jehovah … rod* name used for God in the King James
version of Exodus 3: 2–4; and 4: 2–4; for burning bush,
see Exodus 3: 1–15; the chastening rod of God's occurs frequently in the Bible: see, for instance, Hebrews 12: 5–11.

[16] *bow* allusion to one's children. See Psalm 127: 3–5.

The flame of love shall glance and glow.
Nor let nor hindrance[17] man shall know,
From natal bath[18] to funeral sod;
Perennial shall his pleasures flow
When marriage goes the way of God.

Grant, in a million years at most,
Folk shall be neither pairs nor odd[19] —
Alas! we sha'n't be there to boast
"Marriage has gone the way of God!"

Henry Newbolt (1862–1938)

Born near Wolverhampton in the West Midlands, Newbolt was the eldest of three children of Henry Francis Newbolt (1823–66), an Anglican clergyman, and his second wife, Emily (d. 1921). When he was four, his father died and the family moved to Walsall, north-west of Birmingham, where Newbolt went to the local grammar school, winning a scholarship to Clifton College in Bristol. He became head of the school and went on to Corpus Christi College, Oxford. In 1887 he was called to the bar. In 1889 he married Edina Duckworth (1867–1960), who continued a lesbian relationship with her cousin, Ella Coltman, throughout her marriage, while Newbolt also had a sexual relationship with Coltman. As the *ODNB* says: "The details of this unconventional domestic life seem at variance with Newbolt's standard reputation as a latter-day Victorian, and suggest that he was a more complex figure than is usually supposed." During the First World War Newbolt served in the Admiralty and the Foreign Office. He was knighted in 1915. In 1921 Newbolt chaired the committee that recommended to the government that English literature should replace the classics as the basis for secondary level education. Many of Newbolt's poems use the analogy between schoolboy sports and war, between cricket and battles, and between school loyalty and patriotism. He conflates codes of honour with bravery in combat and team spirit in the games of war and life. He first published a novel, *Taken from the Enemy* (1892), and then a blank-verse tragedy, *Mordred* (1895), but the publication of "Drake's Drum" in the *St. James's Gazette* made his literary name. It was the lead poem in *Admirals All and Other Verses* (1897). Other volumes of poetry followed: *The Island Race* (1898); *The Sailing of the Longships* (1902); *Songs of the Sea* (1904); and *Songs of the Fleet* (1910). No scholarly edition: *Collected Poems* (1910); *Selected Poems of Henry Newbolt*, ed. Patric Dickinson (1981); Susan Chitty, *Playing the Game: A Biography of Sir Henry Newbolt* (1997).

Notes

[17] *hindrance* see BCP on the introduction to the Marriage Service: "If any of you know cause or just impediment, why these two persons should not be joined together in holy matrimony, ye are now to declare it."

[18] *bath* the washing of a newborn child, usually by a midwife; possible reference to baptism, given the context of the poem, as "funeral sod" alludes to the burial of the dead (see BCP).

[19] *odd* late Victorian slang for lesbian.

Vitaï Lampada[1]

There's a breathless hush in the Close[2] to-night—
    Ten to make and the match to win—
A bumping pitch and a blinding light,
    An hour to play and the last man in.
And it's not for the sake of a ribboned coat,   5
    Or the selfish hope of a season's fame,
But his Captain's hand on his shoulder smote
    "Play up! play up! and play the game!"[3]

The sand of the desert[4] is sodden red,—
    Red with the wreck of a square that broke;—   10
The Gatling's[5] jammed and the colonel dead
    And the regiment blind with dust and smoke.
The river of death has brimmed his banks,[6]
    And England's far, and Honour a name,
But the voice of schoolboy rallies the ranks,   15
    "Play up! play up! and play the game!"

This is the word that year by year
    While in her place the School is set
Every one of her sons must hear,
    And none that hears it dare forget.   20
This they all with a joyful mind

Notes

HENRY NEWBOLT

[1] *title* (Lat. the torch of life); a quotation from Lucretius, *De Rerum Naturae* (Lat. on the nature of things; 2. 79): "Some races increase, others diminish; the generations of living things are changed in a short time, and like runners they hand on the torch of life." From *Admirals All and Other Verses* (1897).

[2] *Close* the grounds of Clifton College in Bristol were known as the Close. Clifton was a recent foundation (1862) and unlike the ancient and prestigious public schools such as Eton (founded 1440) and Harrow (1572), Clifton emphasized science and broadened its admission practices to avoid elitism. This paragraph refers to cricket for which Clifton was famous, and the ten runs needed to win the match.

[3] *game* this famous phrase, originally a call for the game of cricket to begin, is applied to playing the game of life, even to the point of death in battle. In *The Spectator* (Nov. 1917 to Feb. 1918) during the First World War there was a series of seventeen letters concerning turning the phrase into Latin, combining schoolboy classics, sports, and warfare (see also n. 21). Among the suggestions were *lude ludum* (Lat. play the game) and *lude juste* (Lat. play fair).

[4] *desert* a reference to the Battle of Abu Klea in Sudan (January 1885) between the British Desert Column (about 1,100) and the forces (about 12,000) of the Mahdi, Muhammad Ahmad (1844–85), religious leader in the Sudan. The British were engaged in the Gordon Relief

Expedition to rescue General Charles George Gordon (1833–85), under siege at Khartoum in Egypt. In the battle, the British square formation broke up, leading to seventy-four losses for the British and over a thousand for the Mahdists. The forces of Field Marshal Garnet Wolseley (1833–1913) to relieve the siege of Khartoum and rescue Gordon arrived "too late" (a phrase that became a watchword of British military failure); Gordon had been killed on 26 January 1885. For Gordon see also n. 17.

[5] *Gatling's ... dead* Newbolt is mistaken: in actuality, it was the Gardner machine gun (invented 1874) that was involved in the battle. However, it proved vulnerable to the desert sand and jammed at the battle of Abu Klea. The Gatling machine gun was invented in America in 1861 and was first used in the American Civil War. In the 1880s it had been widely adopted by the British army, hence Newbolt's confusion. Colonel Frederick Gustavus Burnaby (1842–85) was killed at this battle; he had been educated at Harrow, one of the nine original public schools defined by the Public Schools Act of 1868.

[6] *banks* a metaphoric river, perhaps alluding to the River Acheron on the border of Hell in *Inferno* 3 where the dead wait to be transported across by Charon the boatman; or more likely the Scamander, a river that, full of the dead Trojans in the *Iliad*, speaks to Achilles: "My lovely waters are filled with corpses ... crammed with the dead" (21: 218–20).

Bear through life like a torch in flame,
And falling fling to the host behind—
"Play up! play up! and play the game!"

"He Fell Among Thieves"[7]

"Ye have robbed," said he, "ye have slaughtered and made an end;
    Take your ill-got plunder, and bury the dead:
What will ye more of your guest and sometime friend?"
    "Blood for our blood," they said.

He laughed: "If one may settle the score for five   5
    I am ready; but let the reckoning stand till day:
I have loved the sunlight as dearly as any alive."
    "You shall die at dawn," said they.

He flung his empty revolver down the slope;
    He climbed alone to the Eastward edge of the trees;   10
All night long in a dream untroubled of hope
    He brooded, clasping his knees.

He did not hear the monotonous roar that fills
    The ravine where the Yassîn river sullenly flows;
He did not see the starlight on the Laspur hills,   15
    Or the far Affghan[8] snows.

He saw the April noon on his books aglow,
    The wisteria trailing in at the window wide;
He heard his father's voice from the terrace below
    Calling him down to ride.   20

He saw the gray little church across the park,
    The mounds that hide the loved and honoured dead;
The Norman arch,[9] the chancel softly dark,
    The brasses black and red.

He saw the School Close,[10] sunny and green,   25
    The runner beside him, the stand by the parapet wall,
The distant tape, and the crowd roaring between
    His own name over all.

Notes

[7] *title* the title cites Luke 10: 30, the parable of the good Samaritan. The poem's narrative is based on a sensational murder in what was known as the Great Game, the conflict between Britain and Russia over imperial expansion in disputed areas of what was then Kashmir. Lieutenant George W. Hayward (1839–70) was exploring the mountainous passes in the Pamir region of Kashmir in the areas between Russia, Afghanistan, and India. He left the British army and worked under the auspices of the Royal Geographical Society, receiving their gold medal. However, his remarks about atrocities in the Yasin area, under the supposed control of the Maharaja of Kashmir, Ranbir Singh (1830–85), alienated his supporters so he broke with the Geographical Society and explored on his own. He travelled from Gilgit to Darkot when assassins of local tribal leader, Mir Wali, seized him and executed him on 18 July 1870. Newbolt learned of the story from Frank E. Younghusband's *The Relief of Chitral* (1897). From *Admirals All and Other Verses* (1897).

[8] *Affghan* the Yassîn River in northern Pakistan, bordering on Afghanistan, is one of the tributaries of the Ghizar River, itself a tributary of the Indus. The Laspur hills or mountains border the Laspur River valley.

[9] *arch* the Norman period archway (*c.*1170) in Bristol, part of the gatehouse for the former Abbey, now Bristol Cathedral.

[10] *Close* see n. 2.

He saw the dark wainscot and timbered roof,
    The long tables, and the faces merry and keen;   30
The College Eight[11] and their trainer dining aloof,
    The Dons on the daïs[12] serene.

He watched the liner's stem ploughing the foam,
    He felt her trembling speed and the thrash of her screw;
He heard the passengers' voices talking of home,   35
    He saw the flag she flew.

And now it was dawn. He rose strong on his feet,
    And strode to his ruined camp below the wood;
He drank the breath of the morning cool and sweet;
    His murderers round him stood.   40

Light on the Laspur hills was broadening fast,
    The blood-red snow-peaks chilled to a dazzling white;
He turned, and saw the golden circle at last,
    Cut by the Eastern height.

"O glorious Life, Who dwellest in earth and sun,   45
    I have lived, I praise and adore Thee."
                    A sword swept.
Over the pass the voices one by one
    Faded, and the hill slept.

The Dictionary of National Biography[13]

Sitting at times over a hearth that burns
    With dull domestic glow,
My thought, leaving the book, gratefully turns
    To you who planned it so.

Not of the great only you deigned to tell,—   5
    The stars by which we steer,—
But lights out of the night that flashed, and fell
    To-night again, are here.

Such as were those, dogs[14] of an elder day,
    Who sacked the golden ports,   10
And those later who dared grapple their prey
    Beneath the harbour forts:

Notes

[11] *Eight* the college rowing team.

[12] *daïs* the dons are the teachers who eat at the high table, elevated above the dining hall floor, probably Corpus Christi College hall, Oxford.

[13] *title* the poem was written on 28 April 1896, and derives its title (or subtitle) from the *Dictionary of National Biography* of which Leslie Stephen (1832–1904) was editor (1885–91), succeeded by Sidney Lee. Its sixty-three volumes were published between 1885 and 1900. The poem was later called *Minora Sidera* (Lat. the smaller stars; from the opening lines of Horace's *Epode* 15), followed by the current title. From *Admirals All and Other Verses* (1897).

[14] *dogs* the admirals, explorers, adventurers, pirates, and sea-captains who raided the ports of the enemies of Britain, such as Spain and France, both in Europe and in the Americas. In the poem "Admirals All" (1897)

Some with flag at the fore, sweeping the world
　　To find an equal fight,
And some who joined war to their trade, and hurled　　　15
　　Ships of the line in flight.

Whether their fame centuries long should ring
　　They cared not over-much,
But cared greatly to serve God and the king,
　　And keep the Nelson[15] touch;　　　20

And fought to build Britain above the tide
　　Of wars and windy fate;
And passed content, leaving to us the pride
　　Of lives obscurely great.

The Vigil[16]

England! where the sacred flame
　　Burns before the inmost shrine,
Where the lips that love thy name
　　Consecrate their hopes and thine,
Where the banners of thy dead　　　5
Weave their shadows overhead,
Watch beside thine arms to-night,
Pray that God defend the Right.

Think that when to-morrow comes
　　War shall claim command of all,　　　10
Thou must hear the roll of drums,
　　Thou must hear the trumpet's call.
Now, before they silence ruth,
Commune with the voice of truth;
England! on thy knees to-night　　　15
Pray that God defend the Right.

Notes

Newbolt mentions a number of them: "Effingham, Grenville, Raleigh, Drake, / Here's to the bold and free! / Benbow, Collingwood, Byron, Blake, / Hail to the Kings of the Sea!"

[15] *Nelson* just before the battle of Trafalgar (21 Oct. 1805), Admiral Horatio Nelson (1758–1805) sent the message to the fleet from his flagship *Victory*: "England expects that every man will do his duty." For duty see also HEMANS, n. 1; and CLOUGH, "DUTY."

[16] *title* in the Middle Ages a squire kept an all-night vigil in a church before being invested with the order of knighthood. Victoria's Diamond Jubilee (22 June 1897) invoked the pageantry of empire and the glory of past heroes, but in the months following rebellion erupted in the North-West Frontier in Kashmir, at the Khyber Pass, in the continually unsettled margins of expanding empire. A famous painting by C. R. Leslie (1794–1859), *Queen Victoria in her Coronation Robes* (1838), is sometimes called *The Vigil*, showing Victoria kneeling before the altar in Westminster Abbey.

First printed in *The Island Race* (1898); this poem would later be printed as a leader article in *The Times* on 5 August 1914, the day after Britain declared war against Germany.

Hast thou counted up the cost,
    What to foeman, what to friend?
Glory sought is Honour lost,
    How should this be knighthood's end?   20
Knowest though what is hatred's meed?
What the surest gain of Greed?
England! wilt thou dare to-night
Pray that God defend the Right.

Single-hearted, unafraid,   25
    Hither all thy heroes came,
On this altar's steps were laid
    Gordon's life and Outram's fame.[17]
England! if thy will be yet
By their great example set,   30
Here beside thine arms to-night
Pray that God defend the Right.

So shalt thou when morning comes
    Rise to conquer or to fall,
Joyful hear the rolling drums,   35
    Joyful tear the trumpets call.
Then let Memory tell thy heart;
"England! what thou wert, thou art!"
Gird thee with thine ancient might,
Forth! and God defend the Right!   40

Clifton Chapel[18]

This is the Chapel: here, my son,
    Your father thought the thoughts of youth,
And heard the words that one by one
    The touch of Life has turned to truth.
Here in a day that is not far   5
    You too may speak with noble ghosts

Notes

[17] *fame* for Gordon, see n. 4. General Sir James Outram (1803–63) commanded the forces that defended the city of Lucknow in the Indian Rebellion of 1857.

[18] *title* here as elsewhere Newbolt combines affection for old school ties and friends with Christianity, sport and games-manship, chivalry, and patriotism, carried to the extreme of death in battle. First published in *The Spectator* (10 Sept. 1898) with the following footnote: "Copyrighted in the United States of America by Henry Newbolt." Reprinted in *The Island Race* (1898) with the following endnote: "*Clifton Chapel*. Clifton is one of the two schools from which the largest number of boys passed direct into the R. M. A., Woolwich, and R. M. C. Sandhurst. Thirty-five Old Cliftonian officers served in the late campaign on the Indian Frontier, of whom twenty-two were mentioned in dispatches and six recommended for the Distinguished Service Order. The connection of the school with Egypt and the Soudan is hardly less memorable." The Royal Military Academy (RMA) at Woolwich trained for the navy; the Royal Military College (RMC) at Sandhurst, the army. Ongoing was the first Mohmand Campaign in the North-West Frontier Province of India, in what is now Pakistan. As the poem was being published, Major-General Bindon Blood (1842–1940) was making a major advance. Eight days before this poem was published, the Battle of Omdurman in central Sudan was being fought by an army led by Herbert Kitchener (1850–1916) against Abdullah al-Taashi (1846–99), successor to the Mahdi (see n. 4). For a related tribute to a public school chapel, see also ARNOLD, "RUGBY CHAPEL" (WEB p. 379).

Of manhood and the vows of war
    You made before the Lord of Hosts.

To set the Cause above renown,
    To love the game beyond the prize,   10
To honour while you strike him down
    The foe that comes with fearless eyes:[19]
To count the life of battle good,
    And dear the land that gave you birth,
And dearer yet the brotherhood   15
    That binds the brave of all the earth.—

My son, the oath is yours: the end
    Is His, Who built the world of strife,
Who gave His children Pain for friend,
    And Death for surest hope of life.[20]   20
To-day and here the fight's begun,
    Of the great fellowship you're free;
Henceforth the School and you are one,
    And what You are the race shall be.

God send you fortune: yet be sure,   25
    Among the lights that gleam and pass,
You'll live to follow none more pure
    Than that which glows on yonder brass:
"*Qui procul hinc*," the legend's writ,-
    The frontier-grave is far away—   30
"*Qui ante diem periit:*
    Sed miles, sed pro patria."[21]

Arthur Symons (1865–1945)

Born in Wales, Symons was the son of Mark Symons (1824–98), a Wesleyan Methodist minister and Lydia Pascoe (1828–96). He was privately educated. Symons lived in England, France, and Italy as part of the artistic milieu of the 1880s and 1890s. After editorial work on the quartos of Shakespeare for the editions by Bernard Quaritch (1819–99), he worked for

Notes

[19] *To honour ... eyes* see Aeneas' words honouring Lausus as he slays him: "O pitiful boy, what is there that I, faithful Aeneas, can give to you that suits your bravery? ... But, unhappy one, even in miserable death you can be consoled at least by this, that you fall by the right hand of great Aeneas" (*Aeneid* 10. 826–30).

[20] *life* self-sacrifice for the good of others in imitation of the death of Christ.

[21] *Qui ... patria* (Lat. who, far away from here, died before his time, but as a soldier, and for his native land). This epigraph seems to have been invented by Newbolt, but it is perhaps an echo of Cicero in *On the Extremes of Good and Evil* (*De finibus bonorum et malorum*): "Born not for himself only, but for his native land, and also for his own people" (2. 14. 45). Kipling used Newbolt's Latin phrase at the end of the poem for a memorial plaque in Burwash Church for his son John (1897–1915) who had died in the Battle of Loos (1915). He also used it for an epigraph for "A Little Prep" in *Stalky & Co.* (1899). Newbolt rhymes *patriā* with "far away," two lines earlier, indicating that he is using the unreformed Latin pronunciation of the schools that was undergoing a revision from the 1880s to the new pronunciation agreed on in 1907. Patriotism and classicism that lead to dying in a remote part of the empire are here declared to be wholly English by the rhyme scheme, associating Clifton's British imperial ethic with its classical tradition.

he editorial boards of various periodicals: the *Athenæum* (1891), the *Saturday Review* (1894), and *The Savoy* (1895–96) with W. B. Yeats, Max Beerbohm, and Aubrey Beardsley (whom Symons hired for *The Savoy*). His first volume of poems was *Days and Nights* (1889), followed by *Silhouettes* (1892), *London Nights* (1895), and *Amoris Victima* (1897), all showing his immersion in French writers from Charles Baudelaire to the Symbolists, many of whom he knew and translated. He was a prolific writer of essays, from *An Introduction to the Study of Browning* (1886) to *A Study of Walter Pater* (1932). In *Harpers* he published "The Decadent Movement in Literature" (1893) and to *The Yellow Book* he contributed an essay, "The Symbolist Movement in Literature," later enlarged as an important book (1899). Symons is also known as an important translator from six languages, especially for his French Symbolist poetry. No scholarly edition. Arthur Symons, *The Collected Works of Arthur Symons* (9 vols, 1924); *Arthur Symons: Selected Letters, 1880–1935,* eds Karl Beckson and John M. Munro (1989); *The Memoirs of Arthur Symons: Life and Art in the 1890s,* ed. Karl Beckson (1977); Karl Beckson, *Arthur Symons: A Life* (1987). "Arthur Symons": http://homepages.nildram.co.uk/~simmers/symons.htm.

Pastel[1]

The light of our cigarettes
   Went and came in the gloom:
   It was dark in the little room.

Dark, and then, in the dark,
   Sudden, a flash, a glow,   5
   And a hand and a ring I know.

And then, through the dark, a flush
   Ruddy and vague, the grace—
   A rose!—of her lyric face.

The Absinthe Drinker[2]

Gently I wave the visible world away.
   Far off, I hear a roar, afar yet near,
   Far off and strange, a voice is in my ear,

Notes

ARTHUR SYMONS

[1] *title* in the "Preface" to the second edition of *Silhouettes* (1896), Symons summarizes his rejection of morality in art in favour of the aesthetic impressions of the Decadents: "All art, surely, is a form of artifice, and thus, to the truly devout mind, condemned already, if not as actively noxious, at all events as needless.... However you may try to convince yourself to the contrary, a work of art can be judged only from two standpoints: the standpoint from which its art is measured entirely by its morality, and the standpoint from which its morality is measured entirely by its art. I claim only an equal liberty for the rendering of every mood of that variable and inexplicable and contradictory creature which we call ourselves, of every aspect under which we are gifted or condemned to apprehend the beauty and strangeness and curiosity of the visible world." From *Silhouettes* (1892).

[2] *title* the poem was written after Symons and Havelock Ellis (1859–1939) had sampled absinthe in Paris in 1889–90, when he also met Paul Verlaine (1844–96) and Stéphane Mallarmé (1842–98), French symbolist poets, and Joris-Karl Huysmans (1848–1907), French novelist, best known for *À rebours* (Fr. against nature, 1884). Absinthe is a drink

And is the voice my own? the words I say
Fall strangely, like a dream, across the day;   5
    And the dim sunshine is a dream. How clear,
    New as the world to lovers' eyes, appear
The men and women passing on their way!

The world is very fair. The hours are all
    Linked in a dance of mere forgetfulness.   10
      I am at peace with God and man. O glide,
Sands of the hour-glass that I count not, fall
    Serenely: scarce I feel your soft caress,
      Rocked on this dreamy and indifferent tide.

Javanese Dancers[3]

Twitched strings, the clang of metal, beaten drums,
    Dull, shrill, continuous, disquieting;
And now the stealthy dancer comes
    Undulantly with cat-like steps that cling;

Smiling between her painted lids a smile,   5
    Motionless, unintelligible, she twines
    Her fingers into mazy lines,
Twining her scarves across them all the while.

One, two, three, four step forth, and, to and fro,
    Delicately and imperceptibly,   10
Now swaying gently in a row,
    Now interthreading slow and rhythmically,

Still with fixed eyes, monotonously still,
    Mysteriously, with smiles inanimate,
    With lingering feet that undulate,   15
With sinuous fingers, spectral hands that thrill,

Notes

of green spirits with a high alcoholic content, originally made from green anise and wormwood, itself hallucinogenic. The drink, known as *"la fée verte"* (Fr. the green fairy), had taken Paris's bohemian culture by storm from the 1870s and became a hallmark of Decadent culture in the 1890s. *L'heure verte* (Fr. the green hour) was a frequent subject, as in a number of paintings called *The Absinthe Drinker* – by Edouard Manet (1859), Edgar Degas (1876), Jean-François Raffaëlli (1881), and Félicien Rops (c.1890) and numerous art nouveau posters. From the section titled "Masks and Faces" in *Silhouettes* (1892).

3 *title* the dancers typify Symons's many femmes fatales (Fr. fatal or seductive women). Edgar Degas (1834–1917), French Impressionist artist, painted many canvases of dancers in the 1870s, as instances of arrested movement, captured light, and the ballet as an image of ideal aesthetic life in motion. To Decadent writers of the 1890s, the line of the dance was analogous to the line of verse, especially when taut and twisting in an art nouveau movement. Charles Baudelaire (1821–67), French poet, had related such movement to temptation and erotic love in *"Le serpent qui danse"* (Fr. the dancing snake) from *Fleurs du Mal* (Fr. flowers of evil, 1857). Dancers from Java first performed in Paris in 1889 and became part of the cult of the exotic. First published in *The Book of the Rhymers' Club* (1892) under the title "Javanese Dancers: A Silhouette." Republished in *Silhouettes* (1892), our text.

The little amber-coloured dancers move,
   Like little painted figures on a screen,
   Or phantom-dancers haply seen
Among the shadows of a magic grove.[4]   20

Hallucination[5]

Why is it that I see
Her burning web of hair?[6]
It burns and strangles me.
No, there is nothing there
But sunlight and cool air.   5

And yet I feel it, soft
And warm; and now the wind
Brandishes it aloft.
But is it round my mind
Or round my body twined?   10

I have a deadly fear
When I but think upon
That evil heart in her
Which for more power has gone
Into her hair alone.   15

She has an angel's face.
He will not enter there;
But for his hiding-place,
His fortress and his lair,
Has gone into her hair.   20

There the beast laughs and sits
And twines his web to mesh
The soul into the wits,
The heart out of the flesh:
He twines his web afresh.   25

And I shall never know
If this too shining thing

Notes

[4] *grove* changed in later editions to read:

> In measure while the gnats of music whirr,
>   The little amber-coloured dancers move,
>   Like painted idols seen to stir
>   By the idolators in a magic grove.

[5] *title* From *Knave of Hearts. 1894–1908* (1913).

[6] *hair* a fetish and an erotic preoccupation of the Pre-Raphaelite poets and painters from William Morris's "The Defence of Guenevere" and "Rapunzel" (1858) to Swinburne's *Poems and Ballads* (1866) and Rossetti's "Jenny" and "The House of Life" (1870) – as well as in many paint-ings by Rossetti. Robert Browning had also written of the connection between hair and erotic love in "Gold Hair: A Legend of Pornic" (1864). Loose hair was often associated with Mary Magdalen, as a sign of a fallen woman, and as a name for the rescue homes for prostitutes, "Magdalen Houses." There is also a suggestion here of a connection with the murderous serpents of the hair of Medusa, the sight of which turned the beholder to stone.

[7] *title* heliotrope, usually a violet colour, gave its name to that shade in the 1880s; the white variety, *heliotropium alba*, is a fragrant plant. Heliotrope is also an ingredient in

The wind blows to and fro,
Mocking and comforting,
Is any living thing.   30

I know that I desire
With rapture and despair
To snatch the web of fire
Burning out of the air
And perish in her hair.   35

White Heliotrope[7]

The feverish room and that white bed,
   The tumbled skirts upon a chair,
   The novel flung half-open, where
Hat, hair-pins, puffs, and paints, are spread;
The mirror that has sucked your face   5
   Into its secret deep of deeps,
   And there mysteriously keeps
Forgotten memories of grace;

And you half dressed and half awake,
   Your slant eyes strangely watching me,   10
   And I, who watch you drowsily,
With eyes that, having slept not, ache;
This (need one dread? nay, dare one hope?)
   Will rise, a ghost of memory, if
   Ever again my handkerchief   15
Is scented with White Heliotrope.

Bianca[8]

Her cheeks are hot, her cheeks are white;
The white girl hardly breathes to-night,
   So faint the pulses come and go,
   That waken to a smouldering glow
The morbid faintness of her white.   5

What drowsing heats of sense, desire
Longing and languorous, the fire

Notes

perfume. Here the seduction, mirror, and memory are linked by perfume in synaesthesia, the mingling or cross-activation metaphors, so that sensations of colour are read as scent. From *London Nights* (1895).

[8] *title* the poem is one of a cycle of ten poems entitled "Bianca," this lyric being the first. Bianca was called "Lydia" (also his mother's name) by Symons – she was a dancer at the Empire Theatre in London whom Symons met in 1894 and had an affair with for two years. In *Amoris Victima* (Lat. the victim of love, 1897) he also writes about their love. He later wrote an essay about her, "Lydia" (written December 1920; printed in *Memoirs, 1977*). The images are obsessively repetitive: lips, mouth, fingertips, hands, and throat, as in Swinburne's "Anactoria" and other poems from *Poems and Ballads* (1866). From *London Nights* (1895).

Of what white ashes, subtly mesh
The fascinations of her flesh
Into a breathing web of fire?   10

Only her eyes, only her mouth,
Live, in the agony of drouth,
    Athirst for that which may not be:
    The desert of virginity
Aches in the hotness of her mouth.   15

I take her hands into my hands,
Silently, and she understands;
    I set my lips upon her lips;
    Shuddering to her finger-tips
She strains my hands within her hands.   20

I set my lips on hers; they close
Into a false and phantom rose;
    Upon her thirsting lips I rain
    A flood of kisses, and in vain;
Her lips inexorably close.   25

Through her closed lips that cling to mine,
Her hands that hold me and entwine,
    Her body that abandoned lies,
    Rigid with sterile ecstasies,
A shiver knits her flesh to mine.   30

Life sucks into a mist remote
Her fainting lips, her throbbing throat;
    Her lips that open to my lips,
    And, hot against my finger-tips,
The pulses leaping in her throat.[9]   35

January 18, 1894.

William Butler Yeats (1865–1939)

Born in Dublin to an artist father, John Butler Yeats (1839–1922), and a well-to-do daughter of a merchant in Sligo in the west of Ireland, Susan Mary Pollexfen (1841–1900), Yeats moved to County Sligo where he was raised as part of the Anglo-Irish community. In 1877 when the family moved to London Yeats went to Godolphin School in Hammersmith for four years. The family moved back to Dublin in 1880. After various university and other publications, Yeats started to find his Irish roots in folklore and Irish myth, writing under the influence of

Notes

[9] *1894* all of the poems in the "Bianca" cycle are dated to chronicle the course of the love affair.

Shelley, Blake, and the Pre-Raphaelites. Back in London in 1890, he was involved in the founding of the Rhymers' Club and started a lifelong interest in mysticism and spiritualism. Yeats is most often associated with Modernists like T. S. Eliot (1888–1965) and Ezra Pound (1885–72); however, his career was well established by the end of Victoria's reign. His first substantial publication was *The Wanderings of Oisin* (1889) rooted in Irish mythology, then *Poems* (1895), *The Secret Rose* (1897), and *The Wind Among the Reeds* (1899). In 1889 he met and fell in love with Maud Gonne (1866–1953), Irish nationalist, feminist, and actress, who influenced him for the rest of his life. With Augusta, Lady Gregory (1852–1932), who Yeats met in 1896, he helped found the Abbey Theatre in Dublin (opened 1904). In 1916 Yeats married Georgie Hyde-Lees (1892–1968). He continued to produce plays, essays, and poetry, and in 1923 was awarded the Nobel Prize for Literature. Scholarly Edition: *The Collected Works of W. B. Yeats* (12 vols, 1989–94); *The Variorum Edition of the Poems of W. B. Yeats*, eds Peter Allt and Russell K. Alspach (1968); *The Collected Letters of W. B. Yeats*, eds John Kelly and Eric Domville (3 vols, 1986–94); Terence Brown, *The Life of W. B. Yeats* (2001). Sligo Yeats Society: www.yeats-sligo.com.

The Stolen Child[1]

Where dips the rocky highland
    Of Sleuth Wood[2] in the lake,
There lies a leafy island
    Where flapping herons wake
The drowsy water-rats;   5
There we've hid our faery vats,
Full of berries
And of reddest stolen cherries.
Come away, O human child!
To the waters and the wild   10
With a fairy, hand in hand,
For the world's more full of weeping than you can understand.

Where the wave of moonlight glosses
    The dim grey sands with light,
Far off by furthest Rosses[3]   15
    We foot it all the night,
Weaving olden dances,
Mingling hands and mingling glances
    Till the moon has taken flight;
To and fro we leap   20
    And chase the frothy bubbles,
    While the world is full of troubles

Notes

WILLIAM BUTLER YEATS

[1] *title* the place names are all in counties Leitrim and Sligo in the west of Ireland from where Yeats came. From the *Irish Monthly* (Dec. 1886); reprinted in *Poems and Ballads of Young Ireland* (1888), a compilation by a number of poets, and again in Yeats's *The Wanderings of Oisin and Other Poems* (1889).

[2] *Wood* that is, Slish Wood on the southern shore of Lough Gill, a tree-covered headland that slopes down to the water and Slishwood Island in County Sligo in Ireland.

[3] *Rosses* promontory into Sligo Bay near Sligo Town in the west of Ireland.

And is anxious in its sleep.
Come away, O human child!
To the woods and waters wild   25
With a fairy, hand in hand,
For the world's more full of weeping than you can understand.

Where the wandering water gushes
      From the hills above Glen-Car,⁴
In pools among the rushes   30
      That scarce could bathe a star,
We seek for slumbering trout
      And whispering in their ears
            We give them evil dreams,
            Leaning softly out   35
      From ferns that drop their tears
            Of dew on the young streams.
Come, O human child!
To the woods and waters wild
With a fairy, hand in hand,   40
For the world's more full of weeping than you can understand.

Away with us he's going,
      The solemn-eyed:
He'll hear no more the lowing
      Of the calves on the warm hill side,   45
Or the kettle on the hob
      Sing peace into his breast,
Or see the brown mice bob
      Round and round the oatmeal chest.
For he comes, the human child,   50
To the woods and waters wild
With a fairy, hand in hand,
For the world more full of weeping than he can understand.

The Lake Isle of Innisfree⁵

I will arise and go now, and go to Innisfree,
      And a small cabin build there, of clay and wattles made:
Nine bean rows will I have there, a hive for the honey bee,
      And live alone in the bee-loud glade.

William

Notes ———————————————————————————————————

⁴ *Glen-Car* a lake and waterfall in the valley of the Drumcliff
River, about 13 kilometres north of Sligo Town, in County
Leitrim.
⁵ *title* first published in the *National Observer* (13 Dec. 1890);
reprinted in *The Countess Kathleen and Various Legends and*

Lyrics (1892). Innisfree was an island in Lough Gill (see n. 2).
To hear Yeats read the poem, see LITERATURE: AURAL;
RECORDINGS, YEATS (WEB p. 160).

And I shall have some peace there, for peace comes dropping slow,   5
    Dropping from the veils of the morning to where the cricket sings;
There midnight's all a glimmer, and noon a purple glow,
    And evening full of the linnets' wings.

I will arise and go now, for always night and day
    I hear lake water lapping with low sounds on the shore;   10
While I stand on the roadway, or on the pavements grey,
    I hear it in the deep heart's core.

An Old Song Re-Sung [Down by the Salley Gardens][6]

Down by the salley gardens my love and I did meet;
She passed the salley gardens with little snow-white feet.
She bid me take love easy, as the leaves grow on the tree;
But I, being young and foolish, with her would not agree.

In a field by the river my love and I did stand,   5
And on my leaning shoulder she laid her snow-white hand.
She bid me take life easy, as the grass grows on the weirs;
But I was young and foolish, and now am full of tears.

When You Are Old[7]

When you are old and grey and full of sleep,
    And nodding by the fire, take down this book,
    And slowly read, and dream of the soft look
Your eyes had once, and of their shadows deep;

How many loved your moments of glad grace,   5
    And loved your beauty with love false or true;
    But one man loved the pilgrim soul in you,
And loved the sorrows of your changing face.

And bending down beside the glowing bars
    Murmur, a little sad, *from us fled Love;*   10
    He paced upon the mountains far above,
And hid his face amid a crowd of stars.

Notes

[6] *title* first published in *The Wanderings of Oisin and Other Poems* (1889); given the title "Down by the Salley Gardens" in *Poems* (1895). In *The Wanderings of Oisin* Yeats adds the following comment: "This is an attempt to reconstruct an old song from three lines imperfectly remembered by an old peasant woman in the village of Ballysodare, Sligo, who often sings them to herself." "Salley" is Irish dialect for "sallow" or willow.

[7] *title* first published in *The Rose* (1893).

Rudyard Kipling (1865–1936)

Born in Bombay (now Mumbai), India, Kipling was the son of Alice MacDonald (1837–1910) and John Lockwood Kipling (1837–1911), artist and art teacher. In 1871 Kipling was sent home to live for five unhappy years with a foster family in Southsea. He was then sent to the United Services College, a school for the sons of army officers, the model for his collection of short stories *Stalky and Co.* (1899). He could not obtain an academic scholarship to Oxford or Cambridge, and his parents lacked the financial resources to pay his way. In 1882 he returned to India to work as a journalist, first for the *Civil and Military Gazette* in Lahore (now in Pakistan), and then as editor of *Pioneer* in Allahabad. During this time he wrote poems, collected in *Departmental Ditties* (1886), and short stories that would become *Plain Tales from the Hills* (1888). He returned to England in 1889 as a literary celebrity. In 1892 he published *Barrack-Room Ballads and Other Verses*, a collection of poems in which he continued to experiment with forms of dialect, particularly of British soldiers serving in India. After marrying an American, Caroline Balestier (1852–1939), in 1892, Kipling moved to Vermont, where he wrote his famous children's stories, *The Jungle Book* (1894). He returned to England in 1896, first to Devon, where he wrote his most famous

work, *Kim* (1901), a novel about a young Anglo-Indian orphan who becomes involved in the Great Game between Russia and Great Britain in central Asia. In 1902 he moved to Bateman's, a country house in Sussex, where he resided until his death. Kipling's son John, a second lieutenant in the Irish Guards, died at the age of 18 at the battle of Loos (27 Sept. 1915); thereafter Kipling, filled with grief, modified his views of war and violence, as in the moving elegies "My Son Jack" (1916) and "Epitaphs of the War" (1919). A strong supporter of the British Empire, Kipling was immensely popular during his lifetime; following his death, however, his reputation suffered as he was associated with racist attitudes and jingoism. In 1907 he was the first English writer awarded the Nobel Prize; his ashes are buried in Westminster Abbey. His unfinished autobiography, *Something of Myself*, was published posthumously in 1937. Standard edition: *The Sussex Edition of the Complete Works in Prose and Verse of Rudyard Kipling* (35 vols, 1935–37); *Rudyard Kipling's Complete Verse: Definitive Edition* (1940); *The Letters of Rudyard Kipling* ed. Thomas Pinney (6 vols, 1990–2004); David Gilmour, *The Long Recessional: The Imperial Life of Rudyard Kipling* (2002); "The Kipling Society": www.kipling.org.uk.

Gunga Din[1]

You may talk o' gin and beer
When you're quartered safe out 'ere,
An' you're sent to penny-fights an' Aldershot[2] it;
But when it comes to slaughter
You will do your work on water,   5

Notes

RUDYARD KIPLING

[1] *title* the name Kipling gave to a water carrier named Juma at the siege of Delhi (1857). The name "Gunga" or "Old Gunga" was applied in eighteenth-century maps of India to the Rapnarain River, one of the tributaries of the Ganges; sometimes applied to the goddess of the Ganges. "Din" (Hindi: day). First published in *The Scots Observer*

(7 June, 1890); collected in *Barrack-Room Ballads and Other Verses* (1892), our text. An American collection, *Departmental Ditties, Barrack-Room Ballads and Other Verses*, had been published in 1890.

[2] *o' ... penny-fights ... Aldershot* the speaker is a London Cockney who drops his final consonants (*f, d,* and *g*) and his

An' you'll lick the bloomin' boots of 'im that's got it.
Now in Injia's sunny clime,
Where I used to spend my time
A-servin' of 'Er Majesty the Queen,
Of all them blackfaced crew   10
The finest man I knew
Was our regimental bhisti,[3] Gunga Din.
     He was "Din! Din! Din!
  You limpin' lump o' brick-dust, Gunga Din!
    Hi! slippery *hitherao*![4]   15
     Water, get it! *Panee lao*,[5]
  You squidgy-nosed old idol, Gunga Din."

The uniform 'e wore
Was nothin' much before,
An' rather less than 'arf o' that be'ind,   20
For a piece o' twisty rag
An' a goatskin water-bag
Was all the field-equipment 'e could find.
When the sweatin' troop-train lay
In a sidin' through the day,   25
Where the 'eat would make your bloomin' eyebrows crawl,
We shouted "Harry By!"[6]
Till our throats were bricky-dry,
Then we wopped 'im 'cause 'e couldn't serve us all.
     It was "Din! Din! Din!   30
  You 'eathen, where the mischief 'ave you been?
    You put some *juldee*[7] in it
    Or I'll *marrow*[8] you this minute
  If you don't fill up my helmet, Gunga Din!"

'E would dot an' carry one[9]   35
Till the longest day was done;
An' 'e didn't seem to know the use o' fear.
If we charged or broke or cut,
You could bet your bloomin' nut,
'E'd be waitin' fifty paces right flank rear.   40
With 'is mussick[10] on 'is back,
'E would skip with our attack,
An' watch us till the bugles made "Retire,"
An' for all 'is dirty 'ide

Notes

initial letter *h*. Penny-fights: military slang for inconsequential skirmishes; Aldershot is the main training base for the British army since 1854 in Hampshire, south-west of London.

[3] *bhisti* (Hindi: water carrier).

[4] *hitherao* (Urdu: come here).

[5] *Panee lao* "Bring water swiftly" [author's note]. (Urdu).

[6] *Harry By* "Mr. Atkins's equivalent for 'O brother'" [author's note]. (Urdu: *arré bhai*: come here). Tommy Atkins has

been a generic name for a British soldier from the eighteenth century; *Barrack-Room Ballads* opens with a dedicatory poem, "To T. A."

[7] *juldee* "Be quick" [author's note]. (Urdu: hurry).

[8] *marrow* "Hit you" [author's note]. (Urdu: *maro*: hit).

[9] *dot an' carry one* schoolchild's expression for calculating elementary arithmetic.

[10] *mussick* "Water-skin" [author's note]. (Hindi: made from goatskin); Muslims would reject pigskin, Hindu's calfskin.

'E was white, clear white, inside 45
When 'e went to tend the wounded under fire!
    It was "Din! Din! Din!"
  With the bullets kickin' dust-spots on the green.
      When the cartridges ran out,
      You could hear the front-ranks shout, 50
  "Hi! ammunition-mules an' Gunga Din!"

I shan't forgit the night
When I dropped be'ind the fight
With a bullet where my belt-plate should 'a' been.
I was chokin' mad with thirst, 55
An' the man that spied me first
Was our good old grinnin', gruntin' Gunga Din.
'E lifted up my 'ead,
An' he plugged me where I bled,
An' 'e guv me 'arf-a-pint o' water-green: 60
It was crawlin' and it stunk,
But of all the drinks I've drunk,
I'm gratefullest to one from Gunga Din.
    It was "Din! Din! Din!
  'Ere's a beggar with a bullet through 'is spleen; 65
    'E's chawin' up the ground,
    An' 'e's kickin' all around:
  For Gawd's sake git the water, Gunga Din!"

'E carried me away
To where a dooli[11] lay, 70
An' a bullet come an' drilled the beggar clean.
'E put me safe inside,
An' just before 'e died,
"I 'ope you liked your drink," sez Gunga Din.
So I'll meet 'im later on 75
At the place where 'e is gone—
Where it's always double drill and no canteen;
'E'll be squattin' on the coals
Givin' drink to poor damned souls,
An' I'll get a swig in hell from Gunga Din! 80
    Yes, Din! Din! Din!
  You Lazarushian-leather[12] Gunga Din!
    Though I've belted you and flayed you,
    By the livin' Gawd that made you,
  You're a better man than I am, Gunga Din! 85

Notes

[11] *dooli* (Hindi: covered litter).

[12] *Lazarushian-leather* pun on Gunga Din's state and skin colour: Lazarus (Luke 16) is taken to "Abraham's bosom" or paradise; russian leather is a red-coloured goat or sheepskin dyed brownish-red used in bookbinding and shoe manufacture.

The Widow at Windsor[13]

'Ave you 'eard o' the Widow at Windsor
    With a hairy gold crown on 'er 'ead?
She 'as ships on the foam—she 'as millions at 'ome,
    An' she pays us poor beggars in red.[14]
        (Ow, poor beggars in red!)   5
There's 'er nick[15] on the cavalry 'orses,
    There's 'er mark on the medical stores—
An' 'er troopers[16] you'll find with a fair wind be'ind
    That takes us to various wars.
        (Poor beggars!—barbarious wars!)   10
      Then 'ere's to the Widow at Windsor,
        An' 'ere's to the stores an' the guns,
     The men an' the 'orses what makes up the forces
        O' Missis Victorier's sons.
        (Poor beggars! Victorier's sons!)   15

Walk wide o' the Widow at Windsor,
    For 'alf o' Creation she owns:
We 'ave bought 'er the same with the sword an' the flame,
    An' we've salted it down with our bones.
        (Poor beggars!—it's blue with our bones!)   20
Hands off o' the sons o' the Widow,
    Hands off o' the goods in 'er shop,
For the Kings must come down an' the Emperors frown
    When the Widow at Windsor says "Stop"!
        (Poor beggars!—we're sent to say "Stop"!)   25
      Then 'ere's to the Lodge[17] o' the Widow,
        From the Pole to the Tropics it runs—
     To the Lodge[18] that we tile with the rank an' the file,
        An' open in form with the guns.
        (Poor beggars!—it's always they guns!)   30

We 'ave 'eard o' the Widow at Windsor,
    It's safest to let 'er alone:
For 'er sentries we stand by the sea an' the land
    Wherever the bugles are blown.
        (Poor beggars!—an' don't we get blown!)   35
Take 'old o' the Wings o' the Mornin',[19]
    An' flop round the earth till you're dead;

Notes

[13] *title* nickname of Queen Victoria, who remained in seclusion for almost twenty years after the death of Albert on 14 December 1861. Windsor Castle, where Albert is buried, was her principle residence during this long period of mourning. First published as "The Sons of the Widow" in *The Scots Observer* (26 Apr. 1890); published as "The Widow at Windsor" in *Barrack-Room Verses* (1892); our text.

[14] *red* pun on colour of army uniforms and blood.

[15] *nick* a mark, "VRI," on a horse's hoof, signifying property of the queen (standing for Lat. *Victoria Regina et Imperatrix*: Victoria Queen and Empress).

[16] *troopers* troopships.

[17] *Lodge* the Royal Lodge is a royal residence in Windsor Great Park, 5 kilometres south of the castle; also the Victorian Empire.

[18] *Lodge* a reference to the Masonic Lodge, of which Kipling became a member in 1886.

[19] *Mornin'* see Psalm 139: 9.

But you won't get away from the tune that they play
To the bloomin' old rag over'ead.
(Poor beggars!—it's 'ot over'ead!) 40
Then 'ere's to the sons o' the Widow,
Wherever, 'owever they roam.
'Ere's all they desire, an' if they require
A speedy return to their 'ome.
(Poor beggars!—they'll never see 'ome!) 45

Mandalay[20]

By the old Moulmein Pagoda,[21] lookin' eastward to the sea,
There's a Burma girl a-settin', and I know she thinks o' me;
For the wind is in the palm-trees, and the temple-bells they say:
"Come you back, you British soldier; come you back to Mandalay!"
　　Come you back to Mandalay, 5
　　Where the old Flotilla lay:
　　Can't you 'ear their paddles chunkin' from Rangoon to Mandalay?[22]
　　On the road to Mandalay,
　　Where the flyin'-fishes play,
　　An' the dawn comes up like thunder outer China[23] 'crost the Bay! 10

'Er petticoat was yaller an' 'er little cap was green,
An' 'er name was Supi-yaw-lat—jes' the same as Theebaw's Queen,[24]
An' I seed her first a-smokin' of a whackin' white cheroot,[25]
An' a-wastin' Christian kisses on an 'eathen idol's foot:
　　Bloomin' idol made o'mud— 15
　　Wot they called the Great Gawd Budd[26]—
　　Plucky lot she cared for idols when I kissed 'er where she stud!
　　On the road to Mandalay..

Notes

[20] *title* although Kipling calls the poem "Mandalay," he refers to three locations in Burma: Mandalay, in the centre of Burma, several hundred kilometres up the Irawaddy River, known among the British as the "road to Mandalay"; Rangoon, on the Irawaddy at the intersection of the Yangon and Bango rivers, 31 kilometres from the Gulf of Martaban in southern Burma; and Moulmein, a port city across the Gulf of Martaban. Mandalay was the old capital of Burma from 1860 to 1885 when the Burmese Kingdom was annexed by the British in the Third Anglo-Burmese War (1885–87). The poem is spoken by a fictional British soldier in England who had served in that war. Kipling visited the sites mentioned in the poem in March 1889, recorded in *From Sea to Sea* (1899). Kipling's poem was set to music by Oley Speaks (1874–1948). First published in *The Scots Observer* (21 June 1890); collected in *Barrack-Room Ballads* (1892), our text.
[21] *Moulmein Pagoda* Moulmein, renamed Mawlamyine, is a port city in southern Burma. Probably Kipling refers to the Kyaikthanlan Pagoda dating from 875 CE, whence there is a view of the joining of various rivers and the sea to the west, not the east as in Kipling. At the foot of the

pagoda is the area of the city known as the "Mandalay Ward," though it is more likely that Kipling refers to the city in the north of Burma.
[22] *Flotilla … Mandalay* the flotilla consists of the ships of the Irrawaddy Flotilla Company that plied the river from Rangoon to Mandalay. Rangoon, renamed Yangon, is the largest city in Burma, situated at the mouth of the Irrawaddy River.
[23] *China* thousands of kilometres away, China is not visible from the Moulmein Pagoda; possibly a reference to Indo-China, the French name for south-east Asia, the present Vietnam, Cambodia, and Laos.
[24] *Supi-yaw-lat … Theebaw's Queen* Thibaw (1859–1916) was the last king of Burma who ruled from 1878 until British annexation in 1885. He married Queen Supayalat (1859–1925), and both went into exile in India where Thibaw died. Supayalat returned to Rangoon in 1919.
[25] *cheroot* kind of cheap Indian cigar.
[26] *Gawd Budd* probably the Maha Myat Muni image of the Buddha, the oldest bronze-gilt image of the founder of Buddhism in Burma, dating from before 123 BCE in Mandalay; it is washed daily; a replica is in Moulmein.

When the mist was on the rice-fields an' the sun was droppin' slow,
She'd git 'er little banjo an' she'd sing "Kulla-lo-lo!"[27]   20
With 'er arm upon my shoulder an' 'er cheek agin' my cheek
We useter watch the steamers an' the *hathis*[28] pilin' teak.
    Elephints a-pilin' teak
    In the sludgy, squdgy creek,
    Where the silence 'ung that 'eavy you was 'arf afraid to speak!   25
    On the road to Mandalay . .

But that's all shove be'ind me—long ago an' fur away,
An' there ain't no 'busses runnin' from the Bank[29] to Mandalay;
An' I'm learnin' 'ere in London what the ten-year soldier tells:
"If you've 'eard the East a-callin', you won't never 'eed naught else."   30
    No! you won't 'eed nothin' else
    But them spicy garlic smells,
    An' the sunshine an' the palm-trees an' the tinkly temple-bells;
    On the road to Mandalay . .

I am sick o' wastin' leather on these gritty pavin'-stones,   35
An' the blasted Henglish drizzle wakes the fever in my bones;
Tho' I walks with fifty 'ousemaids outer Chelsea to the Strand,[30]
An' they talks a lot o' lovin', but wot do they understand?
    Beefy face an' grubby 'and—
    Law! wot do they understand?   40
    I've a neater, sweeter maiden in a cleaner, greener land!
    On the road to Mandalay . .

Ship me somewheres east of Suez, where the best is like the worst,
Where there aren't no Ten Commandments an' a man can raise a thirst;
For the temple-bells are callin', an' it's there that I would be—   45
By the old Moulmein Pagoda, looking lazy at the sea;
    On the road to Mandalay,
    Where the old Flotilla lay,
    With our sick beneath the awnings when we went to Mandalay!
    O the road to Mandalay,   50
    Where the flyin'-fishes play,
    An' the dawn comes up like thunder outer China 'crost the Bay!

Recessional[31]

God of our fathers, known of old—
    Lord of our far-flung battle-line,
Beneath Whose awful hand we hold

Notes

[27] *banjo . . . lo-lo* banjo probably refers to a traditional three-stringed Burmese instrument. Her song has not been identified.

[28] *hathis* (Hindi: elephants) trained to move and pile teak logs; Hathi is the name of the old elephant in *The Jungle Book* (1894).

[29] *Bank* the Bank of England building on Threadneedle Street in the City of London.

[30] *Chelsea to the Strand* Chelsea was a middle-class residential borough in south-west London. The Strand is a major thoroughfare in central London, connecting Trafalgar Square and Charing Cross with Fleet Street.

[31] *title* hymn at the end of a religious service when clergy and choir process from the sanctuary. This poem was written for the sixtieth anniversary of Victoria's reign, her Diamond Jubilee. Kipling refused payment for the poem,

Dominion over palm and pine—
    Lord God of Hosts, be with us yet,   5
    Lest we forget—lest we forget![32]

The tumult and the shouting dies—
    The captains and the kings depart—[33]
Still stands Thine ancient Sacrifice,
    An humble and a contrite heart.[34]   10
Lord God of Hosts, be with us yet,
    Lest we forget—lest we forget!

Far-called our navies melt away—
    On dune and headland sinks the fire[35]—
Lo, all our pomp of yesterday[36]   15
    Is one with Nineveh and Tyre![37]
Judge of the Nations, spare us yet,
    Lest we forget—lest we forget!

If, drunk with sight of power, we loose
    Wild tongues that have not Thee in awe—   20
Such boasting as the Gentiles use
    Or lesser breeds without the Law[38]—
Lord God of Hosts, be with us yet,
    Lest we forget—lest we forget!

For heathen heart that puts her trust   25
    In reeking tube and iron shard—
All valiant dust that builds on dust,
    And guarding calls not Thee to guard—
For frantic boast and foolish word,
Thy Mercy on Thy People, Lord!   30
        Amen.

The White Man's Burden

An Address to the United States[39]

Take up the White Man's burden—
    Send forth the best ye breed—
Go, bind your sons to exile
    To serve your captives' need;

Notes

as he did for other poems written for public occasions.
The poem was added to *The English Hymnal* in 1906. First
published in *The Times* (17 July 1897, p. 13).

[32] *forget* see Deuteronomy 6: 12.

[33] *tumult . . . depart* see Job 39: 25.

[34] *Thine . . . heart* see Psalm 51: 17.

[35] *fire* celebratory bonfires to honour the queen on her
Jubilee.

[36] *yesterday* see Psalm 90: 4.

[37] *Nineveh . . . Tyre* cities of extinct empires: the former in
Assyria (now near Mosul, Iraq) fell in 612 BCE to the

Persians; the latter in Phoenicia (now in Lebanon) fell to
the Greeks under Alexander in 332 BCE.

[38] *Gentiles . . . Law* see Romans 2: 14.

[39] *title* written when the USA was first becoming an imperial
power, when it assumed control of Cuba, Puerto Rico,
Guam, and the Philippines following the Spanish-
American War, April to August, 1898. Several writers
answered Kipling ironically: see, for instance, EMPIRE: CEL-
EBRATION; LABOUCHÈRE, "THE BROWN MAN'S BURDEN." First
published in *McClure's Magazine* (New York) in February,
1899; also published in *The Times* (4 Feb. 1899), our text.

To wait, in heavy harness,
    On fluttered folk and wild—
Your new-caught, sullen peoples,
    Half-devil and half-child.

Take up the White Man's Burden—
    In patience to abide,   10
To veil the threat of terror
    And check the show of pride;
By open speech and simple,
    An hundred times made plain,
To seek another's profit   15
    And work another's gain.

Take up the White Man's burden—
    The savage wars of peace—
Fill full the mouth of Famine,[40]
    And bid the sickness cease;   20
And when your goal is nearest
    (The end for others sought)
Watch sloth and heathen folly
    Bring all your hope to nought!

Take up the White Man's burden—   25
    No iron rule of kings,
But toil of serf and sweeper[41]—
    The tale of common things.
The ports ye shall not enter,
    The roads ye shall not tread,   30
Go, make them with your living,
    And mark them with your dead.

Take up the White Man's burden—
    And reap his old reward—
The blame of those ye better   35
    The hate of those ye guard—
The cry of hosts ye humour
    (Ah, slowly!) toward the light:—
"Why brought ye us from bondage,
    Our loved Egyptian night?"[42]   40

Take up the White Man's burden—
    Ye dare not stoop to less—
Nor call too loud on Freedom
    To cloke your weariness.

Notes

[40] *Famine* in the most dire famine in India (1876–78) during British rule, between seven and eight million Indians died. In various famines in different regions of British India between 1878 and 1900, about five-and-a-half million other Indians died.

[41] *serf and sweeper* respectively, low status in medieval Europe and the lowest caste in India.

[42] *night* see Exodus 16: 2–3; the Israelites feared that Moses has misled them when escaping from the Egyptians.

By all ye will or whisper,
    By all ye leave or do,
The silent, sullen peoples
    Shall weigh your God[43] and you.

Take up the White Man's burden!
    Have done with childish days[44]—
The lightly-proffered laurel,
    The easy ungrudged praise:
Comes now, to search your manhood
    Through all the thankless years,
Cold, edged with dear-bought wisdom,
    The judgment of your peers.

45

50

55

WEB p. 498

Lispeth

Lionel Johnson (1867–1902)

Born in Broadstairs, Kent, Johnson was the sixth child of William Victor Johnson (1822–91), a captain in the army, and Catherine Delicia Walters (d. 1903). He was privately educated before entering Winchester College. Thence he entered New College, Oxford on a scholarship, was tutored by Walter Pater, and graduated with a first in classics. In London he moved into Fitzroy House with the Century Guild (Selwyn Image, 1849–1930, and Arthur Mackmurdo, 1851–1942) and in June 1891 was received into the Roman Catholic Church. He also joined the Rhymers' Club and published in their books of 1892 and 1894; he also wrote reviews and essays for *The Academy*, the *Daily Chronicle*, *The Pageant*, *The Savoy*, and *The Spectator*. He published *The Art of Thomas Hardy* (1894), *Poems* (1895), and *Ireland, with Other Poems* (1897). A close friend of Arthur Symons and W. B. Yeats, he was also a drinking companion of Ernest Dowson. He became interested in Irish causes, visited Ireland, and espoused Celticism. These themes, together with his interests in Catholic ritual and theology, as well as his classicism in allusion, learning, and formal restraint, mark his writing. Accordingly he rejected his fellow Decadents' affectation "when emotions become entangled with the consciousness of them." His isolated celibacy and suppressed homosexuality, as well as his alcoholism and religious morbidity, led to depression; his frail health gave way to a series of strokes and an early death. Standard edition: *The Collected Poems of Lionel Johnson*, ed. Ian Fletcher (second edition 1982); *Post Liminium: Essays and Critical Papers*, ed. Thomas Whittemore (1911); Gary Paterson, *At the Heart of the 1890s: Essays on Lionel Johnson* (2007); Richard Whittington-Egan, *Lionel Johnson: The Dark Angel* (2012).

Notes ————————————————————

[43] *God* "gods" when published in *McClure's Magazine*; see n. 39.
[44] *days* see 1 Corinthians 13: 11; for laurel, see HEMANS, n. 17.

The Dark Angel[1]

Dark Angel, with thine aching lust
To rid the world of penitence:
Malicious Angel, who still dost
My soul such subtile violence!

Because of thee, no thought, no thing,   5
Abides for me undesecrate:
Dark Angel, ever on the wing,
Who never reachest me too late!

When music sounds, then changest thou
Its silvery to a sultry fire: 10
Nor will thine envious heart allow
Delight untortured by desire.

Through thee, the gracious Muses[2] turn
To Furies,[3] O mine Enemy!
And all the things of beauty burn   15
With flames of evil ecstasy.

Because of thee, the land of dreams
Becomes a gathering place of fears:
Until tormented slumber seems
One vehemence of useless tears.   20

When sunlight glows upon the flowers,
Or ripples down the dancing sea:
Thou, with thy troop of passionate powers,
Beleaguerest, bewilderest, me.

Within the breath of autumn woods,   25
Within the winter silences:
Thy venomous spirit stirs and broods,
O Master of impieties!

The ardour of red flame is thine,
And thine the steely soul of ice:[4]   30
Thou poisonest the fair design
Of nature, with unfair device.

Notes

LIONEL JOHNSON

[1] *title* the dark angel lurking as the other half of the soul is perhaps drawn from the morality-play character of the Bad Angel in Christopher Marlowe's *Dr. Faustus* (1604), as well as from the fallen angel, Lucifer (Lat. light-bearer) in *Paradise Lost*, 1: 599–600: "Darkened so, yet shone / Above them all th' Archangel." Here the dark angel offers fulfilment of repressed desires that, as in *Faustus*, come at the cost of the immortal soul. From *Second Book of the Rhymers' Club* (1894); reprinted in *Poems* (1895), dated 1893. Our text: 1895.

[2] *Muses* in Greek mythology the Muses are the nine daughters of Zeus and Mnemosyne, each of whom presides over a particular kind of literature and the arts, with Apollo as their leader. Their home was on Mount Parnassus.

[3] *Furies* according to Virgil and Dante, there were three winged Furies whose task was the pursuit and punishment of unavenged crimes; according to the Greek dramatists they fulfilled the same role, though their number is unclear.

[4] *ice* in exploring the *Inferno*, Dante and his guide Virgil pass through burning flames until at the centre of Hell they reach the realm of ice (Cantos 32–34). See also Job 24: 19.

Apples of ashes, golden bright;[5]
Waters of bitterness, how sweet!
O banquet of a foul delight,
Prepared by thee, dark Paraclete![6]   35

Thou art the whisper in the gloom,
The hinting tone, the haunting laugh:
Thou art the adorner of my tomb,
The minstrel of mine epitaph.   40

I fight thee, in the Holy Name!
Yet, what thou dost, is what God saith:
Tempter! should I escape thy flame,
Thou wilt have helped my soul from Death:

The second Death, that never dies,   45
That cannot die, when time is dead:
Live Death, wherein the lost soul cries,
Eternally uncomforted.[7]

Dark Angel, with thine aching lust!
Of two defeats, of two despairs: 50
Less dread, a change to drifting dust,
Than thine eternity of cares.

Do what thou wilt, thou shalt not so,
Dark Angel! triumph over me:
Lonely, unto the Lone I go;   55
Divine, to the Divinity.[8]

The Destroyer of a Soul[9]

To ——

I hate you with a necessary hate.
First, I sought patience: passionate was she:
My patience turned in very scorn of me,

Notes

[5] *bright* Milton refers to the apples of Sodom (see Genesis 13: 12–19: 28) that appeal to the eye but turn to ashes in the mouth (*Paradise Lost* 10: 560–66). Johnson refers to the *poma Sodomorum* (Lat. apples of Sodom) in his Latin tribute to Oscar Wilde for writing *The Picture of Dorian Gray* (1891): "In Honorem Doriani Creatorisque Eius" (Lat. in honour of Dorian and of his creator).

[6] *Paraclete* (Gk. advocate, comforter), one of the titles of the Holy Spirit in Christianity (see John 14: 16), but here a demonic inversion who entices the speaker away from Christ in this stanza's contrast of the heavenly and earthly banquets.

[7] *second ... uncomforted* the "second Death" is the death of the damned soul at the Last Judgement, a fate that the speaker hopes the "dark Angel" will have helped him avoid. The concept of the second death and the related theological notion of double predestination (the elect are predes-

tined to heaven, the reprobate to hell) is explained by St Augustine in *The City of God* (c.410): "For now is the hour when the dead shall hear the voice of the Son of God, and they that hear shall live.... And therefore, when the day of the bodily resurrection arrives, they shall come out of their graves, not to life, but to judgment, namely to damnation, which is called the second death" (20: 9; see also 13: 2; trans. Marcus Dods, 1871). See also Revelation 20: 14.

[8] *Divinity* a Neoplatonic doctrine from the *Enneads* (5. 1. 6) of Plotinus (c.204/5–270): "We first invoke God Himself, not in loud word but in that way of prayer which is always within our power, leaning in soul towards Him by aspiration, alone towards the alone" (trans. Stephen Mackenna, 1918).

[9] *title* in this poem the convention of the Italian or Petrarchan sonnet as a love poem is inverted. The ascription "To—" was deliberately left blank. It alludes to Oscar

That I should dare forgive a sin so great,
As this, through which I sit disconsolate;
Mourning for that live soul, I used to see;
Soul of a saint, whose friend I used to be:
Till you came by! a cold, corrupting, fate.   5

Why come you now? You, whom I cannot cease
With pure and perfect hate to hate? Go, ring   10
The death-bell with a deep, triumphant toll!
Say you, my friend sits by me still? Ah, peace!
Call you this thing my friend? this nameless thing?
This living body, hiding its dead soul?

A Decadent's Lyric[10]

Sometimes, in very joy of shame,
Our flesh becomes one living flame:
And she and I
Are no more separate, but the same.

Ardour and agony unite;   5
Desire, delirium, delight:
And I and she
Faint in the fierce and fevered night.

Her body music is: and ah,
The accords of lute and viola!   10
When she and I
Play on live limbs love's opera!

Ernest Dowson (1867–1900)

The elder son of Alfred Dowson (1843–94), the owner of a dry dock in East London, and Annie Swan (1848/9–95), Dowson attended attended Queen's College, Oxford, but did not complete his second year and left without a degree to work as an accountant at the dry dock. Most of his leisure time was spent, however, with his literary friends at the Rhymer's Club (see John Davidson), meeting at the Cheshire Cheese pub.

He associated especially with Lionel Johnson and fellow Catholics, contributed to *The Yellow Book, The Savoy*, and was assistant editor and wrote for *The Critic* in 1890. With Arthur Moore (b. 1866) he collaborated on two novels, *A Comedy of Masks* (1893) and *Adrian Rome* (1899), and issued his own short stories in *Dilemmas* (1895), and *The Pierrot of the Minute: A Dramatic Phantasy* (1897). He

Notes

Wilde as the "destroyer" of the "soul" of Lord Alfred Douglas (1870–1945). Johnson had met Wilde in Oxford in 1890. In February 1891, Johnson loaned his copy of Wilde's *The Picture of Dorian Gray* (1891) to Douglas, his cousin and a new Oxford undergraduate. Late in June Johnson took

Douglas to meet Wilde in London, their first meeting. From *Poems* (1895), dated 1892.

10 *title* a parody of Arthur Symons's Decadent love lyrics (see SYMONS, "PASTEL"). First published in Johnson's short story "Incurable" in *The Pageant* (1896).

luced several volumes of verse under the uence of Horace and Catullus as well as vinburne: *Verses* (1896), and, posthumously, *Decorations in Verse and Prose* (1899). Following his reception in the Roman Catholic Church in about 1891–92, his verse incorporated themes from the liturgy of the church combined with aestheticism and Decadent themes and images, some drawn from the French Symbolists, like Paul Verlaine (1844–96). When the dry dock business failed in 1894, Dowson moved to Brittany and produced translations for an English audience of Émile Zola (*La Terre*, 1894), Honoré de Balzac (*La Fille aux yeux d'or*, 1896), Choderlos de Laclos (*Les Liaisons dangereuses*, 1898), and others. In 1889 he had fallen in love with 11-year-old Adelaide Foltinowicz (1878–1903), the daughter of a restaurant owner and was devastated when in 1897 she married a tailor. Dowson had dedicated *Dilemmas* and *Verses* to her. Dowson's loss, together with the possible suicide of his father (he had tuberculosis), the actual suicide by hanging of his mother (she also had consumption), his own dissolute lifestyle (alcoholism and prostitution), as well as poverty and his own tuberculosis, in the midst of finely crafted verse and elegant translations, made him almost the quintessential decadent *poète maudit* (Fr. doomed poet). He returned to England, was rescued by Robert Sherard (1861–1943), a friend and biographer of Oscar Wilde, but died six weeks later. Standard editions: *The Poetry of Ernest Dowson*, ed. Desmond Flower (1970); *The Stories of Ernest Dowson*, ed. Mark Longaker (1947); *The Letters of Ernest Dowson*, eds Desmond Flower and Henry Maas (1967); Jad Adams, *Madder Music, Stronger Wine: The Life of Ernest Dowson, Poet and Decadent* (2000); the poems of Ernest Dowson: http://poetry.elcore.net/CatholicPoets/Dowson/index.html.

Non Sum Qualis Eram Bonae Sub Regno Cynarae[1]

Last night, ah, yesternight, betwixt her lips and mine
There fell thy shadow, Cynara! thy breath was shed
Upon my soul between the kisses and the wine;
And I was desolate and sick of an old passion,
    Yea, I was desolate and bowed my head: 5
I have been faithful to thee, Cynara! in my fashion.

All night upon mine heart I felt her warm heart beat,
Night-long within mine arms in love and sleep she lay;
Surely the kisses of her bought red mouth were sweet;
But I was desolate and sick of an old passion,   10
    When I awoke and found the dawn was gray:
I have been faithful to thee, Cynara! in my fashion.

Notes

Ernest Dowson

[1] *title* from the opening of Horace's *Odes*, 4. 1. 3–4: "I am not the same / As in the reign of Cinara, kind and fair"(trans. John Conington, 1865), used by Dowson with symbols typical of the Decadent Movement to set the memory of an ideal love, now impossibly lost, against the present unfulfilling and sordid relationship with a prostitute. The ideal love is reputed to have been Adelaide Foltinowicz (see headnote). The name Cynara was common amongst Roman women. Dowson's metre is based on the French Alexandrine or six-stress line. First published in the short-lived Arts and Crafts periodical, *The Century Guild Hobby Horse* (vol. 6, Apr. 1891, p. 67); reprinted in the *Second Book of the Rhymers' Club* (1894) and then in *Verses* (1896). Our text: *The Poems of Ernest Dowson* (1905).

I have forgot much, Cynara! gone with the wind,[2]
Flung roses, roses riotously with the throng,
Dancing, to put thy pale, lost lilies out of mind;　　　　　　　15
But I was desolate and sick of an old passion,
　　　Yea, all the time, because the dance was long:
I have been faithful to thee, Cynara! in my fashion.

I cried for madder music and for stronger wine,
But when the feast is finished and the lamps expire,　　　　　20
Then falls thy shadow, Cynara! the night is thine;
And I am desolate and sick of an old passion,
　　　Yea, hungry for the lips of my desire:
I have been faithful to thee, Cynara! in my fashion.

Nuns of the Perpetual Adoration[3]

For The Countess Sobieska von Platt

Calm, sad, secure; behind high convent walls,
　　　These watch the sacred lamp,[4] these watch and pray:
And it is one with them when evening falls,
　　　And one with them the cold return of day.

These heed not time; their nights and days they make　　　5
　　　Into a long, returning rosary,[5]
Whereon their lives are threaded for Christ's sake:
　　　Meekness and vigilance and chastity.

A vowed patrol, in silent companies,
　　　Life-long they keep before the living Christ:　　　　　10
In the dim church, their prayers and penances
　　　Are fragrant incense to the Sacrificed.

Outside, the world is wild and passionate;
　　　Man's weary laughter and his sick despair
Entreat at their impenetrable gate:　　　　　　　　　　15
　　　They heed no voices in their dream of prayer.

Notes

[2] *wind* source of the title of Margaret Mitchell's novel *Gone with the Wind* (1937), set in Georgia during the American Civil War (1861–65) and Reconstruction (1865–77), and subsequently made into a famous film by David O. Selznick (1939).

[3] *title* the nuns were probably of the Ursuline order (indicated in early drafts of the poem), who devoted their entire lives to vigil and prayer in adoration of the consecrated bread from the Mass as the presence of Christ. Little is known of the dedicatee, the Countess von Platt, probably Louisa Sobieska (c.1827–97), who married Edouard von Platt (b. c.1820) of the Austrian imperial bodyguard. She was the sister of Charles Edward Stuart (that is, Charles Manning Allen), a somewhat shady inventor of Scottish cultural history and co-author with his brother, John Carter Allen, of *The Costume of the Clans* (1842), more fiction than truth. First published in *The Century Guild Hobby Horse* (vol. 6, Oct. 1891, p. 136) with the title "The Carmelite Nuns of the Perpetual Adoration." With two other poems in the same publication, "Flos Lunae" (Lat. flowers of the moon) and "Amor Umbratilis" (Lat. love in the shade or in private), it made up a group entitled "In Praise of Solitude." Subsequently it was reprinted in the *Mercure de France* (Mar. 1892) with a French translation; in the first *Book of the Rhymer's Club* (1892); and in *Verses* (1896), with slight changes. Our text: *The Poems of Ernest Dowson* (1905).

[4] *lamp* the oil lamp burning before the Sacrament (consecrated bread and wine), indicating the presence of Christ.

[5] *rosary* (from Lat. *rosarium*, rose-garland): Catholic devotional set of prayer beads.

They saw the glory of the world displayed;
    They saw the bitter of it, and the sweet;
They knew the roses of the world should fade,
    And be trod under by the hurrying feet.   20

Therefore they rather put away desire,
    And crossed their hands and came to sanctuary;
And veiled their heads and put on coarse attire:
    Because their comeliness was vanity.

And there they rest; they have serene insight   25
    Of the illuminating dawn to be:
Mary's sweet Star[6] dispels for them the night,
    The proper darkness of humanity.

Calm, sad, secure; with faces worn and mild:
    Surely their choice of vigil is the best?   30
Yea! for our roses fade, the world is wild;
    But there, beside the altar, there, is rest.

Vitae Summa Brevis Spem Non Vetat Incohare Longam[7]

They are not long, the weeping and the laughter,
    Love and desire and hate:
I think they have no portion in us after
    We pass the gate.

They are not long, the days of wine and roses: 5
    Out of a misty dream
Our path emerges for a while, then closes
    Within a dream

Benedictio Domini[8]

For Selwyn Image

Without, the sullen noises of the street!
    The voice of London, inarticulate,
Hoarse and blaspheming, surges in to meet
The silent blessing of the Immaculate.[9]

Notes

[6] *Star* Jesus; the star at Bethlehem indicated the presence of the Christ child to the Magi or Wise Men; Mary is also known as *Stella Maris* (Lat. the "Star of the Sea").

[7] *title* the first poem in *Verses* (1896) is introductory to the volume. The Latin title means "The brief sum of life forbids us the hope of enduring long" (Horace, *Odes* 1. 4. 15). After this epigraphic poem to the volume, a preface follows, entitled "In Preface: For Adelaide." In it, Dowson states, "For I need not write your name for you at least to know that this and all my work is made for you in the first place." For Adelaide Foltinowicz, see headnote. Our text: *The Poems of Ernest Dowson* (1905).

[8] *title* (Lat. the blessing of the Lord). Selwyn Image (1849–1930) abandoned his clerical orders in the Anglican Church and helped found the Century Guild of Artists with A. H. Mackmurdo (1851–1942), co-editing the Guild's periodical, *The Century Guild Hobby Horse*, from 1886 to 1892. First published in *Verses* (1896). Our text: *The Poems of Ernest Dowson* (1905).

[9] *Immaculate* name for Mary, the mother of Jesus. In 1854 Pope Pius IX declared that Mary was conceived without

Dark is the church, and dim the worshippers,
    Hushed with bowed heads as though by some old spell,
While through the incense-laden air there stirs
    The admonition of a silver bell.

Dark is the church, save where the altar stands,
    Dressed like a bride, illustrious with light,   10
Where one old priest exalts[10] with tremulous hands
    The one true solace of man's fallen plight.

Strange silence here: without, the sounding street
    Heralds the world's swift passage to the fire:
O Benediction,[11] perfect and complete!   15
    When shall men cease to suffer and desire?

Spleen[12]

I was not sorrowful, I could not weep,
And all my memories were put to sleep.

I watched the river grow more white and strange,
All day till evening I watched it change.

All day till evening I watched the rain   5
Beat wearily upon the window pane.

I was not sorrowful, but only tired
Of everything that ever I desired.

Her lips, her eyes, all day became to me
The shadow of a shadow utterly.   10

All day mine hunger for her heart became
Oblivion, until the evening came,

And left me sorrowful, inclined to weep,
With all my memories that could not sleep.

original sin, the dogma of the Immaculate Conception. Such a position had been widely held in popular belief and some theological circles (especially the Franciscans) since late antiquity, although it was a matter of controversy in the Middle Ages, with Bernard of Clairvaux (1090–1153), Thomas Aquinas (1225–74), and Bonaventure (1221–74) denying it.

[10] *exalts* in the service of the Benediction of the Blessed Sacrament, a priest elevates the monstrance (a vessel in which a consecrated Eucharistic host is placed) and with it blesses the kneeling people.

[11] *Benediction* a reference both to the service (see n. 10) and to the blessing that the people receive.

[12] *title* according to the medieval physiological theory of the humours, the spleen was supposed to be the source of melancholy and bad temper. Charles Baudelaire (1821–61) and Paul Verlaine both used this title for poems, meaning satiety, bored lack of desire. When republished "(For Arthur Symons)" was added beneath the title. Arthur Symons (1875–1945), English literary critic and interpreter of the Aesthetic Movement and Decadence, edited *The Savoy* (1896), a short-lived journal in which both Dowson and Aubrey Beardsley (1872–98) published. Symons also published a poem called "Spleen," a translation of Verlaine's poem. First published in *Verses* (1896). Our text: *The Poems of Ernest Dowson* (1905).

Villanelle of the Poet's Road[13]

Wine and woman and song,
    Three things garnish our way:
Yet is day over long.

Lest we do our youth wrong,
    Gather them while we may:[14]
Wine and woman and song.

Three things render us strong,
    Vine leaves, kisses and bay;[15]
Yet is day over long.

Unto us they belong,
    Us the bitter and gay,
Wine and woman and song.

We, as we pass along,
    Are sad that they will not stay;
Yet is day over long.

Fruits and flowers among,
    What is better than they:
Wine and woman and song?
    Yet is day over long.

Charlotte Mew (1869–1928)

Mew and her family were left in financial stress when her family, an architect, died in 1898. Several of her siblings were confined as insane. She published a short story, "Passed," in *The Yellow Book* II (1894), a number of stories in *Temple Bar* and elsewhere, and two collections of poems, *The Farmer's Bride* (1916; second edition with additional poems, 1921) and, posthumously, *The Rambling Sailor* (1929). With support from such famous literary figures as Thomas Hardy, John Masefield, and Walter de la Mare, she received a small civil-list pension. She had a close but unrequited attraction to the novelist May Sinclair (1863–1946). She was acclaimed as one of the greatest, though relatively unknown, poets of the 1890s and the Modernist period; to Virginia Woolf she was "the greatest living poetess." She took her life while being treated for depression in a nursing home. Standard edition: *Complete Poems* ed. John Newton (2000); *Collected Poems and Prose* ed. Val Warner (1981); Penelope Fitzgerald, *Charlotte Mew and Her Friends* (1984); "Charlotte's Web": http://studymore.org.uk/ymew.htm.

Notes

[13] *title* a villanelle is a French form consisting of five three-line stanzas and a final quatrain, using only two rhymes. There are two repeating refrains, one at the end of the first stanza, and one at the end of the second. The literary motif is *carpe diem* (Lat. seize the day). First published in *Decorations in Verse and Prose* (1899); our text: *The Poems of Ernest Dowson* (1905).

[14] *may* see also Robert Herrick (1591–1674), "To the Virgins, to Make Much Use of Time": "Gather ye rosebuds while ye may."

[15] *bay* for bay or laurel, see HEMANS, n. 17.

V.R.I.[1]

I   [January 22nd, 1901]

"A Nation's Sorrow." No. In that strange hour
    We did but note the flagging pulse of day,
    The sudden pause of Time, and turn away
Incredulous of grief; beyond the power
Of question or of tears. Thy people's pain   5
    Was their perplexity: Thou could'st not be
God's and not England's. Let Thy spirit reign,
    For England is not England without Thee.
Still Thine, Immortal Dead, she still shall stake
    Thy fame against the world, and hold supreme   10
Thy unsuspended sway. Then lay not down
    Thy sceptre, lest her Empire prove a dream
Of Thine, great, gentle Sleeper, who shalt wake
    When God doth please, to claim another crown.

II   [February 2nd, 1901]

When, wrapped in the calm majesty of sleep,   15
    She passes through her people to her rest,
    Has she no smile in slumber? Is her breast,
Even to their sorrow, pulseless? Shall they weep
And She not with them? Nothing is so strange
    As this, that England's passion, be it pain,   20
    Or joy, or triumph, never shall again
Find voice in her. No change is like this change.

For all this mute indifference of death,
    More dear She is than She has ever been.
    The dark crowd gathers: not "The Queen! The Queen!"   25
Upon its lip to-day. A quickened breath—
    She passes—through the hush, the straining gaze,
    The vast, sweet silence of its love and praise.

To a Little Child in Death[2]

Dear, if little feet make little journeys,
    Thine should not be far;
        Though beyond the faintest star,
        Past earth's last bar,
        Where angels are,   5

Notes

Charlotte Mew

[1] V.R.I. (Lat. Victoria Regina Imperatrix, Victoria Queen Empress). Victoria died on 22 January 1901 and was buried on 2 February 1901. The sonnets were first published in *Temple Bar* (Mar. 1901); republished in *The Farmer's Bride* (second edition 1921).

[2] *title* first published in *Temple Bar* (Sept. 1901).

Thou hast to travel—
Cross the far blue spaces of the sea,
Climb above the tallest tree,
Higher up than many mountains be;
    Sure there is some shorter way for thee,   10
Since little feet make little journeys.

Then, if smallest limbs are soonest weary,
    Thou should'st soon be there;
        Stumbling up the golden stair,[3]
        Where the angels' shining hair   15
            Brushes dust from baby faces.
        Very, very gently cling
        To a silver-edged wing,
            And peep from under.
        Then thou'lt see the King,[4]   20
        Then will many voices sing,
            And thou wilt wonder.
        Wait a little while
        For Him to smile,
            Who calleth thee.   25
        He who calleth all,
        Both great and small,
        From over mountain, star and sea,
    Doth call the smallest soonest to His knee,
Since smallest limbs are soonest weary.   30

At the Convent Gate[5]

"Why do you shrink away, and start and stare?—
    Life frowns to see you leaning at death's gate—
    Not back, but on. Ah! sweet, it is too late—
You cannot cast these kisses from your hair.
Will God's cold breath blow kindly anywhere   5
    Upon such burning gold? Oh! lips worn white
    With waiting! Love will blossom in a night
And you shall wake to find the roses there!"

"Oh hush! He seems to stir, He lifts His Head.
He smiles. Look where He hangs against the sky.   10
He never smiled not stirred, that God of pain

Notes

[3] *stair* in 1880 Edward Burne-Jones, a Pre-Raphaelite, exhibited a painting entitled *The Golden Stairs*, an allegorical painting showing eighteen women, similarly clad in grey-white flowing robes and bearing musical instruments, descending a golden and curved marble stair, possibly suggesting the transition from earth to heaven.

[4] *King* Christ.

[5] *title* Christina Rossetti had published "The Convent Threshold" in *Goblin Market and Other Poems* (1862), stressing the renunciation of earthly pleasures and ideals, and, like Mew, involving lovers' bidding farewell at the entrance to the convent. The Mew family lived near Christina Rossetti in Bloomsbury in the 1890s and they attended the same church, Christ Church, Woburn Square. Mew had visited a convent in Brittany in 1901 and wrote about it in *Temple Bar* (Oct. 1901). First published in *Temple Bar* (Mar. 1902).

With tired eyes and limbs, above my bed—
But loose me, this is death, I will not die—
Not while He smiles. Oh! Christ, Thine own again!"

Song ["Oh! Sorrow"]⁶

Oh! Sorrow, Sorrow, scarce I knew
    Your name when, shaking down the may
In sport, a little child, I grew
    Afraid to find you at my play.
I heard it ere I looked at you;   5
    You sang it softly as you came
Bringing your little boughs of yew⁷
    To fling across my gayest game.

Oh! Sorrow, Sorrow, was I fair
    That when I decked me for a bride,   10
You met me stepping down the stair
    And led me from my lover's side?
Was I so dear you could not spare
    The maid to love, the child to play,
But coming always unaware,   15
    Must bid and beckon me away?

Oh! Sorrow, Sorrow, is my bed
    So wide and warm that you must lie
Upon it; toss your weary head
    And stir my slumber with your sigh?   20
I left my love at your behest,
    I waved your little boughs of yew,
But, Sorrow, Sorrow, let me rest,
    For oh! I cannot sleep with you!

Not for that City⁸

Not for that city of the level sun,
    Its golden streets and glittering gates ablaze—
    The shadeless, sleepless city of white days,
White nights, or nights and days that are as one—
We weary, when all is said, all thought, all done.   5
    We strain our eyes beyond this dusk to see
    What, from the threshold of eternity
We shall step into. No, I think we shun
The splendour of that everlasting glare,

Notes ──────────────

⁶ *title* first published in *Temple Bar* (Aug. 1902).
⁷ *yew* a long-lived evergreen tree, frequently found in graveyards in England, and symbolic of death, as in Thomas
Gray's "Elegy Written in a Country Churchyard" (1751).

⁸ *title* first published in *Temple Bar* (Nov. 1902).

The clamour of that never-ending song.   10
 And if for anything we greatly long,
It is for some remote and quiet stair
 Which winds to silence and a space of sleep
 Too sound for waking and for dreams too deep.

Requiescat[9]

Your birds that call from tree to tree
 Just overhead, and whirl and dart,
Your breeze fresh-blowing from the sea,
 And your sea singing on, Sweetheart.

Your salt scent on the thin, sharp air   5
 Of this grey dawn's first drowsy hours,
While on the grass shines everywhere
 The yellow sunlight of your flowers.

At the road's end your strip of blue
 Beyond that line of naked trees—   10
Strange that we should remember you
 As if you would remember these!

As if your spirit, swaying yet
 To the old passions, were not free
Of Spring's wild magic, and the fret   15
 Of the wilder wooing of the sea!

What threat of old imaginings,
 Half-haunted joy, enchanted pain,
Or dread of unfamiliar things
 Should ever trouble you again?   20

Yet you would wake and want, you said,
 The little whirr of wings, the clear
Gay notes, the wind, the golden bed
 Of the daffodil: and they are here—!

Just overhead, they whirl and dart   25
 Your birds that call from tree to tree,
Your sea is singing on—Sweetheart,
 Your breeze is blowing from the sea.

Beyond the line of naked trees
 At the road's end, your stretch of blue—   30
Strange if you should remember these
 As we, ah! God! Remember you!

Notes

[9] *Requiescat* (Lat. may s/he rest). First published in *The Nation* (13 Nov. 1909).

The Farmer's Bride[10]

Three summers since I chose a maid—
   Too young maybe—but more's to do
At harvest-time than bide and woo.
   When us was wed she turned afraid
Of love and me and all things human;   5
Like the shut of winter's day
Her smile went out, and 'twasn't a woman—
   More like a little frightened fay.[11]
      One night, in the Fall, she runned away.

   "Out 'mong the sheep, her be," they said,   10
   'Should properly have been abed;
But sure enough she wasn't there
Lying awake with her wide brown stare.
So over seven-acre field and up-along across the down
   We chased her, flying like a hare   15
Before out lanterns. To Church-Town[12]
     All in a shiver and a scare
We caught her, fetched her home at last
   And turned the key upon her, fast.

She does the work about the house   20
As well as most, but like a mouse.
   Happy enough to chat and play
    With birds and rabbits and such as they,
   So long as men-folk keep away.
"Not near, not near!" her eyes beseech   25
When one of us comes within reach.
   The women say that beasts in stall
   Look round like children at her call.
   I've hardly heard her speak at all.

Shy as a leveret,[13] swift as he,   30
Straight and slight as a young larch tree,
Sweet as the first wild violets, she,
To her wild self. But what to me?

Notes

[10] *title* the dialect is from the west of England. Some critics have compared the bride with Sue Bridehead in Hardy's *Jude the Obscure* (1895). The poem gave the title to the first volume of Mew's poems, *The Farmer's Daughter* (1916), a volume that had scant success in terms of sales, but that was greatly appreciated in literary circles. When it was first published, it was memorized by Alida Klementaski (1892–1969), who later married Harold Monro (1879–1932): she repeated the poem to him, and he published the collection at his shop in Bloomsbury, London, the Poetry Bookshop, a major publisher of and influence on early twentieth-century poetry. First published in *The Nation* (3 Feb. 1912).

[11] *fay* fairy.

[12] *Church-Town* probably a reference to the village in Somerset in the west of England, though several other villages in Cornwall and Shropshire have the same name.

[13] *leveret* young hare.

The short days shorten, and the oaks are brown,
  The blue smoke rises to the low grey sky,   35
One leaf in the still air falls slowly down,
  A magpie's spotted feathers lie
On the black earth spread white with rime,
The berries redden up to Christmas-time.
  What's Christmas-time without there be   40
  Some other in the house than we!

  She sleeps up in the attic there
  Alone, poor maid. 'Tis but a stair
Betwixt us. Oh! my God! the down,
The soft young down of her, the brown,   45
The brown of her—her eyes, her hair, her hair!

Index of Authors and Titles

Victorian Literature: An Anthology, First Edition. Edited by Victor Shea and William Whitla.
© 2015 John Wiley & Sons, Ltd. Published 2015 by John Wiley & Sons, Ltd.

Index of A